MW01077241

Meditations
in the Book of
PSALMS

Meditations
in the Book of
PSALMS

ERLING C. OLSEN

LOIZEAUX BROTHERS
Neptune, New Jersey

FIRST EDITION 1939
SINGLE VOLUME EDITION 1952
FOURTH PRINTING 1985

Copyright 1941, 1967 by
ERLING C. OLSEN

ISBN 0-87213-680-9

PRINTED IN THE UNITED STATES OF AMERICA

DEDICATION

I have had one major regret in the course of these broadcasts—my mother did not hear any of them. I owe my life to her, and also my first impressions of the Lord. No man had a more faithful or more loving mother. Since her home-going, her memory has been exceedingly precious. Whether or not there is a short-wave "hook-up" in heaven so that the saints hear Gospel broadcasts, we do not know. I am happy to dedicate this book to the memory of my mother, who lived and died in the faith, whose children call her BLESSED.

AUTHOR'S PREFACE

I MUST immediately unload myself of a burden lest anyone get an incorrect impression of this work. This is not an attempt to give an exposition of every verse in every Psalm, nor should it be considered as an expository work at all. I do not consider myself capable of undertaking such a task, to say nothing of the fact that there are already several very excellent works of an expository character on this glorious collection of inspired hymns, including a recent book by my esteemed friend, Dr. Arno C. Gaebelein. This work is only what its title indicates, a series of *meditations* in the book of the Psalms.

Whether any preacher during the Christian era has ever given a consecutive series of addresses on each of the Psalms, I do not know. Of course, there have been published works to which I have already alluded. But of this I am confident—that this effort was the first attempt to present the glories of this matchless collection over the radio.

It was my great privilege to give this series of radio addresses for a period of almost five years, beginning in February, 1934, and ending November 27, 1938. We began broadcasting through WMCA, of New York City, and later expanded to include the stations of the Inter-City Broadcasting System. For a while, these meditations were broadcast over some twenty stations of The American Broadcasting System, but during most of the period, they have been carried over stations of the Inter-City chain, covering the Atlantic seaboard from Washington, D. C., to Maine.

After re-reading these pages, one thing is clear—these broadcasts could never have been given if it were not for the helpfulness of Dr. Harry A. Ironside, pastor of the Moody Memorial Church of Chicago, Illinois, who opened the series and who always was a welcome guest on the radio whenever he was in New York. I am amazed at the number of illustrations that I "lifted" from him. He will forgive me.

One more confession. When I began broadcasting, I had no idea of covering each of the Psalms. I expected to limit the broadcasts to the more prominent or better-known Psalms. It soon became apparent, however, from the interest which developed, that it was desirable to cover all of them. Thus, when we arrived at the 150th Psalm, I went back and covered those that I had previously passed by. I believe that procedure was in the Divine Will also, for I am convinced that I would have been unable to handle those

Psalms without the further background of study, meditation, and prayer which was experienced during the course of the preparation of the messages.

It must be borne in mind that these addresses were prepared not only for Christians in order that their faith and joy in the Lord might be stimulated, but that the gospel should be clearly presented in every address so that the unsaved might know the way of salvation. There is, of course, some repetition. Even preachers repeat themselves, and I am only a layman!

I cannot fully express the deep spirit of thankfulness that possesses my heart that God in His grace ever gave me this privilege. From the letters we have received, I know that men and women have found the Lord as their Saviour. Scores upon scores of ministers have indicated that they have received encouragement in their own souls as they sat by their radios at 9 o'clock on Sunday morning before entering their pulpits to present the message which the Lord had laid upon their own hearts. I know of theological students who received new encouragement to preach the Word as a result of these broadcasts. I have heard from Catholics and have learned of men and women in monasteries and convents who have listened. I have been amazed at the number of professional men, doctors and educators who have written and expressed their pleasure. The broadcasts have appealed to old and young alike. Many Jews have also written in. What a book is the book of the Psalms! How thankful we as the Lord's people should be that it was included in Holy Writ.

At the conclusion of each broadcast, the address that was given was printed in a leaflet and made available to those who wrote in asking for copies. They have therefore had a wide circulation. In reducing them to book form, it has been necessary to eliminate some material in order not to present too bulky a publication. I have wrestled much with the problem of re-editing these 204 messages, but after prayer and consultation with friends, particularly Dr. Wilbur M. Smith of the Moody Bible Institute, to whom I am deeply indebted for help and encouragement (his friendship has been one of heaven's choicest blessings to me) I have sought to maintain the spirit in which the messages were given. Thus, the personal pronoun enters more than I would have otherwise permitted in such a publication.

As indicated in the concluding address, I have devoted no less than one thousand hours of concentrated study on the book of the Psalms since the beginning of this series, and yet, how little has been accomplished. We have not even scratched the surface of this collection of inspired hymns.

The re-editing has been a herculean task, and here I must express my appreciation of the splendid efforts of Miss Clazina Stam, who verified every Scriptural quotation and saw to it that there was uniformity in the presentation of material from a typographical viewpoint; to Miss Alice E. Davies, for her painstaking stenographic efforts; and last, but by no means least, to my wife, who diligently read the final page proofs before publication, after having had to listen to "Psalm Messages" while they were in preparation, "on the air," and later, ad infinitum. Patience *is* a virtue! Despite the fact that the work is far from perfect, I must confess that my own heart has been encouraged afresh in the Lord, as I have re-edited the messages for publication.

May the Lord, who granted the opportunity for the broadcasts, be pleased to add His benediction upon the printed page. May men and women come to know Christ as they peruse these pages. May believers be encouraged in their pilgrim path, and may many preachers, ordained or unordained, find in this work a stimulus to a deeper study of the Word of God and a desire for a more devoted life to the Lord whom we serve. May Jesus Christ be praised!

ERLING C. OLSEN

Two years have elapsed since this work was first published. To confess to many moments of trepidation regarding its acceptance—while in preparation and after printing—is to acknowledge the thoughts of the mind and the emotions of the author's heart. But God has answered prayer. He has been pleased to use this work for His glory. Letters have poured in telling of blessing received. Some have come to know the Lord through its pages. Scores upon scores have told the author that they have used the Meditations for their family worship and devotional periods. Others have stated that they read a meditation on their way to work in the morning and another on their return in the evening. (A particularly good idea when our newspaper headlines are so depressing.) May our precious Saviour be pleased to pour out His blessing on this second edition in even larger measure.

ERLING C. OLSEN.

Scarsdale, N. Y.
October . 1941.

PREFACE TO THIRD EDITION

Thirteen years have elapsed since *Meditations in the Psalms* was first published. It was so well received that a second edition was exhausted four years ago. And still the orders have continued to come in.

The publishers are happy to make this work, which has been a blessing to so many, available once more in this third edition, now for the first time available complete in a single convenient volume.

It is hoped that countless new readers will find real inspiration and refreshment in these pages.

LOIZEAUX BROTHERS, Publishers

New York City
August 1952

Meditations In The Psalms

THE "BLESSED" MAN

THE Book of Psalms is a remarkable book; it has been called the universal book. Someone has designated it the "Peerless Pearl of Scripture." Luther called it "a little Bible." "The Turks, who disclaim both the Old and New Testaments, swear as solemnly by the Psalms of David as by the Alcoran of Mohamet." The Bishop of Derry, when delivering the Bampton Lectures at Oxford University in 1876, said of the Psalms that "they are as near to us as the evangelists themselves." The Book of Psalms is probably the best loved book of all the Bible.

It is to this book that we turn for these matchless words: "The LORD is my shepherd; I shall not want." It is the Psalms to which we go to find an expression of the longing of the human heart for God, for we read in the 42nd Psalm, "As the hart panteth after the water brooks, so panteth my soul after thee, O God." When it comes to penitential sorrow, where is it possible to equal the words found in the 51st Psalm as David therein poured out his heart in anguish to God and cried, "Against thee, thee only, have I sinned. . ."? How can the family relationship, which the believer now enjoys, be more aptly expressed than in the 103rd Psalm? "Like as a father pitieth his children, so the LORD pitieth them that fear him." When it comes to the joy of the forgiveness of sins, it is impossible to find a word so eloquent and so pregnant with meaning as that which David used in the same Psalm when he wrote, "As far as the east is from the west, so far hath he removed our transgressions from us."

Upon the authority of our Lord we have the assurance that He is to be found in the Psalms. There are many who believe that the Psalms are only a collection of poetry, inspired by poets, but on the testimony of our Lord we are assured that the One who inspired Moses, who inspired Isaiah, who inspired all the writers of the Old and New Testaments, is the One who inspired the writers of the Psalms. This testimony is found in that exquisite 24th chapter of the Gospel according to Dr. Luke.

In the 24th chapter of his Gospel, Luke described the meeting of our Lord Jesus Christ with His disciples in an upper room in Jerusalem on the night of His resurrection. The doors were shut and a table was spread before them, when the Lord suddenly appeared in their midst, addressing them in words which He alone could speak, "Peace be unto you." While they were troubled and wondered at the thoughts that arose in their hearts, our Lord continued, "Behold my hands and my feet, that it is I myself: handle me, and see; for a spirit hath not flesh and bones, as ye see me have." When He had thus spoken, He turned about and asked, "Have ye here any meat?" To their astonishment, when they gave Him a piece of broiled fish, and of a honeycomb, He ate it before them. He then said, "These are the words which I spake unto you, while I was yet with you, that all things must be fulfilled, which were written in the law of Moses, and in the prophets, *and in the Psalms*, concerning me."—"Then opened he their understanding, that they might understand the scriptures."

Thus, upon the authority of our Lord Jesus Christ, we are assured that Christ is to be found in the Book of Psalms; in fact, it would be impossible to appreciate the sufferings of our Lord upon the cross and the agony endured by Him, were it not for the Psalms.

The 1st Psalm is in reality the great prefatory Psalm. It is a preface to the entire collection. It is the only* book in all the Bible which opens with the word "Blessed." This Psalm is also a striking study in contrasts. Note, for instance, the first three verses, which read:

> "Blessed is the man that walketh not in the counsel of the ungodly, nor standeth in the way of sinners, nor sitteth in the seat of the scornful.
>
> "But his delight is in the law of the LORD; and in his law doth he meditate day and night.
>
> "And he shall be like a tree planted by the rivers of water, that bringeth forth his fruit in his season; his leaf also shall not wither; and whatsoever he doeth shall prosper."

These verses describe one called the "blessed" man. In the Hebrew, the article is even more definite—"Blessed is *that* man that walketh not in the counsel of the ungodly. . ."

The man of whom the 1st Psalm speaks is none other than the Man, Christ Jesus. There never was a man who failed to walk in the counsel of the ungodly; there never was a man whose sole delight was in the law of the

---

*Some of the New Testament Epistles begin with "Blessed" in the epistle proper, but are preceded by the salutation from the addressor to the addressee.

Lord; there never was a man who meditated in His law day and night. But, our Lord Jesus Christ did. He alone meets the stipulations described herein concerning the man called "blessed."

However, the man who is "in Christ" may also partake of the blessedness described in the opening verses of this Psalm. Strictly speaking the Psalm concerns Christ, but practically speaking it can also be said to describe the believer in Jesus Christ. The godly man of this hour is likewise "blessed," or *happy*, as the Hebrew word also implies. The only truly happy man in this world is the godly man.

It is interesting to observe in this description of the "blessed" man, that we first find a series of negatives. This man does not walk in the counsel of the ungodly; he does not stand in the way of sinners; he does not sit in the seat of the scornful. After this trinity of negatives, we find that this man also possesses positive qualities. "His delight is in the law of the LORD. . ." That word "delight" is interesting, for there are a number of people in this world who take their "religion" sanctimoniously. Almost any Sunday one can go down Park Avenue in New York, and as one observes the people entering the churches, they seem anything but happy; they look as if they are about to "endure" religion for about an hour! One would be tempted to believe that the worship of God was a sad thing, something that required a longdrawn face. On the contrary, the Psalmist declared that the blessed man finds his "delight" in the law of the Lord. The New Testament says of the believer in Christ that he joys in God. That's quite different from being somber. There is no joy in this world comparable to the joy of knowing God. The truly happy man finds his delight, his joy, "in the law of the LORD." In that law he meditates day and night.

This does not mean that the truly happy man should cut himself off from the rest of the world, and spend all his time in the reading of the Bible. We mentioned earlier that this description primarily fits our Lord Jesus Christ. Did He separate Himself from the world of men, retiring to a place where He could study and read the Bible all the days of His life? On the contrary, our Lord led a most active life—He healed the sick; He fed the hungry; He attended a marriage; He sat at the dinner tables of many hosts. Jesus was one of the busiest of men, yet in His law, the law of the Lord, He meditated day and night.

"HE SHALL BE LIKE A TREE. . ."

The godly man's delight is in the law of the Lord—all his actions are motivated by the Scriptures—his every movement finds its genesis in the

Bible. Because his delight is in the law of the Lord; because he meditates in it day and night ". . . he shall be like a tree planted by the rivers of water."

When we consider that it is our Lord Jesus Christ who is spoken of herein, there can be no question of the application of Himself as "a tree planted by the rivers of water." How that reminds us of the tree upon which He hanged.

To some "The cross is nought but a rough plank cut by a Roman axe from a Jewish tree to which justly or unjustly some poor Hebrew criminal was nailed in scorn." Others ". . . would drape it over with ornament to hide its ruggedness." And some ". . . would hew it down with hellish axe," while others ". . . love that naked cross untouched by human art, uncarved—unpolished by the hand of man; just as it stood—outside Jerusalem—where the eternal Son—as a victim went forth to die, ascended it and took with Him our guilt; the Roman cross set on Hebrew soil where Jew and Gentile meet, where earth and heaven come together like converging orbs, henceforth to be one."

When we consider our Lord Jesus Christ as the "tree planted by the rivers of water," what wonderful illumination we receive. But this simile is true also of the believer in our Lord Jesus Christ. He, too, is unmovable, always abounding in the work of the Lord. ". . . like a tree planted by the rivers of water." He shall bring forth his fruit in his season. Not only will he have that fruit which will glorify God, but his leaf—his outward profession—shall not wither, and whatsoever he doeth shall prosper.

That is real prosperity. In a day of disappointment and depression, the truly prosperous man is the godly man—he who finds his delight in the law of the Lord. Everything he does shall prosper. Of course, there are disappointments in life, in many of which the godly man has his share, but in the face of all that is sorrowful, he finds that everything he does shall prosper.

THE UNGODLY MAN

The closing verses of this Psalm contrast the "blessed man" with other men who are called "ungodly." The Psalmist said of them:

> "The ungodly are not so: but are like the chaff which the wind driveth away.

> "Therefore the ungodly shall not stand in the judgment, nor sinners in the congregation of the righteous.

> "For the LORD knoweth the way of the righteous: but the way of the ungodly shall perish."

The words "ungodly" and "sinners" do not necessarily mean what a great many people have read into them. There are men who assume that to be called a sinner necessarily means that they must be criminals. The word "ungodly" and the term "sin" are expressions that are found in the Bible exclusively. They are not synonymous with "crime" and "criminal." A man may be an upright gentleman, he may even be religious, and yet be ungodly. No expression in all the Bible is so terrible in its implication as "the ungodly." That phrase describes all who are outside of Jesus Christ. Every man is ungodly. Man does not possess godliness—he is unlike God; he does not meet the requirements of God.

Irrespective of man's own righteousness, irrespective of his own standing before men—in the sight of God, he is so unlike God's Man that God characterizes him as "ungodly." That, too, is why he is called a sinner, for man has come short of the requirements of God. The ungodly and the sinner are like the chaff, absolutely worthless, which the wind driveth away. They shall not stand in the judgment, but the righteous shall. However, the godly man is not righteous because of his own works. On the contrary, that man has been *constituted* righteous by believing in Jesus Christ our Lord.

The ungodly man shall not stand in the judgment—sinners shall not sit in the congregation of the righteous, "for the LORD knoweth the way of the righteous; but the way of the ungodly shall perish." What is the *way* of the righteous? On the night of the betrayal of our Lord Jesus Christ, in an upper room in the city of Jerusalem, the disciples were gathered about Him. Our Lord told them about His going away. He said that if He went away He would return again and receive them unto Himself. Thomas, one of the twelve, said, "Lord, we know not whither thou goest, and how can we know the way?" To this our Lord replied, "I am *the way*, the truth, and the life: no man cometh unto the Father, but by me." Our Lord Jesus Christ is the "way" of the righteous, but *the way of the ungodly shall perish.*

PSALM TWO

WHEN GOD LAUGHS

THE 2nd Psalm is the first in the group called "Messianic Psalms." Many of the Hebrew doctors of the law have recognized that a large number of the Psalms concern the Messiah. In these Psalms the writer is not speaking about himself. He is recording the language of the

Messiah. It is about the Messiah that these Psalms center. In almost all, if not in every instance, it is the Messiah Himself who is heard speaking. As in every other book of the Old Testament, these Psalms present a conflicting revelation of the Messiah. Some speak of His reign in great power; others tell of His agony and suffering; in fact, there are those in which the Messiah speaks of His sin.

Every Bible-believing Christian believes that his Lord is speaking in these Psalms, prophetically. In some He is the trespass-offering, taking upon Himself the sins of His people, and calling them His own. In others, His glorious reign is the subject. These views can only be harmonized when one understands that there are actually two comings of the Messiah revealed in the Old Testament. His first coming answered to such Psalms as the 22nd where He cries, "My God, my God, why hast thou forsaken me?" and other similar passages, such as Isaiah 53, where it is written, "He was wounded for our transgressions, he was bruised for our iniquities; the chastisement of our peace was upon him; and with his stripes we are healed." All these were fulfilled when our Lord Jesus Christ was crucified between two thieves outside of Jerusalem, almost two thousand years ago.

THE RETURN OF CHRIST

The second coming of the Messiah is the advent when He will fulfill just as literally all of the passages of prophecy relating to His glorious reign as King of kings and Lord of lords.

If it surprises some that there are Psalms in which the Messiah, or the Christ, speaks of His sin, it is of interest to know that there have been doctors among the Jews who have concluded from the study of Isaiah 53 that the Messiah would be a leper, because in that chapter He is spoken of as being "stricken, smitten of God, and afflicted." They based their views upon the then prevalent idea among the Jews that when a man was smitten of God he became a leper. They were not far wrong, for leprosy, in the Scripture, is a type of sin. It is the declaration of the New Testament that the Lord Jesus Christ was made sin upon the cross that we might in turn be made the righteousness of God through Him.

In this 2nd Psalm, which begins with an interrogation but ends with a blessing, we have the resurrection of the Messiah proclaimed, together with a graphic description of His coming in judgment against the nations, and particularly against their rulers and kings.

What a Psalm this is! It opens "Why do the heathen rage, and the people imagine a vain thing?" In twelve short verses the Psalmist presents a tremendous, tumultuous scene, with numerous actors. One cannot read it without being thrilled with the action in it. Here we find armies marching; kings and rulers lead their forces; people riot; counsels are held: while in heaven God is presented as mocking and having the rulers in derision, thundering out His decrees. Anarchy, revolt, bloodshed,—all are described, culminating in the coronation at Jerusalem of Jehovah's anointed ruler, whom He calls His Son, and to whom He demands fealty and devotion from all.

The twelve verses of this Psalm readily divide into four sections or groups, each having three verses. In each group a distinctly different scene is presented, and in each a different speaker is heard.

In the first section we hear an inquirer raising the question, as he describes the armies of earth's rulers in revolt against the Lord and His Christ, the anointed:

> "Why do the heathen rage, and the people imagine a vain thing?
> "The kings of the earth set themselves, and the rulers take counsel together, against the LORD, and against his anointed, saying,
> "Let us break their bands asunder, and cast away their cords from us."

The Gentiles *rage!* What a word! It is the Jewish word "rawgosh" which means *tumultuously assembled.* Here is a riot staged by the Gentiles. But that is not all. In addition, the people, the Jews, imagine a folly. The kings of the earth solemnly assemble themselves. Rulers take counsel together. The great mass meeting of peoples and rulers is held to take action against the eternal God. They maintain that His dominion over them has been in the nature of bands and cords about them. *"Let us break with God"* is the unified cry of this mass of mankind. Incidentally, notice that the plural is used here—"Let us break *their* bands." Evidently the Trinity is also in the first section of this 2nd Psalm.

The first three verses of this Psalm had a partial fulfilment at the first coming of our Lord Jesus Christ. A verse or two from the 4th chapter of Acts will show how the disciples looked at this Psalm. They were forbidden by the rulers of the Jews to speak or teach in the name of Jesus. And, of course, Peter and John answered them, "whether it be right in the sight of God to hearken unto you more than unto God, judge ye. For we cannot but speak the things which we have seen and heard." After further threatening they were allowed to go to their own company, after which we read beginning with the 23rd verse of the 4th of Acts:

"And being let go, they went to their own company, and reported all that the chief priests and elders had said unto them.

"And when they heard that, they lifted up their voice to God with one accord, and said, Lord, thou art God, which hast made heaven, and earth, and the sea, and all that in them is:

"Who by the mouth of thy servant David hast said, Why did the heathen rage, and the people imagine vain things?

"The kings of the earth stood up, and the rulers were gathered together against the Lord, and against his Christ.

"For of a truth against thy holy child Jesus, whom thou hast anointed, both Herod, and Pontius Pilate, with the Gentiles, and the people of Israel, were gathered together.

"For to do whatsoever thy hand and thy counsel determined before to be done."

Thus we know that David wrote this Psalm. We also learn from this passage that the disciples in the early days recognized that this portion of Scripture had its partial fulfilment at the cross of our Lord Jesus Christ when He was crucified. However, a larger fulfilment of this prediction will take place upon the return of our Lord Jesus Christ.

THE STAGE BEING SET

Presiding at a dinner where one of the speakers was the Consul-General of a European country, I learned that he lived only a few city blocks away from our home, so I invited him to drive along with me. On the way home, we had a most interesting conversation regarding the things that are happening at present in the world. We both concluded that the world is in a turmoil—that there are more causes for war, present now, than at any time, and that our whole social and economic system seems to be in a sad state. The same might be said of the spiritual situation. The stage is being set for the first scene of this 2nd Psalm.

At verse 4 the scene quickly changes from earth to heaven. It is a heavenly scene, but it is far from a tranquil one: in fact, it is a heaven thundering with decrees and declarations, in which the God of heaven is presented laughing as if in mockery against the wicked attempts of man to do away with God. It is written: "He that sitteth in the heavens shall laugh; the LORD shall have them in derision. Then shall he speak unto them in his wrath, and vex them in his sore displeasure."

What a description of God!! Some may say, "I want a God whose love is everlasting; whose mercy is unending, but whose wrath is non-existent." Such a God is the production of a distorted mind. He is neither the God of creation nor the God of the Bible. A God who can sit silently by while the earth quakes and reels like a drunken sailor, opening its jaws to devour helpless men, women and children, can sit in the heavens and laugh against man's foolhardy efforts to drive Him out of the universe.

Israel, as well as the Gentiles, sent Jesus Christ back to heaven with this message: "We will not have this man to rule over us." But God bursts forth with His *yet. "Yet have I set my king upon my holy hill of Zion."*

At Jerusalem will our God set His King. No one who has kept abreast of world events, particularly the increase of Jews in Palestine, has any difficulty in observing that the stage is also being rapidly set for this very event when God shall crown His Son upon the holy hill of Zion, the city of Jerusalem.

Commencing with verse 7 we have another scene. Our Lord Jesus speaks. He says: "I will declare the decree: the LORD hath said unto me, Thou art my Son; this day have I begotten thee."

Some may be surprised to find the manifestation of the *SON* in the Psalms. But here it is. Those who are familiar with the New Testament will remember that again and again during the ministry of our Lord a voice was heard from heaven saying, "This is my beloved Son in whom I am well pleased—hear him." In this Psalm our Lord says, "I will declare the decree: Jehovah hath said unto me, Thou art my Son, this day have I begotten thee." If we examine the references in the New Testament which quote this particular verse, we will find that invariably they refer to the resurrection of our Lord Jesus Christ—it was on that day that our God begot Him again from the dead. Then Jehovah said unto Him: "Ask of me, and I shall give thee the heathen for thine inheritance and the uttermost parts of the earth for thy possession."

What a dominion!! What a rule our Lord Jesus Christ is to have some day from His throne seat at Jerusalem! Even all the Gentiles shall be His inheritance—the uttermost parts of the earth shall be for His possession.

What an outlook there is also for the Jewish race upon the return of their Messiah, when He comes to Jerusalem to establish His kingdom.

CLEAR SHINING AFTER RAIN

But this Psalm continues: "Thou shalt break them with a rod of iron; thou shalt dash them in pieces like a potter's vessel." Before our Lord enters into His reign of righteousness, holiness, and peace, He must first break His enemies with a rod of iron,—He must first dash them in pieces like a potter's vessel.

All this speaks of judgment, but this is but one phase of the return of our Lord. The other side may be found in such passages as the 23rd chapter of 2nd Samuel where commencing with verse 1 we have the last words of David:

> "Now these be the last words of David. David, the son of Jesse said, and the man who was raised up on high, the anointed of the God of Jacob, and the sweet psalmist of Israel, said,
>
> "The Spirit of the LORD spake by me, and his word was in my tongue.
>
> "The God of Israel said, the Rock of Israel spake to me, He that ruleth over men must be just, ruling in the fear of God."

And now notice a beautiful simile. It is questionable whether anything comparable can be found in all literature: "And he shall be as the light of the morning, when the sun riseth, even a morning without clouds; as the tender grass springing out of the earth by clear shining after rain."

Is there a sight in all the world comparable to the shining of the sun after the storm? In verse 9 of this Psalm we read of the storm, following which we have the peaceful reign of the Son of Righteousness.

Let us look briefly at the last scene, verses 10 to 12, where the speaker cried out :

> "Be wise now therefore, O ye kings; be instructed. ye judges of the earth.
>
> "Serve the LORD with fear and rejoice with trembling.
>
> "Kiss the Son, lest he be angry, and ye perish from the way, when his wrath is kindled but a little. Blessed are all they that put their trust in him."

Kiss the Son! Yes! Give reverence to the "heir apparent." "Kiss the Son, lest he be angry, and ye perish from the way, when his wrath is kindled but a little." Then follows the closing benediction: "Blessed are all they that put their trust in him," or "Happy are all they that put their trust in him." That is just as true now as it will be then. If we have placed our confidence in the Lord for our eternal welfare, we are indeed happy men.

PSALM THREE

THE WAY OUT OF DEPRESSION

AS WE examine the 3rd Psalm we shall observe that it has an appropriate message for this particular hour. "The Depression Psalm" would be a good title for it.

In the first place, the introduction to the Psalm is illuminating. From it we learn that David wrote it. We can also determine his circumstances as the introduction reveals that it was at the time when he fled from Absalom, his son.

David experienced a revolt in his own family. A man can stand almost anything except his own family turning against him. David tasted such an experience. The irony of it was that Absalom had brought about this revolt. In the olden days it was customary to give a child a name which characterized the youngster, or expressed the circumstances which existed at the time of the child's birth. In this case David had great hopes as he looked into' this child's eyes. He beheld something that reminded him of peace and tranquility; therefore he called the child Absalom, which means "his father's peace."

What a tragedy that a child with a name like that should turn out to be his father's thorn in the flesh. He was the one son who constantly plagued David, yet he was greatly loved by his father.

Absalom was a splendid looking chap. He was the most handsome young man in Israel. From the sole of his foot, even to the crown of his head, there was not so much as a blemish. But the only good thing about him was his name. He stole away the heart of Israel, not only by his beauty, but also by his subtlety, until he seemed to have the whole nation with him; in fact, he had entered into the very court of his father and won over his father's counselor, Ahithophel.

In the 2nd Book of Samuel, and the 15th chapter, we have the record of David's flight from his palace. Beginning with the 23rd verse we learn of much weeping as the king left the palace, passed over the brook Kidron and then went ". . . up by the ascent of mount Olivet, and wept as he went up, and had his head covered, and he went barefoot: and all the people that was with him, covered every man his head, and they went up, weeping as they went up."

This very journey was repeated by our Lord Jesus on the night of His betrayal. He, too, knew what it was to be betrayed by one of His own!

As David journeyed from his palace to the Mount of Olives he observed the revolters—he listened to the jeers of the crowd, and as he sat on the Mount of Olives looking down over the valley he penned his impressions in this Psalm: "LORD, how are they increased that trouble me! Many are they that rise up against me. Many there be which say of my soul, There is no help for him in God." Judging from the phrase "many there be which say of my soul, There is no help for him in God," David must have realized that his enemies concluded that he was in an absolutely hopeless condition. Not only had he a revolt in his own family and had he lost his chief adviser, but his enemies had increased on every hand. They had concluded that God Himself had forsaken David; in fact, there is an old Jewish comment upon this 2nd verse to the effect, that his enemies said, "There is no help for his soul in this world or the next." In other words, they thought he was past redemption. Of course, the many who insisted that David was past redemption were moved to that conclusion by consideration of David's sin.

THE MAN AFTER GOD'S HEART

Atheists delight to call attention to the characters of some of the Bible men. They particularly like to jeer at David saying, "So this is the man after God's own heart—what a man! An adulterer and a murderer." Indeed! But what is so strange about that? All the men whom God ever dealt with, or had to deal with, were sinners. Since he has to deal with you, he will have to deal with a sinner, and that goes for atheists as well.

When the Scriptures say concerning David that he was a man after God's own heart, we miss the entire import of that statement if we think it means design, in the sense that David's heart was like God's heart. Nothing could be more erroneous. The expression is one of direction—not of design. He was a man after (who longed for) God's heart.

While David drew attention in the first two verses of this Psalm to his enemies, in the 3rd he turned about in his distress to his Lord and said: "But thou, O LORD, art a shield for me; my glory, and the lifter up of mine head."

David knew he could not rely upon his army of faithful friends. Therefore he lifted up his heart to his Lord and said: "Thou . . . art a shield for me." As a shield the Lord would stand between his enemies and himself; every dart that his enemies addressed to him would be borne by the Lord. It is the position that God is willing to take.

But more than that, David insisted that as his Lord was his defense so, too, was He his triumph. Thus he called Him "my glory, and the lifter up of mine head." When a man has Christ as his shield, he also has Christ as his victory.

In the 4th verse David gave the panacea for every depression. "I cried unto the LORD with my voice, and he heard me out of his holy hill." It is a pity that we in this nation have lost sight of the fact that this is the only way out of our depression.

There is a worldly philosophy which ridicules a man when he sheds a few tears. Need we be reminded that our Lord knew what it was to shed salty tears? David cried unto the Lord and He heard him. Then to indicate his extreme confidence in the Lord, the next verse reveals a marvelous, tranquil scene. "I laid me down and slept; I awakened; for the LORD sustained me." Most of us when we have a few trials and difficulties are unable to sleep. We toss from side to side, even though before getting into bed we may have poured out our heart unto the Lord, but we do not have confidence enough in Him to rest in the fact that He has heard us.

David when he prayed, rested his case with the Lord. To show his confidence in Him, he lay down and slept. Could we have slept in like circumstances—slept, when we were driven out of our palace—slept when our own family revolted against us—slept when everybody else thought our case was hopeless?

In the New Testament we have a similar scene in the 12th chapter of the Acts of the Apostles. Herod, the king, stretched forth his hands to vex certain of the church. He killed James, the brother of John with the sword, and because he saw it pleased the Jews, he proceeded further to take Peter also." "And when he had apprehended him, he put him in prison, and delivered him to four quaternions of soldiers to keep him. . ."

He might have delivered him to ten thousand soldiers for all it mattered. When God wants a man to witness for him, even a king and an army cannot prevent that man from bearing his testimony.

At any rate, the night before Peter was to be brought before Herod, he was sound asleep between two soldiers, bound with chains. The keepers were before the doors of the prison. If we knew that we were to be brought up on charges the next day before a king who had already slain a fellow-helper of ours, would we have slept the night before? Would we have found it comfortable sleeping between two soldiers, bound with chains, and with a few keepers in front of our prison door?

But Peter was so soundly asleep that when the angel of the Lord came unto him, and a light shined in the prison, even the light failed to awaken him, so that it became necessary for the angel to smite him on the side and raise him up, saying, "Arise up quickly."

While no one would suggest that Peter ever suffered from insomnia, yet on this occasion he enjoyed the soundest sleep. He slept because he rested in the Lord.

"SALVATION BELONGETH UNTO THE LORD"

So David slept; he wakened and wrote: "the LORD sustained me." No wonder he added, "I will not be afraid of ten thousands of people, that have set themselves against me round about." Then he addressed the Lord and said: ". . . thou hast smitten all mine enemies upon the cheek bone; thou hast broken the teeth of the ungodly."

Smiting a man on the cheek bone is not a dignified manner of warfare; it is a sign of contempt. God smote the cheek bone of the enemies of David. He did so literally, for at the height of the battle, Absalom, riding upon his steed through the wilderness, was unable to stoop quickly enough beneath the thick boughs of an oak with the result that his head caught hold of the oak and he hanged in the tree, while his steed ran from underneath him.

David concluded this great depression Psalm by saying: "Salvation belongeth unto the LORD: thy blessing is upon thy people. Selah."

No greater lesson can any man learn than the lesson which David learned, that "Salvation belongeth unto the LORD."

Do we understand what that means? If we are ever to be saved, it must be the work of God. Salvation is His work; it belongs to Him.

Only two men in Scripture used this expression. David was one and the second was none other than Jonah. Both were in such pitiful positions that they rightfully concluded that the deliverance which could come would be by the grace of God. Yes, some scientific smart alecks still ridicule the story of Jonah and the whale but, now that there are in a number of museums specimens of whales that could swallow a dozen Jonahs, that type of ridicule doesn't have its customary effect.

Jonah in "the belly of the whale" had an opportunity to pray. He prayed as only a man in distress can pray. He closed his prayer with: ". . . . I will sacrifice unto thee with the voice of thanksgiving; I will pay that that I have vowed. Salvation is of the LORD."

Irrespective of what our financial or physical circumstances may be, they are not nearly as important as our soul's welfare. The salvation of souls is the work of the Lord. He wrought out that work upon Calvary when in the person of His Son He reconciled us unto Himself, not imputing our trespasses. He has committed unto us the ministry of reconciliation, so that we in His stead invite you to be reconciled to God.

Psalm Four

GODLY GLADNESS

THE 4th Psalm written by David, reads:

"Hear me when I call, O God of my righteousness: thou hast enlarged me when I was in distress; have mercy upon me, and hear my prayer.

"O ye sons of men, how long will ye turn my glory into shame? how long will ye love vanity, and seek after leasing? Selah.

"But know that the LORD hath set apart him that is godly for himself: the LORD will hear when I call unto him.

"Stand in awe, and sin not: commune with your own heart upon your bed, and be still. Selah.

"Offer the sacrifices of righteousness, and put your trust in the LORD.

"There be many that say, who will shew us any good? LORD, lift thou up the light of thy countenance upon us.

"Thou hast put gladness in my heart, more than in the time that their corn and their wine increased.

"I will both lay me down in peace, and sleep: for thou, LORD, only makest me dwell in safety."

There is an introduction to this Psalm which dedicates it to the chief Musician on what is called "Neginoth." That word "Neginoth" is enough to make any Gentile stumble, but a good Jew would know its meaning. It was a stringed instrument, played by the hands alone, such as the harp and the cymbals. This instrument was employed in the use of several Psalms throughout the Psalter such as the 6th, 54th, 55th, 61st, 67th, and

76th. There are those who have suggested that the introductions to the Psalms actually belong to the preceding Psalm as an appendage. Much may be said in favor of that view. However, we shall not spend our time on such an incidental, interesting as it may be; we do better to spend our radio time on the more important parts of the Psalm.

In the first place, it is evident that the Psalm is an evening hymn, for in the 4th verse we read, "Stand in awe, and sin not: commune with your own heart upon your bed, and be still." In the 8th and final verse we read, "I will both lay me down in peace, and sleep: for thou, LORD, only makest me dwell in safety." That last verse reminds one of that fine old prayer which the children love to use:

> "Now I lay me down to sleep,
> I pray the Lord my soul to keep.
> If I should die before I wake
> I pray the Lord my soul to take."

There are some who, having become mature with age, smile at the simplicity of a child, yet how much we learn from observing a child. Our Lord received some children in His midst on an occasion and said, ". . . of such is the kingdom of God . . . Whosoever shall not receive the kingdom of God as a little child, he shall not enter therein." That little evening prayer offered by children ought not to be entirely discarded by us who are older. It is a fine prayer but if we think we are too old to utter it, then at least let us use the words of the 8th verse of this Psalm, "I will both lay me down in peace, and sleep: for thou, LORD, only makest me dwell in safety."

There is no sweeter word in language than the word "Peace." In that connection an interesting item appears in the November (1937) issue of "China's Millions," a publication issued by the China Inland Mission. In an article written by Dr. Northcote Deck, he suggested that the salutation we give to another represents our uppermost thought for that one. He gave a few illustrations—"The practical Englishman says, 'How do you do?' because he is always *doing* things. (Dr. Deck might have added that the American has not enough time to say, 'How do you do?' He says, 'Howdy.') The polite Frenchman with his care for deportment greets one with 'How do you carry yourself?' The ancient Greek with his love for sunshine and gladness had as his greeting, 'Rejoice!' But the Jew, who had been placed by the deliberate choice of God in that little land of Palestine so filled with perilous conditions, had an entirely different greeting. His land had become the battleground between mighty Egypt in the South and successive empires in the North so that the greatest need of Palestine was peace. Thus for the Jew 'Peace' became the national greeting and desire each for the other."

When one Jew meets another he says, "sholem alecheim," and then comes the response from the other, "alecheim sholem." On the lips of a true Israelite who loves his God and His Word, how appropriate is the salutation "Peace." By the way, that word "Peace" was the first word that fell from the lips of the risen Lord as He appeared to His frightened disciples.

"TRIBULATION WORKETH PATIENCE. . ."

But mark in the 1st verse David acknowledged that he was in distress. It was in his distress that he called upon God to give him peace. "Hear me when I call, O God of my righteousness: thou hast enlarged me when I was in distress; have mercy upon me, and hear my prayer."

The other evening a few friends were together and we were talking about patience. I suggested that I had not forgotten a comment I heard in my youth that if one were to ask the Lord for patience he was not to be surprised if God visited tribulation for ". . . tribulation worketh patience. . . ." It is really remarkable how true that principle is. It is not the individual who has an easy task, who has no disturbances or upsets, who manifests patience. It is the man who is in distress. His troubles, disappointments, and tribulations have schooled him to be patient. The more trouble one has, the more patient one is apt to be. Let us not forget, therefore, when we ask for patience—expect to receive tribulation.

But here the Psalmist wrote concerning the Lord's dealings with him that God enlarged him when he "was in distress." I believe that this principle applies even to the present hour. It is a principle that is a problem to the world. For that reason the Psalmist wrote in the 2nd verse, "O ye sons of men, how long will ye turn *my glory into shame?* how long will ye love vanity, and seek after leasing?" One man said to another whom he knew to be serving the Lord, "I cannot understand how you can have so much difficulty since you are so definitely occupied with Christian work. It is an enigma to me. I would think that God would have made the way easier for you." One assumes that if a man lives a godly life God has an obligation toward him, that God is indebted to him, and that He will smooth the man's pathways and so arrange his life that everything will run smoothly. If that were the case we would have still more of what missionaries in China call "rice Christians," those who have confessed faith in Christ simply because of the rice they expect to get from the missionary's compound. If our pathway were strewn with roses and all the difficulties of life vanished in a moment upon receiving Christ, the whole world would receive Him. But our Bible says that those who will live godly in this world shall suffer persecution and that tribulation is a part of the life of every believer.

That which the unsaved considers a shame and which the world cannot understand is the very thing which is the glory of the Christian and the thing he values, for his faith is not based on circumstances nor upon the gifts that God might bestow upon his earthly life but it is based on the eternal love of God which was manifest in the death of His Son and upon what Gladstone called "the impregnable Rock of Holy Writ." Yesterday I saw the picture of a pair of shoes worn by a country pastor in New York State. His post does not provide him with sufficient for the bare necessities of life. Those shoes had large holes in their soles and one was broken in two. Do you think that that man would give up his country parish and cease preaching Christ? A thousand times, No! You say it's a shame. Yes, in one sense it is, but in another it is his glory.

We note from the 3rd verse of this 4th Psalm that the Lord has set apart for Himself the man who is godly. David wrote, "the LORD will hear when I call unto him." That's interesting! To think that the Lord has set apart him that is godly for Himself! How valuable to God is the one who is called a godly man. You will remember our Lord in His great high priestly prayer in speaking to His Father refers to His disciples and those who would believe in Him through the ministry of the disciples as those whom God has given Him. As Christ is God's love gift to us, so we are God's love gift to Christ. That is marvelous! When we look within ourselves we wonder what it is in us that is so precious to our Lord that we have become a love gift from His own Father. I think I know what it is— let me illustrate it by reference to a child.

A little youngster changes the whole atmosphere of a home. Is it not true that sometimes while you are playing with your child you suddenly ask yourself, Is he or she really mine? Is he or she really a part of me? That's it! That little youngster is a reflection of you, is part of you. When God gave to His Son as a gift those who believe on Him, He had in mind that indescribable joy of having a race of people who will manifest the grace and the glory of the Lord Jesus Christ. Parents get a thrill out of the fact that their child resembles them. Many a father in referring to his son, has used with much joy the expression, He's a chip off the old block! So, too, a Christian, by the time God has conformed him to the image of His Son, will be a reflection of Christ. He will be a perfect stone in the building, the spiritual building which the Scripture calls "an habitation of God through the Spirit," and of which our Lord Jesus Christ is the chief cornerstone. Every stone in that spiritual building will reflect the glory of the cornerstone. Every child of God will reflect the glory of our Lord Jesus Christ, for God hath set apart him that is godly for Himself.

But let us look more closely at that word "godly." If there is a passage of Scripture which makes one shudder it is the one found in the last of the New Testament epistles, that little letter written by Jude, wherein the Apostle describes the judgment that shall be visited in the future upon those who have rejected the testimony of God. He writes that this judgment will be executed upon "all, and to convince all that are *ungodly* among them of all their *ungodly* deeds which they have *ungodly* committed, and of all their hard speeches which *ungodly* sinners have spoken against him." How that word "*ungodly*" rings through this passage like the toll of a cemetery bell—ungodly, ungodly, ungodly, ungodly!

But in this 4th Psalm we have some who are spoken of as "godly." They have been *set apart for God* in contrast to the ungodly who have been *separated from God*. What makes a man become godly, a man who previously was ungodly?—for every godly man previously was ungodly. He did not become godly by virtue of his own good works, or his own godliness. He became godly because he received Christ; he believed His Word, and thus was constituted godly through the Holy Spirit's operation. A godly man is therefore one who formerly was ungodly, but by the grace of God has been put "in" Christ. It is by virtue of the godliness of Christ that the man is called godly.

You see, the door is open as wide as the gospel so that any man and every man can enter. That is what makes the gospel of Christ the most wonderful message under the sun. That is why some are perfectly willing to leave family, home, and friends to go out to the darkest part of Africa and live amongst savages or so-called heathen in order that the heathen might also hear of the grace of God that justifies all men from all their sin and sets them apart for God. By the way, "one set apart for God" is the meaning of the word "saint." When we speak of godly men we speak of saints. Concerning such men the Psalmist says that God will hear when they call. No wonder there follows the exhortation, "Stand in awe, and sin not: commune with your own heart upon your bed, and be still." Contemplate the wonderful grace of God that has enabled you, a sinner, but now a believer in the Lord Jesus Christ, to be an heir of God and a joint-heir with Christ. Then "Offer the sacrifices of righteousness, and put your trust in the LORD."

"THOU HAST PUT GLADNESS IN MY HEART"

In the closing section of the Psalm, David called attention to that which begets joy and peace. He wrote, "Thou hast put gladness in my heart, more than in the time that their corn and their wine increased." Whether you are a "New Dealer" and speak of the present business distress as "a recession," or whether you are an "anti--New Dealer," who calls it "a depression"— here, at least, is a passage from which all can profit.

Most of us erroneously assume that joy and serenity come from prosperity. We think the increase of corn and wine symbolizes the acme of all success. It is a sad illusion. If such were the case, the wealthy of our land would be the happiest, but more often they sojourn for a season at Reno and, generally speaking, are the least happy. It is a known fact that a man who lived to be more than seventy years of age, reputed to have given away a million dollars for each year of his life, deliberately took a wet cloth, put it to his side, and then shot himself. A gentleman who probably was this millionaire's closest friend told me that in all the years that he knew this millionaire he never once saw him smile and only once did he laugh and it sounded like the cackle of a rooster! You see, "corn and wine" does not put gladness into the heart, neither does it give peace.

We do not mean to decry riches, nor extol poverty. Poverty is no sure road to peace and gladness. Poverty usually begets sadness. It probably claims as many broken hearts as riches. The mistake is made when we assume that plenty makes for contentment.

This Psalm, in fact this entire Book, declares that gladness and peace come only from God. David said to the Lord, "Thou hast put gladness in my heart . . ." God is the author of peace and gladness. It is the viewpoint of Scripture that "godliness with contentment is great gain."

Because the human heart is treacherously wicked, it does not believe that God is the author of gladness. But sir, whoever you be, millionaire or pauper, rich man or poor man, professional man or manual laborer, God in Christ will put gladness in your heart and peace in your mind, if you but TRUST HIM.

Our Lord said to His disciples, ". . . my peace I give unto you: not as the world giveth, give I unto you." Therefore, "Let not your heart be troubled, neither let it be afraid." Again, He said to them, "In the world ye shall have tribulation: but be of good cheer; I have overcome the world."

God's offer of salvation is to all who will receive by faith His Christ. It is as free as the air we breathe and the sun that warms us and the water that cools us. It is His gift to all who call upon the name of the Lord.

PSALM FIVE—PART ONE

A MORNING HYMN

THE 5th Psalm is another Psalm of David which he dedicated to the chief Musician. In contrast to the preceding Psalm, which we discovered was an evening prayer, this is a morning hymn and, if you please, particularly appropriate to the Christmas season. The first section of the Psalm consists of the first three verses which read:

> "Give ear to my words, O LORD, consider my meditation.
>
> "Hearken unto the voice of my cry, my King, and my God: for unto thee will I pray.
>
> "My voice shalt thou hear in the morning, O LORD; in the morning will I direct my prayer unto thee, and will look up."

These three verses contain a remarkable revelation not only of the grace of God and the glorious person of God, but of the wonderful privilege that is given to a man to address God, to invite Him to give ear, consider, and hearken unto his voice. It ought to be the reverse. We ought to give ear to His words and to consider His meditations and to hearken unto the voice of His cry. Here God listens to a man. But before a man has the right to invite God to give ear to his words, it is necessary for that man to have already heard the Word of God.

Our Lord said, "The hour is coming, and now is, when the dead (that is the spiritually dead, those who are dead in trespasses and sins) shall hear the voice of the Son of God: and they that hear shall live." Again He said, "Verily, verily, I say unto you, He that heareth my word, and believeth on him that sent me, hath everlasting life, and shall not come into judgment; but is passed from death unto life." It is the viewpoint of Scripture that a man by nature and practice is a sinner, that he is dead in trespasses and sins. He has no spiritual life. He has no relationship with God. Any relationship that he might have had previously has been broken because of sin. There is no connection between God and man or rather between man and God. Man could never redeem himself, never pull himself up by his own bootstraps, or raise himself out of his spiritual death. God alone has the power to raise from the dead. It takes equally as much divine power to raise a man who is dead in his sins as it does to raise a man who is physically dead or to heal a man hopelessly ill.

For instance, on one occasion four friends of a paralytic man believed that their friend would be healed if he but came into contact with Christ. Thus they brought him into the presence of Christ. They found the house in which our Lord was speaking so crowded that they had to let their friend down through the roof. When Jesus saw their faith He said to the sick of the palsy, "Son, thy sins be forgiven thee." There were certain scribes present and they said within themselves, "Why doth this man thus speak blasphemies? who can forgive sins but God only?" Of course, our Lord perceived that they so reasoned, thus He asked them, "Whether is it easier to say to the sick of the palsy, Thy sins be forgiven thee; or to say, Arise, and take up thy bed, and walk?" The answer was evident. So our Lord demonstrated that He had the power to forgive sins by saying to the young man, "Arise, and take up thy bed, and go thy way into thine house." And the young man did that very thing.

Faith, therefore, comes by hearing, and hearing by the Word of God. Thus it is written that a man is born again by the incorruptible Word of God which liveth and abideth forever. Now, having heard the Word of God, having received the gospel, having believed in Christ, a miracle transpires in the life of such an individual. He is raised from spiritual death. He receives the forgiveness of sins. There is imparted to him a new life, which is eternal life. He is made a partaker of the divine nature. He becomes a dual personality. There is within him the germ seed of a new life. There is also within him the old nature. The new nature gives him a relationship with God, gives him the privilege of entrance into the presence of God to spread before Him his petitions and ask God to hear and to hearken unto him.

"GIVE EAR . . . CONSIDER . . . HEARKEN"

Notice the language which David employed in this Psalm. Remember this is a morning prayer. "Give ear to my words. . . ." The Word of God is written with the idea of conveying to our minds the personality of God. God is a Spirit and as such He has no body. When we ask God to give us His ear, we do not mean that He has an ear like we have, but we invite Him to listen to our words. But again, ". . . consider my meditation." David, did you mean to ask God to consider your thoughts as you meditate upon Him? That is exactly what David meant. ". . . consider my meditation." "My meditation of him," saith the Scriptures, "shall be sweet. . . ." In another place, the Psalmist said, "Let the words of my mouth, and the meditation of my heart, be acceptable in thy sight, O LORD, my strength, and my redeemer." The meditation is about God, so the Psalmist asked the Father to consider his meditation and to hearken unto the voice of his cry.

These three requests cover the entire sphere of human experience and every conceivable circumstance into which a believer may come. "Give ear to my words" would indicate a time of peace and serenity, a time of normal living and normal experience; "consider my meditation" would cover those periods when we lay aside the usual business of the day, either in the morning or evening, and simply meditate upon the grace and glory of God, whereas "Hearken unto the voice of my cry" would cover those periods of stress and difficulty when we are encumbered with cares and hardly know what to do. How wonderful that we then can cry to God, "Hearken unto the voice of my cry, my King, and my God. . . ."

Note the title David has given to God in this verse, "my King, and my God." This is the Christmas season. When one opens the New Testament Scriptures and reads the opening chapters of Matthew's Gospel, he discovers that the first question is "Where is he that is born King of the Jews?" Again, as one continues in the Gospel records and comes to the last of the Gospels, that written by John, he observes that in the closing verses of the 1st chapter our Lord interviews a man by the name of Nathanael. When Jesus saw Nathanael coming to Him He said, "Behold an Israelite indeed in whom is no guile!" Nathanael said, "Whence knowest thou me?" and the Lord answered, "Before that Philip called thee, when thou wast under the

fig tree, I saw thee." It was impossible from the human viewpoint to have
seen Nathanael under that fig tree, therefore Nathanael immediately responded, "Rabbi, thou art the Son of God; thou art the King of Israel."
That little babe, born in a manger in Bethlehem, is the King of Israel
—is the Lord of glory—is God. It is He to whom David addressed his
prayer when he called Him "my King, and my God." But some may say
Christ was born one thousand years after David wrote this Psalm. Yes,
that is true, but the prophet covered that point when he said, ". . . unto us
a child is born, unto us a son is given . . ." Our Lord Jesus Christ was
always the Son of God, but He became a child. He was always co-existent
with His Father. He was always in the bosom of the Father, but He was
made manifest at Bethlehem when He became the incarnate Word of God,
in order that He might reveal to men the heart of God and give Himself a
ransom for many.

Thus this Christmas as we in memory go back to Bethlehem to look at
the crib and the manger and the surrounding glory of that remarkable sight,
let us not forget that the manger led to the cross. It is the cross that gives
the manger its glory. It is the death of Christ that makes the life of Christ
to become a joy to the believer, for the death which He died justifies a
believing sinner, whereas by itself the life He lived condemns the sinner.

All that God is, Christ is; and all that Christ is, God is. All that we
know or ever shall know about God is revealed in Christ. As we look at
Him in the pages of the four Gospels and the further revelation of the New
Testament epistles we see our King and our God. He is a wonderful God
and a wonderful Saviour!

DIRECTING PRAYER

One further thought before we bring our meditation to a close. In the
3rd verse the Psalmist said, "My voice shalt thou hear in the morning, O
LORD; in the morning will I *direct* my prayer unto thee, and will look up."
There is something interesting about this passage of Scripture which does
not appear on the surface. If we were able to read the Psalm in the Hebrew
language we would immediately recognize that the word translated "direct"
is particularly pertinent. It happens to be a word which was used to describe
the laying in order of the wood used in connection with the sacrifice and the
placing of the victim upon the altar of wood. So we ought to read this 3rd
verse, "My voice shalt thou hear in the morning, O LORD; in the morning

will I *lay in order* my prayer unto thee, and will look up." In other words, the Psalmist was not satisfied with rushing into the presence of the Lord mumbling a few sentences and closing with a hurried "amen," then dashing out to his daily occupation. There was preparation in his prayer. There was a careful presentation of his prayer.

The scene is very much like that when Elijah led the people and the prophets of Baal to Mount Carmel. Elijah said unto the people:

> "I, even I only, remain a prophet of the LORD: but Baal's prophets are four hundred and fifty men.
>
> "Let them therefore give us two bullocks; and let them choose one bullock for themselves, and cut it in pieces, and lay it on wood, and put no fire under: and I will dress the other bullock, and lay it on wood, and put no fire under:
>
> "And call ye on the name of your gods, and I will call on the name of the LORD: and the God that answereth by fire, let him be God. And all the people answered and said, It is well spoken."

You will remember the scene. The prophets of Baal called upon their gods all day long but without avail. Finally as the time of the evening sacrifice was approaching, Elijah said:

> "Come near unto me. And all the people came near unto him. And he repaired the altar of the LORD that was broken down.
>
> "And Elijah took twelve stones, according to the number of the tribes of the sons of Jacob . . .
>
> "And with the stones he built an altar in the name of the LORD: and he made a trench about the altar . . .
>
> "And he put the wood in order, and cut the bullock in pieces, and laid it on the wood, and said, Fill four barrels with water, and pour it on the burnt-sacrifice, and on the wood.
>
> "And he said, Do it the second time . . . Do it the third time . . ."

And they obeyed as he commanded. Then Elijah looked up and addressed his prayer and said:

> "LORD God of Abraham, Isaac, and of Israel, let it be known this day that thou art God in Israel, and that I am thy servant, and that I have done all these things at thy word.
>
> "Hear me, O LORD, hear me, that this people may know that thou art the LORD God, and that thou hast turned their heart back again.

> "Then the fire of the LORD fell and consumed the
> burnt-sacrifice, and the wood, and the stones, and
> the dust, and licked up the water that was in the
> trench.
> "And when all the people saw it, they fell on their
> faces: and they said, The LORD, he is the God;
> the LORD, he is the God."

The scene at Mount Carmel is the scene in this 5th Psalm. *There* was the laying in order of the wood, *here* is careful thought, and quiet meditation in prayer; in *both* there is looking up to God with the assurance that the same God who answered Elijah's prayer with fire will answer David's prayer.

There is no doubt (and I speak to my own heart as well) that if we who have bowed the knee to the Lord Jesus would cease our hustle and bustle in prayer and take time for quiet meditation and careful communion with God in the morning, we too, will have the constant joy of looking up into His face, and never be disappointed.

PSALM FIVE—PART TWO

CAN GOD HATE?

WE have already considered the first three verses of the 5th Psalm which read:

> "Give ear to my words, O LORD, consider my
> meditation.
> "Hearken unto the voice of my cry, my King, and
> my God: for unto thee will I pray.
> "My voice shalt thou hear in the morning, O LORD;
> in the morning will I direct my prayer unto thee,
> and will look up."

In this meditation we shall consider the remaining verses, beginning with the 4th verse, which read:

> "For thou art not a God that hath pleasure in
> wickedness: neither shall evil dwell with thee.
> "The foolish shall not stand in thy sight: thou hatest
> all workers of iniquity.
> "Thou shalt destroy them that speak lies: the LORD
> will abhor the bloody and deceitful man.
> "But as for me, I will come into thy house in the
> multitude of thy mercy; and in thy fear will I worship
> toward thy holy temple.

"Lead me, O LORD, in thy righteousness because of mine enemies; make thy way straight before my face.
"For there is no faithfulness in their mouth; their inward part is very wickedness; their throat is an open sepulchre; they flatter with their tongue.
"Destroy thou them, O God; let them fall by their own counsels; cast them out in the multitude of their transgressions; for they have rebelled against thee.
"But let all those that put their trust in thee rejoice: let them ever shout for joy, because thou defendest them: let them also that love thy name be joyful in thee.
"For thou, LORD, wilt bless the righteous; with favour wilt thou compass him as with a shield."

As we noted previously, this is a morning prayer. In our preceding message we laid particular stress upon the 3rd verse which indicated the thoughtful prayer life of the Psalmist. There is no doubt that every morning he set aside a certain period of time for prayer and that he directed his petitions in an orderly manner with due consideration to the glory of God, the grace of God, and His majesty. All his prayer life found its genesis in the sacrifice. So we, in the sacrifice of our Lord Jesus Christ, find the basis of our approach unto God.

A COLLAPSING CIVILIZATION

In verses 4 to 6, the Psalmist voiced God's attitude concerning those who practice and have pleasure in wickedness, and the abhorrence of God toward the bloody and deceitful man, as well as His hatred toward the workers of iniquity.

Here is a revelation worthy of our consideration. It is generally acknowledged that our boasted 20th century civilization is rapidly coming to a cataclysmic crash. Many of our vaunted hopes for this civilization have already been shattered. The very things for which our forefathers labored and fought, such as their love of liberty, righteousness, and peace, are now being ridiculed. It is but a few generations ago that these things were looked upon as the great bulwarks of progressive appreciation of the responsibilities of man to his fellow-men and as a by-product of the Christian message and the Christian church. This breakdown, however, is not surprising to the man who knows his Bible, but it has been a rude shock to those who looked for great accomplishments and still greater advances in this century. The bloody and deceitful man is now in the place of power and the workers of iniquity are running rampant while the world, mad in its wild rush for pleasure, has come as close as possible to being "sodomite."

One cannot avoid viewing with alarm the condition of the world today. Look at Russia—if one dares to express his opinion of the present regime, or seeks a change or modification of it, he is immediately apprehended and slaughtered. It will never be known how many hundreds of thousands have been murdered in the last two decades in Russia. Take a look at China—it is a serious question whether at any time in the history of the civilized world such an atrocious violation of all decency even in warfare was ever perpetrated upon a people as that which has been visited upon China by a foreign power. The innocent slaughter of multitudes, women and children alike, is enough to nauseate every thinking and honorable person. Look at Spain—blood-drenched everywhere—someone has called it "Hell let loose." Take a look at Germany—does one find conditions different there? Alas, the rise of the bloody and deceitful man is apparent in all too many places in this world. It is a horrible picture and a sad commentary on man's inability to govern himself.

How long God will remain silent is a question no man can answer. As a friend of mine expressed it, "one marvels at the patience of God." But the character of God has not changed one iota. He still abhors the bloody and deceitful man. He continues to have no pleasure in wickedness. The foolish shall not stand in His sight. His hatred for the workers of iniquity has not changed. The only ray of hope which one can observe in this dark picture of our human civilization is the absolute assurance that God will not clear the guilty. Bloody and deceitful men shall have the wrath of God visited upon them. His judgments will sore perplex the workers of iniquity. The reckoning day inevitably comes.

But someone may raise the question—How can God hate; is hatred a characteristic of God? The Bible, which tells us that God is love, also tells us that God is hate. The very perfection of God, which in love expressed itself in the gift of His own Son on behalf of guilty sinners, finds its expression of perfect hatred against the workers of iniquity in judgment.

This 20th century civilization has sought to picture God as a namby-pamby character. Sentimentalism has dulled the hearts of the people, as the unthinking, untaught, and uncommissioned preacher has attempted to present a God contrary to the revelation of Scripture. From the beginning of Genesis to the end of The Revelation the hatred of God against sin has been given equal prominence with the love of God for repentant sinners. The trouble with this generation is that it possesses an inverted mind which has caused it to magnify its own importance and in turn reduced the character of God to a mere idea.

A friend recently suggested that I read an article entitled "An Observer Warns the Church," which appeared in one of the current magazines. If I get time I may read the article, but I answered this friend that I am not overmuch interested in what any observer has to say about the church. Neither am I greatly interested in what any unregenerate person says or thinks about God or His Word or His ministry in this world. For a man to presume to pass judgment upon the acts of God, the Word of God, and the ministry of God is to have an exaggerated ego, a wild vanity, and a distorted imagination. My primary interest is what *God thinks of me* and what *God thinks of the world;* what the Bible has to say about me and what the Bible has to say about the world. In other words, let's practise "thinking straight." The intelligent creature of the dust, fashioned by the hand of God, looks to his Creator and asks, ". . . what wilt thou have me to do?" He does not presume to tell God what he thinks of Him.

Oh, the patience of God, to listen to the braying of so many supposed leaders in this world. Oh, the patience of God, as He looks upon the wickedness of the world, in not immediately expressing His judgment by wiping us out entirely. Oh, the wickedness of man who presumes that he can get away with such an attitude and yet avoid a meeting with the Judge of the universe. But enough of that.

THE WAY OF GOD

David wrote, "But as for me, I will come into *thy* house in the multitude of *thy* mercy: and in *thy* fear will I worship toward *thy* holy temple. Lead me, O LORD, in *thy* righteousness because of mine enemies; make *thy* way straight before my face." Note the frequency of the word "thy" in these verses. It accurately reveals the attitude of a humble worshipper. He enters the house of God in the multitude of God's mercy and in God's fear he worships in God's holy temple. He asks to be led in God's righteousness and that God's way may be straight before his face. God, therefore, has a house—has a temple—has a righteousness which is available to those who will receive it—and He has a way in which He purposes His own should walk—and He has a mercy that transcends all human mercies. One cannot examine these verses without a recognition of the cardinal fact that salvation is of the Lord. It is the wonderful grace of God that answers the prayer of a worshipper who cries, "Lead me, O LORD, in thy righteousness because of mine enemies; make thy way straight before my face."

An illustration or two may prove enlightening. A short while ago one of our listeners wrote about a problem that was perplexing him. He was a Christian man; he had bowed his knees to the Lord Jesus Christ. He was in business and owned a store. He was concerned about keeping his store open on Sunday, the Lord's Day. He wrote to ask for my suggestion. I responded that I could not be conscience for him nor could he be conscience for me. I would not presume to tell him what he ought to do, but that the matter would have to be settled between the Lord and himself, but as the Lord was making him uneasy about it to consider it prayerfully before the Lord. In closing I stated that no man has ever yielded to the pressure of the Holy Spirit without receiving a commensurate blessing from God, who will never be in debt to any man. He wrote me again the other day thanking me for my letter and stating that he had determined by the grace of God to refrain from keeping his shop open on Sunday. Now he has just closed an order which more than compensates him for all the loss suffered since his shop was closed. He added that it has strengthened his faith in prayer and has caused him to rejoice with exceeding joy. You see God has a way and God will lead in righteousness any man who is willing to yield himself to the will of God. As this gentleman has experienced a blessing that more than compensated him for his loss, of course it is to be expected that his heart would be joyful and his spirit happy!

But I also had a letter from another gentleman this past week which brought a note of sadness as well as joy into my heart. This gentleman is a brilliant, educated young Chinese gentleman who has come to a definite knowledge of Christ and an increasing appreciation of His grace, through this ministry over the air. His heart is sad, however, over the plight of his people. He wrote me that at present his home town is a battleground and that he has not heard from his parents since August. But he added a statement in connection with his people which gave me great joy. He wrote, "If it is God's will, let it be done."

It is easy to serve God when He showers us with blessings and when everything our hands find to do prospers, but it is quite another matter to bow before God's will when our hearts are saddened and when the clouds have gathered and our minds are perplexed. No greater expression of faith can any believer render to God than the words which the old patriarch used when he said, "Though he slay me, yet will I trust in him . . ." Job who uttered that wonderful expression of faith did so in the midst of horrible disappointment and bitter woe. He was totally bewildered and had lost almost everything he possessed. But when the final purposes of God were revealed to him the Scripture states that the Lord blessed the latter end of Job more than his beginning and that the Lord turned the captivity of Job and gave him twice as much as he had before. God's grace has not changed. His ways have always been the same. He will give us double for all we suffer. Our obedience to faith is not misplaced.

The Sword of God and His Defense

In the latter part of this Psalm, David vented his imprecations against the wicked. In the 10th verse he wrote:

> "Destroy thou them, O God; let them fall by their own counsels; cast them out in the multitude of their transgressions; for they have rebelled against thee.

> "But let all those that put their trust in thee rejoice: let them ever shout for joy, because thou defendest them: let them also that love thy name be joyful in thee.

> "For thou, LORD, wilt bless the righteous; with favor wilt thou compass him as with a shield."

We will never understand these imprecatory Psalms apart from an appreciation of the absolute justice of God. But notice that David was clearly satisfied to leave the exercise of judgment in the hands of God. It is not for us to take up the sword. The Lord commanded Peter, "Put up thy sword . . ." We do, however, have the right to petition God in respect to our enemies. It is one thing to take the sword in our own hands and quite another matter to pray the Lord to take His sword out of the scabbard. We have a message of blessing in salvation unto the lost. It is not our business, therefore, to vent judgment against any. It is God's business to do that.

Finally, let us look for a moment at a beautiful thought in the 11th verse where David invited the believing sinner, saved by God's grace, to rejoice and shout for joy because God *defends* those who trust Him. It is wonderful to think that God *defends* His own!

While conversing with a gentleman over the phone this past week he told of a minister who called at his office to relate the fact that gossiping tongues were disturbing him. He was resentful about it: it was entirely unwarranted, unfair, and untrue, and he was angry. My friend had said to him, "Sir, if I were to be concerned about everything that is said about me I would be obliged to waste my whole time tracking down the comments and defending myself. I usually smile when I hear gossip and shrug my shoulders and ask, 'What next?' "

You see, God defends His own. It is a good thing that He does. What a mess we would make of our own defense? How vitally important that part of Christ's ministry is to us? For almost two thousand years He has been defending His own at the bar of God's justice. He is the mighty Counsellor, the advocate with the Father, the defender of every believer against the accuser of the brethren. Christ is not only our Saviour but also our advocate with the Father, not only our Lord but also our Counsellor, not only our righteousness but also our defender, not only our joy but also our glory. What Christ is to one He can be to all. If He is not all to you He can be that if you will bow your knee to Him and confess Him Lord.

PSALM SIX

A PENITENTIAL PSALM

WE begin the New Year with the 6th Psalm which in some ways is not particularly appropriate for a New Year's message, for it has much to say about chastisement, rebuke, vexation, death, weariness, groaning, tears, and aging eyes. It would have been more appropriate at a watch night service before the New Year had dawned. Nevertheless, I think we will find much of profit in this inspired song. It was written by David, the sweet singer of Israel.

Strange as it may seem, I invariably think of David as an innocent youth, with a ruddy complexion, full of zeal, and with the smell of the field and his father's sheep in the very weave of his garments. That is a good picture to keep in mind, for it at least will be an encouragement for the New Year.

But David waxed valiant in warfare, mighty in peace and leadership, yet marred his life with sin, and lived to old age when his eyes became dim and his blood no longer could warm him. So whether this be the 31st day of December or the 2nd of January, we need not shut our eyes to reality, nor should we desire to be lulled to sleep through the tickling of the ear by some sophistry of the current brand of human wisdom.

That ought to be a sufficient introduction for this Psalm, so let's get to the heart of the message and see what the Psalm has to say:

> "O LORD, rebuke me not in thine anger, neither chasten me in thy hot displeasure.
>
> "Have mercy upon me, O LORD; for I am weak: O LORD, heal me; for my bones are vexed.
>
> "My soul is also sore vexed: but thou, O LORD, how long?
>
> "Return, O LORD, deliver my soul: oh save me for thy mercies' sake.
>
> "For in death there is no remembrance of thee: in the grave who shall give thee thanks?
>
> "I am weary with my groaning; all the night make I my bed to swim; I water my couch with my tears.
>
> "Mine eye is consumed because of grief; it waxeth old because of all mine enemies.
>
> "Depart from me, all ye workers of iniquity; for the LORD hath heard the voice of my weeping.
>
> "The LORD hath heard my supplication; the LORD will receive my prayer.
>
> "Let all mine enemies be ashamed and sore vexed: let them return and be ashamed suddenly."

PROGRESS IN DOCTRINE AND REVELATION

We will never appreciate the message of any portion of Scripture unless we are acquainted with certain basic Biblical divisions. In the first place, our Bible is automatically divided into the Old and New Testaments, which of itself would indicate a break or a change in God's dealings with the sons of men. The Apostle John accurately described that change when he wrote, ". . . the law was given by Moses, but grace and truth came by Jesus Christ." Thus what was a common experience under the Old Testament economy is rebuked under the New Testament covenant. The law declared, ". . . an eye for an eye, and a tooth for a tooth," but our Lord said, ". . . resist not evil: but whosoever shall smite thee on thy right cheek, turn to him the other also." There is a progress in doctrine and revelation in the Scriptures so that as we consider any part of Old Testament Scripture it is well to look at it in the light of the fuller and more complete revelation through the person and ministry of our Lord and the New Testament Scriptures. This may appear a bit involved, but a little illustration will help.

A short time ago I heard an address given by a man who is an excellent preacher of the gospel. He referred to the case of Elijah on Mount

Carmel and how thoroughly routed were the prophets of Baal on that day and how, when God gave evidence that Elijah was on God's side and the prophets of Baal were not, the prophets of Baal were slain by the children of Israel. This preacher went on to say that all who preach a false message today ought to have the same judgment passed upon them: they should be slain. It may have been a slip of the tongue. He may not have meant what he said. It sounded like a justification of an inquisition. I do not believe the New Testament justifies such a statement. That principle was in vogue under the Old Testament economy. Then the false prophet was to be slain; but in the New Testament an entirely different principle is enunciated. Note what our Lord Jesus said about this in the 13th chapter of Matthew's Gospel, in the second of the seven parables in which He likened the kingdom of heaven unto a man which sowed good seed in his field. He said:

> ". . . while men slept, his enemy came and sowed tares among the wheat, and went his way.
>
> "But when the blade was sprung up, and brought forth fruit, then appeared the tares also.
>
> "So the servants of the householder came and said unto him, Sir, didst not thou sow good seed in thy field? from whence then hath it tares?
>
> "He said unto them, An enemy hath done this. The servants said unto him, Wilt thou then that we go and gather them up?
>
> "But he said, Nay; lest while ye gather up the tares, ye root up also the wheat with them.
>
> "*Let both grow together until the harvest:* and in the time of harvest I will say to the reapers, Gather ye together first the tares, and bind them in bundles to burn them: but gather the wheat into my barn."

This does not mean that we are to condone a false message or a false messenger. Indeed, truth is intolerant, though those whom it possesses are the most tolerant. The other day I read an item in the newspapers reporting excerpts from the 1937 Christmas message of a well-known and popular New York preacher, in which he was reported to have said, "I sometimes hear Him (Jesus) talked about by petty preachers who have relegated Him to a theological creed and made Him quite harmless, praising Him as though He were like a popular cosmetic advertised as colorless, odorless, and guaranteed not to irritate the tenderest skin." Now, that does sound "smart"—but the message of that preacher has been accomplishing that very thing in presenting a Jesus divorced of every irritating Biblical declaration which he calls a "theological creed," but with which God has gloriously surrounded His Christ and His Son in the Scriptures.

Dr. Samuel M. Zwemer, probably the greatest living authority on the Moslem world, wrote a book some time ago, a classic, entitled "The Glory of the Cross." As far as I know, no one has called Dr. Zwemer intolerant, in fact some have thought he has been too tolerant, yet that scholar prefaces or introduces the first chapter of his book, by a quotation from the pen of James Denney in his "Death of Christ." It reads:

> "As there is only one God so there can be only one gospel. If God has really done something in Christ on which the salvation of the world depends, and if He has made it known, then it is a Christian duty to be intolerant of everything which ignores, denies, or explains it away. The man who perverts it is the worst enemy of God and men; and it is not bad temper or narrow-mindedness in St. Paul which explains his vehement language (Galatians 1:8), it is the jealousy of God which has kindled in a soul redeemed by the death of Christ a corresponding jealousy for the Saviour. Intolerance like this is an essential element in the true religion. Intolerance in this sense has its counterpart in comprehension; it is when we have the only gospel, and not till then, that we have the gospel for all."

It is not our business to vent judgment and take the sword in our own hand to slay the false prophet or the exponent of a false religion. It is our business as believers in Christ to sow the good seed of the Word, to cultivate it with prayer, and water it with tears, and then to rest in the absolute assurance that the good seed when it falls into good ground will yield a good crop. Tares will be sown. The enemy will sow them. He always sows them in the field where the wheat is. We are not invited to combat the enemy (except to resist him). We are not called upon, before the harvest, to pluck up the tares which the enemy has sown. This illustrates the development of truth in the Scriptures, "the progress of doctrine," as one has called it.

Thus when we come to a passage like the 5th verse of the 6th Psalm where we read, ". . . in death there is no remembrance of thee: in the grave who shall give thee thanks?" we should remember that the Old Testament saints did not have the fuller revelation which we now have, whereby we know that a believer when he dies goes straight into the presence of the Lord and is at home with the Lord. In the Old Testament when a patriarch died it was said that he "was gathered unto his people," but in the New Testament believers go to be "with the Lord."

God's Character Unchanged

But again we must not assume from what we have just said that the character of God has changed one iota. He is still the righteous God who cannot clear the guilty, who hates sin, who must judge sin, and who corrects His children.

This 6th Psalm is the first in a series of seven Psalms which are called the "penitential Psalms." They are revelations of the moving of heart of a godly man who has sinned, but penitently cries to God for salvation, for cleansing, for deliverance from his sin or from the hand of the enemy.

Here the Psalmist said, "O LORD, rebuke me not in thine anger, neither chasten me in thy hot displeasure." If God were to rebuke us in anger or chasten us in His hot displeasure, where would any of us stand? Has God a displeasure so penetrating that it can be called "hot displeasure?" We, in this day, have lost sight of the righteousness and integrity of God. The Bible gives as much prominence to the fact that God is a consuming fire as it does to the fact that God is love. God does, however, make a distinction between His own and those who are not His own. In dealing with His own, as in the case of David, it is not in anger that He rebukes or in hot displeasure that He chastens. God rebukes and chastens as a father rebukes and chastens his son. There are times when chastening and rebuke are necessary. Failure to do so is to spoil the child. But the exercise of the rebuke and the motivating force behind it, is love. Of course, ". . . no chastening for the present seemeth to be joyous, but grievous: nevertheless afterward it yieldeth the peaceable fruit of righteousness unto them which are *exercised* thereby." David is a perfect example of one who was exercised by rebuke and chastening. As a result he ends his song as a conqueror. He directs his enemies to depart from him because the Lord hath heard his voice, the voice of his weeping, the Lord hath heard his supplications, and the Lord hath received his prayer.

Dr. Ironside, pastor of the Moody Memorial Church, of Chicago, has written an excellent work entitled "Except Ye Repent." The book is a clarion call for the old-time preaching of the gospel that linked repentance with faith. So often in our attempt to honor God's grace we say to a man who has given no evidence of the Holy Spirit's conviction of sin that all he has to do is believe. As a result our churches are filled with men and women who have given a mental assent to the historic and cardinal facts of Christianity, but upon whose life has never come the overwhelming power of the Holy Spirit which moves one to a consciousness of his sin and to cry out ,". . . what must I do to be saved?"

The Apostle Paul declared to the Ephesian elders when he left them for the last time that he had not withheld from them a single thing—he had preached a full gospel. He preached to them repentance towards God and faith in our Lord Jesus Christ. Dr. Ironside in his splendid book discusses the question of social reform which is such a prominent issue at present. He states that applied psychology, psychiatry, and ethical culture will not bring about the new birth and indwelling of the Holy Spirit. Whatever value there may be in the wise use of these systems, so far as combating certain conditions of the mind is concerned, they are utterly powerless to change the heart of man or to produce a new life. Dr. Ironside then refers to an excellent volume written by J. R. Oliver entitled "Psychiatry and Mental Health," and that gentleman, an authority in the field, frankly confesses that, after all, "the varied needs of mankind can best be met by the divine Psychiatrist, the one great Physician of the soul."

THE MORAL PROBLEM OF THE WORLD

The world has a moral problem. We have witnessed a breakdown in the moral life of the world; yea, even in our own country. The moral standards of men in public and political life probably never were as low as they are at this present moment. Men are willing to do almost anything to gain their point, to get control, to possess power. They become politicians instead of statesmen. If those in public life would bow the knee to the Lord Jesus Christ and lay bare their heart and conscience in the presence of God, our whole problem of government and peace would be solved. Righteousness exalts the nation. What is true of the nation and the public servant is equally true of the individual.

Recently I have become increasingly impressed with the mental degeneration which is taking place in our own country. As one drives through the countryside it is amazing to note the increasing number of institutions which are growing up like mushrooms all over the land to house those who are afflicted with mental diseases. Quite frequently (though not always) the breakdown in the mental has been preceded or caused by a breakdown in the moral realm. I chatted with a minister recently, a well-informed gentleman. On the outskirts of the city in which he ministers is one of these large institutions. As we drove around the place I was struck with its size and its numerous buildings. That minister told me that the city is now faced with a dangerous moral problem. Disease has broken out. The Mayor with the members of his Council are almost at their wits' end in their attempt to control it.

This is the first Sunday of January, but our old sins and ways are still with us. This is the beginning of a New Year, but moral declination has not been stopped. There is only one answer to the problem and that is repentance towards God and faith in the Lord Jesus Christ. This Book, the Bible, while it tells of the love of God and the redemptive work of Christ, also cries out on every page against sin. There is only one answer—repentance towards God and faith in the Lord Jesus Christ. So much for the world.

Regarding those of us who do believe, we must confess with shamefacedness that frequently the enemy has conquered and that our flesh has had the upper hand. As we become aware of defeat and failure our very bones become vexed. Ofttimes we water our couch with tears. But how we thank God from the bottom of our hearts that our Lord Jesus Christ is the complete Saviour and that "If we confess our sins, he is faithful and just to forgive us our sins, and to cleanse us from all unrighteousness." Let us not overlook the last part of this passage. He will forgive us our sins, to be true, but more than that He will cleanse us from *all* unrighteousness. One wonders if the moral decline in our nation is not due to the moral decline in the believer's standards of life, or rather his indifference to the high moral standards of Christ. If we who profess His name were fired with the Holy Spirit's power, were careful of our walk, and walked in fellowship and in the path of obedience to Him, the effect would be startling upon our fellow-citizens.

PSALM SEVEN

"A SONG OF THE SLANDERED SAINT"

THE introduction to the 7th Psalm reads, "Shiggaion of David, which he sang unto the LORD, concerning the words of Cush the Benjamite." If you have a name like mine or any other which indicates a Gentile origin you will probably say what I did when I first studied this Psalm—what does "Shiggaion" mean? Of course, if you were fortunate enough to be born a Hebrew you would know, but for the benefit of the rest of us let me quote an excellent introduction to this

Psalm written by Charles Haddon Spurgeon. He says, "As far as we can gather from the observations of learned men . . . this title seems to mean variable songs, with which also the idea of solace and pleasure is associated." There is much to be said in favor of Spurgeon's comment. He continues, "Truly our life-psalm is composed of variable verses; one stanza rolls along with the sublime metre of triumph, but another limps with the broken rhythm of complaint. . . ." He adds, "There is much bass in the saint's music here below," concluding that our experiences are as variable as the weather in England.

There are times, as when my good friend Beverly Shea sings, that I thoroughly enjoy a bass voice. When Spurgeon suggested that there is much bass in the saint's music here below, he referred to the hours of disappointment and grief which ofttimes are movingly characterized in a song which is pitched low in the minor key. But as in the case of one who has been gifted with a bass voice and who has combined it, as Beverly Shea has, with a beautiful Christian character—much joy, comfort, and support through a period of trial is ours. Disappointments are the common lot of all men. Can we soften the disappointments and in turn mellow our own hearts by singing our complaint unto the Lord?

Someone has suggested that this Psalm might be termed "a song of the slandered saint." Recently I had some correspondence with a gentleman who had heard some gossip (about himself) which supposedly came from a certain source and which, his informer told him, also involved certain other people. He immediately wrote to all the people supposedly involved, in the usual attempt to combat the slander that might have been made. I answered, expressing surprise at the contents of his letter. I had never heard anything at any time that even remotely touched upon the things mentioned in his letter. What's more, I also received a copy of a letter which the principal party sent to this gentleman denying the allegation. As I read these letters I thought within myself, Wouldn't it have been better if he had taken the matter and spread it before the Lord instead of spreading it before others? If this 7th Psalm is the song of a slandered saint, David sang it unto the Lord, not to others. Notice the introduction—"Shiggaion of David, which *he sang unto the LORD . . .*"

If you are being slandered by someone, do not get excited, do not get angry and fight back. If you are a child of God, spread the slander before the Lord and leave it there. You will remember that our Lord was slandered and the Scriptures say that He opened not His mouth. If your heart is right before the Lord, you need not worry about slandering tongues. Let us read the Psalm—

"O LORD my God, in thee do I put my trust: save me from all them that persecute me, and deliver me:

"Lest he tear my soul like a lion, rending it in pieces, while there is none to deliver.

"O LORD my God, if I have done this; if there be iniquity in my hands;

"If I have rewarded evil unto him that was at peace with me; (yea, I have delivered him that without cause is mine enemy:)

"Let the enemy persecute my soul, and take it; yea, let him tread down my life upon the earth, and lay mine honour in the dust. Selah.

"Arise, O LORD, in thine anger, lift up thyself because of the rage of mine enemies: and awake for me to the judgment that thou hast commanded.

"So shall the congregation of the people compass thee about: for their sakes therefore return thou on high.

"The LORD shall judge the people: judge me, O LORD, according to my righteousness, and according to mine integrity that is in me.

"Oh let the wickedness of the wicked come to an end; but establish the just: for the righteous God trieth the hearts and reins.

"My defence is of God, which saveth the upright in heart.

"God judgeth the righteous, and God is angry with the wicked every day.

"If he turn not, he will whet his sword; he hath bent his bow, and made it ready.

"He hath also prepared for him the instruments of death; he ordaineth his arrows against the persecutors.

"Behold, he travaileth with iniquity, and hath conceived mischief, and brought forth falsehood.

"He made a pit, and digged it, and is fallen into the ditch which he made.

"His mischief shall return upon his own head, and his violent dealing shall come down upon his own pate.

"I will praise the LORD according to his righteousness: and will sing praise to the name of the LORD most high."

We have a clear demonstration in this Psalm of the wisdom of pouring out our complaint before the Lord. David did not trust in his friends, some of whom, of course, would have come to his defense: he trusted in the Lord. He did not ask his friends to save him from his persecutors. He asked the Lord to save him. There are many characteristics about David which are highly commendable and which we, in this day, do well to adopt. For example, regarding the gossip, David said, ". . . if I have done this; if there be iniquity in my hands; if I have rewarded evil unto him that was at peace with me . . . Let the enemy persecute my soul, and take it . . ." Of course, anybody who knew David knew that instead of attacking King Saul he actually had delivered him. Saul was David's enemy. David was not Saul's enemy. Upon several occasions Saul was delivered into the hands of David, but David never lifted his hand against Saul, but rather allowed him to go scot-free. If I have been an enemy of the King, said David in effect, if I have rewarded evil to any man that was at peace with me, then let the enemy persecute me.

David continued, and in the 6th verse wrote, "Arise, O LORD, in thine anger, lift up thyself because of the rage of mine enemies: and awake for me to the judgment that thou hast commanded." This is another illustration of the principle discussed in the previous Psalm. It is not our business to vent judgment upon an enemy. We have a gospel with a positive message and one that brings a blessing. A Christian should at all times be above petty jealousies and slandering. He should never lower his standards and fight back with the same implements which the enemy used in attacking him. If a sword is to be used, if judgment is to be exercised, let the Lord do it. It is He who shall judge the people, as David said in the 8th verse. What's more, He will also judge David. He will judge you. He will judge me.

DAVID'S RIGHTEOUSNESS

David asked the Lord to judge him according to his righteousness and his integrity. That brings us to a very interesting point. Has a saint any such thing as his own righteousness, and his own integrity? In these broadcasts I have sought to make clear that a man is justified by faith apart from works—that our righteousnesses are as filthy rags in His sight—that a man has no righteousness of his own commendable to God—that the only righteousness satisfactory to God is that which is on a par with His own character —and the only One who had such a righteousness was our Lord Jesus Christ.

The Apostle Paul, in his letter to the Philippians, and in the 3rd chapter, chided those who trusted in themselves. He invited them to compare their lives with his. He said: If you have any confidence in the flesh I have more. I was circumcised the eighth day, of the stock of Israel, of the tribe of Benjamin, an Hebrew of the Hebrews; as touching the law I was a Pharisee; concerning zeal I persecuted the church; and as touching the righteousness which is in the law, I was blameless.

While that was all highly commendable in itself and particularly so concerning man's relationship to man, Paul said, "But what things were gain to me, those I counted loss for Christ." But more than that he said, "I count all things but loss for the excellency of the knowledge of Christ Jesus my Lord: for whom I have suffered the loss of all things, and do count them but refuse, that I may win Christ."

Do Paul and David contradict each other? If Paul had no confidence in his own righteousness and his own integrity, what about David when he said, ". . . judge me, O LORD, according to my righteousness, and according to mine integrity that is in me"? Is this a contradiction? I think not. Grace is free. It is as free as the air we breathe and as the sun which gives its healing rays. Grace is unmerited. It was when we were enemies of God that we were reconciled to Him by the death of His Son. But, asked the Apostle Paul in another place, because we are under grace is that license to sin? God forbid, said he, we that are dead to sin ought not to live any longer therein.

There is laid, therefore, upon the man who has confessed his faith in Christ, and who trusts in the death of Christ for his eternal salvation, a tremendous obligation in connection with his own personal character and life so that he is exhorted to live *as* becometh a saint. We do not live *to* become saints. We live *as* becometh saints. Take the case of one born into a royal family. That person does not live to become a member of that family but his demeanor should be such that it will become a member of a royal family.

To be true, here is where we fail most. I am frank to say that I know enough of myself so as not to lift a finger of accusation against anyone else. But I verily believe that an obligation rests upon us—upon all who have professed the name of Christ, to make certain that our lives manifest the fact that we know Him.

THE BRIDE'S TROUSSEAU

Again in the book of The Revelation, that marvelous closing book of the Bible, an interesting picture is drawn in the 19th chapter which touches on this subject. There we read of the marriage of the Lamb in the heavens. The multitudes praise God and invite each other to be glad and rejoice and give honor to the Lord "for the marriage of the Lamb is come, and his wife hath made herself ready." You see, *she made herself ready*. The bridegroom did not. When I married I did not make ready my bride. I had nothing to do with her trousseau. She made herself ready, she provided her own trousseau. Here is a passage which declares that the bride of the Lord made herself ready and "to her was granted that she should be arrayed in fine linen, clean and white: for the fine linen is the righteousness of saints." If you have a marginal reference Bible you will notice that the word "righteousness" in that passage is more specific than merely describing a character. It refers to "acts done," so that literally translated, it would read that the fine linen is the righteous acts of the saints. Is it possible that the bride of the Lamb weaves her own wedding garment? Of course we cannot dogmatize on that subject. We know she washes her garment in the blood of the Lamb. That is why it is white. But there is a thought in this passage which we would do well to consider. The Bible says that if we judge ourselves we shall not be judged. For example, in my life I do something contrary to Christian standards and I judge myself for it in the presence of the Lord, that is, I say to the Lord—I am sorry, I should not have done it, it was wrong—I have thus judged myself. It is not necessary that I be judged by God later for that sin. The blood of our Lord cleanses from all sin. But if I do not judge my sin I make it necessary for Him to do so. Therefore, for a Christian to maintain his righteousness he should judge himself repeatedly in the presence of the Lord and determine to yield himself to the domination of the Holy Spirit of God.

We have gone into this subject at length because those who believe in the grace of God have been accused of being indifferent about their lives and character. It has been said that they base their faith upon an event that took place in history about two thousand years ago instead of on a living Christ. Indeed, if it were not for the fact that our Lord Jesus Christ is a living Saviour, making continuous intercession for us, we could not be saved to the uttermost as the Scriptures declare we are. Salvation is a wonderful thing. It is complete.

I do trust that those who have not received Christ will take this message to their own heart as well. You cannot save yourself. You cannot make yourself righteous. You are a sinner like the rest of us. You need a Saviour like the rest of us—the Saviour who can save from sin, the only Saviour, the Lord Jesus Christ.

We do not have the time to touch upon all the verses of this 7th Psalm but we have touched upon the general tenor of the Psalm. In closing notice verse 17, which reads, "I will praise the LORD according to his righteous, ness: and will sing praise to the name of the LORD most high."

When there is any singing to be done, any praising to be done, it is to be based on God's righteousness. That righteousness God freely provides.

The Scripture declares that He who knew no sin was made sin for us that we in turn might be made the righteousness of God in Him. The transaction at the cross was a double transaction. Christ took our place and our sins. We now take His place and His righteousness. That is the gospel in a nutshell. Believe it and be saved—receive Him. Let Him live His life in you. Disappointments will come, slandering tongues may gossip about you. What of it? Your defense will be in your God and you will rejoice and praise the Lord and sing praises in His name.

PSALM EIGHT—PART ONE

PERFECTION OF PRAISE

THE 8th Psalm is a masterpiece; its language is beautiful; its message is unique.

I recall when mother took us children to church each Sunday, that I often wondered how it was possible for a preacher to have something new to give each time he preached. Did he ever exhaust his subject? I have since discovered that the difficulty is not there, but rather to get sufficient time to unfold the subject; so vast, indeed, is it. No one has ever exhausted the Bible.

There is enough in this 8th Psalm for ten radio messages. The Psalm begins and ends with the same expression, "O LORD our Lord, how excellent is thy name in all the earth!"

David called the Lord, "our Lord." That is interesting for it denotes faith. It also reveals that it is possible for the Lord to become ours, in an intimate way. There are those who call themselves liberals who ridicule the idea that all men are not the children of God and that it is possible for the Lord to have a relationship to one man but not to another. We have all heard the phrase "the brotherhood of man and the Fatherhood of God." It sounds religious, even Christian, but it is decidedly unscriptural. We are members of the human race, but more specifically a member of our own family, and as such we have a more intimate relationship to our family than we have to all other men. So God, while He is the Creator of all, is not necessarily the Father of all men. It is the Bible view that God is the God and Father of our Lord Jesus Christ, and the God and Father of all those who believe in Him. The Bible declares that we "are all the children of God *by faith in Christ Jesus.*" How does one become a child of God? By faith in Jesus Christ. Those who have faith in Jesus Christ have found an intimate, personal relationship with God which others do not possess. But it is possible for all men to become the children of God. None need be excluded. The invitation is world-wide. It is written: "For God so loved the *world,* that he gave his only begotten Son, that *whosoever* believeth in him should not perish, but have everlasting life."

THE NAME OF GOD

And now note the subject of David's exclamation: "O LORD our Lord, how excellent is thy name in all the earth! who hast set thy glory above the heavens." David had been meditating upon some very important matters.

First, he observed the earth. As he did so he discovered that the name of the Lord is excellent in all the earth.

Second, he learned something about the heavens also, and what is more, even though he lived almost three thousand years ago, he also observed that there was something beyond the heavens. Talk about the scientific accuracy of the Scriptures—it is nothing short of amazing!

Third, moreover, David learned that God has a glory, and that He has set this glory above the heavens. Only an inspired penman could put all' this in a short verse of twenty-one words. This Book is so evidently the Word of God that dull indeed is that spirit which fails to feel the breath of God in it.

Geologist and scientists have searched the earth to know its secrets, its power, its history, and its message. But so often while they stood aghast at the display of law, order, and detail, they failed to observe that God has also written *His name* in all the earth. What did David mean by saying that God had written *His name* in all the earth?

Perhaps we can best answer that question by referring to what our Lord said when two of His disciples informed Him that some Greeks wanted to see Him. This took place on the evening of what we call Palm Sunday. It was thus the beginning of the most important week of our Lord's ministry.

He knew that the plaudits of the crowd that early Sunday morning would lead, not to His coronation, but to His crucifixion. He had stirred the entire countryside. It was not surprising therefore that certain Greeks who had come to worship at the Passover feast should inquire about Him. They asked one of His disciples, saying: "Sir, we would see Jesus." This disciple told another, and both related their request to the Lord. He gave them a startling reply; in fact, one that on the surface seemed ambiguous. The reply was: "The hour is come, that the Son of man should be glorified. Verily, verily, I say unto you, Except a corn of wheat fall into the ground and die, it abideth alone: but if it die, it bringeth forth much fruit." Continuing He said: "Now is my soul troubled; and what shall I say? Father, save me from this hour: but for this cause came I unto this hour." Later in the same talk He said: "Now is the judgment of this world: now shall the prince of this world be cast out. And I, if I be lifted up from the earth, will draw all men unto me."

We concede that this seems a somewhat ambiguous response to the inquiry raised by these Greeks. But when we examine it more closely we shall find instead of it being ambiguous, it is decidedly revealing! Our Lord was reminding these Greeks of the very principle which David had expressed in the opening verse of this Psalm: ". . . how excellent is thy name *in all the earth!*" These Greeks, being Gentiles, did not have a written revelation from God as did the Jews in their inspired writings, but nevertheless, they were not without a witness in that the invisible things of God are clearly *seen*, being *understood* by the things that are made, even His eternal power and Godhead. They were without excuse. Christ invited these Greeks to observe and understand the principles that God had written into nature, where His own name is so excellently revealed. Consider the corn of wheat. In order that it may sustain mankind in the form of bread it is necessary for it to fall into the ground and die; otherwise it is valueless as far as sustaining power is concerned. If it does not fall into the ground and die, it abides alone. Our Lord taught, therefore, that what took place in a corn of wheat was symbolic of His own death and resurrection. Therefore, the principles which are revealed in the Scripture concerning the redemptive work of Christ are the very principles which God has written into creation. Our physical lives are sustained by bread and meat, which are available to us through the death of the grain of wheat and through the death of the animal that becomes our meat.

THE BLOOD "THEORY"

There are those who insist that the Bible is repugnant to them in magnifying the death of our Lord Jesus Christ, and in proclaiming the blood as the basis for redemption. They say: This "theory" belongs to the slaughterhouse age. These men entirely overlook the fact that while this principle of redemption in the Bible is repugnant to their aesthetic nature, they find no such a repugnance when sitting down to a Thanksgiving Day feast to partake of the blessings of the field which God has so richly provided. They could not possibly assimilate their Thanksgiving Day dinner before death and resurrection had taken place, in respect to the food products placed upon the table.

Indeed, practically every principle in the Scripture finds a counterpart in creation. That is not surprising. It is what one would expect. Since God is the author of the Bible, the principles which He enunciates therein must conform to the principles which He has ordained in the operation of creation. As these principles are the same, they become one more link in the great chain of evidence of the inspiration of the Scriptures.

I cannot close this reference to the excellency of His name in all the earth, without drawing attention to Calvary, the place where God most perfectly and most excellently revealed His name. Calvary, in the Hebrew tongue is Golgotha, which means "the place of a skull." Some have suggested that the mount (Mt. Calvary) received its name from the outline which nature carved into it which resembled the form of a man's skull. Others have thought that it was named thus from the fact that it was a burying ground. But whatever it was, it is singular that God revealed unto us His name, His person, His love, His wisdom, and His power so excellently at the place of a skull.

Such a place must have its message. Not only do we find at that cross the provision for our sin, but we will find at that place the answer to every intellectual problem. It is not only when we have come to the end of our sin that we find a ready remedy at Calvary, but when we have come to the end of human reason in its attempt to know God, we find at the place of a skull the revelation of the wisdom of God.

So much for the earth in which His name is so excellently found. In the last half of the 1st verse, David wrote: "who hast set thy glory above the heavens."

The heavens that we see during the day might be called the "first" heaven, the abode of the clouds, the heaven formed by the atmosphere. At night, we are able to penetrate beyond. We discover that the stars have their abode in another heaven. We might call it the "second" heaven. But as every astronomer knows, this whole system of worlds revolves around other worlds and all seem to revolve about a center. If you please, that center is the very throne of the eternal God. How scientifically accurate is David when he said, Thou "hast set thy glory above the heavens." Above the abode of the stars is God's throne. By the side of that throne, on the testimony of Scripture, our Lord Jesus Christ is seated. He is the glory of God. David in another Psalm foresaw the resurrection of Christ. In this 8th Psalm he foresaw the exaltation and ascension of our Lord Jesus Christ. He saw Him seated above the heavens!

THE PERFECTION OF PRAISE

David probably received his inspiration to write this Psalm on an occasion when he sat on the hillsides of Judea looking up into the starry heavens. He studied the heavens through the telescope of faith. My, what he saw that night! He penetrated beyond the heavens to the very throne of God. There he saw the glory of God. That magnificence gave him a study in contrasts. He dropped his "telescope" to gaze at a most helpless sight, a suckling babe. This caused him to write, "Out of the mouth of babes and sucklings hast thou ordained strength because of thine enemies, that thou mightest still the enemy and the avenger."

Our Lord referred to this passage when the Pharisees asked Him to silence the children who were crying out to Him, "Hosanna to the son of David." He answered them, "Yea; have ye never read, Out of the mouth of babes and sucklings thou hast perfected praise?"

Note the liberty our Lord took with this verse. He revealed that when David said, "Out of the mouth of babes and sucklings hast thou ordained strength," this strength of babes lay in their ability to praise Him. Perfection of praise is to be found in the mouth of a babe. How that puts us "grown-ups" to shame. It also reminds us that our Lord said, "Except ye be converted, and become as little children, ye shall not enter into the kingdom of heaven."

I am very fond of the writings of Edmund Flegg. He is a French Jew residing in Paris. Several of his works have been translated into English. His latest, "The Land of Promise," which has an interesting introduction by Ludwig Lewisohn, contains one of the most startling paragraphs I have read in current literature. Mr. Flegg, in his foreword, dedicates this book to his unborn grandson. He informs him that he is about to leave for Palestine to write a life of Jesus. The paragraph reads: ". . . Jesus, Thou who troublest the sleeplessness of my childhood with innocent regrets; Son of Israel, whom Israel denies yet can not ignore, shall I at last know thee through a soul that has learned what it is that estranges me from thee, what it is that draws me to thee? I have searched for thy life in books without number. I only found in them a confused image. Shall I at last meet thee there—see thee face to face, under the horizon upon which thy eyes have gazed?"

Here is an intelligent Jew longing to know the person of Jesus. He reveals that in his childhood there was something about Jesus which was sufficiently captivating to have troubled his sleep with innocent regrets. That is not strange, for there was something fascinating about the personality of Jesus so that children felt perfectly at home in His presence. Is it any wonder the Psalmist wrote, "Out of the mouth of babes and sucklings hast thou ordained strength . . ."

Who of us have not been silenced in our unbelief by the unswerving faith of a child. I shall never forget visiting at the home of some friends where the father was very ill. I had visited the father at the hospital earlier in the day. I decided to drop in at their home later that evening. It was about Christmas time. There are four splendid children in that family. We gathered about the piano and sang a few carols. Some of the children recited the "pieces" they were to give at their Sunday School exercises. Then we all knelt to pray. Upon rising, the mother had a few tears in her eyes. "Chubby," a girl of about eight, said, "Mother, why can't we trust Jesus? He said if we would pray, He would answer. We have prayed that He would heal Daddy." Needless to say, their Daddy became well.

The most remarkable illustration of the truth of the second verse of this Psalm is recorded in the Scripture. It requires that we take the shoes from off our feet. The incident took place in the house of Elizabeth when Mary, her cousin, came to visit her. Both women were great with child. When Elizabeth heard the salutation of Mary as she entered the house, the babe leaped in her womb. Elizabeth, filled with the Holy Ghost, addressed Mary with a loud voice: "Blessed art thou among women, and blessed is the fruit of thy womb. And whence is this to me, that the mother of my Lord should come to me? For, lo, as soon as the voice of thy salutation sounded in mine ears, the babe leaped in my womb for joy." Then Mary gave her magnificat —"My soul doth magnify the Lord . . ." Here was an unborn child, John the Baptist, leaping with joy, bearing his testimony to Christ, who likewise was cradled in the womb of His mother. I know of no greater illustration of David's statement: "Out of the mouth of babes and sucklings hast thou ordained strength." Or, as our Lord added, "perfected praise."

PSALM EIGHT—PART TWO

THE MAN WHOM GOD MADE A LITTLE LOWER THAN HIMSELF

IT is apparent upon a close reading of the 8th Psalm that David was presenting a striking study in contrasts. We have already discussed his first study in which he contrasts the glory of God, which is set above the heavens, with a suckling child. His second study contrasts the glory of the heavens, the moon and the stars, with man. This study commences with verse 3 where we read: "When I consider thy heavens, the work of thy fingers, the moon and the stars, which thou hast ordained; What is man, that thou art mindful of him? and the son of man, that thou visitest him?"

Sometimes man becomes impressed with his own importance. But a visit to the countryside to observe the beauty of the starry heavens has a decidedly sobering effect upon the "ego"! David was a great naturalist. In this Psalm he expressed the viewpoint of a true naturalist, as he was impressed with the Milky Way, the glory of the moon, and the handiwork of God. First he observed the order in creation and was overwhelmed at the worlds within worlds. He then lowered his eyes to behold man. As he did so, he raised the question: "What is man, that thou art mindful of him?"

Look at this word *mindful*. It is a two-syllable word made up of the words *mind* and *full*. When, therefore, David used this word in connection with God's attitude to man, it is evident that he was aware that all of God's mind was centered in man. Has it ever occurred to us that God's mind is full of man? His thoughts and the expression of those thoughts are all occupied with man. It is because God is so "mind-full" of man that David asked the question: "What is man, that thou art *mindful* of him? and the son of man, that thou visitest him?" These are truly logical questions. They demand an answer.

David followed the raising of these questions by a description of the man whom God placed upon the earth. In our English translation of the

Bible we read the following in verse 5: "For thou hast made him a little
lower than the angels, and hast crowned him with glory and honour." It is
interesting to note in passing that David did not entertain any theories of
evolution! He recognized that man was *made*, not evolved. And that man
was *made* "a little lower than the angels."

"MADE A LITTLE LOWER THAN ELOHIM"

Some time ago, I was greatly impressed when my attention was drawn
by a friend to the word in this verse translated *angels*. If any of you are
Hebrews, and have your Hebrew Bible open, you will immediately observe
that David declared that man was made "a little lower than Elohim." Also,
you will recall that Elohim is the first name which is ascribed to God in the
Scriptures. In the very first verse in the Bible we read: "In the beginning
God created the heaven and the earth." The word Moses used in that verse
for *God* is this word *Elohim*. The only place in all the Bible where *Elohim*
is translated *man* is in this 8th Psalm. In all other places, the word is
properly translated *God*. Probably the scholars under King James were
aghast at David's use of the word *Elohim* and thus decided to make use of
its meaning, which is "the strong one"—and applied it to the angels.

What a remarkable person is this man of whom David said that God
had made him a little lower than Himself. This is in perfect accord with
the record in Genesis where the conversation of the Godhead is recorded in
preparation for the creation of man. "Let us make man in our image, after
our likeness . . ." Observe the plural pronouns used in this verse—it is let
us make man in *our* image. A study of both the Old and New Testaments
will reveal that the Godhead is a plurality in unity. Certainly there must
have been One who was co-equal with the Father whom He addressed when
He said *Let us*. I believe the Father referred to Christ—His own Son, in
whose image and likeness man was created.

As we read through this 8th Psalm, it is evident that the man of whom
David wrote was Adam, the man whom God originally created, and who is
the head of our race. God made Adam a little lower than Himself; He
crowned him with glory and honor; He made him to have dominion over
the works of His hands; He put all things under his feet.

It is not necessary to dwell long upon the present man whom we see and
live with. He is anything but crowned with glory and honor. He does not
have dominion over the works of God's hands. He has not all things put

under his feet. In fact, the man whom we see is the extreme opposite. His dignity is impaired, his visage is marred, he is under the domination of the works of God's hands; in fact, he is a slave to the works of his own hands. How evident this is in this mechanical age of which we so greatly boast.

It was God's intention when Adam was placed upon this earth, that he should literally be a god over this creation. He therefore crowned Adam "with glory and honour" and gave him a dignity, if you please, commensurate with his position of complete domination over the sphere in which he was placed.

In the next two verses, 7 and 8, the Psalmist detailed for us the dominions that were placed under Adam's rulership: "All sheep and oxen, yea, and the beasts of the field. The fowl of the air, and the fish of the sea, and whatsoever passeth through the paths of the seas."

Today man is a slave, not a king. I saw a comic strip the other day which showed how clearly man wants to be delivered from his serfdom. It was a picture of a man suddenly awakened by the rude clanging of an alarm clock at 6 A. M. He looked at the clock; attempted to open his eyes wide by rubbing them, when suddenly a flash entered his mind—It's the 30th of May!!—Behold—it's a holiday—He became elated—was tempted to make faces at the old clock—turned himself to enjoy a few more hours of sleep. But before he did, he smiled with that contented expression so aptly put by Webster—"*ain't it a grand and glorious feelin'?*"

Wouldn't it be *grand* if suddenly we were released from servitude and were given the reins of rulership? If, instead of being in constant fear of the beasts of the field, and of all other creation, we should be placed in complete domination over them?

"But We See Jesus"

It would be exceedingly discouraging, if we did not have a further revelation upon this 8th Psalm in the New Testament. It is not pleasant to be reminded of the fall of man, which is so absolutely complete that a little "picayune" insect—a microbe—can attack him. And though he be an almost perfect specimen of human vigor, health, and power, that little microbe can attack him at an unsuspected moment and overpower that powerful man and cause him to lie helpless upon his back. I repeat—it would be most discouraging if no further revelation were given concerning the man whom God intended should rule as a god upon the earth, and who should manifest His glory and honor. I do no dishonor to God in saying that if this were all, then it would be God's defeat, as well as man's failure.

But there is a further revelation. In the 2nd chapter of the letter to the Hebrews, this very passage from the 8th Psalm is discussed and expounded. In the opening verses of that chapter we are exhorted ". . . to give the more earnest heed to the things which we have heard, lest at any time we should let them slip." Knowing that

> "If the word spoken by angels was stedfast, and every transgression and disobedience received a just recompense of reward;
>
> "How shall we escape, if we neglect so great salvation; which at the first began to be spoken by the Lord, and was confirmed unto us by them that heard him;
>
> "God also bearing them witness, both with signs and wonders . . . and gifts of the Holy Spirit, according to his own will?"

Whereupon the inspired writer said, "For unto the angels hath he not put in subjection the world to come, whereof we speak. But one in a certain place testified, saying: (That one is David. That testimony is borne in the 8th Psalm, and the Holy Spirit quotes it), What is man, that thou art mindful of him? or the son of man, that thou visitest him? Thou madest him a little lower than the angels; thou crownedst him with glory and honour, and didst set him over the work of thy hands: Thou hast put all things in subjection under his feet . . ." The Holy Spirit takes cognizance that such is not the case with man now for He immediately adds: ". . . For in that he put all in subjection under him, he left nothing that is not put under him. But now we see not *yet* all things put under him." What then, do we see? Here follows the revelation of Christ—"But we see Jesus. . . ."

He is the man, the God-man through whom God will rescue the man upon whom His image has been marred, and who is now subservient to all things. It is through Christ that God will raise defeated man and put him in the place of exaltation and honor which He originally intended him to have, in fact, even beyond that. To accomplish this purpose, the Holy Spirit said concerning Christ: " . . . we see Jesus, who was made a little lower than the angels for the suffering of death, crowned with glory and honour: that he by the grace of God should taste death for every man."

We have here a declaration that our Lord was made a little lower than the angels for the sole purpose of the suffering of death—that He by the grace of God should taste death for every man. Therefore, on the testimony of the Scripture, God sent His Son to the cross and made Him taste death for *every* man. God made possible the cross of Calvary.

"BECOMING TO GOD"

The preaching of the cross is not appealing to the natural man. To some it seems a defeatist philosophy. To them it is distasteful to think that God had to go to such extremes in order to bring His purposes to pass. Men have thus referred to the cross as "a repulsive sight."

The Scriptures knew that such would be the case; therefore, in verse 10 of the 2nd chapter of Hebrews, God justified Himself by stating through the Holy Spirit, that ". . . It was *becoming to him*, (God) for whom are all things, and by whom are all things, in bringing many sons unto glory, to make the captain of their salvation perfect through sufferings."

It is awesome to consider that the death which our Lord died was absolutely *becoming* to God. In this passage the Holy Spirit gives us to understand that it was becoming to the dignity of God to subject His Son to the indignity of the cross in order that through death He might bring many sons unto glory.

It is disappointing to the spirit of man to contemplate the disaster that sin has wrought in this world, and to consider the pinnacle from which man fell. But it is stimulating to a spirit of worship to contemplate the redemption of man which God wrought out in the death of His Son, and the pinnacle to which man will rise, and in fact already is risen, which is so beautifully expressed by the Holy Spirit through Paul as "seated together in the heavenly places *in* Christ Jesus." Therefore, David in this Psalm also looked into the future to the accomplishments of God's purposes through the man Christ Jesus, and thus closed his Psalm with the same expression with which he opened it—"O LORD our Lord, how excellent is thy name in all the earth!"

There is just one more thought I would like to express before closing our meditation. It refers to the expression ". . . thou hast put all things under his feet." Frequently Christians are so occupied with the things of this world that they do not bear effective witness in harmony with their position in Christ. It is the privilege of every believer in Christ to have all things under his feet rather than to be dominated by things. It has been said that the nobility of ancient Rome had a custom which illuminates this passage. "They wore an ornament in the shape of a moon under the sole of their shoes to show that all worldly things were mutable, and by that little ornament they declared that they lived above the earth—in fact, above the moon."

The application is all too evident. As believers in Christ we have been raised. Our affections should not be set upon the things of this earth, but on the things that are in heaven. We truly should so walk as those ancient aristocrats of Rome walked, with our feet above the moon.

PSALM NINE

WHEN GOD SITS ON HIS THRONE

THERE are times when inquisitiveness pays, as when Moses, upon seeing that strange sight—a burning bush which yet was not burnt, said, "I will now turn aside, and see this great sight, why the bush is not burnt." In response he heard the voice of the Lord and received the call to be the instrument in God's hands to deliver the children of Israel out of the Egyptian bondage. So, at times, it does pay to be inquisitive. But in the case of the inscription given to this Psalm, it seems nothing very much is to be gained. If we knew everything this side of the glory, we would not enjoy the heavens as much as God intends us to enjoy them.

There have been varied suggestions offered by scholars and students as to the application of the word "Muthlabben." Actually the word means "death of the son," but to what son David referred is a great question. I do not know. Some have suggested Goliath, others that little unnamed babe of David's which Uriah's wife bore to him and which died seven days after its birth. Or it might have been some enemy. However, let us not spend time on what we do not know. I admit my ignorance on a great many subjects! There are many things about the Bible that I am most anxious to know but do not know, yet I know that I shall know!

However, let us revel in the knowledge of the things we do know. For instance, I know that I have passed from death unto life, ". . . for I know whom I have believed, and am persuaded that he is able to keep that which I have committed unto him against that day." There are many things about the Lord and my relation to Him, the knowledge of which has produced great joy in my soul so that I am perfectly at peace regarding the things

I do not know. This is one of them. When I see David face to face I shall
ask him whom he had in mind when he wrote this Psalm. If you see him
before I do you might ask him.

GOD'S GREATEST WORK

We have entitled our message on the 9th Psalm, "When God Sits On
His Throne." You say: God always sits on His throne! I am not so sure
about that, any more than I entertain the idea that all our Lord is doing
is sitting on the right hand of God the Father waiting until His enemies are
made His footstool. I believe that God is active in the heavens, just as our
Lord is actively interceding on behalf of His own. But there are times when
He sits on His throne, and when He does we raise the question—What does
God do?

To begin with let us read the first two verses of this Psalm: "I will
praise thee, O LORD, with my whole heart; I will shew forth all thy marvellous works. I will be glad and rejoice in thee: I will sing praise to thy
name, O thou most High." We pause here for a moment and detour from
our subject to consider the perfect illustration we have in these two verses of
the substance of praise. I had occasion this week to write to a gentleman
on this subject. I stated in effect that there are men who revel in their
experiences and others who revel in Christ. There are those whose faith
centers in their experiences and others whose faith centers in Christ. David
never found any occasion to talk about himself. When it came to praise and
witness it was all about the Lord and what He had done. David said, ". . .
I will shew forth all *thy* marvellous works." Salvation is of the Lord. It is
His work. We are simply the beneficiaries.

Dr. Lewis Sperry Chafer gave an address in New York recently entitled
"Justification." In the course of that address he gave forth an expression
which thrilled my soul. In speaking of God's mighty work in justifying a
sinner he said this, "The greatest thing that God ever did or ever will do is
to put a sinner in heaven and make him as perfect as His own Son."

Men sometimes are amazed at this world and well they should be. The
work of God, the power of God manifested in creation, is enough to overwhelm the keenest intellect; but that work is nothing in comparison with
His most marvelous work—justifying a sinner and placing him in the
heavens and making him as perfect as His own Son so that he will forever
and ever be a perfect image of Jesus Christ.

David said, ". . . I will shew forth all *thy* marvellous works. I will be glad and rejoice in thee: I will sing praise to thy name, O thou most High." This praise is the expression of one who knows the Lord. But what about those who are our enemies as well as the Lord's. David had them. We all have them. Concerning them David said in the 3rd verse, "When mine enemies are turned back, they shall fall and perish at thy presence." David was not talking about his own presence but of the presence of the Lord and he continued in verse 4 saying, "For thou hast maintained my right and my cause; thou satest in the throne judging right."

JUDGING RIGHTLY

The first thing we learn therefore about the Lord when He occupies His throne is that He exercises judgment rightly and in so doing, as in the case of David, He maintained David's right and cause while He rebuked the nations, destroyed the wicked, and put out their name forever and ever.

Chiefly, there are two things that transpire when our Lord occupies His throne—the one is justification of His own and the other is the condemnation of His enemies.

Why should one talk so confidently and complacently about God occupying His throne and judging rightly? Is this man so foolish as to presume that his integrity is beyond question and that God is satisfied with him and will find no cause for condemnation in him? To believe such a thing would be the height of folly.

I am frank to say I have not the slightest qualms about the judgment of God, though at the same time I am equally frank in saying that I am just as much a sinner, and inexcusably so, as any other man. My confidence, my willingness to discuss this subject is based not on anything that I have done but on the glorious fact of what the Lord Himself has done.

There is a passage in the 43rd chapter of Isaiah in which our Lord, speaking about the house of Jacob, said, "I, even I, am he that blotteth out thy transgressions for mine own sake, and will not remember thy sins." Was there anything in Israel or in Jacob that caused Him to make such a statement? Absolutely not! Almost in the same breath, in the very last statement of the preceding verse, He said this, ". . . thou hast wearied me with thine iniquities." Yet He continues and says, "I, even I, am he that blotteth out thy transgressions for mine own sake, and will not remember thy sins." That is grace. God did it for His own sake.

When our Lord saves a man and delivers him from judgment, it is solely for our Lord's sake. That is why we rejoice in the future. That is why those who have received Christ have peace and gladness concerning the future, or any future judgment. They believe the Lord who said, "He that heareth my word, and believeth on him that sent me, hath everlasting life, and shall not come into judgment; but is passed from death unto life." If that statement is not true then our Lord Jesus Christ was a liar. Of course, He was not. Then what? He was either telling the truth or He was lying. If He was telling the truth, then every one who has heard the Lord and believed on Him whom God hath sent possesses eternal life now. He will never perish. He will never come into judgment. He *has passed* from death unto life (past tense). When our Lord occupies the judgment seat, He will maintain the right and cause of every sinner who has trusted Him for salvation. He will of course rebuke the nations, He will destroy the wicked and He will put out their name forever. He will exercise His judgment in righteousness.

THE APOSTLE PAUL'S USE OF THE 9TH PSALM

It is interesting to observe how the Apostle Paul made use of the 8th verse of this 9th Psalm where we read, "And he shall *judge the world in righteousness,* he shall minister judgment to the people in uprightness." The Apostle Paul found himself in Athens one day. He was waiting for his friends Silas and Timothy. Paul had just escaped from Berea and his two friends were to follow him. While Paul was waiting for them at Athens, his spirit was moved within him when he saw the city wholly given to idolatry. He reasoned in the synagogue with the Jews and devout persons, and daily in the market place he spoke to all who gave a listening ear. Paul never lost an opportunity. He never wasted a moment. Some of the followers of the several philosophies of the day encountered him and asked, "What will this babbler say? . . . He seemeth to be a setter forth of strange gods: because he preached unto them Jesus, and the resurrection. And they took him, and brought him unto Areopagus, saying, May we know what this new doctrine, whereof thou speakest, is?" Paul stood in the midst of Mars' hill and preached that memorable sermon which has come down through the ages with increasing power. He called attention to the acknowledgment of their ignorance and their religious superstitions when he pointed to the altar which bore an inscription "TO THE UNKNOWN GOD." Paul said,

"Whom therefore ye ignorantly worship, him declare I unto you." Then he went on to show the folly of their reasoning, to suppose that the Godhead was like unto gold or silver, or stone, graven by art and man's device. He said that God overlooked this ignorance in times past but now He commandeth all men everywhere to repent because "he hath appointed a day, *in the which he will judge the world in righteousness* by that man whom he hath ordained; whereof he hath given assurance unto all men, in that he hath raised him from the dead." Notice that this is a direct quotation from the 8th verse of this 9th Psalm. Of course, Paul preached unto them our Lord Jesus Christ. He is the One who will judge the world in righteousness. He is the One about whom David was writing in this Psalm. Well might every unsaved sinner seek to flee from the presence of God, if that were possible. Well might he cry for the rocks and mountains to hide him from the face of Him who sits on the throne in that day when the Lord judges the world in righteousness.

But He will be, as David said in the 9th verse of this Psalm, a refuge for the oppressed, a refuge in times of trouble for those who put their trust in Him. In verse 16 David said, "The LORD is known by the judgment which he executeth," while in the following verse he makes the blunt statement, "The wicked shall be turned into hell, and all the nations that forget God. For the needy shall not always be forgotten: the expectation of the poor shall not perish for ever."

There is one thing which should be borne in mind in any consideration of the judgments of God: it is that the Lord shall judge the world in righteousness. There will be no injustice done. So often I have been asked questions relating to this theme, at times in reference to specific individuals, at other times regarding a whole class of people, as for example, the heathen. What is God going to do about them? Multitudes have never heard the name of Christ. To these questions I invariably respond that God will judge the world in righteousness.

Let us not forget that there are degrees of judgment as there are degrees of sinfulness. Dr. Ironside in his latest book "In the Heavenlies" in touching upon this subject has this to say: "We would not for a moment say everybody is just as corrupt, just as vile, just as wicked, just as despicable as everybody else. That would not be true. And yet if people are dead, they are dead." The Scripture says concerning all that they are dead in trespasses and sins.

In the 16th verse of the 9th Psalm it is written, "The LORD is known by the judgment which he executeth. . ." We are not able always to judge rightly but there is no miscarriage of justice with God. He is known by the judgment which He executeth even as we are known by certain characteristics which are peculiarly ours. Some of us walk a certain way, some write in a certain style. We are all known by the friends we keep. So God is known by the judgments which He executeth. Having executed our judgment upon Christ, we are delivered from judgment.

PSALM TEN

THE SILENCE OF GOD

IN our meditation in the 10th Psalm, the subject, "The Silence of God," meets us at the opening verse—

"Why standest thou afar off, O LORD? why hidest thou thyself in times of trouble?

"The wicked in his pride doth persecute the poor: let them be taken in the devices that they have imagined.

"For the wicked boasteth of his heart's desire, and blesseth the covetous, whom the LORD abhorreth.

"The wicked, through the pride of his countenance, will not seek after God: God is not in all his thoughts.

"His ways are always grievous; thy judgments are far above out of his sight: as for all his enemies, he puffeth at them.

"He hath said in his heart, I shall not be moved: for I shall never be in adversity.

"His mouth is full of cursing and deceit and fraud: under his tongue is mischief and vanity.

"He sitteth in the lurking places of the villages: in the secret places doth he murder the innocent: his eyes are privily set against the poor.

"He lieth in wait secretly as a lion in his den: he lieth in wait to catch the poor: he doth catch the poor, when he draweth him into his net.

"He croucheth, and humbleth himself, that the poor may fall by his strong ones.

"He hath said in his heart, God hath forgotten: he hideth his face; he will never see it.

"Arise, O LORD; O God, lift up thine hand: forget not the humble.

"Wherefore doth the wicked contemn God? he hath
said in his heart, Thou wilt not require it.

"Thou hast seen it; for thou beholdest mischief and
spite, to requite it with thy hand: the poor com-
mitteth himself unto thee; thou art the helper of
the fatherless.

"Break thou the arm of the wicked and the evil man:
seek out his wickedness till thou find none.

"The LORD is King for ever and ever: the heathen
are perished out of his land.

"LORD, thou hast heard the desire of the humble:
thou wilt prepare their heart, thou wilt cause thine
ear to hear:

"To judge the fatherless and the oppressed, that the
man of the earth may no more oppress."

The first thing that impresses one about this Psalm is the fact that it is
anonymously written. There is a big difference between composing a Psalm
or a piece of poetry anonymously and writing a letter anonymously. Joseph
Parker, that witty London preacher, was repeatedly the recipient of anonymous letters. On one occasion some one slipped an anonymous note in with
some notices which Joseph Parker was to read before his address. When he
came to it he stopped and appeared to be reading it intently. It contained
only one word—Fool. The audience was in a dead silence. Finally, Parker
raised his head and said, "My friends, I have had a new experience tonight.
I have received many anonymous letters during my pastorate but this is the
first time I have ever received a letter where the man signed his name but
failed to write the letter."

A TRIPLE THEME

Whoever wrote this 10th Psalm undoubtedly had a reason for keeping
himself in the background; he did not even give the Psalm an introduction.
Whatever might have been his reason, one thing is certain, that the Psalm
discusses a subject which confronts every man almost every day of his life.

At the opening verse we meet the statement, "Why standest thou afar
off, O LORD? why hidest thou thyself in times of trouble?" Then the
writer pointed to conditions existing in the earth, where he found that "The
wicked in his pride doth persecute the poor . . ." He had many things to
say about the wicked besides his pride and the prey upon whom he operates.
He said "the wicked *boasteth* of his heart's desire" and that he blesses the
covetous man, that he is indifferent to the claims of God, and that God is an

alien to his thoughts. The wicked comforts his heart by saying, "I shall not be moved: for I shall never be in adversity." Thus his mouth is full of cursing and deceit and fraud. He sits in lurking places, he crouches, and humbleth himself that the poor may fall. He rejoices in the fact that God has forgotten, that He has hidden His face and that He will never see what the wicked man is doing.

This Psalm has a triple theme: the silence of God, the despair of the humble, and the pride of the wicked. All three go together—the silent heaven, the praying man, and the wicked rascal, indifferent to the claims of God and rejoicing in his wickedness. What a picture! Here then is the beautiful heaven. The sky is gloriously clear. The sun is shining in all its glory. Or it is a beautiful night with the stars twinkling in the deep blackness of the heaven, undisturbed by even a passing cloud. Whether at high noon or at the midnight hour there is an awesomeness about the heaven, a silence about it, which makes it appear that it is a ceiling that can never be penetrated.

Yet here is also a little hovel of a place where the godly man dwells. He is pressed by circumstances and troublous times. He is crying out unto God. But here is also a sumptuous palace in which the wicked man dwells. He purchased the palace with the receipts he has been able to gather in during the night hours while he, secretly, like a lion in his den, waited to catch the poor and bring him into his net to persecute him and take away even what little he possessed, and then let him go, stripped of everything he had. One can almost hear the laughter of the lion as he enjoys his prey, and then lets him go.

What about this triple picture? It is unbalanced. To the thinking man it is a great question mark. To the child of God in circumstances such as we find in this Psalm it also is a question mark, though he is encouraged by the assurance that God will judge righteously. That God can be moved is evident as the oppressed man cries out, "Arise, O LORD; O God, lift up thine hand: forget not the humble." Indeed, as we come to the closing verses of the Psalm, we discover that the Lord has heard the poor man's cry as he triumphantly declares, "The LORD is King for ever and ever . . ."

I can hear someone say, this is all a pretty picture! No wonder the Communists insist that religion is the opiate of the people. It tells the poor, downtrodden worker that he ought to be content with his wages because there is a better day in the future; that he ought not attempt to alleviate his

sufferings and his disappointments because there is to be a heaven hereafter. Indeed, they tell us all the rich preach religion because it gives them
the opportunity to gather in more riches from the purses of the poor.

If there is one thing to be borne in mind it is this, that the rich are not
the only ones guilty of persecuting the poor. I hold no brief for the rich
man who grinds down his servants and employees, but the Communist agi-
tator, the rabble-rouser, the politician who preaches class hatred, are all
equally guilty of persecuting the poor. They lie in wait to grasp the poor
man in order that they may revel in their selfish, devilish pursuits.

THE HEART OF THE TROUBLE

For three thousand years since this Psalm was written men have been
struggling with this triple problem of the wicked, the poor, and the silence
of God. Yet these conditions are still with us. No improvement has been
made. The poor are still with us. Do not let anyone tell you that there ever
will be a time under any type of human government when poverty will be
wiped out. Our Lord said, "Ye have the poor always with you . . ." He
knew more about men than any politician. He knew that the wickedness of
man's heart was incurable. It might be stayed in one place but it would
break out in another. Even if we got rid of the present "sixty rich families"
another group would rise up and grind down the poor. No, the problem
cannot be healed by any man or legislation. The problem is deep-rooted in
the human heart which is so desperately wicked and depraved that no surgeon's knife can remove its cancer nor radium prevent its growth. There is
only one thing to do with a sinful nature and that is to put it to death. That
is exactly what God has done with it. In the death of Jesus Christ God
declared to the world what He thought of sinful flesh. God said that the
human heart was incurably wicked. Even God has never undertaken to
change our human nature. He can, however, impart a new life and that is
exactly what He is doing through the gospel as it is preached and as Christ
is received into a man's life.

That there are multitudes who fear the Lord, and who love His commandments but who are perplexed at the seeming indifference of God to the
inequalities on earth, is conceded. They join with the writer of this Psalm
and say to God, "Why standest thou afar off, O LORD? why hidest thou
thyself in times of trouble?"

There was a time in the early days of my youth when I thought it
was absurd for a Christian to raise such a question in the presence of

God. In the enthusiasm of my new found joy in Christ, I thought it was ridiculous to ask God, Why? Did we not have a prayer-answering God? Had I not experienced answered prayers? To ask God, "Why standest thou afar off?" was a sign of unbelief and lack of trust.

But as I have grown a little older, and the experiences of life have forced me into God's presence many times with an open Bible before me, I have learned a few lessons. I have discovered that the writers of the Psalms frequently asked, Why, O God? Even our Lord, as He hung upon the cross, raised the same question. He cried, "My God, my God, *why* hast thou forsaken me?" Of course, He knew why; yet in the bitterness of the sorrow of separation from His Father He cried out in agony. When He cried for help there was no answer from the blackened heavens. Still He justified His Father when He said, "But thou art holy, O thou that inhabitest the praises of Israel." He made plain the silence of God, and the failure of God to deliver Him. God was holy. Christ was the sinner's substitute. Christ on the cross was, in the eyes of God, the blackest spot in all history. He became the focal point of human sin. He symbolized sin, became identified with the serpent who brought sin into the world. He was made sin. He, therefore, was your substitute and mine. God saw Him as He sees you and me. Some of us, thank God, have come under the shelter of the blood of Christ so that God now sees us in Christ. When God looked down upon His Son on the cross He saw there the personification of human sin. He could not answer the cry of His Son and deliver Him. He had to unsheathe the sword and smite His "fellow." So our Lord justified the silence of God at the time of His death when He said, "But thou art holy, O thou that inhabitest the praises of Israel." Just as the explanation of Christ is clear and satisfies the spiritual heart and mind, so the Bible gives us the only answer for the silence of God in the present age.

I acknowledge that there have been times when I have gone into the presence of my Lord with a Why? upon my lips. Certain problems have come up. A series of circumstances have brought their troubles and one asks the Lord, Why? Where shall we go for our answer? What did Peter say when our Lord asked the disciples, "Will ye also go away?" as they observed the multitude leaving Him because of the words He had spoken. Peter responded, "Lord, to whom shall we go? thou hast the words of eternal life. And we believe and are sure that thou art that Christ, the Son of the living God?"

THE BIBLE'S ANSWER TO "WHY?"

When, therefore, this or any other question comes upon our lips, is the answer to be found in the philosophies of men? Have you ever read in the philosophies of men their ideas of the salvation of God? Have you ever read any of the "baby talk" from the brilliant of this world as they have tried to explain spiritual truth? My little girl, not yet two years of age, knows more about the Lord in her childish faith than the wise of this world. Their hearts and minds have been blinded by the god of this age because of their refusal to believe the gospel.

When a question enters the mind of a Christian and a Why? comes upon his tongue as he looks at world conditions, the Christian finds the answer to his question when he goes to the Word of God. There he discovers that when men rejected Christ they sent Him back to God with this message, "We will not have this man to reign over us." And again, "His blood be on us, and on our children." God has a way at times of taking men at their word. He received His Christ into the heavens. He set Him at His own right hand. Then He began to deal with sinners on the basis of grace. His arm of judgment was stayed by His grace. He also gave men full sway through the world and allowed them to run their lives to suit themselves. Occasionally He interferes in a way which gives evidence that God is still on His throne, but generally speaking the silence of God is the more pronounced revelation of God.

Again, God at times hides Himself even from His own in the time of trouble. What does the Bible have to say about that? Let us look. In the Old Testament the prophet Isaiah explained the failure of God to come to the deliverance of His people in the time of trouble by saying, "For a small moment have I forsaken thee; but with great mercies will I gather thee. In a little wrath I hid my face from thee for a moment; but with everlasting kindness will I have mercy on thee, saith the LORD thy Redeemer."

In the New Testament we learn that there is such a thing as the trial of our faith. Peter said that it is much more precious than gold that perisheth, though it be tried with fire. He suggested to those to whom he wrote that they greatly rejoice, though for a season, if need be, they are in heaviness through manifold trials. He said, that they were to consider that those trials of their faith were precious; that God was trying their faith if perchance there might be found something of praise, and honor, and glory at the appearing of Jesus Christ, "Whom having not seen, ye love; in whom, though now ye see him not, yet believing, ye rejoice with joy unspeakable and full of glory: receiving the end of your faith, even the salvation of your souls."

God tries His people. Sometimes He tries their faith by fire. When He does so it is not with the idea of revelling in their sorrow, but with the idea that there might be found through that testing something that will be to the praise, honor, and glory of God at the appearing of Jesus Christ. The greatest expression of love and service which a child of God can present to his Lord is to be faithful under trial. What honor, what praise, what glory will such a one present to Christ at His appearing. What if we have a little trouble at the present moment? What if the trial of our faith is grievous for a while? Paul said, as he was inspired by the Holy Spirit, that the sufferings of the present moment are not worthy to be compared with the glory that shall be revealed. Our life here is but a few years. Then what? The Christian, perplexed at times by his trials and troubles, rejoices in the One in whom, though not having seen, he yet believes, and in whom he rejoices with a joy unspeakable and full of glory. He knows his Lord will some day appear. Then in the flash of a moment his troubles will be over. His sufferings will never be remembered, so the only thing that he can possibly have that will be to the glory, praise, and honor of God at the appearing of the Lord Jesus is the fact that He trusted God when His face was not clearly seen.

As for the wicked, much is written in this Psalm about his doings here on earth; but when Christ appears the wicked man's day is done. He will be "the forgotten man." I would ten thousand times rather rejoice in Christ now, even though I may at times be perplexed, than to enjoy even for a day the pleasures of sin. Apart from the revelation of God you have no answer to earth's problems nor your sin—but in Christ you will find your problems answered and your sin dealt with.

PSALM ELEVEN

"ANCIENT MODERNISTS" AND
THE "FIRM FOUNDATIONS"

AFTER attempting to cover, in a short period of twenty minutes, Psalms containing eighteen and twenty verses, it is a pleasure to come to a Psalm which has only seven verses, such as the 11th Psalm, in which our meditation will be found. It is another of the Davidic Psalms, in which David said:

"In the LORD put I my trust: how say ye to my
soul, Flee as a bird to your mountain?

"For, lo, the wicked bend their bow, they make
ready their arrow upon the string, that they may
privily shoot at the upright in heart.

"If the foundations be destroyed, what can the
righteous do?

"The LORD is in his holy temple, the LORD'S
throne is in heaven: his eyes behold, his eyelids try,
the children of men.

"The LORD trieth the righteous: but the wicked
and him that loveth violence his soul hateth.

"Upon the wicked he shall rain snares, fire and
brimstone, and an horrible tempest: this shall be the
portion of their cup.

"For the righteous LORD loveth righteousness; his
countenance doth behold the upright."

Whether we turn to the New Testament Scriptures or examine the
books of Moses, or the prophets of Israel, or the Psalms, we find that there
is unity of expression regarding the great fact of salvation. For example,
it is written of Abraham that he believed God and it (that is, his faith)
was counted unto him for righteousness. In the New Testament we read,
"to him that worketh not, but believeth on him that justifieth the ungodly,
his faith is counted for righteousness." Faith is connected with the word
of God. The word and the person of God can never be disassociated. It
is for that reason we sometimes refer to our Lord Jesus Christ as the "living
Word." In fact, it is one of the titles which the Bible gives to Him, "In
the beginning was the Word, and the Word was with God, and the Word
was God." Our Lord Jesus Christ was the visibility of God, the very
thought, the very idea of God, so that all we shall ever know about God is
manifested in Christ. He *is* the living Word. The written Word, the book
we call the Bible, bears its testimony to the living Word and the two are
harmonious.

CHRIST *vs.* RITUALISM

The Psalmist introduced the 11th Psalm, by writing "In the LORD
put I my trust. . . ." David did not put his trust in ritualism. He did not
put his trust in the blood of bulls, goats, lambs, or rams. He knew that
the blood of those animals could not atone for sin. He knew that they
merely portrayed the coming One who, by His own precious blood, would
offer a sacrifice acceptable to God. He is the One to whom Abraham referred when he said, "God will provide himself a lamb for a burnt-
offering. . . ."

This is important, for there are many who place their faith in an institution, in a church, or in a ritual. There are some who believe that as they have been baptized or confirmed, such ritualism makes them children of God. Men are the children of God by faith alone; faith in the Lord Jesus Christ. The Psalmist said, "In the *LORD* put I my trust. . . ." What has been said is not a criticism of the church. The church is a God-given institution, rather a God-designed organism. There are two ordinances in the New Testament: baptism and the Lord's supper, but neither baptism nor the Lord's supper will ever save a soul. Men are saved solely by believing the record that God has given concerning His Son,—that God was in Christ reconciling the world unto Himself. Christ, the just One, died for us, the unjust, that He might bring us to God. So the Psalmist said "In the LORD put I my trust: how say ye to my soul, Flee as a bird to your mountain? For, lo, the wicked bend their bow, they make ready their arrow upon the string, that they may privily shoot at the upright in heart."

While in Chicago last week I heard that the sexton of the Moody Church recently told the pastor, Dr. Ironside, that he had learned a new passage of Scripture. The sexton has a little boy, about four years of age to whom he was teaching the Scriptures. The little fellow quoted the passage, "I will *bust* and not be afraid." We can learn much from children! "I will *trust* and not be afraid," said the Psalmist, but this little four-year-old said, "I will *bust* and not be afraid." When we really *trust* the Lord and our confidence is in Him, *bust* or whatever might come, we will not be afraid. So the Psalmist answered those who suggested to his soul that he flee as a bird to the mountain because the wicked were bending their bow, and making ready their arrow that they might privately shoot at him, "In the LORD put I my trust." You say that's dangerous. At least, I confess that it is daring! But the Psalmist was assured that a thousand should fall at his side, and ten thousand at his right hand but "it" should not come nigh unto him. When you have a God who promises to cover you with His shadow and who declares that He will be your refuge and fortress, you do not have to pay much attention to the wicked who bend their bows and make ready their arrows that they may privily shoot at the upright in heart.

"ANCIENT MODERNISTS"

There is something most interesting in the 3rd verse of this Psalm, "If the foundations be destroyed, what can the righteous do?" Whatever the Psalmist may have had in mind, one thing is sure: That any sound superstructure must have a solid foundation. One cannot build character upon a sandy foundation. The righteous build upon a foundation, which is tried and sure—the Rock, Christ Jesus, and "the impregnable Rock of the Scriptures."

The enemy has not overlooked a single weapon in his attempt to destroy the foundation of the Scriptures! He has been successful in getting many supposedly "intellectual" people to smile at one who makes the statement that he believes the Bible to be the inerrant Word of God. The "dear intellectualist" raises his eyebrows and looks at the man who makes such a confession as if to say, My poor friend, I did not suppose that there were any people left in this world like you! The whole trouble is that these so-called intellectualists have not been keeping up with the times. There never has been a period in human history when such universal testimony to the absolute integrity of this written Word has been unearthed by the spade. The statement of Sir Charles Marston in his recent book entitled "The Bible Comes Alive" is particularly pertinent here. Sir Charles and his party discovered the ancient city of Lachish in the ruins of Palestine. Speaking of a section of the clergy who call themselves "modernists" and who do not believe the Word of God, he suggests that they might make themselves familiar with this advance knowledge if they desire to retain their title, otherwise they have clearly become "ancient modernists." Any man who has kept up with what has been going on during the past ten or twelve years must come to the conclusion by pure logic that the Bible has been affirmed at practically every place where it was previously attacked. "If the foundations be destroyed, what can the righteous do?" Thank God, the foundations have not nor ever will be destroyed.

The more one studies this Bible the more wonderful it becomes. The closer one looks at it the more amazed he is at the absolute care which the Holy Spirit exercised in preserving the Book from error. Let me give you an illustration of what I mean. There is only one miracle which our Lord accomplished during His earthly ministry which is recorded in all four Gospels. All the other miracles are either to be found in one, two, or three of the Gospels. The only miracle which each of the four writers saw fit to include in their Gospels took place when our Lord fed the multitude with the five loaves and two small fishes. Two of the writers, Matthew and John, were witnesses of the event, while the others, Luke and Mark, undoubtedly heard of it from eye-witnesses, yet in each case in speaking of the number fed that day they were careful not to fall into the modern error which refers to the miracle as "the feeding of the five thousand."

One of the greatest Bible teachers of the past generation was Dr. C. I. Scofield. He was greatly used of God in illumining the Word of God. There is an edition of the Scripture which will ever be a great monument to his memory. It is called the Scofield Reference Edition and in it paragraph headings and footnotes have been added by Dr. Scofield in collaboration with several other great Bible teachers of the past and present generations. Dr. Scofield was a lawyer by training. He was also a District Attorney in the State of Texas before he gave his life to the Lord for the public ministry of the Word of God. Despite his legal training and his great gift as a Bible teacher, in each of the four instances in the Scofield Reference Edition where the account of this miracle is found he mentions the number fed as being "five thousand." For example, in St. Matthew's Gospel, the 14th chapter, the account begins with the 15th verse. In the Scofield Reference Edition there is a heading between the 14th and 15th verses reading, "The five thousand fed." Yet in verse 21 St. Matthew says that "they that had eaten were about *five thousand men,* beside women and children." Anyone who has had anything to do with religious work knows full well that the men are in the minority. Since there were five thousand men, beside women and children, we are safe in assuming that there were between fifteen and twenty thousand people fed that day. Yet, isn't it a fact that invariably *we* speak of this miracle as "the feeding of the five thousand?" If any one of the four writers of the Gospels had said that there were only five thousand fed that day, an error would have crept into the record which would have broken down the whole scheme of divine inspiration. Not one of the writers said there were only five thousand fed. When they used the number five thousand they invariably limited it to men. So the foundations can never be destroyed! Because they can never be destroyed the righteous rejoice.

The term "righteous" refers to those who have received Christ as their Saviour, who have believed God's testimony regarding His Son. The term does not refer to those who feel that they are righteous because of what they have tried to do. God declares men righteous because they have believed on His Son. If my righteousness, for instance, were of my own making, I never would face this microphone—I would not waste your time. I would want to hide myself and not be heard. But I rejoice in my salvation because it is God's gift to me. As I have believed His Son, God has declared me righteous. He has declared every sinner righteous who trusted Him. These are the righteous to whom the Psalmist referred when he said, "If the foundations be destroyed, what can the righteous do?" The foundations cannot be destroyed. Every time the foundations have been attacked by the enemy he has been the loser.

WHOM DOES GOD TRY?

But again the Psalmist said, "The LORD is in his holy temple, the LORD'S throne is in heaven: his eyes behold, his eyelids try, the children of men." What a distance is traversed in these verses. First the Psalmist referred to the foundations on the earth and then to the Lord in His holy temple in heaven. The wicked have attempted to attack the foundations on the earth but they cannot attack God in His heavens. The Lord is in His heaven on His throne and there "his eyes behold, his eyelids try, the children of men. The LORD trieth the righteous; but the wicked and him that loveth violence his soul hateth. Upon the wicked he shall rain snares, fire and brimstone, and an horrible tempest. . . ."

This is plain language. The Holy Spirit caused it to be written through the pen of the Psalmist David. It is for the reason expressed in these verses that God pays no attention to the men who stand on street corners challenging God by saying, "If there be a God in the heaven let Him strike me down dead on this corner." Such poor souls do not know that the Lord tries *only* the righteous. He does not bother about the wicked and those who love violence. He knows that there is a day coming when He shall rain upon the wicked snares, fire and brimstone, and an horrible tempest. So He allows the wicked to let off a little steam now and then without paying the slightest attention. Because He pays no attention some men assume He is non-existent.

The righteous are tried. They are subjected to testing because the Lord wants to bring them to a place where they will not trust in themselves but solely in Christ; not in wealth, nor circumstances, nor position, but in the Word of God. He tests the righteous, in order that at the appearing of Christ there may be that which shall be to the praise, and honor, and glory of our Lord.

There are only two classes of people in this world, at least the Bible distinguishes between only two groups—the righteous and the wicked; the saved and the unsaved; the believer and the unbeliever; the godly and the ungodly. *There is no middle class.* With God one cannot straddle the fence. One cannot be partly righteous and partly wicked. We cannot be partly saved and partly lost, partly godly and partly ungodly. We are either one or the other. God has constituted "all under sin" in order that His grace may be freely bestowed upon all.

When we receive the testimony of God concerning His Son, God takes us out of sin and puts us into Christ, out of self and into Him, out of condemnation and into justification. God *constitutes* a sinner righteous because he has believed His testimony concerning Christ.

Concerning the righteous man the Psalmist said in the closing verse of the Psalm, "For the righteous LORD loveth righteousness; his countenance doth behold the upright." There is nothing in the gospel which remotely suggests that as salvation is of grace—therefore the individual who receives it can do just as he pleases. It has been suggested that if we are saved by believing, only, we can be just as wicked as we please and still be saved. Oh, no, it just does not work that way!

Dr. Ironside in his new book, "In the Heavenlies," tells the story of an attempted assassination of Queen Elizabeth. The woman who sought to do so dressed as a man page, and secreted herself in the queen's boudoir awaiting the convenient moment to stab the queen to death. She did not realize that the queen's attendants would be very careful to search the rooms before her majesty was permitted to retire. Hidden there among the gowns they found this woman and brought her into the presence of the queen and took from her the poniard which she had hoped to plant in the heart of her sovereign. She realized that her case, humanly speaking, was hopeless. She threw herself down on her knees and pleaded and begged the queen as a woman to have compassion on her, a woman, and to show her grace. Queen Elizabeth looked at her coldly and quietly said, "If I show you grace, what promise will you make for the future?" The woman looked up and said, "Grace that hath conditions, grace that is fettered by precautions, is no grace at all." Queen Elizabeth caught it in a moment and said, "You are right; I pardon you of my grace." And they led her away, a free woman. History tells us that from that moment Queen Elizabeth had no more faithful, devoted servant than that woman who had intended to take her life.

That is exactly the way the grace of God works in the life of an individual—he becomes a faithful servant of God.

PSALM TWELVE

"GOOD THOUGHTS IN BAD TIMES"

CHARLES HADDON SPURGEON said that the subject matter of the 12th Psalm can readily be kept before the mind's eye if we would entitle the Psalm "Good Thoughts in Bad Times." There is no doubt about our experiencing bad times nor the need for "good thoughts in bad times," but I shall also burden your mind with another title, "Pure Words Refined in the Crucible of Earth." After all, any good thought which we may receive to encourage us in bad times must come from a word that has been tested, tried, and purified. We have reached the stage where a mere man's word cannot produce "good thoughts in bad times." Alas, in spite of the many words to which we have listened for several years as to how we were to enjoy a new economic system which would assure all a good measure of prosperity, we are still plagued with bad times.

A SHORT PRAYER

It is interestingly suggestive that this Psalm opens with these two words, "Help, LORD." One can hardly utter a shorter prayer, at the same time giving evidence of that humility of heart and mind, and that dependency upon God, which would characterize the life of a believer. Here we have a message and the name of the One to whom the message is addressed—yet the Psalmist used but two words. What a volume could be written on those two words!

A man does not usually cry out for help or address his prayer to the Lord unless he is in dire circumstances. It is a drowning man who cries for help. As long as one feels that he can save or extricate himself he does not ask for help. But here the Psalmist cried for help. The very cry presupposed a desperate situation. That brings us to an interesting point. Men are not saved, men do not call upon the name of the Lord, unless they first become conscious of their distress. One does not cry out for salvation until he realizes that he is lost. Thus the first ministry of the Holy Spirit to a soul is to convince that soul of sin, righteousness, and judgment. When a soul has been convicted of sin and realizes its lost condition then the Holy Spirit of God presents the glory of the finished work of Christ as full satisfaction for all sin and complete salvation for the lost soul.

In this Psalm, however, we do not have the cry of a lost soul but the cry of a saved soul who finds himself encumbered by bitter circumstances

that are not to his liking, and which bring increasing cause for distress to
him.

David wrote, "Help, LORD; for the godly man ceaseth; for the faithful fail from among the children of men. They speak vanity every one
with his neighbor: with flattering lips and with a double heart do they
speak." And now read the last verse where David wrote, "The wicked
walk on every side, when the vilest men are exalted."

It has been suggested that David wrote this Psalm when he was persecuted by Saul. Whether that be so or not does not change the message
nor the instruction we can receive from the Psalm. It is a sad hour in the
history of any nation and in the history of the world when godly men
cease and the faithful among the children of men fail and when the vilest
men are exalted; it invariably gives invitation for the wicked to walk on
every side. The analogy is so apparent that one need not elaborate upon
it. The whole world seems to have gone mad. The wickedness of men
in high places—the audacity of dictators and would-be dictators, who from
all appearances are ungodly, is enough to cause men to cry out and say,
"Help, LORD." A few years ago when a voice here and there was heard
calling attention to the rise of dictatorship and the rise of communism,
one was effectively ridiculed by the suggestion that such a one was looking
through colored glasses and seeing everything red. But now the whole
world seems to be gripped by this spirit so that thinking people are at a
loss to know where to turn or what to do, while men's hearts fail them
for fear.

Observe David's familiarity with the "political philosophy" of modern dictators. We have recently been furnished with an example of how
dictators delight to tickle each other's fancy! David said, "They speak
vanity every one with his neighbour: with flattering lips and with a double
heart do they speak."

We ask—Does the Psalmist reveal from whence deliverance from
such treachery is assured? Indeed—from the only One who can deliver,
the One to whom David addressed his prayer when he said, "Help, LORD."

A PRAYER AND A PROPHECY

Before commenting further let us read the Psalm in its entirety:

> "Help, LORD; for the godly man ceaseth; for the
> faithful fail from among the children of men.
> "They speak vanity every one with his neighbour:
> with flattering lips and with a double heart do
> they speak.

"The LORD shall cut off all flattering lips, and the
tongue that speaketh proud things:
"Who have said, With our tongue will we prevail;
our lips are our own: who is lord over us?
"For the oppression of the poor, for the sighing of
the needy, now will I arise, saith the LORD; I will
set him in safety from him that puffeth at him.
"The words of the LORD are pure words: as
silver tried in a furnace of earth, purified seven
times.
"Thou shalt keep them, O LORD, thou shalt preserve them from this generation for ever.
"The wicked walk on every side, when the vilest
men are exalted."

The ray of hope appears in the 3rd verse as the Psalmist wrote, "The
LORD shall cut off all flattering lips, and the tongue that speaketh proud
things: who have said, With our tongue will we prevail; our lips are our
own: who is lord over us?" Who shall do that? The Lord! No injustice
is done to this Psalm, nor to our credulity, in suggesting that it has a peculiar message for our own day. When was there a time when the tongue
prevailed so much as at present? Now one man speaks and a whole nation,
a whole world, gives ear. There was a time when great men spoke with
restrained words. That was when godly men sat in the council chambers
of the nation. But not so now. Restraint upon the tongue has been broken.
The proud boastfully say, ". . . . our lips are our own: who is lord over us?"
But sir, until a man has mastered his lips, he is not fit to exercise mastery
over a whole people.

The first part of this Psalm is a prayer, but commencing with the 5th
verse we have a prophecy. Until we read the 5th verse it would appear
that the Lord looked on inactively and with seeming indifference to what
was transpiring on the earth. But commencing with the 5th verse, the
Lord Himself arises and has something to say. *The last word is always
spoken by the Lord.* Men may use flattering lips and indulge in what
someone has called a "grandiloquent tongue" and revel in the flattery of
one braggart to another, and thus lord it over the poor, the oppressed, and
the godly, but it shall not always be so. The Lord may appear to be indifferent, but all the while He is merely waiting until "the iniquity of the
Amorites" is full. Then He will arise, and when He does, He comes
first to the deliverance of the oppressed, to put the trusting soul in a safe
place.

And now we come to a marvelous verse. Whether these words were
spoken by the Lord or whether they are the expression of the Psalmist,

I do not know, but the statement is gloriously true. It reads, "The words of the LORD are pure words: as silver tried in a crucible of earth, purified seven times."

In the earlier verses we read about flattering lips and a proud tongue, and of course the words that proceed from such a tongue and through such lips are not purified words. Invariably they are the most impure words. But the words of the Lord are pure words. They are without any intermixture of untruthfulness so that they can be absolutely relied upon.

The extent of the purity of the words of the Lord is enhanced by the simile the Spirit used when He said that the words are purified as silver tried in a crucible of earth, not once or twice or even three or four times, but purified seven times. As the words of the Lord have been placed in this crucible of earth, they have been tested by every conceivable formula and fire. Each such testing and fire has demonstrated the purity and perfection of the words.

A crucible is used to pour in molten metal in order to separate the dross from the pure metal. The Bible speaks of a furnace of affliction into which a believer is sometimes called to enter. But there is a marked difference between the purpose of that furnace, in contrast to the crucible through which the Word of the Lord has been purified seven times. Our faith is subject to trial. Our lives are subject to testing. Our works, at the judgment seat of Christ, will be tried by fire and some of us will be saved even as by fire. In each such case, the fire had for its purpose the burning up of the dross in order that there might remain only the purity of life and faith.

But the words of the Lord are pure words. They went through the crucible of earth seven times not that dross might be withdrawn from them but to demonstrate their absolute purity. Each such testing proved the purity of the words. It does not matter from what possible angle one examines the words of God or to what tests the words are put or into what laboratory man may take the words of God and break them apart to examine them under the closest scrutiny, each such examination reveals the purity and the perfection of the words. There is no dross in any part.

The Word of God has been tested in the crucible of earth. That is worthy of note for in another Psalm it is declared, "For ever, O LORD, thy word is settled in heaven." They never tested the Word in heaven. There they know it is settled. It is men on the earth who prepared the crucible of fire in order to test the Word of God. What smart alecks men are!!

PUTTING GOD'S WORD TO THE TEST

But there is another and more glorious way to test the Word of God. Whatever the circumstances into which one may be placed or however trying the situation, the Word of God can be put to the test and it will never be found wanting. The trouble with most of us is that we do not trust Him. We are not talking about unbelievers; we are limiting our comments now to those of us who truly believe. We either think a matter is too great for the Lord to do or too small for Him to consider. But whether the problem is a big one or a little one, we may test the Word of God in the crucible of our experience and we will find it is pure, it is purified silver. Nothing is more pure than purified silver. From the Bible we know that silver is a symbol of redemption and that seven is the number of perfection, so from whatever possible angle we may be called upon to test the Word of God, we will find it gloriously true.

There is a story told about George Mueller, who conducted those great orphanages at Bristol, England, which will ever be a memorial not only to answered prayer but also to the truth of the Word of God. Dr. Arthur T. Pierson, that princely Bible teacher of a generation ago, sat with George Mueller one day. Mr. Mueller was telling of some of the wonderful things that God had done for the orphanages at Bristol. As he talked he was writing. Dr. Pierson noticed that he was having difficulty with his pen-point. In the midst of his conversation Mr. Mueller seemed to lose sight of his visitor. He bowed his head for a moment or two in prayer and then began writing again. Dr. Pierson asked, "Mr. Mueller, what were you praying about just now?" "Oh," Mr. Mueller said, "perhaps you did not notice that I was having trouble with this pen-point. I haven't another and this is an important letter, so I was asking the Lord to help me so that I could write it clearly." "Dear me," said Dr. Pierson, "a man who trusts God for millions of pounds also prays about a scratchy pen-point."

That scratchy pen-point was not too small a task for the Lord. Some might ask—Does the Bible invite us to take even such a problem to the Lord? Indeed it does. It declares, ". . . *in every thing* by prayer and supplication with thanksgiving let your requests be made known unto God . . ." There is not an incident in any Christian's life that is uninteresting or unimportant to God. Many of us have had the joy of testing the Word of God in our own experiences, and have found it to be true. I extend an invitation to you who have not yet trusted the Lord for salvation to commit your soul to His safe keeping. You will then know the joy of a heart which is at peace with God.

PSALM THIRTEEN

HOW GOD CHANGES A WAIL INTO A SONG

WE have entitled our meditation in the 13th Psalm "How God Changes a Wail Into a Song." Others have suggested that the Psalm should be entitled "The How-Long Psalm" or "The Howling Psalm." As we read it we will notice that no less than four times in two verses the Psalmist used the words, "How long?"

> "*How long* wilt thou forget me, O LORD? for ever? *how long* wilt thou hide thy face from me?
> "*How long* shall I take counsel in my soul, having sorrow in my heart daily? *how long* shall mine enemy be exalted over me?
> "Consider and hear me, O LORD my God: lighten mine eyes, lest I sleep the sleep of death;
> "Lest mine enemy say, I have prevailed against him; and those that trouble me rejoice when I am moved.
> "But I have trusted in thy mercy; my heart shall rejoice in thy salvation.
> "I will sing unto the LORD, because he hath dealt bountifully with me."

Those who use the commuting trains on the Erie railroad have noticed that they display car cards carrying interesting sayings or proverbs. You may have noticed the one quoting a Chinese proverb, "A gem cannot be polished without friction, nor man perfected without trials." David had his share of trials. Not a single child of God has been exempt from trials and chastening. We learn from the New Testament that ". . . whom the Lord loveth he chasteneth, and scourgeth *every son* whom he receiveth." That is one way to determine whether or not we are a child of God. If everything goes smoothly and we do not know what it is to be chastened or scourged then it is high time to examine ourselves to determine whether we are in the faith; for trials, sufferings, chastenings, and scourges are the "home training" of every Christian.

GOD NOT THE FATHER OF ALL MEN

I am not talking about all men. I refer only to those who are "in Christ." The Bible makes a distinction between men—those who are in

Christ and those who are not. The Bible has only one message to those outside of Christ and that message is expressed in the word "Believe." The Bible has no other message to any man before he receives the invitation of God to believe the record He has given concerning His Son. Not until one becomes a son *by faith in Jesus Christ* does one have the personal, intimate relationship with God which is of a family character and which involves family training. Men may religiously talk about "the Fatherhood of God and the brotherhood of man," but it is as far from Christian, in fact, as paganism is from the gospel. God is not the Father of all men. Imagine God being the Father of that motley crowd of Japanese soldiers who, according to the Associated Press dispatches from Nanking, have raped every Chinese woman from the ages of sixteen to sixty whom they have encountered. Imagine God being the Father of that vicious group of Nazi adherents who have whisked away into a concentration camp that dauntless, fearless man of God, Pastor Niemoller, even after the Nazi courts have acknowledged that he has completed his sentence—only—because they fear his determination to obey God rather than man. I would hate to think that God was the Father of some men now living in this world. God is the Creator of all men—which is quite another matter. The Bible presents God as the God and Father of our Lord and Saviour Jesus Christ and the God and Father of all who believe in Him. Any attempts to preach anything else is to present a spurious message and another gospel.

As I have gone through these Psalms each Sunday morning I have been much impressed to observe how frequently the Psalmist was in distress and in a disturbed state of mind. Many of God's choicest saints have been pressed from several sides. We may not have been as bold in our prayer as the Psalmist was but do not forget that we are invited to come into His presence *boldly* and to present our petitions before Him. If we are in distress, we have a right to cry to the only One who can deliver us out of our distress.

"How Long . . . ? How Long . . . ?"

David said, "How long wilt thou forget me, O LORD? for ever? how long wilt thou hide thy face from me?" David knew what it was to look up into the heavens and find them absolutely unresponsive to his cry. He could not penetrate the darkness to see the face of Jehovah. Have you had a similar experience? Have you been in a position where, having failed to receive an answer to your cry from the silent heavens, you took counsel with your own soul, you talked to yourself, to your real self, and commiserated on your experiences? Notice will you, that David knew something about that also for he said, "How long shall I take counsel in my soul, having sorrow in my heart daily?"

Could a man of whom God witnessed that he was a man after His own heart, have sorrow in his heart daily? Since he did, then we ought not to complain if we have sorrow in our hearts occasionally.

For the fourth time David said, "How long shall mine enemy be exalted over me?" It is impossible for one to read this Psalm, especially if he is concerned about his own sorrow and disappointments, without concluding that he is not suffering to the same extent as the Psalmist did.

David was a great man from every possible angle. He was strong; even in his youth he possessed amazing strength, which was demonstrated in his care over his father's sheep. He learned the ways of a shepherd with his sheep by actual experience. He was a keen naturalist. He loved the brooks and the still waters. He knew something about the deep ravines of Palestine and the tall cedars of Lebanon. He had a poetic nature and a great gift for expressing his innermost feelings in poetry, song, and music. He had a keen eye and a delightful spirit. Men rallied round him. Of course, he had enemies as well as friends. He knew something of the satisfaction of being raised from a place of obscurity to a place of exaltation, from a despised youngster to a great king. He loved the fellowship of his God. He had a great faith and deep appreciation of spiritual truth. He was a prophet as well as a singer. He had something about him that appealed to people in sorrow so that those who were in distress, disappointments, and in dire circumstances rallied around him. He must have had a cheerful disposition. Yet with all those remarkable characteristics and the great springs that he found in himself, he did not base his faith on his experiences or on anything in himself. He recognized that the deliverer was none other than the Lord. If his eyes were to be lightened or his spirit encouraged the Lord must consider and hear him because he trusted in His mercy.

NORMAL CHRISTIAN EXPERIENCE

Whenever I visit the Moody Bible Institute in Chicago, there is one man whom I particularly delight to engage in conversation. I refer to Dr. Max Reich. He is a Hebrew Christian. He was born a Jew; he is an Israelite in whom there is no guile. He is a Quaker, a very gracious gentleman—a marvelous combination of qualities in one man. He has a deeply spiritual perception of the truth. When at the Institute this past February, Dr. Wilbur M. Smith and I encountered Dr. Reich as we were about to leave one of the Institute buildings. He immediately greeted us and asked if we had any word from the Lord. We said, "No, but we are anticipating a word from you." He went on to tell of his joy in reading the book of Numbers during the early morning of that day. He shared with us the delightful truth he had found in that ancient book. One thing led to another. Just to stir up that saintly gentleman I asked him a question, the answer to which I thought I knew but which I was to learn was only part of the answer. I said, "Dr. Reich, is it correct to say that the experience of Romans 7 is the normal experience of a Christian?" He answered, "The normal experience of most Christians but not normal Christian experience." Then I asked, "Would you say that Romans 8 is normal Christian experience and is it necessary for a Christian to go through Romans 7 before he enters into the joy of Romans 8?"

You who do not know your Bible may think that I am speaking Greek or Latin but if you do not know these two chapters of that great book you ought to make it your business to read them as soon as it is convenient. In the 7th chapter Paul is describing the experience of a man who has been enlightened but who finds that when he wants to do good, evil is present with him. He is constantly annoyed by these two conflicting principles. He finds that he delights in the law of God after the inward man but he sees another principle in his members, warring against the law of his mind and which brings him into captivity to the law of sin. He therefore cries out, "O wretched man that I am! *who* shall deliver me from the body of this death?" Did you notice the pronoun? I had not especially noticed it previously until that good gentleman brought it to my attention. He said that the Apostle Paul then knew that deliverance was not to be found in a ritual nor in a law; he had been brought up on ritualism and on the law, but they only made his heart miserable and his mind wretched and so he cried out not for some *thing* to deliver him but for *some one*. He cried, "O wretched man that I am! *who* shall deliver me from the body of this death?" It was then that he came to that glorious climax when he wrote, "I thank God through Jesus Christ our Lord. . . ." That good Hebrew Quaker continued by saying, "Having found deliverance out of that predicament through a person, Paul rejoices and writes, 'There is therefore now no condemnation to them which are in Christ Jesus.'" We cannot read the 7th chapter of Romans

without sensing the cry or wail of a miserable soul but we cannot enter into
the 8th of Romans without realizing that the man now has a song. He is
not another man. The man in the 7th chapter is one and the same as the
man in the 8th chapter but he now trusts, not in himself, nor in any *thing*,
but he trusts in the matchless person of Jesus Christ.

REJOICING WHILE IN DISTRESS

So as we go back to the 13th Psalm we observe that despite all the
sterling qualities and characteristics which David possessed which ordinarily
would have stamped him as great, he still found that his enemies were triumphing over him. He did not trust in his cunning nor his own power—he
cried to God and said, "Consider and hear me, O LORD my God . . . Lest
mine enemy say, I have prevailed against him; and those that trouble me
rejoice when I am moved. But I have trusted in thy mercy; my heart shall
rejoice in thy salvation." Do you see how this man's wail turned into a
song? It was the same man. The one who wrote the first few verses was
the same who penned the last verses. Mark you, he was *still* in the same
predicament, but he had come to rejoice in the salvation of the Lord. His
faith was not the result of his deliverance but his deliverance was the fruit
of his faith. He trusted in the mercy of God. Because of that trust he
wrote, ". . . my heart shall rejoice in thy salvation." He did not write, "my
heart *is* rejoicing," but he wrote, "my heart *shall* rejoice in thy salvation."
You see, he was still in trouble, though he was coming out of it, but when
he was in distress was the time he trusted. After he had unburdened his
heart to the Lord about his distress, it was then that he wrote, ". . . I have
trusted in thy mercy." From then on he began to come up. He said, because
"I *have* trusted in thy mercy; my heart *shall* rejoice in thy salvation. I
will sing unto the LORD, because he hath dealt bountifully with me." You
see, David was careful in the use of tenses. He did not say, I am singing a
song unto the Lord because He will deal bountifully with me; but he said,
"I *will* sing unto the LORD, because he *hath* dealt bountifully with me."
But some will say, How can a man sing when he is down? You should
rather ask, Who is the man who can sing when he is down? Then we will
be able to answer the question, How can a man sing when he is down?

Those who can sing are those who have trusted in the mercy of the
Lord. They look at encumbering circumstances at times and it causes them
to cry out, "How long?" but after they have poured out their petition unto
the Lord and have cried unto Him they begin to sing, and how they defeat

the enemy by their song! It is reported that Martin Luther once said, "The devil . . . cannot endure sacred songs of joy. Our passions and impatiences, our Alas! (by which he meant our constant crying alas, alas) and our Woe is Me! please the devil well; but our songs and psalms vex him and grieve him sorely." I agree with that great man of God. If we want to vex the devil and grieve him, let us sing our songs of Zion and our hymns of praise. We will discover that in spite of the contradicting and conflicting experiences of life the Lord hath dealt bountifully with us, even as He did with David.

I am glad that David had the varied experiences he did, for we never would have had these Psalms if he had not been sorely tried. Without these Psalms, we who sometimes are in the throes of disappointment and sorrow would have been inclined to ask, Why do we have periods of disappointment and sorrow and why should these things happen to us? They are the common experiences of every believer, they are a part of his training for his future glory. What is more, through these trials the Christian is driven to his knees in order that God may reveal Himself strong on behalf of those who trust Him. Someone once said that "A Christian on his knees can see farther than a philosopher on his tiptoes." The best that unregenerate man can do is to philosophize on the subject of sorrow and suffering. He can use high-sounding words and phrases, but, alas, they are all emptiness. Sir Isaac Newton, great scientist that he was, said, "I can take a telescope and look millions of miles into space, but I can go into my room in prayer and get nearer to God and heaven than I can when assisted by all the telescopes of earth." If you do not know that indescribable joy, may *you* receive Jesus Christ *now* as your Saviour and thereby enter into the joy of communion with Almighty God.

PSALM FOURTEEN

WHAT GOD SAW WHEN HE LOOKED DOWN FROM HEAVEN

THE 14th Psalm is a great Messianic Psalm. It is not a Psalm which would raise one to ecstasy. It is rather one which would produce the opposite emotion. It begins with that familiar expression, "The fool hath said in his heart, There is no God." This does not seem an appropriate statement with which to begin a Sunday morning meditation. But, strange as it may seem, there is a very large company included in this passage.

A short time ago a preacher-friend was telling me of an experience he had at an open-air meeting. Immediately upon finishing he was accosted by a young man who very bluntly stated that he was an atheist. The preacher looked amazed and said, "Indeed, that is quite interesting. I was only reading about you this morning." The young atheist, somewhat surprised, said, "Reading about me?" "Yes," said the preacher. "But, where?" said the atheist. "Why—in the Bible," answered my friend and proceeded to quote "The fool hath said in his heart, no God." Needless to say, that did not rest well upon the astounded countenance of the young atheist!

THE RICH FOOL

It is an interesting study to note in the Scriptures those who are called "fools." For instance, there is the person who believes it is possible to satisfy his soul with the things of this world, the man who thinks that gain is godliness. Speaking in a parable, our Lord said:

> "The ground of a certain rich man brought forth plentifully:
>
> "And he thought within himself, saying, What shall I do, because I have no room where to bestow my fruits?
>
> "And he said, This will I do: I will pull down my barns, and build greater; and there will I bestow all my fruits and my goods.
>
> "And I will say to my soul, Soul, thou hast much goods laid up for many years; take thine ease, eat, drink, and be merry.
>
> "But God said unto him, Thou fool, this night thy soul shall be required of thee: then whose shall those things be, which thou hast provided?"

Our Lord added: "So is he that layeth up treasure for himself and is not rich toward God."

Notice that our Lord spoke of a *certain* rich man who had a parcel of ground which brought forth plentifully. This man made the mistake which so many rich men make, of believing that he could satisfy his soul with the increase of the field, and with material things. When he reached what he believed was the pinnacle of his success he thought within himself, Now from henceforth, I will take mine ease, I will eat, drink, and be merry. What a sad shock when God said to that man, "Thou fool, this night thy soul shall be required of thee." It is pathetic when God calls upon a rich man who has forgotten Him and announces calmly, "This night thy soul shall be required of thee."

You will notice that the man whom the Psalmist calls a fool because he said there is no God, made this decision in his heart, and not in his mind. Atheists labor under the impression that their convictions are the result of pure logic. But the Bible declares that the man who is an atheist is so, not because his mind revolts against God, but because his heart is blackened with sin. It is his heart that controls his thinking. It was out of the heart that there sprang the desire to rid the mind of the thought of the Creator and the obligations of the creature to his Creator. Such a man's heart says to him, "No God." Concerning such individuals the Scripture says: "They are corrupt, they have done abominable works, there is none that doeth good."

LOOKING DOWN FROM HEAVEN

In the next verse there is a further interesting picture—the Psalmist pictured the Lord looking down from heaven upon the children of men, to see if there were any that did understand, and seek after God. This is a most impressive verse, for it presents the Lord in an inquiring position. He ". . . looked down from heaven upon the children of men, to see if there were any that did understand, and seek God."

Man is a religious being. He *seems* to seek after God. He gives the impression that his seeking after God is an intelligent pursuit. Listen to what God thinks of this so-called intelligent pursuit of man after God. "They are all gone aside, they are all together become filthy: there is none that doeth good, no, not one."

We are apt to misapply this passage of Scripture. I would not insult any man's intelligence by saying that there is no such thing as personal righteousness. In fact, there are multitudes of men and women who recognize certain standards of living and adhere to those standards. Indeed, a man may even be religious, with a high standard of morals and ethics, but God witnesses concerning the whole human race—"*They are all gone aside.*" The God who is able to see the heart, and to discern the motives of the heart declares concerning each of us that we have "gone aside" and that we have "together become filthy."

What does this mean? Sin defiles. It has therefore made us valueless to God—or, to use another word, unprofitable. None of us have escaped the defilement of sin. It is as natural for us to sin as it is to breathe, ". . . there is none that doeth good, no, not one."

It is singular that this 14th Psalm is quoted in the 3rd chapter of Paul's letter to the Romans where he gave us God's verdict of the whole human race. In the 1st and 2nd chapters of that Epistle, he took the Jew, with all the revelation of law and ethics that he possessed, and proved to him out of his own Scripture that he was guilty; without excuse. Then, having disposed of religious man, he took the case of an ethical, moral Gentile, and caused him to blush in the presence of an unfolding of his own sin and inconsistency. Finally, he brought in the rest of the human race, and convinced all of sin. When he had done so, he recorded the verdict of God upon the entire race. Beginning with verse 9 of the 3rd chapter, he said: ". . . for we have before proved both Jews and Gentiles that they are all under sin." Then follows a series of quotations out of the Old Testament, many of which were taken from this 14th Psalm. In fact, the opening indictment is this one from the 14th Psalm: "There is none righteous, no, not one: there is none that understandeth, there is none that seeketh after God. They are all gone out of the way, they are together become unprofitable; there is none that doeth good, no, not one."

But why continue? The evidence is so overwhelming that it is irrefutable. But what is most important is that this is the verdict of God, the Judge of all men.

Some of us may be boisterous in the defense of ourselves before men, but when God speaks in the majesty of His own Person, and in the glory of His own character, there is nothing left for us to do but to bow our heads and, in mute silence, acknowledge that the testimony of God is true. It is for that reason that the Apostle Paul added in the 19th verse of the 3rd chapter, "Now we know that what things soever the law saith, it saith to them who are under the law: that every mouth may be stopped, and all the world may become guilty before God."

THE COURT OF GOD AND HIS PROVISION

May I become decidedly personal by asking, Does this testimony that God bears concerning you bring to your own heart an acknowledgment that it is true? If it does, you are just one step away from the Kingdom. While it is God's verdict that "all have sinned, and come short of the glory of God," the very righteousness which condemns us is the prerogative of God that is put at our defense. Let me express it in the language of Scripture: ". . . now the righteousness of God without the law is manifested, being witnessed by the law and the prophets; even the righteousness of God which is by faith of Jesus Christ unto all and upon all them that believe: for there is no difference."

As "there is no difference" in the condemnation of man in that he has "sinned and come short of the glory of God," so the provision that God has made for the justification of man, is available for all. "There is no difference."

If you picture in your mind a court scene, possibly the truth would impress you further. If you wish, put yourself in the court. Upon the bench is the Judge of all the earth. The law has brought in its testimony against you. The evidence has been so overwhelming that the verdict is inevitable. There rises from the bench the Judge of the universe, and He gives as His verdict that you have sinned, and have come short of the glory of His standard. You have not manifested the character of God in your life and conduct. Your own conscience bears witness that the judgment of God is just. But, at the moment when your conscience is overwhelmed, and your head bowed with the burden of your guilt, the very Judge who condemned you offers provision for your redemption and for the clearing of your case in His court.

That scene actually has taken place. The Judge of all the earth, Himself has made provision in the person of His Son. He left the bench, and went to the cross and tasted death for every man. Because He bore the penalty of the law He is now able to sit on that bench and offer to condemned sinners eternal salvation and absolute freedom from the guilt of the law, because His righteousness has been sustained. His grace is able to operate so that He can say to us who have received Christ, that His righteousness is available by faith in Jesus Christ. Previously, we stood condemned in that court, now we stand clothed in a righteousness not our own; it is the righteousness of Christ, and in that righteousness we have been accepted and made perfect. Christ is the satisfaction for our sin and our judgment.

PSALM FIFTEEN

MISAPPROPRIATING SCRIPTURE

IT seems that on the 5th anniversary of the inauguration of President Roosevelt as he returned from attending a special church service, newspaper men approached him for some comment in view of the significance of the day. It is reported that he suggested that this 15th Psalm of David was an appropriate lead for any story they might write. It appears that the Psalm was used during the service. The President went on to suggest that the Psalm would not only be useful as a lead, but if he were a "make-up" editor he would put it at the top of the page. The next morning the "New York Herald Tribune" obliged the President by printing the Psalm upon its front page.

The use of the Psalm by the President immediately gave the press something new to write about. Many columnists took occasion to say something about this Psalm and other portions of Scripture. Dorothy Thompson declared that it is extremely dangerous to quote the Bible in support of one's prejudices because the other side can always find just as appropriate a quotation. She even went so far, and correctly so, as to suggest that the devil can also quote Scripture. But whenever the devil quotes we had better examine closely his quotation. He is a master at misquoting or partly quoting Scripture.

It is to be regretted that a portion of sacred Scripture has been used in this way. The Bible was never written to be handled in a partisan manner, but to be received as it truly is—the Word of God. Irrespective of what office a man may hold, when he drags down the Word of God from the sacred place it occupies one must look askance at such conduct.

The Word of God is the sword of the Spirit. It can be effectively wielded only by a spiritual man as he is guided by the Spirit of God.

America's past greatness was largely the reflection of the dignity of its leaders and the spiritual outlook and respect that both people and leaders gave to the Word of God and to prayerful devotion.

During the Revolutionary War, General Washington's Army was reduced to great straits, and people were greatly dispirited. One of them who left his home with an anxious heart, one day, as he was passing the edge of a wood near the camp, heard the sound of a voice. He stopped to listen and, looking between the trunks of the large trees, he saw General Washington engaged in prayer. He passed quietly on that he might not disturb him and on returning home told his family, "America will prevail," and related what he had heard and seen.

In this serious crisis in the life of our American nation, many of us would take courage were our leaders to adopt the attitude of the Father of our country when this nation was in its earlier distress. What a sight it would be were President, Cabinet, and Congress to unite in prayer imploring divine guidance for the way out of our difficulties.

I listened with much interest to Dr. William Evans, of Los Angeles, as he spoke one night last week in New York City. Commenting upon present conditions in the world, and reminding his audience that "it can happen here," he raised the question—What can we, who are believers in the Lord Jesus Christ, do in this hour? Should we merely fold our arms and rejoice in the fact that we know we are saved and conclude that these things must come to pass—so what of it? Or should we, as he suggested, raise our voice in objection, through the orderly and dignified manner which is offered to us as American citizens, against anything and everything that undermines the great principles of liberty which are dear to the Christian heart, and likewise at every attempt to discredit, misuse, or abuse the Word of God. That good gentleman suggested that we should not only raise our voices in protest, but we should also pray, and bear our testimony to Christ and Christian truth. His words were well spoken and well chosen.

ENTRANCE *vs.* ABIDING IN GOD'S TABERNACLE

The 15th Psalm was written by David. The Psalm reads:

> "LORD, who shall abide in thy tabernacle? who shall dwell in thy holy hill?
>
> "He that walketh uprightly, and worketh righteousness, and speaketh the truth in his heart.
>
> "He that backbiteth not with his tongue, nor doeth evil to his neighbour, nor taketh up a reproach against his neighbour.
>
> "In whose eyes a vile person is contemned; but he honoureth them that fear the LORD. He that sweareth to his own hurt, and changeth not.
>
> "He that putteth not out his money to usury, nor taketh reward against the innocent. He that doeth these things shall never be moved."

The Word of God has a way of getting into the very crevices of the human conscience with terrific convicting power.

But note that David said, "*LORD*, who shall abide in thy tabernacle? who shall dwell in thy holy hill?" You see, the right of ex-communication rests not with man but entirely with the Lord. He it is who governs His own house and who lays down principles and laws which are necessary for relationship with Himself. From David, through the Holy Spirit, we learn what men must possess in order to *abide* in the Lord's tabernacle and *dwell* in His holy hill. Of course, the language of this Psalm is symbolic. The tabernacle of the Lord, and the Lord's holy hill, is His own dwelling-place in the very heavens. Men are invited to have communion and fellowship with God only on the basis of His revealed principles. The Word of God is equally clear in its exclusion of those who have no right to participate in worship because they reject His way, as it is in presenting an open door to all who will worship Him in spirit and in truth.

I have a right to determine who shall enter into my home or who shall come into my office and take my time or participate in my friendship. For instance, one morning this week as I was quite busy at the office I was told that a young man wanted to see me. Through a secretary I inquired of his purpose, for I did not wish to waste any time, but he refused to reveal the reason for his call, insisting that a friend of mine urged him to come to see me. I asked him to wait. He had not waited five minutes when I learned that he was making quite a nuisance of himself. I quickly invited him into my office to find out what he had on his mind. There were two others in my office at the time, but he insisted that he wanted to see me alone—it was important. His whole demeanor was strange. I asked him what friend of mine had urged him to see me. He refused to reveal his name unless I saw him alone. He paraded up and down the office, reminding me that he was a famous jockey—as if that were an excuse for his behavior. I told him I would give him all the time required provided he would reveal the name of the friend who had urged him to see me. He refused to give his name and, of course, I refused to extend the interview.

God has a right to say who shall abide in His tabernacle. There is only one name which gives any man the right to enter the presence of God and that is the name of the LORD JESUS CHRIST. During His earth ministry He was a friend of publicans and sinners. He said He was "the way, the truth, and the life," and the only approach unto God. When men attempt to enter into His presence through any other means than the blood and righteousness of Christ, God refuses to extend an interview, and much less does He allow such to abide in His tabernacle, or to dwell in His holy hill. But when a man receives God's testimony concerning His Son he then has the right of entrance into the presence of God. Thereafter, there are certain principles or rules of conduct which govern his life and which assure him the right of continuous fellowship and communion with God.

RULES OF CONDUCT

Dr. C. I. Scofield, the great Bible teacher, has an interesting comment about the contrast between the message of John's Gospel and that of the First Epistle of John. He said that John's Gospel leads across the threshold of the Father's house; his First Epistle makes us at home there. In the Gospel, therefore, we constantly meet one message, "Believe." Salvation is declared to be ours by faith, apart from works. Our Lord beautifully and simply expressed it when He said, "For God so loved the world, that he gave his only begotten Son, that whosoever believeth in him should not perish, but have everlasting life." You see, God did the giving and now He invites us to receive. We appropriate His gift by faith. But when we come to the First Epistle of John, the writer lays down certain rules of conduct for the believer, to assure him continuous fellowship with God. The Bible has something to say about works, but it never makes the mistake of putting the cart before the horse. It always puts faith *before* works; salvation *before* service; relationship *before* discipleship; sonship *before* friendship.

The things enumerated in this 15th Psalm, applicable to the hour in which they were written, are equally appropriate to the hour in which we live. There can be no doubt that if a Christian is to have fellowship and communion with his Lord there must be a separation from sinful practices and from conduct displeasing to God.

Our *relationship* to God is based on what Christ did for us on the cross, while our *communion* with God rests not only on what Christ is now doing for us, but also on our conduct after we are saved. Let me illustrate. I am a member of my father's house and family by virtue of my birth into his family. Nothing can ever change that relationship, though my father might disown me because of my conduct. But he can never take away the blood relationship which exists between him and me. My conduct may be such that he will drive me out of his house or I may, like the prodigal son, decide to step out and live my own life. Thus my mode of living may deprive me of the friendship and fellowship of my father's house, but it cannot change the fact that I am my father's son. Even so, I am a child of God by new birth, and nothing can change that relationship.

What are the principles that should govern the conduct of a believer in order that he may constantly enjoy the fellowship and communion of God? Our Psalm says he must walk uprightly, he must work righteousness, he must speak the truth in his heart, he must not backbite with his tongue, nor do evil to his neighbor, nor take up reproach against his neighbor, he must not condone sin, he is to be a person in whose eyes a vile person is contemned. You see, there are "do's and don'ts" for *abiding* in God's house. but not for *entrance* into God's house. Again, he must honor them that fear the Lord. That does not mean that he is to be a narrow-minded sectarian, having fellowship and communion *only* with those of his own stripe and type. He is to honor those who *fear* the Lord. That stipulation breaks down the barriers of sectarianism; it makes communion with one another solely on the basis of *fearing* the Lord. The word "fear," used here, of course, means that "reverential awe" which is born in the heart of one who worships and loves the Lord. Let me give you an illustration of this principle. The disciples had been on a missionary tour—or should we call it an evangelistic campaign? They were in the ministry of the Lord. Some time after their return from the trip John thought he saw an excellent opportunity to impress the Lord, so he said to Him, "Master, we saw one casting out demons in thy name, and he followeth not us: and we forbad him, because he followeth not us." Did our Lord say to him, John, that was fine, it was commendable, that spirit of loyalty is a perfect illustration of your love and devotion to me? Indeed not. He said, "Forbid him not: for there is no man which shall do a miracle in my name, that can lightly speak evil of me. For he that is not against us is on our part."

Wouldn't we be a monstrosity if our legs refused to work along with our hands; if they said, we do not like your looks or your silly shape, so we are not going to have fellowship with you?

MISAPPLYING SCRIPTURE

Remember, I am not advocating fellowship with those who *do not fear* the Lord. I am not talking about men who do not believe the Bible, who reject the miraculous, and who refuse to receive Jesus as Lord. We are expressly commanded not to fellowship with any who do not hold the doctrine of Christ. But it is a sin against God to refuse to have fellowship with other born-again believers just because they are not members of our sect.

Another quality that should distinguish a member of the household of faith is expressed in the last line of the 4th verse, "He that sweareth to his own hurt, and changeth not." I am aware that the New Testament tells us to swear not at all. But this passage contains a principle which is applicable to us. If we decide to do a certain thing and vow before the Lord to do it, we should pay our vow and not change our mind about it because the payment is going to hurt.

Another quality of life is given in the final verse where we read, "He that putteth not out his money to usury, nor taketh reward against the innocent." How some of the modern communists and socialists have taken this passage out of its context! Here, say they, is an imperative—a man who wants to have fellowship with God has no right to ask interest on his money. The passage says nothing of the kind, and they willingly or deliberately overlook the teaching of our Lord on this subject which He illustrated in the parable of the ten pounds. The man who held on to his one pound and laid it up in a napkin was severely rebuked for not having made wise use of his talent and multiplying it by getting interest on it. The Bible does not rail against the proper use of money, but it strongly objects to its use for the purpose of usury. Money is not an evil, but the love of money is the root of all evil—whether one has little or much—or none.

Apart from the fact that the principles enumerated in this Psalm govern the believer's conduct in his fellowship with God, they also carry with them temporal and mental rewards. The last verse of this Psalm declares, "He that doeth these things shall never be moved." ". . . godliness is profitable unto all things, having promise of the life that now is, and of that which is to come. This is," said the Apostle Paul, "a faithful saying and worthy of all acceptation."

PSALM SIXTEEN

SEEING THE RESURRECTION OF CHRIST A THOUSAND YEARS BEFORE IT TOOK PLACE

IRRESPECTIVE of what one's view may be on the subject of the inspiration of the Scriptures, at least almost everyone is willing to acknowledge that the Bible is the most unique book ever put into the hands of men. Its expressions, its apt descriptions of important events, its own claims as well as its exquisite language, make this book, though hoary with age, more modern than our daily newspapers. Many of its verses are expressed in such a unique manner that they have been employed by orators and authors who have thereby lifted their otherwise commonplace speeches and writings into the realm of the truly great.

Several years ago I heard Dr. Nicholas Murray Butler, President of Columbia University, give an address of an exhortative type to a gathering of Columbia men. Dr. Butler is known for his excellent addresses, but I observed on that day he went to the Scriptures (without apologizing to the book) and took from it a part of a passage in order to climax his message. He urged Columbia men to so live that when the time of their departure would take place they could say, "I have fought a good fight, I have kept the faith."

The power of the Word of God has also recently been demonstrated by some apt editorials that have appeared occasionally in one of the leading New York metropolitan dailies, "The New York Sun." On Friday, January 9, 1934, this paper carried verbatim a portion of Scripture as it appears in the King James version taken from the 41st chapter of the book of Genesis The editorial was entitled "Zaphnath-paaneah." This striking quotation of how Joseph prepared for the famine that was about to visit the land of Egypt carried a pertinent message to the citizens of the United States in the year 1934, despite the fact that the passage was written almost thirty-five hundred years ago.

The Bible is a living book, as we shall note from our meditation in this 16th Psalm. This is one of the truly great gems of Scripture. It is called "a Michtam of David." It does not take much thinking to discover that this Psalm is not written about David, but about David's Lord, the Lord Jesus Christ. The Apostle Peter, speaking by the Holy Spirit on the day of Pentecost, referred to the 16th Psalm. The multitude that were gathered around the Apostles on the first Pentecost were entirely bewildered as they observed and heard each of the speakers in his own tongue, though the crowd spoke in many tongues and different languages. Peter rose to speak as the leader for the Apostles and said: ". . . Ye men of Judaea, and all ye that dwell at Jerusalem, be this known unto you, and hearken to my words." Peter was using the language of an official manifesto; he spoke by the Holy Spirit. He opened his mouth and the Lord gave the words. Said Peter, ". . . these are not drunken, as ye suppose, seeing it is but the third hour of the day. But this is that which was spoken by the prophet Joel. . . ."

FULFILLED PROPHECY

Before we quote the prophecy of Joel, let's stop and consider the effectiveness of these words *"this is that." This* referred to what was taking place, history in the making. *That* referred to what was written before it became history, and thus it was prophecy. It has been well said that fulfilled prophecy is one of the most potent arguments for the inspiration of the Scriptures. This which the multitude were witnessing and which made them bewildered, Peter said, is that which was spoken by the prophet Joel.

Then he quoted the prophet:

> "And it shall come to pass in the last days, saith
> God, I will pour out of my Spirit upon all flesh:
> and your sons and your daughters shall prophesy,
> and your young men shall see visions, and your
> old men shall dream dreams:
>
> "And on my servants and on my handmaidens I
> will pour out in those days of my Spirit; and they
> shall prophesy:
>
> * * * *
>
> "And it shall come to pass, that whosoever shall
> call on the name of the Lord shall be saved."

Peter continued in that same address and said: "Ye men of Israel,
hear these words: Jesus of Nazareth, a man approved of God among you
by miracles and wonders and signs, which God did by him in the midst of
you, as ye yourselves also know. . . ." I draw your attention to the manner
in which Peter, by the Holy Spirit, completely settled the matter of the
miracle-working power of the Lord Jesus Christ. There are many skeptics
in the land today, not a few of whom occupy supposedly Christian pulpits.
These skeptics deny the miracles of Jesus. They tell us that these miracles
were the "illusions" of the writers of the Gospels, who recorded them in
order to glorify the character of Jesus, about whom they were writing. It
is one matter to stand before an audience in 1934 and deny the historicity
of the miracles of Jesus, but no man would stand up before an audience on
the day of Pentecost and deny them. He might attribute the miracles of
Jesus to Beelzebub, the prince of demons, but no man would deny the miracles of Jesus because they actually transpired and were fully attested.
Peter, standing before an innumerable company, referred to Jesus of Nazareth as ". . . a man approved of God among you by miracles and wonders
and signs, which God did by him in the midst of you . . ." and he added
these significant words: ". . . *as ye yourselves also know*. . . ." There was
no skeptic in that audience. There was not even a Pharisee to object. They
all knew that the miracles and the wonders and the signs had taken place.
The extent of the audience which Peter addressed on that day can be
measured by the fact that no less than three thousand received Peter's
testimony concerning Christ and were born again that day.

"FOR DAVID SPEAKETH . . ."

Now let us examine Peter's reference to the 16th Psalm as he continued his memorable address.

> "Him, (meaning Jesus of Nazareth) being delivered by the determinate counsel and foreknowledge of God, ye have taken, and by wicked hands have crucified and slain:
>
> "Whom God hath raised up, having loosed the pains of death: because it was not possible that he should be holden of it.
>
> "For David speaketh concerning him, I foresaw the Lord always before my face, for he is on my right hand, that I should not be moved:
>
> "Therefore did my heart rejoice, and my tongue was glad; moreover also my flesh shall rest in hope:
>
> "Because thou wilt not leave my soul in hell, neither wilt thou suffer thine Holy One to see corruption.
>
> "Thou hast made known to me the ways of life; thou shalt make me full of joy with thy countenance."

Peter, as a member of the twelve, was an eye-witness to the death and resurrection of our Lord Jesus Christ. No man could be a member of the twelve unless he were an eye-witness, having accompanied our Lord during His public ministry, having seen Him crucified and having later seen Him in the flesh after His resurrection from the dead. Peter knew that the Lord had risen, for he had seen Him, but on this occasion he did not refer to his experience to attest the fact of Christ's resurrection from the dead. He had taken a leaf from the ministry of our Lord on the night of the resurrection. You will recall that our Lord, as he joined the two disciples who were on their way to Emmaus, confirmed their faith in His resurrection from the Scriptures before He allowed the scales to drop from their eyes to witness the resurrection by physical sight.

As a further evidence that David was not writing about himself in the 16th Psalm, the Apostle Peter continued on the day of Pentecost and said: "Men and brethren, let me freely speak unto you of the patriarch David, that he is both dead and buried and his sepulchre is with us unto this day." Certainly, therefore, David was not writing about himself. Of whom then was the Psalmist speaking? Peter continued: "Therefore being a prophet, and knowing that God had sworn with an oath to him, that of the fruit of his loins, according to the flesh, he would raise up Christ to sit on his throne;

he seeing this before spake of the resurrection of Christ, that his soul was not left in hades, neither his flesh did see corruption."

For the summation of all of this; that is, the reference to the prophet Joel and the patriarch David, Peter said:

> "This Jesus hath God raised up, whereof we all are witnesses.
>
> "Therefore being by the right hand of God exalted, and having received of the Father the promise of the Holy Spirit, he hath shed forth this, which ye now see and hear.
>
>   * * * *
>
> "Therefore let all the house of Israel know assuredly, that God hath made that *same Jesus*, whom ye have crucified, both Lord and Christ."

THE BIBLE IS A SUN-DIAL

Considering the limited time that we have for a single meditation in the Psalms, I have gone to an unusual length in the examination of Peter's comment on the 16th Psalm in order that it may be clearly demonstrated that the Psalm literally is a Messianic Psalm and that it concerns the Lord Jesus Christ. Someone may say, and particularly a son of Israel, Why cannot I see equally as clearly as the Apostle Peter that David spoke of Christ when he wrote the 16th Psalm? In answering, let me use the illustration of the sun-dial and suggest that the Bible, particularly the Old Testament, can be likened to a sun-dial. It is not difficult to read the hour marks on a sun-dial. Anybody can read them and at any time, but one can only tell time when the sun shines upon the sun-dial. Thus, while the Bible is the Word of God and can be read by all at any time, only the man who has received the Lord Jesus Christ is able to tell divine time by the Bible. It is only as the "Son" shines upon the pages of Scripture, particularly the Old Testament, that we are able to understand, to see and to appreciate that Christ is to be found on every page of Scripture.

We have but a few moments to briefly touch upon the substance of the Psalm. Note the explicit faith of the substitute for the sinner, who takes the sinner's place where the goodness of God is not available. The sinner's substitute, the Lord Jesus Christ, had never previously been in a place where the goodness of God had not been shining. Prior to that, He had always experienced the Father's smile and the Father's sunshine. On the cross He took the sinner's place and was enveloped in darkness, for He stood in that place where the goodness of God is not available. No wonder He cried "Preserve me O God: for in thee do I put my trust." As He entered the horrible darkness He had an immovable faith and confidence that His Father would preserve Him.

In order to appreciate this 16th Psalm, one must sit down before the cross. He must look at the Word, each verse and syllable, then turn and look at the One on the cross. Then and then only will one appreciate the message of the 16th Psalm.

But again, a careful examination of the Psalm apart from Peter's reference to it on the day of Pentecost, will thoroughly convince one that only Christ could be the speaker. For example, "I have set the LORD always before me; because he is at my right hand, I shall not be moved." The sinner's substitute is now at the right hand of God. Previously, the perfect One became obedient to death in order to redeem the sinner so that the sinner might enjoy the Saviour's heritage, eternal life.

The closing verse of this Psalm is particularly refreshing. Saith the Lord through David, "Thou wilt show me the path of life: in thy presence is fullness of joy; at thy right hand there are pleasures for evermore." That passage is a description of heaven and was spoken by One who always lived there. It is a double assurance to us that if we are to experience the fullness of joy and to have pleasures for evermore, it is not possible apart from a knowledge of the Lord Jesus Christ. Here, therefore, is a testimony of One who knows what heaven is like. It is even more effective than the story Spurgeon tells of a Scotchman who was asked if he were sure he was going to heaven. He immediately replied with much emphasis, "Why, man, I live there already!"

PSALM SEVENTEEN

THE CLIMAX OF LIFE:
LEAVING MONEY OR BEGETTING A NEW LIKENESS

THE 17th Psalm is entitled "A prayer of David." It would be impossible in a short summary to comment on each verse comprising this Psalm, but we shall take time to read it and then lift two or three things out of the Psalm and center our thoughts around them.

> "Hear the right, O LORD, attend unto my cry, give ear unto my prayer, that goeth not out of feigned lips.

"Let my sentence come forth from thy presence; let thine eyes behold the things that are equal.

"Thou hast proved mine heart; thou hast visited me in the night; thou hast tried me, and shalt find nothing; I am purposed that my mouth shall not transgress.

"Concerning the works of men, by the word of thy lips I have kept me from the paths of the destroyer.

"Hold up my goings in thy paths, that my footsteps slip not.

"I have called upon thee, for thou wilt hear me, O God: incline thine ear unto me, and hear my speech.

"Shew thy marvellous lovingkindness, O thou that savest by thy right hand them which put their trust in thee from those that rise up against them.

"Keep me as the apple of the eye, hide me under the shadow of thy wings,

"From the wicked that oppress me, from my deadly enemies, who compass me about.

"They are inclosed in their own fat: with their mouth they speak proudly.

"They have now compassed us in our steps: they have set their eyes bowing down to the earth;

"Like as a lion that is greedy of his prey, and as it were a young lion lurking in secret places.

"Arise, O LORD, disappoint him, cast him down: deliver my soul from the wicked, which is thy sword:

"From men which are thy hand, O LORD, from men of the world, which have their portion in this life, and whose belly thou fillest with thy hid treasure: they are full of children, and leave the rest of their substance to their babes.

"As for me, I will behold thy face in righteousness: I shall be satisfied, when I awake, with thy likeness."

Charles Haddon Spurgeon, commenting upon this Psalm, wrote, "David would never have been a man after God's own heart if he had not been a man of prayer. He was a master in the sacred art of supplication."

PRAYER—A PANACEA

It is absolutely a mistaken notion that every man can pray. God refuses to hear the prayer of those who have not been born again by the Spirit of

God. The only prayer an unsaved man *can* offer unto God, acceptable to Him, is the prayer of the publican, "God be merciful to me a sinner."

There have been some mighty men of prayer. Elijah, for instance, was a great man of faith, a man of prayer. Jonah was a disobedient servant, to be true, but he was a man of prayer.

A. Lindsay Glegg, one of the great laymen of England, has a message on Jonah entitled "Hope for the Backslider," in which he calls attention to the manner in which Jonah closed his prayer. His final cry was, "Salvation is of the LORD." Mr. Glegg says, "That was too much for the fish who said to itself, 'This man is a Calvinist,' and threw him out on to the dry land."

Prayer not only is a dug-out to a Christian, but a mighty weapon, for let us not forget that it is written, ". . . though we walk in the flesh, we do not war after the flesh: (For the weapons of our warfare are not carnal, but mighty through God to the pulling down of strong holds) . . ."

Prayer is also the panacea for despondency. There is much in the world at present that makes for despondency. Many Christians who are not acquainted with their Bible, and God's chart of the course of the ages found in the Bible, are exceedingly depressed and almost driven to despair because of current conditions. But the man who knows his Bible and who is living in intimate fellowship with God daily, knows the truth of what a leading Norwegian theologian recently said, "Living Christianity knows no despondency." The man to whom I refer is one of the brilliant young preachers of Norway. He spent some years in Brooklyn and has recently written a book which he dedicates "to the Unknown America, known to God." In the preface of his book he voices a greeting from the "Unknown Europe, hidden from the shrieking headlines of newspapers, living its rich and victorious life, whatever befalls it." He goes on to explain that "Unknown Europe is the living communion of believers throughout all the nations of what seems to be a dying continent." To those in America who are members of that living communion he points out that we all know "something about the post-war Europe of crazed militarism, bloody revolutions, fanatic nationalism, economic crises, endless and futile conference-talkativeness, appalling hunger and privation. Chaos upon chaos, results of a nonsensical paper called a peace treaty."

But this young man went on to say that few of us in America may "know of the Unknown Europe; the spiritual rebirth of Christianity; the remaining martyrs of Christ in the killing winter storms of Siberia and in Stalin's Moscow; the amazing revivals in the Baltic border states, Poland, and Central Europe; the sturdy, joyous confessors in the totalitarian dictatorship of Nazism; the absolute breakdown of the spineless humanism and rationalism of what used to call itself liberal theology; the God-sent rebirth of personal Christianity in that fortunate, quiet corner of Europe called Scandinavia." Writing of that company of people, he says, "They have not been 're-thinking' Christianity, or been busy remodelling its message. They have *heard* a Word, coming from the Other Side of mere human possibilities. A word from above, lifting them into the *awe*-ful and *joy*-ful presence of *Him* who was, is and ever shall be. There they live and work, there they find courage in persecution, and there the candle of faith is kindled with the flame of hope, unspeakable, and full of glory."

PRESENT-DAY SAINTS AND MARTYRS

All of which is intended to convey that there is in this world a communion of saints, a fellowship of believers that knows no denominational barriers, nor country, nor clime, nor persecution, nor distress, nor famine, nor despondency—they hold the torch high as they rejoice in the knowledge of a living Christ; and while the nations of the earth are reeling like drunken men and the much boasted 20th century civilization is ready to crash, those who have a living faith in the living Christ stand upon a Rock absolutely immovable.

And, by the way, the mention of "re-thinking" Christianity or being busy remodelling its message, which idea was the product of that vicious piece of work entitled "Re-thinking Missions," reminds me of Jonah's experience to which we alluded a moment ago. Jonah received an opportunity to do some *re-thinking* about the mission to which God had called him. He was given another chance but not another message. The message was the same.

I can well imagine that this 17th Psalm is a great source of encouragement to the hearts of the persecuted Christians in Russia, Germany, Spain, China, and other parts of the universe. Such people can enter into the presence of God and cry out, "Hear the right, O LORD, attend unto my (our) cry, give ear unto my (our) prayer, that goeth not out of feigned lips."

And what boldness is manifested when the petitioner asked, "Shew thy marvellous lovingkindness, O thou that savest by thy right hand them which put their trust in thee from those that rise up against them." Whether under the Old Testament or New Testament economy, whether before Christ or after Christ, persecution has frequently been the believer's lot. But God has often demonstrated that He saves by His right hand "them which put their trust in Him from those that rise up against them." You cannot kill a man who has a faith like that. He knows he has eternal life. He knows that if you destroy the body, he still lives. The body is merely a temporary tent that houses the true individual. He cries with confidence in the language of the Apostle Paul, ". . . I know whom I have believed, and am persuaded that he is able to keep that which I have committed unto him against that day." What day? The day to which the Psalmist referred when he closed this 17th Psalm by saying, "As for me, I will behold thy face in righteousness: I shall be satisfied, when I awake, with thy likeness." But we will come back to this thought and have something to say about that glorious hope before bringing our meditation to a close.

For a few moments I want to center our thoughts upon that exquisite 8th verse of this Psalm, where the Psalmist wrote, "Keep me as the apple of the eye, hide me under the shadow of thy wings." I wish I had a physician with me just now to whom I could turn and ask him to describe the apple of the eye. I would like to have a godly scientist, a man who has not only been in the operating room, and who with the skillful use of the knife and his fingers has been able to minister to the physical needs of a sick man, but who also has been in that great hospital called "Christian Soul Care." I refer to such a man as Dr. Howard A. Kelly of Baltimore. Wouldn't I delight to have him here this moment to ask him to describe the wonderful care which the Creator exercised when He designed the human eye. How marvelously protected it is. It is a very delicate part of the body, quite different from the tongue, which is also a delicate and interesting member, and which has a strange capacity for exaggeration, so that when passing over a small cavity it makes one feel that it is a huge canyon—but the eye is so sensitive that a little speck of dust causes havoc. Notice how the eye is protected, not only by the lid, but by the lashes as well. Then, too, the eyes are sunken in, with protecting cheekbone below and forehead above and nose between. But I give up; I am not a physician nor have I had any medical training—the nearest I ever got to one was by marrying a physician's daughter. But this is sure, most of us would rather lose any other member of our body than endure the loss of our eyes.

But the Psalmist referred to a specific part of the eye which is called "the apple of the eye." The phrase is composed of two Hebrew words each having the same sense—indeed it has been called the "black," or the reflection in the eye. In Proverbs 7:9 the same word is translated "black," and in Proverbs 20:20 as "obscure." It is that part of the eye which reflects the man or the girl, whoever it might be, who looks into another's eye and recognizes his or her own reflection; in fact, the Hebrew word has that very thought in it. It has been called "the tenderest piece of the tenderest part of the eye," which is kept most diligently and strongly guarded by nature with "tunicles." David prayed that he might so be kept.

Dr. Alexander MacLaren suggests that "the eye which steadily looks at God can look calmly at dangers." The Psalmist here asked the Lord to keep him as "the apple of the eye." To accomplish that, the eye of the Psalmist must likewise be fastened upon God. When David asked, ". . . hide me under the shadow of thy wings . . ." what a foolish request it would have been if the Psalmist had run away from God's protecting care. On the contrary, here is a beautiful picture—the Psalmist is seen running unto God, getting under His care, bidding Him to hide him under the shadow of His wings, and asking Him to keep him as the apple of the eye.

BOTH EYES ON CHRIST

I have already referred to A. Lindsay Glegg. Let me give you another of his excellent illustrations. He said that some time ago in one of his meetings he asked a Vicar to speak to his people. The Vicar startled the people by the way he began. He said, "I want to give you some good advice. It is this, Don't squint!" Mr. Glegg said his people looked at him and he looked at them and wondered what would be next. The Vicar continued and went on to describe the scene where Peter stepped out of the boat and walked on the sea to meet his Lord. Peter began to sink, you remember, and Christ stretched out His hand and saved him, and brought him back again into the boat. And when they reached the shore the Lord said to His disciple, ". . . wherefore didst thou doubt?" The Vicar told that congregation that the root meaning of the word "doubt" was just this, "looking two ways at once." Were you to ask the Apostle Peter why he began to sink he would undoubtedly have answered that it was because he had one eye upon Christ and the other eye upon the billows and the storm around about him. Lindsay Glegg says that the secret of walking on the water is this—"both eyes on Christ." Thus if you invite the Lord to keep you as the apple of the eye you will have to set your eyes upon the Lord. No man with a living faith in a living Christ will be greatly moved by surrounding disturbances.

In the closing part of the Psalm David contrasted the condition of "the man of the world" as concerning the future, with himself. He said that the men of the world have their portion in this life; their innermost being is filled with hidden treasure; they are full of children and leave the rest of their substance to their babes. In other words, they are men without hope; wealthy men, to be sure, but poverty-stricken as to any faith in a life beyond the grave. By the way, observe that wicked men have a right to earthly things. They spend their youth trying to get somewhere, their middle age in accumulating, and their old age in preparing to distribute their wealth (if any be left), and they pass their substance on to their children, while their children after them vie with each other as to who can spend it most quickly.

David said, "As for me, I will behold thy face in righteousness: I shall be satisfied, when I awake, with thy likeness." You see, David had the same kind of hope that every born-again believer in Christ possesses. John the Apostle said, "Beloved, now are we the children of God, and it doth not yet appear what we shall be: but we know that, when he shall appear, we shall be like him; for we shall see him as he is." Job said, ". . . I know that my redeemer liveth, and that he shall stand at the latter day upon the earth: and though after my skin worms destroy this body, yet in my flesh shall I see God. . ." Abraham looked for a city whose builder and maker was God. Therefore, though he was extremely wealthy he was content to dwell in tents.

Notice the revelation of the future which David had, ". . . I will behold thy face in righteousness . . ." That means that David expected to be an absolutely justified person so that he could look into the face of God and feel perfectly at home in His presence, for when he awakened he would be in the likeness of his Lord. Frankly, I think the most rational thing in the world is to rejoice in the assured promise that a man who has believed in Christ and has committed his life to Him can rest in the hope that he shall be like his Lord in the glory—absolutely justified, declared righteous, and reflecting the very majesty, glory, and righteousness of Jehovah God Himself.

THE SECRET OF A NORMAL SPIRITUAL LIFE

T HIS is a Psalm of fifty verses. We could not hope to begin to cover it with any degree of completeness in less than three to five hours. We shall therefore content ourselves with a few choice "tid-bits" from a sumptuous banqueting table. I shall ask you to look at the first three verses. They read:

> "I will love thee, O LORD, my strength.
> "The LORD is my rock, and my fortress, and my deliverer; my God, my strength, in whom I will trust; my buckler, and the horn of my salvation, and my high tower.
> "I will call upon the LORD, who is worthy to be praised: so shall I be saved from mine enemies."

The first thing that impresses itself upon a mind when reading these verses is the intimacy revealed therein and, secondly, the apparent fact that the Lord is the center of the life described therein, even though the personal pronouns, "I," "my," or "mine," are profusely used, appearing no less than fourteen times in sixty words—a decidedly large percentage.

Let us look at the intimacy revealed in these verses. Intimacy without affection is as flat as an apple pie without salt. The Psalmist said, "I will love thee, O LORD, my strength." Man-made religion has built up a "strange" awesomeness about the Person of the Godhead. Instead of a deep feeling of affection welling up in the heart that can best be expressed by "I will love thee, O LORD," men have developed a fear of God so that they actually shudder in His presence. Our Lord made sinners feel at home in His presence.

THE MAJESTY OF GOD vs. THE MERCY OF GOD

Nothing is more foreign to the writer of this Psalm than shuddering in the presence of the Lord. This does not infer that the Psalmist ever minimized the majesty of His Person; indeed where will we find words that inspire Godly awesomeness as these that are found in this very Psalm?

> "There went up a smoke out of his nostrils, and fire out of his mouth devoured: coals were kindled by it.
> "He bowed the heavens also and came down: and darkness was under his feet.
> "And he rode upon a cherub, and did fly: yea, he did fly upon the wings of the wind.

"He made darkness his secret place; his pavilion round about him were dark waters and thick clouds of the skies."

Could it be possible to describe the majesty of God more terribly? But this revelation of God's character concerns His attitude toward His enemies, not His worshippers.

We could best illustrate the difference by noting the attitude of the unnamed woman who appeared in the house of Simon, the Pharisee, while he performed the part of the host to the Lord Jesus. The woman was a known character. She was unchaste. Yet, she came unostentatiously into the banqueting room. Having heard that He was to be present, she had brought with her an alabaster box of ointment.

As she stood at His feet, behind Him, weeping, her tears trickled down upon His feet. Possessing no other means she wiped those feet with her hair, then kissed them; finally she anointed them with ointment. Of course, it was a shock to the fine sensibilities of the Pharisee, who was a highly respected citizen, and a devout religious leader. Why should it not shock a religious man, who up to that moment had always been impressed with the austerity of God, and His *unapproachable holiness?* Had not the Lord openly appropriated to Himself passages of Scripture from the Old Testament which unmistakably concerned the Messiah? Since the Messiah is the visible revelation of God, surely the acceptance by the Lord of this sinful woman's devotion struck at the very root of Phariseeism.

What did our Lord do? First He related a parable clearly illustrating the true spiritual condition of both His host and the unchaste woman. Then turning to Simon, He said: "Wherefore I say unto thee, Her sins, which are many, are forgiven; for she loved much . . . And they that sat at meat with him began to say within themselves, Who is this that forgiveth sins also?" Upon which our Lord turned to the woman and said: "Thy faith hath saved thee: go in peace."

"Who is this that forgiveth sins also?" He is none other than God, manifest in flesh! All that we will ever get to know about God is revealed in Jesus Christ! His behavior was God-like; His words were God-breathed; His acceptance of the worship of this woman can only be one of two things: either His right as a member of the Godhead, or, the usurpation of a Divine prerogative that is revolting to the extreme and which cries out to high heaven for revenge. No other position is tenable; either Jesus is *God* or else He is a *malefactor!*

But we ask—Did this woman manifest a fear that creates distances, or did she denote by her demeanor that perfect love casteth out all fear? Could not the first verse of our Psalm, "I will love thee, O LORD, my strength" fit perfectly into her mouth? Indeed! That kind of love is the highest devotion a human being can render to God—it is a heart devotion which comes from an appreciation of His grace, which grace has removed the barrier of distance and has brought us into His very presence. How perfectly at home this unchaste woman felt in the presence of Christ, the sinless One!

I have had men say to me, "I can understand Christ, but He seems so different from my conception of God that they seem two distinct Persons." I have invariably replied by quoting the answer of our Lord to this same question which was expressed by Philip, only in slightly different words, "Lord, shew us the Father, and it sufficeth us." Our Lord replied: "Have I been so long time with you, and yet hast thou not known me, Philip? He that hath seen me hath seen the Father; and how sayest thou then, Shew us the Father?"

On another occasion our Lord said: "I and my Father are *one*." The intimacy the believer may have with our Lord, he may also have with the Father.

THE SECRET OF CHRISTIAN LIFE

It is evident that the Lord is the center of the life described in the opening verses of this 18th Psalm. There are many professed Christians who have never learned the secret of such life. Multitudes center their lives in their experiences. The Oxford Group Movement is an example of the effort to center a life in experience. Its activities have been well publicized; its appeal has largely been directed to those who are called "the up and outs" in contrast to the "down and outs." I have observed the movement carefully. I am interested in any effort that purports to present the gospel of our Lord Jesus. I have listened to the testimonies of their adherents. They invariably speak of experiences, some of which are of the most trivial type, and self-centered. But observe that this Psalm, especially verse 2, is concerned with the Lord. The man of whom this passage speaks has found the secret of normal spiritual experience. It is not found in self—it is found in the Lord. He is the center and the circumference. Therefore, David said: "The LORD is my rock, and my fortress, and my deliverer; my God, my strength, in whom I will trust; my buckler, and the horn of my salvation, and my high tower."

Notice how many things the Lord is, to a soul that trusts Him. Is anything more clear than that? The Lord is the center of the life. He is Life itself. But notice also how marvelously the Lord in Himself is the answer to every phase of life. He is "my rock," said David. A *rock* is a foundation—in fact that idea is conveyed in the New Testament in 1 Corinthians 3: 11, where Paul, the Apostle wrote: "For other foundation can no man lay than that is laid, which is Jesus Christ." Is He your foundation? Are we building our life upon *Him?*

Then David also said He is "my fortress." As such, He stood between David and the enemy of his soul. How safe is one when he is sheltered in Him! How aptly is this described by the poet who wrote:

> "O safe to the Rock that is higher than I,
> My soul in its conflicts and sorrows would fly.
> So sinful, so weary, Thine, Thine, would I be.
> Thou blest Rock of Ages, I'm hiding in Thee.
>> Hiding in Thee, Hiding in Thee;
>> Thou blest Rock of Ages, I'm hiding in Thee."

But, more: the Psalmist called Him "my *deliverer.*" What struggles we poor humans have! We strive to overcome our difficulties and trials. We should cease trying and simply trust. We should make Him our victory. In Him is the secret of a victorious life.

Again, David wrote "He is my God, my strength." We have no strength. Our efforts are the feeble expression of a will that desires but which is powerless to act. Note that the inspired writer said "my strength, in whom I will trust . . ." The difference between struggling and trusting is the difference between Christianity and religion! Religion's watchword is "Do"—but Christianity's gospel is "Done."

Finally, David called the Lord "my buckler, the horn of my salvation, and my high tower." A buckler, of course, is a shield to protect one from darts, while upon the battlefield. But what did David have in mind when he wrote He is "the horn of my salvation"? A strange expression! Some will recall that Michelangelo pictured Moses with horns protruding from his forehead! Why do you suppose he did that? The answer is clear. As Moses came down from the Mount where he had been in God's presence, he unconsciously reflected the glory of God, so that his face shone. The elders of Israel asked him to put a veil upon his face for they could not stand in such glory. The reflected glory of God in the face of Moses was expressed in streaks of light blazing from his forehead. These streaks the artist, Michelangelo, pictured as horns. In fact, the words *horn* and *shone* are the same in Hebrew. When David spoke of the Lord as the horn of his salvation he simply used Oriental language. The Lord was the light or the glory of David's salvation.

But the Lord was also David's "high tower." A high tower is a place of defence against an air attack! The Bible speaks of Satan as "the prince of the power of the air!" That is a striking title! It presents a picture quite the opposite from the caricature of the Medievalist—properly scorned by our modern writers and through which millions have been lulled into a false belief that Satan is non-existent.

After this marvelous unfolding of the Lord, is it any wonder that the 3rd verse of our Psalm reads: "I will call upon the LORD, who is worthy to be praised: so shall I be saved from mine enemies." Who else is worthy to be praised?

PSALM NINETEEN—PART ONE

THE PSALM OF THE HEAVENS

THE 19th Psalm, for sheer beauty of literary expression, is without equal, though the entire collection is distinguished by its grandeur in contemplation of the universe.

The Secretary of Agriculture in the present Administration, in a recent book entitled "Statesmanship and Religion," made the following comment regarding the Psalms. "Our pioneer forefathers, confronting physical hazards and obstacles which do not exist for us, had need of all the physical and moral stamina they could summon. It is not surprising that they turned so much to the Psalms of David for spiritual meat and drink. The Psalms seem to typify the rugged individual, fearlessly prepared to meet his God face to face."

Upon reading that paragraph, I was all for wiring the good Secretary, who by the way is a religious man, saying "Splendid!" Indeed that is what our forefathers did. And they prospered! We do well to follow in their steps. But alas, when I came to the last paragraph in his book, I read: "We are no longer faced with the problems of material scarcity. It no longer suffices therefore, to strengthen the spiritual powers of the individual with the simple doctrine of the Psalms of David."

Here we part! It's too bad the Secretary failed to tune in on our Sunday morning meditations in the Psalms. Maybe he might have changed his mind on the spiritual value of the Psalms for our present day! And possibly his agricultural theories also.

You have probably heard it often said that the discovery of Copernicus destroyed the "traditional" way of looking at the heavens. This assertion is true if by traditional is meant "medieval." But it is not true, if by traditional is meant "Biblical." Take this particular Psalm for example. It is the meditation of one who entered into an understanding of creation with deep spiritual intelligence. We shall limit this meditation to the first six verses. These verses read:

> "The heavens declare the glory of God; and the firmament sheweth his handiwork.
> "Day unto day uttereth speech, and night unto night sheweth knowledge.
> "There is no speech nor language, where their voice is not heard.
> "Their line is gone out through all the earth, and their words to the end of the world. In them hath he set a tabernacle for the sun,
> "Which is as a bridegroom coming out of his chamber, and rejoiceth as a strong man to run a race.
> "His going forth is from the end of the heaven, and his circuit unto the ends of it: and there is nothing hid from the heat thereof."

In the New Testament we are told concerning our Lord Jesus Christ that "all things were created by Him, and for Him." We should therefore confidently expect to find in creation a perfect harmony with the revelation of the person, glory, and ministry of our Lord Jesus Christ as contained in the Bible.

THE GLORY OF GOD'S CREATION

The verses we have before us are concerned with the glory of God's creation. Our next meditation will take up the balance of this Psalm, which concerns our Lord's revelation in law, His written revelation. It was Clement of Alexander who said that "the world is God's scripture, the first Bible that God made for the instruction of man."

Upon the blue sapphire of the firmament is spread a sheet of royal paper written all over with the wisdom and power of God. This book of creation is not sold at book stores, but it is to be seen by everyone who lifts his eyes up to heaven. We acknowledge, however, using the language of a scholarly ancient, "that the heavens and the earth, be they ever so diligently read, can never bring a man to the saving knowledge of God in Christ, nor make him perfect, thoroughly furnished unto every good work, which God's other writing, the Holy Scriptures, accomplish." The old adage reads: "Where the philosopher ends, the physician begins." So, where creation ends, revelation begins!

An impartial study of the heavens will bring one to the position which is expressed in the first chapter of Paul's letter to the Romans, where Paul gave several reasons for his loyalty to the gospel by saying, first: ". . . I am not ashamed of the gospel of Christ: for it is the power of God unto salvation to every one that believeth; to the Jew first, and also to the Greek. For therein (that is in the gospel) is the righteousness of God revealed from faith to faith: as it is written, The just shall live by faith." After which he gave as his second reason: "For the wrath of God is revealed from heaven against all ungodliness and unrighteousness of men, who hold the truth in unrighteousness; because that which may be known of God is manifest in them: for God hath shewed it unto them."

But where has God given a revelation, apart from the Bible, which may be known, and which clearly evidences His wrath against "all ungodliness and unrighteousness"? Paul defined the sphere by writing: "For the invisible things of him from the creation of the world are clearly seen, being understood by the things that are made, even his eternal power and Godhead . . ." Thus *all* "are without excuse"!

Now then, let us examine the Psalm more closely. First it is stated: "The heavens declare the glory of God; and the firmament sheweth his handiwork." The word *declare* may be better understood by the use of a synonym, *manifest*. The heavens manifest the glory of God. As the heavens make known the glory of God, we ought to become acquainted with them to learn what is meant by the expression "the glory of God."

The Viewpoint of Our Lord Jesus

The Lord repeatedly referred to creation to illustrate spiritual truth. He is the Lord of creation. We can profit by emulating His method. He had occasion to refer to the lilies of the field in the course of the Sermon on the Mount. He said: ". . . Consider the lilies of the field, how they grow; they toil not, neither do they spin: and yet I say unto you, That even Solomon in all his glory was not arrayed like one of these. *Wherefore*, if God so clothe the grass of the field . . . shall he not much more clothe you, O ye of little faith?" It is clear that our Lord, as He considered the lily, thought of the provision of His Father. Thus we have His viewpoint.

When, therefore, it is our privilege on a marvelous June night to be away from the glare and blaze of the city, let us note the heavens and say with David the Psalmist, "The heavens reveal the glory of God!" Then we should ask ourselves, What is the glory of God? The Bible answers our question—The Lord Jesus is the express image of the Father, and the effulgence of His glory. The glory of God is only clearly and intelligently made known in Jesus Christ. He gives expression to that glory. Therefore, as the heavens manifest the glory of God, they reveal the Person of our Lord Jesus Christ.

That the heavens reveal the Lord Jesus Christ is evident, for it was a star which guided the Magi from the East, and led them to Bethlehem where the Babe was. These wise men carefully read the stars, observed a special significance attached to one, and therefore came to Herod to inquire, "Where is he that is born King of the Jews? For we have seen his star in the east, and are come to worship him."

A study of the heavens is the most ancient branch of science known to man. The very names of the stars are significant, and when stripped of their mythology, evidence that man at one time had a clear understanding of the conflict of the opposing forces of good and evil in the struggle of the crooked serpent and the dual-natured Son of the Virgin for possession of the throne and the crown.

When we look at the Milky Way in the heavens, and remember that astrology calls it the King's Highway, we should think of the King, the Lord Jesus Christ, who is the effulgence of God's glory.

ELOQUENCE OF THE HEAVENS

The 2nd and 3rd verses of this Psalm reveal that the starry heavens have an unusual language. They utter a speech in a dumb but magnificent eloquence. Of their speech it is written, "Day unto day uttereth speech, and night unto night sheweth knowledge. There is no speech nor language, where their voice is not heard."

We moderns often attribute our failure to give attention to spiritual things to the speed of our lives. We might well ask: But where are we speeding to? On the testimony of the Bible, we are speeding to one of two places, either heaven or hell. One can try to smile away the existence of these places, but they still remain! The ceaseless, silent, universal preachings of the heavens are God's messengers inviting attention to the reality of life and of God.

THE SUN A TYPE OF CHRIST

In closing, let me draw attention to what is written concerning the sun —that prince of planets—yet servant of all. The prophet of old used the sun as a type of Christ; for when Malachi, the last of the prophets, closed the Old Testament, he bore this testimony concerning the Christ: ". . . unto you that fear my name shall the Sun of righteousness arise with healing in his wings. . . ."

It is axiomatic that that which makes the night is the absence of the sun! So that which makes this world of ours a night of sin, darkness, rebellion, disappointments, and sorrows—is the absence of our Lord Jesus, who is the Sun of righteousness.

As surely as does the sun each morning make its successive journey and nothing is hid from the heat of it, so our Lord Jesus will one day cause this night of sin to end. His coming will bring in the dawn of a new day— I was almost tempted to say a "New Deal." When this world enjoys the rulership of the King of kings and Lord of lords, it will not be one of trial and error, it will be one of truth and certainty. It ought to be evident that a Bible Christian is not a pessimist! But mark well *where* his hope is placed. The hymn writer put it:

> "My hope is built on nothing less
> Than Jesus' blood and righteousness.
> I dare not trust the sweetest frame
> But wholly lean on Jesus' name.
> On Christ the solid Rock I stand,
> All other ground is sinking sand."

Whether it is peace for the individual or for the world, Christ is the answer to each.

PSALM NINETEEN—PART TWO

THE WRITTEN WORD

I N the first half of the 19th Psalm David gave expression to his thoughts as he contemplated the revelation of God in creation. From the 7th verse to the end of the Psalm, we have his comments concerning the second, and greater revelation of God, namely the Scriptures, the written Word.

At the time when David wrote this Psalm very few of the books of the Bible had been written. The Psalms were only in the course of writing. Many of the great prophets had not yet been born. The Books of the Kings and Chronicles had not been compiled. The major portion of the

Scriptures in the possession of David were the five books of Moses, which are designated the Pentateuch. It was undoubtedly to this collection David specifically referred. I do not believe, however, that it is proper to examine this Psalm from that limited view, but rather to consider the Psalm from the viewpoint of the entire Bible.

THE THREE GREAT DIVISIONS OF THE OLD TESTAMENT

On the evening of the resurrection day, the events of which are recorded in the 24th chapter of Luke, our Lord gave the divine purpose of the entire Old Testament. Commencing with verse 25 of that chapter, our Lord answered the unbelief of the two disciples with whom He journeyed to Emmaus, by saying: ". . . O fools, and slow of heart to believe *all* that the prophets have spoken: Ought not Christ to have suffered these things, and to enter into his glory?" That was our Lord's rebuke to them for their unbelief. Immediately He proceeded to expound the Scriptures. Verse 27 reads: "And beginning at Moses and all the prophets, he expounded unto them in all the scriptures the things concerning himself." That same evening, in the city of Jerusalem, our Lord gave the "eleven" the same exposition. Beginning at verse 44 we read:

> "And he (our Lord) said unto them (the eleven disciples), These are the words which I spake unto you, while I was yet with you, that all things must be fulfilled, which were written in the law of Moses, and in the prophets, and in the psalms, concerning me.
>
> "Then opened he their understanding, that they might understand the scriptures,
>
> "And said unto them, Thus it is written, and thus it behoved Christ to suffer, and to rise from the dead the third day . . ."

Here we have none other than our Lord Jesus Christ, placing in the disciples' hands the "key" to the Old Testament. He said it concerned Him. He also insisted that all things written therein must be fulfilled. He set His seal upon the three great divisions of the Old Testament: the law, the Psalms, and the prophets.

THE NEW TESTAMENT EPISTLES

But someone might ask, What about the New Testament? A word on that may suffice. A few days prior to the resurrection of Christ, in fact, on the very day of His betrayal, our Lord had some things to say concerning a future revelation by the Spirit of God. In the 16th chapter of John's

Gospel, and in the 12th verse of that chapter, our Lord told His disciples: "I have yet many things to say unto you, but ye cannot bear them now." "Many things." That is worthy of note. He added, "but ye cannot bear them now." The disciples could not at that time enter into and understand these "many things." I believe these "many things" to be the future revelation, the New Testament Scriptures. For support of this view, note the following verse in John 16, which reads: "Howbeit when he, the Spirit of truth, is come (the Holy Spirit), he will guide you into all truth: for he shall not speak of himself; but whatsoever he shall hear, that shall he speak: and he will shew you things to come." Thus we have our Lord's prediction concerning the revelation of the Spirit of God about future things that were not then known to the disciples; which very things are revealed in the New Testament epistles and the closing book of the New Testament, the book of the Revelation.

THE FOUR GOSPELS

Beginning with verse 25 of the 14th of John, our Lord announced that the Spirit of God would also provide for that revelation which we have in the four Gospels, all of which concern the things that the disciples had seen and heard during the public ministry of Christ. He said: "These things have I spoken unto you, being yet present with you. But the Comforter, which is the Holy Spirit, whom the Father will send in my name, he shall teach you all things, and bring *all things* to your remembrance, whatsoever I have said unto you."

When, therefore, we read the four Gospels, Matthew, Mark, Luke, and John, we do not need to have doubts concerning the memory of the four writers of those Gospels, two of whom, Mark and Luke, were not even eyewitnesses. John probably was ninety years of age when he wrote. Naturally speaking, John ought to have had a very poor memory, but our Lord did not say that John would be able to recall to his mind all the things which He had said unto the disciples, but that the Holy Spirit *would bring* to John's remembrance whatsoever the Lord had said.

It is for this reason that full weight can be given to such a statement as appears in the 17th chapter of John's Gospel, where it is written, "These words spake Jesus." It was not John's memory that served him to recall the words, it was the Holy Spirit who recalled them to him.

THE LAW OF THE LORD IS PERFECT

And so I have briefly outlined why I believe the complete Scriptures, both Old and New Testaments, to be the written revelation of God. This

19th Psalm is not limited in its view to the books of the Pentateuch, but embraces the entire Bible.

Now note what the Psalmist said concerning this written revelation. Verse 7: "The law of the LORD is perfect, converting the soul. . . ." I do not believe it is possible to convert a soul by any other means. Some professional evangelists seem to think it possible to convert souls by appealing to men through sentimental stories, thus working upon the emotional side of man. But this verse tells us it is the law of the Lord that converts the soul.

Another passage tells us that we are born again by the incorruptible Word of God, which liveth and abideth forever. If a man is converted, or born again, which, while not synonymous terms, yet have much in common, it is a result of the Word of God, which in the 19th Psalm is spoken of as the law of the Lord. Indeed, it is the only thing in this world which is perfect.

The Psalmist continued: ". . . the testimony of the LORD is sure, making wise the simple." How interesting is that statement. We do not know any other place in all the world where we can find a sure foundation upon which to base our confidence for the future, as well as for the present. It is only the testimony of the Lord that is sure and solid. It stands like the rock of Gibraltar. The dashing waves of unbelief cannot disturb nor assail it. About it are strewn the wrecks of time, which cherish the hope that they could destroy its message. It is the *only book* in all the world that claims to be the revelation of God's mind. While men have attempted to destroy it, or ridicule it, it still is the most popular book in all the world. More copies of it are printed than of any other book.

I rejoice that the Psalmist declared that as "the testimony of the LORD is sure," it makes "wise the simple." Men love to be wise, but more often they are wise in their own conceits. If we desire to possess wisdom, we ought to consider what the wisest of men said: "The fear of the LORD is the beginning of wisdom." But the wise man's father said: "The testimony of the LORD" makes "*wise the simple*." You may never have gone through one of the recognized halls of learning—much less graduated! You may not have a single degree behind your name. You may be even a simpleton; yet, if you desire wisdom, the only sure way to its attainment is by a study of the Word of God, and by obedience to the testimony of the Lord.

Again the Psalmist said:

> "The statutes of the LORD are right, rejoicing the heart . . ."

If we have real joy, it is because we have found its source in the statutes of the Lord.

Again David said:

> ". . . the commandment of the LORD is pure, enlightening the eyes."

If we desire to see the future, having eyes that can penetrate through the mists of the present, we will only get such vision by an understanding of the commandments of the Lord.

In the next verse the Psalmist said:

> "The fear of the LORD is clean, enduring forever . . ."

Do we want to be purified? Do we desire to be clean? Then let us "fear the Lord" because His statutes endure forever.

Finally, David said concerning the written Word:

> ". . . the judgments of the LORD are true and righteous altogether."

It is not surprising to find that a "worldly" judiciary is at times subject to disrespect. Innocent men have been made to suffer, while the guilty have gone free. It is not always possible, with our limited knowledge of the human heart, and because of the treachery of influence, to have due justice rendered. But, of this one thing we can be sure, that "the judgments of the LORD are true and righteous altogether."

This written revelation, the Bible, David stated in the next verse, is "More to be desired . . . than gold, yea, than much fine gold. . . ." Even if our dollar contained one hundred per cent of gold and fine gold at that, the worship of that dollar leads to sorrow and disappointment. Such gold is not to be desired nor compared to the revelation of God.

Ah, but David also said of the Word of God that it is ". . . sweeter also than honey and the honeycomb." Did it occur to you that there is something in this world sweeter than honey and the honeycomb? There is! That which is "sweeter" is the testimony of the Lord, the Bible.

> ". . . by them is thy servant warned: (said David) and in keeping of them is great reward."

Is it any wonder that David closed this Psalm by saying this:

> "Let the words of my mouth, and the meditation of my heart, be acceptable in thy sight, O LORD, my strength, and my redeemer."

PSALM TWENTY

ISRAEL'S TROUBLE AND ISRAEL'S DEFENSE

WE have entitled our meditation in the 20th Psalm, "Israel's Trouble and Israel's Defense." This Psalm has a pertinent message for this hour in Israel's history. It has been called Israel's national anthem. It probably was sung when the nation went to war, led by her king. The people took part in the first section of the Psalm, addressing encouragement directly to their king; then all sang the second part, rejoicing together in the salvation of the Lord; then either the priest or the king himself sang the 6th verse, while in the 8th verse the foe's defeat and Israel's victory was announced, whereas the final verse was a prayer to the eternal God.

We have been so accustomed to think of Israel as "a scattered people" that it is difficult for us even now to understand that Israel is actually clamoring for a national home so that she as a nation may participate in the councils of the world. The flag of King David is becoming increasingly familiar, even flying from many ships. We ought therefore to become acquainted with "Israel's national anthem." Some may say, This Psalm refers to Israel, let them enjoy it; there can be no message for us in it. However, I am sure that before we finish with this meditation we will have discovered there is a message in it for us who are not members of the commonwealth of Israel.

ANTI-SEMITISM

Israel is one of the acute problems of the world at the moment. Anti-Semitism has reached alarming proportions. A heart-rending disturbance of the present moment is the vicious attack now being visited upon the Jews in Austria. There are some in Israel who only see the surface disturbances while others, who look underneath the surface for the cause, are recognizing the hand of God in history. I would commend to every Jew, as well as to every Gentile, that fascinating, soul-stirring prophecy of Hosea. It will take about a half-hour to read it but even a mere reading of the prophecy will enable one to understand what is going on today. The true Israelite, the Israelite in whom there is no guile, understands that Israel never suffered at the hands of a Gentile nation except when she had sinned against God. No nation is strong enough to harm Israel when she is in fellowship with God.

But it is well also to bear in mind that there is an underlying principle, or should I use the word *overruling* principle, in Israel's relation to other nations and the relation of other nations to her. In the very first book of the Bible we read these remarkable words:

> "Now the LORD had said unto Abram, Get thee out of thy country, and from thy kindred, and from thy father's house, unto a land that *I will* shew thee:
>
> "And *I will* make of thee a great nation, and *I will* bless thee, and make thy name great; and thou shalt be a blessing:
>
> "And *I will* bless them that bless thee, and curse him that curseth thee: and in thee shall all families of the earth be blessed."

This has been called the Abrahamic Covenant. It is an endless contract. God gave the promise and placed His own personality behind the promise—"I will . . . I will . . . I will . . . I will . . ." Four times God said to Abram "I will." Among the things that He absolutely assured Abram and his posterity was this, "I *will* bless them that bless thee, and curse him that curseth thee: and in thee shall all families of the earth be blessed." There are many people in the world today, and a few leaders, who seem to have entirely forgotten that the 3rd verse of the 12th chapter of Genesis is part of the Word of God. But the principle declared therein has never been abrogated. It has never been repealed. Whenever a nation has blessed the descendants of Abraham that nation has been blessed, witness England and the United States for examples; and whenever a nation has cursed the descendants of Abraham, that nation has in turn been cursed. Because God is true we have no hesitancy in making the prediction that a certain man in this world, and a certain nation, will receive terrific judgment for their present behavior, because God has said, "I *will* . . . *curse him* that curseth thee." When God curses a man and a nation, the result is all too obvious.

But what about Israel? Let us read the Psalm:

> "The LORD hear thee in the day of trouble; the name of the God of Jacob defend thee;
>
> "Send thee help from the sanctuary, and strengthen thee out of Zion.
>
> "Remember all thy offerings, and accept thy burnt-sacrifice; Selah.
>
> "Grant thee according to thine own heart, and fulfil all thy counsel.
>
> "We will rejoice in thy salvation, and in the name of our God we will set up our banners: the LORD fulfil all thy petitions.

"Now know I that the LORD saveth his anointed;
he will hear him from his holy heaven with the
saving strength of his right hand.

"Some trust in chariots, and some in horses: but we
will remember the name of the LORD our God.

"They are brought down and fallen: but we are risen,
and stand upright.

"Save, LORD: let the king hear us when we call."

It is evident from this Psalm that Israel is not spared trouble. Indeed the opening verse refers to the "day of trouble." Possibly the Psalmist had also in mind that day, called by the prophet Jeremiah "the time of Jacob's trouble." A man versed in the study of the Old Testament must acknowledge that what Israel has suffered in the past and what Israel is suffering in the present is mild compared to what Israel shall suffer in the future "in the time of Jacob's trouble." Israel will then be crushed between the upper and nether millstones, between the northern and southern armies, absolutely defenseless, without help from any side—but it is just that moment, called man's extremity, which is God's opportunity. So the Psalm reads, "The LORD hear thee in the day of trouble; the name of the God of Jacob defend thee. . . ."

MODERN MILITARY STRATEGY *vs.* TRUST IN GOD

Israel was never called to rest upon the arm of flesh nor to trust in alliances for her help. In this anthem the people did not ask the king to curry the favor of Gentile nations, but they said, "The LORD (Jehovah) hear thee in the day of trouble; the name of the God of Jacob defend thee . . ." As for the source and place of help, they said—Let Jehovah "send thee help from the sanctuary, and strengthen thee out of Zion. . . ." But I can hear some military strategist say—How ridiculous in this day of modern warfare, when men go down into the bowels of the earth as well as infest the air above, when bombs explode from above and from beneath, how utterly childish to expect to be able to defend without an army, to fight without a sword. Help—Where is it to come from? Oh, if all Israel would realize the truth of this Psalm. If Israel would really bow her knees before God, confess her sin, receive the message of her prophets, and return to the Lord Jehovah whom she rejected, if she would turn to the sanctuary for help—how quickly would her deliverance come. Help for earthly Israel, as well as for the Israel of God, comes from the sanctuary.

Let us stop a moment to draw an application from that which we have already discussed. If the principles enunciated in the opening part of this

Psalm are true concerning earthly Israel, what might be said of their application to the Christian in this day, whose real warfare is not carnal but
spiritual?

In that connection it may not be amiss to direct attention to the
organized effort that has been made to voice objection to the rise of anti-
Semitic feeling. I believe in such effort from the bottom of my heart. I
have no more use for anti-Semitism than I have for the doctrines of demons.
Their source is one and the same. But we have yet to hear of organized
effort to take to task the nations which are persecuting Christians. Whoever heard of raising a united voice against Russia for the slaying of multitudes of innocent men, women, and children, solely because they bowed the
knee to Christ Jesus? Who has organized a movement to express united
antagonism against the Nazi persecution of Christians and when has a voice
been heard against the slaughter of evangelical Christians in other European countries? I am not naive enough to believe that even if such organized objection were articulate it would stop the onslaught, any more than
organized mass meetings against anti-Semitism have succeeded in stopping
the persecution of Jews in Poland, Germany, Austria, and elsewhere. I have
sometimes wondered if the failure of the world to take cognizance of the
persecution of Christians does not lie in the fact that true Christians know
how vain is the help of man. Help must come from the sanctuary; the only
defense we have is the name of the God of Jacob, the God and Father of
our Lord and Saviour Jesus Christ. But what a defense He is! In this day
when the true church of our Lord Jesus is also being persecuted, may she
take courage and learn a lesson from this 20th Psalm and find her help in
the sanctuary and her strength in the Lord.

If we will read this Psalm carefully we will note a wonderful series of
contrasts. We will observe what the people expected of God and what the
people promised the Lord. In the first part of the Psalm they encourage
their king by saying—The Lord hear thee; the Lord defend thee; the Lord
send thee help; the Lord strengthen thee; the Lord remember all thy offerings; the Lord grant thee according to thine own heart; the Lord fulfil all
thy counsel. In the second part the people promised: "*We will* rejoice in
thy salvation;" again, "*We will* set up our banners;" again, "*We will*
remember the name of the LORD our God." There are three things Israel
promised; first, to rejoice in the salvation of God; second, to set up their
banners; and third, to remember the name of the Lord their God. The last
of these three is most interesting for the entire verse reads, "Some trust in

chariots, and some in horses: but we will remember the name of the LORD our God."

This passage of Scripture was vividly impressed on my mind by an experience of a dear old saint of God, who has since gone home to be with his Lord. I refer to Mr. Samuel Levermore whose name some may possibly remember. Mr. Levermore was an Englishman who, together with his wife, felt called during the world war period to do itinerant missionary work in the towns and hamlets of France. They were both well along in years but with "a horse and buggy" they traveled the country-side distributing tracts and speaking to people, at times finding an open home in which to conduct gospel meetings but always having a glorious time in direct house-to-house missionary effort. It was a dangerous undertaking for frequently they were close to the war zone. However, my friend had a strong faith in a mighty God who had promised him, in answer to his prayer for guidance and direction, that "a thousand should fall at his side, and ten thousand at his right hand" but that the pestilence and destruction would not come nigh him. So, when some raised the question as to the wisdom of this undertaking Mr. Levermore would refer them to that promise to which I have just referred which is found in the 7th verse of the 91st Psalm, and then he would follow it up by saying, "Some trust in chariots, and some in horses: but we will remember the name of the LORD our God."

That word "remember" is really a sanctuary word. It might better be translated, ". . . we will *invoke* the name of the LORD our God." How that reminds us of the invocation prayer which usually begins a Christian service but all too often degenerates into mere formality. When we go to church to receive a blessing, do we trust in the preacher's oratory, or the choir's talent, or will we invoke the name of the Lord our God?

The Power of God

Israel recognized that they did not have the equipment or man power comparable to that of their enemies; but they had God. One man with God is an invincible army.

It was interesting to learn recently that an experimenter in the University of California has discovered a new explosive, which is claimed to have sixty times the power of dynamite and from fifteen to twenty-five times that of TNT. He has named it RPX. Originally it had a defect as it was subject to deterioration in storage. But that defect has been overcome, and now it is claimed that it will not lose its power after being kept

for twenty years. But if all the armies of the world were equipped with
RPX, one man with God would still conquer the world. And by the way,
the gospel, which is declared to be the dynamic of God, after twenty centuries has not lost a fraction of its power.

Would God that every Christian availed himself of God's power; would
God Israel would trust God's power. When the outlook is darkest the power
of God still works with miraculous results.

In the days of Elisha the prophet, Ben-hadad, the king of Syria whom
the wicked king Ahab had spared, gathered his hosts and went up and
besieged Samaria. Israel therefore was besieged from without while within
Samaria they suffered from a famine so terrific that the people paid eighty
pieces of silver for an ass's head and mothers boiled the flesh of their children. The king blamed the prophet Elisha for the situation. So the king
sent his lord upon whom he leaned to murder Elisha. When Elisha saw
this messenger he said, "Hear ye the word of the Lord; Thus said the
LORD, Tomorrow about this time shall a measure of fine flour be sold for
a shekel, and two measures of barley for a shekel, in the gate of Samaria."
The servant on whose hand the king leaned, answered Elisha saying, "Behold, if the LORD would make windows in heaven, might this thing be?"
And Elisha answered him, "Behold, thou shalt see it with thine eyes, but
shalt not eat thereof."

What Elisha promised seemed an absurd thing. Imagine being in the
midst of a terrific famine one day and promising that in 24 hours four pecks
of flour would be available for sixty-five cents and eight pecks of barley for
the same price. Ridiculous, said the servant of the king, that might be true
if God opened the windows of heaven and rained down flour and barley.

You who remember this incident as it is written in the 7th chapter of
the 2nd Book of the Kings will recall that four leprous men were at the
entrance to the gate of the city. They were men who were dying with leprosy
and also dying from hunger. What should they do? Enter the city? No,
if they did that they would be slain. Enter the camp of the Syrians? Well,
the Syrians might save them alive. About twilight they went unto the camp
of the Syrians. In the meanwhile the Lord thundered so that He made the
host of Syrians to hear a noise of chariots, and a noise of horses, and the
noise of a great host, and they said to one another, "Lo, the king of Israel
hath hired against us the kings of the Hittites, and the kings of the Egyptians, to come upon us. Wherefore they arose and fled in the twilight, and
left their tents, and their horses, and their asses, even the camp as it was,

and fled for their life." Thus when the four leprous men entered the camp they found it empty of men but filled with provisions. They enjoyed a wonderful banquet. When they finished eating they thought that it was too good to keep to themselves, it was a day of good tidings; so they went to the porter of the city and told the story of what they had found in the camp.

How the mob rushed into the camp of the Syrians and took possession of the fine flour and barley and all else!

The king then appointed the servant who had gone to Elisha the previous day to have charge of the gate through which the people flocked in order to buy food, and the crowd passing through the gate was so unruly that they trod upon this servant and he died as the prophet had said. He saw these things with his eyes but he never ate of them.

When a man trusts and invokes the blessing of God, miracles take place! But when a man refuses God, judgment is inevitable. Which will it be in your case?

PSALM TWENTY-ONE

"THE UNASKED BLESSINGS OF HAPPINESS"

THE 21st Psalm is a companion Psalm to the 20th which we considered in our previous meditation. The 20th Psalm was sung by the people who encouraged their king as he went to war. The 21st Psalm is a return song of triumph. One is a prayer, the other is a thanksgiving Psalm. It is meet when God answers prayer that we offer Him our thanksgiving.

While the 20th Psalm had an immediate application to King David it also has a much larger application to David's Lord, the Messiah. Wonderful as were David and Solomon, both are but feeble types of Israel's true King —David's Lord and David's Son. Here is the Psalm:

> "The king shall joy in thy strength, O LORD; and in thy salvation how greatly shall he rejoice!
>
> "Thou hast given him his heart's desire, and hast not withholden the request of his lips. Selah.
>
> "For thou preventest him with the blessings of goodness: thou settest a crown of pure gold on his head.
>
> "He asked life of thee, and thou gavest it him, even length of days for ever and ever.
>
> "His glory is great in thy salvation: honour and majesty hast thou laid upon him.

"For thou hast made him most blessed for ever:
thou hast made him exceeding glad with thy countenance.

"For the king trusteth in the LORD, and through
the mercy of the Most High he shall not be moved.

"Thine hand shall find out all thine enemies: thy
right hand shall find out those that hate thee.

"Thou shalt make them as a fiery oven in the time
of thine anger: the LORD shall swallow them up
in his wrath, and the fire shall devour them.

"Their fruit shalt thou destroy from the earth, and
their seed from among the children of men.

"For they intended evil against thee: they imagined
a mischievous device, which they are not able to
perform.

"Therefore shalt thou make them turn their back,
when thou shalt make ready thine arrows upon thy
strings against the face of them.

"Be thou exalted, LORD, in thine own strength:
so will we sing and praise thy power."

There is a marvelous message in the opening verse of this Psalm. The
king had returned from his triumph. It would have been natural for the
king to boast of his accomplishments but that is always dangerous business. There is a principle in Scripture which not only has an application
to the believer but also a universal application—God exalts the humble and
puts down the proud. David did not make the mistake of assuming that
the triumph over his enemies was the result of his own powers or that of
his army.

In the previous Psalm the people said, "Some trust in chariots, and
some in horses: but we will invoke the name of the LORD our God." Having invoked the name of the Lord, and the king having triumphed in the
Lord's power, what a mistake it would have been had he come back and
boasted of his triumph or even suggested—We planned it that way, and
don't let anyone tell you otherwise! It is poor business to boast under any
circumstances. But here we read—O Lord, because of thy strength shall the
king rejoice and through thy salvation how greatly shall he rejoice.

Likewise the man who understands the salvation of the Lord will never
boast of his own accomplishments. He will never develop a pharisaical attitude, suggesting that he is glad that he is not as other poor sinners. Indeed,
his joy is in the Lord and his strength is in his God. He knows that if it
were not for the grace of God, salvation would be out of his grasp.

UNASKED BLESSINGS

In the 2nd verse the people said concerning their king, "Thou hast given him his heart's desire, and hast not withholden the request of his lips." We must not go too far afield but we should remind our hearts that our Lord said to His disciples, and through them to us, these pregnant words, "Whatsoever ye shall ask in my name, that will I do, that the Father may be glorified in the Son. If ye shall ask anything in my name, I will do it." Many of us must confess that this is not a reality in our lives. We have asked but we have not received. The fault can never be God's. Our Lord is true to His Word. If we do not receive, then certainly the difficulty is with us—and may each of us search our own heart to determine why God has not answered our prayer, bearing in mind that the people said concerning their king, "Thou hast given him his heart's desire, and hast not witholden the request of his lips."

But God did more than that for the king, for in the next verse, the 3rd verse, we have a most interesting picture of the beneficent grace of God. There we read, "For thou preventest him with the blessings of goodness: thou settest a crown of pure gold on his head." I must confess that this did not convey much to my mind when I first examined it. What could the Psalmist mean when he wrote, "For thou preventest him with the blessings of goodness"? I am indebted to a good Jewish friend for the answer to my question. A couple of years ago at Christmas time this friend presented me with a copy of the Old Testament, translated by Jewish authorities into the English language; it is the Bible which is used in Jewish synagogues. In turning to the 21st Psalm and looking at this verse, I learned a blessed truth, for this passage was translated, "For thou meetest him unasked with the blessings of happiness." How interesting! The Lord met David, unasked, with the blessings of happiness. Is there not a great secret here? "Unasked blessings of happiness." We are so occupied with the things which we have requested God to give us that we are inclined to overlook the blessings He pours upon us without our even asking for them. Have you received any "unasked blessings of happiness"?

But there is still more in this passage of Scripture touching the provision of the Lord on our behalf. There is no doubt that what God did for David He can do and will do and is doing for every soul who has proclaimed his faith in the Lord Jesus Christ. The Father said concerning the Son, "This is my beloved Son, in whom I am well pleased;" and added, "hear ye him." Certainly those of us who have heard Him can expect not only answers to our prayers but also "unasked blessings" from His hand. But here the Psalmist wrote, "Thou meetest him unasked." The Lord met David in the way. David did not ask Him. The Lord met him and bestowed upon him the blessings of happiness or goodness. That is most interesting! The Lord met David unasked. Did you ever have the Lord meet you unasked? Have you ever had an experience where you suddenly discovered that your way was blocked? But you say, That cannot be the same thing that the Psalmist had in mind. Maybe it is—God often meets a child of His and blocks him from straying into the paths of disobedience. While we may think for a moment that the Lord is robbing us of blessing He actually is meeting us with unasked blessings of happiness. In other words, if we really love the Lord and are born again by the Spirit of God, we have been assured the constant communion of the Lord. The path about us has been hedged in by Himself. Frequently He will, Himself, prevent us from going into the paths of disobedience, knowing that such paths, if we tread them, will lead to disappointment and unhappiness. He meets us in our path unasked and carries with Him the blessings of happiness. He does the most astonishing things so that we cry, My God, how wonderful Thou art!

But again, how awe-inspiring to think that not only did God meet David in the way unasked and give him blessings of happiness but He also crowned him with a crown of pure gold.

There is a crowning day coming by and by. The saints of God are not in the majority at the present; they are in the minority, a very small minority; they are not even considered seriously today. May the household of faith be encouraged by the words of our Lord who said, "Fear not, little flock; for it is your Father's good pleasure to give you the kingdom."

Crowns, in the New Testament, are symbols of rewards extended to believers for faithful service to their Lord. We learn from the closing book of the New Testament that the Church triumphant places her crowns at the feet of the Lord. May we have crowns, many crowns, to place at His feet in that day.

DAVID'S GREATER SON

Instead of looking at each of these verses and noting their application to the Psalmist let us look at some of these passages in the light of their larger fulfilment in David's greater Son. For example, in the 7th verse we read, "For the king trusteth in the LORD, and through the mercy of the most High he shall not be moved." In verse 4, "He asked life of thee, and thou gavest it him, even length of days for ever and ever." Certainly these passages are clear references to our Lord Jesus Christ. The fact of the matter is that both the Targum and the Talmud understand that this 21st Psalm refers to the Messiah. Indeed, we might also look at the 3rd verse in its application to Christ and consider the blessings with which the Father met Him, for which He did not ask. Did He ask a crown? No!! He said when He took the cup from His Father's hand, "not my will, but thine, be done." Yet our Lord received a crown. He has been given many crowns. He has been highly exalted, given a name which is above every name, and assured that every knee shall bow and every tongue confess that He is Lord to the glory of God the Father. These are some of the unasked blessings which our Lord received while traveling in the way His Father directed.

Who is the One who has received honor and majesty as indicated in verse 5? To whom did the Father give such dignities? It is all too evident that it is upon the brow of our Lord Jesus Christ. Who is the One mentioned in verse 6 who shall be most blessed for ever? Not David, much as David was a most interesting character. It was the Lord, the One of whom David wrote.

JOY AND SORROW

And now notice the last half of verse 6: ". . . thou hast made him exceeding glad with thy countenance." So often we think of our Lord Jesus Christ as the "man of sorrows and acquainted with grief." He was that. Never once in the Gospel records do we read that He smiled, but we do read that He wept; in fact, several times it is indicated that He wept. But it does not mean that our Lord always wore a sad countenance. As He looked at sin and the sorrows of mankind of course He was sad; but do you think that the children would have romped around Him as they did if He had a long-drawn face? Don't you think He smiled upon them? Do you think that He could have attended a wedding feast and acted as if it were a funeral service? Religious men often wear "long robes and long, sad faces," but our Lord, never! No, our Lord Jesus Christ was not only a man of sorrows but a man of attractive joy, with a compelling personality.

We learn from the 6th verse what made our Lord exceeding glad. ". . . thou hast made him exceeding glad with thy countenance." Our Lord enjoyed the fellowship of His Father, and He bequeathed that joy to His disciples. He said, "These things have I spoken unto you, that my joy might remain in you, and that your joy might be full." If we are to have the fullness of joy we must remember that it is written, ". . . in thy presence is fullness of joy. . . ." Fellowship with Christ always makes a man glad. Someone has recently said "A happy Christian is the only effective defense of Christianity."

But we could go on and observe how wonderfully the things written in this Psalm fit into the mold of Christ. He alone clothes every word with the fulness of meaning, as His brow alone can wear the crown of thorns of the 53rd chapter of Isaiah.

But is there such a thing as making a personal appropriation of these things? The application is all too evident. If our Lord returned thanks to His Father for the blessings of goodness, what might be said about us?

If there is one thing which is pronounced in this Psalm, it is the grace of God and the provisions of God. We read, "*thou* hast . . . *thou* preventest . . . *thou* settest a crown on his head . . . *thou* gavest him length of days . . . *thou* hast laid honour and majesty upon him." The Psalm is filled with what the Father has done for David's greater Son. If our Lord recognized the hand of His Father in blessing how much more ought we.

SELF-OCCUPATION

If a man is occupied with himself, and assumes that he is kept by himself—his life, service, and devotion are the things that are uppermost in his mind, and he thinks those things make him distinctly different from other people. Such a man is impressed with the fact that he does not do things that others do, so he concludes that he is better than the rest. That poor man has never seen the grace or the glory of God. The true servant, the true child of God will do exactly as the Psalmist has expressed in the closing verses of this Psalm when he wrote, "Be thou exalted, LORD, in thine own strength: so will we sing and praise thy power."

One can usually tell a spiritual man by the way he speaks of his Lord and by the absence of exaltation of self. If he sings, if he praises—he sings and praises the Lord. If there is a dirge, it is because he is singing about himself. Oh, what joy there is in singing His praises, and rejoicing in the salvation of the Lord.

Have you observed carefully the tax collector who became a Gospel writer? Matthew, the writer of the first Gospel, was at one time a despised, grafting politician who had sold himself to Rome to collect taxes from his own countrymen. But what a transformation took place in that man's life when the "Stranger of Galilee" met him. He has given his own report of the event in what has been called by Dr. Norborg "the shortest autobiography in world literature." It reads: "And as Jesus passed forth from thence, he saw a man, named Matthew, sitting at the receipt of custom: and he said unto him, Follow me. And he arose, and followed him."

Writing of a number of our present day religious testimonies, Dr. Norborg said, "They are full of ego and self-boisterous pharisaism. The wording of their testimonies betrays that the human element dominates even their discipleship. *They* heard the call, *they* accepted the call, *they* were obedient, *they, they, they*—Oh let us do away with all this self-exaltation and, like the Psalmist and our blessed Lord, say, 'Be *thou* exalted, LORD, in thine own strength: so will we sing and praise *thy* power.' "

PSALM TWENTY-TWO—PART ONE

THE DEATH PSALM

IT was my original intention in our meditations in the Book of Psalms to proceed consecutively. However, considering the particular season of the year, it may be desirable to make a slight change. All Christendom is now considering the Passion of our Lord, and shortly will be observing Holy Week. It occurred to me that it might be interesting, and I trust profitable, to spend the next four Sundays, which will take us to Easter, in a meditation in the 22nd Psalm, the chief of the Messianic Psalms.

The Psalm naturally divides itself into two great divisions, the first of which ends with verse 21. We shall devote three addresses to the first section dealing with the Passion of our Lord; then on Easter Sunday take up the great climax to the Passion, the resurrection of our Lord Jesus Christ.

I have already mentioned that this is the chief of the Messianic Psalms; in fact, it is a whole Bible in one Psalm. If it were the only written message we had of the mind of God concerning His own revelation in the person of His Son, there would be sufficient in it to lead a man from earth to heaven, and give him to understand the great purposes of God in redemption, as well as a marvelous outline of history. All the early fathers of the Church, every Apostle of our Lord, and our Lord Himself, maintained that this Psalm concerns the Christ of God. In the words of the French expositor, Bossuet, "To deny it the world itself is a witness against you." From the very first verse there is scarcely a line which might not have come from the pen of the four evangelists.

Here is no colorless scene. The crucifixion is so vividly portrayed that those of us living almost two thousand years after its event in history can so thoroughly visualize the scene that it is not difficult to hear the spikes being driven into the palms of His hands, or listen to the voice of utter loneliness in the death struggle when our Lord cries, "My God, my God, why hast thou forsaken me?" Even such a rationalist as Schenkel conceded that "*This cry was an entirely credible utterance because it never could have been invented.*"

Before considering the details of the Psalm which so graphically present the crucifixion of our Lord Jesus Christ, may I direct your attention to this significant introduction that appears as the heading of the Psalm?

"To the Chief Musician upon Aijeleth Shahar, A Psalm of David."

Many of us, particularly those of us who are Gentiles, are not inclined to give much thought to those introductions, but an instructed Jew woudl be very careful to observe every word. In the first place, we learn from this introduction that David was the writer of the Psalm.

The critics of Christ have been frantic in their attempt to avoid the logical conclusions to which a study of this Psalm must lead. Any honest study irresistibly concludes that Jesus Christ must be the Son of God; that the Bible must be the Word of God; because the 22nd Psalm was written a thousand years before our Lord was crucified, and every detail of the crucifixion described in the Psalm has been fulfilled to the dotting of the "i" and the crossing of the "t."

Failing in their attempt, these critics have sought to find in the life of David some experience which could fit the description given. Failing in that attempt, they have sought to apply the Psalm to Israel as a nation. But again the detail is so personal and so specific, and the Psalm is so evidently occupied with *one person only*, that such an attempt is all too obvious as having for its purpose the escape from these inevitable conclusions.

This Psalm was written by David, the prophet—he was moved by the Holy Ghost to write of an event of which he had no direct knowledge, and which did not take place until a thousand years after he had written about it. As he penned the Psalm, and wrote its final words, "it is finished," it is most significant and interesting to observe from the manner of his introduction that he entered into the spirit of the Psalm and understood its implications. He sent the Psalm to the chief Musician.

THE CHIEF MUSICIAN

To be exact, the chief Musician is found in the center of the Psalm. He is none other than our Lord Jesus Christ, to whom all Psalms are ascribed. It is He who leads the congregation of the redeemed in this song of redemption.

But, specifically, three men occupied the position of chief Musician at the time David lived—Asaph, Heman, and Jeduthun. The old Jewish rabbis have stated that they believed the Psalms of praise, the Psalms that concern Jehovah, were invariably sent to Heman to be set to music. Heman's home must have been one of the glorious sights in Jerusalem. It is described in the 25th chapter of the First Book of Chronicles, verses 5 to 7. Heman had 14 sons and 3 daughters. What a family! The entire household, saith the Scripture, was "under the hands of their father for song in the house of the Lord, with cymbals, psalteries, and harps, for the service of the house of God, according to the king's order. . . ." He actually had a whole symphony in his home and a great chorus. How readily we can picture the arrival of David's messenger who came to Heman with this Psalm, and how the entire family entered into the spirit of it, setting it to music, and singing it unto the Lord for the first time.

"THE HIND OF THE MORNING"

David understood thoroughly that a musician reading the Psalm would naturally seek to put it in a minor key to a dirgeful tune. The Psalm is so filled with suffering, agony, disappointment, horror, and death that it would be the natural reaction to do so, but David wrote to this chief Musician and in effect said, "before you put this Psalm to music consider the 'hind of the morning,' " which is the interpretation of the phrase, "Aijeleth Shahar." In other words, he invited the chief Musician to go up to the mountains of ʳudea some early morning before the break of day and observe how the ˟ness and the shadows flee away. Then he would notice before the sun ˟ the East, over the mountains there are rays of gray light that pene- ˟ast. These rays form themselves into interesting combinations ˟ʸ are like the horns of a deer. David reminded the Musician that when he put this Psalm to music to bear that scene in mind, for it is not of *a night that has no end that the Psalm consists*, but it describes *a night that has come to an end* through the dawn of a refreshing day, evidenced by the streaks of light in the East announcing that the Sun of Righteousness is about to rise with healing in His wings. Begin the Psalm if you will in the minor key, but close it with a great Hallelujah Chorus!

Let us now consider the Psalm somewhat in detail. The opening words are so evidently the words of our Lord Jesus Christ that there can be no question that it is He who is the speaker; in fact, many believe the entire Psalm was uttered by our Lord upon the cross. One readily observes that the Psalm was intended to be a dialogue between the Father and the Son. But the heavens are silent, so that our Lord conducted a monologue.

Every Christian understands from the Scriptures that our Lord was always the delight of His Father, and that He did the things which were pleasing in His sight. In the light of this Psalm one can thoroughly appreciate why our Lord asked the question recorded in the 12th chapter of John's Gospel and the 27th verse, where it is written:

"Now is my soul troubled; and what shall I say?
Father, save me from this hour: but for this cause
came I unto this hour."

"This hour" refers to His crucifixion—the hour of His death. It is also understandable why our Lord sweat great drops of blood as it were, as He agonized in Gethsemane, pleading with His Father if it were possible to allow the cup to pass from Him, but nevertheless submitting to His Father's will when He added, "Not my will, but thine, be done."

In this Psalm we are transported to the foot of the cross. We are given to understand what our Lord Jesus observed and what He thought as He hung upon that cross.

It is well nigh impossible to analyze the first two verses. "Who ever heard of analyzing a sob?" In these verses our Lord sobs with a broken heart, crying:

"My God, my God, why hast thou forsaken me?
Why art thou so far from helping me, and from the
words of my roaring?

"O my God, I cry in the daytime, but thou hearest
not; and in the night season, and am not silent."

Observe that our Lord, who always had the sweetest communion and fellowship with His Father, finds Himself in a situation whereby it is incumbent upon Him to utter the interrogation "why" on two occasions. *"Why hast thou forsaken me?"* *"Why* art thou so far from helping me?" These words were spoken on the cross as our Lord looked up into a silent heaven. What an agonizing cry must have entered into the ears of His Father, and what must have been the wonderment of the angels who observed the eternal God upon the throne, and yet not one word is addressed to them to seek to deliver the Son of His love from the disaster in which He was found!

Can you imagine our Lord speaking to His Father, and referring to His cry as a "roaring"? What a comfort it has been to me, and I am sure it has been to multitudes of God's people, that our Lord Himself raised a "why" in His Father's ear. It is not always an evidence of unbelief when we find ourselves by force of circumstances, pinched to such an extent that we go into the presence of our Lord and ask Him "why?" Having been tempted in all points like as we, and having raised the question Himself, He is able to enter into our experiences, and thus become to us the God of all comfort.

Jesus Christ—Godlike

However, the third verse gives a revelation of the confidence of our Lord that is nothing short of Godlike. When we cry "why" too often we seek to place the responsibility for our circumstances upon the Lord. But in this verse, despite the agony of Calvary, despite the fact that it was the one and only occasion in all of His ministry and life when He knew what it meant to be forsaken of His Father, yet He does not place the responsibility for the failure to deliver Him upon His Father, for He immediately responds:

> "But thou art holy, O thou that inhabitest the praises of Israel."

The silence of God is thoroughly justified by our Lord on the ground that He who inhabited the praises of Israel is absolutely holy. Some may say, "Well, what has that to do with it?" Very much, indeed. Our Lord on the cross was the sin offering. As He was clothed at His incarnation with the form of man, being made in the likeness of men, so at the cross He was clothed with our sin. As He hung there, He became the representative of every sinner and every criminal in this world. If that is shocking to some, I assure you that it is said in all reverence, and that it is the viewpoint of the Scripture. It is the heart of the atonement. The Bible says that God made Him, Jesus Christ, to be sin for us, He who knew no sin. He took the vilest sinner's place and bore the judgment of the chief of sinners. God's holiness had to be satisfied and judgment had to be borne, so our Lord justified His Father's silence.

In the next three verses commencing with verse 4, our Lord maintains a remarkable distinction between His death and the death of all others preceding Him, who died for a cause or as martyrs.

Sometimes it is said that the death of our Lord Jesus was that of a martyr. From what little study I have given to the history of the martyrs, there is not one single incident in the death of our Lord that remotely resembles the death of a martyr; in fact, in this passage our Lord maintains that He is a victim, not a martyr, and also clearly evidences the purpose of His death:

> "Our fathers trusted in thee: they trusted, and thou didst deliver them.
> "They cried unto thee, and were delivered: they trusted in thee, and were not confounded.
> "But I am a worm, and no man; a reproach of men, and despised of the people."

In verses 4 and 5 He declares that God heard and God delivered the martyrs among the Jewish fathers. In verse 6 He insists He is no martyr; that He is no man; that God did not hear Him; that God could not hear Him; that it was utterly impossible for Him to be delivered.

He presents a contrast that is intensely interesting. "I am a worm —I am not a man; I am a reproach," which word means *disgrace*. I am a disgrace among men; "I am despised of the people." What a combination! What a trinity! Reproach of men; despised of the Jews; forsaken of God!

It is also interesting to observe that our Lord called Himself a "worm." A strange title indeed; in fact, I recall some 15 years ago hearing a preacher say that this is the only time he felt like contradicting the Lord. "On the cross," said he, "I glory in Him; I cannot understand how He could call Himself a worm." That statement left its impress on my mind. I shall never forget it, yet as I heard it there ran through my mind, "Our Lord never made a mistake—there must be some significance to that title." Indeed, upon further study I found that there was a reason for it.

I learned that the word in the Hebrew is "tolahath." It is translated 31 times in the Old Testament by our English word "scarlet" or "crimson." The word is oftentimes used of the "coccus," which students of medicine will recall is the chain-like bacteria—the kind people do not like to have present in their throats in an acute attack of tonsilitis. Doctors refer to the germ as the "streptococcus."

It was from this bacteria that the scarlet dye was obtained for the tabernacle. In Isaiah 1:18 the same word is used, translated "scarlet"—

> "Come now, and let us reason together, saith the LORD: though your sins be as *scarlet*, they shall be as white as snow; though they be red like crimson, they shall be as wool."

It was through His death that our Lord provided the dye that makes possible the removal from the heart and conscience of the red stain of sin. I invite all who are conscious of their sinfulness to observe the extent of God's love and His great provision for cleansing from sin, in the death of His Son. It is the testimony of God that "the blood of Jesus Christ, His Son, cleanses us from all sin." Receive Him as your personal Saviour and enjoy cleansing from sin!

PSALM TWENTY-TWO—PART TWO

"BULLS OF BASHAN"

OUR second meditation in the 22nd Psalm will cover verses 7 to 13, which read:

> "All they that see me laugh me to scorn; they shoot out the lip, they shake the head, saying,
> "He trusted on the LORD that he would deliver him: let him deliver him, seeing he delighted in him.
> "But thou art he that took me out of the womb: thou didst make me hope when I was upon my mother's breasts.
> "I was cast upon thee from the womb: thou art my God from my mother's belly.
> "Be not far from me; for trouble is near; for there is none to help.
> "Many bulls have compassed me; strong bulls of Bashan have beset me round.
> "They gaped upon me with their mouths, as a ravening and a roaring lion."

In this rehearsal on the part of our Lord, it is as if He assumes that His Father could not penetrate the blackness of the heavens to observe the scene and hear the cries of His persecutors. Therefore He describes the scene to His Father. He begins: "All they that see me laugh me to scorn: they shoot out the lip, they shake the head. . . ."

In the 2nd Psalm the Lord is seen sitting in the heavens, about to laugh at the enemies of Christ. That is just recompense for the laughter of His Son's enemies at the cross. When it is considered that all during our Lord's public ministry every footstep was a benediction; that the touch of His hand healed the sick, or gave sight to the blind, or raised the dead; and that every breath he breathed sweetened the atmosphere— it is all the more astounding that at the close of that remarkable three years of ministry men should gather around His cross and laugh in the face of the One who is Creator of the universe—laugh Him even to scorn! As if that were insufficient, they proceed in their darkened conscience to shoot out the lip, and with characteristic movements shake the head and remind Him of His confidence in His Father which He had previously expressed. "He trusted on the LORD that he would deliver him: let him deliver him, seeing he delighted in him."

It was the testimony of God that He found His delight in His Son. The Father broke the silence of heaven several times to announce that fact to men. Our Lord bore witness to this testimony of His Father. The people refuted the witness. They refer now to the pathetic sight upon the cross as abundant evidence that the Father had *no delight* in Him. In this connection there is a passage in the 53rd chapter of Isaiah which becomes unusually precious as we meditate upon it. It is found in the 10th verse.

"IT PLEASED GOD"

In this verse it is written of the despised Messiah, "Yet it pleased the LORD to bruise him. . . ." Look at that word *pleased!* Link it up with this 8th verse of the 22nd Psalm as the witnesses to the crucifixion remind Him that our Lord had said that His Father *delighted* in Him. The witness of the Father was clear during His public ministry. He said concerning His Son, "This is my beloved Son, in whom I am well pleased." But we have also the testimony of Isaiah, that the Father *was pleased* to smite His Son on the cross. "It *pleased* the LORD to bruise him." We know that man's expression of antagonism against Jesus was the result of man's hatred of Him. Even so, the bruising by His Father was the result of His pleasure.

We must not leave this, however, without reminding ourselves of the remainder of Isaiah 53: 10, which reveals to us *why* it was the Father's delight to smite Him at the cross. The prophet continued:

> ". . . he hath put him to grief: when thou shalt make his soul an offering for sin, he shall see his seed, he shall prolong his days, and the pleasure of the LORD shall prosper in his hand."

At the beginning of the verse we find "the pleasure of the Lord" expressed in the judgment which smote our Lord, while at the end of the verse we discover why the Father was pleased to bruise Him; it was in order that "the pleasure of the LORD" should prosper in his hand.

In the 10th chapter of John's Gospel our Lord reveals the safety of His own by saying "no man is able to pluck them out of my hand." Isaiah tells us that the reason the Lord Jesus died was that "the pleasure of the Lord might prosper in his hand." On the authority of our Lord, and of Isaiah, all who are believers in our Lord are this moment in the palm of our Lord's hand, protected from the Adversary of our souls, and we are "the pleasure of the Lord," that should prosper in His hands. Thus one of our titles is "the pleasure of the Lord." It is because we are *His pleasure* that the Father was pleased to bruise His Son.

Now let us return to our meditation in this Psalm. Our Lord acknowledges that His Father did not deliver Him at the cross. He takes two verses, namely 9 and 10, to justify His Father's failure, or, if not to justify, at least to reiterate His absolute confidence in His Father. He reminds His Father: "But thou art he that took me out of the womb: thou didst make me hope when I was upon my mother's breasts. I was cast upon thee from the womb: thou art my God from my mother's belly."

THE VIRGIN BIRTH

The language of our Lord Jesus Christ is exquisite. It can only be understood in the light of the virgin birth. Our Lord is the only Man who could ever say to God, ". . . thou art my God from my mother's belly." It was His pre-incarnation testimony that He would be born of a virgin. Concerning the rest of us it is written: "Behold, I was shapen in iniquity; and in sin did my mother conceive me." But our Lord insists God was His Father while cradled in the womb of the Virgin Mary.

It is sometimes said that only two of the evangelists bear testimony to the virgin birth; that the other two are silent; that none of the writers of the New Testament make any reference to it; and that there are only one or two questionable references to it in the Old Testament. Aside from the fallacy of the statement, the virgin birth of our Lord is such an integral part of the atonement that without it the atonement could have no value. If He had been born as we, then He was a sinner by birth, and could never be a Saviour. As for the virgin birth, I prefer to take the testimony of our Lord as found in this Psalm rather than the testimony of a biologist, or a theologian, or an author—though he be Charles Dickens —none of whom knew anything about it.

STRONG BULLS OF BASHAN

In the next three verses our Lord in most picturesque language describes His enemies gathered at His cross. He says: "Many bulls have compassed me: strong bulls of Bashan have beset me round."

Our Lord frequently spoke in parables. Parables are pictures; in fact, parable language is a perfect language. In this Psalm our Lord uses parable language. As our Lord looks from the cross into the faces of His enemies about Him, He tells His Father that they are like bulls; many bulls; but He also notes among them some who are more ferocious. Those He designates as "strong bulls of Bashan."

You who are familiar with Bible history recall that Og, the King of Bashan, was taken captive by Israel. He was one of the last of the giants. The Bible tells us that his bed was made of iron, and that it was 12 feet long and 6 feet wide. Secular history bears its testimony that his sarcophagus was over 13 feet in length. He ruled over a people of giants. The land also was very fertile; it was known for its prize cattle. Israel had held out to them as one of the rewards for their journey from Egypt that they were to eat "the butter of kine, the milk of sheep, the fat of lambs, and rams of the breed of Bashan. . ."

Some people believe that bull fights originated in Spain or Mexico, but in all probability bull fights were held in Bashan, though in a slightly different manner. It has been suggested that an arena would be made by roping off a certain section of a field, in the center of which would be a huge tree. The day of the bull fight was a great holiday. The hunter was arrayed in a red garment. As the hunter entered the arena one of the prize bulls of Bashan was let loose. The hunter stood in front of the tree. He enticed the bull, until utterly unable to resist any longer the bull leaped at him in one wild dash. Because of his rage, the bull was unable to direct his path. The cleverness of the hunter was demonstrated by his ability at the very last moment to sweep around the tree, thus saving himself. As the bull was unable to change his course, he dashed headlong into the trunk of the tree. To the victor belonged the spoils, and the day was a success when the horns of the bull locked themselves securely into the trunk of the tree.

Our Lord in this Psalm rehearses to His Father the fire in the eyes of His enemies. The antagonism that His enemies expressed against Him is heightened by the fact that hanging upon that cross, where from almost every vein poured forth His precious blood, He seemed to be clothed in a scarlet robe. That sight aroused their deepest hatred against Him. However, our Lord is the victor over the wild bulls. As these strong bulls roar against Him, the best that can be said for them is that they locked their horns into the tree of the cross, but never touched Him.

We heard much from modern theology a few years ago. It is becoming less vociferous. During the past few years it has become increasingly evident that Modernism is hopelessly bankrupt. But there still is nothing that so disturbs a *modern* theologian as to hear or read of the blood of Jesus Christ. Quickly he thrusts it aside as the religion of the shambles, but brushing it aside can never erase God's testimony concerning that blood.

The testimony of the Scriptures is that "without shedding of blood is no remission." Upon the cross our Lord shed His blood. God thereby opened a fount from Immanuel's side, under which sinners may plunge and be washed from their sins and made white.

If you have not availed yourself of the benefits of the death of our Lord, I invite you in His name to become reconciled to God. The cross is an evidence of God's love and the assurance that God will receive any individual who will come in the name of His Son, owning Him as his Saviour.

PSALM TWENTY-TWO—PART THREE

"IS IT NOTHNG TO YOU?"

TODAY (Palm Sunday) ushers in the most solemn season observed throughout Christendom. While many will be reminded in church services this morning of the triumphant entry which our Lord made into Jerusalem, when all the people with the exception of the religious leaders, cried out, "Hosanna! Blessed is he that cometh in the name of the Lord," let it never be forgotten that the voice of the mob is fickle— "The adulation of the multitude is rarely sincere." Indeed ere the week was over that same mob, swayed by their religious leaders, cried out, "Crucify him, crucify him"—Away with this man!

Therefore it is most appropriate that our meditation is in that section of the 22nd Psalm which leads us up to His death, for the first Palm

Sunday led to "Holy Thursday" and "Good Friday." While I acknowledge
that church holy days have been instituted by men rather than by God,
yet this season of the year gives an added opportunity to reach the souls
of men. I like the titles given to the coming Thursday and Friday by my
good Norse ancestors, who taught me about "Skjere" Thursday and "Lang"
Friday. Translated it is "cutting" Thursday, and "long" Friday. There
was a strong tugging at the heart on that Thursday, when our Lord, separated from the world, but closeted with His own, was to have His final
feast with them before the parting of their ways came to pass so that He
could walk alone the path to Calvary. How touching is the manner in
which the Holy Spirit speaks of that hour, when He wrote, "having loved
his own which were in the world, he loved them unto the end." And what
could be said concerning the long, dreary Friday, which witnessed His
crucifixion, His suffering, His humiliation? Oh for a voice to burn into
the hearts of the people the cry of our Lord through the prophet Jeremiah:
"Is it nothing to you, all ye that pass by? behold, and see if there be any
sorrow like unto my sorrow, which is done unto me, wherewith the LORD
hath afflicted me in the day of his fierce anger."

"CRUCIFIED THROUGH WEAKNESS"

For a clearer understanding of the fierceness of Jehovah's anger and
of the affliction in which it was to be expressed, we now turn to the 22nd
Psalm. Verse 14 reads: "I am poured out like water, and all my bones
are out of joint: my heart is like wax; it is melted in the midst of my
bowels."

In 2nd Corinthians 13: 4 it is written that our Lord was "crucified
through weakness." It is an illuminating statement when we consider that
our Lord Jesus Christ is the express image of God and that He upholds
all things by the word of His might. The extent of His abject weakness
is aptly expressed by Him, "I am poured out like water." The extent of
His physical sufferings may be measured by His statement, "All my bones
are out of joint." When we have had a single bone out of joint, whether
in our hand, or our foot, we know the intense suffering caused by it. What
must have been the agony, the physical agony, of our Lord to cause Him
to say, "all my bones are out of joint"? It is as if He were ground between
the upper and nether millstones—as if creation, man and God, expressed
their antagonism against Him. "As a piece of steel that is twisted in an
earthquake as if it were made of paper, so our Lord's body was twisted out
of joint." The physical sufferings were the sorest ever experienced by any

man. But our Lord continues: "My strength is dried up like a potsherd; and my tongue cleaveth to my jaws; and thou hast brought me unto the dust of death."

His strength, He said, was "dried up like a potsherd." What a simile! A potsherd is a piece of pottery or earthenware which is broken because of too much burning. The very fire of God's judgment burned up our Lord's strength. His tongue, always the pen of a ready writer that gave forth the word of God, cleaved to His jaws. That no man could put Him to death, He immediately adds ". . . thou hast brought me into the dust of death."

No one could have taken the life of our Lord; no one had the power to take it from Him. From His Father He received the right to lay it down and to take it again. He voluntarily delivered Himself into the hands of His Father. True, He received from the people the treatment given the sin-offering, but likewise He received from His Father the expressions of justice due unto sin. The Scripture states that "the wages of sin is death." Our Lord paid the wages. In this Psalm He clearly states that sin's wages were given to Him by His Father, the paymaster. No wonder it is written, "It is a fearful thing to fall into the hands of the living God."

We noted in our previous meditation that our Lord called several of the people gathered at the foot of the cross "strong bulls of Bashan." In verse 16 He mentions another group: "For dogs have compassed me: the assembly of the wicked have inclosed me: they pierced my hands and my feet." We do no injustice to Gentiles when we state that the title *dogs* is given to the Gentile nations. You will remember the case of the Syrophenician woman to whom our Lord said, "It is not meet to take the children's bread and cast it to dogs." She responded, "True, Lord, yet the dogs eat of the crumbs which fall from the master's table." The Jews have repeatedly referred to the Gentiles as the "dog" nations. So in picturesque language our Lord refers to the leaders of Israel as "Bulls of Bashan"; to the Gentiles as "dogs"; while His actual executioners He calls "the assembly of the wicked," adding, "they pierced my hands and my feet."

This passage is one of the most potent arguments for the inspiration of the Scriptures. It was written a thousand years before our Lord came into this world; it was written by David, a Jew, who knew only of stoning to death as a means of executing a criminal. Crucifixion was not known at the time David wrote—it was not known for several hundred years after the 22nd Psalm was written. Yet David prophetically recorded our Lord's own words, "they pierced my hands and my feet."

Those pierced hands and feet of our Lord Jesus were offered by Him to His disciples on the night of His resurrection as evidence that He was the very One who formerly walked with them. And the imprints vouchsafed their peace, for with outstretched hands He said: "Peace be unto you." Can any wonder why immediately following, it is added, "Then were the disciples glad when they saw the Lord"? Those pierced hands and feet will remain through all the ages of eternity as constant reminders to the redeemed of the price that was paid for their redemption.

We again call attention to the fact that this passage was written a thousand years before the event took place and that it was literally fulfilled to the dotting of the "i" and the crossing of the "t." By sheer logic one must conclude from this prophetic word that Jesus Christ is the Son of God, and that the Bible is the Word of God.

The next verse, the 17th, makes one almost shudder: "I may tell (or count) all my bones: they look and stare upon me." The iniquity of the human heart could not reveal itself more clearly than in this passage. The New Testament, recording the history of it, states, "the people stood beholding."

Our Lord said, "I may count all my bones." Suffering intensely, yet the deepest humiliation He experienced must have been the indifferent stare of the multitude upon Him, the naked substitute of the sinner. Oh, to remember it was the Creator of the universe who hung there! At the foot of the cross the children of men, made from the dust of the earth, had the effrontery to stand and stare upon the naked Son of God! If that is not sufficient evidence of the depravity of the human heart, what further evidence is needed?

But our Lord continues as He reminds His Father of His pitiful sight: "They part my garments among them, and cast lots upon my vesture." Here is additional evidence of the depravity of man. The soldiers who crucified our Lord turned to the matter of gaining His possessions. They gave no evidence of being disturbed that they were the instruments that brought about the death of the Creator.

It was customary for the soldiers to receive all the possessions of the crucified. In the case of our Lord, He had five garments. There were four soldiers who crucified Him. Each of them took one part of His clothing. The fifth piece, which could not readily be divided without losing its value, became a matter of discussion. Who was to have the seamless robe that the Master had previously worn? They could not amicably settle the matter, so they reverted to gambling for His final possession; therefore our Lord says, "they cast lots upon my vesture."

History bears its testimony one thousand years later that this very thing was done by the four Roman soldiers. Again, could any better evidence be brought that the 22nd Psalm is the Word of God? It cannot be refuted. As only God can predict the future, and having predicted this scene with such minuteness, then the individual crucified and the circumstances of His crucifixion are of great importance. It should spur us on to an understanding of the mystery of the death of that victim.

In the next few verses our Lord gives vent to the final outburst of His heart. Beginning with the 19th verse we read:

> "But be not thou far from me, O LORD: O my strength, haste thee to help me.
> "Deliver my soul from the sword; my darling from the power of the dog.
> "Save me from the lion's mouth . . ."

That brings us to the middle of verse 21. The last half of the verse indicates that God saved Him from the lion's mouth, heard His cry, and answered Him through His resurrection.

Once more our Lord uses parable language. Note how He makes use of animals in describing the bestial participants in His crucifixion. He calls some "bulls"; others "strong bulls of Bashan"; while some He designates as "dogs"; and finally one is called a "lion."

AN AWFUL SCENE

The importance of Calvary, and the death which our Lord Jesus died, is attested to by the participants in that scene, and by the events which took place there. Nothing like it ever happened previously, nor since. All creation was involved. When He was nailed to the cross, the sun was shining in its fulness in order to dry up His strength like a potsherd. Shortly thereafter the heavens blackened—then the thunder roared. The people who gathered, for what to them was to be a great Roman-Jewish holiday, began to feel alarmed. They sought places of safety, but before they had gone very far, the heavens were lit up with streaks of lightning that penetrated the darkness. Then the earth began to quake, and the rocks were rent. The crowd dispelled like ants during a storm! But the greatest miracle of all took place when an unseen hand rent the veil in the Temple from top to bottom which announced to man that God had now opened the way for man to come into His presence.

If ever creation evidenced its interest in any one individual, it did so on this occasion when it would seem that all nature was in a convulsion. Can it be that nature desired to place the responsibility for its thraldom upon Him who hung on that tree? Certainly the presence of thorns upon the rose is the evidence of the curse upon nature. The fact that our Lord wore a crown of thorns seems to indicate that He was bearing nature's curse. Our Lord redeemed creation as well as man. The Scripture tells us that all creation shall be delivered from its groaning, and be brought into the glorious liberty of the sons of God, at the return of our Lord Jesus Christ.

As one stands at the foot of the cross, he not only witnesses the antagonism of men against Christ, but he witnesses the antagonism of nature against Him, and, in addition, as we noticed when we first examined this Psalm, the Father Himself also joined in the attack by pouring upon His Son all the pent-up wrath of the ages of a holy God against sin.

With our naked eye we may not *see* the judgment that God poured out upon His Son, but just as definitely as men expressed their antagonism against Him in the spear wound in His side, and in the print of the nails in His hands, so the testimony of God is that His judgment fell upon His Son.

But it is also the testimony of Scripture that Satan was interested in that cross. "The prince of this world" our Lord called him—he, too, was at the cross. He attempted to find *something,* by which is meant *evil,* in Christ; but our Lord said, "He found nothing in me." If we had eyes to penetrate the spirit world, we would have recognized that Satan, with his army of spirit beings, had gathered about the cross and mocked our Lord to scorn.

As we approach the 21st verse of this Psalm we are conscious that our Lord is aware of the approach of the Satanic powers of darkness. It would seem as if Satan with all his hosts were about to leap upon Him when from the depths of His being He cries out unto God, "Save me from the lion's mouth." We are told that Satan goeth about like a roaring lion, seeking whom he may devour. Before the Satanic powers were about to leap upon Him, our Lord was conscious of their presence, for He said:

> "Be not far from me; for trouble is near; for there is none to help."

In the consciousness that in His deliverance was also the deliverance of His "beloved one," whom He calls His "darling," He cries out unto His Father to deliver Him, for in so doing He would also deliver His "beloved one."

The title "beloved one" applies to those for whom our Lord died. It is a great joy on a Palm Sunday, when the religious world celebrates the triumphal entry into Jerusalem of our Lord, to revel in His greatest triumph which took place when our Lord rode through death. It was at the moment of what seemed to be the triumph of Satanic forces that He was delivered, for He immediately adds in this Psalm, "thou hast heard me from the horns of the unicorns."

This is the first occasion in this entire Psalm when any indication is given that all during the time while our Lord seemed forsaken of God and of man, His Father heard every cry, listened to every expression, and finally came to His deliverance.

He was heard "from the horns of the unicorns." A strange expression, some may say, but perfectly clear to an intelligent Jew. It is a sacrificial expression. The nails attached Him to the cross, but it was our sin that held Him there. It was from that altar that God the Father heard His Son, accepted His death as the atonement for sin, and evidenced that acceptance in His resurrection from the dead.

PSALM TWENTY-TWO—PART FOUR

THE RISEN LORD IN THE 22ND PSALM

WE found the crucified Christ in the preceding verses of this Psalm. This morning we shall also see the risen Christ in the 22nd Psalm. It has been a real delight to learn from many who have listened to this radio program that they have for the first time found Christ in this Psalm. The more I study the Psalms, the more I am inclined to the view that we can find our Lord in most, if not in all, of the Psalms. We shall limit this meditation to verses 22 to 24, though looking once again at the last half of the 21st verse, which reads: "Thou hast heard me from the horns of the unicorns."

To most of us this is an unintelligible remark, but it would not be to an instructed Jew. The horns of the unicorns were located on the altar whereupon the parts of the sacrifice were hung. When our Lord uses the term, He acknowledges the cross to be an altar, and His death a sacrifice.

It was while He hung upon the altar that His Father heard His cry. However, it was no Roman spike that held Him there—it was our sins.

THE MUSIC OF REDEMPTION

Notice how quickly we leave a distressing sight and witness a scene of great joy. In the middle of verse 21 the Psalm abruptly changes from the minor to the major key.

Beyond doubt, the bodily resurrection of our Lord Jesus Christ from the dead is the most established fact of history. It is inconceivable that a fraud could have become so universally proclaimed, or so magnificently praised. No music is comparable to that which is dedicated to the resurrection, not even that for the nativity. It is most appropriate that all nature should burst forth into praise and adoration at Easter time, for in this Psalm the Lord Himself leads the songs of praise in the great congregation. Every detail of what took place the first Easter Sunday sends a thrill through a believer. The three dark days were quickly gone—the Sabbath was over. Very early in the morning as it began to dawn toward the first day of the week, those faithful women went to the sepulchre where He had been laid, and brought with them spices and ointments which they had prepared. Startled, as they approached the garden of Joseph, they discovered the stone rolled away. They entered, but found not the body of the Lord Jesus. They became much perplexed until two men in shining garments stood by them and said, "Why seek ye the living among the dead? He is not here but is risen." Peter and John arrived later—entered the sepulchre and found it empty, as the women had witnessed. Bewildered, but not willing to heed the word of the women concerning the angels' message, they returned to Jerusalem. But Mary Magdalene, to whom our Lord had endeared Himself, stood without the sepulchre, weeping. Suddenly she was accosted by the Lord, who addressed her, "Woman, why weepest thou?" Her eyes dim because of the tears, she supposed Him to be the gardener and asked, "Sir, if you have borne him hence, tell me where thou hast laid him and I will take him away. Jesus said unto her, "Mary"—how that burns into the soul. Oh, man, whoever you are, skeptic, agnostic, indifferent, religious, sinner, saint—note this, while our Lord only spoke one word, what volumes were in that word! What a message—"Mary." Do you understand it? He called one by her own name. Do you know anything in all the world that is more glorifying to God than that one word? Does it touch your heart and give you to understand that He knows *all* about you, your sorrows, your tears, your disappointments, your sin? Ten thousand times better because of what He has done for you, that you recognize in the tone of His voice His recognition of you as one of His own. Mary wished to pour upon Him the reverence due His name, but in rejecting it momentarily He gave a further revelation of the grace of God when He said to her, "Touch me not; for I am not yet ascended to *my* Father: but go to *my* brethren, and say unto them, I ascend unto *my* Father and *your* Father; and to *my* God, and *your* God."

There are two facts in our Lord's message to Mary which also are to be found in the 22nd Psalm. First, He called the disciples "My brethren," and secondly, He announced a new relationship to God for His own for He called God their Father and their God in the same manner in which He spoke of God as His Father and His God.

THE FATHER'S NAME

The 22nd verse of the 22nd Psalm contains the first words of the risen Christ, "I will declare thy name unto my brethren. . . ." From the 17th chapter of John's Gospel, we learn that one of the ministries committed to our Lord was this manifestation of the Father's name. In the sixth verse of that chapter it is written, "I have manifested thy name unto the men which thou gavest me out of the world."

Let us pause a moment while we seek to analyze that statement. Up to that hour no man called God *his* Father. True, the Jews collectively called God the Father of their nation. Again, our Lord in teaching His disciples to pray urged them to begin, "Our Father which art in heaven"—but when our Lord spoke of God, He called Him *His* Father. The Jews recognized that such intimacy revealed relationship, and immediately took up stones to throw at Him because He thereby made Himself the Son of God.

One of the greatest blessings which salvation brings to us who believe is the privilege of looking up and raising our voices in prayer, addressing the great God of the universe as our Father-God. Only those who have received Christ can do so, and only they understand and rejoice in such relationship.

But this is not all that is in this 22nd Psalm. Note that our Lord calls us "My brethren." What condescension that He is willing to call us "brethren," and indeed, to say He is not *ashamed* to call us brethren.

A short time ago an officer of a bank came into my office to see me about some business matters. He seemed also to have something on his mind which he desired to unburden to me. He started rather vaguely as if half ashamed to express it or take my time. I perceived he wanted to tell of an experience in which the Lord had wondrously helped him. Recognizing this, I said to him, "Go on, you need not feel ashamed—I understand your language for I, too, thank God, am a Christian!" My, how relieved he felt. There are many believers in Christ in the business world who seem ashamed to let it be known that they are Christians. Ashamed—how shocking—we ashamed of Christ, who is not ashamed to call us "brethren." One of the most honored New York bankers I know, than whom I do not believe there is a greater—has a most childlike faith in our Lord, for he has a way of speaking of Him which reveals great intimacy.

Never shall I forget a scene I witnessed last summer, which enabled me more fully to appreciate the comment of the Holy Spirit in Hebrews 2:11, upon this 22nd Psalm. I had been invited to speak at an evangelistic rally which was held at the border line of the Harlem section of New York City. The friend who invited me did not give me clear particulars concerning the meeting except to say that there would be approximately two thousand people present, and that the meeting was conducted for the Spanish people in that section of New York City. As I entered the building I went into a side room to meet the gentleman who was to lead the meeting. I found him to be a Mexican, about six feet three inches in height. He informed me that less than ten per cent of the people understood English, and that it would be necessary for me to talk through him as an interpreter. I found that two-thirds of the group were dark-skinned; whereupon the leader acquainted me with the fact that most of them came from the Central and South American countries. While conversing with him in this anteroom I could hear the strains of joyous singing on the part of the multitude that had gathered. They sang in Spanish. I was not able to understand a single word, but they sang tunes with which I was well acquainted. Later we mounted an improvised pulpit. It was almost filthy. I debated in my mind where I might sit down, with at least an assurance that I alone would be occupying the chair. It made me feel creepy—I began to really appreciate the lot of some missionaries. As I looked across the audience I saw a sight which burned itself into my mind. Most of them were serfs. They sang with glee, and whenever the name of our Lord Jesus Christ was mentioned their faces lit up.

I recall how this six-foot-three Mexican introduced me to the audience. To my amazement, as I approached the pulpit they rose to their feet. I am not a midget myself, but as this Mexican gentleman stood at my left, it was necessary for me to look up at him. I opened my Bible to the 3rd chapter of the Gospel according to St. John containing the portion of the Scripture which I desired to present to that audience. I waited a few seconds, rather surprised that the audience did not sit down, as I had assumed that the rising to their feet was an expression of respect to me. So I turned to the leader and asked: "Why don't they sit down?" With a smile he answered: "They will not sit down until after you have read the Scriptures."

As I looked over that audience of "under-privileged" people I thought how marvelous that they knew enough to give respect to our Lord Jesus Christ, to stand while His Word was being read. I have spoken in many churches—some so-called churches of the elite where cultured, refined people attend and usually they remained in their seats while the Word was being read. How the Holy Spirit enlightened my mind that night regarding His comment in the 2nd chapter of Hebrews: "He is not ashamed to call them brethren." We would not have chosen our friends from among that class of people, yet our Lord Jesus Christ, the Creator of the universe, the Lord of glory, is not ashamed to call them brethren!

THE CHIEF SINGER

Now let us look at the last half of verse 22, which reads: ". . . in the midst of the congregation will I praise thee." Have you considered our Lord Jesus Christ as leading a great congregation in songs of praise? That is what this Psalm presents. And it is in harmony with what we learn from the 2nd chapter of Hebrews. You who sing in choruses or lead congregational singing, may it be an added incentive to you, to know that the Lord is the chief Singer, the great choir director. Indeed, no worship, no praise could possibly be acceptable to God unless it went through our Lord Jesus Christ. He is the center of all God's revelation, the center of Christianity. In the 23rd verse we have the various sections of the great choir which our Lord directs. He seems to stand in the midst, instructing each section to render its praise unto God.

In the 24th verse we have the substance of the song of praise, as well as the reason for so much singing at Easter time. "For he hath not despised nor abhorred the affliction of the afflicted; neither hath he hid his face from him; but when he cried unto him, he heard."

He sings and we sing because of His death and His resurrection. Who wouldn't sing upon experiencing the grace of God in their hearts and the assurance that they have been redeemed from sin?

PSALM TWENTY-THREE—PART ONE

THE SHEPHERD PSALM

THE 23rd Psalm undoubtedly is the 'most universal Scripture known, and loved in all lands. Strictly speaking, the 22nd, 23rd and 24th Psalms form an inseparable trinity. These three Psalms present our Lord Jesus in striking manner. In the 22nd Psalm He is the Good Shepherd who gave His life for the sheep; in the 23rd Psalm He is the Great Shepherd, who in resurrection glory leads His sheep; in the 24th Psalm He is the Chief Shepherd who is to return in glory.

Most of us can testify that we have known the Psalm from early childhood. It is the universal Psalm, the pearl of Psalms, the chief Psalm; in fact, one can go on exhausting adjectives in an attempt to express its great message, and still he would only have touched the fringe of its contents. Yet, it is a Psalm of only six verses.

If I were a lawyer pleading the case of the inspiration of the Bible before a tribunal, I think I would say something like this: "Gentlemen, I rest my case upon the 23rd Psalm. Where is it possible to find more beautiful language, more apt illustrations, more infinite love, more clear confidence, than in the few words of this Psalm? If you cannot feel the breath of God in these words, then dull indeed is your intellect and dead are your powers of perception."

THE SHEPHERD-KING

I do not believe God would give a man a brain with which to think if it were not His purpose that through its use man might understand and appreciate God. Nor would He have endowed us with the urge to find out the unknown if He did not some day intend to reveal it to us.

I suppose many more able, prior to my puny endeavors, have sought to find out just when in David's life he wrote this Psalm. My guess is that he wrote it as his strength failed, as his eyes dimmed, and the gray dawn of the life beyond was pressing its influence more consciously upon him.

David was a shepherd lad whom God made king over Israel. If it be so that this Psalm was written toward the close of his life, he never forgot his shepherd days. Only a shepherd could write the 23rd Psalm. It is interesting that the Bible calls those who are pastors of God's people "shepherds" as He calls us who are His children "sheep." I once suggested to a group of theological students that I believe it would be advisable if theological seminaries would provide in their curriculum a six-month period devoted to tending sheep. I think we would then have better pastors—men who would be more fitted to shepherd the flock of God, whom He purchased with the blood of His Son.

Some of the most noted men in the Scriptures were shepherds. Take for instance Moses—who, though he was learned in all the wisdom of the Egyptians—yet after that, God put him in His own training school, which consisted of tending sheep for forty years on the backside of the desert. No wonder Moses was the meekest man in all the earth and became such a great leader.

To appreciate David's first statement in the Psalm when he wrote:

"The LORD is my shepherd; I shall not want,"

one should consider the office of a shepherd. Most of us in Sunday School days learned that the position of a shepherd was a despised one among the Egyptians. When Jacob came down to Egypt and was about to be presented to Pharaoh, Joseph told him that Pharaoh most likely would ask, "What is your occupation?" and suggested that he reply, "Thy servant's trade hath been about cattle from our youth even until now, both we, and also our fathers. . . ." This would influence Pharaoh to allow them to remain in the land of Goshen; "for," said Joseph, "every shepherd is an abomination unto the Egyptians."

In Israel this same disdain toward shepherds was in vogue; in fact, Rabbi Bar Hamma said, "There is no more contemptible office in Israel than that of a shepherd." For Bible evidence of it, look at 1 Samuel 16:1-11 and 1 Samuel 17:15-28, where we learn that in a large family in Israel the task of tending the family sheep was given to the youngest in the family. So unimportant was that youngster that when Samuel, the prophet, went to Bethlehem-judah, to anoint the king whom God desired to reign over Israel in place of King Saul, and called all to worship, Jesse, one of the leading citizens of the village, came with seven of his sons to worship. Each was presented before the Lord, but Samuel replied, "The LORD hath not chosen these." Samuel seemed to be somewhat disturbed, for he addressed Jesse, saying, "Are here all thy children?" to which the father replied, "There remaineth yet the youngest, and, behold, he keepeth the sheep." And Samuel said to Jesse, "Send and fetch him: for we will not sit down till he come hither."

When David was brought before Samuel he was a splendid looking young man, ruddy of complexion, beautiful of countenance, goodly to look upon; and the Lord said to Samuel, "Arise, anoint him: for this is he." Even in the fact of the apparent evidence that God had chosen David to be king over Israel, a short time later when Goliath, the Philistine, was mocking the children of Israel, David, who had been sent by his father with food for his brethren, overheard the prattling against Jehovah, and asked to go out and meet this Goliath, whereupon his older brother severely reprimanded him for his presumption. He took David to task by saying, "Why camest thou down hither? and with whom hast thou left those few sheep in the wilderness? I know thy pride, and the naughtiness of thine heart; for thou art come down that thou mightest see the battle."

How interesting then that the office which was an abomination unto the Egyptians, and which was contemptible to the Jews, is a position to which our Lord is perfectly willing to condescend. "The LORD is my shepherd." Some of us seem to be so impressed with our own importance and position, that we would consider it beneath our dignity to take a lower position or put ourselves in the place of a serf to minister to others. Our Lord never considered His dignity too great to minister to others; in fact, He said, "The Son of Man came not to be ministered unto, but to minister, and to give his life a ransom for many." There we have the action of a true shepherd.

TENDING SHEEP IN A WILDERNESS

Unfortunately most of us in the East, and particularly we urbanites, rarely see a true shepherd, nor observe his dealings with his sheep. The best we can boast is that we have seen a flock of sheep in some neighboring park, with an indifferent sort of a person acting as a shepherd. However, David, who himself was a shepherd, knew what it meant to tend sheep in a Syrian wilderness. It was no park. This old world of ours, while it has many attractions, is, strictly speaking, a wilderness—it certainly is to a Christian.

It was while David was tending his father's sheep in the Syrian wilderness that he came to appreciate the ways of a shepherd. Thus when he came at the close of his life, to review it in retrospect, his mind turned to his shepherd days, for in describing God's dealings with him during his life he said, "Jehovah is my shepherd." That word "shepherd" Hebrew scholars tell us might also be translated "my goer-forth." That is interesting, because it gives evidence that the flock is in transit—that the shepherd is leading his flock through the wilderness. We do not find the sheep in the sheepfold at rest in the fold until we come to the closing verse of the Psalm. The earlier verses present the sheep in transit, on a wilderness journey, being led by a kindly shepherd. He goes before. Nothing can happen to the sheep unless it first happens to him.

Have we considered that the Lord Jesus Christ through life is our Shepherd? He is our goer-forth, He leads our way; He permits nothing to happen in our lives unless it first passes His inspection. I am not referring to mankind in general; I am referring to those whom our Lord specifically calls "My sheep" and of whom He says, "My sheep hear my voice, and I know them; and they follow me and I give unto them eternal life; and they shall never perish, neither shall any man pluck them out of my hand."

Only those who know the shepherd's voice are members of the sheepfold. It is concerning them that it can be said, the Lord is their Shepherd. We can be a member of that sheepfold by a very simple process; by receiving Christ and thus entering into the fold.

"I SHALL NOT WANT"

It is interesting also to notice that the first statement concerning the shepherd in the 23rd Psalm is an incomplete sentence. "The LORD is my shepherd; I shall not want." It is as if David left the sentence incomplete so that we might put in it anything that we might possibly want.

A moment ago, I mentioned that only those whom our Lord calls His own, who have placed their confidence in Him, are entitled to be called His sheep. I recall an illustration that was given by the Pastor of the Moody Memorial Church in Chicago. Dr. Ironside was having a series of meetings in a far western state. He was being entertained in the home of a ranchman who had many large flocks of sheep. His host said to him one evening, "How would you like to spend tomorrow with me, tending sheep?" to which Dr. Ironside responded in the affirmative. They arose early but had not gone very far when Dr. Ironside noticed a sight that moved him. In one of the flocks there was a lamb with six legs, two of which seemed paralyzed. They were the last two. The little lamb seemed to draw these last two legs along after him as he walked. Dr. Ironside turned to his host, and suggested the little creature should not be permitted to live. His host asked him, "Did you ever see a flock of sheep before?" and ere Dr. Ironside had an opportunity to respond, he added, "Evidently you haven't, for the sight that you see is not an uncommon one where there are large flocks. This little lamb is an orphan; its mother is dead. When such a tragedy takes place, it is the shepherd's business to place the orphan lamb with a foster-mother, but invariably the mother sheep recognizes that the orphan does not belong to her, and refuses to nurse or care for it."

The herdsman, who was a true shepherd, continued, "Fortunately for that lamb, one of the lambs of the foster-mother died. The lamb that died was a little farther advanced than this little orphan lamb. When the lamb died we skinned it, removing its skin whole as much as possible. Then we took this skin and put it over the little orphan like a coat. In this case the lamb that died was several inches longer, and, of course, there was nothing left to do but let the hind legs of the lamb that died hang over the back of the lamb that remained alive. We then put the little one with the foster-mother, who sniffed it and seemed to smell her own breed in the coat with which the orphan lamb was clothed. So she accepted the little one and ministered to it as if it were her own."

We are orphans. We did not belong to the flock of which God was the Shepherd, but through the death of the Lamb of God we have been clothed with a garment which enables us to enter into the true fold, and to be ministered to by the true Shepherd. Our Lord Jesus Christ is the Shepherd who gave His life for the sheep. If He is your Shepherd, then you know the joy David so aptly expressed when he said concerning Him, "The LORD is my shepherd."

How personal David becomes in this Psalm. Indeed, salvation is a personal thing. It is true that our Lord bore the sin of the whole world, but we will never understand that death, or appreciate that sacrifice, until we understand that He died for our sins; that He was our substitute; that God so loved us that He gave His only begotten Son that we believing in Him, should not perish, but have everlasting life. No wonder that David added "I shall not want." We, too, need never want since our Lord is our Shepherd.

THE VALUE OF THE LAMB

We have already seen that our Lord is not only the Shepherd, but He is the Lamb. When our Lord was about to enter His public ministry, John the Baptist pointed to Him and said, "Behold the Lamb of God which taketh away the sin of the world."

It might be profitable and interesting to consider our Lord as the *Lamb* of God. Many animals were designated for sacrifice under the old Jewish economy, but the chief of these was the lamb. It would seem as if God had a special claim upon lambs and would impress us with the Lord Jesus as we observe a lamb. There are certain animals which are good only as long as they live, as for example, a dog. There are other animals who have practically no value while they are alive, but are valuable only after they are dead, such as the pig. Yet there are others who have value both dead and alive. This is particularly true concerning the lamb or sheep. In life it provides wool for clothing. In death it provides its meat for food, its skin for parchment, its gut for music. Do you wonder why our Lord is referred to as the Lamb of God? He has provided us with the robe of righteousness to enable us to stand in the presence of a holy God. Through His death He has provided us with meat whereby we may eat and live. As His blood was poured out, it provided the panacea for sin. And, when we consider the parchment it is impossible to overlook the Word of God. The Lamb of God is also the Word of God. Just as perfectly as Christ revealed the Father to us in His life and character just so perfectly does the Bible reveal Christ to us. He is the incarnate Word, the Bible is the written Word, but both the incarnate and written Word are one. And when we consider the gut, who will question the fact that the finest music in the world centers around the Lord Jesus Christ? The sweetest music has come from His death. So Christ is the Lamb as well as the Shepherd.

PSALM TWENTY-THREE—PART TWO

THE SHEPHERD PSALM

A MONG the titles ascribed to our Lord Jesus in the Scriptures, that of the "Shepherd" is exceedingly illuminating; in fact, as we muse on how perfectly accurate David was in his characterization of us as sheep, and of Christ as the Shepherd, our thoughts will run to the "Ancient Hymn" as did Horatius Bonar's, who wrote:

" 'To shepherds first the Heavenly Shepherd came,' or muse upon the Church's old refrain,

'The Lamb redeems the sheep,' or call to mind the old father's words, just such as suits me now:

'Feeding their sheep, they found the Lamb of God.' "

We considered the first verse of the 23rd Psalm in our previous meditation, now let us look at verse 2, which begins: "He maketh me to lie down in green pastures." There are several things in that statement upon which I'd like to comment. I know there are some ministers listening to this radio program—I have heard from many. May I, a layman, be permitted to make a suggestion? If you wish to be faithful to your charge, do note how the true Shepherd leads His sheep. Do not make the mistake of assuming that discussing current magazines, economics, politics, social revolution or what not, is stamping you in your congregation's mind as an alert, currently informed minister. Men do not go to church on Sunday to hear about that which they live with six days a week. They want to hear what God the Lord has to say. Give them the Word of God. Lead them into green pastures. Feed them with that which alone can satisfy a hungry soul—not the husks of discarded, every-day "stuff" which may be all right for swine, but not for sheep. Sheep want to graze in green pastures. If you want to follow the great Shepherd you will do as He did—expound the Scriptures to them.

In David's comment about the Lord and how He leads His sheep, he added what often we overlook: "He maketh me to *lie down* in green pastures." Note the posture which He makes his sheep take after feeding them. He makes them to lie down. A true shepherd will make his sheep rest after eating, so that, lying down in the very grass where they have been grazing they may get the full benefit of the grass they have just eaten. It gives the sheep an opportunity to chew their cud, again and again, in order that the full benefit may be had.

Isn't it true that these lives of ours are so busy as we run hither and yon, that we do not take time to thoroughly masticate what we have received? If we are to enjoy all that is intended for us, it is not only necessary that we feed on the Word, but that we lie down in it. Believer, do you know anything of that? Strange, say you? No, it is not. To lie down is to rest, to lie down in green pastures is to rest in God's Word.

But our Lord does more. Not only does He feed His sheep, then make them to lie down, but He also leads them beside still waters. Note how thoroughly in this Psalm our Lord does it all. We are simply the beneficiaries. We do naught but enjoy His blessing. There is also a great progression in this Psalm. We have relationship in the statement, "The LORD is my shepherd." We have contentment in "I shall not want." We have rest in "He maketh me to lie down." And now we have refreshment in "He leadeth me beside the still waters."

When I came to know Christ as my Saviour, at 17 years of age, I had heard that it was all right for old people to be Christians, but young people want something else. Filled with youth and vigor and the urge to know and see life, I was told youth could never be satisfied with Christ. What nonsense! I have been a Christian for twenty years. I can honestly say there is no joy in all the world comparable to the joy of knowing Christ. There are refreshing wells of joy in being filled with the Holy Spirit; in fact, that is just what the statement means: ". . . he leadeth me beside the still waters."

Those who are acquainted with the Syrian wilderness inform us that these "still waters" were actually wells or pools. We are inclined, upon a hurried glance through the Psalm, to assume that the still waters are *rivers* of water, but we are told that the rivers of that country are polluted and dangerous—that the shepherd after he fed the sheep and saw to it that they had the proper rest, would take them and lead them to pools or wells, and out of these wells he would draw water to quench the thirst of his sheep.

The Scripture speaks of drawing water out of the wells of salvation with joy (Isaiah 12:3). Not only is it necessary to have our hearts and minds filled with the Word of God, but the sheep need the joy of the Holy Spirit. Only as the Spirit ministers the Word do we fully appreciate the green pastures.

STRAYING SHEEP RESTORED

But David continued, "He restoreth my soul." What a statement— "He restoreth my soul." It is not we who restore ourselves. Occasionally I have met some people who believe that they never need to be restored—who think they are perfect in themselves, and do not need this grace of God. But if you are a sheep of His fold, you have within yourself the capability of straying from the fold. It was Aristotle who said of sheep "that they are most sluggish and foolish, aptest of all to wander though they feel no want nor are able to return."

Sheep do not know enough to remain in the fold—the only thing that they seem to know and to do well is to stray from the fold. Even swine know enough when a storm is brewing to run home, and at night will return to their trough; but a sheep cannot do a thing to save itself. None of us is able to keep himself. After we have been saved, if it were not for the tender care of the Lord, there isn't one of us but would have strayed from the fold forever.

It is wonderful to know that if we do stray it is His business to seek us until He finds us and then restore us to Himself. Notice that David said, "He restoreth my soul." No one can do that for you, but Christ can—yea, He does.

The next thing that David said concerning his Lord as a shepherd was ". . . he leadeth me in paths of righteousness for his name's sake." If sheep remain in a certain grazing place for an extended period of time there are paths that are formed leading into the sheepfold, which are made by the continuous coming in and going out of the sheep which are called in the shepherd's language "sheep tracks." We ourselves *do not* walk in paths of righteousness; He leads us. There is an interesting passage in Isaiah 53 regarding this subject where we read: "All we like sheep have gone astray; we have turned every one to his *own* way. . . ." That way is not the way of righteousness. If we tread the way of righteousness it is because of His leading and for His name's sake, that is, for His own glory.

It is our Lord who leads us in paths of righteousness. That reminds us of the value that the New Testament places on the *name* of our Lord Jesus, as a result of which many prayers offered to God in the course of a day are ended, "This do for His name's sake."

In the 10th chapter of John's Gospel we have a beautiful picture of these sheep tracks. In the 9th verse, our Lord said, "I am the door: by me if any man enter in, he shall be saved, and shall go in and out, and find pasture." Going in and out is equivalent to being led in the path of righteousness for His name's sake.

I have some friends who live in Philadelphia—the husband has been engaged for some time past in New York City. They have a son William by name, who is about 18 years of age. He drove his mother to New York one week-end so that the family could spend a little time together. Saturday, Bill drove his mother around New York to see some of its interesting sights. They entered a well-known church building for the purpose of inspecting its architecture. Entering, the mother noticed a text of Scripture inscribed on the wall. Reading it, it seemed to be strange to her, whereupon she turned to Bill, and said, "Have you your New Testament with you?" Bill pulled it out of his pocket, for he is a member of the Pocket Testament League. His mother said, "Now turn to the 10th chapter of John's Gospel,

from which the text on the wall is taken. You read it while I check it with
the inscription for there seems to be something wrong—it just doesn't ring
true." So Bill read from the 1st verse until he came to the 9th verse, which
was the verse that was inscribed on the wall. He read: "I am the door:
by me if any man enter in, he shall be saved, and shall go in and out, and
find pasture." Alas, it was discovered that the passage had been mutilated,
for the inscription read: "I am the door; by me if any man enter in, he
shall go in and out and find pasture." The phrase, "he shall be saved" was
very curiously, and I think designedly, eliminated. The pulpit of that
church is probably one of the best known in this city, yet I question
whether the word "saved" has ever been used from it. I like the word.
There was a time, however, when it did not "register" with me.

In the company of cultured, intelligent, and refined people the use of
it seems to develop a strange kind of repulsiveness, so that one is characterized as "queer," should he blurt out, "I'm glad I'm saved." Instead of
finding a responsive chord he is more apt to be classified as a patient for
an Isolation Hospital, suffering from a contagious and deadly disease.

During these years that I have known the Lord as my Shepherd I have
come to thoroughly appreciate that word "saved." The old hymn writer put
it splendidly when he wrote:

> "I was lost, but Jesus found me,
> Found the sheep that went astray—
> Threw His loving arms around me,
> Drew me back into His way."

The word simply means "safe." That is exactly the meaning of it in the
9th verse of the 10th chapter of John. The scene is that of a sheepfold. We
enter the sheepfold through the door. Our Lord said He is the door. Because He is the door we can go in and out, traveling in the sheep tracks,
perfectly safe and secure, because He leads us in the paths of righteousness
for His name's sake.

"I WILL FEAR NO EVIL"

The absolute confidence that comes from knowing the Lord as one's
Shepherd could not be more perfectly expressed than in the 4th verse of the
23rd Psalm: "Yea, though I walk through the valley of the shadow of death,
I will fear no evil: for thou art with me; thy rod and thy staff they comfort me."

Death is an enemy. It is an enemy to a Christian as well as to a non-believer. It is the most extràordinary experience of life; it is out of tune with everything else in this world. The Bible calls it "the wages of sin," it also declares that by one man's sin death passed upon all men, for that all have sinned. Irrespective of whether we believe the Bible to be the Word of God or not, we must concede that on this subject it has witnessed perfectly. Every graveyard is a testimony to the truth of God in this respect. Every tomb bears its witness that "death passed upon all men, for that all have sinned." There are some who hate to think about death. Others seek to push it aside by saying there is no death—it is a mere error. Again there are others who have sought to remove its reality by insisting that it means cessation of being; that when a man dies, he dies like a dog; it is the end of all things.

The Bible insists, however, that it is a transition from one state to another. It also maintains that there is absolute consciousness upon the part of both the believer and the unbeliever. This is not the place to discuss this with any degree of thoroughness, but our attention should be directed to one thing that is revealed in this 4th verse on the part of David. He said: "Yea, though I walk through the valley of the shadow of death." Here is consciousness! It is not a case of staying in the valley; it is simply a case of walking through a path which leads into another sphere. That is all physical death is. Death to a believer is robbed of much of its sting.

David did not say it is a walk through the "valley of death," but rather through "the . . . shadow of death." It is the unbeliever who goes into the night, but to the believer in Christ, as Paul so aptly expressed it, death means that we are to be at home with the Lord.

Quite true, it means going through a valley; nevertheless that valley leads into the very presence of God. The confidence which David had in the Lord concerning even this journey was due to his own care in tending his father's sheep. Oftentimes in locating a pleasant grazing place for his father's sheep it was necessary to go through the deep ravines of that Syrian wilderness. David undoubtedly got this figure of speech, "the valley of the shadow of death," from his familiarity with these valleys and ravines. The way was beset with difficulties; nevertheless as a true shepherd David would lead his sheep through deep ravines into the next grazing place. His sheep would have absolute confidence in him because he was a true shepherd.

So David said concerning the journey he was about to take through the valley of the shadow of death, he did not fear any evil; the Lord was with him because his Lord was his Shepherd. He said, "for thou art with me," and then added, "thy rod and thy staff they comfort me."

Do we think of the shepherd's rod and the shepherd's staff as sources of comfort? More often we are inclined to think when the Lord uses His rod upon us that it is anything but comforting. Yet David said, "thy rod and thy staff they comfort me." Why did he say so—the answer may be found in the 12th chapter of Hebrews, the 6th verse, which reads: "For whom the Lord *loveth* he chasteneth, and scourgeth every son whom he receiveth." No single son is exempt from scourging. If we have never experienced the scourging rod of God, if we have never been chastised by Him, it is a serious question whether we can call ourselves children of God. The presence of the chastening and the scourging that we have endured are evidences of the fact that we are sheep of His fold. The rod therefore should become a source of great comfort to us; for it bears additional evidence that we are children of God.

So David declared that as he had frequently experienced the rod of God and the staff which drew him back into the way of obedience, they had become a source of comfort to him, as they brought their assurance to him that he was a sheep of the fold, of which the Lord is the Shepherd.

PSALM TWENTY-THREE—PART THREE

THE SHEPHERD PSALM

IN our previous meditation in the 23rd Psalm we concluded with the 4th verse. We shall now consider verses 5 and 6, which read:

> "Thou preparest a table before me in the presence of mine enemies: thou anointest my head with oil; my cup runneth over.
> "Surely goodness and mercy shall follow me all the days of my life: and I will dwell in the house of the LORD for ever."

Our good friends in Eastern lands insist that we in the West are apt to lose sight of the Eastern shepherds' customs when we suggest that with verse 5 of this Psalm the scene changes from a sheepfold to a banqueting house. While it is true that all through the Psalm David used the language of a shepherd, he never lost sight of the fact that the sheep are men and not animals, for you will recall that in verse 3 he said concerning the Shepherd's dealings with His sheep, "He restoreth my soul."

In the former verses of the Psalm we saw that the sheep were in transit; that the Lord was the One who led the way, and who went before the sheep. There can be no doubt as we approach the closing verses of the Psalm that the Shepherd knew all the time that the way He was traveling with His sheep led to the Father's house, where the sheep are to dwell forever.

However, we do not reach the final destination until the close of verse 6. In verse 5 we have the temporary provision that has been made for our entertainment, if you please, pending our arrival in the house of the Lord.

THE LORD'S TABLE

As we examine these two verses we will observe that David is impressed with the provisions which the Shepherd has made for him. So he wrote: "Thou preparest a table before me in the presence of mine enemies." In our study of the Psalms we should bear in mind that David was a prophet. "He foresaw the Lord always before his face," said Peter in Acts 2:25.

David, as a Jew, knew about the table of shewbread used in the worship of the tabernacle. The table of shewbread stood in the holy place. It contained twelve loaves of bread. The loaves were prepared by the Levites. They were called the shewbread, or the Holy Presence bread; they emphasized before God the unity of the twelve tribes of Israel. But David in this Psalm was not talking about a table prepared by the Levites; he saw something entirely different. He saw a table which was prepared by the Lord. It was not prepared in the sanctuary, either, but in the presence of the enemies of David.

Possibly David who was a prophet foresaw the Lord's table, or what is usually referred to as the Lord's supper—the communion table. You will recall that on the night of the betrayal of our Lord Jesus Christ He instituted a supper which from then on has been observed by Christians all through the ages as a memorial. The bread, we are told in Scripture, is to set before us the body of our Lord Jesus Christ which was broken for us, and the wine speaks to our hearts of the blood that He shed, through which we enjoy the very wine of heaven.

David was conscious that the Lord Himself prepared that table; that the Lord was the host, and he (David) was the guest. How precious that is!

The next time it is your privilege to sit at the table of the Lord, do brush aside the thought that it is a church table. It is to be regretted that certain ecclesiastical traditions have been built around that table. But irrespective of that, the next time you sit down to partake of the communion, bear this passage of Scripture in mind, and say, "Thou preparest a table before me." He prepared it—that is the first thing to remember; the second thing to recall is that the table was prepared for you; and finally that He prepared it and set it up in the presence of your enemies. It cannot be made too clear, however, that the table is prepared only for those who are believers in our Lord Jesus Christ.

I am not guilty of mental phantasy or spiritual illusionment when I say that it is my honest conviction that the most remarkable sight that the devil and his demons can ever witness in this world, apart from the cross where they were defeated, is the erection of the Lord's table with a group of believers sitting down at that table, enjoying the fellowship of our risen Lord and of the Father, who made for them this great provision. It is in the presence of the enemies of our soul that God has raised a table. He sets before us on that table His greatest benefactions—the memorials which speak of His own Son, whose flesh is meat indeed and whose blood is drink indeed.

In that connection I recall reading a comment by an old English divine by the name of John Trapp. He lived during the Elizabethan period. I delight in his writings—they are exquisite. Speaking of the wine at the communion table, he has an interesting comment. He writes, "He (our Lord) was in the wine press that we might enjoy the wine cellar." Our Lord was given a cup; He drank it to its bitterest dregs. He was crushed between the upper and nether millstones, and out of the crushing that took place at the cross, where His blood was spilt, and His body broken, there has come forth, for the sons of men who receive Christ as their Lord and Saviour, the very wine of heaven. When we sit down at the communion table, it is not a cup of bitterness; on the contrary it is a cup of joy!

THE OIL-ANOINTED GUEST

David continued his description of the provision of his great Host—oh, if we could appreciate the heart of God, we would then understand that His chief desire is to have communion and fellowship with us. There is nothing in all the world that He loves so much to do as to set a table before us and welcome us into His own presence, and provide us with the bounties of heaven. The creation of worlds and world systems is comparatively nothing alongside the joy that God has in being our Host, and having us as His guests.

In that connection David continued and said:

> ". . . thou anointest my head with oil; my cup runneth over."

We, in the West, might look with some question at this comment of David, "Thou anointest my head with oil," but a word or two respecting it will make this statement most interesting to us. In the 7th chapter of Luke's Gospel, we have a description of a banqueting scene in which our Lord, as a guest, was entertained by a Pharisee, Simon by name. This Pharisee had invited our Lord, and He accepted the invitation and sat down to eat. To the shock of His host, a woman who was a sinner,

> ". . . when she knew that Jesus sat at meat in the Pharisee's house, brought an alabaster box of ointment,
>
> "And stood at his feet behind him weeping, and began to wash his feet with tears, and did wipe them with the hairs of her head, and kissed his feet, and anointed them with the ointment.
>
> "Now when the Pharisee which had bidden him saw it, he spake within himself, saying, This man, if he were a prophet, would have known who and what manner of woman this is that toucheth him; for she is a sinner.
>
> "And Jesus answering said unto him, Simon, I have somewhat to say unto thee. And he saith, Master, say on.
>
> "There was a certain creditor which had two debtors: the one owed five hundred pence, and the other fifty.
>
> "And when they had nothing to pay, he frankly forgave them both. Tell me, therefore, which of them will love him most?
>
> "Simon answered and said, I suppose that he to whom he forgave most. And he said unto him, Thou hast rightly judged.
>
> "And he turned to the woman, and said unto Simon, Seest thou this woman? I entered into thine house, thou gavest me no water for my feet: but she hath washed my feet with tears, and wiped them with the hairs of her head.
>
> "Thou gavest me no kiss: but this woman since the time I came in hath not ceased to kiss my feet.
>
> "My head with oil thou didst not anoint: but this woman hath anointed my feet with ointment."

Here we have a perfect Eastern setting. Suppose you had some friends living in Persia, or Syria. You were planning to pay them a visit; in fact, they had invited you, as soon as you arrived, to make their home your home, and to give them the honor of entertaining you as their guest, further saying that they had planned a dinner in your honor. If it were your first visit to Persia or Syria, you might be shocked a little at their customs. This is what would happen. Upon your arrival, the host would see to it that there would be present at the door certain servants who would pour water in a basin and wash your feet from the defilement of the Eastern sands. Then in the presence of the assembled guests, your host would greet you with a kiss—the usual Eastern salutation—equivalent to our grasp of the hand and the extending of good wishes. Your host would then turn to a shelf whereupon were some bottles containing olive oil, or some other oil. He would pour some of that oil into a little horn. Then he would pour out the oil from the horn on your head. Possibly you wouldn't understand the meaning of it all. But those assembled guests would know by that procedure your host was saying to you, "It is my pleasure to have you in my home. You are my guest; I am your host. These few drops of oil on your head speak to you that this home is your home, and as long as you are in this home the protection of it is yours. Before any harm can come to you, it must first touch me; if necessary I would die before I would permit a sword to touch you."

David was a guest at the table of which the Lord was the Host. The Host had poured the oil upon his head, and thus announced that as long as he is in that house he is perfectly safe. While his enemies may be round about him, before his enemies could touch him they would first have to smite Christ. What safety! What provision! What a Host!

THE TWO SHEPHERD DOGS

As David closed this Psalm, he looked back over the provisions that the Lord had made for him through the wilderness journey; then looking forward, he said,

> "Surely goodness and mercy shall follow me all the days of my life . . ."

If you have seen a large flock of sheep on a journey, you would have noticed that a true shepherd always leads his flock. They crowd around him—they follow him—they know his voice. In the background where oftentimes it is not possible for the shepherd to keep his eye fixed upon those sheep, he has made provision for their care by placing two shepherd dogs as a rear guard. These shepherd dogs know their duty. It is their business to keep the sheep walking in the pathway of the shepherd. When they see any of the sheep commencing to stray, they bark. The barking, very familiar to the sheep, usually brings them back into the right tracks. If by chance the sheep do not heed the barking of the dogs, or if a sheep is wounded, they will bark all the more frequently, thereby drawing the attention of the shepherd, who with his rod and his crook will bring the straying sheep back into the track or minister to the wounded sheep.

Sometimes I think sheep must feel some resentment against these barking shepherd dogs—until they get into their sheepfold, when they would say with David, "surely goodness and mercy have followed me."

These barking dogs—their names are "Goodness" and "Mercy"—have you ever heard them? You certainly have if you are a believer. Sometimes the bark has been a little annoying. But we are assured that all the disappointments of life, all the barking upon the part of the shepherd dogs, will be understood by us when we get to our final destination. We will recognize them as the provision of God for our care. We will then say concerning them, "Surely goodness and mercy have followed us all the days of our life."

At times it may seem rather difficult to reconcile our circumstances and our disappointments so that we might say with David: "Surely goodness and mercy shall follow me all the days of my life." Yet strange as it may seem, those who have suffered the most, and who have cause, naturally speaking, for feeling some resentment are invariably those who take patiently the experiences of life and look beyond the present to the future. On the contrary, we who complain invariably have very little or any cause for complaint. It would appear that the goodness of God, instead of leading us to repentance, makes us callous to His grace.

In this connection a quotation from a letter I received this week will prove interesting. It came from a young woman who has suffered greatly for several years. She writes: ". . . Thank you for your personal message to me. It was very inspiring and the sweet spirit with which it came unfolded many thoughts to me. I continued in that spirit and read your meditation on Psalm 1, and I was assured thereupon regardless of what, of the one fundamental truth, through a spiritual glimpse into the land beyond the ether (if I may put it that way), I shall stand before God, clothed in the glory and beauty of His sparkling righteousness, because of our Lord and Saviour's complete redemptive work. The reality of this has

eased my heart almost completely. And what His faithfulness has done
for me He can in His mysterious way do for others through the power of
His blessed Holy Spirit. . ."

I trust this letter will be a source of comfort to any who may be in
similar circumstances, and who may have wrestled with a question of the
goodness of God.

How impressed I was by this young woman's statement of confidence
that she "shall stand before God, clothed in the glory and the beauty of His
sparkling righteousness."

Then, too, may this letter lead us who do enjoy the blessings of good
health to be more than ever thankful for the goodness and mercy of God
which have followed us all our lives, although at times we have become
indifferent to His blessings.

Finally David looked forward to his dwelling place when he said,

> ". . . I will dwell in the house of the LORD for
> ever."

Upon the night of His betrayal, our Lord and His disciples gathered
round about a table. They were undoubtedly in a very disturbed state of
mind upon learning that one in their midst was to betray Him while all
of them would forsake Him. He turned to them and said:

> "Let not your heart be troubled: ye believe in God,
> believe also in me.
> "In my Father's house are many mansions: if it were
> not so, I would have told you. I go to prepare a
> place for you.
> "And if I go and prepare a place for you, I will
> come again, and receive you unto myself, that where
> I am, there ye may be also."

That is the final abiding place of every believer in Christ. That is
the place to which David looked forward when he said, "I will dwell in
the house of the LORD for ever."

PSALM TWENTY-FOUR—PART ONE

THE MORAL GLORY OF CHRIST

WE now begin our meditation in the last of that great trinity of
Psalms, which set forth the shepherd work of Christ. Beginning
with the 22nd Psalm we saw the Good Shepherd who gave His
life for the sheep; in the 23rd Psalm we found the Great Shepherd who
in resurrection glory leads His sheep through a wilderness journey; and

in the 24th Psalm we shall observe our Lord Jesus as the Chief Shepherd in all the splendor of His moral glory, His ascension, and His exaltation.

When we consider that these Psalms precede the coming of Jesus Christ into this world by one thousand years, it becomes all the more evident that "the Psalms are not only a book of inspired devotion and worship, but also a volume of prophecy in which the sufferings and the glory of the Messiah are revealed."

Were I asked to give a title to this meditation I would suggest "The Moral Glory of the Lord Jesus" for it is He who is the One of whom the Psalm speaks, and who alone "hath clean hands, and a pure heart; who hath not lifted up His soul unto vanity, nor sworn deceitfully."

The Psalm opens:

> "The earth is the LORD'S, and the fulness thereof;
> the world, and they that dwell therein.
> "For he hath founded it upon the seas, and established it upon the floods."

The word "LORD" in the first phrase—"The earth is the LORD'S," is the Hebrew word "Jahveh" which is the redemptive name of God. It is *the Name*—the Name that an orthodox Jew justly reveres; in fact, the Name he never mentions because of its holiness. "Blessed be He"—as the Jew will say. No Jew would read this verse, "The earth is Jehovah's." Instead he would speak of that unspeakable One as "Adonai" which in our English Bible is printed with a capital "L," the balance being in small letters.

At times it is difficult to acknowledge that the earth is the Lord's as one observes the rule of evil, and the seeming indifference of the Lord to what is going on. Yet, the earth belongs to Him. It does not belong to man who so proudly calls it his own, when, alas, he is so frail that he has nothing to say as to how long he may be permitted to live in his domain. This earth is Jehovah's; some day He shall possess it. It is the repeated promise of both the Old and New Testaments. But not only is the earth the Lord's, but also they that dwell therein.

He is the earth's owner in verse 1; in verse 2 He is the earth's creator; in verse 3 He is the earth's priest; in verse 4 He is the earth's only perfect man.

DAVID KNEW CREATION

There are still a few people who believe this earth is the result of evolution. You will notice that these uninformed take their science from

philosophers rather than from those who by virtue of training and study
are qualified as natural scientists. It is one thing to be a philosopher
seeking a way of life, and in so doing to gratify the vanity of human reason by giving it a sop labeled "evolution." But it is quite another matter
to be a scientist wrestling with the secrets of nature, all of whom, with few
exceptions, are believers in fiat creation.

David knew creation, if you please; he knew that Jehovah had founded
this earth upon the seas. Will any geologist question the scientific accuracy
of David's statement? Yet he wrote almost three thousand years ago—a
time when many of our present day egotists believe the world to have been
in the midst of intellectual and scientific darkness, not having the benefit
of our modern institutions of learning, nor our grasp of the mysteries of
knowledge. Oh, well, I suppose man whose breath is in his nostrils ought
to be permitted to display his vanity, if for no other purpose than to reveal
his stupidity!

So much for the creation of the earth and its foundation. A more
penetrating question confronts us in verse 3: "Who shall ascend into the
hill of the LORD? or who shall stand in his holy place?"

I do not believe anyone doubts that the phrase "the hill of the Lord"
is a metaphor speaking of heaven, and that the further question, "who
shall stand in his holy place?" brings us into the very presence of God—
the sanctuary itself.

There is a scene in the Old Testament which will be of help to us in
understanding this verse. Israel was led out of Egypt through the slaying
of the Passover lamb, and by the revelation of God's mighty hand in causing them to walk upon dry ground as they entered into the wilderness on
their journey to the Promised Land. The Lord reminded Moses of the
manner of their deliverance; how He bore them on eagles' wings, and
brought them unto Himself. So the Lord offered a proposition which might
be expressed in the following language: "Hitherto I have dealt with the
nation Israel in grace. Do they wish that I continue on that same basis,
or would they prefer to have a law, the keeping of which will bring them
blessing, the violation of which will bring curses?"

Instead of recognizing that the blessings of God are enjoyed solely as
the result of His grace, Israel proudly answered: "All that the LORD hath
spoken we will do." Immediately the Lord instructed Moses that he was
to be ready against the third day, at which time He would come down in
the sight of all the people upon Mount Sinai. Moses was to set bounds

unto the people round about, and give them the word of warning that they should take heed unto themselves not to touch the mount or the border of it; for whoever should touch it would surely be put to death.

Why do you suppose the Lord gave such instructions to Moses if it were not that the people could not stand in the presence of a holy God? They could not so much as touch the mount upon which he descended or they would meet the wrath of God.

If the people could not approach the border, much less ascend the mountain of the Lord, is it any wonder the Psalmist raised the cry, "Who shall ascend into the hill of the LORD?"

Only one man during the wilderness journey ascended the hill of the Lord. That man was Moses. He stated in Deuteronomy that God would raise up another man like unto him. That man is the Messiah, Jesus Christ the Lord.

There is this distinguishing fact, however, in comparing Moses and Christ—Moses was a servant and as such was ". . . faithful in all his house, as a servant, for a testimony of those things which were to be spoken after; but Christ as a son over his own house . . ." is worthy of infinitely greater respect. He did not require the protection of the Passover lamb; He *was* the Passover Lamb. He was not prevented from entering into heaven because of failure to meet the requirements of God, as Moses was prevented from entering the Promised Land because he smote the rock in the wilderness a second time whereas he had been instructed to speak to the rock and forthwith would come water.

Man loves to boast of his own righteousness, in conversation with other men; nevertheless when he is in the presence of true holiness his mouth becomes sealed. He bows his head and bears his mute testimony that he is a sinner, and that he has no defense. There comes a cry from the heart which sometimes is not able to break through the seal of his lips, and be expressed in audible language, but nevertheless it is just as urgent as when Job said, "Neither is there any daysman betwixt us, that might lay his hand upon us both."

But there are men who are so blind to true holiness that they believe it is possible to find God by searching, and that it is within the realm of possibility that a man might ascend into the very presence of God. Alas, man is unable to mount a single step through his own assistance or through the assistance of any other; he is bowed to the earth; he cannot even look up into the face of God, much less ascend into the hill of the Lord. But who—who shall ascend? Who shall stand in the presence of His holiness?

HE THAT HATH CLEAN HANDS

In verse 4 we have the revelation of One whose moral glory is exquisite; who shines as a white light upon the black pages of human history —the only perfect character that this world has ever witnessed.

His qualifications are aptly expressed in verse 4 where it is stated that he who shall ascend into the hill of the Lord, he who shall stand in His holy place, must be one "that hath clean hands, and a pure heart; who hath not lifted up his soul unto vanity; nor sworn deceitfully."

Clean hands! ! How Pilate sought to clean his hands, and yet all the water in the world could not remove from his fingers the stain of the dripping blood of the Son of God!

The prophet Jeremiah readily pictured the hopelessness of getting clean hands when he said: "For though thou wash thee with nitre, and take thee much soap, yet thine iniquity is marked before me, saith the Lord God."

One would search in vain for any man with clean hands except the Son of Man, Jesus Christ.

A LITERARY MIRACLE

I stated a moment ago that our Lord was the only perfect character this world has ever witnessed. I would like to press that a little further. The old adage is true, "like produces like." Thus in all the myriads of volumes written by man, in none do we find a perfect character portrayed. Every one has at least one stain. How is it that four men, none of whom boasted literary skill, who, if they were our contemporaries, would not even be considered for the Nobel prize for literature—yet they present a perfect character—which is a literary miracle?

Those four Gospels bear the names of four ordinary men. One was a politician, Matthew by name. The second so mediocre that the best designation would be that of a servant, Mark by name. The third, probably the most intellectual of the four, was a physician, by the name of Luke. The fourth was a fisherman, whose name was John.

There is nothing very impressive about these authors, yet they have accomplished what none of the world's great men of letters have ever done —the presentation, or the biography of a perfect character. If we reject the inspiration of the Scriptures, we are logically presented with a still greater miracle in the literary accomplishments of these four men.

Our Lord's life on this earth was scrutinized by bitter enemies. Since the writing of the four Gospels every word has been subjected to the most minute analysis, every motive has been given a laboratory test—yet almost two thousand years of such searching examination by the world's greatest minds has failed to produce a single individual who has accepted the challenge of our Lord when He said: "Which of you convinceth me of sin?"

No man who has had any respect for his intellect has been able to point a finger of suspicion against Him. He hath clean hands! The marvel of it all is that those clean hands could touch human misery and sin, yet remain undefiled, and moreover to the contrary impart healing balm to the one thus touched.

A pure heart and clean hands go together. You cannot have one apart from the other. The heart is not only the seat of affection, it is the very center of one's being, the source of all one's motives. It is out of the heart that there proceed evil thoughts, etc.; in fact, so detestable is it that the prophet suggests—"The heart is deceitful and desperately wicked—who can know it?" It is utterly outside man's capabilities to fathom the depth of corruption that lies in the human heart.

But, blessed be God!—the heart of our Lord Jesus has never been impugned. It is pure.

As for vanity and deceitful swearing, the less said about it the better. All that one can suggest is that the description which the Bible presents of man is correct. His hands have marred and stained everything he has touched.

But there is one Man—the God-Man, Jesus Christ, the righteous, who because of His moral splendor has ascended and stands in the holy place. It is Christ whom I desire to present; it is with Him that I wish you to be occupied, of whom the Psalm speaks.

I cannot close this meditation, however, before calling to attention that it was never God's purpose to send His Son into this world to condemn it; but rather that He should die a death which would forever justify us. Through His coming the panacea is made available for all whose hands are unclean, whose hearts are impure, whose soul is vanity itself, and whose lips have sworn deceitfully!—That panacea is His precious blood poured forth to cleanse us from our sins.

MORE ABOUT THE MORAL GLORY OF CHRIST

OUR previous meditation in the 24th Psalm covered the first five verses. This one will begin at verse 6 to the end, wherein we find the ascension and exaltation of our Lord Jesus Christ.

"This is the generation of them that seek him, that seek thy face, O Jacob. Selah.
"Lift up your heads, O ye gates; and be ye lift up, ye everlasting doors; and the King of glory shall come in.
"Who is this King of glory? The LORD strong and mighty, the LORD mighty in battle.
"Lift up your heads, O ye gates; even lift them up, ye everlasting doors; and the King of glory shall come in.
"Who is this King of glory? The LORD of hosts, he is the King of glory. Selah."

We have already observed that the Psalm could not possibly concern any other than Jesus Christ, our Lord, as He alone of all the sons of men had clean hands and a pure heart; who had not lifted up His soul unto vanity, nor sworn deceitfully. It is He who shall receive the blessing, and through Him those who place their trust in Him, shall share the blessing.

In verse 6 we have a strange statement; in fact, one that has caused no end of difficulty to commentators. It reads: "This is the generation of them that seek him, that seek thy face, O Jacob."

The Psalmist added the word "Selah" which means to pause or read it again. It is so evidently a startling statement that the Psalmist wished all who read it to pause in order to take in its truth.

The great difficulty is due to David speaking of God under the name Jacob. Indeed, upon a casual glance it does seem strange that God, the Lord, should take unto Himself the name of one of the most crooked men in Scripture. The name itself means "Supplanter." If David had said, "This is the generation of them that seek thy face, O Israel," perhaps it would seem plausible, as Israel was the new name that God gave to Jacob after he triumphed over him, which means a "Prince with God." But the Bible does not make any mistakes! Bear that always in mind. As we look more closely at this verse, and remember what preceded it—that only one with clean hands and a pure heart, one who had not lifted up his soul to vanity, nor sworn deceitfully, could ascend the hill of the Lord, or stand in His holy place—it becomes a most glorious revelation.

Everything that Jesus Christ was, Jacob was not. Jacob's hands were soiled, he had a trickster's heart, a vain soul, and as for swearing deceitfully, none could do better. Yet, in the face of all of Jacob's known characteristics, God is pleased to be called by his name in this Psalm. What does this mean, but that our God is so closely identified with His people, that they and He are one. Because of the moral glory of Christ which gave infinite value to His atonement, it is possible for God to call Himself by the name of one whom He transformed from a trickster to be a prince with Himself.

There are many, many people who hide behind the failings of Christians. They seem to delight to refer to the hypocrites in churches, and use such as an excuse, shall I say, for their own hypocrisy. I have yet to meet a Christian (I mean a true believer in Christ) who is satisfied with his own life, and who would not gladly confess his inconsistencies. But remember a true believer is just a witness, not to himself, but to Christ. Can you not look away from the faulty witness and see the One of whom he witnesses?

If you still persist in directing attention to our failures, let this passage in the 24th Psalm put you to silence—that God is our God, by the mere fact that we believe Him. God rejoices to be known by a name that recalls His relationship to sinners. Indeed Christ became sin on the cross to enable Him to become identified with us in our judgment, so that we might be identified with Him in His righteousness.

LIFT UP YOUR HEADS, O YE GATES

Now let us look at the closing verses, which contain the climax of the Psalm. A messenger approaches, raises his voice, and cries: "Lift up your heads, O ye gates; and be ye lift up, ye everlasting doors; and the King of glory shall come in."

We do not know who the messenger is, but we do understand his message. He invites the keeper of the gates to open them as the King of glory is about to enter in. The watchman at the gate responds, "Who is this King of glory?" to which the messenger answers: "The LORD strong and mighty, the LORD mighty in battle."

The same cry is heard a second time, and the same reply is given except that the description of the King is slightly changed to "The LORD of hosts, he is the King of glory."

Of course, the Psalmist is using parabolic language. Those who are acquainted with ancient history will readily recognize the picture. "There is to be seen today at Rome the ruins of Constantine's triumphal arch erected at the time when he entered the city triumphing over Maxentius, which reminds us of the message of this Psalm; in fact, it is well known that it was customary when the Romans would solemnize the entrance of any prince or others they were desirous of honoring, that they would break down the walls, pull off the gates of the city, partly for more free entrance, and partly to show that their city needed no wall nor gates, as long as they had such a guardian or protector within."

From these customs we are enabled to understand this Psalm. Our Lord is seen ascending the hill of the Lord. There is a guardian, watching at the gates. The messenger heralds—"Lift up your heads, O ye gates; and be ye lift up, ye everlasting doors; and the King of glory shall come in." The heavens are about to honor the King—and the gates are to swing open for Him. Did you notice the title—King of glory? "Who is this King of glory?" is the inquiry. None other than the LORD, strong and mighty, the LORD mighty in battle.

THE MAJESTY OF CHRIST

All too often Christians have a very meager view of Christ. They have never read beyond the four Gospels, it would seem. They have saturated their minds with the Christ of Galilee; they have pictured Him as He so often is seen in paintings which, alas, are so evidently a fraud as to deserve no place in a Christian's thinking. Yet it is true, we think of Christ after the flesh, in humiliation, and we seem to pride ourselves on the honor we bestow upon Him in believing Him, to the exclusion of the recognition of Him in His resurrection glory. But remember He will never again be known in humiliation. Do look away and get a glimpse of the full Christ of the Scripture.

Note, for example, that the Apostle Peter, though he had known Christ after the flesh, had touched Him and observed Him, yet before his decease he wished to impress his readers with the fact of the glory of Christ when he writes in the Second Epistle, the first chapter, beginning with the 15th verse, that

> "Moreover I will endeavour that ye may be able after my decease to have these things always in remembrance.
> "For we have not followed cunningly devised fables, when we made known unto you the power and

> coming of our Lord Jesus Christ, but were eye-witnesses of his majesty.
>
> "For he received from God the Father honour and glory, when there came such a voice to him from the excellent glory, This is my beloved Son, in whom I am well pleased."

Peter set the time of this testimony borne to Christ by adding, "And this voice which came from heaven we heard, when we were with him in the holy mount," referring to the Mount of Transfiguration.

If we wish a word painting of the majesty of the Lord Jesus, we go to the first chapter of the Book of Revelation and we will soon rid our mind of the namby-pamby, spineless individual that Christendom has presented to the world as their Christ.

Rev. 1:12-18, reads:

> "And I turned to see the voice that spake with me. And being turned, I saw seven golden candlesticks;
>
> "And in the midst of the seven candlesticks one like unto the Son of man, clothed with a garment down to the foot, and girt about the paps with a golden girdle.
>
> "His head and his hairs were white like wool, as white as snow; and his eyes were as a flame of fire;
>
> "And his feet like unto fine brass, as if they burned in a furnace; and his voice as the sound of many waters.
>
> "And he had in his right hand seven stars: and out of his mouth went a sharp two-edged sword: and his countenance was as the sun shineth in his strength.
>
> "And when I saw him, I fell at his feet as dead. And he laid his right hand upon me, saying unto me, Fear not; I am the first and the last:
>
> "I am he that liveth, and was dead; and, behold, I am alive for evermore, Amen; and have the keys of hell and of death."

Our Lord is very God; He is the ascended Lord, the King of glory, who shall one of these days return to this earth as the King of kings and Lord of lords. Then, and then only, will this poor, weary world know peace.

To declare the fact of the coming again of our Lord Jesus, the Apostle Peter says, is not to present "cunningly devised fables," but rather a divine revelation of God concerning His purpose in His Son which the Apostle himself witnessed in pageant form, to which prophecy bears its double testimony.

In line with David's title of Christ as the King of glory, it is interesting to note in the last book of the Bible, the Book of the Revelation, in the 5th verse of the 1st chapter, He is called *"the prince of the kings of the earth."*

A prince is the heir apparent. He ascends the throne only upon the death of his father, the king, or in the event the king abdicates. Note that our Lord now is called "the prince of the kings of the earth." I dare say the kings of the earth are almost ready to abdicate! Man at last seems on the verge of confessing his total failure, his utter incapability of rulership.

In this connection I cannot refrain from uttering a word of warning. I am not a prophet, nor the son of a prophet, nevertheless, I have observed some things in my studies of the Scripture and in my acquaintance with history. For some time I have felt that a voice should be raised in this hour reminding our own nation of the consequences of its present attitude, especially in its apparent conclusions that our economic ills are due to over-production of farm products and thereby inferentially at least placing upon God the responsibility for our distress, whereas it is evidently man's failure to properly distribute the increase of God's field. Thus we now tell our farmer how much wheat he may raise, how much cotton, how much cattle, etc., etc. We urge him to plow under his fields, slay hundreds of thousands of heads of hogs—as if our troubles were caused by the bountiful benefactions of the creator God, whose goodness is beyond description. I venture to say that it is not strange that out of the West have come reports of droughts, terrific wind storms, and an early siege of the dreaded mormon cricket, the combined results of which efforts may do more in destroying our crops than the economic planning of a "Godless brain trust." Or, it may be just like the Lord to still shower us with His abounding grace in face of all this fanciful planning.

THE KING OF GLORY

How this world needs the King of glory. Who is He? The Lord, strong and mighty, the Lord mighty in battle. The Lord of hosts. Strong and mighty is He, for in the cross He has triumphed over principalities and powers, making a show of them openly. He has broken the strongholds of the wicked one, He has broken the power of cancelled sin, and has set the prisoner free.

In this 24th Psalm the heaven opens to receive Him. Those gates shall open again to allow His coming out as the King of kings and Lord of lords, and to take His rightful place in the affairs of men. This He will do at the very place where men crucified Him and sent a message back to the Almighty God by Him saying, "we will not have this man to reign over us!" But that Man shall reign in true righteousness and peace. Then shall be accomplished what the prophet Isaiah described for us in the 2nd chapter of his prophecy, verses 1 to 5:

> "The word that Isaiah the son of Amoz saw concerning Judah and Jerusalem.
>
> "And it shall come to pass in the last days, that the mountain of the LORD'S house shall be established in the top of the mountains, and shall be exalted above the hills; and all nations shall flow unto it.
>
> "And many people shall go and say, Come ye, and let us go up to the mountain of the LORD, to the house of the God of Jacob; and he will teach us of his ways, and we will walk in his paths: for out of Zion shall go forth the law, and the word of the LORD from Jerusalem.
>
> "And he shall judge among the nations, and shall rebuke many people; and they shall beat their swords into plowshares, and their spears into pruning-hooks; nation shall not lift up sword against nation, neither shall they learn war any more.
>
> "O house of Jacob, come ye, and let us walk in the light of the LORD."

It is because of that hope that a Christian is an optimist in the midst of a world seething in deepest pessimism.

PSALM TWENTY-FIVE

THE SECRET OF GOD

THE 25th Psalm is another of the Davidic Psalms. Incidentally, it is the first of the alphabetical Psalms in which, in its original Hebrew setting, each verse begins with one of the twenty-two letters of the Hebrew alphabet, the consecutive alphabetical arrangement being maintained. It reads:

> "Unto thee, O LORD, do I lift up my soul.
>
> "O my God, I trust in thee: let me not be ashamed, let not mine enemies triumph over me.
>
> "Yea, let none that wait on thee be ashamed: let them be ashamed which transgress without cause.
>
> "Shew me thy ways, O LORD; teach me thy paths.

"Lead me in thy truth, and teach me: for thou art the God of my salvation: on thee do I wait all the day.

"Remember, O LORD, thy tender mercies and thy lovingkindnesses; for they have been ever of old.

"Remember not the sins of my youth, nor my transgressions: according to thy mercy remember thou me for thy goodness' sake, O LORD.

"Good and upright is the LORD: therefore will he teach sinners in the way.

"The meek will he guide in judgment: and the meek will he teach his way.

"All the paths of the LORD are mercy and truth unto such as keep his covenant and his testimonies.

"For thy name's sake, O LORD, pardon mine iniquity; for it is great.

"What man is he that feareth the LORD? him shall he teach in the way that he shall choose.

"His soul shall dwell at ease; and his seed shall inherit the earth.

"The secret of the LORD is with them that fear him; and he will shew them his covenant.

"Mine eyes are ever toward the LORD: for he shall pluck my feet out of the net.

"Turn thee unto me, and have mercy upon me; for I am desolate and afflicted.

"The troubles of my heart are enlarged: O bring thou me out of my distresses.

"Look upon mine affliction and my pain; and forgive all my sins.

"Consider mine enemies; for they are many; and they hate me with cruel hatred.

"O keep my soul, and deliver me: let me not be ashamed; for I put my trust in thee.

"Let integrity and uprightness preserve me; for I wait on thee.

"Redeem Israel, O God, out of all his troubles."

David was a real poet and as such appreciated order. I am inclined to think that the Holy Spirit made use of poetic genius in order to impress us with the fact that the whole of the alphabet was designed for the glory of God.

In the early part of the Psalm, David wrote of his desire for the Lord—

"Unto thee, O LORD, do I lift up my soul.

"O my God, I trust in thee: let me not be ashamed, let not mine enemies triumph over me.

*　*　*　*

"Shew me thy ways, O LORD; teach me thy paths.

> "Lead me in thy truth, and teach me: for thou art
> the God of my salvation; on thee do I wait all the day."

No one can read this Psalm without being impressed with the personal appropriation David made. He called God "my God." He took his position humbly before the Lord and asked Him to teach him, to show him His ways, and to lead him in truth. But as he did so there was a tug at his conscience. How could one who was a sinner, whose life had been marred as frightfully as David's had been, appropriate the Lord as *his* God and ask Him to teach him? Immediately therefore David prayed, "Remember, O LORD, thy tender mercies and thy lovingkindnesses . . ." but "Remember not the sins of my youth, nor my transgressions" but "according to thy mercy remember thou me for thy goodness' sake, O LORD."

One of the chief delights of Satan is to remind one of the sins of his youth, especially if one now has a burning desire for full fellowship with God. It is just another of the tricks of the adversary of our souls to keep us from enjoying the fellowship of God. The Lord has assured us "I will forgive their iniquity, and I will remember their sin no more." If you as a child of God are annoyed by the repeated attempts of the enemy to remind you of your sin, simply refer him to the Word of God, before which he cannot stand. That Word speaks of the grace of God, the gift of Christ, and the blood of Jesus Christ, God's Son, which cleanses us from all sin.

How wonderful is the 11th verse of the 25th Psalm where we read, "For thy name's sake, O LORD, pardon mine iniquity . . ." David freely acknowledged his iniquity. There was no attempt to hide it—God was aware of it. It is folly to try to hide our iniquity from God. He knows our secret sins. The only honorable thing to do is to acknowledge our sins before the Lord and to receive His forgiveness. He offers it to us on the grounds of the righteous atonement for our sin which His own Son provided on the cross.

TEACHING IN THE WAY

Now let us get to the heart of our message. David asked in the 12th verse, who is he "that feareth the LORD?" Do you fear Him? If you do, come near and let's learn what God promises to do for the man who actually fears Him. The inspired penman said, ". . . him shall he teach in the way that he shall choose;" second, "His soul shall dwell at ease . . ." third, ". . . his seed shall inherit the earth;" fourth, "The secret of the LORD is with them that fear him;" and finally, "he will shew them his covenant."

There is a message in this portion of Scripture which would take an eternity to fully appreciate. It speaks of the man who fears the Lord, and of course one cannot fear Him until he has received His testimony; there is no doubt about that. This Psalm is not for an unconverted person. It is for the man who has received Christ, for the one who has been born again by the Spirit of God, who has been introduced into the family of God and therefore is a child of God by faith in Jesus Christ. As such he is teachable. We are told that the fear of the Lord is the beginning of wisdom. All right, how are we to get it? How are we to grow in grace and in the knowledge of our Lord Jesus Christ? By sitting at His feet and learning of Him, for the Psalmist said that such a man shall "he teach in the way that he shall choose." A more accurate rendering of that verse would be "him will he teach in the way he ought to choose."

One of the great problems that confront a young Christian is this— What shall he do with his life? Life is before him. Which way shall he choose? Probably there never was a time in the past fifty years when so great obstacles were presented to a young person getting out of college or school, particularly if that one has received Christ as his Saviour. What shall he do? Which way ought he to choose? Should he become a missionary? Should he go into so-called Christian work, or should he enter secular work, business life, or a profession—what shall he do?

The Lord has said concerning the one who fears Him, "him will he teach in the way he ought to choose." That is a promise of God in the light of which any man who has dared to trust and commit his life into His keeping inevitably concludes that God has led him in the way he ought to choose. He not only will lead, but He will teach him in the way he ought to choose. Teaching is a process. It is a training. The promise of God is that He "will teach him in the way he ought to choose." That is a life training. It is the only safeguard for one who trusts the Lord. If you wish to have perfect peace and quietness in your heart, if you wish to have prosperity, which after all is the actual meaning of the Hebrew word translated "ease," if your soul is to prosper, it is necessary to sit at the Master's feet and learn of Him. There is no incident nor detail in life in which He will refuse to guide and teach you.

I do not believe that there is a place in a Christian's life where the devil appears to trip one so readily as in this matter. Our lives seem to say, We can trust God for eternal salvation but we cannot trust Him to guide our life; we can trust Him for His promise that He will save our soul; we rejoice that we will never know what it is to be condemned in hell, but we cannot have the same trust that He will guide us every moment of every day. That, we say, is our business; we have to fashion our lives. But that is all a mistake. We do not have to do it—and when we do we always spoil it. When we intrude self into our life we mar it. Everything man has ever touched has been marred. God help us to possess our right as His child to commit our life to Him. He has given the assurance that will teach each in the way he ought to choose.

This principle of divine teaching holds true regarding all Christian testimony and activity. I do not believe any man ought to preach the gospel unless he is called of the Lord. I do not believe a man ought to be a missionary unless he is called of the Lord to be a missionary. I do not believe one ought to distribute a tract or speak to an individual about his soul unless he is guided by the Spirit of God. If he is not guided, he performs his ministry and work in the power of the flesh. Such ministry invariably is unfruitful. Let me give you an example of what I mean.

Recently I was invited to speak to a Jewish congregation. A very gracious opportunity was given to me as a Christian to speak to Jews about the Jews and their present plight. There is a passage of Scripture which has a pertinent message regarding a Christian's conduct under all circumstances. It is found in the 10th chapter of 1st Corinthians, the 32nd verse, where we read, "Give none offence, neither to the Jews, nor to the Gentiles, nor to the church of God. . . ." It was an evening I shall never forget. The Rabbi spoke of the service as being "inspiring"—yet some well-meaning but absolutely misguided Christian or Christians thought it was an occasion to slip one over on that company of Jews. They took with them a batch of tracts containing a story entitled, "A HEBREW'S SEARCH FOR THE ATONING BLOOD." They left a number of these tracts in the book racks and even slipped some into the books which of course did not belong to them. Naturally an unpleasant situation developed. A definite offence was given. No person has a right, in my judgment, to give out a tract unless he has been guided, unless he has prayed about the matter and poured forth his heart before the Lord and asked His guidance so that no offence be given. Please bear in mind this is not a criticism of the tract—it is a splendid tract, written by my esteemed friend, Dr. Ironside. But it is a criticism of misguided distribution of tracts. In the first place, as these people were guests, they were guilty of ungracious conduct, they certainly had not grown in *grace,* and secondly, the books in the racks did not belong to them so they were also guilty of failing to recognize ordinary property rights. If we wish to do Christian work, we must be in the center of God's will. The Lord has promised to teach us in the way we ought to choose. Remember, our Lord said to His disciples, ". . . be ye therefore wise as serpents, and harmless as doves." I have related this incident because sometimes more harm than good can come from a zeal which is born of the flesh and not of the Spirit.

THE PROSPERITY OF THE SOUL

In this Psalm the Lord not only gave the promise concerning the man who trusts in the Lord, that God will teach him in the way he ought to go, but we also learn that He will make his soul dwell at ease, or prosper. Is it possible for a soul to prosper? Indeed, it is. The aged Apostle John wrote three tender letters—short, but marvelously sweet. The last of these letters he addressed to a man named Gaius whom he loved in the gospel, saying, "Beloved, I wish above all things that thou mayest prosper and be in health, even as thy soul prospereth." Gaius, therefore, was a man who feared the Lord. We all know how pleasant it is to prosper in business and to have good health, especially so, if we have gone through a period of disturbances, depression, sorrow, or ill-health. What relief, what peace, what gladness possesses a godly soul when his business prospers and his body is in health! But that's nothing compared to the prosperity of the soul. If one truly understands values, he would ten thousand times rather be a pauper as far as temporal things are concerned or an incurable invalid, just as long as he has a rich, spiritually prosperous soul. If we would have a prosperous soul, we must fear the Lord. To fear is to obey Him.

This Psalm has an assurance concerning such that their seed shall inherit the earth. Well do I know that this is an earthly promise to an earthly people and refers particularly to Israel but might it not also be applied to the inheritance of a believer in Christ in this age, or to the head of a Christian family who really fears the Lord?

"THE SECRET OF THE LORD . . ."

In the 14th verse of the 25th Psalm is a remarkable statement. There we read, "The secret of the LORD is with them that fear him. . . ." The secret of the Lord! We sing—"In the secret of his presence, how my soul delights to hide." There is a place called the *secret* place. In the 27th Psalm David wrote, ". . . in the secret of his tabernacle shall he hide me; he shall set me up upon a rock." There is the place of safety, the secret place, to which the believing soul can flee in the time of distress and where he can be perfectly safe and at ease. But there is another thought in this 25th Psalm, "The secret of the LORD is with them that fear him. . ." That is something quite different. What do you suppose the Psalmist mean by "the secret of the LORD"?

In Proverbs, the 3rd chapter, 32nd verse, we read, ". . . his secret is with the righteous." Our Lord said, as recorded in the 15th chapter of John's Gospel, 15th verse, that He would no longer call His disciples servants, "for the servant knoweth not what his Lord doeth:" but thereafter He would call them friends; for all things that He heard of His Father He made known unto them. There you have the secret of the Lord—they are the things which the Lord heard of His Father which He has now made known unto His disciples, whom He calls His friends. It is wonderful to be a servant of the Lord, and to do His bidding, but it is glorious to be His friend and have Him unfold to us the secrets of His Father. These secrets are to be found in the Word of God—this Bible, which is a closed Book to the unbeliever but an open Book to the believing heart. The secret of the Lord enables a child of God to have an equilibrium in the midst of disturbances, to have a quiet mind when the world is upset, to have a quiet conscience and peace in his breast when others are in turmoil.

We have the further statement of this Psalm that God will show to such His covenant, or His agreements, for that is what the word *covenant* means. The Lord will unfold His agreements. He made some of them with the sons of men; He made some with Israel; He made some with His Son. We haven't the time to discuss them; we can merely mention them and suggest a study of the Word of God to observe these agreements so that we might enter into them and rejoice in the promises of the Lord.

What man of you desires to fear the Lord? To you this word is presented. He will teach you in the way you ought to choose; your soul shall prosper; your seed shall inherit the earth; the secret of the Lord is with you; and He will show you His covenants and agreements. That is full salvation. It is all of grace through faith.

PSALM TWENTY-SIX

HOW TO AVOID SLIDING

A HURRIED reading of the 26th Psalm would lead one to the conclusion that the writer had overdone the personal pronoun "I." In twelve verses he used it no less than thirteen times, while "me," "my," and "mine" are to be found in the Psalm a total of fifteen times. Therefore, twenty-eight times in twelve verses David made use of the pronouns "I," "me," "my," and "mine." That's most unusual for David and certainly for anyone who professes humility before the Lord. But as we examine the Psalm more closely we will soon discover a most interesting thing about this matter.

The Psalm reads:

> "Judge me, O LORD; for I have walked in mine integrity: I have trusted also in the LORD; therefore I shall not slide.
> "Examine me, O LORD, and prove me; try my reins and my heart.
> "For thy lovingkindness is before mine eyes: and I have walked in thy truth.
> "I have not sat with vain persons, neither will I go in with dissemblers.
> "I have hated the congregation of evil doers; and will not sit with the wicked.
> "I will wash mine hands in innocency: so will I compass thine altar, O LORD:
> "That I may publish with the voice of thanksgiving, and tell of all thy wondrous works.
> "LORD, I have loved the habitation of thy house, and the place where thine honour dwelleth.
> "Gather not my soul with sinners, nor my life with bloody men:
> "In whose hands is mischief, and their right hand is full of bribes.
> "But as for me, I will walk in mine integrity: redeem me, and be merciful unto me.
> "My foot standeth in an even place: in the congregations will I bless the LORD."

There are very few men in this world who can honestly make use of the words of this Psalm. Most of us must confess that more often than not we have failed miserably in our walk before God.

It has been said that this world has yet to see what God can do through one man who yields himself completely to the Lord. My personal opinion is that the world has seen such a man, at least one such man, and that was the Apostle Paul. The world may have seen others but at least Paul could say, "Be ye followers of me, even as I also am of Christ." This he wrote to the Corinthians while to the Ephesians he said, "Be ye therefore followers of God, as dear children. . . ." In both instances the word "followers" means "imitators." Imagine a man telling others "Be imitators of me, even as I also am of Christ." But it was not vain boasting on the part of the Apostle for he so conducted his life, rather should I say, he so permitted the Lord to live through him, that he could write, "For to me to live in Christ, and to die is gain." This should not be confused with vain glory or pride. There are some men who set themselves up as shining examples but who cannot stand in the piteous light of the scorching rays of God's holiness. You remember the Scotsman who attended prayer meeting in company with his wife. When the hour of testimony arrived he rose and gloriously extolled his own virtues till his wife, Peggy, pulled his coat-tails and whispered, "Sandy, *don't forget, I'm here.*" Yet there is such a thing as personal righteousness without which a testimony becomes as sounding brass and tinkling cymbals.

THE PROBLEM OF SIN AND SLIDING

This Psalm presents a man who invited the Lord to judge him, who declared that he walked before his God in integrity and that he trusted in the Lord—indeed, because of his integrity and his trust in the Lord he confidently expected that he would not slide. It is an interesting expression David used, ". . . I shall not slide."

God must contend with slipping people and sliding saints. At times one gets a rude awakening when he overlooks his feet and fails to watch his step. Some friends of mine use the expression, "Keep looking up." It is most appropriate, for man is the only creature who is able to look up, but it would have been better if they had completed the expression and said, "Keep looking up and watch your step." Faith and walk go hand in hand in spiritual experiences as they do in the matter of the ordinary every-day experiences of life.

I vividly recall a recent "slipping experience" I had. It was a Saturday morning. It had been raining. I parked my car just a short distance from the office and proceeded unconcernedly to walk to our place of business. I was looking "up" all right but I was not watching my step—suddenly I slipped. What a rude awakening I got as my head struck the pavement!

For a moment I wondered where I was. A friend of mine in Chicago heard about it and wrote me. I, in turn, responded that I could thoroughly appreciate that the re-echo of the crash was heard in Chicago for I surely came down with a thump ! ! ! But, sir, did it ever occur to you and has it ever occurred to me that a slip in our moral being, in our Christian walk, inevitably ends in a fall, the repercussions of which echo to the very throne of God? We cannot slip, we cannot fall into sin without that sin striking back at the throne of the eternal God.

The Apostle Paul wonderfully handled the problem of sin in the closing part of the 3rd chapter of his letter to the Romans when he answered the question, How can God be just and the justifier of him which believeth in Jesus? Sin presented a greater problem to God than the creation of universes. God's righteousness and His holiness could never overlook sin nor excuse the sinner. He has written that inexorable law in the entire universe. One cannot break a law of nature without receiving a penalty. As God has embodied that law in His entire creation so, too, has He written the law of the forgiveness of sins by the imputation of the righteousness of God and the remedial effects of a healing balm. In the moral realm that healing balm is the precious blood of the Lord Jesus Christ which He shed on the cross and which enables God to be just and the justifier; the blood sustains His righteousness and permits His mercy to operate. Now God proclaims from heaven the fact that He will justify every individual who believes in Jesus. This justification is without merit on the part of the individual who receives it; it is freely extended by God's grace through the redemption that is in Christ Jesus. That was done nearly two thousand years ago.

But sin still is a problem to God. God well knew that the cross would not change the nature of the individual who believed in Jesus. Man would still have the same old nature he ever possessed—a sinful nature which expresses itself always in sin. In fact, a justified man, by which we mean a Christian, a converted man, a man who has been born again by the Spirit of God, is more plagued about his sin than any other person. His conscience has become more finely tuned. The new nature which has been given to him enters into conflict with his old nature and thereby sets forth the old in its true setting. Frankly, I never knew what sin was nor how wicked and vile it was until I knew Christ as my Saviour.

God knew that there would be times in a Christian's experience when sin would get the upper hand, when he would slip and fall. But, if you please, the moment a Christian sins he sets in motion great activity in the Godhead.

Our Lord Jesus Christ, at the right hand of the Majesty on high, is now performing the work of High Priest. He ever lives to make intercession for those who are in Christ. He has continued that ministry from the moment He was received into the heavens. It has been a continuous ministry, for sin is a continuous problem at the judgment seat of God. Our Lord Jesus Christ is the Advocate with the Father and as such He pleads, on behalf of the Christian, the merits of His own precious blood as the atonement for the sin of that individual Christian. Then the Holy Spirit within the breast of the Christian begins to make such a one feel uncomfortable and will continue to do so until he has confessed his sin before the Lord. When that has been done his fellowship with God is restored by our Lord as his great High Priest. Once again the Christian enjoys communion with God. How absolutely essential, therefore, is it not only to "look up" but to watch one's walk.

ORTHOPEDIC CHRISTIANS

We might raise the question, has our faith penetrated to our feet, or is our faith only a head knowledge, a mental assent to a series of historical facts? Is our faith something that is from the heart? Does it affect our thinking and cause us to think right? No man thinks right about the Scriptures unless he is orthodox. Orthodoxy means right thinking. We speak of orthopedic shoes. They are right-fitting shoes. A Christian ought to be orthopedic as well as orthodox. Right thinking is necessary, but right walking is also an important part of his entire being. A Christian should watch his step as well as keep his upward look. Of course, his eye should be centered upon Christ in the glory. The Scriptures encourages him to do that for it is written, ". . . Looking unto Jesus the author and finisher of our faith; who for the joy that was set before him endured the cross, despising the shame, and is set down at the right hand of the throne of God." We are to look to Him for encouragement and comfort, and at the same time observe that our walk before man is in integrity and in truth. A full experience is the combination of justification by faith and justification by works: justification by faith before God and justification by works before man.

David, the writer of this 26th Psalm, kept those two things clearly in mind and in their proper relationship. That is evident from the way he linked his integrity with his faith, as it appears several times in this Psalm.

For example, in verse 11 we read, "But as for me, I will walk in mine integrity:" and then follows, "redeem me, and be merciful unto me."

The fact that a man is saved by grace, through faith, not of works, lest he should boast, does not mean that thereafter the conduct of his life is not a matter for attention. Indeed, the Scripture immediately following the reference to faith apart from works declares, "For we are *his workmanship*, created in Christ Jesus unto *good works*, which God hath *before* ordained that we *should walk in them*." Our acceptance with God is because of His mercy. As such is the case our walk is a matter of vital importance, in order that we might be in a position to tell others of the wondrous works of God. Let's not forget that if we are to bear an effective testimony before the world our walk must be different from the walk of this world. If it is not, even the world will rebuke us and rightly so, saying, we are not one bit different from them.

Dr. George McNeely recently spoke at the Star of Hope Mission in Paterson, N. J. He said to the Christians in that meeting, "You are a child of the King—behave like one!"

How To Avoid Sliding

In the closing verse of the Psalm David said, "My foot standeth in an even place: in the congregations will I bless the LORD." You see, in this Psalm David cannot get away from the matter of his walk and conduct before men. Neither can we. It is utterly impossible for a Christian ever to get to a place where his walk is of no consequence.

But is there any place of safety? Is there a place where a man may feel certain that his foot will not slip? I believe there is. Do not misunderstand. No man will ever get to the place of sinless perfection in this age. That will never be accomplished until we have been changed into His image and likeness. A man who walks close to his Lord and whose conduct is becoming his Lord is more apt to condemn himself. He never boasts of his walk. He is all too well aware of the imperfections which are unseen by man but which are seen clearly by the eye of a holy God. Sinless perfection is not what we are talking about. We are talking about the "hit or miss" type of Christian experience which characterizes so many people today. Can we avoid that? David said, "My foot standeth in an even place."

I referred earlier to a "slipping experience" in which I slipped because my feet landed on an uneven place. It was a slope, an incline, and I was not expecting it. There is only one even place and that is when both feet are solidly planted on the Rock Christ Jesus, and the impregnable rock of His Holy Word. When our feet are planted on the solid Rock and those feet of ours seek their guidance from the written Word, we will find that we will bless the Lord in the congregations of His saints. Such persons find their affection is in the same place that David's was, as revealed by him in the 8th verse of this 26th Psalm, "LORD, I have loved the habitation of thy house, and the place where thine honor dwelleth."

Fellowship with God and fellowship and communion with His people go hand in hand. The man who is always at the prayer meeting, always at his accustomed place on Sunday mornings and Sunday evenings enjoying the fellowship of kindred minds as they examine the Word of God and behold the beauties of the Lord Jesus Christ, is more apt to have his feet standing in an even place than the man who thinks he can worship God wherever he pleases—at the golf course or at home or in the company of people irrespective of what their views might be concerning the most precious things in life, the Person of Christ and the living Word of God.

If we desire to have a normal, healthy spiritual experience—communion with the Lord, fellowship in His Word, and friendship with His people, are prerequisites. We will then be able to publish with a voice of thanksgiving and tell others the wondrous works of the Lord.

PSALM TWENTY-SEVEN—PART ONE

THE MAN WHO HAD ONLY ONE DESIRE

THE 27th Psalm is another of the beautiful Psalms of David. We shall limit this meditation to the first six verses, which read:

> "The LORD is my light and my salvation; whom shall I fear? The LORD is the strength of my life; of whom shall I be afraid?

> "When the wicked, even mine enemies and my foes, came upon me to eat up my flesh, they stumbled and fell.

> "Though an host should encamp against me, my heart shall not fear: though war should rise against me, in this will I be confident.

> "One thing have I desired of the LORD, that will I seek after; that I may dwell in the house of the LORD all the days of my life, to behold the beauty of the LORD, and to enquire in his temple.

"For in the time of trouble he shall hide me in his pavilion: in the secret of his tabernacle shall he hide me; he shall set me up upon a rock.

"And now shall mine head be lifted up above mine enemies round about me: therefore will I offer in his tabernacle sacrifices of joy; I will sing, yea, I will sing praises unto the LORD."

AN AUDACIOUS STATEMENT

There are two distinct subjects in these verses; the first, David's abiding *confidence*, and the second, the Psalmist's continuous *desire*.

Let us look a moment at his confidence. He said: "The LORD is my light and my salvation. . . ." There is nothing quite so expressive, and at the same time revealing, as this statement: "The LORD is my light and my salvation. . . ." Note that David found his light and his salvation in a *person*, and that person, none other than Jehovah Himself. He did not find light and salvation in a philosophy, in an institution or, for that matter, in a creed. He found it in a person. David was both personal and audacious in this statement. "The LORD *is my* light and my salvation, . . ." Frequently the 1st verse of this Psalm is used as a motto—in fact, part of it—"The LORD is my light," is the motto of Oxford University. Yet it is possible to have something as a motto and yet know nothing of its power. Let me take a moment or two to explain what it means to acknowledge that the Lord is one's light and salvation. First, what is the opposite of light and salvation? Is it not darkness and despair? That is the condition in which the whole world is found, and every individual in it. Man does not in himself possess light, and his failure evidences his need of salvation. Salvation is, therefore, outside of man's range of accomplishment. David knew that. For which reason he declared: "The LORD is my light. . . ." Our Lord Jesus Christ said, ". . . I am the light of the world: he that followeth me shall not walk in darkness, but shall have the light of life." Again He exhorted: ". . . Walk while ye have the light, lest darkness come upon you: for he that walketh in darkness knoweth not whither he goeth."

Here we have a simple test whereby we can determine whether we are walking in the light or walking in darkness. The Lord said, ". . . he that walketh in darkness knoweth not whither he goeth." Do we know where we are going? If we *do not*, then, on the authority of Jesus Christ, we are walking in darkness. If we *do* know where we are going (and let me say this, we *can know*), then it is because the Lord Jesus Christ is our light.

How Can a Man Be Born Again?

But not only did David say, ". . . The Lord is my light," but he also confessed, "He is my salvation." Salvation is the theme of the whole Bible, both of the Old and the New Testaments. The message of the Bible explicitly states that man is a lost creature, but that ". . . God so loved the world, that he gave his only begotten Son, that *whosoever* believeth in him should *not* perish, but *have* everlasting life."

Our Lord gave expression to that exquisite thought in John 3:16, while in conversation with an interesting character, a man named Nicodemus, a Pharisee, and a ruler among the Jews. Nicodemus was a thoroughbred as regards *moral* character. No one could have lifted a finger in accusation against him. He was one of the finest products of the finest religious system ever known to this world. But what did our Lord have to say to him, when Nicodemus sought Him out one evening? Having observed the miracles which our Lord had accomplished, he came to Him saying: ". . . Rabbi, we know that thou art a teacher come from God: for no man can do these miracles that thou doest, except God be with him." Our Lord's reply was baffling. He told that cultured, religious gentleman what very few preachers in this day seem willing to tell the same kind of men. Our Lord said: "Ye must be born again." What does that mean? It is as disconcerting to some as it was bewildering to Nicodemus, who replied, "How can a man be born when he is old? Can he enter the second time into his mother's womb and be born?"

I do not believe that there is a single individual who, had he the opportunity of re-entering into his mother's womb, and being born again, would not take the opportunity.

Our Lord replied to Nicodemus: "That which is born of the flesh is flesh; and that which is born of the Spirit is spirit."

It would do no good to be born again in the usual manner, for it would still be a birth after the flesh. Christ was speaking of a new birth *after* the Spirit. He continued: "Marvel not that I said unto thee, Ye must be born again. The wind bloweth where it listeth, and thou hearest the sound thereof, but canst not tell whence it cometh, and whither it goeth: *so is* every one that is born of the Spirit."

Surely it is a miracle. To be born again by the Spirit of God is, therefore, a definite experience with God, and through it a relationship is established which is just as clear and as definite as when we were born according to the flesh. In support of this, let's look at what is written in the 1st chapter of John's Gospel, beginning with verse 11:

> "He came unto his own, but his own received him not.
>
> "But as many as received him, to them gave he power to become the sons of God, even to them that believe on his name:
>
> "Which were born, not of blood, nor of the will of the flesh, nor of the will of man, but of God."

To be born of God, therefore, is the way by which one enters into the family of God, and becomes a child of God. All of this is accomplished by faith in Christ, which consists of placing one's confidence for eternal salvation in the Person and work of Christ.

In the messages on the 22nd Psalm we observed that David foresaw the crucifixion, the burial, and the resurrection of Christ. He, therefore, as definitely as we in this day, embraced Christ and acknowledged the work of Christ as the basis for his salvation.

Every individual who can say with David, "The LORD is my light and my salvation . . ." can also add, ". . . whom shall I fear?"

Again David said, ". . . The LORD is the strength of my life; of whom shall I be afraid?" Thus the Lord is not only David's confidence, but his very strength and power. David continued: "Though an host should encamp against me, my heart shall not fear: though war should rise against me, in this will I be confident." "In this." In what? In this!—"The LORD is my light and my salvation."

A CONTINUOUS DESIRE

Now let us glance at the next subject, which is also of deep interest. Verse 4 reads: "One thing have I desired of the LORD, that will I seek after. . . ."

Usually an individual possessed of a single-track mind invites upon his head criticism of the so-called liberal-minded. There are some people in this world who think that it is a compliment to be called broad-minded.

Perhaps the most notable character of the past few decades who manifested a single-track mind was President Woodrow Wilson. His enemies berated him for it, while his friends gloried in it. He could only see one thing, thus no obstacle was insurmountable and nothing swerved him. He steadfastly adhered to his idealism.

Now I am not taking sides on the subject of the League of Nations, nor am I expressing what I think of the wisdom of having a single-track mind when it comes to political matters. But what I want to say is this: When it comes to a man's relationship to God, there is no room for anything but a single-track mind. David possessed it! There was only one thing he desired—and it was the supreme motive of his life. He said: I will seek after it. What was it that he sought? What was it that he desired? He expressed it in no uncertain words, saying: ". . . that I may dwell in the house of the LORD all the days of my life. . . ."

That desire would not suit all people! "Church all the days of one's life?" some would say; "It is sufficient for me to go to church *once* on Sunday. Had I to remain in church all the days of my life, whatever would become of me?" But how do you suppose you will enjoy the presence of God in heaven when you do not feel at home in His presence now?

"THE BEAUTY OF THE LORD"

The temple was not yet built when David wrote this Psalm, although the idea of such a building was in David's heart. It was David's son, Solomon, who built the first *temple* for the worship of Jehovah.

Prior to King Solomon's reign the meeting place of the people of God was round the tabernacle, that strange, unattractive dwelling (from the outside), of which the chief article of furniture was the ark of the covenant. The ark was an ordinary box, but made of a particular kind of wood, overlaid with gold, into which were placed the two tables containing the Ten Commandments, Aaron's rod that budded, and the pot of manna. These were to remind Israel of Mount Sinai, the holiness of God, and the provision of God through the priesthood and the manna. But this strange box had a covering of pure gold. Out of the same piece of gold were beaten two cherubims, facing each other and looking toward the covering. This covering was called the mercy-seat. Upon it the high priest placed the blood of the atoning sacrifice. It was from this place that God communicated with the representative of Israel. David desired to learn the *secret* of the place where God dwelt so that he might ". . . behold the beauty of the LORD . . ." Every piece of furniture, every sacrifice, every ritual bespoke the grace and beauty of the Lord.

Contrast that with our own day. We have buildings which we call churches. These buildings are not to be compared with the building to which undoubtedly David referred. The only comparable building to that of which

David spoke is in the heavens, the dwelling-place of God, where our Lord Jesus is *now* seated at the right hand of the Majesty on high. The one all-powerful motive that should govern the life of every believer in Christ is that newborn desire to dwell in the presence of Christ—to dwell where He dwells. For what purpose? For the same purpose which David expressed: " . . . to behold the beauty of the Lord, and to enquire in his temple."

The Person of Christ is all transcending. He is called by scores upon scores of titles, each of which unfolds His beauties, and many reveal His all-conquering work. To enquire in His temple is just another way of saying, I want to know more about the holiness of God and the atoning work of Christ.

Hardly any time remains for comment upon verse 5. "For in the time of trouble he shall hide me in his pavilion: in the secret of his tabernacle shall he hide me; he shall set me up upon a rock."

The tabernacle of God is a safe place of refuge—but what is this about a rock in the tabernacle? There was no visible rock in the tabernacle. Quite true. But there was the invisible Rock of Ages, Christ Jesus the Lord, to whom David referred.

PSALM TWENTY-SEVEN—PART TWO

THE FACE OF THE LORD

BEFORE commenting on the second half of the 27th Psalm, there is a matter in the 6th verse which demands our attention. The verse reads: "And now shall mine head be lifted up above mine enemies round about me: therefore will I offer in his tabernacle sacrifices of joy; I will sing, yea, I will sing praises unto the LORD."

The only sacrifices now acceptable to God are the sacrifices of joy, and the singing of praises. All other sacrifices have ceased. There is an interesting comment about this subject of sacrifices in the 10th chapter of the Epistle to the Hebrews, where we learn that:

> ". . . it is not possible that the blood of bulls and of goats should take away sins.
>
> "Wherefore when he (Christ) cometh into the world, he saith, Sacrifice and offering thou wouldest not, but a body hast thou prepared me:
>
> "In burnt-offerings and sacrifices for sin thou hast had no pleasure.

"Then said I, Lo, I come (in the volume of the book
it is written of me,) to do thy will, O God."

This is a quotation from the Book of Psalms. The last sacrifice of a
blood character that has been accepted by God was the sacrifice of His Son.
It is written concerning that sacrifice that our Lord appeared *once* in the
end of the age ". . . to put away sin by the sacrifice of himself." Therefore, ". . . after he had offered *one* sacrifice for sins for ever, (he) sat
down on the right hand of God. . . ."

It was necessary that our Lord's sacrifice be a blood sacrifice, for the
Scriptures insist: ". . . *without* shedding of *blood* is *no* remission." However, when God accepted that sacrifice all previous sacrificial oblations were
annulled. Any sacrifice offered now, irrespective of by whom offered, is of
absolutely no value. The only sacrifice now possible to offer to God is the
sacrifice of praise, which we are exhorted to render continuously, and which
the last chapter of the letter to the Hebrews declares, is the ". . . fruit
of our lips giving thanks to his name."

Only one class of people can offer that kind of sacrifice—they who have
come under the shelter of the sacrifice of Christ, the Lamb of God, and who
have embraced Him as their offering for sin. Such people can, together with
David, offer up sacrifices of joy; that is, the giving of thanks, the fruit of
one's lips.

THE SONG OF HEAVEN

There is one thing about David which I envy. He said in this Psalm:
"I will sing, yea, I will sing praises unto the LORD." David must have
been a marvelous singer. How I wish I could sing! Some of my friends
would surely take me to task were I to make an attempt at imitating David!!
But I rejoice that the Bible holds out the hope that some day each of the
redeemed of the Lord will be able to sing in that great "Hallelujah Chorus."
There is an interesting thing about that chorus. I may not know the tune to
which the song will be sung, and I am not so sure of the part I shall sing,
but I do know the substance of the song; in fact, the very words of the song!
Let me give it to you (you who are believers ought to become acquainted
with it so that when you get to heaven you will at least be familiar with it);
it is found in the 9th verse of the 5th chapter of the book of The Revelation, where we read, ". . . they sung a new song, saying, Thou art worthy
to take the book, and to open the seals thereof: for thou wast slain, and hast
redeemed us to God by thy blood out of every kindred, and tongue, and

people, and nation; and hast made us unto our God a kingdom of priests:
and we shall reign on the earth."

That is a wonderful song! It is not only one of praise to Christ for
His redeeming work, but it is an acknowledgment that His atonement has
made us "a kingdom of priests;" that is, a people who have the right to
intercede in the presence of God. The song also contains a great anticipation, ". . . we shall reign on the earth."

It should be self-evident that a Bible Christian is the greatest optimist
in the world, but, mark you, his is not a blind optimism, vague as the air,
but it is an optimism which finds its faith in the unerring, eternal Word of
the living God.

THE INCOMPARABLE FACE

Now for a few comments on the latter half of our Psalm. The 8th verse
is very interesting. It reads: "When thou saidst, Seek ye my face; my
heart said unto thee, Thy face, LORD, will I seek." It is evident from
this verse that what the Lord desires of His children is that they should
seek His face. The response should be the same as it was in David's heart:
". . . Thy face, LORD, *will* I seek."

But what is there about the *face* of the Lord? At least, the expression
reveals that God is a person, or that He has revealed Himself in a person.
The Bible declares that person to be Jesus Christ our Lord. There is an
interesting comment on this subject in Paul's second letter to the Corinthians, chapter 4, commencing with verse 3:

> "But if our gospel be hid, it is hid to them that are
> lost:
> "In whom the god of this age hath blinded the minds
> of them which believe not, lest the light of the gospel
> of the glory of Christ, who is the image of God, should
> shine unto them.
> "For we preach not ourselves, but Christ Jesus the
> Lord; and ourselves your servants for Jesus' sake.
> "For God, who commanded the light to shine out of
> darkness, hath shined in our hearts, to give the light
> of the knowledge of the glory of God in the *face of
> Jesus Christ.*"

Consider this last statement in the light of His crucifixion, when men
spat in the face of Christ; when the soldiers wounded His head by placing
a crown of thorns upon Him; when they "plucked the hairs" from His cheek.
It is amazing that the sons of men could be so blind as not to perceive in
that face the glory of God. Of course, our Lord wore a veil, a garment of

flesh, so as to hide that glory, in order that He could have association with men.

If we peruse carefully the record of the sufferings of Christ, we will find that the treatment accorded our Lord was exactly the same treatment that was accorded the scapegoat under the Jewish economy. Indeed, our Lord was the antitype of the scapegoat.

The visage of our Lord which was so scarred during His first advent that the prophet Isaiah said in his 52nd chapter, written seven hundred years before Christ, that it was "marred more than any man," is now manifesting the glory of God.

Probably the greatest incentive to godly living that is set before a believer in Christ is the anticipation that some day he shall see his Lord's face. We have the assurance that when we shall see Him, we shall be like Him; for we shall see Him as He is. I wonder if we appreciate what that means? There is an incident in the Old Testament Scripture that will aid us in understanding it.

After Moses had been in the presence of God, his face reflected the glory of God. That reflected glory was so powerful that the elders of Israel requested Moses to put a veil over his face. Now then, if the reflected glory was so transcendent, what must be the effulgence of Christ from whose face shines, not a reflected glory, but an inherent glory.

It is true that the human mind cannot comprehend glory; but at least God bids us, by faith, to understand that Christ possesses such glory. Furthermore, as recorded in John 17, the Lord prayed to His Father for us who are believers in Christ, in the following words: "And the glory which thou gavest me I have given them; that they may be one, even as we are one." And, again, "Father, I will that they also, whom thou hast given me, be with me where I am; that they may behold my glory . . ." It is simply thrilling to contemplate such a dignity being bestowed upon children of men. Incidentally, the occupation of heaven is revealed by Christ in this prayer; it is this: "Beholding His glory."

However, we cannot pass by this reference to the face of our Lord without directing further attention to what is recorded in the last book of the Bible, describing the attitude of unbelievers to the glory of God upon the face of Jesus Christ. In the book of The Revelation, the 6th chapter, we have this definite statement concerning the world of men who recognize, from the events taking place in the heavens and upon the earth, that the coming of Christ is rapidly approaching, that

> ". . . the kings of the earth, and the great men, and the rich men, and the chief captains, and the mighty men, and every bondman, and every free man, hid themselves in the dens and in the rocks of the mountains;
>
> "And said to the mountains and rocks, Fall on us, and hide us from the face of him that sitteth on the throne, and from the wrath of the Lamb.
>
> "For the great day of his wrath is come; and who shall be able to stand?"

From the testimony of the Scripture, we as individuals can have but one of two attitudes concerning Christ, particularly concerning His face. Either we rejoice in anticipation that we shall see His face and recognize therein the Lord who loved us and gave Himself for us, or we shall be so smitten with horror as we contemplate that face that we will cry for the rocks and mountains to hide us from His face, and from the wrath of the Lamb.

It seems to be forgotten, or designedly overlooked, that the Bible reveals upon the one hand that God is love, and, on the other, that God is a consuming fire. While they are opposite revelations, they are in perfect harmony with each other.

We are urged to flee from the wrath to come, into a place which is a safe haven—the only haven. It is found under the shadow of Calvary's cross, where the fountain was opened from Immanuel's side. Into it the guiltiest and most defiled may plunge and be completely made whole and washed white in the blood of the Lamb.

There is a story told of the colored mammy, who was disturbed by some racket emanating from the kitchen, only to discover that her little pickaninny was wallowing in the flour barrel. "Land sake, sonny," she said, "wat am de matter wid you?" She listened to the boy's tale of woe: he didn't like the little white lads calling him "nigger," so he was going to be like the white boys. His old mammy roared with laughter, then set him on her knees and said, "My boy, you'll never be white, even though you use all de flour in dat barrel. You is black because it's in your blood. But listen, sonny boy, what's more important, de Lord, He done shed His blood at Calvary dat you and me might have our hearts washed white. Better to have black skin and a white heart, dan white skin and a black heart. Sonny boy, dat flour can only white-wash you, but Jesus' blood can wash you white!" Indeed it can, and does.

THE HOPE OF THE WORLD

Verse 11 of our Psalm reads: "Teach me thy way, O LORD, and lead me in a plain path, because of mine enemies." Here the Psalmist took the position of a child and requested that he be instructed by the Lord and that he have the honor of being led by Him. In this verse David revealed the secret of a normal, healthy, spiritual experience. If we, as believers in Christ, are to enjoy all that God has for us, we must take this same position and say, "Teach me thy way, O LORD, and lead *me* in a plain path."

And now for a final word. Let us consider the last two verses of this Psalm. David said: "*I had fainted,* unless I had believed to see the goodness of the LORD in the land of the living. Wait on the LORD: be of good courage, and he shall strengthen thine heart: wait, I say, on the LORD." That exhortation reveals David's great faith when he said he had "fainted" (utterly collapsed) unless he "had believed to see the goodness of God in the land of the living." What land was he talking about? He called it "the land of the living." I believe he was talking about this world of ours. It does now seem to reveal the goodness of the Lord. Certainly at present it reveals chaos, and disappointment, and disturbances that baffle the most capable intellects. Indeed, it is doubtful that one could spend much time in the contemplation of the present conditions on this earth, without inviting the possibility of losing his equilibrium—it's enough to drive a man mad! What is more, the panaceas that some offer for this disturbed old earth of ours are so ridiculous that I feel like using the title which the "New York Herald Tribune" carried for its leading editorial yesterday morning in reviewing the speech of Chancellor Adolf Hitler before the Reichstag on Friday evening. It carried that cryptic, but revealing title, "The Speech of a Fanatic." I think sometimes that the panaceas that are offered for the ills of our world are the *illusions of fanatics.*

The only panacea for this world's ills is that which the Bible offers— namely, the return of our Lord Jesus Christ. It is that event to which David looked when he wrote: "I had fainted, unless I had believed to see the goodness of the LORD in the land of the living."

The "goodness of the LORD." I believe that is more than an attribute of God; it is a personality—the Messiah.

How glad we are that David closed this Psalm by exhorting us to "Wait on the LORD: be of good courage . . ." He repeated, ". . . wait, I say, on the LORD."

PSALM TWENTY-EIGHT

DOES GOD TEMPT MEN?

W E are now to consider the 28th Psalm. Before giving any introductory comments, let us read the Psalm. It has only nine short verses.

"Unto thee will I cry, O LORD my rock; be not silent to me: lest, *if* thou be silent to me, I become like them that go down into the pit.

"Hear the voice of my supplications, when I cry unto thee, when I lift up my hands toward thy holy oracle.

"Draw me not away with the wicked, and with the workers of iniquity, which speak peace to their neighbours, but mischief is in their hearts.

"Give them according to their deeds, and according to the wickedness of their endeavours: give them after the work of their hands; render to them their desert.

"Because they regard not the works of the LORD, nor the operation of his hands, he shall destroy them, and not build them up.

"Blessed be the LORD, because he hath heard the voice of my supplications.

"The LORD *is* my strength and my shield; my heart trusted in him, and I am helped: therefore my heart greatly rejoiceth; and with my song will I praise him.

"The LORD is their strength, and he is the saving strength of his anointed.

"Save thy people, and bless thine inheritance: feed them also, and lift them up for ever."

When I examined this Psalm in preparation for this message, I read through it hurriedly, for the first reading, as I usually do. Immediately there flashed through my mind the question, what could be said about this Psalm? What is distinctive about it; something not to be found in any other Psalm or that we have not previously noted when we have discussed other Psalms? But as I thought a little more, several rays of illumination emanated from other pages of this precious Book, the Bible, to focus their light upon this Psalm.

Before we finish our meditation, we shall discover that this is no ordinary Psalm. It has a message which we can apply to our own hearts and which will be a source of inspiration and encouragement to us now.

FOCUSING GOD'S WORD

The Apostle Peter laid down a principle which, while specifically applying to prophecy, is not without its application to all other subjects revealed in the Word of God. The Apostle, speaking of the prophetic part of the Bible, wrote, ". . . no prophecy of the Scripture is of any private interpretation." Therefore, it is inconsistent to take one passage and magnify it to the exclusion of all other passages that touch upon the same subject. What we should do is to examine all passages on the related subject and focus them all upon the event. In that manner only, can one get a clear outline of prophecy as well as its details. It is simple and clear to any who stop and think. For instance, if we were to describe a chair, we would not spend all our time examining the legs of it; they are only a part of the chair; we would also examine the seat, the back, and every other part. So in prophecy —all the prophetic part of the Scripture on a given subject should be focused on that event.

Incidentally, this is one of the reasons people have stumbled over the Scripture. They have taken a portion and magnified it to the exclusion of other parts; frequently, in fact, totally ignoring the plain teachings of the rest of the Bible. Our Lord said concerning the man who is well versed in the Scriptures, that he ". . . is like unto a man that is an householder, which bringeth forth out of his treasure things new and old" and the Apostle Paul urged us to compare ". . . spiritual things with spiritual;" that is, have one part of the Bible explain the other part.

Let me illustrate this principle. The 3rd verse of our Psalm reads, "Draw me not away with the wicked, and with the workers of iniquity, which speak peace to their neighbours, but mischief is in their hearts." By the way, I saw a cartoon this past week, the inspiration for which undoubtedly came from this verse. It depicted the recent meeting and embrace of Il Duce and the Fuehrer. They were hugging each other in perfect accord, yes, in perfect accord, for each held a dagger pointed into the back of the other—"Draw me not away with the wicked, and with the workers of iniquity, which speak peace to their neighbours, but mischief is in their hearts." When we examine this verse closely we immediately think of another passage, part of the so-called Lord's prayer, that part which reads, ". . . lead us not into temptation, but deliver us from evil . . ." David said, "Draw me not away with the wicked," while our Lord said to His disciples, When ye pray ye are to say, ". . . lead us not into temptation, but deliver us from evil . . ." We should therefore examine this prayer given by the Lord, in order to understand the 3rd verse of the 28th Psalm.

Let me say something else before we go into this matter further. If you still think that this Psalm is an ordinary portion you may be right, but the extraordinary part of it is that it fits perfectly into our ordinary lives; for let's not overlook the fact that our lives are usually made up of many ordinary things. That's just one more reason for finding in this Psalm that which will meet our present need.

DOES GOD TEMPT MEN?

David said, "Unto thee will I cry, O LORD my rock; be not silent to me: lest, if thou be silent to me, I become like them that go down into the pit." Have you ever had such an experience? Of course you have. Have you ever cried unto the Lord? Have you ever asked Him not to be silent? If so, you have had an experience similar to David's. Maybe that will also help us to understand why David should pray, "Draw me not away with the wicked. . ." But, some will ask, Is it conceivable that God would draw men into the paths where the wicked are? If it were impossible for God to lead a man into temptation, why did our Lord teach His disciples to pray ". . . lead us not into temptation. . ."?

Here is a solution to this question—though you may have a better one. Some, if not most of us, are inclined to boast (yes, just a trifle!) particularly when we see others doing things which never occurred to us to do. Let me speak as a "fool." The Apostle Paul resorted to that "pastime" occasionally to show the utter fallacy of some of the modern philosophy of his day. Here as we walk we observe a man coming toward us; he is reeling to and fro. He is hardly able to stand, much less walk straight. He simply cannot seem to keep away from liquor, and I (remember, I am speaking as a fool) say to you, "Humph, liquor is no temptation to me. I would never get into that fellow's shoes. The last thing in the world I'd do would be to get drunk. Liquor holds no interest for me." Now let me tell you what I *actually* say to my own soul since I have come to know the Lord as my Saviour, and have better understanding of my heart. I now say, when I see such a sight, "If it were not for the grace of God I would be that man." You see, I have never been led into that particular path of temptation, undoubtedly because the Lord has kept me from it. I am glad He has never permitted me to be led into it. If He had I am not so sure I would not succumb to it just as others who have been tempted to that extent. It is so easy to boast that we have the power to dominate ourselves. But just let the Lord lead us into a testing place, or, if you please, remove His restraining hand—let Him show us the wickedness of our own heart and the sinfulness of sin and I am sure we would cease all our empty boasting.

Man in his natural state is out of tune with God. It is not surprising that he is all mixed up even on the simplest rules of conduct. He boasts, I am what I am because I am what I am, whereas a Christian says, "By the grace of God, I am what I am."

Now let me give you an example of how the Bible explains itself, as well as present one more evidence of the perfection of God's Word.

Can and does God lead one into temptation? In the 1st chapter of James, verse 13, we read, "Let no man say when he is tempted, I am tempted of God: for God *cannot* be tempted with evil, neither *tempteth* he any man: but every man is tempted, when he is drawn away of his own lust, and enticed." This passage would appear to contradict and make meaningless that phrase in the "Lord's Prayer," ". . . lead us not into temptation . . ." I say it "appears to contradict;" in reality it does not. James says God does not tempt any man nor can He be tempted with evil. But look at the 1st verse of the 4th chapter of Matthew's Gospel where we read, "Then was Jesus led up of the Spirit into the wilderness to be tempted of the devil." Who led our Lord into the wilderness to be tempted? The Holy Spirit. The Holy Spirit is a member of the Godhead, therefore God not only can lead one into temptation, but actually did lead our blessed Lord into the place where He was tempted, or tested.

But here note the perfection of God's Word. God cannot, nor has He ever, tempted any man with evil; but God can and does lead man into the place where he is tempted. So Christ was led up of the Holy Spirit into the wilderness to be tempted. *Tempted* by whom? The devil. Who *led* Him into the wilderness to be tempted? The Holy Spirit. That puts meaning into the phrase of the "Lord's Prayer," ". . . lead us not into temptation, but deliver us from evil. . ." That makes plain the 3rd verse of our Psalm. The principle is in perfect harmony with the passage in James. God never *tempts* any man with evil—Satan does that; but God can and does at times *lead* one into the path where he is tempted of Satan. How wonderfully harmonious is God's Word!

THE USE OF "THE LORD'S PRAYER"

Before we leave "the Lord's Prayer," let me pass on an excellent thought that was given by Dr. Ironside, pastor of the Moody Memorial Church, in Chicago. In fact, from my repeated references to Dr. Ironside in these Psalms, it is evident in what esteem I hold him. Most people never look at the setting when our Lord gave this suggested form of prayer. Has it ever occurred to us that the Lord never intended this to be a public prayer? Let's see what He said about it. In the 5th verse of the 6th chapter of St. Matthew's Gospel, the Lord cautioned the disciples when praying not to be as the hypocrites are, who love to pray standing in the synagogues and in the corners of the streets that they may be seen of men. "But *thou*," said He, "when *thou* prayest, enter into *thy* closet, and when *thou* hast shut *thy* door, pray to *thy* Father which is in *secret;* and *thy* Father which seeth in *secret* shall reward *thee* openly." If this is contrary to anything you have previously learned, remember we are merely quoting the Scripture. You see, we mix things up because we are out of tune with God.

A great many of us even after we have received Christ as our Saviour forget that our natural man is still out of tune with God. When God saves a man—and I use that term advisedly and with great delight, for the word perfectly describes the experience of salvation—He does not *change* his character. He does not *change* his nature. He imparts a *new* nature and a *new* life to the man—that new life is in tune with God while his life in the flesh is out of harmony with God. If one instrument is in tune and the other out of tune you have discord. So, too, in a Christian's life there is discord unless he recognizes spiritual principles. The Apostle Paul discussed this and gave us the secret, the only escape from a disappointing and a discordant experience. Paul said, "I am crucified with Christ: nevertheless I live. . ." That sounds like a contradiction of terms, but it is not. The Apostle continued and said, "yet not I, but Christ liveth in me . . ." What then—what about this "I" and "Christ"? These two lives, these two distinct principles, opposite as the poles, what should our attitude be towards them? The Apostle continued and said, "and the life which I now live in the flesh I live by the faith of the Son of God, who loved me, and gave himself for me." Only by that kind of living is it possible to be in tune with God.

When we are in harmony with God His Word is clear light; we observe every detail of it, and the more we examine it the more perfection will we recognize. Mark you, we are talking now only of those who have been born again by the Spirit of God. We are not talking to any who have not had that experience. One might as well talk about colors to a blind man. Some one has well said, "It is not light that this world needs, it has plenty of light. Light is not the cure for blindness." The cure for blindness is to have that skillful surgeon of the soul, our Lord Jesus Christ, open the eyes of the blind. When *you* are willing to submit to that operation *your* eyes will also be opened. You will then see the flood of light streaming from the pages of the Book we call the Bible. You say, How is the operation performed? It is as simple as A B C. Its principles are exactly the same as in the performance of an operation upon our physical eyes. We commit ourselves to the hands of the surgeon, we trust him. In the language of Scripture it is, "Believe on the Lord Jesus Christ, and thou shalt be saved."

LIFE WITH A CAPITAL "L"

But now let's get back to the 28th Psalm. Note in the 4th verse that we have another of those constantly recurring imprecatory prayers. Concerning the wicked, David said, "Give them according to their deeds, and according to the wickedness of their endeavours: give them after the work of their hands; render to them their desert." Why? Let's read the 5th verse, "Because they regard not the works of the LORD, nor the operation of his hands, he shall destroy them, and not build them up." A moment ago we spoke about the operation that the Physician of the soul is willing to perform. And, sir, whoever you may be, if you go into eternity a lost soul, it is because you have not regarded "the works of the LORD, nor the operation of his hands. . ." Therefore, you will receive the wages which you have earned, which wages Scripture declares is death. You may argue all you will against it, but it is written there in the Book. It is utterly impossible to take it out of the Book. If you go out a lost soul, it is exclusively your own fault. You can go out with tremendous joy if you will submit to the operation of His hand and if you will take cognizance of the works of the Lord.

We know many things David did not know. The great revelations of the New Testament were unknown to him; the wonderful grace of God, how He would take a poor sinner of the Gentiles and put him in the glory, making him as perfect as His own Son; the relationship of Christ to His church—these were all unknown to David. We know much more than he, but we still have many of his problems. We still cry to the Lord, we still present to Him the voice of our supplications. These experiences of ours have been common to the people of God in every age, and for that matter common to all men.

But, here is the distinction between the cry of a blinded heart and the cry of an enlightened heart. We who believe God, may not be able to answer and understand every problem of life, but our cry invariably turns into a song. Without exception we conclude with joy, because the Lord hears and answers the voice of our supplication. Therefore, with David, our hearts greatly rejoice. While we may periodically raise a question and cry with our lips, we invariably end with a song of praise unto the Lord our strength and shield.

That's life with a capital "L." It is the fullness of life. It is that to which our Lord referred when He said, ". . . I am come that they might have life, and that they might have it more abundantly." I would not change places with the most brilliant man or the most honored man in this world who does not know the Christ of God. I would ten thousand times rather be among those of whom David spoke in the closing verse of this 28th Psalm when he wrote, "Save thy people, and bless thine inheritance: feed them also, and lift them up for ever." Why not step out of sin into Christ? It is only one step—it is taken by faith.

PSALM TWENTY-NINE

THE VOICE OF THE LORD

THE 29th Psalm contains the most majestic and terrifying description of a storm to be found in literature.

In some respects it is rather fortunate for us that we live in a part of the world where a little thunderstorm is the nearest approach to our notion of what a hurricane is like. After a lengthy hot spell there is nothing quite so refreshing as an electric storm accompanied by cooling rains. All nature takes on new life, and one can almost hear the trees clapping their hands as if to voice their praise to the Creator. Yet, while our storms in the East are usually of a minor character, I have known of people who are very much afraid at the pealing of a little thunder and the flashing of a few streaks of lightning. I have heard of some timid souls who hide in closets or under the bed, or some other sheltered place, where at least the illumination of the lightning is unable to enter.

However, the storm which the 29th Psalm describes is not that cooling, refreshing summer shower we all love. Neither do I think the hurricanes that occasionally occur in the southern section of our country give us anything but a faint idea of what the Psalmist presented. I shall not soon forget the description a friend of mine gave me of his experiences and the sights that he saw as he went through the hurricane that swept the southeastern coast of Florida some few years ago, after the famous land bubble had burst. He told me of associates who turned white with fright at the lashing of the winds and the devastation that followed. Even that type of storm does not begin to measure in ferocity with the storm which this 29th Psalm describes.

THE MAJESTIC VOICE OF THE LORD

While the scene is one of intense terror, this Psalm is probably the most majestic in the entire collection of one hundred and fifty Psalms. It contains only eleven short verses.

"Give unto the Lord, O ye mighty, give unto the LORD glory and strength.

"Give unto the LORD the glory due unto his name; worship the LORD in the beauty of holiness.

"The voice of the LORD is upon the waters: the God of glory thundereth: the LORD is upon many waters.

"The voice of the LORD is powerful; the voice of the LORD is full of majesty.

"The voice of the LORD breaketh the cedars; yea, the LORD breaketh the cedars of Lebanon.

"He maketh them also to skip like a calf; Lebanon and Sirion like a young unicorn.

"The voice of the LORD divideth the flames of fire.

"The voice of the LORD shaketh the wilderness; the LORD shaketh the wilderness of Kadesh.

"The voice of the LORD maketh the hinds to calve, and discovereth the forests: and in his temple doth every one speak of his glory.

"The LORD sitteth upon the flood; yea, the LORD sitteth King for ever.

"The LORD will give strength unto his people; the LORD will bless his people with peace."

In the first two verses of this Psalm we are exhorted to *give* unto the Lord. My, how it resounds! The Psalmist says *give, give, give*.

When one enters into the New Testament he meets a fuller revelation of the manifestation of God's love. He learns also of an opposite exhortation—*receive*. We are to be the recipients of God's benefits. He is the giver. He is the giver of every good gift. He climaxed His love gifts with the gift of His own Son. We have eternal life by simply believing. Indeed, it is

written, ". . . as many as received him, to them gave he power to become the
sons of God, even to them that believe on his name. . . ."

It is true that at the present time God, in grace, is dealing in benefactions. He is pouring out upon the sons of men the full expression of a
heart overflowing with love to mankind. But, mark you, this age has an
end. By every known law it must come to an end. There must come a day
of reckoning. It isn't pleasant to talk about it—neither is it pleasant to
think about it. Nevertheless, it is inevitable. In the light of that reckoning
day the Psalmist exhorted the particular group of people whom he addressed
to *give, give, give* unto the Lord.

Notice, I said, "to a particular group of people." You will recall how
he addressed them. He calls them "O ye mighty." He is not speaking of
little you and me who make up that vast army of the common people. He
is addressing his exhortation to rulers, potentates, dictators, yes, even presidents; men who by virtue of their position exercise rulership and lordship.
Some of them in the exercise of their office, instead of being servants of God,
assume a position equal to that of God, and act as if they were accountable
to none. It is to this select group of individuals, who call upon common people to give them the glory and majesty due their position, who are themselves called upon in this Psalm to give.

The first Greek translation that was made of the Hebrew Scriptures
gives an interesting translation of this phrase "O ye mighty." It translates
the Hebrew to read, "O ye sons of the Ram." Usually, in a large flock of
sheep, the rams are graced by a bell about their neck. That translation reminds me of a quaint comment an old scholar made when he said, "These
bell-wearers should not cast their noses into the air and carry their crests
higher because the shepherd bestowed a bell upon them, rather than the rest
of the flock."

Government is an institution of God, not of man, although man seems
to think he is its author. There are today those who mock at government.
These communistic people are very aptly described in the 8th verse of that
little Epistle of Jude as being "dreamers" who "defile the flesh, despise
dominion, and speak evil of dignities. But these speak evil of those things
which they know not: but what they know naturally, as brute beasts, in
those things they corrupt themselves." On the other hand, however, rulers
are ministers of God who must themselves in turn account to Him for their
stewardship. It is to that group that the Psalmist addressed his exhortation:
". . . give unto the LORD glory and strength. Give unto the LORD the glory

due unto his name; worship the LORD in the beauty of holiness." It is not possible now to take the time to comment any further upon these verses, though I hesitate to leave without comment, the expression "worship the LORD in the beauty of holiness." I wish you would muse over that phrase in your own meditations. It is rich in interest and blessing.

THE CEDARS OF LEBANON

We leave the exhortation and now enter into the terrific raging hurricane described in the next seven verses, which storm is the result of what is called "The voice of the LORD."

While a man may be possessed of a terrifying voice, his breath is only in his nostrils and he soon passes away; but the voice of the Lord, while terrifying, is majestic.

In order to appreciate the Psalmist's description of the devastation caused by the voice of the Lord, it is necessary to transplant ourselves into the land with which David is familiar. I like the comments on this storm scene given by an ancient scholar, Reuss by name, whose language is exquisite. He writes concerning this storm:

> "There are, properly speaking, two scenes described here, each of which is independent of the other. One passes upon the earth where we see the hurricane raging in a way unknown to our climate. The colossal cedars of Lebanon are slit in pieces; their gigantic trunks are torn from the ground and leap as lightly as the ox on the meadow. The mountain itself groans and trembles, scourged by the tempest. The lightnings furrow a sky darker than the deepest night. Vast deserts, such as that of Kadesh in the South of Canaan where nothing stops the elements, are swept by the hurricane. Their sand becomes a moving sea, the atmosphere an ocean chasing over its tossed bed and sweeping all with which it meets in its passage. The trees which can resist are peeled and stripped bare. Beasts are seized with terror and their convulsive shuddering makes them anticipate the hour of nature."

That description better enables one to appreciate the Psalmist's comment upon the majestic voice of the Lord. Note the 9th verse of the Psalm, which reads: "The voice of the LORD maketh the hinds to calve. . . ." This is not the mere illusion of a poetic mind—it is a biological fact. It is said that the creature which labours the most to bring forth her young is the hind. The Lord had something to say to Job on that subject. In the 39th chapter of the Book of Job these questions are presented to Job by the

Lord—"Canst thou mark when the hinds do calve? Canst thou number the months that they fulfill? or knowest thou the time when they bring forth? They bow themselves, they bring forth their young ones, they cast out their sorrows." It would seem, from this 29th Psalm, that the Lord aids the hind to bring forth her young ones by causing the thunder to roar and the storm to rage so as to lighten her sorrow.

There is one thing I would like to point out in connection with this description of the powerful voice of the Lord expressed by the storm. Have you noticed, in all the description man is nowhere to be found? In fact, he is mute. He has evidently retired from before the terrible majesty of the spectacle.

It is one thing to see a storm and the terrific shuddering of nature upon the silver screen in a movie house, but it is quite another matter to stand before the presence of the powerful voice of God. In grim reality, when a storm rages, man, the timid soul that he is, runs hither and yon seeking a place of safety.

ALL SPEAKS OF HIS GLORY

Before we look at the closing verses of the Psalm, notice the last words of the 9th verse, where we read: ". . . in his temple doth every one speak of his glory." Perhaps some may feel that this description of the majesty of God is terrifying. May I suggest that the God of this universe is the God of the Bible and vice versa, the God of the Bible is the God of the universe. The God whom we worship is a God of majesty and power, but He is a God of love and mercy as well. In fact, the Bible says that He delights to deal in mercy. It is for that reason that the Psalmist said: ". . . in his temple doth every one speak of his glory." Occasionally one meets Christians who boast of their accomplishments, who speak in glowing terms of what they have done and of conquests they have made; but, alas, how evident it is that such persons know nothing of the majesty of the Lord, nor of the true spirit of worship. In His temple every one speaks, not of his own accomplishments, but of God's glory. Some scholars believe that a more literal translation of the Hebrew would make the phrase read: ". . . and everything in his temple speaks of his glory." That, too, is true—the very temple declares and sets forth the glory of the Lord.

Above the awful turmoil of the storm the Lord is seated majestically upon His throne. The closing verse thrills the heart of a believer, "The

LORD will give strength unto his people; the LORD will bless his people with peace." At the beginning of the Psalm we had exhortations addressed to the mighty, to *give* unto the Lord. In the closing verse we have the Lord *giving* unto His people. What is it He gives? He gives strength unto His people, His own strength, if you please; but, what is even more precious, He blesses His people with peace. Peace? Yes. Our Lord said to His disciples, "Peace I leave with you, my peace I give unto you: not as the world giveth, give I unto you. Let not your heart be troubled, neither let it be afraid." This Psalm promises peace in the midst of storm. "The Psalm," said one, "begins with the excellency of glory and it ends with peace in the midst of terror."

PSALM THIRTY

PHANTOM PROSPERITY OR BUILDING ON SAND

TODAY our meditation will be found in the 30th Psalm, which reads:

"I will extol thee, O LORD; for thou hast lifted me up, and hast not made my foes to rejoice over me.

"O LORD my God, I cried unto thee, and thou hast healed me.

"O LORD, thou hast brought up my soul from the grave: thou hast kept me alive, that I should not go down to the pit.

"Sing unto the LORD, O ye saints of his, and give thanks at the remembrance of his holiness.

"For his anger endureth but a moment; in his favour is life: weeping may endure for a night, but joy cometh in the morning.

"And in my prosperity I said, I shall never be moved.

"LORD, by thy favour thou hast made my mountain to stand strong: thou didst hide thy face, and I was troubled.

"I cried to thee, O LORD; and unto the LORD I made supplication.

"What profit is there in my blood, when I go down to the pit? Shall the dust praise thee? shall it declare thy truth?

"Hear, O LORD, and have mercy upon me: LORD, be thou my helper.

"Thou hast turned for me my mourning into dancing:
thou hast put off my sackcloth, and girded me with
gladness;

"To the end that my glory may sing praise to thee,
and not be silent. O LORD my God, I will give
thanks unto thee for ever."

False Prosperity

David was not the last man to confess ". . . in my prosperity I said,
I shall never be moved." Prosperity is a very elusive thing. Some of us
have not even "tasted" it since 1929. For a long time we were assured that
it was "just around the corner," and when what we were told was "prosperity" finally arrived we were informed that it was "planned" that way by
the aid of several "brilliant young brain-trusters" who had suddenly stepped
out of a class-room into the august surroundings of a vast, intricate system
of economy. *They* planned it all right—they immediately went to work on
our "system"—as a two-year-old goes to work on the fine mechanism of a
good watch. They did not discern, however, that their "prosperity" was a
mirage, that it only appeared to be prosperity. What a rude shock those
self-made prosperity planners received when *their* prosperity also proved to
be elusive—a phantom which had no sooner arrived before it disappeared.
Of one thing I am sure—if that crowd of professors will be honest they will
say with David—We, too, in "our" prosperity thought we would never be
moved; but, alas, we built our castles upon sinking sand.

Prosperity is not to be despised, but the experience of the loss of prosperity can be put to real advantage if we will take the place which David
took and which is described in this 30th Psalm. First, note that David
ceased to believe in his own ability. He evidently concluded that it was
impossible to lift one's self up by his own bootstraps, for in the first verse he
wrote, "I will extol thee, O LORD; *for thou hast lifted me up,* and hast not
made my foes to rejoice over me." All of us have foes who watch us like
hawks. Nothing pleases them better than to observe some stumbling on our
part, that they may rejoice over us. But note, David was thankful that his
rise was not due to his own efforts. He was not now climbing a ladder of
his own making, but the Lord lifted him up. When the Lord lifts up an
individual He does not let him down. Such a person can sing with joy in
his heart, "I shall not be moved."

Boasting, then, is not in self—it is in Christ. "I will extol thee, O
LORD . . . " Who is more worthy to receive the praise of His people than

the Lord? David had found himself in distress after he had enjoyed a period of prosperity of his own planning. When he discovered that he was building upon sinking sand he cried unto the Lord. The Lord heard him. The Lord healed him, the Lord lifted him out from the grave and kept him alive. The Lord gave him a song. His experience caused him to appreciate a characteristic of God from which men often shrink. I refer to God's holiness.

In the 4th verse David said, "Sing unto the LORD, O ye saints of his, and give thanks at the remembrance of *his holiness*." The holiness of God does not usually cause a song to rise from the lips of any who really appreciate what holiness means. Since God is holy, He abhors iniquity. Why, therefore, give thanks at the remembrance of God's holiness? Holiness belongs to the Lord, but we are also exhorted to "Follow . . . holiness, without which no man shall see the Lord. . ." How can that make a person sing and give thanks? For our answer, let us look at the 3rd chapter of St. Paul's remarkable "tract" to the Romans, called "The Epistle to the Romans," which had such a devastating effect upon Roman religions that it forever silenced and put them to death.

I am indebted to my friend, Dr. Wilbur M. Smith, of the Moody Bible Institute of Chicago, Ill., for the following excellent observation. If you were to take the 14th edition of the Encyclopedia Britannica and turn to the section devoted to "Roman Religion" you will observe that almost three pages are devoted to the history of Roman religions, prior to the writing of this letter. Then follows a page and a half devoted to the Epistle to the Romans. The Epistle to the Romans eclipsed Roman religions. Nothing further can be written about Roman religions since this Epistle was written. When God speaks He silences man for eternity. There isn't anything to be said after God has spoken! Christ is God's last word to this world. No man has had an authoritative word since our Lord Jesus Christ. All every modern man, either in philosophy or religion, is able to present is to phonograph the religions and philosophies of the ancients which were popular prior to the writing of St. Paul's letter to the Romans. What power there is in the Word of God! That which gave the Roman Epistle such dynamic power was its revelation of the righteousness and holiness of God.

THE DOOM AND THE JUSTIFICATION OF MAN

In the early chapters of the letter, Paul effectively dealt with the cultured, religious Jew; the cultured, refined Gentile; and the renegade Jew and the renegade Gentile: he presented all before God's righteousness, absolutely condemned and doomed. Commencing with the 9th verse of the 3rd chapter he forged a chain of indictments around the neck of every man. Each link in the chain was taken from the Old Testament, many of them from the Book of Psalms. As he forged the links in the chain and placed them around the neck of man it became self-evident that all were under sin. We then learn from the 19th verse of the 3rd chapter that ". . . what things soever the law saith, it saith to them who are under the law: that every mouth may be stopped, and all the world may become guilty before God." To stop the mouth of man is a difficult job. Only God can stop men's mouths. In the 20th verse of this chapter we learn, "Therefore by the deeds of the law there shall no flesh be justified in his sight: for by the law is the knowledge of sin." After that follows the revelation which, seen prophetically by the writer of the 30th Psalm, caused him to sing unto the Lord and give thanks at the remembrance of His holiness. Commencing at verse 21 of Romans 3 we read: "But now a righteousness of God without the law is manifested. . . . Even a righteousness of God which is by faith of Jesus Christ unto all and upon all them that believe: for there is no difference: for all have sinned, and come short of the glory of God." As a result we are now "set right without a cause" by His grace through the redemption that is in Christ Jesus, whom God hath set forth to be a mercy seat, through faith in His blood. The death of Christ justified God for passing over the sins done aforetime by such men as David, Abraham, Moses, Samson, Joseph, Job, and all the other great as well as small characters of the Old Testament times. So important was this fact that the Apostle Paul repeated it in this 3rd chapter of Romans, "To declare," he said, "at this time his (God's) righteousness. . . ." Why? "that he might be just, and the justifier of him which believeth in Jesus."

To some this may seem involved. If so, let us try to make it clear. You and I come through the first two and a half chapters of this letter to the Romans absolutely guilty and condemned before God, with sealed lips and bowed head. The indictments against us are so overwhelmingly attested that there can be no occasion for even attempting a refutation; in fact, we make no plea for we are condemned already. What condemned us? The righteousness of God. What can save and rescue us? Only the righteousness of God. How did God's righteousness come to our rescue? God's righteousness provided a sacrifice in the Person of His own Son, Jesus Christ our Lord, who

Himself was the very righteousness of God, indeed, holiness personified. God caused Christ to be put on the cross to exact from Him the penalty against sin. In so doing He accomplished two things—God justified Himself for seemingly passing over the sins of such men as Moses, David, Elijah, Abraham, and the rest of the Old Testament characters; secondly, God also justified them, and all of us who believe in Jesus. What do we mean by justified? It is to set a person right before God and man. Actually, we have been hailed into court but now we are *set right* before the Judge and before all the spectators in the court, not by virtue of anything we have done but by virtue of what Jesus Christ did. God declares our justification from the heavens. It is upon that declaration that we have placed our faith for the eternal welfare of our souls. We believe that God was in Christ reconciling the world unto Himself. His righteousness which we once feared we now revel in, because it is that which has justified us. His holiness from which we once shrank now is the theme of our song because Christ is our holiness. We have been set right—if you please, as if we had never sinned, and now we have our righteousness in Christ. The work on the cross has been so complete, so marvelous, that God has credited to every sinner who believes in Jesus, a righteousness which we did not have, but which is ours by faith of Jesus Christ.

In the 4th chapter of St. Paul's letter to the Romans we get an amplification of this principle. There we read:

> ". . . to him that worketh not, but believeth on him that justifieth the ungodly, his faith is counted for righteousness.
>
> "Even as David (the writer of the 30th Psalm) also describeth the happiness of the man, unto whom God *reckons* righteousness without works,
>
> "Saying, Happy are they whose iniquities are forgiven, and whose sins are covered.
>
> "Happy is the man to whom the *Lord will not reckon sin.*"

God declares that there are men to whom He will refuse to reckon sin. Is God immoral? Absolutely no! He does so because of the most stupendous fact in history—the death of His Son on a cross. That is real cause for joy —to know that we are clear with God and that God refuses to reckon sin against us. That is enough to cause any man to sing. But we could not sing if salvation were based solely on the love of God, a love which would refuse to send any man to hell. We would fear that kind of spineless love.

It would not be a righteous love; but we rejoice in God because His righteousness has been vindicated by the fact that the penalty for our sin has
already been exacted from our substitute, Jesus Christ our Lord. Sing unto
the Lord? Indeed! Give thanks at the remembrance of His holiness? Certainly! For in a phrase—What we are, Christ became on the cross. What
Christ is, God has given to us. That is salvation: complete, simple, and
glorious.

It is clear that one rejoices in the holiness of God not because of anything he has done, but because everything has been done by Christ. That's
not building salvation on sand. That which is built upon a foundation of
sand collapses in the storm. Salvation built on Christ's death withstands all
storms.

"WEEPING . . . FOR AN EVENING . . ."

But some may say, If a believer rejoices in the holiness of God, what
about times when sorrow and disappointment come? To this the Psalmist
answered: ". . . weeping may endure for a night, but joy cometh in the
morning." The word "night" in the Hebrew does not mean a night of darkness, a continuous night; it means "an evening." So, ". . . weeping may
endure for an evening, but joy cometh in the morning." "Night" characterizes the state of the natural man outside of Christ. We who profess to
know Christ were once of the night. Our Lord told us that men love darkness rather than light because their deeds are evil. In the New Testament,
believers are said to be not of the night but of the day. Believers will never
again enter night. They will never know what darkness is; but there are
experiences in the lives of believers which have their counterpart in the
evening, that period of semi-darkness, of shaded light. Sometimes the Lord
permits periods of evening light for the instruction and edification of His
own, but He assures them that though weeping may endure for an evening,
"joy cometh in the morning." A believer has an abiding joy, his song is
not based on the passing moods of life or on the contradictory experiences
of life. It is based upon something solid, the Word of God and the Person of
Jesus Christ.

In the last two verses of the 30th Psalm David wrote, "Thou hast
turned for me my mourning into dancing: thou hast put off my sackcloth,
and girded me with gladness." For what purpose? "To the end that my
glory may sing praise to thee, and not be silent. O LORD my God, I will
give thanks unto thee for ever."

It is impossible to examine intelligently this Psalm, or for that matter any portion of the Bible, without being overwhelmingly convinced that men are justified by faith, not by works. There can be no room for boasting, it is completely excluded. For a man to boast of his character, his righteousness, or of anything in himself, is to be totally ignorant of himself and the Word of God. May each of us rejoice in the salvation of God which He Himself has provided in Christ.

PSALM THIRTY-ONE—PART ONE

THE ADVANTAGES OF ADVERSITIES

AS the 31st Psalm has 24 verses and contains many interesting things upon which we would like to comment, we shall limit this meditation to the first 14 verses, which read:

"In thee, O LORD, do I put my trust; let me never be ashamed: deliver me in thy righteousness.

"Bow down thine ear to me; deliver me speedily: be thou my strong rock, for an house of defence to save me.

"For thou art my rock and my fortress; therefore for thy name's sake lead me, and guide me.

"Pull me out of the net that they have laid privily for me: for thou art my strength.

"Into thine hand I commit my spirit: thou hast redeemed me, O LORD God of truth.

"I have hated them that regard lying vanities: but I trust in the LORD.

"I will be glad and rejoice in thy mercy: for thou hast considered my trouble; thou hast known my soul in adversities;

"And hast not shut me up into the hand of the enemy: thou hast set my feet in a large room.

"Have mercy upon me, O LORD, for I am in trouble: mine eye is consumed with grief, yea, my soul and my belly.

"For my life is spent with grief, and my years with sighing: my strength faileth because of mine iniquity, and my bones are consumed.

"I was a reproach among all mine enemies, but especially among my neighbours, and a fear to mine acquaintance: they that did see me without fled from me.

"I am forgotten as a dead man out of mind: I am like a broken vessel.

> "For I have heard the slander of many: fear was on
> every side: while they took counsel together against
> me, they devised to take away my life.
>
> "But I trusted in thee, O LORD: I said, Thou art
> my God."

Someone has well said that the Lord probably loves the common people more because He made so many more of them. If that be true, I think we can safely say that the reason so many of the Psalms are occupied with adversity and sorrow and trouble is because much in our lives partakes of adversity, sorrow and disappointment. It is simply amazing how frequently David was in distress—yet he was a man after God's own heart. He was a chosen man. There were also periods of great conquest in his experience. He knew what it was to be exalted, to be raised to a throne from a shepherd's fold; nevertheless, he had plenty of adversity and trouble. We are not unlike him. Our Lord said, "In the world ye shall have tribulation. . . ." If that were all He said, we would have reason to be forlorn, but He added, "be of good cheer; I have overcome the world."

Adversity, sorrow, and trouble are an important part of our child training, as children of God. They develop character. I once heard a gentleman say of another who had no sympathy in his make-up, "'That man never knew what sorrow was. He has never had the mellowing benefit of disappointment." Because sorrow disappointment and trouble have their good work, do not go out looking for them! Personally, I never *pray* for patience though I know the value of patience. If I were to ask the Lord for patience, He would have to send tribulation, for the Scripture says, ". . . tribulation worketh patience. . . ." But if the Lord should send tribulation and adversity, it is the part of wisdom to yield rather than to rebel so that these may have their effectual working in our experience.

AN ABJECT PICTURE

And now notice some of the things that David said about himself and his distress. First, he drew attention to a net that had been laid by his enemies to trap him. Second, he contended that the Lord had considered *his trouble* and had known his soul in *adversity*. Third, his trouble was so overwhelming that his eye was consumed with grief, indeed, his soul and his innermost being as well. Again, trouble and grief were so constantly visited upon him that he said, ". . . my life is spent with grief, and my years with sighing . . ." though he acknowledged that his strength failed him because of his iniquity. He added a few further touches to this picture of adversity by saying that he was a reproach among his enemies, especially among his neighbors. He also was a fear to his acquaintances so that they who saw him fled from him. He was so neglected even by his own that he said, "I am forgotten as a dead man out of mind." To indicate still further his abject state he said, "I am like a broken vessel." If that were not sufficient, he experienced one of the most heart-rending disappointments any man can know—he heard ". . . the slander of many." If that were not more than enough for any man to bear he added that those who slandered him took counsel against him, in fact, they devised to take away his life. Why should a man of God have so much trouble?

Many New Yorkers will remember for a long time the storm which visited the city early last Tuesday evening. It had been raining torrents when suddenly the sun shone through the clouds. Then the God and Father of our Lord and Saviour Jesus Christ went to work and painted for the benefit of all one of the most glorious sunsets that has ever been seen around New York. So glorious was it that the "New York Herald Tribune" two days later devoted an editorial to it. I was driving to Long Island with some friends at the time. We were greatly moved by the sight. Behind us was an array of color produced by the setting sun, and before us was the most beautifully clear rainbow I have ever seen. Neither the sunset nor the rainbow could have been produced without the storm or the clouds. Your life and mine, as believers in the Lord Jesus Christ, will never reflect the full glory of the "Sun of righteousness" unless we know something of adversity.

The Apostle Paul beautifully expressed it when he said, "For unto you it is given in the behalf of Christ, not only to believe on him, but also to suffer for his sake. . . ." And, "If we suffer, we shall also reign with him. . . ."

It is easy to complain against adversity; but God give us grace and wisdom to recognize the hand of the Master as He permits or visits us with adversity.

THE OTHER SIDE OF THE PICTURE

But this is not all that there is in this part of the Psalm. There is another side to this experience. David did not draw a one-sided picture, graphically as he portrayed that side, but he gave posterity a glimpse of the other side whereby he encouraged his soul. Let us look at it.

First of all, he said, "In thee, O LORD, do I put my trust." That is the starting point of all experience with God. To you who have not bowed the

knee to Jesus Christ, may I suggest that no experience with God begins
apart from putting one's trust in the Lord. "Without faith it is impossible
to please him. . . ." God has made salvation so simple and on such a basis
as to make it available to all. It is by faith in Jesus Christ. Do you wish to
begin a life with God? Then begin it as the Psalmist did in the 31st Psalm.
Address the Lord and say, "In thee . . . do I put my trust." That is what
the thief on the cross did. He said, "Lord, remember me when thou comest
into thy kingdom." The answer was immediately given ". . . To day shalt
thou be with me in paradise." Faith begins a life with God. Paradise is the
end of faith's journey.

But again, let us look at some further touches David gave to this other
side of the picture. In verse 2 we read, ". . . be thou my strong rock," and
". . . an house of defence to save me." Verse 3, "For thou art my rock and
my fortress; therefore for thy name's sake lead me, and guide me." Notice
how David covered practically every phase of human life. In this Psalm
is a rock for one who is at sea when all about him are the waters of
adversity. There is also a house of defense when one is on dry land but
surrounded by a host of enemies. There, too, is the fortress into which one
enters to be protected from the slandering onslaught of the unscrupulous
enemy. Again, there is both safety and deliverance when one is led by the
hand of the great Shepherd so that David said, "Pull me out of the net
that they have laid privily for me. . . ." But that is not all. Listen to this:
"I will be glad and rejoice in thy mercy. . . ." What! A man in such sorrow as David was, whose life was spent with grief and his years with sighing, could he say, "I will be *glad* and rejoice in thy mercy. . . ."? Yes, indeed,
and that is what distinguishes a man of faith from a man of this world!
When the man of the world has sorrow he is overwhelmed; but when the
man of faith has sorrow, though he may spend his years in sighing and be
well acquainted with tears, and even have a broken heart, he also will be
glad and rejoice in the mercy of God.

I am reminded of a remark made by my friend, Dr. Homer Hammontree, when he contrasted the white man and the Southern negro. He said,
"When the white man is overwhelmed by trouble he goes out and commits
suicide, but when the colored man has trouble he sits down and sings, or
goes to sleep." The trouble with many of the colored people we see in the
North is that they have tried to ape the white man. That's why we in New
York rarely hear the outburst of unbridled happiness which is so frequently
heard throughout the South.

OUT OF A HAND INTO A LARGE ROOM

A most interesting touch to this other side of the picture is found in the second half of the 8th verse where David wrote, "thou hast set my feet in a large room." In the first place note the contrast in this verse, for in the first half David said, ("Thou) hast not shut me up into the hand of the enemy."

An enemy's hand is a pretty small place—it is a place of excruciating pain. While a man is in the hand of his enemy he is invariably in a most circumscribed place. David contrasted that with the "large room" in which God set his feet.

Charles Spurgeon has an excellent comment on this passage. He says, "God will not let us be shut up but always provides a way of escape." Speaking of the "large room" he says, "Blessed be God for liberty. Civil liberty is valuable, religious liberty is precious, but spiritual liberty is priceless."

The enemy would have deprived David of all liberty, but the Lord not only pulled him out of the net of his enemy and out of the hand of his enemy, (that would only have been partial salvation) but the Lord completed the deliverance by setting David's feet in a large room.

There are some who think when they receive Christ, all that God does on their behalf is to forgive them their past sins. They think that thereafter they have to work out their own salvation with fear and trembling; fear that they might lose their salvation, and trembling that they might be cast into hell. There are many people like that. They think they must keep themselves saved! The Lord did His part, they say, now we must do our part. You have heard of that water-diluted milk of salvation, I'm sure. *If we have any part to perform in salvation it would not be salvation but probation.*

God delivered us out of the hand of the enemy, but He also set our feet in a large room. What did the Psalmist mean by a "large room"? Let us look at a few passages of Scripture. In the 4th Psalm, verse 1, David said, ". . . thou hast enlarged me when I was in distress. . . ." In the 18th Psalm, verse 19, he said, "He brought me forth also into a large place. . . ."

The most interesting incident of all is found in the New Testament, in the 14th chapter of St. Mark's Gospel where we have Mark's record of the last Passover. It was the first day of unleavened bread, the day on which the Passover lamb was to be killed, when the disciples said unto our Lord, "Where wilt thou that we go and prepare that thou mayest eat the passover?" Sending forth two of His disciples, He said unto them, "Go ye into the city, and there shall meet you a *man* bearing a pitcher of water: follow him." I can hear some say, "How would they know which man to follow?" This little touch in St. Mark's Gospel is just another of what Blaunt termed "undersigned coincidences" which evidence the authenticity of the record. If the Lord had said, "Go ye into the city, and there shall meet you a *woman* bearing a pitcher of water: follow her," the disciples probably would have been bewildered. It was customary for women to draw water from the well every morning and evening: it was a rare sight to see a *man* bearing a pitcher of water. Thus the disciples would spot him though there were a million men in the city.

How did our Lord know this man would bear a pitcher of water and be in the city at the very moment the disciples got there? The answer is that the Lord knows our down-sittings and our up-risings. There is not a detail in any man's life of which He is unaware. He knows the end from the beginning. Our Lord said, When you see that man, follow him (they were not to talk to the man who was bearing the pitcher, they were simply to follow him) and wheresoever he shall go in, say ye to the goodman of the house, "The Master saith, Where is the guest-chamber, where I shall eat the passover with my disciples?" And our Lord said, ". . . he will show you a *large upper room* furnished and prepared: there make ready for us."

David said, ". . . thou hast set my feet in a large room." That *large room* in Jerusalem on the night of our Lord's betrayal proved to be the most glorious spot in all the universe. It was a wonderful foreview, a miniature picture of heaven. Notice that the goodman of the house showed the disciples a *large* upper room, *furnished and prepared*. The Lord never delivers a child of His out of the hand of the enemy and then sets him in a small or a barren room. The room is a large guest chamber; you will find our Lord there and you will find that the room is "furnished and prepared."

Later that night our Lord informed His disciples that He was going away to prepare a place for them. "And," said He, "if I go and prepare a place for you, I will come again, and receive you unto myself. . . ." That place is a large room—it will accommodate all the saints of God. Yet it is not so large as to interfere with intimacy of fellowship between the Lord of the house and the individual guests.

That is salvation. It has the promise of the life that now is and the life to come—and causes a man to rejoice in the midst of adversity. In fact, he finds that there are advantages in adversity because they better prepare him to enjoy the "large room" with his Lord.

PSALM THIRTY-ONE—PART TWO

THE SECRET HIDING-PLACE

B EGINNING with the 15th verse of the 31st Psalm, David said:

"My times are in thy hand: deliver me from the hand of mine enemies, and from them that persecute me.

"Make thy face to shine upon thine servant: save me for thy mercies' sake.

"Let me not be ashamed, O LORD; for I have called upon thee: let the wicked be ashamed, and let them be silent in the grave.

"Let the lying lips be put to silence; which speak grievous things proudly and contemptuously against the righteous.

"Oh how great is thy goodness, which thou hast laid up for them that fear thee; which thou hast wrought for them that trust in thee before the sons of men!

"Thou shalt hide them in the secret of thy presence from the pride of man: thou shalt keep them secretly in a pavilion from the strife of tongues.

"Blessed be the LORD: for he hath shewed me his marvellous kindness in a strong city.

"For I said in my haste, I am cut off from before thine eyes: nevertheless thou heardest the voice of my supplications when I cried unto thee.

"O love the LORD, all ye his saints: for the LORD preserveth the faithful, and plentifully rewardeth the proud doer.

"Be of good courage, and he shall strengthen your heart, all ye that hope in the LORD."

In the first half of this Psalm we were presented with a two-fold portrait which David painted of himself; one setting forth his disappointment and trouble and the other his joy and trust in the Lord. With that as a background let us look more closely at the last half of this Psalm.

FATALISM *vs.* CONFIDENCE

In verse 15 David said, "My times are in thy hand:" yet immediately he prayed, "deliver me from the hand of mine enemies, and from them that persecute me." David was not a fatalist. Fatalism is one thing, confidence in a divine plan for one's life is quite another. When David said, "My times are in thy hand:" he expressed his complete confidence that nothing could transpire in his life that would be out of the reach of Jehovah's hand. David temporarily might have been in the hand of the enemy but his times were in the hand of the Lord. In the New Testament this same principle is expressed in the following words, "There hath no temptation taken you but such as is common to man: but God is faithful, who will not suffer you to be tempted above that ye are able; but will with the temptation also make a way to escape, that ye may be able to bear it."

While David had extreme confidence in the Lord it did not prevent him from praying for deliverance from the hand of his enemy and from those who persecuted him. It has sometimes been suggested that the place of trust is a higher one than that of prayer and that to trust the Lord is more commendable than to pray. Any attempt to exalt one side of Christian experience and pull down the other is a mistake. In order to have a well-rounded Christian experience confidence and prayer must go hand in hand. David had great confidence in the Lord. He knew his times were in the hand of the Lord. He knew that death could not visit him unless it was appointed of the Lord: yet he did not take an indifferent attitude or a fatalistic view of life, saying, If anything happens to me God planned it, thus I cannot do anything about it. That's not trust, that's plain indifference. We have a right to trust the Lord but we also have a right to pray. It is only when both are exercised that we enjoy normal Christian experience.

Note the further substance of David's prayer, verse 16, "Make *thy* face to shine upon *thy* servant: save me for *thy* mercies' sake." How interesting to observe the pronouns, *thy* face, *thy* servant, and *thy* mercies' sake. What a book could be written around these three phrases! "Make thy face to shine upon thy servant:" and "save me for thy mercies' sake." Salvation is not because of David's faithfulness but because of God's mercy. It is always thus.

In the following two verses, David prayed down judgment upon his enemies, ". . . let the wicked be ashamed, and let them be silent in the grave. Let the lying lips be put to silence. . . ."

It must not be forgotten in an examination of the Book of Psalms, or for that matter any part of the Old Testament, that a fuller revelation awaits us in the New Testament. That does not mean that the Old Testament is to be discarded. Many Christians rarely read the Old Testament. That is a mistake. All of the Bible was written for our learning and instruction though all of the Bible was not written specifically *to us.* There is a progress of doctrine in the revelation of God's will. The apex of God's revelation is in the Person of Jesus Christ, His Son, our Lord. That does not mean that the words of our Lord are more inspired than the words of His servants, either in the Old Testament or the New. It is intended to convey that there is a progression in revelation that must be understood if we are to have balanced minds and clear thinking in the matter of the Word of God. David prayed for revenge upon his enemies. The New Testament principle bids us to pray for our enemies and to do good unto them that despitefully use us. The one is law, the other grace. The one applied to a past era, the other to this present day.

David knew something also of the grace of God and His future provision for His own. Therefore, he could write in the 19th verse, "Oh how great is thy goodness, which thou hast laid up for them that fear thee; which thou hast wrought for them that trust in thee before the sons of men!" But in the New Testament we have a fuller revelation of this same subject where we read, "Eye hath not seen, nor ear heard, neither have entered into the heart of man, the things which God hath prepared for them that love him. *But God hath revealed them unto us by his Spirit:* for the Spirit searcheth all things, yea, the deep things of God." If you please, the one is elementary and the other a post-graduate course.

THE HIDING-PLACE

The heart of this section of the Psalm is found in the 20th and 21st verses where David said, "Thou shalt hide them in the secret of thy presence from the pride of man: thou shalt keep them secretly in a pavilion from the strife of tongues. Blessed be the LORD: for he hath shewed me his marvellous kindness in a strong city." Evidently there is a place called *the secret of the Lord's presence* while still another place is called *a pavilion.* In one the Lord hides His own from the pride of man and in the other from the strife of tongues. What or where are these places and why should one be used to protect a believer from one ill and the other to safeguard him from another enemy?

First, it is well to bear in mind that we do not hide ourselves. The Lord hides His own. Thus David said, *"Thou* shalt hide them in the secret of thy presence. . . ."* Now look at a few passages of Scripture which will aid us in an understanding of this wonderful revelation. In the 33rd chapter of Exodus Moses prayed the Lord to show him His glory. The Lord said, "Thou canst not see my face: for there shall no man see me, and live." Yet the Lord made provision for Moses saying, "Behold, there is a place by me, and thou shalt stand upon a rock. . . ." David later said "Thou shalt hide them in the secret of thy presence. . . ." Where is that *secret place* and is it the same place to which the Lord referred when He said to Moses, "there is a place by me"? Undoubtedly it is. By that place is a rock. Moses heard God say, ". . . it shall come to pass, while my glory passeth by, that I will put thee in a clift of the rock, and will cover thee with my hand while I pass by. . . ." One who is acquainted with the Bible will have little difficulty in understanding the symbolism which the Lord employed in speaking with Moses. The Rock is Christ. He is the Rock of Ages, cleft for me. Toplady understood it when he wrote that great hymn.

> "Rock of Ages, cleft for me,
> Let me hide myself in Thee;
> Let the water and the blood,
> From Thy wounded side which flowed,
> Be of sin the double cure,
> Save from wrath and make me pure."

The cleft of the rock is the very heart of our blessed Lord. He is now and always has been by His Father's side. We are safely tucked away in the cleft of the Rock and covered by the hand of the Father. "Thou shalt hide them," David said, "in the secret of thy presence . . . "

In another of the great books of the Old Testament, filled with beautiful symbolism, there is also a passage which will aid us in understanding the *secret place.* In the 2nd chapter of the Song of Solomon there is recorded for us a conversation between the bride and the bridegroom. One should never read the Song of Solomon without heeding the injunction given by the Lord to Moses, ". . . put off thy shoes from off thy feet, for the place whereon thou standest is holy ground." In the latter part of the 2nd chapter we are permitted to "listen in" to the bridegroom as He speaks to His bride. Beginning with the closing phrase of the 13th verse He said, "Arise, my love, my fair one, and come away. O my dove, that art in the clefts of the rock," then He asked of her His desire, when He said, "in the secret places of the stairs, let me see thy countenance, let me hear thy voice; for sweet is thy voice, and thy countenance is comely."

In the clefts of the rock is the place of safety, but what about the secret places? In the Authorized Version we read, ". . . in the secret places of the stairs, let me see thy countenance, let me hear thy voice. . . ." In the Hebrew it actually reads, ". . . in the secret of the stairs or, in the recesses of the cliffs, let me see thy countenance, let me hear thy voice, for sweet is thy voice, and thy countenance is comely." David said, "Thou shalt hide them in the secret of thy presence from the pride of man. . . ." There is therefore a secret place by the side of the Lord, where the child of God has the privilege of fellowship and communion with his Lord. He has the right of approach unto the Lord, he knows the "secret stairs" whereby he can enter into communion and fellowship with his Lord. Whether we appreciate it or not it is a fact that the Lord knows no greater joy than that of having His own enter the secret stairs in order that He might see their countenance and hear their voice. May we hereafter more fully appreciate and accept the opportunities that prayer gives to enjoy His presence and to look into His face. It seems too wonderful to believe but there it is in His Word—the Lord loves to hear the voice of His own and rejoices in their countenance.

Let me give you a quaint word on the secret place, which John Trapp wrote some 300 years ago, "In the golden cabinet of Thy gracious providence, where they shall be as safe as if they were in Heaven."

THE CASE OF BISHOP J. TAYLOR SMITH

The man or woman who knows something about communion with God knows that there is one place where pride cannot enter; it is forbidden in the secret place of the Lord. It is only the man who appreciates communion and fellowship with his Lord and who spends much time in prayer, who has the assurance of safety from pride. Let me give you a "modern" illustration.

On our Forum radio period a short time ago it was our pleasure, a pleasure I shall never forget, to interview and have a conversation with Bishop J. Taylor Smith of London. His very countenance reflected the glory of heaven. Dr. Barnhouse said of the Bishop that "we knew he had an old nature like every other Christian, but none of us saw manifestations of it." That is a remarkable testimony, and a true one I believe. One could not be in the Bishop's presence without sensing that he was in the presence of a saintly man of God. I was interested to learn that for years he had made it a practice to get up at four o'clock in the morning in order to have his quiet time with the Lord in prayer and in the reading of His Word. God hid him in the secret of His presence from the pride of man.

Now notice the other place, ". . . thou shalt keep them secretly in a pavilion from the strife of tongues." The good Bishop never appeared annoyed by pride neither was he disturbed by the strife of tongues. He knew that he was called for a task. He performed it in the power of God's Spirit. I was deeply moved when I learned of his death aboard ship as he was sailing from Australia, returning to his earthly home in London. Possibly he little realized that it would be his last sailing and that instead of going from Australia to England he was to go right into the presence of his Lord. Today his body lies buried in the depths of the sea. I remember hearing him one Sunday morning when he was in New York at the Cathedral of St. John the Divine. He was dressed in the robes of his bishopric. If there ever was a non-conformist, I certainly am one, yet as I observed the good Bishop ascend the steps to the pulpit in order to preach, and noticed as the door was shut he knelt in prayer and then rose to preach, I confess that no man ever preached a more glorious gospel message. My heart was moved as I listened to his simplicity of expression, yet his depth of knowledge of spiritual things. Instinctively I lifted up my heart in prayer and thanksgiving, for he was the Lord's man giving the Lord's message. It was evident that he had spent much time in the secret of His presence. Despite the dignity of his position he was most approachable. His demeanor indicated his total lack of pride. If we are to be spared the ravages of the pride of man, we, too, must spend much time in the secret presence of the Lord. There too will we find joy in God through our Lord Jesus Christ. We also will find a pavilion (a cottage or a booth) into which our Lord secretly places us far beyond the strife of tongues.

The last few verses of the Psalm are particularly interesting. While David was in distress in the early part of the Psalm he certainly enjoyed complete deliverance in the latter part of it. He began with tears and ended with a smile. He began with a prayer and ended with praise. He said, "Blessed be the LORD: for he hath shewed me his marvelous kindness in a strong city." In the 8th verse we have the statement, ". . . thou hast set my feet in a large room." We drew an application from that statement to the room in which our Lord enjoyed the last Passover with His disciples. Here, however David speaks of a strong city. Had he become hopelessly confused? Not a bit. Remember, we are heirs of God and joint-heirs with

Jesus Christ. No man in this world, be he ever so rich, compares in wealth with a man who is in Christ. We sometimes sing, "I'm a child of the King." Because of that we enjoy His possessions. The wealthy man usually has a city home, and a country home; in fact he sometimes has several other homes. He hasn't anything on those of us who know Christ as our Saviour! We may be in a circumscribed place now but we still have the benefit of the large room in fellowship with Christ, a secret place and a pavilion. Some day we are going to live in a strong city; it is called the new Jerusalem; it is to descend out of the heavens as we learn from the last book of the Bible. We cannot do more here than merely make mention of it. It would take much time to do justice to the subject.

David was a man of like passions with us. He was not always faithful. He, too, jumped to conclusions as we frequently do. He said, "For I said in my haste, I am cut off from before thine eyes. . . ." How often we have said that, only to learn that speaking in haste means making foolish statements. David learned later that the Lord heard the voice of his supplications.

What is the conclusion of all this? David expressed it perfectly when he wrote:

> "O love the LORD, all ye his saints: for the LORD preserveth the faithful, and plentifully rewardeth the proud doer.
> "Be of good courage, and he shall strengthen your heart, all ye that hope in the LORD."

PSALM THIRTY-TWO—PART ONE

THE BOOKKEEPING OF HEAVEN

THE 32nd Psalm is such a wonderfully inspiring and delightful Psalm that we shall devote two messages to its study, covering the first five verses in this meditation. These verses read:

> "Blessed is he whose transgression is forgiven, whose sin is covered.
> "Blessed is the man unto whom the LORD imputeth not iniquity, and in whose spirit there is no guile.
> "When I kept silence, my bones waxed old through my roaring all the day long.
> "For day and night thy hand was heavy upon me: my moisture is turned into the drought of summer. Selah.

> "I acknowledged my sin unto thee, and mine iniquity
> have I not hid. I said, I will confess my transgressions
> unto the LORD; and thou forgavest the iniquity of
> my sin. Selah."

Upon examining our Bible we note that this Psalm has an introduction which reads "A Psalm of David, Maschil." It is the first of thirteen Psalms which have a similar introduction. The word "Maschil" means knowledge or instruction. Thus, this is a Psalm in which David, possessing certain knowledge, expresses a desire to pass it on to others. It is a Psalm written for our instruction. It contains what I believe is the most important knowledge that can possibly come into the possession of a man.

Then again, this is the second of the Psalms which begin with the word "blessed." In our meditation on the 1st Psalm we mentioned that an apt translation of the Hebrew word would be our English word "happy." Thus, we could read the first two verses of the thirty-second Psalm: "Happy is he whose transgression is forgiven, whose sin is covered. Happy is the man unto whom the LORD imputeth not iniquity, and in whose spirit there is no guile." Indeed, he is a completely happy man. There is no man in this world so happy as is the man who knows that his transgression is forgiven.

SIN AND SINNERS

It is apparent from the first verse of this Psalm that sin is the greatest problem of the universe. We never would have depressions; we never would have droughts; we never would have wars; we never would have troubles in our families; we never would have disappointments, trials or difficulties if it were not for sin. Sin is the most startling fact in the universe. Our liberal theologians and modern thinkers cast a cynical smile at the mention of the word "sin." However, sin is a reality.

All too often people assume that sin and crime and sinners and criminals are synonymous terms. They may be in certain instances. The case of Dillinger is an example where the terms are synonymous, but in the majority of cases the opposite is true. We all know many people whom God calls sinners because they are guilty of sin, but who are by no stretch of the imagination criminals, or guilty of crime. The words crime and criminal appear in every language, but the words sin and sinner belong exclusively to the vocabulary of the Bible. Therefore, in order to know what constitutes sin and who are sinners we must go to the Bible. There we find that a man may be a morally upstanding gentleman, he may even be a religious man, he may attend church regularly, he may contribute to charity and in every way be an exemplary citizen, and yet that man in the sight of God is a sinner. Let me give a specific case: In the tenth chapter of the Acts of the Apostles we find the record of the first Gentile who was converted through the Apostle Peter's ministry. This man lived in Cesarea. His name was Cornelius. He was a centurion of the band called the Italian band. It is written concerning this man, that he was "A devout man, and one that feared God with all his house, which gave much alms to the people, and prayed to God alway." He must have been a marvelous character. There are few like Cornelius now living in the world. But if they lived in droves they would need the same message which Cornelius required in order to be saved. The record in the Book of the Acts states that an angel came to Cornelius and told him to "send men to Joppa, and call for one Simon, whose surname is Peter" and invite him to enter into his home so that the Apostle Peter might tell him words whereby he and all his house should be saved. Peter came, and as he entered he asked why he had been sent for. Then Cornelius acquainted him with the vision of the angel, and stated, "Now therefore are we all here present before God, to hear all things that are commanded thee of God." Peter responded, giving his witness concerning Christ, and in closing his address he said, "To him" (Christ) "give all the prophets witness, that through his name whosoever believeth in him shall receive remission of sins." Could anything be more clear in the case of Cornelius than the fact that he was not guilty of crime? Yet, with all his moral qualities, he still needed the forgiveness of sins. Sin, therefore, is not synonymous with crime. The Bible declares that sin is a nature: that it is the very nature of man.

GOD LIFTS TRANSGRESSIONS

In the first two verses of our Psalm sin is described under three different words—first, as transgression; then, as sin; and finally as iniquity. God has a remedy for each. He has forgiveness for transgression, He has a covering for sin, and He has a method of accounting, in dealing with iniquity.

The word "forgiveness" in the 32nd Psalm has an interesting little message. The word itself *"Nasa,"* means eased, lightened, taken off. Does that convey to our mind what God does with transgressions? You and I are burdened with transgressions. They weigh heavily upon us. The

Psalmist says, Happy is the man whose transgressions are taken off him, lightened from him.

It would be impossible for God to take the load of transgression from any man and throw it into the sea. It would not be consistent with His law of righteousness which He has written into every sphere of nature, where we learn that every transgression receives a just recompense of reward. What, then, has He done with our transgressions? He has eased them. He has taken them from us, but He put them on someone else. That is the gospel! He placed our sins upon the person of His Son and on the cross of Calvary He exacted from Him the penalty of our transgressions. Thus, it is written in the 53rd chapter of Isaiah, that "he was wounded for our transgressions, he was bruised for our iniquities: the chastisement of our peace was upon him; and with his stripes we are healed."

There is in human jurisprudence that which is known as double jeopardy. We heard a great deal about double jeopardy during the time when the 18th Amendment was in effect. We have a rule that a man cannot be held twice for the same transgression. He can only be made to pay one penalty for any one transgression. The State, for instance, cannot ask of him a penalty, and then the Federal Government ask another for the same transgression. This same principle is in effect in divine jurisprudence. God can never hold us in double jeopardy. He cannot ask for a second payment for the same transgression. The Bible declares that He placed all of our sins upon Christ and that Christ paid the penalty for all of them. Therefore, there is offered to us the forgiveness for *all* of our sins. To those who receive that forgiveness there can be no further penalty for sin.

GOD COVERS SIN

So much for transgression. David continued and said, Happy is the man "whose sin is covered." In the New Testament our Lord Jesus Christ is set forth as the covering for our sin. If you have received Christ, He covers you. Thus, as God sees Christ, so He sees you. Let me relate a little incident to illustrate this truth. Returning from a meeting one Sunday evening about 11 o'clock, as I entered our home I was quite surprised to discover on the center of the table a book with a white cover. That particular book was printed in our plant. It should have had a red cover. I was chagrined to notice the white cover and quickly concluded that someone in our plant had made an error. I walked over to the table and picked up the book. As I handled it I thought I was seeing things, for it had the red cover it should have had. I replaced the book on the table. Again it appeared to have a white cover. I was beginning to wonder whether I had failed to follow the Scriptural injunction, "be not drunk with wine, wherein is excess; but be filled with the Spirit"! Then I saw that there was a red bulb in the electric socket. Of course that explained it all. The red rays of light upon the red cover of the book had changed it to a perfect white. Then I remembered with great joy that it is written, "Come now, and let us reason together, saith the LORD: though your sins be as scarlet, they shall be as white as snow; though they be red like crimson, they shall be as wool." But why? The New Testament answers, "the blood of Jesus Christ his Son cleanseth us from all sin." As the red rays made it appear that the book had a white cover, so God as He looks at us through the precious red, shed blood of His own Son does not see upon our heart the stains of sin but He sees a perfect white, the perfectness of His own Son. We are thus covered with Christ.

How God Keeps His Books

The next verse reads "Happy is the man unto whom the LORD imputeth not iniquity, and in whose spirit there is no guile." I have already indicated that God has a method of accounting, to take care of iniquity. In other words, the Godhead has a set of books. You have heard of book-keeping, haven't you? You have also heard that there is a record being kept of everything a man does, which record must meet every man in judg-ment, except the man who is in Christ. But, here is a man whom David calls "happy," because the Lord will not count his iniquity to him. This same subject is developed in the New Testament where we read: "Now to him that worketh is the reward not reckoned of grace, but of debt." In other words, if you work a week, and your boss pays you a salary at the end of that week, he has not given you a gift. He has given you the wages to which you are justly entitled. It is a debt he owes you. The next verse says: "But to him that worketh not, but believeth on him that justifieth the ungodly, his faith is counted for righteousness." There we have the word "counted." God takes that man's faith and credits him on the ledger with righteousness. It is a very old principle of Divine accounting. It is as old as the Book of Genesis; it is as old as Abraham. In the Book of Genesis it is written that Abraham "believed in the LORD, and he (God) counted it to him for righteousness."

Not only does God credit righteousness to the man who believes Christ, but He refuses to charge that man with sin. He has already charged that man's sin to Christ. Is it any wonder that our Psalm reads "Happy is the man unto whom the LORD imputeth not iniquity"? Happy is the man to whom the Lord will not impute (charge) sin. It should be apparent that salvation is of the Lord. It is His work. We simple receive it as His benefaction.

Unfortunately we have not time to touch the 3rd and 4th verses, but there is a statement in the 5th verse which I cannot pass by. David said: "I acknowledged my sin unto thee, and mine iniquity have I not hid. I said, I will confess my transgressions unto the LORD." That is the way. Acknowledge your sins before Him. Do not hide your iniquities from Him. He can see them. You are only hiding them from your own conscience. You are not hiding them from Him. If you acknowledge your sin and believe Christ you will have the same experience which David had.

There is a hymn that I love, entitled "It Is Well with My Soul." I think the 3rd verse is the greatest in all hymnology:

> "My sin, O the bliss of this glorious thought,
> My sin, not in part, but the whole
> Is nailed to His Cross, and I bear it no more.
> Praise the Lord, Praise the Lord, O my soul!"

PSALM THIRTY-TWO—PART TWO

THE POWER OF A LOOK

IN the first five verses of the 32nd Psalm we have a description of the truly blessed man, the man whose "transgression is forgiven, whose sin is covered," the man to whom God absolutely refuses to charge iniquity. These benefactions flow from the grace of God that was manifested at Calvary where the Lord Jesus in His own body bore our sins on the tree.

Commencing with the 6th verse we read:

> "For this shall every one that is godly pray unto thee
> in a time when thou mayest be found: surely in the
> floods of great waters they shall not come nigh unto
> him."
> "Thou art my hiding place; thou shalt preserve me
> from trouble; thou shalt compass me about with songs
> of deliverance."

I do not believe there is anyone in this world who can sing with such joy as the man described in these two verses under the title "godly," the man who has found the Lord to be his hiding-place. He may not sing with the skill and technique of those more gifted and instructed. I, for one, cannot sing a note, and as for carrying a tune I might just as well attempt to carry the Atlantic Ocean in my hand. However, I have often inflicted myself upon my friends by taking refuge behind the exhortation which says, "Make a joyful noise unto God." My friends chide me for my "noise" but they never question that it is a *joyful* noise.

Note that the 6th verse of our Psalm opens "For this shall every one that is godly pray unto thee," with a further statement as to the time—"in a time when thou mayest be found." This takes us back to the first five verses for the cause of which the 6th verse is the effect. There we find that the blessedness of the forgiveness of transgression and the covering of sin gives boldness to pray unto the Lord. It is the godly who shall pray unto the Lord. I like the term "godly."

As we often learn by contrasts, it might be advisable to note what is meant by the term "ungodly." There is nothing that is more terrifying in its revelation of one's position and standing before God than the word "ungodly." That term describes every man who is outside of Christ. It perfectly describes the moral or the immoral, the cultured or the uncultured, it describes all who have refused to receive the testimony that God has given concerning His Son. The only difference between the godly and the ungodly man is that the godly man is the sinner who has been saved by God's grace. That is all! However, it is everything.

In the New Testament we are told that Christ died for the ungodly. From the very moment the ungodly received Christ, the first syllable dropped from the word and they became "godly." That does not mean that we are as perfect as God or that we are like God in certain of His characteristics, but it does emphatically mean that we love the Lord; that we revel in godliness and that we desire, from the bottom of our hearts, to be like the Lord.

"FLOODS OF GREAT WATERS"

Through this Psalm we learn that to the godly man there is a time when the Lord is particularly precious. That time is when "floods of great waters" are compassing the earth. "Floods of great waters" is a figure of speech. It describes a time of disaster and disappointment. We have the assurance that at such a time these "floods" shall not come nigh unto him who is godly. The godly man may be surrounded by "floods of great waters," but as he has his feet on the Rock, there is not—shall I say?—even a bit of spray that can possibly come nigh unto him.

Then, too, it is only the godly man who can sing in the midst of trouble. God gives him a song in the night, therefore his troubles do not overwhelm him. His soul is preserved. He knows the worst thing that can come to him is to be transported from earth to heaven. And as that is the worst than can happen he is more inclined to shout hallelujah, than to go around with a sad countenance and a bewailing tongue.

THE GREAT PROMISE

We have already observed that this is the first of thirteen Psalms in which the Hebrew word "Maschil" is used as part of the title. As the word "Maschil" means instruction, this is a Psalm of instruction. The 8th verse reveals who is the instructor and the course of instruction He gives. I do not think there is a verse in the entire Bible that is more revealing in indicating the relationship that God is desirous of having with His people. "I will instruct thee and teach thee in the way which thou shalt go: I will guide thee with mine eye."

Sometimes I am amused when reading the comments given in certain commentaries. I have almost concluded that it takes learned men to make the most obvious errors. Some commentators suggest that David is the speaker in this verse. If that were the case the Psalm would have a decidedly limited application. Not one of us living at present could claim the promise made in this verse. As for the penetrating powers of David's eyes, I am sure that he needed special glasses to be able to peer through some of the places where even members of his own family traveled. No, this is not a promise of David. It is a promise of the Lord—"I will instruct thee and teach thee in the way which thou shalt go." He does not turn over the instruction to another. He said, "I will instruct thee . . ." You and I have a right, therefore, to claim this promise. We can invite the Lord to instruct us and teach us in the way in which we should go and to guide us with His eye.

"I WILL INSTRUCT THEE"

Three things are promised—first, "I will instruct thee." That is wisdom. The wisest of men once said, "the fear of the LORD is the beginning of wisdom." From what one observes at present he would be inclined to state that we moderns have changed that a little. We now believe that to doubt is the beginning of wisdom. We take pride in our doubts and we actually tickle our fancy in thinking that it is modern to doubt, but old-fashioned to believe.

It rudely shocks some of our freshmen and greatly chagrins our sophists to be informed that doubt is as old as the Garden of Eden. Indeed, as far as man is concerned, doubt is older than faith. The next time someone boastfully informs you that as far as the gospel is concerned he is a modernist, tell him that as for being modern he is decidedly mistaken: that he is more old-fashioned than we who believe. Inform him that his philosophy is as old as Eden and his unbelief is hoary with age. I know the old proverb reads: "He who doubts nothing—nothing knows—"

> "Yet to doubt is not to know;
> To know is not to doubt.
> True knowledge is deliverance from doubt
> And from the bondage which chains the doubter.
> He who winneth this is nobly blest
> For all uncertainty is heaviness of spirit
> And a load by far too grievous to be borne."

The suggestion that James gives in his little epistle is apt and appropriate:

> "If any of you lack wisdom, let him ask of God, that giveth to all men liberally, and upbraideth not; and it shall be given him.
> "But let him ask in faith, nothing wavering."

"I WILL . . . TEACH THEE"

The second promise is this, "I will . . . teach thee in the way which thou shalt go."

How true it is as our Lord Jesus said, "he that walketh in darkness knoweth not whither he goeth." Did you ever meet a man other than a believer in Christ who knew where he was going? Well, if you have, I haven't. But to the godly, the Lord said, "I will . . . teach thee in the way which thou shalt go." None of us know the way except the Lord teach us the way. He has taught us the way.

Let me take you to the 13th and 14th chapters of John's Gospel. The greatest of artists have attempted to paint that scene upon canvas. It vies with Calvary in challenging the world of men. It is in Jerusalem in the place called the "upper room." Our Lord shocked the men who had been closest to Him for three years, by disrobing and putting on the garments of the most menial servant, pouring water into a basin and washing the feet of His disciples. After He finished He said:

> "Ye call me Master and Lord: and ye say well; for so I am.
>
> "If I then, your Lord and Master, have washed your feet; ye also ought to wash one another's feet.
>
> "For I have given you an example, that ye should do as I have done to you."

Then our Lord, troubled in spirit, announced that one of them would betray Him. Everyone was stunned. They looked each to the other. Who could it be? The Christ answered, "He it is, to whom I shall give a sop, when I have dipped it." Judas left the room after he had received the sop. But that is not all. Our Lord revealed that before the night was over they all would leave Him and forsake Him.

I have often wondered, as I have read the record of these events how the disciples maintained their minds. Enough had happened to have caused them to lose all control over their powers of reason. But the Lord comforted their bewildered minds and hearts by saying, "Let not your heart be troubled: ye believe in God, believe also in me." Then He went on to say that in His Father's house were many mansions; He was going away to prepare a place for them, and if He went to prepare a place for them He would come again and receive them unto Himself so that where He was there they might also be. Finally he added, "And whither I go ye know, and *the way ye know*."

Our Psalm reads, "I will . . . teach thee in the *way* which thou shalt go." Thomas said to the Lord that night, "We know not whither thou goest; and how can we know the *way?*" Our Lord replied, "I am the *way*, the truth, and the life: no man cometh unto the Father, but by me."

"I WILL GUIDE THEE WITH MINE EYE"

The next great comfort we receive from this Psalm is this—"I will guide thee with mine eye." We all know of the power there is in a look. Sometimes it is rather disquieting. I was about to state there is nothing as eloquent as a look. I hope it has not been often, but I am sure there have been occasions that we married men can acknowledge when our wives have not said one word but have just given us a glance. That was enough. We knew if that glance were put into words it could fill volumes.

I recall an interesting experience which took place when I was in my teens. It happened during a summer vacation while I was staying in an old-fashioned farmhouse. There were a number of guests at the house.

It was interesting to observe the different manner in which two mothers dealt with their children. Each of these mothers had a boy about nine years of age.

One mother developed a theme song. John invariably got himself into trouble and his mother could be quickly heard saying, "John, stop it, one, two, and if I say three you will get it." It was always, "One, two, and if I say three." But the "three" was never said. None of us expected it and least of all John. The result was that John was constantly in trouble and we heard the theme song all day long. But the other mother had very little to say.

We were sitting on the porch one day, late in the afternoon. I was sitting to the left of this mother while her son, Rudy, sat to the right of her. Not a word was heard of anything of a rebuking character. We were all chatting toegther. Suddenly Rudy excused himself and went upstairs. About ten minutes passed and then Rudy was heard to sing:

"Brighten the corner where you are."

Turning to his mother I asked the why and the wherefore. She said that Rudy had put his leg over the arm of the chair in which he was sitting—which was no place for a leg—and so she merely looked at him and nodded to him to take his leg down. Rudy refused, or at least did not obey immediately, whereupon, she said, "I looked at him once more and the look I gave meant he was to go upstairs and go to bed." Not a word passed, simply the look of the eye and the pointing of the finger. Rudy very meekly and quietly had proceeded upstairs. I thought the punishment too great for the infraction and suggested Rudy should have a little company, so a group of us went upstairs where we found Rudy in bed. In between sucking a lollipop, he was joyfully singing: "Brighten the corner where you are."

THE POWER OF A LOOK

We who are believers in Christ know, too, that sometimes a look has brought us back into the fold. It has often been a glance that has encouraged us or corrected us. The power of a look from the eyes of our Lord Jesus is nowhere so evident as on the night of His betrayal, when He dealt with Peter. Peter did not imagine that he would deny his Lord. He thought our Lord must have been mistaken when He made the assertion that before the cock crowed he would deny Him thrice. But alas, the words of our Lord Jesus Christ were fulfilled. Peter denied any knowledge of the Christ, and upon the third occasion, when a man said concerning him, "this fellow also was with him: for he is a Galilean," Peter said, "Man, I know not what thou sayest." Immediately the cock crew! Then we are told that the Lord turned and looked upon Peter. Some people think that our Lord looked at Peter with an eye of rebuke. I do not think that He did anything of the kind. I have found that, generally speaking, when a man is rebuked he is not often encouraged. He may be cowed for a moment, but it is usually unavailing. The only kind of a look which brings bitter tears to a man is a look of love and devotion. I believe when our Lord looked at Peter that He looked at him with such a look. No wonder we read that Peter went out, and wept bitterly.

We have the assurance from this Psalm that our Lord will guide us with His own eye. Under the circumstances the exhortation found in the next verse is quite appropriate. "Be ye not as the horse, or as the mule, which have no understanding: whose mouth must be held in with bit and bridle, lest they come near unto thee."

The closing verses of the Psalm read: "Many sorrows shall be to the wicked: but he that trusteth in the LORD, mercy shall compass him about." If for no other reason we ought to receive Christ and believe in the Lord on the assurance of that statement. The climax is found in the last verse which reads: "Be glad in the LORD, and rejoice, ye righteous: and shout for joy, all ye that are upright in heart." Whenever I see a Christian with a long face I feel like quoting this last verse of the 32nd Psalm to him. Weeping and lamenting do not belong to a Christian, but joy and rejoicing do, for God has forgiven our transgressions and covered our sin. Why should anyone so blessed, knowing that Christ covered his sin, be other than glad in the Lord. Indeed he ought to shout for joy—as David suggested!

PSALM THIRTY-THREE—PART ONE

LYRICAL EMOTION IN WORSHIP

I T was my anticipation to devote only one message to the 33rd Psalm and I had hoped to center our thoughts upon "The Power of His Breath," from a phrase which appears in the 6th verse of this Psalm where we read, "By the word of the LORD were the heavens made; and all the host of them by the breath of his mouth." However, as I studied the Psalm in preparation for this message I found my heart so stirred with the words of exhortation that appear in the first part of the Psalm that I decided to devote all of this message to the first five verses. Then later we will look at the balance of the Psalm when we shall consider "The Power of His Breath." First of all, let us read the entire Psalm—

"Rejoice in the LORD, O ye righteous: for praise is comely for the upright.

"Praise the LORD with harp: sing unto him with the psaltery and an instrument of ten strings.

"Sing unto him a new song; play skilfully with a loud noise.

"For the word of the LORD is right; and all his works are done in truth.

"He loveth righteousness and judgment: the earth is full of the goodness of the LORD.

"By the word of the LORD were the heavens made; and all the host of them by the breath of his mouth.

"He gathereth the waters of the sea together as an heap: he layeth up the depth in storehouses.

"Let all the earth fear the LORD: let all the inhabitants of the world stand in awe of him.

"For he spake, and it was done; he commanded, and it stood fast.

"The LORD bringeth the counsel of the heathen to nought: he maketh the devices of the people of none effect.

"The counsel of the LORD standeth for ever, the thoughts of his heart to all generations.

"Blessed is the nation whose God is the LORD; and the people whom he hath chosen for his own inheritance.

"The LORD looketh from heaven; he beholdeth all the sons of men.

"From the place of his habitation he looketh upon all the inhabitants of the earth.

"He fashioneth their hearts alike; he considereth all their works.

"There is no king saved by the multitude of an host: a mighty man is not delivered by much strength.

"An horse is a vain thing for safety: neither shall he deliver any by his great strength.

"Behold, the eye of the LORD is upon them that fear him, upon them that hope in his mercy;

"To deliver their soul from death, and to keep them alive in famine.

"Our soul waiteth for the LORD: he is our help and our shield.

"For our heart shall rejoice in him, because we have
trusted in his holy name.

"Let thy mercy, O LORD, be upon us, according as
we hope in thee."

There is not a single passage of Scripture that exhorts us to be "sad"
in the Lord. On the contrary, again and again we are exhorted to "rejoice"
in the Lord. This of course is an opposite view from the seemingly accepted
understanding of worship. Men have always been guilty of inverting the
order of God. It is our nature to mix things up. So we put on a Sunday-
go-to-meeting face as well as Sunday-go-to-meeting clothes. Men think
that in church such clothing and such sanctimonious countenances are
pleasing to God whereas it ought to be apparent to any intelligent being
that it is nothing short of mockery or hypocrisy. If there is a time to
rejoice it is when one is worshipping the Lord. Joy should also characterize our service and devotion to the Lord.

WHO CAN WORSHIP?

This exhortation, this invitation to rejoice in the Lord is definitely
limited. It does not include every man and woman under the sun. It
includes only those who have a relationship with God through our Lord
Jesus Christ. That is the testimony of the Word of God. You may agree
or you may disagree with the statement. I believe it because God has
spoken it. It is consistent with His holiness, with His righteousness, His
love, and His character. God cannot in the very nature of the case accept
the worship of sinful men, neither can He accept devotion as a substitute
for righteousness. Even the worship of a saved man is tainted with sin.
It is necessary for our worship to go through our Lord Jesus Christ in order
that it might be sanctified. Thus we find in the Old Testament the expression, "the iniquity of the holy things." All the instruments which were
used in the worship of Jehovah by the children of Israel had to be cleansed
by an application of the blood of the sacrifices, which was in fact the very
basis of Aaron's high priestly ministry. How then could it be possible for
God to accept the worship of unbelieving men or women? He simply could
not do it.

Even by His enemies our Lord Jesus Christ is conceded to have been
the greatest intellect this world has ever known, the greatest man who ever
lived; yet it was He who said, "I am the way, the truth, and the life: no
man cometh unto the Father, but by me." If there is another way of
approach unto God, our Lord either was deceived or He was a deceiver.

If deceived He could not be the Son of God. If He were a deceiver He could not be a righteous man. Both suggestions are preposterous.

On the testimony of the Word of God it is necessary for a man to be born again by the Spirit of God before he can become a worshipper of God. But our Lord made it clear that He came to seek and save that which was lost. He revealed to a woman of extremely doubtful character the secret and intimacy of worship. The woman of Samaria, because she had a reputation so scandalous that she avoided the women of her town who came twice daily to the well to draw water, went out at the noon hour when no other woman would be at the well-side. Yet it was to her that our Lord said, "God is a Spirit: and they that worship him must worship him in spirit and in truth." He told her that the Father sought such to worship Him. One cannot worship apart from the Holy Spirit, neither can one worship apart from truth. Our Lord Jesus Christ said, "I am . . . the truth . . ." Thus worship is in Christ and through the Holy Spirit. To the men and women who have been born again the privilege of worship causes them to "Rejoice in the Lord."

Notice the exhortation of this Psalm, "Rejoice in the LORD, O ye righteous: for praise is comely for the upright" which means that "praise becometh the upright."

We must, however, make clear the application of the term "righteous." It was never intended to characterize the believer, whether under the Old Testament economy or the New Testament revelation, as being righteous in himself. Indeed not! David described the happiness of the man unto whom God imputeth righteousness without works and Abraham, we are told, was justified by faith apart from works when he believed God's testimony. It is written, "Abraham believed God, and it was counted unto him for righteousness." We who have received Christ as our Saviour are not righteous in ourselves. I for one know my own heart too well to make any such vain boast. We have our righteousness in Christ. That is what causes the heart of a believer to rejoice. It is, therefore, becoming to a justified man to praise the Lord.

How are to praise Him? Well, let's look at David's exhortations to the believers of his day. Beginning with verse 2 we read,

> "Praise the LORD with harp: sing unto him with the psaltery and an instrument of ten strings.
>
> "Sing unto him a new song; play skilfully with a loud noise.

"For the word of the LORD is right; and all his
works are done in truth.

"He loveth righteousness and judgment: the earth is
full of the goodness of the LORD."

It is apparent that when the Psalms were used in worship by Israel
they were always accompanied by instrumental music. Mention is made
of an instrument of ten strings. What it was we cannot say definitely,
but we are acquainted with the harp, so that we know there were at least
two instruments used, possibly more—the harp and the instrument of ten
strings. There was to be skill manifested in the playing of these instruments and there was to be harmony between instrument and voice as praise
was presented to the Lord.

There are some well-taught and devoted Christians who do not believe
that a musical instrument has any place in Christian worship. We have
studiously avoided in these broadcasts any attempt to favor one denomination or one group of believers over another or to speak disparagingly of one
group and commend another. Our sole purpose has been to present Christ
to the hearts of believers that they may rejoice with exceeding joy in their
Lord; and to present Him to the unsaved that they might find Him as their
Saviour. When we touch upon anything that might be a "pet" theory,
please bear with us and above all do not get angry. Some day we will all
see eye to eye on every detail of the Word. I have attended meetings
where instruments were not used when my heart was thrilled and I joined
with great joy in the worship of the Lord. I have also attended meetings
where musical instruments were used when my heart likewise was moved
in devotion and worship of the Lord. So far as I am concerned it is not
a case of preference, but I do want to look at a few passages of Scripture
in the New Testament on this subject of music and song in the worship
of the Lord.

INTELLIGENT PRAYER AND SONG

In the first place, let's look at the 14th chapter of 1st Corinthians,
verse 15, where we have the following inspired words from the pen of the
Apostle Paul, "I will pray with the spirit, and I will pray with the understanding also: I will sing with the spirit, and I will sing with the understanding also." Dr. Archibald T. Robertson, that renowned Greek scholar,
comments upon this passage as follows, "Paul is distinctly in favor of the
use of the intellect in prayer. Prayer is an intelligent exercise of the mind."
Paul also used the same principle in singing for he said, ". . . and I will

sing with the understanding also." Dr. Robertson added, "There was the ecstatic singing like the rhapsody of some prayers without intelligent words. But Paul prefers singing that reaches the intellect as well as stirs the emotions. Solos that people do not understand lose more than half their value in church worship."

Dr. Robertson could have enlarged the sphere of his remarks to include more than solos. A choir can become a source of constant irritation. Let me tell you another of Dr. Ironside's fine stories. It seems that a colored gentleman invited his friend to attend a church service and to make it interesting he said, "We shall have a splendid quartet on that occasion." He met this friend a short time later and asked him why he had not attended. His friend responded, "I did attend but I left before the fight." "The fight?" "Yes," said his friend, "I noticed four men on the platform. One fellow began to shout in a high pitched voice, 'I am the King of glory.' Then another broke in with a deep voice, 'I am the King of glory.' Still a third followed, 'I am the King of glory.' When the fourth said, 'I am the King of glory,' I decided to leave before the fight."

It is interesting to observe in Paul's letter to the Corinthians that he did not write either for or against the use of instruments. He spoke specifically of the voice, whether the inarticulate emotions of the heart or the singing of the lips. In either case he insisted that it be intelligent. The music was to be harmonious and the words intelligent in order that worship might be acceptable to God. It is amazing to say so, but we need to be reminded that God is an intelligent being.

Grant Colfax Tullar, who has written and composed many fine hymns and who listens to our broadcasts regularly, wrote me some time ago and in his letter he said, "It has seemed to me that in our worship through song we have been quite like that preacher of whom the boy said, 'He was all right except that there seemed to be no connection between his tongue and his brain.' "

SINGING WITH GRACE

There is another reference to music in Paul's letter to the Ephesians, 5th chapter, beginning with verse 18, where he said, ". . . be not drunk with wine, wherein is excess; but be filled with the Spirit. . ." Normal Christian experience requires a constant infilling of the Spirit. When a man is filled with the Spirit he exercises himself in spiritual things. This exercise finds its expression in verses 19 and 20 where we read, "Speaking to yourselves in psalms and hymns and spiritual songs, singing and making melody in your heart to the Lord; giving thanks always for all things unto God and the Father in the name of our Lord Jesus Christ. . ."

As the Psalms undoubtedly were originally played on stringed instruments it would appear that musical instruments were used by the early Christians; but that is neither here nor there, the exhortation in this reference is much deeper and more solemn than that. The thing most important is that there be a melody in the heart of the individual. Note that this worship is of kindred minds, for the exhortation is given, "Speaking to *yourselves* in psalms and hymns and spiritual songs, singing and making melody in your heart to the Lord. . ." Thus only Christians can really sing hymns. Notice the phrase "making melody in your heart." Someone has called it the "lyrical emotion of a devout soul." The place for that kind of devotion is in the heart. Indeed, without the heart there is no real worship of God. Whether with instrument or voice or with both, it is all for naught if the adoration is not in and from the heart.

Now let's look at another rich passage of Scripture which adds a further line on this subject. It is found in the 16th verse of the 3rd chapter of Paul's letter to the Colossians where we read, "Let the word of Christ dwell in you richly in all wisdom; teaching and admonishing one another in psalms and hymns and spiritual songs, singing with grace in your hearts to the Lord." Before there can be any teaching or admonishing one another it is necessary that the Word of Christ dwell in one richly in all wisdom. Only then can one sing with grace in his heart to the Lord. The phrase "singing with grace" means "in God's grace." You must be in His grace in order to be able to sing with grace. That kind of singing is melodious and is a source of joy to the Lord who delights in the worship of His people. This passage cuts like a sharp sword the present-day practice in so far as music is concerned in a church or worship service.

The motivating reason behind all this reference to song and music in the worship of the Lord is expressed by David in the 4th and 5th verses of the 33rd Psalm when he wrote, "For the word of the LORD is right; and all his works are done in truth. He loveth righteousness and judgment: the earth is full of the goodness of the LORD." David placed the Word of the Lord, the works of the Lord, and the righteousness of the Lord before the goodness of the Lord. Unless God's righteousness is sustained there can be no display of His goodness. Justice precedes mercy. That is why the cross is absolutely indispensable in any appreciation and reception of the goodness of God. You cannot appeal to the goodness of God until you have understood His righteousness. It was His righteousness that designed the cross and the transaction which took place on that cross. It is written ". . . wthout shedding of blood is no remission." There can be no experience of the goodness of God until one has been justified freely by His grace through the redemption that is in Christ Jesus. Thus there can be no relationship with God apart from Jesus Christ.

THE POWER OF HIS BREATH
PSALM THIRTY-THREE—PART TWO

IN this final meditation in the 33rd Psalm, we shall center our thoughts around the phrase ". . . the breath of his mouth," which appears in the 6th verse. We have therefore entitled this address, "The Power of His Breath." We shall examine only a few verses commencing with verse 6:

> "By the word of the LORD were the heavens made; and all the host of them by the breath of his mouth.
>
> "He gathereth the waters of the sea together as an heap: he layeth up the depth in storehouses.
>
> "Let all the earth fear the LORD: let all the inhabitants of the world stand in awe of him.
>
> "For he spake, and it was done; he commanded, and it stood fast.
>
> "The LORD bringeth the counsel of the nations to nought: he maketh the devices of the people of none effect.
>
> "The counsel of the LORD standeth for ever, the thoughts of his heart to all generations.
>
> "Blessed is the nation whose God is the LORD; and the people whom he hath chosen for his own inheritance."

There is no book like the Bible. It is so different from any of the writings of men that it is in a class entirely by itself, irrespective from what viewpoint the book is examined. Edward FitzGerald has a famous line in his work entitled "Letters." It is particularly pertinent here. He said, "The power of writing one fine line transcends all the Able-Editor ability in the ably-edited Universe." In the light of that statement what a mine is the Word of God. It abounds with fine lines. Where, for example, is it possible to find anything that equals the 6th verse of this Psalm, "By the word of the LORD were the heavens made; and all the host of them by the breath of his mouth"? Or, the 9th verse where we read, "For he spake, and it was done; he commanded, and it stood fast"? If for no other reason, a man ought to read the Bible to enjoy its superb literary style and should he approach the Bible in a spirit of humility he will find it to be, as it truly is, the Word of God.

We begin the consideration of this portion of the Psalm by looking a moment at the last half of the 5th verse which reads, ". . . the earth is full of the goodness of the Lord." Undoubtedly much can be found in our experiences that would cause us to question that statement. There is so much sorrow, so much unpleasantness, so much wickedness in this world that it is difficult to reconcile the actual situation as we see it with the statement David made, that "the earth is full of the goodness of the LORD."

MAN IN GOD'S MIND

In that connection let us examine another passage found in the 8th Psalm where the Psalmist raised the question before the Lord, "What is man, that thou art mindful of him?" The Psalmist did not question the fact that God's mind is full of man but he asked the question, "What is man?" What is there about man that God's mind is full of him? God's thoughts are concerned with man and everything He does is performed with man in mind. I confess that there are occasions when it does not appear as if God's mind is full of man, but when we divorce ourselves from a petty personal viewpoint and sit on a mountain top and look at the world from a proper perspective we will confess without hesitation that in everything God has ever done in creation, in redemption, in the expression of His love, in every display of His character, He has had man supremely in mind. It was for that reason that our Lord Jesus Christ was made for a little season a little lower than the angels in order that He might taste death for every man and thereby raise man into his proper place in the economy and purpose of God.

Now then, let us look at the statement, "the earth is full of the goodness of the LORD." Since God's mind is occupied with man, it is not surprising that the earth, one of the smallest planets, if not the smallest, should be the sphere for the display of the goodness of the Lord since the earth is the sphere where man is supreme. I repeat, if one should divorce himself from his petty personal position he would confess that the earth *is* full of the goodness of the Lord. The channel through which God's goodness has been displayed is the Person of our Lord Jesus Christ. The place where it was poured out was the cross of Calvary.

Someone has said that every human being stands with all the wealth of divine love concentrated on him, and tells the following story to illustrate that fact. Standing on the top of the Cheviot hills, a little son's hand in his, a father taught the measure of the measureless love of God. Pointing northward over Scotland, then southward over England, then eastward over the German Ocean, then westward over hill and dale, and then, sweeping his hand and his eye round the whole circling horizon, he said, "Johnny, my boy, God's love is as big as all that!" "Why, father," the boy cheerily replied, with sparkling eyes, "then we must be in the very middle of it!" We will get a more spectacular display of the grace of God in the future but we shall never get a greater outpouring of His goodness than that which He meted out to us when He sent His Son to the cross. The cross will always be supreme.

After establishing the fact that the earth is full of the goodness of the Lord, David said, "By the word of the LORD were the heavens made; and all the host of them by the breath of his mouth. He gathereth the waters of the sea together as an heap: he layeth up the depth in storehouses." David expressed in a few well-chosen words what many scientists have not been able to determine by laborious study and by the examination of books upon books written by other scientists.

There is a portion in the New Testament from which I would like to quote. In the 3rd verse of the 11th chapter of Hebrews we read, "Through faith we understand that the worlds were framed by the word of God. . . " We do not understand "fiat creation" from any other source, only through faith. We do not get it from a study of the science of men. We understand and know it through faith. Now ". . . faith cometh by hearing, and hearing by the word of God." So if a man has faith it is because he has heard God speak. When, therefore, David said that the heavens were made by the word of the Lord and all the host of them by the breath of His mouth, he made that statement because he was inspired by the Spirit of God. David heard the Lord and believed Him. No man knows how or when this world was created for the simple reason that no man was there when it happened. It is the testimony of Christ that God made the world by His Word. That may seem irrational to the wise of this world who could labor for millions and millions of years, and yet be unable to produce by their research so glorious a statement as that which appears in the very opening page of our Bible. In matchless words we read, "In the beginning God created the heaven and the earth." From the

33rd Psalm and other passages of Scripture we learn that He created these by the word of His mouth, "For he spake, and it was done; he commanded, and it stood fast."

MAN'S BREATH *vs.* GOD'S BREATH

To believe in creation by divine decree has appeared to some people to be unscientific, and as a result they have closed the Bible and refused to believe it. If you are a member of that group, listen to what I am about to say. You and I are the most helpless, hopeless creatures in this world. It takes us longer to become self-sustaining and self-sufficient than any other creature God ever made. Few of us were able to support ourselves until we were in our late teens and most of us had to wait until our late twenties, and there are a lot of people who never get to the place where they are independent of the services and the care of loving hands. The thing that keeps us alive is the breath in our mouths, yet it is the weakest thing we possess. We have very little power in our breath, though some shallow-thinking people have developed a boisterous display of wind as their mouths become a "cave of the winds." But there is just a breath between every man and death—only a breath—that is all. When it stops, we are immediately obliged to lay down everything, whether we want to or not, and the body that formerly was strong, doing our bidding, falls like a helpless wet rag. No wonder the Word of God chides us for ever fearing what a man can do. Man is a mere powerless breath which he does not even own or control.

But contrast that with the power of God's breath. Some entirely ignore the statement in the 33rd Psalm as being merely poetic. Some suggest that David was only a poet. Some conclude that when he wrote these transcendently "fine lines" he was merely playing with words. But an illustration or two of the power of God's breath will either cause such to eat their words or stamp them as those who refuse to exercise the simplest rules of logic.

Let us consider an attested incident in history which is of remarkable importance. Our Lord had entered into Capernaum. It was noised about that He was to be in a certain house. Immediately many were gathered toegther to hear Him. The crowd was so great that there was no room to receive them, no, not so much as about the door. Our Lord preached the Word unto them. Though you may disregard the fact that our Lord Jesus is the very Word of God, the *logos*, the very idea of God, you cannot get away from the fact that He was preaching the Word of God to the crowd gathered at that house. There were some friends of a man in Capernaum who was sick of the palsy, who had heard of the healing power manifested by our Lord upon the sick. They mutually agreed that, if their palsied friend could get near this miracle-working Jesus, he would be healed.

We do not know what conversation took place between the sick man and his friends, but we do know that they picked up the bed upon which he lay and sought to gain entrance into the house where our Lord was. They were hindered by the great crowd. But they were not to be thwarted. They proceeded to the roof and then, through an opening, let down the bed whereon the sick of the palsy lay. If you can picture that scene it will fascinate you. Our Lord saw the faith of the four friends and so, addressing the man who was sick and absolutely helpless, said, "Son, thy sins be forgiven thee." Immediately a theological discussion took place because there were a number of theologians present in the house. Some suggested that "this man" (Jesus) was blaspheming, ". . . who can forgive sins but God only?" Our Lord sensed their reasoning and asked, "Why reason ye these things in your hearts?" Then He put a proposition in logic to them. He asked which was easier, to say to this man sick of the palsy, impotent, unable to move—and remember he had been that way for years—he could not have gotten into the house unless his friends brought him—which was easier to say, "Arise and take up thy bed, and walk?" or, "Thy sins be forgiven thee. . . ?" Of course, it was so crystal-clear that no response came from that critical audience. But our Lord added, ". . . that ye may know that the Son of man hath power on earth to forgive sins," and then, turning to the sick of the palsy, He said, "I say unto thee, Arise, and take up thy bed, and go thy way into thine house." There was such an exhibition of power in the words which our Lord Jesus spoke, unmatched by the skill and scientific knowledge of all physicians, then or thereafter, that the man immediately rose up, took up his bed, and went forth before the crowd gathered in that house. He walked out through the door. Everyone in the house acknowledged that they had seen something and they glorified God, saying, "We never saw it on this fashion." Neither have we. Those people saw a display of "the power of his breath."

Again we refer to another incident witnessed by friend and foe alike. It happened in Bethany. A beautiful home was located there in which two sisters and a brother lived. The brother was desperately ill. His illness proved fatal. Prior to his death, word had been sent to our Lord that he was sick. As far as the sisters were concerned, He seemingly paid no attention to their message. Friends came to comfort these sisters and mourn with them but their Lord did not come. They buried their brother, sealed the tomb, and went home and wept some more. Four days later our Lord appeared in Bethany. There was an exchange of words between the sisters and our Lord. Then our Lord asked concerning the brother, "Where have ye laid him?" They said, ". . . come and see." Then an interesting thing took place—a most interesting thing. Our Lord "wept." The Jews said, "Behold how he loved him!" There were also some critical "scientists" there who said "Could not this man, which opened the eyes of the blind, have caused that even this man should not have died?" Our Lord groaned in His spirit. They came to the grave. It was a cave and a stone lay upon it. Our Lord said, "Take ye away the stone." If I may be permitted to paraphrase, one of the sisters of the dead man said, "Lord, aren't you making an unreasonable request? Putrefaction has already taken its toll. If we roll away the stone the stench which will come from the tomb will be nauseating." Our Lord rebuked the sister saying, "Said I not unto thee, that, if thou wouldest believe, thou shouldest see the glory of God?" They took the stone away from the place where the dead was laid. Jesus then lifted up His eyes and said, "Father, I thank thee that thou hast heard me. And I knew that thou hearest me always: but because of the people which stand by I said it, that they may believe that thou hast sent me." When He had thus given thanks in prayer He cried with a loud voice, "Lazarus, come forth." And the man who was dead came forth, bound hand and foot in graveclothes. That's power—"the power of his breath."

Our Lord in three words accomplished something which all the scientists with all their powerful medicines have been unable to accomplish and will never be able to accomplish. There has never been a case, authenticated as is this record, where a man rose from the grave after he had been dead four days, when his body was stinking from the putrefaction that had already set in. That is power.

"HE SPAKE . . . IT STOOD FAST"

Who is this One who had such power in His breath? I for one do not have the slightest trouble in recognizing that He was the same One who exercised the same power when He caused the heavens to be made and all the hosts of them. Then, too, He spake and it was done. He commanded and it stood fast. Some say it is unscientific to believe in "fiat creation."

Yes, it is, if we consider the science which is of and by men. It may be unscientific to unbelieving scientists, but it is just like God to those of us who have come to know Him as He is revealed in Jesus Christ.

But David had some other things to say about that subject in this Psalm. Evidently David knew that there would be a conflict between science, falsely so-called, and the Bible record. Who will win out in this controversy? In the 10th verse of the 33rd Psalm we read, "The LORD bringeth the counsel of the nations to nought: he maketh the device of the people of none effect." Contrast that with the next verse, "The counsel of the LORD standeth for ever, the thoughts of his heart to all generations." In other words, David said, that every attempt upon the part of man or a group of men to understand creation or the plan of God or the purposes of God, be it the most brilliant expression by the most brilliant minds, would come to nought. Their science would not stand from one generation to another. The ideas, their counsels, their deliberations, the "consensus of their scholarship" would not be eternal. They would be just like themselves, a mere breath. Our Lord has made the devices of the people to be of none effect, but through all generations the counsel of the Lord standeth forever. We can hardly blame the Psalmist for his burst of praise which appears in the 12th verse, "Blessed is the nation whose God is the LORD; and the people whom he hath chosen for his own inheritance."

PSALM THIRTY-FOUR—PART ONE

ADULLAM'S D.D.D. FOUR HUNDRED

HERE is another Psalm so beautiful and refreshing that it is impossible to do it justice in one message. We will limit this message to the first six verses. I am sure we will find a blessing for our souls by a mere reading of them.

> "I will bless the LORD at all times: his praise shall continually be in my mouth.
>
> "My soul shall make her boast in the LORD: the humble shall hear thereof, and be glad.
>
> "O magnify the LORD with me, and let us exalt his name together.
>
> "I sought the LORD, and he heard me, and delivered me from all my fears.
>
> "They looked unto him, and were lightened: and their faces were not ashamed.

"This poor man cried, and the LORD heard him,
and saved him out of all his troubles."

A PERFECT PSALM

This Psalm, like all the rest of the Psalms, was written originally in
Hebrew. When translated into another tongue, it sometimes is not possible to preserve the native beauty of the Psalm. I recall some quaint
expressions my mother frequently used when we were mere children which
have a particular charm in the Norwegian language, but when translated
into English they fall as flat as the proverbial English joke. So, too, in
translating from the Hebrew into the English, some of the charm of the
original Psalm is missed. For instance, as we open our English Bible to the
thirty-fourth Psalm we would not be able to determine that David built
this Psalm about the Hebrew alphabet. If we were to hear a venerable Jewish rabbi refer to this Psalm as an alphabetical Psalm we would
probably wonder to what he was referring. When David wrote this Psalm
he cast its meter about the twenty-two letters of the Hebrew alphabet. In
its construction and composition his Psalm is perfect, as it contains the
letters of the alphabet, from Aleph to Tau as the Hebrew would say, or
from A to Z as we Americans would put it. Thus, this Psalm fits into every
experience of life.

Incidentally, without being charged with being too fanciful, I like to
think of the Semitic alphabet as being God-designed. Its last letter is Tau.
When written in symbol it forms a cross. The ills and the disappointments
of this world will all be over when Israel, nationally, comes to the Cross
and beholds that it was there that Jehovah's Fellow, as their prophets
entitled the Messiah, was pierced and wounded in the house of His friends.

The Psalm has two distinct applications, one historic and the other
prophetic; one to David and the other to Christ.

DAVID'S SOCIAL REGISTER

Considering the Psalm from David's own experience, and thus historically, we can gain great profit and learn many lessons. Considering it
prophetically, from the viewpoint of our Lord Jesus Christ, we will enter
into the joys and blessings of a more devoted worship of the Lord.

This Psalm, like a number of others, has an introduction to it which
enables us to picture the historic setting. This introduction reads: "A Psalm
of David, when he changed his behaviour before Abimelech; who drove him
away, and he departed."

In the 21st chapter of the First Book of Samuel we get the setting and the actual background for this Psalm. David fled from the face of King Saul though he knew, as a result of the prophet Samuel's anointing, that he was Jehovah's chosen king. He came to Nob, where he met Ahimelech, the priest, and begged of him five loaves and received the shewbread for himself and his little group of famished followers. Then he begged a spear, and much to his surprise he received the sword which had belonged to Goliath, the Philistine, whom he had slain. Can you picture David with the sword of a giant? But of all places to flee, David went straight to Gath! He went into the land of the Philistines and directly to the king, whose servants immediately recognized the stripling to be none other than David, who had slain Goliath. David became sore afraid and changed his behaviour, feigning himself to be mad, scrabbling upon the doors of the gate and otherwise acting as a madman. This caused the king to be angry with his servants and he gave them instructions that David be driven out of the city.

David fled to that never-to-be-forgotten place, the cave of Adullam, at which place his friends joined him when they heard of his whereabouts. The record in First Samuel reads: "And every one that was in distress, and every one that was in debt, and every one that was discontented, gathered themselves unto him; and he became a captain over them. . . ."

There were about four hundred men. I wonder if the social register containing New York's "Four Hundred" received their idea from the group gathered in David's cave of Adullam. You and I would have to be "well" born, possess a lot of money and boast of a cultural, blue-blood background to break into New York's "Four Hundred." However, all that was required to "break" into David's select four hundred were three D's—distress, debt, and discontentment. But what a meeting took place with those four hundred "DDD's," with David as their captain.

If you are in distress; if you recognize your obligation to God and how you are in debt to Him; if you are discontented with this world, its empty hopes, and its vanishing mirages—pray sir, come to the 34th Psalm, where you will find the most helpful and encouraging message.

David told that four hundred at Adullam in the 1st verse of this Psalm: "I will bless the LORD at all times: his praise shall continually be in my mouth."

"David could be a homeless exile, a proscribed wanderer, or a king upon the throne of Israel, yet in any situation he could sing, for the springs of divine melody are in the secret of divine communion, not in human circumstances."

To us who are Christians—not mere church members—but men and women who have been born again and who know Christ as our Saviour—may this example of David be an inspiration to us. He said: "I will bless the LORD at all times: his praise shall continually be in my mouth."

We may be in the cave of Adullam today, with a great company of others who are in debt, in distress, and discontented, but tomorrow He may transport us into His own presence and place us upon the throne. We will find our task made lighter, shall I suggest, even glorious, if we will do as David did—bless the Lord at all times and let His praise be continually in our mouth.

There is a lasting impression upon my heart and mind as a result of reading about a certain martyr, whom history does not even name. He was about to be burned at the stake and, when given an opportunity to speak a final word, he said: "I am sorry that I am going to a place where I shall be ever receiving wages and do no more work."

How true it is that when we are in His presence we shall be continually receiving the benefactions of His grace and dwelling in His sunshine. It will be easy to praise Him then, but how privileged we are to praise Him now in the midst of sorrow, distress, debt, and discontentment. A spiritual man finds His praise perpetual; afflictions cannot quench it, temporal circumstances and position cannot augment it. It is paramount, above all circumstances and changes, for it is the Holy Spirit Himself who is the spiritual man's spring and power of joy. A true test of a spiritual state is the ability of the believer to praise the Lord at all times.

But I can hear someone saying, "That is a splendid theory, but what if you were out of a job not knowing from where your next meal would come?" Spurgeon, in the earlier days of his ministry, was preaching on the faithfulness of God in time of trial. His grandfather sat on the platform behind him. He suddenly rose up and came to the front of the pulpit and said, "My grandson can preach this as a matter of theory, but I can tell you it as a matter of experience, for I have done business upon the great waters and have seen the works of the Lord for myself."

HEAVEN BEFOREHAND

The 3rd verse of our Psalm reads: "O magnify the LORD with me, and let us exalt his name together." In the communion of kindred minds and spirits there is strength. An old English clergyman in commenting upon this verse, said that "by so doing," that is, magnifying the Lord and exalting His name together, "we begin heaven beforehand." There is great joy experienced by a group of believers in Christ, exchanging their experiences and praise, and together magnifying the Lord and exalting His name.

I particularly enjoy the 4th and 6th verses of this Psalm. If ever a man was in difficulty and presented a distressing picture, David, in the court of the king of the Philistines, was all of that—feigning madness—yet crying unto the Lord from the bottom of his heart, so that when the king bade him depart he proceeded immediately to the cave of Adullam to further pour out his heart unto the Lord and cry unto Him. As a result, the Lord delivered him from all of his fears and out of all his troubles.

None of us have been promised exemption from troubles. In fact, the Scripture says, "In the world ye shall have tribulation." Our Lord was the One who said that, but He added, "but be of good cheer; I have overcome the world." If you are compassed about with fears or burdened with a multitude of troubles so that even your countenance seems to have the word "distress" written all over it, may I suggest that the cure is to do exactly as David did—seek the Lord and cry unto Him.

I have already mentioned that this Psalm has a prophetic outlook as well as an historic background. This is not strange. It is not unique to this Psalm. It is true of much of the Old Testament. It records events that happened thousands of years ago, yet, through the history and the record of events that are past, the Holy Spirit announced and presented a prophetic message, so that when we come to the close of the Old Testament, the Book of Malachi, we have water-marked into the record the impress of the Messiah, the Christ of God. Thus in this 34th Psalm, the Holy Spirit, taking the experiences of David and having him give expression to his own heart and the trials of his own life, guided and led David to write the prophetic record of Christ, as well. It is for that reason that we can look at this Psalm from the viewpoint of our Lord Jesus Christ. The Holy Spirit has commented in the New Testament on this 34th Psalm and declared it to be a prophecy of our Lord.

A BONE OF HIM SHALL NOT BE BROKEN

The 19th chapter of St. John's Gospel specifically details for us the record of the crucifixion. There we read that when our Lord knew that all things were accomplished, and that the Scripture might be fulfilled, He said, "I thirst." Someone took a sponge, filled it with vinegar, and with a little hyssop, put it to His mouth. It was then that He said, "It is finished:" and bowed His head, and gave up the ghost. The Jews, therefore, because it was the preparation prior to a high feast day, insisted that the bodies of Christ and the two thieves crucified with Him should not remain upon the cross on the Sabbath day. Thus, they besought Pilate that the legs of the three might be broken. The soldiers were so instructed and proceeded to break the legs of the first, and of the other, but when they came to our Lord they saw that He was dead already, and therefore did not break His legs. Little did those soldiers realize that their very movements were directed by God, and that their reactions to breaking the legs of our Lord were prophesied by the Psalmist a thousand years before Calvary. We read in the 36th verse of the 19th chapter of St. John's Gospel that

> ". . . these things were done, that the scripture should
> be fulfilled, A bone of him shall not be broken."

The 20th verse of the 34th Psalm reads: "He keepeth all his bones: not one of them is broken."

Thus Christ is presented in this Psalm, and that most marvelously. We can therefore place these very words into His mouth—

> "I will bless the LORD at all times: his praise shall
> continually be in my mouth.
> "My soul shall make her boast in the LORD: the
> humble shall hear thereof, and be glad."

Our Lord invites us who have been redeemed by His Cross to join Him in praising the Lord, by saying: "O magnify the LORD with me, and let us exalt his name together."

In the 22nd Psalm, and the 22nd verse, it is written: "I will declare thy name unto my brethren: in the midst of the congregation will I praise thee." There our Lord is seen in the midst of the congregation. When we see that, we will understand the glory of worship.

The fifth verse of our Psalm is particularly inspiring: "They looked unto him, and were lightened: and their faces were not ashamed." It is the sinner, unforgiven, who is ashamed in the presence of Christ, but the sinner who is covered by the blood of the sacrifice of Christ looks unto Him and is lightened.

Our closing verse reads: "This poor man cried, and the LORD heard him, and saved him out of all his troubles." David was poor, we are poor, but none are as poor as Christ was. We are told that, though He was rich, yet for our sakes He became poor, that we through His poverty might be rich. Troubles? How our Lord was compassed about with them. He, too, cried unto the Lord. The Lord heard Him and saved Him out of His troubles. As a result we take courage and rejoice in Christ.

PSALM THIRTY-FOUR—PART TWO

MINISTERING ANGELS

WE shall not touch upon each of the remaining verses of this Psalm. Rather, we shall choose a few and press their refreshing drink between our lips, for "God has left us His Word as our heritage."

Irrespective of the viewpoint from which one may examine the Bible —literary, historic, or as God's Word—it is the outstanding miracle of all ages. This old world would be poor indeed were it deprived of the Bible, and when it comes to intellectualism, no man who does not have a close acquaintance with the Bible can possibly call himself an "intellectual." The Bible is both ancient and modern. It is more up-to-the-minute and more accurate than "Time," the modern, weekly news magazine. This past week the editors of that periodical issued the finest broadside I have seen advertising a magazine. In it they raised the question, "Does 'Time' make errors?" to which they answered—"Yes. Occasionally 'Time' slips, and the mistakes that call forth the greatest fire from readers are on the subjects of science, medicine, and the Bible." If we desire to know what is going on in this modern age of ours, we must become better acquainted with the Bible!

The 7th verse of the 34th Psalm reads: "The angel of the LORD encampeth round about them that fear him, and delivereth them."

I realize we are living in a decidedly material age and that to talk about angels seems to bring us into the realm of the ethereal. Angels? Did you ever meet one?

The Bible has much to say about angels and, whether we know it or not, another heritage of every believer in Christ is to have an angel of the Lord encamp round about him and deliver him from evil.

All the angels I have ever seen painted by men are sort of effeminate creatures with wings and a halo—anything but the beings the Bible presents them to be.

In the 1st chapter of the letter to the Hebrews we have a great dissertation upon angels. In this chapter the angels are compared with and contrasted to Christ so that the supremacy and excellency of Christ may be known. In the last verse of that chapter we have revealed to us one of the ministries of the angels. There we read: "Are they not all ministering spirits, sent forth to minister for them who shall be heirs of salvation?"

Angels therefore are the servants of believers. They minister to them. They are never worshipped. They worship the Lord and, as God's servants, minister to us who are heirs of God's salvation. They encamp round about the believer as our Psalm indicates. We may not see them. They are spirits, and spirits are unseen, but, nevertheless, they are real.

Frequently, in both the Old and New Testaments, angels appeared visibly in the form of men, acting as servants of God and ministering to God's own. The Jews highly reverenced angels. They knew them to be God's messengers, and that their message was steadfast and that every disobedience received a just recompense of reward. They counted themselves honored to have a visit from an angel.

ENTERTAINING THE LORD

Probably the greatest revelation about angels appears in the 18th chapter of the Book of Genesis, where the Lord Himself appeared in the form of an angel, accompanied by two other angels. He paid Abraham a visit, and as a friend communed with Abraham about the impending destruction of Sodom. When Abraham, sitting in his tent door, noticed the three approaching men, he bowed himself to the ground and invited them to be his guests. To Abraham was given the great honor of entertaining the Lord and two of His angels.

From then on, the Jews have been zealous in entertaining strangers. In olden times, in their synagogues throughout Judea, a section was set apart for strangers. As the ram's horn was blown to announce the Sabbath, men went with quick steps to the synagogue. When the doorkeeper noticed a stranger he would ask his occupation and seat him among men of his own trade. After the synagogue service the members of the congregation would vie with each other for the privilege of entertaining the stranger in their midst, for they knew that their forefathers, in entertaining strangers, frequently entertained angels unawares.

How different from our present-day churches! Usually the stranger is shunned, and as for entertaining him at dinner after the meeting, such church etiquette is frowned upon. But try it some time. You may get a great blessing.

However, whether or not we have ever entertained an angel unawares, in entertaining a stranger we can be assured upon the testimony of the Bible that we, as believers in Christ, have angels as God's messengers ministering to our needs.

The 8th verse of our Psalm reads: "O taste and see that the LORD is good: blessed is the man that trusteth in him."

Let a man once taste that the Lord is good and he will no longer be content with the tasteless things of this world. "Taste and see"—that is an invitation. It is David's invitation; it also is our Lord's. It is the invitation of one who has already tasted the goodness of the Lord for himself. If you have never tasted nor seen—Come! You, too, will then know the blessedness of "the man that trusteth in him."

". . . There is no want to them that fear him. The young lions do lack," said David, "and suffer hunger: but they that seek the LORD shall not want any good thing."

To those who have never tasted the goodness of the Lord it may seem absurd to say, "there is no want to them that fear him." If you have such a notion, how I would delight in taking you to some men I know who rejoice in Christ with exceeding joy, yet who are compassed about with trials of life which would completely discourage another. I am thinking now of a man, in whose presence I have always received great blessing in noting his cheery disposition and thankful spirit to God; yet this man was so sorely pressed financially this past winter that he and his family sat in their home with overcoats about them to keep warm, having no coal to put on a fire. You could not have determined from the behavior of either that man or his wife that they lacked anything. Indeed, they lacked nothing, for in having Christ they had *all*. Everything, without Christ, is emptiness; but Christ, even without anything else, is complete satisfaction.

A TRUE TUTOR

Commencing with verse 11 to the end of the Psalm we, as children, are invited to sit in on a truly great lesson, taught by a superior pedagogue. Verse 11 reads: "Come, ye children, hearken unto me: I will teach you the fear of the LORD." The fear of the Lord is declared to be "riches, and honour, and life." Do we know of anything more desirable than riches, and honor, and life? The Jews to this day count a man's master or tutor worthy of more respect than his father, for as one of their ancients said, "his father has given him only his being, but the other his well-being."

At Christmas-time a couple of years ago I was delightfully surprised by a gift I received from a member of our sales' staff, a splendid young Jewish chap. This Jewish salesman invariably remembers me at Christmas. This particular year he came into my office with the usual beaming smile upon his face and said, as he left a parcel, "I think you'll get a 'kick' out of what I put on the fly-leaf of one of the books in the package."

I hope you are not too old to get a thrill out of opening a Christmas package. Upon arriving home, his was the first one I opened. I found three books. Two were commentaries on Genesis and Exodus by the Chief Rabbi of the British Empire, and the third a book by Farbridge, "The Renewal of Judaism." The fly-leaf of the latter had this inscription:

> "To Rabbi E. C. Olsen
>
> Respectfully,
>
> M. S. Jacobson
>
> (page 42)"

I have been called "Reverend," "Doctor," "Dominie," and what-not, but that was the first time I was ever called "Rabbi." I quickly noted the reference for an explanation of the title, so I thumbed the pages to find it. There I learned that a disciple of Rabbi Meir emphasized the fact that if a Jew is taught wisdom by a Gentile he must call him "Rabbi—my master."

Here in this 34th Psalm we have the wisdom of a true Rabbi. Do we desire life, do we want many days, do we desire to see good? Then hearken! The Psalmist said:

> "Keep thy tongue from evil, and thy lips from speaking guile.
> "Depart from evil, and do good; seek peace, and pursue it.

"The eyes of the LORD are upon the righteous, and
his ears are open unto their cry."

These instructions are given only to those who are called "the righteous." When studying the 32nd Psalm we learned that such a man is
righteous, not as a result of what he himself does, but because of what the
Lord has done for him. The principle of the entire Bible from Genesis to
Revelation is just this, that God credits righteousness to the man who believes and trusts Him. It is written that Abraham believed, and that it
(his faith) was counted to him for righteousness.

It is, therefore to those who in simple faith have trusted the Word of
God for their salvation, that it is written: "Thy eyes of the LORD are upon
the righteous, and his ears are open unto their cry."

A RIDDLE OF LIFE

The 17th verse of our Psalm reads: "The righteous cry, and the LORD
heareth, and delivereth them out of all their troubles." There are many
who cannot understand why a Christian should have troubles. If, as the
Christian maintains, he is a child of God by faith in the Lord Jesus, how
is it that God does not throw about him a hedge protecting him from trials?
Would not that be an evidence to an unbeliever that God is true and His
Word dependable? Would he not then turn to the Lord? My answer to
that is—First, God sent His Son into this world almost two thousand years
ago. He demonstrated by overwhelming logic and evidence through His
miracles that He was God manifest in flesh. Did the world fall down and
embrace Him? Indeed not! They gave Him a cross! Men do not believe
to the saving of their souls by *seeing;* this to the contrary to everything
they say. Seeing, to them, is not believing. The kind of belief that saves is
that which is born by *hearing* the Word of God! Second, if Christians were
spared trials or troubles I am inclined to think we'd have multitudes who
would resemble what they call in China "rice Christians," Chinese who have
seemingly confessed Christ in order to get some rice to eat. No, Christians
are not spared the trials of life! It is written that our Lord Jesus said concerning His Father, which is in heaven, that "he maketh his sun to rise on
the evil and on the good, and sendeth rain on the just and on the unjust."

Christians who are sorely pressed by life's trials and difficulties, should
observe the teaching of this Psalm: "The righteous cry, and the LORD
heareth, and delivereth them out of all their troubles." We are invited to

cry. He answers us; His ears are open to our cry, and He promises us that He will deliver us out of all our troubles. Some day He will do that completely when He takes us to His heavens.

The 19th verse of our Psalm assures us that "many are the afflictions of the righteous." Christians, instead of being spared troubles, are assured that they will have *many* afflictions. But I do not know of one but who has, through afflictions, come to know the Lord better. Take Job as an example. No one, except the Lord, suffered such afflictions as he did. Yet, what happened to Job? Did he not receive the greatest revelation a man can receive when he said to the Lord: "I have heard of thee by the hearing of the ear: but now mine eye seeth thee"? Did Job get puffed up about his revelation? Indeed he did not, for he immediately added: "Wherefore I abhor myself, and repent in dust and ashes." That is what trials and difficulties did for Job. He came to know the Lord and, through knowing Him, knew himself. How encouraging it is therefore to read in the closing verses of the Book of Job that ". . . the LORD turned the captivity of Job . . . also the LORD gave Job twice as much as he had before."

David closed this wonderful Psalm: "The LORD redeemeth the soul of his servants: and none of them that trust in him shall be desolate."

PSALM THIRTY-FIVE

CHRISTIAN GRACE—A FORGOTTEN VIRTUE

THE 35th Psalm is an earnest prayer by a depressed soul. There is not much one can say about the historic setting of the Psalm. We know that it was written by David, who undoubtedly described his own experience when he was persistently pursued by King Saul.

I am not prepared to state that the Psalm has a further application to the Person of our Lord Jesus Christ, though there are some statements which are strikingly appropriate to our Lord, as for instance the 11th verse, where we read, "False witnesses did rise up; they laid to my charge things that I knew not." Then again the 17th verse contains language which reminds one of the 22nd Psalm, which Psalm unquestionably refers to our Lord. The 17th verse reads, "Lord, how long wilt thou look on? Rescue my soul from their destructions, my darling from the lions."

UNPREJUDICED BIBLE STUDY

There is always a danger that one might seek to stretch the Scriptures to fit into some preconceived idea. If there is a book which ought to be handled reverently and without prejudice it is the Bible. There is really only One who can expound its glories and reveal its meaning—the Holy Spirit. The Holy Spirit has been given to all believers. His anointing assures us that we need not that any man teach us. The Holy Spirit will be our teacher. But this promise must be considered in the light of other passages. The Word of God is intended to develop a Christian into a well-balanced individual. It is essential that we avoid extremes. The assurance to which I have just referred appears in the 27th verse of the 2nd chapter of the 1st Epistle of John, where we read, "But the anointing which ye have received of him abideth in you, and ye need not that any man teach you: but as the same anointing teacheth you of all things, and is truth, and is no lie, and even as it hath taught you, ye shall abide in him." This promise should be read in the light of the 4th chapter of Ephesians. There we learn that the risen Christ gave to His church apostles, prophets, evangelists, pastors and teachers, "For the perfecting of the saints, for the work of the ministry, for the edifying of the body of Christ . . ." Evidently the Lord bestowed gifts upon certain chosen men, including the gift of teaching. In bestowing these gifts He sets a man apart for Himself and presents that man—teacher, evangelist, or whatever he may be—to the whole body of Christ, the church. These gifted men are given in order that Christians might be perfected, that they might be instructed in the Word, and that the enire body might be edified.

There is no contradiction between these two passages. There is perfect harmony. A Christian need not be deceived by any false doctrine or any false spirit. He has the Holy Spirit within him, who will guard him against false spirits and false doctrines if the individual will yield himself to the ministry of the Spirit of God.

This same tendency to stretch Scripture is manifested in many ways. A current example appeared on the front pages of some of our morning newspapers this past week. It seems that out in Cleveland there is a youngster referred to as a "minister." He is eight years old. He even has the title "Reverend" prefixed to his name. He performed a wedding ceremony —which proved to be a good publicity stunt. By the way, our Lord never sought publicity nor did He ever hire a publicity agent! It is true that our

Lord Himself said, in referring to a little child, ". . . of such is the kingdom of heaven" but it should also be remembered that the Holy Spirit through the Apostle Paul cautioned Timothy to lay hands suddenly on no man and, for a place of leadership in the church, he was not to sanction a novice. *There never was but one Samuel.*

There is a certain school that claims to find in every portion of Scripture some direct application to our Lord Jesus Christ, but an examination of our Lord's teaching would avoid that error. On the day of His resurrection our Lord gave an enlightening exposition of the Scriptures to two disciples as He journeyed with them on the way to Emmaus. He first chided them for their slowness of heart to believe *all* that the prophets had spoken. He asked them, "Ought not Christ to have suffered these things, (that is, the death and the ignominy of the cross) and to enter into his glory?" Before they could answer He proceeded to give an exposition of the Scripture for, ". . . beginning at Moses and all the prophets, he expounded unto them in all the Scriptures *the things* concerning himself." There are in the Old Testament certain *things* that concern Christ—none other—and it was to *these things* that our Lord referred and which He presented to those disciples in order that they might understand the Scriptures. So, in the absence of any definite reference in the New Testament, it is inadvisable to state that what is found in this 35th Psalm applies to our Lord. This is a long introduction, but I trust it has been worthwhile.

DAVID *vs.* CHRIST

We shall not take time to read the Psalm in its entirety. Rather we shall read the first 9 verses in order that we may get an idea of the general tenor of the Psalm—

> "Plead my cause, O LORD, with them that strive with me: fight against them that fight against me.
>
> "Take hold of shield and buckler, and stand up for mine help.
>
> "Draw out also the spear, and stop the way against them that persecute me: say unto my soul, I am thy salvation.
>
> "Let them be confounded and put to shame that seek after my soul: let them be turned back and brought to confusion that devise my hurt.
>
> "Let them be as chaff before the wind: and let the angel of the LORD chase them.

"Let their way be dark and slippery: and let the angel
of the LORD persecute them.

"For without cause have they hid for me their net
in a pit, which without cause they have digged for my
soul.

"Let destruction come upon him at unawares; and
let his net that he hath hid catch himself: into that
very destruction let him fall.

"And my soul shall be joyful in the LORD: it shall
rejoice in his salvation."

Here is another of those portions of Scripture which will lead us into
hopeless entanglement unless we observe the principle of comparing spiritual
things with spiritual. In the first place, I do not believe that any Christian
has a right to pray as David prayed in this 35th Psalm. Because David
was permitted to do so does not gives us license to do the same. David
never had the benefit of the revelation we now have. He saw the cross, to
be true, but not as clearly as we see it. He saw the Lord, but never in His
incarnate glory. He knew very little about the matchless grace of God
which is now manifested as a result of the death of Christ. He could sing
Psalms, but he never knew the joy of singing such a song as

"When I survey the wondrous Cross
On which the Prince of Glory died;
My richest gain I count but loss,
And pour contempt on all my pride."

David knew nothing of the soul-thrilling experience that comes by
singing,

"Just as I am, without one plea,
But that thy Blood was shed for me,
And that Thou bid'st me come to Thee;
O Lamb of God, I come, I come."

David merely saw the cross in anticipation, not in history. Even the
disciples having our Lord Jesus personally in their midst and constantly
expounding the Scriptures unto them—even they could not understand or
grasp the cross until it had become history. It is the cross which illumines
the pages of the Old Testament.

It is also necessary to bear in mind that a new principle of conduct
has been invoked as a result of the cross. The law was given by Moses, but
grace and truth came by Jesus Christ. David could pray and sing the 35th
Psalm, but an enlightened Christian cannot. When he is subjected to persecution or misunderstanding or is pushed about by his enemies, he has not
the privilege nor the right to pray down judgment upon his enemies. The
Scripture bids him to do the extreme opposite. If a man asks him to walk
a mile, he is to go two. If a man smites him on one cheek, he is to turn

the other. He is to pray for them that despitefully use him. He is to do exactly as Stephen did when he was stoned to death for his testimony for Christ. He is to kneel down and cry, "Lord, lay not this sin to their charge." In simple words, he is to emulate his Lord. This is a "forgotten" virtue which God intended should distinguish a Christian from all other men of the world.

This does not mean that a Christian should be a namby-pamby, vacillating type of individual; one need only casually examine the ministry of our Lord Jesus Christ to refute such an idea. He never "pulled his punches," if I may use a modern vulgar expression, nor did He ever adjust His message to suit the convenience of the moment. For instance, He was not a modernist in Galilee and a fundamentalist in Jerusalem. He was not all things to all men. He did not carry water on both shoulders. Yet, He never carried a chip on His shoulder nor did He resort to vindictiveness.

It is helpful to observe the language of the Apostle Peter in referring to our Lord's conduct before men. Let us look at his exact words, commencing with the 21st verse of the 2nd chapter of his first letter, where he exhorted believers in the following language:

> "For even hereunto were ye called: because Christ also suffered for us, leaving us an example, that ye should follow his steps:
>
> "Who did no sin, neither was guile found in his mouth:
>
> "Who, when he was reviled, reviled not again; when he suffered, he threatened not; but committed himself to him that judgeth righteously . . ."

What a contrast to that which is found in the 35th Psalm. Our Lord never threatened, never reviled—but He committed Himself to Him who judgeth righteously. But we must do David justice also. David did not revile when he was reviled, for he said that he behaved himself as though he had been a friend or brother to his enemy; but the difference between David and the Lord was in this: David prayed down judgment upon his enemies while our Lord committed judgment to Him who judgeth righteously.

FOLLOWING CHRIST

So ought we to do. Our Lord has given us an example. We ought to follow in His steps. Only a born-again man can follow in His steps. No one else can. Our Lord is not an example to an unsaved man. He is an example to a saved sinner. To an unsaved sinner He can only be a Saviour or a Judge, but after a man has received Christ as his Saviour, then our Lord becomes his example. This cannot be made too clear. If you reverse the order it means condemnation, not salvation nor justification. If you have taken Christ as your example and not as your Saviour, He thoroughly condemns you by His life, but if you have received Christ as your Saviour He invites you to follow in His steps.

Probably a large percentage of our radio audience is composed of men and women who profess to know the Lord as their Saviour. The conduct and behavior of our Lord before men and God becomes the standard for your life and mine. If I were asked what I considered the saddest situation in the church of Jesus Christ on earth today, I should say it is the lack of love for fellow-believers. Have you ever noticed how frequently our Lord on the night of His betrayal commanded His disciples to love one another? Our Lord said, "If a man love me, he will keep my words: and my Father will love him, and we will come unto him, and make our abode with him." Again He said, "This is my commandment, That ye love one another, as I have loved you." That is the standard. Again He said, "Ye are my friends, if ye do whatsoever I command you." Knowing the dullness of mind of the disciples, as well as the dullness of our minds He repeated, "These things I command you, that ye love one another."

Our Lord said that this was a *new* commandment. Sometimes we forget that. We act as if we lived under the old commandment of an eye for an eye and a tooth for a tooth. But we now live under a new commandment. We are to love one another as our Lord loved us. By this, that is by our love for one another, our Lord said the world would know that we are His disciples. That, I repeat, is the saddest situation in the Christian church today. I am not talking about professing Christendom. I am talking about the church of our Lord, that body made up of men and women who have been born again and are members of His body. It is an everlasting shame upon us and a sin against our Lord that we fail to show love and affection for other believers in Christ. How Satan must gloat to see Christians "scrapping" with each other. It's a disgrace! It's a sin! It's a dishonor to the Lord! If you have been guilty, get on your knees and confess your sin and ask God for grace to love all believers in Christ. There are also believers who refuse to have fellowship with other believers, and so conduct themselves as if they were members of the choicest part of His body while

the rest of us, well, we are just His feet. However, I would be happy to
be a part of His feet, for it is written that God ". . . hath put all things
under his feet, and gave him to be the head over all things to the church,
which is his body, the fulness of him that filleth all in all." If believers in
Christ, true born-again people, would cease their bickering and unpleasantness with one another and unitedly determine by God's grace to be obedient
to their Lord's command, this world would then be able to see that we are
His disciples. The result would be astounding—a true Holy Spirit revival
would ensue.

WASHING FEET

But some may ask, What about times when a fellow-believer has fallen
into difficulty, or sin, or disobedience—what should our attitude be then?
Should we pull up our skirts, refuse to have communion or fellowship with
that individual, pass him by as if he were the world's worst, and then
begin talking about him to everyone we know? When our Lord had finished
washing the disciples' feet, He said, "Ye call me Master and Lord: and ye
say well; for so I am. If I then, your Lord and Master, have washed your
feet; ye also ought to wash one another's feet. For I have given you an
example, that ye should do as I have done to you." Again the Apostle
Paul in his letter to the Galatians said, "Brethren, if a man be overtaken
in a fault" (you must not forget that little word "if") "if a man be overtaken in a fault, ye which are spiritual . . ."—what should you do, talk
about him? Oh, no! ". . . ye which are spiritual, restore such an one in
the spirit of meekness; considering thyself, lest thou also be tempted." That
is a forgotten Christian virtue. May God help us to reclaim it and so let
the world see a true disciple of Jesus Christ.

PSALM THIRTY-SIX

"THE FOUNTAIN OF LIFE"

THE 36th Psalm was written by David. In the introduction he presented himself as ". . . the servant of the LORD"—a most suggestive
title. Many men in this world delight in honorable titles. The more
that can be prefixed to a man's name, the more impressive he seems to
appear. But here is a *King* of a great people who spoke of himself as the
servant of the Lord.

There is no room for high-sounding titles in the presence of God. One
might be a Right Honorable, or a Right Reverend, or the great and mighty

Lord so-and-so, all of which I suppose is necessary in this distorted world of ours, but nothing matches the dignity, the simplicity, and the glory of the title given to a true man of God when he is called "the servant of the Lord." Even our Lord humbled Himself and became a servant of all.

TWO CLASSES OF PEOPLE

Let us see what David, "the servant of the LORD," had to say in this Psalm—

> "The transgression of the wicked saith within my heart, that there is no fear of God before his eyes.
>
> "For he flattereth himself in his own eyes, until his iniquity be found to be hateful.
>
> "The words of his mouth are iniquity and deceit: he hath left off to be wise, and to do good.
>
> "He deviseth mischief upon his bed; he setteth himself in a way that is not good; he abhorreth not evil.
>
> "Thy mercy, O LORD, is in the heavens; and thy faithfulness reacheth unto the clouds.
>
> "Thy righteousness is like the great mountains; thy judgments are a great deep: O LORD, thou preservest man and beast.
>
> "How excellent is thy lovingkindness, O God! therefore the children of men put their trust under the shadow of thy wings.
>
> "They shall be abundantly satisfied with the fatness of thy house; and thou shalt make them drink of the river of thy pleasures.
>
> "For with thee is the fountain of life: in thy light shall we see light.
>
> "O continue thy lovingkindness unto them that know thee; and thy righteousness to the upright in heart.
>
> "Let not the foot of pride come against me, and let not the hand of the wicked remove me.
>
> "There are the workers of iniquity fallen: they are cast down, and shall not be able to rise."

In the first four verses of this Psalm David described those whom he called "the wicked." He said their transgressions found an echo within his own heart. As he observed the wicked and rebellious man he concluded within his own heart that the transgression of the wicked was due principally to the fact that there was "no fear of God before his eyes." That charge, incidentally, is the closing accusation in the chain of indictments forged around the conscience of every man in the 3rd chapter of Paul's letter to the

Romans. There it is written that the climax of sin is the total lack of the fear of God before the eyes of men.

As a result of this blindness David noted that the wicked "flattereth himself in his own eyes." That led to the heaping up of iniquity upon iniquity until the mouth of the wicked became a cesspool of all evil. At no time could he find relaxation from the constant expression of wickedness which led him even to devise mischief upon his bed. This picture drawn by David is a dark portrait and one which naturally causes a man to rebel.

The Bible knows of *two classes* of people *only*. The righteous and the wicked. The righteous are not divided into grades nor the wicked into different groups. There are only two divisions in the sight of God. A man is either wicked or he is righteous. A man is either condemned or he is justified. A man is not "pretty good" or "slightly bad." He is either just or unjust. If he is not just and righteous, then he is unjust and unrighteous. It is a simple statement, yet the most difficult for man to accept because he has been so occupied with himself. Having shut out the thought of God, he compares himself with his own ilk, forgetting that God's only standard of righteousness is that which was manifested in His own Son. Either you are as righteous as Christ or you have missed the mark. Of course, it is apparent that no man in himself could be as righteous as Christ. Men are constituted righteous by the atonement of Christ, even as men are condemned already because they have not believed in the name of the only begotten Son of God. The absolutism of the Bible and the gospel is that in which a saved man rejoices and at which an unsaved man rebels. Yet in the very nature of the case it could never be otherwise, for what communion hath light with darkness? But enough of the wicked—let us look at what David had to say about the Lord.

THE PROVISIONS OF THE LORD

In the next few verses David made these statements, "Thy mercy, O LORD, is in the heavens; and thy faithfulness reacheth unto the clouds. Thy righteousness is like the great mountains; thy judgments are a great deep: O LORD, thou preservest man and beast."

The mercy of the Lord is no mere drop. It is so overpowering that it reaches into the heavens. We are saved not for time only, but for eternity. God's mercy takes one right into the heavens.

Recently I heard of a gospel worker who walked up to two men and handed each a tract. One of the men smiled and asked, "Life insurance?" The Christian worker replied, "Yes, for time and eternity."

God's faithfulness is not only manifested in the care of His own on the earth but His faithfulness reaches unto the clouds. There is no power in heaven or earth that can break God's faithfulness to His own. His righteousness which He bestows upon men who believe in Christ is so complete a covering, that it is like a great mountain. ". . . where sin abounded, grace did much more abound. . . ." Again, His judgments are so certain that the depths of them cannot be sounded. Yet this never disturbs a believer because the Lord Himself preserves man and beast. No wonder the Psalmist said, "How excellent is thy loving-kindness, O God! therefore the children of men put their trust under the shadow of thy wings." The shadow of His wings is not only a comforting place but a safe place, a place of trust and gladness and refuge.

The New Testament clearly reveals the significance of the phrase, "the shadow of His wings," for our Lord as He wept over the city of Jerusalem cried, "O Jerusalem, Jerusalem, thou that killest the prophets, and stonest them which are sent unto thee, how often would I have gathered thy children together, even as a hen gathereth her chickens under her wings, and ye would not!" Our Jewish friends who are suffering untold hardships from the hand of cruel inquisitors should ponder these words of our Lord, and then take courage in the words which immediately followed when He said, "Behold, your house is left unto you desolate. For I say unto you, Ye shall not see me henceforth, till ye shall say, Blessed is he that cometh in the name of the Lord." And may God haste that day!

The children of men who place their trust "under His wings," find it also to be a place of satisfaction where the Lord abundantly satisfies with the fatness of His house. That is a strange expression. We are told that "Among the nations of antiquity, fat was regarded as the richest part of animals and therefore became synonymous as the best and prime of everything." Undoubtedly there is an allusion by David to the offerings of the Lord. These offerings enabled the priests to enter into the tabernacle and minister, but they also provided for their sustenance and upkeep. So our Lord Jesus Christ fulfilled this double feature. He is not only the door by which we enter into the fold, but He is the lamb upon whom the believer feasts. But there is more than rest and provision for the believer, under the shadow of the wings of the Lord. There God also makes His people to drink of the river of His pleasures, for, said the Psalmist, ". . . with thee is the fountain of life. . . ."

"THE FOUNTAIN OF LIFE"

This passage I consider the heart of the Psalm. So many people think of God only at the time of extremity. When a man is about to die, a pastor is called to minister and to be a comfort to the man ere he passes out of the present into the hereafter. A jazz-band will never play hymns unless a ship has struck an iceberg. Men never associate God with pleasure. When men think about God it is because of the nearness of death. The thought of God does not beget pleasure in the human breast. It begets fear. But here is a passage in which David, addressing God, said, ". . . and thou shalt make them drink of the river of thy pleasures. For with thee is the fountain of life. . . ."

Men are very short-sighted. They are occupied solely with the passing things of this world, this little span called life. They entirely forget the meaning of eternity. It is amazing how many men make preparation for their families in the event of death but make absolutely no provision for themselves. Undoubtedly they think it is the part of wisdom to enjoy one's self to the fullest and then at the last moment call upon God for salvation. It does not seem to occur to men that God can be associated with pleasure, that there is such a thing as "godly pleasures," and that life, the fountain of life, the wellspring of life is with the Lord and with Him only. Never, until we walk in His light, is it possible to see light or life in its proper perspective.

Some of us have been on both sides of the fence; we've tasted and experienced the pleasures of this world and we have since tasted and experienced the pleasures of the Lord. Please at least give us credit for having a fair amount of judgment. One usually doesn't give up a good thing for a poor one. Indeed, without contradiction, the pleasures of sin cannot even be compared with the sufferings of the people of God, much less with their pleasures! The hymn writer was correct who wrote:

> "Turn your eyes upon Jesus,
>   Look full in His wonderful face,
> And the things of earth will grow strangely dim,
>   In the light of His glory and grace."

Speaking of judgment and a proper perspective and seeing light in His light, I was greatly moved this past week by a letter I received from a young girl who had just graduated from high school. She won a high honor award which carried with it a prize of $100. This young lady, still in her teens, expressed on behalf of herself and her family her joy and pleasure in these Psalm programs. Already in her teens she has learned the wisdom of recognizing the source of life and the responsibility and privileges extended to those who know God. She sent me $10, a tithe, and asked me to put it to whatever work or use I designated, as it was being given to the Lord. That girl has already placed her trust under the shadow of the wings of her Lord. She has drunk from the river of His pleasure. She has already tasted the fountain of life and because she is walking in His light she sees life clearly and in its true perspective.

Even from the viewpoint of pure logic, how much wiser is this girl than that vast multitude of high school girls and boys who, because of their families' neglect of God and His Word, spend their time and lavish their affections upon that which is not bread, but a stone.

How wise was David, this servant of the Lord, to close this Psalm with a prayer for the continued enjoyment of God's lovingkindness; then for preservation from pride of self and the hand of the wicked; finally pointing to the end of those who because of their refusal and rebellion against God are cast down and unable to rise.

From any viewpoint, sin is a hard taskmaster while God is a gracious Father to those who have bowed the knee to Jesus Christ and have received God's Son as their Saviour.

It is only when one walks in the light as He is in the light that one is able to see light and know anything about the fountain of life.

PSALM THIRTY-SEVEN—PART ONE

HOW GOD UNRIDDLES HIS PROVIDENCE

IN the case of the thirty-seventh Psalm, we shall limit our meditation to the first ten verses which read:

> "Fret not thyself because of evildoers, neither be thou envious against the workers of iniquity.
>
> "For they shall soon be cut down like the grass, and wither as the green herb.
>
> "Trust in the LORD, and do good; so shalt thou dwell in the land, and verily thou shalt be fed.
>
> "Delight thyself also in the LORD; and he shall give thee the desires of thine heart.

"Commit thy way unto the LORD; trust also in him; and he shall bring it to pass.

"And he shall bring forth thy righteousness as the light, and thy judgment as the noonday.

"Rest in the LORD, and wait patiently for him: fret not thyself because of him who prospereth in his way, because of the man who bringeth wicked devices to pass.

"Cease from anger, and forsake wrath: fret not thyself in any wise to do evil.

"For evildoers shall be cut off: but those that wait upon the LORD, they shall inherit the earth.

"For yet a little while, and the wicked shall not be: yea, thou shalt diligently consider his place, and it shall not be."

The twenty-fifth verse gives us a clue as to when David wrote this Psalm. There we read: "I have been young, and now am old; yet have I not seen the righteous forsaken, nor his seed begging bread." David was old; therefore, his counsel, as given in the first ten verses, came from the lips of a venerable old man whose experiences gave him the right to be a tutor.

LIFTING THE MIST

Probably one of the greatest riddles of the universe is the seeming prosperity of the wicked. It makes some envious—others perplexed. I have often been asked, "If there is such a personality as God whom you claim the Bible presents as being definitely occupied with this world, is it not strange that evil frequently goes on with fervor, oftentimes unpunished, whereas the righteous man faileth?" There are enough riddles in this universe to baffle the mind of the thinker who is deprived of Bible revelations. In his despair he often expresses his complete disgust with the indifference of Providence, as Pompey said when beaten by Caesar, "There is a mist over the eye of Providence."

The 1st verse of our Psalm exhorts us to fret not because of evil-doers, nor to be envious "against the workers of iniquity." It is apparent that to fret over this condition is natural—to express envy is but the manifestation of one's ego. Why not? Take the case of Brooklyn's recent $427,000 theft. What precision was apparent. How readily did those thieves execute their plans, and surely it looks as if they were 100 per cent successful. If God is in the world how can we account for such happenings?

Contrast these men with the hard-struggling men and women whose honesty is beyond question yet whose success is failure. Is there not an answer somewhere to these riddles? Thank God, there is a solution and it is with singular joy that I pass it on to you. To put it briefly—"it is alone, in the sanctuary, that absolute satisfaction is given the puzzled soul."

In the 73rd Psalm this subject is presented clearly. There the Psalmist said his "feet were almost gone;" his "steps had well nigh slipped," for he "was envious at the foolish" when "he saw the prosperity of the wicked." He observed the wicked; saw, too, the anguish of the righteous. How reconcile it? Asaph said, "When I thought to know this, it was too painful for me; *until* I went into the sanctuary of God; then understood I their end." In the sanctuary, God unriddles His providence and explains the inexplicible.

To give a feeble illustration, there is the remark of a contemporary of Queen Elizabeth who said that Elizabeth, when she was in prison, envied the milkmaid, but if she had known what a glorious reign she was to have afterwards for forty-four years she would not have envied the milkmaid.

"Fret not." Why? "For they shall soon be cut down like the grass." When we understand the latter end of a believer in Christ, at home with his Lord, and contrast that with the awfulness of the latter end of the unbeliever, we are thoroughly appeased. What if the righteous suffer? What if the wicked prosper? It is eternity that counts!

WHAT ABOUT HELL!

"Moderns" sneer at "hell"—laugh it out of existence. However, such attempts are but the confession of a riddled brain and spirit. Hell is so logical, not to say Scriptural, as to be overwhelmingly demonstrable. Take a look at the misery in life! Look at our asylums, our hospitals, our penitentiaries and slums; look at disease and debauchery. If there is no such place as hell, pray sir, where does all this "hell on earth" come from, or lead to?

The whole thing baffles a thinking man. It is a riddle no man can solve by searching or learning. It is solved in the Bible alone. It is in this Book that God reveals His mind and it is therein that the glory of a heaven with the Lord is unfolded. That does give courage, and should. It gives great joy in facing death, knowing that to be absent from the body is to be at home with the Lord.

While we are first exhorted negatively, that is, to "fret not," we are presented in this with several positive exhortations:

> Verse 3 asks us to "Trust in the LORD."
> Verse 4 to "Delight . . . in the LORD."
> Verse 5 to "Commit" our "way unto the LORD."
> Verse 7 to "Rest in the LORD" and, finally, to "wait patiently for him."

To trust in the Lord should be quite natural and easy, for who could be better trusted?   Yet the most difficult task for any soul is to "trust in the Lord."

Notice the third verse says: "Trust in the LORD, and do good." That is God's order. Never reverse it. Always keep both together. Trust; then do; but you will never trust if you put doing before trusting. Works follow faith, never precede faith. If you "Trust in the LORD, and do good" the promise is given, "so shalt thou dwell in the land, and verily thou shalt be fed."

The assertion that I am about to make will be laughed at by some, but it comes from one whose business is primarily economic, whose office is in what is called the "Wall Street" district and who loves business. I believe from the bottom of my heart that our economic ills would fly away like the chaff before the wind were we to experience a general revival in our land, a turning to God and a crying out to Him for salvation. What America needs today is *CHRIST*—not the Christ of modern theology but the Christ of the Bible, the Saviour from sin. What America needs, the world needs. In fact, it is either the Christ or—shall I say it—the antichrist. The choice is narrowing daily.

I recall a visit to my office of a banker from a city in Pennsylvania. This gentleman came to see me regarding the bond account of his institution. We exchanged greetings and began to chat about every-day things, when this banker proceeded to tell me about an experience that seemed to weigh heavily upon him. I noted a little hesitancy. The shocking part of the mockery of our lives is that we talk glibly about almost everything, but feel it an intrusion to speak of vital things to one another. What shams our lives sometimes are!

This gentleman told of backing his car out of the garage, at the rear of his home, one morning on his way to his office. Suddenly he felt the rear wheels pass over what seemed to be a small mound. Intuitively he called loudly to his wife asking about his only daughter, a child of about five—as he sat in his seat, almost stunned. Sure enough, he had accidentally run over his own child. Does a man think of business in such a moment? Indeed not! He picked up his child, placed her in the rear of his car and drove furiously to the nearest hospital. His child was rushed into the operating room. Her head was badly lacerated. The surgeons began operating. The father was told there was little hope, as the surgeons confessed that aid for the child was outside of their realm and required the intervention of another Hand. The banker began to hesitate as he proceeded, saying, "I wonder if you understand me—I began to pray." I responded, "Go ahead, do not hesitate—I thoroughly understand your language for I, too, being a Christian, know the power of prayer." How relieved that gentleman became as he told me of his fervent prayer for his child, as she lay between life and death. Then with great enthusiasm he reported, "God marvelously answered my prayer. My child is perfectly well and the only evidence of the accident is a slight scar on her forehead."

As I listened to this gentleman speaking hesitantly, I could not resist thinking why is it when discussing the deeper things of life and one's relationship to God it seems necessary to apologize. Apologize?—for speaking about the most vital things in life? When our life here is merely a sojourn, and that trinity of questions presses itself upon our hearts and minds for a solution: Where did I come from? Why am I here? Where am I going? I do not apologize for saying that what this country requires more than a "New Deal," a "Square Deal," or any other kind of a "deal" is that we, individually, turn back to the God of the Bible.

DELIGHT IN THE LORD

The exhortation of the fourth verse of this Psalm is particularly noteworthy:

> "Delight thyself also in the LORD; and he shall
> give thee the desires of thine heart."

Have you found your delight in the Lord? Or is your delight in the things of the world? What are the desires of your heart? Here is an assurance that such desires shall be realized if you delight yourself in the Lord. I have occasionally stated during the course of these broadcasts that there are far too many people who take their religion, so to say, decidedly too sadly. It almost seems as if it were a heavy burden upon them. One feels

like shaking such a person and exhorting him to cheer up. The Lord does
not demand that we come into His presence with a sad countenance. The
Bible says, "Delight thyself also in the LORD," and what is more, "Commit
thy way unto the LORD; trust also in him; and he shall bring it to pass."

Bringing this meditation to a close, I invite your attention to a few
comments on verses 7 and 10. We are exhorted to "Rest in the LORD, and
wait patiently for him." Finally we are informed, "For yet a little while, and
the wicked shall not .be: yea, thou shalt diligently consider his place, and
it shall not be." To "Rest in the Lord" is to place one's entire body, soul,
and spirit confidently in His keeping. True rest is enjoyed only when that
is done. To "wait patiently for Him"—have you ever asked yourself just
what that means? Does it mean we are to fold our hands and wait patiently
for death, as some people mistakenly think? Indeed not!

The Scripture gives a beautiful example of waiting for the Lord, in the
case of the Thessalonians to whom Paul wrote in his first letter that he gave
thanks to God always for them, making mention of them in his prayers,
remembering their "work of faith, and labour of love, and patience of hope
in our Lord Jesus Christ, in the sight of God and our Father." He stated
that the fervency of the devotion of these people, as a result of the Apostle's
preaching, had become known everywhere. Paul said:

> "For they themselves shew of us what manner of
> entering in we had among you, and how ye turned
> to God from idols to serve the living and true God;
>
> "And to wait for his Son from heaven, whom he
> raised from the dead, even Jesus, which delivered
> us from the wrath to come."

That's it—"to wait for His Son from heaven." That event is spoken of in
the Scripture as the blessed hope of the believer—to wait patiently for the
Lord, as the Psalmist exhorts us to do, and to confidently anticipate the
return of the Lord Jesus Christ.

Now I know that many false prophets have arisen and I also am aware
that there is a large group of misguided zealots who have made all sorts of
predictions regarding the coming of Christ and, in fact, distorted every doctrine of the Scripture. It is not surprising to find that such is the case. It
merely behooves us to study the Bible for ourselves and to understand what
the mind of our Lord is. There we learn not only that He promised to
return to receive us unto Himself, but also that the apostles and prophets
bear witness to the fact that the Lord will come for His own, and then He
will return physically and bodily to this world to reign as the absolute mon-

arch of the world. Then, and then only, will this poor old sorrow-stricken world know God's "deal," and not man's. It will not be a failure. When that event will take place *no one knows*. We are simply told to watch, wait, and be ready. In fact, we are told that "in such an hour as ye think not the Son of man cometh."

When the disciples, moved by their Jewish heritage, and hopes of the Messianic age, pressed our Lord, after His resurrection, for an answer to their burning question as to when He would restore again the Kingdom to Israel, He responded to them as follows:

> ". . . It is not for you to know the times or the seasons, which the Father hath put in his own power.
>
> "But ye shall receive power, after that the Holy Ghost is come upon you: and ye shall be witnesses unto me both in Jerusalem, and in all Judæa, and in Samaria, and unto the uttermost part of the earth."

After our Lord said this, He was caught up into the heavens and a cloud received Him out of the sight of the gazing disciples. As they looked in wonderment at the ascension of Christ, the Scripture records for us that two men in white apparel appeared, and said to the disciples: ". . . Ye men of Galilee, why stand ye gazing up into heaven? This same Jesus, which is taken up from you into heaven, shall so come in like manner as ye have seen him go into heaven."

If any man goes beyond these statements, which are quotations of Scripture, he is a zealot, lacking knowledge. No man knows the day, nor the hour, but we do know that the promise is sure that He will return. He is coming for His own, and that coming may take place in a hundred years; it may take place in a thousand years. However, we have the assurance that He will return. It is the believer's joy and privilege to wait patiently for the Lord. When that day does come, the 10th verse of our Psalm will be fulfilled, which says: "For yet a little while, and the wicked shall not be: yea, thou shalt diligently consider his place, and it shall not be."

PSALM THIRTY-SEVEN—PART TWO

WHY PRAYERS AT TIMES ARE UNANSWERED

WHEN we considered the first ten verses of the thirty-seventh Psalm, it was my intention to pass over the remaining verses. However, I have received so many interesting letters the past week, which indicated that great blessing was enjoyed from our meditations on the first ten verses, that I feel constrained to comment upon at least a few of the remaining verses.

THAT PERPLEXING QUESTION

It was not surprising to note that in a large number of the letters the same perplexing problems which confronted David are still afflicting many people. Why do the ungodly prosper, while the righteous man faileth? It is a very disturbing problem, but as we observed, the riddle is solved when we enter into the sanctuary and see the end of the unbeliever.

Let me read you a few sentences out of one of the letters I received, which is typical of many. This gentleman asks:

> "Why do the ungodly flourish, while Christian people do not? Why? Why? I have prayed for several years about a matter that means a great deal to me in my little way. Yet no answer. Now it looks as if I shall lose it all. I am like David, old and gray-headed. Still I pray for deliverance in this special matter, but no answer. Yet I can say that 'Thou art righteous.' The Scripture cannot be broken. There is a reason somewhere—yet no deliverance comes to me. I go into the sanctuary to pray therein, but yet how does that help me in my difficulty? Business has fallen off, while the ungodly flourish."

This gentleman added that blessing had come to his own soul as a result of our recent meditations. Yet, there is that pressing, seemingly unanswerable question, Why is there no answer to my prayer?

I have given much thought to this subject, and on two occasions recently, have preached on it in churches in Paterson and Philadelphia. Before seeking an answer to this question, let us look at a few verses from this thirty-seventh Psalm as a background to this subject. Verses 16 and 17 read:

> "A little that a righteous man hath is better than the riches of many wicked.
> "For the arms of the wicked shall be broken: but the LORD upholdeth the righteous."

Then verses 23, 24 and 25, where we read:

> "The steps of a good man are ordered by the LORD: and he delighteth in his way.
> "Though he fall, he shall not be utterly cast down: for the LORD upholdeth him with his hand.
> "I have been young, and now am old; yet have I not seen the righteous forsaken, nor his seed begging bread."

Finally, commencing with verse 35, David said:

> "I have seen the wicked in great power, and spreading himself like a green bay tree.
>
> "Yet he passed away, and, lo, he was not: yea, I sought him, but he could not be found.
>
> "Mark the perfect man, and behold the upright: for the end of that man is peace.
>
> "But the transgressors shall be destroyed together: the end of the wicked shall be cut off.
>
> "But the salvation of the righteous is of the LORD: he is their strength in the time of trouble.
>
> "And the LORD shall help them, and deliver them: he shall deliver them from the wicked, and save them, because they trust in him."

I address my remarks particularly to those who have already received the Lord Jesus Christ as their Saviour and Lord, yet who have found the trials and difficulties of life exceedingly perplexing; such as this gentleman, part of whose letter I have read. At the same time, you who have not confessed Christ, listen with us, for I believe you, too, will be interested and, I trust, led to acknowledge Christ.

There was a time when I thought to raise the question, "Why?" in the presence of God was to express unbelief and therefore it was dishonoring to the Lord. However, as I have read and re-read the Psalms and other portions of the Scripture, I have concluded that it is natural to ask such questions. I have noted that David was frequently in disturbing situations and time and again cried unto God for deliverance and many times asked Him the Why? of his circumstances. He also lamented that God seemed to be so far from him. I would remind you that even our Lord Jesus, prophetically, in the 22nd Psalm, raised this question to God and, historically, did so on the cross, where He asked, "My God, my God, *why* hast thou forsaken me?" Of course, our Lord knew why, for He immediately answered His own question, by saying, "But thou art holy, O thou that inhabitest the praises of Israel." Yet for our sakes I believe He raised the Why? to His Father, that we should not be overcome by disappointment and distress.

We are of like passions with David. We have our perplexing problems. We have our difficulties. Sometimes they seem almost overwhelming. Think, in such moments, of the challenge that our Lord Jesus Christ gave to Peter and His other disciples, when He noticed how many followers left Him because of the difficulty in understanding His word. Christ said, "Will ye also go away?" as He saw the multitudes turn from Him. Peter responded, "Lord, to whom shall we go? thou hast the words of eternal life. And we believe and are sure that thou art that Christ, the Son of the living God." Let us raise the same question again, "*To whom shall we go?*" Do we know of any place or any individual in this world to whom we may go with the perplexing trials and difficulties of life and receive a solution? Try it some time and note how readily you will return, thoroughly disheartened that others have had the same experience and are *seeking*, but have never found, the solution to the same problems. *Seeking, seeking—but never solved.*

"DESTITUTE, AFFLICTED, TORMENTED"

The 23rd and 24th verses of our Psalm read:

> "The steps of a good man are ordered by the LORD: and he delighteth in his way.
> "Though he fall, he shall not be utterly cast down: for the LORD upholdeth him with his hand."

I again take you to the experiences of the gentleman, part of whose letter I read. It is evident that he is a good man; that is, he is a believer in our Lord Jesus Christ. Of such a man the Scripture says, his "steps are ordered by the LORD" and that "the LORD upholdeth him with his hand." Yet this gentleman raises the question—"Why? What about my business which has fallen off? What about the difficulties that I am experiencing with my property?—It looks now as if I shall lose everything."

For an answer to his problem let us look at the eleventh chapter of the letter to the Hebrews, one of the most interesting books in the New Testament. In that chapter we have what has been called the "Hall of Fame by Faith." We have the names of the men and women who accomplished great exploits by faith. By faith is meant that in obedience to God's word they went forth and accomplished those things which God had bidden them to do. The first few verses of that chapter define faith. There we read:

> "Now faith is the substance of things hoped for, the evidence of things not seen.
> "For by it the elders obtained a good report.
> "Through faith we understand . . ."

Thus we know what faith is, what it accomplishes, and how it enables us to understand the mysteries of life. Following that declaration about faith there appears a long list of men and women whose deeds are recorded for us in the Old Testament.

But in verse 36 we learn of an unnamed group, called "others," about whom it is written that they endured trials "of cruel mockings and scourgings, yea, moreover of bonds and imprisonment: "they were stoned, they were sawn asunder, were tempted, were slain with the sword: they wandered about in sheepskins and goatskins; being *destitute, afflicted, tormented*." That unnamed group were able, by faith, to bear their sore trials, persecutions, afflictions, and torments just as definitely as did Abraham, Isaac, Jacob, Moses and Joseph accomplish their mighty works by faith. What is the testimony of the Holy Spirit concerning the group that was stoned and that was destitute, afflicted, and tormented? They were believers. They were devout in their love and devotion to the Lord. What about them? The Bible says concerning them, that of them "the world was not worthy; they wandered in deserts, and in mountains, and in dens and caves of the earth." They all received a good report through faith. What does this all mean? It means that God has always had among His children those who faced terrific trials, and from all outward appearances they bore no evidence of having the blessing of God upon their lives. They were so precious to Him that He said, "the world was not worthy" of them.

I have met Christians in difficulties. I know a few of the difficulties and trials of a Christian's life myself, but I have met few who could fit into the 11th chapter of Hebrews amongst those who were destitute, tormented, and afflicted. Evidently to suffer afflictions is not a new thing for God's people.

That Home in Bethany!

So much for evidence, first, that the problems and difficulties of our lives are no different from the experiences of other ages; second, that God does not look upon the outside, but the inside: He looks at the heart, not at one's dress and outward adornment; finally, that disappointments, trials, and afflictions are equally as glorifying to God as when some outstanding hero of faith performed great exploits that broke into the record.

Now let us come to a specific instance. In Bethlehem, some twenty miles from Jerusalem, was a home where our Lord often retreated, the home of Mary and her sister, Martha, and Lazarus. He found there a delightful oasis in the desert of this world. I do not believe it was a pretentious house, but rather, a modest one. Only three lived in the home, the two sisters and their brother. Suddenly, sickness enters into that home. Lazarus is abed. Can you see Martha hustling about to get a cure for her brother's ills? Can you see Mary sitting by the bedside, unfolding to her brother some of the preciousness of Christ that she had learned of Him as she sat at His feet? Alas, her brother became worse. Their confidence in Christ was so deep and abiding that they sent a messenger to the Lord, saying, "Lord, he whom thou lovest is sick." I believe that that expression is one of the deepest, concerning faith, that it is possible to find in Scripture. They neither asked the Lord to heal their brother, nor invited Him to their home. Their confidence in Christ was so real, it was sufficient just to mention that Lazarus was sick. That is faith. Have you ever prayed like that? What happened? Our Lord received the messenger, and sent him back with His response— "This sickness is not unto death, but for the glory of God, that the Son of God might be glorified thereby."

When the messenger arrived with this message from the Lord, can you see how quickly the gloom was driven out of that home? Do you see Martha hustling to tell Mary, and Mary quietly, yet jubilantly acquainting her brother with the good news that the Lord said his sickness was not unto death, but for the glory of God?

If you were in like circumstances would you be thrilled at such a message? But alas, their brother became worse—their faith was tested sorely— finally, the death rattle was heard and Lazarus died. What do you think those sisters thought? What would you think? Of course, you would ask questions. WHY? WHY? WHY did He say Lazarus would not die? WHY did He not come? WHY? WHY? Thank God the record tells us why, but they knew nothing of it at that time.

THE LORD JESUS GLAD WHILE HIS OWN ARE SAD

Now let me complete the scene. It is several days later. The Lord is still with His disciples in the same place as when the messenger came from Bethany. To His disciples He announces, "Let us go into Judæa again." They ask Him why. He informs them, finally, that their friend Lazarus is asleep, and He is going that He may awaken him out of sleep. Strange, Lord, say they, "If he sleep, he shall do well." Then Christ says plainly, "Lazarus is dead," and adds an amazing statement, saying, "I am glad for your sakes that I was not there, to the intent ye may believe."

The Lord glad He was not there? Did it ever occur to you, that the Lord said He was *glad* that He was not there, in Bethany, where His three friends were undergoing terrific disappointment and a testing of faith? My, what a contrast! The Lord glad—His own loved ones in Bethany, sad. Why was He glad, in the case of Lazarus? He answers His disciples, saying, "I am glad *for your sakes* that I was not there, to the intent ye may believe." In other words, He permitted disappointment to come into those few lives, to teach a most important lesson to twelve men. He permitted suffering in some, for the encouragement of others. That is a glorious principle of faith. Our Lord knew that those disciples would have their trials of faith later on, so, through this experience of Lazarus, Martha, and Mary, He was preparing them for their disappointments. Actually He implied to them, If you have sore trials; if you pray and there seems no answer to your prayer; if you question the goodness of God—remember Lazarus and that little home in Bethany—"Weeping may endure for a night, but joy cometh in the morning." When our Lord arrived in Bethany, He met the cry of the sister, "Lord, if thou hadst been here, my brother had not died." As a result of the sorrow which came into that home we have been enriched beyond measure by the words that came from our Lord's lips, when He said, "I am the resurrection, and the life: he that believeth in me, though he were dead, yet shall he live: and whosoever liveth and believeth in me shall never die."

In all sincerity I ask you—after Christ had raised Lazarus from the dead and given him back to those sorrowing sisters, do you suppose they would have missed the disappointments of those trial-days for the joy that they later experienced? The answer is too obvious.

So I say to you who are sorely pressed by life's sorrows and disappointments—true, you have prayed; yet it seems as if He has either not heard or is indifferent to your cry. It *seems* so, but you should see His plan. Now you may not see it, but later you shall, just as surely as did those two sisters and that brother.

If we weighed eternity properly we would consider it an honor to suffer for His name's sake now.

Are the steps of a righteous man ordered by the Lord, as our Psalm assures us? Were they ordered in Lazarus' case? It did not seem so, for a time, but it was gloriously evidenced later.

Are our steps as believers ordered by the Lord? He said they are. Will we, therefore, thank Him, instead of being disturbed?

Finally, why all these experiences of life for the believer in Christ? The answer is given in the closing verse of this Psalm—". . . the salvation of

the righteous is of the LORD: he is their strength in the time of trouble."
Salvation is of the Lord, not of us, our works or our deeds—a thousand
times, no!! It is of the Lord. Thus we would urge you who have not yet
confessed Christ, to receive and believe Him; then when your trials come,
you shall know Him as your strength "in the time of trouble."

PSALM THIRTY-EIGHT

SORROW FOR SIN—WHAT PLACE HAS IT
IN A MODERN WORLD?

T HE 38th Psalm is exceeded, as a penitential outburst from a sorrow-
ing heart, only by the 51st Psalm. It will be helpful as we read the
Psalm to observe how a sorrowful spirit affected the physical well-
being of the Psalmist. A broken-hearted man is never a physically well man.
I have no doubt that many will find their own experience written in this
Psalm, which reads:

> "O LORD, rebuke me not in thy wrath: neither chasten
> me in thy hot displeasure.
>
> "For thine arrows stick fast in me, and thy hand press-
> eth me sore.
>
> "There is no soundness in my flesh because of thine
> anger; neither is there any rest in my bones because of
> my sin.
>
> "For mine iniquities are gone over mine head: as an
> heavy burden they are too heavy for me.
>
> "My wounds stink and are corrupt because of my fool-
> ishness.
>
> "I am troubled; I am bowed down greatly; I go mourn-
> ing all the day long.
>
> "For my loins are filled with a loathsome disease: and
> there is no soundness in my flesh.
>
> "I am feeble and sore broken: I have roared by reason
> of the disquietness of my heart.
>
> "Lord, all my desire is before thee; and my groaning
> is not hid from thee.
>
> "My heart panteth, my strength faileth me: as for the
> light of mine eyes, it also is gone from me.
>
> "My lovers and my friends stand aloof from my sore;
> and my kinsmen stand afar off.
>
> "They also that seek after my life lay snares for me:
> and they that seek my hurt speak mischievous things,
> and imagine deceits all the day long.

"But I, as a deaf man, heard not; and I was as a dumb man that openeth not his mouth.

"Thus I was a man that heareth not, and in whose mouth are no reproofs.

"For in thee, O LORD, do I hope: thou wilt hear, O Lord my God.

"For I said, Hear me, lest otherwise they should rejoice over me: when my foot slippeth, they magnify themselves against me.

"For I am ready to halt, and my sorrow is continually before me.

"For I will declare my iniquity; I will be sorry for my sin.

"But mine enemies are lively, and they are strong: they that hate me wrongfully are multiplied.

"They also that render evil for good are mine adversaries; because I follow the thing that good is.

"Forsake me not, O LORD: O my God, be not far from me.

"Make haste to help me, O Lord my salvation."

It is advisable to keep in the back of our minds the words of the Psalmist found in the 18th verse, ". . . I will be sorry for my sin." First, we desire to call attention to the two types of sorrow. Then we shall look specifically at the substance of this Psalm. It is not unusual for men to be exceedingly sorrowful for their sin. The sorrow may be good; and again, it may not be good. It may reveal a true heart of repentance, but it could also reveal a heart of stoical indifference. All too frequently men have been sorry that their sin has become known rather than exhibiting genuine sorrow for their sin. Likewise, men have been sorry for the disastrous results that followed their sin though they did not repent of the sin which in reality was responsible for the loss that followed.

Sorrow for Sin

A perfect example of this type of sorrow may be observed in the case of Esau. The Scripture designates Esau as a profane person. Do not get the idea that he used profanity. When the Bible calls a man profane it is because that person has lost all appreciation of true spiritual values. A man may be a cultured, refined gentleman—distinguished for his use of beautiful English; he may frown upon profanity as an expression of an uncouth nature and yet he may be a profane person; he may be entirely devoid of any understanding of spiritual things and occupied solely with the things of the earth. Esau was that type of profane person. For *one* morsel of meat he sold his birthright. Men today sell their lives for even less than that for which Esau sold his birthright. Even in our land of the "brave and the free," men are all too willing to sell their civil liberty for a mess of pottage or relief from a little poverty. Poverty is far from the worst affliction a man can experience. Many of our greatest leaders were reared in poverty. The loss of self-respect and the urge to work is far worse.

Esau sold his birthright for one morsel of meat. Afterward when he would have inherited the blessing that came with the birthright he was rejected, for Jacob had already received it. Esau found no place of repentance, though he sought it *carefully* with tears. Here was a man who was sorry for his sin. He wept bitter tears over the results of his sin, but found no place of repentance though he sought it carefully.

Now note the contrast in the case of the Apostle Peter. Peter was a brawny fisherman. Undoubtedly the smell of the salt was on his garments. One needed to be in his presence for only a few moments to observe that his language betrayed the fact that he was a fisherman. Impetuous though he was, he had many fine qualities. His brother, Andrew, was not only a partner in his "fish business," but a joint occupant of Peter's home. They lived together. Peter was a married man. He either had an excellent mother-in-law or he was easy to get along with, for it appears that his mother-in-law lived with them. However, let's not forget his wife, Mrs. Simon Peter. Dr. Scroggie says that she must have been a fine wife for she did not raise an objection to Peter bringing along an unexpected Guest for dinner when her mother lay sick abed with a fever!

Peter was also a devout man. I have no doubt he dearly loved the Lord, but it was not until the wee hours of the morning of his Lord's passion that he learned the lesson that spiritual victories are not won by the arm of flesh, and that brawn and sinews are not the weapons of a spiritual man. He undoubtedly was shocked out of his complacency, yet not convinced of his weakness, when the Lord had said earlier that evening, ". . . this day, even in this night, before the cock crow twice, thou shalt deny me thrice." That strong seaman wilted before a maid. The Apostle denied his Lord. A little later, when some suggested that his speech betrayed him, that he was a Galilean and one of the band who followed the Lord, Peter reverted to the fiery vocabulary of his fisherman days—he began to curse and to swear saying, "I know not this man of whom ye speak." Immediately while he yet spoke, the cock crew the second time. Then what happened? The

Bible description of the scene is graphic! The Lord was inside the palace of the high priest. When the cock crew for the second time the Lord turned and looked upon Peter. I wish it were possible for some artist to paint that scene, giving us the benefit of the expression upon the Lord's face, and that which was upon the face of His enemies and also on the Apostle Peter's. As Peter met his Lord's look he remembered the Lord's words, and went out, and wept bitterly. I do not believe that Peter wept because he was found out, but rather because he had so bitterly disappointed his Lord and betrayed Him. Peter's tears evidenced true repentance.

Dr. Harry Rimmer's new book, "The Crucible of Calvary," which I greatly enjoyed, speaks of Peter and his tears, as follows: "The eye can see more than the lips can ever utter. The tears of the contrite are sweet in the eyes of God; the weeping of a penitent heart is acceptable to the Almighty as the only offering He can receive. So in that bitter bath of hot and blinding tears, Peter was transformed and reborn. In after years Peter had occasion to bless God for the burning experience of that dark hour. Peter came out of the Crucible of Calvary, saved." Dr. Rimmer further comments: "We have met men in the ministry who have denied Christ with a more shameful defection and a more reprehensible cowardice than ever marked the action of Peter, because they were afraid to be thought 'back numbers.'" Then he makes this indictment, "After Satan found how impossible it was to assail the strongholds of Christian faith from the outside, he joined the church and proceeded to capture our seats of learning." We might add to Dr. Rimmer's comment that Satan's emissaries even this very morning will occupy many supposedly Christian pulpits. We cannot point the finger of scorn at Peter, but we can profit from his experiences. Peter was moved by godly sorrow which led to true repentance.

CONFESSION OF SIN

But notice the order which David observed in the 18th verse of the 38th Psalm, "For I will declare my iniquity; I will be sorry for my sin." Men find it difficult to confess their sins. I think that is true of Christians as well as non-Christians. It is true of the saved man as well as of the unsaved man. How often have you substituted a true confession of your sin before the Lord for an *absolutely evasive* prayer, "Lord, forgive us our sins." The hymn, "If I have wounded any soul today . . . Dear Lord, forgive" may be a splendid theme song, but it is neither honest nor Biblical. The

New Testament Epistles urge a Christian to *confess* his sins. Whenever the problem of sin enters a Christian's life, God does not urge him to ask for the forgiveness of sins. Listen to what He does say, "If we (Christians) *confess* our sins, he (God) is faithful and just to forgive us our sins, and to cleanse us from all unrighteousness."

Dr. Wilbur Smith, of the Moody Bible Institute, told me that Heinrich Meyer, the great German theologian, directs specific attention to the phrase "our sins" in this passage, maintaining that it requires the naming of each one before the Lord. Dr. A. T. Robertson, the great Greek scholar, translates the passage "If we keep on confessing *our sins.* . . ."

Now let us look specifically at this Psalm. It is very evident that David made his complaint before the Lord. He did not answer his critics nor his enemies. In that respect he emulated his Lord. Our Lord was dumb before His accusers. He answered them not a word. David said, "But I, as a deaf man, heard not; and I was as a dumb man that openeth not his mouth. Thus I was as a man that heareth not, and in whose mouth are no reproofs." That attitude was manifested by our Lord and also by David against those who made accusations. In the case of our Lord, of course, the accusations were untrue. In the case of David, some probably were true, but many were not true. David knew about his sin and he confessed it before the Lord.

THE LORD'S DEALINGS WITH HIS OWN

No man wept more bitter tears for his sin against God than did the writer of this 38th Psalm. So depressed was he about his disobedience and the pricking of his conscience by God that he said, ". . . thine arrows stick fast in me, and thy hand presseth me sore." God did that to one who served and loved Him. God is harder (I use that word advisedly) on His own than He is on the world. He will stick His arrows in their conscience and He will press them sore with His hands. So sorely was David pressed that he was physically ill. There was no soundness in his flesh, there was no rest in his bones. His wounds were like an open sore, but he recognized that his corruption was due to his own foolishness. He was depressed—he was bowed down—his mourning was not only during the night season, but all the day long. While he was a strong man, he was feeble and sore broken. His eyes had no light in them. He was a pathetic sight.

Immediately, his enemies took advantage of his distress. They laid snares for him, they spoke mischievous things about him. Then they increased their imaginations, and magnified his disobedience. What imaginations an enemy can develop in attempting to do another harm!! David said they imagined deceits all the day long. Should he have justified himself against their attacks? Should he have defended himself against their unwarranted assertions? What a mistake he would have made had he done so! He confessed his sin before the Lord. His sin was ever before him. He bowed his heart and conscience before God, but he paid no attention to his enemies. He allowed them to exaggerate his sin and imagine deceits against him. As far as they were concerned he was a deaf man and a mute. But he did something that was most important and absolutely essential. He poured out his heart before the Lord—he confessed his sin to Him.

This past week we received several letters from people who are in distress. In most of the cases their circumstances are the direct result of their own disobedience to God's Word. There are others listening in, who have had similar experiences, but have not expressed them. I must confess that an examination of my own life and the lives of hundreds of others has led me to the conclusion that with few exceptions when a believer gets into trouble it is because of his own disobedience to the Word of God. What should be our attitude in such situations? Exactly that which David manifested in this Psalm. Pour out our heart to the Lord, confess our sin before Him, be sorry for it, quit it by His grace, and ask Him to dominate our life, place our case in His hands, and trust Him for the forgiveness He has promised and the cleansing He has assured and the strength He will give. Then go on rejoicing in the knowledge of a Saviour who saves unto the uttermost all those who come unto Him.

SAVING FAITH

This message must not close, however, without making a matter clear to those who have not bowed the knee to Jesus Christ. Sorrow for sin and confession of sin, while important and in a measure a prerequisite, must not be looked upon as a means of salvation. You could be sorry for your sins throughout all the ages of eternity, but that would never save you. Your confession of sin will never save you. There is only one thing that saves and that is the blood of our Lord Jesus Christ. It is the blood that maketh atonement for the soul. Sorrow for sin is good, confession of sin is admirable, but both are insufficient apart from faith in the Lord Jesus Christ.

Repentance is important, it is a prerequisite. But Paul preached a powerful gospel; a two-edged sword was always in his hand. He preached repentance toward God and faith in the Lord Jesus Christ. You cannot separate them. Repentance without faith will never avail. Repentance with faith will always avail. I love the words of Toplady's immortal hymn, "Rock of Ages." You will remember the second and third stanzas read:

> "Not the labor of my hands,
> Can fulfill Thy law's demands;
> Could my zeal no respite know,
> Could my tears forever flow,
> All for sin could not atone,
> Thou must save, and Thou alone.

> "Nothing in my hand I bring,
> Simply to Thy cross I cling;
> Naked, come to Thee for dress;
> Helpless, look to Thee for grace;
> Foul, I to the fountain fly,
> Wash me, Saviour, or I die."

There we have the gospel in poetry. Salvation from eternal death can only come by an application of the Lord's own blood shed on Calvary's tree. There is only one fountain "for sin and for uncleanness." It is available to all who want to be clean.

PSALM THIRTY-NINE

A DIRGE THAT ENDS WITH A SMILE

THE 39th Psalm is dedicated by David to Jeduthun, one of the chief Musicians of Israel. We have already observed that there were three men who occupied the position of chief Musician during the days of David, the King. They were Asaph, Jeduthun and Heman. I do not believe that any of us have ever heard the singing of sacred music comparable to that of David's reign. Jeduthun was an instructor in music. He led the Levites in the singing of their praises. His name is quite interesting. It means "praise-giver."

A DIRGE FOR A PRAISE-GIVER

As one hurriedly reads through this 39th Psalm he is rather surprised that David should have chosen Jeduthun as the one to whom the Psalm should be sent, since it is more in the nature of a dirge than a Psalm of praise. Yet I am sure that by the time we complete our meditation all will agree that David used keen judgment and undoubtedly was directed by the Holy Spirit when he sent this Psalm to the "praise-giver," Jeduthun, for while it begins with a dirge, it ends with joy.

Commencing with the 1st verse, we read:

> "I said, I will take heed to my ways, that I sin not with my tongue: I will keep my mouth with a bridle, while the wicked is before me.
>
> "I was dumb with silence, I held my peace, even from good; and my sorrow was stirred.
>
> "My heart was hot within me, while I was musing the fire burned: then spake I with my tongue,
>
> "LORD, make me to know mine end, and the measure of my days, what it is; that I may know how frail I am.
>
> "Behold, thou hast made my days as an handbreadth: and mine age is as nothing before thee: verily every man at his best state is altogether vanity. Selah.
>
> "Surely every man walketh in a vain shew: surely they are disquieted in vain: he heapeth up riches, and knoweth not who shall gather them.
>
> "And now, Lord, what wait I for? my hope is in thee."

This brings us to the end of the seventh verse. Let us stop there and note some of the things mentioned in these earlier verses. I particularly like the self exhortation that David expressed when he stated: ". . . I will take heed to my ways, that I sin not with my tongue: I will keep my mouth with a bridle, while the wicked is before me. I was dumb with silence, I held my peace. . . ."

Notice how distinctly personal the Psalmist was in these verses. He was not occupied with the sins and shortcomings of others. He was not using the transgressions of others as a cloak behind which he might hide—rather he recognized his sin and acknowledged that the Lord alone was his hope. So often men seek to hide behind the transgressions of others. You have frequently heard men say when invited to consider Christ, "Oh well, the church is full of hypocrites," as if they were thus excused because of the transgressions of others. The message of this Psalm may be directed to all of us, individually. We, too, will be wise if we take heed to our ways; if we see to it that we sin not with our tongue. What a lot of sorrow we would thus save ourselves!

A FOUR-FINGERED LIFE

I like David's attitude which he expressed in the 4th verse, when he asked: "LORD, make me to know mine end, and the measure of my days, what it is; that I may know how frail I am."

Occasionally, when listening to the boastings of man it would seem as if he were thoroughly oblivious to his frailty. Most of us spend our days as if we were accountable to none, as if this life were all that was offered to us. Not so with David who requested the Lord to show him several things—first, that he might know his end; second, that he might know the measure of his days; finally, that he might know how frail he was.

Have we ever considered these things? Have we ever asked ourselves the question, What is my end? Wouldn't we like to know the measure of our days? If we did know, I am inclined to think it would change our behavior, and possibly the entire course of our lives. In the midst of life how differently we would act if we recognized that our strength lay alone in the grace of God, who gives us the breath of life.

In the 5th verse David said: "Behold, thou hast made my days as an handbreadth; and mine age is as nothing before thee: verily every man at his best state is altogether vanity. Selah."

We have already noted that this Psalm begins with a dirge. Now a dirge is not a very pleasant tune on a Sunday morning, yet I know of no better time to be reminded that one's life is but a handbreadth, in other words, only four fingers broad. Will you bear that metaphor in mind? When next you look at your hand, say to yourself, there is the measure of my days. Then ask yourself, to what use am I to put my four-fingered life?

Themistocles died when he was almost 107 years of age. He was grieved to go and said, "Now I am to die when I begin to be wise." How essential, therefore, that we take heed of the priceless possession we have. In the sight of God and in comparison to eternity, David was accurate when he said, "mine age is as nothing before thee." How true it is that ". . . every man at his best state is altogether vanity."

When the Psalmist said that "every man at his best state is altogether vanity," he was expressing the divine view of our righteousness. Bear in mind, it is of our righteousness, that is, the good which we accomplish, which, measured by every standard of human morality, glorifies us, that David said "it is altogether vanity." Another passage of Scripture maintains that "our righteousnesses are as filthy rags" in His sight? Does that mean that God honors or commends a man because of his sin? A thousand times, no! We are to understand by that remark that the only thing that can possibly be satisfactory to God is absolute perfecion. It is apparent that nothing but perfection can satisfy God.

You do not suppose that the great Paderewski would be interested in listening to the playing of a novice, or that Michelangelo could have thrilled over the scrawling of a kindergarten child of six. As an artist demands perfection—so God is satisfied only with perfection. Anything less perfect than God is sin. Everything lacking perfection is marred and spotted. Is it any wonder that the Bible says "our righteousnesses are as filthy rags?" Such is the viewpoint of God, whose eyes penetrate into the deepest recesses of the human heart, thereby analyzing both the act, and the motive behind the act, and concluding that the very best man can produce, is in His sight "as filthy rags."

THE GOSPEL

What should we do under the circumstances? David answered that in the 7th verse of this Psalm. He asked "what wait I for?" and answered, "my hope is in thee."

The gospel is good news to the man who will acknowledge that the Bible description of him is true. God does not desire the death of any sinner. He did not send His Son into the world to condemn the world; but that the world through Him might be saved. So God offers to every man His gift, which is eternal life through Jesus Christ our Lord. From such a man He removes his transgressions and clothes him with the righteousness of Christ, which is the perfection of God.

Now we look at the 6th verse for a moment or two, and as we do, try to visualize it in your mind. It is an interesting characterization of man: "Surely every man walketh in a vain shew: surely they are disquieted in vain: he heapeth up riches, and knoweth not who shall gather them."

Did you ever see a mannequin parading before an amused and interested people? Her head is held high, she struts along like a peacock all decked in garments, but not her own. For a moment she may proudly strut about, but alas, her strutting is but a vain show. Such is the picture David presents of vain man. He says of such a man, "he heapeth up riches, and knoweth not who shall gather them." That man may get the Police Department to put up "No Parking" signs in front of his mansion, so that his chauffeur may with ease drive him up to his door, while the doorman awaits upon his honor. He may provide what one very rich man did for his children—as one of his own expressed to a friend of mine when she said, "Our father gave us gold plates on which to eat our food, yet in reality we never had a father. Even at the dinner table we children dared not raise a voice or address him, so engrossed was he with big business." Were I to mention the name of this father you would immediately recognize the truth of the Psalmist's statement, when he said, "he heapeth up riches, and knoweth not who shall gather them." That gentleman's estate has been depleted by all sorts of suits by his heirs. How often does the man who heaps up riches overlook the fact that he is working for death, that he is laboring for that which he cannot hope to enjoy. Alas, alas, what a vain show. Such a man has entirely overlooked the goodness of our God, who giveth to all men all things richly to enjoy.

David conceded that this description of man was true concerning him, so he cried out in the 7th verse "Lord, what wait I for?" He answered, "my hope is in thee." Then he invited the Lord to do certain things for him. He asked, "Deliver me from all my transgressions: make me not the reproach of the foolish. Remove thy stroke away from me. . . ." In the 11th verse, he acknowledged: "When thou with rebukes dost correct man for iniquity, thou makest his beauty to consume away like a moth: surely every man is vanity. Selah." "Deliver me from all my transgressions. . . . Remove thy stroke away from me." These two urgent requests can be presented by you and me in this day, just as surely and with just as definite results.

Finally this vain show of man drove David to pray, and his prayer is recorded in the last two verses of our Psalm.

> "Hear my prayer, O LORD, and give ear unto my cry;
> hold not thy peace at my tears: for I am a stranger
> with thee, and a sojourner, as all my fathers were.
> "O spare me, that I may recover strength before I go
> hence, and be no more."

Let me give a more literal translation of the Hebrew text of the 13th verse. In our English Bible, we read: "O spare me, that I may recover strength, before I go hence, and be no more."

You who are Israelites, and have the Hebrew Psalm before you, will bear with me when I state that scholars are agreed that a desirable translation of the text would read: "Look away from me, that I may recover my smile, before I go hence, and be no more."

That almost seems like a contradiction of facts—"Look away from me, that I may recover my smile or my brightness." If David had written, "Look on me that I may recover my smile" most of us would agree, but "Look away from me" does seem an odd request. What does it mean? That prayer of David is the heart of the gospel! Let's look at a comparable New

Testament scene. It is perfectly analogous to this one. It is the parable our Lord told for the benefit of those who "trusted in themselves that they were righteous, and despised others." It is recorded in the 18th chapter of St. Luke's Gospel. Our Lord said:

> "Two men went up into the temple to pray; the one a Pharisee, and the other a publican.
>
> "The Pharisee stood and prayed thus with himself, God, I thank thee, that I am not as other men are, extortioners, unjust, adulterers, or even as this publican.
>
> "I fast twice in the week, I give tithes of all that I possess."

Note that this man while praying believed that he was addressing God, yet invited God to look *at him* in contrast to "this publican" by his side. He may have been a Pharisee, a doctor of the law with a D.D. degree, yet he had not the slightest acquaintance with the holiness of God as revealed in the Mosaic Law.

Of the publican, a despised man, the Lord said: "And the publican, standing afar off, would not lift up so much as his eyes unto heaven, but smote upon his breast, saying, God be merciful to me a sinner." Concerning this publican our Lord said, "I tell you, this man went down to his house justified rather than the other. . . ."

We Gentiles have badly misapplied that Scripture. How often in missions are derelicts invited to go up to the penitent bench and pray, "God be merciful to me a sinner." But for all that, probably ninety-nine out of one hundred have not the slightest appreciation of the import of that prayer.

The Pharisee of whom the Lord spoke directed attention in his prayer to his own works, while the publican was saying exactly what David said in this Psalm—Look away from me, for a look at me will consume me; will cause me to lose my smile; will make me to become frail. Look away from me, not at me. Thus, when the publican prayed, "God be merciful to me a sinner" he completed the scene which David began, when he said, "Look away from me," for the publican was using intelligent spiritual language, directing the Lord to look at the mercy seat within the temple, upon which was placed the blood of the sacrifice—Look away from me, but look upon Christ. So to paraphrase the prayer of the publican, he said, in so many words, Lord, look away from me, but look upon the mercy seat.

When that was done, both David and the publican recovered their strength and regained their smile. Their countenance brightened. Such is the experience of every man who has received the testimony that God has given concerning His Son.

PSALM FORTY—PART ONE

THE SONG OUR LORD JESUS SINGS!

DURING this series of meditations in the Psalms, we have considered some marvelous Psalms, such as the 8th, 16th, 23rd and others. Great as they are, none surpass the 40th Psalm.

We will limit this message to the first eight verses of the Psalm, which read:

> "I waited patiently for the LORD; and he inclined unto me, and heard my cry.
>
> "He brought me up also out of an horrible pit, out of the miry clay, and set my feet upon a rock, and established my goings.
>
> "And he hath put a new song in my mouth, even praise unto our God: many shall see it, and fear, and shall trust in the LORD.
>
> "Blessed is that man that maketh the LORD his trust, and respecteth not the proud, nor such as turn aside to lies.
>
> "Many, O LORD my God, are thy wonderful works which thou hast done, and thy thoughts which are to us-ward: they cannot be reckoned up in order unto thee: if I would declare and speak of them, they are more than can be numbered.
>
> "Sacrifice and offering thou didst not desire; mine ears hast thou opened; burnt-offering and sin-offering hast thou not required.
>
> "Then said I, Lo, I come: in the volume of the book it is written of me,
>
> "I delight to do thy will, O my God: yea, thy law is within my heart."

On several occasions during the course of these broadcasts I have used the expression, "Messianic Psalms." That term has been used to describe those Psalms, universally recognized, in which the Messiah is the speaker, or in which the Messiah is presented. The 40th Psalm is a Messianic Psalm. While David was the inspired penman, he was not speaking of himself, he voiced the language of the Christ. At least seven of the Psalms are quoted or referred to in the New Testament. These Psalms are the 12th, 16th, 22nd, 40th, 69th, 109th and 110th. Of this group none is given as much space as the quotation from the 40th Psalm. We have, therefore, the authority of the Holy Spirit Himself that the speaker in this Psalm is not David, but Christ.

Before we look at the New Testament reference to the 40th Psalm I would like to quote from the writings of that venerable Irish prelate, Dr. William Alexander, whose writings on the Psalms have been my great delight. He was the Archbishop of Armagh and the Primate of all Ireland. He delivered a series of scholarly and spiritual addresses at Oxford University in 1875, giving what is known as Bampton lectures, on the general theme, "The Witness of the Psalms to Christ and Christianity." I have been moved deeply as I have read his lectures, noting the exquisite language he used and the evident deep insight that he had into the Scriptures. As he delivered his closing address, in an auditorium crowded with clergymen and students, he quoted, for the benefit of the clergy, the remark of that great scholar, now almost forgotten, Salmasius, who, when in the sight of death, exclaimed: "Ah! I have lost the immensity of that most precious thing, time. If I had but one year more it should be spent in studying the Psalms and St. Paul's Epistles." The aging bishop then said, "As the evening of my days draws on, that opportunity has been given to me." Finally, turning to the great company of university students who packed the gallery, he said: "The sight of that gallery is one that I can never forget. My sons! love and study the Psalms. You will discover that it will indeed requite studious regard with opportune delight. In it you will find Him whom it is best to know, Jesus, your Lord and your God."

I do trust our meditations in the Psalms have brought many to know our Lord Jesus Christ. As this great clergyman said, He is to be found in the Psalms.

THE SPIRIT'S ILLUMINATION OF THE 40TH PSALM

Upon the testimony of the Holy Scriptures, our Lord Jesus is to be found in the 40th Psalm. Let us, therefore, examine that testimony, which appears in the 10th chapter of the Epistle to the Hebrews. I would urge a careful reading of that chapter, which reveals the value of the sacrifice of Christ and the purposes of God in that sacrifice.

We learn from that portion of Scripture what ought to be self-evident —that the blood of bulls and of goats cannot possibly take away sins. But we all have sins, and they must be removed. What then? It is just here that the Spirit refers to the 40th Psalm saying, concerning our Lord as

He entered into this world, that ". . . Sacrifice and offering thou wouldest not, but a body hast thou prepared me: in burnt-offerings and sacrifices for sin thou hast had no pleasure. Then said I, Lo, I come (in the volume of the book it is written of me), to do thy will, O God."

This, you will recognize, is a quotation of part of the 40th Psalm. Thus, Christ is the speaker. It is He who said, "Lo, I come . . . to do thy will, O God." What that will is, we have revealed to us in what immediately follows in the 10th chapter of Hebrews. It is written: "By the which will we are sanctified through the offering of the body of Jesus Christ once for all." Furthermore, it is written that ". . . after he had offered one sacrifice for sins for ever, sat down on the right hand of God. . . . For by one offering he hath perfected for ever them that are sanctified."

Christ came to do the Father's will, because the blood of bulls and of goats could never take away sin. A body was prepared Him for that purpose. The Father's will was that He offer His body in death, as a sacrifice for sin. That sacrifice was so stupendous it had to be made just once, and through it He forever put away sins—your sins and my sins; but more than that, He perfected us forever. You ask how? The Bible answers, by His offering. There is only one remedy for sin, only one "cleanser" for sin, it is the blood, the precious blood of Jesus Christ, God's Son!

Is it any wonder that our entire civilization has changed as a result of Christ's coming into this world, though such is but a mere by-product of His coming? That cross, that sacrifice upon the cross, is God's answer to sin. It is God's provision for the sinner. All we need to do is to receive that provision, and return thanks unto God.

It may surprise some who have casually read the 40th Psalm, who have not gone beyond the surface and therefore labor under the impression that David was speaking of himself, to now learn that our Lord is speaking of His own experience; that it was He who waited patiently for His Father, and that He had to go down into a horrible pit and from it be lifted out by His Father, who in turn set His feet upon a rock and established His goings.

Those of you who are familiar with your Bible will recall that it was said of our Lord Jesus Christ, by the soldiers who entered into the temple to lay hands upon Him and to bring Him before the proper tribunal for trial, "Never man spake like this man." They were held breathless by Him, spellbound, in fact; so that their hands became powerless and they returned to their superiors with their task unfinished. Their only defense was, "Never man spake like this man." From the time our Lord Jesus Christ spoke, until this very day, the words of men have been but sounding brass and tinkling cymbals. Where have you ever heard words such as, "I am the way, the truth, and the life: no man cometh unto the Father, but by me"? or "In my Father's house are many mansions. . ." ? or that exquisite gospel message, that "God so loved the world, that he gave his only begotten Son, that whosoever believeth in him should not perish, but have everlasting life"?

But have you noticed how repeatedly our Lord spoke in parables? Parables are pictures. They are used to symbolize or to describe deep experiences. Thus in the 40th Psalm, our Lord speaking of the agony of the cross, used a picturesque parable. Consider what He said, when He cried, "I waited patiently for the LORD . . ." Does there flash into your mind a picture of the scene at Calvary just as our Lord was about to die? The forsaken Son of God is hanging there alone, but for the few soldiers who remain at the foot of His cross. The mob has already dashed for shelter, thoroughly frightened by the disturbances of nature. Can you not hear Him cry, "I waited patiently for the LORD"? He was not disappointed, for He added, "and he inclined unto me, and heard my cry." After that, He spoke of His glorious resurrection. He declared His Father brought Him out. In speaking of His death, our Lord described it as "an horrible pit." I think we will find it interesting to examine the word "pit," and thereby observe why our Lord used it. An incident in the Old Testament will aid us.

You will recall that Joseph was sold by his brethren, who were incensed against him. But before they sold him they stripped him of his coat of many colors, and then cast him into a pit. That pit was empty: there was no water in it. While he was in that pit his brethren sat down to eat bread. Then they lifted up their eyes and beheld a company of Ishmaelites coming towards them. Judah finally persuaded his brethren to sell Joseph to these men. In the casting of Joseph into the pit by his brethren we have a picture of Calvary.

You will remember that the Gospels also record the earlier scene at Calvary. While our Lord was hanging upon the cross, the people sat down idly to watch the proceedings, absolutely indifferent to the fact that they were crucifying the Lord of glory. The Scripture states they did it in ignorance. Our Lord was cast into a horrible pit. He describes it as "miry clay." He was in that pit for three days and three nights. But He was not left there. He was raised from the dead. In the 40th Psalm He spoke of His Father's resurrection of Him, saying, "He brought me up also" and then the Father set His feet upon a rock, and established His goings.

THE LAMB AND THE SONG OF THE LAMB

I am particularly impressed with the 3rd verse of this Psalm, which reads: "And he hath put a new song in my mouth, even praise unto our God: many shall see it, and fear, and shall trust in the LORD."

Possibly, few of us realize that our Lord Jesus sings, and that He has a new song. That is because, all too often, we have a limited view of the ministry of Christ at Calvary. We are inclined to look at it exclusively from the side of suffering and humiliation. We seem to have lost sight of the God ward aspect of the cross.

It is written that our Lord endured the cross and despised its shame for the joy that was set before Him. Thus our Lord saw something beyond the cross. It is also written that because of His voluntary humiliation, "God . . . hath highly exalted him, and given him a name which is above every name," assuring Him "that at the name of Jesus every knee should bow," and "every tongue . . . confess that Jesus Christ is Lord, to the glory of God the Father." How I long for the moment when all the world will bow their knees and confess with their lips the Lordship of Christ.

Raised from the dead, the Father gave Christ a new song. In the 22nd Psalm our Lord is heard singing this song, offering praises unto His Father in the midst of the entire company of the redeemed. In the book of The Revelation, which is the last book of the Bible, we discover a great company joining in a great song. It is recorded in the 15th chapter of that book, commencing with the 3rd verse.

> "And they sing the song of Moses the servant of God, and the song of the Lamb, saying, Great and marvelous are thy works, Lord God Almighty; just and true are thy ways, thou King of saints.
>
> "Who shall not fear thee, O Lord, and glorify thy name? for thou only art holy: for all nations shall come and worship before thee; for thy judgments are made manifest."

Did you notice that they sing the song of Moses, the servant of God, and the song of the Lamb? The song of Moses is found in the 32nd chapter of

Deuteronomy. Moses *composed* that song. The song of the Lamb is mentioned in the 40th Psalm. The Lord was *given* that song. Its theme is "praise unto our God." He said, "many shall see it, and fear, and shall trust in the LORD."

WE, TOO, MAY HAVE A NEW SONG

Because the Lord had these experiences on the cross, as described in the 40th Psalm, we, who are believers in Christ, can now say the same things. We have been brought up out of a horrible pit of miry clay. We have had our feet placed upon the Rock, and our goings established. We have had a new song placed in our mouths. It is a song of praise unto our God.

I do hope you have noticed, as we have commented upon these early verses of the 40th Psalm, that our Lord ascribes every act of deliverance to His Father. He heard His cry. He inclined His ear to Him. He brought Him up. He set His feet upon a rock. He established His goings. He put a new song in His mouth. Do you wonder why the theme of the song is praise unto His Father. What the Father did for Christ Jesus His Son, His Son does for us. The Father did all for Christ. Christ does all for us. Cease, therefore, your vain struggle and trust Him for His salvation, which is complete and perfect.

It is good to read and re-read the 5th verse, especially in these days when we seem to think we have so much trouble and difficulty. There we are told: "Many, O LORD my God, are thy wonderful works which thou hast done, and thy thoughts which are to us-ward: they cannot be reckoned up in order unto thee: if I would declare and speak of them, they are more than can be numbered." If we would sit down to number the blessings that the Lord has showered upon us, what praise we would render! We would have to confess that they are more than can be numbered.

We have only begun to enter into the glories of the 40th Psalm. But in closing, let me say this, in the 22nd Psalm we have a description of Calvary and the crucifixion of the God-Man, Christ Jesus, in the sight of man. All the historical details are found there, though the Psalm was written approximately a thousand years before His nativity in Bethlehem. In the 40th Psalm we have God's viewpoint of the atonement. In it is found "*the crucifixion of the will in the sight of God.*" Christ said, "Lo, I come to do thy will." That *will* involved His death—through which He put away sin and thereby enabled God to justify the sinner.

PSALM FORTY—PART TWO
"GOOD NEWS"

IN our previous meditation we considered the first eight verses of this Psalm. We observed that this is a Messianic Psalm, a Psalm in which Christ is the speaker, though David is the writer.

We learned also that more space is devoted to this Psalm in the New Testament than to any other. If the amount of space devoted to a specific reference in sacred Scripture is an indication of the value of it, then the 40th Psalm is of major importance.

We further noted that our Lord, in the first eight verses of this Psalm used parable language to describe His death, burial and resurrection, which historic facts form the basis of what the Bible calls "the gospel." That Christ died, that He was buried and that He was raised from the dead are irrefutable facts of history. They are substantiated by the application of every recognized rule of historic criticism which has been in use for centuries in determining the accuracy and validity of any ancient historic event.

A NEW WORD

I recall hearing that prince of linguists, the late Dr. Robert Dick Wilson of Princeton and Westminster Theological Seminaries. He once said to a New York audience, "There is no man living who knows enough to assail the historical accuracy of the Old Testament." What Prof. Wilson said about the Old Testament is true also regarding the New Testament.

While the facts of Calvary and of the resurrection of our Lord Jesus Christ are the most established facts of history, the historic facts are not "the gospel." That Christ died is history—we do not require the Bible to tell us that. History is its own witness. But that Christ died for our sins according to the Scriptures is a revelation of God, and it is that which constitutes the gospel. It is the greatest piece of news this world has ever heard.

I have a friend who is a missionary in Africa, a man I sincerely love and admire. His name is Sir John Alexander Clarke. He has been decorated several times by the King of the Belgians for his ministry in the Belgian Congo. A few years ago he visited our country, at which time he related many interesting experiences.

On many occasions I have listened to him with keen delight as he would describe his thrilling experiences with big game. In fact, we have in our home one of his trophies, which he presented to Mrs. Olsen and me as a wedding gift. But, thrilling as his hunting stories were, they faded and vanished alongside of the one I am about to re-tell to you. He entered Africa and went into the Katanga district before copper was discovered there. In fact, he was probably the first white man to visit that area of Africa. Like all pioneer missionaries, he literally had to take the language of the natives from out of their own lips, and then reduce the phonetic syllables to writing. Of course, months were spent before he was able to converse sufficiently to acquaint the African chief and his tribe with the purpose of his coming.

He told me of his long search for a native word that would convey to the minds of these primitive Africans what the English word "gospel" means to us.

One day he was stirred by the beating of drums. Coming out of his tent he saw a wild scramble of men all heading for the hut of their village chief. Then he heard a strange cooing coming from over the hills. He joined the crowd about the African chief. Presently from the distance the cooing became articulate. Mr. Clarke heard a word for the first time, and immediately noted a decided relaxation of the tenseness that had possessed the men of the village tribe and their chief from the moment the cooing was heard.

Finally the messenger arrived. Then, while all listened in perfect silence, he told his tale. A feud of long standing had existed between the chief of this tribe and the chief of another tribe. The messenger had left two weeks previously as an envoy of peace, with an offering to settle the quarrel. He was now returning with the news that the offering had been accepted, and that peace now reigned where formerly strife prevailed. As the messenger came over the hills he cried but one word. I shall not disturb the sensitiveness of your ears this morning by trying to pronounce the word the messenger used, but translating it into English it means "good news." It was the first time my missionary friend had heard it. His heart was thrilled. He begged of the chief the privilege of speaking to his tribe. So, seated about a camp fire he told the chief and his men of the "good news" of the gospel, using as an illustration the messenger who had just returned, and quoting that very familiar verse from the prophet Isaiah—"How beautiful upon the mountains are the feet of him that bringeth good tidings, that publisheth peace; that bringeth good tidings of good, that publisheth salvation; that saith unto Zion, Thy God reigneth!"

The gospel, therefore, is good news—the good tidings of peace and the acknowledgment that God reigns. That Christ died is a fact of history with which the entire civilized world is acquainted, but the gospel proclaims God's viewpoint of what actually transpired upon the cross when our Lord Jesus Christ died.

THE "WATER-MARKED" CROSS

In this connection, I think it will be interesting to bear in mind the contrasts of viewpoint between the 22nd Psalm and the 40th Psalm, which we are now considering. In the 22d Psalm we have the crucifixion scene. It is so wonderfully presented in detail that there cannot be the slightest doubt that the writer is occupied with presenting death by crucifixion. David wrote that Psalm a thousand years before the nativity of Christ in Bethlehem, yet the details of the cross are so clearly water-marked into the text that, as we take that Psalm and stand at the foot of the place called Mount Calvary, we are compelled to acknowledge that the crucifixion at Calvary is that of which the prophet spoke in the 22nd Psalm. However, the viewpoint is that of the historic cross, the manner of His death and the circumstances surrounding it. It is entirely from the viewpoint of a tragedy on earth.

In the 40th Psalm we have the divine viewpoint of the cross. "In it we find the crucifixion of the will in the sight of God." Our Lord said, "Lo, I come to do thy will." It is that viewpoint of the cross that forms the gospel which the Holy Spirit has woven about the facts of His death, burial and resurrection. The Apostle Paul clearly defined it in his first letter to the Corinthians, where he wrote:

> " . . . I declare unto you the gospel which I preached unto you, which also ye have received, and wherein ye stand . . .
> "For I delivered unto you first of all that which I also received, how that Christ died for our sins according to the scriptures;
> "And that he was buried, and that he rose again the third day according to the scriptures . . . ."

This is the viewpoint which is presented in the 40th Psalm. It is God's estimate of the sacrifice of Christ. With this in mind, let us read from this 40th Psalm commencing with verse six, to and including verse ten:

> "Sacrifice and offering thou didst not desire; mine ears hast thou opened: burnt-offering and sin-offering hast thou not required.
> "Then said I, Lo, I come: in the volume of the book it is written of me,

"I delight to do thy will, O my God: yea, thy law is within my heart.

"I have preached righteousness in the great congregation: lo, I have not refrained my lips, O LORD, thou knowest.

"I have not hid thy righteousness within my heart; I have declared thy faithfulness and thy salvation: I have not concealed thy lovingkindness and thy truth from the great congregation."

It is a delight to contrast the prerogatives of God, appearing in these verses, with the works of God that appear in the first three verses of this Psalm.

In our previous meditation we particularly stressed the fact that our Lord in the early verses of this Psalm is occupied with what the Father did for Him: He heard His cry; He brought Him out of the horrible pit; He set His feet upon a rock; He established His goings; He put a new song in His mouth. It is our Lord's testimony of the work that was accomplished by His Father at the cross.

In verses 8 to 10 our Lord is again speaking to His Father, but on this occasion He is extolling the glorious character and prerogatives of God, His Father. Notice the things He speaks of in these verses—

"I delight to do *thy will*"

"*thy law* is within my heart"

"I have not hid *thy righteousness* within my heart"

"I have declared *thy faithfulness* and *thy salvation*"

"I have not concealed *thy lovingkindness* and *thy truth* from the great congregation."

We shall comment very briefly upon a few of these seven prerogatives of God.

The Lord said, "I delight to do *thy will*" and, "*thy law* is within my heart." Our Lord Jesus Christ alone could say those things. In fact, He also said to His Father just before the cross, as related in the 17th chapter of John's Gospel: "I have glorified thee on the earth. I have finished the work which thou gavest me to do." No *man* could ever say, "I delight to do thy will." Our Lord was pleased to go to Calvary because He knew it was there He would accomplish His Father's will to redeem this sin-stricken world. He also said, "thy law is within my heart."

THE PURPOSE OF THE LAW

Do you remember what God did with the law of the Ten Commandments, or at least what He instructed Moses to do with them? When I hear certain religious leaders express their beliefs in the phrase "Do good and be good," I feel like suggesting that they sit at Moses' feet and learn of him. Moses received from the hand of Jehovah two tables of stone, upon which were inscribed the Ten Commandments. Coming down from the mount, where he had been in Jehovah's presence, he was shocked as he observed the idolatry of his people. They had violated the very first commandment. Did Moses go to Aaron, the elders, and the entire company of Israelites, and say, Here is God's law—strive to keep it—this is what God demands of you—be good and do good? He did nothing of the kind. He took those two tables and dashed them to pieces upon the foot of the mountain. Why? Why did he not give them the law? Of course, a legal mind would immediately respond, Why give a law-breaking people a law and ask them to keep it? They had already broken it. Moses knew, therefore, that they could never be justified by the works of the law. What happened? God graciously made a provision for the sinning Israelites. He gave Moses a ceremonial law and instructed him in the building of a tabernacle, where He would meet with the representative of the Israelites. He provided sacrifices which had to be slain, whose blood would be placed upon the mercy seat in order that God could have fellowship with a sinful people. What happened to the law? Second tables were prepared and upon them the Ten Commandments were re-written. Then the Lord gave Moses specific instructions regarding them. He was to place the law within a wooden box overlaid with gold, which box was called the ark of the covenant. That ark of the covenant, which had a covering of gold called the mercy seat, upon which the blood of the sacrifice was placed, became a sort of safe deposit box for the safekeeping of the law.

Our Lord said He had the law within His heart. He alone kept the law. Because He had that perfect moral character He was able to be the perfect sacrifice.

In verse 10 our Lord said, "I have not hid thy righteousness within my heart." What does that mean? "Thy righteousness." Evidently, God has a righteousness. Indeed! and it is that righteousness that He bestows upon every believer who receives Christ as his sacrifice for sin.

Let me quote a verse or two from the New Testament, where the same principle that I have just outlined is declared, regarding the law of God's righteousness. After all, I know of no more important question than the one of knowing how to be saved and how God can justify or clear a man who is a sinner.

In Paul's letter to the Romans, chapter 3, verse 19, we read: "Now we know that what things soever the law saith, it saith to them who are under the law: that every mouth may be stopped, and all the world may become guilty before God." In that verse we have God's design in the giving of the law. Where there is no law sin cannot be charged, for there is no transgression. Thus God gave the law to Moses to charge the Israelites with sin, and, through the Israelites, to charge all the world with sin. Every mouth is stopped—all the world is guilty.

Paul concluded his great masterpiece of divine jurisprudence in the first three chapters of the letter to the Romans by saying: "Therefore by the deeds of the law there shall no flesh be justified in his sight: for by the law is the knowledge of sin."

But, if this were all, we might despair, for all the striving in the world would not help in wiping out transgression. Can you imagine Warden Lawes of Sing-Sing welcoming a prisoner who has been judged by the law and sentenced to pay its penalty, by saying, "Young man, come into my office. I want to read to you the law—this do, and you shall be free to live." "Oh, Warden," the prisoner would say, "that is fine. You mean to say all I have to do is to be good and do good? Great! I'll try from now on. Goodbye, Warden. I am glad you helped me so and showed me the way of freedom." I need not add what the Warden would reply. It's all too obvious!

Sin must be paid for. The law was given to prove we are sinners, but that is no gospel. The gospel follows in the next few verses in that letter to the Romans, where we read:

> "But now the righteousness of God without the law is manifested, being witnessed by the law and the prophets;
> "Even the righteousness of God which is by faith of Jesus Christ unto all and upon all them that believe: for there is no difference:
> "For all have sinned, and come short of the glory of God."

PSALM FORTY—PART THREE

THE TESTIMONY OF GOD AND CREATION TO CALVARY

THE 40th Psalm is not only a piece of poetry, but a divine revelation. For our third meditation in it we will begin reading at verse 11:

> "Withhold not thou thy tender mercies from me, O LORD: let thy lovingkindness and thy truth continually preserve me.

"For innumerable evils have compassed me about: mine iniquities have taken hold upon me, so that I am not able to look up; they are more than the hairs of mine head: therefore my heart faileth me.

"Be pleased, O LORD, to deliver me: O LORD, make haste to help me.

"Let them be ashamed and confounded together that seek after my soul to destroy it; let them be driven backward and put to shame that wish me evil.

"Let them be desolate for a reward of their shame that say unto me, Aha, aha.

"Let all those that seek thee rejoice and be glad in thee: let such as love thy salvation say continually, The LORD be magnified.

"But I am poor and needy; yet the Lord thinketh upon me: thou art my help and my deliverer; make no tarrying, O my God."

The depth to which our Lord Jesus went is aptly described by Him as "an horrible pit," out of which His Father brought Him, through resurrection. Such is the substance of verse 2, where it is written, "He brought me up also out of an horrible pit . . ."

THE IMPORTANCE OF CALVARY

The central message of Christianity is the cross of our Lord Jesus Christ. Without the cross there is no such thing as "Christianity." All of the Old Testament writers look forward to the cross: all of the New Testament writers look back to the cross. The cross is the turning point of God's revelation and dealings with the sons of men. It is the apex of His revelation. It was our Lord Himself who said, on the night of His betrayal, as the shadow of the cross was deepening across His spirit, ". . . Father, the hour is come; glorify thy Son, that thy Son also may glorify thee . . ."

Surely it is evident from this passage quoted from the 17th chapter of John's Gospel that the event which was about to take place was of such tremendous importance to the Godhead that our Lord Jesus, addressing His Father, said, "Father, *the hour* is come." "*The hour*"—a very definite, specific time. Upon the testimony of the Bible, that hour was the supreme hour in the ministry of Christ. It was the hour for which the world was spun into space. It was the hour for which He came into this world. It was the hour when the Lord Jesus, who knew no sin, became sin. Fathom that if you can! I cannot, but I believe it and greatly rejoice in it.

Christ was made sin that we might be made the righteousness of God in Him. As righteousness was foreign to us, so sin was foreign to Him, but, as a believer in Christ has been made righteous, so Christ was made sin. This may appear to be a simple statement, but, as we contemplate what it means, we learn that it is probably the most astounding statement that has ever been made.

When we stand at the foot of the cross, with the 22nd Psalm before us, comparing the prophecy made therein with the crucifixion scene, we then confess that the one is prophecy, the other history. But to penetrate through the scene, to the heart of the gospel, is given only by God the Holy Spirit, through the Scriptures.

In these closing verses of the 40th Psalm we have such a revelation. Here is described the inmost feeling through which our Lord went as He hung upon the cross. The reality of the sufferings of Christ are graphically portrayed in the 11th and 12th verses.

It is true that others have suffered the torture of physical death and that thousands upon thousands have been crucified and have probably experienced equally excruciating physical pain as did our Lord Jesus Christ, but what distinguishes the death of our Lord from the death of every other man is the fact that every other man has died *because of* sin, whereas Christ died *for* sin.

A STRANGE PRAYER

In the 11th verse, our Lord cried,

> "Withhold not thou thy tender mercies from me, O LORD: let thy lovingkindness and thy truth continually preserve me."

That is a strange prayer when it is considered that the Father broke the silence of heaven several times during the public ministry of Christ by saying, "This is my beloved Son, in whom I am well pleased." It is the testimony the Father gave concerning His Son, yet the Son cried,

> "Withhold not thou thy tender mercies from me, O LORD: let thy lovingkindness and thy truth continually preserve me."

It was during the period when our Lord was on the cross that the attitude of the Father changed.

Frequently it is said that the Father turned His back upon the Son, but such is nowhere to be found in the Scriptures. Who ever heard of a judge turning his back upon the guilty as he pronounces sentence? When our Lord hung upon the cross He symbolized sin. God the Father, who is the Judge of all the earth, exacted from Him the penalty of sin. That penalty is death. Thus our Lord Jesus died.

In order to consider the reality of the cross, let us look at our Lord's cry, in verse 12: "For innumerable evils have compassed me about: mine iniquities have taken hold upon me, so that I am not able to look up; they are more than the hairs of mine head: therefore my heart faileth me."

What a statement! "My iniquities have taken hold upon me." Such hold was so pronounced that He said, "I am not able to look up" and the iniquities so numerous that they are more than the hairs of His head. So real was the transaction of Calvary that as our sin, yours and mine, and the sin of the universe, was placed upon Christ, He actually called them His own, referring to them as "His iniquities." But notice His language: they "have taken hold upon me." The Hebrew word used in this verse, which is translated "taken hold," is an intensely interesting one. It means "reach," as swallowing waves, to "fall upon," as in the case of a blessing or a curse. Thus the waves of human sin are seen rolling upon our Lord Jesus. We also see here what is presented in the 3rd chapter of the letter to the Galatians. Christ was made a curse for us, for it is written, "cursed is every one that hangeth on a tree . . ." How accurate, therefore, is the Scripture—"mine iniquities have taken hold upon me."

Our Lord Jesus Christ is the personification of God's righteousness. The life He lived upon the earth demonstrated His sinless perfection. There was such a marked distinction between the life He lived and the life of other men, that our Lord Jesus appears as the only white page in the history of man upon the earth. No intelligent man has ever raised a finger of accusation against our Lord. He distinguished Himself from others when He said to a group of Pharisees, ". . . Ye are from beneath; I am from above: ye are of this world; I am not of this world."

It cannot be stated too emphatically that our Lord Jesus was the sinless, perfect One. What perfection He possessed! We get a beautiful example of the moral glory of our Lord in the case of the miracle He performed in healing a leper, described in the 8th chapter of Matthew's Gospel. It took place immediately after He delivered what is universally called the Sermon on the Mount. We are told He came down from the mountain and that great multitudes followed Him. Suddenly there came a leper and worshipped Him, saying, "Lord, if thou wilt, thou canst make me clean." The Scripture says Jesus put forth His hand and touched the leper, saying, "I will; be thou clean." And, the record reads, "immediately his leprosy was cleansed."

There are a number of interesting things to note in connection with this record. The leper violated the law of Moses when he came out of his seclusion and entered into the mob. He had but one thought—*he must be made clean*. He had a strong faith—*the Lord could make him clean*. But the law of Moses clearly stated that if a leper approached other people or if other people approached a leper he was to raise his voice and cry, "unclean, unclean," thereby warning others to avoid his uncleanness. It was absolutely prohibited for any other than a priest to touch a leper. Our Lord was never a priest while He was on the earth. Priesthood remained with the Levites. Our Lord touched this man, full of leprosy, yet He was not contaminated by the leprosy. He had within His body that cleansing virtue which healed the leprous man and made him clean. Our Lord when He touched the leper touched sin, but it did not defile Him. On the contrary, His touch made the leper clean.

Our Lord on the cross did not change His character. He always was the Son of God's love, the sinless, perfect One, but upon the cross He became sin. He was made sin—the sin of the universe was placed upon Him. There was no sin *in* Him: the sin was *placed upon* Him. He was weighed down by these sins. They were so numerous they were more than the hairs of His head. While He had no sin in Him, the sin of others took hold upon Him so that He was not able to look up.

THE THREE CROSSES

Perhaps we can illustrate this thought by asking you to recall that. our Lord was crucified between two thieves. There is no doubt that these thieves were sinners. The Lord was in the center. At first both derided Him, but suddenly one had a change of heart—or, should I say, a deep sense of sin. He turned to the thief on the other side of the Lord and said, "Dost thou not fear God, seeing thou art in the same condemnation? And we indeed justly; for we receive the due reward of our deeds . . ." but he said concerning the Christ, who hung on the middle cross, "this man hath done nothing amiss." Then, addressing the Lord, that dying thief prayed, "Lord, remember me when thou comest into thy kingdom." Our Lord responded, "Today shalt thou be with me in paradise."

Look at those three crosses. On the one hangs a sinner, unrepentant— he has sin *in*, and *upon* him. On the other side of Christ is the sinner who cried to the Lord for salvation—he had sin *in* him, no doubt about it, but his sin was transferred to Christ. He had no sin *on* him, but there was sin *in* him. Christ, who hung upon the middle cross, had no sin *in* Him, but taking the sin of the confessed thief and the sin of the universe, He had sin *upon* Him. Hanging there upon the cross He paid sin's penalty.

We cannot fathom the anguish of heart that our Lord endured as He became sin. We can only learn by comparisons and contrasts. We have never known what it is to possess righteousness. We have never been in contact with a truly righteous man. Our thinking is sin, our lives are sinful; but Christ, the sinless One—oh, the horror that must have possessed Him when sin took hold upon Him!

Of course, our Lord understood it was necessary that He go to the cross and that He suffer the penalty of sin, in order that He might be the Saviour of the world, especially them that believe, but that does not change nor detract from the reality of His spiritual suffering. Is it any wonder He cries out in the 13th verse: "Be pleased, O LORD, to deliver me: O LORD, make haste to help me." Is it any wonder He also cries, "Let them be ashamed and confounded together that seek after my soul to destroy it; let them be driven backward and put to shame that wish me evil. Let them be desolate for a reward of their shame that say unto me, Aha, aha."

Occasionally men revolt against the imprecatory words of Christ given in the Psalms. They ask, Where is the evidence of love in such expression? Evidently, these men are entirely ignorant that grace must reign through righteousness, and that just as definitely as God is love, just so definitely is He also a consuming fire. The answer to those who hold such a thought is an appeal to the record of what actually transpired. Those who jeered at Christ when He was crucified—were they later ashamed? Were they confounded together? Were they driven back? Were they put to shame? Were they made desolate because of their shame in crying out to Him in the manner in which they did?

What is the record? If we only had the testimony of the miracles in creation at the time our Lord was crucified, we would have sufficient to inform us that His death was not the death of an ordinary man. Let me enumerate some of these miracles.

When our Lord was crucified it was high noon. Suddenly the heavens became black, the thunder roared, and the lightning flashed across the heavens. You say that is nothing unusual. That could take place at any time. But there was something so unusual about that storm that the multitudes who previously sat with stoic indifference ran for shelter. The centurion who supervised the crucifixion and had to remain through this dreadful scene, as he observed all of nature in revolt, and listened to the words of Christ as He hung upon the cross, said, "Truly this man was the Son of God."

The greatest miracle of all took place in the sanctuary, the temple in Jerusalem. An unseen Hand reached into the very holy of holies and there rent the veil that separated that place from the outer sanctuary— rent it in twain from the top to the bottom, God having thus demonstrated that the way into His holiest presence was now made manifest, because of the death that our Lord died.

How confounded, how ashamed, how distressed His enemies became! They who previously cried, "Aha, aha," who chided Him, saying, "If thou be the Son of God, come down from the cross," were all driven back. That afternoon, when all the earth seemed to be in convulsion, the blackest page of human history was written. But out of it has come the shining of a new day. The Sun of righteousness arose with healing in His wings. The Lord was magnified.

PSALM FORTY-ONE

THE BETRAYED AND THE BETRAYER

THE 41st is the last Psalm of the first section of the Book of the Psalms. The Psalms, instead of being one complete book, actually contain five books. Where each ends and the other begins, is easily recognized by the repetition of the phrase, "Amen, and Amen," which we will note appears as the closing statement of this 41st Psalm.

In the very beginning of our series of meditations in the Psalms we called attention to the universality of this marvelous collection of inspired poems and revelations. They fit into every situation, into every life, and into every age. There is no clime nor people where their message does not bring tremendous comfort. Yet as we have traveled through these Psalms we have learned one great lesson; that is that our Lord Jesus is as definitely found in this portion of Scripture as in any other. We have His own authority that He is found in the Psalms by the statement He made on the night of His resurrection when He opened the understanding of the disciples, that they might understand the Scriptures.

> "And he said unto them, These are the words which I spake unto you, while I was yet with you, that all things must be fulfilled, which were written in the law of Moses, and in the prophets, and in the *Psalms*, concerning me.
>
> " . . . Thus it is written, and thus it behoved Christ to suffer, and to rise from the dead the third day:
>
> "And that repentance and remission of sins should be preached in his name among all nations . . . "

In this 41st Psalm we will "find" our Lord Jesus. The Psalm begins with a beatitude and ends with a doxology.

> "Blessed is he that considereth the poor: the LORD will deliver him in time of trouble.
>
> "The LORD will preserve him, and keep him alive; and he shall be blessed upon the earth: and thou wilt not deliver him unto the will of his enemies.
>
> "The LORD will strengthen him upon the bed of languishing: thou wilt make all his bed in his sickness.
>
> "I said, Lord, be merciful unto me: heal my soul; for I have sinned against thee.
>
> "Mine enemies speak evil of me, When shall he die, and his name perish?
>
> "And if he come to see me, he speaketh vanity: his heart gathereth iniquity to itself; when he goeth abroad, he telleth it.
>
> "All that hate me whisper together against me: against me do they devise my hurt.
>
> "An evil disease, say they, cleaveth fast unto him: and now that he lieth he shall rise up no more.
>
> "Yea, mine own familiar friend, in whom I trusted, which did eat of my bread, hath lifted up his heel against me.
>
> "But thou, O LORD, be merciful unto me, and raise me up, that I may requite them.
>
> "By this I know that thou favourest me, because mine enemy doth not triumph over me.
>
> "And as for me, thou upholdest me in mine integrity, and settest me before thy face for ever.
>
> "Blessed be the LORD God of Israel from everlasting, and to everlasting. Amen, and Amen."

"TURNING HIS BED IN SICKNESS"

It has been well said that, "for pregnancy of expression, beauty of illustration, power of condensing maxims of spiritual life, there is nothing to be compared with the Psalms, which are attributed to David." While David was a warrior, there is abundant evidence throughout the record of these Psalms that he possessed touches of tenderness beyond the tenderness of even a woman.

Where, for example, is it possible to find words more tender than in the 3rd verse of this Psalm, which contains a promise to "him that considereth the poor"? "The LORD will strengthen him upon the bed of languishing: thou wilt make all his bed in his sickness." The Hebrew word used by David, translated "thou shalt make," has in it the thought of "turning," so that one might well paraphrase the passage by saying, "Thou art wont to soothe him, as one soothes a sick man, who turns his whole bed over and over, that he may lie more softly and get some rest."

But let us examine the first three verses more carefully. There is a blessing upon him "that considereth the poor." There is the assurance that the Lord will deliver such in the time of trouble, that He will preserve him and keep him alive, that he shall be blessed upon the earth, and that he will not be delivered unto the will of his enemies. Please do not limit the word "poor" to a matter of money. The greatest mistake is apt to be made if we think that "the poor" are only those who lack the wherewithal to provide for some of the comforts of life which are given to those who are possessed of this world's goods. For example, did not our Lord speak of those who were poor in spirit, and say concerning them: "Blessed are the poor in spirit; for theirs is the kingdom of heaven."

No indeed! "The poor" in this Psalm are not limited to those who are "penniless." Poor indeed is that man who, though possessed of millions, and houses and goods, yet does not know the peace of heart and conscience which comes from the assurance of sins forgiven. Poor indeed is any man who does not know the Lord Jesus as his Saviour and his Lord. All the wealth of this world, without Christ, would be abject poverty. Blessed is the man who does know Him as his Lord and Saviour, and is considerate of those who know Him not, those who are truly poor. Blessed is the man who makes known to poor, wretched men the goodness of God that leadeth them to repentance, the grace of God that bringeth salvation, and the peace of God that bringeth assurance and quietness. It is of such a one that the promise is made: ". . . the LORD will deliver him in time of trouble." It is of such a one that the promise is given: "The LORD will strengthen him upon the bed of languishing . . ." and He will even turn his bed in his sickness.

The 3rd verse indicates the extent to which the great God of the universe is willing to condescend to serve those who are His own. Not only does He cause the sun to rise in the morning and set in the evening; not only does He cause it to shine upon the good and the evil; not only does He give the increase of the field and shower it with refreshing rains, but He is so specifically interested in those who are His own that He assures them that He will make their bed in sickness.

Our Lord has never promised us freedom from suffering or from sickness. If He had, this passage would be absolutely meaningless. If there were no such thing as trouble; if there were no such thing as sickness; if there were no such thing as languishing; if there were no such thing as despair, these three verses would have no meaning at all.

THE BETRAYAL OF CHRIST

In this Psalm, however, we not only get an exhortation and a promise of blessing to those who consider the poor, but light is thrown on a touching incident in the ministry of Christ. He Himself later appropriated a verse from this Psalm and applied it to Himself. It is John, the writer of the fourth Gospel, who records the circumstances for us in the 13th chapter of his book. What a penman is the Holy Spirit! Graphically does He portray the event, so that while it took place almost two thousand years ago, the description of it is so real that it transports the reader to the very scene.

It is the last night our Lord is spending with His disciples before His passion. He shocks them by disrobing after supper and putting upon Himself the garment of the most menial servant. Then He takes a basin and fills it with water. To the amazement of the disciples He begins to wash their feet and wipe them with the towel wherewith He was girded. Peter refused Him, saying: "Lord, dost thou wash my feet?" It was only upon the insistence of our Lord: "If I wash thee not, thou hast no part with me" that Simon Peter acquiesced to the ministry of our Lord. After He had completed the ceremony, our Lord Jesus said,

> "Ye call me Master and Lord: and ye say well; for so I am.
> "If I then, your Lord and Master, have washed your feet; ye also ought tó wash one another's feet.

"For I have given you an example, that ye should do as I have done to you.

"Verily, verily, I say unto you, The servant is not greater than his lord; neither he that is sent greater than he that sent him.

"If ye know these things, happy are ye if ye do them."

Then, to the consternation of the twelve, He said:

"I speak not of you all: I know whom I have chosen: but that the scripture may be fulfilled, He that eateth bread with me hath lifted up his heel against me.

"Now I tell you before it come, that, when it is come to pass, ye may believe that I am . . . ."

You will recognize that this is a quotation from the 41st Psalm, the 9th verse, where it is written:

"Yea, mine own familiar friend, in whom I trusted, which did eat of my bread, hath lifted up his heel against me."

All the civilized world has condemned Judas, the betrayer and the traitor of his Lord. But mark you, this 41st Psalm reveals to us another company of people whose guilt, if not on a par with that of Judas, is equally condemning. In the 7th and 8th verses, we are told,

"All that hate me whisper together against me; against me do they devise my hurt.

"An evil disease, say they, cleaveth fast unto him: and now that he lieth he shall rise up no more."

It is true that Satan put it in the heart of Judas to betray the Lord, but there was another company of people who conspired with him for a certain price that he might betray his Master and Friend to them. Little did they realize that that event would be the subject of myriads and myriads of sermons, and that it would be indelibly left in the record, never to be wiped out!

Of course the room was in turmoil when our Lord revealed that a betrayer was in their midst. Each disciple looked to the other, wondering of whom He spake. There was leaning on His bosom at that time, John, the beloved disciple. Simon Peter beckoned John and suggested that he ask the Lord of whom He spake, and then John, lying upon the breast of the Lord Jesus, feeling the throb of Deity's heart, asked, "Lord, who is it?" to which the Lord responded,

"He it is, to whom I shall give a sop, when I have
dipped it . And when he had dipped the sop, he gave
it to Judas Iscariot, the son of Simon.

"And after the sop Satan entered into him. Then
said Jesus unto him, That thou doest, do quickly."

But there was not a man at the table who knew to what intent our
Lord spake this unto Judas. The Bible is an Eastern book, that is, its
setting is in the East. Thus, many of the customs of the East prevail in it.
We are able to get some precious glimpses into the written Word when
we are acquainted with Eastern customs and scenes. A missionary who
labored in Persia for some little time told of an incident in his experience
that has enabled me more fully to appreciate the record of the betrayal
of Christ by Judas.

A native of Persia in goodly humor chided the missionary by saying,
"You Westerners have a very limited knowledge of the Bible. It is we
here in the East, knowing the customs of the East, who see and appreciate
its message. I want to prove my assertion to you. Will you come to my
home," specifying a certain evening, "and be my guest at dinner? Then
I will give you the sop." The missionary said a cold chill ran up his spine,
"Give me the sop?" What could he mean? To the missionary, the sop
had always symbolized the betrayal of Christ, but the Persian assured
the missionary he would see a message in it that he probably hadn't seen
previously, and so he accepted the invitation.

The night of the dinner arrived; the friends came, and the missionary
was the guest of honor. They all squatted on the floor. In the center
was a huge bowl containing the choice meal of the evening. After grace
had been said, the host tore off a piece of bread. It was not a loaf such
as we have in the West, but a flat, pancake-shaped bread. He took this
strip, made it into the form of a cone and then dipped into the bowl in
the center and "fished out" the choicest piece of meat in the dish. Turning
to the missionary, with all the grace of the Orient, he said, "I hereby give
you the sop." The missionary took it. Then the host continued, "Let
me tell you what I have done. These assembled guests are friends of
mine. I wanted to introduce you to them, and them to you, and so I
arranged this dinner. You are our guest of honor. All these guests know
that when I, as the host, give the sop to a specific guest, I have singled
that one out as the honored guest of the evening."

Immediately, the missionary perceived a new meaning to the 13th
chapter of John's Gospel, and began to appreciate, as I have appreciated
since hearing this story, the wonderful, undying love of our Lord Jesus

Christ. Now I can understand why the disciples were unable to fathom that it was Judas who was about to betray their Lord, for when He gave him the sop, He singled him out as the guest of the evening. It seems as if our Lord was extending to His own familiar friend a last expression of love before that one went to his traitorous task.

Only God could act as Jesus did. This was not the action of a mere man. There never was a man who could act as this Man did. It was the action of God. Jesus Christ is the God-Man. One cannot explain Him. or understand Him, upon any other basis.

Later on, that evening, after our Lord had completed His agony in Gethsemane, Judas led a band of people into the garden and betrayed the Lord to the multitude through the sign of a kiss. Treacherous, you say. Yes indeed! But I ask, just how would we have greeted Judas? I daresay our indignation would rise and we would have given an outlet to it by addressing Judas in some such way as this, You Scoundrel! You dare to kiss me, in order that you may do your despicable task!

But our Lord is not such as we. Oh, the magnitude of His love! He addressed Judas, saying: "Friend, wherefore art thou come?" Friend! Can anyone question who Jesus is? Must we not confess, as did the centurion—"Truly this was the Son of God."

It is fitting that we close with the doxology, which appears as the last verse of the 41st Psalm, "Blessed be the LORD God of Israel from everlasting, and to everlasting. Amen, and Amen."

PSALM FORTY-TWO—PART ONE
"PANTING LIKE A DEER"

THE Book of the Psalms actually is a collection of five books. Each book ends with the phrase, "Amen, and Amen." We completed our meditation in the first book, when we considered the 41st Psalm, wherein is found the prophecy of the betrayal of Christ by Judas. The 42nd Psalm is a superb piece of inspired literature. Because of the many subjects mentioned therein, and their importance, we shall limit this meditation to the first five verses, which read:

> "As the hart panteth after the water brooks, so panteth my soul after thee, O God.
> "My soul thirsteth for God, for the living God: when shall I come and appear before God?
> "My tears have been my meat day and night, while they continually say unto me, Where is thy God?

"When I remember these things, I pour out my soul
in me: for I had gone with the multitude, I went
with them to the house of God, with the voice
of joy and praise, with a multitude that kept holyday.

"Why art thou cast down, O my soul? and why art
thou disquieted in me? hope thou in God: for I shall
yet praise him for the help of his countenance."

PSALM SINGING

After the Psalmist wrote the Psalm, he sent it by the hand of a messenger to one of the chief Musicians. At the time, three men occupied that position—Asaph, Jeduthun, and Heman. This Psalm was to be sung by the sons of Korah; therefore, it went to Heman, who was a descendant of Korah. If you have a good memory you will recall from Sunday school days that Korah perished in the rebellion against Aaron, but some of his sons remained faithful to Jehovah God. There are several Psalms dedicated to the sons of Korah. Each have a plaintive message that is unusually characteristic and interesting. Then again, the word "Maschil" is the Hebrew word for "instruction." This Psalm, therefore, is not merely words to be set to music, not mere idle singing; it contains a message of instruction.

Living in such an age as we do, where the radio has brought the message of song to millions who never had the pleasure previously of attending concerts, we have about concluded that the singing of our choral societies, the melody of our symphonies, and so on, could never have been equaled in any generation, but I would love to have been present when the sons of Korah sang this beautiful Psalm. I am inclined to the view that had we that privilege we would all concede that we had never heard singing like that of the sons of Korah.

The writer of this Psalm craved the communion of the Eternal One; he longed for the heart of God.

He used the simile of a deer pursued by a hunter, and how this deer craves refreshing water to quench his thirst. He likened the panting of the deer to his own heart, longing and thirsting after God. It would be difficult to find a more beautiful picture in all of literature:

"As the hart panteth after the water brooks, so panteth
my soul after thee, O God."

There are several things about that simile which are apparent even on the surface. In the first place, this craving after God is on the part of one who already knows God. It was because the Psalmist knew the Lord that he craved His fellowship. Men who do not know the Lord do not crave His fellowship.

CRAVING FOR GOD

The one great indictment that can be made against our present age is the fact that men have lost their thirst for God. Our age boasts of its infidelity. It seems to pride itself on its unbelief, and with great ado it has ruled God, or the personality of God, out of its sphere of thinking. Not so with the man who knows God. His heart craves for fellowship with the Eternal One. It is the most glorious privilege of the sons of men to have communion and fellowship with the great God of the universe. It ought to be apparent that such was the purpose of God in creating man; that He might have a company of people who would love His fellowship and delight in His presence. How sin has spoiled the fellowship and ruined the communion! But the heart of God craves for fellowship with men, and as an evidence of it He gave His only begotten Son to the world, that whosoever believeth in Him should not perish, but have everlasting life.

It is evident that there are times in the experience of a man who knows God when his God seems to be afar off and when his enemies chide him. As his circumstances seem to belie his friendship with God, his enemies say, Where is his God?

But let us look at this picture once more. The Psalmist said:

> "As the hart panteth after the water brooks, so panteth
> my soul after thee, O God."

The writer of this Psalm was a naturalist—a true naturalist. He never worshipped creation; he worshipped the God of creation. As he entered into the woods, he did not worship the trees, nor the beasts of the field, but he saw in the provisions of the forest, and in the care of the animals, the provisions of God, and the care of the Creator. As he considered the animals, and the beasts of the field, he observed in their movements that which was typical of the experience of his own heart. So, to describe the craving of his heart for God, he went into the woods and noted the panting of the red deer.

It is particularly appropriate that our meditation in the 42nd Psalm comes in the fall of the year. Every hunter loves the months of October and November. It is the season of the year when he dons his Nimrod outfit, takes his gun, and treks into the woods to seek his prize. As the hunter goes into the woods to get his deer, he observes the movements of that strange, yet lovable creature. The deer naturally is hot and dry, but when hunted he becomes extremely thirsty. He senses danger, he seeks a place of shelter, he is entrapped, he pants frightfully like a dying man panting for a drop of cooling water. The hart longs for the cooling streams of the forest where he may quench his terrific thirst. Just as that deer pants when he is pursued by a hunter, and is in a place of danger, "so panteth my soul after thee, O God," said the Psalmist.

We, too, are in the land of the enemy. How evident this is. We are pursued on all sides by circumstances that sometimes are bewildering. We, too, in our despair cry out for our God, as the writer did in the second verse: "My soul thirsteth for God, for the living God: when shall I come and appear before God?" He proceeded to state: "My tears have been my meat day and night, while they continually say unto me, Where is thy God?" Notice how carefully he chose his words. He did not say his soul *hungered* for God, but he said, "My soul thirsteth for God." A man can go weeks, yea months, without food, but he cannot go very long without water. To describe his soul's longing for God, he said that his soul thirsted for God. For fear anyone might misunderstand him, he qualified that longing of the soul, by saying it was "for the living God."

How precious that is to every believer in the Lord Jesus Christ, for he remembers that he does not worship a dead Saviour, a buried Christ, but he worships a risen, ascended, and living Lord. His heart thrills at the message the risen Lord gave to John, the Evangelist, as it appears in the 1st chapter of the book of The Revelation, when the Lord laid His right hand upon John, and said unto him: "Fear not; I am the first and the last: I am the living one, that was dead; and, behold, I am alive for evermore, Amen; and have the keys of hell and of death." Our Lord Jesus Christ on the cross died, literally died. He paid the penalty of sin, that we might live. God the Father opened the tomb and raised Him from the dead, seating Him at His own right hand, from whence our Lord is looking forward to the time when His enemies shall be made His footstool.

When the Psalmist cried, and said that he thirsted for the living God, he expressed his faith in the Eternal One, the living God.

There is no joy in all the world that compares with the joy so aptly described by the writer as the time when he is to appear before God. How that encourages a Christian, for he knows it is written that "when he shall appear, then we shall also appear with him in glory."

It is also interesting to note that the Psalmist said: "My tears have been my meat day and night, while they continually say unto me, Where is thy God?"

Many a hunter has borne witness that as the deer is pursued, and he suddenly realizes that he cannot escape from the huntsman, his eyes become watery, and it seems as if the deer is about to shed tears. The Psalmist used that simile when he said: "My tears have been my meat day and night."

Human tears are salty, and salt intensifies thirst. A beautiful paraphrase of this verse has been given by an old Jewish rabbi: "My tears have been my *dry bread* day and night." I cannot think of anything that would more intensify thirst for a man already thirsty than to feed on dry bread.

Finally the Psalmist said: "When I remember these things, I pour out my soul in me: for I had gone with the multitude, I went with them to the house of God, with the voice of joy and praise, with a multitude that kept holyday." In other words, he recalled the time when his heart was overwhelmed, when he was filled with joy, and when he joined the great multitude in Israel who went up to the house of God with the voice of joy and praise, with that great company that kept holyday.

A Holyday vs. a Holiday

How we have changed Sunday from a holyday to a holiday! Whereas, in the early period of our nation's history men laid aside their duties on Sunday and joined with the multitude to go up into the house of God, to hear His Word expounded and join in the singing of praises, now the great multitudes join in doing almost everything under the sun but going to the house of God. Yet the man who knows God appreciates that there is no fellowship in all the world that is as precious, as deep, and as real as the fellowship of kindred minds as they gather about the Person of Christ.

Those who have listened to the broadcasting of these Psalms know that this man is not a preacher in the accepted sense of the word. He is a business man; he has a very busy life. Practically every Sunday, in addition to this radio broadcast, I have the honor and privilege of preaching His Word in various churches throughout the East. Sometimes, I also have been able to squeeze in a meeting or two during the week. Frequently on Sunday, traveling to different churches to preach, I drive for the sake of convenience. Driving home at the close of the day, I meet a great crowd of motorists. I have observed the expressions upon the faces of the occupants of other cars. They have been out for a day's ride, and are coming home tired and weary.

While I have frequently returned home, almost exhausted, after preaching two or three times on a Sunday, yet the exhaustion is different, as accompanying it there is a deep satisfaction which surpasses anything else in this world, in knowing that I have been in association and fellowship with those who know the Lord Jesus as their Saviour, who rejoice in the salvation of our Lord, and who delight in His Word. If you do not know that joy I invite you to receive the testimony that God has given concerning His Son. This is the testimony: "He that hath the Son hath life; and he that hath not the Son of God hath not life."

Acknowledge Him as your Lord, receive Him as your Saviour. Then you too will have the joy of His fellowship. You will want to go with the multitude to the house of God to join with them in the voice of joy and praise.

There may be times, as the Psalmist described in the 5th verse, when your circumstances will cause you to be downcast. Probably every one of us have known occasions when our song has been lost. What then? Let us do just as the writer of this Psalm did. Say to our own souls, as he did: "Why art thou cast down, O my soul? and why art thou disquieted in me? hope thou in God: for I shall yet praise him for the help of his countenance."

PSALM FORTY-TWO—PART TWO

"THE PANACEA FOR A DEPRESSED SPIRIT"

IN many Psalms the language is parabolic. The psalmists frequently used a picture language. That also was the method our Lord employed during His public ministry.

Thus as we read from verse 6 of the 42nd Psalm, let us take note of the meaningful language used—

> "O my God, my soul is cast down within me: therefore will I remember thee from the land of Jordan, and of the Hermonites, from the hill Mizar.
>
> "Deep calleth unto deep at the noise of thy waterspouts: all thy waves and thy billows are gone over me.

"Yet the LORD will command his lovingkindness in the daytime, and in the night his song shall be with me, and my prayer unto the God of my life.

"I will say unto God my rock, Why hast thou forgotten me? why go I mourning because of the oppression of the enemy?

"As with a sword in my bones, mine enemies reproach me; while they say daily unto me, Where is thy God?

"Why art thou cast down, O my soul? and why art thou disquieted within me? hope thou in God: for I shall yet praise him, who is the health of my countenance, and my God."

THE LIVING WORD

One thing about the Bible that distinguishes it from any other book is its vitality. For instance, take this 42nd Psalm. It was written approximately three thousand years ago. It is hoary with age, yet there is something about this Psalm that fits in perfectly with our own present-day experiences. The Bible is always fresh. If you wish to observe the contrast between the living Word and the ordinary words of man, visit any public library that retains newspapers for several decades. Ask to see a copy of a newspaper, published say about thirty years ago. It is so out of date, its whole style is so different from our modern way, that it is startling to note the contrast. A few weeks ago I was calling on a friend of mine at his place of business and he happened to be occupied for the moment. While waiting, one of his associates showed me a copy of the "New York Journal" dated in 1901, which he had dug up in his apartment the night before. It was the issue that brought the news of the death of Queen Victoria. Well, it was quite amusing to turn the pages of that paper, noting the typography of it and the "ads." My, it seemed archaic!

Not so with the Bible. It has a message for today, as it had a message for the age during which it was written. No other book compares with it. In the Psalms, the experiences of David and others seem to be our own experiences. His vicissitudes of life seem analogous to ours. Some days we are happy, at other times we are sad. Sometimes we are so depressed it seems impossible to smile. These experiences are nothing new. The Psalmist knew about them. He knew what it was to have a depression too, but, fortunately for him, he also knew the remedy for such experiences. Indeed, while the Bible is one of the oldest books, it is so distinctly modern that it comforts us "moderns," along life's pathway. What is more, its message and ministry extend today beyond anything that the greatest visionary ever dreamed possible.

This past week I was particularly thrilled to read in an English periodical about a number of wealthy Chinese Christian laymen in Shanghai who have set up a Christian broadcasting station. Who would have dreamed that such a thing would take place in the land of China? These Chinese Christians maintain an eight-hour program daily, with some items in English and some in the Mandarin dialect. When the proprietors heard that the reception in the distant western province of Szechwan was poor, they contributed $30,000 to provide a new short-wave installation. When I read that item, I said, "Thank God for Chinese Christian laymen!"

The Bishop of Fukien, in writing about the broadcast, said—

> "I listened to an evangelistic service in Mandarin. A hymn was beautifully sung as a tenor solo; a passage of Scripture was read and then an address was given. Being in Mandarin I could not understand much of it but I can never describe the thrill it gave me to hear the name of Jesus recur over and over again and to think of the very atmosphere reverberating with His name, even to remote Szechwan."

As I read of the Bishop's thrill, I could almost feel it in my own being as I thought of a "thrill" I had a short time ago. I was in Chicago over Labor Day week-end. On Sunday evening I tuned in to a radio program. On one of Chicago's stations the voice of a Chinese gentleman was giving forth the gospel. The outline of his message was as clear as any gospel message I have ever heard from the lips of our great American preachers. He began by saying that there were some things in life we could do without, but that there were other things in life that are so essential it is utterly impossible to do without them. He then applied that to the Scripture. He began quoting passages of the Bible. He did it as skilfully as a master. His first quotation was that verse in the book of Hebrews, ". . . without faith it is impossible to please him (God). . . ." He stressed the importance of faith and the decree of God that a man must have faith if he is to please Him. Then he followed it with that imperative word that without holiness ". . . no man shall see the Lord." "Of course," said this Chinese preacher, "none of us possess holiness—on the contrary, we are sinful." Then he led his audience to the cross, where sin is removed, and reminded his radio listeners that the Scripture says that without the shedding of blood there is no remission of sin.

Who would have thought that the day would ever come when a native of China would enter a studio in Chicago and broadcast through the air the unsearchable riches of Christ? Miracle? Certainly it is a miracle.

Somehow we seem to be occupied with the Chinese today, but you will probably be interested in another incident. A few weeks ago a friend of mine who is a missionary in Manchoukuo, the former province of Manchuria, wrote of a certain Mr. Wang, who lives six miles from the mission station and who called on my friend and his family. He conversed about the things of the Bible. He had brought with him a Bible he had purchased three years previously. This gentleman is a very wealthy Chinese. He owns the entire village where his home is located. He invited the missionary and his co-workers to come to his home and address his household. The missionary told me that the household alone made a good-sized congregation. However, this Chinese master, while anxious to hear the Word of God and to have his household learn about the Bible, has himself not opened his heart to receive Christ. I responded to the letter, telling my friend, the missionary, that the next time he had an occasion to speak to Mr. Wang to tell him that there is a young man in the western world whose business life daily brings him in contact with what is going on in the economic life of this world, who would very definitely pray for Mr. Wang, that he might come to know the Lord Jesus as his Saviour. And when I hear that he has received Christ I shall offer up a word of thanks that God has saved him by His grace!

In Exile

These few, scattered experiences from different parts of the world must impress upon us the universality of the message of the Bible. The message of this Book is today as powerful as it ever was.

We today can appreciate and enter into the Psalmist's experiences from the words that he penned: "O my God, my soul is cast down within me: therefore will I remember thee. . . ." Were you ever downcast? If you never have been, you are indeed a very strange person. When you are downcast, do you do as the Psalmist did? Do not forget God in a time like that. It is so easy to forget Him and it is so easy to conclude that He has forgotten you. At a time like that, the panacea for a depressed spirit is what the Psalmist offered herein, when he said, "therefore will I remember thee." To remember God in such a time is like pouring oil upon troubled waters. However, this writer is specific. He said, "I will remember thee from the land of Jordan, and of the Hermonites, from the hill Mizar."

Now, of course, an instructed Israelite can understand more readily than we this reference to the land of Palestine, yet even we Gentiles, who have received Christ, can receive blessing from these similes. Who does not know that Jordan is the river of death? Many of the Negro spirituals are built around this view of Jordan. The land of Jordan, therefore, could well represent the land of death. Then there is the land of the Hermonites and the hill Mizar. Every one who has traveled through Palestine brings back tales of white-capped Mount Hermon, clothed with the light of heaven reflected from her snows. The Psalmist's vista was from the valley of death to the mountain of God's throne and from that little hill Mizar. He was bringing to his remembrance the times of refreshing he had while enjoying the full fellowship of his God.

In the 7th verse of this Psalm we get an unusual picture of anguish and distress. "Deep calleth unto deep at the noise of thy waterspouts: all thy waves and thy billows are gone over me." Could a storm be more graphically pictured? Could you imagine a scene of more terrifying distress than this? "Deep calleth unto deep at the noise of thy waterspouts. . . ." In other words, there is a judgment from beneath and a judgment from above, one calling to the other to vent its force upon the Psalmist, who adds, "all thy waves and thy billows are gone over me."

JONAH AND THE FORTY-SECOND PSALM

At the very beginning of this meditation we directed attention to the universality of these Psalms. They fit into every age and every experience of life. Let me prove that by asking you to look at a much maligned book of the Old Testament called Jonah. You surely have heard of the prophet Jonah. To many skeptics, that seems to be the only book in the Bible. The critics were more sure of themselves a few hundred years ago. We have come a long way since then. We have learned a lot about whales during the last couple of hundred years. In fact, in quite a number of museums there are specimens of whales that could house Jonah and his whole family, if he had one. The finest sermon ever preached on Jonah is found in Melville's classic "Moby Dick."

The prophet Jonah described in his little book the experiences he had when attempting to go counter to God's instructions. He did not wish to go to Nineveh, so he went to Joppa and found there a ship going to Tarshish. He paid his fare and immediately went to his berth, where he slept soundly. He never knew what seasickness was, or that the sea was in an unusual uproar. Finally, the mariners of the ship, sensing that there was something unusual about the storm, concluded that some one in their midst was to blame. Jonah was dragged out of his berth. Then they cast lots. The lot fell upon Jonah. He confessed to the seamen his disobedience to God and urged them to cast him overboard. But God had prepared a huge fish, and into the belly of that fish Jonah went. Of course, a smart college freshman may not believe this to be a scientific fact. Could it possibly be that a fish could swallow a man and not digest him? Well, Jonah is not the only undigested miracle which has happened in this world. What about that modern illustration of the same miracle, the Jewish race. Certainly the Jews have been cast into the sea of the Gentile nations for almost two thousand years, yet the Gentiles have never been able to digest the Jew. A Jew is just as definitely a Jew today as he ever was. He can never become anything else and woe be to any Jew who tries to be anything but a Jew. His whole heritage rebels against it. Jonah presents no greater problem to the mind than do the Jews.

While Jonah was in the belly of this fish, undigested, he had opportunity to think about the 42nd Psalm, the very Psalm in which we are meditating this morning. In fact, in the 2nd chapter of his book he quotes from this Psalm. Let me quote one or two verses from that chapter. You will then note the acquaintance Jonah had with this Psalm and how he takes expressions from it, applying them to himself. Jonah said—

> "I cried by reason of mine affliction unto the LORD, and he heard me; out of the belly of hell cried I, and thou heardest my voice.
>
> "For thou hadst cast me into the deep, in the midst of the seas; and the floods compassed me about: *all thy billows and thy waves passed over me.*"

Jonah knew what it was to have all God's billows and God's waves pass over him!

CHRIST IN THE FORTY-SECOND PSALM

But there can also be a further application of this passage of Scripture. The Psalmist was not only describing his own experience—Jonah was not alone in sharing this experience. There was a greater than the Psalmist, and a greater than Jonah, who knew of the same distress. I refer to our Lord Jesus. He knew what it was to have the waves and billows of God's judgment pass over Him. The deluge fell upon Him at the cross. It is impossible to understand the cross apart from this. In fact, because He bore the judgment of sin, you and I are spared that experience, if we take our refuge in Christ.

Finally, it is interesting to observe that the Psalmist did not allow his distress to overwhelm him, for in verse 8 he wrote—"Yet the LORD will command his lovingkindness in the daytime, and in the night his song shall be with me, and my prayer unto the God of my life."

What comfort has come out of this passage to multitudes of distressed people. Lovingkindness in the daytime, a song in the night, and a prayer unto God—that is my idea of a happy life—happy in the midst of distress because our Lord gives us a song in the night. No one but a Christian can sing in distress, can sing in the night. You have heard it said, "Character is what a man is in the dark." So a song in the night is what a Christian is in distress.

The Psalmist, in the closing verses, encouraged his own heart not to be downcast nor disquieted, but to hope in the eternal God. Because He commands His lovingkindness in the daytime and gives a song in the night, he added, "I shall yet praise him, who is the health of my countenance, and my God." If you should be in distress this morning—if you should feel downcast and disheartened, I invite you to come to Christ, receive Him as your own Saviour and your Lord. You will then discover that you will yet praise Him, for He thus becomes the health of your countenance and your God.

PSALM FORTY-THREE

THE GOD FOR DEPRESSIONS

ONE must be in a proper mood to consider a doleful Psalm such as the 43rd, which reads:

"Judge me, O God, and plead my cause against an ungodly nation: O deliver me from the deceitful and unjust man.

"For thou art the God of my strength: why dost thou cast me off? why go I mourning because of the oppression of the enemy?

"O send out thy light and thy truth: let them lead me;
let them bring me unto thy holy hill, and to thy tabernacles.

"Then will I go unto the altar of God, unto God my
exceeding joy: yea, upon the harp will I praise thee,
O God my God.

"Why art thou cast down, O my soul? and why art
thou disquieted within me? hope in God: for I shall
yet praise him, who is the health of my countenance,
and my God."

Here is a sad Psalm for sad people. While there is an abundance of
fanfare and much noise in this world there is also a vast army of sad
hearts. Thousands crowded about one of the corners of New York City
this past week to watch a young man dangling from the ledge of the seven-
teenth floor of a New York hotel. For hours he stood there threatening to
jump to his death and finally did, just two minutes before the Police and
Fire Departments had put out a net that would have saved him.

Sad hearts? The world is filled with sad hearts. That young man left
behind him a family whose hearts were subjected to a terrific strain. They
pled with him for hours to refrain from carrying out his intention. There
was a crowd at the foot of the building watching with intense eagerness
the actions of a single man. Some were amused, some were entertained.
Others, it would appear, stayed for hours to satisfy their morbid appetites
for feasting upon other people's grief. Yet there must have been men and
women in that crowd whose hearts were stirred and who were reminded of
their own troubles. This world is a vale of sorrows. But there was One who
walked its sands who was called "a man of sorrows." He bore our griefs
and carried our sorrows to the cross, and because He was a man of sorrows and acquainted with grief, He can now succor all those who come unto
Him with their troubled hearts and minds.

A SURE CURE FOR SAD HEARTS

In this 43rd Psalm, the Psalmist once again is found conversing with
himself—having a sort of "soul conversation." He evidently recognized that
he was a trinity; that he had a spirit, soul, and body. His soul was indeed
sorrowful. His body evidenced it also. However, he had a hopeful spirit
which helped him to bear a burdened soul and body. He recognized that
the spirit was supreme. It was his spirit that talked with his soul and
said, "Why art thou cast down, O my soul? and why art thou disquieted
within me?" Before he gave his soul an opportunity to tell of its sorrows

and woes, he pushed down a big, heaping tablespoonful of spiritual tonic, encouraging his soul to "hope in God." He knew the disease, but he also knew the cure. What's more, he knew the reaction that would take place in his own soul once it had assimilated the tonic, for he said, "for I shall yet praise him, who is the health of my countenance, and my God." A sickly soul can be encouraged only by a great big dose of faith in God. When such a soul drinks from that fountain it will readily recover its health and once again rejoice in the knowledge of the One whom the writer called "the God of my strength."

Through the kindness of a friend I have just come into possession of an old volume entitled "Memories of Gennesaret." It is the kind of a book that smells musty—it is so old. Most men would have paid little or no attention to it and many a housewife would object to giving it a place on the bookshelf. The odor was sufficient to cause one to leave it alone, but as I glanced through its pages I discovered some exceedingly choice things expressed in exquisite language. A chapter is devoted to the resurrection from the dead of the daughter of Jairus. You will remember Jairus was a ruler of the synagogue. His little daughter of twelve years of age, his only child, was desperately ill. The ruler of the synagogue, when he learned of our Lord's presence, came running and fell down at His feet and besought Him greatly that He would come into his house and lay His hands on her. Alas, in the interval the daughter who had previously gladdened his home had died. The writer of this book introduced his chapter devoted to this incident in the life of our Lord with a few lines of poetry entitled "The Only Daughter."

> "Fondly I prized that lovely mind
>   Where all was gentle, sweet, and mild;
> A thousand blooming flowers entwined
>   The earth-bower of my sainted child!
>
> "Forth sped the doom—'Return to dust!'
>   In the cold grave my treasure lies;
> I was a traitor to my trust,
>   I got it not to idolize!
>
> "Hush, breaking heart, that pines and weeps,
>   Laughing the holy word to scorn,
> 'The maiden is not dead but sleeps:'
>   You'll meet her on the Heavenly morn!"

This gifted writer drew many lessons from that home and its experiences. One exhortation suggested that we learn the nature of real sorrow.

Let me quote some of his lines because they proved such a blessing to my heart, and I trust they will to yours as well.

"He who wept at the grave of Lazarus does not forbid *Tears*. They are holy things, consecrated by Incarnate tenderness. Let the world, if they may, condemn it as unmanly to grieve,—or, worse, let them seek oblivion of their trials in the giddy round of its pleasures and follies, and make the grave of their dead as soon as may be 'the land of forgetfulness.' He encourages no such cold and stern stoicism. But, on the other hand, neither does He countenance overmuch sorrow. True Christian grief is calm, tranquil, chastened. The noisy, wailing, mimic crowd are spurned from the scene. If they had been the tears of a Martha or Mary, He would have held them as sacred;—but being the hollow echoes of unfeeling hearts, He says, '*Give place: why make ye this ado and weep?*'

"Jesus, on every occasion in His public ministry, stamps with His abhorrence all *pretence*. He dislikes *unreality*, what is made to *appear* gold which is tinsel;—whether it be simulated joy, or simulated piety, or simulated tears. That is a poor sorrow which expends itself in funeral trappings,—which is measured by doleful looks, and passionate words, and mourning weeds. True grief is not like the stream which murmurs and frets because it passes over a shallow bed;—that which is deepest makes least noise. Inconsolable sorrow is unbecoming the Christian. To abandon one's self to sullen gloom, moping melancholy and discontent, is sadly to miss and mistake the great design of trial. God sends it to wake us up to a sense of life's realities—not to fold our hands, but to be more in earnest than ever in our work and warfare. Oh! when He sees meet to enter our households, and, as the Great Proprietor of life, to reclaim His own, be it ours to thank Him for the precious loan, to acknowledge His right and prerogative to recall the grant. 'The Lord loveth a cheerful giver.' Although it was in a trial, of which, God forbid any of us should ever know the bitterness, I know not in all Scripture a more touching picture of this silent acquiescence in God's sovereign will than we have in the case of a parent who had seen his two worthless children smitten down before his eyes, and yet of whom we only read that 'AARON HELD HIS PEACE.' "

May these lines be a benediction to those who have had real sorrow enter into their homes, particularly if a loved one has been taken away. ". . . why go I mourning because of the oppression of the enemy?" The Psalmist knew what it was to be sorrowful. Sorrows are the common lot of man. None of us are exempt. When our heart is heavy and our sorrows are burdensome and we do not know where to turn, we should do exactly as the Psalmist did, go into the presence of God and speak to Him. We will soon discover that God has a purpose in the ministry of suffering; that He wants us in His presence, to enjoy His fellowship and He to enjoy ours, so that we may know the wellsprings of joy and understand that the highest and best moments of a man's life are those in which he has a quiet, undisturbed, intimate fellowship with the eternal God in Christ.

INWARD OR REFLECTED LIGHT

Now note the earnest plea found in the 3rd verse of this Psalm, "O send out thy light and thy truth: let them lead me; let them bring me unto thy holy hill, and to thy tabernacles."

It has often been said, although erroneously so, that there is a spark of the divine in every man, and that it needs only to be fanned into a flame which will light up the entire man. That is a Satanic lie. Men do not possess a spark of the divine unless they have been born again by the Spirit of God through the operation of the Word of God and by faith in Jesus Christ. The Lord taught Moses what was in the breast of every man, when He commanded him, "Put now thine hand into thy bosom." Let's not forget that the bosom is the central part of a man, the very heart of his being, that which accurately portrays what he is. The Scripture notes that Moses "put his hand into his bosom: and when he took it out, behold, his hand was leprous as snow."

It may not be pleasant, but we might just as well face the fact. In the sight of God, morally, every one of us is a leper. If we should put our hand into our bosom as Moses did and should then look at our hand we would find it as leprous as snow. But I am delighted that the Lord did not stop there with Moses. He had another lesson to teach him. So the Lord said a second time, "Put thine hand into thy bosom again." We are told that Moses "put his hand into his bosom again; and plucked it out of his bosom, and behold, it was turned again as his other flesh." When a man has been born again by the Spirit of God he can touch his bosom the second time and have the same experience Moses did, for that which the Holy Spirit placed within him upon believing is not only a spark of the divine nature, but a very part of it. It is of that which the Apostle John wrote when he said, "Whosoever is born of God doth not commit sin; for his seed remaineth in him: and he cannot sin, because he is born of God."

A discouraged soul would remain forever in the abyss of disappointment if he were to look within himself for light to drive away the gloomy shadows of disappointment. The Psalmist said, "O send out *thy* light and *thy truth:* let *them lead* me; let *them bring* me unto *thy* holy hill, and to *thy* tabernacles."

It was George Mueller, of Bristol, England, I think, who followed the practice in his morning devotions, as soon as he had dressed, to sit down with an open Bible in order that God's light and truth might shine into his heart and upon his mind, and only after reading would he have his devotions in prayer. All too often people pray without reading the Word of God. The Psalmist said, "O send out *thy* light and *thy* truth. . . ." God's light and His truth are to be found only in His Word. When the light of God's truth shines into the darkened and discouraged breast, then the clouds are dispelled and the gloom vanishes. The result will inevitably be the same as that which the writer experienced which he expressed in this Psalm. He was led by them directly to the place called God's "holy hill" and His "tabernacles."

We were driving along the new Merritt Highway the other evening, returning to New York after dinner, when Thomas Rees, that charming young Englishman who gave such a rousing testimony on our Forum broadcast recently, said, "Ah, I've got a fine illustration for you." I had already called his attention to the reflections of light streaming from the road reflectors along the edges of the road which lit up the contour of the highway—only to have Mr. Rees tell me that this method of road lighting was extensively used in England. But said he, "Those little disks called 'road reflectors' have no light in themselves; they merely reflect light from borrowed light—only as the rays of light from the headlights of your car play upon the reflectors do they prove to be a guide in the dark. Isn't that true of us? We have no light in ourselves. It is only as God sends out His light and His truth that we can be led in the right path." A few minutes later Mrs. Olsen added a further thought as she drew attention to the varying degrees of light which were apparent—some of the reflectors farthest away gave the brightest light, some gave no light at all, while others gave only a little light. It is only as the 'road reflectors' are properly and fully focused *directly* to the headlights that they give the maximum of light. How true of us! If we are to be shining lights in this world, we must look full into His wonderful face on which abides "the light of the knowledge of the glory of God. . . ." In Psalm 34:5 we read, "They looked unto him, and were lightened: and their faces were not ashamed." A more expressive translation of David's words would be, "They looked unto him, and were radiant: and their faces were not ashamed."

ACCEPTABLE SACRIFICES AT GOD'S ALTAR

It is most interesting to note that the Psalmist leaned for guidance upon God's light and His truth, and that he confidently prayed that these might lead him to God's holy hill and tabernacle, there to come before the altar of God, who was his exceeding joy. At that place he enjoyed the most holy contemplation. He called for his harp to join him in praise of his God.

No unsaved, unconverted man can approach the *altar* of God. He must face the *bar* of God. An altar requires a sacrifice. God alone provided the sacrifice in the person of His Son. Now, as a result of His death, we can come before the altar of God with either our broken and contrite hearts to receive restoration; or with our bodies, presenting them to Him for consecration, which of course is the only intelligent service a Christian can offer; or we can come continually by Christ with "the sacrifice of praise to God continually, that is, the fruit of our lips giving thanks to his name."

Perhaps we have observed sufficient in this short Psalm to enable us to understand more fully why the Psalmist should have encouraged his disquieted soul, as he did in the closing verse of this Psalm when he said: "Why art thou cast down, O my soul? and why art thou disquieted within me? hope in God: for I shall yet praise him, who is the health of my countenance, and my God."

PSALM FORTY-FOUR—PART ONE

"AN OLD, OLD STORY"

AS the 44th Psalm in which our meditation is found this morning is divided into two parts, and each contains a profitable message, we shall limit this morning's meditation to the first eight verses which form the first section. Next Sunday we shall examine the remainder of the Psalm as we consider a strange but constantly recurring subject, "Shaking Heads at Sorrowing Saints." The first eight verses read:

> "We have heard with our ears, O God, our fathers have told us, what work thou didst in their days, in the times of old.

"How thou didst drive out the heathen with thy hand, and plantedst them; how thou didst afflict the people, and cast them out.

"For they got not the land in possession by their own sword, neither did their own arm save them: but thy right hand, and thine arm, and the light of thy countenance, because thou hadst a favour unto them.

"Thou art my King, O God: command deliverances for Jacob.

"Through thee will we push down our enemies; through thy name will we tread them under that rise up against us.

"For I will not trust in my bow, neither shall my sword save me.

"But thou hast saved us from our enemies, and hast put them to shame that hated us.

"In God we boast all the day long, and praise thy name for ever. Selah."

There could scarcely be a more timely theme for this boasted enlightened modern age of ours than to be reminded about certain things that even three thousand years ago were considered an old story. We are supposed to be an advanced people, and so super-intelligent that we have discarded all that our fathers and grandfathers ever held dear, and now we venture to sea without chart or compass. Frankly, I invariably have to smile when listening to some young college sophomore talk about "our new day" and "philosophize" on any and every conceivable subject. But if, instead of swallowing it whole, you "roll" it under your tongue, you'll soon realize that it is the same old pill, only this time it has a sugar coating. If what the world is witnessing now is an expression of our modern philosophy of living, then men ought to be ready to listen to what even the Psalmist considered an old story in his day.

THE PASSOVER STORY

The Psalmist wrote, "We have heard with our ears, O God, our fathers have told us, what work thou didst in their days, in the times of old." After which he enumerated some of the things that God did in those good old days; how He drove out the heathen from the land and gave it to Israel for an inheritance. The Psalmist is careful to remind us that the children of Israel did not get the land in possession by their own sword, and that it certainly was not their own arm that saved them. Rather was it the right hand of God and His arm which provided the victory. Again the Psalmist insisted that Israel enjoyed these expressions of God's power solely because God had "a favour unto them."

Even to this day the children of Israel go back to the Book of Exodus for "An Old, Old Story," as annually each Jewish family celebrates the Passover. The father, the head of the household, with his children and grandchildren seated about him, delightfully rehearses it for their benefit, that they, in turn, may pass on to the next generation that page in the history of Israel when there was no doubt that God performed miracles. Israel at that time was a feeble, enslaved people. They had no army and they had no weapons for warfare worthy of the name. They were in bondage and sore distressed. They were considered the offscouring of the earth. Yet they humiliated and defeated the most powerful nation on the earth and caused all other peoples to tremble before them as they triumphantly left Egypt, marched through the wilderness, and on into the promised land. That group of defenseless, ill-prepared people, with no provision save the clothing on their backs and the shoes on their feet could never have subdued their enemies apart from the mighty right hand of the eternal God. The God of Israel was a miracle-working God.

"We "moderns" do not believe in miracles today. We're too intelligent to "digest" miracles. But every Jew and every Egyptian that lived in that day knew that God was a miracle-working God, and furthermore that He displayed His power in miracles on the behalf of the children of Israel solely because they had found favor with Him.

You can imagine some youngish-smart-alecky Jewish lad at Passover season turning to his father or grandfather as he listens to the story of the exodus, breaking in with a question, Why doesn't God do the same things today? Such a one would be sure to take the position that never having seen a miracle, he does not believe in miracles. He uses that Missourian expression "Show me," and proudly adds, "Only then I will believe."

But modern unbelief isn't new, nor the absence of miracles an unusual thing, for even three thousand years ago the Psalmist wrote, "We have heard with our ears, O God, our fathers have told us, what work thou didst in *their days*, in the times of old." God was not doing those works in the Psalmist's day, nor is He, in fact, doing them today. This is not the day of miracles. Neither was it in that day. Indeed, as one studies the Scriptures carefully, he is impressed with how few miracles have taken place in the history of this world. He also discovers that miracles were concentrated into two specific eras of history only, with very few exceptions. One covered the period from the exodus to Israel's entrance into the promised land. The second was from the time of the ministry of our Lord Jesus Christ on earth through the early days of the church's history. To be true there were occasional miracles between those periods, just as there have been a few scattered miracles since the days of the apostles. But, generally speaking, the miracles of God can be placed in two great periods of time. Men in subsequent ages have been called upon to believe that God did previously display Himself in miracles. From the time of Moses to the time of Christ, Israelites were asked to believe the record of the miracles that were performed during the time of the exodus. Christians today are enjoined to believe the record found in the Gospels and the Acts of the Apostles concerning the miracles accomplished during the Lord's ministry and through the lives of the apostles.

There are some people who believe that God intended miracles to take place in every age. There is no sound reason, they say, why miracles should not take place today. That is why we have so many cults, all of which promise healing for the body. But God does not work that way to-day. Occasionally He may. But, generally speaking, God is not now dis-playing His miraculous powers as He did during the Lord's ministry and at the time of the exodus. God never wastes power. Neither does He gratify the idle curiosity of the natural man. But He has given sufficient evidence of His power so that every honest-thinking man is overwhelmingly con-vinced of the might of God, while the unbeliever is thoroughly condemned for his reasoning and disbelief. But someone may ask, Did not our Lord say to His disciples, "He that believeth on me, the works that I do shall he do also; and greater works than these shall he do; because I go unto my Father"? To what did our Lord refer as "greater works" than those which He did?

Let me give an example from the Scriptures. The disciples, empowered by the Holy Spirit, did a "greater work" on the day of Pentecost than did our Lord during all His earthly ministry. Never in all the public ministry of our Lord were three thousand people born again on a single day or, for that matter, in all the three years of His ministry. But on the day of Pentecost there were about three thousand souls added to the company of believers who gladly received the word preached. No greater miracle has ever been witnessed than when a soul dead in trespasses and sins is raised into newness of life. Only the Word of God can raise a soul from spiritual death to spiritual life. That's a miracle!

SALVATION BY GRACE

But let us also notice some things that are found in the 6th, 7th and 8th verses of this 44th Psalm. There the writer, speaking on the behalf of himself and Israel, made these interesting comments, "I will not trust in my bow, neither shall my sword save me. But thou hast saved us from our enemies, and hast put them to shame that hated us." And then, as would naturally be expected, he added, "In God we boast all the day long, and praise thy name for ever."

There are a goodly number of professed Christians who never read the Old Testament. They think the Old Testament was written exclusively by the Jews and for the Jews, and that the New Testament was written entirely by the Gentiles and for the Gentiles. Nothing could be more inaccurate. While all the Bible was not written *to* us in this day, all the Bible was written *for* us; therefore we read in the New Testament, "For whatsoever things were written aforetime (that is, the Old Testament books) were written for our learning, that we through patience and comfort of the scriptures might have hope." We are also told that those things which happened then should be considered ensamples and the record of them was written for our admonition. The Apostles together with our Lord preached exclusively from the Old Testament Scriptures. The Old Testament is a mine of spiritual truth. The principle of salvation by grace apart from works of the law is clearly enunciated in the Old Testament. In this 44th Psalm the writer said he did not trust in himself. Neither did the Israelites trust in themselves. They trusted in the Lord. They boasted not in anything they accomplished. They boasted in God all the day long. Their boast in God and praise of His name was not limited to one day in seven; indeed, it is written, "In God we boast all the day long, and praise thy name for ever."

A gentleman recently came to my office to see me. He has had much difficulty, and in that I deeply sympathize with him. His disappointments and difficulties urged him to find an anchor for his soul. Like many people in like circumstances he went from one thing to another. I asked him pointedly, "Do you know the Lord as your Saviour?" He answered, "I think so." Then I asked him if he was married and he answered affirmatively, in a positive tone of voice. Then I said, "It is interesting to contrast your responses to the two questions I have just asked. You didn't say, 'I think I'm married.' You knew you were married. But when it came to knowing Christ, you evidently do not know Him, for there is a doubt in your own mind, so you answered, 'I think so.' " He smiled and got the point. I proceeded to make clear to him why he had given such an answer to my question. It was because he was not trusting exclusively in the Lord. Oh, yes, he was *trying* to be good. He said he was regularly reading the New Testament. He had gone to several men, preachers and otherwise, seeking help, and all the while he was running around in circles instead of going directly to the fountain head of all help, the Lord Jesus Christ Himself.

Is it possible to know God? Indeed, it is. St. John wrote his Gospel that we might believe that Jesus is the Christ, the Son of God; and that believing we might have life through His name. Then John wrote his first Epistle to believers that they might know that they have eternal life. Our Lord, in prayer to His Father, said, ". . . This is life eternal, that they might know thee the only true God, and Jesus Christ, whom thou hast sent." When men trust in other things, good in themselves, they are not believing and trusting in God. Salvation is of the Lord. It is by grace. There is nothing we can possibly do to merit it. The children of Israel knew that it was not their bow or sword that delivered them from the Egyptian bondage. They knew it was solely due to the fact that they had found favor with God. Their boast was not in their accomplishments. They boasted all the day long in God and they revelled in the knowledge of God.

So from the 44th Psalm we learn the principle of grace. If we are ever to know salvation and to experience eternal life it will only be when we cease trying and eternally trust. In other words, there is nothing to do, for it is all done. It is an old, old story, but it is always new, because it is true.

We were driving along the road the other evening, with my little youngster strapped into her seat right by my side. My wife and I were singing to her "The Old, Old Story." Again and again she asked for it, in her sweet, high-pitched, childish voice, saying, "More old, old 'tory." That little youngster was drinking it in. The Gospel is good news, it is old, but it is ever new, and the more you hear it and embrace it the more you revel in it. If you will believe on the Lord Jesus Christ you will be saved. If you do so, you will find that the old, old story is "the power of God unto salvation to every one that believeth . . ."

PSALM FORTY-FOUR—PART TWO

SHAKING HEADS AT SORROWING SAINTS

OUR meditation again takes us to the 44th Psalm, which discusses two separate and distinct subjects. There is a sharp break in the Psalm commencing with verse 9. This meditation on the last part of the Psalm we have entitled "Shaking Heads at Sorrowing Saints," based particularly on the 14th verse, which reads, "Thou makest us a byword among the heathen, a shaking of the head among the people." Commencing with verse 9, we read:

"But thou hast cast off, and put us to shame; and goest not forth with our armies.

"Thou makest us to turn back from the enemy: and they which hate us spoil for themselves.

"Thou hast given us like sheep appointed for meat; and hast scattered us among the heathen.

"Thou sellest thy people for nought, and dost not increase thy wealth by their price.

"Thou makest us a reproach to our neighbours, a scorn and a derision to them that are round about us.

"Thou makest us a byword among the heathen, a shaking of the head among the people.

"My confusion is continually before me, and the shame of my face hath covered me.

"For the voice of him that reproacheth and blasphemeth; by reason of the enemy and avenger.

"All this is come upon us; yet have we not forgotten thee, neither have we dealt falsely in thy covenant.

"Our heart is not turned back, neither have our steps declined from thy way;

"Though thou hast sore broken us in the place of dragons, and covered us with the shadow of death.

"If we have forgotten the name of our God, or stretched out our hands to a strange god;

"Shall not God search this out? for he knoweth the secrets of the heart.

"Yea, for thy sake we are killed all the day long; we are counted as sheep for the slaughter.

"Awake, why sleepest thou, O LORD? arise, cast us not off for ever.

"Wherefore hidest thou thy face, and forgettest our affliction and our oppression?

"For our soul is bowed down to the dust: our belly
cleaveth unto the earth.
"Arise for our help, and redeem us for thy mercies'
sake."

Upon a hurried reading, one could hardly be blamed for concluding
that the Psalm presents a contradiction. The first half closes with a note
of praise to the Lord and a boast in Him for His deliverance and good
favor, whereas the last half actually takes the Lord to task (if I may use
that expression) for failing to come to the aid of His suffering people. In
fact, the Psalmist becomes so bold as to say, "Awake, why sleepest thou,
O Lord? arise, cast us not off for ever."

A more bold statement would be difficult to imagine. It is one thing
for the Lord to address us as He does in the New Testament letter to the
Ephesians, "Awake thou that sleepest, and arise from the dead, and Christ
shall give thee light." It is quite another story for a man to address God,
"Awake, why sleepest thou . . . ?"

"THOU HAST . . ."

Here are some of the charges against the Lord that the writer of this
Psalm made—in verse 9 he said, ". . . *thou* hast cast off, and put us to
shame . . ." In verse 10 he again places the responsibility on the Lord,
"*Thou* makest us to turn back . . ." In verse 11, "*Thou* hast given us like
sheep appointed for meat; and hast scattered us among the heathen." Verse
12, "*Thou* sellest thy people for nought . . ." Verse 13, "*Thou* makest us
a reproach to our neighbours, a scorn and a derision to them that are round
about us." Verse 14, "*Thou* makest us a byword among the heathen, a
shaking of the head among the people." It is to be expected that a people
who endured such contradictions would be in a state of utter confusion.
One would suppose that the Lord would never deal with His children in
such manner unless it were due to their sin and rebellion, and then only as
a last resort to bring His people back to Himself. But in this particular
case sin and rebellion are not the causes, for in verse 17 we read, "All this
is come upon us; yet have we not forgotten thee, neither have we dealt
falsely in thy covenant." And in verse 18, "Our heart is not turned back,
neither have our steps declined from thy way . . ."

Our examination of this Psalm, I sincerely trust, will change the
minds of some, for all too many have jumped to the conclusion, whenever
they have seen a saint or a group of God's people suffering disappointments,
sorrows, and heart-breaking experiences, that they have been disobedient.

God is chastening such, they say; as if God held a big stick in His hand ready to beat any child of His who did anything contrary to the spirit of His grace. Those of us who are real parents never treat a child of ours in such fashion. Yet we assume that God deals with His children in that manner! What an insult to an intelligent God. Ah, no! If we, being sinful, know how to give good gifts to our children, how much more is that true of the Lord, in dealing with those whom He has called His own.

THE HOLY SPIRIT'S USE OF THIS PSALM

This is a difficult Psalm. Indeed, if it were not for a direct quotation from it in the New Testament, we would be hopelessly at sea regarding its message. But the Holy Spirit never left a loose end in the Old Testament without taking it up in the New Testament and bringing it to a beautiful conclusion. I recall a smile I enjoyed some time ago, while reading an application for a position by one who undoubtedly was a so-called "old maid," in which she wrote that she had "neither beads nor bangles nor loose ends."—No, there are no loose ends in the Bible.

One cannot help raising questions as one examines the Old Testament. The Old Testament is full of questions, but as one turns to the New Testament the answers to these questions are found. So in this case, the Holy Spirit through the pen of the Apostle Paul made reference to this 44th Psalm in the 8th chapter of Romans, one of the great chapters of the Bible.

There is not a single Christian, I think, who has not at one time or another in his experience found the 8th chapter of Romans a great encouragement for his faith. It is a thrilling chapter. It begins with the glorious statement, "There is therefore now no judgment to them which are in Christ Jesus." That is enough to make any man glad. And the chapter ends with an even more glorious statement: that nothing, *nothing*, I repeat again, *nothing* "shall be able to separate us from the love of God, which is in Christ Jesus our Lord." Yet in that 8th chapter of Romans one finds words such as these—suffering, groanings, infirmities, persecutions, nakedness, peril, and sword. Indeed, it is just here that the Holy Spirit, in verse 36 of the 8th chapter of Romans, quotes from the 44th Psalm, "As it is written, For thy sake we are killed all the day long; we are accounted as sheep for the slaughter." For whose sake? For the Lord's sake. Those persecutions and distresses did not come upon the Apostle

Paul and others associated with him in the early days of the Christian church because of any disobedience to the Lord, but, on the contrary, because of their faithfulness to the Lord. So far as the world was concerned, the apostles and early Christians were counted as sheep for the slaughter. But someone may ask, do you mean to suggest that God would permit a child of His to undergo such disappointments? To which I reply, How can one arrive at any other conclusion after an examination of the 44th Psalm and the 8th chapter of Romans? But let me hasten to add that every man in the midst of such experiences will say the very thing that Paul wrote in this 8th chapter of Romans: "For I reckon that the sufferings of this present time are not worthy to be compared with the glory which shall be revealed in us."

So it is not extraordinary to find that the experiences of God's people run through the whole scale, from the highest to the lowest. What is more, and possibly a little surprising to some, the Lord's people frequently are called to pass through experiences from which the world is exempt. Witness what took place the night following that great miracle when our Lord fed five thousand men, besides women and children, with five barley loaves and two small fishes. The multitudes who were fed returned to their homes on foot, safely and without distress; but the disciples, who were commanded by our Lord to get into a boat and to go to the other side of the sea, that night had the most harrowing experience ever endured on the Gennesaret Lake as they fought against an overpowering storm. But there were compensations! I do not believe that one of those twelve men would have preferred the safety enjoyed by the multitude. The storm enabled them to see the Lord in all His glory and power when He walked on the sea, stilled the storm, and quieted the waves, so that they all gladly received Him into the boat and worshipped Him, saying, "Of a truth thou art the Son of God."

There is a tremendous descent from the first part of this Psalm to the last. At the beginning of the Psalm, a high note of joy is struck, but before the Psalm ends one hears a deep lamentation and prayer. The extent to which the writer of this Psalm sank is aptly expressed in verse 14 to which we previously alluded, where the Psalmist wrote, "Thou makest us a by-word among the heathen (or nations), a shaking of the head among the people."

Now then, with the background of the 8th chapter of Romans in our minds and understanding that disappointing experiences may be visited upon some of the people of God, not because of any sin, but rather for the glory of God and the accomplishment of His great will and purpose, let us not be so ready to pass judgment upon the Christian in our circle who may be in distress. Above all, let us not shake our head at him and say in our hearts, if not with our lips—Poor fellow, I wonder what he has been up to now.

In the 44th Psalm, the shaking of the head and the calling by name of God's people was done by the heathen and the unbeliever. Oh, of course, the Psalm is particularly Jewish. The children of Israel for many generations have known what it has meant to be a byword among the nations and to have the Gentiles shake their heads at them. They have been, to use the language of another, "The common butt of every fellow's arrow." The same author suggests that those whose "heads were the emptiest, wagged them at the separated people." Persecution is always done by empty-headed men. Sometimes it expresses itself by the sword—but frequently by the butt of ridicule.

I have known men who have wagged their heads at saints even when those saints were not in trouble. But let me be clear—I do not mean dead saints! God is not the God of the dead. He is the God of the living. A saint in the Bible is a man who believes in Jesus Christ. God calls him a saint because He has separated that man unto Himself. A saint is an enigma to the natural man. He is so unaccustomed to seeing a saint walk around in this old world that it is to be expected that the unconverted look at a Christian and wonder what kind of a missing link he is. And by Christian I do not mean the fellow who simply has "the label on the bottle," but I mean the man who is truly a believer.

Those who know the Lord Jesus Christ and are living separated lives in accordance with the position presented in the New Testament, have had business friends and associates and social friends say to them and about them, Well, he is a fine fellow in lots of ways, but I cannot make him out. He does not seem to do anything. He doesn't smoke, he doesn't dance, he doesn't attend the theatre, he just does not do anything. Poor fellow, what a morbid type of a life he must lead; yet he seems to be happy. That is shaking heads at happy saints. Some think that to believe the Bible and to be an old-fashioned Christian, one must throw his intelligence to the winds. But please bear with us. We have not gone stark mad. We have come into possession of a life not our own, but imparted to us by God's grace and that life has given us tremendous joy. And as we behold our

Lord in all His glory and revel in the knowledge of His saving grace, the things of earth have become strangely dim.

PERSECUTIONS AND GOD'S ULTIMATE PURPOSE

But this 44th Psalm and the 8th chapter of Romans are not occupied with that type of shaking heads, nor do they describe the lot of the godly man who is having happy fellowship with his Lord and on whom the blessings of the Lord are continuously being poured. Rather, this Psalm and the 8th of Romans are occupied with the child of God who is in distress, the one to whom everything seems to have gone wrong. Sorrow upon sorrow has entered his life. Sometimes he himself is unable to reconcile his circumstances with his assured standing in the presence of God. Of course, the world mocks such a man and shakes its head against him.

Paul knew what it was to have sorrow. In fact, the Word of God says, ". . . all that will live godly in Christ Jesus shall suffer persecution.' If that word is true, as every other word in the Scripture is true, it means that if we are not suffering persecution, we are not living godly lives. It is inevitable.

But there is another and very timely message in this Psalm that can be applied to the church as a body, to believers as a group, and to the Jews as a company of people. All Bible-believing people know that Israel is yet to enter upon her worst period of suffering and persecution. Today it is so apparent that a blind man can see it coming. But let not the church believe that she is to be exempt in this day. There is as much hatred in the heart of a Hitler, a Stalin, and a Mussolini, against a true Christian as there is against a Jew. Such men know that they cannot dominate a Christian who takes his orders from God and His Word. The Communist hates the church of Christ.

One can burn Rome and blame it on Christians as Nero did and one can cut off the heads of Christians as was done to the Apostle Paul—but all hell can never stamp out God or His Word or prevent His people from yielding obedience to God. All over this world, the Christian, as well as Israel, is being pressed from all sides. But let it not be forgotten that the God to whom this Psalm was prayed and sung, the God whom the Psalmist urged to rise and deliver His people for His mercies' sake, is not One who is indifferent to the circumstances of the Jew nor to the problems of the Christian. Some day He shall arise. One of these days He *will* redeem His people and deliver them from the land of the enemy. His own people will be redeemed and God will vent His wrath upon their enemies. Let the world shake its head at the believer. Only the man who believes God and His Word has his feet on the ground and knows that nothing can separate him from the love of God which is in Christ Jesus his Lord. He therefore rejoices in tribulation and joys in his God.

PSALM FORTY-FIVE—PART ONE

THE NUPTIAL PSALM OF THE KING

THE 45th Psalm is a masterly piece of literature. If you have your Bible open before you, which I think is a more excellent way to enjoy our broadcasts, you will observe that this Psalm like many of the others has an illuminating introduction. It reads: "To the chief Musician upon Shoshannim, for the sons of Korah, Maschil, A Song of loves."

THE LILY SONG

The word "Shoshannim" means lilies. It is the Jewish word for that spring flower. It is also the name of a six-stringed instrument. It is thus a lily song, but it is also a song of loves. It is intended for the spring of the year, but more particularly for a wedding feast. Tradition has it that David wrote this Psalm and sent it to the chief Musician so that the sons of Korah might sing it at the nuptial feast when his son Solomon was married to the daughter of Pharaoh. There are those who have advanced the thought that Solomon himself wrote it, as the message resembles that of the song of Solomon. However, "while the verbal critic notices that the writer, whoever he might have been, claims for himself a happily conceived strain, a poem flowing with felicitations not laboriously hammered, but with ease coming with the exuberance of a fountain that boils and bubbles," a Christian will immediately recognize the higher inspiration of prophecy. He will observe in the 45th Psalm an objectively Messianic Psalm of transcendent importance. By Messianic we mean that the Psalm is occupied with presenting the Christ of God.

There is so much in this Psalm that to do it justice we must devote two messages to it. I intend, therefore, to limit this morning's message to the first seven verses, which read:

> "My heart is inditing a good matter: I speak of the
> things which I have made touching the king: my tongue
> is the pen of a ready writer.

"Thou art fairer than the children of men: grace is poured into thy lips: therefore God hath blessed thee for ever.

"Gird thy sword upon thy thigh, O most mighty, with thy glory and thy majesty.

"And in thy majesty ride prosperously because of truth and meekness and righteousness; and thy right hand shall teach thee terrible things.

"Thine arrows are sharp in the heart of the king's enemies; whereby the people fall under thee.

"Thy throne, O God, is for ever and ever: the sceptre of thy kingdom is a right sceptre.

"Thou lovest righteousness, and hatest wickedness: therefore God, thy God, hath anointed thee with the oil of gladness above thy fellows."

Those of you who read this Psalm carefully will agree that it cannot be accommodated to David or to Solomon or to any other prince in Israel. In the 6th verse the title "God" is ascribed to the One who is addressed. It

This Psalm is only intelligible upon two suppositions. *First*, that the One praised and extolled in this Psalm is none other than the Lord Jesus. This is the viewpoint of the New Testament Scripture as we will notice later when we quote from the Epistle to the Hebrews. *Second*, that which is discussed in this Psalm is the love of the Lord Jesus for His own, under the imagery of the bridegroom and the bride. This matter we will present more fully in our next meditation.

FEEDING THE HEART

Let us examine each verse specifically. The Psalmist said:

"My heart is inditing a good matter: I speak of the things which I have made touching the king: my tongue is the pen of a ready writer."

I was interested in noting that the Psalmist said his heart was *inditing* a good matter. That word *inditing* in the Hebrew is usually used in connection with the digesting of food, but here it is applied to the heart. Food is essential to our physical well-being, but the heart also requires food—not the husks that men usually feed it, but rather the heart needs to feed upon the Lord. The matter with which the Psalmist was feeding his heart and by which he was sustained, is a good matter. He explained what it is, as he wrote: "I speak of the things which I have made touching the king is written, "Thy throne, O God, is for ever and ever . . ."

. . ." And in so doing his tongue was the pen of a ready writer. The Psalmist likened his tongue to the scribe whose pen glides across the pages of the scroll recording the word of God.

The writer is the Holy Spirit. The tongue is that of the Psalmist. The Holy Spirit took possession of the tongue of this man and caused him to glorify and to unfold the glories of the Son of God. And the picture that the Psalmist painted of the King is one that thrills the heart of every Christian.

Of course, the King is none other than the Lord Jesus. Any other view would be unintelligent as the King is called "O God" in the 6th verse where it is written:

> "Thy throne, O God, is for ever and ever: the sceptre of thy kingdom is a right sceptre.
>
> "Thou lovest righteousness, and hatest wickedness: therefore God, thy God, hath anointed thee with the oil of gladness above they fellows."

This very passage is quoted in the 1st chapter of the Epistle to the Hebrews and is there applied to Christ. In fact, the Holy Spirit introduces the quotation by saying, "But unto the Son he saith, Thy throne, O God, is for ever and ever: a sceptre of righteousness is the sceptre of thy kingdom." Here is God speaking with God. It is God, the Father, addressing God, the Son.

THE MANY-TITLED CHRIST

Our Lord has many titles ascribed to Him in the Scripture, but His chief titles are Prophet, Priest, and King. Each of these titles fit into a specific phase of His ministry. During His public ministry, which culminated at the cross, He was robed as a prophet and spoke as the messenger of God. Now at the right hand of His Father in the heavens He is the Priest, garbed in priestly robes, interceding and offering the worship of His people to His Father. However, just as certainly as His ministry as a prophet ceased when He entered into His priestly ministry in the heavens, so His priestly ministry will likewise cease some day. When that takes place He will appear in the scarlet robes of a king to reign as the King. Do not dismiss the thought by assuming that His kingship is a spiritual matter and His domain a spiritual one. On the contrary, His kingship is political and His kingdom is on the earth. This earth of ours is rapidly setting the stage for the advent of the Son of God who will come to reign as King of kings and Lord of lords.

This is not a wild dream of a visionary. It is the expressed declaration of the Word of God. Let me quote you just one passage that appears in the 11th chapter of the book of The Revelation, the last book of the Bible. In the 15th verse of that chapter we find this statement: "The kingdoms of this world are become the kingdoms of our Lord, and of his Christ; and he shall reign for ever and ever."

It is to be regretted that because our Lord has not yet come, many Christians have spiritualized various references in both the Old and New Testaments, which refer to the Messianic reign of our Lord, so that they cease to think of it as a literal kingdom, but rather as a spiritual dominion. It is the very mistake that the Israelites made and which caused them to fail to recognize our Lord as their Messiah when He came the first time.

THE TWO COMINGS OF CHRIST

Throughout the whole of the Old Testament, on almost every page may be found some reference to the anointed One, the Christ. Therefore the Israelites, when our Lord did come, were in an expectant mood anticipating the coming of "the anointed."

When the wise men from the East arrived at Herod's palace in Jerusalem, having been guided by a strange and new star, they asked him "Where is he that is born King of the Jews?" Could anything be more apparent than the fact that even these Magi knew something about the Messiah and that their knowledge of Him centered about His kingship.

Herod was disturbed and called in the chief priests and the scribes and inquired of them where their king was to be born. They answered quoting from one of their prophets, "In Bethlehem of Judæa." For thus it is written, "And thou Bethlehem, in the land of Juda, are not the least among the princes of Juda: for out of thee shall come a Governor, that shall rule my people Israel." The wise men went immediately to Bethlehem and saw the Lord Christ and worshipped Him. This is one of the strangest records in history.

When our Lord Jesus entered into His public ministry. He was heralded by John, His forerunner, of whom the prophets also spoke. John preached, saying "Repent ye: for the kingdom of heaven is at hand." He electrified the entire coast of Judea. Multitudes of people gathered round about him. The leaders of the people were strangely impressed. They inquired of him, "Art thou he that should come, or do we look for another?"

John witnessed, saying, that he was merely a voice crying in the wilderness, "Prepare ye the way of the Lord, make His paths straight."

When our Lord entered into His public ministry, Israel was unable to reconcile her views of a Messiah who was to come in splendor and glory, with what they actually saw with their eyes. Jesus of Nazareth was a disappointment to Israel, but this very disappointment, this very rejection was as clearly stated in the Scripture as the references to His divine glory and respendent reign.

We are told by the Apostle Peter that the prophets who wrote the Old Testament Scripture were perplexed by two diverse views of the Messiah.

On the one hand were statements concerning His humiliation, His rejection, and His death. On the other hand were statements concerning His glory, His splendor, and His reign. What every prophet of the Old Testament was prevented from knowing was simply this, that there are two comings of Christ. He came the first time and every prediction made concerning Him with reference to His suffering and humility was fulfilled. Take the 22nd Psalm and the 53rd chapter of Isaiah and go to the foot of the cross with them and you will find that everything stated therein concerning His was actually fulfilled to the dotting of the "i" and the crossing of the "t."

Is it logical to suppose that the eternal God would send His Son into this world to fulfill these predictions of His rejection and then fail to send His Son into this world again to fulfill every other prediction made concerning Him?

The Bible declares that Christ appeared once to put away sin by the sacrifice of Himself and unto them that look for Him He shall appear the second time apart from the sin offering unto salvation. When our Lord Jesus comes the second time He will fulfill literally the exhortation in the 45th Psalm, which reads,

> "Gird thy sword upon thy thigh, O most mighty, with thy glory and thy majesty.
> "And in thy majesty ride prosperously because of truth and meekness and righteousness; and thy right hand shall teach thee terrible things."

At that time He will also fulfill the judgment expressed in this same Psalm where it is written, "Thine arrows are sharp in the heart of the king's enemies; whereby the people fall under thee." Then will all of the nations join with the Psalmist and say concerning the anointed One, "Thou art fairer than the children of men: grace is poured into thy lips: therefore God hath blessed thee for ever."

At the present time there are multitudes out of every nation and people and tongue who have recognized in the Lord Jesus Christ all that it written in this Psalm. They have recognized that grace was poured into His lips and that God has blessed Him, above all others forever. I bid you to notice that the Psalmist said concerning Christ, "grace is poured into thy lips." I think the most beautiful word in language is the word "grace." From it we get our word "graciousness." To learn what grace is it is necessary to observe Christ!

THE PREACHER OF NAZARETH

Do you recall the first time our Lord Jesus preached in His native village of Nazareth? Considerable space is devoted to it in the 4th chapter of St. Luke's Gospel. Our Lord had already stirred the countryside by healing the sick, causing the blind to see, and the lame to leap with joy. As He returned to His native village the multitudes asked Him to perform some miracle for their gratification. They gathered in the synagogue and the Lord mounted the rostrum. He was given a scroll of Scripture. It contained the writings of the prophet Isaiah. Our Lord found the place where it is written and He began to read:

> "The Spirit of the Lord is upon me, because he hath anointed me to preach the gospel to the poor; he hath sent me to heal the broken-hearted, to preach deliverance to the captives, and recovering of sight to the blind, to set at liberty them that are bruised.
>
> "To preach the acceptable year of the Lord ... "

Then He closed the scroll and gave it to the minister and sat down. The eyes of the multitudes were on Him. The Scripture says the eyes of all were "fastened" on Him. He began to say unto them "This day is this scripture fulfilled in your ears. And all bare him witness, and wondered at the gracious words which proceeded out of his mouth."

I would it were our privilege to have heard our Lord's message on that Sabbath day. We, too, would undoubtedly have wondered at the gracious words that proceeded out of His mouth.

Grace! How enriched is this world because of the words of grace our Lord spoke, for example, to Nicodemus, when He said: "For God so loved the world, that he gave his only begotten Son, that whosoever believeth in him should not perish, but have everlasting life."

Grace! What words of grace He poured into the ears of that woman whose life had been marred, Neither do I condemn thee: go, and sin no more."

Grace! What of these words to broken discouraged men: "Come unto me, all ye that labour and are heavy laden, and I will give you rest. Take my yoke upon you, and learn of me; for I am meek and lowly in heart: and ye shall find rest unto your souls. For my yoke is easy, and my burden is light."

Grace! What about these words to a sin-sick soul: "Son, thy sins be forgiven thee."

Ah! Whoever you may be, your life will be enriched beyond measure if you allow the Son of God to pour into your heart these words of grace. Remember, it is written that He came not to condemn the world but that the world, through Him, might be saved. By receiving Him, that blessing will be yours!

PSALM FORTY-FIVE—PART TWO

THE NUPTIAL PSALM—THE KING'S GARMENTS

WE have already devoted one message to the 45th Psalm, one of the truly great Psalms of this Book. While this second meditation more specifically covers verses 8 to 11, for the sake of continuity we will read from the 1st verse to and including the 11th:

> "My heart is inditing a good matter: I speak of the things which I have made touching the king: my tongue is the pen of a ready writer.
>
> "Thou art fairer than the children of men: grace is poured into thy lips: therefore God hath blessed thee for ever.
>
> "Gird thy sword upon thy thigh, O most mighty, with thy glory and thy majesty.
>
> "And in thy majesty ride prosperously because of truth and meekness and righteousness; and thy right hand shall teach thee terrible things.
>
> "Thine arrows are sharp in the heart of the king's enemies; whereby the people fall under thee.
>
> "Thy throne, O God, is for ever and ever: the sceptre of thy kingdom is a right sceptre.
>
> "Thou lovest righteousness, and hatest wickedness: therefore God, thy God, hath anointed thee with the oil of gladness above thy fellows.

"All thy garments smell of myrrh, and aloes, and cassia, out of the ivory palaces, whereby they have made thee glad.

"Kings' daughters were among thy honourable women: upon thy right hand did stand the queen in gold of Ophir.

"Hearken, O daughter, and consider, and incline thine ear; forget also thine own people, and thy father's house;

"So shall the king greatly desire thy beauty: for he is thy Lord; and worship thou him."

CHRIST IN THE PSALMS

From the message He gave to His Apostles on the night of His resurrection, as recorded in the 24th chapter of the Gospel according to St. Luke, we have the authority of our Lord Jesus Christ Himself that He is to be found in the Book of Psalms. We also have the authority of the Holy Spirit on this same subject, for in the 1st chapter of the New Testament epistle to the Hebrews the Holy Spirit specifically quotes from the 6th and 7th verses on this 45th Psalm and maintains that the testimony stated therein was given by God the Father to His Son. It was He who said, "Thy throne, O God, is for ever and ever."

We have already noted that this Psalm is a nuptial Psalm, unfolding to us the love of our Lord for His own, under the imagery of the bridegroom and the bride.

A favorite hymn of mine is one by Henry Barraclough, entitled "Ivory Palaces." Mr. Barraclough composed this hymn after listening to a sermon on the 8th verse of the 45th Psalm by the late Dr. J. Wilbur Chapman.

In whatever hymn book you find this song, the following invariably appears under the title:

"Suggested by a sermon by Dr. J. Wilbur Chapman on Psalm 45, verse 8, in which Christ is pictured coming out of the ivory palaces of heaven to redeem mankind, clothed in garments which are perfumed with myrrh for beauty, with aloes for bitterness and with cassia for healing, the fragrance of which remains to tell of His near presence."

In that brief paragraph we have the outline of the message of the 45th Psalm. Our Lord Jesus is seen coming out of the ivory palaces clothed in garments which exude fragrance. This, of course, brings us to the consideration of the glory of our Lord prior to His incarnation while still abiding in the ivory palaces.

The cornerstone of Christian truth is the character and person of our Lord Jesus Christ. It is He who makes Christianity. Christianity should never be confused with a system of religion. On the contrary, it is the unfolding of the person of Christ. The world has its religions; Christianity is Christ. It is the declaration of Scripture that our Lord Jesus is the visibility of God, the very effulgence of His glory and the express image of His person. As such, He has always been in the bosom of His Father. It is written in the 1st chapter of St. John's Gospel that, "No man hath seen God at any time; the only begotten Son, which is in the bosom of the Father, he hath declared (or manifested) him."

It was the learned Nicodemus, a shining light is an otherwise mediocre Sanhedrin which ruled when our Lord ministered upon the earth, who came to our Lord by night and said to Him, ". . . Rabbi, we know that thou art a teacher come from God: for no man can do these miracles that thou doest, except God be with him." To this our Lord responded, ". . . No man hath ascended up to heaven, but he that came down from heaven, even the Son of man which is in heaven."

To the natural, unregenerate man, our Lord's statement is not only involved and bewildering but also wholly unintelligent. Such a man might well ask, Who is this Son of man? Whence did He come down from heaven? How, if it is of Himself He is speaking, could it be said "even the Son of man which is in heaven"? Was He not upon the earth at that time? I answer, indeed, He was. It is all the more evident that our Lord Jesus cannot be accounted for by any other view but that He is God the Son. Granted this view, His message becomes intelligent and glorious. From any other viewpoint His message is meaningless nad bewildering.

He said He came down from heaven. As to the glory our Lord had prior to His incarnation, while He dwelt in the heavens by His Father's side, an interesting light is given to us in the 17th chapter of St. John's Gospel. There our Lord prayed. It was the night before His crucifixion. In that prayer, among other things, He said, addressing His Father, "I have glorified thee on the earth. I have finished the work which thou gavest me to do. And now, O Father, glorify thou me with thine own self with the glory which I had with thee before the world was."

What a witness this is from the lips of our Lord Himself concerning His position in the ivory palaces, even before the world was. Language could not be plainer in its insistence upon the Deity and glory of our blessed Lord. Such being the case, it is shocking that man neglects to consider Christ. Should it not be our task to find out the purpose of His coming and the result of His ministry? From earliest childhood, every Sunday school pupil learned, or at least was taught, from his catechism that "The first purpose of man is to glorify God and to enjoy Him for ever." How far short we have come of that standard is too evident to require any comment.

COMING OUT OF THE IVORY PALACES

But mark, this 45th Psalm is unfolding the glory of the Christ who is seen coming out of the ivory palaces. He is seen clothed with garments. It is the testimony of Scripture that our Lord became a man when He clothed Himself with our likeness, with a body of flesh and blood such as we possess, so that He could touch our lives at the very places of our living. I delight to think of our Lord Jesus clothed with a physical body, so as to have communion with man where man dwells. He thus enabled man to touch Him and to handle Him. Yet, because He was clothed with a body like unto ours many failed to observe Him. Some thought of Him only as the carpenter's son; others saw Him as a miracle worker; many others confessed that He was a prophet; rulers acknowledged He was a good man. However, with the eye that penetrated beyond the outward form of flesh, there were those who beheld His glory, as of the only begotten Son of the Father, full of grace and truth.

To illustrate what I mean, let us examine the case of the young man born blind who had received sight by a miracle of Christ. After this young man was cast out of the synagogue because of his defense of Jesus, our Lord found him and asked him, ". . . Dost thou believe on the Son of God?" The young man responded, "Who is he, Lord, that I might believe on him?" To this question our Lord replied, "Thou hast both seen him, and it is he that talketh with thee." The record reads that the young man said, "Lord, I believe." And then he worshipped Christ. Indeed, it was just such a revelation of God that our Lord Jesus came into this world.

THE FRAGRANCE OF CHRIST—MYRRH

It will be of interest to consider the Psalmist's references to the fragrance of the spices that exude forth odors from His garments. The 8th verse of our Psalm reads: "All thy garments smell of myrrh, and aloes, and cassia, out of the ivory palaces, whereby they have made thee glad." These spices remind us somewhat of the gifts the wise men brought to the cradle of our Lord. They presented unto Him their gifts, as they opened their treasures. The gifts consisted of gold, frankincense, and myrrh. To the spiritual mind these gifts speak not only of the adoration of the Magi but also of the glory of our Lord. Here in the 45th Psalm His garments smell of myrrh, aloes, and cassia.

Myrrh was used for two specific purposes, first, for beauty; and secondly, for burial. Striking, isn't it! Not only is there that about the garments of our Lord which speaks to us of the beauty of holiness and the beauty of a glorified manhood, but there is also that which reminds us of death. Our Lord took possession of that body in order to accomplish His Father's will. Through that body He offered Himself as the sacrifice for sin. Our Lord expressed the supreme purpose of His incarnation when He said: "I came not to be ministered unto, but to minister, and to give my life a ransom for many."

It is possible to contrast the birth of our Lord Jesus as He came into this world of ours with the birth of other men. We are born to live. True, because of sin we die, because of the eternal edict of God that by one man's sin many were constituted sinners, and so death has reigned as a result of sin. However, there is in the breast of every man that which strives to live and fights against death. Man was born to live—he wants to live. ". . . all that a man hath will he give for his life."

However, our Lord Jesus was born to die. The odor of myrrh that came from His garments spoke of the purpose of His coming. It is the death of our Lord Jesus that has brought joy into the world, for through that death God has been able to receive sinful man and to justify him by His grace and righteousness. He exacted from His own Son the penalty of sin, and because of this He offers eternal life to you and me through Jesus Christ our Lord.

THE FRAGRANCE OF CHRIST—ALOES

His garments also smell of aloes. As the hymn writer put it, aloes speaks of bitterness. There was that about the life of our Lord Jesus which is perfectly adapted to the symbolism of aloes. Isaiah spoke of Him as the "man of sorrows" and the One "acquainted with grief." It is often said that life is sweet, but let it not be forgotten that it has also its bitterness. From the cradle on, through the various stages of human life until the grave, it is given to the sons of men to taste of the bitterness of circumstance and life. Our Lord was a "man of sorrows." He was "acquainted with grief." He could enter, therefore, into the griefs of men and sympathize with them. What a perfect man was Christ! He could sit at the banqueting table of a wedding feast as is recorded in the 2nd chapter of John. He could supply for that nuptial feast the very wine that maketh the heart of man glad, but He could also stand beside the tomb in which were the remains of a beloved brother. In fact, one of the sisters of Lazarus, who stood by the Lord at the grave, rebelled against the injunction of Christ when He ordered her to roll away the stone from the grave. She responded, "Lord . . . he hath been dead four days." As the friends of the bereaved noted the expression upon the face of our Lord Jesus, a true man of sorsows, they said, Could not this man who caused the blind to see, could not He have prevented the death of this man? For they noted that from the eyes of our Lord trickled salty tears. It is written "Jesus wept." How a Christian rejoices, that in the midst of tears, death, and sorrow, our Lord revealed His power and Deity, as He cried with a loud voice, "Lazarus, come forth" and he who was dead arose to life again. From that incident have come these words which have brought comfort and cheer to the ears and hearts of many millions of people when our Lord said: "I am the resurrection, and the life: he that believeth in me, though he were dead, yet shall he live: And whosoever liveth and believeth in me shall never die."

THE FRAGRANCE OF CHRIST—CASSIA

His garments also give forth an order of cassia, which was used as a healing balm. One of the ministries ascribed to our Lord Jesus as found in the prophet Isaiah is to "bind up the brokenhearted." Indeed, the ministry of our Lord Jesus has so blessed this universe that every step He took was a benediction and every breath He breathed sweetened the atmosphere. He has bound up the brokenhearted. Where previously there was discord, lack of harmony, disappointment, and sorrow, there now is the quietness, harmony, the joy and the peace of Christ. Is it any wonder that the Psalmist was so enrapt as he wrote of the coming of Christ out of the ivory palaces?

Is it any wonder that in verses 9 to 11 he called attention to the multitudes that had gathered about Him, under the imagery of an Oriental nuptial gathering? It is written, "Kings' daughters were among thy honourable women: upon thy right hand did stand the queen in gold of Ophir."

In this parabolic and picturesque language is found the love of our Lord Jesus Christ. Is it any wonder we have in the 10th verse this exhortation? "Hearken, O daughter, and consider, and incline thine ear; forget also thine own people, and thy father's house. . . ."

To most of us Gentiles this is rather difficult to understand, but to those instructed in Bible history and sacred writings it is exquisite. When Israel conquered the nations they often led captive some of the women. Frequently these women became the wives of the men of Israel. But before they could come into the family of an Israelite they had to solemnly forswear their own people and their father's house. This has a spiritual lesson for us. When a man receives Christ, the Bible declares that a marvelous transformation takes place. He will live a new life from that time forth. His feet will travel in a different direction. His delights will be in a different sphere. The whole complex of his life is changed. The Apostle Paul put it graphically when he stated ". . . God forbid that I should glory, save in the cross of our Lord Jesus Christ, by whom the world is crucified unto me, and I unto the world." Thus it is easy to understand the exhortation, "forget . . . thy father's house" and the assurance, "So shall the king greatly desire thy beauty: for he is thy Lord, and worship thou him."

This same principle appears in the case of the sons of Zebedee, and the Apostle Peter. Our Lord found these men and took them from their occupation as fishermen. He said, "Follow me, and I will make you fishers of men." The whole complex of their lives changed. They became as our Lord indicated, "fishers of men." So with every individual who has received Christ, their whole scheme of life is changed. They are called new creatures in Christ. What a transformation! If you will receive Christ as your Lord and Saviour, and worship Him, as we are exhorted to do in verse 11, you too will experience the same transformation. In fact, you will believe that the sun shines brighter and that the grass seems more green. Your whole manner of life will be different. Your friends and your family will recognize it and you will strive to glorify the Lord who purchased your salvation upon the cross of Calvary.

Psalm Forty-six—Part One

GOD IS OUR REFUGE—A Thanksgiving Message

THANKSGIVING Day is an American institution. Once a year we Americans are reminded, by the proclamations of the Governors of our various states, that we have cause for thanksgiving to the Almighty for His benefactions. It is a splendid idea. It would be equally desirable were we to set apart a day, at least once a year, as a national day of prayer. *

It may seem fantastic to some to suggest that the difficulties and ills of the present hour can be met and conquered through prayer, but the testimony of the ages bears its universal acknowledgment to the truth of the fact.

In our own land we are not without a witness. On Thursday of this week the families of our country will gather in their homes and, with a sumptuous spread before them, will recall the struggles of the early Pilgrims. These Pilgrim fathers had many difficulties to encounter, but with true perseverance and steadfast faith and prayer they were not overcome by their difficulties but rather they overcame their difficulties. They recognized, however, that the accomplishment was a result of the blessings of the eternal God and thus they set aside a day for thanksgiving to the Creator God for His benedictions and blessings.

We have had our problems during this past year. There are many yet to be solved, but the grace of God has once more been evident. There is not a family that will gather on Thursday but it can extend thanks to God for His grace. Yet I am confident, were our nation, from its President down to its humblest citizen, to pray unitedly for God's blessing upon our land, confessing both our national and individual sins, such prayer would not go unanswered.

Would to God more of our national leaders were praying men. Many economists have drawn our attention to the strides that England has made in getting out of this depression, strides that we in America must confess we have not attained. Might not the answer to our failure lie in the spiritual realm?

Several friends have told me that every day that Parliament is in session a number of the members, irrespective of party affiliation, gather for a session of prayer in which they earnestly implore God's guidance and bless-

---

* It was the Great Commission Prayer League which advocated November 25 as a National Day of Prayer.

ing upon their deliberations. There are several in that body who are outstanding lay-preachers. Were our incoming Congress a praying Congress, we would need have no fear about the coming session. What is true about Congress is also true of each citizen. As individuals neglect God, so do nations. It is well therefore for the nation and for the individual to return to God.

A THANKSGIVING PSALM

It seems fitting at this Thanksgiving season that our Meditation in the Book of Psalms is found in the 46th Psalm, a Psalm in which appears "a strain of grandest power and most abundant blessing to the soul whose refuge is in the living God." While in this Meditation we will not comment upon more than a few of the verses of this Psalm, it will be appropriate to quote the entire eleven verses—

> "God is our refuge and strength, a very present help in trouble.
> "Therefore will not we fear, though the earth be removed, and though the mountains be carried into the midst of the sea;
> "Though the waters thereof roar and be troubled, though the mountains shake with the swelling thereof. Selah.
> "There is a river, the streams whereof shall make glad the city of God, the holy place of the tabernacles of the most High.
> "God is in the midst of her: she shall not be moved: God shall help her, and that right early.
> "The heathen raged, the kingdoms were moved: he uttered his voice, the earth melted.
> "The LORD of hosts is with us; the God of Jacob is our refuge. Selah.
> "Come, behold the works of the LORD, what desolations he hath made in the earth.
> "He maketh wars to cease unto the end of the earth; he breaketh the bow, and cutteth the spear in sunder; he burneth the chariot in the fire.
> "Be still, and know that I am God: I will be exalted among the heathen. I will be exalted in the earth.
> "The LORD of hosts is with us; the God of Jacob is our refuge. Selah."

THE TWO METHODS OF BIBLE STUDY

There are two methods of approach to, and use of, the Scriptures. First, there is what we might designate the exact method. This is the method which the scholar uses to determine the exact purpose of the writing and its particular place in the great structure of the Bible. Were we to pursue this method in our approach to the 46th Psalm, we would have to note that a strict application of its contents looks forward to the Messianic or millennial age, that age which prophets, bards, and poets have dreamed of for centuries. It is the age when the God of Jacob, the Lord of hosts, is seen in the midst of His people upon the earth.

The other method of Bible study is to apply the spiritual lessons to present-day situations, and thus have the heart feed upon the spiritual. It is the latter method which we shall employ this morning.

I would that the first verse of our Psalm might appear as a text, or motto, in every home in our land, and that each of us applied its message to our own circumstances. The Psalmist said, "God is our refuge and strength, a very present help in trouble." Oh, that I could burn that verse into every heart! "God is our refuge." A refuge is a safe haven from a storm. Some men take refuge in position, in wealth, in friendships and in associations, but alas, alas, precious as friends are in times of distress, important as wealth is in periods of depression, powerful as position is in the hour of need, there comes a time in every life when wealth, position, friends, and associations, everything in fact, fails, and grim reality stares us in the face. When health is gone, and wealth cannot buy another day, and business problems can no longer ask for our time, it is then that man is faced with the claims of eternity. Happy is that man who can then say with the Psalmist, "God is *my* refuge and strength, a very present help in trouble." But, mark you, our Psalm has an assurance for the present as well as for the future. It is written "God *is* our refuge and strength." At this moment God can be that to every man, and God is that to every believer in the Lord Jesus.

THE TOLL OF THE DEPRESSION

The past few years have taken a terrific toll of lives. Some men have been so overwhelmed that they were unable to resist the urge to end it all. Well do I remember a man who came to my home one evening last spring to discuss his financial problems with me. He had lost heavily in business and in his security holdings. In a desperate plunge to recoup his losses, he over-extended himself. Whereas he formerly had several hundred thousand dollars as a reserve, he now had but fifteen thousand dollars and his business was yielding him a small salary of fifty dollars a week. He was restless, his face was drawn and his hair almost white. I would have guessed him to be a man about seventy to seventy-five years of age. I asked his age, and was shocked when he answered "fifty-one." He had a wife but no children. He said to me, "I would feel greatly relieved were I, upon leaving your home, to be run over by a passing automobile." That man did not have God as his refuge and strength in the time of trouble. He had trusted in uncertain riches and position.

While many other men would be extremely happy with a reserve of fifteen thousand dollars and an income of fifty dollars a week, this man, because of the contrast between what he formerly had and what he was now receiving, was desperate. I repeat he trusted in uncertain riches and position, but how unstable they were in a time of distress!

Some men grapple with moral problems and seek refuge in all sorts of ways except the only way. It is alone at Calvary that sin is dealt with and pardon extended. It is alone in Jesus Christ that man receives power to overcome sin. It is alone in God that man can find a safe refuge from the storm, and strength to overcome his difficulties.

When we are in good health and position it is easy to forget God and to conclude that our refuge lies in our own strength and ability and state. Yet, it is when we least appreciate Him, that we most need Him.

How Christians Meet Reverses

It has been my privilege to know families who have faced distressing situations as a result of the present depression, yet their solace has been in Christ. Oh, Christian friend, whoever you are or wherever you may be, do not think it is strange that you are experiencing trials and troubles. Indeed, this Psalm acknowledges the existence of trouble. Why speak of God as a present help in trouble, if there were no such thing as trouble?

Our Lord Jesus stated to His disciples: "In the world ye shall have tribulation: but be of good cheer; I have overcome the world." I have seen Christians in trouble. I have seen non-Christians in trouble. If I ever desired a proof of the joy there is in Christ, observing the attitudes of each would be sufficient for me.

I have already related the experience of a man who was not a Christian. Let me tell you of one who is a devoted follower of our Lord. This gentleman is in financial distress. There was a time when his business flour-ished, and there seemed to be no dark could upon the horizon. In fact, he, like many of us, concluded there would never be such a thing as a dark cloud. He was a good man, gave liberally, raised a beautiful family, a jolly, happy individual. I shall never forget, however, when, at the close of a service I was conducting in a suburban church, he came to me seeking a few moments of my time. We retired to the pastor's study. He could not contain himself any longer. He was a man of mature years, yet he broke down and sobbed like a child. He had lost everything. Yet there broke through the sob, like a rainbow after a storm, a gleam of hope and joy, as he clasped my hand and said, "I do not mean to complain. My Lord has been gracious to me heretofore—He will see me through now." Courage like that comes only from a faith that can remove mountains. How well it is written in the 2nd verse of this Psalm, "Therefore will not we fear, though the earth be removed, and though the mountains be carried into the midst of the sea. . . ."

I am a lover of old books. Just this week I received one from the other side of the Atlantic. It is about one hundred years old, written by a bishop of the Anglican church. In a chapter devoted to evidences of Christianity, he contrasts and compares the lives and deathbeds of some Christians with those of some unbelievers. He wrote of the death scenes of the two most noted unbelievers of the past centuries—Thomas Paine and Voltaire. Both records are well known. Alas, alas, what hopeless creatures were they! But show me a Christian who ever lamented on a dying bed his belief in the revelation of the gospel. Such a man cannot be found. I myself have witnessed such scenes. If ever I needed an urge to a more devoted discipleship to our Lord, those scenes supplied it. Indeed, whether in life or in death there can be but one safe haven of refuge. The Psalmist declared it when he said, "God is our refuge and strength."

AN ANTIPHONAL PSALM

The 46th Psalm, like all other Psalms, was set to music to be sung by the choirs of Israel. This particular Psalm, as its introduction indicates, undoubtedly was intended for the virgins who composed the soprano choir, to be sung antiphonally to the male choir. It is a Psalm whose strains reach up unto the heights. Trouble may be apparent in the first three verses of the Psalm, but joy immediately follows. In the 4th and 5th verses of the Psalm we read "There is a river, the streams whereof shall make glad the city of God, the holy place of the tabernacles of the most High. God is in the midst of her; she shall not be moved: God shall help her, and that right early."

We mentioned earlier that there was an exact method of approach to this Psalm and a spiritual method. Were we to use the exact method, we would have to call attention to the fact that this city, the city of God, the holy place of the tabernacles of the most High, was none other than Jerusalem. Some day, in answer to the prophets' predictions, God will be in the midst of her, and out of her shall flow streams of living water.

But our Lord Jesus used the river as a figure of speech and applied it to the abundant life of the spiritual man. The occasion when He used it is recorded in the 7th chapter of St. John's Gospel. Our Lord was in the temple. It was the last day of the feast of the tabernacles. The multitudes were crowded into the temple and all about Jerusalem. The last day was the great day of the feast. It was then that the Lord Jesus stood and cried: "If any man thirst, let him come unto me, and drink. He that believeth on me, as the scripture hath said, out of his innermost being shall flow rivers of living water."

Did you note that our Lord "cried"? It is very rare that such a statement is recorded of our blessed Lord. Evidently the message was of extreme importance. The message was in the nature of an invitation. It was wide enough to include every man. He said, "If any man thirst . . ." The only limitation was that the man should thirst. To such a man the Lord said, "let him come unto me, and drink." Since the time our Lord extended that invitation, millions upon millions of people have come to Him and have drunk of the water of life. They have quenched their thirst. But that is not all the gospel has to offer. Our Lord not only assured us that the thirsty man could come unto Him and drink, and be satisfied, but He went a step further and said, "He that believeth on me, as the scripture hath said, out of his innermost being shall flow rivers of living water."

The joyful and satisfied man is the man who has received Christ as his Lord and Saviour and who thereby has quenched his thirst and is now living the more abundant life. I close by reminding you that it is written: ". . . the wages of sin is death; but the gift of God is eternal life through Jesus Christ our Lord" who said, ". . . I am come that they might have life, and that they might have it more abundantly."

PSALM FORTY-SIX—PART TWO

"BE STILL"

WHILE we have already given one address on the 46th Psalm, I wish to look at it again before proceeding further in our "Meditations in the Book of Psalms." As we read the Psalm observe the unusual activity described therein. It is like a continuous roar of peals of thunder.

"God is our refuge and strength, a very present help in trouble.

"Therefore will not we fear, though the earth be removed, and though the mountains be carried into the midst of the sea;

"Though the waters thereof roar and be troubled, though the mountains shake with the swelling thereof. Selah.

"There is a river, the streams whereof shall make glad the city of God, the holy place of the tabernacles of the most High.

"God is in the midst of her; she shall not be moved: God shall help her, and that right early.

"The heathen raged, the kingdoms were moved: he uttered his voice, the earth melted.

"The LORD of hosts is with us; the God of Jacob is our refuge. Selah.

"Come, behold the works of the LORD, what desolations he hath made in the earth.

"He maketh wars to cease unto the end of the earth; he breaketh the bow, and cutteth the spear in sunder; he burneth the chariot in the fire.

"Be still, and know that I am God: I will be exalted among the heathen, I will be exalted in the earth.

"The LORD of hosts is with us; the God of Jacob is our refuge. Selah."

We devoted the previous message to the first five verses, but more specifically to the first phrase which reads, "God is our refuge and strength, a very present help in trouble."

AN IMPERATIVE COMMAND

We shall now consider the latter half of the Psalm, focusing our minds on the 10th verse which contains the unusual command:

"Be still, and know that I am God: I will be exalted among the heathen, I will be exalted in the earth."

When God addresses such a message it behooves us to give it our very best attention. Let us examine what precedes this command.

It is hardly necessary to call attention to the fact that what precedes this exhortation is a description of terrific judgments. The 6th verse resembles a huge battlefield, "The heathen raged, the kingdoms were moved: he uttered his voice, the earth melted." Every word in that verse is like a bombshell. The tramp of armies can be heard—the ragings of nations peal forth like thunder—kingdoms are collapsing—the very foundations of earth seem to give way. In the midst of that catastrophe there is a place of refuge, a haven of rest and of peace. It is written, "The LORD of hosts is with us; the God of Jacob is our refuge."

That which is described in these verses is what we were told during the World War was the complete justification of that terrific toll of lives. Beautiful rhetoric indeed it was—"*This is the war to end war.*" Alas, it seems now but to create mockery in the breast of the world. In two decades there have been planted the seeds of jealousies and hatreds that have caused the nations of the world to arm to the teeth. Hardly an issue of any leading newspaper of the world has been printed the past few months but it has contained glaring front-page headlines on the preparations for war which are taking place in the world. Every traveler returning from Europe relates tales of tension and distress amongst the nations there and almost to a man they conclude that war seems inevitable.

Evidently our Lord was an infinitely better judge of human nature than some of our leading pacifists and self-styled humanitarians who have insisted that at last war had been outlawed by the nations. It was our Lord who said,

> ". . . ye shall hear of wars and rumours of wars; see that ye be not troubled: for all these things must come to pass, but the end is not yet.
>
> "For nation shall rise against nation, and kingdom against kingdom; and there shall be famines, and pestilences, and earthquakes, in divers places.
>
> "All these are but the beginning of sorrows."

Do not misunderstand me. Every effort should be expended to assure and preserve peace, and every sincere effort devoted to such ends should be encouraged. But as long as human nature is what it is, war can never be entirely banished out of this world. Furthermore, the Bible declares that the particular characteristic of this age is that which is aptly expressed in the phrase ". . . *ye shall hear of wars and rumours of wars.*" It is the blind pacifist who fails to understand the simple, clear message of the Scripture upon this subject.

This world of ours would be poor indeed, were that the sole outlook for the future. I thank God that some day there *shall* be a war to end war. But that war has not yet taken place. It is the war described in this Psalm. It is the great battle between God and the armies of men. The result will be terrific desolations upon the earth. In fact our Psalm, in its 8th verse, invites us to look at the disaster: "Come, behold the works of the LORD, what desolations he hath made in the earth." It is after He has made this desolation that it is written, "He maketh wars to cease unto the end of the earth; he breaketh the bow, and cutteth the spear in sunder; he burneth the chariot in the fire."

The statesmen of the nations are at present faced with terrific problems. They need our prayers. There is hardly a nation upon earth but is faced with turmoil from within and possible attack from without. Such a condition requires a most skillful handling of the ship of state. While we are pressed with problems and difficulties, I am far from a pessimist. I am a realist to the marrow, to be sure, but a "hope-ist" at the time when the night becomes the darkest.

This is not a new problem. One of the more famous quotations from the Bible by Isaiah, the prophet, resolves itself about this same problem, when there comes from the voice of the inquirer, "Watchman, what of the night?" to which the watchman responds, "The morning cometh, and also the night." The watchman who replied to the burning question of the inquirer was not like the proverbial ostrich who hides his head in the sand to escape the furor of the oncoming storm. He was a realist, for he added, "and also the night," but his eyes could pierce through the blackness of the night and observe the gray dawn of the morning, for he maintained that, "The morning cometh"!

Yes, "The morning cometh," the morning of peace and of tranquility, the morning of joy and of gladness when He, the Prince of Peace, shall come. Then, and not until then, will He make wars to cease!

This entire Psalm is devoted to, and is occupied with, the return of our Lord in power and in great glory. We shall not, however, discuss this particular phase of the message, but shall do as we did in the previous address, attempt to apply the principles and lessons of this Psalm to present-day problems and conditions with which each of us is confronted, hoping thereby to get some spiritual blessing.

"BE STILL, AND KNOW"

Thus we shall take the 10th verse out of its true context, which looks forward to a restored earth in blessing and grace, with the Lord Himself in the midst of the city, and, instead, apply it to our circumstances.

It is a great message. "Be still, and know that I am God. . . ." Frankly I do not know a more difficult task. We all seem to delight to talk, to defend ourselves, to justify our failures, to condone our defeats, to controvert our neighbors, but the injunction is clear and emphatic "Be *still*—and know that I am God."

We Americans have learned after years of leanness that "activity is not necessarily a sign of progress." Indeed, apart from the mechanical strides in the realm of inventions and designs, we must confess that instead of progress we have really been slipping quite fast. Oh, I know that even now there are still one or two die-hard evolutionists who chant, "Every day in every way we are getting better and better." That's partly true, but its application is not always so correct. We are getting better and better in learning methods of destruction. We can, and have, devised machines to go faster and faster in their destructive powers. We have devised chemical combinations that can wipe out a nation in a day. But it is a serious question whether this can properly be called constructive progress.

The physician agrees with the message of this Psalm. He knows the value of quietness as a remedy for a disturbed and a disordered constitution. What a message this is—"be still, and know that I am God"!

What is true about the world is equally true of the individual. We, too, are faced with problems in our own lives and troubles of every description. The message to us as individuals is just the same, "Be still." But this is more than cessation of activities. It is more than the stopping of frets and worries. It is a positive as well as a negative message. It is—*"be still, and know that I am God."*

"Know that I am God," yes, that is the greatest revelation that can come to any soul. Our Lord Jesus gave evidence of its great value in His high priestly prayer addressed to His Father. It is recorded in the 17th chapter of St. John's Gospel where we read, ". . . this is life eternal, that they might *know* thee the only true God, and Jesus Christ, whom thou hast sent." When we have learned that lesson it gives great courage. It was the Apostle Paul who said: ". . . I *know* whom I have believed, and am persuaded that he is able to keep that which I have committed unto him

against that day." It was the Apostle John who wrote, "Beloved, now are
we the sons of God, and it doth not yet appear what we shall be: but we
know that, when he shall appear, we shall be like him; for we shall see him
as he is."

THE NEED TO "BE STILL"

The importance of true knowledge is all too evident to warrant comment, but the application of such knowledge is very often lacking.

Let me relate a little incident which undoubtedly will illustrate the
thought that is expressed by the Psalmist, "Be still, and know that I am
God." Some time ago I received a letter from a radio listener. It was
written by a woman who, it was evident, was faced with difficulty. She
began her letter as follows: "Will you kindly give me your opinion concerning the employment of childless married women with husbands earning fine
salaries, while single, self-supporting women and men with families are
forced to sit idle, many undergoing dire circumstances?"

I have studiously avoided a discussion of social and economic problems in our radio "Meditations in the Psalms." In the first place most of
us get enough of that six days of the week; but more important, I believe
a true understanding of the gospel is the answer to every problem. Yet, I
confess that the opening sentences of the letter induced me to read on. Most
of us find it difficult to stifle inquisitiveness altogether—men at any rate!
So I learned that her question was not an abstract one, but presented her
own case. She was a school teacher out of a position. She was incensed that
in the town where she lived the members of the Board of Education, when
a vacancy occurred, gave it to a married woman and more often to someone
related to one of the members of the Board, or a friend of the Board. She
became so incensed that she wrote an article which condemned this practice
and sent it to the town newspaper, which printed it. The newspaper signed
it in big letters "Town Teacher."

Of course, the Board concluded that she was the writer. They questioned her, but she refused to admit her authorship. She then joined the
Taxpayers' Association and began to raise riot. Needless to add, this
teacher is still without a job. She wonders why. She asked "What can I
do?" and finally ended her letter by stating: "Your talks over the radio are
lovely but can I accept them if it does not work in my own life? I want
something that works in my own life. I cannot be 'without God and hope'

but I feel that religion must work in the *individual's own* life to be effective. Others' experiences do not help me unless I get the *same* results."

What that lady needs to learn is the lesson of the 10th verse of this Psalm, "Be still, and know that I am God." I'll confess it is no easy lesson to learn!

Let me press the subject a little closer home. I daresay that if the principle of this verse were practiced in our homes, many, many of the problems of marital life would never arise. Oh, I know it is a hard thing to be still when you know you are right, but more often than otherwise, we are the most vociferous when we have the weakest defense. Instead, therefore, of criticizing the times and the circumstances and what not for our difficulties and problems, why not do as God invites us to do in this verse—"Be still, and know that I am God."

But, I hasten to explain that this exhortation is a limited one. It is addressed to those who know God. If you have not been born again, if you do not know the Lord Jesus as your own Lord and Saviour, this lesson is meaningless, though the principle may be worthwhile. If you wish to know God, you need not go very far. You may find snatches of revelation of His power and deity in all the realms of creation but you will never find God in creation. You may even hear His voice in the thunder, but you will never see Him. To know God is to know an individual, a person, not merely a power. This is the testimony of Christianity which makes its message unique —that the person of God is revealed in His Son Jesus Christ our Lord.

And I dare to say that one cannot read the claims of our Lord, as contained in the Gospels, without being aware that He claims Himself to be God, for He said, "he that hath seen me hath seen the Father. . . ." Again, He said, "I and my Father are one." It would seem that pure logic would drive a man to either one of two conclusions. Either Jesus Christ is God, as He declared Himself to be, or He was the world's greatest impostor. But I cannot leave that without this further comment. If He were an impostor, the world has a still greater miracle to explain. The miracle of literature. It would be next to impossible to determine the number of books that have been written, but of this there can be no doubt—in all the literature of the world, not one single perfect character has been portrayed. The literary geniuses of the world have failed to depict a perfect man. But what geniuses failed to do, four men have accomplished, none of whom had any literary talent and only one of whom could be called an educated man. Matthew, a former politician, Mark, an indifferent helper, Luke, a physician, and John, a fisherman, each have presented a miracle of literature—a portrayal of a perfect Man! If Jesus Christ is not God, as someone once put it, we ought to bow before the four men who portrayed Him. If you wish to know God, you must consider Christ.

THE FUTURE EARTH

Finally, our Psalm contains a great promise. The Lord said: "I will be exalted among the heathen, I will be exalted in the earth." It is quite evident such is not the case now. This is man's day. It is a day of sin, a day of contradictions. Evil is upon the throne, while righteousness is on the scaffold. But it shall not always be so. The nations of the earth will one day exalt Him. That exaltation will take place upon the earth.

Now, however, it is given to you and to me, as individuals, to glorify God. We glorify Him when we believe the record that He has given of His Son. And this is the record that God gave of His Son, "that God hath given to us eternal life, and this life is in his Son. He that hath the Son hath life; and he that hath not the Son of God hath not life."

PSALM FORTY-SEVEN

THE PSALM WITH A CHRISTMAS MESSAGE

THE Psalm to which we desire to direct our attention this morning is the 47th, which contains nine short verses. It is primarily a Psalm of praise. As we read the Psalm, note the frequent exhortation to praise contained therein.

"O clap your hands, all ye people; shout unto God with the voice of triumph.

"For the LORD most high is terrible; he is a great King over all the earth.

"He shall subdue the people under us, and the nations under our feet.

"He shall choose our inheritance for us, the excellency of Jacob whom he loved. Selah.

"God is gone up with a shout, the LORD with the sound of a trumpet.

"Sing praises to God, sing praises: sing praises unto our King, sing praises.

"For God is the King of all the earth: sing ye praises with understanding.

"God reigneth over the heathen: God sitteth upon the throne of his holiness.

> "The princes of the people are gathered together, even
> the people of the God of Abraham: for the shields
> of the earth belong unto God: he is greatly exalted."

From time to time, during the course of these Meditations in the Psalms, we have directed our attention to two specific viewpoints, the first being the universality of this great collection of Biblical poems. Beyond a doubt, it represents the most beloved part of the Scripture. It seems as if the Psalmist has touched our lives in a most unusual manner and that he has expressed perfectly the conflicting emotions that we experience, and that he has done so infinitely more aptly than we ever hoped was possible to express in language.

Of course, this evidences divine authorship and the inspiration of the Holy Spirit. The Book of Psalms, like every other portion of the Bible, is God-breathed. The Psalmists were moved by the Holy Spirit. While their personality is never lost, and in a true sense the words are their own, it was the Spirit of God who guided their writing, and in a more true sense the words are God's words. For this reason, though the Psalms are hoary with age, there is nothing "antique" about them. They are as alive and as fresh today and vibrating with vitality and life as the day they were written.

In addition to the universality of the Psalms, we have also called attention to the Messianic message of the Psalms. Like all other portions of the Old Testament Scripture, the Person who is presented in the Psalms is none other than the Lord Jesus Christ. Many of the Psalms are Messianic in their outlook, pointing forward to the time when the Messiah shall reign as the absolute monarch of the world. The 47th Psalm points to that era.

THE FAMOUS FIRST CHRISTMAS MESSAGE

It is somewhat coincidental that we should consider the 47th Psalm at this particular season of the year. Very shortly, Christendom will once more call to mind the birth of our Lord Jesus Christ. That great story which never grows old will once more be told. The famous Christmas carols will be sung. Wherever the name of our Lord Jesus has become known, the details of His birth and the startling testimony of nature and the angels will be brought afresh to thrill minds and hearts. Will you consider this 47th Psalm in the light of the Christmas message?

> "O clap your hands, all ye people; shout unto God
> with the voice of triumph.

> "For the LORD most high is terrible; he is a great
> King over all the earth."

Let us look at the testimony of St. Luke concerning the manner of our Lord's coming into this world. We are told that the angel Gabriel was sent from God unto a city of Galilee, named Nazareth. He was sent to a virgin espoused to a man whose name was Joseph, of the house of David; and the virgin's name was Mary. The angel came unto her with a strikingly strange salutation. "Hail, thou that art highly favoured, the Lord is with thee: blessed art thou among women."

Now, of course, it is difficult for us to imagine the reception that Mary gave to the salutation of the angel. However, every instructed Israelite at that particular time knew that the prophet Isaiah had declared that a virgin should give birth to a son and that this son would be Immanuel, God with us. I do not think that it is inconceivable that in the breast of every virgin in Israel the hope was cradled that perchance she might be the most honored among women.

Mary was troubled at this saying of the angel, and cast in her mind what manner of salutation this should be. The disturbed expression led to that sincerely comforting message from Gabriel, as he addressed it to Mary when he said,

> "Fear not, Mary: for thou hast found favour with God.
> "And, behold, thou shalt conceive in thy womb, and
> bring forth a son, and shalt call his name JESUS.
> "He shall be great, and shall be called the Son of the
> Highest: and the Lord God shall give unto him the
> throne of his father David:
> "And he shall reign over the house of Jacob for
> ever; and of his kingdom there shall be no end."

There were several promises made by the angel to Mary, and in observing these promises bear in mind what is also written in the Scripture, that every word spoken by an angel "was steadfast, and that every transgression and disobedience received a just recompense of reward." Here are the promises:

> First, that Mary would give birth to a son.
> Second, His name would be called Jesus.
> Third, He would be great.
> Fourth, He would be called the Son of the Highest.
> Fifth, The Lord God would give unto Him the
> throne of His father David.

> Sixth, He would reign over the house of Jacob for
> ever.
> Seventh, of His kingdom there would be no end.

Let us look at the actual historical record. Mary did give birth to a son. She did call His name Jesus. There is no doubt about it, He was and is "great." No sensible, sane person would question that His greatness far surpasses the combined greatness of all other great men. Again, He was called the Son of the Highest. Thus, four of the promises of the angel Gabriel were literally fulfilled, to the dotting of the "i" and the crossing of the "t." But the angel also made three other promises which have not yet been fulfilled. These promises are as follows,

> One, "The Lord God shall give unto him the throne of
> his father David."
> Two, "he shall reign over the house of Jacob for ever."
> Three, "of his kingdom there shall be no end."

What kind of loose thinking do you suppose must take place to arrive at the conclusion that while the first four promises were literally fulfilled the last three are not to be literally fulfilled? Indeed, the only sane view that any sound-thinking man can take is that just as definitely as the first four promises were fulfilled, so the last three shall likewise be fulfilled. Our Lord is to have the throne of His father David. He is to reign over the house of Jacob forever, and of His kingdom there shall be no end. He will some day, therefore, be recognized as the universal Messiah. He shall have the throne of His father David. His father David had his throne in Jerusalem. Our Lord shall reign over the house of Jacob forever, but the confines of His kingdom shall not be limited to Palestine, but will extend throughout the earth, for it is written, "of his kingdom there shall be no end."

GOD'S PLAN FOR THIS EARTH

With the message of Gabriel in mind, let us focus our thoughts upon the 47th Psalm.

> "O clap your hands, all ye people; shout unto God with
> the voice of triumph.
> "For the LORD most high is terrible; he is a great
> King over all the earth."

Who is the Lord most High? None other than the Christ of God. What are the confines of His kingdom? The whole earth. What will take place when He reigns as King over all the earth? The 3rd verse of this Psalm declares it: "He shall subdue the people under us, and the nations under our feet."

Some of us Gentiles may not like what I am about to say, but too many of us who are Christians (of course, there is a tremendous difference between a Gentile and a Christian—all who are not Jews are Gentiles, but only those who have received and embraced Christ are Christians) have assumed that God has cast away His ancient people, Israel, for all time. How anyone can arrive at such a conclusion is beyond me, when the Scripture is so clear as to what God intends to do in this earth of ours. Let me give you the plan of God. It was expressed by James, the apostle, who presided over the first council of the church. The record of it is found in the 15th chapter of the Acts of the Apostles. This council was held in Jerusalem. The great, pressing question was this, What relationship should the Gentiles have in the church of God? After listening to the testimony of the various apostles, James concludes the decision of the council, and gives his summation. He said:

> "Men and brethren, hearken unto me:
>
> "Simeon (Peter) hath declared how God for the first time did visit the Gentiles, to take out of them a people for his name.
>
> "And to this agree the words of the prophets; as it is written,
>
> "After this I will return, and will build again the tabernacle of David, which is fallen down; and I will build again the ruins thereof, and I will set it up:
>
> "That the residue of men might seek after the Lord, and all the Gentiles, upon whom my name is called, saith the Lord, who doeth all these things."

How definite is the plan of God. At the present time, God is taking out of the Gentiles a people for His name. In fact, it was from this incident that the word *church* became the accepted designation of the group of people gathered unto the name of our Lord Jesus. The word *church* comes from the Greek word *ecclesia*, meaning "called out ones." God is now calling out of the Gentiles a people for Christ's name. They are Christians. They compose the invisible church. When this task has been completed, in agreement with the words of the prophets, He will return and build again the tabernacle of David, which is fallen down. He will build the ruins, and set it up, that the blessings of Abraham might come on all Gentiles. What a glorious plan God has for this earth!

It is to that period that this 47th Psalm refers. When the Psalmist said, "He shall subdue the people under us, and the nations under our feet," he referred to the domination of the nations under the leadership of Christ by Israel. Any other viewpoint of the 47th Psalm could not possibly be entertained. The Jews some day will cease to be the tail of the nations. They will become the head of the nations, with their Messiah reigning from Jerusalem. This may not please Fuehrer Hitler, but, then, someone should give that man a Bible! Israel shall join hands in that great kingdom. This is further evidence by the comments in the closing section of this Psalm, in the 8th and 9th verses, which read, "God reigneth over the heathen: God sitteth upon the throne of his holiness. The princes of the people are gathered togethered together, even the people of the God of Abraham: for the shields of the earth belong unto God: he is greatly exalted." We Gentiles should be honest and confess that the "heathen" mentioned in this Psalm are the Gentile nations, and that the references to "the princes of the people are gathered together, even the people of the God of Abraham . . ." applies to the Israelites.

GOD'S "NEW DEAL" GOVERNMENT

Do not get the mistaken notion that this reign will be a despotism. It will be a theocracy! That is the "New Deal" this poor world needs. Despotism has failed. Monarchy has proved deficient. Democracy has been weighed in the balances and found wanting. Communism, Fascism, Hitlerism, or any other form of human government, is destined to failure. There is only one hope for this old world of ours, and it is theocracy, the rulership of our Lord Jesus, as the Anointed of God, over the nations of the earth.

This is not the dream of a visionary. It is the expressed declaration of the Word of God. It is to be found on almost every page of Scripture. What an era of peace, joy, and gladness it will be! It is to that age the angel Gabriel referred in his salutation to Mary. It will be an era of tremendous joy. Look, for instance, at the 6th and 7th verses of our Psalm. They read, "Sing praises to God, sing praises: sing praises unto our King, sing praises. For God is the King of all the earth: sing ye praises with understanding."

In two short verses the exhortation to sing is found five times. The song is a song of praises. The praise is offered to God, who is the King of all the earth. We are exhorted to sing praises with understanding.

Now then, I hope we have made it quite clear during the course of our meditation that this Psalm focuses upon the kingdom reign of our Lord

Jesus, upon the Messianic age, the time when our God shall reign as King of all the earth. However, does that mean we poor mortals who live in the present age are to fold our hands and sit down and mope? Indeed not! There is also a spiritual message in this Psalm that carries its exhortation to our own hearts in this particular hour, for which reason I want to take the exhortation that appears in the 6th and 7th verses and consider it for the present moment. The exhortation is to sing praises unto God. I hardly need to tell you how enriched this world has become as a result of what took place that first Christmas day. Man received a new song. The angels gave the substance to the song, "Glory to God in the highest, and on earth peace, to men of good will." From that day to this very hour, Christianity has brought a song into the world, but more particularly into the heart of every believer in Christ.

Art, (literature, music, and all the higher sciences in which man's soul is permitted to express itself, have all become greatly enriched and lifted into the sphere of ecstasy, as a result of the coming of our Lord Jesus. Song? Where can you hear such chords and strains as in the great "Hallelujah Chorus"? Where has it been possible to find comfort and cheer comparable to that which comes from the hymns of Christendom? They are not in the minor key. They are in the major key. They express the gladness of the human heart, because that heart has found its resting place in God, its Creator, Redeemer, and Lord. How the heart responds to that glorious hymn,

> "All hail the power of Jesus' name!
> Let angels prostrate fall;
> Bring forth the royal diadem
> And crown Him Lord of all.
>
> "O that with yonder sacred throng
> We at His feet may fall,
> We'll join the everlasting song,
> And crown Him Lord of all."

There may be hours of perplexity which will bring a note of sadness into the breast of the believer, yet even in such an hour it is written, He giveth a "song in the night. . . ." Yes, indeed, this world has been enriched by the songs of praise unto our God.

But there is an exhortation in our Psalm which reads, "sing ye praises with understanding." Here is no ordinary singing or joining in with the multitude because of a delightful tune. Here is singing with the understanding and songs wherein we consider the words, as well as the music. Only the

man who has been born again and whose life has been touched by the Lord
Jesus can sing the songs of praise unto our God with understanding.

Some of us have not been blessed with the gift of melody. I once heard
Dr. Ironside, who is pastor of the great Moody Memorial Church, in Chicago, say that sometimes the urge to sing so overwhelms him, he is driven
into the woods, where only the birds are privileged to hear him sing. That
struck a responsive chord in my own heart. Unfortunately, I have occasionally forgotten that I was in an audience, while thrilled to the marrow
over the words of a hymn, but I was soon rudely shocked by those about
me casting unadmiring glances my way! However, I am glad it is written
that we are to make a joyful noise unto the Lord, and that our singing
should be from the heart. It is then that it is with understanding.

May I suggest to those who may not have a song in your heart, a song
of praise unto God, that the wells of joy will be yours upon receiving the
testimony of the gospel. Christ Jesus, received by you as your Lord and
Saviour, will bring this song into your heart.

PSALM FORTY-EIGHT

THE FUTURE CITY OF THE GREAT KING

WE are now to consider another great Psalm, in fact, a most appropriate Psalm for the day in which we live. For some weeks the
whole world has been on edge. The nerves of the nations have
been worn to a frazzle while the eyes of all turned to Prague, to Berlin, to
London, to Paris, to Berchtesgaden, to Rome, and to Godesberg, as each
vied with the other in what was almost certain to terminate in a clash.
Washington was also a place of great tenseness. All the world held its
breath, wondering what would take place. Were the nations of the earth
again to engage in another World War? And, if so, would it accomplish
what many people fear—the utter collapse of our civilization? Who knows?
But of this we are assured; neither London, nor Paris, nor Berlin, nor Godesberg, nor Rome, nor Washington, compares with a city which the Psalmist
extolled in the 48th Psalm when he wrote:

> "Great is the LORD, and greatly to be praised in the
> city of our God, in the mountain of his holiness.
>
> "Beautiful for situation, the joy of the whole earth, is
> mount Zion, on the sides of the north, the city of the
> great King.

"God is known in her palaces for a refuge.

"For lo, the kings were assembled, they passed by together.

"They saw it, and so they marvelled; they were troubled, and hasted away.

"Fear took hold upon them there, and pain, as of a woman in travail.

"Thou breakest the ships of Tarshish with an east wind.

"As we have heard, so have we seen in the city of the LORD of hosts, in the city of our God: God will establish it for ever. Selah.

"We have thought of thy lovingkindness, O God, in the midst of thy temple.

"According to thy name, O God, so is thy praise unto the ends of the earth: thy right hand is full of righteousness.

"Let mount Zion rejoice, let the daughters of Judah be glad, because of thy judgments.

"Walk about Zion, and go round about her: tell the towers thereof.

"Mark ye well her bulwarks, consider her palaces; that ye may tell it to the generation following.

"For this God is our God for ever and ever: he will be our guide even unto death."

What a Psalm for the nerves of today! One can almost hear in it the tramp of soldiers, the massing of troops, the drawing of battle lines, the cries of distress, the explosions of a naval conflict, the parading of dictators and kings. But, thank God, one can also hear the wild scramble of the invaders as they retreat in distress before the revelation of the One called "The Great King." Here the sabre-rattling of all time is silenced before the Lord, and peace finally reigns. It is a good Psalm to examine in a time of distress.

But note, here is a Psalm which in its introduction is also called "a Song." It was given to the sons of Korah who participated in the worship of Jehovah. It is a patriotic song as well as a spiritual Psalm for the earthly people of God.

ISRAEL *vs.* THE CHURCH

In this connection there is a matter which may require clarification. It is essential that we think straight, walk straight, and even sing straight. For instance, there are some hymns written by men and women who evidently knew little or nothing about their Bibles. Many of these writers failed to recognize the simple distinction between the Old and the New Testaments, between Israel and the church of Christ. Israel had a Saviour, a Book, and a land. The Christian has a Bible and his Christ, but no land. Israel was an earthly people—Christians are a heavenly people. The prophet of old was a patriot—the man of God today is an ambassador. Ambassadors never meddle in the politics of the land of their ambassadorship. The preacher of today, if he is true to his calling, has one task, *only one*—to preach the unsearchable riches of Christ and to make the way of salvation plain. The prophet in the Old Testament not only led the people into the path of obedience to the Lord, but invariably led the nation to a political domination over its enemies. Politics had a place in the preaching of the prophets; it has no place in the ministry of the Christian messenger.

This 48th Psalm therefore, when it speaks of Zion and Jerusalem, does not refer to the church and the heavens. The Psalm is occupied with an earthly city, described in verse 2 as "Beautiful for situation (or elevation), the joy of the whole earth. . ."

Neither Rome, London, Berlin, Paris, nor Washington can be termed "the joy of the whole earth." The "joy of the whole earth" in the future will be Jerusalem. So it is both advisable and appropriate for us to examine this Psalm and learn something about the city which some day will come into its designated place of exaltation.

But, let me say this—one can never separate a Jew from his religion. The Gentile nations have never been able to assimilate the Jew. Even such a melting pot as the United States never has and never will be able to assimilate the Jew. The Jew insists, and rightly so, that he is a nationalist of the nation of his citizenship; but he is also a Jew. That strange phenomenon of all times is a miracle; a definite, unanswerable proof of the inspiration and accuracy of the Bible. The situation exists because of the determinate counsel and foreknowledge of God. It is as impossible to stamp out the Jew in this world as it is to stamp out God. God has a purpose in that people. He will bring His purpose to pass. So, it is good and timely to consider this Psalm, especially in the light of the things which are transpiring at the present moment.

Now then, here is a matter of extreme importance in considering the subject of this Psalm. The very first word is an expression of praise, "Great is the LORD. . . ." The trouble with this world is not that they have placed God second. Indeed, they have excluded Him entirely. He is not even considered last. He is *never* considered. When Chamberlain and

Hitler met this week, I dare say it was not suggested that they open their discussions with prayer, asking the Lord for His guidance, though thank God multitudes of God-fearing people in this world have been praying about that meeting, including the wife of the British Prime Minister, whom one of our American "lady" columnists inadvisedly took to task for so doing. The problems of Europe could be amicably settled in short order if men would only give God His place in this world. Thus, it is interesting to observe the order found in this Psalm. First, we have the Lord, and then an exhortation to praise the Lord, and finally the designated place where praise is to be offered.

Concerning that place, it is written, it is "Beautiful for situation," it is the "joy of the whole earth," it is "the city of the great King. God is known in her. . . ." That, however, did not prevent the kings of the earth from assembling themselves together with a view to disturbing the inhabitants of the city as on previous occasions. But alas, a striking transformation had taken place in the city. God was there. First they marveled, then were troubled, whereupon they quickly retreated. Fear took hold upon them, overpowering their strength, as they recognized that God had established His name in that city.

And then the scene changes. The people within the city think of the lovingkindness of God. They praise Him. The praise vibrates to the ends of the earth. Mount Zion rejoices and her people are invited to walk around Zion, to count her towers, to mark well her bulwarks, and to consider her palaces. Finally, the Psalm closes as it begins, with a recognition of God's place in the nations of the earth—"For this God is our God for ever. . . ."

As the Psalm specifically refers to the city of Jerusalem, it is primarily intended for the Jewish nation. It probably refers to a specific time in the history of that nation when the people sang this song with great joy, but it also has a prophetic message. The Bible has much to say about the future glory of Jerusalem. In fact, the peace of the world is definitely linked up with what will transpire in that city and in the land of Palestine.

JESUS CHRIST IN HISTORY

Now, without going too far afield, we shall call attention to a few things which we do well to carefully bear in mind. There are certain historical facts which no right-thinking man controverts. The facts are so abundantly attested that they are unanswerable. They are, first, that Jesus Christ lived on this earth in the land of Palestine some nineteen hundred years ago. Second, that the life He lived was so absolutely perfect that it still remains the most remarkable that has ever been witnessed in this world. Third, this Jesus of Nazareth had some things to say about Jerusalem and the temple therein, some of which were literally fulfilled forty years later to the dotting of an "i" and the crossing of a "t." His prediction regarding the temple was minute. He said that not one stone of that magnificent structure would be left upon another. The disciples immediately raised the question, What about the future? Whereupon He outlined what would transpire on the earth during His absence, for He had already let it be known that He would return to His Father's house. Fourth, He also described the events that would transpire immediately prior to His return to this earth, which conditions should be considered as a sign of His near approach. Fifth, He was taken by wicked hands and crucified, and buried in a rich man's grave. But He arose from the dead and showed Himself alive after His passion by many infallible proofs. Finally, one day, He took His disciples out to the Mount of Olives. There He outlined the whole course of gospel preaching, saying that it would begin at Jerusalem, penetrate all of Judea, then go into Samaria, and then unto the uttermost parts of the earth. The disciples asked, What about the restoration of the kingdom to Israel? Our Lord answered, "It is not for you to know the times or the seasons, which the Father hath put in his own power. But ye shall receive power, after that the Holy Ghost is come upon you: and ye shall be witnesses unto me. . . ."

Then a most extraordinary sight greeted their eyes. This Jesus with whom they had been intimately associated for three years; this Jesus who had such a tremendous hold upon them, even though He again and again jolted them with a statement that bewildered them; this Jesus whom they had forsaken in the moment of His passion; this Jesus in whom they revelled upon recognizing Him after His resurrection—this Jesus was taken up from them into the heavens. They saw Him ascend. They saw a cloud receive Him out of their sight. And, as they stood steadfastly gazing into the heavens, suddenly two men in white apparel appeared unto them and said, "Ye men of Galilee, why stand ye gazing up into heaven? this same Jesus, which is taken up from you into heaven, shall so come in like manner as ye have seen him go into heaven." The Scripture states they "returned to Jerusalem with great joy. . . ."

The disciples, at the time when our Lord left them, were all Jews. Later on, the Gentiles began to hear the gospel. Then a problem arose. Had God turned to the Gentiles? If so, what about the Jews? What about the relationship between Jews and Gentiles who received Christ? The 15th chapter of the Acts of the Apostles answers these questions. From it we learn that James, the apostle, arose before the assembled brethren and declared that God was now visiting the Gentiles, "to take out of them a people for his name." And after this, that is, when He has finished that task, He will "return, and will build again the tabernacle of David, which is fallen down. . . ." He will build again the ruins thereof and will set it up, "That the residue of men might seek after the Lord, and all the Gentiles," upon whom the name of the Lord is called.

So you see, Christians in the 1st century believed that the Lord would return, at which time He would establish the throne of David and would build the ruins of the city, for the great purpose that blessing through Israel might be poured out upon the Gentiles and that all might call on the name of the Lord. I never think about the future without a prayer in my heart that God may hasten the time when these things will actually transpire. No Christian has a right, and certainly no sane Christian will ever take it upon himself, to set the time when this event shall take place. We do not know the day nor the hour. But in His Word our Lord has given us certain definite predictions which He urged us to consider as signs of His near approach. One of these signs relates to the activity in the city of Jerusalem and in the land of Palestine.

THE PEACE OF JERUSALEM

With each passing year of the past two decades, Jerusalem and the land of Palestine have come more and more to the forefront. Multitudes of Jews have returned to the land. Problems have arisen which seem almost insurmountable. But, the land is vibrating with activity, pointing its sure testimony to the fact that God is interested in it and that some day an event of utmost importance will take place within its borders. If you please, that event will put fresh meaning into this 48th Psalm. It will enable the ancient people of God to sing it with a new fervor and a new spirit. No wonder we are urged in the Word to pray for the peace of Jerusalem, which is equivalent to praying for the return of our Lord Jesus Christ, for the peace of Jerusalem is linked up with the return of the Prince of Peace. When Palestine and Jerusalem have peace, then the whole world will enjoy that same tranquillity. But it is all because "Great is the LORD, and greatly to be praised in the city of our God. . . ."

At the present time this all seems like a dream. There are so many matters that need to be settled before peace, real peace, can be enjoyed. But I dare say when God moves, He moves with startling rapidity and with terrific might.

Let me give you an example. One of the greatest ships afloat is the Queen Mary. It was scheduled to sail from its pier in New York at 4.30, Wednesday afternoon. Massive as is that ship, it was unable to sail as scheduled and did not leave until the next morning at 5.30—because a mere wind, which we called "a tornado," prevented its sailing.

When our Lord returns, He will sweep the world with might and power, He will crush every rebellion, and rule with a rod of iron. The kings of the earth then assembled will be troubled. We can thoroughly appreciate and understand the phrase used in the 5th and 6th verses of this Psalm where we read, "They . . . hasted away. Fear took hold upon them there, and pain, as of a woman in travail." That is what is in store for some of our modern, maddened, self-intoxicated, blood-thirsty rebels called dictators.

But we must not close this message without a mere personal word. The world is made up of men. The problem of the world is the problem of men; the very forces in the world are those that dominate men. The problems that confront the world are the problems that confront men. I suggest that you, as an individual, will never know peace in your troubled breast, any more than this world will know peace in this troubled age, until you open your heart to receive Him who not only is the Prince of Peace, but the Saviour of your soul. It is of no avail to fight against Him. What is more, it is no use trying to solve your own problems. They defy solution. The nations of the earth one day will be obliged to bow the knee and confess Him as the Lord of lords and King of kings, but it is your privilege and mine to gladly acknowledge Him *now* as our Lord and as our Saviour. Then, as every Christian will confess, there is experienced in the heart the peace of God which passes understanding. That peace is a symbol of the peace that this world will some day enjoy when God is in His right place.

Until the Lord occupies the right place in our heart, in our thinking, and in our life, we will never know what it is to really live and rejoice and sing with a heart of gladness and a mind at peace and rest.

PSALM FORTY-NINE—PART ONE

TRADING ON BORROWED WISDOM OR
RESTING ON ANOTHER'S DEATH

THE 49th Psalm contains twenty verses. We shall limit this meditation, however, to the first eight verses. Those who are acquainted with their Bible will immediately recognize that this Psalm presents the great facts of death, redemption, and resurrection.

> "Hear this, all ye people; give ear, all ye inhabitants of the world:
> "Both low and high, rich and poor, together.
> "My mouth shall speak of wisdom; and the meditation of my heart shall be of understanding.
> "I will incline mine ear to a parable: I will open my dark saying upon the harp.
> "Wherefore should I fear in the days of evil, when the iniquity of my heels shall compass me about?
> "They that trust in their wealth, and boast themselves in the multitude of their riches;
> "None of them can by any means redeem his brother, nor give to God a ransom for him:
> "(For the redemption of their soul is precious, and it ceaseth for ever:)"

It is certainly apparent that here is a message addressed to all mankind. It is not alone given to Israel, but also to all the inhabitants of the world, "Both low and high, rich and poor, together." In the councils of God there is no distinction between "low and high, rich and poor." The Bible divides the world of mankind into three great divisions. There is first the Jew, constantly referred to as God's "chosen" people. Then there is the great mass of Gentiles, who comprise the larger portion of the people. The third class is made up of individuals out of both the Jews and Gentiles. They are the people who have received Christ and embraced Him as their Lord and Saviour. They form what the New Testament is pleased to call "the church" of the Lord Jesus Christ, the church of which He is the Head.

It is hardly necessary to impress upon you the fact that the Bible knows only about one church. To unbelievers, particularly critical unbelievers, it seems a monstrosity that the so-called Christian church is broken up into almost a thousand pieces. Well might the question be raised, where is there any evidence of the oneness of believers in Christ? Did not Jesus pray that all believers might be one? Yes, our Lord actually did that in His high priestly prayer recorded in the 17th chapter of John's Gospel. He prayed for all believers. He asked His Father, "That they all may be one; as thou, Father, art in me, and I in thee, that they also may be one in us: that the world may believe that thou hast sent me."

How is it possible to reconcile that for which the Lord prayed, and which is unfolded in the Scriptures, with what one actually sees in existence in this world? The answer is that there is no reconciling them—they are two different diverse things. The church of which the Bible speaks is not the visible church—it is the invisible church. That church is called the body of the Lord Jesus. The members of that church may have their membership on the rolls of some earthly church but, mark you, membership in a local church is no assurance that one's name is "written in the Lamb's book of life." Even in the company of twelve disciples one was a devil!

The church of our Lord Jesus Christ, of which He is the Head, includes as its members every born-again man or woman who has believed in the Lord Jesus, irrespective of what denomination he or she may be a member on earth. I hope I have made that clear and that you understand that God has divided this world into Jew, Gentile, and the church of our Lord Jesus. Apart from this division the Bible does not know of the social distinctions that exist between the various classes of people.

A UNIVERSAL MESSAGE

This Psalm has a universal message. It is addressed to "Both low and high, rich and poor. . . ." All the inhabitants of the earth are invited to listen to the words that proceed out of the lips of the Psalmist when he states, in the 3rd and 4th verses, "My mouth shall speak of wisdom; and the meditation of my heart shall be of understanding. I will incline mine ear to a parable: I will open my dark saying upon the harp."

The New Testament reveals Christ as the wisdom of God. He is the One whose mouth speaketh wisdom, and the meditation of whose heart is of understanding. He, too, spoke in parables and uttered things which had been kept secret.

Frankly, while it may not be particularly comforting to us in the 20th century to be informed that the wisdom of this present age is but a phonograph of earlier centuries, yet such a fact cannot be denied. We have been trading on borrowed wisdom. During the four centuries preceding the coming of our Lord Jesus, man was given an opportunity to speak. In no other time in man's history did he speak as loudly. It was the springtime of human wisdom. That period is invariably referred to as the "era of the philosophers." At the close of that period our Lord Jesus appeared on the scene. It is quite interesting to observe that during those four centuries when the vast majority of philosophers lived, there was not a visit from an angel, nor any word from the eternal God. In Bibliology that period is called "the four centuries of silence." It covers the years between the close of the Old Testament and the opening of the New Testament Because God was silent, man had an opportunity to speak the loudest, but as soon as our Lord Jesus came the tongue of man was silenced. Never before did man listen to such wisdom as was expressed by Him. Well did those soldiers say concerning Him, "Never man spake like this man." The words of our Lord Jesus have echoed through the centuries, and are as powerful today as they ever were, for the words of our Lord Jesus are the words of God. The beginning of wisdom is the fear of the Lord. Our Lord's mouth spoke forth wisdom and revealed the great purposes of God in redemption.

The Iniquity of Our Heels

In the 5th verse of our Psalm an unusually quaint saying is found: "Wherefore should I fear in the days of evil, when the iniquity of my heels shall compass me about?"

The Psalmist was expressing confidence against the day when the iniquity of his heels should compass him. "The iniquity of his heels" is a phrase pregnant with meaning. It is, of course, an oriental expression. Sin clings to the heels of a man as dust covers the heels of the Eastern traveler, shod only with sandals. Usually upon the return of a member of the household, or upon the arrival of a guest, a servant awaits at the door, unfastens the sandals, and washes the defiled feet. The Psalmist has a Redeemer. He does not fear against the day when men's sins shall be manifested, when they will no longer be able to shake the dust from off their feet. Comforting indeed is the possession of confidence against that day. But it is not the result of anything the Psalmist did, nor anything that we might do for ourselves, nor that another man might do for us. Indeed, in the following verses it is revealed that,

> "They that trust in their wealth, and boast themselves in the multitude of their riches;

> "None of them can by any means redeem his brother,
> nor give to God a ransom for him:
> "(For the redemption of their soul is precious, and
> it ceaseth for ever:)"

These three verses give me great delight. They contain a very important message. It is evident that it is impossible to buy salvation. What is more, it is impossible for any other man, or relative, to aid, or to give to God a ransom for his brother. The redemption of the soul is so precious, that once it is paid, it ceases forever. It is done once and for all! Who is able to redeem us? It is here that the gospel of our Lord Jesus comes in with tremendous power. He had no sins of His own. His life was spotless. Even the critics of our Lord concede that much. The judge who sentenced Him said, "I find no fault in this man." One of the thieves who was crucified with Him said, ". . . this man hath done nothing amiss." In fact, the centurion who supervised the crucifixion said, "Truly this man was the Son of God."

If you possessed all the money in the world you could not, with all that wealth, purchase your own salvation or the salvation of any other. The scripture contains the edict that "without shedding of blood is no remission" of sins. This is a message for "Both low and high, rich and poor, together."

The gospel exerts a powerful leveling process. It takes a man steeped in wealth and high in the world's esteem and brings him down to the level of the poor man and the man of low estate. Certainly it is evident that we brought nothing into this world and we cannot take anything out with us. Sometimes great men or wealthy men have conceded that the testimony of God concerning their souls was true, and have received the Lord Jesus as their Saviour.

The late J. Pierpont Morgan certainly was a man of high estate and one of the world's richest men. However, with all his riches and with all the advantages of his birth, Mr. Morgan had to come by the same way every sinner comes. His confidence in the Lord Jesus was very aptly expressed by him in the preamble to his will. Because of this declaration, a tract was issued entitled, J. Pierpont Morgan's Greatest Transaction. The preamble of this will reads as follows:

> "I commit my soul into the hands of my Saviour, in
> full confidence that having redeemed it and washed
> it in His most precious blood, He will present it
> faultless before the throne of my Heavenly Father;
> and I entreat my children to maintain and defend,
> at all hazard, and at any cost of personal sacrifice,

the blessed doctrine of the complete atonement for
sin through the blood of Jesus Christ, once offered,
and through that alone."

Frankly, I have never read a clearer testimony concerning unswerving faith and confidence in the value of the atonement of our Lord Jesus. J. Pierpont Morgan acknowledged that his soul was stained with sin, but had been washed and redeemed. Nothing could take the stains of sin out of his soul but the precious blood of our Lord Jesus. Nothing is able to take the stains of sin out of my soul or your soul but that same precious blood. But mark you, as the noted financier expressed in his will, something even greater than that is done—the presentation of that washed and cleansed soul faultless before the throne of our heavenly Father. I do not know whether the children of the late Mr. Morgan have given ear to the entreaty of their father, and "maintained and defended, at all hazard, and at any cost of personal sacrifice, the blessed doctrine of the complete atonement for sin through the blood of Jesus Christ, once offered, and through that alone." No greater entreaty could be laid at the door of any soul.

But there are men who are willing to maintain and defend, at all hazard, and at any cost of personal sacrifice, the blessed doctrine of the complete atonement for sin through the blood of Jesus Christ, once offered, and through that alone.

THE CASE OF JOHN AND BETTY STAM

All the civilized world listened this past week with breathless interest to the news flashes of the death of two fine young missionaries, brutally murdered by a band of Chinese Communists. I refer to the late Mr. and Mrs. John C. Stam. It was with great relief that we learned that the little babe, Helen Priscilla, three months of age, was found, and from all reports, was well and unharmed. Here were two young people in their late twenties, who cast aside every offer that this world presented them, and in devotion to their Lord went forth into dark places, treacherous places, in order to make the name of our Lord Jesus Christ known. I knew John Stam personally for fifteen years. I watched that young man grow. I observed the devotion that he had for his Lord. I know his family very well and have had close fellowship with them these past fifteen years. I never expect to know as large a family whose every member is wholeheartedly yielded to the Lord, and whose whole purpose in life is "to maintain and defend, at all hazard, and at any cost of personal sacrifice, the blessed doctrine of the complete atonement for sin through the blood of Jesus Christ, once offered, and through that alone." His family has given a marvelous testimony to the grace of God.

The memory of December 13th will never be wiped out of my mind. The father of John Stam was visiting in New York. One of his sons phoned me, and told me that his father expected to visit with me, at my office, and that they had just heard of the death of their brother and his wife—would I break the news to his father? The first words from the lips of the father as he entered my office were these, "Have you heard any news?" I responded, "Yes." "Tell me what it is," said the father. When I told him that he had the honor of being the father of a son and daughter-in-law who had given their lives for the Lord, he answered, with tears in his eyes, "I can say 'the Lord gave and now the Lord hath taken away,' yet, while it hurts, I can add, 'blessed be the name of the Lord.' "

Of course, there was a deep wound in this father's heart. We can sympathize, though we cannot enter into his sorrow. But through it all there was the abiding consciousness of the joy that is in Christ, in the fact that his son, John, had gone forth to make the name of the Lord Jesus known among the heathen. Only the previous night he had prayed for the captors of his son, that they might come to know the same Lord whom he and his family served.

The day after the news came of the death of these two missionaries I received in the mail a letter from John Stam. It was quite evident that he knew of the dangers in Tsingteh, the place from which he was taken captive. His letter was written from Wuhu on November 10. He wrote of the raids by Chinese bandits then. He asked prayers for a native Chinese Christian, by the name of Mr. Lo, who was about to move to another district. Mr. Lo's wife, he said, "was inclined to be on the fearful side." Then he ended: "Pray that both they, and we, may know the truth of that verse, 'God hath not given us the spirit of fear.' Praise God for such a gospel as we have to preach."

Here were a young man and a young woman who willingly devoted their lives in order that others, not as fortunate as we in multitudinous opportunities of hearing the gospel, might have a chance to hear the good news that the sacrifice of Christ atoned for sin.

The soul of a man is precious. Our Lord asked the question, ". . . what shall a man give in exchange for his soul?" The soul of a man must be valuable if the redemption of that soul is precious.

I have often said, and love to repeat it, that God robbed heaven of its glory when He sent His Son into this world. He sent Him for the express purpose of redeeming man's life from destruction. What a gift God gave to this world on the first Christmas Day!

Because the redemption of man's soul is precious, the Psalmist says it ceaseth forever. It is finished. It was completed when the Lord Jesus died on the cross and cried out, "It is finished." Since that hour there has been placed in the breast of every believer the urge to make the gospel of our Lord Jesus known to those who know Him not.

I do wish I could impress upon each of you the necessity of personally receiving the testimony God has given concerning His Son, that you may have the assurance of the redemption of your soul. May we make sure that we are not placing our confidence in our wealth, nor boasting ourselves in the multitude of our riches, but that we are placing our trust in the sacrifice of our Lord Jesus and our boast in the multitude of the riches of God's grace.

PSALM FORTY-NINE—PART TWO

REDEEMED FROM THE POWER OF THE GRAVE

IN our previous meditation in the 49th Psalm we touched upon the first eight verses, beginning with the universal exhortation to all people to give ear, and ending with the statement that no man can by any means redeem his brother, nor give to God a ransom for him, because the redemption of the soul is precious and it ceaseth forever.

We shall now consider the balance of the Psalm, commencing with verse 10:

> ". . . wise men die, likewise the fool and the brutish person perish, and leave their wealth to others.
> "Their inward thought is, that their houses shall continue for ever, and their dwelling places to all generations; they call their lands after their own names.
> "Nevertheless man being in honour abideth not: he is like the beasts that perish.
> "This their way is their folly: yet their posterity approve their sayings. Selah.
> "Like sheep they are laid in the grave; death shall feed on them; and the upright shall have dominion over them in the morning; and their beauty shall consume in the grave from their dwelling.
> "But God will redeem my soul from the power of the grave: for he shall receive me. Selah.

"Be not thou afraid when one is made rich, when
the glory of his house is increased;

"For when he dieth he shall carry nothing away:
his glory shall not descend after him.

"Though while he lived he blessed his soul: and men
will praise thee, when thou doest well to thyself.

"He shall go to the generation of his fathers; they
shall never see light.

"Man that is in honour, and understandeth not, is
like the beasts that perish."

We shall not attempt to comment on each of these remaining verses
of this Psalm, but rather take two or three of the peak passages and press
their message to our hearts and minds.

It is quite evident that the Psalmist was declaring the absolute equality
of man when it comes to the matter of death. It has often been said that
all men are born equal. But that is far from a fact. All men are born in
the usual manner. All enter the world without anything, but there is no
equality apart from that. Certainly there is a vast distinction between
being born into a royal family or a family of wealth and distinction, and
the birth of the large majority of us who constitute the common people.
However, at death something quite different takes place. Irrespective of
the family relationship, irrespective of whether an individual is a member
of a royal family or of the common people—each dies and leaves everything
behind. How true it is as the Psalmist expressed it in the 10th verse:
". . . wise men die, likewise the fool and the brutish person perish, and
leave their wealth to others."

There is a certain glamour about gathering wealth and building large
estates and having dwelling places called after our names. Nevertheless,
all that striving is vain. After one has acquired wealth and has risen to
a high position and even perchance has gained great wisdom so that the
world literally sits at his feet and listens to the outpouring of his wisdom—
What of it? It is only for a passing day. When night comes, the tongue
is silent, the wealth is left behind, the dwelling places are vacant, and the
individual is gone. How true that the one who fails to make preparation
for such an event, while spending all his time in the way of getting position,
wealth, buildings, and land, is traveling the way of mere folly.

Men are laid in their graves, whether in "potter's fields" or in million-
dollar mausoleums. Death feeds on all. Yet there is a vast distinction
between men in death. A man goes out of this world either saved or lost.

He will either rise with the righteous dead or he will rise with the wicked dead. He either leaves this world to go home to be with the Lord or he leaves this world a lost, wandering soul. Such is the testimony of the Bible, the only book in all the world which speaks with authority on the subject of what is beyond the grave.

PULLING THE CURTAIN ASIDE

Our Lord Jesus, during the course of His public ministry, gave a revelation of what transpires beyond the grave, in that compelling story of Lazarus and the rich man.

The rich man fared sumptuously every day. Lazarus was a mere beggar who sat at the gate of the wealthy man and ate the crumbs that came from his table. Even the dogs came and licked his sores. But it came to pass that they both died. What happened then? Let us hear the words of our Lord Jesus. Regarding the beggar He said, "And it came to pass, that the beggar died, and was carried by the angels into Abraham's bosom . . ." Concerning the rich man He said, "the rich man also died, and was buried . . ." With the exception of the fact that the onlookers were not able to see the angels who carried the soul of the beggar into Abraham's bosom, man witnessed these facts. The rich man and the beggar died. It is a question where the beggar was buried, or that he ever was buried. The rich man, however, was buried. We can readily imagine the costly funeral service held for him. But what was beyond? Here is where the Lord pulls the curtain aside and allows us to see.

Our Lord was speaking and He said:

> "And in hell he (the rich man) lift up his eyes, being in torments, and seeth Abraham afar off, and Lazarus in his bosom.

> "And he cried and said, Father Abraham, have mercy on me, and send Lazarus, that he may dip the tip of his finger in water, and cool my tongue; for I am tormented in this flame."

Some will say that this is merely figurative speech. But what is figurative speech? It is symbolic language. But what is a symbol? Is it not like the shadow, compared to the reality? Conceded that this is picturesque, parbolic language, yet it cannot be denied that our Lord thus depicted terrific sufferings. Again, He thereby revealed beyond a shadow of reasonable doubt that there was consciousness after death upon the part of the rich man and upon the part of the beggar. And what makes hell?

Memory! The one was in comfort and glory, while the other was in torment. I beg of you to bear in mind that it was our Lord Jesus who gave us this unfolding.

The rich man recognized Lazarus, who was but a beggar when upon the earth and asked Father Abraham to send Lazarus, that he might dip the tip of his finger in water, and cool his tongue. What did Abraham say? According to our Lord, this is what he said:

> "Son, remember that thou in thy lifetime receivedst thy good things, and likewise Lazarus evil things: but now he is comforted, and thou art tormented.
>
> "And beside all this, between us and you there is a great gulf fixed: so that they which would pass from hence to you cannot; neither can they pass to us, that would come from thence."

Then in his desperation, the rich man spoke to Abraham and said,

> "I pray thee therefore, father, that thou wouldest send him to my father's house:
>
> "For I have five brethren; that he may testify unto them, lest they also come into this place of torment."

Quite frequently it has been maintained that if one only rose from the dead to tell us what takes place there, the world would strain to hear about it. If such an experience did occur, it would be on the front page of every newspaper; it would be broadcast over every radio station. Man would then be informed on the subject which so perplexes him. But what does Abraham answer? Listen to our Lord: "Abraham saith unto him, They have Moses and the prophets; let them hear them." To which the rich man responded, "Nay, father Abraham: but if one went unto them from the dead, they will repent." But Abraham replied, "If they hear not Moses and the prophets, neither will they be persuaded, though one rose from the dead."

It is a fact, that no man has ever been convinced by what he has seen. Saving faith does not come by sight. Faith, born only by sight, is valueless to the saving of the soul. Nowhere in Scripture is it said that a man saw, and then believed. This is what it does say, ". . . faith cometh by hearing, and hearing by the word of God." A man is saved by believing. *After* he believes he sees. The order is never reversed. How true, as Abraham remarked,

> "If they hear not Moses and the prophets, neither will they be persuaded, though one rose from the dead."

Our Lord Jesus arose from the dead. He was seen by upwards of five hundred men at one time, during the forty days after His resurrection. Before He ascended, He demonstrated by many infallible proofs that He had risen from the dead. But does man now believe, because Christ rose from the dead? Not at all! Yet, that Christ rose from the dead is not a matter of belief; it is a fact of history.

Christ did not say the rich man was in hell because of his riches, nor Lazarus in paradise because of his poverty. That which caused these men to be in opposite conditions was their attitude to the Word of God. "They have Moses and the prophets; let them hear them. . . If they hear not Moses and the prophets, neither will they be persuaded, though one rose from the dead." Lazarus was saved because he believed God's Word. The rich man was lost because he did not believe. You and I are either saved or lost for the same reason.

PSALM FIFTY—PART ONE

WHEN GOD SPEAKS

SINCE it is true that "Man shall not live by bread alone, but by every word that proceedeth out of the mouth of God" we ought to examine with more than ordinary care the message of the 50th Psalm, for practically the entire Psalm is devoted to the spoken word "out of the mouth of God" as recorded by His servant, Asaph, who was one of the three great song leaders of Israel during David's reign. The Psalm reads:

"The mighty God, even the LORD, hath spoken, and called the earth from the rising of the sun unto the going down thereof.

"Out of Zion, the perfection of beauty, God hath shined.

"Our God shall come, and shall not keep silence: a fire shall devour before him, and it shall be very tempestuous round about him.

"He shall call to the heavens from above, and to the earth, that he may judge his people.

"Gather my saints together unto me; those that have made a covenant with me by sacrifice.

"And the heavens shall declare his righteousness: for God is judge himself. Selah.

"Hear, O my people, and I will speak; O Israel, and I will testify aaginst thee: I am God, even thy God.

"I will not reprove thee for thy sacrifices or thy burnt-offerings, to have been continually before me.

"I will take no bullock out of thy house, nor he goats out of thy folds.

"For every beast of the forest is mine, and the cattle upon a thousand hills.

"I know all the fowls of the mountains: and the wild beasts of the field are mine.

"If I were hungry, I would not tell thee: for the world is mine, and the fulness thereof.

"Will I eat the flesh of bulls, or drink the blood of goats?

"Offer unto God thanksgiving; and pay thy vows unto the most High:

"And call upon me in the day of trouble: I will deliver thee, and thou shalt glorify me.

"But unto the wicked God saith, What hast thou to do to declare my statutes, or that thou shouldest take my covenant in thy mouth?

"Seeing thou hatest instruction, and castest my words behind thee.

"When thou sawest a thief, then thou consentedst with him, and hast been partaker with adulterers.

"Thou givest thy mouth to evil, and thy tongue frameth deceit.

"Thou sittest and speakest against thy brother; thou slanderest thine own mother's son.

"These things hast thou done, and I kept silence; thou thoughtest that I was altogether such an one as thyself: but I will reprove thee, and set them in order before thine eyes.

"Now consider this, ye that forget God, lest I tear you in pieces, and there be none to deliver.

"Whoso offereth praise glorifieth me: and to him that ordereth his conversation aright will I shew the salvation of God."

We are told by Hebrew scholars that the verbs in the first verse of this Psalm should be in the present tense, rather than in the past tense. It is not that the mighty God *hath* spoken and called the earth, but rather that the mighty God, even the Lord, *speaketh* and *summoneth* the earth from the rising of the sun unto the setting thereof.

There is another noteworthy fact in this opening verse which in our English translation is not quite as impressive. The Authorized Version reads, "The mighty God, even the LORD, hath spoken. . ." In the Hebrew it reads, "El Elohim Jahve speaketh . . ." which literally translated would be "God, God(s) (uni plural of El) Jehovah, speaketh . . ." In the Old

Testament God is given several names. Each of these names connotes a specific characteristic of God. The first name of God that we find in the Bible is Elohim. It appears in the opening verse of the Bible, which reads, "In the beginning God (Elohim) created the heaven and the earth."

In this 50th Psalm we have *El Elohim Jahve*, which while it is accurately translated *the mighty God, even the LORD*, is more impressive in the Hebrew, to the spiritual mind. It is God, the all-mighty One, the all-powerful One who is about to speak in this Psalm. But it is also interesting to observe that the Psalmist introduces God not alone as the mighty God but also by that other name, probably His greatest name, which no Jew ever allows to pass his lips: the name of Jehovah. Invariably the Jew substitutes the name Adonai for the name Jehovah. Jehovah is too holy a name to pass human, sinful lips, they say. The use in this Psalm of the name Jehovah linked with Elohim implores us to understand that the One who is about to speak and before whom is a tremendous audience is not only the all-mighty, all-powerful God, the Creator of the universe, but also the holy God, the unapproachable God. He is the One whose eyes are too holy to behold sin.

Here is another interesting thing. The first time the name Jehovah is used in the Bible is in connection with the creation of man, as recorded in the 2nd chapter of Genesis. That use of the name would indicate that Jehovah is the special name of God in His relationship to men. Actually, the word *Jehovah* means "the self-existent One," but the word also has in it the thought of revelation and manifestation. It is written that when God called unto Moses out of the midst of the burning bush, commissioning him to go unto Pharaoh and to deliver the children of Israel out of the Egyptian bondage, Moses said unto God, "Behold, when I come unto the children of Israel, and shall say unto them, The God of your fathers hath sent me unto you; and they shall say to me, What is his name? what shall I say unto them?" To this question God answered, "I AM THAT I AM . . . Thus shalt thou say unto the children of Israel, I AM hath sent me unto you."

But there is even more than that in the name Jehovah. There is in it a very strong inference of a future revelation, so that the answer of God to Moses' question could as well be translated, "I will be that I will be . . . thus shalt thou say unto the children of Israel, *I will be* hath sent me unto you." Indeed, I have in my library a copy of an English edition of the Old Testament, translated by Jewish scholars exclusively. It was given to me by a Jewish gentleman for whom I have the highest esteem. In it this passage in the book of Exodus is translated just as I have given it to you. Therefore the name itself indicates a future revelation of Jehovah to men. It is the testimony of the New Testament that this is the very thing that God has done in Jesus Christ. Thus, according to New Testament teaching, the Lord Jesus is none other than the Jehovah of the Old Testament.

It is of further interest to note that Jehovah is the redemptive name of God, the name God invariably employs in speaking of and revealing Himself in this great task of the redemption of man from the power, and the guilt, and penalty of sin.

There is so much in the opening verses of this Psalm that, frankly, I hardly know where to begin or how to present it in some orderly manner which will enable us to retain in our minds a sense of the majesty and the mercy of the eternal God and also to gain some impression of His ultimate purpose in this world.

In a large measure, we in this age are better able to understand the message of this Psalm than our forefathers and the ancient sages. It is only in the last two decades that man has made extensive use of the discovery that it is possible to put sound on light waves so that the voice can travel around the whole globe in a flash of a split second. Previously the world had no tangible evidence that it was possible for one man to speak and yet be heard by all peoples in all parts of the earth. Now we know through radio how closely the nations have been brought together. It is now possible to know immediately what is transpiring in other parts of the world. The variations of time do not make the slightest difference. In some parts of the earth there is the rising of the sun, in other parts the setting thereof, and in still other parts it is high noon. Yet today we hear the voice of one man speak and it reverberates around the whole earth. All of us were impressed this past week when we saw how one man could disturb the whole earth. Such being the case now, of a mere man, what will it be when Almighty God, even the Lord, speaks! He will call upon the whole earth to listen to what He has to say. There will be no rabble-rouser or sword-rattler in that great audience. The Lord demands silence. All the world is called upon to listen to Him. Now the opposite is a fact. God is silent—man speaks. But while God may be silent, He is far from being asleep.

Let us never assume that because God is silent now, He will remain silent forever. In a very real sense He has already spoken in the written

Word which we call the Bible, but one day He will speak aloud. When He speaks it will not be from Munich. God will speak out of Zion, the place which He calls "the perfection of beauty," and from whence our God shall shine. It is to be expected that the Lord would return to Zion for it was in that place where "the princes of this world" crucified "the Lord of glory." It was there that man sent this message back to the heavens, "We will not have *this man* to reign over us." If God did not send His own Son back to that very spot where He was rejected, and there demand obedience to Him, the eternal God would be defeated. The idea is preposterous and inconceivable.

While we are unable in this meditation to examine the message of God found in this Psalm there is one other introductory matter that requires attention. It is this—God does not keep any man in suspense or in ignorance of His message. Suspense is terrible. The world was in suspense during a large part of the past week. We did not know what would transpire. We did not know what a certain man would say or decide. We were not sure whether he would be satisfied with the offer made to him; whether it would gratify his vanity and soothe his ambitions, or spur him on to further madness. But God has not left us in ignorance of His purpose or His message or the things that will take place in the future. If we want to know what the Lord shall speak some day which will be heard by the whole earth read the 50th Psalm. He has given us the advance "press release," if you please. He gave it to the generations that preceded us in order that they, too, might not forget God.

INVERTED THINKING

This 20th century has devised an "apology" for God. They have made a mechanical robot and labeled him God. And so our thinking is inverted.

Let me give you an example of inverted thinking. The other evening my wife and I took a walk along Fifth Avenue. We passed by one of New York's great churches. On its bulletin board were the topics the minister will preach on today. His morning message was entitled "Christianity on Trial." I stopped, looked at the bulletin board again, and pondered on that subject title. The more I thought of it the more absurd it became. Unwittingly, that minister gave evidence that he had neither gotten his message from the Word of God, nor intelligently prayed before the Lord about it. Imagine if you can a more clear evidence of the lopsided, shallow thinking of today, which supposes that it is possible for God to be on trial, for the Bible to be on trial, for Christianity to be on trial! Sir, it is not God nor Christ nor the Bible nor Christianity which is on trial—it is you, I, and every other member of this human race. Oh, for a voice that would be heard above all this 20th century rabble, that would call men back to God and to the Bible. It is a Godless civilization that is on trial. It has been weighed in the balances and found wanting, and its future brings forebodings.

But there are some people in this world (thank God, there are a number of them) who have absolutely no fear for the future though they know exactly what will transpire. They have no fear because they believe God and the record He has given concerning His Son: that God was in Christ reconciling the world unto Himself. God has already provided the redemption, and now all that He asks of mankind is to believe Him, to receive His mercy, and then to praise and glorify Him. Simple! It is the least we can do. It is not a case of earning one's salvation, but of receiving a free gift and then manifesting a spirit of devotion to the One who loved us and gave Himself for us. But the same Lord who died on the cross, and permitted men to spit at Him and pluck hairs from His cheek, and whose back the Roman soldiers scourged, that same despised Nazarene, is the Almighty. Some day He will speak out of Zion and will not keep silent. Fire shall devour before Him, and it shall be very tempestuous round about Him when He calls to the heavens and to the earth for an accounting and to enter into the judgment before Him.

It is inevitable that it be so. Everything within a man bears testimony that it must be so. Sin must some day be dealt with in judgment. Righteousness must fill the whole earth. These things demand that "God shall come, and shall not keep silence. . ."

PSALM FIFTY—PART TWO

THE JUDGE'S PRONOUNCEMENTS

THERE are a number of cutting words in this 50th Psalm which do not find their way into many, if any, of the pulpits of our fashionable churches today. The October issue of the "Reader's Digest" contained an excellent attempt to put in succinct word pictures some of the cartoons that have recently appeared in the "New Yorker," all of which touched upon what they termed "the foibles of the upper crust." One of the group was a typical fashionable church scene. The service was finished in fitting style, the crowds poured out in their fine array. A gentleman in a top hat turned to his wife and speaking of the preacher said, "Everything considered, he preaches a remarkably good sermon. It is so hard to avoid offending people like us." But the Word of God has no fear of offending people, as is evident from this 50th Psalm.

In this Psalm, the scene is a judicial one. A subpoena has been issued and served upon each individual, making it mandatory for all to be present to hear what God, the Judge of all, shall say. Note will you that there are two classes of people ordered to appear before God—one called "saints" and the other "the wicked." In the 5th verse God delineates saints as those who have made a covenant with Him by sacrifice.

Notice also that before God has anything to say to the wicked, He pronounces His verdict upon His saints who have made a covenant with Him by sacrifice.

Since we learned from verse 7 that God is prepared to testify against those who have made a covenant with Him by sacrifice, may I ask the question—What do you suppose will be the experience of those who have no such relationship with God because they have no sacrifice? Since God declares that He will testify against His covenant people, then, what about those who are not members of that covenant?

Let us look at a New Testament word about this same matter. The Apostle Peter in his first letter, the 4th chapter, commencing with the 17th verse wrote, "For the time is come that judgment must begin at the house of God: and if it first begin at us, what shall the end be of them that obey not the gospel of God? And if the righteous scarcely be saved, where shall the ungodly and the sinner appear?"

So in this 50th Psalm, God judges His own covenant people before He passes judgment upon those who are outside of that covenant.

A FORM OF GODLINESS ONLY

Israel even in her earliest history, made the mistake of assuming that a ritual was satisfying to God; that a *form* of worship was all that God required. But all the blood of bullocks, and goats, and fowls could never atone for a man's sin. First there had to be a deep consciousness in the breast of the offerer that he was a guilty, undeserving sinner, and that his sacrifice was presented to declare emphatically that his sin demanded death and his only hope of pardon lay in the death of his substitute. The substitute was *typified* by the animal sacrifices which God required of Israel, but the true sacrifice by which atonement was to be made had to be provided by God Himself. That is exactly what Abraham told his son would take place, when Isaac asked his father—Here's the wood and the fire, but where is the lamb for a burnt-offering? Abraham answered, "My son, God will provide himself a lamb for a sacrifice. . ." From John the Baptist we learn that our Lord Jesus Christ was that Lamb, for John testified of Him, saying, "Behold the Lamb of God, which taketh away the sin of the world."

In verses 14 and 15 we are told what God requires of His own people. "Offer unto God thanksgiving; and pay thy vows unto the most High: and call upon me in the day of trouble: I will deliver thee, and thou shalt glorify me." Remember, these words were addressed to those whom God called His "saints." God did not say that to an unsaved person nor to anyone who failed to come with a sacrifice. Indeed, He did not address "the wicked" in this Psalm until the 16th verse. Prior to that He is seen judging those who have already called upon His name. To use a parallelism, if a man, who has already received Christ as his Saviour, wants to know the will of God for his life and to have the blessing of God upon it, he is required first to offer unto God his thanksgiving; second, he must pay his vows unto the most High. If he does these he has the assurance that if he will call upon the Lord in the day of trouble, the Lord will deliver him. All God will require for that deliverance is an expression of praise that will glorify Him. But I can hear someone ask, Do you mean that vows apply to a Christian? Are vows mentioned in the New Testament? Are they not limited to the Old Testament and to Israel?

Quite true, but the character of God has not changed. He does not condone sin in His people today nor is He less concerned about it than He was in the days when He delivered Israel out of the wilderness and brought them into the Promised Land.

THE SECRET OF BLESSING

Yieldedness to the Lord is still the sole basis upon which the blessing of God falls upon a man who has already embraced Jesus Christ as his Saviour. If your life and mine are devoid of the blessing of God it behooves us to examine our lives to determine what is preventing the blessing from being experienced by us. As far as I know there are only two reasons; one, the will of God, and the other, the sin of the Christian. There are times when God withholds blessing from a child of His in order to test that individual so that He may purify his faith even as by fire. The case of Job was a perfect example of that. Such a man, however, wiii continue to praise God, for he knows his heart is right with God. But very frequently our sin is to blame for our failure to enjoy all that God intended us to have.

We ought never to quote only part of God's promises. For instance, we have no right to say that it is written, ". . . call upon me in the day of trouble: I will deliver thee, and thou shalt glorify me." We should quote the entire statement, "Offer unto God thanksgiving; and pay thy vows unto the most High: *and* call upon me in the day of trouble: I will deliver thee, and thou shalt glorify me."

THE THREAT OF GOD

In this Psalm, God has also some things to say to the wicked. God groups in that classification all who have not come under the shelter of the blood of the sacrifice He provided. God knows only two classes of people in this world—the righteous and the wicked, the saved and the unsaved. If you have never received the Lamb of God as your sacrifice, then, hear what God has to say to you, especially to you who have a form of righteousenss and godliness but who do not have the motivating power of the Holy Spirit to put the form into practice. Listen, "What hast thou to do to declare my statutes, or that thou shouldest take my covenant in thy mouth? Seeing thou hatest instruction, and castest my words behind thee." That is God's indictment against every man and woman who has failed to receive His Word. A man can do only one of two things—either receive the Word of God or reject it. One can take it and be obedient to it, or cast God's words behind his back. One can welcome the instruction of God or hate it.

But I would not be faithful to my God, to you, nor to my own conscience, if I did not add this further word. In the 22nd verse of this Psalm, the same God, loving, kind, and faithful to His promise, who provided the sacrifice when we had none, who provided us with righteousness when we were sinners, that same God who declared that God is love, made this statement, "Now consider this, ye that forget God, lest I tear you in pieces, and there be none to deliver."

This does not "set well" with a 20th century "churchy" crowd of people who have a namby-pamby sort of God who they seem to think does not bat an eyelash against sin. But the God with whom you and I must deal said, "Now consider this, ye that forget God, lest I tear you in pieces, and there be none to deliver." This principle is not limited to the Old Testament, it is found in the New Testament as well. It is part of the very character of God. Sin is high treason against God.

But you say: I do not believe the Bible to be the Word of God. That does not excuse you one iota. You are then guilty of making God a liar. If that does not strike at the very heart of God's throne, what does? You may say: I cannot believe all the Bible. Then I ask, Have you ever read it? In my experience I have found that those who do not believe the Bible know little or nothing about it. Those who have poured their hearts and minds over the Book have bowed before it enjoying its perfections and beauties.

PSALM FIFTY-ONE—PART ONE

SETTING THE FIFTY-FIRST PSALM IN ALLEGRO—"Haydn"

WE COME now to the 51st Psalm; an extremely interesting Psalm. Every student of divine writ loves it; every critic and scoffer knows it. Every devout believer comes to this Psalm in full consciousness that sin may be forgiven, in fact, entirely blotted out, and the joy of restored fellowship experienced.

The critic, however, points a finger of scorn and says, A man after God's own heart?—what a contradiction! If the writer of this Psalm was guilty of adultery and murder, was not his character a contradiction of the character of God? Every bit of that criticism is true, yet the sneer may not always be sincere. It is not entirely out of the realm of possibility that the sneerer is himself hiding behind the sin of David, so that his own sin may not be seen. I particularly enjoy the comment of Carlisle upon this Psalm, when he wrote,

> "David had fallen into sins enough, blackest crimes. Unbelievers sneer and ask 'Is this your man according to God's heart?' The sneer seems to me but a shallow one. What are faults, what the outward details of a life, if the inner secrets of it, the remorse . . . and the never ended struggle of it, be forgotten? Of all acts, is not for a man repentance the most divine? The deadliest sins were the same supercilious consciousness of no sin. . . . David's life and history, as written for us in those Psalms of his, I consider to be the truest emblem ever given of a man's moral progress and warfare here below. All earnest souls will ever discern in it the faithful struggle of an earnest human soul towards what is good and best. Poor human nature! Is not a man's walking, in truth, always that: —a succession of falls? Man can do no other."

THE PENITENT'S PRAYER

We will not, of course, be able to cover this Psalm in one short meditation, but we shall content ourselves by considering the first seven verses, which read:

> "Have mercy upon me, O God, according to thy lovingkindness: according unto the multitude of thy tender mercies blot out my transgressions.
>
> "Wash me throughly from mine iniquity, and cleanse me from my sin.
>
> "For I acknowledge my transgressions: and my sin is ever before me.
>
> "Against thee, thee only, have I sinned, and done this evil in thy sight: that thou mightest be justified when thou speakest, and be clear when thou judgest.
>
> "Behold, I was shapen in iniquity; and in sin did my mother conceive me.
>
> "Behold, thou desirest truth in the inward parts: and in the hidden part thou shalt make me to know wisdom.
>
> "Purge me with hyssop, and I shall be clean: wash me, and I shall be whiter than snow."

Like many other Psalms previously considered by us, this Psalm has an introduction that places the event at a specific time in the writer's history. The introduction to this Psalm is as follows: "To the chief Musician, A Psalm of David, when Nathan the prophet came unto him, after he had gone in to Bath-sheba."

We may not have sinned in the manner in which David did, but that each of us has sinned is evident. Were the eternal God to flash upon a screen a record of our lives we would have to bow our heads in shame.

But where should the sinful man go? To whom should he turn when his conscience has pricked him so that his heart is fairly bleeding with regret? The answer is specific. It is given in the 1st verse of our Psalm. David went to God, and poured out his heart to the Lord and begged His mercy. Let us look at this verse. "Have mercy upon me, O God, according to thy lovingkindness: according unto the multitude of thy tender mercies blot out my transgressions."

THE ONLY PEOPLE WHO CAN CONFESS
SIN AND RECEIVE REMISSION

There is just one specific class of people, to whom the promise is extended that if they confess their sins, God is faithful and just to forgive their sins, and to cleanse them from all unrighteousness. Oftentimes I have heard preachers say to a mixed audience that if they would confess their sins God would forgive them. That may sound true but the fact of the matter is, it is decidedly unbiblical and there is not a scintilla of truth in the statement. Not a single passage of Scripture can be found to support it. The Bible speaks of two classes of people—the one it designates as "saved," and the other it designates as "lost." Thus there are saved people and lost people. We are either saved or lost. If we are saved, it is by virtue of the fact that we have received Christ. If we are lost, it is because we have not received Christ. From the minute one receives Christ as his Lord and Saviour he receives the forgiveness of sins. This comes not from confession of sins, but from receiving Christ. In addition, he also receives redemption and the gift of eternal life; and then there is given the gift of the Holy Spirit, just to mention a few of the things that become ours the minute we receive Christ.

Now then, for those of us who have received Christ as our Lord and Saviour, that fact does not mean that from then on we do not sin. On the contrary, sin is more apparent to the man who has received Christ than to the man who has not received Christ. That can readily be demonstrated. The farther away a man walks from the light the less he can detect the inconsistencies of his life; whereas, the closer a man walks to the light the more inconsistencies he can see. We learn by contrasts. Thus light brings to light the hidden recesses of human sin that would otherwise not be revealed. What then, after a man has received Christ, should he do, if perchance he sins? It is then that "confession" of sin is called for. The statement of Scripture, that if "we" confess our sins they will be forgiven, is limited to a specific group—to those who have already received Christ. If "we" confess our sins, He is faithful, because of family ties, and just, because of the death of Christ, "to forgive us our sins, and to cleanse us from all unrighteousness."

In the 2nd verse of our Psalm, David asked, "Wash me throughly from mine iniquity, and cleanse me from my sin." Thus you will note that David not only requested the Lord to blot out the record of his transgressions, but he also asked Him to enter into his heart and wash him thoroughly from his iniquity and cleanse him from his sin. There we have the evidence of true repentance.

In the 4th verse David recognized what every true Christian must recognize—that all sin strikes at the very heart of God. It is true, as David stated, "Against thee, thee only, have I sinned, and done this evil in thy sight. . . ." Sin strikes at the very throne of God. David, of course, sinned against his fellow-man, but the transgression went even further, so that in reality he had sinned against God.

At times our courts of human jurisprudence can be tampered with so that justice is not done, but at the bar of God that is unthinkable. Yet, blessed is that man who has a daysman, a counselor, to intercede for him. Job gave expression to the need of such an One, when he said,

> "If I wash myself with snow water, and make my hands never so clean;
> "Yet shalt thou plunge me in the ditch, and mine own clothes shall abhor me.
> "For he is not a man, as I am, that I should answer him, and we should come together in judgment.
> "Neither is there any daysman betwixt us, that might lay his hand upon us both."

But there is such an One, now fully revealed in the Scripture, whose work it is to do just that. John, the beloved apostle, referred to Him when he wrote, ". . . if any man sin, we have an advocate with the Father, Jesus Christ the righteous. . . ."

The Psalmist was not giving us mere poetry in the 5th verse, when he said, "Behold, I was shapen in iniquity; and in sin did my mother conceive me." He was expressing a fact. We were shapen in iniquity. We were conceived in sin.

Godliness is what characterizes our Lord Jesus. His is the character that manifests God. It is His character we need. Anything less is sin. Measured by His standard, "all have sinned, and come short of the glory of God. . . ." There is, therefore, a distinction between crimes, vices, and sins. They are the objects of three sciences, respectively, jurisprudence, ethics and theology.

SETTING THE 51ST PSALM IN ALLEGRO

But let's not look at this Psalm exclusively from the dark side of human sin, but rather at the grace of God that shines through it. Such words as mercy, lovingkindness and tenderness, joy and gladness, are to be found in this Psalm. When the great Austrian musician, Franz Joseph Haydn, was asked why his sacred music was so joyful, he answered that it was "because God was so good that he would even set the 51st Psalm in Allegro."

Would to God men would understand His grace; that it is His desire that man should enjoy His mercy, revel in His lovingkindness, and bask in the sunshine of His tender care. It is His delight to take a life, stained and marred by sin, and make it an object upon which to display His grace. To every cry such as David's "Purge me with hyssop, and I shall be clean: wash me, and I shall be whiter than snow," there is the ready response, "Come now, and let us reason together, saith the LORD: though your sins be as scarlet, they shall be as white as snow;" for, "the blood of Jesus Christ His (God's) Son cleanseth us from all sin." Is it any wonder that the Apostle Paul cried out, "God forbid that I should glory, save in the cross of our Lord Jesus Christ. . . ."

PSALM FIFTY-ONE—PART TWO

THE INALIENABLE RIGHTS OF A BELIEVER

THERE are many interesting and instructive lessons to be learned from a study of the 51st Psalm, part of which we have already considered.

During our previous message we covered the first seven verses. We will, therefore, begin reading from verse eight, and as we do, will you kindly bear in mind that this is the prayer of a man who already knows the Lord, but as a result of specific sin his fellowship with God and the joy and communion which comes from fellowship has been broken. Therefore, after confessing his sin and pleading for its expiation, he asks:

"Make me to hear joy and gladness; that the bones which thou hast broken may rejoice.

"Hide thy face from my sins, and blot out all mine iniquities.

"Create in me a clean heart, O God; and renew a right spirit within me.

"Cast me not away from thy presence; and take not thy holy spirit from me.

"Restore unto me the joy of thy salvation; and uphold me with thy free spirit.

"Then will I teach transgressors thy ways; and sinners shall be converted unto thee.

"Deliver me from bloodguiltiness, O God, thou God of my salvation: and my tongue shall sing aloud of thy righteousness.

"O Lord, open thou my lips; and my mouth shall shew forth thy praise.

"For thou desirest not sacrifice; else would I give it:
thou delightest not in burnt-offering.

"The sacrifices of God are a broken spirit: a broken
and a contrite heart, O God, thou wilt not despise.

"Do good in thy good pleasure unto Zion: build thou
the walls of Jerusalem.

"Then shalt thou be pleased with the sacrifices of
righteousness, with burnt-offering and whole burnt-
offering: then shall they offer bullocks upon thine
altar."

HAVING A BIBLE AS A COMPANION

Among the many things that are apparent from a mere reading of this
Psalm is the fact that joy and gladness are the inalienable rights and possessions of the man whose sins are forgiven and whose fellowship is with
the Lord. All too frequently the notion is prevalent that being a Christian
is the pastime of the aged and decrepit. All too often it has been said that
the period in which we live is so sophisticated, cultured, and intelligent that
modern American youth requires something of a thrill in order to satisfy
the craving of its youthful persuasion. As for finding any thrill in the
knowledge of God, and in the growth in God's grace, the mere suggestion
of it usually brings forth a cynical smile.

In a very definite way, I have dealt with youth for the past two
decades. I can say without fear of contradiction, Give me a young person
devoted to Christ and I will show you a youth who is living a one hundred
per cent life, thrilled to the overflowing in the knowledge of the truth.

New Year's Eve I was in Philadelphia. I met some friends for dinner
at a downtown hotel, along about six o'clock in the evening. There were
six of us at the table. Unless you were close enough to hear the conversation you might not have guessed that all of us were Christians, rejoicing
in God's grace and in the friendships we had with each other, for somehow the notion prevails that to be a Christian requires one to be sober, and
long-faced, and to parade about with the general appearance of bearing the
weight of the world upon one's shoulders. Well, we, on the contrary, were
truly hilarious.

I was to stop at that same hotel overnight. Thus after dinner, about a
quarter to eight o'clock, I went upstairs to get my coat and hat, while the
rest of the group waited in the lobby. Knowing where I was to spend the
evening, I hurriedly put on my coat and tucked a Bible under my arm,
while the elevator waited. When I got on it, I was evidently such a monstrosity that the bell-hop running the elevator looked at me as if he were

a human question mark, and then asked, "Where in the wide world are you going with a Bible on New Year's Eve?" I answered that I knew of no better companion on New Year's Eve than a Bible. Quick as a flash, he answered, "That may be true, but it is the last thing in the world I would want on New Year's Eve."

The fact was, I spent New Year's Eve at a watch-night service in one of Philadelphia's prominent and active churches, the Tenth Presbyterian Church, of which Dr. Donald Grey Barnhouse is pastor, who, by the way, is now making a tour of mission stations in the Orient. The church, therefore, was without its pastor, but that had no effect on the crowd that was present. There were at least six hundred people attending. The service began at eight o'clock, with an interruption at ten o'clock which lasted for about one hour, during which time light refreshments were served. Then we returned to the main auditorium to continue with the services. At 11:30 communion was served, ending about two minutes after the New Year had come in. In the earlier period, several hundred people had given short, but interesting testimonies of God's goodness and grace to them during the past year, which, by the way, is exactly what the 107th Psalm bids us to do, where we read:

> "O give thanks unto the LORD, for he is good: for his mercy endureth for ever.
> "Let the redeemed of the LORD say so, whom he hath redeemed . . .
> "Let them exalt him also in the congregation of the people, and praise him in the assembly of the elders."

More than half of that congregation was young people. It would have been easier to find a needle in a haystack, than to have found a person in that audience with a long-drawn face. Everybody was having a glorious time of fellowship. If you will pardon the modern vernacular, "I had the time of my life." When I returned to my hotel room no man in this world was more truly joyful and thankful and I can assure you there was not a trace of a headache the next morning!

David, the Psalmist, knew that very same joy. Sin, however, had marred it so that he felt as if his bones were broken. Thus he cried out for a restoration of his previous joy, when he prayed: "Make me to hear joy and gladness; that the bones which thou hast broken may rejoice."

Another thing that is apparent upon a mere reading of this Psalm is this: It is the business of every believer to teach others the way of salvation. David said: "Restore unto me the joy of thy salvation; and uphold me with thy free spirit. Then will I teach transgressors thy ways; and sinners shall be converted unto thee." The joy of an individual is infectious. Any man who knows the Lord ought to be joyful. There is no room for "calamity howlers" here. With joy restored to David, he declared that he was then able to teach transgressors the ways of God.

A KING AS A PREACHER

David was not a priest. He was just a king. That, however, did not deter him from teaching transgressors the way. There were priests and Levites at the time who performed their task, but that did not mean that David had no business to teach transgressors the way. We have made a mistake in assuming that it is solely the preachers' task to give forth the message of the gospel. Thank God for faithful preachers. I know a host of them, and many are my intimate friends, yet I revel in every opportunity to witness for my Lord and teach transgressors the way. One does not have to be a theologian to be able to tell a sinner that Jesus Christ said, "I am the way, the truth, and the life. . . ." It does not take a course in theology to understand what that means. Words can be no plainer. Jesus Christ said that He is the way to God. No other way ever leads to God. Sometimes that does sound simple—almost bewilderingly simple. Because of it, there are those who think a man must be queer, to be able to joy in God and to find delight and pleasure in telling others of the way of salvation.

I recall reading some years ago with much amusement an attempt to explain the spiritual mind, by Henry L. Mencken, who was then editor of "The American Mercury," a magazine no one would ever charge with propagating "fundamentalism." A more liberal work would be hard to find.

Yet Mencken, who delighted to cast gibes at those who were old-fashioned enough to believe the Bible, invariably concluding that they were members of the "Society of Ignoramuses," was faced with a problem in analyzing the mind of his Baltimore neighbor, Dr. Howard A. Kelly of Johns Hopkins.

Mr. Mencken stated that he admired Dr. Kelly; that he had visited at his home several times and always enjoyed the occasion, but invariably he had to listen to Dr. Kelly explain his simple faith in Christ. He could not call Dr. Kelly an ignoramus, for he well knew that he is one of our outstanding men of science, having been greatly honored both at home and abroad. But then, in typical "Menckenian" fashion, he concluded Dr. Kelly had an unusual brain; it was divided into two parts! The one part functioned abnormally, yes, even brilliantly. It was with this part of his brain that Dr. Kelly worked when delving into scientific matters. However, the other half of his brain was sub-normal, and it was with that half that Dr. Kelly worked when he studied the Bible!

It is just as easy to tell a blind man the glories of color as it is to tell a natural man the glories of spiritual things in Christ. But, as the man who sees revels in color, so the man who has had his eyes opened to the glory of God in the face of Jesus Christ is thrilled by the joy of the revelation of God in Christ, and by the fellowship and communion he has with the eternal God. I make bold to say that no man is living a normal life, or is enjoying all that God intended him to enjoy until he has received Christ, and rejoiced in the grace of God. There is nothing drab nor dreary about the Christian life. However, a Christian life cannot be lived apart from Christ. As a friend of mine put it, "Don't try to live the Christian life until you first have the Christian life to live." He was absolutely correct.

In closing, may we briefly call attention to that which is discussed in verses 14 and 15 of our Psalm. In the last half of the 14th verse, David said, ". . . my tongue shall sing aloud of thy righteousness," and then in the 15th verse, he invited the Lord to open his lips and added, "my mouth shall shew forth thy praise." May I repeat that, "my tongue shall sing aloud of thy righteousness" and "my mouth shall shew forth thy praise." David had no righteousness of his own. David was a sinner, overwhelmed with sin. Nothing he could do, and nothing any other man could do, could deliver him from his sin. He said, "my tongue shall sing aloud of *thy* righteousness," not his own righteousness! Alongside of this Psalm I love to place a quotation from the 4th chapter of the New Testament letter of the Apostle Paul of the Romans, where it is written: "Now to him that worketh is the reward not reckoned of grace, but of debt. But to him that worketh not, but believeth on him that justifieth the ungodly, his faith is counted for righteousness."

THE PRINCIPLE OF THE GOSPEL

That is a glorious principle. It is "Not by works of righteousness which we have done, but according to his mercy he saved us. . . ." Our simple faith in our Lord Jesus, apart from any work, God counts for righteousness.

This is not only a New Testament principle; it is an Old Testament principle as well. For that reason, Paul continues, in the 4th chapter of his letter to the Romans:

> "Even as David also describeth the blessedness of the man, unto whom God imputeth righteousness without works,
>
> "Saying, Blessed are they whose iniquities are forgiven, and whose sins are covered.
>
> "Blessed is the man to whom the Lord will not impute sin."

David, of course, knew the blessedness of the man to whom God imputeth righteousness without works, for he was such a man. No wonder he said, "my tongue shall sing aloud of thy righteousness." A spiritually instructed Christian never calls attention to himself, but a well-taught Christian will sing aloud of the righteousness of God, which he has received as a free gift of God, simply because he has believed the Scripture. Is it any wonder the Psalmist said, "my mouth shall shew forth thy praise"? David did not boast of himself. Neither have we anything to boast of in ourselves, but we have much for which to return thanks and to sing His praises.

PSALM FIFTY-TWO

"A GREEN OLIVE TREE IN THE HOUSE OF GOD"

LIKE many others of the Psalms of David, we are able to get from the introduction to the 52nd Psalm some interesting light as to the historic circumstances when he wrote the Psalm. Therefore, in reading the Psalm I shall begin with the introduction. It is a very short Psalm.

> "To the chief Musician, Maschil, A Psalm of David, when Doeg the Edomite came and told Saul, and said unto him, David is come to the house of Ahimelech."
>
> "Why boasteth thou thyself in mischief, O mighty man? the goodness of God endureth continually.
>
> "Thy tongue deviseth mischiefs; like a sharp razor, working deceitfully.
>
> "Thou lovest evil more than good; and lying rather than to speak righteousness. Selah.
>
> "Thou lovest all devouring words, O thou deceitful tongue.

"God shall likewise destroy thee for ever, he shall take thee away, and pluck thee out of thy dwelling place, and root thee out of the land of the living. Selah.

"The righteous also shall see, and fear, and shall laugh at him:

"Lo, this is the man that made not God his strength; but trusted in the abundance of his riches, and strengthened himself in his wickedness.

"But I am like a green olive tree in the house of God: I trust in the mercy of God for ever and ever.

"I will praise thee for ever, because thou hast done it: and I will wait on thy name; for it is good before thy saints."

When I first read this Psalm in preparation for this message I am frank to tell you that I wondered what comment I could make that would be timely, instructive, and interesting. Yet I long ago arrived at a place in my thinking where I have learned from actual experience that the portion of Scripture which seems to have the least appeal undoubtedly is one of unusual interest. It is for that reason I have been obliged to disagree with the position of that noted German theologian, Karl Barth. While he is a very striking character, and has done an unusual piece of work in Germany, I have had to part company with his theology, when he insists that only that portion of Scripture which speaks to him is the Word of God. He does not say that the rest of Scripture cannot be the Word of God to others to whom it may speak, but it is not the Word of God to him. That is a very subtle teaching, but it is contrary to the expressed declaration of the Bible, where it is written: "*All* scripture is given by inspiration of God, and is profitable for doctrine, for reproof, for correction, for instruction in righteousness: That the man of God may be *perfect, thoroughly* furnished unto all good works."

For that reason we can come, as we have, to the Psalms that were written three thousand years ago, and find in them a ministry that will be of decided help to us in our own individual lives in this 20th century. Please do not misunderstand me. All Scripture was not written *for* us. There are portions of Scripture that were specifically written for a certain company of people. For instance, all of the Old Testament was written primarily for Israel. But all Scripture is profitable for us and is equally inspired. Because all Scripture is equally inspired, the Bible is a living organism, vibrating on each page with the Spirit of God.

This long, preliminary word of explanation as an introduction to this 52nd Psalm has been given in anticipation that some may raise the question, Of what value to us is the record of a squabble (a private quarrel, if you please) that existed between David and an Edomite, by the name of Doeg, a servant of King Saul?

In answering such a question, will you notice that in the introduction to this Psalm there is the Jewish word "Maschil." It appears in a number of Psalms. The introduction to this Psalm reads: "To the chief Musician, Maschil, A Psalm of David. . . ."

Up to the past week I labored under the impression that the word "Maschil" simply meant instruction or learning. In other words, this is an instructive Psalm. But during the past week I came across a very interesting explanation of the word. A certain contemporary writer, a brilliant Jew who resides in Paris, is quite a favorite of mine. Whenever there is an announcement of a new book written by him I invariably get possession of it. Last month a New York publisher announced that he expected to have a new book available January 4th, written by this Parisian Jew. The title of the book is very gripping. It is "*JESUS.*" I have not finished reading it, but during the course of the early chapters it was interesting to learn that he viewed the word "Maschil" as we would the word "parable."

You will recall that our Lord constantly spoke in parables during His public ministry. Parables are illustrations. Our Lord spoke in parables in order to illustrate certain truths or principles. Thus, wherever the word "Maschil" appears as a heading to a Psalm, we can apply this principle, and examine it as a poem with a moral.

Here is a story, the record of an actual happening, but it is not written as mere history. It has some underlying principles, most extraordinarily presented, which reveal the mind and purpose of God. Thus, as we approach this Psalm we learn that while the facts apply to David in his controversy with Doeg, the principle of God's hatred for sin is apparent. His insistence upon the recognition by the sinner of his sin, as well as God's dealing with him, as a sinner, are also amply demonstrated.

Then too we discover an individualism in this Psalm, which clearly indicates that God deals with this race as individuals and, finally, that there is judgment expressed against the wicked, while marvelous promises are given to the righteous.

THE FACT OF SIN

Let us take some of these facts and note how they are presented in the Psalm. First, the hatred of God for sin. The Psalmist said, "Why boastest thou thyself in mischief, O mighty man?" Because the goodness of God endureth continually, is no reason for thy boastfulness, for God shall destroy thee for ever and pluck thee out of thy dwelling place, and root thee out of the land of the living.

The second thing we learn from this Psalm is that God deals with us as individuals. We hear much in the present time about rugged individualism, and also that which is in contrast to it—regimentation.

When it comes to man's relationship with God there is no regimentation. Each of us, as individuals, must face the inevitable. We are responsible to the eternal God for the manner in which we have conducted our lives, and for the stewardship of that which has been committed to us.

Finally, this Psalm expresses the assured judgment of those whom the Scripture calls the wicked and the assured blessing of those whom the Scripture calls the righteous. We have tried to make clear many times during the course of these meditations, who are the wicked and who are the righteous.

THE FACT OF JUDGMENT

All sin strikes at the throne of God. We are, therefore, each of us, sinners; but there is a distinction between sinners. There are those who still retain their sin; there are others who have gotten rid of their sins by believing in Jesus Christ and personally appropriating His death as the sacrifice for their sin. To those who have received Christ, righteousness is extended because they have believed the record God gave of His Son. That is what makes us righteous. Thus it is not because of what we have done, but because of His mercy.

That which saved the firstborn in Israel was the blood of the paschal lamb. That which protects us who have received Christ, is the precious blood of Him, who is called in the Scriptures "The Lamb of God, who beareth away the sin of the world." On those who refuse to receive God's mercy, judgment will be inflicted, even as it was inflicted upon the person of Christ. The penalty of sin must be borne either by you, as an individual, or by your substitute, Jesus Christ. Those who have received Christ, have the promise of being eternally in the presence of God, even as David had the assurance that he would be like a "green olive tree in the house of God. . . ."

Let me relate something quite interesting. Studying this Psalm I was impressed with the simile David used, when speaking of his abiding eternally in the house of God. Said David, "I am like a green olive tree in the house of God." That is a rather strange figure of speech, isn't it? What did David mean by its use?

Every orthodox Jew values the inspired revelation. It is a delight to him to expound its treasures. Knowing a splendid young Jewish man who has a father-in-law who is like a patriarch of old, I asked him to inquire of his father-in-law what the teachings of the ancients among Israel are on these words. I am indebted to him for much help. The olive tree resembles the lilac tree when in full bloom. It is laden down with white flowers. The olive tree was, of course, abundant in Palestine. It must have been a beautiful sight when these trees were laden with white flowers.

But David said, "I am like a *green* olive tree in the house of God," reminding us of the olive *leaf* which is green above, but silver below. The spiritual mind revels in this symbolism, as it recalls that silver was used for redemption money. Underneath, therefore, was redemption, whereas, above, was vibrating, pulsating life.

From the time of the flood, the olive branch has been a symbol of peace. But what is even more interesting is this—when Solomon built the temple, cedar wood was used throughout, yet when it came to the Holy of holies, the two cherubims, whose outstretched wings reached from wall to wall, were made of the wood of the olive tree; and for the entrance in that holy place, where only the high priest could go, once a year, and then only with the blood of the sacrifice, he made the doors of olive wood. Every student of Scripture knows too that olive oil has been used throughout, as a symbol of the Holy Spirit.

David, being a prophet, foresaw the building of the house of God, the temple, which his son, Solomon, built after him. Undoubtedly, he knew the plans for the use of the wood from the olive tree. When, therefore, he uses the simile, "I am like a green olive tree in the house of God . . ." he reveled in the glory of being in the very presence of the Holy One, at peace with God and filled with the Holy Spirit, because of the redemption provided for him.

"I WILL PRAISE THEE FOR EVER"

It is easy to understand why the Psalmist closed this Psalm by saying: "I will praise thee for ever, because thou hast done it: and I will wait on thy name; for it is good before thy saints." When we have such a glorious hope as David possessed, it isn't difficult to face the vicissitudes of life, its disappointments, and perplexities. Indeed, as the Apostle Paul put it, ". . . we glory in tribulations also. . . ."

Allow me to give a modern illustration of the fortitude such a hope gives. All of you, undoubtedly, have fresh in your minds the brutal murder of those two young missionaries in China, Betty and John Stam. I noticed, with much pleasure, tne pictures that appeared in the New York papers this past week of the little orphaned babe, Helen Priscilla. John had written a letter after the capture, to the headquarters of the China Inland Mission, at Shanghai. The other day I received a copy of that letter, which was sent from the Mission. This letter perfectly illustrates the courage that comes from knowing the Lord. It is dated December 6, 1934, from Tsingteh, in Anhwei Province, China:

> China Inland Mission,
> Shanghai.
>
> Dear Brethren:
>
> My wife, baby, and myself are today in the hands of the Communists, in the city of Tsingteh. Their demand is twenty thousand dollars for our release.
>
> All our possessions and stores are in their hands, but we praise God for peace in our hearts and a meal tonight. God grant you wisdom in what you do, and us fortitude, courage, and peace of heart. He is able—and a wonderful Friend in such a time.
>
> Things happened so quickly this a.m. They were in the city just a few hours after the ever-persistent rumors really became alarming, so that we could not prepare to leave in time. We were just too late.
>
> The Lord bless and guide you, and as for us, may God be glorified whether by life or by death.
>
> In Him,
>
> (Signed) JOHN C. STAM.

What an evidence this letter gives of the courage a Christian possesses when faced with a problem that involves life or death!

PSALM FIFTY-THREE

THE REMEDY FOR THIS WORLD'S ILLS

IN my judgment there is no better way to begin the Lord's day than to gather ourselves about one of the great Psalms of David. We have now come in our studies to the 53rd Psalm. Its opening verse may not seem particularly appropriate. But then, we are reminded that "All scripture is given by inspiration of God, and is profitable . . ." so that we can find some instruction, and possibly a little correction, as we undertake a meditation in this Psalm, which reads:

> "The fool hath said in his heart, There is no God.
> Corrupt are they, and have done abominable iniquity:
> there is none that doeth good.
>
> "God looked down from heaven upon the children of
> men, to see if there were any that did understand,
> that did seek God.
>
> "Every one of them is gone back: they are altogether
> become filthy; there is none that doeth good, no,
> not one.
>
> "Have the workers of iniquity no knowledge? Who
> eat up my people as they eat bread: they have not
> called upon God.
>
> "There were they in great fear, where no fear was:
> for God hath scattered the bones of him that en-
> campeth against thee: thou hast put them to shame,
> because God hath despised them.
>
> "Oh that the salvation of Israel were come out of
> Zion! When God bringeth back the captivity of his
> people, Jacob shall rejoice, and Israel shall be glad."

Those of you who are acquainted with the Scriptures will remember that this Psalm is given considerable space in the New Testament. The Holy Spirit, therefore, has stamped this Psalm as one which requires our study and one which has an unusual message. Strange as it may seem, there are undoubtedly more atheists in the world at present than in any previous age.

It is not my wish to give much time to the matter of atheism, but I would like to quote a comment, written by a very learned man, some forty years ago. He called attention to the various views concerning creation. He said, There is the polytheistic, which insists that "nature is the work of a plurality of gods." Then there is the pantheistic, which holds "that nature and God are the same"; that there is no distinction between God and the universe. Then there is the agnostic, which acknowledges that "nature is," but that is all that any agnostic, knows; whether there is a God or not, he does not know. He will not go as far as the atheist, and say that there is no God. The agnostic simply shrugs his shoulders: "I don't know anything; I never knew anything; I don't expect to know anything." Then there is the theistic view, which is the viewpoint of every Christian, and of every Jew who believes the Scriptures, and though it may surprise some, this scholar said that "It is the view which has been held by the greatest, the wisest, and best of mankind from the remotest ages of which we have any

record." The atheist insists there is no God. "Nature exists, but there is no
God. . . . Nature is a building without an architect; a design without a
designer; a kingdom without a ruler; a family without a father."

To me it has always been quite interesting to observe how the atheist
knows there is no God. In the language of another, we might raise a few
questions. "Has he been to see? He was born yesterday and will die tomorrow. His little life is confined to this one world. Even of this world
he knows but a part. He owns that everything around him is full of mystery. He confesses he knows next to nothing; yet he knows there is no
God. He cannot climb to heaven to ascertain whether there be a God or
not. He cannot assert that he has seen His throne and found it empty;
but he knows there is no God. He knows! We may be permitted to question his knowledge. How does he know there is no God? He infers it from
the existence of evil. But were you to ask him, 'Does he know the history
and destiny of evil?' he would confess his ignorance. About the only thing
an atheist knows is that there is no God."

THE HEART OF AN ATHEIST

However, the Scripture is very careful in its diagnosis of the atheist
and his reasoning, by stating, "The fool hath said *in his heart,* There is no
God." No one ever came to that conclusion by an operation of the intellect. It is not by a mental process that a man concludes that there is no
God. Nature itself is sufficient answer to any inquiry of the mind. But the
man who says there is no God, has concluded it *in his heart.* It is from
that cesspool of iniquity that he repeats, like a parrot, "No God; No God."
The Scripture says, "The heart is deceitful above all things, and desperately
wicked: who can know it?" The physician may know something about the
operation of the heart; the psychologist may observe certain reactions that
come from the heart; the psychiatrist may conclude certain details; but all
that any of them are able to determine relates to the actions of the heart
and the expression of the movements of the heart; as respecting the actual
motives, they can be of no help. The study of the heart is so profound that
the Scripture is careful to ask, "who can know it?" It is written that
". . . man looketh on the outward appearance, but the LORD looketh on
the heart." It is He alone, who can read and understand the heart.

Concerning the heart of an atheist, whom the Scripture calls a fool, it
witnesses, "Corrupt are they, and have done abominable iniquity: there is
none that doeth good."

However, this Psalm is not occupied exclusively with the atheist; in fact, it devotes only one verse to him. The Psalm enlarges its scope. In the 2nd verse, we have the scrutinizing eye of the Holy One looking down from heaven upon the children of men. He looks to determine if *any* did understand and if *any* did seek after God. As God is the Creator of man, He has a right to inquire as to the understanding of His creatures, and whether they are sufficiently interested in Him to seek Him.

RUNNING AWAY FROM GOD

Again and again men insist that they have been seekers for truth. But the Scriptures say that "there is none that seeketh after God." From Adam right down to the present generation, man has been running *away* from God, and not *toward* God. That was abundantly demonstrated at the cradle of human history, when the woman yielded to the suggestion of the serpent, and Adam joined in the transgression. They suddenly realized that they were naked, and in their distress they busied themselves about the Garden, seeking a covering. Fig leaves were chosen and sewed together, which provided a temporary covering, but when the Lord God came down in the cool of the day, seeking His creatures, it is written that the Lord God called unto Adam, and said unto him, "Where art thou?" Adam had already heard the voice of the Lord God, and he and his wife "hid themselves from the presence of the Lord God amongst the trees of the garden." It is quite evident that Adam and Eve were running *away* from God. It is equally evident that God was seeking His sinning creatures. Adam never would have found God. The sons of Adam have, ever since, sought refuge from God by hiding behind all kinds of trees, but not one provides a shelter. It was the Lord God who sought His sinning creatures. He found them, successfully got a confession from them, and then Himself provided a covering, a coat of skins, which necessitated the slaying of a lamb, or some other creature.

But we leave the matter of God's verdict concerning us (it's too true to be comfortable) and proceed to the remedy. After one has recovered from a disease, he is quite prone to talk about his former illness; its gravity, the operation, and all that, but while he was ill, what most concerned him as he looked up into the face of the physician, was the remedy, his only question being, Doctor, what have you that can make me well?

THE HOPE OF THIS WORLD

This is a sick world! An opiate may help temporarily, but what is needed is beautifully expressed in the last verse of our Psalm: "Oh that the salvation of Israel were come out of Zion! When God bringeth back the captivity of his people, Jacob shall rejoice, and Israel shall be glad." Let me remind you that this is a Psalm of David. When it was written, Israel was entering into her greatest glory. Israel was not in captivity. Yet David cried, "When God bringeth back the captivity of his people, Jacob shall rejoice, and Israel shall be glad." There isn't a doubt that David was a prophet. He foresaw the scattering of Israel among the nations even before it took place. He also hoped for Israel's return.

What is the remedy for this world? Just this, "that the salvation of Israel were come out of Zion!" Mark you, I said "world." The remedy, for an individual, lies in his receiving Christ as his Lord and Saviour, thereby acknowledging God's verdict as just; but the remedy for this world lies in the salvation of Israel, which will come out of Zion.

PSALM FIFTY-FOUR

A MELODY OUT OF A DISCORD

WE now come to a short Psalm with a long introduction. The 54th Psalm contains only seven verses, but the introduction reads, "To the chief Musician on Neginoth, Maschil, A Psalm of David, when the Ziphims came and said to Saul, Doth not David hide himself with us?"

If in your youth you did not attend Sunday school regularly, or since then you have not kept up your familiarity with Old Testament history through the systematic reading of the Bible, this introduction will appear to you to be a jumble of words. But if you are now attending Sunday school, or if you remember your Bible history from Sunday school days and since then have kept your mind keen and alert through constant reading of the Old Testament, then the picture that is presented in the introduction to this Psalm will greatly enhance your appreciation of the Psalm itself.

"TIME OUT" FOR PRAISE

This little hymn was composed by David after he had experienced one of his many miraculous deliverances from what appeared to be certain disaster and imminent death. Whenever he passed through an experience of that kind he always took "time-out" to collect his thoughts, to set them in order, to put them into verse and either set the words to music or have them set to music, so that he might properly and intelligently praise his God for the deliverance which was extended to him.

We in America, particularly we in the East and specifically we New Yorkers, live a hustle-bustle sort of life. We are constantly on the go. We may not be going to any specific place but still we rush. The "itch" to go gets into the very fibre of our being so that we hardly have time to sleep, much less do we have any time to devote to orderly praise unto God for His blessings and benedictions.

Some friends came in for dinner the other evening; a fine young couple who plan to spend some four months in New York City for study and meditation in the Word of God. They related a little of their experiences since their arrival about a fortnight ago. One of their pastimes has been to watch the faces of people who walk our streets. One day, strolling through Central Park, they discovered a rare sight—they actually saw a man who had a smile on his face, the first smile they had seen on a pedestrian's face since their arrival in the city. It is amazing how we rush about with a stern look on our faces, rarely, if ever, softening our expressions with a smile. God never intended that men should live a hectic life, at least, not Christian men. When our Lord saw the disciples tired, He invited them to come apart into a desert place and rest awhile. When a believer has experienced a great blessing and benediction from his Lord the least he can do is to take "time out" to thank God and to praise His name.

David sent this 54th Psalm to the chief Musician with specific instructions that it was to be accompanied by stringed instruments, for that is the meaning of the phrase, "on Neginoth." But David did not desire the Psalm to be mere words, sung to the accompaniment of stringed instruments just to while away the time. Therefore, as the song contained a needed message which could form the basis of instructions for the child of God, David also added the word "Maschil" in the introduction, which word means *instruction*. God is an intelligent Being. Worship should be the intelligent occupation of a spiritual heart and mind. A song, therefore, must be intelligent as well as musical before it can be used in the worship of the Lord.

In this introduction David also clearly revealed the historic setting of the Psalm. It was at the time when David fled from the city of Keilah upon learning that the inhabitants were about to deliver him up, whereupon he went into the wilderness of Ziphim. But there the dwellers of the wilderness betrayed him, yea, even pledged themselves to capture him. They were also talebearers, for they sent this message to Saul, "Doth not David hide himself with us?" From all outward appearances, therefore, it looked as if David were cornered. Every possible avenue of escape was closed. But sudden deliverance came to him, for as Saul was about to pursue him, Saul learned of the successes of the advancing Philistine armies, so that he was obliged to reverse his course and leave David alone. When a man has been delivered from certain death, whether in the spiritual or in the physical realm, he has real cause for thanking and praising God. That is why David wrote this Psalm:

> "Save me, O God, by thy name, and judge me by thy strength.
>
> "Hear my prayer, O God; give ear to the words of my mouth.
>
> "For strangers are risen up against me, and oppressors seek after my soul: they have not set God before them. Selah.
>
> "Behold, God is mine helper: the Lord is with them that uphold my soul.
>
> "He shall reward evil unto mine enemies: cut them off in thy truth.
>
> "I will freely sacrifice unto thee: I will praise thy name, O LORD; for it is good.
>
> "For he hath delivered me out of all trouble: and mine eye hath seen his desire upon mine enemies."

We have already noticed that this experience of which David wrote was one of several narrow escapes from what appeared to be certain death. All his life he had to be on the alert; the enemy was repeatedly at his heels or trying to make him stub his toes. It is well for us to bear this in mind, for it helps to reconcile our experiences with what was endured or enjoyed by the Lord's people in ages past. No Christian ever gets to the stage where he is entirely free of temptations from within or without, or where he ceases to be encumbered with difficulties and trials. They appear at the most unexpected moments and they often break out everywhere, like the measles.

Have you ever noticed a little phrase which appears in St. Luke's Gospel in the record of the temptation of our Lord by Satan? You will remember that our Lord was driven by the Spirit into the wilderness. After being there forty days He was tested by Satan, who could find no flaw in Him. It was then that it was written, "And when the devil had ended all the temptation, he departed from him *for a season*." Satan did not leave Him forever. He merely departed from Him *for a season*. Neither will he leave you and me alone for more than a season. He may take to his heels like a defeated foe at times, but don't lull yourself to sleep when Satan does so, by assuming he will never return. He will leave you alone "for a season" only; he is sure to try his wiles on you again.

THE NAME OF THE LORD

Now let us look at the message of the Psalm. What ought one to do when he is in trouble? David opened this Psalm by praying, "Save me, O God, by thy name, and judge me by thy strength." The word "judge" is sometimes translated "right," so that the Psalm in some versions reads, "Save me, O God, by thy name, and right me with thy might," or, "by thy strength grant me justice." You will remember that it is written, "Some trust in chariots, and some in horses: but we will remember *the name* of the LORD our God." It is also written, "*The name* of the LORD is a strong tower: the righteous runneth into it, and is safe."

What power there is in the name of God! For instance, after the resurrection of our Lord Jesus Christ, "Peter and John went up together into the temple at the hour of prayer, being the ninth hour." And as they did so they discovered "a certain man lame from his mother's womb." He was carried by friends who laid him daily "at the gate of the temple which is called Beautiful, to ask alms of them that entered into the temple." When the lame man saw Peter and John about to go into the temple, he asked an alms of them. Neither Peter nor John were men of wealth. When they died they did not leave a large estate, or even a small one, but they left an invaluable heritage to all the world.

Peter was the spokesman on this occasion and, with John, fastening his eyes on the lame man said to him, "Look on us." Of course, the man gave heed, confidently expecting to receive something from them. Then Peter said, "Silver and gold have I none; but such as I have give I thee: In the name of Jesus Christ of Nazareth rise up and walk." And the Scripture declares that Peter

> ". . . took him by the right hand, and lifted him up: and immediately his feet and ankle bones received strength.

> "And he leaping up stood, and walked, and entered
> with them into the temple, walking, and leaping, and
> praising God:
>
> "And all the people saw him walking and praising God:
>
> "And they knew that it was he which sat for alms
> at the Beautiful gate of the temple: and they were
> filled with wonder and amazement at that which had
> happened unto him."

But they were guilty of making the same error a mob always makes. They assumed that Peter and John had miraculous power: but the power was in the word Peter had spoken, and that word was, "In *the name* of Jesus Christ. . . ."

David prayed, "Save me, O God, by *thy name*. . . ."

When a man appeals to the name of the Lord he *will* experience deliverance from the power of inescapable death. When one is hemmed in by circumstance, as David was on this occasion, there is only one thing to do. To look around will bring disappointment. To seek a way out through a friend is to experience disillusionment. But to look up and call upon the name of the Lord is to enjoy victory. David also said, "Hear my prayer, O God: give ear to the words of my mouth." Whereupon he called attention to his circumstances as he rehearsed them before the Lord.

> "For strangers are risen up against me, and oppressors
> seek after my soul: they have not set God before them.
> Selah.
>
> "Behold, God is mine helper: the Lord is with them
> that uphold my soul.
>
> "He shall reward evil unto mine enemies: cut them
> off in thy truth."

Then said David, "I will freely sacrifice unto thee: I will praise thy name, O LORD; for it is good." Finally, he closed the Psalm by saying, "For he hath delivered me out of all trouble: and mine eye hath seen his desire upon mine enemies."

It was Job who said, "Though he slay me, yet will I trust in him. . . ." It is difficult, if not impossible, to praise God when one is hemmed in by distresses and circumstances. The most we can do is to trust God in the midst of disappointment, and the least we can do is to cry out to Him in the hour of trial. But after He has delivered us, the least we can do is to praise the Lord for His goodness and His marvelous deliverance.

PSALM FIFTY-FIVE

THE WINGS OF A DOVE

W E come now to the 55th Psalm. It is quite long. We shall take time to read only a few of its verses. It divides itself, in my judgment, into three sections, the first of which includes verses 1 to 7, describing the cry of a man whose experiences almost overwhelmed him. In his depression he cried for wings like a dove.

> "Give ear to my prayer, O God; and hide not thyself from my supplication.
> "Attend unto me, and hear me: I mourn in my complaint, and make a noise;
> "Because of the voice of the enemy, because of the oppression of the wicked: for they cast iniquity upon me, and in wrath they hate me.
> "My heart is sore pained within me: and the terrors of death are fallen upon me.
> "Fearfulness and trembling are come upon me, and horror hath overwhelmed me.
> "And I said, Oh that I had wings like a dove! for then would I fly away, and be at rest.
> "Lo, then would I wander far off, and remain in the wilderness. Selah."

The second section of the Psalm includes verses 12 to 14, where the Psalmist informs us that his terrific disappointment came through the rebellion of a bosom friend. He said:

> "For it was not an enemy that reproached me; then I could have borne it: neither was it he that hated me that did magnify himself against me; then I would have hid myself from him.
> "But it was thou, a man mine equal, my guide, and mine acquaintance.
> "We took sweet counsel together, and walked unto the house of God in company."

The third section of this Psalm expresses the Psalmist's confidence in the One who is able to deliver. In succeeding verses he said:

> "As for me, I will call upon God; and the LORD shall save me.
> "Evening, and morning, and at noon, will I pray, and cry aloud: and he shall hear my voice. . . .
> "Cast thy burden upon the LORD, and he shall sustain thee: he shall never suffer the righteous to be moved."

THE TREMBLING OF A SAINT

There isn't any doubt that David referred to the experiences he underwent as a result of the rebellion of Absalom, his own son, in which Ahithophel, his counselor and guide, joined with Absalom. A man can stand almost anything better than betrayal by one of his own family, or a close adviser or friend.

David had a few faithful friends about him, but, comparatively speaking, he stood alone. His few faithful friends were dependent upon him, rather than he dependent upon them. As he looked at the increase of his enemies he realized that he was trapped, that he could not possibly escape. In his distress he could only look in one direction. It was upward, and as he did so he desired to flee, to rise from earth's distress. He expressed the urging of his heart when he cried: ". . . Oh, that I had wings like a dove! for then would I fly away, and be at rest."

THE SUFFERING OF A SAINT

Bear in mind that this was the experience of a man who already knew God. As one considers his experiences, he may raise the question that has been raised from the beginning of creation, Why does a righteous man suffer? Here was not the suffering of a guilty man; it was the suffering of an innocent man. Here was not the suffering and disappointment of an unbeliever; it was the disappointment of a believer.

Are we, as believers in the Lord Jesus Christ, exempt from tribulation and difficulty? A thousand times No! The fact is, that the Christian is subject to trials and difficulties beyond anything that is experienced by an unbeliever. One may raise the question, Why? but the *fact* still remains.

It would be wrong to assure any of you that if you receive Christ as your Saviour you will be freed from the tribulations and trials of life. We can assure you, however, that if you will receive Christ you will be eternally saved, and God will bestow upon you a righteousness which you never had and never could possibly have. It is the righteousness of His own Son. We can assure you that God will deal with you in grace, but that does not mean that He will shelter you from every trial and difficulty; in fact, He will give you the honor of remaining faithful to Him under trial, which is one of the greatest honors that man could ever render to his God.

Did you ever ask why David specifically desired the wings of a dove? Why not another bird? A dove has always symbolized peace, and a dove is a peaceful bird even in flight. I recall reading that a dove has unusual stamina. It has a way of flying that is quite interesting. Nearly all other birds fly with both wings, and when tired either rest on a rock or some other place. Quite naturally that places the bird at a disadvantage if pursued, but in the case of a dove, it is said that when it becomes tired it folds up one wing, resting it, while with the other wing it proceeds on its flight.

At least there isn't any doubt that David wished to fly away, so as to escape his predicament and be at rest. But there never has been a set of wings provided for any man to escape his circumstances except the wings of faith, which enable a man to fly out of the present and into the beyond, into the very courts of the eternal God. While he may be pressed about the circumstances, so that they almost overwhelm him, he can find rest in the house of the Lord, gathered about the person of the Lord Jesus.

The second section of this Psalm relates to the character of the opposition that was expressed against David. Speaking of his close counselor, he said, "It was not an enemy that reproached me; then I could readily have borne it. It was not one that hated me; then I could have hid myself. But it was a man so close to me as to be my guide and counselor. We had sweet counsel together, and even walked unto the house of God in company; yet he lifted up his heel against me."

Undoubtedly many of you have had similar experiences. You have placed confidence in a friend and a counselor. You had become so close you regarded that individual as a confidant, but lo, something happened. The friendship was broken, and you learned that the confidence was misplaced, and you had bitter heartaches.

David's betrayer was a man with whom he had walked together to the house of God. May I go so far as to suggest that you cannot afford to place your confidence even in a Christian! I have many, many friends. I value their friendship highly, but I would not for a moment base my faith upon my fellowship with my friends. There comes a time in a man's life when he is face to face with God, and the only One in whom he can place implicit confidence is the eternal God Himself. He will be deceived if he places his faith in another. The Scripture says, Cursed is he that placeth his trust in the arm of flesh. That is strong language, but that is what the prophet Jeremiah said. We do not wish to deprecate friendship. God forbid. It is one of the sweetest things this side of heaven. But if you place your confidence in God you will never be disappointed.

In that connection, one cannot refrain from thinking of the experiences of our Lord Jesus with His betrayer. Judas was a man with whom He had had familiar friendship, who did eat bread with Him, and with whom He had sweet counsel. Yet that man lifted up his heel against Him. He betrayed Him for a mere thirty pieces of silver and climaxed the betrayal with a kiss!

THE PRAYER OF A SAINT

Fortunately for David, he knew One who could deliver him, and he knew how to cry to Him. Let us see what David did. He said: "As for me, I will call upon God; and the LORD shall save me. Evening, and morning, and at noon, will I pray, and cry aloud: and he shall hear my voice."

Prayer is a remarkable thing. Of course, to the unbeliever prayer seems a mockery. Why pray? But to a true Christian, who knows the Lord as his Saviour, prayer is not only an opportunity of presenting before the Lord the requests of the heart, but it also presents an avenue whereby the heart can pour out its affection upon the person of the Lord Jesus. It is the opportunity for worship. Prayer should be the constant occupation of a believer.

We come now to the closing section of the Psalm. It is the most comforting part of the whole Psalm. The 22nd verse enjoins us, "Cast thy burden upon the LORD" and it assures us, "and he shall sustain thee" and it comforts us by saying, "he shall never suffer the righteous to be moved." To those who are burdened, here is a message from One who is able to lift the burden, and what is more, He is very willing to bear it for you. Our Lord is the Burden-bearer. Oh, do not be unwise. Do not continue to bear it alone. Tell Him about it, and cast it upon Him. You thereby do Him no injustice; you do Him the greatest honor by casting your burden upon Him. He has promised that He will sustain you, and, what is more, He assures you that He will never suffer the righteous to be moved.

PSALM FIFTY-SIX

A BOTTLE FOR TEARS, OR A WAY OF ESCAPE

A S we read the 56th Psalm we will immediately recognize that it is a prayer. The introduction places the event at the time when David was in the hands of the Philistines, when they took him in Gath. In this case, David's prayer was in the nature of a cry. The introduction to the Psalm calls it the cry of a dove. With that in mind, let us attempt to picture the scene as we read the Psalm:

> "Be merciful unto me, O God: for man would swallow me up; he fighting daily oppresseth me.
>
> "Mine enemies would daily swallow me up: for they be many that fight against me, O thou most High.
>
> "What time I am afraid, I will trust in thee.
>
> "In God I will praise his word, in God I have put my trust; I will not fear what flesh can do unto me.
>
> "Every day they wrest my words: all their thoughts are against me for evil.
>
> "They gather themselves together, they hide themselves, they mark my steps, when they wait for my soul.
>
> "Shall they escape by iniquity? in thine anger cast down the people, O God.
>
> "Thou tellest my wanderings: put thou my tears into thy bottle: are they not in thy book?
>
> "When I cry unto thee, then shall mine enemies turn back: this I know; for God is for me.
>
> "In God will I praise his word: in the LORD will I praise his word.
>
> "In God have I put my trust: I will not be afraid what man can do unto me.
>
> "Thy vows are upon me, O God: I will render praises unto thee.
>
> "For thou hast delivered my soul from death: wilt not thou deliver my feet from falling, that I may walk before God in the light of the living?"

Again, like so many of the previous Psalms, there is much that suggests itself, even from a mere reading of the Psalm. We shall content ourselves, however, by calling attention to some of the more apparent truths. For example, look at verse 3, where David said: "What time I am afraid, I will trust in thee."

To be able to trust God at all times is the privilege and right of every believer, but it is particularly when we are afraid, or placed in circumstances that seem so dire as to offer no way of escape, that we are completely thrown upon the Lord. It is at such a time that He becomes exceptionally precious. Then we get to understand His marvelous care and love manifested toward us. It is well to bear in mind the next time any one of us is placed in a similar position, that David had the same experience, and we, too, ought to try his remedy—trust in the Lord!

We have already referred to the martyrdom of John and Betty Stam. As the news of the details come through, we learn of their confident trust in the Lord. For instance, there is the incident at the time John stopped on his journey at a store, which proved to be the post office also. The shopkeeper asked him, "Where are they taking you? Where are you going?" to which John Stam replied, "We do not know where they are going, but we are going to heaven." That certainly is a modern example of what David stated in verse 3: "What time I am afraid, I will trust in thee." Such courage is not born in the individual, it is not the product of the individual. It comes solely as a result of confidence and trust placed in the Lord.

THE WORD OF GOD

In the 4th verse of our Psalm we have a declaration of David's abiding confidence in God. He said: "In God I will praise his word, in God I have put my trust; I will not fear what flesh can do unto me." I do not know what haven you have, but there certainly is no safer haven than to trust in His Word. And yet the most difficult task any man is called upon to do is to trust implicitly in the Lord. Invariably we seek visible means of escape; we trust friends—and yet who has ever been a greater friend than God, or who is more able to deliver than the Lord? David said: "I will praise his word." That is quite interesting, isn't it? He would "praise his word." In another Psalm he said: "For ever, O LORD, thy word is settled in heaven."

David, of course, believed in the verbal inspiration of the Bible, but we must bear in mind that at the time David wrote this Psalm very little of what we call the Bible was in his possession. There were only the five books of Moses, the Books of Joshua and the Judges, and possibly one or two other books, including, undoubtedly, the Book of Job—but beyond that we cannot say specifically. Yet, with even such a limited written revelation, David said: "I will praise his word."

How much more cause *we* have to thank God for His Word, the most precious thing we have in life. We are told that "The entrance of thy word giveth light. . ." and that the beginning of wisdom is the "fear of the Lord." The Bible abounds in promises, promises such as we drew attention to in our comments on the 55th Psalm, where we are told to cast our burden upon the Lord, and are given the assurance from Him that He shall sustain us and not permit the righteous to be moved. That is a marvelous promise.

But there is a surprisingly large group of people who read such a promise in Scripture and yet do not appropriate it. More often than otherwise we read these promises and we rejoice in them to a certain degree, but we rarely, if ever, apply them to ourselves and our own circumstances. Let me illustrate what I mean. My good friend, Dr. Isaac Page, of the China Inland Mission, dropped in at my office this past week and told a humorous story about an English curate, who labored in a parish composed mostly of poor people. His recompense was a mere stipend. On one occasion, however, there came into his congregation a stranger who, after listening to his sermon, felt so refreshed by it that he sent him a check for five pounds. The good curate had never previously seen a check for such a large amount. He took it to the bank the next day, approached the teller's window, and passed his check through. The teller examined it, looked all over the front of it and was perfectly satisfied with it. Then he turned to the reverse side and noticed that the check was not endorsed. He returned it to the curate and suggested to him that it was necessary that it be endorsed, whereupon the clergyman wrote the following lines: "I heartily endorse this check," and gave it to the teller. "Oh," said the teller, "put your name on it."

Well, that is exactly like a great number of people who are in difficulties. They believe these promises were written—oh, no doubt about it; they heartily endorse every promise of Scripture, but they rarely take these promises and apply them to themselves. They do not put their own signature to them, and thereby endorse them.

PERSONAL, APPROPRIATING FAITH

Let me give you a little personal witness. I am sure that I am like a multitude of people. I was brought up in a Christian home; from a child I knew the gospel story. My mother had given it to me; my Sunday school teachers had drilled it into me. There never was a time when I doubted that Jesus Christ was God, nor did I ever question that the Bible was the Word of God. Neither did I have any doubt concerning the fact that our Lord died for the sins of the world, and that He arose physically from the grave. Never for a moment did I question these facts. They seemed, even to my young mind, amply supported by every possible test that could be applied to past historical facts to determine their validity. But, believing all of that, I still was lost; I still needed to be saved. It was not until I personally appropriated for myself the death that our Lord Jesus died that I knew what it was to be saved, and knew what it was to have eternal life. That is what it means to endorse a promise of God.

A BOTTLE FOR SAINTS' TEARS

Having received Christ, you will find that the Bible abounds in promises; promises that assure you of deliverance from difficulty, trials, and temptations; promises that God will sometimes permit you to go through difficulties, though assuring you that He will keep you; promises that although everything seems dark about you, He will never, no never, leave you, nor forsake you. These are all very precious promises to a believer who finds himself in the need of comfort.

In the 5th and 6th verses David said: "Every day they wrest my words: all their thoughts are against me for evil. They gather themselves together, they hide themselves, they mark my steps, when they wait for my soul." David was a marked man; his enemies watched him, they sought an occasion to trap him and to find cause for rebuke, but with very little success. To be in the hand of an enemy is not pleasant experience, and wandering in the camp of the enemy, instead of among familiar home surroundings, is to experience a loneliness that can only be described by the word *wanderings*. David said in verse 8: "Thou tellest my wanderings." Can we appreciate what it means; that God knows about our wanderings? He knew David's. He knows ours. We can expect the blessing of God and the care of God to be manifested over us to the same extent as it was over David. Thus, if you seem to be wandering, I do trust it will be a source of comfort to you to know that God knows about your wanderings. If you are so depressed, so lonesome, and so in need of comfort that you cannot restrain your tears, David gives you further assurance. He said: "put thou my tears into thy bottle . . ." What an interesting expression that is!

That David was a fighter is too apparent to need comment. Everything about him showed the heroic; yet, great as David was, he knew what it was to shed tears. Tears are nature's safety valve. When oppressed with sorrow and disappointment, it is a tremendous relief just to cry. The Scripture calls the Lord Jesus "a man of sorrows, and acquainted with grief."

Tears are an expression of affection, as well as a manifestation of sorrow and disappointment. In the case of David, in the 56th Psalm, tears were a manifestation of disappointment, of a longing for fellowship with his Lord. Do you think that a man ever sheds tears under such circumstances, without God taking recognition of them? Indeed, David informed us that God has a bottle in which He stores up the tears of the saints, for he suggested, "put thou my tears into thy bottle: are they not in thy book?"

WIPING AWAY SAINTS' TEARS

Some time ago I was greatly impressed by reading a touching expression from the pen of that very gifted man, Horatius Bonar, whom some of you will remember as the writer of many fine Christian hymns. Bonar wrote, "The tearless dry no tears." How true it is! All one has to do is to go to some friend or acquaintance who has never had the experiences that you have gone through; and your tears, to that friend or acquaintance, are a mockery. He cannot understand them. No, the tearless dry no tears. It is only those who have had like experiences who are able to sympathize, comfort, and enter into our own sorrows. Our Lord Jesus Christ enters into our experiences. The Scripture says that "He was tempted in all points like as we, yet without sin." And because of this He is able to succor all those that come unto God by Him, seeing He ever liveth to make intercession for us. How pleasant it is to read that among the things God has promised in the Scripture is that He shall wipe away our tears!

And now, for a closing comment may we notice a thing or two found in the 13th verse. David said: "For thou hast delivered my soul from death: wilt not thou deliver my feet from falling, that I may walk before God in the light of the living?" Here is a comment especially to those of you who have received Christ as your Saviour and who know the Lord Jesus as your own Lord. Don't you suppose that the One who delivered your soul from death is able to keep your feet from falling? This constantly stumbling, defeated type of Christian experience is not what God intended you to have. The One who is able to deliver you from death is able to keep your feet from falling. He desires that you walk before Him in the light of the living. Here, right in this life, you and I have the privilege of so walking before God that others may recognize that we are living epistles, representing the Lord Jesus Christ. God grant that each of us in our own lives may faithfully reveal Him and that those without may recognize that Christ lives in us.

PSALM FIFTY-SEVEN

"THE ANNOUNCEMENT OF THE DIVINE PRESENCE ON OUR EARTH"

THE 57th Psalm has much in common with the 56th; in fact, the subject is the same. The Psalm is a prayer. The opening words are identical: "Be merciful unto me, O God . . ." It is not a very long Psalm. It has eleven short verses, which read:

> "Be merciful unto me, O God, be merciful unto me:
> for my soul trusteth in thee: yea, in the shadow of
> thy wings will I make my refuge, until these calamities
> be overpast.
>
> "I will cry unto God most high; unto God that per-
> formeth all things for me.
>
> "He shall send from heaven, and save me from the
> reproach of him that would swallow me up. Selah.
> God shall send forth his mercy and his truth.
>
> "My soul is among lions: and I lie even among them
> that are set on fire, even the sons of men, whose teeth
> are spears and arrows, and their tongue a sharp sword.
>
> "Be thou exalted, O God, above the heavens; let thy
> glory be above all the earth.
>
> "They have prepared a net for my steps; my soul is
> bowed down: they have digged a pit before me, into
> the midst whereof they are fallen themselves. Selah.
>
> "My heart is fixed, O God, my heart is fixed: I will
> sing and give praise.
>
> "Awake up, my glory; awake, psaltery and harp: I
> myself will awake early.
>
> "I will praise thee, O Lord, among the people: I will
> sing unto thee among the nations.
>
> "For thy mercy is great unto the heavens, and thy
> truth unto the clouds.
>
> "Be thou exalted, O God, above the heavens: let thy
> glory be above all the earth."

Were we to paraphrase the 1st verse it would read something like this: "Be full of mercy unto me, O God, be full of mercy unto me: for my soul trusteth in thee: yea, in the shadow of thy wings will I make my refuge, until these calamities be overpast."

"GLORYING IN TRIBULATION"

Some people have developed a complaining spirit because of the trials and circumstances of life, particularly because of the hardships that have developed as a result of the lengthening depression. However, I am again and again reminded that it is the man who has some real hardships to endure who actually makes no complaint.

For instance, a very interesting letter came this week from a gentleman residing in Florida, who formerly lived in New York. About three years ago an operation was performed on his right eye. After two similar operations a third one was resorted to, at which time the eye was removed. Shortly afterward he lost the sight of his left eye, so that for the past two and a half years he has been blind. He has written to me several times. Each letter has a ring about it that I wish I could convey to you. There is not a word of lamentation; on the contrary, there is every evidence that despite his affliction he still praises the Lord. Some time ago he wrote that while he had not seen the sun since August 1st, 1932, God had been very good to him. Despite his misfortune, he immediately took to developing a scheme to enable him to write. He made a small drawing-board in the form of a square. He tacks his paper to the board and writes as best he can, and the fact is, his letters are more legible than many I receive from people who have the sight of both eyes!

One paragraph in his letter was especially fine. He wrote: "I trust you may be able to read this letter written by one of God's redeemed ones who, while not able to see the natural sun, has been in touch with the Sun of Righteousness many years."

Don't you think that we, who are blessed with health and strength and many other blessings of life, complain all too frequently? Can not we take a lesson from those who are truly afflicted, and who yet rejoice in the mercy of God?

Last week the newspapers played up the story of the honest sandwich man, Frank Greges, who found and returned securities worth $42,000. There was one little reference that I particularly enjoyed. You recall he got a job with the brokerage house on Wall Street which owned the securities. As an added celebration, that firm had a luncheon brought in from a restaurant for Greges. As he ate, he remarked, "It is a long time since I prayed, but last night I said, 'Thank you, Lord.' " How long is it since you returned thanks for God's bounties?

THE EXTENT OF GOD'S MERCY

The Lord never exhausts His mercy. It is written that His mercy is "from everlasting to everlasting upon them that fear him . . ." and that He crowns a life with "lovingkindness and tender mercies . . ."

When David cried, "Be merciful . . ." he had the thought of the mercy seat in mind. He desired God to remember the blood of the sacrifice that had been slain. We Gentiles, on the contrary, invariably look upon the word as if it contained the idea that God should excuse us from our sin and refuse to exact its penalty. The fact is, the penalty has already been exacted through the death of His own Son. Therefore God can deal in mercy. Yea, He deals liberally in mercy.

Notice also the place of refuge David chose. He said, ". . . in the shadow of thy wings will I make my refuge, until these calamities be overpast." Those who have studied the Bible with any degree of care have received a rich recompense in discovering that God is the answer to every disappointment, and that He has a special revelation for every circumstance. For example, here is a picture of a helpless little chick in a calamity. The winds roar; the storm rages. Where is a place of safety? There is no safer place in the world for the little chick to be than under the wings of the mother hen. Safe under the shelter of its mother's wing the storm has no alarm for the chick.

In this Psalm the eternal God, of whom it is written that the heaven of heavens cannot contain Him, is likened by David to a mother hen. Under His wings you and I may find a place of refuge in the time of calamity. Why is it that the gentleman to whom I referred earlier, deprived of his livelihood because of a physical affliction, has not a word of lamentation, but on the contrary expresses himself with joy and gladness? It is because, in his calamity, he has found a refuge in the shadow of the wings of the Almighty. If you are in the midst of perplexities and calamities you may be assured that God will do for you what He did for David. He will shelter you from the force of the storm and you will find that there is a place of refuge in the shadow of His wings.

THE HOPE OF THIS WORLD

In bringing our message to a close, will you observe the note of hope and optimism David sounded as he ended the Psalm. There is calamity in the first verse, but there is a marvelous reign of peace, splendor, and joy in the closing verses. David said: "I will praise thee, O Lord, among the people: I will sing unto thee among the nations . . . Be thou exalted, O God, above the heavens: let thy glory be above all the earth."

Many of us are looking forward to exactly what David wrote about in the closing verses of the Psalm. This poor old world seems to be in a very bad way. It hasn't a song. Its opiates have worn off, so that its tragic plight seems more apparent. Nations are bewildered, almost staggering, because of the failure of their leaders to cope with its problems. Hardly a nation is exempt from internal disorder. The spectre of gathering war clouds in the Orient and in Europe, adds to the disturbance.

Is there any good news to be given to our distressed world? Indeed there is! When the event happens, it will be the greatest bit of news ever to be heard. Last week Edwin C. Hill, over the radio, answered the question as to what he considered would be the greatest bit of news ever to be broadcast. He replied, "The announcement of the divine Presence upon our earth." How true! That will be the answer to all our distressing situations—the return of our Lord Jesus Christ in glory, to reign as the Prince of Peace, when "Of the increase of his government and peace there shall be no end . . ." To those who are believers in the Lord Jesus Christ, the very thrill of the closing verses of this Psalm will cause us to rejoice.

At the time of the presence upon our earth of the eternal Messiah, there will be fulfilled in its most glorious application the climax of this Psalm: "Awake up, my glory; awake, psaltery and harp: I myself will awake early. I will praise thee, O Lord, among the people: I will sing unto thee among the nations." No man who knows the Scripture and revels in the glorious promises found therein can be pessimistic. He must be optimistic, as in his breast he harbors the hope, which the Apostle Paul put so clearly, when he wrote:

> "For the grace of God that bringeth salvation hath appeared to all men,
>
> "Teaching us that, denying ungodliness and worldly lusts, we should live soberly, righteously, and godly, in this present world;
>
> "Looking for that blessed hope, and the glorious appearing of the great God and our Saviour Jesus Christ . . ."

PSALM FIFTY-EIGHT

AN IMPRECATORY PSALM

IN some respects the 58th Psalm is a strange Psalm. It is in the nature of an imprecatory prayer and for that reason it is called an "imprecatory Psalm." There are several Psalms of the same character. This Psalm reads:

"Do ye indeed speak righteousness, O congregation? do ye judge uprightly, O ye sons of men?

"Yea, in heart ye work wickedness; ye weigh the violence of your hands in the earth.

"The wicked are estranged from the womb: they go astray as soon as they be born, speaking lies.

"Their poison is like the poison of a serpent: they are like the deaf adder that stoppeth her ear;

"Which will not hearken to the voice of charmers, charming never so wisely.

"Break their teeth, O God, in their mouth: break out the great teeth of the young lions, O LORD.

"Let them melt away as waters which run continually: when he bendeth his bow to shoot his arrows, let them be as cut in pieces.

"As a snail which melteth, let every one of them pass away: like the untimely birth of a woman, that they may not see the sun.

"Before your pots can feel the thorns, he shall take them away as with a whirlwind, both living, and in his wrath.

"The righteous shall rejoice when he seeth the vengeance: he shall wash his feet in the blood of the wicked.

"So that a man shall say, Verily there is a reward for the righteous: verily he is a God that judgeth in the earth."

Now for a definition of the word "imprecatory". Surely we have all heard it used many times, as applied to some Psalms. The critic has taken occasion to verbally lash the writer of the Psalms for these outbursts. It has been said that they do not manifest the love of God, or the love one man should have for another; on the contrary, they show forth anger, judgment, and evil. There we have the meaning of the word "imprecatory". It means to invite or to pray that judgment or evil may befall an individual or a whole company of people. Thus an imprecatory Psalm is one invoking evil. As we read through this Psalm we will find that David was praying to the Lord, invoking Him to express judgment upon those whom he calls "the wicked." The judgment requested is terrific! That brings us to a very interesting subject—Is God Love?

It is true that God is love, infinite love; but it is equally true that our God is a consuming fire. It it dishonest to take one revelation of the character of God as given in the Scripture and refuse to accept another revelation.

Bear in mind that nowhere in the world, save in the Bible, can one find a revelation of the love of God. Look at creation for a moment. Where is there any revelation of God's love in creation? True, there are certain revelations of His benefactions, but haven't you often observed that nature reveals a strange, uninterested Creator; a Creator who manifests a striking indifference to the affairs of men; a Creator who permits droughts, famines, pestilences, etc. This Creator sometimes reveals Himself in a storm, on which occasion not the slightest evidence of His love is manifested, but on the contrary, there seems to be a cruel manifestation of hate.

For instance, here is a man walking down the street, or I should say, attempting to walk. He is so inebriated he cannot walk a straight line. He reels to and fro. He has been eating husks, fit only for swine. He is wallowing in the mire of human degradation, but as the storm rages he is laughingly indifferent to it and the storm seems to be indifferent to him. The lightning strikes and the thunder peals. Suddenly there appears a woman with a helpless little babe in her arms; the wife of the drunkard. The lightning streaks and, lo, it smites the helpless babe cradled on its mother's breast, while the drunken father careens carelessly down the street. Where is there in this any revelation of God in nature, as a just Creator, a loving Father, and a helping Saviour? We search in vain in all of creation for any revelation of a God of love.

However, in the Bible we find that God "so loved the world, that he gave his only begotten Son, that whosoever believeth in him should not perish, but have everlasting life." As a manifestation of that love He placed His Son upon the cross and exacted from Him the penalty of sin in order that He might redeem mankind, so that His righteousness and holiness might be upheld, while His love is given an opportunity for manifestation and operation. Oh, the silly thinking that believes that because God has manifested His love, He has ceased to hate sin, or that He has forever stayed His hand of judgment.

This Psalm deals with the subject of judgment. David is not exacting the judgment. He is merely praying for judgment. David is unable to judge righteously, but he calls upon God, the Judge of all the earth to do so.

PAUL AT MARS' HILL

In that connection, let us examine that interesting sermon which the Apostle Paul preached on Mars' hill. The disciples had conducted Paul to Athens and left him there to wait until Silas and Timothy were come. While Paul waited for them his spirit was stirred in him when he saw the city wholly given to idolatry. Therefore, he reasoned in the synagogue with the Jews and with the devout persons, and in the market place with those who met with him. Then certain philosophers of the Epicureans and of the Stoics encountered him. Some asked: "What will this babbler say?" Others said: "He seemeth to be a setter forth of strange gods: because he preached unto them Jesus, and the resurrection." These philosophers finally took him, and brought him to Mars' hill, saying: "May we know what this new doctrine, whereof thou speakest, is? For thou bringest certain strange things to our ears: we would know therefore what these things mean."

Then Paul stood in the midst of Mars' hill, and said:

"Ye men of Athens, I perceive that in all things ye are too religious.

"For as I passed by, and beheld your devotions, I found an altar with this inscription, TO THE UNKNOWN GOD. Whom therefore ye ignorantly worship, him declare I unto you.

"God that made the world and all things therein, seeing that he is Lord of heaven and earth, dwelleth not in temples made with hands;

"Neither is worshipped with men's hands, as though he needed any thing, seeing he giveth to all life, and breath, and all things;

"And hath made of one blood all nations of men for to dwell on all the face of the earth, and hath determined the times before appointed, and the bounds of their habitation;

"That they should seek the Lord, if haply they might feel after him, and find him, though he be not far from every one of us:

"For in him we live, and move, and have our being; as certain also of your own poets have said, For we are also his offspring.

"Forasmuch then as we are the offspring of God, we ought not to think that the Godhead is like unto gold or silver, or stone, graven by art and man's device.

"And the times of this ignorance God winked at; but now commandeth all men every where to repent;

"Because he hath appointed a day, in the which he will judge the world in righteousness by that man whom he hath ordained; whereof he hath given assurance unto all men, in that he hath raised him from the dead."

Notice that the crux of that sermon centers around the assurance that God, on an appointed day, will judge the world in righteousness, and that He will do so by a Man whom He hath ordained; and that Man is He whom God raised from the dead, even our Lord Jesus Christ.

Judgment Is Sure

It is not my intention to scare any man, but I would be untrue to my God, and to you, if I did not emphasize and reiterate that God will one day judge this world in righteousness. Granted, it does not appear so at the present time, as the wicked prospers and spreads himself like a green bay tree. Very often he is the leader of his district or a powerful politician, and when the poor demand an expression of justice he mocks and laughs, as if all the power in heaven and earth rested in his lap. Do you think that the eternal God is going to permit that endlessly? Don't you think this whole world cries out for that day when God will judge the world in righteousness? Then He will do what David prayed for in this 58th Psalm. At that time even the 10th verse will be literally fulfilled, where it is written: "The righteous shall rejoice when he seeth the vengeance: he shall wash his feet in the blood of the wicked."

We hasten to add, however, that no man in this world has the capability to express righteous judgment. There is only one person who can be trusted to do so, and that one is our Lord Jesus Christ, who said, during His public ministry, ". . . the Father judgeth no man, but hath committed all judgment unto the Son; that all men should honor the Son, even as they honour the Father."

Judgment! That is an awful word, and sometimes it falls upon unsuspecting ears. For example, John the Baptist, coming out of the wilderness of Judea, cried, "Repent ye: for the kingdom of heaven is at hand." John was the Lord's forerunner. He was the one of whom the prophet Isaiah wrote, saying, "The voice of him that crieth in the wilderness, Prepare ye the way of the LORD. . . ." All of Judea came out to hear him and many were baptized, confessing their sins.

However, when John saw many Pharisees and Sadducees coming to his baptism he spoke an unexpected message to them. The Pharisees and Sadducees were religious leaders. The Pharisees held to the letter of the law. They boasted of their own righteousness and the accomplishments of their own character, whereas the Sadducees not only did the same, but also were the so-called liberals of the day, who denied the miraculous. They did not believe in the resurrection of the body. They scoffed at the infallibility of the Scriptures, even as some of our so-called preachers do at the present time. But you would have supposed that of all men the religious leaders were "the righteous," comparatively speaking, at least. But what did John say to them? This is what he said: "O generation of vipers, who hath warned you to flee from the wrath to come?" That is strong language. Did you notice that John said: "who hath warned you to flee from the wrath to come?"

The age in which we live is the age of God's grace. His hand of judgment has been stayed. But it will not always be stayed. The sword shall not always rest in the scabbard. Some day it will be unsheathed, and what a day that will be, when God reveals the secrets of men's hearts. None of us could stand in His presence for a moment. His holiness would consume us. However, God has provided a haven of refuge, under the shelter of the shadow of Calvary's cross. There the penalty of sin was exacted, through the death of His Son, of whom it is written that He was "delivered for our offences, and was raised again for our justification. Therefore being justified by faith, we have peace with God through our Lord Jesus Christ. . . ." Our Lord Jesus said: "Verily, verily, I say unto you, He that heareth my word, and believeth on him that sent me, hath everlasting life, and shall not come into judgment; but is passed from death unto life."

PSALM FIFTY-NINE

CAN A MAN HAVE GOD FOR HIS DEFENSE?

AGAIN we come to a Psalm which has presented a problem to many people. The language appears so strange; it is vituperative, and they point to "the philosophy of Jesus" who suggested that we should love our enemies and do good to them that despitefully use us. On previous occasions we have seen that there is a progress of revelation in the Bible. Failure to recognize this progression will lead one into hopeless difficulties.

When I use the word "progression" do not assume that I mean *evolution*. There is development in man's life from babyhood, to childhood, to manhood, to maturity. This development or growth is to be found in all creation as our Lord expressed it when He said, ". . . first the blade, then the ear, after that the full corn in the ear." Of course, we are exhorted to grow in grace and in the knowledge of the Lord. That is not evolution, that is progression. We did not grow *into* grace. We are in grace already by having received God's gift but we grow *in* grace and *in* the knowledge of our Lord Jesus Christ. In creation, while everything is after its kind, there is growth within the kind, but there is no jumping from one kind into another kind. That is the missing link which will never be found.

An enlightened Christian cannot pray the full 59th Psalm because of the further revelation that is found in the New Testament. We now are called upon to pray for our enemies, but thank God we can also pray for deliverance from them. Let me give you an illustration.

Recently I was in Chicago and had a delightful time. I am grateful to my friend, Dr. Wilbur M. Smith, who arranged a splendid gathering for Saturday evening. There was Dr. Houghton, the president of the Moody Bible Institute, Dr. Wilbur M. Smith, and his father, Mr. Thomas Smith, Dr. Homer Hammontree, who I think is this country's greatest song leader, and then, to the surprise of us all, Dr. "Mel" Trotter, who does such a great piece of work in Grand Rapids, Michigan, and whose evangelistic efforts have been singularly honored by God. Dr. Trotter related a story which fits in perfectly here. He told of a gentleman who formerly was a prize-fighter, a big strapping fellow. That man was saved. (I hope you like the language. I love it, though there was a time when I did not. The word *saved* then did not find a responsive chord in my being, but it does now because I know of no word that better describes what actually takes place when a man receives Christ.) Anyway, this prize-fighter received Christ and was saved. What a transformation took place! He had a "little bit" of a wife. You know very often big men have small wives. She was quite annoyed with her husband for having received Christ. He refused to go to places she enjoyed. She wanted him to go here, there, and everywhere he formerly went with her. But now he insisted that he did not wish to follow those paths. He wanted to walk in the path of obedience to God's will. Some women can get very angry, and this little lady certainly did. She made his life miserable. One day she even took a big broom and beat him. She knocked him on the floor, and what a trouncing that wife administered to the former prize-fighter! While she was administering her punishment, the door opened and in walked an old friend. This friend looked at the former prize-fighter lying on the floor and said, "Do you mean to tell me that you, a former prize-fighter, would permit your little wife to beat you with a broom as she has done?" Immediately came the response, "That's about all the heaven she will ever get so she might just as well have a good time now." You could be assured nothing like that would have happened before his conversion to Christ!

So much for the introduction to our message. The Psalm reads:

"Deliver me from mine enemies, O my God: defend me from them that rise up against me.

"Deliver me from the workers of iniquity, and save me from bloody men.

"For, lo, they lie in wait for my soul: the mighty are gathered against me; not for my transgression, nor for my sin, O LORD.

"They run and prepare themselves without my fault: awake to help me, and behold.

"Thou therefore, O LORD God of hosts, the God of Israel, awake to visit all the heathen: be not merciful to any wicked transgressors. Selah.

"They return at evening: they make a noise like a dog, and go round about the city.

"Behold, they belch out with their mouth: swords are in their lips: for who, say they, doth hear?

"But thou, O LORD, shalt laugh at them; thou shalt have all the heathen in derision.

"Because of his strength will I wait upon thee: for God is my defence.

"The God of my mercy shall prevent me: God shall let me see my desire upon mine enemies.

"Slay them not, lest my people forget: scatter them by thy power; and bring them down, O LORD our shield.

"For the sin of their mouth and the words of their lips let them even be taken in their pride: and for cursing and lying which they speak.

"Consume them in wrath, consume them, that they may not be: and let them know that God ruleth in Jacob unto the ends of the earth. Selah.

"And at evening let them return; and let them make a noise like a dog, and go round about the city.

"Let them wander up and down for meat, and grudge if they be not satisfied.

"But I will sing of thy power; yea, I will sing aloud of thy mercy in the morning: for thou hast been my defence and refuge in the day of my trouble.

"Unto thee, O my strength, will I sing: for God is my defence, and the God of my mercy."

The mere fact that one cannot as a Christian use all the words of this Psalm as a prayer does not mean that we cannot derive some benefits from a study of the Psalm. Listen to the words of Charles Haddon Spurgeon in his introductory comments on this Psalm. He said, "Strange that the painful events in David's life should end in enriching the repertoire of the national minstrelsy. . . . Had David never been cruelly hunted by Saul, Israel and the church of God in after ages would have missed this song." Then I like his further comment, "The music of the sanctuary is in no small degree indebted to the trials of the saints. Affliction is the tuner of the harps of sanctified songsters." These are excellent words and the thought is beautifully expressed.

"HOLY HUMOR"

It is equally true now as it was in David's time that God can use trials and disappointments and painful experiences as the basis of a great burst of praise due to the result of His deliverance. Let me give you an illustration that came out of a letter from a missionary couple connected with the China Inland Mission. In it they described the tribulations of difficulties that have arisen as a result of Japanese occupation of the territory in which their station is located. They were very careful as to who was allowed to enter the compound. They permitted only terrified women and children to come in. They kept out soldiers with the exception of the officers. One morning there was a knock on the outer gate and when they went to open it there was the young man who customarily brought water to the compound. "I am alive," he gasped as he stepped into the safe shelter of the compound, "and I am trusting in Jesus now, for He saved my life. I hid under the straw in the room when the soldiers came in, and prayed Jesus to save me. All the other men in the room were shot but though the straw was poked I was not discovered—the Lord saved me and I belong to Him now."

Some of you may have noticed the item that appears in this week's issue of "Time," the weekly news magazine, reporting a letter sent by that faithful German pastor, Niemoeller, whom the ungodly regime of Germany has kept in a concentration camp because he refuses to obey man rather than God. "Time" entitled the article, "Holy Humor." The letter was written to his wife and part of it read, "I think my imprisonment belongs to the holy humor of God. First the mocking laughter 'Now we've got that fellow'; and then the imprisonment; and what are the consequences? Full churches, a praying community. To get bitter about such things would be shameful ingratitude." Thank God for a man like Pastor Niemoeller. Would God there were more like him.

God Shall Laugh at Them

There are several things in this 59th Psalm that are a source of encouragement to the Lord's people who may be in trial at this moment. It is true that some people develop a martyr complex; they think that the enemy is pursuing them all the time; they become so occupied with themselves that their faith is self-centered. I am not talking of or to that type of person—they need no encouragement but rather a severe rebuke.

Did you notice what David said in this Psalm? His enemies were not lying in wait for his soul because of his transgression or his sin or any fault in him, but his enemies were lying in wait for his soul because God had anointed him to be king over Israel.

David graphically described his enemies in this Psalm and said, ". . . they make a noise like a dog . . . they belch out with their mouth: swords are in their lips. . . ." They behave in that manner because they said, Who doth hear?—who knows anything about it?—God does not indicate that He is interested—let's get rid of this fellow—who will know the difference? To that kind of reasoning the Psalmist said, "But thou, O LORD, shalt laugh at them. . . ." Some may not like the thought that God one day will laugh at the wicked but that is the testimony of the Bible. Even in the 2nd Psalm it is written, "He that sitteth in the heavens shall laugh: the Lord shall have them in derision."

Look at the few men in this world today who are responsible for the sorrow and distress of nations and peoples; do you think that God is indifferent to the cry of these multitudes, particularly His own, against the oppression of these men? Do you think that God is an idol made of wood and stone, and that He has no eyes to see nor ears to hear? Sir, I would infinitely rather believe that God shall laugh some day at the wicked and shall have them in derision and that He will vent His wrath against all who justly deserve His wrath. I believe in hell as well as in heaven. No man can believe the Bible without believing in both places. There are those who have tasted of hell here and now. There are others who have tasted of heaven here and now. Those who have had a taste of heaven now, look forward with greater anticipation to the fullness of joy when they shall actually and physically be in the heavens. Those who endure hell now on the earth assume that it is possible to get away from it. Some have gone so far as to commit suicide, jumping out of the windows of hotels and other places. But if hell on earth has been painful and agonizing, what must it be when the bottomless pit is opened!

But we do not wish to be occupied with either heaven or hell in this meditation; rather let us stress things as they now are. David, in the midst of dire circumstances, was pleased to wait upon the Lord, and because of the strength of the Lord, he said, "God is my defence." In verse 9 he said, "God is my defence" and in verse 16, "thou hast been my defence" and in verse 17, "I will sing: for God is my defence. . . ." Is it possible for a man to have God as his defense? Physical suffering and deliverance from physical torture is not the supreme thing in this world. Indeed it is not. Our Lord said, "Be not afraid of them that kill the body, and after that have no more that they can do. But I will forewarn you when ye shall fear: Fear him, which after he hath killed hath power to cast into hell; yea, I say unto you, Fear him."

I repeat, can a man have God for his defense? We shall speak from the spiritual viewpoint, which of course is supreme. The answer to that question is found in a marvelous chapter of the Bible, the 8th of Romans, wherein, after a magnificent declaration of the work of God in the gospel on the behalf of those who believe in Christ, the Apostle Paul by the Holy Spirit, raised a few questions. In verse 31 of this 8th chapter he asked, "What shall we then say to these things? If God be for us, who can be against us?" Notice how Paul answered the question, "He that spared not his own Son, but delivered him up for us all, how shall he not with him also freely give us all things?" Again a question follows, "Who shall lay anything to the charge of God's elect?" Shall God, who alone possesses the right to make a charge? Shall God? The Apostle Paul replied, "It is God that justifieth." After God has justified a sinner and cleared him entirely because of his faith in Christ, will God bring anything to the charge of the justified man? That is unthinkable. But again, Paul asked, "Who is he that condemneth?" Shall it be Christ? To answer this Paul enumerated the things our Lord has done on the behalf of those who have received

Him. Shall Christ condemn? He that died, yea rather, that is risen again, who is even at the right hand of God, who also maketh intercession for us? Preposterous! Since God has justified us He certainly will not make any charge against us. He is our defense. Since Christ has died for us will He condemn us, especially when we bear in mind that He is risen again and is now in the heavens at the right hand of God, making intercession for those who receive Him?

Can a man have God for his defense? Indeed, if that man has come under the shelter of the shed blood of Jesus Christ His Son. But more than that. The Apostle Paul continued in his letter to the Romans, "Who shall separate us from the love of Christ? Shall tribulation, or distress, or persecution, or famine, or nakedness, or peril, or sword?" He answered, No, "in all these things we are more than conquerors through him that loved us" and closed the chapter with these words, "For I am persuaded, that neither death, nor life, nor angels, nor principalities, nor powers, nor things present, nor things to come, nor height, nor depth, nor any other creature, shall be able to separate us from the love of God, which is in Christ Jesus our Lord." Can a man have God for his defense? He can! How can he? The answer is simply this—by believing on the Lord Jesus Christ. God becomes our justifier, Christ our Saviour, our intercessor, our deliverer. Nothing shall be able to separate us from the love of God which is in Christ Jesus.

PSALM SIXTY

WHEN GOD SHAKES THE EARTH

BEFORE making any comment on the 60th Psalm let us read it and note the emphasis placed by the Psalmist upon the One responsible for the situation in which the people were then found:

> "O God, thou hast cast us off, thou hast scattered us, thou hast been displeased; O turn thyself to us again.
>
> "Thou hast made the earth to tremble; thou hast broken it: heal the breaches thereof; for it shaketh.
>
> "Thou hast shewed thy people hard things: thou hast made us to drink the wine of astonishment.
>
> "Thou hast given a banner to them that fear thee, that it may be displayed because of the truth. Selah.
>
> "That thy beloved may be delivered; save with thy right hand, and hear me.

"God hath spoken in his holiness; I will rejoice, I will divide Shechem, and mete out the valley of Succoth.

"Gilead is mine, and Manasseh is mine; Ephraim also is the strength of mine head; Judah is my lawgiver;

"Moab is my washpot; over Edom will I cast out my shoe: Philistia, triumph thou because of me.

"Who will bring me into the strong city? who will lead me into Edom?

"Wilt not thou, O God, which hadst cast us off? and thou, O God, which didst not go out with our armies?

"Give us help from trouble: for vain is the help of man.

"Through God we shall do valiantly: for he it is that shall tread down our enemies."

It interested me to read that Dr. Franz Delitzsch, the brilliant Hebrew Christian scholar of the 19th century, who has sometimes been called "The Christian Talmudist," and who was Doctor and Professor of Theology in the University of Leipzig from 1867 to 1890, in his classic work on the Psalms refers to this 60th Psalm as one that was "sung at military exercise after a lost battle." It immediately brought to mind an incident in the Book of Joshua of which I recently read in the course of my evening devotions. It took place shortly after the historic conquest of Jericho. Joshua, the leader of Israel, sent men from Jericho to Ai, which the Bible locates as being beside Bethaven, on the east side of Beth-el; and he said to these men, "Go up and view the country. And the men went up and viewed Ai. And they returned to Joshua, and said unto him, Let not all the people go up; but let about two or three thousand men go up and smite Ai; and make not all the people to labour thither, for they are but few."

Joshua took the advice of those men and sent about three thousand to besiege the city. About thirty-six were killed while the remaining members of the "expeditionary force" retreated rapidly to the camp, and the hearts of the people melted and became as water. "Joshua rent his clothes, and fell to the earth upon his face before the ark of the LORD until the eventide, he and the elders of Israel, and put dust upon their heads." Then Joshua addressing the Lord said, "Alas, O Lord GOD, wherefore hast thou at all brought this people over Jordan, to deliver us into the hand of the Amorites, to destroy us? would to God we had been content, and dwelt on the other side Jordan!" Even in the mind of such a godly man as Joshua there was that which immediately placed the cause for the disaster upon God. It was again a case of failing to distinguish between cause and effect.

The Lord said to Joshua, "Get thee up; wherefore liest thou thus upon thy face?" Then followed the recitation of the cause for the defeat. "Israel," God said, "hath sinned, and they have also transgressed my covenant which I commanded them: for they have even taken of the accursed thing, and have also stolen, and dissembled also, and they have put it even among their own stuff." Therefore, the children of Israel "could not stand before their enemies, but turned their backs before their enemies, because they were accursed:" and the Lord said to Joshua, "neither will I be with you any more, except ye destroy the accursed from among you." Thus you see it was not the time to pray, it was the time to do some judging. When the guilty one was discovered, he was exposed and made to bear the penalty of his sin. After the execution of judgment the Lord said to Joshua, "Fear not, neither be thou dismayed: take all the people of war with thee, and arise, go up to Ai: see, I have given unto thy hand the king of Ai, and his people, and his city, and his land. . . ."

I have given this long introduction for one primary reason: we are faced with a most important Psalm for it touches upon an age-old subject which has once more lifted its wicked head in the earth. All over this world we are witnessing the rise of anti-Semitism. In the first place, never has a Bible-believing Christian persecuted a Jew. A man cannot be a Bible-believing Christian and persecute the Jew for his Lord was a Jew according to the flesh; and the New Testament letters which he reverences as equally inspired with the Old Testament were written by Jews.

The one great Apostle who is called the Apostle to the Gentiles was a Jew by birth, so that a Christian (remember I am referring now to a Bible-believing Christian) acknowledges that everything he has in this world that is precious to him from the spiritual viewpoint has come down through the Jewish nation, because God was pleased in the exercise of His divine prerogative to choose that nation to be the custodian of His revelation and the people through whom the Anointed of the Lord would come. In addition they were to be a steadfast testimony to the unity of the Godhead, and what must necessarily follow, a testimony against all the nations who serve any but the true God. Whenever Israel has been persecuted the persecutors have always been other than Bible-believing Christians. The Apostle Paul said he could wish himself accursed, if that were possible, if through that means he could win his own countrymen to a knowledge of Christ.

We want to extract a message from this Psalm that will be a comfort to every Jew, a source of encouragement to every Christian, and a rebuke to every man who has not yet bowed the knee to Jesus Christ.

GOD IS ON HIS THRONE

In the first place, notice that David knew full well that God was on His throne and as far as he and his people were concerned nothing could transpire without the knowledge of God. It is only when God is displeased with His people that they suffer. God cannot then bless them. But mark you, in the 4th verse of this Psalm it is written, "Thou hast given a banner to them *that fear thee,* that it may be displayed because of the truth." So you see there was a "remnant" in that day in the midst of national backsliding that still remained true and who feared the Lord. There is a "remnant" today also. To them the Lord has given a banner which will protect them and which is to be displayed about them because of His eternal truth. The Lord does that in order that those who fear Him, whom He calls His beloved, may be delivered and saved by the right hand of God.

GOD'S PLAN FOR THIS EARTH

Now the 2nd verse of this Psalm is particularly interesting in view of what transpired a week ago. You will remember how a large part of our nation was disturbed by a radio broadcast which was so realistically enacted that many people forgot that it was only an "act." Well, that is what people deserve for listening to that kind of program on a Sunday! If they had been in the house of the Lord they would not have heard the fantastic things that were presented. Those who were not permitted by force of circumstance to be in a church could have tuned in to a good gospel program; they would then have heard old-fashioned hymns, and the preaching of the old-fashioned gospel, and their nerves would have been quieted. They would have enjoyed an evening in the good old-fashioned American way. Call it "puritanical" if you please, but it was and still is a better method than the "crazy" modern way that seems to possess many in our present generation. But, if a few men can scare a multitude of people by stage-acting a fantastic dream, what will be the result when the Lord causes the earth to tremble?

Notice, will you, verse 2 where we read, "Thou hast made the earth to tremble; thou hast broken it: heal the breaches thereof; for it shaketh." Professor Delitzsch gives a fine rendering of this verse. He translates it, "Thou hast made the land to tremble; Thou hast rent it; heal the breaches thereof; for it tottereth!!" Note the word *tottereth.* This whole civilization seems to be *tottering* at the present moment, but there is coming a day when our God *shall* shake the earth and cause it to reel like a tottering, drunken man. That will be a time when men will have cause to cry out for fear! It will not be a visitation from Mars—it will be a visitation from God!

GOD WILL REJOICE

Notice the last half of this Psalm. "God," said the Psalmist, "hath spoken in his holiness; I will rejoice. . . ." The Psalmist reported God as saying, "I will rejoice." Isn't that interesting? In the previous Psalm, the 59th Psalm, we learned that God will "laugh" at the wicked, but in this 60th Psalm we learn that God will "rejoice" in His ancient people, Israel. Indeed, more than that, He said, "I will divide Shechem, and mete out the valley of Succoth." That may surprise some of our ungodly smart Alecks of today, who in high places think the division of the earth is to be made in accordance with their national pattern. But back in that old book of the twice-told law, Deuteronomy, there is this statement, "When the Most High divided to the nations their inheritance, when he separated the sons of Adam, he set the bounds of the people according to the number of the children of Israel."

In other words, this earth cannot have an era of lasting peace until everything is in its proper order and in its proper place. As long as Israel is out of her place the world will be in turmoil. God divided to the nations their inheritance on the basis of the number of the children of Israel. That is what the Psalmist confirmed in this 60th Psalm as he recorded the Lord's words, "I will divide Shechem, and mete out the valley of Succoth. Gilead is mine, and Manasseh is mine; Ephraim also is the strength of mine head; Judah is my lawgiver; Moab is my washpot; over Edom will I cast out my shoe. . . ." There you have the complete divorcement of the Edomites! God has a plan for Palestine. It is not a partition plan either! Only God can handle the Palestinian problem. Even a reservation in Lower California is not in the "scheme" of God. Man can think up more crazy-quilt patchwork solutions for this world's problems while blinding his eyes to the plan of God! Palestine is promised to Israel. She will get it when the Lord returns.

And now one final word. The Psalmist said, "Give us help from trouble: for vain is the help of man." Indeed, it is. Then David closed the Psalm with this great cry, "Through God we shall do valiantly: for he it is that shall tread down our enemies."

PSALM SIXTY-ONE

THE HERITAGE AND THE INHERITANCE

THE 61st Psalm is another short Psalm, containing only eight verses. It is a composition intended to be played on a stringed instrument. Sometimes I wish it were possible to play and sing these Psalms as they must have been played and sung in David's time, and thereby musically interpret them. It is surely impossible that these Psalms could be interpreted by a female dancer such as a Park Avenue, New York church decided to exhibit last Sunday!

It is interesting to note the detours which certain members of the clergy make in order to entertain an audience. It is my experience that it is unnecessary to entertain a person to get him to come to church. There is nothing so satisfying to a hungry human heart as a simple proclamation of the Word of God.

Not having the stringed instruments, and not knowing the composition actually prepared for this Psalm, we cannot sing it and interpret it musically but, thank God, we can give an unfolding of the spiritual truth found in this Psalm.

"Hear my cry, O God; attend unto my prayer.

"From the end of the earth will I cry unto thee, when my heart is overwhelmed: lead me to the rock that is higher than I.

"For thou hast been a shelter for me, and a strong tower from the enemy.

"I will abide in thy tabernacle for ever: I will trust in the covert of thy wings. Selah.

"For thou, O God, hast heard my vows: thou hast given me the heritage of those that fear thy name.

"Thou wilt prolong the king's life: and his years as many generations.

"He shall abide before God for ever: O prepare mercy and truth, which may preserve him.

"So will I sing praise unto thy name for ever, that I may daily perform my vows."

It was an outstanding English clergyman who made the suggestion to a group of ministers that if they wished to preach to filled churches they should preach to broken hearts. What tragedies we humans experience. How often we find ourselves in trouble. At times we do not seem to know where to turn. How thankful we should be that David in this Psalm told us where a broken-hearted individual may go.

ATTENDING TO PRAYER

You will note that David was in prayer. He cried unto God and asked Him to attend unto his prayer. I love that word "attend." It not only has in it the thought of hearing, but it also expresses the idea of acting—having heard our prayer God acts upon our request.

The extremity of David's position is graphically presented in the 2nd verse, which reads: "From the end of the earth will I cry unto thee, when my heart is overwhelmed: lead me to the rock that is higher than I." That is a beautiful metaphor. In the next verse David indicated that it applied to a person, for he said: "For *thou* hast been a shelter for me, and a strong tower from the enemy."

The expression "the rock" is constantly ascribed to Deity in the Scriptures. During the wilderness journey Moses smote the rock, and as a result the children of Israel drank of the water that flowed from it. The Apostle Paul referred to that incident. What he had to say about it is quite interesting and enlightening. It is found in the 10th chapter of Paul's first letter to the Corinthians.

> "Moreover, brethren, I would not that ye should be gnorant, how that all our fathers were under the cloud, and all passed through the sea;
>
> "And were all baptized unto Moses in the cloud and in the sea;
>
> "And did all eat the same spiritual meat;
>
> "And did all drink the same spiritual drink: for they drank of that spiritual Rock that followed them: and that Rock was Christ."

David asked his God to *lead* him to the Rock. What a picture! This is not a case where David flies, or runs, to the Rock, but he cries in his deep need to the eternal God to lead him. David was a true sheep. A sheep does not know the way. He must be led. Like a sheep of the pastures David asked the Father to lead him to the Rock, and about that Rock he said, it is "higher than I." A rock is intended to provide a shelter from the storm; but a rock is also a strong tower to protect one from the enemy.

In verse 4 David said: "I will abide in thy tabernacle for ever: I will trust in the covert of thy wings. Selah." David was a man of hope. A true Bible-taught Christian is a man of hope. He knows his destination.

His ticket is purchased, stamped, and paid for. His destination is in the heavens with his Lord. With great confidence he rejoices in anticipation of the time when he will abide in the tabernacle of his Lord forever.

The Heritage of a Saint

But notice the last half of verse 5 where it is written: ". . . thou hast given me the heritage of those that fear thy name." There is a distinction between heritage and inheritance. At times the words may be synonymous but there is a shade of meaning in each that is interesting to observe. We have an inheritance in Christ. It is said we are heirs of God, and joint-heirs with Jesus Christ. As such, we will receive tangible evidences of possession. Heritage, however, may at times be intangible, such as, for instance, the heritage of family, the entrance into the family life, and the background of a family, which at times cannot be measured in terms of possessions. Heritage also has in it the idea of the enjoyment of the inheritance. It may be one thing to have an inheritance, and quite another matter to enjoy the inheritance. When we read: "thou hast given me the heritage of those that fear thy name," it is evident that the writer enjoyed a family relationship in the household of God by virtue of the reverence given to the name of God, who gives one the right of enjoyment of all that is in store for a saint.

We have already looked at a Scripture which declares that we who are in Christ, that is we who have received Christ, are heirs of God, and joint-heirs with Jesus Christ. That inheritance is a very definite, tangible something. The Lord said that the cattle on a thousand hills and the silver and gold were His. Because they belong to Him, they belong to us who are in Christ. It may be true that someone else is at present enjoying them. It may likewise be true that a great many of the wicked are enjoying the cattle on the hills and the silver and gold. However, some day the true believer in Christ will enter into his inheritance. I believe the inheritance is material as well as spiritual. God will have no saints in heaven who are paupers! While He may *now* have a great number of choice saints in poorhouses, some day He will give them their inheritance. They will be transported out of the poorhouses into the mansions of glory. What is more, the shock of the change of circumstances will not affect their mental equilibrium. They will not go mad with riches. They will have a body like unto our Lord's own body, which fits into the environment of heaven. Remember it is written: "Eye hath not seen, nor ear heard, neither have entered into the heart of man, the things which God hath prepared for them that love him. But God hath revealed them unto us by his Spirit: for the Spirit searcheth all things, yea, the deep things of God."

Before we came to know the Lord as our Saviour we did not have the slightest notion what God had in store for those who love Him, but because we have received Christ, and having received Christ we have received His Spirit, we now rejoice in the knowledge of the things that we, as children of God, shall inherit. If on no other basis than that of profit and loss, every man should receive Christ. There is no doubt, in my judgment, that if men only knew what God has in store for those who love Him, they would love Him from the bottom of their hearts.

Psalm Sixty-two

AN EXHORTATION FOR EACH OF US

AS one glances over the 62nd Psalm he is amazed to note how many subjects David covered in a short Psalm of twelve verses. Note the expanse of subject matter found therein.

"Truly my soul waiteth upon God: from him cometh my salvation.

"He only is my rock and my salvation; he is my defence; I shall not be greatly moved.

"How long will ye imagine mischief against a man? ye shall be slain all of you: as a bowing wall shall ye be, and as a tottering fence.

"They only consult to cast him down from his excellency: they delight in lies: they bless with their mouth, but they curse inwardly. Selah.

"My soul, wait thou only upon God; for my expectation is from him.

"He only is my rock and my salvation: he is my defence; I shall not be moved.

"In God is my salvation and my glory: the rock of my strength, and my refuge, is in God.

"Trust in him at all times; ye people, pour out your heart before him: God is a refuge for us. Selah.

"Surely men of low degree are vanity, and men of high degree are a lie: to be laid in the balance, they are altogether lighter than vanity.

"Trust not in oppression, and become not vain in robbery: if riches increase, set not your heart upon them.

"God hath spoken once; twice have I heard this; that power belongeth unto God.

> "Also unto thee, O Lord, belongeth mercy: for thou
> renderest to every man according to his work."

In approaching this Psalm to classify it, one is presented with quite a task. There are so many subjects in it, that it is difficult to place it under any particular heading. There is in it, for instance, that which resembles an imprecatory Psalm. This is evidenced in verses 3 and 4 where we read: "How long will ye imagine mischief against a man? ye shall be slain all of you: as a bowing wall shall ye be, and as a tottering fence. They only consult to cast him down from his excellency: they delight in lies: they bless with their mouth, but they curse inwardly. Selah."

THE GLORY OF GOD

But imprecation is only one subject upon which David touched in this Psalm. The one I particularly delight to discuss is the marvelous revelation of God found in it. Take, for instance, such passages as:

> "Truly my soul waiteth upon God: from him cometh
> my salvation.
> "He only is my rock and my salvation; he is my
> defence . . .
> "My soul, wait thou only upon God; for my expecta-
> tion is from him.
> "Trust in him at all times; ye people, pour out your
> heart before him: God is a refuge for us."

How evident it is from these quotations that David was presenting the personality of the Godhead. Let me quote another: "It has often been said that the sublime idea of one spiritual God came to the Hebrews from nature. But why did not other races see His name in the starry heaven like David? When Israel was given up to his own instinct he was always returning to Baal, or Moloch; to the cruelties and obscenities of alien gods and altars. The chief witnesses of Jehovah were His martyrs. Israel was the prophet of Theism, not because of race instincts, but in spite of them —not by the inspiration of the voice of nature, but against it."

No man can read this 62nd Psalm, bearing in mind the pantheistic ideas of the age in which it was written, without glorying in the matchless revelation of the eternal personal God so gloriously portrayed therein. What is more, there is in each verse a clear, unmistakable evidence that the writer of the Psalm knew that eternal God. That kind of knowledge, said our Lord Jesus, is eternal life.

Notice that David was not praying in this Psalm. He was not making a single request. He was simply extolling the greatness of God, glorying in His person, and exhorting his own soul to find rest in God. Particularly pertinent is the phrase in the 5th verse: "My soul, wait thou only upon God. . . ."

They that trust in the Lord, trust in Him *alone*. You cannot trust in the Lord and rest upon the arm of flesh at the same time. It has been said that "He that stands with one foot on a rock and another foot upon a quicksand will sink and perish as certainly as he that standeth with both feet on a quicksand."

When God is your Rock, you have *both* feet upon the Rock even though you are like the good old colored woman who said, "I may tremble on the Rock, but the Rock never trembles under me."

MAN'S REMEDIES *vs.* GOD'S CHRIST

Another subject in this Psalm, upon which we should spend a few moments, relates to the conclusion at which David arrived, which is expressed in the 9th verse, where it is written: "Surely men of low degree are vanity, and men of high degree are a lie: to be laid in the balance, they are altogether lighter than vanity."

That is a statement of fact. It indicates that He who examines the motives of the heart of man, rather than the outward expressions, declares that all men are on the same level of vanity. There are no distinctions here. Whether an individual be one of low degree or of high degree, both are lighter than vanity.

Just now it seems to be a pastime of some to heap all manner of invectives upon those who are of high degree or great position. One voice cries out ". . . Salvation can only be had in the sharing of wealth." Another insists that it is not a matter of sharing wealth, but of sharing income. Still another, a clergyman, used to shout, "In silver lies our redemption." The fact of the matter is that salvation is in none of these, neither the salvation of the individual, nor of society. While we may see some distinction in men, and assume that by the simple process of equalizing wealth we can bring man into a paradise; in God's sight sin is the cause of inequalities. So long as sin reigns, just so long will these situations exist. It is sheer nonsense to talk about sharing wealth, with the sharing in the hand of a politician. It is the same as expecting a Millennium without the Messiah. Sin will reign, until our Lord Jesus Christ Himself rules over this world as King of kings, and Lord of lords.

In the meanwhile, the exhortation of this Psalm still holds: "Trust not in oppression, and become not vain in robbery: if riches increase, set not your heart upon them." This is a very pertinent and worthwhile exhortation. To the man of power, the Scripture says, "Trust not in oppression." To the man who is striving, the Scripture says, "become not vain in robbery." To the man who has seen his riches increase, the Bible says, "set not your heart upon them."

There will always be those who lead, and those who oppress, and those who possess riches. There will always be the temptation to those in leadership to trust in oppression; to those in struggle to trust to robbery, whether it be legal or illegal; and there will always be the temptation to the man of wealth to trust in his riches. However, the Scriptures say to one, "Trust not in oppression," to the other "become not vain in robbery," and to the third, "set not your heart upon" your riches.

THE POWER OF GOD

In closing, the Psalmist brought out two striking facts. First, "God hath spoken once; twice have I heard this; that power belongeth unto God." Second, ". . . unto thee, O Lord, belongeth mercy." These two statements contain a wealth of knowledge. All who are exercised by them will be enriched, and will not be disturbed by the passing, depressing moments. Come what may, they know that power belongeth to the Lord. The most difficult lesson for any man to learn is that "power belongeth unto God."

Let me quote another Psalm, in this connection. In the 100th Psalm, verse 3, it is written: "Know ye that the LORD he is God: it is he that hath made us, and not we ourselves; we are his people, and the sheep of his pasture." When a man knows that the Lord is God, he also knows that power belongs to Him.

Finally, a word about the second fact which David stated ". . . unto thee, O Lord, belongeth mercy." Just as power belongs to God, so mercy belongs to Him. Mercy is one of the most precious words in our vocabulary. It is written, "But God, who is rich in mercy, for his great love wherewith he loved us, even when we were dead in sins . . . hath raised us up together with Christ. . . ." He has saved us by His grace. In fact, "The LORD is merciful and gracious, slow to anger, and plenteous in mercy." His mercy is from everlasting to everlasting upon them that fear Him. How true it is—"Not by works of righteousness which we have done, but according to his mercy he saved us . . . "

THE WISDOM OF RECEIVING CHRIST IN ONE'S YOUTH

IN our meditation in the 63rd Psalm we shall limit our comments to the first eight verses, which read:

> "O God, thou art my God; early will I seek thee: my soul thirsteth for thee, my flesh longeth for thee in a dry and thirsty land, where no water is;
>
> "To see thy power and thy glory, so as I have seen thee in the sanctuary.
>
> "Because thy lovingkindness is better than life, my lips shall praise thee.
>
> "Thus will I bless thee while I live: I will lift up my hands in thy name.
>
> "My soul shall be satisfied as with marrow and fatness; and my mouth shall praise thee with joyful lips:
>
> "When I remember thee upon my bed, and meditate on thee in the night watches.
>
> "Because thou hast been my help, therefore in the shadow of thy wings will I rejoice.
>
> "My soul followeth hard after thee: thy right hand upholdeth me."

While it is true that God is the Creator of all men, and as such He has a certain relationship with man, in a more personal and distinct manner He is the God and Father of our Lord Jesus and the God and Father of all those who believe in Him. Like David, they can say from the bottom of their hearts, "O God, thou art my God."

Note that David said, "early will I seek thee." I do not believe this limits the matter of time to one specific day as, for instance, "early (in the morning) will I seek thee." Rather, it describes the relationship that existed in the early days of David's life.

It has been said that approximately ninety per cent of those who have received Christ as their Saviour have received Him before they were 24 years of age. It seems apparent therefore, if these figures are accurate (and I do not know of anything that would lead me to question them), that the older a man or a woman becomes, the more difficult it is for him or her to be saved. I do not know the reason. All I know is that it is a fact that the overwhelming majority who have received Christ received Him in their youth. Receiving Christ in one's youth is not only a great joy but also a tremendous privilege. It gives one a foundation for life which is very difficult to overestimate. Coming to know the Lord in one's youth enables one to grow in grace and in the knowledge of the Lord, as well as to have one's faith strengthened as the years go by.

For instance, it was my privilege recently to speak at the Second Presbyterian Church, in Princeton, N. J., where a number of Princeton undergraduates were present. I met a fine group of young fellows, all of whom had definitely received Christ as their Saviour and who knew the joy of salvation. My, how I enjoyed the experience! It was a pleasure to listen as they told of their experiences and described the general conditions at the University. You could not shake the faith of that group of fellows by any type of ungodly philosophy that any ungodly professor could give. They know that the Bible is true and that Jesus Christ is the Son of God, because they have definitely come into a relationship with the Lord.

"Ruled With a Rod of Words"

Last week I received a very encouraging letter from a friend who is a missionary in Jehol Province, in Manchuria. Some people think of missionaries as a very uninteresting lot of people, and that a missionary's life is an uninteresting one. I have never found it so and, what is more, my friends who are missionaries give evidence of living a life which makes our city environment and its confining limitations look pretty small.

At any rate, this missionary wrote that the Lord was giving him and his family overweights of joy. Recently, quite a number of souls have turned to the Lord from idols. He told of one family, some of whom are now staying with him and who give him great joy. To quote from his letter:

"Over twenty years ago my wife sowed the good seed in the heart of a young girl scarcely in her 'teens. She is now the mother of several children, the eldest being older than the girl was when my wife first spoke to her of the Lord Jesus. All these years she has been ruled with a rod of words (and words can be sharper than a sword, you remember!) proceeding out of the mouth of a tyrant of a mother-in-law. But in her heart the little wife knew the Lord Jesus as her Friend, and now that she has given several sons to the family, she is allowed to open her mouth! Well, the upshot of it all is, she has persuaded the whole family to turn to God. Do you wonder our hearts are happy?"

The letter continues: "The old mother-in-law, who is one of those staying with us, is quite a comical old dame of seventy odd summers. Bob (one of the missionary's sons) went up in the car to fetch her. They live in the country about thirty or forty miles out. She had heard about motor cars, of course, but never dreamed of riding in one, and surprise knew no bounds when she found the thing could fly. Chinese carts do about three miles an hour. Imagine her feelings to find herself in an infernal machine doing thirty miles an hour! But the poor old dear nearly burst her skin when she suddenly saw a train as they were entering the city. All she could say was 'That thing! That thing!' She had heard of terrible dragons belching out fire and brimstone, but here was one before her very eyes; and with such a long tail, too! It happened to be a freighter."

Apart from the indication there is in this letter that a missionary has a human soul, and can enjoy himself even in a heathen country, what I was particularly interested in noting was the strength this young woman received in knowing Christ, which strength enabled her to meet the trying circumstances of later life, and which finally led her to become the victor over those circumstances and bring even her critics to the foot of the cross.

"In the Sanctuary"

Then said David, "my soul thirsteth for thee, my flesh longeth for thee in a dry and thirsty land, where no water is. . . ." Sometimes this world seems to have an interesting glamour about it, but it is merely a mirage. One soon find the wells of this world empty. When a soul has tasted the joy of knowing the Lord, there is no doubt that this world loses its attraction. The reason for this is so marvelously expressed in the 2nd verse, where David said: "To see thy power and thy glory, so as I have seen thee in the sanctuary."

In the Old Testament the building of a sanctuary was evidently such an important matter that minute details were given concerning it. Not a single iota was left to the imagination of man. Every article of furniture was thoroughly described, the dimensions were given, as well as the color of the fabrics to be used. Every detail was given by God to Moses. But when you come into the New Testament you are startled to discover that not one single line is given, by intimation or definite expression, telling how an earthly sanctuary should be built. I doubt if you will find a single reference to the building of any church. When our Lord said to Peter, ". . . upon this rock I will build my church; and the gates of hell shall not prevail against it," He did not refer to a building of brick and mortar: He referred to that spiritual body composed of every believer in our Lord Jesus.

called out of this world to be members of His body. That body is the church.

Of course, we do not wish to decry churches or the building of churches. God forbid! I thoroughly enjoy entering into an appropriate building set aside for the worship of the Lord. But it does not make any difference whether we meet with a handful of people in a home, provided we are gathered unto the name of our Lord Jesus; for worship is not now at a specific place, such as indicated in the Old Testament. All worship now is in the heavenly sanctuary.

PEACE IN THE NIGHT

Before closing, may we consider verses 6 and 7, where David said:

> "When I remember thee upon my bed, and meditate on thee in the night watches.
> "Because thou hast been my help, therefore in the shadow of thy wings will I rejoice."

A believer in our Lord Jesus Christ is greatly blessed, and, of course, David was as much a believer in our Lord as you and I who have received Him. He looked forward to Christ. We look back to Him. Every believer has many advantages, the chief of which is the abounding joy in the knowledge of the Lord; and next to that, I would say is the peace that possesses his soul. To enumerate these blessings would be quite a task. True peace in the night seasons demonstrates its quality.

David said, ". . . I remember thee upon my bed, and meditate on thee in the night watches." If a Christian has a sleepless night he can enjoy himself by meditating upon his Lord in the night watches. It is an infinitely greater joy than being plagued by a disturbed conscience. Someone has made the statement that "a man is what he is in the night."

If your conscience has disturbed you and the burden of guilt rests heavily upon your heart, listen to the invitation of our Lord when He said, "Come unto me, all ye that labour and are heavy laden, and I will give you rest." It was the Apostle Paul who said, "This is a faithful saying, and worthy of all acceptation, that Christ Jesus came into the world to save sinners; of whom I am chief."

And now, just a word on the 8th verse: "My soul followeth hard after thee: thy right hand upholdeth me." Someone has said, "this is a marvelous unfolding of grace." All will remember the opening lines of the 2nd

verse of Charles Wesley's immortal hymn, "Jesus, Lover of My Soul." This
verse begins:

> "Other refuge have I none;
> Hangs my helpless soul on Thee."

Even that does not adequately express the depth of meaning of
David's language in this Psalm.

There is an old Jewish translation of this 8th verse, which reads: "My
soul fast to thy skirts would cling." That's it! You who are acquainted
with the Gospels recall the woman who had an infirmity for twelve years,
who concluded, "If I may but touch his garment, I shall be whole." All it
required was a touch of the hem of His garment. Then her disease vanished through the influx of His saving, healing virtue. Oh, that we may
not only touch His garment, but do as David encouraged his own heart:
"My soul fast to thy skirts would cling."

PSALM SIXTY-FOUR

THE SNOOPING OF SINNERS AT THE SINS OF SAINTS

A GOOD title for this meditation on the 64th Psalm, I think, is "The
Snooping of Sinners at the Sins of Saints." Whether you like the
title or not, I am sure you will enjoy the Psalm, which reads:

> "Hear my voice, O God, in my prayer: preserve
> my life from fear of the enemy.
> "Hide me from the secret counsel of the wicked;
> from the insurrection of the workers of iniquity:
> "Who whet their tongue like a sword, and bend
> their bows to shoot their arrows, even bitter words:
> "That they may shoot in secret at the perfect: sud-
> denly do they shoot at him, and fear not.
> "They encourage themselves in an evil matter: they
> commune of laying snares privily; they say, Who
> shall see them?
> "They search out iniquities; they accomplish a diligent
> search: both the inward thought of every one of
> them, and the heart, is deep.
> "But God shall shoot at them with an arrow; sud-
> denly shall they be wounded.
> "So they shall make their own tongue to fall upon
> themselves: all that see them shall flee away.
> "And all men shall fear, and shall declare the work
> of God; for they shall wisely consider of his doing.
> "The righteous shall be glad in the LORD, and shall
> trust in him; and all the upright in heart shall glory."

The *sins* of saints are a matter of concern to God as they are a problem and a sorrow to the saints, though an occasion for much gloating upon the part of unregenerate sinners.

David knew something about this experience. Therefore, in this Psalm he cried out to God to preserve his life from the fear of the enemy. He also told about the secret counsels of the wicked and how they "whet their tongue like a sword, and bend their bows to shoot their arrows, even bitter words. . . ." What a description of the cutting power of a word! Many of God's people have felt it and would rather have taken some physical punishment than the cutting words of their enemies.

Now sin *was* a problem to God just as sin *is* a problem to man. Can you imagine what a world this would be if there were no such thing as sin, and no such person as a sinner? But sin not only presented a problem to God, but in a definite way involved the very throne of God, for the obvious reason that God was pleased to go along with men who were sinners and, indeed, even referred to one of them as a man after His own heart. If a man is known by the friends he keeps, God also is known by His friends.

That there were some men who were called friends of God is evident. Abraham, for example, was called a friend of God. Yet atheists and unbelievers delight to remind us that Abraham was a liar and on several occasions lacked the courage of a man when he hid behind the skirts of his wife. Neither have these critics overlooked the crookedness of Jacob, who was said to have been "a prince with God." And David has always been a choice morsel under their tongues. They delight to impress us with the fact that David was an adulterer and a murderer, yet he was the one of whom it is written that he was a man after God's own heart!

God was not unmindful that a serious moral charge was laid at His throne for having friendship with men of the character of those whom we have already enumerated. Indeed, one major reason why our Lord Jesus Christ came into this world and was nailed to the cross was to justify God from this attack upon the part of the enemies of God and the enemies of God's people. Our Lord's death on the cross justified God as well as the sinner! Christ's death on the cross has set God right before the world as it has set sinners right before God. That phase of our Lord's ministry is the testimony of the 25th and 26th verses of the 3rd chapter of the Epistle to the Romans, where we learn that God set forth our Lord Jesus Christ to be a mercy-seat "through faith in his blood, to declare his (God's) righteousness for the remission of sins that are past, through the forbearance of God. . . ." Thus God had friendship with sinful men such as Abraham, Isaac, Jacob, Moses, and David, in anticipation of what Jesus Christ would do on the cross. It was not that God overlooked their sin, but that He knew provision would be made for it, for He Himself would provide the Lamb. Therefore our Lord was called by John the Baptist, "the Lamb of God, which beareth away the sin of the world."

SAINTS AND SAINTLINESS

God has been more mindful of the sins of His saints than have any of the enemies of His saints. But we must make clear what we mean by "saints." The Bible calls every man a saint who has received Jesus Christ as his Saviour. Men are "called saints," as the Scripture puts it. A saint is a man who has been separated unto God by the death of Jesus Christ. The fact that he has been "called" a saint has *nothing to do with his character*. It has *everything to do with his position!* It is a positional word exclusively, just as the office of president is a positional office. A man occupies the chair of president solely because of his calling and election. After his election he can be one of two things: he can either be a good president, true to his office, true to his calling; or, he can be a bad president, untrue to his calling, and untrue to his office. Even so, a believer in Christ is called a saint. It is his position by virtue of what Christ has done. The believer can be faithful and saintly in his behavior or he can be unfaithful and unsaintly in his behavior.

When a saint is unfaithful and unsaintly there are repercussions which are immediately felt at the very throne of God, where the Lord sits on the right hand of the Majesty on high. In fact, for almost two thousand years our Lord has been carrying on a continuous work in the heavenly sanctuary, ever living to make intercession for His sinning saints. Even this day He is washing the defiled feet of sinning saints, as He did in symbol on the night of His betrayal when He washed the disciples' feet with water that was in a basin.

Now saints sin, for they are as much in the flesh as all other men, and because of the presence of a new nature their flesh, if anything, is more sensitive to sin.

The words of that splendid young Norwegian philosopher, Sverre Norborg, Professor of Philosophy at the University of Minnesota, are thought-provoking. He said, "A Christian is not a fortunate person who has never done anything wrong or who has attained a high point on the ladder of holiness. True Christianity does not consist in anything we have done, but rather in what God has done in and for us."

It is a sad fact that many Christians do not live the Christian life. They neither claim their possessions in Christ nor seem interested in appropriating the power that God has made available to every Christian to live as becometh saints. I am also aware that Christians can be guilty of snooping and talking about other Christians, even as the unbeliever. I do not know of anything so unbecoming to Christian conduct as for one Christian to talk about another Christian. Of course, none of us would do anything of that kind!! It is always the other fellow who does it. Would to God many of us would adopt the idea of a great Bible teacher of a generation ago who would walk out of the room, wherever he might be, when one Christian began gossiping about another. I do not know who is the author of this statement, but it is good: "We should talk to our neighbors *about God;* and talk *to God* about our neighbors."

There is nothing quite so effective as preaching a sermon to one's self! In the course of prayer recently I mentioned a man of God before the Lord, a man who needed to be taken down a peg or two for his own good; at least, *I thought, so,* but I soon ceased that line of attack, as the Spirit of God suddenly said to me, Haven't you enough difficulties of your own, not to be concerned about another's shortcomings? Needless to say, I dropped that line of approach.

SNOOPING SINNERS

In this 64th Psalm and the 6th verse, David described the snooping of sinners against saints when he wrote, "They search out iniquities; they accomplish a diligent search: both the inward thought of every one of them, and the heart, is deep." To this the Psalmist immediately added, "But God shall shoot at them with an arrow; suddenly shall they be wounded. So they shall make their own tongue to fall upon themselves: all that see them shall flee away."

There is a great lesson in this Psalm for the workers of iniquity whose hatred for God and His people is all too evident. Of course, they feel justified in their attack. The poison of hatred has successfully blinded their eyes so that self-justification can readily be argued with great persuasion by them. Let me give you an extreme incident which took place this past week and which every decent man must deplore. When a youth still in his teens, undoubtedly crazed by overwhelming emotions which were put into force by dire circumstances, unfortunately shot the secretary of the German Embassy in Paris, it brought a repercussion throughout all Germany in the vilest kind of violence against a people whose only blame was that they were born Jews. Yet to this wicked, Satanic-inspired expression, no less a personality than the Propaganda Minister sought to justify the violence with these words, "While I would not have done as the people did yesterday, yet I admit that inwardly I stood completely on the side of the people." Oh, the reasoning of wicked men! But hear what this 64th Psalm has to say, "God shall shoot at them with an arrow; suddenly shall they be wounded. So they shall make their own tongue to fall upon themselves: all that see them shall flee away." Someone has said that the wheels of God grind slowly, but they grind exceeding sure.

But let's not shoot our arrows across the sea from a safe place in the United States, for there is nothing heroic about facing a foe with an ocean between. This 64th Psalm has a message for every man right in our midst. We have given the Bible definition of a saint. Now I must give you the Bible definition of a sinner. God only sees two classes of people—saints and sinners—only two. A saint, we learned, is a man who has been justified by faith in Jesus Christ through the redemption accomplished at the cross. A sinner from the Bible viewpoint is a man who is less perfect than God.

When a rich young ruler came running to our Lord and fell down before Him asking, "Good Master, what shall I do that I may inherit eternal life?" our Lord's first response was this, "Why callest thou me good? there is *none* good but one, that is, God." That means every man is a sinner. It is inevitable, for God cannot in the very nature of His being accept anything less perfect than He is. In this book, the Bible, *the question of sin cuts deep*, even going so far as to state that if we have respect to persons we commit sin and are convicted of the law as transgressors, for "whosoever shall keep the whole law, and yet offend in one point, he is guilty of all." These are solemn words. They constitute every man a sinner. There is only one remedy for sin. As the hymn-writer put it:

> "There is a fountain filled with blood
> Drawn from Immanuel's veins;
> And sinners plunged beneath that flood
> Lose all their guilty stains.
>
> "The dying thief rejoiced to see
> That fountain in his day;
> And there may I, though vile as he,
> Wash all my sins away.

> "E'er since, by faith, I saw the stream
> Thy flowing wounds supply
> Redeeming love has been my theme
> And shall be till I die.
>
> "Then in a nobler, sweeter song
> I'll sing Thy power to save
> When this poor, lisping, stammering tongue
> Lies silent in the grave."

PSALM SIXTY-FIVE

A SPRING PSALM

THE 65th Psalm seems to have in it the idea of the spring season of the year, when suddenly everything desires to burst out in praise and in newness of life. We shall not consider the entire Psalm, but merely a few of the verses around which we will center our thoughts. The Psalm opens with an exhortation to praise.

> "Praise waiteth for thee, O God, in Sion: and unto thee shall the vow be performed.
> "O thou that hearest prayer, unto thee shall all flesh come.
> "Iniquities prevail against me: as for our transgressions, thou shalt purge them away.
> "Blessed is the man whom thou choosest, and causest to approach unto thee, that he may dwell in thy courts: we shall be satisfied with the goodness of thy house, even of thy holy temple."

Let us stop there for a moment and see if we cannot find a delightful morsel in it. In the first place notice the opening words, "Praise waiteth for thee, O God . . ." In another Psalm it is written, "Whoso offereth praise glorifieth me . . ." No greater tribute can any human being offer than to praise the Lord.

THE CASE OF FANNY CROSBY

Today (March 24) is the anniversary of the birth of Fanny Crosby. If any might have had cause to complain, it was she. Born with eyesight, she lost it when she was six months old. She lived to reach almost ninety-five years. When she was old enough to understand, her mother told her she would never see the faces of her friends, the flowers of the field, the blue of the skies, nor the golden beauty of the stars. So she made up her mind to store away a little jewel in her heart, which she called "Content." This was the comfort of her whole life. She was of a happy, contented disposition and refused to be pitied because of her great affliction, and when only eight years old wrote:

> "O what a happy soul am I!
> Although I cannot see,
> I am resolved that in this world
> Contented I will be.
>
> How many blessings I enjoy
> That other people don't,
> To weep and sigh because I'm blind,
> I cannot and I won't."

Why do you suppose Fanny Crosby could write, "O what a happy soul am I!" The secret lay in her faith in Christ and her vision of Him which enabled her to write, "Praise Him! Praise Him! Jesus, our blessed Redeemer." Let none suppose their circumstances so dire that they have cause to cease to praise Him. To the man or woman who has received Christ as his or her Saviour, there is written this great injunction:

> "Be careful for nothing; but in every thing by prayer and supplication with thanksgiving let your requests be made known unto God.
>
> "And the peace of God, which passeth all understanding, shall keep your hearts and minds through Christ Jesus."

Then again, notice that it is written, "Praise waiteth for thee, O God, *in Sion.*" I need not remind those who are acquainted with the Bible that God never makes a mistake; that He is well able to express Himself in language that can be easily understood; neither does He interchange expressions that are not synonymous. For instance, when speaking of Zion, He is not speaking of heaven; when speaking of Jerusalem He is not speaking of the glory; when speaking of Israel He does not mean the church.

Unfortunately, Protestantism has approached the Old Testament in a strange way, attempting to take out of it all the blessings and applying them to Christians generally, and it has been very careful to leave the curses and the hard things right where they belong in the Old Testament, insisting that they all refer to Israel and the Jews. Of course, the attempt is absurd. If the judgments belong to Israel, so do the blessings.

True, the Old Testament was written to the Israelites, and all of it concerns the children of Israel, but we learn from the New Testament that ". . . whatsoever things were written aforetime (that is, in the Old Testament) were written for our learning, that we through patience and comfort of the scriptures might have hope." We also know, from our Lord's handling of the Scriptures, that Christ is as surely outlined in the Old Testament as He is now to be found in the New Testament. In fact, it is utterly impossible to appreciate the message of the Old Testament if you fail to see Christ therein.

But when the Psalmist said, "Praise waiteth for thee, O God, in Sion" he meant just exactly what he said. He was particularly referring to the city of Sion or Jerusalem, in Palestine, where the Israelites gathered for the celebration of their various feasts and rejoiced in the bountiful provisions of the eternal God.

"THE MAN WHOM THOU CHOOSEST"

In the 4th verse the Psalmist was undoubtedly speaking of the high priest, who was chosen among men to approach unto God. We know from the New Testament that such privilege is now extended to every believer in our Lord Jesus. That is what makes the gospel of our Lord Jesus so precious. Think of it—we who are Gentiles in the flesh, who at one time were without hope and without God in the world, strangers from the covenants of promise, aliens from the commonwealth of Israel—we *now* have been made nigh through the blood of Christ. As the high priest was blessed in having the privilege of entering into the presence of the Lord through the blood of the sacrifice, so we, who have received Christ, have likewise been blessed. We, too, know what it is to be satisfied with the goodness of the house of God.

Commencing with the 8th verse, this Psalm extends its horizon beyond the confines of Jerusalem, as you will note while we quote from the 8th verse to the close of the Psalm:

> "They also that dwell in the uttermost parts are afraid at thy tokens: thou makest the outgoings of the morning and evening to rejoice.
> "Thou visitest the earth, and waterest it: thou greatly enrichest it with the river of God, which is full of water: thou preparest them corn, when thou hast so provided for it.
> "Thou waterest the ridges thereof abundantly: thou settlest the furrows thereof: thou makest it soft with showers: thou blessest the springing thereof.
> "Thou crownest the year with thy goodness; and thy paths drop fatness.
> "They drop upon the pastures of the wilderness: and the little hills rejoice on every side.
> "The pastures are clothed with flocks; the valleys also are covered over with corn; they shout for joy, they also sing."

In these verses God is pictured as the Benefactor who waters the earth, enriches its yield and crowns the year with His goodness. The

Psalmist has pictured a fertile field, pastures clothed with flocks, valleys covered with corn, and the increase of the earth verily shouting for joy as they revel in the glory of the beneficent Creator, God.

What an indictment this Psalm brings against the new type of economics that has for its basic philosophy the destruction of God's bounties.

I believe that the church ought to be separate from politics, that it should have nothing to do with politics, and that the man of God should attend to his own "knitting," and that is preaching the Word of God. However, just as strongly as I am convinced of that position, equally persuaded am I that, individually or nationally, one cannot violate the laws of God in nature and expect to escape the penalty. This nation shall not escape the judgment of God for its ungodly, vicious attempts to place the responsibility for our distress at the throne of a beneficent Creator who has blessed this country with the increase of the field. For a nation, professing to be Christian, to proceed from the viewpoint that God has given us too much, and therefore, in order to hold up prices, we should destroy His benefactions, is to be guided by men whose minds must have lost their equilibrium.

All of us can forgive errors of judgment. All of us can forgive errors in the field of experimentation, but who will forgive such a wicked procedure? Is it any wonder that our wheat belt suffers from a terrific drought? Is it any wonder that even now, right at the threshold of the spring planting season, we read of frightful dust storms in the Midwest? I was interested to read that the Administration has now decided to permit the farmer in the wheat belt to be released from further restriction. But, alas, it does not seem to have been urged by an acknowledgment of sin, but rather for fear that it will be blamed if further droughts should again plague our land.

THE THEME SONG OF THE 65TH PSALM

It would be an excellent idea, I think, if in the Department of Agriculture, and in Congress, and in the White House, someone would print in large letters the substance of the closing verses of this Psalm:

"*Thou* visitest the earth, and waterest it: *thou* greatly enrichest it with the river of God, which is full of water: *thou* preparest them corn, when *thou* hast so provided for it.

"*Thou* waterest the ridges thereof abundantly: *thou* settlest the furrows thereof: *thou* makest it soft with showers: *thou* blessest the springing thereof."

Who is it that does all this? Thou—the eternal God. The word "*thou*" seems like a theme song, running on through the Psalm, as God is extolled as the "*Great Giver*." The New Testament declares that He is the giver of every good gift. What sin, therefore, must it be to flaunt our wisdom in the face of God and to say that His benefactions are too much. If He were to withhold His hand of blessing, where would we be?

Before closing, let me refer you to the 5th verse of our Psalm, which reveals to us the place of confidence. There it is written: "By terrible things in righteousness wilt thou answer us, O God of our salvation; who art the confidence of all the ends of the earth, and of them that are afar off upon the sea . . ."

To place confidence in any other but our Lord is to misplace such confidence. Do not trust in riches, in the arm of flesh, or in any other thing, but rather place your confidence in the eternal God, the God of our salvation. You will never be disappointed. You will never be confounded. You will always be at peace in your heart. You will have a song in your mouth. You will find that the passing circumstances of earth will not disturb you. You will be able to rejoice in tribulation. You will find "that all things work together for good to them that love God, to them who are the called according to his purpose."

The Lord has a way of making all things abound to His glory. A few months ago our newspapers carried big headlines about a lost airplane—forced down just north of Albany, N. Y., in a snow-storm. For days everyone waited, almost breathlessly, for some news. And there was great joy when those men were rescued. One of the passengers was a born-again Christian. During their distress he led each of the others to Christ. Oh, yes, when men are in distress, then it is so apparent that God alone is their hope. But don't wait until then. Acknowledge Him now as the God of your salvation.

PSALM SIXTY-SIX

THE CHRISTIAN LIFE WITH CHRIST

WE come now to the 66th Psalm, which reads:

"Make a joyful noise unto God, all ye lands:
"Sing forth the honour of his name: make his praise glorious.
"Say unto God, How terrible art thou in thy works! through the greatness of thy power shall thine enemies submit themselves unto thee.

"All the earth shall worship thee, and shall sing unto thee; they shall sing to thy name. Selah.

"Come and see the works of God: he is terrible in his doing toward the children of men.

"He turned the sea into dry land: they went through the flood on foot: there did we rejoice in him.

"He ruleth by his power for ever; his eyes behold the nations: let not the rebellious exalt themselves. Selah.

"O bless our God, ye people, and make the voice of his praise to be heard.

"Which holdeth our soul in life, and suffereth not our feet to be moved.

"For thou, O God, hast proved us: thou hast tried us, as silver is tried.

"Thou broughtest us into the net; thou laidst affliction upon our loins.

"Thou hast caused men to ride over our heads; we went through fire and through water: but thou broughtest us out into a wealthy place.

"I will go into thy house with burnt-offerings: I will pay thee my vows,

"Which my lips have uttered, and my mouth hath spoken, when I was in trouble.

"I will offer unto thee burnt-sacrifices of fatlings, with the incense of rams; I will offer bullocks with goats. Selah.

"Come and hear, all ye that fear God, and I will declare what he hath done for my soul.

"I cried unto him with my mouth, and he was extolled with my tongue.

"If I regard iniquity in my heart, the Lord will not hear me:

"But verily God hath heard me; he hath attended to the voice of my prayer.

"Blessed be God, which hath not turned away my prayer, nor his mercy from me."

The 1st and 2nd verses of our Psalm contain an interesting exhortation: "Make a joyful noise unto God, all ye lands; sing forth the honour of his name: make his praise glorious." That exhortation has fallen on deaf ears. While there are multitudes who rejoice in Christ and praise the Lord, yet, comparatively speaking, they are in the minority, so much so that oftentimes for one to give expression to his praise is to cause people to look upon him as somewhat of a freak.

Today, for one to rejoice in Christ is to present himself before the world as a monstrosity, but there is a day coming which is expressed in the

4th verse of our Psalm, when all the earth shall worship the Lord and sing unto Him—they shall sing to His name.

It might be advisable for some of the more vociferous critics of the Bible and Christianity to sober their minds by reading the 7th verse of the 66th Psalm, where it is written: "He (the Lord) ruleth by his power for ever; his eyes behold the nations: let not the rebellious exalt themselves. Selah." Now it does seem, from a surface examination, that the wicked exalts himself and that everything is on the side of the superficial, whereas righteousness, holiness, and fellowship with God are looked upon as being *passé*. But that shall not always be so.

We have not time, of course, to comment specifically on every verse in this Psalm. I want, however, to bring out two further thoughts. First, the necessity for individual experience, and second, the question of prayer, answered and unanswered. In the 16th verse the Psalmist said:

"Come and hear, all ye that fear God, and I will declare what he hath done for my soul."

Irrespective of what church you are a member, I suggest that the most important thing in life is your personal relationship with Christ. Have you, in simple faith, received Christ as your Saviour? If you have, then you have passed from death unto life. The Scripture has promised you eternal life, in fact, you now have it, and I am sure there wells up in your heart a desire to do just what the Psalmist said in the 16th verse: "Come and hear, all ye that fear God, and I will declare what he hath done for my soul."

In the following verse, verse 17, the Psalmist gave the substance of his testimony. He said: "I cried unto him with my mouth, and *he* was extolled with my tongue." I have been to a number of meetings where testimony is permitted, in fact where it is customary, and I have observed that very often folk think that testimony means to be given an opportunity to tell all about themselves. However, the Psalmist said, ". . . he (meaning the Lord) was extolled with my tongue." One can invariably tell a Spirit-filled man by his testimony. He will speak of the glories of his Lord. He will not talk of himself, but he will talk of Christ. There never was, and never will be, a subject as interesting, as fascinating, or as joyful as the subject of the Person of Christ and what He has done for us as individuals.

THE SUBJECT OF PRAYER

Now for a few words on the subject of prayer. In the 18th verse the Psalmist said: "If I regard iniquity in my heart, the Lord will not hear me . . ." In the 19th verse he said: "But verily God hath heard me: he hath attended to the voice of my prayer." He closed the Psalm by saying: "Blessed be God, which hath not turned away my prayer, nor his mercy from me."

Our Lord said, "Ask, and it shall be given you, seek, and ye shall find; knock, and it shall be opened unto you . . ." He also said to His disciples on the night of His betrayal: "Verily, verily, I say unto you, Whatsoever ye shall ask the Father in my name, he will give it you. Hitherto have ye asked nothing in my name: ask, and ye shall receive, that your joy may be full."

The first thing we should remember on the subject of prayer is this— only the believer can pray. He only has the right of prayer. Our Lord said to His disciples, "Hitherto have *ye* asked nothing in my name: ask, and *ye* shall receive, that *your* joy may be full."

The Bible has much to say about prayer. It speaks about answered and unanswered prayer. It indicates why prayer is answered and why prayer is not answered.

It must be noted that only the prayer that is offered in the name of our Lord Jesus is acceptable. Our Lord says, "Whatsoever ye ask the Father in my name, he will give it you." Bear in mind that the Lord said, "Whatsoever ye shall ask the Father in my name, he will give it you." He did not say, "Whatsoever you pray the Father, he will give it you." Many Christian people think that is what He did say. But He said, "Whatsoever ye shall ask the Father in my name." What does it mean to ask "in the name" of the Lord? Does it mean that we simply rattle off our requests to the Father and end up with, Father, this we pray in the name of Jesus or in Jesus' name? A thousand times No!

A prayer, to be offered in the name of the Lord, is a prayer that the Lord Himself could offer. When we make a request in His name, we come in all the perfection of that name; we come in His stead and ask exactly what the Lord would ask, under our circumstances. That type of prayer never goes unanswered. There are times when we may not see an immediate answer to our prayer. But, remember, our Lord said, ". . . not my will, but thine be done." That is the way to pray in His name.

In our Psalm we have a basic principle of prayer. The Psalmist said, "If I regard iniquity in my heart, the Lord will not hear me." It simply means this, that if sin is in our life, as a believer in Christ, we have no right to prayer. Our business is to confess our sin, and to be assured that He has promised to be faithful and just to forgive us, and when we have confessed our sins we are in a position to pray. If we harbor sin and iniquity and if we harbor evil against another, that iniquity is robbing us of the right of prayer. It is also written that when we pray we should pray in faith, believing. One must pray with confidence that the Lord will do as He promised and there is no doubt but that He does it every time.

PSALM SIXTY-SEVEN

A BENEDICTION

THAT delightful little Psalm, the 67th, contains seven short verses, but it is filled with hope, praise, and joy. The divine penman has given us a wonderful illustration of what praise is and can be. The Psalm reads:

"God be merciful unto us, and bless us; and cause his face to shine upon us; Selah.
"That thy way may be known upon earth, thy saving health among all nations.
"Let the people praise thee, O God; let all the people praise thee.
"O let the nations be glad and sing for joy: for thou shalt judge the people righteously, and govern the nations upon earth. Selah.
"Let the people praise thee, O God; let all the people praise thee.
"Then shall the earth yield her increase; and God, even our own God, shall bless us.
"God shall bless us; and all the ends of the earth shall fear him."

In the Old Testament we frequently find the Lord appearing in human form and conversing with the sons of men. Take, for instance, the case of the visitation of the Lord, in company with two men who came to Abraham's tent door and for whom Abraham spread a delicious Eastern meal.

Later on in the course of that visit the Lord spoke directly to Abraham and said, "Shall I hide from Abraham that thing which I do . . . ?" Then the Lord acquainted Abraham with His purpose and His plans for the destruction of Sodom and Gomorrah. There followed that marvelous audacity that comes by faith, of pleading and reasoning with the Lord for the saving of those cities, if peradventure there were ten righteous in the city, for Abraham asked, "Wilt thou also destroy the righteous with the wicked?" As a result of that intercession, the Lord promised Abraham that if ten righteous men were to be found in the city it would be spared. Finally, it is written, "And the LORD *went his way,* as soon as he had left communing with Abraham: and Abraham returned *unto his place.*"

There is every indication in the record that the Lord appeared in the form of man, but there is no doubt that the outward form of a man did not hide from the eyes of Abraham the fact that it was the Lord. Thus it would seem that all these prior appearings of the Lord in the Old Testament simply paved the way for the Incarnation when our Lord took on Himself a body of flesh and bones and dwelt among the sons of men, so that men could look up into His face and say, ". . . we beheld his glory, the glory as of the only begotten of the Father, full of grace and truth."

When, therefore, the Psalmist said, "God be merciful unto us, and bless us; and cause his face to shine upon us . . ." he visualized the personality of God and presented the Lord in visibility.

THE WAY OF THE LORD

In the 2nd verse, of the 67th Psalm, the Psalmist gives us the end for which he craved the mercy and blessing of God. He says, "That *thy* way may be known upon earth, *thy* saving health among all nations." You will remember that after the Lord had left Abraham, following His interview regarding the destruction of Sodom, the Scripture said, "The LORD *went his way* . . . and Abraham *returned unto his place.*" What do you suppose the Psalmist had in mind when he wrote, "That *thy way* may be known upon earth . . ."? The *way* of the Lord *is* in the sanctuary, for which reason the writer said, "I was glad when they said unto me, Let us go into the house of the LORD," for there the Psalmist was able to behold the beauty of the Lord, and to enquire in His temple.

A way is a road that leads from the place of departure to the place of desire. Every sane-thinking person wants to know the way from earth to heaven. Are there many ways, or is there but one way? The Psalmist said, "God be merciful unto us . . . That *thy* way may be known upon earth . . ." That would seem to indicate that the Lord has a way and man has a way. Furthermore, that the Lord knows but one way and that way is *His* way. Everyone who is a born-again Christian recalls the statement of our Lord which He made to His disciples when He was about to leave them. He said He was going to His Father's house, in which were many mansions. While there, He would prepare a place for them, and just as assuredly as He went, He would return and receive them unto Himself, that where He would be, there they might be also. Then, with startling significance, He added, "And whither I go ye know, and *the way* ye know." Thomas asked, "Lord, we know not whither thou goest; and how can we know the way?" Our Lord responded, "I am the way, the truth, and the life: no man cometh unto the Father, but by me."

Now back to our Psalm. The Psalmist prayed that God would be merciful unto the children of Israel, and that He would bless them and cause His face to shine upon them. For what reason? "That *thy* way may be known upon earth, thy saving health among all nations." That verse is a window through which we may view the purpose and plan of God. The Psalmist looked far beyond the first appearing of Christ to His second coming and the glorious reign of splendor which the Lord shall have upon the earth. When that takes place, Israel will come to know "the Way"; that is, they will come to know the Christ, who is God's "Way."

Now notice what results from this revelation. The Psalmist prayed for a demonstration of God's saving health among all nations. When Israel is restored to her own land and her Messiah is revealed unto her, then the blessings of Abraham shall come upon all the Gentiles and they shall enjoy the saving health of the eternal God. All this is in the future, as we have already seen. But we, now, individually, who have received Christ, have come to know His saving health. We know what it is to have a sin-sick soul healed by the sympathizing physician; we know what it is to have balm poured into open wounds that have been made by the hard task-master of sin; we know what it is to be raised from death to life. We know this *now*.

"LET ALL THE PEOPLE PRAISE THEE"

Note the exhortation of the 3rd verse, which reads, "Let the people praise thee, O God; let all the people praise thee." There are, strange to say, many people, Christian people, who labor under the impression that the business of praising the Lord is exclusively the right of the preacher. Here the Psalmist said, "Let *all* the people praise thee." May I reverently say that no individual can take your place and praise the Lord for you. You are to have that great pleasure and privilege yourself. We have raised all sorts of traditions that seem to elevate the minister and separate him from the people. In fact, some preachers feel that they are the exalted ones, and that the rest of the congregation should minister unto them. That characteristic is the extreme opposite of what our Lord said was to characterize a minister of His. He said:

> "Ye know that the princes of the Gentiles exercise dominion over them, and they that are great exercise authority upon them.
> "But it shall not be so among you: but whosoever will be great among you, let him be your minister;
> "And whosoever will be chief among you, let him be your servant. . ."

The Psalmist not only said, "let all the people praise thee," but he also said, "let the nations be glad and sing for joy: for thou shalt judge the people righteously, and govern the nations upon earth." How clear it is from this passage that the writer rejoiced in the second coming of Christ. He rejoiced in anticipation of the time when the people shall be judged righteously and the nations shall understand what good government actually is. Then the nations will be glad. War songs will be completely forgotten; nations will not rejoice in their power, measured by the number of men under arms, or the number of aeroplanes, or the size of their battle fleets. Nations will be glad in the Lord and sing for joy. Can you imagine what a glorious sound it will be when nations will join in the singing of such hymns as:

> "There is a fountain filled with blood,
> Drawn from Immanuel's veins,
> And sinners plunged beneath that flood
> Lose all their guilty stains."

What a contrast between that song and the usual war songs. Man will rejoice then, not in arms nor in war, but in the Lord, and will sing His praise.

Now I am not a visionary, but I do look forward to the time to which all the prophets bear witness, when the Lord Jesus Himself will reign as King of kings and Lord of lords. "Then," as the Psalmist said, "shall the earth yield her increase; and God, even our own God, shall bless us." There will be no dust storms, no famines, no pestilence nor earthquakes, no more tears, in fact, for God shall wipe them all away. The earth will yield her increase, and all creation will join with redeemed men and women to sing the praise of their Creator and Redeemer. Trees will clap their hands, the very stones of the earth will cry out, and the field will yield her praise in the form of her increase.

THE MILLENNIUM BLESSING

The closing verse of our Psalm has an anticipatory benediction. The Psalmist said, "God shall bless us; and all the ends of the earth shall fear him." God has always dealt in blessing. In that hour when our Lord Jesus shall reign as King of kings and Lord of lords, the blessing of God, that maketh rich and that addeth no sorrow, will be poured out upon all the inhabitants of the earth. We are told that all service and all play, whether of child or grown-up, will be centered around the fact of God's blessing. Even the horses shall have on their harness the words, "HOLINESS UNTO THE LORD."

However, bright as the future is to the man who believes in God's Word, his blessing does not belong exclusively to the future. He now enjoys the fellowship of God, the communion of saints, the forgiveness of sins, the blessings of God's Holy Spirit. Yes, he even rejoices in tribulation also, " . . . knowing that tribulation worketh patience; and patience, experience; and experience, hope: and hope maketh not ashamed; because the love of God is shed abroad in our hearts by the Holy Ghost which is given unto us."

PSALM SIXTY-EIGHT

DAILY LOADINGS OF BENEFITS

TO do justice to the various subjects discussed in the 68th Psalm would take a volume, so we shall content ourselves with a sweet morsel here and there, scattered throughout the Psalm, which will cause us more fully to understand the purpose of God and His ways. We shall limit our reading to the first six verses:

> "Let God arise, let his enemies be scattered: let them also that hate him flee before him.
> "As smoke is driven away, so drive them away: as wax melteth before the fire, so let the wicked perish at the presence of God.
> "But let the righteous be glad; let them rejoice before God: yea, let them exceedingly rejoice.

"Sing unto God, sing praises to his name: extol him
that rideth upon the heavens by his name JAH, and
rejoice before him.
"A father of the fatherless, and a judge of the widows,
is God in his holy habitation.
"God setteth the solitary in families: he bringeth out
those which are bound with chains: but the rebellious
dwell in a dry land."

There are many authorities who believe that this Psalm was sung
when the ark of the covenant was moved from place to place. There is a
striking similarity between the opening verse of the Psalm, "Let God arise,
let his enemies be scattered . . ." and that which actually took place when
the children of Israel broke camp and proceeded on their journey. As the
cloud rested above the camp, which cloud made visible the presence of God,
the nation rested; but as the cloud would arise from above the ark it was a
signal for the people to move forward. Then the attendants would break
up camp, take the various articles of furniture used in tabernacle worship,
wrap each carefully, and finally the ark would be lifted, borne by those
who were commissioned to carry it. Then Moses would address the ark
and say, "Rise up, LORD, and let thine enemies be scattered; and let them
that hate thee flee before thee." When the journey was completed and
the ark rested in its proper place, Moses would say, "Return, O LORD,
unto the many thousands of Israel."

THE ARK OF THE COVENANT

As the ark preceded the march of the children of Israel, it spread
terror into the hearts of the enemies of Israel, but it made the children of
Israel glad. So in the 3rd verse of our Psalm David wrote: "But let the
righteous be glad; let them rejoice before God: yea, let them exceedingly
rejoice." Then there followed the exhortation to "Sing unto God, sing
praises to his name: extol him that rideth upon the heavens by his name
JAH, and rejoice before him. A father of the fatherless, and a judge of
the widows, is God in his holy habitation."

This brings us to a very interesting subject. On previous occasions
we have discussed the imprecatory Psalms, wherein the Psalmists invited
God to express Himself in judgment against His enemies. In this Psalm
we are faced with somewhat the same situation. David prayed God to
drive away His enemies, to melt them as wax melteth before the fire; while
in the same breath he exhorted the righteous to rejoice. However, notice
that the righteous do not rejoice in the judgment extended upon the wicked,
but the righteous rejoice before God.

A Christian who knows his Bible rejoices in his Lord. When he calls out for judgment upon the wicked, he invites the Lord to do the judging. He does not do it himself, for he is aware that such is mere tongue-lashing. This world is to be judged; no intelligent person questions it. But by whom is it to be judged? Shall it be by a man of the cloth, or the Man of God? The Apostle Paul, when preaching on Mars' hill said, "God . . . hath appointed a day, in the which he will judge the world in righteousness by that man whom he hath ordained;" the One of whom He hath given assurance unto all men, in that He hath raised Him from the dead. How thankful we should be that it is the Lord Jesus Christ who will judge this world. His pronouncements will not be in demagogism—they will be in righteousness. God will not judge the world according to man-made standards. He will judge it in righteousness, by that man, Jesus Christ, whom He hath ordained.

When that hour comes, every believer in Christ (men and women out of every denomination) who has, with child-like confidence, trusted Christ for salvation, will rejoice; not because the wicked are judged, but that thereby the Lord will beget increasing glory to Himself. Their song, as we find it in the 4th verse of our Psalm, will be one of praise unto the name, that matchless name of Jehovah, the redemptive name which God was pleased to reveal to the children of Israel.

The Christian understands that the Jehovah of the Old Testament is the Lord Jesus of the New Testament, because having observed the Jehovah in the Old Testament and having observed the Lord in the New Testament he has found one and the same Person—the One who is filled with mercy, though wielding His sword in righteousness.

To substantiate that statement look at verses 18 to 20 of our Psalm, where it is written:

> "Thou hast ascended on high, thou hast led captivity captive: thou hast received gifts for men: yea, for the rebellious also, that the LORD God might dwell among them.
> "Blessed be the Lord, who daily loadeth us with benefits, even the God of our salvation. Selah.
> "He that is our God is the God of salvation; and unto GOD the Lord belong the issues from death."

THE HOLY SPIRIT'S USE OF THE 68TH PSALM

Now with these three verses in mind, let us go to the New Testament Epistle to the Ephesians. We will note therein what the Holy Spirit, through the pen of the Apostle Paul, has to say about these verses in the

68th Psalm. We now read from the 4th to the 8th verse of the 4th chapter of Ephesians:

> "There is one body, and one Spirit, even as ye are called in one hope of your calling;
> "One Lord, one faith, one baptism,
> "One God and Father of all, who is above all, and through all, and in you all.
> "But unto every one of us is given grace according to the measure of the gift of Christ.
> "Wherefore he saith, When he ascended up on high, he led captivity captive, and gave gifts unto men."

Now we skip to verse 11 and read through to the 13th:

> "And he gave some, apostles; and some, prophets; and some, evangelists; and some, pastors and teachers;
> "For the perfecting of the saints, for the work of the ministry, for the edifying of the body of Christ:
> "Till we all come in the unity of the faith, and of the knowledge of the Son of God, unto a perfect man, unto the measure of the stature of the fulness of Christ. . ."

Observe that the 8th verse of the 4th chapter of Ephesians is a direct quotation from the 18th verse of the 68th Psalm. David said in that verse: "Thou hast ascended on high, thou hast led captivity captive: thou hast received gifts for men . . ."

Of whom was David speaking? The Apostle Paul, through the Holy Spirit, tells us it is the Lord Jesus, for he declares: "(Now he that ascended is he also that first descended into the lower parts of the earth. He that descended is the same also that ascended up far above all heavens, that he might fill all things.)"

In other words, the Jehovah of the Old Testament is the Lord Jesus of the New Testament! It is He who first descended into the lower parts of the earth, in order to deliver those who were held captive. Then He *ascended*, taking with Him the spoils of His triumph. Now from that high, exalted place in the heavens He has given gifts to men. To some He has given the gift of apostleship; to some, that of evangelist; to some, pastors; and to others, teachers. For what purpose? For the perfecting of the saints, for the work of the ministry, for the edifying of the body of Christ.

There are two further subjects in this Psalm which we desire to touch upon before bringing our meditation to a close. If you will read the Psalm, you will observe that in the English we have two names for the Almighty; the name God, and the name LORD, beside, of course, the name JAH, which appears in verse 4 and which is a transliteration, not a translation. But could we read this Psalm in the original Hebrew, we would recognize several names of the Godhead. He is called by the name "Elohim" in verse 2; He is called by the name "Adonai" in verse 11; "El Shaddai" in verse 15; "Jehovah" in verse 17; "JAH" in verse 4 and in verse 19, and "El" in verse 20.

Here then is a Psalm in which all the characteristics of the Almighty are revealed. As Elohim, He is the strong one, a refuge of strength. As Adonai, He is the master, the one to be obeyed and to be served, and also the one to lead. As El Shaddai, He is the Almighty, the all-sufficient one, the one who comforts and strengthens. As Jehovah, He is the Redeemer, the ever-revealing God, the one constantly referred to as "I Am." The name "JAH" is the contraction of Jehovah. All these names of God unfold the fact that He is able to meet all our needs under every circumstance of life.

The second subject we wish to discuss centers about the 19th verse, which reads: "Blessed be the Lord, who daily loadeth us with benefits, even the God of our salvation."

There is no depression with God. There are no periods or cycles of prosperity, followed by depressions, which in turn are followed by recovery, and then again by prosperity. God is daily loading us with His benefits. Did you note David said, "daily"? Not now and then, but daily. Not occasionally, but always. His benefits are not given sparingly—He loadeth us! Isn't that wonderful?

But we raise the question, are we being loaded daily with His benefits, and if not, what is wrong? Certainly it cannot be said of everyone that he is loaded down with God's blessings. Nor can it be said that God is at fault. Well, what is wrong with us, if we are not loaded down with blessings?

Just this—if we are not just now loaded with His benefits, so that we feel like joining with David in saying, "Blessed be the Lord," we are so filled up with other things that there is no room for His blessing. We cannot load a container that is already filled. If self is enthroned, if we fill all, then we have no room for His load of blessings. However, if we are empty, then we are in proper condition to be filled with His benefits. When there is none of self in our lives it can be all of Christ. If, as believers in Christ, we desire to be filled with all the fulness of God, I pray that we may yield to Him. He will fill us to overflowing.

PSALM SIXTY-NINE—PART ONE

HOW CHRIST CALLED OUR SINS HIS OWN

THE most important season in the year to Christendom is that which is called the Lenten season. The greatest day of the year is Easter Sunday, which commemorates the triumph of our Lord Jesus Christ over death and the grave. Before the triumph, however, there was His passion, when He suffered all the tortures of hell in order to redeem us from our sin.

While our Lord hung upon the cross He gave utterance to seven famous sayings. These sayings of Christ have formed the basis of many volumes and countless sermons. We learn, however, from the Old Testament scriptures, that our Lord had much more to say, which mortal man was not privileged to hear, as He hung upon the cross. Such Psalms as the 22nd and the 69th compose the utterances of our Lord as He made known to His Father His anguish and sufferings.

That Christ is to be found in the Psalms can readily be demonstrated. Someone has said, "From the reported words of our Lord Jesus, given to us in the four Gospels, we learn that He used the Psalms in devotion, in testings, in the wilderness, in parables, in argumentative discourses, and in prophetic application. Our Lord employed the Psalms at the Passover, in the high priestly prayer in John 17, on the cross, and on the resurrection day." Thus we might say, from the beginning of our Lord's public ministry until His resurrection day, He lived in the Psalms and they were the source of His constant companionship.

We shall also observe as we continue our meditation in the 69th Psalm that it is just as important as the 22nd, and equally as expressive and quite as minute in its description of the sufferings of Christ. Of course, David wrote the Psalm, but by no stretch of the imagination is it possible to find in the experience of David anything that remotely resembles the sufferings described in this or in the 22nd Psalm. David was a prophet. He was merely the penman. He was recording the words of our Lord Jesus. It is our Lord who is the speaker in the 69th Psalm.

With that as an introduction, let us read carefully the first nine verses:

> "Save me, O God; for the waters are come in unto my soul.
> "I sink in deep mire, where there is no standing: I am come into deep waters, where the floods overflow me.

"I am weary of my crying: my throat is dried: mine eyes fail while I wait for my God.

"They that hate me without a cause are more than the hairs of mine head: they that would destroy me, being mine enemies wrongfully, are mighty: then I restored that which I took not away.

"O God, thou knowest my foolishness; and my sins are not hid from thee.

"Let not them that wait on thee, O Lord GOD of hosts, be ashamed for my sake: let not those that seek thee be confounded for my sake, O God of Israel.

"Because for thy sake I have borne reproach; shame hath covered my face.

"I am become a stranger unto my brethren, and an alien unto my mother's children.

"For the zeal of thine house hath eaten me up; and the reproaches of them that reproached thee are fallen upon me."

You who are familiar with the New Testament will recognize that several quotations appearing in the New Testament have been taken from this section of the Psalm.

The 4th verse is quoted in the 15th chapter of John's Gospel, the 8th verse is fulfilled in the 7th chapter of John's Gospel, and the 9th verse is quoted in the 2nd chapter of the same Gospel. Part of the 9th verse is also found in the 15th chapter of Paul's letter to the Romans.

In the 2nd verse of this Psalm there is pictured, as clearly as language possibly can, our Lord Jesus taking the sinner's place; actually he is seen coming to the very place where the sinner's feet stand and becoming encompassed about with the very circumstances that surround the sinner. There is no *standing* in mire; there can only be sinking. As our Lord Jesus had to take the place of the sinner in order to provide redemption through His blood, He must take my place; He must take your place; He must come to the very spot where we are and our sins must become His own. Why was it that He sweat, as it were, great drops of blood, on the night prior to His crucifixion, as He cried, "O my Father, if it be possible, let this cup pass from me: nevertheless not as I will, but as thou wilt"? For an answer, one has but to read the 3rd verse of this Psalm, where our Lord said, "I am weary of my crying: my throat is dried: mine eyes fail while I *wait* for my God." It is as if we can already hear our Lord saying, "My God, my God, why hast thou forsaken me?"

Not only does our Lord take the sinner's place, His feet sinking in mire, His heart weary with crying, His throat parched, His eyes dimmed with the mists of tears as His Father seemed so far away from Him, but as He sees a group of enemies near at hand, He cries out, "They that hate me without a cause are more than the hairs of mine head: they that would destroy me, being mine enemies wrongfully, are mighty. . . ."

Notice, our Lord said that they are His enemies wrongfully. Little did those men at the cross, who witnessed the crucifixion of our Lord, or the religious leaders of Israel who mocked Him, or the Roman soldiers who crucified Him—little did any of them realize that they were crucifying the Lord of glory. They were urged on by the hatred of sin against holiness, and in order that the divine counsels of God might be fulfilled. Because of the blindness of their hearts our Lord prayed, "Father, forgive them; for they know not what they do." The New Testament goes so far as to say that none of the princes of this world knew who our Lord Jesus Christ was, for had they known it, "they would not have crucified the Lord of glory." Those who were the enemies of our Lord were His enemies wrongfully. How numerous they were! He said they were more than the hairs of His head. Because our Lord became sin on the cross, His enemies were in comparison "mighty."

CRUCIFIED THROUGH WEAKNESS

But some may ask, "How is it possible to reconcile the view of Christ being God manifest in flesh and thus, of course, equal with God, with the statement of Christ in this Psalm, when He said His enemies were 'mighty.'" You say, if He is God, His enemies would vanish as the chaff on the wings of the wind.

Indeed, it is possible to reconcile this which seems irreconcilable. The facts cannot be disputed. His enemies were mighty. They did triumph over Him as He hung on the cross; at least, so it appeared to the onlooker. However, let it not be forgotten that our Lord Jesus once said: "Therefore doth my Father love me, because I lay down my life, that I might take it again. No man taketh it from me but I lay it down of myself. I have power to lay it down, and I have power to take it again. This commandment have I received of my Father." Unless there was first the willingness on the part of our Lord to yield His life, there never would have been the crucifixion scene. However, because He yielded Himself to do His Father's will, he was helpless while on the cross, and His enemies, in comparison, mighty. Thus it is written in 2nd Corinthians 13:4, "For though he was crucified through weakness, yet he liveth by the power of God."

I am particularly impressed with the 5th verse of this 69th Psalm, where the Lord said, "O God, thou knowest my foolishness; and my sins are not hid from thee." For two thousand years no man who has had any respect for his intellect, has dared charge our Lord Jesus with sin. But some might ask, What do you mean when you say our Lord is the speaker in this verse? Just this: the fact of Calvary is not a sham or mirage. It is an actual fact. Christ making atonement for sin was a reality. The New Testament declares that He who knew no sin was made sin for us that we might be made the righteousness of God in Him. As Christ restored that which He took not away, that is, restored to us a righteousness which we never had, so Christ had to take your sins and mine, your foolishness and mine. These sins became such an integral part of Him that He called them "my sins, and my foolishness." Our Lord was the substitute for the sinner. He had to take the sinner's place and, in so doing, He took upon Himself all of the sinner's sin. In the 53rd chapter of Isaiah it is written, "Surely he hath borne *our* griefs, and carried *our* sorrows . . . and the LORD hath laid on him the *iniquity of us all.*" The iniquity of us *all* was laid upon Christ. He bore *our* sins "in his own body on the tree." Can you fathom that? When you do, you will understand the mystery of the gospel.

The prayer of our Lord Jesus, found in the 6th verse of this Psalm, is most impressive. He prayed: "Let not them that wait on thee, O Lord GOD of hosts, be ashamed for my sake: let not those that seek thee be confounded for my sake, O God of Israel."

There can be no doubt that there is a mystery about the cross. It is confounding to the natural man to understand our Lord Jesus and His death, and he almost turns away ashamed. Our Lord understood this, and on the behalf of those who could not understand, who could not reconcile the shame of Calvary with a conquering Messiah in whom the prophets of the old Testament had gloried, our Lord prayed to His Father, "Let not them . . . be confounded for my sake . . . Let not them that wait on thee, O Lord GOD of hosts, be ashamed for my sake."

But why? Our Lord gave the answer in the following verse, where He said, "Because for thy sake I have borne reproach; shame hath covered my face." For *whose* sake did our Lord Jesus bear the reproach of Calvary? For His Father's sake; for the sake of His Father's love for mankind; for the sake of justifying His Father.

THE SHAME OF CALVARY

Notice also the language which our Lord used ". . . shame hath covered my face." Men spat upon the face of our Lord Jesus; they plucked the hairs from His cheek; they smote Him with the palms of their hands; they crowned His head with thorns, so that from every vein burst forth blood; His face was a horrible sight. He said *"shame* hath covered my face." However, while at Calvary His face was covered with shame, there now appears upon that very face of our Lord the eternal glory of the eternal God. What is more, the next time this world sees the face of our Lord the glory of it will be so transcendent that His enemies will cry to the rocks and mountains to hide them from the face of Him who sits upon the throne, and from the wrath of the Lamb.

A STARTLING PROPHECY

For our closing comments in this meditation we will consider verses 8 and 9: "I am become a stranger unto my brethren, and an alien unto my mother's children. For the zeal of thine house hath eaten me up; and the reproaches of them that reproached thee are fallen upon me." Need I remind you of the startling, accurate fulfillment of this statement in the life of our Lord? Here is a Psalm that was written a thousand years before Christ came. It contains so striking a contrast to what one would expect, that it must have seemed incredible at the time of writing. Could it be possible that the Messiah, the anointed of God, would become a stranger unto His brethren and an alien unto His mother's children?

If it were not for the historic record we have in the Gospels, this prophecy would seem weird and fantastic. However, it foretold the event accurately. In Mark 3:21 we have its fulfillment: "And when his friends heard of it, they went out to lay hold on him: for they said, He is beside himself." "He is beside himself" is just another way of saying that our Lord was mentally deranged. Alas, alas, how accurate was the Psalmist's prediction.

However, it ought not to have caused anyone to stumble; for another, who was a type of the Messiah, had a similar experience. I refer to Joseph, the son of Jacob. He was sold by his brethren. He was stripped of his coat of many colors, which emphasized his father's love for him. He was left as dead. He was sold to the Egyptians, but he became the saviour in Egypt, and was recognized by his own brethren after his exaltation, and in his glory he became the saviour of his own people.

The parallel between Joseph and Christ is so clear, that it hardly needs a comment. Our Lord was rejected by His own. He has been exalted. He is now offered to the Gentiles as their Saviour, but some day, and I pray that it will be soon, He shall be Israel's Lord and Saviour and then they will mourn for Him as the brethren of Joseph did, but He will be glorified in their midst and this earth will finally enjoy its Millennium.

In the 9th verse we have another prophecy of the ministry of Christ. It reads: "For the zeal of thine house hath eaten me up; and the reproaches of them that reproached thee are fallen upon me." The fulfillment is found in John 2:14 where the record of our Lord's first purging of the temple is given. He found

> ". . . those that sold oxen and sheep and doves, and the changers of money sitting:
>
> "And when he had made a scourge of small cords, he drove them all out of the temple, and the sheep, and the oxen; and poured out the changers' money, and overthrew the tables;
>
> "And said unto them that sold doves, Take these things hence; make not my Father's house an house of merchandise.
>
> "And his disciples remembered that it was written, The zeal of thine house hath eaten me up."

PSALM SIXTY-NINE—PART TWO

"I WAS THE SONG OF THE DRUNKARDS"—JESUS CHRIST

RECENTLY I came into possession of a reprint of an interesting clipping from the London "Times," quoting the Bishop of Chelmsford. The Bishop had the following to say:

> "I have often thought that when the longed-for revival of religion takes place it will probably come through a re-discovery of the Bible. There are a great many religious movements agitating the Church more or less at the present time, and I might say jostling one another for pre-eminence, but the history of religious revivals seems to me to indicate that the revival does not take the form of the successful competitor in this contest for supremacy. It is always something new and quite unexpected.
>
> "A re-discovery of the Bible will be the thing of all others which will bring new life and new hope into us. People today are looking for a lead and for a guide, and though the opinion may be a very old-fashioned one, I am, myself, firmly of the opinion that

> the bewilderment which is so characteristic of life today will be only dispersed when we can again be described as a Bible-reading nation."

What the Bishop had to say concerning England applies equally to our own country. Our bewilderment will be dispersed where we again become a Bible-reading nation. I thoroughly agree with the Bishop that the longed-for revival will take place through a re-discovery of the Bible. My personal opinion is that it has already started, as all over this land there are genuine efforts being expended, through Bible conferences, to preach the unsearchable riches of Christ.

ANOTHER FULFILLED PROPHECY

Our previous meditation ended with the 9th verse. Thus, we shall commence reading from the 10th verse and will continue to verse 17:

> "When I wept, and chastened my soul with fasting, that was to my reproach.
> "I made sackcloth also my garment; and I became a proverb to them.
> "They that sit in the gate speak against me; and I was the song of the drunkards.
> "But as for me, my prayer is unto thee, O LORD, in an acceptable time: O God, in the multitude of thy mercy hear me, in the truth of thy salvation.
> "Deliver me out of the mire, and let me not sink: let me be delivered from them that hate me, and out of the deep waters.
> "Let not the waterflood overflow me, neither let the deep swallow me up, and let not the pit shut her mouth upon me.
> "Hear me, O LORD; for thy lovingkindness is good: turn unto me according to the multitude of thy tender mercies.
> "And hide not thy face from thy servant; for I am in trouble: hear me speedily."

If there is one thing that is evident from a reading of this Psalm it is this—that the sufferings of our Lord Jesus were terrific. Weeping, chastening, and fasting seemed to be His portion. How accurate, therefore, is the statement of Isaiah in the 53rd chapter, referring to our Lord Jesus, "He is despised and rejected of men; a man of sorrows, and acquainted with grief. . . ."

It is evident from this Psalm that our Lord found it an impossibility to satisfy everybody. In the Gospel of Matthew, our Lord indicated the futility of trying to do so, by saying:

> "But whereunto shall I liken this generation? It is like unto children sitting in the markets, and calling unto their fellows,
>
> "And saying, We have piped unto you, and ye have not danced; we have mourned unto you, and ye have not lamented.
>
> "For John came neither eating nor drinking, and they say, He hath a devil.
>
> "The Son of man came eating and drinking, and they say, Behold a man gluttonous, and a winebibber, a friend of publicans and sinners. But wisdom is justified of her children."

Whether our Lord came eating or drinking or whether He made sackcloth His garments, He was a proverb to the multitudes.

The descriptive language of the 12th verse hardly needs a comment. There our Lord said: "They that sit in the gate speak against me; and I was the song of the drunkards."

"They that sit in the gate" is an Oriental expression used to denote the rulers of the people. How true it was that the rulers spoke against our Lord. Not only the rulers, however, but our Lord went a step further and said, "I was the song of the drunkards."

In the day that our Lord was crucified He was "the song of the drunkards." The sad fact is that He still is to this very day.

It is written, "men swear by the greater. . . ." You never heard a drunkard swear by the name of George Washington, or Abraham Lincoln, or Buddha, or Confucius. Whenever a name is taken in vain, it invariably is the name of our Lord Jesus. A drunken man, or a swearing man, thereby is giving an unconscious witness to the glory and deity of our Lord. Have you ever asked yourself why this is so? If you do, and then take sufficient time to seek an answer to your question, you will be led to acknowledge the Lordship of Jesus Christ.

Notice also how our Lord directed His prayer to His Father, in the 13th verse, where He said, ". . . my prayer is unto thee, O LORD, in an acceptable time:" and then He cried:

> "O God, in the multitude of thy mercy hear me, in the truth of thy salvation.
>
> "Deliver me out of the mire, and let me not sink: let me be delivered from them that hate me, and out of the deep waters.
>
> "Let not the waterflood overflow me, neither let the deep swallow me up, and let not the pit shut her mouth upon me."

Our Lord frequently spoke in parables. The language He used when addressing His Father on this occasion was parabolic. Incidentally, parable language is the most perfect human language, as it not only clothes a naked thought, but it adds a background which gives a more perfect setting to our thoughts than the language which we are accustomed to use in everyday speech.

Notice our Lord said, "Let not the waterflood overflow me. . . ." How this brings to mind another verse, which is found in the 42nd Psalm, where our Lord is also the speaker, and said: "Deep calleth unto deep at the noise of thy waterspouts: all thy waves and thy billows are gone over me." When the waterspout of God's judgment burst upon our Lord Jesus it met the force of the geyser from below, so that it seemed for a moment as if He would be swallowed up by it. How we thank God that instead of being swallowed up by death, He actually spoiled the powers of death and "made a shew of them openly, triumphing over them" in the cross.

The last phrase of the 15th verse of the 69th Psalm is particularly significant. It reads, "let not the pit shut her mouth upon me." The word *pit* is a synonym for *grave*. Just as our earth seems to have thrived on human blood since it first tasted of Abel's blood, with the result that ever since it seems to possess a craving for blood, so the jaws of death seemed set to swallow our Lord Jesus. Our Lord went into the pit, the abode of the dead. He had to do so. As the penalty of sin is death, and as corruption follows in its wake, it was not sufficient that Christ died; He had to be buried. So at the cross the grave craved its victim, perchance it could corrupt Him and hold Him. But, as Jonah could not be digested by the whale, so that finally the whale vomited up Jonah and cast him on dry land, so death could not assimilate our Lord Jesus. The jaws of death were opened to receive our Lord, but it had to let Him go forth as its conqueror.

PSALM SIXTY-NINE—PART THREE

THE CRUCIFIED CHRIST IN THE 69TH PSALM

BEFORE proceeding with the third section of this Psalm I desire to present a background, in order that we may more fully appreciate the passion of our Lord Jesus and the tremendous love that God has for the sons of men.

All of Christendom is ushering in the commemoration of so-called Holy Week. In almost every church some reference will be made this morning to the triumphal entry of our Lord Jesus into the city of Jerusalem. The writers of the Gospels, with a wonderful economy of words, have suggested to us the atmosphere of the city. As another recently wrote, "Classical literature contains nothing so vivid as the Gospel account of the events that led up to the crucifixion, and as we read them the background, never described but always suggested, is the tense, nervous atmosphere of Jerusalem."

From the early morning of that first Palm Sunday to the end of the following Sunday the tension in the city of Jerusalem was almost indescribable. Events passed with startling rapidity, yet it is possible for us to calmly observe those events, even though they are separated from us by nineteen hundred years.

"THE CEREMONY OF THE SECOND COMING"

Were we privileged to be in Jerusalem today, and were we to attend the Armenian Church of St. James, we would witness what is known as "The Ceremony of the Second Coming." Travelers who have returned bearing reports of this ceremony state that the church is darkened, that all pictures and all decorations in the church are covered with a veil, while the altar is hidden behind a tapestry. A bishop holds a key in his hand while another bishop, hidden from the congregation, stands behind the tapestry. A dialogue ensues between the bishops. The one behind the tapestry asks for admittance, while the other asks who it is that calls. Finally, the bishop who is outside chants, "Open unto me the gates of righteousness: that I may enter into them, and give thanks unto the Lord." Then the curtain is slowly withdrawn and at the same time the veils covering the pictures are pulled aside and the church is illumined by the lights of candles. Impressive as such a sight would be were we privileged to be there, it is nothing in comparison to that which actually occurred at the time of our Lord's entry into Jerusalem.

When He arrived, the whole city was excited. He came in riding upon an ass, with a colt, the foal of an ass. Multitudes preceded Him, while other multitudes followed Him. They spread their garments in the way. Some cut down branches from the trees, and strawed them in the way, while they all cried: "Hosanna to the son of David: Blessed is he that cometh in the name of the Lord: Hosanna in the highest."

Matthew, the writer of the first Gospel, tells us that when He came into Jerusalem all the city was moved, saying, "Who is this?" while some responded, "This is Jesus the prophet of Nazareth of Galilee." Our Lord went into the temple of God, and cast out all that sold and bought in the temple, and overthrew the tables of the moneychangers, and the seats of them that sold doves. This was the second purification of the temple. To justify His action, our Lord quoted from Isaiah, saying, "It is written, My house shall be called the house of prayer; but ye have made it a den of thieves."

As usual, the blind and the lame came to our Lord and He healed them. In one corner of the temple was a group of bewildered men; chief priests and scribes. They had seen the wonderful things our Lord did for the sick and the lame, and they had listened to the children singing, "Hosanna to the son of David." They were not only bewildered, but they were sore displeased. Matthew tells us that they said to the Lord, "Hearest thou what these say?" and our Lord answered, quoting from the Psalms, "Yea; have ye never read, Out of the mouth of babes and sucklings thou hast perfected praise?"

Were we able to transport ourselves into the crowd on that first Palm Sunday our ears would tingle with the song of the children, as they took it from the disciples and those that gathered about our Lord as He entered into the city. We might have been tempted to ask, Who taught them that song? Who composed it? If we had no acquaintance with the Old Testament we would be bewildered, but if we knew our Book of Psalms we would immediately recognize that the multitude, including the children, were singing from the 118th Psalm, the same Psalm from which the bishop behind the tapestry hiding the altar in the Church of St. James, chants, "Open unto me the gates of righteousness: that I may enter into them, and give thanks unto the Lord."

Let me quote a verse or two from it, in order to deepen our impression of the background of that first Palm Sunday. As you read this quotation you will recognize a familiar passage of Scripture. I do trust that hereafter, every time you read it, you will remember that it refers to the first Palm Sunday and that its further fulfillment will take place when our Lord, for the second time, will ride into Jerusalem for His true inaugural as King of kings, and Lord of lords. I now quote from the 24th verse of the 118th Psalm:

> "This is the day which the LORD hath made; we will rejoice and be glad in it.
> "Save now, I beseech thee, O LORD: O LORD, I beseech thee, send now prosperity.
> "Blessed be he that cometh in the name of the LORD . . ."

Thus far, we have merely given a background to the events which transpired on that first Palm Sunday. Now let us return to the 69th Psalm, in order that we may observe the movements within the very heart of our Lord and listen to His voice as He expresses Himself to His Father. While His mercy manifested itself in the healing of the blind and sick, there must have been running through His mind the approaching shadows of Calvary. It is a mercy of God that we are spared the knowledge of what the future holds in store for us. It is certain that some of us would not be able to bear the thought were we aware of things before they transpire. Our Lord, however, was not spared the knowledge of the future. He knew, on the very morning He rode so triumphantly into Jerusalem, that before the week was over He would be led outside the walls of the city and there be crucified! He also knew that the same mob would cry out "Crucify him, Crucify him."

This has been a long introduction. We now shall read from verse 18, of the 69th Psalm, up to and including verse 28. As we read, we shall hear a message from the lips of our Lord Jesus that some may not have thought of—that may even be foreign to any previous idea some have had of what our Lord uttered, when He was upon the cross, in His prayer to His Father.

"Draw nigh unto my soul, and redeem it: deliver me because of mine enemies.

"Thou hast known my reproach, and my shame, and my dishonour: mine adversaries are all before thee.

"Reproach hath broken my heart; and I am full of heaviness: and I looked for some to take pity, but there was none; and for comforters, but I found none.

"They gave me also gall for my meat; and in my thirst they gave me vinegar to drink.

"Let their table become a snare before them: and that which should have been for their welfare, let it become a trap.

"Let their eyes be darkened, that they see not; and make their loins continually to shake.

"Pour out thine indignation upon them, and let thy wrathful anger take hold of them.

"Let their habitation be desolate; and let none dwell in their tents.

"For they persecute him whom thou hast smitten; and they talk to the grief of those whom thou hast wounded.

"Add iniquity unto their iniquity: and let them not come into thy righteousness.

> "Let them be blotted out of the book of the living,
> and not be written with the righteous."

In this section of the Psalm there are two main subjects. One: the sorrow and anguish of our Lord's heart, coupled with the treatment He received while hanging upon the cross. Two: His strange outbursts of imprecations.

"MY REPROACH, SHAME, AND DISHONOUR"

When our Lord rode into Jerusalem the adulation of the mob rang in His ears, but He also knew that His enemies lurked at every street corner, in every road, and in every corner of the temple. They were waiting for an opportunity to leap upon Him. He knew that before the week would close, the hour would arrive which He Himself called, "Satan's hour." To the casual observer it would seem as if our Lord should have been thrilled with the reception He received, but alas, He was aware that soon the hour would come when He would be pressed to cry out, in the language of our Psalm, "Thou hast known *my reproach*, and *my shame*, and *my dishonour.* . . ." When our Lord refers to His indignities while upon the cross, He calls them His *reproach*, His *shame*, and His *dishonour*.

In the 21st verse it is written, "They gave me also gall for my meat; and in my thirst they gave me vinegar to drink." That was the prophecy. It was written a thousand years before Calvary. The actual historical record of the fulfillment of that prophecy is found in the 27th chapter of Matthew's Gospel, verses 33 and 34: "And when they were come unto a place called Golgotha, that is to say, a place of a skull, they gave him vinegar to drink mingled with gall: and when he had tasted thereof, he would not drink."

It is impossible, by any logical reasoning to arrive at any other conclusion than that the 21st verse of the 69th Psalm is a prophecy of what took place at the crucifixion. Logic must also lead one to the conclusion that this prediction of the very ingredients that composed the drink given to our Lord stamps the Bible as true and furthermore, that all that is written about the person of our Lord Jesus is true, so that one must acknowledge Him to be what He claimed to be—the Son of God.

Granted that this reasoning is logical there can be no difficulty in understanding the imprecations that follow in this Psalm. What is more, there is no such thing as a contradiction between these imprecations of Christ and His plea to His Father for His executioners, when He cried: "Father, forgive them; for they know not what they do." If the Father had not answered our Lord's prayer that afternoon there would have been none left alive. But because He did, multitudes from that hour to this have enjoyed the forgiveness of sin. However, to the unrepentant and recalcitrant individual, or nation, who rejects Christ and His mercy, there can be only one thing left and that must be judgment. To apologize for judgment is to be untrue to God's Word.

PSALM SIXTY-NINE—PART FOUR

THE RISEN CHRIST IN THE 69TH PSALM

FROM the very break of gray dawn this morning (Easter) until the late hours tonight there will be sounded in almost every city of our land, and in practically every country in the world, that glorious fact of history ". . . now is Christ risen from the dead, and become the firstfruits of them that slept." I intend to present the resurrection of Christ, from the closing verses of the 69th Psalm. I shall attempt again to develop a background for our approach to the Psalm in the story of the resurrection.

THE CITY OF JERUSALEM

The events that have changed the whole course of human History took place in and about the city of Jerusalem, a city that disappoints almost every traveler. It will surprise some to know that the city itself could be put into Central Park in New York City with ample room to spare. In fact, when we bear in mind that "in the course of our Lord's travels He was never more than 130 miles from Jerusalem, and that only once when He journeyed to the borders of Tyre and Sidon . . ." we suddenly become conscious that it must be the Man, not His environment, that accounts for the power of the gospel. "What is more," we are told, "a careful check of the four Gospels will reveal that our Lord's ministry was limited to no more than eighteen villages or towns," yet out of the confines of one life and one death within that area have come blessings to the universe.

If there is one thing the Gospel records convey to our mind, it is the unusual stillness that rested over Jerusalem from the hour of His burial until that early Easter morning. The disciples had lost all hope. Not one of them remembered our Lord's promise of His resurrection. It would seem that not one of them dreamed of it. The only group to remember His words

was the chief priests and the Pharisees who came to Pilate the day after
the crucifixion and said:

> "Sir, we remember that that deceiver said, while he
> was yet alive, After three days I will rise again.
>
> "Command therefore that the sepulchre be made sure
> until the third day, lest his disciples come by night,
> and steal him away, and say unto the people, He is
> risen from the dead: so the last error shall be worse
> than the first."

Pilate responded to them and said: "Ye have a watch: go your way, make
it as sure as ye can." They went and made the sepulchre sure, sealing the
stone and setting a watch. Yet, while a group of the enemies of Christ
remembered His words that He would arise, not a single one of the disciples recalled it. They were, of all men, most dejected, broken, and
despondent.

THE EASTER SUPPER

On this Easter Sunday, from the early hours of dawn every born-again
Christian rejoices in the resurrection of our Lord. However, there was no
rejoicing among the disciples on that first Easter morning. In fact, the
gloom among them was very heavy. It was not until late that night when
our Lord gloriously revealed Himself to the eleven who were gathered about
a supper table with a delicate spread thereon, that the disciples, devoid of
an appetite, at last found joy. They were at first afraid, supposing that they
had seen a spirit or a ghost, but when He invited them to behold His hands
and feet, and said, ". . . a spirit hath not flesh and bones, as ye see me
have" then suddenly they recognized Him and with joy embraced Him,
until He graciously asked, "Have ye here any meat?" The record in Luke's
Gospel reads: ". . . they gave him a piece of a broiled fish, and of an
honeycomb. And he took it, and did eat before them."

Some years ago I taught a delightful little Bible class in the home of
some friends who lived in the Washington Heights section of New York
City. One evening we were discussing the resurrection of Christ, when a
church officer, who was present, asked, "Mr. Olsen, do I understand you to
say that Christ arose in a body of flesh and bones?" I answered, "That is
exactly what the Bible says and that is just what I do mean." Then he
added, "I always thought Christ arose in the spirit." I asked if he had
ever read about the supper consisting of broiled fish and honeycomb which
the disciples had spread on that first Easter Sunday night. "Yes," said he,
"but Christ never partook of that supper."

Now some may wonder that a church officer could raise such a question, but when I read to him the account of that supper from the Gospel according to Luke, 24th chapter, particularly the 43rd verse which reads, "He (meaning Jesus) took it, (that is, the broiled fish and honeycomb) and did eat before them" his eyes almost popped out of their sockets and he would not believe that I was reading correctly until he looked at the very page.

Actually, I was not surprised, for I have heard and still hear of supposedly outstanding ministers in our famous churches who talk on Easter Sunday about the resurrection of Jesus, and all they have in mind is the resurrection of His spirit, whatever that might be. His spirit was never buried. How could there be a resurrection of the spirit? It was the body that was buried and it was in His body that He arose. Jesus Christ arose from the grave, clothed in the same body with which He was buried—a body of flesh and bones.

In the closing verses of this great Psalm, there's a complete reversal of musical key, as in the 22nd Psalm. The Psalm opens with a dirge but it ends with a great outburst of praise.

Beginning with the 29th verse the change of key is noted. I again ask you to bear in mind that it is our Lord Jesus who is the speaker. It is He who said:

> ". . . O God, set me up on high.
> "I will praise the name of God with a song, and will magnify him with thanksgiving.
> "This also shall please the LORD better than an ox or bullock that hath horns and hoofs.
> "The humble shall see this, and be glad: and your heart shall live that seek God.
> "For the LORD heareth the poor, and despiseth not his prisoners,
> "Let the heaven and earth praise him, the seas, and every thing that moveth therein.
> "For God will save Zion, and will build the cities of Judah: that they may dwell there, and have it in possession.
> "The seed also of his servants shall inherit it: and they that love his name shall dwell therein."

When our Lord said to His Father "O God, set me up on high," He looked beyond the resurrection to the ascension. He left His Father's throne in order to become manifest in flesh. This He did in order that He might be the propitiation for our sins. He went to Calvary and paid the penalty of sin. He was buried, and on the third day He arose again from the dead. However, the promise of His Father was not only that He would raise Him from the dead but that He would exalt Him to His own right hand to be a Prince and a Saviour.

THE SINGING SAVIOUR

I delight in the change of key, beginning with the 30th verse of our Psalm, after the sorrow and pain which our Lord endured and which He expressed to His Father while on the cross. The 30th verse reads, "I will praise the name of God with a song, and will magnify him with thanksgiving." Our Lord Jesus is the singing Saviour.

It has been said that, "He is the only One of the sons of men to sing on both sides of the sea of death. On the night of His betrayal He led His choir of eleven fishermen in the singing of a hymn, (I should say in the singing of several hymns) as at the beginning of the passover feast our Lord sang with His disciples those great Hallelujah Psalms, 113 and 114, and then upon finishing the feast He led them in Psalms 115 to 118." After His death and resurrection He led the host of God's redeemed ones in a glorious song of praise. It is in harmony, therefore, with the fact of His resurrection that Easter has produced the finest of Christian music.

It is delightful to think of our Lord Jesus singing songs of praise unto the name of His Father and leading the great host of redeemed men and women in the singing of these songs. Notice to what extent our Lord will increase the throng. In the 34th verse He said: "Let the heaven and earth praise him, the seas, and every thing that moveth therein." Thus we not only find our Lord leading the sons of men in the songs of praise, but as He also redeemed creation from her thraldom and bondage, so all of it shall burst forth with songs of praise.

Recently, Mrs. Olsen and I drove up from Washington. On our way we stopped off at Longwood, where Mr. Pierre du Pont has his estate and those magnificent gardens which are opened to the public at certain hours. As we walked in to the main hothouse we were met by a riot of color, and strains of music from an organ. I have never seen such a display of flowers. I have seen many of the flower shows held in New York but nothing compared with this sight. The glory of that display so gripped my heart that it was difficult to find words to speak.

As I looked at that sight I thought of John's description of the place where our Lord was crucified, which is found in the 19th chapter of his Gospel, the 41st and 42nd verses: "Now in the place where he was crucified there was a garden; and in the garden a new sepulchre, wherein was never man yet laid. There laid they Jesus. . . ." I turned to Mrs. Olsen and said, "This is the closest I have ever been to heaven." Oh, the glory of God's handiwork. Great indeed it is, but when one couples His handiwork with His wounded hand the heart leaps up in praise to our God for His love.

Yet, as my soul basked itself in the presence of God's glory in creation, I thought of an editorial that appeared in the "New York Sun" the previous day. It was singular that it should appear in that paper on the celebration of Good Friday. I refer to the editorial headed "Obituary," where the editor of that great paper chided Clarence Darrow for his tragic surrender which is so graphically evidenced in the obituary that the well-known lawyer himself had dictated. Mr. Darrow wrote: "All my life I have been seeking some definite proof of God—something I could put my finger on and say: 'This is fact.' But my doubts are at rest now. I know that such fact does not exist. When I die—as I shall soon—my body will decay. My mind will decay and my intellect will be gone. My soul? There is no such thing."

What a conflict of thoughts gripped my mind. Here I was in a garden that the hands of men had gathered together, but the hand of God had grown, perfumed, and painted. Yet a supposed intelligent man cries out, "Where is God?"

Now notice the time when creation shall sing her praises to God, led by the Lord Jesus. It is expressed in verses 35 and 36 of our Psalm: "For God will save Zion, and will build the cities of Judah: that they may dwell there, and have it in possession. The seed also of his servants shall inherit it: and they that love his name shall dwell therein."

If there is one thing for which I long it is that hour when God will save Zion, when He will gather both Jew and Gentile unto the Person of our Lord Jesus and when all shall acknowledge His Lordship. Then He shall reign as King of kings and Lord of lords. At that time even creation will join in the singing of His praises, for as the Lamb of God He is worthy to receive the praises of all creation.

PSALM SEVENTY

A TWICE-TOLD PSALM

LIKE many other Psalms, the 70th Psalm's inscription is both interesting and illuminating. This one reads, "To the chief Musician, A Psalm of David, to bring to remembrance." Then follows the Psalm, which is composed of five short verses, reading:

> "Make haste, O God, to deliver me; make haste to
> help me, O LORD.

> "Let them be ashamed and confounded that seek after
> my soul: let them be turned backward, and put to
> confusion, that desire my hurt.
> "Let them be turned back for a reward of their
> shame that say, Aha, aha.
> "Let all those that seek thee rejoice and be glad in
> thee: and let such as love thy salvation say con-
> tinually, Let God be magnified.
> "But I am poor and needy: make haste unto me, O
> God: thou art my help and my deliverer; O LORD,
> make no tarrying."

There are a number of interesting questions that arise in our minds as we examine this Psalm. In the first place, it is practically a repetition of the closing verses of the 40th Psalm. Thus we ask, Why should David make a separate Psalm of it? Was it not sufficient that he gave the substance of it previously? Why did he repeat it?

"To Bring to Remembrance"

There is not the slightest doubt in my mind but that David had a specific reason for repeating this section of the 40th Psalm and for writing it separately. In fact, the inscription throws light on it, for David said that he wrote it "to bring to remembrance." It evidently contains something that is of such importance as to make it advisable to bring it to our remembrance. Of one thing we can be sure, each remembrance of it will bring a blessing.

During the course of our meditation in the 40th Psalm we pointed out that it was a Messianic Psalm; that is, that David was not writing about his own experiences, but about the experiences of our Lord, and that it was the Lord, Himself, who was the speaker in the Psalm. These verses com-posing the 70th Psalm are, therefore, the words of our Lord Jesus. He uttered them while in communion with His Father, as He hung upon the cross.

It was for this reason that David suggested that it be brought to our remembrance. We cannot be reminded of it too often. In the communion service this very same thought of "remembrance" is used. Paul said, con-cerning the communion, or the Lord's Supper ". . . as often as ye eat this bread, and drink this cup, ye do shew the Lord's death till he come," while our Lord, when He instituted the feast, said ". . . this do in remembrance of me."

It is to be regretted that the communion table has become the center of division among Christendom, whereas it should be the place of fellowship. I have not forgotten the first time that it was my privilege, as a young man, to gather with a group of the Lord's people about the communion table and enjoy the memorials of the broken bread and the wine, which brought afresh to my heart the fact of Christ's love for me, manifested in His death. From that very first occasion until this hour, whenever I have had the privilege of partaking of the Lord's Supper, those memorials upon the table have reminded me anew of the Person and work of our Lord Jesus Christ. How true, therefore, were the words of our Lord to His disciples, when He said, "this do in remembrance of me."

David requested the chief Musician to set the 70th Psalm to music, so that it might be sung separately, in order to bring to the remembrance of the Israelites, and God's people throughout the generations, the fact of the sufferings of Christ. It was He who cried:

> "Make haste, O God, to deliver me; make haste to help me, O LORD.
> "Let them be ashamed and confounded that seek after my soul: let them be turned backward, and put to confusion, that desire my hurt.
> "Let them be turned back for a reward of their shame that say, Aha, aha."

The gospel of Christ is a marvelous message. Certain historical facts form the background of the message. The coupling of these historical facts with the declaration of the Scripture concerning their significance is found, or should be found, in every gospel message. These facts and these revelations are as follows: That Christ died for our sins *according to the Scriptures;* that He was buried; that He was raised again from the dead on the third day *according to the Scriptures.*

Here are three simple facts of history: Christ died; Christ was buried; Christ was raised again. They are irrefutable facts of history, more completely attested than a great many events which we take for granted. Woven about these historical facts is the revelation of God that Christ died for our sins, that is, His death was in accordance with the doctrine of Scripture; likewise, that in His resurrection there was the revelation of God's purpose; that He was raised from the dead *according to the Scriptures.* It is incumbent upon a man of God that he preach that message. There have been thousands of books written about the gospel. There have been millions of sermons preached about Christ and His death. Yet all ministry that is faithful to Christ grows out of these three simple facts: Christ's death, His burial, and His resurrection. Therefore, in every presentation of the gospel there is the recurring remembrance that Christ suffered upon the cross. Is it any wonder, therefore, that the Psalmist David, guided by the power of the Holy Spirit, took out of the 40th Psalm this little record of the anguish of heart of our Lord and placed it separately, in order that we might more readily bring it to our remembrance?

That which gives freshness to any ministry of God's Word is the constant remembrance of the sufferings of our Lord. When a man has been thrilled by the knowledge of what Christ has done for him, that man is urged on by the overwhelming power of the Holy Spirit, to bear to others a witness concerning the value of the death of Christ.

Occasionally in broadcasting these messages I have made reference to a few of the many interesting letters I have received from our radio audience. This week I was particularly impressed by a letter which came from a young man living in St. Louis who had heard our broadcast when it came over a local St. Louis station some time ago. His letter contained a reference which impressed me with the distinction between ministry born of love, and ministry born of profession. Let me quote from this letter, though you will pardon the personal references:

> "I am a graduate of a theological seminary and never had an ounce of inspiration for the preaching of Christianity until I heard you, and now, after a number of years, am getting back to teaching a Bible class of boys. I pray that I will be able to impart some of the infectious zeal which your spoken and written words impart."

It is a pretty sad state of affairs when a man can go through a theological seminary and not once receive an ounce of inspiration for the preaching of Christianity. Is it any wonder that many of our churches are empty? Is it any wonder that many of our ministers are lacking in power? What we need is a vision of Christ as He is to be found in the Word of God.

Now let us look at the 4th verse of this Psalm. Our Lord, continuing in His prayer, said, "Let all those that seek thee rejoice and be glad in thee: and let such as love thy salvation say continually, Let God be magnified." Here are two things for which our Lord prays, on the behalf of those that seek God. First, "Let all those that seek thee rejoice and be glad in thee. . . ." Second, "let such as love thy salvation say continually, Let God be magnified."

No man has ever honestly sought the Lord but that he found Him, or rather, he was found of the Lord. As a result of that meeting between the Lord and the seeking sinner there came to pass a meeting of minds, which gave the latter a joy and gladness he did not previously possess. The source of joy is in God. Thus it is written, "we . . . joy in God. . . ." That is quite the opposite of the natural man who does not like to retain God in his knowledge.

By way of illustration, let me relate an interesting story which I heard two weeks ago from the lips of a man who knew intimately the one about whom the story is told. A short time ago one of America's most successful business men committed suicide. He left a note to the effect that his work was done and thus, Why live? This gentleman had given away an average of one million dollars a year for each of his seventy-two years of life. My informant told me that he knew this gentleman intimately for years, and was in his office only two weeks before the fatal event. From the conversation which ensued at that time, it was apparent that this business leader planned to inflict death upon himself. If money and possession of riches and the power that wealth gives to an individual can make a man happy, certainly that man should have been extremely glad. Yet, said my informant, in all the years that he had known him, with all the wealth he possessed, this fabulously rich man never once smiled. Only once did he try to laugh and then, I was told, it sounded like the crowing of a rooster.

What a contrast to those who know Christ as their Lord and Saviour! I know many who have been deprived of the benefits of this world's goods, but who are so filled with joy in the knowledge of their Lord that their joyfulness is infectious. You cannot be in their presence without feeling it and partaking of it. How true that a man's life does not consist in the abundance of the things which he possesses. No man really *lives* until he comes to know the Lord as his Saviour.

"GLORIFYING GOD"

The second request of our Lord, on the behalf of those who seek God, is, "let such as love thy salvation say continually, Let God be magnified."

A most illuminating verse of Scripture is the last verse of the 1st chapter of Paul's letter to the Galatians. In the earlier verses of that chapter he related the record of his persecutions of Christians and his zeal for his own religion and the traditions of his fathers. Then follows a terse report of his conversion, his meeting with the Lord, his visit to Jerusalem, his association with the apostles, and the joy of Christians everywhere, over his salvation. Many of them had not seen him face to face, but only heard,

"That he which persecuted us in times past now preacheth the faith which once he destroyed." Then follows that enlightening passage, "And they glorified God in me." The climax of a man's ministry is reached when those to whom he ministers glorify God because of his ministry. How readily can we thus understand why our Lord prayed, "let such as love thy salvation say continually, Let God be magnified."

But the confines of that prayer are not limited to ministers of the gospel, as in the case of Paul, the apostle, and multitudes of others who have followed him in faithfully presenting Christ to the people. Our Lord said, "let such as love thy salvation say continually, Let God be magnified." That means you and me; indeed, all who love His salvation. Note, too, we are called upon to say continually, "Let God be magnified." That does not limit the praise to occasions of prosperity, but goes on continually.

PSALM SEVENTY-ONE

A MESSAGE FOR ALL AGES, OR
DOES LIFE BEGIN AT FORTY?

I HAVE an idea that the writer of the 71st Psalm composed it in late middle age, or when he was fast approaching old age, for he talks about his youth and also about his coming old age.

You, of course, have heard of that popular phrase, "Life begins at forty," but I am inclined to the view that those who make much of that phrase are trying to effectively evade the sudden realization that half, if not more than half, of one's life has already passed and gone.

Isn't life interesting? In our childhood we ape our elders. When we get into our late 'teens the calendar seems to roll around with annoying slowness. We cannot wait until we reach our 21st birthday to announce to our family that a full-fledged young man is now a member of the household, or that a young maiden has come into her womanhood. During the twenties life seems so tremendously interesting—everything has a glamour about it. But as soon as we have turned thirty, the calendar suddenly seems to acquire a terrific speed. Then the near side of forty approaches with a shock and we observe that the waist-line has increased and a few gray hairs have made their appearance, and we raise the question, What about the future?

As I am soon to reach the fortieth milestone I can understand why a man who does not know Christ is trying to live in a fool's paradise by saying, "Life begins at forty."

A PSALM FOR YOUTH

In this Psalm, which opens with a prayer, "In thee, O LORD, do I put my trust: let me never be put to confusion" the Psalmist looked back upon his youth, for in the 5th and 6th verses he said:

> "For thou art my hope, O Lord GOD: thou art my trust from my youth.
>
> "By thee have I been holden up from the womb: thou art he that took me out of my mother's bowels: my praise shall be continually of thee."

We who have had the privilege of being brought up in Christian homes can never sufficiently praise the Lord for our heritage. From my early youth, because of a godly mother, the name of the Lord Jesus has been revered in our home. From childhood I recall the delightful Sunday school days. How I have praised my Lord that He found me and that I came to know Him when I was in my 'teens. Nothing in this world is comparable to the privilege of knowing Christ in one's youth and determining, by His grace, to make the Lord our trust and to seek to bear witness to His grace.

In the 3rd verse the Psalmist continued his prayer and said, "Be thou my strong habitation, whereunto I may continually resort...." A beautiful picture, isn't it? The language used is both picturesque and significant. The writer realized that he lived in a world contradictory to God. The New Testament informs us that the "... whole world lieth in the lap of the wicked one." The Psalmist described life in the world, its traps and its snares, but he appreciated the fact that he had to have someone to whom he could go, who would be to him a strong habitation, and he had to have someone to whom he could go continually.

There is a New Testament passage I would like to place alongside the 3rd verse of our Psalm. The passage is in the closing verses of the 4th chapter of the letter to the Hebrews, where we read:

> "Seeing then that we have a great high priest, that is passed into the heavens, Jesus the Son of God, let us hold fast our confession.
>
> "For we have not an high priest which cannot be touched with the feeling of our infirmities; but was in all points tempted like as we are, yet without sin.

"Let us therefore come boldly unto the throne of
grace, that we may obtain mercy, and find grace to
help in time of need."

Isn't that a marvelous place of refuge? That place is vouchsafed to
every believer in Christ. Now then, the next time you are in a place of need
do not go around complaining about your troubles or seeking someone to
share them, for you will be terribly disappointed. Go right into the presence
of God and there, in the name of your great High Priest, the Lord Jesus,
claim the mercy and help that God has assured you He will give to
you when you come into His presence. If we continually resort unto that
strong habitation, we will join with the Psalmist, as he wrote in the 8th
verse, "Let my mouth be filled with thy praise, and with thy honour all the
day."

A FORWARD LOOK

In the early verses the Psalmist reminded the Lord of his youth,
whereas in the 9th verse he looked forward to the future and prayed:

"Cast me not off in the time of old age; forsake me
not when my strength faileth.
"For mine enemies speak against me; and they that
lay wait for my soul take counsel together,
"Saying, God hath forsaken him: persecute and take
him; for there is none to deliver him."

In the New Testament it is written that our adversary, the devil, goeth
about as a roaring lion, seeking whom he may devour. The thing that
bothers me is to observe, very frequently, that that old devil, the serpent,
and Satan, delights to disturb and plague a believer when either his health
or strength fails, or if perchance his circumstances seem to indicate that
God has forsaken him.

If you who are perplexed by your circumstances, the outward appearances of which seem to indicate that the Lord has forsaken you, and you
feel that you are being pursued by the enemy, let me give you a passage of
Scripture which I hope you will never forget. It is found in the 25th chapter
of the First Book of Samuel. It was uttered by a woman by the name of
Abigail. Her words were spoken to David in the time of his youth. Commencing with the middle of verse 28 we read: ". . . for the LORD will
certainly make my lord (David) a sure house; because my lord (David)
fighteth the battles of the LORD, and evil hath not been found in thee all
thy days." Abigail continued in the 29th verse, "Yet a man is risen to
pursue thee, and to seek thy soul . . ." referring, of course, to King Saul.
And now this is the part of the verse I want you to embrace and make yours

forever: "but the soul of my lord (David) shall be bound in the bundle of life with the LORD thy God; and the souls of thine enemies, them shall he sling out, as out of the middle of a sling."

Beginning at the 14th verse of the 71st Psalm, the Psalmist revealed a situation that is unusually interesting. He declared:

> "But I will hope continually, and will yet praise thee more and more.
>
> "My mouth shall shew forth thy righteousness and thy salvation all the day; for I know not the numbers thereof.
>
> "I will go in the strength of the Lord GOD: I will make mention of thy righteousness, even of thine only."

A normal Christian life, as the years roll by, should develop the same characteristic that possessed the writer of this Psalm when he said: "But I will hope continually, and will yet praise thee more and more."

The closer a man walks with God the more sin he sees in himself; the farther away, the less sin he sees. The closer a man is in fellowship with the Lord the more surely will he speak of the righteousness of his Lord; not his own, but the righteousness of the Lord.

I have suggested that I believe the Psalmist wrote this Psalm in late middle life, or in early old age, because he looks back on his youth, and forward to his old age. The forward view is expressed in verse 18, where he wrote: "Now also when I am old and greyheaded, O God, forsake me not; until I have shewed thy strength unto this generation, and thy power to every one that is to come."

"GREAT AND SORE TROUBLES"

There is no excuse for a Christian to live in the past, or to feed upon his past experiences. The present should always be the time of hope and fellowship with the Lord, and should be devoted to service to Him. A Christian should live in the present, and rejoice in hope of the future. That does not mean that the Christian is spared trials and difficulties, for in the 20th verse the Psalmist said: "Thou, which hast shewed me great and sore troubles, shalt quicken me again, and shalt bring me up again from the depths of the earth."

In this same verse of this Psalm, the writer looked forward to something beyond death. He had great faith in God, therefore he said, "Thou, which hast shewed me great and sore troubles . . . shalt bring me *up* again from the depths of the earth." In other words, the Psalmist believed in the resurrection of the dead. He did not have the hope that we Christians now have, in the coming of the Lord. Our Lord promised to come again, and receive *us unto Himself.* He never indicated when that would take place. He simply told us to watch, wait, and be ready for it. There is to be one generation of Christians who will be spared the valley of the shadow of death: they will go directly into the presence of their Lord.

PSALM SEVENTY-TWO

A PSALM FOR THE KING OF KINGS

WHILE there are 150 Psalms and we speak of the collection as the "Book of Psalms," nevertheless, there are actually five books. The first book ends with Psalm 41. Each of the books end in almost identical language. The 72nd Psalm ends the second book, and you will note that the closing verses read:

> "Blessed be the LORD God, the God of Israel, who only doeth wondrous things.
>
> "And blessed be his glorious name for ever: and let the whole earth be filled with his glory; Amen, and Amen.
>
> "The prayers of David the son of Jesse are ended."

A PSALM FOR A KING

This 72nd Psalm was written by David. It has an inscription reading: "A Psalm for Solomon." Solomon was David's son, who followed him upon the throne. Oh, you say, everybody knows that. Indeed? Let's see.

As a friend of mine is planning to make a trip to Palestine, accompanied by his wife, his brother gave him a book entitled, "So you are going to the Mediterranean?" by the travel writer, Clara E. Laughlin. Describing Palestine, particularly Cana of Galilee, Miss Laughlin states that Cana is seven and a half miles beyond Tiberias, and then comes this suggestive sentence, "If I add that Cana is where Christ performed His first miracle and at the marriage feast turned water into wine, please do not take it as an insult to your intelligence. Remember," says Clara Laughlin, "I have recently been in Palestine and heard tales upon tales of visitors—college bred, many of them—who had no notion why people visit the Garden of Gethsemane, who Judas Iscariot was, or what makes Bethlehem sacred."

David knew Solomon would take his throne, because the Lord had made certain promises concerning the glory of Solomon's kingdom. Thus David opened his Psalm by saying:

> "Give the king thy judgments, O God, and thy righteousness unto the king's son.
>
> "He shall judge thy people with righteousness, and thy poor with judgment.
>
> "The mountains shall bring peace to the people, and the little hills, by righteousness.
>
> "He shall judge the poor of the people, he shall save the children of the needy, and shall break in pieces the oppressor.
>
> "They shall fear thee as long as the sun and moon endure, throughout all generations.
>
> "He shall come down like rain upon the mown grass: as showers that water the earth.
>
> "In his days shall the righteous flourish; and abundance of peace so long as the moon endureth."

Let us stop there for a moment. It is apparent that David looked beyond Solomon, his son, to his greater Son, of whom the Scriptures constantly witness, for it is about the kingdom reign of the Messiah that this Psalm was actually written.

Only the other day I read a terse sentence that succinctly describes this Psalm. It was this—that this Psalm was penned by a king for a king and concerns the King of kings.

While Solomon enjoyed a reign of splendor and peace, and there can be no doubt that this Psalm was dedicated to him, yet he did not have the dominion which is described by David in the 8th verse, where we read: "He shall have dominion also from sea to sea, and from the river unto the ends of the earth." The extent to which this kingdom is to be increased is further evidenced from the comments in the next three verses, reading:

> "They that dwell in the wilderness shall bow before him; and his enemies shall lick the dust.
>
> "The kings of Tarshish and of the isles shall bring presents: the kings of Sheba and Seba shall offer gifts.
>
> "Yea, all kings shall fall down before him: all nations shall serve him."

Here we have the homage paid to David's greater Son. Even the kings of Tarshish and of the isles of the sea shall bring presents unto Him. In fact, ". . . all kings shall fall down before him: all nations shall serve him." This brings us to a very interesting subject. I have tried to make it clear, during the course of these broadcasts, that at the present time God is doing a specific work in this world. It is not a spectacular work. To use the language of James the apostle, recorded in Acts 15, He is taking out of the Gentiles a people for the name of His Son. This company of people, the New Testament declares, is composing the body of Christ, called the church, which, when completed, will be presented to Him as His bride. That is what God is doing at the present time. He is saving individuals out of every race and clime. I repeat, it is not a spectacular work. But there is coming a day when the Lord will cease to deal with men as individuals; when He will expand His domain to nations. Then, instead of doing a quiet work, as He is now doing, the Lord will give a spectacular display of power and of glory. I refer to the Millennial reign of our Lord Jesus Christ.

All the prophets, many a poet, and many a painter, have vied with each other in describing the hope that rests in the bosom of every man, that some day this world shall have an era of peace and splendor the like of which it has never known, and in which period, as the prophet Micah declared: ". . . they shall sit every man under his vine and under his fig tree; and none shall make them afraid: for the mouth of the LORD of hosts hath spoken it." But the question is, when shall this take place and what will bring it about? Well, let's see if we can find an answer.

The present depression has lasted almost six years. Certainly it is the worst one we have known anything about. It is not surprising that due to the distress of multitudes there have arisen men who promise—I was almost going to say, the earth; but who are impotent to make their promises good. We listen to demagogues in every sphere of human activity and each promises that he will make every man a king. Will this day of peace and splendor, plenty and abundance, come about through the promises of any man? No indeed! There is only One in whom we can have confidence; who shall judge the people in righteousness and the poor in judgment; who will be able to deliver the needy when he crieth; who will redeem their soul from deceit and violence and provide corn and fruit in every city, so that each city will flourish like the grass of the earth. That one is He of whom the Psalmist wrote in the 17th verse: "His name shall endure for ever: his name shall be continued as long as the sun: and men shall be blessed in him: all nations shall call him blessed."

Of whom was the Psalmist speaking? Of Solomon? Oh, no! He meant the One whose name shall *never be forgotten,* and all nations shall call Him blessed.

THE CHRIST OF GOD

The Bible, from the beginning of Genesis to the end of Revelation, is occupied with an unfolding of the plan and purposes of God. As we read through this book we discover that the plan and purposes of God are centered in one person. In Genesis He is called the seed of the woman; in Exodus He is the passover; in Leviticus He is the burnt offering to the Lord; in Numbers He is the brazen serpent; in Deuteronomy He is the rock; in Joshua He is the leader of His people; and so we could go through the Old Testament into the New Testament, to the very last book of the Bible, and in each we can find this one person, who though His names seem almost endless, is none other than our Lord Jesus. He is the fulness of the Godhead bodily. He is the effulgence of God's glory. He upholds all things by the word of His might. It is concerning Him, that David wrote in the 72nd Psalm, "His name shall endure for ever. . . ." He is the King of kings, and the Lord of lords. He is not only the King, but the King's Son, and the extent of His domain will be from sea to sea, and from the river unto the ends of the earth.

This is not the wild dream of an imaginative mind. It is the expressed declaration of Scripture. This is the day to which every born-again, Bible-instructed Christian looks forward with tremendous delight. We have a description of His coming in the last book of the Bible, the Book of the Revelation, where John wrote what he saw while on the Isle of Patmos, when God gave him a revelation of the future in a sort of pageantry. In the 19th chapter of the Revelation, beginning with the 11th verse, we read:

> "And I (John) saw heaven opened, and behold a white horse; and he that sat upon him was called Faithful and True, and in righteousness he doth judge and make war.
>
> "His eyes were as a flame of fire, and on his head were many crowns; and he had a name written, that no man knew, but he himself.
>
> "And he was clothed with a vesture dipped in blood: and his name is called The Word of God.
>
> "And the armies which were in heaven followed him upon white horses, clothed in fine linen, white and clean.

> "And out of his mouth goeth a sharp sword, that with it he should smite the nations: and he shall rule them with a rod of iron: and he treadeth the winepress of the fierceness and wrath of Almighty God.
>
> "And he hath on his vesture and on his thigh a name written, KING OF KINGS, AND LORD OF LORDS."

Then in the 21st chapter, beginning with the 1st verse, John said:

> "And I saw a new heaven and a new earth: for the first heaven and the first earth were passed away; and there was no more sea.
>
> "And I John saw the holy city, new Jerusalem, coming down from God out of heaven, prepared as a bride adorned for her husband.
>
> "And I heard a great voice out of heaven saying, Behold, the tabernacle of God is with men, and he will dwell with them, and they shall be his people, and God himself shall be with them, and be their God.
>
> "And God shall wipe away all tears from their eyes; and there shall be no more death, neither sorrow, nor crying, neither shall there be any more pain: for the former things are passed away.
>
> "And he that sat upon the throne said, Behold, I make all things new. And he said unto me, Write: for these words are true and faithful."

In the 22nd chapter, beginning with verse 1, John further described the glory of the future, by saying:

> "And he shewed me a pure river of water of life, clear as crystal, proceeding out of the throne of God and of the lamb.
>
> "In the midst of the street of it, and on either side of the river, was there the tree of life, which bare twelve manner of fruits, and yielded her fruit every month: and the leaves of the tree were for the healing of the nations.
>
> "And there shall be no more curse: but the throne of God and of the Lamb shall be in it; and his servants shall serve him:
>
> "And they shall see his face; and his name shall be in their foreheads.
>
> "And there shall be no night there; and they need no candle, neither light of the sun; for the Lord God giveth them light: and they shall reign for ever and ever."

While we do not see an era of peace today, nor a period wherein righteousness flourishes, yet we have a hope, steadfast and sure, that some day when the coming of the Lord takes place this world will enjoy a great time of peace and righteousness.

But I am tremendously interested in the 15th verse, where David said:

> "And he shall live, and to him shall be given of the gold of Sheba . . ."

We all hear much about money at the present time, and we have a certain school of economists who think that the nation's gold should be in possession of the Government, not the individual. In fact, today we dare not possess any gold coin; all of it must be in the possession of the United States Treasury. There are other economists who insist that this is not the best procedure, as it places our gold in the hands of men who might be swayed by political advantage. But in our Psalm we are told that the gold of Sheba shall be given to Him, our Lord Jesus, in that day.

Sheba is a very interesting place. You will remember that the Queen of Sheba came to Solomon and was impressed with his great learning and with the glory of his kingdom. Sheba means "an oath." How interesting that the gold of Sheba is to be placed in the hands of our Lord. He is the only one who ever kept an oath and whom we can trust to keep an oath. He alone will be able to deliver the poor and the needy and, in fact, supply the wants of the wealthy at the same time. With a Central Bank in Jerusalem, with our Lord in possession of the gold, this world will then know what it is to have a perfect banking system!

THE THEME SONG OF THE PSALM

Before bringing our Psalm to a close, I suggest that you, at your convenience, underscore two phrases in this Psalm and note their contrast. They occur with the regularity of a theme song throughout the Psalm. One refers to the Lord and what "He shall" do, and the other to the people and what "they shall" do. For instance, it is said of Him that

> He shall judge the people in righteousness.
> He shall judge the poor.
> He shall save the children of the needy.
> He shall break in pieces the oppressor.
> He shall come down like rain.
> He shall have dominion from sea to sea.
> He shall spare the poor and needy, and redeem their soul.
> He shall live.

And concerning the multitudes of the people, it is written:

> They shall fear Him.
> They that dwell in the wilderness shall bow before Him.
> His enemies shall lick the dust.
> The kings shall bring presents.
> All the kings shall bow down before Him.
> All nations shall serve Him.

No wonder the Psalmist closed this second book of the Psalms with: "Blessed be the LORD God, the God of Israel, who only doeth wondrous things. And blessed be his glorious name for ever: and let the whole earth be filled with his glory. . . ."

Meditations In The Psalms

THAT EVER-PERPLEXING PROBLEM

THE 73rd Psalm, which begins the third book of the Psalms, was not written by David, but by Asaph, who was one of the three chief singers, or choir leaders, in Israel at the time of King David's reign. It is interesting to observe that the singing of the Israelites, in connection with divine worship, was never placed on the basis of professionalism. Asaph sang unto the Lord for the joy of singing. He was a choir leader who not only reveled in the quality of tone and the character of his choir from a musical viewpoint, but who knew the Lord and rejoiced in the knowledge of God's grace.

THE PROBLEM

Yet Asaph, like multitudes of others down through the ages, was perplexed with a problem that defied solution. Thus he said:

"Truly God is good to Israel, even to such as are of a clean heart.

"But as for me, my feet were almost gone; my steps had well nigh slipped.

"For I was envious at the foolish, when I saw the prosperity of the wicked.

"For there are no bands in their death: but their strength is firm.

"They are not in trouble as other men; neither are they plagued like other men.

"Therefore pride compasseth them about as a chain; violence covereth them as a garment.

"Their eyes stand out with fatness: they have more than heart could wish.

"They are corrupt, and speak wickedly concerning oppression: they speak loftily.

"They set their mouth against the heavens, and their tongue walketh through the earth.

"Therefore his people return hither: and waters of a full cup are wrung out to them.

"And they say, How doth God know? and is there knowledge in the most High?

"Behold, these are the ungodly, who prosper in the world; they increase in riches.

"Verily I have cleansed my heart in vain, and washed my hands in innocency.

"For all the day long have I been plagued, and chastened every morning.

"If I say, I will speak thus; behold, I should offend against the generation of thy children."

Let us stop there. In this Psalm Asaph has presented a universal problem, a problem which, as I have already stated, seems to defy solution. This problem is not to be solved by a study of facts, nor by any study of God's apparent dealings as the governor of the universe.

We quoted only the first fifteen verses of the Psalm. They present the problem. Asaph possessed a logical mind. He saw the difficulty and groped for its solution. The solution, however, is not to be found by the exercise of the intellect, any more than one can rationalize love. Love defies the mathematician to understand its movements. Man, who glories in the supposed possession of a logical mind, thinks that everything must be reasoned out. He concludes, therefore, that if a man suffers, he suffers because of his sin; if another prospers and enjoys riches, it is because he has not sinned. That seems logical, but it is not true!

Asaph said, "When I thought to know this, it was too painful for me . . ." I can picture Asaph looking at the outward appearances. Not only was his mind absolutely bewildered, but his heart also was pained.

The contradictions of life are so abounding, that there can be no solution to them unless we do exactly what Asaph did. He said, "When I thought to know this, it was too painful for me: until I went into the sanctuary of God; then understood I their end."

THE ONLY SOLUTION

I do not believe any man suffered more, in one day, than did Job, that godly, righteous man. Probably the saddest picture that is to be found in all literature, outside of Calvary, is the picture of Job sitting among the ashes. We read in the 2nd chapter, verse 9: "Then said his wife unto him, Dost thou still retain thine integrity? curse God, and die." But Job responded: "Thou speakest as one of the foolish women speaketh. What? shall we receive good at the hand of God, and shall we not receive evil? In all this did not Job sin with his lips."

Asaph knew about Job's history and similar situations. He saw the wicked prosper. He also saw the righteous suffer. But to try to find an answer to the problem was impossible, until he went into the sanctuary of God. It is only in the presence of God that one gets a proper answer to the perplexities of life, both concerning the present and the future. Until a man has entered into the sanctuary of God, the world is absolutely a mocking, defying question mark. Sin, righteousness, and judgment are words that defy man's intellect. Man can find the answer to them, only in the sanctuary of God. Someone said to me recently, "You do not know what trouble is. Everything seems to go so easy for you." I responded, "If you only knew how frequently I have gone into His presence with a burdened heart. If it were not for the comfort and the knowledge I receive in His presence, life would often be dismal." I, too, would be inclined to ask the same question Asaph asked in this Psalm. But when a man enters into the sanctuary of God he has the joy of communing with God, of knowing the mind of God, of understanding His will, and of learning that life does not consist in what we eat or wherewithal we are clothed, but that it consists in the knowledge of God.

If there is any one thing for which I thank my God, next to the fact of salvation, it is the great privilege of having a godly mother. Trouble? That dear soul knew what trouble was. She knew what it was to have four little children, a husband in a hospital, and just fifty cents in her pocketbook. However, she had a faith that could move mountains. She had a love for her Lord that shone in her face. She went into the sanctuary with her problems.

So the writer of the 73rd Psalm, when he was troubled and perplexed, went into the sanctuary of God. There he saw that God had set the wicked in slippery places, and that they were about to be cast down into destruction, and brought into desolation. When Asaph *learned* that, he said in verse 21: "Thus my heart was grieved, and I was pricked in my reins. So foolish was I, and ignorant..."

A PERSONALLY CONDUCTED TOUR

But I love the closing verses of this 73rd Psalm, beginning with verse 24, where Asaph wrote: "Thou shalt guide me with thy counsel, and afterward receive me to glory." What a heritage belongs to the child of God!

There is not one of us but is desperately in need of counsel. The counsel of man is faulty. The counsel of a friend ofttimes is helpful and precious, but it is inadequate. But the counsel of God is sure and perfect.

What a privilege. What a heritage for man in this day to have the Lord to guide him with His counsel, and then afterward to receive him to glory.

Notice how personal Asaph became when he said: "Thou shalt guide *me* with thy counsel, and afterward receive *me* to glory." When one is possessed with that hope, one is able to bear the disappointments of life, even though they cut into the heart. There may be a number of things he does not understand, but he rests, in joy and peace, in the faith that afterward he will be received into glory.

Some years ago I heard an interesting story. Whether it is true or not I do not know. It came out of Russia, long before the Communistic regime. It seems that a certain atheist was parading up and down the country-side, pouring out his verbiage against the very thought of God and ridiculing all those who believed in God. On one occasion he addressed a group gathered in a large hall. He stirred them to a high pitch and then hurled an invitation to God, that if there were a God, He should reveal it by smiting him to death. Of course, God did not do that, and so he turned to his audience and said, "See, there is no God."

A little Russian peasant woman, with a shawl about her head, arose to speak. She addressed her remarks to the speaker and said, "Sir, I cannot answer your arguments. Your wisdom is beyond me. You are an educated man. I am merely a peasant woman. With your superior intelligence, will you answer me one question? I have been a believer in Christ for many years. I have rejoiced in His salvation and I have enjoyed my Bible. His comfort has been a tremendous joy. If, when I die, I come to learn that there is no God; that Jesus is not the Son of God; that the Bible is not true and there is no salvation, nor heaven, pray sir, what have I lost, by believing in Christ during this life?" The room was still. The audience grasped the woman's logic and then they turned to the atheist, who by that time was swayed by the woman's simplicity, and in quiet tones he responded, "Madam, you won't stand to lose a thing." Then answered the peasant woman, "You have been kind in answering my question. Permit me to ask another. If, when it comes your time to die, you discover that the Bible is true; that there is a God; that Jesus is His Son and that there is a heaven and a hell; pray sir, what do you stand to lose?" The logic was so overwhelming that the crowd leaped to its feet and shouted in ecstasy. The atheist had no answer. It is only in the sanctuary that one understands the ways of God.

Asaph added one more word that is also interesting. It is in verse 25: "Whom have I in heaven but thee? and there is none upon earth that I desire beside thee."

We have heard all sorts of questions as to where heaven is. If heaven is up, and as our earth is like a globe, it is up in one place and down in another. How man reasons! Heaven is where the Lord Jesus is, His presence is what makes heaven. The Lord said, when He was about to leave His disciples, ". . . I go to prepare a place for you. And if I go and prepare a place for you, I will come again, and receive you unto myself, that where I am, there ye may be also." A believer in Christ has great joy in the hope that he will be brought into His presence and that he will see the glory of God in the face of Jesus Christ. Each of us who has been redeemed by the grace of God can also say from the bottom of his heart, as Asaph did in the 73rd Psalm, ". . . there is none upon the earth that I desire beside thee."

PSALM SEVENTY-FOUR

WHAT ABOUT THE JEW?

BEFORE entering into our meditation on the 74th Psalm I want to quote from a letter received this past week. It came from a little girl, who wrote:

> "I was listening to your sermon on the radio this morning, we enjoyed it so much that my mother would like you to send her three copies of it. This is the first time we have heard you and we think you are 'splendent.' I am 11 years old and just got a radio for my birthday."

Let none suggest that the Psalms are intended for old people only! They meet the need of everybody—young or old, black or white. The Psalmists have struck a chord that finds a response in the human heart, in its desire to know the truth, through all the perplexities of life. And when the heart has come to know the truth, it rejoices with a joy that is unspeakable and full of glory in the knowledge of the Lord God.

Like the 73rd Psalm, the 74th is ascribed to Asaph. It has an introduction reading, "Maschil of Asaph," which means it is a Psalm of instruction. That is exactly what it is. In many ways it is an unusual Psalm.

Because of its predictive element, some people have attempted to prove that it was written at much later period. But I believe that God can

prophesy an event hundreds and even thousands of years before it takes
place! The Psalm opens:

> "O GOD, why hast thou cast us off for ever? why doth
> thine anger smoke against the sheep of thy pasture?

> "Remember thy congregation, which thou hast pur-
> chased of old; the rod of thine inheritance, which thou
> hast redeemed; this mount Zion, wherein thou hast
> dwelt.

> "Lift up thy feet unto the perpetual desolations; even
> all that the enemy hath done wickedly in the sanc-
> tuary.

> "Thine enemies roar in the midst of thy congregation;
> they set up their ensigns for signs.

> "A man was famous according as he had lifted up axes
> upon the thick trees.

> "But now they break down the carved work thereof at
> once with axes and hammers.

> "They have cast fire into thy sanctuary, they have
> defiled by casting down the dwelling place of thy name
> to the ground.

> "They said in their hearts, Let us destroy them to-
> gether: they have burned up all the synagogues of God
> in the land.

> "We see not our signs: there is no more any prophet:
> neither is there among us any that knoweth how long.

> "O God, how long shall the adversary reproach? shall
> the enemy blaspheme thy name for ever?

> "Why withdrawest thou thy hand, even thy right hand?
> pluck it out of thy bosom.

> "For God is my King of old, working salvation in the
> midst of the earth."

WHAT ABOUT THE JEW?

We have entitled this meditation: "What about the Jew?" All will
agree that Christendom has developed a selfish attitude toward the gospel.
Some professing Christians believe that the Lord Jesus belongs exclusively
to the Gentiles. Thus, they think that it is quite all right to send missionaries to China, Africa, and the islands of the sea; but because the Jew
rejected Jesus of Nazareth and refused to own Him as their Messiah, God
has entirely wiped out the Jewish nation as far as any relationship to Himself is concerned. Therefore, the average Christian says in effect, Let us
have nothing to do with the Jew.

Nothing could be further from the truth. Every true Christian who knows his Bible and understands the way of salvation, rejoices in the fact that the blessings he has received have all come through those who were Jews according to the flesh. Our Lord was a Jew according to the flesh. Every writer, but one, of the New Testament Books was a Jew. But somehow, because we are living nineteen hundred years from those events, we Gentiles have assumed that God sent His Son into this world for our particular benefit only. In fact, Christendom has practised, if not actually believed, that its duty is to persecute the Jew because of his rejection of Jesus. Is it any wonder that many Jews have come to despise the name of Jesus, considering all they have suffered in the name of Christianity? But a true Christian never persecutes a Jew.

It is of Israel that the sweet singer wrote when he cried "O GOD, why hast thou cast us off for ever? why doth thine anger smoke against the sheep of thy pasture?" Then the Psalmist called upon the Lord to "Remember thy congregation. which thou hast purchased of old; the rod of thine inheritance, which thou hast redeemed; this mount Zion, wherein thou hast dwelt."

In the New Testament letter to the Romans, in the 11th chapter, we learn a few things about Israel which are very important. Beginning with the 1st verse Paul wrote:

"I say then, Hath God cast away his people? God forbid. For I also am an Israelite, of the seed of Abraham, of the tribe of Benjamin.

"God hath not cast away his people which he foreknew. Wot ye not what the scripture saith of Elias? how he maketh intercession to God against Israel, saying,

"Lord, they have killed thy prophets, and digged down thine altars; and I am left alone, and they seek my life.

"But what saith the answer of God unto him? I have reserved to myself seven thousand men, who have not bowed the knee to the image of Baal.

"Even so then at this present time also there is a remnant according to the election of grace."

Israel rejected her opportunity and as a result of it the Gentiles have had the gospel preached unto them, but, said the Apostle Paul in the eleventh verse of the same chapter, ". . . Have they (that is Israel) stumbled that they should fall? God forbid: but rather through their fall salvation is come unto the Gentiles. . ." and then he added this significant verse: "Now if the fall of them (that is the Israelites) be the riches of the world, (that is the Gentiles who have had offered to them the riches of the grace of God) and the diminishing of them the riches of the Gentiles; how much more their fulness?" Then in verse 15 he said: "For if the casting away of them (which is Israel) be the reconciling of the world, (that is the Gentiles) what shall the receiving of them (Israel) be, but life from the dead?"

Let it not be forgotten that Israel is still the people of God in a unique way and in a special manner. Israel has been cast aside for the time being, in order that the Gentiles may have the grace of God preached to them, through the redemption there is in Christ. But the hour will come when God will cease to deal with the Gentiles (as He did in the casting away of the Jews as a nation) and He will then revert to the Jews. Paul tells us that when the Lord God shall receive Israel as a nation, the result will be life from the dead. The greatest era of peace, joy, and gladness in this world awaits the time when Israel takes her rightful place among the nations. This world will never know peace, this world will never know true prosperity, until the nation of Israel is back in her own land and enjoys the blessing of the presence of her Lord.

At present, and for some long period in history, the anger of the Lord has smoked against the sheep of His pasture, as Asaph said in the 74th Psalm, but Asaph cried out, "Remember thy congregation, which thou hast purchased of old; the rod of thine inheritance, which thou hast redeemed. . ." Israel is His inheritance—His own people.

WE, TOO, ARE GOD'S INHERITANCE

In even a more definite way God has purchased us and redeemed us, and we now are also the rod of His inheritance. By "we" I mean those of us, whether Jew or Gentile, who have received Christ, who have acknowledged that we were in desperate need of a Saviour, that the Lord Jesus was that Saviour, and that by His death He purchased our redemption. So we have been redeemed, and, oh the glory of it, we became His inheritance.

Occasionally Christian people say (and they have said it honestly) that they could not understand why the Lord loved them so, or why He had done so much for them. Well, there is a reason why God loves us. Back in the Old Testament He said, concerning Israel, that He loved them *because* He loved them, and that, of course, is why anybody loves. But why should God display His grace and love upon us, unworthy though we are and sinful though we are? A verse or two in the 1st chapter of the letter to the Ephesians will clear up this matter for us. In the 15th verse of the 1st chapter Paul prayed and said:

"Wherefore I also, after I heard of your faith in the Lord Jesus, and love unto all the saints,

"Cease not to give thanks for you, making mention of you in my prayers;

"That the God of our Lord Jesus Christ, the Father of glory, may give unto you the spirit of wisdom and revelation in the knowledge of him:

"The eyes of your understanding being enlightened; that ye may *know* what is the *hope of his calling,* and *what the riches of the glory of his inheritance in the saints."*

Notice that Paul wanted the eyes of our understanding to be enlightened, that we might know what is the hope of God's calling and what are the riches of the glory of God's inheritance in the saints. It is easy to understand what is our inheritance in Christ, as Christians. We have a goodly heritage. We are heirs of God and joint-heirs with Jesus Christ. By the way, I am so glad this inheritance of ours cannot be taxed away from us, aren't you? But why did God love us? Because He finds in us something that He wants. It is so precious in His sight that He calls it His inheritance. You, I, and all who have received Christ as Lord and Saviour become an inheritance to God. Do not go around, therefore, saying that you cannot understand why God loves you. Do not get a mistaken notion concerning your worthlessness to God. You are truly very valuable in His sight if you have received Christ. You are so valuable that He gave His Son in order that He might redeem you. What shall we then do? Simply love Him, and seek to walk worthy of the high calling of God in Christ.

"THE RIGHT HAND OF GOD"

Now let us return to the 74th Psalm, and as we do so let us not forget that the congregation of which Asaph spoke is Israel. Israel is God's purchased congregation; Israel is also the rod of His inheritance. But in verse 2 Asaph also links the people with the land when he said, ". . . this mount Zion, wherein thou hast dwelt." The Gentiles have had Palestine for a long time, but Palestine actually belongs to the Jew. Therefore, Asaph prayed to God and said: "Lift up thy feet unto the perpetual desolations; even all that the enemy hath done wickedly in the sanctuary." In verse 5, Asaph wrote of the time when a man was made famous because of his contribution to the building of the temple, but since then a man became famous because he broke down the carved work that was once erected.

In the 10th verse Asaph prayed: "O God, how long shall the adversary reproach? Shall the enemy blaspheme thy name for ever?" Finally, in the 11th verse he challenged the Lord by saying: "Why withdrawest thou thy hand, even thy right hand? Pluck it out of thy bosom."

The one of whom the Psalmist spoke in the 11th verse under the title "even thy right hand," is the Lord Jesus, I believe, or, if you please, the Messiah of Israel. Let me give you my authority. In the 53rd chapter of Isaiah, which is also concerned with the Lord, we read, "Who hath believed our report? and to whom is the *arm* of the LORD revealed?" After that the prophet Isaiah described the humiliation of the one who was offered for the transgression of the nation. Need I remind you, who know your Bible, that our Lord has been exalted to the *right hand* of God, where He now is a Prince and a Saviour? What light that fact sheds upon this 11th verse of the 74th Psalm. "Why withdrawest thou thy hand, even thy right hand? Pluck it out of thy bosom."

Let us place a New Testament passage of Scripture alongside of this verse in the 74th Psalm so that we may see how beautifully the Old Testament is fulfilled in the New, and that we may observe the unity which exists between the Psalmist and the writers of the Gospels. In the 8th verse of the 1st chapter of John's Gospel we read, "No man hath seen God at any time, the only begotten Son, who is in the bosom of the Father, he hath declared (or manifested) him." Notice that it is written in John's Gospel that the only begotten Son is in the bosom of the Father, while in the 74th Psalm Asaph cried to God that He pluck out His right hand from His bosom. How wonderful! Now our Lord has returned to heaven. He is seated at the right hand of His Father. But as surely as God is God, He will answer the cry of the Psalmist. He will again pluck out of His bosom His right hand, the Messiah of Israel, the Lord of glory. When that happens then that which is described in the 12th verse will take place. It reads: "For God is my King of old, working salvation in the midst of the earth."

THE HORN OF THE WICKED
vs.
THE HORN OF THE RIGHTEOUS

THE 75th Psalm is a short Psalm of ten verses, written by Asaph. It is dedicated to the chief Musician and it abounds in the thought of the expression of judgment. It reads:

"Unto thee, O God, do we give thanks, unto thee do we give thanks: for that thy name is near thy wondrous works declare.

"When I shall receive the congregation I will judge uprightly.

"The earth and all the inhabitants thereof are dissolved: I bear up the pillars of it. Selah.

"I said unto the fools, Deal not foolishly: and to the wicked, Lift not up the horn:

"Lift not up your horn on high: speak not with a stiff neck.

"For promotion cometh neither from the east, nor from the west, nor from the south.

"But God is the judge: he putteth down one, and setteth up another.

"For in the hand of the LORD there is a cup, and the wine is red; it is full of mixture; and he poureth out of the same: but the dregs thereof, all the wicked of the earth shall wring them out, and drink them.

"But I will declare for ever; I will sing praises to the God of Jacob.

"All the horns of the wicked also will I cut off; but the horns of the righteous shall be exalted."

Not only is this a Psalm of judgment, but it is a Psalm of thanksgiving; in fact, the opening verse is a beautiful expression of thanksgiving.

We shall place a verse or two from the New Testament Scriptures alongside of the 1st verse of our Psalm, in order that we may better understand that the giving of thanks should be a normal expression of a Christian's life. In the 5th chapter of Paul's letter to the Ephesians we are exhorted to give thanks "always for all things unto God and the Father in the name of our Lord Jesus Christ." In the 4th chapter of Paul's letter to the Philippians we are urged to be careful for nothing; but in everything by prayer and supplication with thanksgiving let our requests be made known unto God. And the peace of God, which passeth all understanding, shall keep our hearts and minds through Christ Jesus. Another passage of Scripture in the 3rd chapter of Paul's letter to the Colossians has a bearing on the same subject also. We are exhorted in that chapter that whatsoever we do in word or deed we are to "do all in the name of the Lord Jesus, giving thanks to God and the Father by Him."

All three passages indicate that the normal expression of a believer's life should be a constant giving of thanks to God for His marvelous benefactions. Let us stop there, and comment on one of these verses. I refer to the one which Paul wrote to the Philippians, in which we are exhorted to be careful for nothing. What an indictment against us. We are concerned about everything. But we are told to be careful for nothing; but in everything, that means in every part of life—social, religious, business, or whatever it might be—in everything, by prayer and supplication, mingled with thanksgiving, we are to let our requests be made known to the Lord.

A Christian should never rise in the morning, nor retire in the evening, without expressing a note of praise, in prayer to the Father, for His graciousness in the privilege of knowing Him and Christ Jesus the Lord. Is it any wonder, therefore, that the Psalmist declared: "Unto thee, O God, do we give thanks, unto thee do we give thanks: for that thy name is near thy wondrous works declare."

That is exactly the position Paul took in his letter to the Romans, where he declared that while the Jews received the written Word and were the custodians of the divine revelation and therefore responsible to God for their stewardship, nevertheless the Gentiles were without excuse "Because that which may be known of God is manifest in them; for God hath shewed it unto them." Then he demonstrated how God has shown Himself unto the Gentiles, by adding, "For the invisible things of Him (God) from the creation of the world are clearly seen, being understood by the things that are made, even his eternal power and Godhead; so that they are without excuse . . ."

The revelation of God in creation manifests a personality and indicates that this personality is endowed with power and might and that He rules in absolute righteousness. The very sun that shines, and the glittering stars of the glory, and every blade of grass bear their silent message that the name of God is near at hand.

THE JUDGMENTS OF GOD

At the beginning I mentioned that this Psalm was a Psalm of judgment. It actually was written about the future, from a time point of view, as it looks forward to the occasion of the revelation of Christ, when the wicked shall be subject to judgment, and the righteous shall rejoice in the presence of their Lord. In fact, it is none other than the Lord Himself who speaks, beginning at the 2nd verse, where it is written:

> "When I shall receive the congregation I will judge uprightly.
>
> "The earth and all the inhabitants thereof are dissolved: I bear up the pillars of it. Selah.
>
> "I said unto the fools, Deal not foolishly: and to the wicked, Lift not up the horn:
>
> "Lift not up your horn on high: speak not with a stiff neck.
>
> "For promotion cometh neither from the east, nor from the west, nor from the south.
>
> "But God is the judge: he putteth down one, and setteth up another."

We can receive a much needed word of exhortation and instruction from this portion of Scripture. In the first place, may I hasten to explain what the Psalmist means by saying, "Lift not up the horn . . ." It is very interesting. I confess I used to stumble over it and wonder what it meant. The Psalm ends with a somewhat similar expression, where we read: "All the horns of the wicked also will I cut off; but the horns of the righteous shall be exalted."

Most of us have imagined that the only one who has horns is the one who has been pictured and caricatured as Satan, who invariably is represented with horns, hoofs, and a tail. Of course, the caricature is ridiculous and is merely a hangover from the medieval ages—but just what has the Psalmist in mind when he writes of the horns of the wicked, and the horns of the righteous? I may shock you in suggesting that you have a horn and I have a horn, and while it may not be visible to you and to me, it is invariably visible to someone else.

The word horn as used by the Psalmist is merely a figure of speech, describing glory. When, therefore, Asaph wrote of the horns of the wicked, he was speaking of the glory of the wicked, and when he wrote of the horns of the righteous, he meant the glory of the righteous. The wicked glory in their sin; the righteous glory in the righteousness of the Lord.

Who Does the Promoting?

Then notice something in verses 6 and 7, which I think warrants our consideration. In those verses we read: "For promotion cometh neither from the east, nor from the west, nor from the south. But God is the judge: he putteth down one, and setteth up another."

Most of us think promotion comes from our own efforts, and some of us think that men are put up, or set down, by their own efforts, or by the efforts of a political machine. However, the Psalmist said, "God is the judge: he putteth down one, and setteth up another."

This principle applies not only to the political, but it applies to every sphere of life. If you have a place of honor, remember God is Judge. Let us trust Him.

Now a comment or two upon the 8th and 9th verses of our Psalm which brings our message to a close. The reason we are to trust in the Lord is expressed in verse 8, where we read: "For in the hand of the LORD there is a cup, and the wine is red; it is full of mixture; and he poureth out of the same: but the dregs thereof, all of the wicked of the earth shall wring them out, and drink them. But I will declare for ever; I will sing praises to the God of Jacob."

The Psalmist, of course, used parable language. He pictured the Lord with a cup in His hand, and in it there was wine. It was red. We are told by the prophets that that which is referred to as wine is the fierceness of the wrath of Almighty God. I know we are living in an age which is called the enlightened 20th century. How distasteful it would be if a Fifth Avenue or Park Avenue preacher were to talk to his highly cultured, intellectual, wealthy, self-satisfied congregation about the fierceness of the wrath of Almighty God. We speak now of the love of God. We have relegated the wrath of God to the dark ages. Men now think it is their business to speak in glowing terms of the love of God, and to assume that God could never be anything but love. Oh, the namby-pamby type of preaching in which some preachers glory. Any man who stands in the pulpit, behind an open Bible, and declares that there is no such thing as the wrath of God, is unfaithful to the Lord, unfaithful to the Book, unfaithful to his congregation, and unfaithful to himself.

There is in the hand of the Lord a cup of wine, which is red. The dregs of that cup shall be wrung out upon the wicked of the earth. There is no doubt that God will judge the world in righteousness.

PSALM SEVENTY-SIX

HOW GOD MAKES THE WRATH
OF MAN TO PRAISE HIM

SOMEONE has suggested that the age in which we live might be
called the Vitamin Age. If it were possible, I think some men would
give up the habit of eating if they could get predigested vitamin
pills. There are some preachers, also, who boast of sermons in vitamin
capsules. I heard of a minister who recently made the statement that he
could pack more into a short sermon of some fifteen minutes than any
man on the public platform today. He may have said it with a twinkle
in his eye, but when it comes to a short sermon, the Apostle Paul still holds
the honors. However, as far as I know, Paul never boasted of the brevity
or length of his sermons. Do not misunderstand. The Apostle Paul did
not limit his message to short sermons. At Troas he once preached to a
large congregation till midnight when he was rudely interrupted because a
young man had sunk down in sleep and fallen down from the third loft only
to be taken up dead. After the chap was raised from the dead Paul went
on preaching till the break of day. So Paul holds the record for the shortest
and longest of sermons.

"... THE UNKNOWN GOD"

The shortest sermon he preached is recorded in the 17th chapter of
Acts. It took only two minutes to deliver, that is if Paul happened to be
a slow speaker. I doubt if any man put more meat into a sermon of any
size than did the Apostle Paul in his message at Mars' hill. Paul was a
great man, a man fully yielded to the Lord! Paul has given the world an
opportunity to see what God can do through a man fully yielded to the
Lord.

If you will pardon the bluntness of the language, he was no numb-
skull. I find myself repeatedly apologizing at least to my own heart for
some of the sermons I hear—they are so empty. They evidence the lack
of preparation by the preacher. They are presented on such a low level
of intelligence that it is an insult to the gospel of the grace of God which
is declared to be the expression of God's wisdom! Some people seem to
think that God puts a premium on ignorance. Oh, no! Paul was a mighty
man and he was as alert as a fox. He never wasted a moment. He had
trouble with his eyes as a result of seeing the Lord in His ascension glory,

but he made excellent use of what eyesight he had. He puts all of us to shame.

Paul went to Athens because of the persecution which was visited upon him by the Jews of Thessalonica who had learned that Paul's ministry in Berea was being received by the Bereans as they examined the Scriptures and learned that what the Apostle Paul preached agreed thoroughly with the writings of the Old Testament prophets. When some of the brethren at Berea heard of the advancing army of persecutors they immediately sent Paul away. He was conducted to Athens where he was to wait for the coming of Silas and Timotheus.

Paul made good use of his eyesight while in Athens. Before long an opportunity was presented to address a large group of Athenians. In doing so this is what he said, "Ye men of Athens, I perceive that in all things ye are too religious. For as I passed by . . ." (R. V.).

How significant that is! We never stand still, we pass by. We are either going ahead or falling behind. But as Paul "passed by" he saw some things for, said he, I "beheld the objects of your worship." He thus noticed two things. He observed that the Athenians were too religious. Is that possible? Yes! Then Paul also noticed the objects of their worship. Of the latter he said, "I found an altar with this inscription, TO THE UN-KNOWN GOD."

Now then with this scene at Athens as a background, let us read the 76th Psalm in which our meditation is found. You will immediately observe an amazing contrast:

> "In Judah is God known: his name is great in Israel.
> "In Salem also is his tabernacle, and his dwelling place in Zion.
> "There brake he the arrows of the bow, the shield, the sword, and the battle. Selah.
> "Thou art more glorious and excellent than the mountains of prey.
> "The stouthearted are spoiled, they have slept their sleep: and none of the men of might have found their hands.
> "At thy rebuke, O God of Jacob, both the chariot and horse are cast into a dead sleep.
> "Thou, even thou, art to be feared: and who may stand in thy sight when once thou art angry?
> "Thou didst cause judgment to be heard from heaven; the earth feared, and was still;
> "When God arose to judgment, to save all the meek of the earth. Selah.

"Surely the wrath of man shall praise thee: the remainder of wrath shalt thou restrain.

"Vow, and pay unto the LORD your God: let all that be round about him bring presents unto him that ought to be feared.

"He shall cut off the spirit of princes: he is terrible to the kings of the earth."

In Athens God was "*unknown.*" In Judah God is "*known.*" What an effective testimony that man by wisdom knew not God. Athens with its great seats of learning was the epitome of human wisdom. In Judah, where God's name was known, the knowledge of God was by revelation. It is only as God reveals Himself that He is known. Man cannot find God by searching along the human wisdom route.

"IN JUDAH IS GOD KNOWN . . ."

At Athens Paul rebuked the Athenians for failure to recognize the revelation of God in this created world. There was no reason for the altar bearing the inscription "TO THE UNKNOWN GOD." God had revealed, was still revealing, His might, His power, and His personality in the visible creation. They were without excuse.

But there is one place above all others where God is known. The Psalmist said it was Judah. If there is a place in this world where its people are inexcusable for their failure to recognize the Lord, that place is Palestine, and if you please, in Judah. It was from the tribe of Judah that our Lord came. He made His dwelling-place in Zion. The inhabitants of Jerusalem and the environs of Judea alone had the opportunity to see the Lord's Christ.

The coming of our Lord to Zion was such a stupendous event that, since His coming, the whole world goes back in their faith or in their pilgrimage to the mount outside the gates of Jerusalem. The shocking thing about that place is the name given to it in Holy Writ some sixty years after our Lord's death. There are people today who are amazed that of all places in the world, Jerusalem has continuously been a place of controversy. One would have assumed that our Lord's breath had sweetened the air and that His footsteps had been such a benediction that Jerusalem, true to its name, would have been the most peaceful place on earth. But this Bible knows the end from the beginning, as well as all the time between. So in the last book of the Bible, the book of The Revelation, the city of Jerusalem is spoken of as "the great city, which spiritually is called Sodom and Egypt, where also our Lord was crucified."

It seems particularly appropriate, therefore, that in this Psalm we should find the words "Surely the wrath of man shall praise thee (God): the remainder of wrath shalt thou restrain." It was at Jerusalem where the wrath of man waxed hottest and it was at that place above all others that God made the wrath of man to praise Him. In man's wrath our Lord was crucified, but to the everlasting glory of God it was at that hour that God made man's wrath to praise Him; for Calvary, the place of human tragedy, became the place where Divine reconciliation was accomplished.

Frequently the work of the Lord has been hindered in this world. Sometimes it has been hindered by the Lord's people, as for example when the Lord had to rebuke Peter for objecting to Calvary, saying to him, "Get thee behind me, Satan: thou art an offence unto me: for thou savourest not the things that be of God . . ." More often the work of the Lord has been hindered by Satan's emissaries in this world. But even then, "Surely the wrath of man shall praise" the Lord.

Of course, it is evident that the 76th Psalm celebrated a deliverance of Israel from her enemies which was clearly wrought by the hand of God. Thus it is no surprise to find that the occasion was used as an opportunity to sing a song of praise to God. Observe that in speaking of Jerusalem and Zion the Psalmist in verse 3 said, "There brake he (that is, the Lord) the arrows of the bow, the shield, and the sword, and the battle." The victory was gotten in Jerusalem. The Psalmist, of course, specifically referred to a previous hour in Israel's history which we shall not take the time to examine. The Psalms, with hardly an exception, have a spiritual import. Thus they have lived throughout the centuries. In a deeply spiritual sense, God got Himself a great victory at Jerusalem. He will get Himself another great victory at Jerusalem. It was at Jerusalem that our Lord "spoiled" principalities and powers and there He made a show of them, openly triumphant over them in Christ. I repeat, God Himself got a great victory at Jerusalem. There the Lord's Christ bruised the head of the serpent, though in doing so the serpent bruised Christ's heel. There God shall get Himself another victory when He reveals for the second time the Son of Man, the Redeemer of the world. And His dwelling-place again will be in Zion.

THE WRATH OF GOD

Note also what the Psalmist said about the might of the Lord which was manifested at the time of the deliverance. The Psalmist said of God,

"Thou art more glorious and excellent than the mountains of prey." Jerusalem is surrounded by mountains. These mountains have not infrequently been used as hiding places for the enemies of Israel. At times within the wall of the city the people seemed almost helpless but the Psalmist said, "Thou art more glorious and excellent than the mountains of prey." Turning to the New Testament we observe that this same principle still applies, for in the 1st Epistle of John, chapter 4, verse 4, we read, "Ye are of God, little children, and have overcome them: because greater is he that is in you, than he that is in the world."

No wonder the Psalmist wrote in verses 5 and 6, "The stouthearted are spoiled . . . At thy rebuke, O God of Jacob, both the chariot and horse are cast into a dead sleep." Again, is it any wonder that he immediately adds of God, "Thou, even thou, art to be feared; and who may stand in thy sight when once thou art angry?"

In the Bible it is written, "It is a fearful thing to fall into the hands of the living God." Recently there appeared a cartoon in one of the English papers in which the artist depicted Hitler approaching the gates of heaven. To his great surprise who should stand at the gates but St. Peter, with a hooked nose betraying his Jewish origin. Hitler, whose hair stood on end, addressed St. Peter and said, "Vat, you here?" Sir, I believe the grace of God is so great that even if that man were this day to repent and receive Christ as his Saviour there would be eternal salvation for him. If he does not, he will learn that it is a fearful thing to fall into the hands of the living God for ". . . who may stand in thy sight when once thou art angry?"

In the 8th and 9th verses of this 76th Psalm the Psalmist said, "Thou didst cause judgment to be heard from heaven; the earth feared, and was still, when God arose to judgment, to save all the meek of the earth." It ought to be evident to all that the world in which we live is antagonistic to God. The whole world, as the Bible puts it, lieth in the lap of "the wicked one." Satan despises every Bible-believing Christian. He will vent his wrath not only against the Jew, who gave birth to the Son of God, but also against every born-again Christian. The wicked in this world have no more use for a Christian than they had for our Lord at the time of His rejection. But the world has had demonstrated repeatedly that it is impossible to kill a man whose faith is in Jesus Christ. There have been moments when wickedness appeared to triumph and the people of God were made to suffer in the throes of persecution but there has always come the hour when even the patience of God came to an end.

The goodness of God leadeth men to repentance. At times men have taken advantage of the goodness of God. They have assumed that His silence meant that He was non-existent but they only awakened with sadness of heart. No man has been able to stand in His sight when once God displayed His anger. Someone may ask, Is it possible for God to be angry? Sir, the question evidences a woeful lack of observation. Again and again, this created earth of ours has given evidence of the anger of God. The very bowels of the earth have seemed to belch forth His anger. If God permitted and still permits the earth to show forth His anger, it is for the purpose of acquainting men with the fact that God is a consuming fire, as well as a God of love. The fields that blossom in the springtime give evidence of the grace and love of God but that display is no assurance that a storm will never break. The fact that God is silent while revealing His matchless love should never be taken as assurance that He is too loving, too kind, and too tender to be angry.

The last two verses of this 76th Psalm contain a solemn warning both to the Christian and to the rulers of the earth. From the 13th chapter of St. Paul's letter to the Romans, we learn that rulers are ministers of God. God instituted human government. Every man who occupies a governmental office is a minister of God. He is as accountable to God for the faithful discharge of his ministry, as a believer is accountable to God for his faithfulness in the discharge of his Christian obligations. To the Christian, or to the believer, whichever you wish, the Scripture says, "Vow, and pay unto the LORD your God . . ." I have previously in these broadcasts discussed the subject of vows. It is sufficient to say now that a believer has an obligation. Having received Christ as his Saviour, he should recognize that his entire being belongs to the Lord. Every moment of his life and every dollar he earns should be put under the Lordship of Christ.

To the rulers there is a solemn warning in the last half of the closing verse of this Psalm. God is "terrible to the kings of the earth." Some of the rulers of this world assume that they hold the reins of government by their own right and power—that they will never be taken to task or to judgment. But this book, the Bible, says that God is "terrible to the kings of the earth." Let us not forget that to whom much is given, of him much shall be required. I realize that this message is not being heard by any of the rulers of the earth, with the possible exception of some of the lesser officeholders in these United States, but every man in the seat of governmental authority is a minister of God, accountable to Him. If our governmental servants recognized their position, I am sure they would be less apt to use their office for personal gain or for any other selfish interest. God will exact an accounting from every man who occupies any place in the government of this world.

After Munich comes the Great White Throne. Not only after Munich, but after every life that has not sought shelter under the atoning blood of God's Lamb, shed at Calvary almost nineteen hundred years ago.

PSALM SEVENTY-SEVEN

SOLVING THE QUESTION OF PARENTS AND CHILDREN

THE 77th Psalm is another poem composed by Asaph, which he dedicated to his associate in the office of chief Musician, namely, Jeduthun. He, together with Asaph and Heman, composed the trio who acted as the chief Musicians during the reign of King David. Jeduthun's name means *praise-giver* or *laudatory*.

In ancient days the names that were given to children invariably gave expression to the hope of the parents, or to a particular idea the parents had in mind. When this little child was born, his parents undoubtedly were thankful from the bottom of their hearts for a gift from the Lord. They must have dedicated that child immediately to the Lord and hoped that he might be used to sing forth the praises of Jehovah. Thus they called him the *praise-giver*, which in Hebrew is Jeduthun.

Now that brings us to an interesting subject—the question of the relationship of parent and child. Has the Bible anything to say on the subject? Knowing that men are prone to dash in where angels fear to tread, I am going to take a chance and give expression to my thoughts on the subject.

CHRISTIAN HOUSEHOLDS

In the first place, the New Testament particularly mentions the household of believing parents. A very interesting passage is found in the 16th chapter of the Acts of the Apostles. Paul and his friend, Silas, were cast into prison at Philippi, because of their faithfulness to the Lord in the preaching of the gospel. The magistrates who sentenced them charged the jailer to keep them safely. The jailer, having received such a charge, thrust them into the inner prison and made their feet fast in the stocks. I am going to assume that the majority of you are acquainted with the Roman type of prison. Thus, you can well appreciate that being thrust into the inner prison and having their feet placed in the stocks was not a pleasant situation for Paul and Silas.

At midnight (we will have something more to say about that later on) Paul and Silas prayed and sang praises unto God, and the prisoners heard them. Suddenly there was a great earthquake, so that the foundations of the prison were shaken, and immediately all the doors were opened, and everyone's bands were loosed. The keeper of the prison, who awakened out of sleep, saw the prison doors open, and recognized his responsibility. He pulled out a sword and would have killed himself, supposing that the prisoners had fled. However, Paul cried out and suggested that he do himself no harm, for the prisoners were safe. Then the jail-keeper called for a light, and sprang in and, trembling, fell down before Paul and Silas and brought them out and said, "Sirs, what must I do to be saved?" Wouldn't you delight to go to prison because you preached the gospel, and wouldn't you love to have the privilege of hearing your jailer ask you what he must do to be saved? I don't mean that you should go out and violate some law and have yourself cast into prison, but you can, in a measure, imagine the joy that Paul and Silas must have experienced when their jailer asked, "what must I do to be saved?"

Then follows that memorable answer by Paul, "Believe on the Lord Jesus Christ, and thou shalt be saved, and thy house."

If my memory serves me correctly, this is the first occasion that the expression, "and thy house" is found in the New Testament. What did Paul have in mind when he added, "and thy house"? I think we can answer that by observing the further things that transpired at that time. Immediately, Paul and Silas spoke unto the prison-keeper the word of the Lord and they spoke to all in the jail-keeper's house. All were evidently convicted of sin and realized how unjustly Paul and Silas had suffered. So they took them and washed their stripes. Then Paul and Silas were brought into the jailer's home, and the keeper "set meat before them, and rejoiced, believing in God *with all his house.*"

What I think on the subject, as to assurance that every member in a household will be saved just because the head of the household is saved, I shall not say. I merely give this suggestion for you to study the subject further—that on this occasion Paul said that the way to be saved was to believe on the Lord, and that this applied to the head of the household as well as to every member of it. But let us not forget that every member heard and believed. Of one thing I am sure—God honors the preaching of His Word to the salvation of souls. Furthermore, He honors believing prayers and the faithfulness of Christian parents in the bringing up of their children in the admonition and nurture of the Lord.

AN EXAMPLE

Let me offer you a modern illustration of this view. I know of a family where every member rejoices in the faith of Christ, even as did every member of the household of the Philippian jailer. I refer to that interesting family, the Stam family of Paterson, N. J., of which John Stam was a member. You will recall he gave his life in China, in the course of his duty as an ambassador of Jesus Christ. I know of no large household, though there may be many others, where God is so singularly honored as in that family. And I truly believe that this is so because of the faithfulness of both the mother and father in that household, their steadfastness to the Lord, their devotion to Christ, and the manner in which they have brought up their family. I think, beyond a doubt, that I speak the mind of both mother and father, that they praise the Lord from the bottom of their hearts and give thanks to Him for the privilege of rearing such a family, where every member rejoices in Christ and where each in his own way is witnessing for Christ.

Thus we can find a modern example of a Christian home, and the influence which is exercised in that home by a godly mother and father. Please do not misunderstand me, I am sure that this is not the only case. I am satisfied that there are many families listening to this program who can testify to the same blessing that has come to the Stam family, because of the faithfulness of godly parents.

So, in the family into which Jeduthun was born, there was such joy and gladness, that these parents dedicated their child to the Lord and called him the "praise-giver." They also gave him the name "Ethan," which means *strong*.

Occasionally I have mentioned the influence of a godly mother in our home. I hope I do not bore you by referring to her once more. Mother was never given to many words. She rarely said much, but what she said was worthwhile. I do not know from where I get my verboseness, but it certainly does not come from my mother's side. I recall the evening I returned home, after I had received the Lord Jesus as my Saviour. One of my sisters had come home earlier and informed mother that I had received the Lord Jesus. I was but seventeen years of age at the time, and strange as it may seem, mother never said a word to me. However, some time later, she said something that has forever left its impression upon my mind. On that occasion she took me aside and told me that before I was born she prayed to the Lord that she might have a son and if He would give her a son she would in turn give that son to Him. Thus, from the moment I was born she dedicated her son to the Lord and asked the Lord that He might use that child in the ministry of His Word. When mother revealed that to me she added these simple words, "And now my Lord has answered my prayer."

May I particularly impress upon the hearts and minds of you Christian mothers and fathers that you recognize the heritage that is yours in your children, by bringing them up in the fear of the Lord and presenting Christ to them right early. God will answer your prayer and undoubtedly will allow you the joy of knowing that your children, in turn, will delight to present Christ to someone else.

While I have spent much time just on the introduction of the 77th Psalm, yet I am not finished with it. I have already mentioned that Jeduthun's name means *praise-giver*. Isn't it strange, that to the man whose name is *praise-giver* there should be dedicated a Psalm which opens with an outburst of tears? That brings us to another interesting subject.

Life is a mixture of tears and gladness. None of us are spared tears, and it is questionable whether any of us are refused a measure of joy. However, it is my humble judgment that the deepest praise is offered in tears. Therefore, it is not surprising that Asaph, when he wrote this Psalm, which undoubtedly reflected his own experience, should have dedicated it to the praise-giver. Now let us read the Psalm. It has twenty verses, but we shall limit our reading to the first fifteen verses:

> "I cried unto God with my voice, even unto God with my voice; and he gave ear unto me.

> "In the day of my trouble I sought the Lord: my sore ran in the night, and ceased not: my soul refused to be comforted.

> "I remembered God, and was troubled: I complained, and my spirit was overwhelmed. Selah.

> "Thou holdest mine eyes waking: I am so troubled that I cannot speak.

"I have considered the days of old, the years of ancient times.

"I call to remembrance my song in the night: I commune with mine own heart: and my spirit made diligent search.

"Will the Lord cast off for ever? and will he be favourable no more?

"Is his mercy clean gone for ever? doth his promise fail for evermore?

"Hath God forgotten to be gracious? hath he in anger shut up his tender mercies. Selah.

"And I said, This is my infirmity: but I will remember the years of the right hand of the most High.

"I will remember the works of the LORD: surely I will remember thy wonders of old.

"I will meditate also of all thy work, and talk of thy doings.

"Thy way, O God, is in the sanctuary: who is so great a God as our God?

"Thou art the God that doest wonders: thou hast declared thy strength among the people.

"Thou hast with thine arm redeemed thy people, the sons of Jacob and Joseph. Selah."

How many of us have had similar experiences! We are forced by circumstances to go into the presence of God and to cry out aloud to Him with our voices, as Asaph did in this Psalm.

Now I know that there are some who feel that to complain is unbecoming to a Christian. May I suggest that even such a man as Asaph said he complained to God. I am glad that our Lord knows what we are, and how thankful we should be that He understands our frame, and remembers that we are but dust. I can assure you who are troubled, that when you complain in the presence of your Lord, He is not disturbed by your complaint.

The language that Asaph used in the 6th verse is particularly significant, where he stated: "I call to remembrance my song in the night: I commune with mine own heart: and my spirit made diligent search."

When I related the conversion of the Philippian jailer, I mentioned that I intended later to comment on the fact that Paul and Silas sang at the midnight hour. I had in my mind then, the phrases that appear in verses 2 and 6 of the 77th Psalm, where Asaph said: "My sore ran in the night, and ceased not:" and, "I call to remembrance my song in the night."

It was the Bishop of Derry who made the statement, "Our nights are spiritual tests, perhaps truer and subtler than our days." The night season is used by the wicked in the pursuit of their wickedness; whereas the night season should be used by a Christian, when he is in difficulty, in the pursuit of his Lord.

Our Lord Jesus laid stress upon the depth of sin, by reminding us that a man can sin in his heart and in his thoughts, though he may not be guilty of the overt act.

I am sure you will agree with the Irish bishop, who also added:

> "Experience shows us the dangers and the fascinations of the region of thought. There is an inner world of sin. There the ambitious can surround himself with the images of a splendor and power which he can never attain. There a feeble hatred can exchange its pointless pen and blunted sarcasms for epigrams which make an enemy's face blanch and his nerves quiver ... There the voluptuous can scent the bouquet of the wine of sin, without the vulgarities and disappointments which are the portion of those who drain the cup to its burning lees."

The shocking part and the truth of the matter is that the night is the season when temptation does its deadliest work—"When the mind is turned in on itself and its true character revealed."

SIN

If we would only realize that it is just as sinful to think evil as to do evil, then I am sure we would appreciate why it is that the Lord Jesus said, "Ye must be born again." The wickedness of man is exceedingly great. It is not possible for man to wipe out the thought of sin, for when he least expects it, it manifests itself. How often haven't you heard of the terrific outburst of violent language which pours forth from the lips of cultured, refined people as they come out of the ether, after an operation. Why do you suppose such language proceeds out of lips that never used the language? The answer is found in the Bible. The heart is the source, and of the heart it is written that it is desperately wicked—who can know it? Someone may ask, Am I responsible for that? In a measure you may not be, but you are responsible if you neglect the salvation of God which is offered to you. You are responsible if you fail to recognize that what God says about you is true.

Psalm Seventy-Eight—Part One

A PSALM OF NEEDED INSTRUCTIONS

THE 78th Psalm is a Psalm of seventy-two verses, so that we could not begin to cover it in one address. It contains so many interesting things that it will be profitable and worthwhile to spend two or three meditations on it.

The Psalm is another of the instructive poems written by Asaph. The first eight verses read:

> "Give ear, O my people, to my law, incline your ears to the words of my mouth.
>
> "I will open my mouth in a parable: I will utter dark sayings of old:
>
> "Which we have heard and known, and our fathers have told us.
>
> "We will not hide them from their children, shewing to the generation to come the praises of the LORD, and his strength, and his wonderful works that he hath done.
>
> "For he established a testimony in Jacob, and appointed a law in Israel, which he commanded our fathers, that they should make them known to their children:
>
> "That the generation to come might know them, even the children which should be born; who should arise and declare them to their children:
>
> "That they might set their hope in God, and not forget the works of God, but keep his commandments:
>
> "And might not be as their fathers, a stubborn and rebellious generation; a generation that set not their heart aright, and whose spirit was not stedfast with God."

There are several interesting things found in that introduction. In the first place, notice the manner in which we are introduced to the Psalm. It is written: "Give ear, O my people, to my law: incline your ears to the words of my mouth." Here, therefore, the Psalmist is acting as a prophet, speaking the words of the Lord and commanding the people to give ear to the law and to incline their ears to the words that proceeded out of His mouth. There can be no doubt that the Lord Himself was the speaker. The exhortation to give ear was limited to that company of people whom He addressed as, "O my people."

The prophet on this particular occasion is presenting a message to the Jews who were and still are, in a peculiar manner, the people of God.

THE WORDS OF HIS MOUTH

There is another interesting thing in the 1st verse of our Psalm. The Lord asks us to incline our ears to the words of His mouth. It was Charles Haddon Spurgeon who once said, "Men lend ears to music, how much more then should they listen to the harmonies of the gospel; they sit enthralled in the presence of an orator, how much rather should they yield to the eloquence of heaven."

It particularly impresses me that the Lord invites us to incline our ears to the words of His mouth. Sometimes we employ familiar language in speaking of God, but let us never forget His glory and majesty. Earthly rulers and dignitaries possess majesty; how much more, therefore, the eternal God. I have been interested to observe the contrast between the words of men in high office and esteem, and those of the eternal God. Take our own land, for instance. We have a President. He occupies the highest office in the land. Occasionally he gives one of his fireside chats over the radio, when he either summarizes the accomplishments of his Administration or outlines his proposed plans for the future. However, I think I do him no injustice by stating that on such occasions his language is general, not specific; and at times we are left in doubt, as citizens of this country, as to what we should expect of the Administration. Even the President's friends, not to say his enemies, have pointed out this particular fault. Yet this is not singular with our President; in fact, the same characteristic is found in the rulers of other nations. Rarely does the president, the king, or the dictator speak directly to the people. The result is that we have what we call in this country a White House spokesman. We citizens are dependent upon what we receive through newspaper reports, press conferences, and every other conceivable avenue. Not so with God. He does not need a spokesman. He invites us to incline our ears to the words of His mouth. His dignity is the greatest; yet He condescends to men of low estate.

Notice also that in the 2nd and 3rd verses it is indicated what His mouth will speak. It is written:

> "I will open my mouth in a parable: I will utter dark sayings of old:
>
> "Which we have heard and known, and our fathers have told us."

This passage in the 78th Psalm is applied to our Lord Jesus Christ and fulfilled in His public ministry as we find it in the New Testament. In the 13th chapter of St. Matthew's Gospel, where we have the record of the seven parables outlining the mysteries of the kingdom of heaven, we read in verses 34 and 35:

> "All these things spake Jesus unto the multitude in parables; and without a parable spake he not unto them:
>
> "That it might be fulfilled which was spoken by the prophet, saying, I will open my mouth in parables; I will utter things which have been kept secret from the foundation of the world."

Now a parable is merely a story or an illustration. The 78th Psalm is also a parable. As the prophet referred back to the history of Israel he made application of it to present conditions. That is what makes the Word of God living. We can come, as we do this morning, to the 78th Psalm, which is now almost three thousand years old—yet there is in it that which is the breath of God, which makes its throb with life, so that it is as fresh in its application today as at the time it was written.

You will notice that the Lord Jesus was called upon to utter dark sayings of old. It was Lord Bacon who said, "Old wood is best to burn, old books are best to read, and old friends the best to trust."

Our Lord said that the "scribe which is instructed unto the kingdom of heaven is like unto a man that is an householder, which bringeth forth out of his treasure things new and old."

THE INSTRUCTION OF CHILDREN

The Psalmist also said, "We will not hide them from their children, shewing to the generation to come the praises of the LORD, and his strength, and his wonderful works that he hath done. For," he continued, "he (the LORD) established a testimony in Jacob, and appointed a law in Israel, which he commanded our fathers, that they should make them known to their children."

The Jewish rabbis have a strict custom and method in the instruction of their children according to their age and capacity. At five years of age they become sons of the law and are expected to read it. At thirteen they become sons of the precept and are expected to understand the law. At fifteen they become disciples of the Talmud, and they are expected to delve into the deeper points of the law, even into the Talmud itself. At the Passover it is the youngest child of the house who asks the father questions.

It is the child who asks, "Why is it called the Passover?" and the father responds, "Because the angel passed over us when He slew the Egyptians and destroyed us not." It is the youngest child who asks, "Why do we eat unleavened bread?" to which the father responds, "Because we were forced to hasten out of Egypt." It is the youngest child who still further asks, "Why do we eat bitter herbs?" and the father responds, "To remind us of our affliction in Egypt." That type of conservative training from earliest childhood must bear its fruit, and does bear it in future life. It was Mr. Spurgeon who said, "Children ought to be taught to magnify the Lord" and that "The best education is education in the best things. The first lesson in a child's life should be concerning his mother's God. Teach a child what you will, if a child learn not the fear of the Lord he will perish for lack of knowledge."

The purpose of all this child-training is explained in verses 7 and 8, where it is written, "That they might set their hope in God and not forget the works of God, but keep his commandments . . ." and further, that they "might not be as their fathers, a stubborn and rebellious generation; a generation that set not their heart aright, and whose spirit was not stedfast with God."

Let us examine these reasons a bit more closely. First, it is stated that children should be taught the Word of the Lord and the works of the Lord, in order that they might set their hope in God. Even the Communists have recognized the value of child-training. It is a well-known fact that they delight to take a child in its early years and fashion its mind so that in later years it may adhere to the principles of Communism. How necessary, therefore, that those who are Christians teach their children the Word and works of the Lord, so that their children might set their hope in God. Now, I do not mean by that that a person is a Christian because he is born into a Christian family. An individual becomes a Christian when he receives Christ as his Saviour, but there is no time limit, either from the viewpoint of youth or that of age. It is an established fact that the overwhelming majority of those who are believers in Christ have come to that decision in their early years. What a reason, therefore, for instructing our children in the Word and works of the Lord, in order that they might set their hope in God. All too soon they will be faced with the problems of life and they will discover that the things in which they set their hope (unless their hope be in the Lord) are without foundation. But what a joy, from childhood on, to have one's hope set in the Lord.

Then we note that we are to instruct children in the Word of the Lord and the works of God, in order that they might not forget His works.

A child's mind is never so fascinated as when it hears of the works of the Lord as recorded for us in the Scriptures. Who of us cannot bear testimony to impressions from childhood which we received when we first heard the story of Daniel in the lions' den, or of David when he slew Goliath, or of Moses in the ark of bulrushes? Invariably a child's mind absorbs these stories so that they become a vital part of their being, and occasionally they express themselves in a way that strikes us as being humorous, but really indicates a deep thoughtfulness that enables us to understand why our Lord said, "Except ye . . . become as little children, ye shall not enter into the kingdom of heaven."

An amusing little incident occurred at the time of the last election for Governor in New York State, when Robert Moses ran against Herbert Lehman. A little child, just three years of age, had been particularly impressed with the story of Moses in the ark of bulrushes, and whenever her mother or grandmother would relate the story and show her the picture of it, the little child would say, "Moses 'c'ying.' " Thus on election morning when this little child's father proceeded to the polls to vote, she wanted to accompany him, and she even insisted upon going into the voting booth with him. As she entered the place she shouted, "I vote for Moses." The next day her mother informed her Moses had been beaten, whereupon she looked up into her mother's face and said, "Moses 'c'ying.' "

Do you think any child would ever forget, if properly taught, that God knew all about that crying babe in an ark of bulrushes? Will it forget that it was God who sent Pharaoh's daughter to the riverside, and then touched her heart? Will the child ever forget that God used the circumstances of that childhood to bring great glory to His own name? Those Old Testament facts of history, as well as the New Testament records, reveal to us the works of God. What a comfort they prove in later years, when we are faced with difficulties and trials of every conceivable nature. What a joy to remember the works of God and to appropriate His promises to our own circumstances.

Another reason why children should be instructed in the Word and works of God is that they might keep His commandments. It was the Psalmist who said, "Thy word have I hid in mine heart, that I might not sin against thee." Sin is a hard taskmaster. The wages of sin is death.

The path of sin is strewn with disappointments and hardships. How necessary, therefore, that we should be instructed in the Word of the Lord and in His works, in order that when temptation arises we may meet it, not in our own power, but in the power of the Word of God.

In verse 8 we learn of another good reason why we should be instructed in the Word of God. It is in order that we might not be a stubborn and rebellious generation, as were the fathers of Israel who died in the wilderness because they stubbornly refused to believe God. The Lord help us to profit from the instructions contained in His Word.

PSALM SEVENTY-EIGHT—PART TWO

"CAN GOD FURNISH A TABLE IN THE WILDERNESS?"

THERE is sufficient in the 78th Psalm to form the basis of at least ten messages, but we shall try to boil it down to three. In doing so, I wish in this meditation to call attention to the reception that the people of Israel gave to the revelation of God, and in the final meditation we shall discuss specifically what the Lord did to restore His people to fellowship with Him.

THE DECLINE OF ISRAEL

It was a fact, as the Psalmist declared, that the children of Ephraim turned back in the day of battle, and kept not the covenant of God, and refused to walk in His law, and forgot His works, though His works were marvelous displays of power. He divided the sea. He caused them to pass through dry land. He made the waters to stand as an heap. He led the nation in the daytime and in the night seasons. He clave the rocks in the wilderness and gave them drink. He caused streams to pour out of the rock. Yet, with all His great care and His provision, they sinned more and more by provoking Him in the wilderness. They even tempted the Lord in their heart, asking meat for their lust, as they raised the question, "Can God furnish a table in the wilderness?"

It seems striking that any man, or any group of men, would ever raise the question, "Can God?" Yet we are just as guilty of questioning the power and love of God and the provisions of God as were those old Israelites. "Can God furnish a table in the wilderness?" It is an interesting question, isn't it?

As we think about it, let us try to visualize the scene. It is a wilderness—barren, disappointing, unattractive. No pathways are laid out and every step seems to invite further difficulties. Is it possible to have a table in such a place? Is it possible to have communion with God and to be sustained by Him? Can God meet all the needs of man when he is in the wilderness? For, of course, a table speaks of communion and sustenance. In other words, can God supply a table for a man when he is in desperate circumstances, or do circumstances prevent God? It would seem that the mere raising of the question would provide its own answer, for if He be God then certainly there can be no limitation upon His power. The only question that can be raised concerns His love, His affection, and His benefactions. Granted the Lord is God, then He is all powerful. But in raising the question "Can God?" men seem to doubt His love and grace.

There are multitudes who have come to know God through Jesus Christ who can bear testimony that they have frequently been called upon to travel through a wilderness. In fact, the wilderness is the symbol for the actual walk of a Christian in this world. Yet through the wilderness walk God has furnished a table.

In the case of Israel, whose history is recorded for us by one of their own in the 78th Psalm, it would seem that they professed godliness in order that they might experience some benefactions of God. But as for trusting Him when things did not look bright, that was quite another matter.

The first accusation the Psalmist made against them is found in the 9th verse, where he said: "The children of Ephraim . . . turned back in the day of battle." The next thing is described in the following verse: "They kept not the covenant of God, and refused to walk in his law." It is not surprising, therefore, that it is written, "They forgat his works, and his wonders that he had shewed them." In these verses I think we have a picture, true to life, of the decline of a soul. First, there is the refusal to participate in the battle, and the refusal to keep the covenant and to walk in His law and, finally, to forget His works.

"BECAUSE THEY BELIEVED NOT . . ."

If any of you have the notion that living a Christian life is like lying on a bed of roses you are sadly mistaken. You will find it requires more than blood in your veins to withstand the battle. But how thankful we are that we do not stand in our own strength, for the power of the Holy Spirit is at our disposal. What a joy to know that when the way seems darkest the opportunity is brightest for God to reveal His works.

What happened in the case of Israel is familiar to all of us. While the Lord led His people, as the Psalmist described in verses 12 to 16, yet they sinned more and more against the most High. They even tempted God. But what a surprise they received when the fire of the Lord was kindled against Jacob and the anger of God was exhibited. Notice *why* God's anger was exhibited. In verse 22 it is written: "Because they believed not in God, and trusted not in his salvation . . ."

Just before our Lord was crucified He revealed to His disciples that the Holy Spirit would be sent into this world to do three things: to convict men of sin, of righteousness, and of judgment. Lest they develop a mistaken notion as to what was meant by sin, our Lord immediately added, "Of sin, because they believe not on me."

It does not matter how perfect a life one may have lived; if one does not receive Jesus Christ as his Saviour, he is lost.

The Scripture is careful to tell us that the fire of God was kindled against Israel because they believed not in Him and trusted not His salvation. What is more, the failure to trust the Lord was in the face of a marvelous display of God's mercy. He commanded the clouds from above, and opened the doors of heaven and made manna to rain down upon them, and had given them of the corn of heaven, and caused men to eat angels' food. He also caused an east wind to blow in the heaven, and by His power He brought in the south wind. He rained flesh also upon them as dust, and feathered fowls like as the sand of the sea. He let it fall in the midst of their camp, round about their habitations. They did eat and were well filled; for He gave them their desire. Yet in verse 32 it is written: "For all this they sinned still, and believed not for his wondrous works."

But what happened? In verse 34 it is written: "When he slew them, then they sought him: and they returned and enquired early after God. And they remembered that God was their rock, and the high God their redeemer."

FLATTERING MOUTHS AND LYING TONGUES

Men delight to talk about the love of God, while they "soft pedal" the wrath of God, yet it is a fact that when the sun shines men do not call upon God. It is when the winds roar and the storms rage that men cry out to Him. Take the Titanic, for instance. What gaiety was aboard the ship! No one thought of God. But just as soon as that big ship struck the iceberg, and there suddenly was a consciousness of danger, the music changed from jazz to "Nearer, My God, to Thee," and men, women, and children all over the ship cried out unto God. What a revelation concerning the heart of man! Man waits until disaster comes before he inquires concerning God. How much better to call upon Him when the sun shines, so that we may acknowledge Him in the morning of our lives, the high noon of our experience, and the sunset hours of our lives.

But note, in verse 36 of the 78th Psalm it is written: "Nevertheless they did flatter him with their mouth, and they lied unto him with their tongues." Some may say, But that might have been true some thousands of years before the Christian era, but nobody flatters the Lord with their mouth and lies unto Him with their tongues now. You can go into many churches on a Sunday morning and listen to flattering lips and lying tongues! Much of it will emanate from the choir. As a friend of mine put it some time ago, "The cheapest thing ever done is to get paid for singing lies to God." What a testimony to the wickedness of the human heart, and what evidence that we need a Saviour who can cleanse us from our sin.

PSALM SEVENTY-EIGHT—PART THREE

THE PROVISION OF GOD FOR THE SIN OF HIS PEOPLE

WE now come to our closing message in the 78th Psalm, in which we shall discuss what the Lord did to restore His people to fellowship with Him. For a starting point, let us read a few verses, commencing with verse 34:

> "When he slew them, then they sought him: and they returned and enquired early after God.
>
> "And they remembered that God was their rock, and the high God their redeemer.
>
> "Nevertheless they did flatter him with their mouth, and they lied unto him with their tongues.
>
> "For their heart was not right with him, neither were they stedfast in his covenant."

What a commentary on the human heart are those four verses! In the next two verses we read what God did. It is written:

> ". . . he, being full of compassion, forgave their iniquity, and destroyed them not: yea, many a time turned he his anger away, and did not stir up all his wrath.
>
> "For he remembered that they were but flesh; a wind that passeth away, and cometh not again."

Again and again throughout the gospel records it is said that our Lord had compassion on the people. Here, in the 78th Psalm, we find He is *full* of compassion, despite the fact that the people repeatedly sinned against Him. They, like us, were full of sin, but He was full of compassion. And, as evidence of that compassion, He forgave their iniquity and destroyed them not.

Many of you have heard of the heroic manner in which John and Betty Stam went to their death in China. John Stam's favorite passage of Scripture is found in the 3rd chapter of Jeremiah's Lamentations, verses 22 to 24, where we read:

> "It is of the LORD'S mercies that we are not consumed, because his compassions fail not.
>
> "They are new every morning: great is thy faithfulness.
>
> "The LORD is my portion, saith my soul; therefore will I hope in him."

What a passage for a life text! What a comfort to be reminded that His compassions fail not and that they are new every morning.

"A WIND THAT PASSETH AWAY"

Not only did the Lord forgive the iniquity of the children of Israel, but He turned His anger away. How marvelous that God is willing to turn His anger from us, for, as verse 39 indicates: ". . . he remembered that they were but flesh; a wind that passeth away, and cometh not again."

By the way, here is an interesting description of man, "a wind that passeth away, and cometh not again." If we are honest, we must confess that it is true. Yet some people dare not think straight about life and death. Therefore they lull their souls to sleep by grasping the straw of transmigration, whereby they hope that after death their souls will move out of one body into another, and probably by the time their souls have migrated out of a dozen bodies they may appear, finally, as a peaceful cow. Don't laugh at the suggestion. One does not have to live in heathendom to lull their conscience to sleep in that manner.

Only last Sunday a young girl of seventeen, whose father is the son of a minister, came into our home for a visit. I learned that even at that early age she had already embraced Buddhism, believing it to be a logical religion, for, said she, "I despise the idea that there is such a thing as the forgiveness of sin, where one is relieved of the judgment of sin by another's death." I responded, "Yet you think it is reasonable to believe that through transmigration you will gradually purify your own soul," adding, "it cannot be done." I suggested that the root of her difficulty was not mental, but spiritual, and that the source of it was a darkened heart, and that only the Holy Spirit could illumine a soul and bring that soul to Christ. To this she answered, "I hate the words, 'I can't' and despise hearing about the Holy Spirit." Of course, I had only one passage of Scripture in mind when I listened to her response, and remember, she was but seventeen years of age, a native American, brought up in a so-called Christian home. One does not have to go to heathen lands to observe Satanic delusions.

Some years ago I was riding through the country with a few friends. We passed a field where some cows were grazing. One of them said, "My, I'd love to be a cow, for they appear to be so peaceful." Trying to be humorous, I responded, "But wouldn't you hate to be as dumb looking as cows?" But immediately my own heart was pricked by a reminder of what the Lord said through the prophet Isaiah:

> "Hear, O heavens, and give ear, O earth: for the LORD hath spoken, I have nourished and brought up children, and they have rebelled against me.
>
> "The ox knoweth his owner, and the ass his master's crib: but Israel doth not know, my people doth not consider.
>
> "Ah sinful nation, a people laden with iniquity, a seed of evildoers, children that are corrupters: they have forsaken the LORD . . ."

If such a statement could be made concerning Israel, it is a thousand times more true concerning us Gentiles. Oh, that we too might heed the Word of the Lord, when He said: "Come now, and let us reason together . . . though your sins be as scarlet, they shall be as white as snow; though they be red like crimson, they shall be as wool."

Then we are so prone to boast because we are in good health, but remember what the Lord said about us in the 78th Psalm, that we are as "a wind that passeth away, and cometh not again." How that deflates our inflation!

"HE LED THEM ON SAFELY"

Beginning at verse 52 we have another instance of what the Lord did to restore His people to fellowship with Himself. We read there:

> ". . . (He) made his own people to go forth like sheep, and guided them in the wilderness like a flock.
>
> "And he led them on safely, so that they feared not . . ."

What the Lord did for Israel in the years long ago, He is able to do for us in this day. He makes His own people to go forth like sheep and He has promised to guide them in the wilderness like a flock and lead them on safely. I believe in the safekeeping of a believer in Christ, but the "safekeeper" is Christ, and not ourselves. It is said of Israel by the Psalmist, that "he led them on *safely*, so that they feared not . . ." Our Lord Jesus used somewhat the same language when He said, concerning those of us who have received Him, "My sheep *hear my voice*, and *I know them*, and *they follow me:* and *I give* unto them eternal life; and *they shall never perish*, neither shall any man pluck them out of my hand." And, as if that were not all, our Lord added, "My Father, which gave them me, is greater than all; and no man is able to pluck them out of my Father's hand. I and my Father are one."

There are multitudes of Christians who believe that they are saved by virtue of what they do, whereas the Bible is as clear as crystal that a man is saved not by what he does, but by what Christ did.

"He Brought Them to . . . His Sanctuary"

In verse 54 of the 78th Psalm we have another of the many things that the Lord did for His sinful people. There we read:

> "And he brought them to the border of his sanctuary, even to this mountain, which his right hand had purchased."

It is interesting to note how carefully the Psalmist wrote of this, in stating that the Lord brought Israel to the *border* of His sanctuary; He did not bring them into the sanctuary. He merely brought them to the border.

However, let us contrast that with what we now enjoy in Christ. One of the miracles which took place at the time when our Lord Jesus died took place in the temple. An unseen hand rent the veil that separated the holy place from the "Holy of holies" from the top to the bottom. We are told that God thus signified that the way into the "holiest of all" was thus made manifest, or open. Therefore, we in this generation who receive the testimony that God has given concerning His Son, have a privilege that no Israelite ever enjoyed, of entering directly into the presence of God, into that place which was symbolized by the "Holy of holies." We may enter either for the purpose of worship or for intercession. We are invited to come with boldness into His presence and make our requests known unto God.

In the New Testament letter to the Hebrews we learn that the veil in the temple, which barred the way into the holiest place, foreshadowed the body of Christ, which He offered in sacrifice. Now the veil is rent because God came out to man in the death of Christ, and laid bare His own breast to the gaze of sinful man. And, as God has come out to man at Calvary, man is invited to come to God through Calvary. We are not only invited to the border of the sanctuary; we are invited to come into the sanctuary itself.

PSALM SEVENTY-NINE

"THE HEATHEN IN GOD'S INHERITANCE"

THE 79th Psalm is another Psalm ascribed to Asaph, who, as we have noted previously, was one of the chief singers who led the congregation of Israel during the time of King David's reign. Asaph not only was a skilled musician, but he possed a deep spiritual understanding of the ways of God and the longing of the human heart for fellowship with God. In this particular Psalm its musical strain is in the nature of a wail. It is not a Psalm where praise rises to the heavens with great hallelujah outbursts, or where the heart is flowing over with thanksgiving unto God; but it is a lamentation, a dirge, because of the dire straits which Israel specifically was in as a result of the defilement of Jerusalem by the Gentiles. Before commenting on the Psalm, may we read it. It has thirteen verses:

> "O God, the heathen are come into thine inheritance; thy holy temple have they defiled; they have laid Jerusalem on heaps.
>
> "The dead bodies of thy servants have they given to be meat unto the fowls of the heaven, the flesh of thy saints unto the beasts of the earth.
>
> "Their blood have they shed like water round about Jerusalem; and there was none to bury them.
>
> "We are become a reproach to our neighbours, a scorn and derision to them that are round about us.
>
> "How long, LORD? wilt thou be angry for ever? shall thy jealousy burn like fire?
>
> "Pour out thy wrath upon the heathen that have not known thee, and upon the kingdoms that have not called upon thy name.
>
> "For they have devoured Jacob, and laid waste his dwelling place.

"O remember not against us former iniquities: let thy tender mercies speedily prevent us: for we are brought very low.

"Help us, O God of our salvation, for the glory of thy name: and deliver us, and purge away our sins, for thy name's sake.

"Wherefore should the heathen say, Where is their God? let him be known among the heathen in our sight by the revenging of the blood of thy servants which is shed.

"Let the sighing of the prisoner come before thee; according to the greatness of thy power preserve thou those that are appointed to die;

"And render unto our neighbours sevenfold into their bosom their reproach, wherewith they have reproached thee, O Lord.

"So we thy people and sheep of thy pasture will give thee thanks for ever: we will shew forth thy praise to all generations."

THE PLIGHT OF ISRAEL

Asaph gave expression to a lamentation because Jerusalem was being trodden under foot by Gentiles. Some may raise the question, What has that to do with me? I answer, It has much to do with the world; therefore, it ought to have much to do with you, for whether you like it or not, Israel is a peculiar people unto God.

It is quite true, as the Apostle Paul declared, that because Israel rejected the Lord Jesus, they have been temporarily set aside so that we Gentiles might enjoy the salvation of God. However, let no one be so ignorant as to assume that God has forgotten His inheritance in Israel, for that nation is yet to enjoy its greatest glory under the reign of David's greater Son, the King of kings and Lord of lords. With that in mind as we examine the Psalm, I want to point out the historic setting, but at the same time seek to find a message for our own hearts and for our own circumstances that will aid us in coming to a full knowledge of the truth as it is in Christ, that we may rejoice in the Lord.

To begin with, let us look at the 1st verse, where the Psalmist said, "O God, the heathen are come into thine inheritance; thy holy temple have they defiled; they have laid Jerusalem on heaps." In the 2nd and 3rd verses the Psalmist described the defilement of Jerusalem; he saw the dead bodies of the servants of the Lord strewn over the land, and he saw Jerusalem as a fountain of blood, and the dead in the city more numerous than it was possible to bury.

Profane as well as sacred history tells us of many occasions when blood flowed in Jerusalem, but it is a serious question whether any period of distress was comparable to the time when Titus, the Roman general, laid waste that city in A. D. 70, at which time the words of our Lord were fulfilled to the dotting of the "i" and the crossing of the "t," when He said concerning the temple that not one stone would be left upon another. But before Israel will enjoy the blessing of God, in full possession of her land, she will undergo severe persecution and distress far more terrible than at any previous period in history.

That statement might have been seriously questioned a few years ago, but no one who is acquainted with what is now transpiring in the world will hesitate to receive it. Who could have realized, for example, that such hatred would ever be manifested against the Jew as has been witnessed in Germany during the past year?

"THE HEATHEN IN GOD'S INHERITANCE"

But our Psalm calls attention to the fact that the heathen (the Gentiles) are in the place called the inheritance of God. "O God," said Asaph, "the heathen are come into thine inheritance; thy holy temple have they defiled; they have laid Jerusalem on heaps." Is that of any interest to us? Indeed it is, for we have a comparable situation in our present day. Just as Jerusalem is referred to as the inheritance of God, so the professing church of Jesus Christ in the earth can be referred to as the inheritance of God. And when we examine the professing church of Jesus Christ in this world, we can as definitely say to God as did Asaph in this Psalm, "O God, the heathen are come into thine inheritance . . ."

The sad part of Christendom, as we observe it at the present time, is the fact that one can go from church to church and seek to get a message that will meet the heart's crying need of God, and instead of being given bread one will be given a stone; instead of being given a "Thus saith the Lord," one will be given the guesses of a science falsely so-called. How true such a statement is, is all too apparent to need any confirmation, but, as an example, I might refer to a letter which I received from one of our listeners in Philadelphia. She told of a young grandson who had returned from Sunday school. As the child spoke of certain pictures he had seen at Sunday school, the grandmother asked the youngster, "What were the pictures you saw?" and he responded, "A movie of Mickey Mouse." When his grandmother displayed amazement he immediately said, "Grandma, *ours is a modern* Sunday school."

Some may suggest that this is an isolated case, but I do not think so. How true that today we might cry out even as the Psalmist did almost three thousand years ago, "O God, the heathen are come into thine inheritance . . ." While we lament the fact that the "world" has come into the organized church, and in many cases even into the pulpit, such a situation does not disturb the faith of a believer in Christ. The fact is, he has been warned again and again in the Scripture that such a thing would take place. For example, in the Apostle Paul's second letter to the Corinthians, in the 11th chapter, we are cautioned: "For if he that cometh preacheth another Jesus, whom we have not preached, or if ye receive another spirit, which ye have not received, or another gospel, which ye have not accepted, ye might well bear with him." Right at the beginning of the Christian era there were already some in the professed Christian church who preached another Jesus, were energized by another spirit, and proclaimed another gospel. Should we be surprised to find a comparable situation in our churches today? Indeed not, for the apostle, in the 13th verse of the 11th chapter of 2nd Corinthians, said:

> "For such are false apostles, deceitful workers, transforming themselves into the apostles of Christ.
>
> "And no marvel; for Satan himself is transformed into an angel of light.
>
> "Therefore it is no great thing if his ministers also be transformed as the ministers of righteousness; whose end shall be according to their works."

A true believer in the Scripture is not surprised at this situation. As he examines it, he concludes that it is a natural sequence. Since the gospel is true, it is not amazing that the Devil, whether you believe in him or not, is occupied with a counterfeit gospel. This entire world of ours is a religious world. On the one side is the eternal God, in Christ, beckoning men and women to worship Him, while on the other side is Satan, whom the Bible calls "the god of this age," beckoning men and women to worship him. Well might we add with the Psalmist, "O God, the heathen are come into thine inheritance . . ."

ISRAEL'S INIQUITIES

Now let us notice the cause for this strange situation in Jerusalem over which Asaph lamented. In verse 4 he said, "We are become a reproach to our neighbours . . ." In verse 5 he asked, "How long, LORD? wilt thou be angry for ever?" In verse 6 he invited the Lord to pour out His wrath on them that had not known Him, and in verse 8 he pleaded with God not to remember against Israel former iniquities, but rather to let His tender mercies speedily come to their aid, for, said Asaph, "we are brought very low."

You will notice that in the case of Israel her distress could be laid to her iniquities. So I believe that the troubles of the Christian church may be laid to our iniquities. Well might we take the same position as Asaph has done in the 79th Psalm and confess our sins before the Lord and invite Him to pour out His tender mercies upon us.

However, in the midst of the lamentation there is a ray of light. In the 9th verse of this Psalm, Asaph said: "Help us, O God of our salvation, for the glory of thy name: and deliver us, and purge away our sins, for thy name's sake."

What a passage! The Psalmist pleaded for a revelation of the tender mercies of the Lord, not on any basis of human merit, but on the basis of unearned grace. He asked for help, not for Israel's sake, but for the glory of the Lord's own name. He prayed for deliverance and for the purging of Israel's sins, not for their sake, but for the sake of the name of the Lord. How that reminds us of the New Testament. It touches our daily prayer life as we come into the presence of our Lord and pray for cleansing from the defilement of sin, as we pray for the blessing of God, and for the help of God, not for our sake, not for any merit in ourselves, but for the sake of the name of our Lord. How valuable is the name of our Lord Jesus Christ!

To you who have not acknowledged the Lord Jesus Christ, I can only say that no amount of lamentation on your part can avail. No amount of praying can save you. No tears, no human effort of any kind can remove the guilt of sin. Only the sacrifice of Christ avails for guilty men. We are not saved by anything we do. We are not urged to pray to be saved. We are invited to believe and receive Christ, and we *shall* be saved. Then, because we are saved by grace, we can pray. But the order should never be reversed.

The last verse closes with a note of hope:

> "So we thy people and sheep of thy pasture will give
> thee thanks for ever: we will shew forth thy praise to
> all generations."

What a future for Israel—she will yet show forth the praise of God to all generations.

PSALM EIGHTY

"THE MAN OF GOD'S RIGHT HAND"

THE 80th Psalm is a delightful Psalm. This Psalm is closely related to the 79th. Both are in the minor key and are intended for lamentations. However, there is a marked difference between the two. In the 79th Psalm the writer was more occupied with Jerusalem the city, and the nation as a whole, whereas in the 80th the Psalmist concerned himself with the individual. Because of this, it is a very personal Psalm. We can find much in it of profit to ourselves.

In the first six verses the Psalmist wrote:

> "Give ear, O Shepherd of Israel, thou that leadest Joseph like a flock; thou that dwellest between the cherubims, shine forth.
>
> "Before Ephraim and Benjamin and Manasseh stir up thy strength, and come and save us.
>
> "Turn us again, O God, and cause thy face to shine; and we shall be saved.
>
> "O LORD God of hosts, how long wilt thou be angry against the prayer of thy people?
>
> "Thou feedest them with the bread of tears; and givest them tears to drink in great measure.
>
> "Thou makest us a strife unto our neighbours: and our enemies laugh among themselves."

What a message is to be found in this portion of the Psalm! There is the prayer to God, under the title of "Shepherd of Israel," to give ear to the lamentation of His people, with a reminder of His relationship with His people. Said Asaph: "Give ear, O Shepherd of Israel, thou that leadest Joseph like a flock; thou that dwellest between the cherubims, shine forth."

It is singular that Asaph should remind the Lord that He was a Shepherd to Joseph, especially considering the situation in which the nation Israel was found; for, despite the contradictory circumstances that took place in Joseph's life, there was abundant evidence later that through all those vicissitudes the Lord was definitely leading Joseph.

The eternal God frequently is referred to under the title of "Shepherd." In fact, our Lord Jesus took this title unto Himself. In the 10th chapter of John's Gospel He said: "I am the good shepherd: the good shepherd giveth his life for the sheep."

Under the Old Testament economy the sheep gave their lives for the shepherd, but in the New Testament manifestation of God's grace the Shepherd gave His life for the sheep. As one meditates upon the title of "Shepherd" as applied to the Lord Jesus, his heart leaps with thanksgiving. Oh, the wonder that we can have such precious intimacy and fellowship with the Lord as is so beautifully exemplified in the dealings of a shepherd with his sheep.

Mark you, the Psalmist not only gave the Lord the title of "Shepherd of Israel," but he reminded the Lord of His active relationship with Joseph, for he said: ". . . O Shepherd of Israel, thou that *leadest* Joseph like a flock . . ."

There is a wealth of meaning embodied in the word *leadest*. "Thou that *leadest* Joseph like a flock." Here God is seen actively engaged in the work of a shepherd and dealing with Joseph like the sheep of His flock. In that word *leadest* there is all that is involved in the tender care of a shepherd over his sheep. Here we see:

> The shepherd feeds his sheep.
> He watches over his sheep.
> He defends them.
> He seeks to reduce them when they wax fat.
> He shears them of their wool so that their fruit may be enjoyed.
> He handles them tenderly and carefully.
> He cures them when they are ill.
> He washes them when they are defiled.
> He leads them when they are going through dangerous paths.
> He even carries them when their pathway is too encumbered with difficulties for their feet to tread safely.

Everything that a good shepherd does for his sheep the Lord did for Joseph, and what the Lord did for Joseph He does for every believer in Christ this very day. We who know the Lord, as we contemplate Him, should raise our hearts in praise and thanksgiving for such a shepherd-like Saviour.

CONVERSION: THE WORK OF THE LORD

In the 80th Psalm, the relationship between the Lord and Israel, His people, had been broken off because of sin and failure. Therefore, the Psalmist prayed for a restoration of the former relationship. He invited the Lord not only to give ear, but to *shine forth*. Four times in this Psalm Asaph invited the Lord to *shine forth*.

Asaph was aware that there was a thick cloud between Israel and the Lord. He wished the Lord to remove that cloud, to shine forth in His own glory and mercy, for when that takes place Israel is glad. What is true of Israel is true of us.

Another interesting thing is to be found in verse 3, where the Psalmist invited the Lord to accomplish something in the lives of the individuals of Israel, when he cried out: *"Turn us again, O God, and cause thy face to shine; and we shall be saved."* Incidentally, this verse is the theme song of the Psalm, for it is to be found three times; in verse 3, again in verse 7, and finally in verse 19. Each time there is the invitation: "Turn us again, O God, and cause thy face to shine; and we shall be saved." As I was interested in that phrase, "Turn us again," I decided to look it up in the original Hebrew. I discovered that the word "turn" in Hebrew is *shoov*. I learned that the word means *to convert* or *to change*. I also noted that several times in the Old Testament, in our English version, the word is translated by the English word "convert." For instance, in the 51st Psalm, verse 13, we read: "Then will I teach transgressors thy ways; and sinners shall be *converted* unto thee." Again in the 19th Psalm, verse 7, we read: "The law of the LORD is perfect, *converting* the soul . . ." In each, there is that same Hebrew word *shoov*. We could go on and mention several other instances where the same word is used and translated *convert*.

Thus, Asaph asked the Lord to convert Israel, to cause His face to shine, and when He does, Israel shall be saved. What was true about Israel is true about us sinners of the Gentiles. But, mark you, conversion is a work of the Lord. Asaph said, "Convert us again." We cannot convert ourselves. That is the work of the Lord.

There is one other matter in connection with the first portion of the Psalm that should be considered before passing on to the next section. In verse 4, Asaph asked how long the Lord would retain His anger against His people, and in verse 5 he stated that the Lord fed them with bread of tears, and their drink likewise was composed of tears.

There is no prosperity for a child of God out of the will of God. If we do not walk in the light, as He is in the light, we do not have fellowship with the Lord. We are not in the sunshine of God's grace. When we walk afar off we invite dangers. Frequently it becomes necessary for the Lord to mingle our bread with tears. Likewise, He causes our drink to be filled with tears. It is a serious situation for a Christian to walk apart from his Lord. If we are in circumstances where our bread is bitter and our water accentuates our thirst, it might possibly be due to our failure to walk in His way. If such is the case, God help us to do just what Asaph did in this Psalm—invite the Lord to cause His face to shine upon us once more.

"A VINE OUT OF EGYPT"

In the second section of the 80th Psalm, beginning with verse 8, Asaph spoke of Israel under the imagery of a vine. Commencing with verse 8 we read:

> "Thou hast brought a vine out of Egypt: thou hast cast out the heathen, and planted it.
>
> "Thou preparedst room before it, and didst cause it to take deep root, and it filled the land.
>
> "The hills were covered with the shadow of it and the boughs thereof were like the goodly cedars.
>
> "She sent out her boughs unto the sea, and her branches unto the river."

Notice how the Psalmist called attention to the carefulness of the husbandman in cultivating His vine. He brought Israel out of Egypt. He called Israel a vine. This is also beautifully set forth in the 5th chapter of Isaiah, where in verse 7 we read: "For the vineyard of the LORD of hosts is the house of Israel, and the men of Judah his pleasant plant . . ." In that same prophecy the Lord raised the question, "What could have been done more to my vineyard, that I have not done in it?" In the 80th Psalm we learn that the Lord brought them out of Egypt. He cast out the inhabitants of the land in order to plant Israel in the Promised Land. He caused the vine to take deep root and fill the land. All the neighboring peoples enjoyed the blessings of Israel's presence in the land. As a result of the prosperity of God, Israel's boughs were sent out unto the sea and her branches unto the river. But Israel failed the Lord bitterly. The Lord, as the husbandman, sought fruit from His vine, but, instead of finding pleasant fruit, He found His vine brought forth wild grapes.

What happened is clearly presented to us in verse 12 of our Psalm. The Lord broke down the hedges about the vine, so that the boar of the wood wasted it and the wild beast of the field devoured it. God caused fire to destroy the very vine He had planted. He laid the entire land waste because of the sin of His people.

A vine is of no value except to bear fruit. The wood of the vine is worthless except for the fire. It cannot be used to make anything. A vine, therefore, is only valuable to the extent it yields fruit. God sought fruit from Israel but, instead, He found wild grapes. But God has another vine.

CHRIST, THE VINE

We mentioned at the beginning of our study that the title "Shepherd" is ascribed to our Lord Jesus in the New Testament. Therefore it was He who led Joseph like a flock. It is also interesting to find, in the New Testament, that our Lord takes unto Himself the title of "the vine." In the Gospel according to John, our Lord employs the same imagery which Asaph used in the 80th Psalm, in referring to Israel. In the 15th chapter of St. John's Gospel our Lord said: "I am *the true vine*, and my Father is the husbandman." He also added, "I am the vine, ye are the branches . . ." By "ye" He meant those who confessed Christ as their Saviour and acknowledged Him as their Lord. We are cautioned by our Lord to abide in the vine, for, as we abide in the vine and He abides in us, the fruit of the vine becomes a joy to the Father's heart.

Our Lord is the vine, we are the branches. A branch does nothing but bear fruit. It takes the sap from the vine and has the honor of yielding luscious fruit. God is never disappointed in His Son; in fact, He is the only One of whom He witnessed, ". . . in thee I am well pleased." We can bring honor to our Lord by abiding in Him, so that the vine, Christ, may have His fruit displayed in our lives.

There is one more subject in this Psalm we should note before closing. In verse 14, the Psalmist cried out: "Return, we beseech thee, O God of hosts: look down from heaven, and behold, and visit this vine . . ." God will indeed answer that prayer. The Lord Jesus *will* return to this earth. He *will* visit Israel once more.

That it is of the Messiah that the Psalmist was pleading is evident from verses 17 and 18, where he prayed: "Let thy hand be upon the man of thy right hand, upon the son of man whom thou madest strong for thyself. So will not we go back from thee: quicken us, and we will call upon thy name."

PSALM EIGHTY-ONE

"THE FINEST WHEAT AND THE BEST HONEY"

THE 81st Psalm bears the interesting inscription: "To the chief Musician upon Gittith." We find a similar inscription to the 8th Psalm. The title "Gittith" was probably given to a musical instrument which was used in the home of Obed-edom, the Gittite, during the time that the ark of the covenant rested in his house.

God blessed that man's house while the ark was on his premises, so that it is well within the realm of possibility that great joy prevailed in his home. And where there is joy there is usually a song. So the Psalms that have the inscription "Gittith" are Psalms of praise, reminding us of the great joy that abides in a home where the Lord is honored and worshipped.

"SING ALOUD UNTO GOD"

It isn't surprising, therefore, that in the 81st Psalm we find an exhortation to "Sing aloud unto God," accompanied with an invitation to the musicians to play upon the timbrel, the harp, and the trumpet.

> "Sing aloud unto God our strength; make a joyful noise unto the God of Jacob.
> "Take a psalm, and bring hither the timbrel, the pleasant harp with the psaltery.
> "Blow up the trumpet in the new moon, in the time appointed, on our solemn feast day.
> "For this was a statute for Israel, and a law of the God of Jacob.
> "This he ordained in Joseph for a testimony, when he went out through the land of Egypt: where I heard a language that I understood not.
> "I removed his shoulder from the burden: his hands were delivered from the pots.
> "Thou calledst in trouble, and I delivered thee; I answered thee in the secret place of thunder: I proved thee at the waters of Meribah. Selah."

Notice that the little word "Selah" is found at the end of the 7th verse. There has been much discussion as to the meaning of the word, but at least everyone is agreed that it was intended to atract attention, to invite the reader to reconsider the subject and to enjoy its message. Thus we will reconsider these few verses.

In the first place, as we have already suggested, there is the exhortation to "Sing aloud unto God our strength: make a joyful noise unto the God of Jacob."

God gave Israel a song, as He wanted His people to sing, for a singing nation is always a happy nation. So a singing Christian is always a happy Christian.

The 6th verse of the 81st Psalm is interesting, where the Lord said concerning Israel: "I removed his shoulder from the burden: his hands were delivered from the pots." That is extraordinarily interesting, for it touches us right at our daily tasks.

If you are burdened with a heavy load, and the grind of everyday life is becoming monotonous, may I suggest, even if He does not remove the burden at the present moment, that some day you will know for a reality that the Scripture is true when it suggests that the "sufferings of this present time are not worthy to be compared with the glory which shall be revealed in us." I have quoted the 18th verse of the 8th chapter of Romans. Will you note that I have quoted it accurately! The Apostle Paul was not talking of the glory which shall be revealed *unto us,* but he talked of the glory which shall be revealed *in us.*

In the 7th verse the Lord reminded Israel of His work for them, in saying: "Thou calledst in trouble, and I delivered thee; I answered thee in the secret place of thunder; I proved thee at the waters of Meribah. Selah." You who are familiar with the Old Testament, particularly the wanderings of Israel, will recall what the Lord had in mind and to what event He referred. You know what comfort you have received from God's dealings with Israel. To you who are troubled, may I suggest that when your waters are bitter and trouble encompasses you and there seems to be the constant roaring of thunder, so that you question whether you can even hear the voice of God, may it be a source of comfort to you to know that if you will only call upon Him He will hear you. All you have to do is to test Him. Pour out your trouble to Him, call upon Him, and see if He will not shine upon you in His grace.

"OPEN THY MOUTH WIDE"

Commencing with the 8th verse we have the second division of the Psalm, which is another exhortation by the Psalmist, in the name of the Lord. We shall read, commencing with verse 8 to the end of the Psalm:

> "Hear, O my people, and I will testify unto thee:
> O Israel, if thou wilt hearken unto me;

> "There shall no strange God be in thee; neither shalt
> thou worship any strange god.

> "I am the LORD thy God, which brought thee out of
> the land of Egypt: open thy mouth wide, and I will fill
> it.
>
> "But my people would not hearken to my voice; and
> Israel would none of me.
>
> "So I gave them up unto their own hearts' lust: and
> they walked in their own counsels.
>
> "Oh that my people had hearkened unto me, and Israel
> had walked in my ways!
>
> "I should soon have subdued their enemies, and turned
> my hand against their adversaries.
>
> "The haters of the LORD should have submitted them-
> selves unto him: but their time should have endured
> for ever.
>
> "He should have fed them also with the finest of the
> wheat: and with honey out of the rock should I have
> satisfied thee."

This exhortation is addressed to the Lord's ancient, earthly people, Israel, but let none of us think that its application to our own circumstances is unwarranted. If we only knew the grace of God and His love, we would more readily respond to the message contained in the 10th verse, where the Lord said: ". . . open thy mouth wide, and I will fill it."

That, of course, is figurative speech, but we know its import. Just as surely as He said He would fill every open mouth of Israel, so He will fill our mouths, if we will only open them wide enough. The sad thing is that we have been guilty of the same transgressions as the children of Israel. Thus the Lord can say about us, as He did about Israel, ". . . my people would not hearken to my voice; and Israel would none of me."

JEHOVAH-JESUS

We also should notice the heartfelt compassion and disappointment expressed by the Lord in the 13th verse, where He said: "Oh that my peo-ple had hearkened unto me, and Israel had walked in my ways!" Doesn't that remind us of the time when our Lord Jesus wept over the city of Jerusalem, as He left the temple for the last time. At that time He said:

> "O Jerusalem, Jerusalem, thou that killest the prophets,
> and stonest them which are sent unto thee, how often
> would I have gathered thy children together, even as a
> hen gathered her chickens under her wings, and ye would
> not!
>
> "Behold, your house is left unto you desolate.
>
> "For I say unto you, Ye shall not see me henceforth,
> till ye shall say, Blessed is he that cometh in the name
> of the Lord."

By the way, as we read that quotation from the closing verses of the 23rd chapter of St. Matthew's Gospel, did we get the significance of what our Lord Jesus said, concerning Jerusalem: "how often would I have gathered thy children together." What does that mean? It means that He who was known as Jehovah, in the Old Testament, who constantly sought to gather His people together, is none other than the Lord Jesus Christ. Thus, it is our Lord Jesus who is the speaker in the 13th verse of the 81st Psalm, which reads: "Oh that my people had hearkened unto me, and Israel had walked in my ways!"

We must take a message for our own heart from this portion of the Word, for we professed Christians, in my judgment, are much more guilty than Israel ever dreamed of being. With the revelation of the full grace of God, we have been indifferent and callous. Undoubtedly our lack of power and influence over the lives of others is traceable to our own failure to walk before the Lord. As God said of Israel, in the last verse of the 81st Psalm, that He would have fed them the finest of the wheat, and with honey out of the rock would He have satisfied them, so we, too, may enjoy the finest of the wheat and the honey out of the rock, if we walk in fellowship with our Lord and are obedient to Him.

By the way, notice something in that last verse which, at first, may seem far fetched, but upon further consideration we think otherwise. In that verse we have the food which God would have given to Israel, which He speaks of as the finest of the wheat and honey out of the rock. What is meant by those two things—the finest of the wheat and the honey out of the rock? Did the Lord merely mean the wheat that grows out of the ground, and the honey the bee puts in the rock? No, indeed!

In the 12th chapter of St. John's Gospel our Lord spoke of Himself as "a corn of wheat." He said, in the 24th verse of that chapter: "Verily, verily, I say unto you, Except a corn of wheat fall into the ground and die, it abideth alone: but if it die, it bringeth forth much fruit." He gave that statement in answer to a company of Greeks who had come to Jerusalem to worship at the feast, and who inquired of one of His disciples, "Sir, we would see Jesus." That may seem a strange answer to the inquiry, but just as our Lord told those Greeks that if a corn of wheat die, it bringeth forth much fruit, so that message is true today.

If we are to see the Lord, we are to see Him as a corn of wheat that went into the ground and died. Through His resurrection He became the bread of eternal life to everyone who appropriates Him. So when God promised that He would feed the children of Israel the finest of the wheat, He was speaking of His own Son. Each of us, who have appropriated the Lord Jesus Christ as the bread of God, can bear testimony that we have enjoyed Him as the finest of the wheat.

Then, honey out of the rock. What about that? The Lord is spoken of constantly in the Scripture as the rock of our salvation, and that title is particularly ascribed to the Lord Jesus Christ. The honey speaks of sweetness. It is not an artificial sweetness, but it is natural sweetness. Invariably, throughout the Scripture, honey is the symbol for joy. It is only the Christian who knows true, natural joy, not a joy that is pumped up and self-generated, that oftentimes is merely a covering for sorrow. True joy is deep, and its source is an abiding knowledge of Christ Jesus, our Lord. To you who know Him not, all I can say is—taste Him; appropriate Christ as the bread of God. As you do, you will find He not only sustains, but He will give you joy, abounding joy. That is what you will receive, simply by believing that God so loved you that He robbed heaven of its glory, when He sent His Son to die for your sins.

PSALM EIGHTY-TWO

WHEN GOD JUDGES THE JUDGES

THE Bible is a very interesting book. I can hear some of you saying, That is not an original thought. I confess that it is not, but now and then certain portions of Scripture impress themselves upon our minds in a way that makes that statement fresh and timely. I was impressed with the fact in reading over this 82nd Psalm, in which our meditation will be found. When I first read the Psalm it did not seem to contain much of interest that would lend itself to a radio program. My first impression was to pass it by and take the next Psalm, yet I felt a little convicted as I turned the page, so I went back and re-read the Psalm. As I read, and meditated in it, what wonderful things I found lying beneath the surface.

Some years ago I visited a friend of mine who was a student at the Moody Bible Institute. He said something to the effect that salvation is free. It is ours, simply because our Lord finished the work. But, said he, a knowledge of the Scripture comes by the sweat of the brow and by much knee practice. It is because most of us do not take time in the presence of our Lord, or time to study the Scripture, that we are unable to see its beauty.

So as we read the 82nd Psalm, which is composed of eight short verses, notice the many subjects touched upon therein. This is another of the Asaphic Psalms:

> "God standeth in the congregation of the mighty; he judgeth among the gods.
>
> "How long will ye judge unjustly, and accept the persons of the wicked? Selah.
>
> "Defend the poor and fatherless: do justice to the afflicted and needy.
>
> "Deliver the poor and needy: rid them out of the hand of the wicked.
>
> "They know not, neither will they understand; they walk on in darkness: all the foundations of the earth are out of course.
>
> "I have said, Ye are gods; and all of you are children of the most High.
>
> "But ye shall die like men, and fall like one of the princes.
>
> "Arise, O God, judge the earth: for thou shalt inherit all nations."

Charles H. Spurgeon has an interesting note on this Psalm, which is worth quoting. Says Spurgeon:

> "Asaph's sermon before the judges is before us in the 82nd Psalm. He speaks very plainly and his song is rather characterized by strength than by sweetness. We have here a clear proof that all Psalms and hymns need not be direct expressions of praise to God. We may, according to the example of this Psalm, admonish one another in our Psalms. Asaph, no doubt, saw round him much bribery and corruption and while David punished it with sword, he resolved to scourge it with a prophetic Psalm. In doing so the sweet singer was not forsaking his profession as a musician for the Lord but rather was practically carrying it out in another department. He was praising God when he rebuked the sin which dishonoured Him and if he was not making music he was hushing discord when he bade them to dispense justice with impartiality."

In that brief paragraph by Spurgeon we have a synopsis of the contents of the 82nd Psalm. The sweet singer of Israel addressed his Psalm particularly to the rulers and judges of the people. What he said to them may be said with even greater force for the hour in which we live, for if there is one thing that is disturbing to common decency these days it is the corruption of our courts.

Recently I asked Dr. Herbert Lockyer, of Liverpool, England, what were his impressions of our country, particularly from a political viewpoint. He had been in our country for almost eight months, during which time he had traveled about twenty thousand miles and visited the major cities of the Midwest and East. In response to my question, he stated that what had impressed him most was the moral corruption among American politicians. Said he, "We in England would never stand for such a situation as you have in America." Then he cited a case of four magistrates of a certain eastern city, who had just been indicted for bribery. He said, "We never hear of anything like that in our country."

His comment was very interesting, and in the light of the 82nd Psalm takes on particular significance. It is no secret that in a large number of cases, our politicians select our judges. One only has to be in court for a short period to observe the influence the politician exercises over the court.

THE BUSINESS OF THE CHURCH

Now then, let us look more closely at the first two verses of this Psalm. Before we do so, however, may I preface my remarks with a statement which I desire to make as clear as I know how. I do not believe that it is the business of the church to meddle in politics. Therefore, I do not believe that it is the business of the preacher to meddle in politics. I do not believe that the church of our Lord Jesus Christ has any right to do any other business than to preach the gospel. I do not believe the church should be occupied with social service, or seek to make politics clean, or strive for the enactment of certain laws designed to improve the moral character of individuals by a series of prohibitions. I do not believe that character or morals can be legislated. I am a firm believer in the gospel of the grace of God and in the redemption which our Lord Jesus accomplished on the cross. Thus in every broadcast I have endeavored to present the gospel as clearly as I know how. Yet, while I appreciate that it is my business, as a minister of the gospel, to present to the unsaved the way of salvation, let no one in authority assume that God is any the less occupied with the affairs of the sons of men, or that government is not under His jurisdiction, or that presidents, statesmen, governors, and judges are not responsible to God. The Bible is very clear in stating: ". . . there is no power but of God: the powers that be are ordained of God . . . For he (that is, the one in authority) is the minister of God . . . for good. But if thou do that which is evil, be afraid; for he beareth not the sword in vain: for he is the minister of God, a revenger to execute wrath upon him that doeth evil." Because of this passage in the 13th chapter of Paul's letter to the Romans, all Christians are called upon to pay ". . . tribute to whom tribute is due; custom to whom custom; fear to whom fear; honour to whom honour."

Authority, vested in a judge or ruler, makes that judge or ruler accountable to God for his judgeship or his rulership. Therefore, Asaph said: "God standeth in the congregation of the mighty; he judgeth among the gods." It is interesting to note that Asaph spoke of judges as "gods," for they stand in the place of God to exercise judgment. Yet, in the presence of these "gods," God standeth in the congregation. If you have ever visited a court, you know that the people in the courtroom arise while the judge enters and must not be seated until the judge sits down on his bench. I thoroughly believe that if our judges were aware that God is *standing* in the court, upon the behalf of His creatures, there would be less corruption in our courts. Note that God is not sitting on the bench with the judge, He is standing with His congregation before the judge. What an awakening some of our judges will have when God demands an account of their stewardship!

Thus, Asaph said: "How long will ye judge unjustly, and accept the persons of the wicked?" Then he gave his instructions: "Defend the poor and fatherless: do justice to the afflicted and needy. Deliver the poor and needy: rid them out of the hand of the wicked." It was Rutherford, I think, who once said that judges "are not the creatures of kings, to execute their pleasures, and do not derive their power from the monarch, but are authorized by God Himself, as much as the king, and are, therefore, bound to execute justice, whether the monarch desires it or no."

When, therefore, the Holy Spirit energized Asaph to write the 82nd Psalm and then to preserve it for the future posterity, He did so because God has an interest in the affairs of the sons of men. Rulership and government are in the hands of Almighty God, and while for the moment He has given it to the sons of men, they hold it in stewardship and must account to Him for their reign.

As one reads this Psalm and then observes what is taking place in the world, one must conclude that we are living in a misgoverned world.

THE TRUE JUDGE

How true is Asaph's comment in verse 5, "They know not, neither will they understand; they walk on in darkness: all the foundations of the earth are out of course." The only one who can judge righteously is the One who is able to detect the motives of men's hearts as well as their actions, and discern distinctly between right and wrong. That one is none other than the Lord Jesus Christ, who said:

> ". . . the Father judgeth no man, but hath committed all judgment unto the Son:
>
> "That all men should honour the Son, even as they honour the Father. He that honoureth not the Son honoureth not the Father which hath sent him."

During His public ministry, our Lord Jesus did not exercise authority or judgeship, for He came not to condemn the world, but that the world through Him might be saved. He is to exercise judgeship and rulership when He returns the second time. Therefore He said, as recorded in the 8th chapter of St. John's Gospel, the 15th and 16th verses:

> "Ye (meaning earthly judges) judge after the flesh; I judge no man.
>
> "And yet if I judge, my judgment is true: for I am not alone, but I and the Father that sent me."

He it is who will some day judge this world in righteousness. God speed the day!

Now let us look at the 6th and 7th verses of the Psalm, where it is written:

> "I have said, Ye are gods; and all of you are children of the most High.
>
> "But ye shall die like men, and fall like one of the princes."

It is interesting to observe how our Lord made use of the 6th verse of the 82nd Psalm. In the 10th chapter of St. John's Gospel, our Lord Jesus said:

> "I and my Father are one.
>
> "Then the Jews took up stones again to stone him.
>
> "Jesus answered them, Many good works have I shewed you from my Father; for which of those works do ye stone me?
>
> "The Jews answered him, saying, For a good work we stone thee not; but for blasphemy; and because that thou, being a man, makest thyself God.
>
> "Jesus answered them, Is it not written in your law, I said, Ye are gods?
>
> "If he called them gods, unto whom the word of God came, and the scripture cannot be broken;

"Say ye of him, whom the Father hath sanctified, and sent into the world, Thou blasphemest; because I said, I am the Son of God?

"If I do not the works of my Father, believe me not.

"But if I do, though ye believe not me, believe the works: that ye may know, and believe, that the Father is in me, and I in him."

Thus, when Asaph wrote, in the 82nd Psalm: "I have said, Ye are gods; and all of you are children of the most High" he reminded the rulers of Israel that their position, where they acted as gods, exercising judgment, made them responsible to the most High. When our judges recognize that they are responsible to the most High, that they hold in their hands the sword of judgment and that they wield it in the place of God, they will exercise justice, mercy, and truth. This does not presuppose that a judge cannot make a mistake, but when a judge recognizes his position and his duty, then the governed are glad. It was said of Francis the First, of France, that when a woman kneeled before him to beg justice, he bade her stand up, for, said he, "Woman, it is justice that I owe thee, and justice thou shalt have; if thou beg anything of me, let it be mercy."

THE PANACEA FOR CORRUPTION

Human nature has not changed one iota since the fall of our first parents, Adam and Eve. Corruption has broken out, even among men of high place, in every generation. In David's time there was corruption and bribery. Therefore, Asaph wrote that "ye shall die like men, and fall like one of the princes."

In our own day corruption is also apparent. Frequently men in high places act as if they were responsible to no one but themselves. Yet, the Scripture is as true today when it says: "ye shall die like men, and fall like one of the princes."

If the 82nd Psalm ended with the 7th verse, we should have occasion to be disquieted. To contemplate that with all the passing years, approximately one thousand years from the time Asaph wrote the Psalm to the coming of Christ, and approximately two thousand years since His coming —that in all those three thousand years human nature has not changed one iota, ought to be sufficient to discourage anyone who dons the garb of a reformer. Yet, the reformer seems to profit less from his experience and from the experience of history than any other individual in the world. A Christian is not a reformer. He is a preacher of a gospel. The gospel is good news to the sinful man. It tells him that God is able to righteously save people, on the ground that His Son paid the penalty of sin. That settles the matter of the individual's relationship to God. As for the family of men, and the relationship of individuals to society, we thank God that the 8th verse will some day be fulfilled, where Asaph cried: "Arise, O God, judge the earth: for thou shalt inherit all nations."

The Christian whose faith embraces the return of the Lord Jesus to judge the world and inherit the nations looks beyond the present to the future, to the return of the Man of God, who will rule as King of kings and Lord of lords and whose rule will be in righteousness and truth only.

PSALM EIGHTY-THREE

A SLEEPING SAVIOUR

THE content of the 83rd Psalm is so timely as to create the impression that it was written yesterday, whereas in fact, it is several thousands of years old.

It is the last of the Psalms ascribed to Asaph. It is in the nature of an invitation to God, who alone is known by the name Jehovah, to reveal Himself on the behalf of His people, that men may know that He is the most High over all the earth.

Of course, the Psalm has a distinctly Israelitish color and primarily concerns that nation. At the present hour the Jew once again occupies the front pages of our newspapers. The past two or three years have seen a concerted effort upon the part of one of the major powers to definitely extinguish the influence of the Jew in that particular land. The reports that have come out of that country have reverberated throughout the world, so that all nations are interested in observing these conditions and are raising a number of questions as to their solution.

Therefore this Psalm is so timely, that as we read a few of its verses I am sure you will agree that it almost appears as if the writer lived in our own day and as if he were jotting down the circumstances that are taking place this very hour. We shall look now at the first five verses:

> "Keep not thou silence, O God: hold not thy peace, and be not still, O God.
>
> "For, lo, thine enemies make a tumult: and they that hate thee have lifted up the head.

> "They have taken crafty counsel against thy people,
> and consulted against thy hidden ones.
>
> "They have said, Come, and let us cut them off from
> being a nation; that the name of Israel may be no more
> in remembrance.
>
> "For they have consulted together with one consent:
> they are confederate against thee . . ."

Repeatedly I have stated that the Bible has much to say about the Jewish question. Any honest, clear-thinking student of the Bible must confess that the prophets of the Old Testament, our Lord Jesus Christ, and the writers of the New Testament were all in accord in voicing the prediction that Israel is yet to enjoy her greatest hour of prosperity and peace and that when she does, the nations of the earth will be blessed, for the blessings of Abraham must flow to all the nations of the earth.

THE PRESENT AND FUTURE WORK OF GOD

That event, however, requires the return of Israel's Messiah, whom we believe to be our Lord Jesus. Israel does not believe Him to be the Messiah and therefore has rejected His claim. Nevertheless, even her own prophets bore witness that the Messiah would be rejected and afterwards received. Because of the rejection by Israel of her Messiah, the Gentiles, who previously had no covenant relationship with God, were extended the gift of God's grace and eternal salvation.

At the present time God is taking out of the Gentiles a people for His name and, as James the Apostle said in the first council of the church, at Jerusalem, which record is found in the 15th chapter of the Acts of the Apostles,

> ". . . to this agree the words of the prophets; as it is
> written,
>
> "After this (that is, after the taking out of the Gentiles
> a people for His own name) I will return, and will
> build again the tabernacle of David, which is fallen
> down; and I will build again the ruins thereof, and I
> will set it up:
>
> "That the residue of men might seek after the Lord,
> and all the Gentiles, upon whom my name is called,
> saith the Lord, who doeth all these things."

To leave Israel and David's throne out of our calculation is to disregard a large portion of the Scripture. The Scripture says, ". . . that blindness in part is happened to Israel, until the fulness of the Gentiles be come in." Therefore any attempt on the part of any people toward persecution of the Jews, must be deplored by every Christian.

It might not be inadvisable, were those who are persecuting the Jews to bear in mind that all other nations who previously have persecuted the Jews have gone into oblivion.

There can be no doubt that the Lord will answer the prayer of the petitioner in this 83rd Psalm. Some day He will refuse to keep silence and hold His peace, rising up to express Himself in judgment, as He did to all of the nations and kingdoms mentioned in the 6th to 11th verses of this Psalm.

While the majority of the Psalms concern Israel's relationship to the Lord, and many of them look forward to the future, yet at all times we can examine these Psalms and find a message for our own hearts and for the hour in which we live. Thus, let us look at this Psalm more carefully and apply the principles of it to our own hour.

Notice that the Psalmist invited the Lord to cease His silence and to no longer hold His peace.

For well nigh two thousand years the heavens have been silent. Except for an occasional burst of fury upon the part of nature, there is very little evidence from the silent heavens that God is interested in the affairs of this world or that He is specifically interested in those who claim to be the children of God because of their faith in the Lord Jesus Christ.

A SILENT HEAVEN AND A SLEEPING SAVIOUR

Because the heavens have been silent, the enemies of God have assumed that He either is non-existent, that He is incapable of delivering His people, or that He is indifferent to the affairs of men. Thus, in examining this portion of Scripture we may raise the question, Why does God keep silent and why does He hold His peace? In the first place, God is silent in order to give man every opportunity to express himself, thereby making man his own judge of his own incapabilities.

Secondly, the Lord is silent regarding the affairs of men because this is the hour of His grace, when He is extending the gift of His salvation to all who will trust Him by faith. His hand of judgment has been temporarily stayed because His hand of grace is extended; His grace is free and unmerited and therefore His hand of judgment cannot express itself. However, the Bible is equally clear that this age of grace will come to an end, when His sword will be unsheathed and judgment will fall wherever it is due.

It can also be said that God frequently is silent even on behalf of His own people. Undoubtedly, we who love our Lord Jesus and rejoice in His salvation acknowledge that there have been occasions in our lives when our Lord did not seem to answer our prayer, and when He appeared to keep silent. Each of us have had occasions where we have sought the mind of the Lord, but He has not revealed it to us. We cried to the heavens, but they were silent. Why should God be deaf to the cry of His people?

The Lord frequently appears to be asleep, (I say that reverently) in order to try, or test, the faith of those who are His own. I need give only one illustration to emphasize this fact. In the 8th chapter of St. Mathew's Gospel we have the record of a storm which tried the patience of the disciples. They were on a ship, in company with the Lord Jesus. He was in the hinder part of the ship, asleep. There arose a great tempest in the sea. The disciples struggled against the tempest, yet our Lord slept on, until the disciples were so overwhelmed and overpowered by the storm that they awoke Him and said, "Lord, save us: we perish." Our Lord awakened out of His sleep, and answered, "Why are ye fearful, O ye of little faith?" He then rebuked the winds and the sea, with the result that a great calm enveloped the sea, so that the disciples marveled, saying, "What manner of man is this, that even the winds and the sea obey him!"

Were we to have the privilege of interviewing any one of those disciples who were aboard the ship that day, and were we to ask, Which would you have preferred—that the sea be calm at all times, as if you were basking in the Lord's grace all through the journey, or would you rather have suffered the experience of feeling as if you were left alone, struggling for very life itself, and then have the Lord demonstrate His power, through which He revealed Himself to be the Lord of all comfort? I doubt that any one of us would expect to receive an answer other than, A thousand times would we have preferred to endure the storm, in order to see the glory of God. Why did the Lord permit the storm to take place? For no other purpose than to strengthen the faith of those weak disciples. Thereafter, whenever they were in a place of danger or a period of distress, they could look back to that incident with much comfort, in remembering how the Lord delivered them. It would give them courage, and faith to understand and know that the Lord was with them at all times, even when the rage of the storm was fiercest.

When, therefore, the heavens seem silent and your prayers seem unanswered, don't be disturbed or distressed, providing your own heart is right with the Lord. He may be trying your faith in order that He may have an opportunity to reveal His power and His glorious person to you. Then you will do exactly as those disciples did: you will marvel at the Man whose name is "the Lord Jesus."

We could go on and mention several other reasons why the Lord appears to be silent, but I think we have seen sufficient to be a source of comfort to any who are sorely tried.

THE ONENESS OF GOD AND HIS PEOPLE

There is one other fact revealed in the early part of this 83rd Psalm upon which we should spend a moment or two. In the 2nd verse we are introduced to a people spoken of as the enemies of the Lord. They are said to hate the Lord. Now, they have no way of expressing their hatred against the Lord Himself. His throne is so far beyond the range of men, that even were they to take all of their TNT and make one explosive bomb with it, it would hardly reach the fringe of the clouds, much less disturb the Almighty. Therefore, the enemies of the Lord express their hatred for Him, against His people, which brings us to a most interesting subject.

As the enemies of God express their wrath against His people, thereby revealing that God and His people are one, so God recognizes that He and His people are one. Take the case of Saul of Tarsus. If ever there was a man who hated the church of our Lord Jesus, that man was Saul of Tarsus. But, that noonday when he journeyed toward Damascus, he was smitten by a light, above the glory of the noonday sun, and he heard a voice speaking unto him, "Saul, Saul, why persecutest thou me?"

As Saul was a devout religionist, how could he persecute God? He believed his actions were in defense of God. Yet he heard that strange voice from heaven, saying, "Saul, Saul, why persecutest thou *me?*" He responded and asked, "Who art thou, Lord?" and the Lord answered, "I am Jesus whom thou persecutest: it is hard for thee to kick against the pricks." But Saul had never persecuted the Lord Jesus: he persecuted those who were the followers of the Lord Jesus. However, by persecuting the followers of our Lord Jesus, he was persecuting the Lord. What a comfort that should bring to each of us who love the Lord and who have received Him as our Saviour—to know that He has constituted us a part of Himself. Nothing, therefore, can befall us, but it befalls Him. He and His people are one.

The Psalmist used an expression, concerning the Lord's people, that is exceedingly precious. He spoke of them to the Lord as "thy hidden ones."

Why do you suppose he used such language, for of course, language is always descriptive of fact? What is it that the Lord wishes to convey to our minds, by speaking of us as His "hidden ones." A hiding-place actually accomplishes two things. First, it provides a safe haven of rest, where an individual may enjoy peace and quiet. Second, it provides a place of safety and preservation when the enemy pursues.

A number of passages of Scripture could be brought to focus upon this thought. David, the Psalmist, elsewhere stated, ". . . in the time of trouble he shall hide me in his pavilion: in the secret of his tabernacle shall he hide me; he shall set me up upon a rock." Our Lord Jesus, prophetically speaking through the Scriptures, said, ". . . in the shadow of his hand hath he hid me . . ." I refer also to that passage in Paul's letter to the Colossians, 3rd chapter, where he wrote, concerning those who are in Christ:

> "Since ye then be risen with Christ, seek those things which are above, where Christ sitteth on the right hand of God.
>
> "Set your affection on things above, not on things on the earth.
>
> "For ye are dead, and your life is *hid with Christ in God*.
>
> "When Christ, who is our life, shall appear, then shall ye also appear with him in glory."

As we have read this passage, we can say a hiding-place is used for another purpose. It is for temporary seclusion, pending the time when the individual will be revealed. Every born-again Christian has his life hid with Christ in God. The world does not know that. It does not see any evidence of it. But the Bible declares it to be a blessed fact.

If you are outside the place of refuge and have no hiding-place from the wrath to come, our Lord invites you to come under the shelter of His own precious blood, which He spilled on the cross for your sin and mine. There you will find refuge. You will not only find a safe haven from the storm, but you will find a precious Saviour who will be your guide through life, who will give you peace and who will comfort you with the knowledge that your life is hid with Him in God. Some day He will reveal Himself in glory; and when He reveals *Himself* in glory, He will reveal *you* in glory.

That is the grace of God. There is no message that compares with the gospel of the grace of God. It cost the death of His Son, but it is ours without money and without price. It is as free as the air we breathe. It is ours when we receive it and appropriate it.

PSALM EIGHTY-FOUR—PART ONE

THE PLACE OF REST

THIS past week produced a great number of interesting letters in reference to the 83rd Psalm, which we discussed last Sunday. A number of Jewish people found interest in the comments regarding their status in the world at present and God's plan for that nation in the future. One Jewish man inquired whether there are many Christians who view the Scriptures as I do and who look forward to the coming of Israel's Messiah, when we shall, together, rejoice in the grace of God. I responded in the affirmative, saying that every Bible-believing Christian loves the Jew and rejoices in the promise of the return of our Lord, but also wants him to come to Christ now.

It is easy to see how it is that this question is raised, for much of Christian profession is merely Church-ianity, without Christ and the Bible. That' which makes Christianity is Christ, and you cannot have Christ apart from the Bible. You cannot take a portion of the Bible, you must take it all. From Genesis to Revelation, through all the sixty-six books, there is that constant breath of God's approval, witnessing concerning His grace and His own purpose in this world.

As I receive such inquiries, there is an urge in my heart to pray for the speedy return of our blessed Lord. He promised it in the closing verses of the Bible, saying, "Surely I come quickly" and we respond, "Even so, come, Lord Jesus." In the meanwhile, may the Lord find us faithful in witnessing for Him.

A BEAUTIFUL PSALM

We are to consider a very delightful Psalm. Were I asked which Psalm I like most I would hardly know what to say, I have so many favorites. This 84th Psalm is one of them. It is a beautiful Psalm, so beautiful that we shall devote three meditations to it. Let me read it in its entirety, although I will comment only on the first four verses:

> "How amiable are thy tabernacles, O LORD of hosts!
>
> "My soul longeth, yet, even fainteth for the courts of the LORD: my heart and my flesh crieth out for the living God.
>
> "Yea, the sparrow hath found an house, and the swallow a nest for herself, where she may lay her young, even thine altars, O LORD of hosts, my King, and my God.

"Blessed are they that dwell in thy house: they will be still praising thee. Selah.

"Blessed is the man whose strength is in thee: in whose heart are the ways of them.

"Who passing through the valley of Baca make it a well; the rain also filleth the pools.

"They go from strength to strength, every one of them in Zion appeareth before God.

"O LORD God of hosts, hear my prayer: give ear, O God of Jacob. Selah.

"Behold, O God our shield and look upon the face of thine anointed.

"For a day in thy courts is better than a thousand. I had rather be a doorkeeper in the house of my God, than to dwell in the tents of wickedness.

"For the LORD God is a sun and shield: the LORD will give grace and glory: no good thing will he withhold from them that walk uprightly.

"O LORD of hosts, blessed is the man that trusteth in thee."

Observe that this Psalm has an interesting introduction. It is dedicated "to the chief Musician upon Gittith, A Psalm for the sons of Korah."

In previous meditations we learned that the word Gittith probably represents a type of instrument which was used in David's day and which received its name from Obed-edom, the Gittite, in which home the ark of the covenant rested for a little while. The ark symbolized the presence of the Lord with His people. Undoubtedly Obed-edom enjoyed the presence of God in his own home in an unusual manner. Where the Lord is present there is peace, joy, and a song. In the home of every God-fearing man there is a song. Thus, Psalms that were to be played on the Gittith invariably were Psalms of praise and adoration.

Certainly there must be some suggestive message in that this Psalm, together with a few others, was for the sons of Korah. Certain Psalms are known as Davidic Psalms, others are given the title, Asaphic Psalms, and still others, Korahitic Psalms. Each of these groups have certain characteristics familiar to each. There are the Davidic Psalms, in which David speaks of the glory of his greater Son. There are the Psalms of Asaph, "that delve into every problem of life and give us light to be exercised thereby." Then there are the Psalms for the sons of Korah, in which "the love of God's house is ardent and the pain of separation from its services keenly felt."

It was Korah who led the rebellion against Moses and Aaron, saying unto them: "Ye take too much upon you, seeing all the congregation are holy, every one of them, and the LORD is among them: wherefore then lift ye up yourselves above the congregation of the LORD?" As a result of this rebellion and gainsaying God demonstrated, in judgment, that Moses and Aaron were His own choice for ministry and intercession. Judgment fell upon Korah and his associates when the earth opened her mouth and swallowed them up.

How interesting it is, that there were sons of Korah who did not follow their father in his rebellion. In these Psalms, dedicated to the sons of Korah, there is the longing for the house of God and for the worship of God, which was refused to their father and his associates because of their rebellion. What is more, it is interesting that God did not charge the sons with the rebellion of their father, but gave them to continue in the happy service of the tabernacle. Sir, even if your father sins, it is no excuse for you to do so.

THE TABERNACLES OF THE LORD

Now let us look more closely at the first four verses. The Psalm opens with: "How amiable are thy tabernacles, O LORD of hosts!" Do we love the house of the Lord? Do we enjoy the fellowship of the Lord's people? I am aware, of course, that the tabernacle in the Old Testament was quite a different building from the churches in our cities and villages, which have been in existence since the beginning of the Christian era. In the tabernacle of the Old Testament God promised to dwell, to commune with the representatives of Israel, to receive the worship of the people through chosen representatives, and to pour out blessing upon the whole people. Is it any wonder that the Psalmist said, "How amiable (how inviting, how beautiful) are thy tabernacles, O LORD of hosts!"

You will observe that the writer spoke of "tabernacles," so that he had in mind not only the earthly tabernacle, but he was also occupied with the heavenly tabernacle. He was looking beyond (understanding the symbol of the earthly tabernacle and entering into the heavenly tabernacle) to behold the beauty of the Lord.

Strictly speaking, our church buildings are not the habitation of God. We have been accustomed to think of the church building as the house of God. But you will look in vain in all of the New Testament for the slightest intimation that a church building is the house of God. What is more, you will never find even one suggestion that any group of believers in Christ should erect a church, much less will you find any instructions as to how that church building should be erected, or what furniture should go into it. But, in the Old Testament there was not a single detail left to the sons of Israel. Moses was informed how to build the tabernacle, what size to make it, the material that should be used, and every article of furniture that should go into it. Why do you suppose that such instruction is lacking in the New Testament?

The Old Testament abounds in symbolism. Everything therein symbolizes deeper truths. In the New Testament we have the fulfilment of the symbolism. Thus we know that the tabernacle was built according to the pattern that God showed to Moses in the heavens. Now, however, the symbolism is no longer required, for the worshippers enter, by faith, into the very presence of God, and behold ". . . the glory of God in the face of Jesus Christ." Whereas, in the Old Testament, God dwelt in a building called the tabernacle, in the Gospels He dwelt in the body of His Son, but now He dwells in the body of every believer. Thus when a group of believers gather together for worship, for praise, and for testimony, they are called "the church." So a church is a group of people, not a building. If we who know Christ as our Saviour would only realize that these bodies of ours are tabernacles of the Holy Spirit and that God dwells in them, I think our whole manner of life would be different and we would be more careful of our walk.

In olden times there was only one place of worship. That was in Jerusalem. Even our Lord Jesus acknowledged that. When Israel was out of Jerusalem, she missed the ritual of the temple. Then the heart of every true Israelite longed, yea, even fainted, for the courts of the Lord.

THE LIVING GOD

Now, however, it is no longer in Jerusalem, nor in Samaria, that worship is to be offered, but, as our Lord said, the hour has now come, "when the true worshippers shall worship the Father in spirit and in truth: for the Father seeketh such to worship him." Therefore, we in this age, wherever we may be, and where there are two or three gathered together in the name of the Lord Jesus, may offer praise and worship, for by faith we enter into heaven itself. It is written that we are now seated together in heavenly places in Christ Jesus, blessed with every spiritual blessing.

If an Israelite's soul longed, and his heart fainted, for the courts of the Lord, how much more should we seek to abide in His presence and enjoy the courts of the Lord.

The extent of a true Israelite's longing for the courts of his Lord is graphically portrayed by the phrase, "my heart and my flesh *crieth out* for the living God."

Many of us are occupied with either a dead Christ or an historic Christ. I know Christ died, and, of course, I love the record of the historic Christ of the Gospels, but, if that were all we had, we would have no gospel. We have a living Christ, risen and glorified in the heavens, who, when received as Saviour and Lord, invites us to have fellowship with Him. That is what Paul, the Apostle, had in mind when he wrote, "I count all things loss for the excellency of the knowledge of Christ Jesus my Lord. . ."

Our Lord, in the 17th chapter of John's Gospel, gave us the definition of eternal life, when He said, ". . . this is life eternal, that they might know thee the only true God, and Jesus Christ, whom thou hast sent."

The Psalmist used beautiful language in the 3rd verse, where he said: "Yea, the sparrow hath found an house, and the swallow a nest for herself, where she may lay her young, even thine altars, O LORD of hosts, my King, and my God."

The sparrow symbolizes the poor. The sparrow is found in almost every country in the world; so, too, we find the poor everywhere. The sparrow is the cheapest of birds, yet not a single sparrow falls to the ground, but that the heavenly Father is aware of it; so our Lord assured us that not a hair of our head would be disturbed without His Father's knowledge.

An outstanding characteristic of the swallow is its wanderlust. It roams everywhere. Yet we seldom see a swallow alone. They always fly in flocks. We might call them social birds.

There are some people in the world who delight in being alone. They seem to be able to enjoy themselves when alone. There are others who delight to have companies of people about them and who rejoice in friendships. We call the latter "gregarious."

However, both the sparrow and the swallow have found the house of the Lord a desirable resting-place, a place of safety where none can harm them. The swallow has built a nest for herself and places her young therein, fully assured that no harm will befall them. It was in the altars of the

Lord's house that these birds found their rest. So we find our rest in that which is symbolized by the altar, which, of course, is the death of our Lord Jesus Christ.

Notice, too, how personal the Psalmist became in the 3rd verse? He spoke of the Lord of hosts as "my King, and my God." Is He your God, in an intimate, personal manner? If He is, then you have eternal life. If you cannot say so, you may this moment have eternal life if you will receive His grace. All you have to do is to believe and to receive Christ. Then the blessing mentioned in verse 4 will be yours, as well as ours, for the Psalmist said: "Blessed are they that dwell in thy house: they will be still praising thee."

PSALM EIGHTY-FOUR—PART TWO

THREE TREES OR
"THE VALLEY OF MULBERRY TREES"

I N our former meditation we commented upon the first four verses, which read :

"How amiable are thy tabernacles, O LORD of hosts!

"My soul longeth, yea, even fainteth for the courts of the LORD: my heart and my flesh crieth out for the living God.

"Yea, the sparrow hath found an house, and the swallow a nest for herself, where she may lay her young, even thine altars, O LORD of hosts, my King, and my God.

"Blessed are they that dwell in thy house: they will be still praising thee. Selah."

Now we shall notice the message that is found in the next three verses. They read:

"Blessed is the man whose strength is in thee; in whose heart are the ways of them.

"Who passing through the valley of Baca make it a well; the rain also filleth the pools.

"They go from strength to strength, every one of them in Zion appeareth before God."

Of all the creatures of the earth the offspring of man is the most helpless. Many years are required before the individual is self-supporting and self-sustaining. When that time arrives, there begins the ceaseless struggle to maintain one's physical life, to ward off disease, to strive for mastery and through the strife to seek an answer to a few questions that intrude themselves into our minds, such as, Where did we come from? Why are we here? Where are we going?

Ere we know it, some disease enters in, gains a hold, and finally lays us low. Or in the bloom of youth or in strong manhood we are stricken, through an accident, and whisked out of the here to go—Where? Were we deprived of the Bible, and were we to exercise our reason only, we would be so baffled by the conflicting circumstances of life that it would be very difficult to keep our reason on an even keel. The disappointments of life, the perplexities, and the unsolved mysteries, would be enough to drive one mad. Yet, this thing called life not only has given us reason, but it has provided us with an organ we call the heart, which enables us to have kindly feelings toward each other and, indeed, deep unquenchable affection. Couple this reason of ours with this heart of ours, and house it in a body that from the very moment of our birth contains the seed of corruption which will finally smite us in death, and one must cry out, To whom shall we go? Who has the words of eternal life to answer these perplexing problems that arise in our hearts and minds?

You may bury your mind in the study of philosophy or lull your conscience to sleep in a false paradise of amusement or self-indulging pleasure, but you will search in vain for true happiness until you have found the One who made you after His own image.

Therefore, the Psalmist said: "Blessed is the man whose strength is in thee (the Lord); in whose heart are the ways of them."

"THE VALLEY OF BACA"

There is no denying that the most perfect day in a man's life was the day he was born, for from then on he is headed for the grave. The helplessness of man is readily appreciated when one considers that one can take the finest specimen of human physique, with muscles like iron and with a constitution that appears impregnable, and yet let a germ smite him, a germ that it would take a microscope to see, and that germ will prove the victor. How helpless are the sons of men. How much are we in need of a strong One who will be our strength. The Psalmist said, "Happy is the man whose strength is in the Lord; in whose heart are the ways of them. Who passing through the valley of Baca make it a well; the rain also filleth the pools."

None of us are spared disappointments or sorrows. Into every life there comes what is aptly described as the rain. We may have sunshine at times, but the clouds gather and the rains fall. Unless our hearts are established in the Lord, we will not be able to smile and have a joyful countenance in the midst of the rainy season. As the Bible is its own best commentary, we go to it to determine what the writer had in mind by the expression, "the valley of Baca." Some translations use the phrase, "the valley of mulberry trees." Baca means *weeping*. Thus, the valley of Baca is the valley of tears and weeping. It is a valley of bitterness, reminding us of a place that Israel called by the name of Marah, which means bitterness. We find in the 15th chapter of Exodus that Marah was a stopping-place in Israel's journey through the wilderness.

In the early part of the chapter we read that Moses led the nation in a song of praise unto the Lord. Great joy was the portion of the people as they sang unto Jehovah, because of their wonderful deliverance from Pharaoh and the Egyptian hosts who were drowned in the Red Sea. After the celebration, Israel proceeded on their journey. They went into the wilderness of Shur, traveled three days, but found no water. Suddenly they came to a place where they saw water. Oh, said the people, now our thirst will be quenched. When we remember that they had traveled for three days without water, we can appreciate how delighted they must have been to see water.

But oh, the sorrow and bitterness that took hold of the people when they observed that the waters were bitter. They were unable to drink. In fact, they expressed their disappointment by calling the place Marah, which means bitterness. Immediately the people began to murmur to Moses and said, "What shall we drink?" Moses cried unto the Lord. In answer, the Lord showed Moses a tree, which when he had cast it into the waters, they were made sweet. Wonderful experience, wasn't it? As a result, Moses made a statute and an ordinance, for there the Lord proved Israel and said, "If thou wilt diligently hearken to the voice of the LORD thy God, and wilt do that which is right in his sight, and wilt give ear to his commandments, and keep all his statutes, I will put none of these diseases upon thee, which I have brought upon the Egyptians: for I am the LORD that healeth thee."

THE THREE TREES

Now then, let us go back to our Psalm and see if we cannot find the significance of the language which the Psalmist used. Again we read verses 5 and 6 of the 84th Psalm: "Blessed is the man whose strength is in thee: in whose heart are the ways of them. Who passing through the valley of Baca make it a well; the rain also filleth the pools." In other words, even those whose strength is in the Lord may go through a wilderness or come to a place of bitterness, yet, through the bitterness they have have found something, or someone, if you please, who has turned the bitter waters into sweet waters. They understand that even in the place of bitterness there is a well, from which one can draw out the sweet waters of salvation.

The Bible has quite a little to say about trees. It was the fruit of a tree, when eaten, that caused sin to enter into this world. It was a tree that was used by Adam and Eve, as a hiding-place from the face of a seeking God; but the Lord God sought and found His creatures. God has a third tree. It is the tree called Calvary. Upon that tree Christ our Lord was made a curse. He drained the bitterness to the last dregs. Because He drank those dregs, the bitter experiences of life are made sweet to all who have received Christ; who have taken the cross by faith.

The Bible makes much of the cross of our Lord Jesus. It was Paul, the Apostle, who said, "God forbid that I should glory, save in the cross of our Lord Jesus Christ," for that cross crucified Paul unto the world, and crucified the world unto Paul.

One whose strength is in the Lord is filled with happiness, he is able to endure the bitterness of life and still retain a smile. If you desire an example, take the case of Fanny Crosby, blind soon after birth, yet with no bitterness in her heart. Filled with the knowledge of Christ, she rejoiced and gave the world songs that have cheered multitudes of Christians in their journey from earth to heaven. What made the bitter waters sweet for Fanny Crosby? The tree of Calvary and the Christ who hung upon that tree. The place of bitterness was made a well, out of which she drank waters that quenched her thirst. The very rains that ordinarily bring disappointments fill the pools, so that there is an overflowing abundance of joy.

The cross of our Lord Jesus will make bitter waters turn sweet. The bitter experiences of life will then be borne in the knowledge that the morning cometh soon, when it shall be our joy to receive from our Lord's hand a crown of rejoicing.

"EVERY ONE"—NONE MISSING

In bringing our meditation to a close note the 7th verse, which reads: "They go from strength to strength, every one of them in Zion appeareth before God." Bearing in mind what we have already said, that the preceding verses are occupied with those whose strength is in the Lord, consider this 7th verse, "They go from strength to strength, every one of them in Zion appeareth before God." They may pass through the valley of tears and bitterness, but they never stay there. They *pass through* the valley on the way to Zion, to appear before God.

It will be a source of comfort to those who are now going through bitterness, to know that the 84th Psalm promises that the man whose strength is in the Lord merely *passes* through the valley of bitterness. He is not destined to remain there. You are merely going through the valley of bitterness and, as you do, you will go from strength to strength as you depend upon the Lord God.

To the Christian whose strength is in the Lord, a period of bitterness is merely temporary and transitory. The assurance is given to them that they will appear before the Lord, in Zion.

There is a beautiful touch in the last phrase of this 7th verse. It is this—that *"Every one* of them in Zion appeareth before God." Not a single one will be left in the valley of bitterness.

If you are fainthearted and have any doubts about your salvation, whether you will hold out till you get to the glory with your Lord, may this be a source of assurance and comfort to you, that the Psalmist said, concerning those whose strength is in the Lord, that every one of them in Zion appear before God.

In the 17th chapter of John's Gospel, our Lord gave an account of His stewardship to His Father. Incidentally, He gave a ray of light regarding ourselves, who believe in Him in this day, which is exceedingly precious. Beginning at verse 9 of that chapter, our Lord said:

> ". . . I pray not for the world, but for them which thou hast given me; for they are thine.
>
> "And all mine are thine, and thine are mine; and I am glorified in them.
>
> "And now I am no more in the world, but these are in the world, and I come to thee. Holy Father, keep through thine own name those whom thou hast given me, that they may be one, as we are.
>
> "While I was with them in the world, I kept them in thy name: those that thou gavest me I have kept, and none of them is lost, but the son of perdition; that the scripture might be fulfilled."
>
> * * * *
>
> "Neither pray I for these alone, but for them also which shall believe on me through their word . . ."

Observe that the Lord kept every one, except the son of perdition. The Psalmist said, concerning those whose strength is in the Lord, "they go from strength to strength, every one of them in Zion appeareth before God." Salvation is of the Lord. It is absolutely a finished work. He accomplished it on the cross. He paid the penalty of sin. He purchased *eternal* redemption. To those who receive Him and believe Him, He has promised, on His own Word which cannot fail, that He will present each before His Father's throne, absolutely faultless and without sin. As He kept all that the Father gave Him during His early ministry, do you suppose His Father will lose any for whom Christ prayed? Every one will appear in Zion, the city of God, and therefore appear before the eternal God. That is salvation. That is the gospel, which is the greatest message that has ever been preached to men.

PSALM EIGHTY-FOUR—PART THREE

THE DOORKEEPER—FIRST IN AND LAST OUT!

COMMENCING with verse 8, of the 84th Psalm we read:

"O LORD God of hosts, hear my prayer: give ear, O God of Jacob. Selah.

"Behold, O God our shield and look upon the face of thine anointed.

"For a day in thy courts is better than a thousand. I had rather be a doorkeeper in the house of my God, than to dwell in the tents of wickedness.

"For the LORD God is a sun and shield: the LORD will give grace and glory: no good thing will he withhold from them that walk uprightly.

"O LORD of hosts, blessed is the man that trusteth in thee."

The subjects the Bible covers are so numerous one could almost say that it is difficult to think of any subject that is not discussed or touched within the covers of that wonderful book. Yet, while a myriad of subjects is discussed, the one great theme of the Bible is aptly expressed in that familiar phrase, "Man's complete ruin in sin and God's perfect remedy in Christ." We might even boil that phrase down by declaring that the Bible is concerned with "the Person of Christ." On almost every page of Scripture the Lord Jesus Christ may be found in prophecy, in type, or in song. He is the central person of the Godhead. All that any of us will ever get to know about God is known through Christ, for He is declared to be the visibility of God and the express image of His person. Concerning the Father in His own person, we are told that "No man hath seen God at any time; the only begotten Son, which is in the bosom of the Father, he hath manifested him."

BEHOLDING THE FACE OF CHRIST

Observe that the Psalmist spoke of God under the titles, "O LORD God of hosts," also "O God of Jacob," and finally "O God our shield." This is not vain repetition. Each phrase reveals a certain characteristic of God. He is the Lord God of hosts, yet He is the God of Jacob. He is Lord over hosts, but He also is Lord to a single individual. This latter relationship is beautifully expressed in the further title "O God our shield." A shield protects. It is used to prevent darts from smiting us. In these titles of God, there is a message for our hearts today as well as for Israel at the time the Psalm was written.

The request that the Psalmist made to God emphasizes what I have just said regarding Christ as the manifestation of God. In the 9th verse we read: "Behold, O God our shield, and look upon the face of thine anointed." Every student of the Bible knows that the title "Christ" means "The anointed one." Thus when the Psalmist said ". . . look upon the face of thine anointed" he was asking God to look upon the face of Christ. But why this invitation to look upon the face of Christ, the anointed of God?

Perhaps I can best express that by relating an interesting question which my wife raised. After I had conducted the services at a certain church and we had returned home, my wife asked, "How is it that invariably, when you lead a congregation in prayer, you invite God to look at His own Son? It seems to me that the Father knows the glories of His Son better than we and does not need that we call His attention to Him."

That was an intelligent question and I enjoyed responding to it. If there is one thing I love in public ministry, it is the privilege of leading a congregation in prayer before the Lord. I believe the highest expression of love that one, who has been redeemed by the blood of Christ, can offer to God is the worship of the individual's heart. If we multiply that so that a church or body or company of believers, gathered together for worship, is led by one in that company, we have the highest form of devotion to God.

What does it mean to worship? It is a serious question how much any of us know about the subject of worship. It is a mistaken notion to call a preaching service a worship service. I know it is done constantly. True worship is to present to the Father the praise and adoration of the redeemed heart. In doing so, the heart pours out its affection upon the

Father because of the work of His Son and the ministry of the Holy Spirit. Thus, I delight in presenting the praise of God's people, and, in so doing, invite the Lord to behold the glories of His own Son.

The Bible speaks specifically of our Lord Jesus as the Son of the Father's delight. God frequently testified concerning Him "This is my beloved Son, in whom I am well pleased. . ." Our Lord is the Son of God's love. He is the only begotten of the Father, full of grace and truth. All of the Father's mind is centered in the Son. No redeemed individual, who is taught in the Word of God, will ever come into the presence of God upon any other ground than that of the atoning blood of the Lord Jesus Christ. Coming upon that ground, no redeemed individual will call attention to himself. He calls attention to the glories of Christ. Thus, when the Psalmist invited God to look upon the face of His anointed he was doing what the Christian is invited to do in this present day, that is, to call attention to the glories of His own Son. Therefore, you and I may invite the Father to look at Christ and remind Him that we are in Christ. What a joy it is to consider that God thus sees us in Christ. As He looks at us He sees the face of His only begotten Son. That, I believe, is the heart of worship and the greatest service any individual can render to God.

But there is another reason for the Psalmist to pray "look upon the face of thine anointed." Through all eternity we will never forget Calvary. In fact, our Lord said it was for Calvary that He came into this world. Thus, as we worship and behold the face of God's anointed, we should never forget what undoubtedly the Father always beholds—the sufferings of Christ, so graphically pictured in the Holy Spirit's account of the treatment accorded to Christ. For instance, in St. Mark's Gospel, the 14th chapter and the 65th verse, we read concerning Christ's treatment before the tribunal of the high priest, "And some began to spit on him, and to cover his face, and to buffet him, and to say unto him, Prophesy: and the servants did strike him with the palms of their hands." That face that was covered by men and enveloped in the clouds of judgment, so marred as to resemble but little the face of a man, now reveals the glory of God. Do you think God will ever forget Calvary as He looks upon the face of His Christ, the anointed? But mark well, for God to behold the face of His anointed is not to provoke Him to judgment, but rather to revel in the obedience of His Son to His will in order that thereby God could justify every sinner who receives His grace.

A DAY IN THE LORD'S COURTS

In the 10th verse the Psalmist said: "For a day in thy courts is better than a thousand. I had rather be a doorkeeper in the house of my God, than to dwell in the tents of wickedness." I question whether any individual in his sane mind would arrive at any other conclusion than that which is expressed by the Psalmist. Yet we can understand how some people react to spiritual things. If I may be permitted to refer to my own experience, there was a time when church attendance and fellowship with Christians was about the last thing in the world that would interest me. I wanted to enjoy "life," the pleasures of this world, its amusements. I wanted a business career. I enjoyed the type of friends with which I was associated. Occasionally I went to church, but only to satisfy my mother. As for going to a prayer meeting, that was inconceivable, and certainly it was no place where anyone could have any pleasure. *Now*, my entire viewpoint is changed. There is nothing I enjoy as much as the fellowship of God's people, worship with His people, and the place of prayer. The happiest hours of my life have been spent in prayer meetings. I know some people cannot understand that—yet I think I am normal! The world has many pleasures to offer one and there are certain indulgences which are quite interesting. For example, there are many good things that I enjoy: good music, good books, good sports, and good friends. I also enjoy my business. Yet, I confess before you that there is not a thing that I enjoy half as much as fellowship with God in the midst of His people. I wholeheartedly agree with the Psalmist when he said, "a day in thy courts is better than a thousand. . ."

Why do you suppose this change takes place? Solely because one comes to understand that he was a sinner and needed a Saviour; and then in simple faith, believes that God so loved him that He gave His only begotten Son that he might have eternal life. Having received Christ, we now have a *capacity* for the enjoyment of fellowship with God, which only redeemed people possess.

If you will receive Christ as your Saviour, you, too, will have that capacity whereby you will enjoy the fellowship of God. There will be no place in the world that will hold such attraction for you as the courts of the Lord.

Now notice the closing phrase of the 10th verse where the Psalmist said, "I had rather be a doorkeeper in the house of my God, than to dwell in the tents of wickedness." There we have a direct expression of choice. That brings us to an interesting subject.

It is my firm belief that no man will be eternally lost except he *chooses* to be lost, and that no man will be saved except he *chooses* to be saved. I am well aware that the man who is outside of Christ is dead in trespasses and in sins, and I understand that salvation is the work of the Lord, but you and I must *choose*. It is a case of *choosing* between Christ and Barabbas, as Pilate offered to the people at the time of Christ's trial. Whom will ye serve? The Psalmist said his *choice* was the Lord who is a sun and shield, and that he would rather be a doorkeeper in the house of God than dwell in the tents of wickedness. To some it may appear that the Psalmist did not have very high ambitions. The idea of being satisfied with the position of a doorkeeper! Well, I am not so sure that the Psalmist's ambitions were of the low kind. Of course, he presenting a contrast. If it came to a choice between dwelling in the tents of wickedness or being a doorkeeper in the house of the Lord, he would far rather be a doorkeeper in the house of the Lord.

THE DOORKEEPER

The job of doorkeeper is not to be despised! The other day I came across an interesting thought. It was the brain-child of a brilliant scholar who lived about three hundred years ago, John Trapp. His writings have been a source of joy to me. In commenting on this 9th verse of the 84th Psalm, he said, "A doorkeeper is the first one in and the last one out." I do not know how you feel, but after reading that statement, I am all for being a doorkeeper!

But another thought impresses itself upon the mind, as we think of the title "doorkeeper." Our Lord Jesus said "I am the door: by me if any man enter in, he shall be saved . . ." There is only one door, and that door is Christ. If you ever expect to be saved and enter into heaven, you can only do so through Christ. That is the testimony of God. No mere man is the door. Christ is the door. How wonderful that we can be "door*keepers*." We can *keep* the testimony of Christ, as the door, so clear, and keep the door so wide open that the wayfaring man can be led by us, through the door, into the presence of God. Christ is the door, but unless you and I make it our business to tell others about the door, they will never get to know the way. What an honor it is, therefore, to be a door*keeper*.

The other day I received a letter from a friend of mine, the man who led me to Christ. In answering it, I told him that I have never forgotten the words he spoke to me, more than twenty years ago, to the effect that now that I had received Christ I had experienced only one half of the joy God intended for me. I would receive the other half when I had led my first soul to Christ. There was much truth in what that man told me. It is a great joy to be a doorkeeper in the house of the Lord.

Now notice the provision of God on the behalf of His people, as expressed in verse 11 where the Psalmist said: "For the LORD God is a sun and shield: the LORD will give grace and glory: no good thing will he withhold from them that walk uprightly." That passage was written more than twenty-five hundred years ago, and yet the promise is as true today as it was then. To those who trust in God and walk uprightly, the Lord is a sun and shield. But in addition He gives grace and glory and promises not to withhold any good thing. That is a blank check, if you please. It is the heritage of every God-fearing Christian man. Is it any wonder that the Psalmist ended this delightful Psalm with the statement "O LORD of hosts, happy is the man that trusteth in thee."

If you wish to be happy, trust in Him. That ought not to be difficult, for who can be trusted as God can be trusted. Why not, this very day, place your confidence in Christ? Trust in Him. Receive Him as your Saviour. Then, on the testimony of this Psalm, you will be a happy man.

PSALM EIGHTY-FIVE

THE SCAPEGOAT

I N our series of meditations in the Book of Psalms, we arrive at the 85th. It has thirteen verses. I hope you are not superstitious. However, if you do not like the fact that the Psalm has thirteen verses, be relieved to know that a Hebrew translation carries fourteen verses because it considers the inscription to the Psalm as verse 1!

Like several of the Psalms we have recently considered, this one is dedicated to the chief Musician for the sons of Korah.

> "LORD, thou hast been favourable unto thy land: thou hast brought back the captivity of Jacob.
>
> "Thou hast forgiven the iniquity of thy people, thou hast covered all their sin. Selah.
>
> "Thou hast taken away all thy wrath: thou hast turned thyself from the fierceness of thine anger.

"Turn us, O God of our salvation, and cause thine anger toward us to cease.

"Wilt thou be angry with us for ever? wilt thou draw out thine anger to all generations?

"Wilt thou not revive us again: that thy people may rejoice in thee?

"Shew us thy mercy, O LORD, and grant us thy salvation.

"I will hear what God the LORD will speak: for he will speak peace unto his people, and to his saints: but let them not turn again to folly.

"Surely his salvation is nigh them that fear him; that glory may dwell in our land.

"Mercy and truth are met together; righteousness and peace have kissed each other.

"Truth shall spring out of the earth; and righteousness shall look down from heaven.

"Yea, the LORD shall give that which is good; and our land shall yield her increase.

"Righteousness shall go before him; and shall set us in the way of his steps."

Most of us have our ups and downs. One day we are on the mountain top, enjoying the rare air and atmosphere of that exalted place, only to find that the next day we are deep down in the valley of despair. Of course, normal Christian experience does not take *circumstances* into consideration. Paul the Apostle was just as fervent in writing to the Ephesians, Philippians, or Colossians while he was a prisoner in the city of Rome as he was when addressing the multitudes on Mars' hill.

When the heart is set upon its Redeemer, circumstances are not as important as they appear to be on the surface. While tribulations, trials, and distresses take place, the heart is anchored in a haven of peace when it rests upon the finished work of our Lord Jesus Christ.

"THOU HAST CARRIED AWAY OUR SINS"

The Psalmist in this 85th Psalm based his request to God to revive the people again, so that they might rejoice in Him, on the fact of His former goodness to His people. Thus, in the opening verses of the Psalm, he wrote:

"LORD, thou hast been favourable unto thy land: thou hast brought back the captivity of Jacob.

"Thou hast forgiven the iniquity of thy people, thou hast covered all their sin. Selah."

Let us examine this for a moment, because it necessarily looks back into the distant past and claims a right to implore the blessings of God because of what He did at that time.

Repeatedly I have stated during these broadcasts that certain Psalms have a definite Israelitish color. Every one of them was written by a Jew. While many concern the Anointed of God, there are others which are occupied with the position of the people in respect to their land. Just as God brought back the captivity of Jacob in a previous day, so He *will* again bring back the captivity of His people.

News coming out of the land of Palestine shows us that it is nothing short of a miracle that Palestine has been changed from a desolation into a fertile garden. Palestine is an important place. It contains the city of the great King. As one observes the present activity in that land there necessarily burns in the heart of every true Israelite, and in the heart of every Bible-believing Christian, the glorious hope of the anticipation of millennial days.

But that is not what I wish to consider now. I want to present a message from this Psalm and make its application to our own day.

You will observe that God's favor is spoken of in verse 1, while His anger is reported in verses 3 and 5. While they seem to be contradictory characteristics, there is abounding evidence in nature that at times God smiles upon us in the sunshine of His grace, while at other times His anger rages in the storm. To question the right of God to manifest His sunshine, or His anger, is to lose sight of the fact that we are the creatures and He the Creator.

The favor of God is best evidenced to the Psalmist by the fact that He forgave the iniquity of the people and covered their sin. Let us look at that evidence for a moment.

The Hebrew word which is translated *forgiven* literally means Thou hast *borne* or *carried away* the iniquity of Thy people. The Psalmist clearly pictured what took place on the day of atonement, when a live goat, called the scapegoat, was taken, and the priest poured over its head the record of the past sins of Israel. After he had completed that task, the sin literally being transferred to the scapegoat, the goat was led into the wilderness by the hand of a fit man, to be lost forever.

Identification and Substitution

In that interesting ceremony there is a beautiful picture of what took place when our Lord Jesus died. You will remember that John the Baptist said concerning Him: "Behold the Lamb of God which taketh away (or beareth away) the sin of the world." Our Lord Jesus was made the scapegoat. He bore our sins. He took those sins, carried them away and literally buried them in the wilderness of God's "forgettery."

But notice one other fact in connection with that interesting ceremony. There was identification with the scapegoat on the part of the people through their representative. The people knew that they had sinned. They knew that they deserved judgment, and they knew that the penalty of sin was death. However, the penalty was transferred to a substitute.

God has never changed His attitude toward sin. Sin is high treason against heaven. Yet it is a common occurrence to every individual every day of the year. The measure of God's hatred for sin can easily be determined by the extent of the sufferings of Christ. He, as the representative of the sinner, bore the judgment due to sin. The same judgment that caused Christ to cry, "My God, my God, why hast thou forsaken me?" will be borne by every individual who does not appropriate the death of Christ on his own behalf. You may not agree with it, but it is God's Word.

You may either receive Christ or reject Him. If you receive Him, God will do for you what He did for the children of Israel. He not only provided a scapegoat who carried their sins into the wilderness, but He also covered their sins. Notice the Psalmist said, ". . . thou hast covered all their sin."

That reminds us of a passage in the New Testament where it is written, ". . . the blood of Jesus Christ . . . cleanseth us from all sin." All sin must mean all sin. It cannot mean anything less than all. There is no such distinction as good sins or bad sins, big sins, or little sins. All is sin, and the blood of Jesus Christ, God's Son, cleanseth us from all sin.

THE IMPELLING GOSPEL

Why do you suppose men and women count not their lives dear, leaving friends and family to go to the darkest corners of the earth to tell to those we call the heathen the news that God in Christ offers them full salvation?

Just now I am thinking of a man whom I love sincerely. He is attractive in appearance; so attractive that were you to see him you would immediately turn, look at him, and almost intuitively say, There is a real man. This morning he is in Africa. A few years ago he was in our country.

On one occasion he was playing golf with a group of men connected with the New York Stock Exchange or Stock Exchange firms. One man in the group turned to my friend and said, "Mr. Clark, why do you want to return to Africa? Aren't there enough heathen in this country? I could bring you to the floor of the Exchange and show you a goodly company of heathen that need the message you bring." My friend responded that there are hundreds of men in New York City who know the gospel of the grace of God and are telling others of it, but what about those black men in Africa who have little opportunity to hear it? Aren't they entitled to hear that same message you have heard dozens of times, but to which you have paid no attention? There is no doubt that my friend, had he gone in for a business career, would have been a tremendous success. However, he turned his back upon success, as men call it, and went to Africa to tell the black man the glorious news that our Lord Jesus carried away our sins and will cover us with His righteousness if we will receive Him. Isn't that a wonderful message?

But I can hear someone say, Must *I* not *do* something? Sir, the thief who died on the cross never heard a sermon, never went to church, never received communion, and was never baptized. Yet, because he turned to our Lord who hung upon the cross and said to Him, "Lord, think of me when thou comest into thy kingdom" that thief, who in this generation would be called a Dillinger, was promised by Christ, "Today shalt thou be with me in paradise." That gangster went with Christ to paradise simply because he acknowledged the Lord. He did not do a thing. Christ did it all.

Before I close I want to draw your attention to the 8th verse, where the Psalmist said, "I will hear what God the LORD will speak: for he will speak peace unto his people, and to his saints . . ."

On the night of our Lord's resurrection, the disciples were gathered in the upper room in the city of Jerusalem. The doors were shut for fear of the people. Then to the shock and surprise of the disciples, the Lord Jesus appeared in their midst. I wish I were an artist and could paint the expressions on the faces of the disciples as they looked upon the form of the risen Lord. They thought they were seeing a ghost. Their minds had been bewildered during the course of the day as they heard others say they had seen the risen Christ. But *they* had not seen Him. Yet here He was right in their midst. Without a doubt, were He an ordinary man He would have rebuked them, saying, What fine friends you turned out to be. Not one of you stood by me. Not one of you had the backbone to stand against the crowd. You all turned and fled. Did He say anything of the kind? A thousand times NO! He said just what the Psalmist in this 8th verse of the 85th Psalm expressed when he wrote, "I will hear what God the LORD will speak: for he will speak peace unto his people, and to his saints . . ." What were the words that proceeded from the lips of the risen Lord, when He saw His disciples for the first time? He said *"Peace be unto you."* Then He showed them His hands and His side as if to confirm the fact that peace had been made.

Our Lord speaks the same message today—"Peace be unto you." I can hear someone say, Oh, but the Psalmist said, "for he will speak peace unto his people, and to his saints . . ."; one has to be a saint before he can have peace. You are correct; peace and sainthood go together, but you do not have to die to become a saint. Nor to be a living saint do you need to go about with a long-faced sober countenance. The Bible calls every believer in Christ a saint. The word *saint* means nothing more nor less than a separated one. A saint is a man or woman separated unto Christ. While God has some saints in His presence, He has many saints on earth who are still walking around in shoes. You do not become a saint by being good, but if you are a saint you will want to do good. Since Christ brings peace to your heart, and forgives your iniquities, you will want to give Him the worship of your heart and the service of your hands. This is all He asks; but before He wants anything from you He wants to give you His salvation. Will you receive Him *now* as your Saviour and Lord?

PSALM EIGHTY-SIX

IS PRAYER A POWER OR A FANTASY?

T HE 86th Psalm is called "A Prayer of David." In the opening verse David petitioned the Lord, saying:

> "Bow down thine ear, O LORD, hear me: for I am
> poor and needy."

The subject of prayer is one of intense interest. There are some who question its power. There are others who insist that it is merely the pastime of an imbecile mind. There are yet others who believe that prayer is the avenue of the soul's approach unto God.

OUR LORD, A MAN OF PRAYER

As one reads the Gospels he is impressed with the fact that our Lord was a man of prayer. In very few instances do we have the subject matter of His prayers. However, in the few that we do have we discover that the substance of our Lord's prayers was quite different from the substance of our prayers. In no case did our Lord ask the help of His Father as we ask God to aid us. Our Lord is all powerful in His own person. He is God manifest in the flesh. It is evident therefore that He did not pray in order to be sustained, or in order to receive help. Only on one occasion did He pray in a manner indicating that His Father possessed a power He Himself did not have. That was on the occasion of the agony in the garden, when He asked if it were possible that the cup, which symbolized "the judgment of God," be removed from Him. Yet He immediately added, "nevertheless not as I will, but as thou wilt." This instance clearly indicated the subjection of our Lord to His Father's will.

In the Gospel according to Luke, in the 11th chapter, we are informed that "it came to pass, that, as he (our Lord) was praying in a certain place, when he ceased, one of his disciples said unto him, Lord, teach us to pray, as John also taught his disciples" whereupon our Lord gave them that prayer, sometimes called the Lord's Prayer, but which more accurately is the disciples' prayer. Our Lord could never utter the petitions He asked His disciples to pray, such as "Forgive us our debts, as we forgive our debtors." Our Lord almost exclusively used prayer as an avenue of fellowship between His Father and Himself.

WHO CAN PRAY?

In the 86th Psalm, David, being a man of like passions with us, used prayer as a combination of petition and fellowship. There are so many sides to this subject of prayer that it is impossible to cover it with any degree of thoroughness in the short period of time we have. Sufficient to say that prayer is a vital part of a Christian's life.

That brings us to the first fact regarding prayer. Only a Christian can pray. A church member is not necessarily a Christian; but only those who have a relationship to God, by faith in Jesus Christ our Lord, can pray. Such are the very words of the Lord, who said, " . . . no man cometh unto the Father, but by me." However, that does not mean that if you are outside of Christ (that is, if you have not definitely received Christ as your Lord and Saviour) you are beyond the benefit of prayer.

Very often the prayers of a righteous man have brought great blessing upon another who did not pray, nor could pray.

For example, in the 2nd chapter of St. Mark's Gospel, we have the record of the healing of a paralytic man. We are told that his friends, four of them, brought him, urged by an assured, conscious faith that the Lord would heal their sick friend. The Scripture is clear to state, that "When Jesus saw *their* faith (notice the plural), he said unto the sick of the palsy, Son, thy sins be forgiven thee." At least we can say that this man was an unpardoned sinner when his friends brought him in.

After He had forgiven the sins of the sick man, He demonstrated to the group in the room that He had the power on earth to forgive sins, by healing the man of paralysis.

Someone asked this question of a friend of mine, who in turn presented it to me. "Has a Christian the right to pray for the unsaved, in view of the fact that our Lord said, in John 17, that He does not now pray for the world; He only prays for those who are His own in the world?" I responded, "Yes, for our Lord in that same chapter said: 'Neither pray I for these alone (that is, the eleven disciples gathered about Him), but for them also which shall believe on me through their word . . .' "

Thus, our Lord was praying for those who would become Christians through the testimony of the apostles and others who followed. If we, as believers in our Lord Jesus, would recognize the potency of prayer on the behalf of others, we would be amazed at the results of our faith.

A Scientist's View on Prayer

In that connection, a paragraph or two on the subject of prayer from the recent book entitled "Man, the Unknown," by Dr. Alexis Carrel, famous surgeon of the Rockefeller Institute, will be of interest. Dr. Carrel in his book does not present himself as a Christian, yet he acknowledges the potency of prayer in the healing of disease. Regarding it, the eminent physician said:

> "Prayer should be understood, not as a mere mechanical recitation of formulas, but as a mystical elevation, an absorption of consciousness in the contemplation of a principle both permeating and transcending our world. It is incomprehensible to philosophers and scientists, and inaccessible to them. But the simple seem to feel God as easily as the heat of the sun or the kindness of a friend."

The doctor goes on to say, "There is no need for the patient himself to pray, or even to have any religious faith. It is sufficient that someone around him be in a state of prayer." Speaking of the results in miraculous healings, he says, "They show the reality of certain relations, of still unknown nature. They open to man a new world." On this subject of the efficacy of prayer, he states that his conclusions are based on the observation of patients who have been cured almost instantly from various infections, such as tuberculosis, abscesses, cancer, etc. In quoting Dr. Carrel, I have not done so in order to go outside of the realm of Scripture for evidence of the efficacy of prayer, but refute the notion that prayer is merely the pastime of an imbecile mind, as is so often suggested by psychologists, sociologists, physiologists, and others.

So much for the matter of prayer and who can pray. Now notice the attitude of prayer, as we have it in the 1st verse of this 86th Psalm. You will observe that David addressed the Lord, saying: "Bow down thine ear, O LORD, hear me . . ." Again in the 6th verse he cried: "Give ear, O LORD, unto my prayer; and attend to the voice of my supplications."

It is quite evident that David was conscious of the personality of God whom he speaks of in that great, all-inclusive title of "Jehovah," and whom Christians understand to be none other than the Lord Jesus Christ.

Oh, the audacity of faith in action, when it lifts up its voice and invites God to bow down His ear and attend to the voice of our supplications.

It is clear to you, I think, that I believe in the majesty of Christ. A gentleman sent me a postcard, asking for some copies of last Sunday's meditation. As I read the contents of his card, it was as if a knife pierced into my heart because of the glib manner in which he spoke of the Lord Jesus Christ. I found it necessary to suggest that he failed to recognize the majesty of the Lord Jesus Christ, for he constantly and familiarly used the name Jesus. I reminded him that, as far as we know, no disciple ever addressed the Lord as Jesus. They addressed Him as Lord, or Master. Since our Lord's exaltation, following His humiliation upon the cross, He has been given a name which is above every name, of which the Scripture says, that at the name of Jesus every knee shall bow and every tongue confess that He is *Lord*, to the glory of God the Father.

The majesty of the person of Christ, the exalted Lordship of His position in the Godhead, is indescribable; yet we can, with the sincerest of intimacy, have fellowship with Him. When we consider the majesty of the Lord and then recognize that it is our right to address the Lord as

David did, we suddenly become conscious of the privileges of a Christian in this matter of prayer and the attention that God will give to the prayers of His children. When next you pray, I do trust that this consciousness will permeate your soul so that you may realize that you are in the presence of the great God of the universe.

THE SUBSTANCE OF PRAYER

Now regarding the substance of prayer. David said, "I am poor and needy." You are, and I am. We need to pray. We need the help of God. But David continued, praying for the preservation of his soul, for, said he, "I am holy . . ." What, David, didn't you make a mistake? You are a sinful man. You are not holy. You even committed adultery and you murdered a man. Aren't you mistaken when you say, "Preserve my soul; for I am holy . . ."? Were we to put that question to David I have no doubt as to his answer. He would say, I am not talking about my own righteousness. I am talking about what *I am to God*. By the use of the word *holy* I am referring to the fact that I have been set apart for God. Lest you have any notion that I am trusting in my own righteousness, please continue to read what I have to say in the 2nd verse, ". . . save thy servant that *trusteth* in thee."

The gospel of the grace of God is the power of God unto salvation to every one that believeth. I rejoice in it because I find that God, in the death of His Son, has made provision so that I can stand in His presence. He has provided me with a holiness I never had and never could have by anything I have done or ever could do, so that now I can stand in His presence. He has clothed me with His Son. That is what the Word of God teaches. "As he is," says the Scripture, "so are we in this world." That is what makes the gospel so powerful. God offers us complete redemption from sin, from the consequences of sin, and from the power of sin, through the sacrifice of His Son, and He also provides the right to stand in His presence, so that we can say as David said, ". . . I am holy: O thou my God, save thy servant that trusteth in thee."

As to the frequency of prayer, David said in the 3rd verse of this 86th Psalm, ". . . I cry unto thee daily." As to the glory of the grace of God, in the 5th verse David said: ". . . Thou Lord, art good, and ready to forgive; and plenteous in mercy unto all them that call upon thee."

We have already noted that prayer not only enables us to present our petitions before the Lord, but it also provides an opportunity for fellowship with God. Our prayer should not be devoted exclusively to petitions. They should be mingled with thanksgiving, even as the Apostle Paul declared in his letter to the Philippians, writing:

> "Be careful for nothing; but in every thing by prayer and supplication with thanksgiving let your requests be made known unto God.
>
> "And the peace of God, which passeth all understanding, shall guard your hearts and minds through Christ Jesus."

In the 8th verse David gave us an example of how to praise God in prayer, saying: "Among the gods there is none like unto thee, O Lord; neither are there any works like unto thy works." In the 10th verse he said: "For thou art great, and doest wondrous things: thou art God alone." Again, in the 12th and 13th verses he said:

> "I will praise thee, O Lord my God, with all my heart: and I will glorify thy name for evermore.
>
> "For great is thy mercy toward me: and thou hast delivered my soul from the lowest hell."

We will never know the joy that prayer can offer until we, as believers in Christ, take advantage of it as an opportunity to pour out our heart's affection upon the person of our Lord Jesus Christ.

Psalm Eighty-Seven

LOW BIRTH, HIGH BIRTH, NEW BIRTH—WHICH?

THE 87th Psalm is more of a song than a Psalm. It was intended for the sons of Korah. In many ways it is a strange Psalm. It reads:

> "His foundation is in the holy mountains.
>
> "The LORD loveth the gates of Zion more than all the dwellings of Jacob.
>
> "Glorious things are spoken of thee, O city of God. Selah.
>
> "I will make mention of Rahab and Babylon to them that know me: behold Philistia, and Tyre, with Ethiopia; this man was born there.
>
> "And of Zion it shall be said, This and that man was born in her: and the highest himself shall establish her.
>
> "The LORD shall count, when he writeth up the people, that this man was born there."

> "As well the singers as the players on instruments shall
> be there: all my springs are in thee."

Were I to ask for a word or a phrase to aptly describe this Psalm, I think most people would suggest "jigsaw." Undoubtedly, most of you worked out one or more jigsaw puzzles when they were so popular a few years ago. When all broken up into small bits it looked as if it were utterly impossible to put the pieces together to make a perfect design. But with patience and ingenuity each of the sections were pieced together, and when finally we inserted the last one in its proper place we were able to get a clear view of the whole picture.

DIFFICULT SCRIPTURES

To some people the entire Bible is a jigsaw puzzle, absurd as that idea is; it is difficult for some to put anything together. But there is no need to deny that there are things in the Scripture that are difficult to understand. The Bible freely acknowledges that to be the case. For instance, in the Old Testament we have an explicit statement that there are some things that are not revealed. In Deuteronomy, chapter 29, verse 29, it is written: "The secret things belong unto the LORD our God: but those things which are revealed belong unto us and to our children for ever . . ." In the New Testament we find a similar statement. In Peter's second letter, the Apostle acknowledged that some of the writings of Paul were hard to be understood. Let me read you what Peter had to say regarding them: ". . . our beloved brother Paul also according to the wisdom given unto him hath written unto you; as also in all his epistles, speaking in them of these things; in which are some things hard to be understood, which they that are unlearned and unstable wrest, as they do also the other scriptures, unto their own destruction."

Peter acknowledged that there were some things in Paul's writings that were hard to be understood. What should one do about them? Seek to wrest the Scriptures? Indeed not, if we are wise and instructed. Peter said that he "unlearned and unstable wrest (Paul's writings), as they do also the other scriptures, unto their own destruction." The wise and godly pass over the portion that is not clear, perfectly satisfied to leave it with the Lord, knowing that the Bible is the Word of God, that it was written by holy men of God as they were moved by the Holy Spirit. Therefore, it is utterly inconceivable that any man or group of men would ever know all there is to be known about any passage of Scripture. That is what distinguishes the Bible from every other book in the world. All other books or other writings can be thoroughly mastered, because they are the works of man. Because they are the works of man, man can understand them; but the Bible is the work of the Holy Spirit and, therefore, is beyond human wisdom.

When we approach a portion of Scripture which seems, on the surface, hard to be understood, we should present the matter to the Holy Spirit and ask for His guidance.

THE HOLY CITY

Now let us look at this Psalm a little more closely. The first three verses are the exuberant expressions of a patriot. As, for instance, in "America, the Beautiful," the writer is enrapt and enthralled with the glories of our land, so the Psalmist was enrapt and enthralled with the glories of the city called Zion. The city is built in a mountain range— very unusual type of mountain range. They are called the "holy mountains." What makes any city holy? What makes any individual holy? Holiness is nothing drab. I am aware that some people think that an individual, to be holy, must have a long-drawn countenance, marked with sadness. That is is a sadly mistaken notion. That may be a mock holiness, but never true holiness. Holiness simply means that an individual is separated unto God and belongs to the Lord. His joy is not in the things of this world; his joy is in the Lord and in Christ. Such a person is enjoying true happiness.

Thus, when the Psalmist said that the city has its foundations in the holy mountains, he was not talking about a drab country, but a country that had been set apart for God. In that country, set aside for God, there is a city. As one approaches its gates, they swing open to invite the visitor in. Concerning that city, and particularly the gates of that city, the Psalmist said, "The LORD loveth the gates of Zion more than all the dwellings of Jacob." There is no place in the world of which the Lord is as fond as the city of Zion. That city is called the city of God. The Psalmist said, "Glorious things are spoken of thee, O city of God."

Christendom seems to have gone through the Old Testament with a fine comb. Wherever it has found a blessing, it has applied it to the church; to the believer in this particular age. Wherever it has found a curse or judgment, it has magnanimously applied it to Israel, the ancient people of God. How gracious and kind Christendom has been! For instance, I was looking at a Bible this past week in which, concerning this particular Psalm, there is an italic comment at the head of it which reads, "the seat and glory of the church."

Now if you did not study this Psalm, you might think that whoever put that heading in knew what he was about, and that the Psalm concerned the church, the bride of Christ. But you won't find the church, or the bride of Christ in this Psalm. When the Old Testament speaks of Jerusalem and Israel, let us be honest and admit it concerns Israel according to the flesh, and Jerusalem, the city of Palestine. I know that the average Christian thinks that Zion is heaven. You may call it so. Heaven is heaven by any name you may term it, but when the Bible speaks of Zion it is speaking of Jerusalem. Jerusalem is the city which is in the heart of this 87th Psalm. The Lord loves the gates of Jerusalem more than the dwellings of Jacob. Of that city the Psalmist said, "Glorious things are spoken of thee."

Anyone acquainted with the Old Testament will acknowledge that there was a time when glorious things were spoken of Jerusalem. Take the reign of Solomon, for instance. A glorious reign and a wonderful city. But for almost two thousand years the city has been desolate, with devastation written all over. During the past decade a marvelous transformation has taken place. Where thorns and thistles grew, roses now bloom. Where barren wastes and wilderness formerly appeared, orchards are springing up. In fact, Palestine is probably the only country in the world which has escaped the ravages of the depression these last six years.

"THE KING OF GLORY"

However, when the Psalmist said, "Glorious things are spoken of thee . . ." he was not speaking of the revival that is now taking place in Jerusalem; he was talking about that day when, in the language of the 24th Psalm, the crier will say, "The earth is the LORD'S, and the fulness thereof; the world, and they that dwell therein." Then will come the message from the forerunners of the coming King, who will cry to those who watch at the gate, "Lift up your heads, O ye gates; and be ye lift up, ye everlasting doors; and the King of glory shall come in." Then the keepers at the gate will ask the advancing messengers of the King, "Who is this King of glory?" They will respond, "The LORD strong and mighty, the LORD mighty in battle." Then follow other messengers, who herald the approach of the King and join with the former group, crying, "Lift up your heads, O ye gates; even lift them up, ye everlasting doors; and the King of glory shall come in." Again, the gatekeepers ask, "Who is this King of glory?" to which the response will come, "The LORD of hosts, he is the King of glory."

The Bible is clear that some day the gates of Jerusalem shall be flung open wide and the King of glory will come in, followed by His host of redeemed ones. Then will take place the triumphal entry of the Lord, of which the first Palm Sunday was but a mere shadow and a miniature pageant.

Beginning with the 4th verse, the Psalmist continued:

> "I will make mention of Rahab (which, is Egypt) and Babylon to them that know me: behold Philistia, and Tyre, with Ethiopia; this man was born there.

> "And of Zion it shall be said, This and that man was born in her: and the highest himself shall establish her.

> "The LORD shall count, when he writeth up the people, that this man was born there."

One of the really fine books on the Psalms, which is now unfortunately out of print is a work written by Dr. J. J. Stewart Perowne, who was Dean of Peterborough. Writing on this 87th Psalm, he said:

> "Foreign nations are here described, not as captives or tributaries, not even as doing voluntary homage to the greatness and glory of Zion, but as actually incorporated and enrolled, by a new birth, among her sons. Even the worst enemies of their race, the tyrants and oppressors of the Jews, Egypt and Babylon, are threatened with no curse; no shout of joy is raised in the prospect of their overthrow, but the privileges of citizenship are extended to them, and they are welcomed as brothers. Nay, more, God Himself receives each one as a child newly-born into His family, acknowledges each as His son, and enrolls him with His own hand in the sacred register of His children.

> "It is this mode of anticipating a future union and brotherhood of all the nations of the earth, not by conquest, but by incorporation into one state, and by a birthright so acquired, which is so remarkable. In some of the Prophets, more especially in Isaiah, we observe the same liberal, conciliatory, comprehensive language toward foreign states, as Tyre and Ethiopia, and still more strikingly toward Egypt and Assyria. But the (87th) Psalm

stands alone amongst the writings of the Old Testament in representing this union of nations as a new birth into the city of God.

"This idea gives it a singular interest, and clearly stamps it (this Psalm) as Messianic. It is the Old Testament expression of the truth which St. Paul declares, when he tells us that in Christ 'there is neither Greek nor Jew, Barbarian, Scythian, bond nor free;' or when he writes to the Gentile church at Ephesus, 'Now therefore ye are no more strangers and foreigners, but fellow-citizens with the saints, and of the household of God.'

"It (this 87th Psalm) is the first announcement of that great amity of nations, or rather of that universal common citizenship of which heathen philosophers dreamt, which was 'in the mind of Socrates when he called himself a citizen of the world,' which has 'become a commonplace of the Stoic philosophy, which Rome accomplished, so far as the external semblance went, first by subduing the nations, and they by admitting them to the rights of Roman citizenship.' But the true fulfillment of this hope is to be found only in that kingdom which Christ will set up. He will gather into His commonwealth all the kingdoms of the earth. He will make men one, members of the same family.

"It is evident, that the hope of the Jewish singer is no false hope; that there is a Father in heaven who cares for all, whatever name they bear. Thus the Psalm will receive a better and higher fulfilment than that which lies on the surface of its words. It will be fulfilled in Christ.'"

In these words Dr. Perowne has given a clear picture of the teachings of the 87th Psalm. Men are born into the kingdom of God by faith in the Lord Jesus Christ. Indeed, I enjoy the words of another English writer who wrote three hundred years ago, "No birth is equal to a new birth in Christ."

Some people boast of their birth, their culture, their breeding, and their refinement. In fact, one would suppose they had selected their parents and station in life. How proud the flesh can be; yet the Bible says all flesh is as grass, and that which is born of the flesh is flesh. But whether we have had a low or a high birth, if we have not had a new birth in Christ, we do not know what it is to be well-born. If we have been born again in Christ, we will not glory in our fleshly birth; we will glory in our spiritual birth. Such is the mark of a true Christian.

PSALM EIGHTY-EIGHT

THE WAILING PSALM

T HE 88th Psalm is a most unusual Psalm. It is the darkest, saddest Psalm in all the book. As someone once said, "It is one wail of sorrow from beginning to end. It is the only Psalm in which the expression of feeling, the pouring out of the burdened heart before God, fails to bring relief and consolation."

In the oldest book of the Bible we have an evidence that almost from the beginning of time man was born to sorrow. In the 5th chapter of the Book of Job, the 7th verse, we read: "Yet man is born unto trouble, as the sparks fly upward."

But here is an unusual Psalm, for while we can find a number of Psalms which begin with a lamentation, there is only one such Psalm that ends with the wail still being heard. All other Psalms that begin with sorrow end with joy.

As the 88th Psalm is unique, we ought to give it our special attention. It is a little long, but it will pay us to read it.

> "O LORD God of my salvation, I have cried day and night before thee:
> "Let my prayer come before thee: incline thine ear unto my cry;
> "For my soul is full of troubles: and my life draweth nigh unto the grave.
> "I am counted with them that go down into the pit: I am as a man that hath no strength:
> "Free among the dead, like the slain that lie in the grave, whom thou rememberest no more: and they are cut off from thy hand.
> "Thou hast laid me in the lowest pit, in darkness, in the deeps.
> "Thy wrath lieth hard upon me, and thou hast afflicted me with all thy waves. Selah.
> "Thou hast put away mine acquaintance far from me; thou hast made me an abomination unto them: I am shut up, and I cannot come forth.
> "Mine eye mourneth by reason of affliction: LORD, I have called daily upon thee, I have stretched out my hands unto thee.
> "Wilt thou shew wonders to the dead? shall the dead arise and praise thee? Selah.
> "Shall thy lovingkindness be declared in the grave? or thy faithfulness in destruction?

"Shall thy wonders be known in the dark? and thy
righteousness in the land of forgetfulness?

"But unto thee have I cried, O LORD; and in the
morning shall my prayer prevent thee.

"LORD, why castest thou off my soul? why hidest thou
thy face from me?

"I am afflicted and ready to die from my youth up:
while I suffer thy terrors I am distracted.

"Thy fierce wrath goeth over me; thy terrors have cut
me off.

"They came round about me daily like water; they
compassed me about together.

"Lover and friend hast thou put far from me, and mine
acquaintance into darkness."

Those of you who have been brought up in the Church of England will
recall that the 88th Psalm is quoted during Holy Week. That might give us
a clue as to the meaning of the Psalm. At least, it would give an idea what
one group in Christendom thought of it. Incidentally this is another in the
series of Psalms which is a monologue. It was intended for a dialogue, but
the fact is, only one member speaks, while the other is terribly silent.

"STRONG CRYING AND TEARS"

We will observe, however, as we examine the Psalm, that there is a ray
of light that penetrates through the darkness, which enables us to understand that here is an example of what was in the mind of the writer of the
New Testament letter, the Epistle to the Hebrews, when he wrote, concerning our Lord Jesus, that ". . . in the days of his flesh, when he had offered
up prayers and supplications with strong crying and tears unto him that
was able to save him from death, and was heard in that he feared . . ." If
that statement seems strange, let me immediately quote what the Spirit of
God added, when He wrote, saying: "Though he were a Son, yet learned he
obedience by the things which he suffered; and being made perfect, he became the author of eternal salvation unto all them that obey him . . ."

We are dealing with a Psalm that corresponds to what Paul calls
strong meat. It is intended for those who are fully grown and matured. As
a babe in Christ, we desire the sincere milk of the Word, that we may grow
thereby. But as we grow in grace, and in the knowledge of the Lord, it is
expected that we will mature and be able to enjoy the deep things of God
which, the more one meditates upon, the more one marvels at the wonders
of the Bible, and the glorious grace of our God in the revelation of Jesus
Christ.

In the 53rd chapter of Isaiah, we have a prediction concerning the suffering Saviour, which will enable us to better understand the cry and the wail of the 88th Psalm. The opening verses of this chapter of Isaiah read:

> "Who hath believed our report? and to whom is the arm of the LORD revealed?
>
> "For he (that is, the Lord) shall grow up before him (that is, the Father) as a tender plant, and as a root out of a dry ground: he hath no form nor comeliness; and when we shall see him, there is no beauty that we should desire him."

Thus the Holy Spirit describes the reception given to our Lord Jesus by His own according to the flesh, which was fulfilled to the dotting of the "i" and the crossing of the "t." There was no beauty in Him. They did not desire Him. He did not possess that outward form of comeliness that is so attractive to the human eye. In fact, they said concerning Him, "Is not this the carpenter's son?" and "How knoweth this man letters, having never learned?" But, mark you, there is a touching reference to the character of our Lord Jesus, when the prophet said: "he shall grow up before him as a tender plant, and as a root out of a dry ground."

It is amazing that it should be written, concerning our Lord, that He shall "grow up" before the Father as a tender plant, which, of course, refers to His earthly ministry. Now a tender plant is never intended for a wilderness. It just does not belong there. It is not its environment. So our Lord did not belong here. His environment was heaven. He must have been uncomfortable in the presence of sin. But how wonderful that the prophet went on to say, that He is "as a root out of a dry ground." What do you suppose the Holy Spirit had in mind by that language? Some say it refers to the deadness of David's posterity. Might it not also refer to something else? Our Lord Jesus was different from any of the sons of men. We have been curiously wrought in the heart of the earth. We belong to the earth. We are made of the dust of the earth. Our roots are in the earth; but not so with our Lord Jesus. He is as a root out of a dry ground. He sustained His life from above and not from beneath. Continuing in the 53rd chapter of Isaiah, in the 3rd verse, we read: "He is despised and rejected of men; a man of sorrows, and acquainted with grief: and we hid as it were our faces from him; he was despised, and we esteemed him not." That verse speaks of just what we find in this 88th Psalm. Christ is a man of sorrows and the one acquainted with grief.

"OUT OF PLACE"

There are many things, particularly pleasures and associations, in life, that are perfectly fitting and proper for the worldly or earthly person. There is nothing evil or wrong about them, yet, a Christian in fellowship with his Lord feels out of place in such situations. I recall one which I was in a short while ago. There was nothing particularly evil about it, but it was just not the place I'd choose to be in if the Lord came. The result was that I felt uncomfortable. It was a relief when I got out of the place. I did not violate any fundamental law of God. I merely was in a place where the Lord Jesus Christ was not honored, but rather, where men and women tried to lull their consciences to sleep. As I sat in that room I could understand, in a measure, considering His matchless, sinless person, what our Lord must have endured to live in a world contrary to God. No wonder the Bible calls Him the man of sorrows, and one acquainted with grief. It was impossible that His life be otherwise.

BORN TO DIE

The extent and the character of that sorrow and grief with which He was acquainted is realized as we read the 88th Psalm. The Psalmist said:

"... I have cried day and night before thee:
"Let my prayer come before thee: incline thine ear
unto my cry;
"For my soul is full of troubles: and my life draweth
nigh unto the grave."

These words are the words of our Lord Jesus Christ, the man of sorrows, and the one acquainted with grief. How accurate are the words of our Lord, when He said, "my life draweth nigh unto the grave." Our Lord alone, among the sons of men, was born to die. We are born to live, and yet we are shockingly disappointed at the short span of our life. He was born to die and His life drew nigh unto the grave. In the 4th verse, He said: "I am counted with them that go down into the pit: I am as a man that hath no strength: free among the dead, like the slain that lie in the grave, whom thou rememberest no more: and they are cut off from thy hand." Of course, none of us can appreciate the agony of soul our Lord endured, which caused Him to cry out in this fashion.

There is so much in this Psalm, I hardly know what to pass over and what to comment upon. For instance, take again the 4th verse: "I am counted with them that go down into the pit: I am as a man that hath no strength . . ." If David or some other psalmist wrote this of himself, it would not be extraordinary; but these are the words of our Lord. It is astonishing that He should be counted with them that go down into the pit; that He should be as a man that hath no strength. If that seems incomprehensible to some, consider our Lord as He hung upon the cross. They nailed Him to the tree. They spat upon Him. They jeered at Him and cast all manner of mock salutations at Him, and then they pierced Him. Yet there was not one single evidence from Him that He possessed a power that could smite His enemies into the dust by just a spoken word; no evidence that He was the Lord of glory, the One who upholds all things by the word of His might. Oh, how accurate, therefore, is the New Testament when it states that "He was crucified through weakness . . ."

When we consider all Christ is, the mystery of Calvary will ever be the grandest theme of human mind and contemplation. There is only one way of explaining or understanding Calvary; that is to understand God's redemptive plan—that God was in Christ, reconciling the world unto Himself. To accomplish this redemption our Lord Jesus Christ was made sin for us, He who knew no sin, in order that we, in turn, might be made the righteousness of God in Him. Put in common language, He took our place in order that we might share His place with Him. To take our place, He had to take our sin. He had to pay the penalty of our sin. He had to experience the sufferings which the sinner would experience because of sin. He had to taste death.

When one thus understands Calvary, he forever becomes a worshipper of the Lord.

Psalm Eighty-nine—Part One

THE SONG BEGUN ON EARTH
AND CONTINUED IN HEAVEN

THIS 89th Psalm is quite long. It has fifty-two verses. We could not begin to cover it in one message, so that we shall devote another meditation to it, limiting this one to the opening verses. It is called a Psalm of instruction. It is ascribed to Ethan, the Ezrahite.

The Psalm opens with a song. It reads:

"I will sing of the mercies of the LORD for ever: with my mouth will I make known thy faithfulness to all generations.

"For I have said, Mercy shall be built up for ever: thy faithfulness shalt thou establish in the very heavens.

"I have made a covenant with my chosen, I have sworn unto David my servant,

"Thy seed will I establish for ever, and build up thy throne to all generations. Selah."

I do not believe that the speaker is the same in the first two verses as in the 3rd and 4th verses. It appears from the 1st and 2nd verses that the speaker is the writer of the Psalm, whereas in the 3rd and 4th and some of the following verses the Psalmist is recording the language of the Lord, as the Lord Himself is the speaker.

Let us look at the 1st verse and note its message. Said Ethan, the Psalmist, "I will sing of the mercies of the LORD for ever." Frequently, during the course of these meditations in the Psalms, we have observed that God provides a song for His people, even in the night.

All the world understands the influence of good music. Any normal individual thoroughly enjoys a symphony conducted by an artist, in which trained, artistic players join together in presenting a harmonious rhythm of musical glory. I shall have to confess that much of what is called music I am not able to appreciate, but I am aware that some of our hymn writers have attempted to ape "Broadway," by giving us some jazzy hymns.

However, the singing heart is a joyful heart. To sing a song from the heart drives away the shadows, relieves the burden, and ministers a balm to the distressed spirit. Usually men sing after they have gotten out of some difficulty; but that which distinguishes a Christian from all others is the fact that he can sing in the midst of trial and disappointment. "He giveth songs in the night."

The finest music that has ever been produced centers around the fact of the coming of Christ, His death, and His resurrection. At least, to my own heart all other music fades into silence alongside of the glorious strains of a gospel song.

"THE MOST BEAUTIFUL HYMN"

Dr. Hugh R. Munro recently wrote an article entitled, "The Most Beautiful Hymn," in which he gave, as his judgment, a hymn that was composed by Bernard of Clairvaux, of France, in the 12th century, as being the pre-eminent Christian hymn. It has many verses, but I want to quote only two:

> "Jesus, Thou Joy of loving hearts,
>   Thou Fount of life! Thou Light of men!
> From the best bliss that earth imparts
>   We turn unfilled to Thee again.
>
> "Thy truth unchanged hath ever stood;
>   Thou hearest those that on Thee call;
> To them that seek Thee Thou art good;
>   To them that find Thee All in all!"

Whatever be your choice hymn, there is no doubt that to the redeemed heart the center of joy is in the person of the Lord Jesus Christ. You will observe that just as the heart of a Christian today finds the acme of joy in the person of Christ, so the Psalmist found his joy and his song in the Lord Himself. Thus he wrote in the opening verse, "I will sing of the mercies of the LORD for ever: with my mouth will I make known thy faithfulness to all generations."

THE SINGERS AND THEIR SONGS

There is so much in this first verse, it has seemed to me as I have thought upon it that every word has depths that are unfathomable. "I will sing." Who will sing? Who can sing? The redeemed soul! Who are the redeemed? Those who have received Christ as their Lord and Saviour! Who may receive Him? *Whosoever will!* Does it make any difference how bad or how good an individual has been? Not the slightest! ". . . all have sinned, and come short of the glory of God"! What must I do to be saved? Simply this—"Believe on the Lord Jesus Christ, and thou shalt be saved"! What happens when I do that? The Bible says that I pass out of death into life; out of self and into Christ; out of condemnation and into the glorious liberty of the sons of God! Is it any wonder that every soul who knows and has had that experience, joins with the Psalmist in the 89th Psalm, when he said, "I will sing"!!

What is the substance of the song? What you and I have done? A thousand times NO! Our religion, our devotion, or our good deeds? Again, a thousand times NO! What is the substance of the song of the redeemed? The Psalmist gave it, saying, "I will sing of the mercies of the LORD . . ." Is God merciful? I need only quote one passage of Scripture—"But God, who is rich in mercy, for his great love wherewith he loved us, even when we were dead in sins . . . hath raised us up together (with Christ), and made us sit together in heavenly places in Christ Jesus: that in the ages to come he might shew the exceeding riches of his grace in his kindness toward us through Christ Jesus."

When a man becomes conscious of the super-abounding mercy of God he ceases to talk about himself. On the contrary, he begins to extol his Lord. I appreciate that there are many well-meaning (though untaught) Christians, who boast of their experiences, who make much of their devotion and their good deeds. The fact is, that they have never stayed long enough in the presence of their Lord, nor meditated sufficiently in the Bible, to understand, first, their own sinfulness, their depravity, their own incapabilities; and, second, the glorious person of the Lord Jesus Christ, and the wonderful grace of our God, not only in forgiving our trespasses, but in actually accepting us in the beloved Son, so that every redeemed individual stands in the presence of God as perfect as His own Son.

If that strikes some as being more glorious and more wonderful than you have ever dreamed possible, I assure you that it is actually the teaching of the Scriptures. You and I are halting, stumbling, and disappointing, even to our own selves. Yet God has received us in Christ, and has given us a position in His grace whereby He has justified us from all sin from which we "could not be justified by the law of Moses." It is any wonder that the Psalmist said, "I will sing of the mercies of the LORD"? How long? He said, "for ever." How long will a Christian sing? Just as long as the Psalmist said, "for ever." When we come into the presence of our Lord and when these eyes shall behold His glory, we will join in the song which is found in the 9th verse of the 5th chapter of the book of The Revelation, the last book of the Bible, where it is written: "And they sung a new song . . ." But, mark well, as we examine the subject of the new song, we find it is the same song that has been sung in the heart of every believer since he was redeemed, for, said John, the writer of The Revelation:

> "They sung a new song, saying, Thou (our Lord Jesus) art worthy to take the book, (the title deed to the earth), and to open the seals thereof: for thou wast slain, and hast redeemed us to God by thy blood out of every kindred, and tongue, and people, and nation;
>
> "And hast made us unto our God a kingdom of priests: and we shall reign over the earth."

Now then, coming back to the 1st verse of the 89th Psalm, Ethan, the writer, said not only that he would sing of the mercies of the Lord forever, but he would also with his mouth make known the faithfulness of his God to all generations. Again I repeat what I have already stated, that the substance of the *song* of the redeemed is the mercy of the Lord, so the substance of the *message* of the redeemed soul is the faithfulness of God. Let me illustrate what I mean, by an incident I have mentioned before.

Some years ago I was employed by the United States Steel Corporation. We had a large office; I should judge there were at least seventy-five desks in the one room. Most of the desks were of the double type; that is, one man sat on one side and another on the other side. I was seated at such a desk. There was a young man opposite me. One morning this young man said, like a thunderbolt out of a clear sky, "Mr. Olsen, I just cannot understand how you can say that you *know* you are saved. I think it is presumptuous for a man to say so. I do not believe any of us will ever get to know whether or not we are acceptable to God until after our death, when our life will be weighed in the balance, and if our good deeds overbalance our bad deeds, we will then be privileged to enter into heaven."

It may be that there are many who have much the same thoughts as were expressed by that young man. If you have such thoughts, listen to my response. I asked him one question. It was this, "Can God be trusted?" He responded, "Why, I never said that He cannot be trusted." I asked him another question, "Do you believe God is able to speak clearly and plainly what He means?" Again he stated, "I have never questioned that. I was talking about what you think and say." I answered, "I know you don't, but I ask again, 'Can God be trusted when He makes a statement?'" "Certainly," was the answer. Then I said, "Listen to what God says in the 10th chapter of Paul's letter to the Romans, verses 9 and 10."

> "That if thou shalt confess with thy mouth the Lord Jesus, and shalt believe in thine heart that God hath raised him from the dead, *thou shalt be saved.*
>
> "For with the heart man believeth unto righteousness; and with the mouth confession is made unto salvation."

Then I said to that young man, "The Bible says that if I confess with my mouth the Lord Jesus (and that I have done and am doing), and if I will believe in my heart that God raised Christ from the dead (and I certainly do), I shall be saved. I believe God is able to say what He means, don't you?" That young man looked astounded.

The accusation that God is making today against men and women who have heard the gospel and who have not received Christ is this, (it is found in the 10th verse of the 5th chapter of the 1st Epistle of John)—

> ". . . he that believeth not God hath made him a liar; because he believeth not the record that God gave of his Son.
>
> "And this is the record, that God hath given to us eternal life, and this life is in his Son.
>
> "He that hath the Son hath life; and he that hath not the Son of God hath not life."

Finally I suggested to that young man that if I did not believe God I would make Him a liar. It would be equivalent for me to say that God cannot be trusted. To which he responded, "Now I see what you mean by saying that you *know* you are saved." Indeed, I know, because God said I would be saved if I believed and confessed the Lord Jesus Christ. No wonder the Psalmist said in this 89th Psalm, "with my mouth will I make known thy faithfulness to all generations."

THE FAITHFULNESS OF GOD

God is faithful to His Word. He is faithful to His Son. God will be faithful to every individual who will believe His Word. I close by giving a specific invitation to you who have not yet confessed with your mouth the Lord Jesus, and believed in your heart that God hath raised Him from the dead. I invite you now to do that very thing this moment. Turn to whoever is by your side, and say, "I believe and receive the Lord Jesus Christ as my Saviour and my Lord." If you do that and believe that God raised Christ from the dead, then, on the testimony of God, "thou shalt be saved." I repeat, God is faithful to His Word. He will save you as He has saved every individual who dared to believe His Word.

Before I close, may I say just a word regarding the 2nd verse, where the Psalmist wrote: "For I have said, Mercy shall be built up for ever: thy faithfulness shalt thou establish in the very heavens." It is great to think that "Mercy shall be built up for ever . . ." that is, that mercy always exceeds one's need or, to put it in the language of the New Testament, "where sin abounded, grace did much more abound . . ." It is also comforting to observe that the Lord's faithfulness shall be established in the very heavens. Not only on earth, but when we get into His presence, we will find that His faithfulness to His promise is established in heaven as well. What a gospel! It befits the great person of the eternal God!

PSALM EIGHTY-NINE—PART TWO

WHEN GOD MAKES AN AGREEMENT— DOES HE KEEP IT?

O
UR first meditation on the 89th Psalm was limited specifically to the 1st and 2nd verses, which read:

> "I will sing of the mercies of the LORD for ever: with my mouth will I make known thy faithfulness to all generations.

> "For I have said, Mercy shall be built up for ever: thy faithfulness shalt thou establish in the very heavens."

Now we shall attempt to cover the next eighteen verses.

THE DAVIDIC COVENANT

The 3rd and 4th verses of the Psalm will help us get a proper perspective of the general theme of the Psalm. There we read:

> "I have made a covenant with my chosen, I have sworn unto David my servant,

> "Thy seed will I establish forever, and build up thy throne to all generations."

Now a covenant is an agreement. In these verses the Lord affirms that He had made an agreement or a contract with David, who was king over Israel and who was a servant of the Lord. In this contract God swore. That is quite a strong word. God swore to David that He would accomplish certain things. The complete details of that contract are found in the 7th chapter of the 2nd Book of Samuel.

When God makes a contract or an agreement with any group of men or any specific man, it behooves us to examine that contract. The chief stipulation in the agreement was this, "Thy seed (that is, David's family) will I establish for ever, and build up thy throne to all generations." This contract is known as "The Davidic Covenant."

Now David was an interesting character. He was the youngest son of a large family. He was taken by the Lord from a sheepfold and put upon the throne of Israel. His predecessor was King Saul, a man after Israel's choice. They chose King Saul because he was good-looking, attractive, tall, and handsome. Saul was the kind of man who would not only engage the eye of a woman, but he would be the ideal of any man. Every one acclaimed him and he began his reign with every hope of success. All the while God had a man. He was a mere stripling. God was training that boy for rulership. His training school was out in a wilderness, tending his father's sheep. When the time of God's appointment came, that young lad, ruddy-cheeked and with the smell of the field on his garments, was taken from the training school and put upon the throne. God said, concerning him, This is the man "after mine own heart . . ."

While David sinned (and so has every other man) and at times disappointed the Lord, as every other servant of God has disappointed Him, nevertheless, David's heart was right. He loved the Lord from the bottom of his heart. His reign and kingdom evidenced his fellowship with the Lord. God therefore swore to David that He would perpetuate his throne, that He would build it up to all generations, and that He would establish his family forever.

THE RUIN OF THE THRONE—AND THE POWER OF GOD

Anyone familiar with the history of the Jewish people will recall that very few generations passed before the kingdom was rent in twain, ten of the tribes forming the Northern Kingdom and the remaining two tribes, the Southern Kingdom, commonly called Judah, and, as every school boy knows, or should know, no king has reigned on David's throne for more than two thousand years.

When Ethan wrote the 89th Psalm, the throne of David had either already toppled or was ready to fall; certainly, at least, every one knew that its collapse was at hand. Yet, Ethan wrote, quoting the words of the Lord to David. That brings up the question of the faithfulness of God to His own promises. From a first glance at the Psalm it would appear that there is a break, commencing with verse 5 up to and including verse 17, for no reference is made in these verses to the fulfillment of the promise that God made to David. On the contrary, these verses have no relation to the promise that God made to David.

It has been said, "as you examine the Psalm, you are struck with the suddenness with which the promise of God is introduced into the Psalm and then to observe how it stands alone, with a brevity that is almost startling, while the Psalmist proceeds to comment upon the faithfulness and the power of the One who made the promise to David." For instance, let us read a few of these verses. The 5th verse reads: "And the heavens shall praise thy wonders, O LORD: thy faithfulness also in the congregation of the saints." Again, the 8th verse reads: "O LORD God of hosts, who is a strong LORD like unto thee? or to thy faithfulness round about thee?" And then, commencing with verse 9, the Psalmist directed attention to the power of God, manifested in creation. He said: "Thou rulest the raging of the sea: when the waves thereof arise, thou stillest them." Again, in verse 12:, "The north and the south thou hast created them: Tabor and Hermon shall rejoice in thy name."

How interesting that in this Psalm, where the promise God made to David as to the perpetual character of his kingdom was spoken of, when that kingdom was either ready to collapse or had collapsed, the Psalmist should call attention to the faithfulness of God. What is more, not only did he call attention to the faithfulness of God, but he demonstrated that God has the power to keep His Word. That is interesting and presents a problem comparable to that which exists in our own lives this very day.

This problem may be briefly stated in the form of a question. How can anyone recognize the faithfulness of God, in view of the apparent contradictions of life? If you are a Jew, you may ask the question, How can it be reconciled that God promised David that he would have a King who would forever sit upon his throne, a direct heir, and yet that throne has been empty for more than two thousand years?

Though the circumstances seem contrary, the fact is, they can easily be reconciled. To do so, let us go to the opening statement of the New Testament. The very first words from the pen of Matthew, the writer of the first Gospel, are these: "The book of the generation of Jesus Christ, *the son of David,* the son of Abraham." From that first verse on through the twenty-seven books of the New Testament, until we come to the very close of it (which closing statement has the promise of the Son of David, Jesus Christ, that He will come again) the whole content of the New Testament is concerned with the One who is the promised heir to the throne of David.

There is an element in life which seeks to break down God's plan. The Bible calls that element sin. Sin strikes at the throne of God. Sin hinders the will of God. Sin has marred the creation of God. Sin robs a man of his likeness to God. Sin leaves chaos and disruption in its wake. Sin overthrew the throne of David. Sin is responsible for the fact that the throne of David has been unoccupied for two thousand years. Sin is responsible for every ill and disappointment in this world. Laugh at it, if you will; philosophize it out of your thinking, if you care to; but the stark, bold fact of sin crouches at your own feet. However, sin cannot thwart the purpose of God. Because of the promise God made to David, that He would perpetuate his throne and that He would establish it for all generations, the New Testament has introduced the son of David, Jesus Christ, our Lord, who is also the son of Abraham.

To prove that Jesus Christ is the legal and rightful heir to the throne, two genealogies are given: one in Matthew's Gospel and the other in that of Luke. In one, we have His genealogy through Joseph's line, while in the other we have the genealogy through the line of Mary, His mother's line. Both of them traced their ancestry back to David; one through Solomon, the legal heir to the throne, and the other, through Nathan, who possessed the blood-right to the throne.

There never has and never will be any other who has both the legal and the blood-right to the throne of David. Jesus Christ our Lord possesses it. In the New Testament there is a promise, that just as our Lord Jesus Christ left this world, leaving it from Mount Olivet, and being caught up into the heavens, so He will return to the very place from which He left, and He will establish the throne of David forever. In the 16th verse of the 15th chapter of The Acts of the Apostles, we have this statement: ". . . I will return, and will build again the tabernacle of David, which is fallen down; and I will build again the ruins thereof, and I will set it up . . ."

THE POWER OF FAITH

Now let us go back to our Psalm. The Psalmist, after bringing in the Davidic covenant, which to all intents and purposes was not being fulfilled, called attention to the might of God in creation to strengthen the heart of the believer. Faith looks beyond circumstances, to the one who possesses all power in heaven and in earth.

Faith uses obstacles as stepping-stones to God. Faith removes the mountains of doubt and makes them ladders into His presence. Faith could cause Stephen, the first Christian martyr, to disregard the stones that were hurled at his body, and the gnashing teeth of his antagonists, because he, being "full of the Holy Spirit, looked up stedfastly into heaven, and saw the glory of God, and Jesus standing at the right hand of God." Faith enabled him to endure the stones, the trials, and the taunts and jibes of his enemies, so that he could turn to that group and say, "Behold, I see the heavens opened, and the Son of man standing on the right hand of God."

Now we see clearly why the Psalmist, upon introducing the promise of God to David, could leave it seemingly unconnected and proceed to write of the power of God and His faithfulness? After he had done that, he returned in verse 18 and said: "For the LORD is our defence; and the Holy One of Israel is our king."

PLACING THE BLAME ON GOD

I N giving the third and final message on the 89th Psalm, we want to center our thoughts around the 35th verse which reads:

> "Once have I sworn by my holiness that I will not lie unto David."

In our two previous meditations on this 89th Psalm, we have endeavored to set forth the historical setting, stating that the throne of David had already fallen or was tottering, and yet, despite this fact, the whole theme of the Psalm relates to the promise which God had given to David, that He would perpetuate his throne and family line.

We also considered the details of the covenant itself and why the Psalmist, after enumerating them, proceeded to extol the faithfulness of God and the power of God.

THE PROMISES OF GOD

There is a very interesting dialogue, which occupies the major section of the Psalm, in which the voice of the Lord is heard. This dialogue commences with verse 20 and continues to practically the close of the Psalm. Let us read a few verses, commencing with verse 20, in which the Lord speaks, stating:

> "I have found David my servant; with my holy oil have I anointed him:
>
> "With whom my hand shall be established: mine arm also shall strengthen him.
>
> "The enemy shall not exact upon him; nor the son of wickedness afflict him:
>
> "And I will beat down his foes before his face, and plague them that hate him.
>
> "But my faithfulness and my mercy shall be with him: and in my name shall his horn be exalted.
>
> "I will set his hand also in the sea, and his right hand in the rivers.
>
> "He shall cry unto me, Thou art my father, my God, and the rock of my salvation.
>
> "Also I will make him my firstborn, higher than the kings of the earth.
>
> "My mercy will I keep for him for evermore, and my covenant shall stand fast with him."

We have read as far as verse 28. Let us stop there and notice some of the things that the Lord Himself has said. First, notice the frequency of the promises of God, expressed by the phrases, "I will" and "I have." Take the case of the phrase "I have." God says: "I have found David . . . I have anointed him." Now notice the frequency of the phrase "I will."

> "I will beat down his foes . . .
> I will set his hand also in the sea . . .
> I will make him my firstborn, higher than the kings of the earth . . .
> My mercy will I keep for him . . .
> His seed also will I make to endure."

Then, after enumerating the things that the Lord has already done, and the promises for the future expressed by the phrase "I will," commencing with verse 30, a responsibility is enjoined upon the descendants of David.

> "If his children forsake my law, and walk not in my judgments;
> "If they break my statutes, and keep not my commandments;
> "Then will I visit their transgression with the rod, and their iniquity with stripes.
> "Nevertheless my lovingkindness will I not utterly take from him, nor suffer my faithfulness to fail.
> "My covenant will I not break, nor alter the thing that is gone out of my lips.
> "Once have I sworn by my holiness that I will not lie unto David.
> "His seed shall endure for ever, and his throne as the sun before me.
> "It shall be established for ever as the moon, and as a faithful witness in heaven. Selah."

In these verses we note that while many of the promises that God made were based on His own prerogative, still some of the blessings that would be enjoyed were based on the faithfulness of the descendants of David. Failure to meet these requirements would entail punishment. Nevertheless, even if the children of Israel failed, God would remain true to His covenant to David, for He said in verses 34 and 35: "My covenant will I not break, nor alter the thing that is gone out of my lips. Once have I sworn by my holiness that I will not lie unto David." Here is the promise: "His seed shall endure for ever, and his throne as the sun before me. It shall be established for ever as the moon, and as a faithful witness in heaven."

THE WORK OF GOD

After God thus speaks, another voice is heard, and that voice has the audacity to speak to God and to remind Him of what *He has done*. That is interesting. God promised He would do certain things—I will be faithful to David; I will keep my promise to him; I will establish his seed for ever. Yet, another who intrudes, commencing with verse 38, dares to charge God with responsibility for the collapse of the throne. Let us read, commencing with verse 38:

> ". . . *thou hast* cast off and abhorred, *thou hast* been wroth with thine anointed.
>
> "*Thou hast* made void the covenant of thy servant: *thou hast* profaned his crown by casting it to the ground.
>
> "*Thou hast* broken down all his hedges; *thou hast* brought his strong holds to ruin."
>
> * * * *
>
> ". . . *thou hast* made all his enemies to rejoice.
>
> "*Thou hast* also turned the edge of his sword . . ."

What audacity that speaker had who dared to place the responsibility for the collapse of the throne of David upon the Lord!

If my memory serves me, there is only one other comparable situation in the Bible, the record of which is found in the 32nd chapter of the book of Exodus. The conversation there is between the Lord, on one side, and Moses on the other. The situation was as follows: The children of Israel had broken the law in a most abominable manner. They had forgotten all about the fact that God had led them out of Egypt, and because Moses tarried in the presence of God, they decided that he had gone forever. They had to have something to worship, so they suggested to Aaron, Make us gods. He did so, and then said, "These be thy gods, O Israel, which brought thee up out of the land of Egypt." And they built an altar, and rose up early in the morning and offered burnt-offerings, and peace-offerings. Then we have this statement: "and the people sat down to eat and to drink, and rose up to play."

The play referred to was probably the vilest expression of degraded morality that is found in the Scripture. The result, of course, was that the Lord became angry with the people and said to Moses: ". . . get thee down; for *thy* people which *thou* broughtest out of the land of Egypt, have corrupted themselves . . . I have seen this people, and, behold, it is a stiff-necked people . . ." God also said to Moses: "Now therefore let me alone, that my wrath may wax hot against them, and that I may consume them:

and I will make of thee a great nation." Yet Moses had the audacity to say: ". . . LORD, why doth thy wrath wax hot against *thy* people, which *thou* hast brought forth out of the land of Egypt with great power, and with a mighty hand?"

Did you observe that God said, concerning Israel, Moses, they are thy people; while Moses in effect, said, No, they are not; they are Thy people.

The result of this intercession upon Moses' part brought a remarkable change, for in the 14th verse of this 32nd chapter of Exodus we have this statement: "And the LORD repented of the evil which he thought to do unto his people."

In the 89th Psalm we have a comparable situation. Said the Lord—I promised David; I will not lie— ". . . I have sworn by my holiness that I will not lie unto David. His seed shall endure for ever, and his throne as the sun before me." Yet, there is one who intercedes, saying the responsibility for the collapse of David's throne, for the dispersion of the children of Israel, for their becoming a reproach to their neighbors, belongs to God for, said he, "thou hast done it." This one, who has the audacity to so speak, says in the 49th and 50th verses:

> "Lord, where are thy former lovingkindnesses, which thou swarest unto David in thy truth?
>
> "Remember, Lord, the reproach of thy servants; how I do bear in my bosom the reproach of all the mighty people; . . ."

I believe, that the 50th verse of this Psalm indicates who the speaker is who dares to say to God that He is responsible for Israel's disturbances. It is the One who said: ". . . I do bear in my bosom the reproach of all the mighty people . . ." Who bore the reproach? Can it be any other than the Lord Jesus Christ. "The reproaches of them that reproach thee," said He in another Psalm, "are fallen upon me."

WHO IS RESPONSIBLE WHEN ISRAEL IS PERSECUTED?

This Psalm, particularly this dialogue, is extremely interesting and timely. If there is any one thing that is established in the Bible it is this, that faithfulness to God, upon the part of Israel, would be rewarded by the abundant blessing of God, whereas unfaithfulness to God would cause the Lord to pour out His judgments.

Just now, the Jews are feeling the oppression of the enemy once again. All the civilized world has joined with the Jew in expressing indignation against this oppression; but I say with all kindliness that Moses and every prophet who followed him has borne a unanimous testimony to the truth of this 89th Psalm, that the Lord Himself is responsible when Israel feels the edge of the enemies' sword.

All the protest meetings in the world will never accomplish for Israel what God said He would do whenever they would return unto the Lord and obey His voice. The promise of God which we find in Deuteronomy 30 is still true:

> "That then the LORD thy God will turn thy captivity, and have compassion upon thee.
>
> *   *   *   *
>
> "And the LORD thy God will put all these curses upon thine enemies, and on them that hate thee, which persecuted thee.
>
> *   *   *   *
>
> ". . . for the LORD will again rejoice over thee for good, as he rejoiced over thy fathers . . ."

Let it never be forgotten that history has a way of repeating itself. The very gallows that Haman had built for Mordecai, the Jew, in Queen Esther's time, became the gallows upon which Haman was hanged instead of Mordecai, but this came about because of what is written in the 3rd verse of the 4th chapter of the book of Esther, where we read: ". . . there was great mourning among the Jews, and fasting, and weeping, and wailing; and many lay in sackcloth and ashes."

"My Firstborn, Higher Than the Kings of the Earth"

Now then, let's drop the subject of Israel for a moment, and see if we Gentiles who have confessed the Lord Jesus as our Lord and Saviour, can find a blessing from this portion of Scripture.

Did you notice as we read the 27th verse, that God said, concerning the one who will sit on David's throne, ". . . I will make him my first-born, higher than the kings of the earth." I hardly need impress upon you that this promise refers to none other than our Lord Jesus Christ. It is He who is the first-begotten from the dead. It is He who at present is the Prince of the kings of the earth, the heir-apparent to all earthly thrones. But some day (and we pray it will be in the very near future) the kings of the earth will be obliged to abdicate their thrones, and the Prince will become the King of kings, and the Lord of lords. It is He who is David's greater Son. He shall reign on David's throne as the Prince of Peace, as the beloved of the Father, and as the Saviour of the world.

Is it any wonder, therefore, that the Lord declares, beginning at verse 34 of this 89th Psalm:

> "My covenant (or my agreement) will I not break, nor alter the thing that is gone out of my lips.
> "Once have I sworn by my holiness that I will not lie unto David.
> "His seed shall endure for ever, and his throne as the sun before me."

The God who said, I will not lie unto David, said to David's Son, yet David's Lord, in Psalm 2, verse 8: "Ask of me, and I shall give thee the Gentiles for thine inheritance, and the uttermost parts of the earth for thy possession." That One is our Lord Jesus Christ, of whom it is written in Luke's Gospel, the 2nd chapter, that when He was but a child, Mary and Joseph brought Him to Jerusalem to present Him to the Lord; and while there in the temple, Simeon, a just and devout man—the Holy Spirit having revealed unto him that he should not see death, before he had seen the Lord's Christ—took the child up in his arms, and blessed God, saying:

> "Lord, now lettest thou thy servant depart in peace, according to thy word:
> "For mine eyes have seen thy salvation,
> "Which thou hast prepared before the face of all people;
> "A light to lighten the Gentiles, and the glory of thy people Israel."

PSALM NINETY—PART ONE

MOSES—THE MAN AND HIS GOD

THE 90th Psalm is the beginning of the fourth book of the Psalms. There are five books, all told. The fourth begins with the 90th Psalm, and ends with the 106th Psalm.

Note that this is not a Psalm written by David, but rather it is a prayer written by Moses, the man of God. We shall read the Psalm, before commenting upon it:

> "LORD, thou hast been our dwelling place in all generations.
> "Before the mountains were brought forth, or ever thou hadst formed the earth and the world, even from everlasting to everlasting, thou art God.
> "Thou turnest man to destruction; and sayest, Return, ye children of men.
> "For a thousand years in thy sight are but as yesterday when it is past, and as a watch in the night.

"Thou carriest them away as with a flood; they are as a sleep: in the morning they are like grass which groweth up.

"In the morning it flourish, and groweth up; in the evening it is cut down, and withereth.

"For we are consumed by thine anger, and by thy wrath are we troubled.

"Thou hast set our iniquities before thee, our secret sins in the light of thy countenance.

"For all our days are passed away in thy wrath: we spend our years as a tale that is told.

"The days of our years are threescore years and ten; and if by reason of strength they be fourscore years, yet is their strength labour and sorrow; for it is soon cut off, and we fly away.

"Who knoweth the power of thine anger? even according to thy fear, so is thy wrath.

"So teach us to number our days, that we may apply our hearts unto wisdom.

"Return, O LORD, how long? and let it repent thee concerning thy servants.

"O satisfy us early with thy mercy; that we may rejoice and be glad all our days.

"Make us glad according to the days wherein thou hast afflicted us, and the years wherein we have seen evil.

"Let thy work appear unto thy servants, and thy glory unto their children.

"And let the beauty of the LORD our God be upon us: and establish thou the work of our hands upon us, the work of our hands establish thou it."

We have already seen that this 90th Psalm is a prayer. Psalms, therefor, can be used for prayer, as well as praise. In fact, in my own prayer life I find myself again and again reverting to the Psalms, in order to express to the Lord those strange emotions that enter into the human heart.

"THE MAN OF GOD"

Here is a prayer which has been preserved for posterity. I like its title, "A Prayer of Moses the man of God." That's interesting—Moses, the man of God. Moses was the man who had that marvelous experience of speaking with God, face to face, even though at times it was through a thick cloud. Moses also was the man who said to his people, "The LORD thy God will raise up unto thee a Prophet from the midst of thee, of thy brethren, like unto me; unto him ye shall hearken . . ." Thus Moses was a type of that Prophet that God would raise up. Israel expected Him from that time on, and whenever anyone arose who had an extraordinary minis-

try, they asked, "Art thou that prophet?" as they did in the case of John
the Baptist. However, the Prophet of whom Moses spoke was none other
than the Lord Jesus Christ.

But not only was Moses a prophet; he was a man of God. One does
not have to be a prophet to be a man of God. If such were the case, how
few of us would have the honor of being called "a man of God." But,
whether it has ever occurred to us, you and I may be called by that title,
if we embrace, by faith, the privileges that are ours in Christ. It is for that
reason that Paul wrote to his young friend, Timothy, and said: "All scripture is given by inspiration of God, and is profitable for doctrine, for reproof, for correction, for instruction in righteousness: That the man of
God may be perfect, throughly furnished unto all good works."

There are so many things in this Psalm on which I would like to comment, that we shall limit this meditation to the first two verses. Let us
read them again.

> "LORD, thou hast been our dwelling place in all gene-
> rations.
> "Before the mountains were brought forth, or ever thou
> hadst formed the earth and the world, even from ever-
> lasting to everlasting, thou art God."

What a wonderful way to address the Lord! What intimacy is revealed! What expressions that demonstrate true humility! Did you observe
the manner in which Moses addressed the Lord? No pronoun is used. He
did not say, "My LORD" or, "Our LORD." He just said, "LORD."

The disciples came to our Lord on one occasion and asked Him to
teach them to pray, whereupon He said unto them, "When ye pray, say,
Our Father which art in heaven, Hallowed be thy name. Thy kingdom
come. Thy will be done, as in heaven, so in earth." However, here in the
90th Psalm, Moses did not address the Lord, calling Him "Our LORD."
He just said, "LORD," as if to indicate wonderful intimacy.

You may recall that our Lord Jesus did the same on the eve of His
crucifixion, when He lifted up His eyes to heaven, and said, "Father, the
hour is come . . ." He did not say, "My Father," nor did He say, "Our
Father." He simply addressed Him "Father." Besides revealing intimacy
of relationship, this manner of salutation indicates calm possession of spirit,
and a deep adoration of God the Father. I wonder if we realize that it is
possible for us in this generation to have that same intimate relationship
with God, so that we may look up into His face and call Him "Father."
In that salutation there is also revealed the glory of the person of God,

and the wonderful privilege the sons of men possess, who have been redeemed by the precious blood of Christ.

"LORD, THOU HAST BEEN OUR HOME"

But here in Moses' prayer, he said to the Lord, "LORD, thou hast been our dwelling place in all generations." That is a strange way to speak of the Lord "thou hast been our *dwelling place.*" If Moses had said to the Lord, Thou hast been our God in all generations, we would not have any difficulty in agreeing with him; but he said, "thou hast been our dwelling place." What is a dwelling-place? It is a home, is it not? Thus, Moses said, "LORD, thou hast been our *home* in all generations."

Abraham was the first to be called "an Hebrew." He received the name Hebrew, from the fact that he was a traveling man. It ought not to be surprising that Jews have become such prosperous traveling salesmen! God called him to leave his family, his home, and his city, and to go out to a place that He would show him; and Abraham went out, not knowing whither he went. From then on, to the end of his life, Abraham lived in a tent. Though very rich in possessions, he never had a palatial home such as some of our more wealthy folk have. He did not even have so much as an apartment, which some of us less fortunate ones in New York City have. Abraham lived in a tent, to indicate that he had no certain dwelling-place here and that he "looked for a city which hath foundations, whose builder and maker is God."

Moses also had a very strange experience. He, too, never had a certain dwelling-place, from his very birth even unto his death, and he did not so much as own a burial place, so that God buried him in His own cemetery. When Moses was born, he was such a goodly child to look upon that his mother refused to give heed to the edict of Pharaoh to slay all male children. She made her babe a little ark, put him into it, and then put the ark in the river, praying to her God that the child would be picked up by someone who would care for it. You will remember how Pharaoh's daughter came down to the riverside. She saw this strange floating cradle and suggested to one of her maidens that she fetch it. When she opened it she saw the child, and, behold, the babe wept. She had compassion on him and said, "This is one of the Hebrews' children." Then said Moses' sister, who had watched the proceedings, "Shall I go and call to thee a nurse of the Hebrew women, that she may nurse the child for thee?" Pharaoh's daughter said to her, "Go" and she went to call the child's mother. Pharaoh's daughter, said to Moses' mother, "Take the child away and nurse it for me, and I will give thee thy wages." Moses' mother took the child and when he grew she brought him to Pharaoh's daughter, and he became her son, and she called his name Moses for, said she, "I drew him out of the water." Thus, from the moment of his birth, Moses had no certain dwelling-place.

May I digress here a moment? Moses may have had a floating cradle as a babe, but his dwelling was in God, and God took care of him. While the child floated in the river, God arranged everything, even to seeing that his mother would receive wages for doing the thing she most wanted to do —nurse her own little babe.

I read an interesting comment concerning this episode from the pen of a learned Jew. Said he, "Our children ask our fathers, 'Why was Moses nursed by a Hebrew woman and not by Pharaoh's daughter?' whereupon the elders of Israel respond, saying, 'The mouth that was one day to converse with God could not defile itself with the impure milk of an Egyptian.'" I do not know how much such a statement means to you, but oh, what a message! What an exhortation to us, who love the Lord Jesus Christ, to drink the sincere milk of the Word, that we may grow thereby, and that our mouths may be clean, so that we may converse with God.

Moses had no certain dwelling-place even in the court of the Pharaohs, for he soon found himself on the backside of a desert mountain tending sheep. Later he was put at the head of Israel as they came out of Egypt; and even then he dwelt with Israel in tents, all during the wilderness journey. Moses never knew what it was to have a certain dwelling-place. Is it any wonder, therefore, that he wrote, "LORD, thou hast been our *dwelling place* in all generations." The home of the soul is in the glorious person of the Creator and Redeemer, God. The soul of an individual is never at rest until it has found its dwelling-place in God.

THE MAN MOSES AND THE SECRET OF HIS LIFE

Observe further how in verse 2 Moses carefully distinguished between the Creator and His creation; between nature and nature's God; between the author and the author's book; for this world, if you please, is a book of God. Moses, therefore, was as clear a scientist in his thinking as he was a theologian.

Moses, beyond contradiction, was one of the world's greatest men. There is not a man on earth at present who could hold a candle to him. Our statesmen would not even qualify as kindergarten teachers in the art of statecraft if Moses were present, and when it comes to the perplexing question of the farm and farm products, our AAA schemes, crop-destruction programs, processing taxes, and slaughtering of live-stock seem like nursery-room pastimes, compared with the simple method that Moses instituted for feeding a nation traveling in a wilderness for forty years. Our manufacturers, particularly of shoes and clothing, are just pikers alongside of the manufacturer whose clothes and shoes did not show wear at the end of forty years' constant use; and yet Ingersoll had the temerity to go up and down this country for years, lecturing on "The Mistakes of Moses," at a couple of dollars a head, while empty-headed people applauded with delight.

The more I think of Moses and how he led the children of Israel for forty years, the more I admire him and the bigger he looms. What is it that distinguishes him from the brand of statesmen we have with us at present? Just this—Moses was a man of God. Moses knew God. Moses trusted God. He knew that God was distinct from His creation, though He was Lord of creation.

There is a very interesting telescope in the Bible by which it is possible to measure the greatness of Moses, and through which evidence abounds of his knowledge of God. In the 12th chapter of Numbers, the 3rd verse, it is written: "Now the man Moses was very meek, above all the men which were upon the face of the earth."

Would God our statesmen and leaders were a bit like Moses, even a little bit. But allow me to come closer. Would God you and I were like Moses, even a little bit.

The secret of Moses' life lay in his knowledge of God, as expressed in this 2nd verse of the 90th Psalm. I know that there are some rattle-brained folk who, when one asks, Do you know God as He is revealed in Jesus Christ His Son? proudly answer, Nature is my god. But not so with Moses. He knew God was distinct from His creation, for he wrote: "Before the mountains were brought forth, or ever thou hadst formed the earth and the world, even from everlasting to everlasting, thou art God."

In closing, let me direct attention to the harmony between this verse in the 90th Psalm and a few verses in John's Gospel where, concerning our Lord Jesus Christ, it is written:

> "In the beginning was the Word, and the Word was
> with God, and the Word was God.

"All things were made by him; and without him was not any thing made that was made.

* * * *

"And the Word was made flesh, and dwelt among us, (and we beheld his glory, the glory as of the only begotten of the Father,) full of grace and truth."

Should someone ask, How can I know God? the answer is found in the words of John's Gospel, chapter 1, verse 12, which reads: ". . . as many as received him, to them gave he power to become the sons of God, even to them that believe on his name . . ."

PSALM NINETY—PART TWO

THE INESCAPABLE FACT OF GOD!

WE limited our initial meditation in the 90th Psalm to the first two verses, which read as follows:

"LORD, thou hast been our dwelling place in all generations.

"Before the mountains were brought forth, or ever thou hadst formed the earth and the world, even from everlasting to everlasting, thou art God."

Last Sunday I visited some friends who listened to this broadcast. During the conversation one friend mentioned something I thought was particularly interesting and significant.

There is no doubt that both Moses and Abraham possessed great wealth, yet they lived in tents. They did so, as the Bible tells us, to indicate that they "looked for a city which hath foundations, whose builder and maker is God." They gave abundant testimony that they were strangers and pilgrims here. This friend reminded me that our Lord Jesus was the perfect antitype of both Moses and Abraham. Our Lord was rich. He was so rich that He held the wealth of the world in His hands. By the mere spoken word, He could have built mansions that would have made the homes of our richest people look like dilapidated East Side New York tenements. Yet, all during His public ministry He had no certain dwelling-place. He Himself said, "The foxes have holes, and the birds of the air have nests; but the Son of man hath not where to lay his head." His dwelling-place was in God, His Father. How significant, therefore, is that passage of Scripture which declares that ". . . though he was rich, yet for your sakes he became poor, that ye through his poverty might be rich."

Continuing our studies in this 90th Psalm, observe the note of instruction that appears, commencing with verse 3 up to and including verse 12. These verses read:

> "Thou turnest man to destruction; and sayest, Return, ye children of men.
>
> "For a thousand years in thy sight are but as yesterday when it is past, and as a watch in the night.
>
> "Thou carriest them away as with a flood; they are as a sleep: in the morning they are like grass which groweth up.
>
> "In the morning it flourisheth, and groweth up; in the evening it is cut down, and withereth.
>
> "For we are consumed by thine anger, and by thy wrath are we troubled.
>
> "Thou hast set our iniquities before thee, our secret sins in the light of thy countenance.
>
> "For all our days are passed away in thy wrath: we spend our years as a tale that is told.
>
> "The days of our years are threescore years and ten; and if by reason of strength they be fourscore years, yet is their strength labour and sorrow; for it is soon cut off, and we fly away.
>
> "Who knoweth the power of thine anger? even according to thy fear, so is thy wrath.
>
> "So teach us to number our days, that we may apply our hearts unto wisdom."

If there is any one thing that characterizes the age in which we live it is the utter disregard of God upon the part of men. The sad fact is, whether we like it or not, that it has reached the stage where it almost seem necessary to apologize when the fact of God is "intruded" into a conversation. We have become so absorbed with our materialistic view of life that even to suggest faith in God is to cause the eyebrow of the highbrow to be lifted in amazement, and yet not a single, solitary one of us will escape a meeting with God.

"THOU TURNEST MAN TO DESTRUCTION"

Will you observe three things that Moses stated concerning God's relationship to man. First, "Thou turnest man to destruction." Second, "Thou carriest them away as with a flood." Third, "Thou hast set our iniquities before thee, our secret sins in the light of thy countenance."

I welcome the opportunity this Psalm presents to discuss the matter of God's rights and God's judgment. We have a constitution in this country, though I'm aware that it seems to have become "the forgotten document" to our particular brand of contemporary politicians. Nevertheless, that instrument pledges certain rights to the individual citizen which are sacred and oftentimes implored. When they are implored we speak of our constitutional privileges, or the violation of our constitutional rights. To the same extent, we might speak of the constitutional rights of God. However, I hasten to add that God's rights are not subject to change. His constitution is permanent. It is an everlasting document. It cannot be tinkered with. It cannot be abrogated, and, try as you will, you cannot avoid it. God has certain specific rights in the world and in the individual life. This is not a popular subject, and a considerable proportion of our ministers have concluded that it is more becoming to the gospel to speak of God's love than of His righteousness. To even suggest that God has certain rights in the individual life is to violate the modern conception of Christianity.

They be blind leaders of the blind, who shut their eyes to the obvious evidences in this world of men concerning God's rights. Will you note, for instance, the first thing that Moses stated in this 90th Psalm concerning God's rights. Said he, "Thou turnest man to destruction . . ." Now the word "destruction" in the Hebrew literally means *crumbling to dust.* We may, therefore, read this phrase, "Thou turnest man to dust." You may argue from now to the day of your death that there is no God and that you are the master of your own destiny and the captain of your own soul, and that you will live as you please and do as you please; but you have not one word to say when that hour arrives when God exercises His divine right to turn you to dust. You will not be able to extend your life by one single moment of time. You cannot defeat God's purposes even if you leave provisions in your will that you wish your body burned and the ashes distributed over the face of the sea. God still possesses the right to turn His creatures to the dust of the earth. It is well for us never to lose sight of it.

It is a point of wisdom, in business, to prepare for possible future contingencies. No successful business man shuts his eyes to the future. Of course, the present is important, but the obligations and possibilities of tomorrow are equally as important as the opportunities of the present. No business can survive when its executives give no consideration to the future. If that be so in business, how much more true is it in the realm of our individual lives? We undoubtedly think it is so important that those of us who are married invariably have provided for our wives and families through the setting aside of an estate or through life insurance. Sir, if you have made provision for your family and your wife, your business and your social relationships, pray by what law of reason have you excluded your own soul—the most valuable thing you possess in life?

The 3rd verse of this 90th Psalm ascribes to God the right to turn man to dust—to say, "Return, ye children of men." Let us never forget it. To forget it, to neglect it, or to reject it is a tragedy, and is the biggest error of our entire lives. So much for the right of God to turn man to the dust of the earth.

"THOU CARRIEST THEM AWAY AS WITH A FLOOD"

In the 5th verse of our Psalm Moses said, "Thou carriest them away as with a flood." The interesting thing about that phrase is the fact that in the Hebrew it is expressed by only one word. I do not know whether it is possible to find in the English language a comparable word except it be the word *gone*. If we wish to meditate upon the figure that was in the mind of the writer of this Psalm, it will be necessary for us to watch a torrent sweep by, and as we observe it sweeping by say to ourselves, There is my life flowing away; the water that is gone never returns. To give double emphasis to the illustration, Moses continued and said, "They are as a sleep: in the morning they are like grass which groweth up. In the morning it flourisheth, and groweth up; in the evening it is cut down, and withereth. For we are consumed by thine anger, and by thy wrath are we troubled."

Some may cringe under this type of preaching; some may rebel against this idea of God; some may go so far as to say, If that is the kind of personality that God has I will have nothing to do with Him. But we have as little possibility of avoiding a meeting with God as a little twig that is in the pathway of the sweeping torrent has of avoiding the torrent's force. Wisdom is not evidenced in anger. It is evidenced in the acknowledgment of the truth.

The evidences that abound in this world, of the inexorable law of God, are so profuse that the man who does not profit by them can be characterized by one word only, which word I leave you to supply. Not only is there abounding evidence in the Bible (which we believe to be the Word of God) as to the inescapable judgment of God, but this very earth of ours is also filled with substantiating evidences so that one cannot escape the conclusion that the God of the Bible and the God of creation is one and the same person, and the character of God as revealed in the Bible is the character of God as revealed in creation. Thus, we are doubly without excuse if we neglect the salvation of God. Judgment is just as sure as the day of our birth. It is unthinkable, unreasonable, and un-Biblical to suppose that any will escape it.

"OUR INIQUITIES . . . OUR SECRET"

The final statement we shall consider now is expressed in the 8th verse, "Thou hast set our iniquities before thee, our secret (sins) in the light of thy countenance." One may wipe out of his mind, if he will, his iniquity, but one will never succeed in hiding it from God. We may cover it up from our fellow-man and closest friend, but it is written, "Thou hast set our iniquities before thee." We may harbor in our breast a secret that we would not dare to reveal to a soul, yet, though it is closeted in the darkest corner of our heart and conscience, it is written, "Thou hast set our iniquities before thee, our secret (sins) in the light of thy countenance." There isn't a man but will acknowledge that he would be absolutely silenced and abashed were another permitted to see what God alone can see in the light of His countenance. There we have the secret of God's judgment. But, in presenting this message of God's judgment, I would be untrue to God, and to my own heart and yours, if I did not explain the provision of God against His judgment.

It is written of the Lord, "Thou art of purer eyes than to behold evil . . ." Sin is the most talked of thing in this world, and yet the most neglected subject in the world. Time was when men hesitated to attend a church service because there they heard of their sins. But, alas, sin is now an untouchable subject in many of our churches. The fact is that while our clergymen have eliminated the sin theme from the pulpits, our motion picture producers have put it on the screen, and they have been ably assisted by the stage. It was Shakespeare who wrote, "Few love to hear the sins they love to act."

The shocking fact is that we cannot do anything about sin. We cannot remove a single stain of sin from our conscience, nor blot it out of the record of God, by anything we can ever possibly do. There is only one thing which can remove sin, and that is the precious blood of our Lord Jesus Christ. That is the testimony of God. Therefore it ought to be apparent that there is only one person in all the world who can do anything about sin, and that person is God.

A little while back I said that it was unthinkable, unreasonable, and un-Biblical to suppose that any will escape judgment. God knew that, and He knew that there was nothing we could do about it, so He did something about it! What He did is recorded in the four Gospels—Matthew, Mark, Luke, and John. He sent His Son into this world to take the sinner's place, and upon the cross He exacted from Him the judgment due sin. That judgment was so terrific that the Bible witnesses that the entire earth was enveloped in darkness while our Lord hung upon the cross. The judgment was so terrific that our Lord cried out, "My God, my God, why hast thou forsaken me?" Thus our Lord bore the judgment of sin. Because He did that, the gospel may be preached. The gospel, in simple terms, is this: If you will, you may take your place under the shadow of Calvary, and you will thereby escape the judgment of your sin. You can escape it, because another bore it; that Holy One, our Lord Jesus Christ. Thus, it is written, "There is therefore now no judgment to them which are in Christ Jesus." Again it is written, "How shall we escape, if we neglect so great salvation . . . ?"

Do not rebel against God because of your sin. Do not rebel against God because of the judgment due your sin, but receive His invitation, when He says, ". . . him that cometh to me I will in no wise cast out." Under the shadow of Calvary you will find eternal redemption from sin, from the guilt of sin, from the power of sin, and some day from the very presence of sin. May God help you to embrace Christ as your Saviour.

PSALM NINETY—PART THREE

SEVENTY YEARS—AND THEN WHAT?

WHILE we have already given two meditations in the 90th Psalm, I think that there is a further lesson to be gotten from the Psalm. So let us read commencing with the 9th verse:

> "For all our days are passed away in thy wrath: we spend our years as a tale that is told.
>
> "The days of our years are threescore years and ten; and if by reason of strength they be fourscore years, yet is their strength labour and sorrow; for it is soon cut off, and we fly away.
>
> "Who knoweth the power of thine anger? even according to thy fear, so is thy wrath.
>
> "So teach us to number our days, that we may apply our hearts unto wisdom.
>
> "Return, O LORD, how long? and let it repent thee concerning thy servants.

"O satisfy us early with thy mercy; that we may rejoice and be glad all our days.

"Make us glad according to the days wherein thou hast afflicted us, and the years wherein we have seen evil.

"Let thy work appear unto thy servants, and thy glory unto their children.

"And let the beauty of the LORD our God be upon us: and establish thou the work of our hands upon us; yea, the work of our hands establish thou it."

SPENDING A THOUGHT

There are several things in these verses that are most interesting. The first is the statement, "we spend our years as a tale that is told." The second relates to the average span of life, how quickly it is brought to a close, and how swiftly we fly away. The third is an exhortation to teach us to number our days. Finally, the closing petition of the Psalm, where Moses invited the Lord to do two things; to let His work appear unto His servants, and to let the beauty of the Lord be upon us and to establish the work of our hands.

Let us look at these things a little more closely. In the Authorized Version, the phrase that appears at the close of the 9th verse reads, "we spend our years as a tale that is told." Consulting your Bible you will notice that the last three words are in italics, which means that the translators inserted these words to give sense to the phrase. Actually, it would read, "we spend our years as a tale." Now a tale is a story. In the Hebrew the word "tale" has in it the idea of a single thought. Thus the phrase could be translated, "we spend our years as a thought." This idea of life is also found in Homer. Thought is often used as a symbol for speed. There is nothing as swift as thought. While it takes a ray of light, headed for this earth of ours from the nearest star, traveling at the rate of 186,324 miles per second, $6\frac{1}{4}$ years to reach us, in quicker time than it takes to tell, our thoughts can go from earth to heaven. Our life is so short a span that it is merely a thought. Yet the striking thing about it all is that most of us, if not all of us, spend more time on this little span of life than about the eternity that lies just beyond the grave. We slave, we work, we heap up riches, we strive to raise a family. Oh, how much time we put on this little span of life, which Moses said runs to about threescore years and ten, and which might run to eighty years if the individual possesses a strong and healthy constitution. But what if it runs to a hundred years? What is a hundred years compared to the endless period of eternity?

TWENTY-FOUR PRECIOUS HOURS

Is it not a fact that we spend about 23½ hours a day on this short span of life, and give the Lord probably one-half hour a day. One-half hour? Why, some of us do not even give Him a minute a day. Stop a moment, and take an inventory of your life. If you happen to be a business man, you probably work 8 hours a day; you probably take 1½ hours going to and from your business; about 2½ hours for eating, and reading your paper; you take probably another 2 hours listening to the radio; 8 hours of sleep; another half-hour to see that you are properly cleaned, and the balance of 1½ hours you devote to learning, or to amusements, or anything to while away the time.

Moses said, ". . . teach us to number our days, that we may apply our hearts unto wisdom." David said, "The fear of the LORD is the beginning of wisdom . . ." How much time, during the course of one day, do we devote to the Lord, to fellowship with the Lord in prayer, to reading His Word, to studying the revelation of God in creation, to helping someone else come to know the grace of God? What unprofitable servants the best of us are, and what can be said about the rest of us who are average mortals! Some have probably not given God a few seconds a day, while others really think they pay God a compliment when they spend between sixty and ninety minutes, once a week, in church. Yet Moses prayed "teach us to number our days, that we may apply our hearts unto wisdom." One of my secretaries at the office suggested—What about the Christmas season? How many hours do we spend Christmas shopping, sending Christmas cards, running hither and yon, trying to get ready for Christmas—and, behold, if we have not forgotten entirely the Christ who made Christmas possible. Oh, if each of us who love the Lord Jesus Christ would recognize the claims that He has upon us so that we might live lives so filled with the Spirit of God that the joy of our hearts might flow into the lives of others!

"THY WORK . . . OUR WORK"

But I ought not to forget that we are rapidly approaching the Christmas season, which is a glad time of the year. Thus, we should not give too much that will lead one to feel disturbed and distressed, for even the 90th Psalm contains the petition, "Make us glad according to the days wherein thou hast afflicted us . . ." So if I have afflicted you for half of this meditation, I hope during the balance of it to make you glad. The way to make

a person really glad is expressed in the closing verses of this Psalm, where
Moses prayed:

> "Let thy work appear unto thy servants, and thy glory
> unto their children.
>
> "And let the beauty of the LORD our God be upon us:
> and establish thou the work of our hands upon us; yea,
> the work of our hands establish thou it."

Will you notice the order of these requests. "Let *thy* work appear unto
thy servants"—that is the first request; while the last request is, "yea, the
work of *our* hands establish thou it." Thus we have, first, the *Lord's* work,
and last, *our* work, and in between, the glory and beauty of the Lord. Now
let us go to the New Testament for a passage of Scripture that will throw
light on this order.

In the 2nd chapter of Paul's letter to the Ephesians, commencing with
verse 8, we read:

> "For by grace are ye saved through faith; and that not
> of yourselves: it is the gift of God:
>
> "Not of works, lest any man should boast.
>
> "For we are his workmanship, created in Christ Jesus
> unto good works, which God hath before ordained that
> we should walk in them."

The order in Ephesians is exactly the order that appears in the 90th
Psalm. Salvation is by grace through faith. That is the work of the Lord.
It is written, "Salvation belongeth unto the LORD . . ." It is His work.
He planned it. He prepared it. He completed it. When our Lord Jesus,
on the cross, cried, "It is finished," He met every claim of righteousness
against sin. On the cross He became the depositary of sin. All the sin of
the universe was laid upon Christ. He bore the judgment due sin. Because
He bore the judgment, none of us need bear our judgment, none of us need
bear our sin, none of us need suffer for our sins. He suffered, the just One,
for us, the unjust, that we might be brought unto God. Again I repeat, He
became the depositary of the sin of the world. He became the depositary in
order that He might be the channel through which the beauty and the
glory of God might flow upon all who believe.

If we are to be saved it will be through the work of our Lord. That
work has been done. We are saved by grace through faith; and that not
of ourselves: "it is the gift of God: not of works, lest any man should
boast." Therefore Moses prayed, "Let thy work appear unto thy servants,

and thy glory unto their children." That is wonderful, is it not—to let the glory of God in the work of salvation be so apparent in our lives that our children may behold its glory, and that the beauty of the Lord may be upon us. I am afraid there are very few of us who have embraced it by faith. I know some people who live so close to the Lord that you can actually behold the beauty of the Lord upon their countenance. They manifest the fact that they know the Lord. But that is a rarity. The rest of us, who so miserably fail our Lord, may take courage in the fact that some day the beauty of the Lord shall be upon us, and the glory of His salvation will be manifested in our countenance.

PSALM NINETY-ONE—PART ONE

A CHRISTMAS MESSAGE FROM THE NINETY-FIRST PSALM

LAST year we gave a Christmas message from the 47th Psalm; so, strange as it may appear, we can find real Christmas joy in the Psalms, as well as in the Gospels of Matthew and Luke. For this Christmas we consider the 91st Psalm.

I know some very devout, godly Christians who do not celebrate Christmas. They believe, and rightly so, that the observance of that day dates back long before the Christian era. They have noted the various customs associated with the Christmas season, such as the decorating of trees and the gathering of Yule logs, all of which are hangovers from paganism. These customs can be traced back to the earliest periods of civilization. There are others who suggest that our Lord could never have been born on December 25th, and they maintain that December 25th was set apart to celebrate the birth of the supposed virgin-born son of the Babylonian queen of heaven; all of which is undoubtedly true. It can be safely said that the Bible does not clearly indicate the exact day when our Lord Jesus Christ came into the world. It can also be said with great confidence that the Bible, particularly the New Testament epistles, is occupied with the death of the Lord Jesus Christ, and the resurrection and exaltation of our Lord, rather than His birth.

But it can also be said with great force that if He had not been born into the world He could never have died; so that we are justified in considering His birth, as well as His death. I hope I never get too old to enjoy those marvelous, stirring records of the birth of our Lord Jesus found in the Gospels, and to enter into the joy that the angels expressed when all of nature gave testimony to His appearance, and when the shepherds on the Judean hills thrilled with ecstasy as they observed the Christ-child.

If our Lord's return is delayed, and He allows me to grow stoop-shouldered and gray-haired, I hope I shall always revel in that beautiful expression of faith, confidence, and joy, which was the portion of Simeon of old, of whom the Scripture witnesses that he was a just and devout man, waiting for the consolation of Israel. It was revealed unto him by the Holy Spirit that he should not see death before he had seen the Lord's Christ. He came, by the Spirit, into the temple; and when the parents of our Lord brought the child Jesus into the temple, to do for Him after the custom of the law, Simeon took the babe up in his arms and blessed God, saying, "Lord, now lettest thou thy servant depart in peace, according to thy word; for mine eyes have seen thy salvation, which thou hast prepared before the face of all people; A light to lighten the Gentiles, and the glory of thy people Israel."

There is probably not one single individual but who would envy the privilege that Simeon had in taking that babe in his arms; that babe, of whom the Scripture witnesses that prior to His incarnation He spun the ages into their course and created the universe. That babe was God manifest in the flesh; and the man, Simeon by name, whom He created from the dust of the earth, had the joy of holding that babe in his arms. The Holy Spirit revealed unto him that the babe was the Salvation of God.

"CHRIST IN US, THE HOPE OF GLORY"

Wouldn't you love to have had that privilege? I quickly add, however, that you and I who are believers in our Lord Jesus Christ have a joy that Simeon did not have. Simeon had the pleasure of holding the babe in his arms; but Christ now lives, by faith, in the breast of every believer. That event takes place the moment a sinner receives Christ; then the Lord Jesus comes into the heart and lives there, by His Holy Spirit, so that we can say, Christ in us, the hope of glory.

Therefore, while I repudiate the notion that is so prevalent in Christendom that it is our privilege at the Christmas season to receive the Christ-child into our hearts, I want to emphasize the fact that the Christian has perpetual joy by having Christ in his heart 365 days in the year, and an extra day every four years.

"THE SECRET PLACE"

That is a long preliminary to our Psalm. The 91st Psalm is such a wonderful Psalm, we shall not deprive ourselves of the pleasure of looking at it more closely. For that reason, we will devote another meditation to it. We shall limit this one to a few comments from the early verses.

You will observe it opens: "He that dwelleth in the secret place of the most High shall abide under the shadow of the Almighty." The 2nd verse is a personal testimony, where the Psalmist said:

"I will say of the LORD, He is my refuge and my fortress: my God; in him will I trust." Then another voice is heard, commencing with the 3rd verse, saying:

> "Surely he shall deliver thee from the snare of the fow-
> ler, and from the noisome pestilence.
>
> "He shall cover thee with his feathers and under his
> wings shalt thou trust: his truth shall be thy shield and
> buckler.
>
> "Thou shalt not be afraid for the terror by night; nor
> for the arrow that flieth by day;
>
> "Nor for the pestilence that walketh in darkness; nor
> for the destruction that wasteth at noonday."

In the 1st verse we have a definite statement of fact and principle, prevalent in both the Old and New Testaments. I believe the Holy Spirit is the speaker, saying, "He that dwelleth in the secret place of the most High shall abide under the shadow of the Almighty." There is marvelous imagery in this 1st verse. The most high God is pictured as having a secret place, into which a specific company of people enter and dwell, and therein they find that the Almighty casts a shadow of protection over them. Nothing disturbs them; nothing harms them; no fear nor disappointment enters therein.

Let us look at the verse from the New Testament viewpoint. But before we do, let me comment upon the Old Testament viewpoint. Moses knew that God had a secret place. He inquired to know it and to see it. The record of his inquiry is found in the 33rd chapter of the book of Exodus. There Moses said to the Lord: "Now therefore, I pray thee, if I have found grace in thy sight, shew me now thy way, that I may know thee, that I may find grace in thy sight . . ." The Lord said to Moses, "My presence shall go with thee, and I will give thee rest." However, Moses was not satisfied with the presence of the Lord. He wanted to see the secret place. Finally God acquiesced, and said, "I will do this thing also that thou hast spoken . . ." Then the Lord provided a safe place for Moses. In the 21st verse of the 33rd chapter of Exodus we read:

> "And the LORD said, Behold, there is a place by me, and thou shalt stand upon a rock:
>
> "And it shall come to pass, while my glory passeth by, that I will put thee in a clift of the rock, and will cover thee with my hand while I pass by:
>
> "And I will take away mine hand, and thou shalt see my back parts: but my face shall not be seen."

Wonderful experience, wasn't it? There was a clift in the rock, in which God hid Moses. Hiding in the clift of that rock, Moses saw the glory of God.

Now for the New Testament viewpoint of this 1st verse of the 91st Psalm. The New Testament presents Christ as the Rock. He is also the chief cornerstone, the altogether lovely One. On the cross, Christ, as the Rock, was cleft, the heart was wounded, and the very bosom of God was laid bare to the gazing eyes of the sons of men.

THE VIRGIN-BORN SON

God came out to the sons of men, in Christ, at the incarnation at Bethlehem. The mystery of the incarnation cannot be fathomed. We cannot tell the how nor the wherefore, nor explain the details, of how God came into the womb of a woman, and by His Holy Spirit formed a body in that womb, and then had His own Son take possession, and enter into that body, and be born, as other men are born, and be cradled on the breast of a woman. It is a mystery no man can solve, but like Simeon of old and the wise men of the East, it is the glorious privilege of the sons of men to worship the One who was born.

This morning, before the broadcast, I glanced over a paragraph in that fascinating new book, "Man, the Unknown," by Alexis Carrel, one of the outstanding scientists of this generation. Speaking of the human brain, Dr. Carrel says, "Our knowledge of this intricate subject is still rudimentary. We understand less . . . how thought is born."

If we do not know how thought is born, how ridiculous for any to ask us to explain the virgin birth of Christ.

As God came out to the sons of men, in the incarnation, so He laid bare His own heart in the death of His Son. There He revealed His secret place. It is now the privilege of every individual, Jew or Gentile, black or white, whoever he may be, without regard to race, creed, or color—it is the privilege of everyone, who receives the testimony of God concerning His Son, to find the secret place in the torn breast of the Son of God, and rest therein.

The Scripture states, concerning every believer, that he is "in Christ." Christ is in us; but so, too, are we in Christ. Christ is the secret place of the most High, and because we are in Christ, the shadow of the Almighty rests over us.

GOD'S CARE OF HIS OWN

But I mentioned earlier that another voice is heard, commencing with verse 3. One who knows, says:

> "Surely he shall deliver thee from the snare of the fowler, and from the noisome pestilence.
>
> "He shall cover thee with his feathers, and under his wings shalt thou trust: his truth shall be thy shield and buckler.
>
> "Thou shalt not be afraid for the terror by night; nor for the arrow that flieth by day;
>
> "Nor for the pestilence that walketh in darkness; nor for the destruction that wasteth at noonday."

What wonderful promises! Take the one in the 4th verse, "He shall cover thee with his feathers, and under his wings shalt thou trust . . ." There we have the Lord likened unto a mother hen, who takes her brood under her wings to protect them from the oncoming storm. Anyone who has raised chickens knows that a mother hen senses an approaching storm with uncanny precision. If a hen can possess such intuition, what may be said of the Lord, who knows the end from the beginning and who knows all about every storm that might possibly approach. What a wonderful Saviour is Jesus our Lord!

PSALM NINETY-ONE—PART TWO

THE PSALM THE DEVIL QUOTED

THE 91st Psalm is a dialogue, with several participants. Undoubtedly, it is the Holy Spirit who speaks in the 1st verse, saying: "He that dwelleth in the secret place of the most High shall abide under the shadow of the Almighty."

Here is an interesting fact regarding this 1st verse. The promise is given that "He that dwelleth in the secret place of the most High *shall abide*

under the shadow of the Almighty." I want to call attention to the word
"abide." In the Hebrew, a beautiful thought is expressed. The word literally means *stay overnight* as, for example, when a guest arrives at our
home, and we invite him to stay overnight, to enjoy the peace and the
shelter of our home.

Every Christian knows that this world is a night. We live in the night
season. How wonderful that they who dwell in the secret place of the
most High, shall spend the night under the shadow of the Almighty.

In the 2nd verse, we have the personal testimony of the writer of the
Psalm: "I will say of the LORD, He is my refuge and my fortress: my
God; in him will I trust."

Beginning with verse 3, to and including the 13th verse, the Holy Spirit
is again the speaker. Certainly, it is the voice of one who definitely knows
the grace of God and the wonderful care that the Lord manifests over those
who are His own. Then, commencing with verse 14 to the end of the Psalm,
the eternal God Himself is the speaker.

THE PSALM THE DEVIL QUOTED

In our previous meditation we considered the first six verses, so that
we will commence with verse 7. There we read:

> "A thousand shall fall at thy side, and ten thousand at
> thy right hand; but it shall not come nigh thee. Only
> with thine eyes shalt thou behold and see the reward
> of the wicked.
>
> "Because thou hast made the LORD, which is my
> refuge, even the most High, thy habitation;
>
> "There shall no evil befall thee, neither shall any
> plague come nigh thy dwelling.
>
> "For he shall give his angels charge over thee, to keep
> thee in all thy ways.
>
> "They shall bear thee up in their hands, lest thou dash
> thy foot against a stone.
>
> "Thou shalt tread upon the lion and adder: the young
> lion and the dragon shalt thou trample under feet."

This section of the Psalm revolves about the 9th verse, which reads:
"Because thou hast made the LORD, which is my refuge, even the most
High, thy habitation . . ."

I was amused by a comment I found in a publication that was issued
in 1889, to the effect that "a certain German physician in St. Petersburg
recommended this 91st Psalm as the best preservative against cholera."

The Psalm actually is the most wonderful prescription any physician has even given for a patient, faced with or in the midst of difficulties.

It is essential to the well-being of us humans that we breathe clear air, and that we eat good, substantial food and enjoy some measure of exercise. It is considered a point of wisdom to keep away from an individual who has a contagious disease, and certainly being in the midst of a pestilence is not a safe place. But here is a statement that the one who has placed his trust in the Lord will not be afraid "for the terror by night; nor for the arrow that flieth by day; nor for the pestilence that walketh in darkness; nor for the destruction that wasteth at noonday." Pestilence and destruction take their terrific toll of life, for it is written: "A thousand shall fall at thy side, and ten thousand at thy right hand; but it shall not come nigh thee."

The individual who has placed his trust in God, sees destruction all about him; he sees the reward of the wicked; they fall on all sides; but with great confidence he rejoices in the grace of God, as none of these things touch him.

This 91st Psalm is very interesting, if for no other reason than the fact that Satan was acquainted with it, so well acquainted that he quoted part of it to our Lord Jesus Christ. It would appear that Satan thought the Psalm concerned Christ, particularly the 11th and 12th verses, where it is written: "For he shall give his angels charge over thee, to keep thee in all thy ways. They shall bear thee up in their hands, lest thou dash thy foot against a stone." You remember the occasion. Our Lord, at the very beginning of His public ministry, was led into the wilderness by the Spirit, to be tested of the devil; and when He had fasted forty days and forty nights,

> ". . . he was afterward an hungred.
>
> "And when the tempter came to him, he said, If thou be the Son of God, command that these stones be made bread.
>
> "But he answered and said, It is written, Man shall not live by bread alone, but by every word that proceedeth out of the mouth of God.
>
> "Then the devil taketh him up into the holy city, and setteth him on a pinnacle of the temple."

Satan evidently had been reading the 91st Psalm! There is one thing about the devil that interests me. While his dupes, his emissaries, and his preachers, who occupy some of the so-called best pulpits of the land, have doubts about the inspiration of the Scripture, and doubts about the Bible being the Word of God, one thing is sure, their master, Satan, has no doubts about the Word of God. Satan knew that the 91st Psalm was in the Old Testament. He was well acquainted with it, for when he took our Lord into the holy city, and set Him on a pinnacle of the temple, he said:

> "If thou be the Son of God, cast thyself down: for it is written, He shall give his angels charge concerning thee: and in their hands they shall bear thee up, lest at any time thou dash thy foot against a stone."

You will observe that the deceiver, the devil, left out a very important phrase from the 11th verse, as that verse reads: "For he shall give his angels charge over thee, *to keep thee in all thy ways.*"

If this portion of the Psalm specifically applies to our Lord, let it not be forgotten that it also has a broader application to include every believer in Christ. Each individual believer in Christ is precious to God. Thus, what is written in this portion of the Psalm could also apply to us. God has not promised to keep us if we walk in Satan's way. Satan knew enough about the ways of the Lord to realize that he could not use the whole of verse 11, in quoting it to our Lord, because what he was offering was not in the way of the Lord.

Should there be some who do not believe in a personal devil, and who think that the notion of such a being is rank childishness, I suggest that you actually manifest the power of that being over your own mind, by his very successful attempt to lull your intellect and spirit to sleep concerning his own existence. It is the blind who cannot see. The most active individual in this world is the one of whom the Bible speaks as "that old serpent, called the devil . . ." There is so much evidence of his presence round about us that one does not even have to look at somebody else to see it. We need only look into our own heart and life to observe how active Satan is. One thing is sure, our Lord recognized that Satan was a person, who in turn recognized the inspiration and power of the Word of God.

THE MINISTRY OF ANGELS

Let us leave Satan for a while, remembering that the Apostle Paul declared in the closing chapter of his letter to the Romans, "And the God of peace shall bruise Satan under your feet shortly." Let us hope it will be very shortly.

Now let us discuss some equally interesting creatures. The promise is given, in this 91st Psalm, that the Lord God "shall give his angels charge over thee, to keep thee in all thy ways." Undoubtedly, Satan was correct in his assumption that this was a promise given to our Lord Jesus Christ.

During the public ministry of our Lord Jesus, angels had a prominent part. They ministered to Him several times. More than twelve legions of angels, our Lord said, stood ready to deliver Him from the hands of His enemies, were it not for the plan of God to provide for our redemption. As a legion is six thousand, that means that more than seventy-two thousand angels were ready to come to His aid.

Let me speak now specifically, concerning our relationship to angels. In the last verse of the 1st chapter of the letter to the Hebrews, Paul writes, concerning the angels: "Are they not all ministering spirits, sent forth to minister for them who shall be heirs of salvation?"

A friend of mine refers to angels as the domestic servants of heaven. In a measure, that is true; but their ministry is not limited to heaven. The heir in the home of wealth and position, such as, for instance, in the home of a king, not only has the fellowship of that home, but invariably he has a retinue of servants to watch over him and see to it that he has everything he needs and the protection he requires. Because we are heirs of salvation, God has sent forth His angels, who are ministering spirits, to minister unto us.

It is amusing to observe the impressions that men have about angels. Whenever I have seen an angel pictured, the artist seems to have labored under the impression that they were effeminate-looking creatures with wings, long hair, and an innocent feminine face. Possibly, that's why some men glibly refer to their wives as angels—sometimes! But the fact is, the Bible never speaks of angels in the feminine gender. Better get rid of the notion that angels are beautiful women, or that any woman is an angel. Our Lord said that the angels neither marry nor are given in marriage. While it cannot be said that they are either male or female, yet, whenever they are spoken of in Scripture, the Bible always uses the masculine gender, and whenever they appeared in bodily form, they always appeared to the individual in the form of men.

Very few of us who know the Lord Jesus Christ are aware of His wonderful provision for us. Each believer has a group of angels, whose business it is to minister to him. Thus, in the 91st Psalm, we read that God has given "his angels charge over thee, to keep thee in all thy ways. They shall bear thee up in their hands . . ." Isn't that interesting? Angels have hands, though we cannot see them. If there is a stone in your pathway, they are so careful about you, that they put their hands forth to prevent you from stumbling over a little stone, and when you meet the larger problems of life, they are there to minister to you, for the Scripture continues, "Thou shalt tread upon the lion and adder: the young lion and the dragon shalt thou trample under feet." Why has God so blessed the believer in Christ? Why should we be different from the rest of the world? Is it because of good works on our part? God forbid that any should ever get that impression. The reason is stated in verse 14: "Because he hath set his love upon me, therefore will I deliver him: I will set him on high, because he hath known my name."

The Bible says, "If any man love not the Lord Jesus Christ, let him be accursed . . ." but the Bible is also clear, that we love Him, because He first loved us. It is because we love the Lord, that God promises to deliver us. More than that, in the 15th and 16th verses, He says:

> "He shall call upon me, and I will answer him: I will be with him in trouble; I will deliver him, and honour him.
> "With long life will I satisfy him, and shew him my salvation."

PSALM NINETY-TWO

THE ABSURDITY OF "TRYING" TO BE A CHRISTIAN

THE 92nd Psalm which contains fifteen brief verses has an interesting inscription, which reads, "A Psalm or Song for the sabbath day." Here then is a Psalm that was used as a song in connection with Israel's worship on the Sabbath day.

"THE SABBATH DAY" *vs.* "THE LORD'S DAY"

Before we read the Psalm, may we stop a moment and explain the difference between the Sabbath day and the Lord's day. Anyone who has even a speaking acquaintance with the Old Testament, will recognize that God set apart the seventh day of the week for rest, and He called it the Sabbath day. Even to this day, Israel observes Saturday as the Sabbath. Occasionally, I hear Christians referring to Sunday as the Sabbath day, but that is not correct. Sunday is the Lord's day. It is the first day of the week. We Christians do not observe the Sabbath day. The Sabbath is a part of the old economy, expressed in the law of the Ten Commandments. Since the resurrection of our Lord Jesus Christ, the first day of the week has taken on a new significance.

For example, in the 16th chapter of the first letter to the Corinthians, Paul gives us certain instructions regarding Christian conduct on the Lord's day. There we read:

> "Now concerning the collection for the saints, as I have given order to the churches of Galatia, even so do ye.
>
> "Upon the *first* day of the week let every one of you lay by him in store, as God hath prospered him . . ."

In the Acts of the Apostles, the 20th chapter, we learn how the Apostle Paul conducted himself on the first day of the week, as well as how the Christians in Troas observed the day. In the 7th verse of the 20th chapter, we read:

> "And upon the first day of the week, when the disciples came together to break bread, Paul preached unto them, ready to depart on the morrow; and continued his speech until midnight."

Thus, the first day of the week was set aside by Christians to observe the resurrection of our Lord Jesus and to break bread, that is, to have the communion service, and the preaching of the Word of God.

WHO CAN PRAISE?

So much for the distinction between the Lord's day and the Sabbath day. Now let us read this interesting 92nd Psalm:

> "It is a good thing to give thanks unto the LORD, and to sing praises unto thy name, O most High:
>
> "To shew forth thy lovingkindness in the morning, and thy faithfulness every night,
>
> "Upon an instrument of ten strings, and upon the psaltery; upon the harp with a solemn sound.
>
> "For thou, LORD, has made me glad through thy work: I will triumph in the works of thy hands.
>
> "O LORD, how great are thy works! and thy thoughts are very deep.
>
> "A brutish man knoweth not; neither doth a fool understand this.
>
> "When the wicked spring as the grass, and when all the workers of iniquity do flourish; it is that they shall be destroyed for ever:
>
> "But thou, LORD, art most high for evermore.
>
> "For, lo, thine enemies, O LORD, for lo, thine enemies shall perish; all the workers of iniquity shall be scattered.

"But my horn shalt thou exalt like the horn of an unicorn: I shall be anointed with fresh oil.

"Mine eye also shall see my desire on mine enemies, and mine ears shall hear my desire of the wicked that rise up against me.

"The righteous shall flourish like the palm tree: he shall grow like a cedar in Lebanon.

"Those that be planted in the house of the LORD shall flourish in the courts of our God.

"They shall bring forth fruit in old age; they shall be fat and flourishing;

"To shew that the LORD is upright: he is my rock, and there is no unrighteousness in him."

The first three verses of the Psalm are actually a prelude. Observe that the Psalmist said, "It is a *good* thing to give thanks unto the LORD, and to sing praises unto thy name, O most High . . ." The Bible teaches that only redeemed individuals can offer praise or sing praises to God. Until an individual has embraced the Lord Jesus Christ as his or her Saviour and has known what it means to pass out of death into life, he or she cannot offer praise unto God. The one who has been redeemed by the precious blood of our Lord Jesus Christ has been made a worshipper, and he has a right and liberty to enter into the very holiest presence and there extend his praise unto God.

In the 13th chapter of Hebrews, the 15th verse, we read: "By him (our Lord Jesus) therefore let us offer the sacrifice of praise to God *continually*, that is, the fruit of our lips giving thanks to his name." Observe that praise-giving on the part of a Christian is not limited to one day of the week. He is called upon to offer the sacrifice of praise to God continuously, and who of us, who have that privilege, but understands the Psalmist when he said: "It is a good thing to give thanks unto the LORD, and to sing praises unto thy name, O most High . . ."

Will you also observe that, while the Psalm was intended for the Sabbath day, the 2nd verse implies that for one to sing on the Sabbath it is necessary to sing every day, for the 3rd verse reads: "To shew forth thy lovingkindness in the morning, and thy faithfulness every night, upon an instrument of ten strings, and upon the psaltery; upon the harp with a solemn sound."

In King David's time, as we well know, the instrument of ten strings was most popular. Possibly it has a significance—a spiritual significance.

We are to show forth His lovingkindness in the morning and His faithfulness every night, upon an instrument of ten strings.

Dr. Lockyer has an interesting booklet on the 3rd verse of the 92nd Psalm. He seems to find in the verse the suggestion that the number ten carries with it some interesting significance. He points to the ten fingers of our hands and the ten toes of our feet, conveying the impression that our whole life and body should prove to be an instrument for the praises of God. What a privilege, to have the praise of God vibrating in our bodies in a symphony of rapturous glory!

"THE WORK OF GOD"

But the thing I want to stress in this Psalm is in the 4th verse, where the Psalmist said: "For thou, LORD, hast made me glad through thy work: I will triumph in the works of thy hands."

The Lord Himself is the source of joy, for it is written, ". . . thou, LORD, hast made me glad . . ." The means through which the gladness has come to the Psalmist is the consciousness of the completion of that which he calls "thy work."

A friend called at the office the other day, and we went out and had a delightful luncheon together, during which he directed my attention to a passage of Scripture which he considered to be the greatest passage in the entire Bible. He referred to verse 29 of the 6th chapter of John's Gospel, where our Lord, responding to the inquiry, "What shall we do, that we might work the works of God?" said, "This is the work of God, that ye believe on him whom he hath sent." Will you bear that answer in mind, as we consider this 4th verse of the 92nd Psalm, "thou, LORD, hast made me glad through thy work: I will triumph in the works of thy hands."

Observe the subtlety of the question presented to Christ, "What shall we do, that we might work the works of God?" If the work be of God, it certainly is presumptuous to assume that "we" might work the works of God. Our work, of necessity, must be man's work, whereas those inquirers recognized that there is that of which the Psalmist speaks as being God's work. Something that He has done—something that is His own. Now the notion that these people had, who inquired of our Lord Jesus, was not limited alone to the company of people who asked the question.

A ruler once came to our Lord Jesus, in fact, ran to Him, kneeled before Him, and prayed Him, saying, "Good Master, what shall I do that I may inherit eternal life?" There again is that strange notion that one must do something to inherit eternal life; that we must work the works of God. Our whole system of religious thinking seems to be based on the false premise that it is possible for us to work a work that will be satisfactory to God; whereas it is utterly impossible to offer anything to God that is the work of our hands, because it must of necessity be tainted with sin. Thus, when our Lord Jesus responded to the inquiry, "What shall we do, that we might work the works of God?" He said, "This is the work of God, that ye believe on him whom he hath sent."

This past week, I received a letter from a gentleman who stated he was trying to be a Christian. Imagine that! As if it were possible to be a Christian by anything we could ever do. I had to write him, informing him that men are Christians, not by trying, but because they have received Christ. If you tried to live a Christian life for a thousand years, that would not make you a Christian. You cannot live a Christian life until you have Christ! You might just as well try to drive an automobile that does not have a drop of gas in the tank and expect it to travel at the rate of eighty miles an hour!

There is a phrase in Scripture that I love. It is "Salvation belongeth unto the LORD." Salvation is God's work. It was completed when our Lord Jesus said on the cross, "It is finished." Nothing can possibly be added to it. Nothing can be taken from it. God evidenced His satisfaction with it when He raised our Lord Jesus Christ from the dead and exalted Him to His own right hand to be a Prince and a Saviour. The work of God in the present age characterizes the ministry of God in every age. It is that which was so marvelously expressed by our Lord Jesus, "This is the work of God, that ye believe on him whom he hath sent." Whether we like it or not, the work of God is to make us believe in Christ.

But here is a statement in the 92nd Psalm, where either David or Moses was speaking saying: ". . . thou, LORD, hast made me glad through thy work: I will triumph in the works of thy hands." If the work of the Lord is to believe on Him whom He hath sent, is it possible that David or Moses, or even Abraham, could have believed on the Lord Jesus Christ before He came into this world? How could they believe, when our Lord Jesus had not yet appeared? We can best answer that by having the Lord Jesus Christ answer the question. In the 5th chapter of John's Gospel, our Lord said to the people:

> "Do not think that I will accuse you to the Father: there is one that accuseth you, even Moses, in whom ye trust.

"For had ye believed Moses, ye would have believed
me: for he wrote of me.

"But if ye believe not his writings, how shall ye believe
my words?"

Therefore if any one believes the writings of Moses, he must believe
our Lord Jesus Christ, for Moses wrote of Christ. Now let us take a man
like Abraham, who lived ages before Moses saw the light of day. In the
8th chapter of John's Gospel, our Lord Jesus again said to the people:
"Your father Abraham rejoiced to see my day: and he saw it, and was
glad."

Is it any wonder that the Psalmist, writing in the 92nd Psalm, said,
"thou, LORD, hast made me glad . . ." when Abraham rejoiced to see
Christ's day. For our Lord said he saw it and was glad. When our Lord
made this statement the people said, "Thou art not yet fifty years old, and
hast thou seen Abraham?" to which our Lord responded, "Verily, verily,
I say unto you, Before Abraham was, I am." The fact of the matter is,
that the only thing which can give true gladness is the knowledge of the
work of the Lord.

THE FACT OF JUDGMENT

There is one other fact in this Psalm upon which we should comment.
In the closing part of it the writer contrasted the doom of the enemies of
the Lord with the glory of those who love Him. We are told that "The
righteous shall flourish like the palm tree . . ." for they are planted in the
house of the Lord and "They shall still bring forth fruit in old age . . ."
The reason is expressed in the final phrase of the Psalm, where it is written,
"To shew that the LORD is upright . . . and there is no unrighteousness
in him."

That brings us to the question, as to whether God is righteous in the
exercise of judgment against those whom He calls the workers of iniquity.
Sometimes I have felt that in the preaching of the gospel we have sought
to make much of the grace of God, while on the other hand we have soft-
pedalled the note of judgment. For one to suggest that he believes in a
literal torment is to invite the gnashing of teeth and the sarcasms of unbelief. But whether we like it or not, the Bible clearly teaches that those who
reject the salvation of God will be eternally banished from the presence of
God and will eternally suffer the tortures of hell. Yet the fact that God will
extend His judgment upon those whom He calls the wicked is no reflection

upon His righteousness, for in the exercise of judgment His righteousness will be made manifest.

There are certain inevitable laws in this universe, from which neither man nor beast can escape. For instance, ". . . whatsoever a man soweth, that shall he also reap." If one sows to the flesh, he shall reap corruption. If one sows to the Spirit, he shall reap life. That law is definitely written in every part of our being. For instance, were we to take a little pin and prick the tips of our fingers, blood would immediately pour forth. We cannot violate a law of nature without receiving a just recompense of reward. How then is it possible to escape the penalty of sin? "God is not a man, that he should lie . . ." It will be utterly impossible to bribe His court of judgment.

The Apostle Paul, when preaching on Mars' hill, declared that God was commanding all men, everywhere, to repent, and the reason was expressed as follows: "Because he hath appointed a day, in the which he will judge the world in righteousness by that man whom he hath ordained; whereof he hath given assurance unto all men, in that he hath raised him from the dead."

Those Grecians could not stand that type of preaching, for when they heard of the resurrection of the dead, some of them mocked and others said, "We will hear thee again of this matter." However, we have no record that Paul ever returned to Mars' hill. You may mock at the Word of God; you may neglect salvation, and suggest that you will hear of the matter again; but it is inevitable that judgment follows the rejection of our Lord Jesus Christ. God grant therefore that you may receive Christ now.

PSALM NINETY-THREE

WHEN THE LORD GOD OMNIPOTENT SHALL REIGN

THE 93rd Psalm is one of the shortest of the collection and yet, with all its brevity, someone has said it is "probably the noblest, poetically, in the entire collection, glorifying God as the Lord of Creation."

Examining your Bible you will observe that this Psalm is without an inscription. Actually, in the Hebrew, it does not have an inscription, but in the Septuagint Version of the Old Testament, which was used at the time of our Lord's ministry on earth, there appears a very interesting heading, which reads, "A Psalm of David for the Day before Sabbath when the

earth became inhabited." From that reference it would seem that the
Psalm was sung in the synagogue on Friday, as a memorial of the creation,
especially of man. But as one observes the Psalm, with only a degree of
care, one is immediately impressed with the fact that it is more concerned
with the new creation than with the old. Thus, it is a prophetic Psalm,
looking forward to the time when the Lord God omnipotent shall reign.

THE DEATH OF KING GEORGE V

I am thankful that, in the providence of God, we have this particular
Psalm for our consideration this morning. Had we considered it last Sunday the Psalm would not have meant as much to me as it does this morning. Somehow the death of King George V and the accession to the throne
of King Edward VIII adds peculiar, timely significance to this Psalm. Let
us read the Psalm. It has only five short verses.

> "The LORD reigneth, he is clothed with majesty; the
> LORD is clothed with strength, wherewith he hath
> girded himself: the world also is stablished, that it can-
> not be moved.
>
> "Thy throne is established of old; thou art from ever-
> lasting.
>
> "The floods have lifted up, O LORD, the floods have
> lifted up their voice; the floods lift up their waves.
>
> "The LORD on high is mightier than the noise of many
> waters, yea, than the mighty waves of the sea.
>
> "Thy testimonies are very sure: holiness becometh thine
> house, O LORD, for ever."

All the world was shocked when the announcement of the death of
King George V was made on Monday. Hardly a day had passed, before
attention was transferred from the dead king to the new ruler, the former
Prince of Wales. On Wednesday morning, January 22nd, an interesting
ceremony took place in the city of London, proclaiming Edward VIII as
the new king and emperor. I cannot begin to describe the thrill that went
through my being, when our alarm-clock awakened me at 5 o'clock that
morning and I jumped out of bed to tune in on the proceedings. One could
hear easily the tramping of the soldiers, the roaring of the guns, the blare
of the trumpets, the arrival of celebrities, climaxed with the proclamation
that "the high and mighty Prince Edward Albert Christian George Andrew
Patrick David is now, by the death of our late sovereign of happy memory,

become our only lawful, rightful liege-lord, Edward VIII, by the grace of God, King of Great Britain, Ireland and the British Dominions beyond the Seas, Defender of the Faith, Emperor of India." I do not know how many of you got up early enough in the morning to listen to that remarkable proclamation, culminating with the singing of "God Save the King" but if you were too lazy to get up you missed a rare proceeding. It was an example of the old pomp and ceremony that has been used in England for about a thousand years.

For several reasons I was interested in that proceeding. First, because I thought of the 93rd Psalm, and the opportunity I was to have this morning to present God's message from that Psalm. Second, I was impressed with the fact that "the high and mighty" go by the way of all the sons of men. Death is no respecter of persons. Then I was impressed with the speed with which one king is set down and another is exalted. There goes up the cry, "The King is dead" while, in the next breath, there arises the shout, "Long live the King." How much this reminds us that men are flesh, and that it is appointed unto men once to die, whether they be commoners or princes. I was also interested in the proceeding, because of the many names the former Prince of Wales has and likewise the many titles of which he is now the sole possessor.

"THE LORD REIGNETH"

Now let us look at the Psalm, in the light of these happenings: "The LORD reigneth, he is clothed with majesty; the LORD is clothed with strength, wherewith he hath girded himself: the world also is stablished, that it cannot be moved." Then there speaks another member of the Godhead, saying: "Thy throne is established of old: thou art from everlasting." That same voice is heard throughout the balance of the Psalm. Here, therefore, is a short song, rising to heights of lyric exultation, in meditating upon the reign of Jehovah; and I question whether it can be equalled in any other part of the Book.

As I heard that early morning proclamation, when the Prince of Wales became Edward VIII, I thought of the time when the heavens are to be opened, and when out of those silent clouds shall come the blare of trumpets, announcing the approach of the King of kings and Lord of lords. As Enoch of old prophesied, the Lord will come with ten thousands of His saints; and in that great company will be those who have been redeemed by His precious blood; who will participate with Him in the announcement to the world, which God Himself will make concerning His Son. "Yet have I set my king upon my holy hill of Zion. I will declare the decree: . . . Thou art my Son; this day have I begotten thee. Ask of me, and I shall give thee the nations for thine inheritance, and the uttermost parts of the earth for thy possession." What a Hallelujah chorus will be raised to the high heavens when all the hosts of God's redeemed children will sing, The Lord God omnipotent reigneth, King of kings and Lord of lords.

A Bible-believing Christian cannot be pessimistic as he looks into the future, even though there are many things upon earth that present a dark picture. He cannot be pessimistic, with the certain knowledge that some day this world will witness the proclamation from heaven of our Lord Jesus Christ as the eternal Messiah, King of kings and Lord of lords. Neither will he mourn the fact that the one who is spoken of in the Bible as the prince of the air, and the god of this age, will be dethroned.

Again let us look at the Psalm more closely. The Psalmist actually saw the reign of the Lord on earth, for he said, "The LORD reigneth . . ." That is in the present tense. There is that about the Bible that looks at the future and speaks of it as in the present, because of the certainty with which the prophecy will become history. Today we do not see the Lord reigning. Today sin is on the throne; man reigns. However, some day the princes of this earth, the high and mighty, will abdicate their thrones and our Lord will reign.

"EYEWITNESSES OF HIS MAJESTY"

Observe the Psalmist's description of the person of Christ, as contained in this 93rd Psalm, where he said, "he is clothed with majesty; the LORD is clothed with strength, wherewith he hath girded himself . . ."

Speaking of the glory of Christ, the Apostle Peter, in his second letter, made a most interesting comment. Because Peter knew that he must die the death of a martyr before entering into the presence of his Lord, he said: "I will endeavour that ye may be able after my decease to have these things always in remembrance. For we have not followed cunningly devised fables, when we made known unto you the power and coming of our Lord Jesus Christ, but were eyewitnesses of his majesty."

The Psalmist, in the 93rd Psalm, said, "he is clothed with majesty;" while Peter, fully a thousand years later, said, "we were eyewitnesses of his majesty." Peter, when did you witness the majesty of our Lord? Did He not come in humiliation? Was He not the Son of man? Was He not called ". . . the carpenter's son?" How then could you have witnessed His majesty? The Apostle Peter responds, saying: "For he received from God the Father honour and glory, when there came such a voice to him from the excellent glory, This is my beloved Son, in whom I am well pleased." But, Peter, where did you hear that voice? Peter replies: "And this voice which came from heaven we heard, when were with him in the holy mount."

In the 17th chapter of St. Matthew's Gospel we have the record of that event. There we read that our Lord was transfigured "before them: and his face did shine as the sun, and his raiment was white as the light. And, behold, there appeared unto them Moses and Elias talking with him." Luke tells us in his Gospel that they talked together about the death our Lord was to die at Jerusalem.

THE CONFLICT OF THE TWO SEEDS

Now let us examine the 2nd verse of the 93rd Psalm, where the Father speaks to the Son, saying, "Thy throne is established of old: thou art from everlasting." Yet in the 3rd and 4th verses we learn of an attempt that was made to usurp the throne, for we read:

> "The floods have lifted up, O LORD, the floods have lifted up their voice; the floods lift up their waves.
>
> "The LORD on high is mightier than the noise of many waters, yea, than the mighty waves of the sea."

It would be easy to demonstrate, that from the time when the first promise of a Redeemer was made, until the cross of our Lord Jesus Christ, Satan, with his princes and powers, sought to prevent the appearance of the coming One. When the seed of the woman finally came upon the scene, the antagonism was expressed through the medium of King Herod, who slew every man-child within a certain border, thereby hoping to destroy the seed of the woman. Again and again during the public ministry of our Lord Jesus, Satanic forces took possession of men and caused them to pick up stones to throw at Him, but our Lord walked peacefully through the mob. Ineffective was every attempt until the time when our Lord witnessed, This is Satan's hour— ". . . the prince of this world cometh, and *findeth* nothing in me." Upon the cross, our Lord Jesus Christ bore the brunt of the attack of the serpent, who assumed that he had finally conquered the seed of the woman. But alas for him, the place where he assumed that he had triumphed was the place of his defeat; for, while our Lord Jesus was wounded unto death, He was raised from the dead. The cross has become the symbol of the triumph of the seed of the woman over the serpent. At the cross the floods rose and the waves roared, seeking to envelop our Lord, but "the high and mighty Prince" was mightier than the noise of many waters, yea, than the mighty waves of the sea, so that He is now clothed with majesty and with strength.

Before bringing our message to a close, I direct attention to the 5th verse, where the Psalmist said: "Thy testimonies are very sure: holiness becometh thine house, O LORD, for ever."

A son of Abraham can understand far better than we Gentiles what must have vibrated through the breast of the Psalmist when he wrote, "holiness becometh thine house, O LORD, for ever." He knows from the testimony of his own historians, that the house which was intended to be God's house was desecrated, it had become a den of thieves. But an hour is coming when that house will be re-established upon Mount Moriah and from it shall go forth the Word of the Lord. And out of that revived Temple will go forth not only the testimonies of Jehovah, but the holiness of the house will become it forever.

PSALM NINETY-FOUR

THE PSALM WITH A VENGEANCE—
AND THE GOSPEL FOR TODAY!

AS we consider the 94th Psalm we will discover that it has in it a note of sadness. Just as life has its sorrow as well as gladness, its disappointments as well as opportunities, so we must be honest with ourselves and with each other and face the facts of life as they are presented to us. It is for that reason that we draw attention to this 94th Psalm, which begins with a cry for vengeance and ends with the assurance that the vengeance will be exercised by the Lord our God. So despondent is the writer of this Psalm, that he penned these words, found in the 17th verse: "Unless the LORD had been my help, my soul had almost dwelt in silence." Before making an attempt at applying the principles of this Psalm to the present day and our own circumstances, I shall briefly outline the contents of the Psalm.

In the 93rd we were occupied with the majesty of the Lord and His reign in strength and power. It is quite interesting therefore to find that the next Psalm is occupied with the judgment of God, for actually, when the Lord reigns, His judgment will be operative, and so we have the cry of the first four verses of this 94th Psalm:

> "O LORD God, to whom vengeance belongeth; O God, to whom vengeance belongeth, shew thyself.
> "Lift up thyself, thou judge of the earth: render a reward to the proud.
> "LORD, how long shall the wicked, how long shall the wicked triumph?
> "How long shall they utter and speak hard things? and all the workers of iniquity boast themselves?"

This certainly is a familiar note, isn't it? I am positive that all of us at sometime have raised the same question which is heard in this Psalm.

This past week I had a letter commenting on an item which appeared in one of the western papers, containing a statement I made some time ago.

Before I tell you further about this letter, the mention of a western paper brings to mind an interesting clipping I received yesterday from a friend of mine in Chicago. The clipping consisted of a cartoon which appeared on the editorial page of the Chicago Daily News on Wednesday, February 5th, drawn by Vaughn Shoemaker, head cartoonist of that paper. In the foreground was a sketch of the sky line of Chicago, while in the background, towering over the buildings, was the familiar pose of Dwight L. Moody, his right hand pointing to the heavens, while in his left appeared an open Bible. In the lower righthand corner were the words, "Moody Centenary Jubilee Celebration," while a caption appeared above the cartoon, reading, "Chicago Needs Another."

When a great daily newspaper acknowledges that Chicago needs another sound, heaven-sent evangelist with an open Bible, proclaiming the glorious gospel of the Lord Jesus Christ, I think that's news!! I make bold to say, New York needs such an one; so do Boston and Philadelphia and Washington—our whole country needs one. God grant that such an one may soon be heard above the rabble and tinkling cymbals of these days. There was no uncertain note in D. L. Moody's ministry. He had a whole Bible and a crucified, risen Saviour for every needy sinner. No sickening ethics and pseudo-political harangue ever fell from Moody's lips. He preached Christ and Him crucified, and such a message we need today.

Getting back to the letter of which I was about to tell you, the writer lamented conditions that exist in our country today, and could not understand why the heavens are silent, while the wickedness of man seemingly triumphs. The one thing we need to remember is the fact that it is not our business to judge. This is the hour of God's grace. This is the time when God is justifying the ungodly who take refuge in the sacrifice of His beloved Son. He is offering pardon, He is not punishing. To those who know Him, He has committed the glorious privilege of presenting Christ to souls crushed by the weight of guilt and sin. It is written, ". . . as he is, so are we in this world." When He was here He said, ". . . I judge no man." He declared that His Father had not sent Him into the world to condemn the world; but that the world through Him might be saved. We do well to bear this in mind, for not only will we be better able to conduct ourselves in accordance with the Scripture, but we will also be better able to understand the seeming indifference of the Godhead to what is transpiring in the world. This is not the day of the vengeance of the almighty God. This is the day of His grace. But he is a very unwise man who spurns the grace of God and who assumes that because judgment and vengeance is postponed, it thereby infers that it is forever cancelled. The sword may be in the scabbard, but it shall be unsheathed, and when it is, we will learn that just as God was gracious in love, so He is stern and righteous in judgment.

WHAT GOD MUST SEE AND HEAR

As I think of this Psalm, particularly the 5th verse, which reads: "They break in pieces thy people, O LORD, and afflict thine heritage," I am reminded once again of the wave of anti-Semitism that is sweeping the world. This is not a new experience for evidently the same situation existed at the time when this Psalm was written. How blind were those who persecuted, for they reasoned, as is expressed in the 7th verse: ". . . The LORD shall not see, neither shall the God of Jacob regard it." How utterly foolish is such a comment, for, as the Psalmist said: "He that planted the ear, shall he not hear? he that formed the eye, shall he not see? . . . The LORD knoweth the thoughts of man, that they are vanity."

Now let me take this portion out of its context and apply its principles to the present day. It is really surprising how little we seem to learn from the experience of others. It appears that we must experience the fire before we are satisfied that one cannot touch it without being burned. Throughout the pages of Holy Writ, again and again we have the record of the overthrow of civilizations, of cities and of peoples, because of their sin and disobedience, yet the very same sin and disobedience are exhibited in our own generation, and, in fact, in our own lives.

The other afternoon as I was looking out of the window of my office and observing the beautiful view of New York Harbor, I thought of the restfulness that such a sight brings to the mind. There was evidence of God's handiwork; there were the ships plying the river, and the many evidences of man's work upon the earth; and yet, while it gave to my mind a restful benediction, I thought of the One who planted the ear and who formed the eye, and what He must hear and see. One does not have to be a prude, or have a pharisaical attitude to the rest of mankind, in commenting upon the sin and the debauchery that every city of our land, and of the world, produces and harbors. I know too much of my own heart, and of the sinfulness of my own nature, to ever point a finger of scorn at another individual. But, just as my heart is grieved over what I have found in my own life, so my heart is grieved as I contemplate the lives of those who live in our cities.

In a measure we can understand that which must have gripped the prophet Isaiah, when he wrote: "In the year that king Uzziah died I saw also the Lord sitting upon a throne, high and lifted up, and his train filled the temple." Isaiah observed the adoration and worship that was given to the Lord by the seraphims, who cried saying: "Holy, holy, holy, is the LORD of hosts: the whole earth is full of his glory." As Isaiah pondered that vision he said: "Woe is me! for I am undone; because I am a man of unclean lips, and I dwell in the midst of a people of unclean lips: for mine eyes have seen the King, the LORD of hosts."

Anyone who has had a vision of the eternal God in all His glory will cry out in the same language that Isaiah used. Before there is the consciousness of sin in another, there is that heartrending consciousness of sin 'n self. When that consciousness possesses our soul, and the heart cries out to God as Isaiah did, we will experience the cleansing from defilement and sin that Isaiah enjoyed, when one of the seraphims ". . . having a live coal in his hand, which he had taken with the tongs from off the altar:" laid it upon Isaiah's mouth, and said, "Lo, this hath touched thy lips; and thine iniquity is taken away, and thy sin purged."

Is it any wonder that the Psalmist, in the midst of an outburst for vengeance and of pleading to God for the expression of judgment against the oppressors of His people, should find occasion to express a word of thanks as he contemplated his own heart and his own experience, and thus wrote, in verses 12 and 13,

> "Blessed is the man whom thou chastenest, O LORD,
> and teachest him out of thy law;
>
> "That thou mayest give him rest from the days of ad-
> versity, until the pit be digged for the wicked."

May I suggest a word to those who already know the Lord Jesus Christ as Saviour, and who have felt the chastening hand of God from time to time. In the letter to the Hebrews, we are told that "no chastening for the present seemeth to be joyous, but grievous: nevertheless afterward it yieldeth the peaceable fruit of righteousness unto them which are exercised thereby." If you are enduring chastening now, consider it a blessing. Be exercised thereby, for you will have "rest from the days of adversity . . . For the LORD will not cast off his people, neither will he forsake his inheritance."

THE MAN WHOM CHRIST CALLED A FOOL

Now a word to you who are pursuing a path of indifference to spiritual things and to the claims of God upon the human life. We cannot be unmindful of the exhortation contained in the 8th verse of our Psalm, where it is written: "Understand, ye brutish among the people: and ye fools, when will ye be wise?"

Will you look at that question, "ye fools, when will ye be wise?"—but wait a moment—I have better sense than to call another man a fool, but the Bible calls certain people "fools."

The Man who spake as never man spake occasionally allowed the word *fools* to fall from His lips. What makes a man a fool? Suppose, for instance, you have had a friend to whom you have gone, and whom you have acquainted with your difficulties. He gave you some suggestions, yet you hesitated to take them. He then turned to you and said, Friend, do not be foolish; take my advice. Why did he make such a comment? For your own good; to help you avoid unnecessary pitfalls. Why did our Lord Jesus Christ call some people "fools"? In order that others might be prevented from traveling that path which leads to the loss of sound judgment. Take the case of the man who came to our Lord Jesus and said, "Master, speak to my brother, that he divide the inheritance with me." On the surface that sounds like a reasonable request, but our Lord, who knows the inner thoughts of men's hearts, saw through that request and knew that it was the expression of a covetous nature. Thus He answered, ". . . Take heed, and beware of covetousness: for a man's life consisteth not in the abundance of the things which he possesseth." Then our Lord spoke a parable, in which He told of a certain rich man, whose ground brought forth bountifully. The rich man said to himself:

> "What shall I do, because I have no room where to bestow my fruits?
>
> "And he said, This will I do: I will pull down my barns, and build greater; and there will I bestow all my fruits and my goods.
>
> "And I will say to my soul, Soul, thou hast much goods laid up for many years; take thine ease, eat, drink, and be merry."

But God said unto him:

> "Thou fool, this night thy soul shall be required of thee: then whose shall those things be, which thou hast provided?"

On the authority of our Lord Jesus Christ, that man is a fool who spends his time gathering the things of this world and assumes that such is the primary purpose of life, and whose sole ambition is a high position in this world. What a sad commentary!

God grant that if you have neglected your soul, while seeking worldly things for the future, you may this moment be wise and instructed, and receive the salvation of the Lord, which is offered as freely as the air we breathe. It is offered to you on the basis of what Christ did on the cross. He paid the penalty of sin. He made the atonement for you. His blood is the only basis of approach to God. Your sin has been settled by the sacrifice of our Lord Jesus Christ. If you will receive Him, then He will blot out your transgression forever.

PSALM NINETY-FIVE

IS HILARITY IN WORSHIP IRREVERENT?

THOSE who know Dr. Harry Ironside, pastor of the Moody Memorial Church in Chicago, know that besides being an able Bible expositor, if not the greatest in our country, he also has a keen sense of humor. He tells a story of a Scotch lady, who arose in a meeting of the "kirk" to express her resentment against the inroads of modern ideas in church construction. It seems that the meeting had been called to discuss the matter of putting stained-glass windows in the new "kirk" that was being built. "Indeed," said this Scotch lady, "we should have none of this man-made glass. We ought to be satisfied with the plain glass that God has made."

Then, of course, you have heard of some folk who insist on singing the Psalms of David to the tunes that David wrote for them. It would be interesting if we did have the tunes in our possession, but, as we do not, we shall have to be content with the language of the Psalms, perchance their exuberance may give us some appreciation of the hilarity which oft-times characterized the worship of the godly Israelite. The 95th Psalm abounds in praise. It opens with a high note of praise and ends with a word of exhortation from the mouth of God. Let us read the Psalm before commenting upon it.

> "O come, let us sing unto the LORD: let us make a joyful noise to the rock of our salvation.
>
> "Let us come before his presence with thanksgiving, and make a joyful noise unto him with psalms.
>
> "For the LORD is a great God, and a great King above all gods.
>
> "In his hand are the deep places of the earth: the strength of the hills is his also.
>
> "The sea is his, and he made it: and his hands formed the dry land.
>
> "O come, let us worship and bow down: let us kneel before the LORD our maker.
>
> "For he is our God; and we are the people of his pasture, and the sheep of his hand. To day if ye will hear his voice,
>
> "Harden not your heart, as in the provocation, and as in the day of temptation in the wilderness:
>
> "When your fathers tempted me, proved me, and saw my work.
>
> "Forty years long was I grieved with this generation, and said, It is a people that do err in their heart, and they have not known my ways:
>
> "Unto whom I sware in my wrath that they should not enter into my rest."

THE NOTE OF JOY IN WORSHIP

In preparation for our meditation I read an interesting paragraph from the writings of Dr. Alexander MacLaren, whom some of you good Britishers will surely remember. Speaking of the exhortation to praise found in the first two verses of our Psalm, he says that they give a "striking picture of the joyful tumult of the Temple worship. Shrill cries of gladness, loud shouts of praise, songs with musical accompaniments rang simultaneously through the courts, and to Western ears would have sounded as din rather than as music, and as more exuberant than reverent. The spirit expressed is, alas! almost as strange to many moderns as the manner of its expression. That swelling joy which throbs in the summons, that consciousness that jubilation is a conspicuous element in worship, that effort to rise to a height of joyful emotion, are very foreign to much of our worship. And their absence, or presence only in a minute amount, flattens much devotion and robs the Church of one of its chief treasures. No doubt there must often be sad strains blended with praise. But it is a part of Christian duty, and certainly of Christian wisdom, to try to catch that tone of joy in worship which rings in this Psalm."

I trust that we shall catch some of that tone of joy which so apparently must have possessed the writer of this Psalm. All too often we have been so impressed with the solemnity of worship that many are shocked when it is suggested that the child of God has a right to approach God with a note of praise upon his lips. Here then, in this Psalm, in the first place is a call by the Psalmist for community worship.

No joy that I know of is comparable to that of meeting with a group of people who love the Lord Jesus Christ, irrespective of what label they may have of a denominational character. It is the acme of joy to go to church. It is not a duty—it is a delight.

We who have come to know the Lord find a response in our heart to that invitation that the Psalmist made when he said, *"come, let us* sing unto the LORD: *let us* make a joyful noise to the rock of our salvation. *Let us* come before his presence with thanksgiving, and make a joyful noise unto him with psalms." The reason for all this was beautifully expressed by the Psalmist when he said, "The LORD is a great God, and a great King above all gods." What a contrast! Whether they be the gods of philosophy or the gods of heathendom, they are without ears to hear, and eyes to see, or heart that can be moved by the pleadings of human-kind. There is no God but the Lord, and there is no king save Him.

HIS PASTURE AND HIS SHEEP

In the 4th and 5th verses the Psalmist said: "In his hand are the deep places of the earth: the strength of the hills is his also. The sea is his, and he made it: and his hands formed the dry land."

There is no doubt in the mind of the writer of this Psalm that "all things were made by him; and without him there was not any thing made that was made." Whether we enter into a cave and explore the wonders of

God's creative hand, or stand at the foot of the Swiss Alps and observe the strongest barrier against invasion ever known, or travel the seas and see God's wonders in the waters, or trek across the sands of the Sahara or our own desert places, we cannot get away from the handiwork of God. Were we to raise the question, To whom does all this belong? our hearts must respond, in the language of the Psalmist, in this 95th Psalm, They are His; He made them; He formed them; they belong to Him who is our God. We are wise, therefore, to consider that we are the people of His pasture, and the sheep of His hand.

I like the analogy that the Psalmist made in speaking of those who worship the Lord as being the ". . . people of his pasture, and the sheep of his hand." The New Testament uses the same type of language. In the 10th chapter of John's Gospel the Lord said, "I am the door of the sheep . . . by me if any man enter in, he shall be saved, and shall go in and out, and find pasture." Our Lord Jesus is conceded to be the finest character this world has ever seen—even His enemies confess that, and His own people according to the flesh are rapidly acknowledging Him as their greatest prophet. No man ever spake as He spake; and yet He said, "I am the door; by me if any man enter in, *he shall* be saved, and shall go in and out, and find pasture." Now, either our Lord Jesus Christ told the truth in that statement, or He was the world's greatest impostor, deserving no consideration, for He was trifling with the souls of men. But who will question the truth of the words of our Lord Jesus Christ? If we are to find pasture we can only find it through Him.

To be "the people of his pasture" is, therefore, to be believers and followers of our Lord Jesus Christ. But the Psalmist not only wrote that we were the people of His pasture, but that we were the sheep of His hand. Notice how our Lord employed the same symbolism, saying, "My sheep hear my voice, and I know them, and they follow me: and I give unto them eternal life; and they shall never perish, neither shall any man pluck them out of *my hand*. My Father, which gave them me, is greater than all; and no man is able to pluck them out of my Father's *hand*. I and my Father are one."

TRAITS OF SHEEP

Now let us go back to the 7th verse of the 95th Psalm. There the Psalmist said, "For he is our God; and we are the people of his pasture, and the sheep of his hand." Well, what is expected of sheep? Perhaps everyone concedes that it is no compliment to be likened unto sheep, for sheep are the dumbest of all animals. You cannot trust sheep alone. A dog or a cat will find its way home, but no one ever heard of a sheep who knew how to get back to the fold. Sheep seem to know only how to walk in their own way, and that means they lose their way. But here in the 10th chapter of John's Gospel our Lord Jesus said, "My sheep hear my voice, and I know them, and they follow me . . ." Observe that He said, they "hear my voice." Now notice the last phrase of the 7th verse of the 95th Psalm, and what follows: "To day if ye will hear *his voice*, Harden not your heart, as in the provocation, and as in the day of temptation in the wilderness: when your fathers tempted me, proved me, and saw my work. Forty years long was I grieved with this generation, and said, It is a people that do err in their heart, and they have not known my ways . . ."

That is a sad commentary. The language is familiar to every student of the Scripture. It refers to that period of forty years of wandering that Israel experienced between the time they left Egypt and the time they crossed into the promised land. Forty wasted years in a wilderness. Why? Simply because they hardened their heart and refused to hearken to His voice. The most difficult thing for us to do is to be obedient to the voice of the Lord and not provoke Him. For that reason I cannot scathingly denounce Israel for their behavior during the wilderness journey. There are some preachers who seem to take a delight in criticizing certain characters of both the Old and New Testaments, wherever those characters were disobedient to their calling. But I dare say that if the spotlight of God were flashed upon their lives, and the record written and preserved for time and eternity, they would squirm. I am positive they would never again raise their voice in criticism of another. It is for that reason that whenever a word of exhortation is given, it must be addressed to the one giving it also.

PSALM NINETY-SIX

A PSALM WHICH OUGHT TO GIVE
EVERY LIVING PERSON A THRILL ! ! !

THE 96th Psalm is a wonderful Psalm to read when perchance you wake up feeling ill or indifferent or downcast. Before you finish reading it you will feel an overwhelming surge through your whole being and a desire to join in a joyful expression of praise.

In the worship of Israel there was what was known as the ark of the covenant, or the ark of God. It formed a most important part of the tabernacle worship, while Israel was traveling in the wilderness, and likewise, in taking possession of the promised land. The ark was a box. In itself it had no covering. It was made of a specific type of wood and overlaid with gold. The dimensions of it were given minutely by God to Moses, and Moses saw a pattern of it while he was in the mount, receiving his instructions from Jehovah God. The ark became the depository of certain valuable articles; first, the two tables of stone, upon which the finger of God had written the Ten Commandments; second for preservation as a memorial, there was a pot of manna, that strange food that God had provided for the children of Israel during their forty years of wilderness journeying; finally, there was a rod, called Aaron's rod. Aaron, the brother of Moses, was the first high priest. The rod was to be preserved, because when a controversy arose in Israel as to whether only one family had the right of priesthood, God demonstrated to Israel that Aaron was His chosen priest, by having a dead piece of wood suddenly break forth into life and bud. In addition to being a depository of these articles, the ark represented the mystical presence of Jehovah amongst His people. However, in order that God could commune with men, He provided a covering for the box which was made of pure gold, and in addition, beaten out of one piece, there protruded the forms of two angels, facing each other and looking down upon the covering. This covering or lid was called the mercy seat, for it was upon it that the high priest placed the blood of the sacrifice. God promised to commune, from above the mercy seat, with the representatives of His people. Not only did God give specific instructions as to how it was to be built, and what was to be placed in it, but He commanded that the ark should only be carried by the Levites as Israel traveled from place to place.

At the time this Psalm was written the ark rested in the home of a man known as Obed-edom, the Gittite. David determined that it should be brought to Jerusalem and placed in a tent which he had erected for it in Jerusalem.

Now let us read a few verses from the 15th chapter of the 1st Book of Chronicles, commencing with the 25th verse, so as to get the historic setting:

> "So David, and the elders of Israel, and the captains over thousands, went to bring up the ark of the covenant of the LORD out of the house of Obed-edom with joy.
>
> "And it came to pass, when God helped the Levites that bare the ark of the covenant of the LORD, that they offered seven bullocks and seven rams.

"And David was clothed with a robe of fine linen, and all the Levites that bare the ark, and the singers, and Chenaniah the master of the song with the singers: David also had upon him an ephod of linen.

"Thus all Israel brought up the ark of the covenant of the LORD with shouting, and with sound of the cornet, and with trumpets, and with cymbals, making a noise with psalteries and harps."

Then in the 16th chapter, commencing with verse 1, we read:

"So they brought the ark of God, and set it in the midst of the tent that David had pitched for it: and they offered burnt-sacrifices and peace-offerings before God.

"And when David had made an end of offering the burnt-offerings and the peace-offerings, he blessed the people in the name of the LORD.

"And he dealt to every one of Israel, both man and woman, to every one a loaf of bread, and a good piece of flesh, and a flagon of wine.

"And he appointed certain of the Levites to minister before the ark of the LORD, and to record, and to thank and praise the LORD God of Israel.

* * * *

"Then on that day David delivered first this psalm to thank the LORD into the hand of Asaph and his brethren."

At the close of that day we learn that "all the people said, Amen, and praised the LORD." That was a glorious day. It was a holy day, and one filled with tremendous praise.

I trust that we may catch some of the same spirit of joyful praise which possessed the people on that day, even though we do not have an ark to look upon and to gather about, and though we do not have a company of priests and Levites with singers to lead us in song and in music.

As I have already said, the ark symbolized the mystical presence of Jehovah God amongst His people. It therefore typified the ultimate purpose of God to clothe Himself with our humanity in order that He might have fellowship with the sons of men. Isaiah declared that when such an event took place, the One who came would be called Immanuel, which means God with us. That One, the New Testament declares, is our Lord Jesus Christ. Thus the ark typified Christ. Therefore, while we do not have the symbolism that David and Israel had at that time, we have the substance of the symbolism, and by faith we may gather round about the Lord Jesus Christ to offer our praise and thanksgiving.

A THRILLING PSALM

That is a long introduction to our Psalm. Now let us read it:

> "O sing unto the LORD a new song: sing unto the LORD, all the earth.
>
> "Sing unto the LORD, bless his name; shew forth his salvation from day to day.
>
> "Declare his glory among the heathen, his wonders among all people.
>
> "For the LORD is great, and greatly to be praised: he is to be feared above all gods.
>
> "For all the gods of the nations are idols: but the LORD made the heavens.
>
> "Honour and majesty are before him: strength and beauty are in his sanctuary.
>
> "Give unto the LORD, O ye kindreds of the people, give unto the LORD glory and strength.
>
> "Give unto the LORD the glory due unto his name: bring an offering, and come into his courts.
>
> "O worship the LORD in the beauty of holiness: fear before him, all the earth.
>
> "Say among the heathen that the LORD reigneth: the world also shall be established that it shall not be moved: he shall judge the people righteously.
>
> "Let the heavens rejoice, and let the earth be glad; let the sea roar, and the fulness thereof.
>
> "Let the field be joyful, and all that is therein: then shall all the trees of the wood rejoice
>
> "Before the LORD: for he cometh, for he cometh to judge the earth: he shall judge the world with righteousness, and the people with his truth."

Isn't this a wonderful Psalm? Can't you feel some of the vibration in your own breast as you contemplate its historical setting and enter into its joyous anticipation? It would appear to me as if the Psalmist overflowed with joy as he cried out, "O sing unto the LORD . . ." There is no note of sadness here.

THE NEW SONG

Were we to ask the Psalmist, What are we to sing? I think he would reply, "O sing unto the LORD a new song." A new song? Yes, a *new* song. If we turn the page of our Bible, we discover that in the 98th Psalm there is that same exhortation to sing a new song. It is an interesting study to observe the frequency of mention in the Bible of the new song. Let me quote just one, taken from the last book of the Bible, the book of The Revelation. In the 5th chapter of that book, the Apostle John described

the sight he saw in the heavens, as the glorified representatives of the redeemed were gathered before the Lord Jesus, the Lamb of God. Then he
said, "they sung a new song . . ." John recorded the words of that new
song. Here they are—"They sung a new song, saying, Thou art worthy
. . ." Who is worthy? The Lamb in the midst of the throne. Who is the
Lamb? The One who nineteen hundred years ago was introduced as "the
Lamb of God, which beareth away the sin of the world." But listen further:
they sung a new song, saying, "Thou art worthy to take the book, and to
open the seals thereof: for thou wast slain, and hast redeemed us to God by
thy blood out of every kindred, and tongue, and people, and nation; and
hast made us unto our God a kingdom of priests: and we shall reign on (or
over) the earth." So we have the substance of the new song.

Of course, the song is sung unto the Lord. The song speaks of His
accomplishments, and the death He died; that He was slain so that He
might redeem us to God, that is, buy us back to God. He did so, by the
blood of His cross. Those who are redeemed are from every kindred and
tongue, and people, and nation. What is more, our Lord has made us to
be a kingdom of priests. Thus we have the right to enter into His presence,
worship Him, extol Him, and glorify His name. And as for the future, we
are to have the pleasure of reigning with Him over the earth.

Some may say that this is all beautiful, but it is spiritual, while I have
been using terms that seem to imply operations in the physical realm. But
bear in mind that the words I have been using have been quoted from the
eternal Book, the Bible. I, for one, rejoice in the fact that some day this
world shall witness the return of the Prince of Peace, and I am as happy
as a lark to think that I shall be amongst the redeemed who will reign with
our Lord over this earth at that time. I would not exchange my privilege
to reign with Christ when He returns for Edward VIII's right to England's
throne; for his throne will mean nothing at his death; he will not be able
to reign forever, nor will he have a thing to say as to when it shall end.
But the throne of the Lord shall be from everlasting to everlasting. What
a joy it will be to reign with Christ. The new song speaks of the time of
rulership by our Lord Jesus Christ over the earth. The Psalmist wrote in
this 96th Psalm, "sing unto the LORD, all the earth." That is no small
company of people. It is not an exclusive group. The entire earth is invited
to sing unto the Lord. And what are we to do? The 2nd to the 4th verses
enjoin us to "bless his name; shew forth his salvation from day to day;
declare his glory among the nations, his wonders among all people. For

the LORD is great, and greatly to be praised: he is to be feared above all gods."

THE PERSON AND WORK OF CHRIST

Now just one more matter before we bring this message to a close. In the 11th verse of the Psalm we read, "Let the heavens rejoice, and let the earth be glad; let the sea roar, and the fulness thereof." In the 12th verse, "Let the field be joyful, and all that is therein: then shall all the trees of the wood rejoice . . ." Isn't that wonderful language? All creation is delivered from the bondage. There is no depression here. Here is prosperity and blessing. But all rejoicing is done, according to the 13th verse of the Psalm, "Before the LORD." Why? ". . . for he cometh, for he cometh to judge the earth: he shall judge the world with righteousness, and the people with his truth." God speed the day when that shall be accomplished.

Perhaps we now feel like adding our voice to that of Israel on that day when the Psalm was written, as the ark was brought into the tent pitched for it at Jerusalem, when all the people shouted "Amen," and praised the LORD.

PSALM NINETY-SEVEN

THE COMING KING, AND THE
MANNER OF HIS COMING

AS we examine the 97th Psalm we will recognize that it, too, is occupied with the rulership of Jehovah over the earth. The Psalm reads:

> "The LORD reigneth; let the earth rejoice; let the multitude of isles be glad thereof.
>
> "Clouds and darkness are round about him: righteousness and judgment are the habitation of his throne.
>
> "A fire goeth before him, and burneth up his enemies round about.
>
> "His lightnings enlightened the world: the earth saw, and trembled.
>
> "The hills melted like wax at the presence of the LORD, at the presence of the Lord of the whole earth.
>
> "The heavens declare his righteousness, and all the people see his glory.
>
> "Confounded be all they that serve graven images, that boast themselves of idols: worship him, all ye gods.

"Zion heard, and was glad; and the daughters of Judah rejoiced because of thy judgments, O LORD.

"For thou, LORD, art high above all the earth: thou art exalted far above all gods.

"Ye that love the LORD, hate evil: he preserveth the souls of his saints; he delivereth them out of the hand of the wicked.

"Light is sown for the righteous, and gladness for the upright in heart.

"Rejoice in the LORD, ye righteous; and give thanks at the remembrance of his holiness."

There are two ways to approach any part of the Scripture, and particularly the Psalms. We may seek to determine the viewpoint of the Psalmist and to understand the historical import of it, or we may study the Psalm for our own spiritual nourishment. It is well to understand these viewpoints and never to mix them; for while it is important that the spiritual life be nourished and fed by the spiritual ministration from any part of God's Word, yet we need to be instructed in the way of truth, so that we may adhere to the injunction of the Apostle Paul to rightly divide the word of truth. Paul wrote to his young friend Timothy, urging that he rightly divide the word of truth. In order to do so, he suggested, "Study to shew thyself approved unto God, a workman that needeth not to be ashamed, rightly dividing the word of truth."

Let us look at that exhortation, because it will aid us in understanding the message of this 97th Psalm. Paul instructed Timothy to "study." Now study may be delightful when we enjoy the subject, but there is no doubt that study requires the labor of brain, the looking into problems in order to gain the ability to recognize a difference between two things that appear to be alike. Timothy was to study; first, to show himself approved unto God, and second, that he might be a workman that needed not to be ashamed.

The man of God who is called to preach the Word, who studies and meditates in it in order that he may know the mind of the Spirit, is approved unto God. He is also a workman; that is, just as the carpenter is a workman and his skill with his tools is manifested in the beautiful cabinetwork that he does, so the books of the Bible are the tools of the man of God, and he should be so well acquainted with his Bible that he appears, to all who hear him, to be a workman that needeth not to be ashamed of the message he presents, because he has studied the Word and rightly divided the word of truth.

THE COMING KING AND THE MANNER OF HIS COMING

This is a long introduction to our study of the 97th Psalm, but I have in mind the necessity of emphasizing that this Psalm is not presenting something that took place in the past, though the language employed is in the present tense, for actually the Psalmist was looking beyond the past and the present, into the future. He was writing about events in the future, using the present tense, as if they were actually transpiring while he was writing. In the mind of God, when He decrees an event, the certainty of that event is so apparent that He may speak of it in the present tense, though it may not actually be fulfilled for several thousand years.

So, here, the Psalmist was writing about the Kingdom reign of Jehovah on the earth. It has not yet taken place. It will take place in the future. All the world is headed for it, if we can understand and appreciate what is going on right now in the world. I question whether there ever was a period in history when things were so topsy-turvy. All the world seems seated on a keg of dynamite. The only redeeming feature of it is the fact that men are aware that they are seated on the keg. Everywhere there is the cry for a form of government that will be world-wide in its scope, and which will be headed by one capable of rightly distributing the necessities to all, so that we may enjoy peace and comfort. It does not matter what we think of Stalin, Hitler, Mussolini, or even our own Roosevelt; but, if the best qualities of these men and one hundred others were to be found in a single man, the world would still look in vain for a capable and competent world-ruler. There is only one who is capable—the Lord Jesus Christ Himself. This world will know and experience that type of government when He returns to this earth as the absolute Monarch of the world; the King of kings and Lord of lords; Israel's long-expected Messiah, the Church's glorious Lord. Of course, it is the viewpoint of the New Testament that the One who is presented under the title of the Lord Jesus Christ is the same person referred to in the Old Testament under the title of Jehovah.

A description of the manner in which the Lord will return is found in this 97th Psalm, commencing with verse 2:

> "Clouds and darkness are round about him: righteousness and judgment are the habitation of his throne.

"A fire goeth before him, and burneth up his enemies round about.

"His lightnings enlightened the world: the earth saw, and trembled.

"The hills melted like wax at the presence of the LORD, at the presence of the Lord of the whole earth."

This is picturesque or parabolic language, but, just as a parable is a shadow of an actuality, so this language is a shadow of what will actually transpire. If these words convey anything, they convey the fact that our Lord will return in judgment. That may not be nice to hear, but the Scripture is as clear as crystal that the coming of our Lord Jesus Christ will take place in judgment. Any honest thinking leads to the same conclusion. I do not know a man who is willing to stake his reputation, by prophesying what will take place in this world during even the next five years. Some people are afraid to think of it. I learned last week of a man who committed suicide because he feared that everything was going to seed and that this country was inevitably headed for Communism. His may have been an extreme case. I am not venturing the suggestion that we are heading for anything of the kind. However I am saying that the only person in the world who can look into the future with absolute complacency is the man who believes the Bible.

THE TWO SCHOOLS OF INTERPRETATION

At the beginning of our meditation I called attention to the necessity of rightly dividing the word of truth. There are two schools of interpretation concerning future events. There is one school which believes that, through the preaching of the gospel, the world will get better and better and better, and finally, the whole universe will be converted to the gospel, and when that takes place the King Himself will return. I do not like to ridicule a viewpoint, I do not think that we have a right to do that; but, my! what a long, long, long time we will have to wait, for with two thousand years already of the propagation of the gospel, I am afraid that we are a very great distance from the accomplishment of that goal.

The other school of interpretation declares that it is their viewpoint that the Bible teaches that the Kingdom will be established by the coming of the Lord Jesus Christ. The world will not be prepared for Him, if by preparation we mean that they will be waiting with open arms for Him.

The world will be unprepared, yet He will take possession of it. When He comes, conditions are disturbed (men's hearts have failed them for fear) and the love of many has waxed cold; so that the Lord raises the question, Will He find faith on the earth when He returns? This school declares that the coming of the Lord Jesus Christ will take place at a specific time in history, which no one knows except God Himself; and with that coming, the visible appearance of the Lord Jesus Christ will be ushered in; the Bible speaks of it as the Kingdom reign of our Lord.

The other day, a certain clergyman sent me a leaflet describing what he calls a "vital religion" for the followers of Christ. He called it "A Kingdom of God Movement" and he declared that the objectives of the movement are "a regenerated, social and economic Christianity with world-wide cooperation, based on Christ's Golden Rule." He declared that Christian principles can be successfully applied to the world economic system, so as to bring nearer the Kingdom of God on earth. He invited co-laborers to join the movement, to learn how to cooperate in preparing the way for the promised "BRANCH" King in God's Kingdom.

When I read that leaflet I thought: Would to God someone would give that man a New Testament with all twenty-seven books that comprise it, that he might understand that Christians do not have a thing to do with this world economic system. All that Christians are called upon to do in this generation is to preach the gospel. As far as this world economic system is concerned, the Bible is clear that such is under the domination of the one who is called "the god of this age" and "the prince of the power of the air," who is none other than Satan, himself. I have no hesitancy in stating that Christian principles cannot be successfully applied to the present system of world economics. It will need a regenerated system, and that will only take place through the coming of the Lord Jesus Christ in great power and great glory.

Let us note this 97th Psalm, to find out what will happen when the Lord reigns. Verse 8 reads: "Zion heard, and was glad; and the daughters of Judah rejoiced because of thy judgments, O LORD." Now one may spiritualize Zion and the daughters of Judah, but then he is not handling the Scripture honestly. Zion is Jerusalem, and the daughters of Judah are the Jews. At the coming of the Lord, Zion will hear and be glad; and the daughters of Judah will rejoice. All of Jerusalem will say, "For thou, LORD, art high above all the earth: thou art exalted far above all gods."

THE PRESERVATION OF HIS SAINTS

There are one or two other things in this Psalm upon which we should comment before bringing our message to a close. In the 10th verse there is an exhortation, the principle of which can be applied to the present time. There we read, "Ye that love the LORD, hate evil . . ." There is not a doubt that we, who love the Lord, should actually *hate* evil. Our testimony would be more convincing and more powerful, if we, who profess to love Him, would keep His commandments. His commandments are not grievous. We are called upon to love one another, to eschew evil, and to avoid conformity to this world. We are urged to bear our witness for Christ, to love our fellow-men and to present Christ to them. Such a life is not without its great compensation.

In the same verse we read, "he preserveth the souls of his saints; he delivereth them out of the hand of the wicked." The New Testament calls every believer in the Lord Jesus Christ a saint, although it is equally clear that a lot of us are not saintly. A saint, according to the New Testament, is any man or woman who has received the Lord Jesus Christ as his or her Saviour. It simply means that they are set apart for God. If you have received Christ you are His saint for you belong to Him, and you belong to Him by right of purchase.

This statement in the 97th Psalm is reflected in every other portion of Scripture. We are assured that the Lord "preserveth the souls of his saints." To preserve is to keep. Thus, the Lord will keep His saints. We do not keep ourselves. My! how glad we should be about that, for, if salvation depended upon our keeping and our preservation, it would not last very long. But because it depends entirely upon His keeping and His preservation, our salvation will last for time and eternity. I hope that this is an encouragement to each of you who have received Christ.

Not only does God promise to preserve the souls of His saints, but He also promises to deliver each from the hand of the wicked. So you see, here is preservation and deliverance. Preservation assures us of eternal salvation. Deliverance assures us of victory. When we understand these things, then it is quite natural to enter into the closing exhortation of the Psalm, which reads, "Rejoice in the LORD, ye righteous; and give thanks at the remembrance of his holiness."

"A SINGING MILLENNIAL PSALM"

THE very fine letters I have received recently are certainly appreciated. One in particular did my heart much good. It came from my friend, Dr. A. C. Gaebelein, who listened in last Sunday morning to the comments on the 97th Psalm. You who are acquainted with Dr. Gaebelein, know that for more than fifty years he has borne his faithful testimony to the Word of God, up and down this country. His letter said something I greatly enjoyed. In speaking of this particular group of Psalms, which we are now considering, he said that he calls Psalms 95 to 100, "The Singing Millennial Psalms."

It is not surprising that we find the 98th Psalm opening with "O sing unto the LORD a new song; for he hath done marvellous things . . ." Before we read the Psalm in its entirety, I shall comment on what is meant by the word "millennium." The word actually is a compound Latin word, made up of *mille* meaning *a thousand*, and *annus* meaning *years*. In other words, the millennium is a period of one thousand years. The phrase "one thousand years" is found several times in the last book of the Bible, the book of The Revelation. Let's read a few verses from the 20th chapter of that book:

> "And I saw an angel come down from heaven, having the key of the bottomless pit and a great chain in his hand.
>
> "And he laid hold on the dragon, that old serpent, which is the Devil, and Satan, and bound him *a thousand years,*
>
> "And cast him into the bottomless pit, and shut him up, and set a seal upon him, that he should deceive the nations no more, till *the thousand years* should be fulfilled: and after that he must be loosed a little season.
>
> "And I saw thrones, and they sat upon them, and judgment was given unto them: and I saw the souls of them that were beheaded for the witness of Jesus, and for the word of God, and which had not worshipped the beast, neither his image, neither had received his mark upon their foreheads, or in their hands; and they lived and reigned with Christ *a thousand years.*
>
> "But the rest of the dead lived not again until *the thousand years* were finished. This is the first resurrection.
>
> "Blessed and holy is he that hath part in the first resurrection: on such the second death hath no power, but

they shall be priests of God and of Christ, and shall reign with him *a thousand years*."

Observe that the phrase "a thousand years" is found several times in tihs portion. It refers to the age when the Lord Jesus Christ shall reign as the absolute Monarch of the world. Poets, philosophers, and artists have vied with each other in attempting to picture a period when the strife and struggle of life will be over; when disturbances will no longer take place; when everything will be calm and peaceful and all will have their own home and garden and live like lords in their own domain. It seems that in the breast of man there lies the hope that some day this world will enjoy an extraordinary era of peace. The Bible bears testimony to that same era and declares it to be a period of one thousand years when the Lord Jesus Christ shall reign as the Prince of Peace. Indeed, of that period and that which follows, Isaiah wrote: "Of the increase of his government and peace there shall be no end, upon the throne of David, and upon his kingdom, to order it, and to establish it with judgment and with justice from henceforth even for ever."

In our previous meditation we spent some time explaining the two views that are held respecting these future events. One insists that through the preaching of the gospel and the receiving of Christ, the whole world will be saved and enjoy that era of peace and gladness; the other insists that nothing of the kind will take place, that the coming of the Lord Jesus Christ in judgment will usher in this period of Kingdom rulership. We shall not go over that again, except to remind ourselves of what Dr. Gaebelein has said regarding Psalms 95 to 100. They are songs that will be sung during the millennial reign of the Lord Jesus Christ.

The Psalm reads:

"O sing unto the LORD a new song; for he hath done marvellous things: his right hand, and his holy arm, hath gotten him the victory.

"The LORD hath made known his salvation: his righteousness hath he openly shewed in the sight of the heathen.

"He hath remembered his mercy and his truth toward the house of Israel: all the ends of the earth have seen the salvation of our God.

"Make a joyful noise unto the LORD, all the earth: make a loud noise, and rejoice, and sing praise.

"Sing unto the LORD with the harp; with the harp, and the voice of a psalm.

"With trumpets and sound of cornet make a joyful
noise before the LORD, the King.

"Let the sea roar, and the fulness thereof; the world,
and they that dwell therein.

"Let the floods clap their hands: let the hills be joyful
together

"Before the LORD; for he cometh to judge the earth:
with righteousness shall he judge the world, and the
people with equity."

When we consider that this Psalm is a millennial Psalm, with the
nation of Israel back in her own land, in Jerusalem; the Temple restored;
and with ten Gentiles taking hold of the skirt of one Jew, and saying to that
Jew, in the language of Zechariah the prophet, "We will go with you: for
we have heard that God is with you"—and when we consider the wave of
anti-Semitism that is now sweeping the world, we are forced to acknowledge
that a miracle must take place, before ten Gentiles of various nations will
grasp hold of the skirt of one Jew, and say to that man, "We will go with
you: for we have heard that God is with you." No wonder the Psalmist
said, in verse 1 of the 98th Psalm, "O sing unto the LORD a new song;
for he hath done *marvellous* things: his right hand, and his holy arm, hath
gotten him the victory."

GOD'S RIGHT HAND

Need we be reminded that this is the work of the Lord. It is He who
hath done marvelous things. It was His right hand and His holy arm that
got Him the victory. He will change the condition of the world. The deliverance comes, not by virtue of any inherent value in the Jew or the Gentile,
but it comes by virtue of the eternal decree of God, and the revelation of
His right hand and His holy arm. It is He who has gotten the victory.

In the 2nd and 3rd verses the Psalmist wrote:

"The LORD hath made known his salvation: his righteousness hath he openly shewed in the sight of the
heathen (or nations).

"He hath remembered his mercy and his truth toward
the house of Israel: all the ends of the earth have seen
the salvation of our God."

I repeat what I have said before: The man who knows the Lord as
his Saviour and knows the Scripture and the plan which God has for this
world, which is yet to be accomplished, *cannot be a pessimist*. He is the
only one who can look at the events that are transpiring at the present time

and keep his equilibrium. Without a fear or a qualm he knows that the counsel of God will stand and that His purposes will be accomplished.

But it is our desire not only to observe the proper setting of this Psalm from a historical viewpoint, but also to enter into the joy that is expressed therein. We are informed by the Apostle Paul in his letter to the Romans, ". . . that blindness in part is happened to Israel, until the fulness of the Gentiles be come in." Because of their rejection of Christ, the Jewish nation has been temporarily set aside. God is now dealing primarily with Gentiles. Yet out of both Jews and Gentiles He is calling a people for His own name. The New Testament describes that company of people as the Body of Christ—the Church of the living God. When that work has been completed, God will once more deal with Israel as a nation. When that takes place, the Bible says that it will be like "life from the dead."

As the Psalmist rejoiced in the wonderful things of the Lord, so we too can sing unto the Lord a new song—"for he hath done marvellous things: his right hand, and his holy arm, hath gotten him the victory."

Will you observe that the writer spoke of God's right hand and His holy arm as the means which produced the victory. Bear that in mind while we consider a question which the prophet Isaiah raised in the 53rd chapter: "Who hath believed our report? and to whom is the arm of the LORD revealed?" Then the prophet described the suffering Messiah, saying:

> ". . . he shall grow up before him as a tender plant, and as a root out of a dry ground: he hath no form nor comeliness; and when we shall see him, there is no beauty that we should desire him.
>
> "He is despised and rejected of men; a man of sorrows, and acquainted with grief: and we hid as it were our faces from him; he was despised, and we esteemed him not.
>
> "Surely he hath borne our griefs, and carried our sorrows: yet we did esteem him stricken, smitten of God, and afflicted."

You have undoubtedly observed, from this quotation from Isaiah, that the arm of the Lord is synonymous with the Lord Jesus Christ. Who hath believed our report? To whom hath the arm of the Lord been revealed?

Thus, when the Psalmist said in this 98th Psalm, "O sing unto the LORD a new song; for he hath done marvellous things: his right hand, and his holy arm, hath gotten him the victory" the spiritual mind can understand that he is referring to Christ. It is through the Lord Jesus Christ that God has gained His great victory.

How evident it is that the time of which the Psalmist was speaking is a time of great gladness. We are able to see the salvation of God. We are invited to make a joyful noise unto the Lord. There will be singing, the playing of harps, and the voice of the Psalm. There will be trumpets and the sound of the cornet. All will make a joyful noise before the Lord the King for, said the Psalmist in the closing verse: ". . . he cometh to judge the earth: with righteousness shall he judge the world, and the people with equity."

The bulwark of any government is its righteousness. When a government judges the people with equity and righteousness, the people rejoice, but when a government is based on the selfish desires of a specific group, so that its wishes are inflicted upon others, or the one governing seeks to feather his own nest, the people are in despair.

Observe that what brings about the tremendous outbursts of joy expressed in this 98th Psalm, is the fact that the Lord cometh to judge the world with righteousness and the people with equity.

PSALM NINETY-NINE

THE MAJESTY AND HOLINESS OF GOD

THE 99th Psalm reminds us of an incident which happened in the life of Moses, the man of God, which I think will place us in a better frame of mind for approaching this remarkable Psalm.

Moses, when he became of age, refused to be called the son of Pharaoh's daughter. Having spent forty years in the court of Pharaoh, he spent another forty years on the backside of a desert, tending the flock of Jethro, his father-in-law. While leading the flock, he came to a place called Mt. Horeb. There the angel of the Lord appeared unto him in a flame of fire out of the midst of a bush. Moses observed that the bush burned, yet it was not consumed. Strange phenomenon indeed! Thus Moses said, "I will now turn aside, and see this great sight, why the bush is not burnt." When he did, God called out of the midst of the bush, and said, "Draw not nigh hither: put off thy shoes from off thy feet, for the place whereon thou standest is holy ground." From that time forward, the religious East has always approached the presence of God with unshod feet.

If there ever was a Psalm where the injunction applies to remove one's shoes from off one's feet because the ground is holy, that Psalm is the one which we are about to consider. In fact, a great expositor has called this 99th Psalm an earthly echo of the hymn that the seraphims sing in the heavens; the hymn to which Isaiah referred to, when he wrote:

> "In the year that King Uzziah died I saw also the Lord sitting upon a throne, high and lifted up, and his train filled the temple.

> "Above it stood the seraphims: each one had six wings; with twain he covered his face, and with twain he covered his feet, and with twain he did fly.

> "And one cried unto another, and said, Holy, holy, holy, is the LORD of hosts: the whole earth is full of his glory."

This 99th Psalm, though it has only nine short verses, contains three references to the holiness of God, just as the seraphims cried, "Holy, holy, holy . . ." Let us read the Psalm:

> "The LORD reigneth; let the people tremble: he sitteth between the cherubims; let the earth be moved.

> "The LORD is great in Zion; and he is high above all the people.

> "Let them praise thy great and terrible name; for it is holy.

> "The king's strength also loveth judgment; thou dost establish equity, thou executest judgment and righteousness in Jacob.

> "Exalt ye the LORD our God, and worship at his footstool; for he is holy.

> "Moses and Aaron among his priests, and Samuel among them that call upon his name; they called upon the LORD, and he answered them.

> "He spake unto them in the cloudy pillar: they kept his testimonies, and the ordinance that he gave them.

> "Thou answeredst them, O LORD our God: thou wast a God that forgavest them, though thou tookest vengeance of their inventions.

> "Exalt the LORD our God, and worship at his holy hill; for the LORD our God is holy."

We shall center our thoughts as briefly as possible upon the general structure of the Psalm, in order that we may spend as much time as we have available for a consideration of the holiness of God.

In the first place, this Psalm, like the several preceding, is another of what Dr. A. C. Gaebelein has called "The Singing Millennial Psalms." Observe that the Lord is actually reigning on the earth. Because He is visible, people tremble. Someone has said the Psalmist "does not call on man to bow before a veiled majesty;" but before God, who has revealed Himself in stupendous acts, and has thereby made Himself a name. This is gloriously expressed in verse 3, where we read: "Let them praise thy great and terrible name . . ."

No mortal can possibly contemplate a grander theme than the Person of the Godhead. In this Psalm the glory and majesty of the Lord so beggar description that the Psalmist contents himself with speaking of His name, as being "great and terrible." The Lord's person is manifested in One whom the Psalmist speaks of as the King. The presence of the King on the earth institutes the reign of Jehovah, and because the Lord is exalted as our God on the earth there is the exhortation to the people to worship "at his holy hill," for He is holy.

"ENTHRONED BETWEEN THE CHERUBIMS"

Observe, in verse 1, that when the announcement is made that the Lord reigneth, with the consequent injunction to the people to tremble, it is written that the Lord "sitteth between the cherubims . . ." So marvelous is this revelation of God, that the Psalmist invited the earth to move at the presence of the Lord. But note the place where the Lord is seated: "He sitteth between the cherubims . . ." If we were to go to a Hebrew lexicon, in order to delve into the meaning of the Hebrew verb *yashab*, translated *sitteth*, we would observe that it has in it the thought of enthronement. Thus the Lord is enthroned between the cherubims. An instructed Israelite would understand that better than we Gentiles.

In a study of a previous Psalm we described that interesting article of furniture which was used in tabernacle worship by Israel, called "the ark of the covenant." It symbolized the presence of Jehovah among His people. It had a covering, called the mercy seat, made out of pure gold, and out of that same gold there were beaten the angelic forms of two cherubims. They faced each other and looked down upon the mercy seat. The high priest, on the day of atonement, walked into the holy of holies, where the ark was situated, and sprinkled the blood of the atoning sacrifice before the ark and on the mercy seat. When that was completed, God promised to pardon their sins and commune with the representative of Israel in that matchless, holy place.

In the 1st chapter of Hebrews we learn that when our Lord ascended on high, after His resurrection, His Father said to Him, "Sit thou at my right hand, until I make thine enemies thy footstool." Our Lord is now seated in the presence of His Father, and, if you please, between the cherubims. He is there for two reasons, first, until His enemies be made His footstool, and, second, as a continuous testimony to the fact that the work that He accomplished on the cross is absolutely satisfactory to God. Redemption is full and complete. He now sits there, having purged us from our sins.

Now it ought to be apparent that the majesty of the Creator is so transcendent that no creature can stand in His presence. Moses wanted to see more of God, but God answered, "Thou canst not see my face: for there shall no man see me, and live." The majesty, the glory, and the indescribable holiness of God is so pronounced that a sinner must flee to a place where he may hide himself from the presence of such glory. But in this Psalm, while the people are invited to tremble, observe that in verse 5 they are also called upon to come so close to His presence that they are asked to worship at His footstool. The acme of God's grace is exhibited when a sinful man is invited to come to God's footstool and worship before His presence.

While at present our Lord Jesus is seated at the right hand of God in the heavens, it is but a temporary throne. He is there only until His enemies are made His footstool. In the 99th Psalm we find Him on the earth, and the place of worship is at Zion, which is called "his holy hill." That which will characterize the reign of our Lord on the earth is His holiness and His forgiving grace. Three times over, in this Psalm, He is spoken of as "holy," while in verse 8, we are reminded that the Lord our God was a God who forgave; though He did take vengeance against their inventions.

GOD'S FORGIVING GRACE

That brings us to the two great subjects. First, the fact of God's forgiving grace; and second, the glorious fact of His holiness.

In this Psalm reference is made to God's dealings with the children of Israel, particularly as manifested through Moses, Aaron, and Samuel, wonderful names and wonderful persons. They interceded for Israel. They were priests and prophets of the most High. God answered, when they interceded, and forgave the sins of His people, though He took cognizance of their deeds. Someone will say, How is it possible to reconcile the fact of

God's forgiveness of sin, when yet He takes cognizance of their deeds? I read a helpful comment on this subject which came from the pen of Alexander MacLaren. Speaking of this characteristic of God, he said, "The great principle, firmly grasped and clearly proclaimed by the singer, is that a holy God is a forgiving God—But God loves too well to grant impunity . . . Forgiveness is something far better than escape from penalties. It cannot be worthy of God to bestow or salutary for men to receive, unless it is accompanied with such retribution as may show the pardoned man how deadly his sin was."

I think every individual who has experienced the joy of the forgiveness of sins never loses sight of the fact that he was and is a sinner, by nature and by deed. The fact of his sin, though pardoned and forgiven, never leaves his mind. In fact, it is impossible to approach the presence of God, though in full consciousness that we have been forgiven, without recognizing that we are sinful. So often people assume that because we say that we are saved and that we know the Lord, it means that we profess to live a life without sin. Nothing could be further from the truth. We are sinners, but we are sinners saved by grace. That is the distinction. But some may ask, What should a person do to receive the forgiveness of sin? Let me take you to a passage of Scripture that will clearly answer that question. In the 10th chapter of the Acts of the Apostles and the 43rd verse, (Simon Peter is the speaker, and he is addressing a group at the house of Cornelius, a centurion) speaking of our Lord Jesus, Peter said: "To him give all the prophets witness, that through his name whosoever believeth in him shall receive remission of sins."

Observe that Peter said, "Whosoever believeth in him shall receive remission of sins"? *Whosoever* means anybody. It is just as wide as it is possible to make any invitation. Peter also declared that all the prophets gave witness, "that through his name whosoever believeth in him shall receive remission of sins." So if we believe in the Lord Jesus, then on the authority of God's Word and the testimony of the Apostle Peter, we shall receive the forgiveness of sin.

GOD'S HOLINESS

Now we come to the fact of God's holiness. Frequently, on a Sunday morning, a church service opens with that glorious and awe-inspiring hymn, "Holy, Holy, Holy, Lord God Almighty!" How is it possible for a company of people to sing about the holiness of God? The Bible says that His is too holy an eye to behold sin, and that He will by no means clear the guilty. If there is any one thing that man fears, it is the holiness of God. I remember that from earliest childhood I never wanted to think about it. It bothered me. Holiness? Why that is the extreme opposite of everything that I am. How is it possible to find any joy in the contemplation of the holiness of God? There is only one thing it can possibly bring to heart and mind; that is a dreadful fear. Well, strange as it may seem, while at one time I feared the holiness of God, now the very contemplation of His holiness gives me tremendous joy. But why, you may ask, is the characteristic of God which is so disturbing to the natural man, the very characteristic that is a delight to the spiritual man? Because it was God's holiness and His righteousness that demanded that sin be punished and the penalty exacted. It was God's holiness that provided the ransom, through the death of His Son. It was God's holiness that sent His Son into this world, to be born in the womb of a virgin. It was God's holiness that sent Him to the cross, and it is God's holiness that clears every individual who embraces by faith the death of our Lord Jesus Christ.

PSALM ONE HUNDRED

A DOXOLOGY FOR A SPRINGTIME ORATORIO OR THE GLORIOUS FACT OF GOD'S GOODNESS

FOR some little while past, in our meditations in the Book of Psalms, I have been confronted with the difficulty of trying to condense a message on a long Psalm into a short period of twenty minutes; so that it is a delightful change to come to a Psalm that has only five verses in it. We ought to be able to do a little more than skim over the surface. The 100th Psalm, in which our meditation is found reads as follows:

"Make a joyful noise unto the LORD, all ye lands.

"Serve the LORD with gladness: come before his presence with singing.

"Know ye that the LORD he is God: it is he that hath made us, and not we ourselves; we are his people, and the sheep of his pasture.

"Enter into his gates with thanksgiving, and into his courts with praise: be thankful unto him, and bless his name.

"For the LORD is good; his mercy is everlasting; and his truth endureth to all generations."

The mere reading of the Psalm indicates that it is one of praise, a most appropriate Psalm for a Sunday morning, and particularly a Sunday morning in the springtime. As a young man's heart seems to develop a strange exuberance in the spring season, I certainly hope that we will experience that indescribable joy and good feeling that possess a soul when it feels like making a joyful noise unto the Lord.

To begin with, this Psalm has been called a doxology. It actually ends a certain section of the Psalms, or series of Psalms, which has had as its basic theme, "The Kingdom Reign of our Lord Jesus Christ."

I shall not spend much time in reminding you that the Bible abounds in predictions concerning the glory that this world will some day enjoy under the rulership of the King of kings and Lord of lords.

For instance, when we approach the Old Testament for the first time we are impressed with two contradictory lines of prediction concerning the One of whom the prophets speak as "The Coming One." In the breast of every true Israelite there is the hope that the Messiah will some day appear and that their nation will enjoy their own land and become a blessing to all nations of the world. That hope is based on one of these lines of prediction in the Old Testament. The second line centers around a suffering Messiah who would bear the sin of the nation, who would be the antitype of every sacrifice, and who would meet the demands of a holy God. In the New Testament, particularly in the Gospels, we find that our Lord Jesus Christ fits perfectly into every prediction made concerning a suffering Messiah. Every detail concerning His reception, the type of ministry He would give, the rejection by the people, the mode of His death—every detail was fulfilled to the dotting of the "i" and the crossing of the "t." When we come to the end of the Gospel record, we raise the same question that the disciples raised to their Lord after His resurrection, when they asked, "Lord, wilt thou at this time restore again the kingdom to Israel?" Our Lord answered that it was not for them "to know the times or the seasons, which the Father hath put in his own power. But," said he, "ye shall receive power, after that the Holy Spirit is come upon you: and ye shall be witnesses unto me both in Jerusalem, and in all Judæa, and in Samaria, and unto the uttermost part of the earth." As we proceed into the Acts of the Apostles and the New Testament Epistles, we find that our Lord outlined perfectly the gospel ministry. It began in Jerusalem, spread throughout Judea, and on into Samaria, and finally into every corner of the earth.

All of the New Testament books join with the Old Testament in holding out the promise that just as precisely as was every prediction concerning the suffering Messiah fulfilled, so every prediction concerning the glorious reign of the Messiah and the exaltation of the Jewish nation will be fulfilled.

"A JOYFUL NOISE"

Now these Psalms that we have been considering, particularly from the 95th to the 100th, are all occupied with the glorious reign upon the earth, of the King of kings and Lord of lords. To understand the character of these Psalms better, we might consider them in the nature of an oratorio, with the 100th Psalm as a doxology to the oratorio. It is a gloriously fitting climax and seems to sum up all that has been previously sung. This of course means that the Psalm specifically refers to that period of history in the future, when our Lord, as King of kings and Lord of lords, will reign on the earth. But that should not deter us from entering into the joy that this glorious Psalm of praise expresses. Let us look at the Psalm carefully.

In the first place, we are invited to make a joyful noise unto the Lord. The invitation is broad. It is written, "Make a joyful noise unto the LORD, *all ye lands.*" I do not know how you feel, but I thrill to the marrow when I hear a trained choir sing with perfect harmony and rhythm. You may not like to have that described as a joyful "noise." But imagine that choir multiplied so as to take in all lands and that you were suddenly to tune in and hear the entire world offering its praise unto God. That will give you some idea of the future glory that awaits this world. You had better get in on it immediately and join with those who have received Christ as their Saviour and who know what it is to be redeemed from sin and to enjoy even now the throb in our breast in response to the invitation to make a joyful noise unto the Lord.

"YE ARE MY FRIENDS . . ."

I think that the first verse of this Psalm expresses the heart's adoration unto the Lord. Verse 2 reads, "Serve the LORD with gladness: come before his presence with singing." That emphasizes that while solemnity and order ought to be observed in the house of the Lord, it should not be forgotten that God loves a singing heart, and we are to come into His presence with singing. Note that worship and service go hand in hand. We cannot serve the Lord until we have given Him the adoration of our heart. Let us put the first thing first. Let us not put the cart before the horse. We serve the Lord because we love to serve Him and because He saved us by His grace. We do not serve in order to be saved—we serve because we are saved.

But God did not save men in order to make them servants. He has myriads of servants that can serve Him better than men; angels in His presence always do His bidding, which is more than any of us have done, even at our best. It is friendship, love, and devotion that God desires from the sons of men, as we learn from the New Testament.

The words were spoken by our Lord on the night of His betrayal, as He left the upper room in Jerusalem, having finished the passover supper, and proceeded to the Garden of Gethsemane. On that journey, during the quiet midnight hours when the Judean stars were shining in their brilliance and all creation seemed to hold its breath, wondering what man would do to the Creator, the stillness of the hour was broken only by His voice as He spoke to His disciples, who listened in breathless silence—"These things have I spoken unto you, that my joy might remain in you, and that your joy might be full. This is my commandment, That ye love one another, as I have loved you. Greater love hath no man than this, that a man lay down his life for his friends. Ye are my friends, if ye do whatsoever I command you. Henceforth I call you not servants; for the servant knoweth not what his lord doeth: but I have called you friends; for all things that I have heard of my Father I have made known unto you."

THE GOODNESS OF GOD

What a searching question the Psalmist addressed to us, "Know ye that the LORD he is God: it is he that hath made us, and not we ourselves . . ." Frequently we act as if we had made ourselves. Haven't you heard of a "self-made man"? How we love to tickle our fancy! Yet our Lord said, "Which of you by taking thought can add one cubit to his stature?" As long as we cannot, by taking thought, add one cubit to our stature, let's not talk about being "the master of our fate and the captain of our soul."

By virtue of the fact that God has made us, we belong to Him. When we couple that with the fact that He died for us and purchased us with the precious blood of His Son, then we must agree that He is entitled to our lives. We should delight in the knowledge that we are the sheep of His pasture.

Considering His claims upon us let us do exactly as the Psalmist suggested in the 4th and 5th verses, "Enter into his gates with thanksgiving, and into his courts with praise: be thankful unto him, and bless his name. For the LORD is good; his mercy is everlasting; and his truth endureth to all generations."

PSALM ONE HUNDRED ONE

A PSALM FOR A KING

T HE 101st Psalm was written by a king for a King; it reads:

"I will sing of mercy and judgment; unto thee, O LORD, will I sing.

"I will behave myself wisely in a perfect way. O when wilt thou come unto me? I will walk within my house with a perfect heart.

"I will set no wicked thing before mine eyes: I hate the work of them that turn aside; it shall not cleave to me.

"A froward heart shall depart from me: I will not know a wicked person.

"Whoso privily slandereth his neighbour, him will I cut off: him that hath an high look and a proud heart will not I suffer.

"Mine eyes shall be upon the faithful of the land, that they may dwell with me: he that walketh in a perfect way, he shall serve me.

"He that worketh deceit shall not dwell within my house: he that telleth lies shall not tarry in my sight.

"I will early destroy all the wicked of the land; that I may cut off all wicked doers from the city of the LORD."

Some people believe that David wrote this Psalm just before he ascended the throne; others assert that it was written shortly after he became king. It appears to me that the latter is the proper view. Of one thing we may be sure: the Psalm outlines clearly what David expected to accomplish as king. Observe that he addressed certain instructions to his own heart before he proceeded to outline how he would purge his court. With this in mind, we can expect to find interesting, homely exhortations to right living, particularly as it applies to a king, or a person in authority. But if these exhortations apply to a king they should likewise apply to his subjects. Therefore, we may approach this Psalm and receive a word of encouragement and instruction for our own souls.

Usually I live with a Psalm for a week, in preparation for these Sunday morning meditations. Thus it is not strange that I seek to translate the happenings of the week in the terms of the Psalm we are to consider. Last Friday an incident took place which helped me understand this Psalm. I was having lunch with some delightful friends, including Dr. Homer Hammontree, and Dr. Wilbur M. Smith. Dr. Smith related an incident in the life of the present King of England, told by Mr. Lunt Geoffrey, who was the secretary of the Junior Work of the Church Missionary Society. He said that the chaplain of Dartmouth College in England, where the Prince of Wales was educated, was examining and preparing the boys for confirmation. He made a custom of taking each boy, individually, for a half-hour talk on very serious subjects. When the Prince came up for confirmation the chaplain was somewhat doubtful as to how much the boy should be told. He wrote to one of his tutors at the palace, asking him to put the matter before the King. In response, the chaplain received a personal letter from the King himself, saying that he was to tell the Prince just exactly what he told the others, and that he might send word of the exact day and hour at which this talk was to take place, as he, the King, wished to spend that time in prayer, because the fate of empires would depend on what was said during that half-hour.

In this 101st Psalm we have just such a message; though it came from the pen of the king himself, David, the son of Jesse. In the first place, David said, "I will sing of mercy and judgment . . ." No throne can be stable unless mercy and judgment are the foundations of that throne. Then David, speaking of himself, said, "I will behave myself wisely in a perfect way . . . I will walk within my house with a perfect heart. I will set no wicked thing before mine eyes . . . I will not know a wicked person." Let us stop a moment and consider these things.

"A CHEAP RIGHTEOUSNESS"?

I have heard it said that we who preach that a man is constituted righteous on the basis of receiving Christ as his Saviour present a cheap gospel. A young man I knew turned to his sister, who was witnessing to him about Christ, saying, "I do not want any of your cheap righteousness. I believe righteousness comes by hard work—by a life of constantly doing good. What you present as 'the Gospel' is the cheapest thing I know anything about. Away with that kind of cheap righteousness." I have heard that same idea, expressed in slightly different words, even from ministers; the inference being of course that righteousness is the result of works; that righteousness comes from character building; it is not a free gift.

In a measure, I suppose, some such criticism may be lodged by an individual who does not understand the gospel. But when it comes from a clergyman, I feel like suggesting that he get himself a New Testament and read it, instead of so-called modern books on religious thinking. The Bible is as clear as crystal, that a man is justified by faith, apart from works. It goes so far as to state that "by the deeds of the law there shall no flesh be justified in his (God's) sight . . ." It is written, that it is "Not by works of righteousness which we have done, but according to his mercy he saved us . . ." It is also written that "by grace are ye saved through faith; and that not of yourselves: it is the gift of God: not of works, lest any man should boast." If it be presumed that because salvation is a free gift, and the sinner who receives Christ is immediately justified from all things from which he could not be justified by the law of Moses, that such means that he has come in possession of a cheap righteousness, may I very kindly, but emphatically, state that the righteousness with which every individual in Christ has been clothed, is the result of the most priceless thing in this universe. That righteousness was purchased by the life-blood of our Lord Jesus Christ—it cost the very glory of heaven for a sinner to be justified through Christ.

But I am aware that there are some people who reason that because they are saved by grace they may do as they please. I have known of professed Christians, who would not admit this, but whose lives speak boldly in defense of that theory. Such an individual is a disgrace to the Christian church. While the Scripture is clear that "we are saved by grace through faith" and "Not of works, lest any man should boast . . ." we are dishonest if we end the quotation there. The Spirit of God continued, through the pen of the Apostle Paul, by writing, "For we are his workmanship, created in Christ Jesus unto good works, which God hath before ordained that we should walk in them." It is the solemn duty of every Christian, after he has received Christ, to ". . . be careful to maintain good works."

Faith precedes works; the order is never reversed. Because we are saved, we are expected to walk honorably. Thus David wrote in this Psalm, "I will behave myself wisely in a perfect way . . . I will walk within my house with a perfect heart." Now that does not mean that we are going to satisfy everybody, for it seems to be the indoor sport of the world to criticize a Christian. Furthermore, there are a lot of people who think that because an individual has professed Christ, they must therefore take advantage of him. That is not what I mean. David knew what it was to have one even in his own household turn against him, for his son Absalom lifted up his heel against his father; while our Lord said, ". . . a man's foes shall be they of his own household." But David knew that it was necessary, if his kingdom were to endure, that he conduct himself wisely within his own house. If he did so, it would be much easier to deal with outside problems. So we find in this Psalm some very excellent and timely exhortations.

Notice verse 4, where David said, "I will not know a wicked person." It has often been said that a man is known by the friends he keeps. How much we would spare ourselves if we were careful of our friendships and associations! How true it is that many a young life has been ruined because of undesirable friends and associations. You cannot be in the company of a wicked person, that is in association and friendship with him, without being contaminated. You have thereby already placed yourself in a difficult, compromising position.

CHRISTIAN CONDUCT

David added, There is another person I do not want to have around me; that is the one who privately slanders his neighbor. Here is an exhortation that each of us can take to our own heart. Have we ever listened to gossip? Oh yes, we were told it was a secret, ye we turned about to whisper it to someone else, and added a few more details. By the time the story had been told a dozen times, we couldn't even recognize it as the one we first heard. I know of a man who at times made it uncomfortable for his host or guests. When either his host or guests would begin gossiping about some-one, he would immediately rise from his chair and leave the room. If any-one should be clear of gossip, it is a Christian. But I am sorry to say that some Christians are not altogether free from that type of thing. I do pray that if we have been guilty, we will present the matter before our Lord now, and vow by His help never to be a tool of gossip again.

Now let us look at verse 7, where David said, "He that worketh deceit shall not dwell within my house: he that telleth lies shall not tarry in my sight." One almost feels like raising the question, David, who were your friends?—Did you have any left?—You must have been frightfully lone-some. Now we do not always call them that, but a lie by another name is still nothing but an outright untruth.

Just to assure you that this message is not limited to the Old Testa-ment, let us read a few passages from the New Testament. Before we do, let me state clearly that the exhortations we are about to read are addressed to those who have received Christ, who have acknowledged Him as their Lord. There is no denying the fact that the unregenerate man cannot do anything that will please God. The Bible is emphatic, ". . . they that are in the flesh cannot please God." The first thing an unsaved man is called upon to do is to receive Christ as his Saviour and Lord. Until he does that, the Bible has no message for him except judgment. However, we who have received Christ as our Saviour, have the following exhortations addressed to us, which I have taken from the 12th chapter of Paul's letter to the Romans, commencing with the 9th verse:

1—Let love be without dissimulation. (In other words, do not base your love on selfish motives.)
2—Abhor that which is evil.
3—Cleave to that which is good.
4—Be kindly affectioned one to another with brotherly love.
5—In honour preferring one another.

How does that sound? If we have been disturbed because somebody else always gets the limelight, remember, it is written, ". . . In honour preferring one another." Again, we read: "Not slothful in business; fervent in spirit; serving the Lord . . ." These are fine exhortations, aren't they? There is plenty of room in which to develop a godly character here, but we cannot develop a godly, spiritual character, until we have been born again. Remember, we grow in grace and in the knowledge of our Lord Jesus Christ. We do not grow *into* grace, but we are expected to grow and develop *in* grace.

In this same chapter of the Roman Epistle, we are called upon to rejoice in hope; be patient in tribulation; continue in prayer; distribute to the necessity of saints; and be given to hospitality.

There are many more exhortations in this 12th chapter of the New Testament letter to the Romans, but we have quoted sufficient to sustain the view that the principles advanced in the 101st Psalm are perpetuated in the New Testament. To insist that Christian righteousness by the constituted act of God is a cheap righteousness, is to profess ignorance of God and His holy Word.

PSALM ONE HUNDRED TWO—PART ONE

"A SPARROW ALONE ON THE HOUSE TOP"

THE 102nd Psalm has an introduction which reads as follows, "A Prayer of the afflicted, when he is overwhelmed, and poureth out his complaint before the LORD."

At first glance it would seem that here is a prayer anyone could offer who is afflicted, or who finds his troubles overwhelming to him, so that he is urged to utter his complaint before the Lord. But as we read the Psalm carefully we will discover that this is not an ordinary prayer of an ordinary man, but it is an extraordinary prayer by an extraordinary Man. I think we shall be convinced before we finish that this is one of the prayers which our Lord Jesus Christ offered to His Father while in the days of His flesh.

In the 5th chapter of the Epistle to the Hebrews, beginning at the 7th verse, it is written of our Lord Jesus Christ, "Who in the days of his flesh, when he had offered up prayers and supplications with strong crying and tears unto him who was able to save him from death, and was heard in that he feared; though he were a Son, yet learned he obedience by the things which he suffered; and being made perfect, he became the author of eternal salvation unto all them that obey him . . ."

Here we have a direct statement in the New Testament from which we learn that during the days of our Lord's flesh He offered prayers and supplications with strong crying and tears. The sufferings at Calvary were not a sham. They were real. In this 102nd Psalm we undoubtedly have one of the prayers which our Lord offered with supplication and strong crying and tears. I repeat that no ordinary man could offer such a prayer as is found in this Psalm, for observe that the eternal God, to whom the prayer is offered, hears the suppliant and answers Him immediately, by saying, commencing with verse 25:

> "Of old hast thou laid the foundation of the earth: and the heavens are the work of thy hands.
>
> "They shall perish, but thou shalt endure: yea, all of them shall wax old like a garment; as a vesture shalt thou change them, and they shall be changed.
>
> "But thou art the same, and thy years shall have no end."

The Holy Spirit has used this quotation from the 102nd Psalm in the New Testament, and maintains that it is the Father's testimony concerning His Son.

In the 1st chapter of the Epistle to the Hebrews, we find a marvelous word-portrait of our Lord Jesus Christ. To prove the sonship and deity of Christ, the Holy Spirit went to the Psalms, and specifically to this 102nd Psalm, for in the 10th to the 12th verses He definitely quotes the 25th to the 27th verses, and declares that they are the testimony of God the Father concerning His own Son.

"THE MOST REMARKABLE OF ALL PSALMS"

We shall limit this meditation, to the prayer that our Lord offered; while in the following one we shall consider the answer that God the Father gave to His prayer. Now let us turn to the Psalm and read the first 11 verses:

> "Hear my prayer, O LORD, and let my cry come unto thee.
>
> "Hide not thy face from me in the day when I am in trouble; incline thine ear unto me: in the day when I call answer me speedily.
>
> "For my days are consumed like smoke, and my bones are burned as an hearth.
>
> "My heart is smitten, and withered like grass; so that I forget to eat my bread.
>
> "By reason of the voice of my groaning my bones cleave to my skin.
>
> "I am like a pelican of the wilderness: I am like an owl of the desert.
>
> "I watch, and am as a sparrow alone upon the house top.
>
> "Mine enemies reproach me all the day; and they that are mad against me are sworn against me.
>
> "For I have eaten ashes like bread, and mingled my drink with weeping.
>
> "Because of thine indignation and thy wrath: for thou hast lifted me up, and cast me down.
>
> "My days are like a shadow that declineth; and I am withered like grass."

It was Adolph Saphir, that prince of expositors, who said, "I doubt whether, without apostolic teaching, any of us would have had the boldness to understand it (this Psalm): for in many respects it is the most remarkable of all Psalms—the Psalm of 'The Afflicted One'—while His soul is overwhelmed within Him with great affliction, and sorrow, and anxious fear."

I have frequently commented upon the wonderful high note of praise and song which is found in the Psalms; but here and there, such as in the 22nd and this 102nd Psalm, we find Psalms that are written in the minor key. They are sorrowful dirges. Remember, our Lord Jesus was called "the man of sorrows" and the one "acquainted with grief." Furthermore, in that strange book called the "Lamentations of Jeremiah," we have this call to the multitude, who indifferently pass by the suffering one, "Is it nothing to you, all ye that pass by? behold, and see if there be any sorrow like unto my sorrow, which is done unto me, wherewith the LORD hath afflicted me in the day of his fierce anger."

Of course, it was our Lord Jesus Christ who, prophetically, spoke in the book of Lamentations. Here, in the 102nd Psalm, we get an insight into the extent of the sorrow of "the man of sorrows."

"THE MAN OF SORROWS"

In the first place our Lord invited His Father not to hide His face from Him in the day of trouble. Let us stop here a moment. "Hide not thy face from me. . ." Have we ever prayed like that? Have we ever known what it is to have trouble and then discover, as we poured out our heart before the Lord, that the heavens seem to be made of brass and that it was utterly impossible to penetrate the awful silence? Have we ever experienced such sorrow that we wondered how God could silently look on and observe our experiences? May it be a source of comfort to know that our Lord can understand perfectly how we feel, for He was tempted in all points, but, of course, without sin. Because of that, "he is able to succor all them that are tempted."

Just as definitely as God evidenced to His Son that He heard Him and that He understood His affliction; just so definitely can we be assured that God hears us and that He is not unmindful of our disappointing experiences. While we may not have the pleasure of an immediate answer to our agonizing prayer, nevertheless this fact is sure—God hears the aching heart-cry of His people.

Will you observe the language that our Lord used to describe His suffering. He said:

> ". . . my days are consumed like smoke, and my bones are burned as an hearth.
>
> "My heart is smitten, and withered like grass; so that I forget to eat my bread.
>
> "By reason of the voice of my groaning my bones cleave to my skin."

Here we have a picture of abject poverty. We have a description of the emaciated form of a man, whose condition is due solely to suffering. That is the extent to which our Lord Jesus Christ suffered; He, the just one, for us, the unjust, so that He might bring us unto God.

Will you also observe that our Lord is the recipient of the outburst of wrath from two sources. First, in verse 8, He said, "Mine enemies reproach me all the day; and they that are mad against me are sworn against me." Here we have man expressing his antagonism against God, and venting that displeasure upon the person of His Son. But in verses 9 and 10 we find that the Father added His wrath. In those verses we read, "For I have eaten ashes like bread, and mingled my drink with weeping. Because of *thine* indignation and *thy* wrath: for *thou* hast lifted me up, and cast me down." Do not allow anyone to suggest that the sacrifice of Christ was not the most stupendous event in history! Do not allow anyone to suggest that the sufferings of Christ were superficial and not actual!

Our Lord suffered as no man suffered. He was ground between the upper and nether millstones. As He hung upon the cross it seemed as if He were suspended between heaven and earth. Earth rejected Him, saying, "We will not have this man to reign over us." What a picture of human nature one gets as he reads the records of the Gospels, and observes the antagonism that was expressed by the multitudes against the Lord Jesus Christ. Thus, if you please, our Lord was unfit for earth. But, as the waves of the rebellion of man rose up to overwhelm Him, He met from above the increasing tempo of God's wrath and indignation, for he was the sin-offering, so that He literally became unfit for heaven. The Father vented His wrath against sin by smiting His Son. All this was done in order that we might never know what it is to be judged for our sin, that we might never know what it is to face death, eternal death, which is separation from God.

Our Lord Jesus, in the quotation from the book of Lamentations we noted a few moments ago, suggested that a comparison be made of His suffering with the suffering of others. The question is raised, ". . . see if there be any sorrow like unto my sorrow . . ."

"A PELICAN—AN OWL—A LONELY SPARROW"

Now let us go back to the 102nd Psalm, to get a picture of suffering and loneliness which cannot be equalled in all of literature. In verse 6, our Lord said:

> "I am like a pelican of the wilderness: I am like an owl of the desert."

and, in verse 7:

> "I watch, and am as a sparrow alone upon the house top."

By the way, in an interesting translation of the Psalms by Hebrew scholars, which I received from a fine young Jewish business associate of mine, I noticed that they have translated verse 7 thus:

> "I watch, and I am become like a (night-) bird sitting alone upon the house top."

Someone once said that "sadness and solitude go together—we plunge into the lonely places when we give voice to our grief." Dr. Thompson, an authority on Palestine and the customs of the people, speaks of the characteristics of these creatures to which our Lord referred when He expressed His solitude. Of the pelican Dr. Thompson said that it is the most sombre and austere bird he ever saw. Of the owl he wrote that it is always found in places of ruin, and of the sparrow he remarked that when one of them loses his mate, which is an everyday occurrence, he will sit on the housetop alone and lament by the hour.

Now the Bible declares that our Lord Jesus Christ is the Creator, for it was by Him that God made the earth. Everything that was made—He made it. It was made by Him and for Him. If we better understood creation, we would observe that all of creation manifests in some way the glorious person and work of Christ. Haven't you wondered why there are such creatures as pelicans and owls? Well, I sometimes think that possibly the Lord made them in order that we might better understand the extent of His sorrow.

One thing I particularly delight to dwell upon is the statement, "I watch, and am as a sparrow alone upon the house top." This is very interesting, because at the paschal season Jerusalem was crowded. Droves of people came from all over Judea and elsewhere, and swarmed into the city. All met each other. There was great joy everywhere. Were you there, you'd say it would be impossible to be alone—and yet, here was our Lord watching the procession, like a sparrow alone on the housetop lamenting its sorrow in solitude.

You and I will never know the depths of sorrow our Lord Jesus experienced; for He always was the Son of His Father's love. He, only, knew what it was to enjoy the Father's smile and fellowship, until at the cross He experienced that awful separation. There was none to whom He could turn. He could not turn to His disciples. They seemed at that time to be the weakest of all men. They had left Him and fled. He had lost the fellowship of His Father and the fellowship of His friends. He was like a sparrow alone on the housetop. The house was desolate and empty. There was no fellowship to be had in the house. The only place He could go was on the top of the house, there to watch the proceedings, and meditate on His sorrow, and pour out His complaint before the Lord.

PSALM ONE HUNDRED TWO—PART TWO

A PRE-EASTER ANNOUNCEMENT OF THE RESURRECTION OF CHRIST, IN THE 102nd PSALM

WE have already discussed the first half of this truly remarkable Psalm. We found that it was one of the prayers that our Lord Jesus uttered during the days of His flesh. No ordinary man could pray in the words of this Psalm.

For the third consecutive Easter, we have given a resurrection message from the Book of Psalms. Many may think this is rather strange. Some undoubtedly believe that the only place from which an Easter message can be taken is from the four Gospels—Matthew, Mark, Luke, and John, as they give us the historical facts of the physical resurrection from the dead, of our Lord Jesus Christ. But as we observed last year and the previous year, the fact of the resurrection was expected long before the event took place. The writers of the Old Testament rejoiced in and looked forward, with happy anticipation, to that event around which the whole of Christianity is built.

Among the writers of the Old Testament who rejoiced in the resurrection of Christ was David, the author of the majority of the Psalms. In this 102nd Psalm we have a pre-announcement of the resurrection of Christ. It is a wonderful Psalm. Note the resurrection message as we read from verse 18 to the end of the Psalm:

> "This shall be written for the generation to come: and the people which shall be created shall praise the LORD.
>
> "For he hath looked down from the height of his sanctuary; from the heaven did the LORD behold the earth;
>
> "To hear the groaning of the prisoner; to loose those that are appointed to death;
>
> "To declare the name of the LORD in Zion, and his praise in Jerusalem;
>
> "When the people are gathered together, and the kingdoms, to serve the LORD.
>
> "He weakened my strength in the way; he shortened my days.
>
> "I said, O my God, take me not away in the midst of my days: thy years are throughout all generations.
>
> "Of old hast thou laid the foundation of the earth: and the heavens are the work of thy hands.

"They shall perish, but thou shalt endure: yea, all of them shall wax old like a garment: as a vesture shalt thou change them, and they shall be changed.

"But thou art the same, and thy years shall have no end.

"The children of thy servants shall continue, and their seed shall be established before thee."

It would take too long to point out in detail the wonderful facts that are announced in this Psalm, written almost a thousand years before the Lord Jesus came into the world, so that we shall draw attention to one or two things only.

WHY CHRIST DIED

First, notice the statement of our Lord in verse 23, "He weakened my strength in the way; he shortened my days." To whom was our Lord referring? The context indicates that it was none other than His Father. It was not the hand of man that put our Lord Jesus Christ to death. Man was guilty of His crucifixion, to be sure, but it was God the Father who put Christ to death. God was tremendously interested in that cross. On it, the most stupendous event in history took place. It was the hour to which our Lord referred when He said, on the night of His betrayal, "Father, the hour is come . . ." The eternal God sapped the strength of our Lord, during that never-to-be-forgotten journey from Pilate's judgment hall to Calvary's hill, so that it was necessary for a colored man, a Cyrenian, to carry His cross, and to follow Him on the Via Dolorosa. And, at the cross, God the Father shortened the days of our Lord Jesus Christ. But why should His days be shortened? Wasn't His life this world's greatest benefaction?

Again we refer to the 53rd chapter of Isaiah, that marvelous prophecy of the Messiah, written seven hundred years before the Lord Jesus came into this world. In the 8th verse of that prophecy it is written concerning the Lord, "He was taken from prison and from judgment: and who shall declare his generation? for he was cut off out of the land of the living: for the transgression of my people was he stricken." There we have the reason for the shortening of the days of our Lord. They were shortened because of the transgressions of the people; in order that our Lord might put away sin by the sacrifice of Himself.

How wonderful it is, as we go back to this 102nd Psalm, that we are able to hear our Lord's agonizing prayer. Of course He was conscious of the suffering! Of course He understood that He was about to pay the penalty of sin! Of course He realized that soon the face of His Father would be enveloped in the shadows and darkness, and He would no more be able to look up into His face and behold a smiling countenance of intimate fellowship! But as He contemplated the darkness enveloping Him, the excruciating consciousness of the fact that He was about to be made sin overwhelmed Him so, that He cried out, as in verse 24 of the 102nd Psalm: "O my God, take me not away in the midst of my days: thy years are throughout all generations."

THE FATHER'S ANSWER TO THE PRAYER OF CHRIST

And now we come to that delightful part of this Psalm, which, the Holy Spirit has informed us in the New Testament, is God the Father's own testimony concerning His Son. It was the Father's answer to the agonizing prayer of His Son, who was about to be made sin. What a comforting answer to His prayer it must have been. What an encouragement it was, when our Lord heard this wonderful response from His Father, commencing with the 25th verse: "Of old hast thou laid the foundation of the earth . . ."

Let us stop there a moment. Who laid the foundation of the earth? Our Lord Jesus Christ. Who said so? God the Father. Who was there when it happened? The eternal God. It is God the Father who is witnessing in this Psalm to the fact that our Lord Jesus is the Creator.

I should like to invite skeptics to read the four Gospels, and to do so with an open mind, seeking to know the truth. These records, the most marvelous pieces of literature that have ever been written, bear inherent evidence of authenticity and accuracy. One cannot read these records with an open mind without coming to the conclusion that Jesus Christ is God manifest in the flesh. Again and again He demonstrated that He was the Creator. He took five loaves and two small fishes, and by the simple method of division and subtraction He actually multiplied the bread and the fishes and He fed the multitude. He evidenced the fact that He was the Son of God by raising several from the dead, by healing all manner of diseases, by silencing the waves and the winds. I repeat that no man can approach the four Gospels with an open mind without coming to the conclusion that Jesus Christ is the Son of God, the Creator. Here in the 102nd Psalm is the same testimony, written hundreds of years before the Lord Jesus Christ came into the world. The Psalm records for us the very words of God when He answered His Son. He said: "Of old hast thou laid the foundation of the earth: and the heavens are the work of thy hands."

Thus our Lord not only formed the earth but likewise the heavens. What a wonderful revelation creation manifests of the power and deity of God. It almost appears that creation is eternal. It has been the same for thousands of years. Why, a seed that a man plants will grow into a huge tree that will outlast him, and the house he builds will be a memorial to his name. That is why men love to build estates and love to have statues built. They want their names to remain alive after they die. They are envious of creation. They want to live. But here is a statement from the lips of God concerning His Son; reminding Him that He is the Creator of the earth, and that the heavens are the work of His hands. Then the Father continued, saying to His Son:

> "They shall perish, but thou shalt endure: yea, all of them shall wax old like a garment; as a vesture shalt thou change them, and they shall be changed.
> "But thou art the same, and thy years shall have no end."

Now let us look at that marvelous New Testament book, the Epistle to the Hebrews. In that book we find that the Holy Spirit, to demonstrate the deity and sonship of Christ, goes to this 102nd Psalm and mentions that these words were addressed by God to His Son. In verse 8 of that 1st chapter we read: "But unto the Son he saith, Thy throne, O God, is for ever and ever: a sceptre of righteousness is the sceptre of thy kingdom." In verses 10 to 12 He added:

> "And, Thou, Lord, in the beginning hast laid the foundation of the earth; and the heavens are the work of thine hands:
> "They shall perish; but thou remainest; and they all shall wax old as doth a garment;
> "And as a vesture shalt thou fold them up, and they shall be changed: but thou art the same, and thy years shall not fail."

Here then is not the testimony of man. Here is the testimony of the Holy Spirit to show that the words used in the 102nd Psalm are actually God's witness concerning His own Son. The eternal God was giving to His Son His pre-Easter announcement of His resurrection.

THE UNCHANGING CHRIST

We may not be able to contemplate the joy and strength that our Lord must have received from this testimony, but we can at least rejoice in it.

To be told that He would endure; that He would outlive and change creation, so that it would manifest His wonderful glory; to be told that His years shall have no end; these things must have been a marvelous encouragement to our blessed Lord as He faced Calvary.

Only God can prophesy the future, and here is a statement telling of the resurrection of Christ long before He even died; long before He even came into the world. What a statement—"thou art the same . . ."

In the letter to the Hebrews we read, "Jesus Christ the same yesterday, and today, and for ever." He is the only One who is the same. He never changes. He is God manifest in the flesh, and the fact of His resurrection from the dead is a glorious announcement of the emancipation of every individual, previously bound by sin and circumstances, who will confess Christ.

So, this wonderful Easter morning, God grant that if you are in despair and the future holds no particular light for you, and if by chance your eyes are dimmed with tears, you may be comforted as was Mary Magdalene, who stood before the sepulchre weeping, that early Easter morning, wondering where the body of her Lord had been taken.

When the angels asked, "Woman, why weepest thou?" she replied, "Because they have taken away my Lord, and I know not where they have laid him." She turned herself about and saw Jesus standing, and knew not that He was the Lord. Our Lord also asked her, "Woman, why weepest thou? whom seekest thou?" Supposing Him to be the gardener, she said, "Sir, if thou have borne him hence, tell me where thou hast laid him, and I will take him away." Then our Lord said just one word, but what a word! In the tone of His voice there was the immediate knowledge that *He* knew everything. Our Lord turned to her and said, "*Mary*." When she heard her name spoken by the risen Lord she turned and said, "Rabboni; which is to say, Master."

There are multitudes who live on this earth who have heard the risen Lord whisper into their ears the very same message that He whispered to Mary. We know Him because He first knew us. We have bowed our knee and acknowledged that He is the master of our soul and the Lord of our life. If you have not yet done so, if you have not made Him the master of your soul and the Lord of your life, I know of no better time to do so than this early morning hour on an Easter Sunday.

PSALM ONE HUNDRED THREE—PART ONE

IS THE HEALING OF THE BODY INCLUDED
IN CHRIST'S ATONEMENT?

NEXT to the 23rd Psalm, the 103rd is probably the most familiar in the entire Psalter. It contains twenty-two short verses, but we shall content ourselves at this time with an examination of the first five verses, which form a prelude to the Psalm. They read:

> "Bless the LORD, O my soul: and all that is within me, bless his holy name.
> "Bless the LORD, O my soul, and forget not all his benefits:
> "Who forgiveth all thine iniquities; who healeth all thy diseases;
> "Who redeemeth thy life from destruction; who crowneth thee with lovingkindness and tender mercies;
> "Who satisfieth thy mouth with good things; so that thy youth is renewed like the eagle's."

The mere reading of these verses ought to be sufficient to arouse the dormant heart to an expression of thanksgiving unto the Lord. An examination of the entire twenty-two verses would reveal that while the Psalm is addressed to the Lord, and David not only invited his own soul but the soul of every individual, including the very hosts of heaven, to join with him, not one single petition is to be found in the Psalm.

This Psalm therefore is a perfect expression of worship. Multitudes look upon prayer solely as an avenue of approach unto God in order to ask the Lord for certain benefactions. It is true that prayer involves petition, but if our prayer life consists solely of petitions, we do not know the real secret of prayer. Prayer offers a greater opportunity to pour out one's heart affection upon the Lord and to worship Him.

Someone once said that in this Psalm David "was carried out of himself as far as the heavens." It *is* possible for the soul and spirit of man to be transported out of this environment into the very presence of God. Now it is one thing to dream dreams, to fall asleep and dream of a wonderful environment and feel yourself transported into that environment; that phenomenon may give one a momentary thrill, until someone jostles him and he awakes to behold it was only a dream; but prayer opens an avenue for the soul to enter into the very presence of God. That transportation is not a dream or a fantasy. It is an actual fact.

And so it has been the delight of the redeemed heart, in every age, to rise above environment and enter into the very presence of the Lord to praise and to worship Him. Unless we have used prayer with that thought in mind, we have yet to tap its wonderful treasures.

Here is a Psalm of worship. It of course was set to music and sung before the Lord. Thus it is possible to use Psalms and hymns as an expression of our adoration and praise unto the Lord.

Observe that David suggested certain things to his own soul. He said, "Bless the LORD, O my soul: and all that is within me, bless his holy name." What an occupation! Some people reserve worship for Sunday only, but actually one can be occupied with the Lord every minute of the day and every day of one's life. And when we know the Lord Jesus Christ as our Saviour, we always find a ready response in our heart at any time, to the invitation to join in His praise and say with David, "Bless the LORD, O my soul: and all that is within me, bless his holy name."

Note also that this Psalm is occupied with the Lord. There are many people occupied with *doing* something and with *working* for the Lord, so to speak, who have entirely lost sight of the fact that the chief occupation of a redeemed life should be the contemplation, adoration, and praise of God. Just to go into His presence to exalt His name in glorious adoration is to render to the Lord the highest service.

"BLESS THE LORD, O MY SOUL . . ."

In verse 2 David suggested, "Bless the LORD, O my soul, and forget not all his benefits . . ." It is so easy to forget. In fact, if we happen to get a streak of rainy weather, we entirely forget the glorious days of sunshine we had a few days previously. So in connection with our lives—when in the midst of disappointments, sorrows, and trials, we cry out to the Lord, asking His help and blessing; but when the blessings come in a uniform measure, and we have enjoyed them for a length of time, we forget that we received them exclusively because of His grace. Have we ever promised to do something if the Lord would do something for us ? When the Lord had fulfilled His part of the bargain by giving us His benefaction and blessing, did we forget even to thank Him?

But David continued, addressing his soul, "Bless the LORD, O my soul . . . who forgiveth all thine iniquities; who healeth all thy diseases; who redeemeth thy life from destruction; who crowneth thee with loving-

kindness and tender mercies; who satisfieth thy mouth with good things
. . ." Observe that it is the Lord who does all these things. We have
nothing to do with them. David had nothing to do with them. Nothing
David could possibly do would ever enable him to receive the forgiveness
of all his iniquities. He could not, if he employed the most skillful physician, be healed of all his diseases. He could never crown his own life with
lovingkindness and tender mercies. He could not satisfy his mouth with
good things continuously. These are the benefactions of the Lord. He is
the author of them. He offers them to every individual who trusts Him
and believes Him and responds to his invitation.

Let us look at these things a little more closely and in more detail.
Notice that the first thing that David had to say about God's benefactions
related to the forgiveness of sins. He stated that God forgives all iniquities;
not some—not many—but all—every single one of them. The New Testament counterpart of this message is found in the 1st Epistle of John, where
we read that ". . . the blood of Jesus Christ his (God's) Son cleanseth us
from *all* sin." Again we have that little word "all." It is little, but what
a difference it makes! If God would only forgive part of our iniquity, if He
would forgive the major part of our sins, it would not be of any avail, for
the Scripture says, " . . . whosoever shall keep the whole law, and yet offend
in one point, he is guilty of all." Just one sin is enough to keep us out of
heaven. Just one sin is enough to mar our fellowship with God. Just one
sin is sufficient to bring disaster and disappointment into our life. Take the
case of our first parents. They disobeyed only one command. They partook of the fruit of the tree of knowledge of good and evil, which God
specifically commanded they were not to do. But every ill, every dis-
pointment that ever entered into the human heart, every sickness, every
death, every graveyard, can be traced to that one sin of disobedience.

We are not conscious, I am afraid, of the far-reaching effect of sin, and
its terrific results. However, we are offered, as a free gift, the forgiveness
of all sins, absolutely complete and full. There is only One who can forgive sin. That One is none other than God. Thus if you are burdened with
the consciousness of sin, and sin seems to lie heavy on your heart and mind,
I suggest that irrespective of how black your sins might be, the Lord Jesus
Christ, God's Son, will cleanse you from *every* stain of sin.

THE HEALING MATTER—MORAL

Further, note that David addressed his soul, saying, "Bless the LORD, O my soul . . ." for the Lord "healeth all thy diseases." This brings us to that very interesting subject of disease and its healing.

In what is probably the oldest book in the Bible is recorded a controversy between Satan on one hand, and God on the other. Job, who was a perfect and upright man, who feared God and eschewed evil, was the subject of the controversy. Because of Job's devotion to God, the Lord placed a hedge about him. Satan suggested that the real reason Job praised the Lord was because God had placed this hedge about him and blessed him. Take it away, said Satan, and see how quickly Job will curse you. So the Lord said to Satan, All right, you go down, and all Job hath is in thy power; but do not touch him. Satan did not waste a single day. He brought destruction, disappointment, sorrow, and death into Job's life in one day, yet Job maintained his integrity. When he received the final news of the loss of his children, "Job arose, and rent his mantle, and shaved his head, and fell down upon the ground, and worshipped. And said, Naked came I out of my mother's womb, and naked shall I return thither: the LORD gave, and the LORD hath taken away; blessed be the name of the LORD." And the Scripture says, "In all this Job sinned not, nor charged God foolishly."

But Satan was not satisfied. He again had occasion to bring up the subject of Job's devotion, and this time he said to the Lord, ". . . all that a man hath will he give for his life. Put forth thine hand now, and touch his bone and his flesh, and he will curse thee to thy face." Whereupon the Lord said to Satan, "Behold, he is in thine hand; but save his life." How Satan plagued Job's body—but you remember the story, I need not rehearse it. However, I want to call your attention to the principle that Satan enunciated when he said to the Lord, ". . . all that a man hath will he give for his life." It is not surprising therefore that this viewpoint has been adopted by various cults and religious systems. They all offer health of body and mind, if one follows their principles. It is amazing what a man is willing to give when the promise is held out that he may have health in exchange for sickness. Very often these cults quote this 103rd Psalm to sustain the view that there is complete healing from all bodily ills.

Now this passage is clear. Here is a definite statement from David that the Lord "healeth all thy diseases . . ." but if we assume that David was talking exclusively about bodily ills, we are mistaken. Old age is a disease of the body, and none are exempt from its ravages. So we ask, when David addressed his soul, O my soul, bless the Lord because "he healeth all thy diseases," to whom did he address this statement? To his body? No—to his soul. He said, "Bless the LORD, O my soul . . . who healeth all thy diseases . . ."

This passage not only refers primarily to the soul, but *exclusively* to the soul. No human physician knows how to deal with the soul, or what to prescribe for it. That soul is so desperately wicked, so incurably diseased that the most skillful surgeon could not remove the cancer of sin from it. It is a hopeless case. There is only one physician who is able to deal with the ills of the soul and to heal its diseases, and that one is the Great Physician, the Lord Jesus Christ. So this passage refers to a moral disorder, not a physical one.

THE HEALING MATTER—PHYSICAL

But I want to take this occasion to discuss the subject of the healing of bodily ills. History tells us that the Apostle Paul was a little hunchback; that his bodily presence was weak; that he had a disease of the eyes which made it difficult for him to see. Many hold that this disease was caused by the brilliant, dazzling glory that Paul saw when the Lord revealed Himself, that high-noon hour on the road to Damascus. An inference of Paul's difficulty is found in his letter to the Galatians, to whom he wrote, saying that their love for him was so manifest that he could bear them witness that, if it were possible, they would have plucked out their own eyes and given them to him. So we see the great Apostle Paul was not exempt from physical suffering and physical ills.

Again, it appears from the Scripture that Timothy, Paul's intimate companion, was annoyed with a chronic ailment; Paul suggested, in fact commanded, that Timothy take a little wine for his stomach's sake, and his "often infirmities." Timothy was a marvelously devoted servant of the Lord, and of Paul, his father in the faith—yet it is evident that he was often ill, for Paul spoke of *"often* infirmities." We could go on and tell about others of whom the Scripture witnesses that they were sick. To deny sickness is to deny the Word of God.

One other thing is sure; sickness is no respecter of persons. Sickness enters the home of sinner and saint alike. But God in His infinite grace has provided in the forces of nature that which counteracts disease, and He has also seen to it that the earth bears chemicals and herbs that minister healing to the human body.

While the Lord is able to heal without the use of means, it cannot be denied that even He at times used means. We could of course give some incidents where an individual, past human help, in answer to prayer, was healed without the use of means. However, to assert from these instances that healing of the body is vouchsafed for us in the atonement of Christ, is to shut one's eyes to the plain teachings of Scripture. If there were no such things as bodily ailments and diseases, there would be no such thing as death; at least no Christian would die. As far as I know, every one of the previous generation has died, saint and sinner alike, even those who insisted that they had the key to health!

So let us not distort Scripture, nor assume that when the Scripture mentions "diseases" it is talking exclusively of bodily ailments. Very frequently the Scripture refers to the diseases of the soul and heart, which are far more alarming and devastating.

We close this meditation with a comment upon the 5th verse. It reads, "Who satisfieth thy mouth with good things; so that thy youth is renewed like the eagle's." Was David talking about his physical body or his physical mouth? Or that as far as his physical life was concerned, his youth should be "renewed like the eagle's"? If we think so, we have missed the vital point of this portion of Scripture.

David knew what it was to grow old; but he had a youthful soul, with a full degree of vitality, even in old age, because he knew the Lord, and the Lord satisfied his mouth with good things. In order to indicate the perennial youthfulness of his soul, he went to the eagle, saying that as an eagle has its youth renewed, so the youthfulness of his soul was renewed.

The eagle is a wonderful bird. It is the only bird that soars in a straight line, the only bird that can look at the glory of the sun and not be blinded by it, or even blink an eye. The eagle soars to great heights, and presents a wonderful picture of the redeemed soul. The redeemed soul can go straight into the presence of God. He can look up at the glory of the Son of God, the Lord Jesus Christ, and not be blinded by His glory; in fact, the redeemed soul delights to look up into His face. The abode of the redeemed soul is the highest place in the heavens.

Men have tried to find out the reason for the long life of the eagle, and among the things they have discovered is the fact that the eagle is able to masticate its food even in old age. It has been suggested that when the eagle gets old, and its beak becomes long, so that it finds it difficult to open its mouth, it takes its prey between its beak and dashes it against the rocks, breaking it into small pieces. While the eagle is doing that, it is automatically breaking off its beak. It again becomes short, and it finds that it can open its mouth like a young fellow once more. When the soul that waits upon the Lord is fed by the Word of God, it will be sustained, and its youth will be constantly renewed like that of the eagle.

To you who think you are getting old, and to those who have already reached quite an age, may I suggest that the fountain of youth is in the presence of our Lord Jesus Christ, where you may feast upon the good things He has prepared for you.

PSALM ONE HUNDRED THREE—PART TWO

WHERE SIN IS FOREVER SEPARATED
FROM THE SINNED

THE 103rd Psalm may be divided into three sections: the first ending with verse 5, second with verse 18, and the third comprising the balance of the Psalm. We will limit this meditation to the second section, beginning with verse 6 and ending with verse 18, which reads:

"The LORD executeth righteousness and judgment for all that are oppressed.

"He made known his ways unto Moses, his acts unto the children of Israel.

"The LORD is merciful and gracious, slow to anger, and plenteous in mercy.

"He will not always chide: neither will he keep his anger for ever.

"He hath not dealt with us after our sins; nor rewarded us according to our iniquities.

"For as the heaven is high above the earth, so great is his mercy toward them that fear him.

"As far as the east is from the west, so far hath he removed our transgressions from us.

"Like as a father pitieth his children, so the LORD pitieth them that fear him.

"For he knoweth our frame; he remembereth that we are dust.

"As for man, his days are as grass: as a flower of the field, so he flourisheth.

"For the wind passeth over it, and it is gone; and the place thereof shall know it no more.

"But the mercy of the LORD is from everlasting to everlasting upon them that fear him, and his righteousness unto children's children:

"To such as keep his covenant, and to those that remember his commandments to do them."

The first thing we should consider is found in the 7th verse, where we
read: "He made known his ways unto Moses, his acts unto the children of
Israel." I do not think that this is mere poetry, nor that David simply
sought to avoid repetition. On the contrary, a marvelous truth is presented
in this 7th verse. It indicates that there is a lesser and a higher degree of
revelation, and that one may enjoy a greater unfolding of the person and
ministry of the Lord, above that which is enjoyed by the multitude. Thus
David said, "The LORD made known *his ways* unto Moses, *his acts* unto
the children of Israel." The children of Israel merely knew His acts; they
saw the display of His power, but Moses saw His glory.

"SHEW ME THY WAY . . ."

Now let us examine the historical record which will illumine this passage. In the 33rd chapter of Exodus there is an interesting conversation between the Lord and Moses, to which I have previously referred. Moses said
to the Lord, "See, thou sayest unto me, Bring up this people (that is,
Israel): and thou hast not let me know whom thou wilt send with me. Yet
thou hast said, I know thee by name, and thou hast also found grace in my
sight." Evidently Moses reasoned that as the Lord knew him by name and
he had found grace in His sight, he ought to pray for a knowledge of God
and an expression of His grace. So he prayed, "shew me now thy way
. . ." What did Moses mean when he asked God to show him His way?

I believe the answer is found in the 14th chapter of St. John's Gospel.
The chapter describes an event which took place in an upper room in the
city of Jerusalem, where our Lord and His eleven disciples were gathered.
The time—the night of the betrayal. There was as much bewilderment in
the hearts and minds of those eleven disciples as there was in the heart and
mind of Moses. They too had heard from the Lord that they had found
grace in His sight, and of course He knew them by name, because He called
them by their names. But, as in the case of Moses, these eleven disciples
wanted to know more. Thus, when our Lord said to them, ". . . I go to
prepare a place for you. And if I go and prepare a place for you, I will
come again, and receive you unto myself, that where I am, there ye may be
also," one of the eleven, Thomas by name, asked, "Lord, we know not
whither thou goest; and how can we know the way?" Then our Lord gave

that memorable response, "I am the way, the truth, and the life: no man cometh unto the Father, but by me."

Now let us go back to the Old Testament. We find Moses asking God, "shew me now thy way, that I may know thee, that I may find grace in thy sight . . ." Hitherto, the knowledge had been on the side of the Lord toward Moses. The Lord had said to Moses, "I know thee by name, and thou hast also found grace in my sight." But Moses wanted to know God. He wanted to know His way. So the Lord answered Moses, "My presence shall go with thee, and I will give thee rest." But Moses was evidently dissatisfied with the response, and continued, ". . . I beseech thee, shew me thy glory." To this the Lord said, "I will make all my goodness pass before thee, and I will proclaim the name of the LORD before thee; and will be gracious to whom I will be gracious, and will shew mercy on whom I will shew mercy . . . Thou canst not see my face: for there shall no man see me, and live." But a provision was made. The Lord said, "Behold, there is a place by me, and thou shalt stand upon a rock: and it shall come to pass, while my glory passeth by, that I will put thee in a clift of the rock, and will cover thee with my hand while I pass by: and I will take away mine hand, and thou shalt see my back parts: but my face shall not be seen."

Now we can understand why David wrote in this 103rd Psalm, probably as much as five hundred years later, "He made known *his ways* unto Moses, *his acts* unto the children of Israel." David was talking about that time when God put Moses in the cleft of the rock, covered him with His hand, and gave him to see His way, as He passed by. If we did not have the New Testament, it would be difficult to understand this, but the New Testament throws a flood of light upon the event. Our Lord said to His disciples, "I am the way, the truth, and the life . . ." Therefore when Moses said to God, "shew me now thy way . . ." he was actually asking God to show him His Christ, His anointed. Oh, you say, that is far-fetched. Well now, let us see how far-fetched it is.

In the 5th chapter of St. John's Gospel, our Lord is heard speaking to the Pharisees. He challenges them to search the Scriptures, and raises the question, "Do not think that I will accuse you to the Father: there is one that accuseth you, even Moses, in whom ye trust. For had ye believed Moses, ye would have believed me: for he wrote of me." That ought to satisfy the inquiring mind, and make it clear that when Moses asked God to show him His way, he asked to see Christ, who is *the Way* of God. Note our Lord said, He was *the* way—not *a* way. There are many people who think that there are a thousand and one ways to God, but that is not so.

ONLY ONE WAY

This past week I had luncheon with Dr. Ironside, pastor of the Moody Memorial Church of Chicago. There were several in the group. Dr. Ironside had just returned from a three-months' trip, which included Palestine. He told of meeting a jolly Franciscan monk, who was lamenting the attitude of the respective groups in Palestine who insisted that they were proclaiming the only right way. Here was one insisting this is the sepulchre where Christ was laid, another insisting this is the sepulchre, and a tnird insisting that this is the sepulchre where He lay. The monk, turning to Dr. Ironside, said, "You look like an American. My, how I wish I were back in America. I lived in Washington for a time, and back in your country a man can think as he pleases, but out here he dare not express an opinion. Everybody insists that he is right and the other fellow is wrong." Dr. Ironside was in company with another gentleman, who broke in and said, "But, actually, there is only one way," whereupon the jovial monk said, "Now let us have none of that. Let us be broadminded." However, Dr. Ironside said, "My friend meant that there is only one way to God, and that way is the Lord Jesus Christ," and the monk said, "Indeed, I can say Amen to that."

To put it in the language of another friend, Dr. Barnhouse, there may be ten thousand ways to Christ, but there is only one way to God, that is, through our Lord Jesus Christ. Each one of us has had a different experience in coming to a knowledge of Christ, but we all bear witness that we came to know God through Jesus Christ alone. While we would never dare presume to say, We are the way, our Lord Jesus Christ could say, "I am the way."

Incidentally, notice that Moses, in his prayer, asked God to show him His *way;* whereas David, in the Psalm, said, "God made known his *ways* unto Moses . . ." In the prayer it is in the singular, while in the Psalm it is in the plural: His ways. When Moses came to know God's way, he also came to know His ways. For the way of the Lord is Christ, while the ways of the Lord are the ways of Christ. When we know the ways of God, we do not need to see His acts. Moses had intimate fellowship with God, whereas the children of Israel, who walked far off, merely saw the display of God's power. The five thousand whom our Lord Jesus Christ fed with five loaves and two small fishes saw His acts, but they knew nothing of His ways.

"As Far as the East is From the West . . ."

Now let us continue in this wonderful Psalm, and get to know something of the ways of the Lord. We read in verse 8: "The LORD is merciful and gracious, slow to anger, and plenteous in mercy." But mark you, if we assume from that verse that God never gets angry, notice that David has a qualifying statement in the next verse, saying: "He will not always chide: neither will he keep his anger for ever."

This passage is an indication that God mixes judgment with mercy, but let no one assume that He will exclude judgment. God has a right to be angry because of our sin. We have been disobedient to Him, and that is putting it mildly! Yet, by His grace, we are reminded that "He hath not dealt with us after our sins; nor rewarded us according to our iniquities. For as the heaven is high above the earth, so great is his mercy toward them that fear him. As far as the east is from the west, so far hath he removed our transgressions from us."

It is interesting to observe, in this Psalm, what is written concerning God's attitude toward our sins. In verse 3 we read, He "forgiveth." In verse 10 we read that He has "not dealt with us after our sins; nor rewarded us according to our iniquities." In verse 12, ". . . he removed our transgressions from us." That word *removed* represents God's attitude toward our sins. Speaking of this fact, Charles Spurgeon said, "O glorious verse, no word even upon the inspired page can excel it! Sin is removed from us by a miracle of love! What a load to move, and yet it is removed so far that the distance is incalculable."

I believe, however, that in this passage there is an additional thought, apart from the fact of the distance which God has separated us from our sins. You will remember the little line that goes, "East is east and west is west, and never the twain shall meet." It is utterly impossible to calculate the distance between east and west, for we have nowhere from which to begin. The thing that impressed itself upon my mind, as I have studied this verse, is the fact that my sin has been separated from me, by the act of God, as far as the east is from the west; and just as east is east and west is west, and never the twain shall meet, so my sin and I will never meet again. I do not know how much comfort that thought is to you, but to me—I almost feel like becoming a shouting Methodist—I mean the old-fashioned kind! My sin has been removed. God removed it. I will never meet it again. Do you know any other message that can give such joy as the knowledge this message brings?

There is a delightful translation of this passage which reads, "As far as the sunrise from the sunset, so far has He removed our transgressions from us." Here is the same thought expressed in different words. The sin and the sinner are forever separated. But it was His work, not ours. God put it away, by placing it upon His own Son, and he exacted from Him the penalty due sin.

The other day I read an interesting illustration of this fact in an article written by Captain Reginald Wallis, of Dublin, Ireland. It seems that a minister was boarding at a certain farmhouse. Early one morning the farmer beckoned the minister to follow him to the chicken-house. There on the nest sat a hen, with a brood of chicks peeping out from under her wings. "Touch her," said the farmer. As he did so, he found that she was cold. "Look at the wound in her head," continued the farmer, "a weasel has sucked all her blood from her and yet she never moved, for fear that the little beast would get her chicks." That is exactly what the Lord did. He paid the penalty of sin. He gave His blood in order that we might be spared the judgment due sin. What a picture of the death of our Lord Jesus.

The Psalmist continued, speaking of God's wonderful compassion: "Like as a father pitieth his children, so the LORD pitieth them that fear him." That pity, or compassion, is based on the fact that God knows our frame. He is mindful that we are made of the dust of the earth, and that our glory is like the grass and flower of the field. If we wish to get an understanding of God, who He is, what He is like, and what motivates His being, we must consider our Lord Jesus Christ, whom the Scriptures declare to be God manifest in the flesh. If we wish to understand His compassion and His pity, we will observe it in the way He sees the multitude. The Scripture says that "He had compassion on them, and viewed them as sheep without a shepherd." Notice Him in the case of the woman whom the Pharisees brought into His presence; a woman with a dark stain of sin on her life. Did He smite in judgment? No. He had pity on that woman, for He knew her heart, and so, after he invited her accusers by a soft-spoken but penetrating word to examine their own consciences, they made haste to get out of His sight. Then our Lord looked up at that woman and asked, "Woman, where are those thine accusers? hath no man condemned thee? She said, No man, Lord. And Jesus said unto her, Neither do I condemn thee: go, and sin no more." That is God. That shows His pity and compassion for the sinner.

So, we can go through the ministry and life of our Lord Jesus Christ and receive a perfect representation of God. He is the One to whom we must go. He is the One to whom judgment has been committed. He is either our Saviour or our Judge. Which will He be, in your case?

PSALM ONE HUNDRED THREE—PART THREE

WHO RULES OVER EARTH'S KINGDOMS?

NOW for our third and last message from the 103rd Psalm. We have commented on the first eighteen verses of this great Psalm; so that we shall now give consideration to one of the greatest calls to public praise that is to be found in the entire Bible. Beginning with verse 19, we read:

> "The LORD hath prepared his throne in the heavens; and his kingdom ruleth over all.
>
> "Bless the LORD, ye his angels, that excel in strength, that do his commandments, hearkening unto the voice of his word.
>
> "Bless ye the LORD, all ye his hosts; ye ministers of his, that do his pleasure.
>
> "Bless the LORD, all his works in all places of his dominion: bless the LORD, O my soul."

The Book of Psalms corresponds to our hymnbook. Each of these great Psalms was set to music, and sung during the worship by Israel.

If we consider the opening verses of this Psalm as a prelude to a great oratorio, then we must consider these closing verses as a grand finale. In the opening verses David called upon his own soul to bless the Lord. His whole being was urged to join in the praise of the Lord. But in the closing verses he invited all created beings, as well as created things, to join in one great burst of praise.

I love to consider this Psalm as an oratorio. Toward the close of it, the chief Musician is observed leading the great hosts in an offer of praise unto the Lord. First he invites the angels in heaven to bless the Lord. Then he turns to earth and asks all the hosts and His ministers to join in a song of praise, and finally he calls on all creation to express their adoration to their Creator; and for fear that any may think they are overlooked, he calls upon all things in all places in the dominion of God to bless the Lord. I hope we can feel some of this exuberant joy as we contemplate this Psalm. All Israel must have rejoiced when they heard this Psalm sung in their worship period.

WHO RULES OVER ALL?

Let us look at this section with a little more care. In verse 19 we have an interesting statement. There we read, "The LORD hath prepared his throne in the heavens; and his kingdom ruleth over all." We must acknowledge that it does *not appear* to be so at the present time. All the world had its attention drawn this past week to the triumph of the Italian forces in Ethiopia. The headlines of every paper blazoned the announcement of the success of the intruder who smashed everything in his way to gain possession of the land of Ethiopia. Yet in this Psalm we are told that "The LORD hath prepared his throne in the heavens; and his kingdom ruleth *over all*." I do not know all the details that led up to the trouble in Ethiopia, except as they appeared in the press and periodicals. But I do know that every unprejudiced, honest-thinking man rebels at the manner in which the land of Ethiopia was conquered. After two thousand years of gospel ministry, after hundreds of years of so-called western civilization, we must again hang our heads in shame because of ruthless exploitation by the sword and mailed fist. It does not *appear* as if God's kingdom ruleth over all. Once again western civilization has given an exhibition that might is right, and if press reports are correct, a whole nation expressed itself in ecstasy over the slaughter of innocent victims.

It is not my business to meddle in the affairs of the world. I trust I know my place as a Christian; that it is my business to preach the gospel, and woe is me if I preach not the gospel. But indignation must well up in the breast of every individual against such ruthlessness. Yet some may ask, But how can you justify God? How can you reconcile this passage of Scripture in the 103rd Psalm with what actually is transpiring on this earth? Evidently, say they, the 19th verse of this Psalm is not true. While we are expected to believe the first half, as we cannot see into the heavens, we cannot be expected to believe the last half, when we observe what is going on. The Lord may have prepared His throne in the heavens, we do not know, we have never seen it, but it is far from the truth to suggest that God's kingdom ruleth over all.

To all of this we answer that it is possible to justify God. It may seem strange for a man to presume to justify God. Is He not able to justify Himself? Yes, He is! Yet we have the privilege of justifying God. In the 7th chapter of St. Luke's Gospel and in the 29th verse it is written, "And all the people that heard him, and the publicans, *justified* God, being baptized with the baptism of John. But the Pharisees and lawyers rejected the counsel of God against themselves, being not baptized of him." The context of that chapter will indicate that the "him" is John the Baptist. So there is such a thing as a man justifying God; even as there is that in the gospel which enables God to justify men. Those who gave heed to the preaching of John the Baptist justified God against the day when He expressed His judgment upon those who disobeyed Him—in this case the Pharisees, the religious leaders of the people, and the lawyers. Do not think that those lawyers were the same as lawyers in the present age. Those lawyers were doctors of the law of God; doctors of the Scripture. If they lived today, we would call them the Reverend Doctor so-and-so.

That there is no evidence at the present time that the 19th verse of the 103rd Psalm is true, we freely admit. This is man's day. It is also Satan's hour. The Bible presents Satan as "the prince of this world" and "the god of this age." It also declares that ". . . the whole world lieth in the lap of the wicked one." In fact, you will remember that during the temptation of our Lord Jesus Christ in the wilderness, Satan took our Lord Jesus up into an exceeding high mountain, and showed Him all the kingdoms of the world and the glory of them, and said unto our Lord, "All these things will I give thee, if thou wilt fall down and worship me." Our Lord did not dispute with him and say, Satan, you are mistaken; these kingdoms of the world do not belong to you; they belong to My Father, and because they belong to My Father, they are Mine. Our Lord did not dispute with Satan on the question of the truthfulness of his comment. Our Lord merely turned to him and said, "Get thee hence, Satan: for it is written, Thou shalt worship the Lord thy God, and him only shalt thou serve."

The Bible specifically declares that this world's kingdoms are under the jurisdiction of Satan, the prince of the power of the air. The kingdoms of this world have not yet become the kingdoms of our Lord and of His Christ, nor has He entered into His reign as yet. Thus we are not surprised at the conditions that exist in this world, nor have we any difficulty in reconciling the 19th verse of this 103rd Psalm with what actually is transpiring on earth.

But there is a limit to the power of Satan, and there is coming a day when the kingdoms of this world will become "the kingdoms of our Lord, and of his Christ; and he shall reign for ever and ever." How this world needs Him! This world needs Him to reign as King, just as we need Him to reign as Lord in our lives.

The 103rd Psalm was not only written for the time in which David lived, nor for the time in which we live, but this Psalm is part of the eternal Word of God. It will be sung once again in this world when our Lord reigns as absolute monarch of the world. At that time the Ethiopians will not be disturbed by a black-shirt dictator, nor will any son of Israel be subject to persecution by the hand of a brown-shirt dictator, nor will labor be oppressed by capital, nor will capital be at the mercy of labor's grasping; all will be under the domination of the King of kings and the Lord of lords, and equity will characterize His rule. When that time arrives, then it will be true that God's kingdom "ruleth over all"—and the redeemed of the Lord will join together in one great burst of praise.

A GREAT CALL TO PRAISE

Now look at the 20th verse, "Bless the LORD, ye his angels, that excel in strength, that do his commandments, hearkening unto the voice of his word." I wish we had time to consider the angels, but when we get to the 104th Psalm another opportunity will be given to discuss these marvelous creatures. Sufficient to state now that the angels excel in strength. They obediently fulfill the commandments of God, and they hearken to the voice of His Word. We who know Christ, or profess to know Him, must confess that we frequently are weaklings; that we do not avail ourselves of the strength of the Holy Spirit, which is at our disposal. We must also acknowledge that we frequently violate His commandments, and hearken not unto the voice of His Word. The angels do not have the glorious privilege we have, of knowing what it is to have been redeemed from sin and ushered into a relationship with God far more intimate and far superior to that which they enjoy. Oh to be more conscious of our glorious privileges as believers in Christ!

Then follows a call to all the hosts to join in praise to God. There is a company too, known as ". . . ye ministers of his, that do his pleasure." That's an interesting phrase, "Ye ministers of his, that do his pleasure." This passage of Scripture does not eliminate the multitude who sit in the pews, nor does it refer alone to the minister in the pulpit. On several occasions in the Gospels it is written, concerning certain women who followed our Lord Jesus, that they "ministered to him." They gave of their substance, and He, the Lord of glory, was pleased to accept it.

The Psalmist brought his song to a close by saying, "Bless the LORD, all his works in all places of his dominion: bless the LORD, O my soul." I can hear someone say, Do you mean to tell me that the works of God can worship and praise the Creator? Yes, and if you are surprised, I remind you of two incidents: one in the Old Testament and the other in the New Testament. Remember Balaam's ass? Balaam was a prophet, a disobedient prophet. He was supposed to be a man of intelligence and of keen perception, and a man of honor: but his ass, who was but a beast of burden, could see what Balaam could not see. God loosed the tongue of that ass, to rebuke his master. Since God could loose the tongue of a dumb animal to rebuke a disobedient servant, He will have no difficulty in loosening the tongues of dumb animals to join with all His redeemed in praise of His name.

In the New Testament you will remember the Pharisees who objected to the shout of the multitude of our Lord's disciples as they hailed our Lord's entry into Jerusalem on His triumphal journey. The Pharisees even asked our Lord to put a stop to their outburst, but our Lord answered, "I tell you that, if these should hold their peace, the stones would immediately cry out." Since the stones recognize their master and are ready to praise Him, how much more should we who are endowed with greater intelligence.

Note that David ended this 103rd Psalm exactly as he began it, with an exhortation, addressed to his own soul, to render a word of thanksgiving unto the Lord. I question if there is a phrase in all the Bible which is so full of meaning as the phrase, "bless the LORD, O my soul." Apart from the worship and adoration that the hosts of heaven render to God, and that all creation extends to Him; apart from the importance of public worship and praise; unless we individually and personally possess that urge in our own soul to bless the Lord, we have yet to know what it is to have fellowship with God.

Then too, how thankful we should be that worship is not limited to public gatherings. Think what the aged and the sick, and the infirm would suffer if worship was limited to a group or public meeting. Thank God, we can individually worship Him as we invite our own soul to bless the Lord.

PSALM ONE HUNDRED FOUR

THE MINISTRY OF ANGELS

WHILE we will observe a close connection between the 103rd and 104th Psalms, we shall also note a marked distinction between the two. Each of these Psalms opens with an exhortation, addressed by the writer to his own soul, to bless the Lord; and each ends with the same strain. However, whereas the 103rd Psalm is occupied with God's dealings with men, and particularly as the Redeemer of men; in the 104th Psalm we find that the Creator, in all His glory, and the provision He has made in creation, is the subject of the Psalm. The Psalm begins:

"Bless the LORD, O my soul. O LORD my God, thou art very great; thou art clothed with honor and majesty.

"Who coverest thyself with light as with a garment: who stretchest out the heavens like a curtain:

"Who layeth the beams of his chambers in the waters: who maketh the clouds his chariot: who walketh upon the wings of the wind:

"Who maketh his angels spirits; his ministers a flaming fire:

"Who laid the foundations of the earth, that it should not be removed for ever."

Observe how the Psalmist in these verses is occupied with the greatness and majesty of the person of God. I have frequently stated, in the course of these broadcasts, that the greatest occupation of the human mind is the contemplation of the glory and majesty of God.

THE MAJESTY OF CHRIST

Occasionally, during the ministry of our Lord Jesus Christ, both the multitudes of Judea and the disciples, who were closer to the Lord, had an opportunity to see a display of the deity of the Lord Jesus Christ. In the healing of the sick, the raising of the dead, the feeding of the multitudes with but five loaves and two small fishes, the discerning eye could have recognized the Lord of glory, dwelling in what appeared to be mortal flesh. On one occasion during the public ministry of our Lord three of the disciples had a marvelous opportunity to behold the glory and majesty of the person of Christ. That experience was so wonderful and awe-inspiring, that one of the three, Peter by name, wrote years later:

". . . we have not followed cunningly devised fables, when we made known unto you the power and coming of our Lord Jesus Christ, but were eye-witnesses of his majesty.

"For he received from God the Father honor and glory, when there came such a voice to him from the excellent glory, This is my beloved Son, in whom I am well pleased.

"And this voice (says Peter) which came from heaven we heard, when we were with him in the holy mount" (that is, the mount of Transfiguration).

Three men had the privilege to observe the majesty of Christ and to listen to the voice of God, coming out of the excellent glory, addressed to them, and speaking of Christ, saying, "This is my beloved Son, in whom I am well pleased . . ."

Now we are faced with two propositions: either Peter and the other two disciples, James and John, were the perpetrators of the worst fraud that has ever been exercised on men, or they reported accurately what actually transpired on the mount of Transfiguration, and they had an experience the like of which only few men have enjoyed—men such as Moses, Abraham, and Isaiah, who saw the Lord in His glory and had the opportunity of hearing Him speak in human language, so that they could understand and appreciate His message.

I repeat, that the greatest and most beneficial occupation of the human mind is the contemplation by that mind of the person and glory of the eternal God as He is manifest in Jesus Christ. It is the viewpoint not only of the New Testament but of the Old Testament as well, that God can only be known through His Son. In the Old Testament He is spoken of under the title Jehovah, and in the New Testament under the title of the Lord Jesus. He is one and the same person. He is the visibility of God. He is the express image of His own person. He upholds all things by the word of His power. It is concerning Him that the Psalmist said, "thou art very great; thou art clothed with honour and majesty. Who coverest thyself with light as with a garment . . ."

When our original parents were formed, God the Father said to the other members of the Godhead, "Let us make man in our image, after our likeness . . ." The Scripture is careful to state that when God created man out of the dust of the earth and breathed into him the breath of life and man became a living soul, his clothing was not made with hands, but his clothing was the light, for he was made in the likeness of God. As Adam was clothed in light and needed no garment to cover him, so the Lord Jesus Christ, on the mount of Transfiguration, was covered with light. Our Lord was clothed with glory. It was not until man sinned that he became aware of the fact that he was naked, and then sought to clothe himself. The very fact that each of us is obliged to wear clothing to cover our nakedness, is abundant evidence of the truth of the Bible, that man lost the image of God when he sinned in the Garden of Eden.

But, as God is described in this 104th Psalm as being clothed with light as with a garment, so it is the hope, born of the Scriptures, of every individual believer in Christ, that some day he shall again be clothed in light.

THE MINISTRY OF ANGELS

The majesty of the Creator and the marvelous provisions that God has made in creation, occupied the pen of the writer of this 104th Psalm. It is impossible, in the short space of twenty minutes, to touch even briefly upon the contents of the Psalm, but there are some things I must at least comment upon. First, we have the majesty of God, about which I have already spoken, and second, in verse 4, the Psalmist wrote: "Who maketh his angels spirits; his ministers a flaming fire . . ."

If we were to examine this Psalm with the care it is entitled to have, we would note that not only is the glory and majesty of God presented, but creation, the angels, and the sons of men are likewise the subjects of the Psalm. I want to touch on each of these three. For the moment, the angels, then creation, and then man.

In the first place, let me remind you that angels are not a company of effeminate-looking beings with wings and long hair, hovering around in a love scene. That may be the conception that medieval artists had, but it is not the Biblical view. Wherever we find the angels spoken of in the Old Testament, or the New Testament, we never find the feminine gender used. Angels are always referred to in the masculine gender. When they appeared to men, they appeared as men; notably in the case of the angels who came to Abraham's tent door to tell him of the impending destruction of Sodom and Gomorrah. One of the group was none other than the Lord Himself, under the title, The Angel of the Lord.

While angels have made their appearances in the form of men, more specifically they are ministering spirits. They merely took possession of a body when they came visibly in contact with men. The Old Testament abounds with the ministry and visitations of angels. In the Gospels, again and again, we find the mention of angels in connection with the ministry of our Lord Jesus Christ. They were present at His temptation; they were present at His resurrection; they were present at His ascension. They always appeared in the form of men. When we read the Acts of the Apostles, we observe again that the ministry of angels is mentioned. When we come to the New Testament letter to the Hebrews, in the 13th chapter, the 2nd verse, we observe that Christians are exhorted to entertain strangers who may come in their midst. Says the writer, "Be not forgetful to entertain strangers: for thereby some have entertained angels unawares."

But that to which we want to call attention, specifically, is the fact that the Holy Spirit made reference to this 104th Psalm in the letter to the Hebrews. In the closing verse of the 1st chapter, we read of the angels: "Are they not all ministering spirits, sent forth to minister for them who shall be heirs of salvation?"

On the basis of this New Testament quotation, we make this statement: that the angels are ministering spirits, sent forth to minister unto them who shall be heirs of salvation. Now we know that an heir to an earthly throne is surrounded by ministering servants who watch over him day and night to see that no harm befalls him, to see to it that he is properly sustained, and that his needs are met. The heir apparent to the throne finds himself encompassed by ministering servants. The Bible says, concerning the angels, that they are ministering spirits; if you please, they are our servants. They occupy the same position in relation to those who are the heirs of salvation as do the servants in connection with the heir apparent to the throne. So, instead of the notion that seems to be prevalent that each of us has an angel watching over us, every born-again Christian has a whole retinue of angels to guard over him and to minister to him. They have been definitely sent forth by God to do this.

There is one further thought in connection with angels, to which I would like to draw attention. Since God sends forth His angels to be our ministering servants, then certainly we must be most valuable in His sight. There is a dignity about the person whom God encircles with a group of angels, which dignity surpasses any imagination of the human mind. That dignity answers every question that can be raised concerning man; who he is, what he is, and what is intended for him. In addition to ministering to believers, the angels extol God's glory and do His bidding. Their dwelling-place is in the heavens and, as a good friend of mine has often said, "Angels are the domestic servants of heaven." Their delight is to do the will of God.

MAN AND CREATION

So much for the angels. Let us now take a moment for the subject of creation. There are some people who insist that creation, or nature, is their God. There are also some Christians who have entirely shut their mind to the fact of God's glorious revelation in creation. Nowhere in the entire Bible do we find any attempt to unite God and creation. They are separate. There is a great gulf fixed between them. As creation, or nature, is the work of the Creator, God has given in nature a demonstration of His power, of His might, and of His wisdom. The keener the spiritual mind is, the more will it observe that nature bears testimony to the very principles of revelation which are found in the Scriptures. He will discover that the book of creation and the book of revelation are written by the same hand. But what folly to suggest that nature is our god. To all such, I would like to suggest that they examine more closely and they will observe that the laws written in nature are inexorable and that nature reveals many inequalities. Look at the stormy ravages that nature, as they say, visits upon creation. Is there any revelation of God's love in creation? We search in vain for it. We find only a revelation of God's might and power. We must go to the Bible for a revelation of God's love.

While we may read in this 104th Psalm some wonderful things about God's creation, we close by drawing attention to a few things concerning man. In verse 23 we read, "Man goeth forth unto his work and to his labour until the evening." That describes man perfectly. Let us not forget that the sleep of a laboring man is sweet. It is only the man who goeth forth unto his work and to his labor until the evening, who is able to enjoy the provision that God has made, even in his own nature. He finds cause to thank God, even for sleep.

The Psalmist brought the Psalm to a close by saying:

"I will sing unto the LORD as long as I live: I will sing praise to my God while I have my being.

"My meditation of him shall be sweet: I will be glad in the LORD.

"Let the sinners be consumed out of the earth, and let the wicked be no more. Bless thou the LORD, O my soul. Praise ye the LORD."

Observe that the Psalmist found joy in God. Do we joy in God, or do we fear Him, in the sense of hating to think of His name? Do we love the fellowship and communion of the Lord, because our joy centers in

Him? It is either one or the other. When nature gives expression to anger and revulsion, by the thunder that roars and the lightning that streaks and the earth that quakes, do we find ourselves trembling, or do we find ourselves possessed of a peace that passeth all understanding? To have peace is the divine right of every individual who has trusted Christ for eternal salvation. That man or woman looks beyond nature to nature's God. He knows that some day he shall behold the face of the One by whom all things were created and for whom all things were made.

PSALM ONE HUNDRED FIVE

THE JEWISH PROBLEM

JUST a glance through the 105th Psalm will indicate that it is occupied primarily with the record of God's dealings with Israel in the land of Egypt, centering about the controversy between Moses and Pharaoh, which led finally to the deliverance of the children of Israel out of Egypt. It is a wonderful Psalm to read at the Passover season of the year, and even to this day, the Jewish race rejoices in the Psalm with each recurring Passover season. We shall read a few verses as an introduction to this meditation, limiting our reading to the first twelve verses:

> "O give thanks unto the LORD; call upon his name: make known his deeds among the people.
> "Sing unto him, sing psalms unto him: talk ye of all his wondrous works.
> "Glory ye in his holy name: let the heart of them rejoice that seek the LORD.
> "Seek the LORD, and his strength: seek his face evermore.
> "Remember his marvellous works that he hath done; his wonders, and the judgments of his mouth;
> "O ye seed of Abraham his servant, ye children of Jacob his chosen.
> "He is the LORD our God: his judgments are in all the earth.
> "He hath remembered his covenant for ever, the word which he commanded to a thousand generations.
> "Which covenant he made with Abraham, and his oath unto Isaac.
> "And confirmed the same unto Jacob for a law, and to Israel for an everlasting covenant:
> "Saying, Unto thee will I give the land of Canaan, the lot of your inheritance:
> "When they were but a few men in number; yea, very few, and strangers in it."

This is a memorial Psalm, looking back to a finished redemption, when the mighty arm of God was laid bare and enabled a nation to leave its captivity in a single day. This is quite evident when you look at verse 6, "O ye seed of Abraham his servant, ye children of Jacob his chosen"; verse 23, "Israel also came into Egypt; and Jacob sojourned in the land of Ham"; verse 43, "And he brought forth his people with joy, and his chosen with gladness . . ." In each of these passages the Psalmist referred to Israel. It is utterly impossible to read the church into this Psalm. The church is a New Testament body, which began at Pentecost and which will be completed when the Lord Jesus Christ returns to receive His own unto Himself.

"HIS NAME," "HIS DEEDS," "HIS WONDERS," ETC.

While the Psalm concerns Israel, I am sure that even the most zealous Israelite will have no objection if we take a sweet morsel from their delightful table of good things, for there are certain principles in this Psalm which are applicable to every age and to certain people in each age. The exhortations to give thanks, to make His deeds known, to sing unto Him, to glory in His holy name, and to seek His face, are exhortations we do well to heed.

If we were to take a pencil and go through this Psalm and underscore, in the twelve verses we read, the pronoun "His," as used in reference to the Lord, we would get a wonderful Bible lesson. In verse 1 we have His name and His deeds. In verse 2 we have His wondrous works. In verse 3 His *holy name*. In verse 4 His strength and His face. In verse 5 His marvelous works, His wonders, and the judgments of His mouth. In verse 6 His chosen. In verse 7 His judgments. In verse 8 His covenant. In verse 9 His oath. In fact we could go through the whole Psalm like this and find a wonderful unfolding of the person of God, in relation primarily to the children of Israel, and through them to the nations of the world.

The children of Israel were to give thanks unto the Lord and to call upon His name. They were to make His deeds known among the people. They were not to talk about themselves; they were to talk about the Lord. They were not to sing about themselves; they were to sing about Him. They were not to talk about their own powers, but about His work, and they were to seek His strength and His face. That brings us to a very interesting subject.

Occasionally I have mentioned, during the course of these broadcasts, that there is a passage of Scripture in which I greatly delight. That passage is, "Salvation belongeth unto the LORD . . ." That doctrine permeates the entire Bible. Salvation is God's work. He planned it. He purposed it. He brought it to pass. He bestows it. It is not our work. It is His work. We are not the masters of our souls, nor the captains of our salvation. If we were, it would be a sorrowful mess we would make of it.

The salvation of which the Bible speaks is perfection in every detail because it is His work. You may center your faith in your own experiences; some people do. You may center your faith in the person of Christ, as other people do. I know some people who are occupied with their experiences, and get together to talk about their experiences. Thy share their experiences and seek to mold their lives to conform to what they call the Christ-life. While that phrase sounds religious, and even sounds like Christianity, there is not one iota of Christianity in it. Christianity is Christ. When our faith is centered in Christ, we discover that there is an urge in our own breast to do the very things that the Psalmist called upon Israel to do in the early verses of this Psalm. We will delight to call upon His name. We will delight to sing His praises. In fact, we will glory in His holy name.

THE JEWISH PROBLEM

I want to devote the major part of our meditation to Israel and what we call the Jewish problem. Anyone, even with limited information at his disposal, must be aware of the fact that there is an increasing rise of anti-Semitism in the world today, probably more so than at any time in our generation. It is not limited to one place or to one country, and it cannot be said that even we in this country are entirely free from it. Just why does this feeling arise against the Jew? Why should these people be different from all other peoples in the world? Why is it that the nations of the world have not been able to assimilate the Jew? The Jew may change his name a hundred times, and may even join some of the exclusive Gentile clubs, but at heart that man is a Jew, and will always be a Jew. When we consider the rising tide of anti-Semitism let us bear in mind this 105th Psalm, particularly verses 12 to 15: "When they (Israel) were but a few men in number; yea, very few, and strangers in it (that is, in the land of Canaan). When they went from one nation to another, from one kingdom to another people; He (the Lord) suffered no man to do them wrong:

yea, he reproved kings for their sakes; saying, Touch not mine anointed, and do my prophets no harm."

This passage shows us the protection that God placed around the descendants of Abraham at a certain period in their history. Whether the people were few in number or many, I do not believe the principle is different. God could just as well protect a whole nation as a little clan. There was a time in Israel's life when no man could do them wrong. There was a time in Israel's experiences when God would not even permit a king to do them any harm. He decreed, "Touch not mine anointed, and do my prophets no harm." Has God changed? Is God less powerful today, than He was in that early period of Jewish history? Is God's arm shortened, that He cannot save? Has He lost His affection for the children of Israel? These are interesting and timely questions.

Let us look at verse 16 of this Psalm, where it is written, "Moreover he called for a famine upon the land: he brake the whole staff of bread"— referring to the famine that was in the land of Canaan. Why did He do it? There is only one answer. He loved Israel with an everlasting love. He chose that nation for a specific purpose, or rather, purposes. He made that nation the depository of His divine revelation. He gave to that nation the privilege of giving birth to the Messiah; out of their loins the Holy One of God appeared. He called that nation out of the midst of idolatry and the worship of many gods, to be a faithful witness to the fact that there is only one God, and His name One. But that nation upon whom He placed His affection woefully rebelled against Him, disappointed Him, and disobeyed His commandments. Israel was never in trouble, Israel never was persecuted, Israel never knew what it was to lose an encounter with an enemy, until she disobeyed the commandments of God.

So I would say to the modern Jew, without attempting or implying any justification of the acts of the persecutor—I say it with all the love that it is possible to put into a voice—that I believe you are suffering today because of your disobedience to God. The generation that said, "We will not have this man to reign over us" and ". . . His blood be on us, and on our children" left a terrific heritage to the coming generations. Of course, God knew that the nation would reject His anointed. The prophets of the Old Testament foretold it. Those who bore testimony to His coming also predicted that they would despise and reject Him. They knew and foretold this rebellion upon the part of Israel. But mark you, God has a purpose in it all, and the persecutor will not escape until he has paid the utmost **farthing.**

THE CASE OF JOSEPH

Now notice verse 17, where we read: "He (the Lord) sent a man before them, even Joseph, who was sold for a servant . . ."

Let us not forget that it was actually Joseph's brothers who sold him. And we must not forget that it was jealousy which led Joseph's brothers to be put him in a place to be sold. Through several dreams that Joseph related to his brethren, it was evident that God intended that he should reign over them and that his brethren should give obedience to him. They did not like it. They rebelled against it and finally, in their jealous anger, they put him in a pit, from which he was sold to the Gentiles. Now it is interesting to consider how God makes the wrath of man to praise Him, for while it was wrath that caused Joseph to be sold, yet the 17th verse of the 105th Psalm informs us that God was moving in a mysterious manner, His wonders to perform. He sent Joseph into Egypt before his father and his brethren. The one whom they rebuked, and who was sold to the Gentiles, later became the great deliverer of the nation in a time of deep sorrow and affliction.

Our Lord Jesus Christ is the perfect antitype of Joseph. He, too, was rejected by His brethren and sold to the Gentiles. It was the hand of Gentiles that put Him to death; but, as in the case of Joseph God caused the wrath of man to praise Him, so in the case of our Lord Jesus Christ, God caused the wrath of man to glorify Him, because the death that our Lord died was in the determinate counsel and foreknowledge of God. Just as Joseph was separated from his brethren for a period, and they assumed him to be dead, so Christ has been separated from His brethren, the Jews, and many among them assume Him to be dead. Yet, He is to be the deliverer through whom the nation Israel is to know liberty and glorious freedom, just as Joseph proved to be the deliverer of his brethren in that far away period in Israel's history.

When God overruled in the case of Israel's rejection of Joseph, and placed Joseph in Egypt, where he married a Gentile bride, He opened the way for Israel's going into Egypt. After the death of Joseph, a new Pharaoh arose, who did not know Joseph, and who made the tasks of the sons of Israel, in Egypt, to be encumbered with difficulties, the like of which the nation had not previously experienced. Let's not forget that we learn from verse 25 of the 105th Psalm, that it was God who turned the hearts of the Egyptians against the nation Israel, for it is written, "He turned their heart to hate his people, to deal subtilly with his servants." That is important in any consideration of the problem of the Jew, even today. While the New Testament informs us that the Lord has temporarily ceased His dealings with Israel nationally, it also emphatically teaches that God and His ancient people cannot be separated. But pity the man or the nation that persecutes the Jew, even if that nation be the instrument in God's hand to bring judgment upon His ancient people; for everyone who knows anything about sacred history will understand that while it was God who turned them, the Egyptians whom He used to judge His people became the objects of God's own judgments, which were more severe than those which Israel endured.

Just as God took Israel out of Egypt and led them into the wilderness, and finally into the promised land, the God who caused that to be brought to pass will some day call His own from the four corners of the earth and He will lead them back into their own land. The nations that persecuted His people will in turn experience the judgment and wrath of God. No one who is acquainted with the Bible, unless he deliberately refuses to receive it, can shut his eyes to the fact that the darkest hours of Israel's suffering lie before her. I am sorry to tell you who are Jews that the sufferings you have endured are as nothing compared to the sufferings you shall yet endure.

However, there is coming an hour in your history when, hemmed in on all sides by the enemy, you will find that there is no place, no arm, upon which you may lean. In desperation you will turn to God, whom your forefathers long ago served and honored, and you will cry out to Him, and in answer to your prayer He will send a deliverer out of Zion, and place you as head of the nations, instead of the tail. He will give you to put your enemies to flight and exalt you so that through you the blessings of Abraham may come upon the Gentiles and all the people that call on God's name. In closing, I suggest that you have an individual responsibility now, just as every Gentile is individually responsible to the One, Jesus of Nazareth, whom the New Testament declares is the anointed of God. He is the anointed Prince and the Saviour. His resurrection from the dead sealed His Saviourhood and His princely title. He will give repentance to Israel, and He extends His salvation to you now, as He does to every individual (irrespective of race, creed, or color) who will receive Him.

PSALM ONE HUNDRED SIX—PART ONE

SEEING vs. BELIEVING

IN our series of meditations in the Book of Psalms we come now to the 106th Psalm, which closes the fourth book of the Psalms. There are a number of interesting things in this Psalm on which we should comment—for that reason we shall devote three addresses to it.

There is a close relationship between this and the previous Psalm. This Psalm continues the review of the history of the children of Israel. Psalm 105 more specifically refers to the revelation of power on the part of the Lord, while the Israelites were in Egypt; whereas the 106th, generally speaking, concerns the wilderness journey which lasted forty years. That journey on the part of Israel very frequently symbolizes our own experiences in life. For that reason we can go to this Psalm and discover that the principles find their application in our own day and experiences. So much for an introduction to this Psalm. Now let us read the first twelve verses:

> "Praise ye the LORD. O give thanks unto the LORD; for he is good: for his mercy endureth for ever.
>
> "Who can utter the mighty acts of the LORD? who can shew forth all his praise?
>
> "Blessed are they that keep judgment, and he that doeth righteousness at all times.
>
> "Remember me, O LORD, with the favor that thou bearest unto thy people: O visit me with thy salvation;
>
> "That I may see the good of thy chosen, that I may rejoice in the gladness of thy nation, that I may glory with thine inheritance.
>
> "We have sinned with our fathers, we have committed iniquity, we have done wickedly.
>
> "Our fathers understood not thy wonders in Egypt; they remembered not the multitude of thy mercies; but provoked him at the sea, even at the Red sea.
>
> "Nevertheless he saved them for his name's sake, that he might make his mighty power to be known.
>
> "He rebuked the Red sea also, and it was dried up: so he led them through the depths, as through the wilderness.
>
> "And he saved them from the hand of him that hated them, and redeemed them from the hand of the enemy.
>
> "And the waters covered their enemies: there was not one of them left.
>
> "Then believed they his words; they sang his praise."

While the literary value of the Bible cannot be minimized, the Book was given not to be admired but to be received as the Word of God; that we might come to know Him of whom the Scriptures witness. Thinking along these lines, I was reminded of an illustration used by Captain Reginald Wallis. He tells that an actor and an aged minister were present at a gathering of some very distinguished people. The host asked the actor to recite, and by request he recited the 23rd Psalm. He did it magnificently and was well applauded. He then went over to the minister and asked him to recite the same piece. The minister was a godly man and recited it in his own way. When he finished there was no applause, but many cheeks were wet. The actor went over to the minister and said, "I know the *Psalm,* but you know the *Shepherd.*"

THE VOICE OF THE LORD

A mere intellectual knowledge of the Bible, valuable and interesting though it may be, is not sufficient. These printed words that appear in our Bible come to us in the name of the Lord. When we recognize and hear the voice of the Lord, through the written Word, then we have come to grasp the true purpose of the Book. Now let us see if we can discern the voice of the Lord as we contemplate this 106th Psalm. It is given today to the sons of men to know God; even as men like Moses, David, Isaiah, Paul, and Peter knew Him. We may not have the privilege of touching the hem of His garment; we may never have seen Him as Paul saw Him, nor have the experience of Moses and Isaiah, but we can say, from the bottom of our hearts, that we know whom we have believed, and are persuaded that He is able to keep that which we have committed unto Him against that day.

The Psalmist declared that the Lord is good. His goodness is expressed in His mercy, and His mercy endureth forever. So often people do not like to retain the thought of God in their knowledge. He is the last person they ever consider. They dislike the thought of God. Life seems to be glorious now; there is a glitter and gaiety about it. To think about God, to these people, is to think about death. That is a silly notion. To think about God is to live; to know God is eternal life. To the man who knows God, death is not something to be feared. He does not think about God in view of death, but he thinks about God because of His goodness, which goodness is expressed in His mercy.

LORD, REMEMBER ME

There are a few things in the early part of this Psalm to which we draw attention specifically. First, note in verse 4 that the Psalmist became exceedingly personal when he lifted up his heart in prayer, saying, "Remember me, O LORD, with the favour that thou bearest unto thy people: O visit me with thy salvation . . ." Of what does this remind us? "Remember me." It seems as if we can hear the voice of the one who was crucified with our Lord Jesus. He could not kneel before Him. He could not run an errand for Him. He could not even touch Him with his hand; all he could do was to turn his head and speak with his mouth. His only request was, "Lord, remember me when thou comest into thy kingdom." If we were to dig into the meaning of the word "remember," we would discover that there is in it the idea of thinking. The Psalmist and the penitent thief invited the Lord to "think" of them. On the testimony of the Bible, God's thoughts are occupied with man. In the 8th Psalm there is this inquiry, "What is man, that thou art *mindful* of him? And the son of man, that thou visitest him?" Let me change that so we can get its full significance. "What is man, that Thy mind is full of him?" God's mind is occupied with man, and when He created man He created him because He was *mindful* of him. The heart of the Creator responds with joy when any child of the dust lifts up his heart in prayer, simply asking, "Remember me." We all recall the answer of our Lord, given to that dying thief—hands stained with sin, conscience undoubtedly borne down with the weight of blood-guiltiness, a disreputable character—yet our Lord turned to him and said, ". . . Today shalt thou be with me in paradise." That man, who went from a prison to a cross, went from the cross to Paradise, because he threw himself upon the mercy of God and acknowledged the Lordship of Christ.

FOR HIS NAME'S SAKE

Another thing we should note is found in the 8th verse. It is necessary to read the 7th also, in order to get the context:

> "Our fathers understood not thy wonders in Egypt; they remembered not the multitude of thy mercies; but provoked him at the sea, even at the Red sea.
> "Nevertheless he saved them for his name's sake, that he might make his mighty power to be known."

This Psalm was written by a Jew, who was looking back on the familiar history of his people. He was calling attention to the failure and rebellion of his fathers. But notice what he wrote, in verse 8: "Nevertheless he saved them for his name's sake, that he might make his mighty power to be known."

Look at the phrase, "for his name's sake." God did not save Israel for Israel's sake. God did not display His mercy for their sake. He did it for His own name's sake. In the New Testament we are met with the development of the phrase, "for his name's sake." Our Lord said, "Hitherto have ye asked nothing in my name: ask, and ye shall receive . . ." Why? For the sake of the name of the Lord.

When God saves a man He saves him for the sake of His name; for the value of His name. What a wonderful name He has.

There is one more thing to which we call attention. God made His power known by rebuking the Red Sea, and allowing Israel to go through on dry land, and then having the waters envelop the enemies of Israel who followed behind them. When Israel was on the other side of the sea, and their enemies were buried at the bottom of the sea and not one of them remained, verse 12 tells us, "Then believed they his words; they sang his praise." When Israel believed God's Word, they sang His praise. That is true now. When a man believes God's Word he sings the praises of God. But someone may say, Well, if I could see the display of power that Israel saw—if I had the same experience, of course I would believe. Yes, that may be true. In fact, that is exactly what Thomas said. Ten of his best and closest associates told him that they had seen the Lord, had eaten with Him, and that He was risen from the dead. Yet Thomas said, "Except I shall see in his hands the print of the nails, and put my finger into the print of the nails, and thrust my hand into his side, I will not believe."

We should observe why Thomas refused to believe the testimony of ten competent witnesses. There was only one reason, and it is the same reason that prevents any man today from believing. Thomas did not believe because he said, "I will not believe." Man disbelieves because of a stubborn will. He refuses to receive the testimony of competent witnesses.

Although Thomas said, "I will not believe," at least he made it his business to be present the following Sunday night, when the disciples met again with their risen Lord. Wouldn't you have loved to have been present, to look at Thomas and notice the gaze and the stare in his eyes and the bewildered expression on his face, when he turned to look upon the risen Lord and heard Him speak, saying, "Thomas, reach hither thy finger, and behold my hands; and reach hither thy hand, and thrust it into my side:

and be not *faithless*, but *believing*." And Thomas, enrapt by the sight of the risen Christ, cried out, "My Lord and my God."

If a man will come to God with his doubts, if he will come to the Bible, particularly to the four Gospels, reading the record therein with an open heart, desiring to know the truth, he will know the truth, and the truth will make him free, indeed. Then he too will sing God's praises.

PSALM ONE HUNDRED SIX—PART TWO

THE MAN WHO STOOD IN THE BREACH

WE have already observed that the 106th Psalm is occupied with the history of Israel; particularly the wilderness journey. We found that the principles of this Psalm find their counterpart in our own experiences. This is not surprising, as human nature has not changed one iota since the Psalm was written or since the events discussed in the Psalm took place. The last verse on which we commented was the 12th verse, reading, "Then believed they his words; they sang his praise." That is always true. When a man or woman believes God's Word, his or her whole outlook on life changes. There is hope and optimism. There is joy and gladness in the soul. That joy must find an outlet, and it usually does so through songs of praise.

The shocking part of the record found in this 106th Psalm is that the 13th verse contains this startling fact: "They soon forgat his works; they waited not for his counsel . . ." It would be difficult to find two verses in Scripture that present so sharp a contrast as do verses 12 and 13 of this Psalm. In the 12th verse we find faith and joy, while in the 13th we have unbelief and disaster. Then note what follows. When man forgets God's works and refuses to wait for His counsel, the very same situation develops as that which is recorded in this Psalm, from verse 13 to 26, which read:

> "They soon forgat his works; they waited not for his counsel:
> "But lusted exceedingly in the wilderness, and tempted God in the desert.
> "And he gave them their request; but sent leanness into their soul.
> "They envied Moses also in the camp, and Aaron the saint of the LORD.
> "The earth opened and swallowed up Dathan, and covered the company of Abiram.

"And a fire was kindled in their company; the flame burned up the wicked.

"They made a calf in Horeb, and worshipped the molten image.

"Thus they changed their glory into the similitude of an ox that eateth grass.

"They forgat God their saviour, which had done great things in Egypt;

"Wondrous works in the land of Ham, and terrible things by the Red sea.

"Therefore he said that he would destroy them, had not Moses his chosen stood before him in the breach, to turn away his wrath, lest he should destroy them.

"Yea, they despised the pleasant land, they believed not his word:

"But murmured in their tents, and hearkened not unto the voice of the LORD.

"Therefore he lifted up his hand against them, to overthrow them in the wilderness."

We have frequently referred to two passages of Scripture to aid us in the study of the Psalms. In the 15th chapter of Paul's letter to the Romans, the 4th verse, we read, "For whatsoever things were written aforetime were written for our learning, that we through patience and comfort of the scriptures might have hope." Again, in Paul's first letter to the Corinthians, 10th chapter, 11th verse, we read, "Now all these things happened unto them (Israel) for ensamples: and they are written for our admonition . . ." So the 106th Psalm was written for our learning, for our admonition, for our comfort, that we, by the Scriptures, might have hope for the future and fashion our lives thereby.

So let us take the principles found in this portion of Scripture, to determine if they have a message for our own time. The Psalmist declared that the majority were on the side of unbelief. He said, "*They* soon forgat his works; *they* waited not for his counsel . . . *They* envied Moses . . . *They* made a calf . . . *They* forgat God their saviour . . . *They* despised the pleasant land, *they* believed not his word . . ." It is a trite thing to say, but it is true, that the voice of the mob is rarely, if ever, the voice of God, and that the pathway in which the majority travel is not the pathway of obedience to God but rather the highway of disobedience. There were, of course, faithful men in Israel at the time. There were Moses and Aaron and Joshua and Caleb; but the vast majority lent their strength to the agitators and to the unbelieving leaders who envied Moses and Aaron, and they disbelieved God and put everything in the pathway of God's anointed leaders to make their task heavy and cause the people to suffer. It is a strange thing to note that the nation which once believed God and saw His wonderful works in the land of Ham should so soon forget God, forget His works, reject His counsel, and disobey His commands. But has it ever been otherwise? Who was it that rejected our Lord Jesus Christ? Who were the leaders that caused the people to shout, "Crucify him, crucify him." They were the scribes and Pharisees, the religious leaders of the people, who suggested that the indictment against Christ be changed from blasphemy to political aspiration and insurrection, in order that the true complaint might be obscured so that their desire might be gratified. That was nineteen hundred years ago.

"THERE SHALL BE FALSE TEACHERS"

But let us get a little closer home, and see if conditions have changed. In so doing let us look at a passage written by Peter. In fact, they are the last recorded inspired words that we have from the pen of that mighty Apostle. Peter said that he wrote to stir the followers of Christ to remembrance, and to endeavor that they might, after his death, recall that he informed them that just as there were, in a previous era, false prophets among Israel, which caused Israel to stumble, so "there *shall be* false teachers among you, who privily shall bring in damnable heresies, even denying the Master who bought them and bring upon themselves swift destruction. And," said Peter, "many shall follow their pernicious ways . . ." Did Peter tell the truth?

About two weeks ago at a convention of one of the evangelical denominations a group of men, claiming to sit as a court of Jesus Christ, passed judgment upon another group of men, members of the same body, and stripped them of their rights and privileges of conscience. All this because that small group of men had the audacity to attack some of the leaders of that denomination and expose their treacherous betrayal of the Lord, by permitting men to be sent as well as to remain on the mission field who do not hold the faith of Christ. When a friend of mine had the courage, as a minister of that body, to openly declare that the decision and act of the ecclesiastical court was blasphemy, and the crowd at the convention learned of it, the crowd roared, demanding that he be put out. That, in an assembly of supposedly Christian gentlemen, who met together to further the ministry and gospel of Jesus Christ our Lord!

Have conditions changed? Have we profited by the experiences recorded in the Old Testament? Have we come to understand that the only ground of fellowship is in obedience to God and His Word, and that joy comes only when one believes God's Word and obeys Him?

There is another word in this Psalm that should never be forgotten. It should be sounded in the ear of every religious leader in this country who has lost his message, and who has left the high plane of preaching Christ and Him crucified. When Israel murmured in their tents and hearkened not unto the voice of the Lord, the 26th verse tells us what took place: "Therefore he (God) lifted up his hand against them, to overthrow them in the wilderness . . ." The price of disobedience to God is ever the same —God's standard never changes.

THE MAN WHO STOOD IN THE BREACH

But we ought not to close this meditation without giving a word on what is the heart of the 106th Psalm. In verse 23, we read, "Therefore he (God) said that he would destroy them, had not Moses his chosen stood before him in the breach, to turn away his wrath, lest he should destroy them." Here was one man, Moses, the leader of the people, who stayed the judgment of God. The people murmured against God; they expressed their anger to Moses. It was Moses who bore the brunt of their attack. He stood, as the Scripture says, "in the breach." If it were not for Moses and the intercession he made, every last one of them would have been smitten in God's wrath.

What a wonderful man Moses must have been. Is it any wonder that the nation Israel still reveres that wonderful name. But let us get the full picture. Moses said, "The LORD thy God will raise up unto thee a Prophet from the midst of thee, of thy brethren, like unto me; unto him ye shall hearken . . ." Concerning that prophet, the Lord said to Moses, "I . . . will put my words in his mouth; and he shall speak unto them all that I shall command him. And it shall come to pass, that whosoever will not hearken unto my words which he shall speak in my name, I will require it of him." That Prophet, like unto Moses, is none other than the Lord Jesus Christ. He too stood "in the breach." From the one side He took the antagonism of the people, the outburst of sin against righteousness; from the other side, He took the wrath of God and the judgment of righteousness against sin. He was literally ground between the upper and nether millstones. Were He not in the breach, not a single one of us would have been able to stand in the presence of God and rejoice in the knowledge of God our Saviour. What a wonderful Saviour is Jesus our Lord!

My friend Dr. Wilbur Smith mentioned something to me the other evening, which was thought-provoking. We were talking about the 21st verse of this 106th Psalm, which reads, "They forgat God their saviour, which had done great things in Egypt . . ." Dr. Smith asked if I had looked into the meaning of the original Hebrew word translated *forgat*. Then he went on to say that the word "shakach" in the Hebrew text means *to mislay*. Actually, one cannot forget God, at least, not one who has known Him; but we can *mislay* Him; we can put Him aside. But, mark, we can never mislay God, and leave empty the place in our life that He formerly occupied. If we mislay God, someone else, or something else, comes in and takes possession of the place that God occupied in our life. It is possible to mislay God and put religion in His place. It is possible to mislay God and put service in His place. It is possible to mislay God and put self in His place. If we have mislaid God, let us open our hearts once again to allow the Lord to have His proper place in our life and affection.

PSALM ONE HUNDRED SIX—PART THREE

THE ONE FAILURE OF MOSES

FOR the third and final Meditation in the 106th Psalm, we shall begin reading at verse 32:

> "They angered him also at the waters of strife, so that it went ill with Moses for their sakes:
>
> "Because they provoked his spirit, so that he spake unadvisedly with his lips.
>
> "They did not destroy the nations, concerning whom the LORD commanded them:
>
> "But were mingled among the heathen, and learned their works.
>
> "And they served their idols: which were a snare unto them.
>
> "Yea, they sacrificed their sons and their daughters unto devils,
>
> "And shed innocent blood, even the blood of their sons and of their daughters, whom they sacrificed unto the idols of Canaan: and the land was polluted with blood.
>
> "Thus were they defiled with their own works, and went a whoring with their own inventions.

"Therefore was the wrath of the LORD kindled against his people, insomuch that he abhorred his own inheritance.

"And he gave them into the hand of the heathen, and they that hated them ruled over them.

"Their enemies also oppressed them, and they were brought into subjection under their hand.

"Many times did he deliver them; but they provoked him with their counsel, and were brought low for their iniquity.

"Nevertheless he regarded their affliction, when he heard their cry:

"And he remembered for them his covenant, and repented according to the multitude of his mercies.

"He made them also to be pitied of all those that carried them captives.

"Save us, O LORD our God, and gather us from among the heathen, to give thanks unto thy holy name, and to triumph in thy praise.

"Blessed be the LORD God of Israel from everlasting to everlasting: and let all the people say, Amen. Praise ye the LORD."

There are three things in this remaining part of the Psalm which we shall consider. First, that which is found in the 32nd and 33rd verses, where, because of the sin of a whole people, one man failed and suffered irreparable loss. Second, that which is found in the 40th verse, where we learn that the wrath of the Lord was kindled against His people so that He actually abhorred His own inheritance. But we ought not to leave this meditation with a black picture in our minds. Therefore we shall close it with a consideration of the 44th and 45th verses, where we read:

"Nevertheless he regarded their affliction, when he heard their cry:

"And he remembered for them his covenant, and repented according to the multitude of his mercies."

Let us take these things in order. First, the failure of Moses.

THE FAILURE OF MOSES

You have heard of the mistakes of Moses, that is, the *supposed* mistakes of Moses; those things that the infidel, Bob Ingersoll, ridiculed at so much per head. Moses made no mistakes in his writings. The works of Moses, the five books ascribed to him, are the inspired, inerrant Word of God. The record found therein can stand every test, and each such test will reveal the wonderful perfection of that portion of Scripture; even as such tests reveal the perfection of every other portion of the Bible. So, we are not talking about the *mistakes* of Moses, but *the one failure* of Moses.

Israel angered the Lord at the place called the waters of strife, so much so, that it went ill with Moses for their sakes. They provoked Moses, so that he spoke "unadvisedly" with his lips. The historical record of it is found in the 20th chapter of Numbers.

The whole congregation of Israel came into a place called Zin. It was a desert place and they could find no water. The congregation got up in arms. They gathered themselves together against Moses and against Aaron. The Bible says that the people chode with Moses, saying, "Would God that we had died when our brethren died before the LORD! And why have ye brought up the congregation of the LORD into this wilderness, that we and our cattle should die there? And wherefore have ye made us to come up out of Egypt, to bring us in unto this evil place? it is no place of seed, or of figs, or of vines, or of pomegranates; neither is there any water to drink. And Moses and Aaron went from the presence of the assembly unto the door of the tabernacle of the congregation, and they fell upon their faces: and the glory of the LORD appeared unto them."

What an experience that must have been! Out of that glory the Lord spoke unto Moses, and said, "Take the rod, and gather thou the assembly together, thou, and Aaron thy brother, and speak ye unto the rock before their eyes; and it shall give forth his water, and thou shalt bring forth to them water out of the rock, so thou shalt give the congregation and their beasts drink."

Now observe that the Psalmist tells us that Israel angered the Lord at the waters of strife. I want you to notice the graciousness of the Lord. You could not tell from the record of the comments of the Lord to Moses, that is found in Numbers, that God was angry with them. What wonderful grace! What a wonderful God is our God. He gave no evidence of being angry with His people; but He simply told Moses to go to a certain rock, and speak to it, and out of it would gush forth waters that would satisfy the congregation and their cattle.

But Moses, though he was the meekest man in all the earth, could not stand the rebellion of Israel any longer. He took the rod, as he was commanded, and gathered the congregation together. What a tongue-lashing Moses gave that congregation! Let me read it, "Hear now, ye rebels; must *we* fetch you water out of this rock?"

"And Moses lifted up his hand, and with his rod he smote the rock twice: and the water came out abundantly, and the congregation drank, and their beasts also."

What's wrong with that picture? Two things. First, Moses could no more fetch water out of the rock than you or I could. God said *He* would cause water to come out of the rock. Second, Moses, instead of doing as God commanded him to do; that is, simply speak to the rock, actually smote the rock with the rod, not only once, but twice. The water came forth, but the Lord immediately addressed Moses and Aaron, and said, "Because ye believed me not, to sanctify me in the eyes of the children of Israel, therefore ye shall not bring this congregation into the land which I have given them."

Now note what the 32nd and 33rd verses of the 106th Psalm say. "They angered him also at the waters of strife, so that it went ill with Moses for their sake: because they provoked his spirit, so that he spake unadvisedly with his lips." Israel had sinned many, many times, yet God, on equally as many occasions, forgave them; but here, Moses made just *one mistake,* simply speaking unadvisedly with his lips and smiting the rock when he was told to speak to it, and for that, would we say, little infraction, Moses was forbidden to lead the people into the Promised Land. He died, as we know, before the people got there and he was buried by the hand of God. His was the only funeral service that God ever conducted. He performed the part of the undertaker.

God gave Moses to see the land, but He did not permit him to enter. Why do you suppose God was so harsh with Moses and so liberal with the people? May I suggest two reasons. First, because Moses failed to glorify God, as the Lord said to him, "Because ye believed me not, to sanctify me in the eyes of the children of Israel . . ." Second, because of the added responsibility that devolved upon Moses as the leader of the people and as a result of the direct revelations he received from the Lord. Let us look at this because it is most important.

". . . THAT ROCK WAS CHRIST"

The rock that Moses smote, while it appeared to be an ordinary rock found in the desert, had a tremendous significance, as we learn from the New Testament. In the 10th chapter of Paul's first letter to the Corinthians, we read that: ". . . they (Israel) drank of that spiritual Rock that followed them: and that Rock was Christ." That rock which Moses smote was Christ. So says the Scripture.

On a previous occasion, when the nation needed water to quench their thirst, God told Moses to *smite* the rock and water would gush forth; but on this occasion God told Moses to *speak* to the rock, not to smite it. But Moses smote it a *second time*. Because of that, he was forbidden to enter and lead his people into the land. Does that convey any thought to us? Yes, this: Just "as it is appointed unto men once to die, but after this the judgment: so Christ was once offered to bear the sins of many; and unto them that look for him shall he appear the second time, *apart from the sin-offering*, unto salvation."

Christ suffered once; the judgment of God fell upon Him once. He was to bear the sin of the world only once. He can never be smitten the second time. Christ died in judgment. He put away sin by the sacrifice of Himself. He will never die again for the sin of the world. From the very moment He paid the penalty of sin, He is to be worshipped and implored by those of us who have received Him. He is now the High Priest; He never again will be the sacrifice.

That is a wonderful thought; for as Christ will never again pay the penalty of sin, so God will never exact from us the penalty of our sin. He exacted from His Son the penalty due our sin. God expressed His satisfaction with it by raising Christ from the dead and exalting Him to His own right hand. Our sin is forever put away, but, not by our virtue, not by the work of our hands, not by any merit of our doing. It was done by the completed sacrifice of Christ. It does not have to be done a second time.

Abhorring His Own Inheritance

Now let us continue to the second subject. In verse 40 we read: "Therefore was the wrath of the LORD kindled against his people, insomuch that he abhorred his own inheritance." Things must have gotten to a frightful stage for God to abhor His own inheritance! We learn from verse 37 that Israel sacrificed their sons and daughters unto demons, and that the land was polluted with blood. The land became a stench in the nostrils of God.

I prefer not to dwell on the sins of a former generation, but I should like to apply this portion of Scripture to our own day. Every informed man or woman, who knows anything about the condition of the professing church of Jesus Christ in this world, will acknowledge that we have not profited from the sins of Israel. We may not sacrifice our sons and daughters in the same way that Israel did, but we freely give them to the world and to the "god of this age." I am afraid that there is just as much cause for God to feel nauseated about the professing church today, as in the case of Israel at the time of which this Psalm speaks. If we only knew the day of our visitation! If only the professing church knew that her place is not *of* the world, though *in* the world as a witness for Christ. It is not her business to mix in the political or social life of this world. It is her business to witness about her rejected Lord. What a travesty, when we consider that the church, which is presented in the New Testament as the bride of Christ, is actually wooing the world and finds herself in the embrace of the world that crucified her Lord, to whom she is betrothed, but who, because of His rejection, is absent in the glory. But enough of that. It is too heart-sickening to dwell on at length, except to remind those who are part of it that God's judgments never change.

THE WONDERFUL GRACE OF GOD

And now we hasten to the last part of our meditation. In the 44th verse, we find, "Nevertheless he (God) regarded their affliction, when he heard their cry: and he remembered for them his covenant, and repented according to the multitude of his mercies." He caused them to be saved, to give thanks to His holy name, and to triumph in His praise. Here is something on which we can pause for a moment or two with great joy. Note, first, the fact that they cried. They were brought so low that they cried unto God. He noticed their affliction, when He heard their cry. Was it ever otherwise? What a wonderful God is our God. He heard their cry, He regarded their affliction, He remembered His covenant, He repented. *He did it all.* God never forgets His covenant.

From the New Testament we learn that God has a new covenant, a covenant in which He entered into an agreement with His Son and in which agreement we are the beneficiaries. The covenant provided that Christ was to die and pay the penalty of sin. For that, He was to be exalted to be a Prince and a Saviour. The beneficiaries of the covenant are all those who come under the shelter of the sacrifice of Christ, and the inheritance is eternal life through faith in Jesus Christ. God will never forget His covenant. Christ sealed it with His own blood. Let us thank Him and praise Him and bless His name forever, and, as the Psalmist reminds us in the closing verse of the 106th Psalm, ". . . let all the people say, Amen. Praise ye the LORD."

PSALM ONE HUNDRED SEVEN

A PSALM WITH A MESSAGE FOR AMERICA TODAY

IN our series of meditations in the Book of Psalms we now come to the beginning of the fifth book.

This 107th Psalm is of timely interest. It has a strain in it that recurs with such rhythmic frequency as to leave no doubt as to its central message. The theme to which I refer is first found in the 8th verse, "Oh that men would praise the LORD for his goodness, and for his wonderful works to the children of men!"

We do not have time to read all of the forty-three verses that compose this Psalm, but if we read at least the first twenty-one they will give us an appreciation of the general tenor of the Psalm and its theme song:

"O give thanks unto the LORD, for he is good: for his mercy endureth for ever.

"Let the redeemed of the LORD say so, whom he hath redeemed from the hand of the enemy;

"And gathered them out of the lands, from the east, and from the west, from the north and from the south.

"They wandered in the wilderness in a solitary way; they found no city to dwell in.

"Hungry and thirsty, their soul fainted in them.

"Then they cried unto the LORD in their trouble, and he delivered them out of their distresses.

"And he led them forth by the right way, that they might go to a city of habitation.

"Oh that men would praise the LORD for his goodness, and for his wonderful works to the children of men!

"For he satisfieth the longing soul, and filleth the hungry soul with goodness.

"Such as sit in darkness and in the shadow of death, being bound in affliction and iron;

"Because they rebelled against the words of God, and contemned the counsel of the most High:

"Therefore he brought down their heart with labour; they fell down, and there was none to help.

"Then they cried unto the LORD in their trouble, and he saved them out of their distresses.

"He brought them out of darkness and the shadow of death, and brake their bands in sunder.

"Oh that men would praise the LORD for his goodness, and for his wonderful works to the children of men!

"For he hath broken the gates of brass, and cut the bars of iron in sunder.

"Fools because of their transgression, and because of their iniquities, are afflicted.

"Their soul abhorreth all manner of meat; and they draw near unto the gates of death.

"Then they cry unto the LORD in their trouble, and he saveth them out of their distresses.

"He sent his word, and healed them, and delivered them from their destructions.

"Oh that men would praise the LORD for his goodness, and for his wonderful works to the children of men!"

It is not known exactly when this Psalm was written, but it is safe to conclude that it was some seven hundred to a thousand years before our Lord Jesus Christ came into the world. Thus it is more than twenty-five hundred years of age, but I am sure, as we continue our meditation in it, we shall discover that it has a distinct message for the very hour in which we live. First, let us look at the opening verses.

THE CHARACTER OF GOD

Observe that the exhortation is found right at the beginning, to give thanks unto the Lord on the basis of the fact that He is good, and that His mercy endureth forever. We are told in another passage of Scripture that it is the goodness of God which leadeth a man to repentance. One of the things we need to know is the character of Almighty God. It would almost seem evident that the God of the universe is good; but a vast number of people have an erroneous impression of the character and personality of God and are unable to think of Him in terms of goodness. They picture Him as a stern ruler without one iota of mercy and kindness about Him; He is enthroned in darkness and thunderings; He is surrounded by a retinue of angels whose sole business it is to discharge judgment; He sits as an angry Being, ready to have the sword fall upon innocent victims and to cast them into a lake of fire. These people go so far as to picture Him as indulging in roaring laughter over the destruction of the poor and the innocent.

While this picture was originally developed in the medieval ages by a powerful institution that desired to keep its subjects in ignorance and bondage, nevertheless, even in this 20th century, the idea is not entirely eliminated from the minds of a great multitude of people. It is not surprising that communists and atheists love to dwell on this caricature of God. The only book in the world that purports to speak in the name of God is the book we call the Bible. While the wrath of God is clearly revealed in the Scriptures, He is possessed of a righteousness far superior to anything man has ever known. He is also good and His mercy endureth forever.

The only people who know anything about the goodness and mercy of God are those referred to in the 2nd verse of this Psalm, where the exhortation is found: "Let *the redeemed* of the LORD say so, whom he hath redeemed from the hand of the enemy . . ." Now a redeemed man is one who has tasted of the goodness of God and who has experienced His mercy. The picture conveyed by the word "redeemed" is an interesting one. I hope that few of you have had the experience of being obliged to go to a pawnshop in order to pawn an article. At any rate, the usual custom is to leave the article with the pawnbroker. He pays you a price which is but a percentage of the real value of the article. He, in turn, gives you a ticket which enables you, when you have the wherewithal, to redeem the article and take it out of the hand of the pawnbroker.

The Bible uses this picture because it conveys actually what transpires. If you please, the devil is the pawnbroker. I have no difficulty in believing in a personal devil because I see his handiwork and ministry almost every moment of every day. Frankly, we have literally sold ourselves to the pawnbroker. We are slaves to sin. We cannot redeem ourselves for we do not have the wherewithal. However, the God who created us, seeing His possession was in the hand of the pawnbroker, went directly into the marketplace and there paid the purchase price for the redemption of the slaves in the sin market. The purchase price was the blood of the Lord.

Those of us who have received the redemption of God to enjoy the liberty of free re-born men, have found that God is good, for He has redeemed us. We have also discovered that His mercy endureth forever; for the redemption that was purchased for us is eternal and can never be broken. If you have yet to experience that liberty, I invite you to receive the Redeemer's salvation and come to know what it is to pass out of death and out of the slave market into the atmosphere and presence of the eternal God. Words cannot describe the marked change that takes place in the life of an individual who experiences that transformation.

While this Psalm specifically concerns Israel, I do not think that any of the children of Jacob will object to our application of it; for as we learn from verses 3 to 7, the redeemed of the Lord come from all lands; from the east, and the west, the north, and the south. They, like Israel, "wandered in the wilderness in a solitary way; they found no city to dwell in.

Hungry and thirsty, their soul fainted in them. Then they cried unto the LORD in their trouble, and he delivered them out of their distresses. And he led them forth by the right way, that they might go to a city of habitation."

THE 1936 DROUGHT

Now let us go to the second section. Reading from verse 9 to verse 15, we learn that "(God) satisfieth the longing soul, and filleth the hungry soul with goodness. Such as sit in darkness and in the shadow of death, being bound in affliction and iron; because they rebelled against the words of God, and contemned the counsel of the most High . . . he brought down their heart with labour; they fell down, and there was none to help. Then they cried unto the LORD in their trouble, and he saved them out of their distresses. He brought them out of darkness and the shadow of death, and brake their bands in sunder. Oh that men would praise the LORD for his goodness, and for his wonderful works to the children of men!"

What does all this mean? Simply this: the history of man is replete with failures and restorations, and we find this repeated again and again in this Psalm. First, we have a description of God, rich in goodness and mercy, anxious to have fellowship with the children of men, constantly giving a demonstration of His wonderful works to the children of men. However, they rebel against Him and refuse His counsel. Because of that, they are brought low until they get to a place where they cry out to God in their trouble and He finally saves them from their distresses.

We have a famous expression that "history repeats itself." What has been, is; what is, has been; and what is, will be. In other words, we are like sheep. You see, we are so dumb that we haven't the sense to profit from our own mistakes or those of others.

May I become personal and come right down to our present day. Every newspaper in this country has blazoned across its front pages the record of the terrific heat wave that has swept our land, which has left destruction and death in its wake. A serious depression has been visited upon this country since 1929. Though some folks believe it is over, the vast majority know that it is not. During these seven years, since 1929, do you think that our country as a nation has recognized that "Every good gift and every perfect gift is from above and cometh down from the Father of lights, with whom there is no variableness, neither shadow of turning"? Do you think that we as Americans, individually or collectively, have recognized the hand of God in judgment? Do you think that we have been brought down sufficiently low to cry out unto God that He might once again restore us to a place of prosperity, and joy, and gladness so that we can praise Him and revel in His wonderful name and in His wonderful works to the children of men? The answer is too obvious. Every man and woman knows that instead of any contrition of heart there is the extreme opposite. There is even a spirit of boastfulness over what little improvement there has been, which spirit has been so aptly expressed even by one in a high position as "we planned it that way."

But let us look a little further. We here in the east, and along the Atlantic seaboard, have no idea of the devastation that has been raging in the wheat belt, except from newspaper accounts and a few pictures that have found their way into the press. I do not wish to appear as a calamity howler, for I know only too well that God is good and His mercy endureth forever, and that He waits patiently for men to repent before He expresses Himself in judgment. However, I must confess that I would not be surprised if God withholds His blessing from the earth in order to bring us back to an acknowledgment of His goodness and mercy. When I think of the wickedness of men in high places, I say *wickedness*, in what has been called the "philosophy of scarcity," when by government edict men have plowed under their fields of cotton and wheat and other foodstuffs, and men have literally slain livestock, it is not surprising that God withholds His refreshing rains. I do not desire to be intruding a politically partisan comment here; I am not interested in politics from that viewpoint and I do not believe it is the business of a preacher to meddle in politics; but I cannot avoid speaking the evident truth that this nation, from its President down, cannot smile away the responsibility of such godless, wicked doings.

A WARNING MESSAGE TO AMERICA

In the wheat belt, in 1933, we received a warning, and again in 1934. Do you think we heeded? Indeed not. Do you think we got to a place where we discarded the "philosophy of scarcity" and recognized that God is the giver of every good gift and that He alone can give of the increase of the field? Did we cease our wicked doings? Indeed not. Instead, we spoke in high sounding phrases about "economic royalists" and blamed everybody and everything for our circumstances—except our own sins. May I suggest that all Americans, I mean you and I, do exactly that which is described in verse 13 of this Psalm; that we cry unto the Lord in our trouble. There is no doubt that He would bring us out of our distresses. He would then break the bands of our afflictions and bring us into a wide place where we might see the works of the Lord and rejoice in His name.

Let us not forget that there is a definite comment regarding a situation similar to our present circumstances, commencing with verse 31, where we find the same theme song, "Oh that men would praise the LORD for his goodness, and for his wonderful works to the children of men!" Then follows the exhortation "Let them exalt him also in the congregation of the people, and praise him in the assembly of the elders. He turneth rivers into a wilderness, and the watersprings into dry ground; a fruitful land into barrenness . . ." Why? "for the wickedness of them that dwell therein." Just as God will turn a fruitful land into barrenness because of the wickedness of the people that dwell therein, so upon their repentance He will turn the wilderness into a standing water, and the dry ground into watersprings, so that the people may sow the fields, and plant vineyards, which may yield fruits of increase. He will bless them also that they will be multiplied greatly; and He will suffer not their cattle to decrease. That kind of blessing only comes when a nation bows itself before God and repents of its wickedness. Would to God America would do that!

PSALM ONE HUNDRED EIGHT

THE BEST REMEDY FOR A FLUTTERING HEART

WE have a very interesting Psalm for our meditation; one that fills the heart with exuberance and joy. It is particularly appropriate for a Sunday morning. I refer to the 108th Psalm. I hope you are not superstitious, for it has thirteen verses. However, it is the kind of Psalm that will enable you to have a smile on your face even if ten mirrors break into a thousand bits, or a dozen black cats cross your path, or you walk under ten ladders. The fact is, that if your heart is fixed, as was David's who wrote this Psalm, circumstances do not mean a thing. Let me read the Psalm first:

"O God, my heart is fixed; I will sing and give praise,
even with my glory.
"Awake, psaltery and harp: I myself will awake early.

"I will praise thee, O LORD, among the people: and
I will sing praises unto thee among the nations.

"For thy mercy is great above the heavens: and thy
truth reacheth unto the clouds.

"Be thou exalted, O God, above the heavens: and thy
glory above all the earth;

"That thy beloved may be delivered: save with thy
right hand, and answer me.

"God hath spoken in his holiness; I will rejoice, I will
divide Shechem, and mete out the valley of Succoth.

"Gilead is mine; Manasseh is mine; Ephraim also is
the strength of mine head; Judah is my lawgiver;

"Moab is my washpot; over Edom will I cast out my
shoe; over Philistia will I triumph.

"Who will bring me into the strong city? who will lead
me into Edom?

"Wilt not thou, O God, who has cast us off? and wilt
not thou, O God, go forth with our hosts?

"Give us help from trouble: for vain is the help of man.

"Through God we shall do valiantly: for he it is that
shall tread down our enemies."

We of course recognize immediately, upon reading the Psalm, that
much of it is concerned with God's ancient people, Israel. We will have
something to say about them later, but let me first of all do as the Scripture
invokes us to do—draw water from the wells of salvation with joy—for the
first half of this Psalm contains a wonderful exhortation to praise.

A FIXED HEART

The first thing we should notice is the fact that David said his heart
was fixed. By the way, the first five verses of this Psalm are to be found
almost verbatim in verses 7 to 11 of the 57th Psalm. At the time we discussed that Psalm we did not comment specifically upon those verses, so
that we will not be repeating ourselves by directing attention now to this
wonderful statement.

What do you suppose David meant when he said his heart was fixed?
God had said, concerning David, that he was a man after His own heart.
When God so testified concerning David, He was not describing his uprightness, He was talking about the direction of David's heart and David's
mind. David desired the heart of God. He constantly went *after* it. He
loved the fellowship of the Lord.

However, in this Psalm David said, "O God, my heart is fixed;" and, because it was fixed, "I will sing and give praise, even with my glory." It is interesting to note the root meaning of the Hebrew word that David employed, which is here translated *fixed*. I found that the Hebrew word was "kuwn," which comes from a primitive root, meaning to prop up, to erect, to stand perpendicular. In other words, David's heart was upright; it was in a straight perpendicular line. David knew that there was a straight line to God, and that it was unnecessary to go in circles. He knew there was a straight pathway from his heart into the very presence of God, where the other end of the perpendicular line terminated. God said that David was a man after His own heart. David said, "O God, my heart is fixed . . ." There was a straight line between God and David. I trust this conveys an impression to your mind, so that you too may recognize that it is the privilege of every man, as was given to David, to have his heart fixed definitely. These hearts of ours need something to keep them steady. How they can fluctuate! You young folk know what I mean. The passing of a young lady or a young man has a tendency to make that little thing we call the heart fluctuate; just like every passing wave has a tendency to make the movement of the compass fluctuate. However, when the ship is sailing a straight course, it is due to the fact that the skipper has set his compass to that course, and, having done that, it is set and does not fluctuate. Thus, when our heart is set upon God there is no fluctuation. *Now, variety may be the spice of life, but it is the curse of Christian experience.* We ought not to have the up-and-down experience; one day up on the mountain top and the next day down in the valley. When one's heart is set in a straight line and is perpendicular to God, it does not make the slightest difference what our circumstances are. There will always be the urge to sing and give praise to Him.

SINGING WITH OUR GLORY

David said, ". . . I will sing and give praise, even with my glory." I wonder what he meant by the expression "my glory." Someone has suggested that he meant his best member, and undoubtedly referred to his tongue. The Hebrew word "kabowd" which is here translated *glory* is made up of two syllables, the first of which is *ka*. It can be used in either one of two senses It can be used in a bad sense, to mean burdensome, severe, and dull, and it can be used in a good sense, to mean numerous, rich, and honorable. Thus, at times it can be a weight, burdensome and heavy, and at other times it can express quality and glory. With that in mind, let us see the picture that David draws. ". . . my heart is fixed;" and, because my heart is fixed, "I will sing and give praise, even with my glory." There is a close relationship between the tongue and the heart. The tongue is one's glory, for it expresses the thoughts and the intents of the heart. After all, glory is the display of power and of character. It is brilliance, something that cannot be seen or felt apart from its brilliance. For instance, our Lord Jesus is presented in the Scripture as the glory of God. We cannot see God with the naked eye. He is a Spirit and cannot be seen. God is only visible in Christ. Thus, Christ is the glory of God—the effulgence of God. Everything we know about God is revealed in Christ, so that if we have come to know Christ we have come to know the Father also. There is perfect harmony between the two. One is indescribable and the other is tangible. One is a Spirit and the other is a body. Thus, when David said, I will sing with my glory, he was inviting that member which gives voice to the throb of the heart, to join with it in praise, to demonstrate to God that his heart was fixed. When we consider that the tongue can very often be a burdensome member and a decidedly heavy weight, it ought to be a means of encouragement and exhortation for us to know that the only way we can control our tongue is by having our heart set upon God. Our Lord said that out of the heart proceed evil thoughts and all manner of wickedness; so likewise, out of a renewed heart, filled with joy and gladness in God, the mouth expresses the sacrifice of praise, which is acceptable to God.

Observe also that in the 2nd verse David invited his instruments, the psaltery and harp, to join with him, as he arose early in the morning to praise his Lord among the people. That surely conveys to our mind that God is entitled to have the very best in His service. Nothing is too good to be used in God's service.

Don't you like the suggestion that David made in the 3rd verse, when he said, "I will praise thee, O LORD, among the people: and I will sing praises unto thee among the nations." After all, is there any music in the world that is so soothing to the heart and to the troubled mind as the great, solid Christian hymns, the wonderful songs that are associated with the coming of our Lord Jesus Christ? Music? There is no music in the world to be compared with that which is concerned with the expression of the heart's adoration of God for the gift of His Son. Let us sing heartily, so that the nations may come to know about Him.

Now a word or two about the 4th verse, where we read, "For thy mercy is great above the heavens: and thy truth reacheth unto the clouds." Let me interpose a personal word here. There is only one Being in all the world who knows this heart and life of mine better than I do myself, and that is the eternal God. I have lived with this heart long enough to know that I have never gone through a single day without finding cause for severely rebuking it. There has never been a day lived that I have been thoroughly satisfied with the accomplishments of this life. I know that God demands perfection. Nothing but perfection can ever satisfy a holy God. He does not find it in me, nor can He find it in you. He has only found it in Christ. He is the only perfect Man. What about me? What about you? Do you think that God is going to be more satisfied with my life than I myself, or with your life than you are with it? Indeed not! Then what? Just this: the very mercy that God has been displaying in my life and in your life, which enables you and me *right here* to have the sweet, conscious peace of God because we have received His testimony concerning His Son —that mercy will meet us in the glory. It is not only expressed on the earth, but it is great *above* the heavens. That enables a man to look up into the face of God, and, by faith, to feel perfectly at home in the presence of a holy God, whose eyes cannot behold sin. Wonderful grace—wonderful truth. When an individual is conscious of that, he joins with David as he expressed himself in the words of the 5th verse, "Be thou exalted, O God, above the heavens: and thy glory above all the earth . . ."

"MY WASHPOT" AND "MY SHOE"

In the last half of the Psalm we have some interesting metaphors. God said:

> ". . . I will divide Shechem and mete out the valley of Succoth.
> "Gilead is mine; Manasseh is mine; Ephraim also is the strength of mine head; Judah is my lawgiver;
> "Moab is my washpot; over Edom will I cast out my shoe; over Philistia will I triumph."

We do not have the time available to discuss these individually, but every Jewish heart that revels in the antiquity of his people, and the wonderful dealings that God has had with his people, understands the symbolism used in this Psalm. At least, he should understand it, for not only are there names of the various members of the Jewish economy, such as

Ephraim, Manasseh, and Judah, but there is even mention of others, such as the Moabites and Edomites, and reference is also made to the land, that land over which God will triumph, as is expressed "over Philistia will I triumph."

May we spend our closing moments on two of these expressions? One is, "Moab is my washpot;" and the other, "over Edom will I cast out my shoe. . ."

What about Moab and Edom? The Moabites, who were the descendants of Moab, were a stumbling-block to Israel. They caused Israel to indulge in horrible impurity. Isn't it interesting, therefore, that of the nation which caused Israel to sin, the nation which enjoyed sin and brought defilement to Israel, God should say, They shall be My "washpot." In other words, God is going to clean up Moab, and He is going to do such wonderful things for them that, instead of being the cause of sin and impurity, Israel will be able to enjoy the fellowship of the Moabites; and as they come in contact with them, cleanness and purity and holiness will be the result. By the way, that is the very effect every Christian should have upon those with whom he comes in contact.

Then God said, "over Edom will I cast out my shoe . . ." To understand what is meant by that expression, one must go to the East. Edom was the nickname for Esau. His descendants came to be known as Edomites. Esau despised his birthright; he sold it to his brother Jacob. Because he despised his birthright, he was deprived of all the privileges connected with it. There is a striking significance about the throwing away of a shoe. Let me refer to a portion from one of the most wonderful short stories ever written; a true love story. The book I refer to is the Book of Ruth. Boaz, who was Ruth's lover, wanted to redeem the land, the field of Naomi, Ruth's mother-in-law. He could not, for while he was near of kin, he was not the nearest kinsman. But the nearest kinsman said, "I cannot redeem it for myself, lest I mar mine own inheritance: redeem thou my right to thyself; for I cannot redeem it." In the 7th verse of the 4th chapter of Ruth, we read, "Now this was the manner in former time in Israel concerning redeeming and concerning changing, for to confirm all things; a man plucked off his shoe, and gave it to his neighbour: and this was a testimony in Israel. Therefore the kinsman said unto Boaz, Buy it for thee. So he drew off his shoe."

God is going to restore Edom. Esau lost his birthright; he lost its privileges; but God is going to redeem it and give him back everything he lost, and, believe it or not, the Edomites and Israelites will dwell together in perfect harmony in the land of Palestine.

How will it be accomplished? Can it be done through diplomatic channels? Can it be done through the League of Nations, or any mandate of the League? Can it be accomplished by the good intentions of what is probably the most honorable diplomatic nation in the world? No! In the 12th verse we read, ". . . vain is the help of man." However, in the closing verse David said, "Through God we shall do valiantly: for he it is that shall tread down our enemies." It does not make any difference to Israel who her enemies are, for if she trusts in God she will find that she will tread down all her enemies. What a message this 108th Psalm has for Israel today. But alas, that nation, not unlike the so-called Christian nations, is depending upon the help of man, instead of trusting God. Are you doing the same in your individual life? "Cease ye from man, whose breath is in his nostrils . . ." Instead, trust the living God, who cannot lie, and who said, "He that hath the Son, hath life; and he that hath not the Son of God hath not life."

PSALM ONE HUNDRED NINE

THE STRANGEST PSALM OF ALL, AND PETER'S USE OF IT

A CRITIC has said, concerning the 109th Psalm, that it contains a "pitiless hate, a refined and insatiable malignity." These are very strong words—yet I must confess that I am not surprised, for this 109th Psalm is not only the last, but the most terrible, of all the imprecatory Psalms.

A STRANGE PSALM FOR DIVINE SERVICE

Before we read a few of its verses, may I call your attention to the fact that this Psalm contains an inscription reading, "To the chief Musician, A Psalm of David." From that inscription we learn two things: first, it was intended to be sung in divine service. It may not be easy to imagine a whole nation singing such dreadful imprecations as are found in this Psalm, yet there can be no doubt that the Psalm was intended for just such a purpose. Then, we learn from the title that it was a Psalm of David. Anyone who is acquainted with the history of David knows that revenge was as far from the mind of David as anything could possibly be. David would not even smite King Saul, when he knew Saul sought his blood. While he was a man of war, yet he possessed a beautiful spirit; he was a man of tender heart and he greatly loved music. Thus we raise the question, how could a man like David write such a Psalm, and why should it be sung in the house of God? We will discuss these questions later. Let us read a few of its passages. The Psalms contains thirty-one verses, but we shall content ourselves with reading the first sixteen verses. They will be sufficient to give us an idea of the character of the Psalm.

"Hold not thy peace, O God of my praise;

"For the mouth of the wicked and the mouth of the deceitful are opened against me: they have spoken against me with a lying tongue.

"They compassed me about also with words of hatred; and fought against me without a cause.

"For my love they are my adversaries: but I give myself unto prayer.

"And they have rewarded me evil for good, and hatred for my love.

"Set thou a wicked man over him: and let Satan stand at his right hand.

"When he shall be judged, let him be condemned: and let his prayer become sin.

"Let his days be few; and let another take his office.

"Let his children be fatherless, and his wife a widow.

"Let his children be continually vagabonds, and beg: let them seek their bread also out of their desolate places.

"Let the extortioner catch all that he hath; and let the strangers spoil his labor.

"Let there be none to extend mercy unto him: neither let there be any to favor his fatherless children.

"Let his posterity be cut off; and in the generation following let their name be blotted out.

"Let the iniquity of his fathers be remembered with the LORD; and let not the sin of his mother be blotted out.

"Let them be before the LORD continually, that he may cut off the memory of them from the earth.

"Because that he remembered not to shew mercy, but persecuted the poor and needy man, that he might even slay the broken in heart."

PETER ON "JUDAS IN THE 109TH PSALM"

You who are familiar with the Bible recognize immediately that Peter quoted from this Psalm, when he rose up in the midst of the disciples, shortly after our Lord had ascended into the heavens, and said, "Men and brethren, this scripture must needs have been fulfilled, which the Holy Ghost by the mouth of David spake before concerning Judas, which was guide to them that took Jesus." Then Peter went on to say that Judas purchased a field with the reward of his iniquity, that is, the thirty pieces of silver, and "falling headlong, he burst asunder in the midst, and all his bowels gushed out," and, what is more, Peter added, "It was known unto all the dwellers at Jerusalem; insomuch as that field is called in their proper tongue . . . The field of blood." Such being the case, Peter said, "it is written in the book of Psalms, Let his habitation be desolate, and let no man dwell therein: and his bishoprick let another take."

As a result, Matthias was chosen to take the place of Judas in the company of the twelve who could bear witness that they had been associated with the Lord Jesus from the baptism of John unto the very day that He was taken up into heaven. The point I wish to make is this: it seems evident that Peter placed his stamp upon a part of the 109th Psalm; that is, the 8th verse, and declared that it was written concerning Judas, and that when David wrote it he was moved by the Holy Spirit of God. David was not talking about any enemy of his; he was writing about Judas, who would be the betrayer of our Lord Jesus Christ.

The man or woman who has bowed the knee to Jesus Christ—acknowledging Him as Lord, and who has come to know what the Bible has to say about the death of Christ; that individual sees, in the circumstances surrounding the rejection and crucifixion of Christ, the revelation oι hearts: first, the heart of mankind, which expressed itself in indiff... and in wickedness and atrocities which have never been equaled. Second, the heart of Satan was revealed. He had found an avenue for his hatred of Christ, in one who formerly sat within the inner circle. He took possession of that man, Judas, and controlled and dominated him in his vindictiveness against the Lord Jesus Christ. When Satan had accomplished his purpose, Judas was a spectacle of broken humanity going out into the night and committing suicide. Not only was the heart of man and the heart of Satan revealed, but the heart of God was also revealed, for the Bible declares that our Lord Jesus Christ was in the bosom of the Father. Thus the gospel is sometimes called the gospel of the bosom of God. As our Lord was in the bosom of His Father, God laid His heart bare in the person of His Son. And as Satan laid bare his heart in the person of Judas, so that we know the motives that actuated Satan, and the wickedness that pervaded his character;

so, in Christ, we see the heart of God, and the righteousness and the loving-kindness that motivate God.

Our Lord Jesus Christ, in the midst of that scene, was ". . . brought as a lamb to the slaughter, and as a sheep before her shearers is dumb, so he openeth not his mouth." Not only is the heart of God revealed through the actions of His Son, but, in forsaking His Son, God demonstrated His love and affection for the whole of the human race. Unless He had forsaken His Son and exacted from Him the penalty for sin, this world would not be a fit place for any man to live in.

Therefore we may view this 109th Psalm, if not entirely, at least partially, as being the utterance of our Lord Jesus Christ concerning Judas, the blackest character this world has ever known. If such is the case, it is easy to understand the 6th verse of the Psalm, where we read, "Set thou a wicked man over him: and let Satan stand at his right hand."

PERFECT HATE

There is such a thing as perfect hate, as well as perfect love. In the New Testament letter to the Hebrews, in the 10th chapter, the 30th and 31st verses, we read, "For we know him that hath said, Vengeance belongeth unto me, I will recompense, said the Lord. And again, The Lord shall judge his people. It is a fearful thing to fall into the hands of the living God." I want to repeat that last sentence, "It is a fearful thing to fall into the hands of the living God." Too often we lose sight of the fact that God is righteous and that His judgments are sure. We are too prone to think of Him in terms of mercy, grace, and kindness, without ever considering the characteristic of vengeance. Do we need to apologize for God, because of His vengeance? Why, the idea of a man apologizing for God! But some will say, That is not our concept of God; that is the concept of an ancient people. We do not think of God in terms of vengeance, of wrath, or imprecatory Psalms; we think of Him as merciful and loving; He overlooks the faults and iniquities of man. I answer: if you were to take vengeance and judgment from the Bible, you would not have any Bible left: it would fall like a house of cards. There is a perfect hate, as there is a perfect love. If perfection in love is as grand as we have experienced, who have placed our trust in Christ, let it not be forgotten that there is also perfection in wrath. An evidence of that is found in this Psalm.

Irrespective of who the author of this Psalm may be, can you imagine a man saying, concerning another, ". . . let his prayer become sin. Let his days be few . . . Let his children be continually vagabonds, and beg . . . Let his posterity be cut off . . ."? But that, I think, is what happened in the case of Judas.

In the beginning of our meditation I raised two questions, How could a man like David write such a Psalm, and why should it be sung in the house of God? Of course, I believe that this 109th Psalm is as definitely inspired as any other portion of Scripture. David wrote it under the guidance of the Spirit of God. But why should he write it? To that, I reply: in order that men might understand the wrath of God, as well as the grace of God: wrath against His enemies, but grace to those who love Him.

While part of the Psalm is devoted to imprecations, let us not forget that there are other parts which speak of His grace toward His children. For instance, look at verse 21, where we read, "But do thou for me, O GOD the Lord, for thy name's sake: because thy mercy is good, deliver thou me." Again, in verse 28, "Let them curse, but bless thou: when they arise, let them be ashamed; but let thy servant rejoice" and finally, in the 30th and 31st verses we read, "I will greatly praise the LORD with my mouth; yea, I will praise him among the multitude. For he shall stand at the right hand of the poor, to save him from those that condemn his soul." Thus the Psalm is occupied with the grace of God toward His children, as well as the judgment of God poured out upon His enemies. Note an interesting contrast before we discuss the second question. Verse 6 reads, "Set thou a wicked man over him: and let Satan stand at his right hand." Then, in verses 30 and 31, we read, "I will greatly praise the LORD with my mouth; yea, I will praise him among the multitude. For he shall stand at the right hand of the poor, to save him from those that condemn his soul." This world is divided into two great camps: one consists of those who are on the side of the Lord, and the other consists of those who are on the side of Satan. Whom have you at your right hand?

However, why should a whole nation sing a song such as this 109th Psalm? I seriously question whether any one of us would care to sing it; it seems so foreign to us. The average congregation sings of the grace of God and of His salvation. Nevertheless, who of us would feel concerned if the enemies of our soul and the enemies of God were forever destroyed? Let me cite you an example. Take the case of the kidnapping of the Lindbergh baby. The man who conceived that crime perpetrated a most hideous thing, so that the hearts of the entire nation rose in an expression of sympathy to the father and mother who lost their loved baby. However, the hearts that expressed sympathy found in them the impulse to cry out for the life of the man who did the crime. Almost to a man, there was the feeling that the penalty fitted the crime. "It cannot be denied that we wish well for all mankind," to use the language of another, "but for that very reason we sometimes blaze with indignation against the inhuman wretches by whom every law which protects our fellow creatures is trampled down and every dictate of humanity is set at naught."

If God has placed that hate in the human breast, do you think that there is any difficulty in reconciling the wrath of God, when one considers that He is able to see what no human eye can see. For example, what do you think God sees in just one city, for instance in New York, when the shadows of night fall and all the leeches of humanity come out of their hiding? You could not stand such a sight; you would be horrified; yet God must look at it night after night. Were it not for His grace (for He is not willing that any man should perish) His judgment would have been displayed long ago. The fact of delayed judgment, however, is far from an assurance of no judgment at all. God is extending His grace at the present hour. He has given to man the privilege of preaching Christ and His gospel, in order that as many as possible be saved from the wrath to come. Thus I say to you, that while the church of Jesus Christ delights to sing His praise and those good old gospel hymns that have been the means of the salvation of multitudes of sinners, the triumphant church will find it no less difficult or joyful to sing when the hour of God's judgment shall break upon the world.

Let me take you back to the 2nd Psalm, where the question is raised, "Why do the heathen rage, and the people imagine a vain thing? The kings of the earth set themselves, and the rulers take counsel together, against the LORD, and against his anointed, saying, Let us break their bands asunder, and cast away their cords from us." Then from the heavens we get this response. "He that sitteth in the heavens shall laugh: the Lord shall have them in derision. Then shall he speak unto them in his wrath, and vex them in his sore displeasure." Just because that hour has been delayed, let us not labor under the false hope that it will never take place. Just now the wicked laugh at God. That is not a matter of concern, in one sense of the world, for man's breath is in his nostrils. He is here today and gone tomorrow. He is like the flower and grass of the field. However, it *is* a matter of deep concern when God sits in the heavens and laughs. What a thought—that God will laugh at the wicked and vex them in His sore displeasure.

The Bible not only presents a God of love, who gave His own Son that we might have fellowship with Him, but it presents that same God as a God of wrath, who will pour out His sore displeasure upon those who have despised His grace. That is not only true, collectively and nationally, but it is also true individually. I do no injustice to the gospel by suggesting that you flee from the wrath to come, so that you may be able to say with David "I will greatly praise the LORD with my mouth; yea, I will praise him among the multitude." For He shall stand at my right hand, to save me from those that condemn my soul.

PSALM ONE HUNDRED TEN—PART ONE

A GREAT MESSIANIC PSALM

WE are now to consider the 110th Psalm, which, by the way, is quoted more frequently in the New Testament than any other. From these quotations we can gather what our Lord Jesus Christ and the Holy Spirit have to say concerning the author of the Psalm and the subject of the Psalm.

I suppose it is futile to raise the question of favorite Psalms or favorite verses, but, from a viewpoint of the exceeding greatness of our Lord's person, I love the 110th Psalm and consider it my favorite. Let us read it. It is short, containing only seven verses:

"The LORD said unto my Lord, Sit thou at my right hand, until I make thine enemies thy footstool.

"The LORD shall send the rod of thy strength out of Zion: rule thou in the midst of thine enemies.

"Thy people shall be willing in the day of thy power, in the beauties of holiness from the womb of the morning: thou hast the dew of thy youth.

"The LORD hath sworn, and will not repent, Thou art a priest for ever after the order of Melchizedek.

"The Lord at thy right hand shall strike through kings in the day of his wrath.

"He shall judge among the heathen, he shall fill the places with the dead bodies; he shall wound the heads over many countries.

"He shall drink of the brook in the way: therefore shall he lift up the head."

This is another Psalm of which David is the author, but we learn from the lips of our Lord Jesus that David was writing in the Holy Spirit; that is, he was not writing about himself or some other human king, but he was writing about the Messiah. In the 22nd chapter of Matthew, our Lord is found questioning the Pharisees, and, in doing so, He makes use of this 110th Psalm. Commencing with verse 41 of Matthew 22, we read: "While the Pharisees were gathered together, Jesus asked them, saying, What think ye of Christ? whose son is he? They say unto him, The son of David." Our Lord asked, "How then doth David in spirit call him Lord, saying, The LORD said unto my Lord, Sit thou on my right hand, till I make thine enemies thy footstool? If David then call him Lord, how is he his son?" The divine comment upon that questioning is this, "And no man was able to answer him a word, neither durst any man from that day forth ask him any more questions." What a wonderful testimony that scene is of the power of the Word of God, and what a demonstration that the last court of appeal is the Bible. There is no arguing about it: it is the constitution of God's kingdom, and no amendment can be added to it.

THE INSPIRATION OF THE PSALMS

Thus, first of all, we learn that David wrote this Psalm by the Holy Spirit. That brings up another question which one of our listeners raised, as to whether all of those Psalms are inspired. Indeed they are. So is the entire Book, for all Scripture is given by inspiration of God; not just some, but all Scripture. These Psalms are not mere poetry. They are inspired revelations from God. Here is a Psalm where David writing by the Holy Spirit, has recorded for us one of the many interesting dialogues that are found in the Psalms, where the several members of the Godhead converse. Thus, when the Psalm opens, "The LORD said unto my Lord, Sit thou at my right hand, until I make thine enemies thy footstool" David recorded what the Holy Spirit heard the eternal God say unto His Son; and David said concerning His Son, that He was Adonai—my Lord. One member of the Godhead, therefore directs His word to the other member, saying, "Sit thou at my right hand, until I make thine enemies thy footstool."

That brings us to another passage of Scripture, for we learn from the New Testament letter to the Hebrews that this statement was never made concerning an angel, but it was made concerning our Lord Jesus Christ, and it was made to Him upon His resurrection from the dead. Let me take you to the 10th chapter of the book of Hebrews, where the Holy Spirit takes several quotations from the Psalms, and applies them to the Lord Jesus Christ. In the 10th verse of that chapter we observe that ". . . we are sanctified through the offering of the body of Jesus Christ once for all." Then, we learn that "every priest standeth daily ministering and offering oftentimes the same sacrifices, which can never take away sins . . ." This, of course, refers to the ritualism of Moses and the daily Levitical offerings. The fact that they were repeated is clear indication that these offerings could never take away sins. In the 12th verse of this letter to the Hebrews, the Holy Spirit contrasts the sacrifices offered in the temple with the one sacrifice of Christ upon the cross, by saying, "But this man (that is, Jesus Christ), after he had offered one sacrifice for sins *for ever*, sat down on the right hand of God; from henceforth expecting till his enemies be made his footstool." Thus, our Lord Jesus expects God the Father to literally fulfill the promise that the Father gave to Him, which is recorded in this 110th Psalm. It is, therefore, a Messianic Psalm. It concerns the Lord Jesus Christ.

THE TWO VIEWS OF THE OLD TESTAMENT

Some people cannot understand how a Psalm can concern Christ and still be encumbered with imprecations. It appears foreign to them to have judgments proceed from His lips. They cannot reconcile such a presentation of Christ with that which they have come to know about Him from the four Gospels.

How I wish I could make each see clearly that the Old Testament is occupied with two comings of the Messiah. There are two lines of prediction. They are the extreme opposite of each other. They became a source of difficulty, not only to the writers who recorded them, but to the godly, and the scribes and Pharisees, who studied them. One line speaks of His humiliation, of His suffering, of the beauty of His character as a servant of the Lord, binding the brokenhearted, preaching peace to captives, not even breaking a bruised reed nor quenching a smoking flax. Alongside of that type of prediction are the references concerning His majesty, His glorious reign in power, how He would subdue His enemies and rule over them with a rod of iron, and of the increase of His government, of which there would be no end, to order and establish it.

Because of these two diverse lines of reference to the Messiah, the rabbis invariably spiritualized His sacrificial death and His coming in weakness. They believed only that He would come in power and great glory and majesty. Therefore, when our Lord came, they were unable to understand Him. They could not reconcile Him with their traditions of the Messiah. Of course, if they had only had their Bibles open and looked at these passages, and then compared them to our Lord Jesus, they would have found that He fulfilled them perfectly and literally.

But, what is happening today? There are great numbers of people in Christendom who believe in the humiliation of Christ, and in the sacrificial death of Christ, solely because they are *facts of history*—not because they were prophecies. That group does not believe that our Lord is coming in great power and glory, and that He will exercise judgment and will rule with a rod of iron and trample His enemies underfoot. They think these things are spiritually and refer to the triumphs of the church, and ought not to be taken literally concerning Christ Himself. However, just as definitely as our Lord Jesus Christ had His garments parted from him, and just as surely as His whole body was a mass of blood as He hung upon the cross bearing the judgment due sin, so, literally and definitely, will our Lord Jesus some day fulfill the predictions made concerning His glorious reign.

Let me quote a passage from the Old Testament, which describes His coming in glory and vengeance. I take you to the 63rd chapter of Isaiah, where a voice is heard crying, as he observes the returning, conquering hero, "Who is this that cometh . . . his garments dyed in blood, with his apparel glorious, and traveling in the greatness of his strength?" The answer comes, "I that speak in righteousness, mighty to save." Then the further question is asked, "Wherefore art thou red in thine apparel, and thy garments like him that treadeth in the winepress?" And the answer is given, "I have trodden the winepress alone; and of the people there was none with me: for I will tread them in *mine anger,* and trample them in my *fury;* and their blood shall be *sprinkled upon my garments,* and I will stain all my raiment. For the day of vengeance is in mine heart, and the year of my redeemed is come." Continuing, He declares, "I will tread down the people in mine anger, and make them drunk in my fury, and I will bring down their strength to the earth." Shocking words, aren't they? Do you know that there are a multitude of Christians who are horrified when someone suggests that these words will proceed out of the mouth of our Lord Jesus Christ? They have been accustomed to think of Him as the lowly Nazarene. They think only of His coming in weakness. While that was true concerning His first coming, it will never be so when He takes up the rulership of this world and reigns in the midst of His enemies. No man will then pluck the hairs from His face nor smite His cheek.

But let us get back to our Psalm. In our English translation it is difficult for us to visualize the picture, when we read, "The LORD said unto my Lord, Sit thou at my right hand, until I make thine enemies thy footstool." This seems a strange contradiction of terms, but if we had a Hebrew Bible we would observe that it reads, "Jehovah said unto Adonai," which might be translated, "The LORD said unto my Master." But when did He say this?

Let me take you to the cross. What a scene! Yet the angels had to view it, and the eternal God, Jehovah Himself, had to see it. There was our Lord hanging upon the cross. A horrible sight! His form was so terribly distorted, one found it difficult to recognize it as that of a man. At the foot of the cross were some Roman soldiers, selfish and grasping. They gambled for the only possessions He had in the world—His own garments. A little farther the rulers of Israel are found mocking Him, by inviting Him to come down and demonstrate that He is the Christ. By His side was a rebel, paying for his crime, who taunted Him also, declaring, "If thou be the Christ, save thyself and us." Then there was the crowd that came to enjoy a Roman holiday, absolutely indifferent to the sufferings of the Christ. On the outskirts of the crowd were His disciples, broken and disappointed; every one of them had forsaken Him. The Father looked on the scene in silence at the beginning. Suddenly it appeared as if nature expressed antagonism against Christ. Then the Father exacted from Him the penalty of sin, *but* God raised Him from the dead, and said to Him, "Sit thou at my right hand, *until* I make thine enemies thy footstool." Note that His present throne is not a permanent one. Our Lord is exalted now, for He is the risen Lord in the glory. He is the imperial Prince of glory, but His is but a temporary throne, *until* the Father makes His enemies His footstool. There is a time element about His presence in the heavens now. It is only until His Father shall make His enemies His footstool. I know of no expression which so definitely indicates subjection, as when the Father said to His Son, "I (will) make thine enemies thy *footstool*." This is just as much a part of the gospel as the facts of our Lord Jesus Christ's death and it needs to be emphasized in our preaching today. Paul the apostle did so, as you would observe were you to read his address on Mars' hill.

"THE FOOLISHNESS OF PREACHING"

That reminds me of something. Did you note the publicity which a certain New York rector received because he advocated a moratorium on preaching? I think he suggested a period of two years. Of course, if he had reference to the pseudo-economic and social propaganda which is being preached from many of the pulpits of our land, I am with him one hundred per cent, but if he referred to the gospel of our Lord Jesus Christ, I would remind the distinguished cleric that, even though I am a layman without theological training, it is written, "For after that in the wisdom of God the world by wisdom knew not God, it pleased God by the foolishness of preaching to save them that believe." If you prefer a more literal translation of the Greek text, it would be, "it pleased God by the foolishness of the thing preached to save them that believe." That foolish thing is the cross of Jesus Christ. It is a scandal to some, and foolishness to others; but it is the wisdom of God and the power of God to them that believe.

The Greek word used by the Apostle Paul and translated *foolishness* also means silliness and absurdity. In other words, the gospel to the natural man is silly; it is absurd and foolish. Absurd, yes; it is absurd to believe that the death of one man atones for the sin of the whole world and that an individual does not have to do a single thing to merit salvation, but to receive the death of that one man. Yes, that does sound absurd, but, when you understand that the Man who died was God manifest in the flesh, and when you come to realize that God knows the human heart better than anyone else, and that He found and still finds it a cesspool of iniquity, then you can understand that the gospel is not only the power of God, but it is the expression of His divine wisdom.

Let me give one more comment on the 110th Psalm, before we leave it. It is quite apparent that we have not been able to cover it with any degree of thoroughness, so that we shall devote another meditation to it.

Notice verse 2, where we read, "The LORD shall send the rod of thy strength out of Zion: rule thou in the midst of thine enemies." Here is one more passage that states the place from which our Lord shall reign. I am aware that there are many people who assume, that as Zion is the city of God, it is heaven. You know that song:

> "We're marching to Zion,
> Beautiful, beautiful Zion;
> We're marching upward to Zion,
> The beautiful city of God."

The writer of that hymn assumed that Zion was heaven, but Zion is Jerusalem, the city of the great King. Out of Zion, out of Jerusalem, shall Jehovah send the rod of His strength, and He shall commission His Son to rule in the midst of His enemies.

In the midts of a world which is so disturbed that is is well-nigh impossible for a European dictator or ruler to go to sleep for fear his kingdom will be gone when he awakens, it is well for us to become acquainted with what the Bible has to say about the future. Mussolini may think that Rome will become the center of the universe, Stalin undoubtedly hopes that Moscow will become the center, and, of course, Herr Hitler thinks he should have some say, but there is only one place from which God will reign, and that is Jerusalem. From the land of Palestine will come forth the rod of His strength. Once again the East will hold sway over the nations of the earth. That is a big subject, and I do not intend to discuss it now, but I simply wish to impress upon our minds that it is the man who knows his Bible who undoubtedly is the best informed man as to the outcome of this terrific strife for power that is being waged in our day. Man may not be willing to acknowledge it, but it is becoming increasing apparent that, as far as government in the world is concerned, man is an abject, pitiful failure.

But God has a man, the Man, Christ Jesus; He is the answer to the world's need; but, specifically, now He is the answer to the need of the human heart. If you do not know the peace of God, nor the joy of the forgiveness of sin, you will find, upon receiving Christ as your Lord, that He gives peace, offers pardon, and completely satisfies the heart of man.

PSALM ONE HUNDRED TEN—PART TWO

THE ONLY MEDIATOR THAT CAN PRACTISE AT HEAVEN'S THRONE

IN our previous meditation I mentioned that the 110th Psalm is one of the great Messianic Psalms, and that it is quoted more frequently in the New Testament than any other; even though it is but a brief Psalm of seven verses. In our first meditation we considered the message contained in the opening verse, where it is recorded, "The LORD said unto my Lord, Sit thou at my right hand, until I make thine enemies thy footstool." We found that this was the Father's testimony to His Son and that it was given upon His resurrection from the dead, when He was exalted to the right hand of God.

There is today in the heavens a man, seated at the right hand of the throne of the Almighty. It is well to bear that in mind in any consideration of life. Whether it be our own lives, individually, or as members of the human race, we ought to remember that He is God's anointed—the chosen Man. He is the *Man* Christ Jesus. He is the God-Man. The Bible declares that there is only "one mediator between God and men, the man Christ Jesus . . ." He is the only approach unto God. We cannot come to God apart from Him. That makes the message of Christianity a narrow message, to be true, but the most important message that any creature could ever hear. If the Bible is true in this statement that there is only one mediator, and that one the man Christ Jesus, then there *is* no other mediator, and anyone trusting any other mediator is making the most disastrous mistake a human being can ever make.

THE COMING KING AND HIS PEOPLE

Again, in our contemplation of this verse we found that our Lord Jesus has been given a temporary throne and that some day He shall relinquish that throne and take possession of His own throne, and that will take place when His enemies shall be made His footstool. In that connection there is a very interesting passage in the last book of the Bible, The Revelation, which passage has always been a source of pleasure to me, for it contains a title of our Lord Jesus Christ which is intensely significant. In the 5th verse of the 1st chapter, which contains part of the salutation, we find this statement, "And from Jesus Christ, who is the faithful witness . . ." Thus, the book of The Revelation comes not only from God the Father, but from the Lord Jesus Christ as well. Among the titles given to Him in that passage are: "*the faithful witness,*" "*the first begotten of the dead,*" "*the prince of the kings of the earth.*" God has never had a more faithful witness to Himself than His own Son, Jesus Christ our Lord. He is the first begotten of the dead. Of course, others were raised before Him; in fact, He raised them from the dead, but they died afterwards. He is the firstfruits of the resurrection. Death has no more claim upon Him. But notice that He also has the title "the prince of the kings of the earth." Kings are not popular today, but we have a brand new type of kings. We call them dictators. However, what goes for kings is true of dictators. The prince is the heir apparent to the king's throne. Frankly, I would hate to be a king with the consciousness that my eldest son, the prince, is simply waiting around for my death or for my abdication so that he may become king in my stead.

Isn't that just the attitude of the prince? There is nothing very much else he can do.

Now then, our Lord Jesus is called "the prince of the kings of the earth." Our Lord, therefore, is the heir apparent to every throne of every king in this world. That is God's statement. How I wish I could ring it into the ears of all the dictators in this world, and remind them that while they may think they have great power, they are mere puny humans in the sight of God, and the throne they occupy will one day be occupied by our Lord and Saviour Jesus Christ. Some day He will take His possession and rule as the King of kings and Lord of lords. When He does, He shall rule in the midst of His enemies, as we learn from the 2nd verse of the 110th Psalm. Won't that be pleasant for the enemies of our Lord!

Now look at verse 3, where it is written, "Thy people shall be willing in the day of thy power, in the beauties of holiness from the womb of the morning: thou hast the dew of thy youth." Of course, this is picturesque language, but one can see a marvelous revelation in it. Here is a people, not willing at one time, but now willing. They freely offer themselves in the day of His power, and, what is more, their devotion will be expressed in holiness, and with the holiness they will enjoy the fellowship of the exalted Christ who possesses the dew of youth.

Commencing with verse 4 we are introduced to another situation:

> "The LORD hath sworn, and will not repent, Thou art a priest for ever after the order of Melchizedek.
>
> "The Lord at thy right hand shall strike through kings in the day of his wrath.
>
> "He shall judge among the heathen, he shall fill the places with the dead bodies; he shall wound the heads over many countries.
>
> "He shall drink of the brook in the way: therefore shall he lift up the head."

Isn't that an interesting statement—"The LORD hath sworn, and will not repent . . ." That is very strong language. It is such an astounding statement that it is not surprising that the Holy Spirit has referred to it several times in the New Testament. In the 5th chapter of the letter to the Hebrews, we read:

> "For every high priest taken from among men is ordained for men in things pertaining to God, that he may offer both gifts and sacrifices for sins;

"Who can have compassion on the ignorant, and on them that are out of the way; for that he himself also is compassed with infirmity.

"And by reason hereof he ought, as for the people, so also for himself, to offer for sins.

"And no man taketh this honour unto himself, but he that is called of God, as was Aaron.

"So also Christ glorified not himself to be made an high priest; but he that said unto him, Thou art my Son, to day have I begotten thee.

"As he saith also in another place, Thou art a priest for ever after the order of Melchisedec."

Again, in verse 10 of the same chapter we read concerning Christ, ". . . Called of God an high priest after the order of Melchisedec." And in the 7th chapter of Hebrews we read the following concerning this man Melchisedec. He is called "king of Salem, priest of the most high God . . ." He met Abraham returning from the slaughter of the kings, and blessed him. Abraham in turn gave him one-tenth of all he possessed. Melchisedec, we are told, "without father, without mother, without descent, having neither beginning of days, nor end of life; but made like unto the Son of God; abideth a priest continually." Some have assumed that Melchisedec was the Son of God, but the Bible says he was "made like unto the Son of God . . ." He was a priest-king. He was king of righteousness, king of peace, a priest of the most high God. Abraham gave him one-tenth of all he possessed. Thus, the Holy Spirit argues in the 7th chapter, "consider how great this man was, unto whom even the patriarch Abraham gave the tenth of the spoils." For "verily they that are of the sons of Levi, who receive the office of the priesthood, have a commandment to take tithes of the people according to the law, that is, of their brethren, though they come out of the loins of Abraham . . ." Here was one who was not counted from them, and who received tithes from Abraham, who, in turn, is blessed of him, and the Scripture says, "And without all contradiction the less is blessed of the better."

Conscience and Atonement

What does all this mean, anyway? Just this. There is born in the breast of every man that thing we call conscience. The Hottentot possesses it, the primitive African gives evidence of having it; cultured or uncultured, all have this thing we call conscience. Conscience acts as God's watchdog.

When it is functioning properly it accuses the individual of sin. Conscience does one of two things: it either accuses or excuses. If conscience has become seared by habitual sin in the individual, it frequently excuses rather than accuses; but when conscience performs normally it always accuses him. You know what I mean. Let me illustrate. You are driving along the road, an open road, and even the air seems to fill you with exhilaration. There is hardly anyone on the road and you step on the gas, and you take a look at the speedometer and it registers 60, 65, yes, even 70 miles per hour. You go along merrily, until suddenly you look up in your mirror and you see a police officer trailing behind. Just as soon as you see that officer, it conveys a message to your conscience and you know you have violated the speed laws.

Conscience sometimes drives some people to suicide. Conscience is God's policeman. May I be very frank? Let conscience have its good work. You cannot run away from it. You may think you can, but, in addition to that policeman in your own heart, there is a recording station in the heavens which records your deeds in the books of heaven, and there is not a thing you can do to blot them out, except one thing I will tell you of in a minute.

Perhaps you have heard of the motorist who was driving his automobile through an intersection of the city and deliberately passed a red light. He heard a familiar whistle and the order, "Pull up to the side." The police officer parked his motorcycle with much deliberation, then walked over to the bewildered motorist and slowly placing one foot on the running board and one elbow on the door of the car, and looking up at the confused motorist said, in an Irish brogue, "What's the matter, didn't you see the light?" The motorist responded, "Yes, but I did not see you." That is like a lot of people we know. They think they can get away with it, but it is impossible. Sin is high treason against heaven, and you must face that problem of sin.

There is also born into the breast of every individual something else that no other creature under the sun possesses. It is more than the consciousness that we have violated the laws of God, it is the fact that we know atonement must be made and that someone must intercede for us. We can go to the darkest corners of the earth; we can go to the most primitive and savage people in the world, and we will find that consciousness in the breast of every individual. The result is that witchcraft, priestcraft, and other vicious things and systems have been invented to appease the conscience. The most despicable thing in this world is priestcraft, but the most wonderful thing is priesthood. There is as much difference between the two as day and night.

We need a Priest; we need an Intercessor. When our Lord Jesus Christ died on the cross and put away sin by the sacrifice of Himself, God said to His Son, I have sworn, and will not repent, "Thou art a priest for ever after the order of Melchizedek." Our Lord Jesus Christ is now in the heavens, and while He is waiting until His enemies are made His footstool, He is not idle. He is doing the work of a priest.

"WHILE WE WERE YET SINNERS . . ."

The other day I read of an incident which took place during the Revolutionary War. A minister of the gospel, by the name of Peter Miller, labored in Pennsylvania. He had a neighbor who was constantly a source of annoyance and who did everything in his power to hinder the ministry of Peter Miller. One day Miller learned that his neighbor had gotten into difficulties with the Constitutional Army. He had been tried for high treason and found guilty. Immediately Miller went by foot a distance of twenty miles to intercede for his neighbor with General Washington. He got his interview and presented his plea. Washington turned and said, "Sir, I am afraid there isn't a thing I can do for your friend. The case was clear and he was guilty." "But," said Miller, "I beg your pardon, General, he isn't my friend. He is my worst enemy." Washington looked at Miller in amazement. "He is your enemy and you come this distance to intercede for him? That puts a different light on the subject." Then, after listening a while longer, he wrote out a pardon and handed it to Miller. The preacher walked as fast as his feet could carry him for another fifteen miles, to the place where the execution was to take place. He saw that the scaffold was erected and the crowd was around it. Dashing through the mob, his neighbor, about to be hung, spied him and railed at him, "You scoundrel, you came all the way to this place in order to make my death worse, if possible." But Miller handed the pardon to the officer, who was about to hang him, who in turn, delivered it to his enemy. That, in a measure, is what our Lord has done for us. We were enemies of God. The Bible says, ". . . when we were enemies, we were reconciled to God by the death of his Son . . ." Not only did He die for us, but He is ever interceding for us. No child of God can ever be lost as long as his High Priest lives.

PSALM ONE HUNDRED ELEVEN

THE MAJESTIC PERSON OF GOD

THE 111th Psalm and the two following begin with the expression "Praise ye the LORD." The word in the Hebrew, in all three cases, is the same word, and literally means *hallelujah;* thus this Psalm begins a trinity of hallelujah Psalms, and, as we might expect, each contains reasons for an outburst of praise on the part of God's people.

This particular Psalm is devoted to a description of the character of God. Well might we stop and contemplate some of the things that are mentioned herein concerning God. May we read the Psalm at this time:

"Praise ye the LORD. I will praise the LORD with my whole heart, in the assembly of the upright, and in the congregation.

"The works of the LORD are great, sought out of all them that have pleasure therein.

"His work is honourable and glorious: and his righteousness endureth for ever.

"He hath made his wonderful works to be remembered: the LORD is gracious and full of compassion.

"He hath given meat unto them that fear him: he will ever be mindful of his covenant.

"He hath shewed his people the power of his works, that he may give them the heritage of the heathen.

"The works of his hands are verity and judgment; all his commandments are sure.

"They stand fast for ever and ever, and are done in truth and uprightness.

"He sent redemption unto his people: he hath commanded his covenant for ever: holy and reverend is his name.

"The fear of the LORD is the beginning of wisdom: a good understanding have all they that do his commandments: his praise endureth for ever."

GOD, AND THE HUMAN INTELLECT

As this 111th Psalm is a declaration of the majesty and the glory of the person of God, it offers an opportunity for the heart and the mind to contemplate God. The mind of man cannot possibly be devoted to a greater or a more majestic theme. For the individual who has embraced Jesus Christ as his or her Saviour, no more delightful occupation can be imagined;

but neither can it be denied that there are vast multitudes of people to whom a contemplation of God brings terror and distress to the heart and mind. They are much like the group of whom the Apostle Paul wrote in his letter to the Romans, that, as they did not like to retain God in their knowledge, God gave them over to a reprobate mind.

It is not in our province to enter into a dissertation on the mind of man, except to say that when God created man, He created him in His own image and likeness. He therefore gave that man a wonderful mind and intellect; so wonderful a mind that, when God caused the animals to pass before Adam, he named each one of them and the name Adam ascribed to the animals has come down from that day to this. But not only was that mind able to comprehend the created beings on the earth, but it was so constructed and constituted that it could also undertake a contemplation of God.

But when man sinned he lost the consciousness of God in his soul; he lost the desire of fellowship with God; in fact, his every motive seemed bent on trying to get away from God, if that were at all possible. Thus, in the fall of man, his entire being became involved in sin and suffered in consequence. The mind of man became dulled by sin and unbelief and, if anything, through the long period of human history the intellect became more dulled and the soul more blind, so that, in fact, man refused to retain God in his knowledge. The extent of that decline is well expressed in the Scriptures, where we read that ". . . the natural man receiveth not the things of the Spirit of God: for they are foolishness unto him: neither can he know them, because they are spiritually discerned."

Who of us are not acquainted with men and women who seem to have keenness of perception and an active mind in almost every range of human intellect, but whose brain is befuddled when it comes to any knowledge of God or of spiritual things. There is something lacking; there is something that does not function. That which is lacking is supplied when the individual receives Christ as his or her Saviour, since among the gifts that such a one receives is the "mind of Christ." What a wonderful phrase that is, "the mind of Christ." Think of it, "the mind of Christ!" The mere mention of the fact seems to overwhelm one. A great number of people think that faith is a matter of the heart, exclusively; that it is a matter of maudlin sentiment and that it is not based on fact or reason. While it is true that man believes in his heart, nevertheless, much Scripture is devoted to the subject of man's mind and reason. Thus a spiritual mind desires to contemplate the person of God; and to such a one it is the most natural thing to find the word *hallelujah* or the phrase "Praise ye the LORD" right at the beginning of this Psalm, with the further comment, "I will praise the LORD with my whole heart, in the assembly of the upright, and in the congregation." Notice, it takes a whole heart to do that.

There is one thing that should be noted about the expression, "I will praise the LORD with my whole heart, in the assembly of the upright, and in the congregation" in that it seems to open wide the door for the expression of praise upon the part of the individual members of the congregation, as they gather for worship and praise of the Lord. In most churches the people have very little to say; it is the minister who does all the talking and now some congregations are not even permitted to sing, as they have choirs and special singers to do that for them. All that is expected of such congregations is that they sit in dull silence, and yet that same congregation will rise to its feet and read responsively such a Psalm as this 111th Psalm. I wonder, sometimes, if we haven't made a mistake in limiting the work of the Holy Spirit to just one man in the congregation, who gets paid for doing the speaking. I do not mean to say that a man hasn't any right to get paid; the Bible is clear that ". . . the labourer is worthy of his hire" and that ". . . they that preach the gospel shall live of the gospel" but, in a praising congregation, we invariably find a powerful demonstration of the Holy Spirit's presence. In that kind of congregation even the preacher finds it easier to expound the Word of God and to preach the gospel of Jesus Christ.

Recently I heard of a humorous incident which took place in the life of a young minister who wrote to a more experienced servant of God asking some advice regarding the ministry. He received the following reply, "Dig deep, keep the fences tight, and tie up the old bull." It so happened that the reply was intended for a young farmer, who had also asked for advice and the answers were put into the wrong envelopes! Yet the advice given the preacher may not have been altogether inappropriate. Well, so much for who should praise the Lord in the congregation of the people.

CHRIST, THE CROSS, AND GOD

Now let us note the contents of the 2nd and 3rd verses, where we read: "The works of the LORD are great, sought out of all them that have pleasure therein. His work is honourable and glorious: and his righteousness endureth for ever." I wonder if there isn't a distinction between the works of the Lord in verse 2 and the work of the Lord in verse 3. There is a specific work that God has accomplished which is distinct from the many other manifestations of His power, and that one work is the atonement which He wrought on Calvary in the person of His Son. It is my judgment that it was of that work of which the Psalmist was writing, when he said, "His work is honourable and glorious: and his righteousness endureth for ever." Concerning that work, the Psalmist said it was honorable and glorious. Does it seem strange that he should use the adjective *honorable* concerning the work of Christ on the cross? The cross of Christ, to this very day, is an accursed thing to multitudes of people, and the idea of atonement by blood is scoffed at and ridiculed by many so-called cultured people as absolutely offensive to their esthetic tastes. Yet the Bible declares, concerning the death of Jesus Christ, that, as far as God the Father is concerned, it was becoming to God ". . . in bringing many sons unto glory, to make the captain of their salvation perfect through sufferings." Yes, the work of God at Calvary was an honorable one, as well as glorious, and the righteousness with which He clothes the believing sinner as a result of Christ's death "endureth for ever" as the Psalmist declared.

The character of God is revealed in the manifestations of His dealings; so we read, ". . . the LORD is gracious and full of compassion. He hath given meat unto them that fear him: he will ever be mindful of his covenant." Everything that is written about God in this 111th Psalm fits perfectly into the life and ministry of the Lord Jesus Christ and, thus, if we want to know the character of God, it is necessary to contemplate the person of Jesus Christ. Take for example the two factors contained in the 4th verse. First, the Lord is gracious, and then He is full of compassion. Were we to examine the four Gospels, we would see how wonderfully this fits into the life of Christ. We read about His viewpoint of humanity as He looks over the multitude, "he was moved with compassion on them, because they fainted, and were scattered abroad, as sheep having no shepherd." Then again we see Him in the synagogue at Nazareth, where He expounded the Scriptures to His own neighbors. The divine comment is given in Luke 4:22, "And all bare him witness, and wondered at the gracious words which proceeded out of his mouth."

Now take the 5th verse of the 111th Psalm, "He hath given meat unto them that fear him . . ." Remember how the Lord fed the five thousand with five barley loaves and two small fishes, and how a goodly number of them followed Him the next day, apparently trying to convey the impression that they were interested in Him. But our Lord said, "Ye seek me, not because ye saw the miracles, but because ye did eat of the loaves, and were filled. Labour not for the meat which perisheth, but for that meat which endureth unto everlasting life, which the Son of man shall give unto you: for him hath God sealed." Thus, if we wish a revelation of God, we will find it in the person of Jesus Christ.

THE BEGINNING OF WISDOM

Bringing our meditation to a close, I want to spend a moment on the last verse of this Psalm, where we read, "The fear of the LORD is the beginning of wisdom: a good understanding have all they that do his commandments: his praise endureth for ever." Observe that the fear of the Lord is the *beginning* of wisdom. Not mere understanding of the multiplication table, not simply appreciation of science, nor a familiarity with the rules of grammar, but the fear of the Lord is the beginning of wisdom. The more brilliant a man becomes and the more of an authority he gets to be in any sphere of learning, if that individual has never learned the fear of the Lord he has not even begun to know wisdom. The very first lesson in wisdom, the Bible says, is the fear of the Lord. We should not read into the word *fear* something that God never intended to convey. Fear does not mean trembling in His presence, nor hiding one's self from Him, as if to draw back or to shun Him. Invariably, when the Bible speaks of the fear of the Lord, it speaks both of the childlike trust a babe reveals while in the arms of its mother and the hesitancy of a loving child to do anything contrary to that love. The fear of the Lord is trusting Him, loving Him, and committing our whole being to His control.

PSALM ONE HUNDRED TWELVE

ANTHROPOLOGY FROM GOD'S VIEWPOINT

ANY contemplation of God on the part of the believing mind and heart is a definite cause for a word of praise and thanksgiving to God. The 112th Psalm, which we are to consider, centers around the ..ian that feareth the Lord and delighteth greatly in His commandments. Thus, while the first of the three Hallelujah Psalms (111, 112, 113) concerns God, the second is centered in man. All agree that man is also an interesting subject.

Now let us read the Psalm:

> "Praise ye the LORD. Blessed is the man that feareth the LORD, that delighteth greatly in his commandments.
>
> "His seed shall be mighty upon earth: the generation of the upright shall be blessed.
>
> "Wealth and riches shall be in his house: and his righteousness endureth for ever.
>
> "Unto the upright there ariseth light in the darkness: he is gracious, and full of compassion, and righteous.
>
> "A good man sheweth favour, and lendeth: he will guide his affairs with discretion.
>
> "Surely he shall not be moved for ever: the righteous shall be in everlasting remembrance.
>
> "He shall not be afraid of evil tidings: his heart is fixed, trusting in the LORD.
>
> "His heart is established, he shall not be afraid, until he see his desire upon his enemies.
>
> "He hath dispersed, he hath given to the poor; his righteousness endureth for ever; his horn shall be exalted with honour.
>
> "The wicked shall see it, and be grieved; he shall gnash with his teeth, and melt away: the desire of the wicked shall perish."

It is easy to recognize that this Psalm is concerned with man; or more specifically with one type of man, although both types are mentioned in the Psalm. It surprises some to know that there are two types of men, for they think that all men are born equal and that, therefore, all men are one. I am not so sure that all men are even born equal; but I am absolutely sure that God speaks of two types of men. One type, called blessed, are those who fear the Lord; the other type, called wicked, are those who do not fear God. In every part of the Bible we distinctly find these two types of men. Some times the one is called the seed of faith and the other the seed of the flesh; at times the one is called righteous and the other unrighteous; again, the one is spoken of as the believer and the other as the unbeliever; on still other occasions the Bible speaks of the justified and the condemned; and finally there are those who are called saved, while the others are lost. A man finds himself in one or the other of the two groups. Either he is in one camp or the other; he cannot be on the fence, having one foot in saved territory and the other in the abyss of the lost while his head and heart swing between the two. Man is either justified or condemned; saved or lost. I trust I have made that clear, but let me press the subject. Where do *you* stand? To which group do *you* belong?

This 112th Psalm declares that the man who feareth the Lord is blessed. Happy, therefore, is the man who feareth the Lord; who delighteth greatly in His commandments. That's the first thing the Psalmist said about the believing man—that the man who loves God is happy. He is in possession of a deep, abiding, inward joy which is not subject to fluctuations due to varied experiences of life. Human happiness is declared to be changeable; now you have it and now you don't. The philosophy of this world is best expressed in that familiar phrase in the Constitution which guarantees to every American "the pursuit of happiness." The Constitution does not *guarantee* happiness to *any* American citizen, but it assures to every citizen the right to the *pursuit* of happiness. A pursuit is simply a race; and what an elusive thing is this matter called happiness, after which multitudes of people are running. Only in the Bible is a man assured of the possession of happiness. It declares that happiness comes as a direct result of fearing the Lord and delighting in His commandments.

THE BLESSINGS OF A BLESSED MAN

Now notice a few other things the Psalmist said concerning this happy man. In verse 3 we read that "Wealth and riches shall be in his house: and his righteousness endureth for ever." But I can hear someone say, Why, there's so-and-so, he is a Christian, but certainly wealth and riches do not dwell in his house. Why, he is so close to the poorhouse as to probably be its next guest. He surely hasn't much of this world's goods. May I assure you that, in the house of any man who fears the Lord and delighteth in His commandments, wealth and riches dwell which are infinitely more valuable and more tangible and certainly more stable than the riches and wealth that seem to dwell in the house of the worldly rich. I think we have all experienced, during the past few years, how absolutely unstable are the so-called riches which express themselves in money or goods or stocks or bonds. One may be poor so far as this world's goods are concerned, and yet wealth and riches dwell in his house. Someone put it pointedly, when he said, "You cannot starve a man who is feeding on God's promises."

But, again, the Psalmist said, concerning the man who fears the Lord, that there arises a light in the darkness and He is gracious and full of compassion. Observe that to the man who fears God there is no exemption from darkness. There are some people who think that when a man embraces

Christianity, his life should become a bed of roses; that such a one will never have any difficulties and that everything will be smooth and even. The truth of the matter is, that there enter into such a life all the varied experiences that are common to all men, plus still greater difficulties, because the Devil realizes that this man is his enemy. But what distinguishes a Christian from a non-Christian is that, in the hours of darkness and disappointment, there is a wonderful light in the midst of the darkness. That light is the effulgence of the presence of the One who said, "I will never leave thee, nor forsake thee." What a marked difference His presence makes.

Observe that God says further, concerning the man who trusts in the Lord, "Surely he shall not be moved for ever: the righteous shall be in everlasting remembrance." Surely he shall not be moved forever. You will observe that it does not read that he won't be moved for a short time, but he will not be *moved forever*. Satan may tempt him and play havoc with him for a time; he may even sift him like wheat, as he did Peter, but he cannot move that man *forever*. But another thing is said concerning the man who fears the Lord, which I believe is the heart of this Psalm. In verse 7 we read, "He shall not be afraid of evil tidings: his heart is fixed, trusting in the LORD."

Recently I read an interesting statement from the pen of that mighty man of God, who died a short time ago, Dr. F. B. Meyer. He said that there could not be evil tidings to the soul which has fixed its trust in the Lord, for every messenger that comes into his presence with a dispatch, brings tidings of what has been permitted or done by our Father. No tidings can be evil to him whose heart is fixed, trusting in the Lord. What makes a man unmovable by evil tidings? Is it because he is indifferent to the experiences of life? No, indeed, it is because his heart is fixed, trusting in the Lord. I love the further words of Dr. Meyer when he said that the man who trusts God *knows* that all things must be working for good in his behalf, for even "in the hieroglyphics, he detects his Father's handwriting; in the mysterious figure standing on the shore, veiled in morning mist, he beholds the Lord who died for him." Well did someone say, concerning these things, that one may not always understand, but he can always trust. Was it not Job who declared, "Though he slay me, yet will I trust in him . . ." Remember, men of one idea are irresistible; so, a man whose whole motive of life is to trust God is like Gibraltar, you cannot move him.

THE OTHER MAN

But there is another man spoken of in this Psalm. He is called an enemy of the righteous and is referred to as "the wicked" one. Concerning him it is said, ". . . he shall gnash with his teeth, and melt away: and the desire of the wicked shall perish." There are two classes of people in this world and only two. In the first group are those who believe on the Lord Jesus Christ, and who, thereby, are saved; in the second group are those who do not believe on the Lord Jesus Christ, and who, thereby, are damned. That's a broad statement. I would not dare make it—but the Bible declares it. What is more, it's not our business to defend it, nor to apologize for it, nor to soften its evident meaning. It is our business to present it; to preach it so clearly that the reaction will be the extreme opposite of what took place in King's Chapel, as related by that eminent Harvard Professor of Philosophy, Dr. George Santayana, in his latest book, "The Last Puritan." Speaking of the services in King's Chapel, Santayana wrote, "The music was classical and soothing; the service High Church Unitarian, with nothing in it either to discourage a believer or to annoy an unbeliever . . . The sermon was sure to be pleasantly congratulatory and pleasantly short . . . An Easter sermon on the Resurrection might prudently avoid all mention of Christ or the Trump of doom startling the dead. Instead, the preacher might blandly describe the resurrection of Nature in the Spring, the resurrection of science in the modern world, and the resurrection of heroic freedom in the American Character."

The subtle sarcasm in Santayana's words is not overdrawn, there are many "King's Chapels" in this day. It was our Lord who said, ". . . he that believeth not is condemned already, because he hath not believed in the name of the only begotten Son of God." Our Lord told Nicodemus, one of the most cultured men of his day "Except a man be born again, he cannot see the kingdom of God." Of course, Nicodemus was bewildered. To be born again was a new philosophy to him; how could a man be born when he was old?

Our Lord addressed this statement to the most cultured gentleman of his day, a man of wealth, a man of religious convictions, a man of social position, a man who had everything in this world but new birth. He could enter into the choicest places and into the finest society of his day, but he could not enter into the Kingdom of God. Why? Because he was not born again. How can a man be born again? By believing the testimony of the Word of God concerning Jesus Christ.

PSALM ONE HUNDRED THIRTEEN

"WHO IS LIKE UNTO THE LORD . . ."

OUR meditation is found in the 113th Psalm which is the last of a group of three Psalms each beginning with the word "Praise." While it is the last of that group, it also is the beginning of a series of Psalms, called by the Jews of all time, the "Hallel" Psalms, which were sung on the solemn feast days of the Hebrew people. This particular Psalm is not recited, however, on the Jewish "Day of Atonement." The doctors of Israel prefer not to use the 113th Psalm "on the Day of Atonement, because of its cheerful strains of praise which do not seem appropriate for the solemnity of the Day of Atonement." But on the three great feast days and at each new moon, this particular Psalm is sung or recited in the home of every orthodox Jew.

Observe, as we read the Psalm, that there is not a single note of sadness to be found in it.

> "Praise ye the LORD. Praise, O ye servants of the LORD, praise the name of the LORD.
>
> "Blessed be the name of the LORD from this time forth and for evermore.
>
> "From the rising of the sun unto the going down of the same the LORD'S name is to be praised.
>
> "The LORD is high above all nations, and his glory above the heavens.
>
> "Who is like unto the LORD our God, who dwelleth on high,
>
> "Who humbleth himself to behold the things that are in heaven, and in the earth!
>
> "He raiseth up the poor out of the dust, and lifteth the needy out of the dunghill;
>
> "That he may set him with princes, even with the princes of his people.
>
> "He maketh the barren woman to keep house, and to be a joyful mother of children. Praise ye the LORD."

When an individual has come to know God as He is revealed in Christ, there is a constant urge to fulfill the exhortation of the 113th Psalm, "Blessed be the name of the LORD from this time forth and for evermore. From the rising of the sun unto the going down of the same the LORD'S name is to be praised."

THE WORK OF GOD TO NEEDY SOULS

There are several interesting subjects in this Psalm. First, the glory of God; the majesty of God. Then, His exaltation high above the heavens. He is presented as "The Incomparable One" as the Psalmist raised the question, "Who is like unto the LORD our God, who dwelleth on high . . ." In addition to this exaltation and praise to the Creator, we get a revelation of His condescending grace, when He humbled Himself in order to behold things, not only in heaven, but on the earth. But we also discover why He humbled Himself, for we learn in verses 7 and 8 that, "He raiseth up the poor out of the dust, and lifteth the needy out of the dunghill; that he may set him with princes, even with the princes of his people." That's a transformation, isn't it? Here is a man who formerly was poor; who dwelt in the dust of the earth; the fact of the matter is, he found himself in a dunghill, a needy man; but now, because God humbled Himself, He has taken that poor and needy one, a dweller of the dunghill, and made him to be set with princes, even with the princes of His people.

A friend of mine, a Jewish gentleman, reminded me of the similarity between the Jewish words for feast and feet, stating that, in the Jewish prayer book, where these "Hallel" Psalms are found, mention is made of the feet of the Israelites as well as the feast days of Israel. The feet of the wandering Israelite seemed lighter, as he journeyed to Jerusalem to enjoy the feasts of Jehovah. Just so, the feet of the believer in this age, somehow, are lighter and the journey less arduous as he contemplates the fact that he is on his journey home to enjoy the presence of the Lord.

BARREN SOULS AND JOYFUL MOTHERS

I want also to call attention to a wonderful message which is conveyed in the closing verse of this Psalm, where we read, "He maketh the barren woman to keep house, and to be a joyful mother of children. Praise ye the LORD." I had lunch with a friend of mine, this past week. She is a maiden lady in her late seventies. She had just returned from spending a week with the matron of a poorhouse in one of the smaller villages in New York State. While there, she brought her usual cheer to the inmates of that institution, who are living out their closing days on earth in not too sumptuous surroundings. That woman's face just lit up with joy as she related the experiences of the week. I know there are multitudes whom God has

touched through the ministry of that handmaiden of His. She fits perfectly into the 9th verse of the 113th Psalm, where we read, "He maketh the barren woman to keep house, and to be a joyful mother of children . . ."
Despite the fact that certain women substitute poodle dogs for children, there is no doubt that the acme of a woman's life is reached when she has a babe in her arms. There is not a joy in the world, humanly speaking, comparable to the joy of a mother caring for her little babe. May I take this passage of Scripture and apply it to the spiritual realm, for there is no denying that many things that transpire in our lives find a counterpart in our spiritual relationships with God. Let me address a word directly to you who have received Christ as your Saviour. I refer again to the words which fell from the lips of the gentleman who led me to Christ. Said he, "You have now received one-half of the joy that God has in store for you. You will receive the other half when you lead your first soul to Christ." Have you ever questioned in your mind as to why God permits you to live on this earth after He has saved you by His grace? Why didn't He take you to heaven immediately? He wanted to give you the joy of having children, spiritually speaking. He wanted to give you the indescribable pleasure of leading a soul to Christ and applying the Word to others' hearts and lives in order that they may be cleansed and made instruments fit for the Master's use.
Dr. F. B. Meyer has written "God can make barren souls authors of life to thousands." The woman to whom I referred a moment ago has no children, humanly speaking, but what a host of children she has in the spiritual realm. But, mark you, in the spiritual realm "souls are only born to those who cannot live without them." I can hear someone say, particularly married folks, mothers and fathers: I haven't time. I have work in my own home which must be done. Yes, that is important, to be true, I would not gainsay it for a moment. But, until you have extended your family relationships so that they include others who have been led into the kingdom of God through your ministry, you do not know what it is to live a full Christian life. I again think of my friends, the Stams. I love to enter their home. I have rejoiced in its fellowship many years. The Stams are a big family, but neither the mother nor the father have been so occupied with their own as to exclude the poor and needy. Because they have been faithful to the poor and those in want who needed the gospel, their own home has been gloriously blessed, so that every member of it is devoting his or her life to making the gospel of Jesus Christ known.

If your life has been barren, God help you to plead with Him, just as Hannah pleaded with the Lord to remove her reproach. In answer to her prayer she gave birth to Samuel. But remember that when she gave birth to Samuel she gave him to the Lord. Have you done that, you mothers and fathers? Have you given your children to God, or are you so selfish that you must have them in your own grasp? Those who, like Hannah, give their Samuels to God, like her, will also break forth and sing, "My heart exulteth in the LORD, mine horn is exalted in the LORD . . . because I rejoice in thy salvation."

And now, one word to you who have not yet opened your heart to receive Christ. God has humbled Himself, despite your indifference. He still pleads with you. He wants to enter your life and make that life conform to His glory. You cannot live a life comparable in fullness of joy to the life that God wants you to lead as you yield yourself to Him.

PSALM ONE HUNDRED FOURTEEN

MOUNTAINS THAT SKIPPED AND SEAS THAT FLED

AS a Gentile in the flesh I must confess much ignorance of the manners and customs of the Jews. I have, however, noticed an interesting thing in that interesting people. Their songs, at least those which I have heard either over the radio or elsewhere are invariably pitched in the minor key. That should not be surprising, when one considers their history which is replete with suffering.

The 114th Psalm which we are to consider, I am confident, was never put to music in the minor key. A mere reading of the Psalm increases the tempo of the heart-beat, so that it is self-evident that it must have been pitched in the major key and with a decidedly fast tempo. It is the kind of song that would have the tendency to sweep one off one's feet. So, as we read this Psalm, notice the hidden movement which is yet so readily perceptible, and which someone once said, "Moves fast with the swiftness of a bird flapping its wings."

"When Israel went out of Egypt, the house of Jacob from a people of strange language;
"Judah was his sanctuary, and Israel his dominion.
"The sea saw it, and fled: Jordan was driven back.
"The mountains skipped like rams, and the little hills like lambs.

> "What ailed thee, O thou sea, that thou fleddest? thou
> Jordan, that thou wast driven back?
> "Ye mountains, that ye skipped like rams; and ye little
> hills, like lambs?
> "Tremble, thou earth, at the presence of the Lord, at
> the presence of the God of Jacob;
> "Which turned the rock into a standing water, the flint
> into a fountain of waters."

It was interesting to learn from a news article the other day, that there is a group of middle-aged men and women, who meet together regularly in the city of Brooklyn, who call themselves "The Lost Chord League." These men and women have suffered the loss of their larynx because of throat cancer. By the skillful help of a physician, they have been taught to speak without vocal cords. It is said that the patients are taught to swallow air and belch it forth, at the same time formulating sounds with the forced up air. I read the report with a great deal of interest, for I can think of few things that an individual needs more than the power of speech. Men of science are to be congratulated, in having discovered that God has so constructed the human body that, when one's larynx has been removed, the balance of the human body can be employed to emit articulate sounds, so that the worst that can be said about the individual who speaks without his larynx is that he sounds as if he has a cold. Here is a Psalm which indicates that all creation has a voice.

A PSALM OF THE EXODUS

Of course this Psalm, strictly speaking, belongs to Israel. In the Jewish ritual it is set aside for the eighth day of the "Feast of the Passover." Every descendant of Jacob knows, and every Gentile at least ought to have a speaking acquaintance with, the works of God at the time of the exodus; but here, in this short Psalm of eight verses, the Psalmist has brought together "in a miniature picture, majestic and charming," the entire history of the exodus. Observe that Israel went out of Egypt; the house of Jacob left a people of a strange language. Every Bible student knows that God instructed Abraham, Isaac, and Jacob that they were not to go down into Egypt; but, when the aged Jacob heard that his son Joseph was there, he pleaded with God to allow him the privilege of going down to Egypt that he might see his son whom he had thought dead. God gave Jacob permission to go down; but what suffering it entailed for future generations because Jacob pleaded with God to put aside His directive will, and to give him permission to go down to Egypt.

There is such a thing as God's directive, revealed will, and there is also such a thing as God's permissive will. We may have the choice of either. We may be obedient to His direct will, suffering what appear to be difficulties and disappointments, but what actually are but stepping-stones to a further revelation of His grace and glory; or we may take His permissive will, which seems to be the road of least resistance, but which we will discover leads to endless difficulties, if not for ourselves, then certainly for someone else. What then? There is only one thing to do—get out of Egypt. I am addressing Christians. I am talking to men and women who have received Christ—and who know what I mean. Egypt is a symbol of this world. The Christian is said to be *in* it, but not *of* it. The Christian who is *of* it as well as *in* it is a monstrosity; but the Christian who is *in* the world and yet not *of* it is a living testimony to the saving grace of God. When Israel went out of Egypt, leaving a people of a strange tongue, Judah became the sanctuary of God and Israel became His dominion. And when this happened the Psalmist said, "The sea saw it, and fled: Jordan was driven back. The mountains skipped like rams, and the little hills like lambs." If we have a love for the poetical, we will have little difficulty in recognizing in the language of the Psalm a perfect unfolding of what happens to difficulties when an individual becomes the sanctuary of God and when his life is under the dominion of God.

Judah became the sanctuary of God. You know what a sanctuary is. It is a dwelling-place, a temple of God, the place where God is pleased to dwell. God does not dwell in temples made with hands. You can erect the most stately church building, you can put paneled walls and stained-glass windows in it, you can put all the religious paraphernalia in it you want, but that does not make it the temple of God; it does not thereby become the sanctuary of God. The people who attend and come together as a body of believers in Jesus Christ constitute a local church. God wants to dwell among His people. He did not want Israel down in Egypt, so He led them out of that strange land in order that He could have fellowship with His redeemed people.

But the New Testament makes it even more personal and individual. It declares that the bodies of those who have received Christ are the temples of the living God. What a statement! I wonder how much we think of it. If we thought enough about it, it would be utterly impossible but that our lives would be different. Imagine, our bodies the temples of the living God. God, by His Spirit, dwells in our bodies. When that is true, I repeat, difficulties skip away, just as the mountains skipped like rams and the little hills like lambs when Israel left Egypt under the guidance of God. Even when the sea saw Israel coming it fled, and Jordan, which, you remember, always symbolizes death, was driven back. So the Psalmist raised the question, "What ailed thee, O thou sea, that thou fleddest? thou Jordan, that thou wast driven back? Ye mountains, that ye skipped like rams; and ye little hills, like lambs?" What was the matter? The hills seemingly stand impregnable, and the flood has tremendous devastating powers. You cannot fight against the forces of nature and expect to conquer, but you can find a way out, whereby the very forces that conquer you and have conquered you, the very difficulties that dog your feet and make your life miserable, will skip away and tremble at the presence of the Lord, at the presence of the God of Jacob.

I haven't any doubt that Pharaoh had a competent force of military strategists who were acquainted with every inch of land leading in and out of Egypt. They must have laughed up their sleeves at the seeming folly of Moses and Israel, who insisted that they must leave Egypt to go out into the wilderness in order to worship their God. I can hear those worldly wise Egyptians saying to Pharaoh, Let them go. We will get them. Why, there isn't an engineer in the whole crowd. They haven't the material to build a bridge to cross the Red Sea, and you know that the way they are going leads directly to the sea, and even if they could get across they would head directly into a devastating wilderness. Let them go. That will probably stop this plague that has beset our land. Give them a couple of days' head start, then we will follow. Just leave this conquest to us. Here is a perfect setting for a perfect victory. There is no danger involved for us. Why, none of the Israelites are possessed of weapons. They cannot fight back. It is such a perfect setting for a victory that we suggest that you ride before us. With our horsemen we will catch them very quickly. Did the Red Sea ever fail us? Has anyone ever conquered the wilderness? Of course not!

But what happened? "What ailed thee, O thou sea, that thou fleddest?" Pharaoh and his military strategists failed to consider God. The very elements they expected would prevent Israel, were the elements with which they themselves were destroyed.

THE PRESENCE OF THE LORD

It does make a tremendous difference when God is present. Our Lord said to His disciples, on one occasion, "In the world ye shall have tribula-

tion . . ." None of the sons of men are exempt from it, and not a single
believer can avoid it. Our Lord said very definitely, "In the world ye shall
have tribulation:" but He added this, "be of good cheer; I have overcome
the world." For "God is able to make all grace abound toward you; that ye,
always having all sufficiency in all things, may abound to every good work
. . ." That is a wonderful promise! Child of God, you may draw upon it at
any time and you will find there is always a balance left at the bank of
heaven. This 7th verse becomes the solution of every problem confronting
the individual life. "Tremble, thou earth, at the presence of the Lord, at
the presence of the God of Jacob . . ." If you are encompassed about with
difficulties; if they seem immovable; if they loom so large that they appear
as mountains before you, remember that if you trust God the earth will
tremble and the mountains will be removed, for, in the presence of God,
every difficulty vanishes.

Now notice the 8th verse, the closing verse of the Psalm, where we
learn of one of the great accomplishments of God during the wilderness
journey of Israel, when He turned the rock into a standing water, the flint
into a fountain of waters. That's a miracle. It is a miracle, someone once
said, we all need to experience. Let us see the picture. Here is a huge rock
at the foot of which Israel is gathered, their tongues are hanging out and
their lips are parched. Their hearts are hardened; they begin to grumble,
"Would God that we had died in . . . Egypt!" Dying by thirst is a frightful,
lengthy, torture. Moses, of course, pleaded with God. God said—Do you
see that rock before you? Gather Israel together, take that rod which you
have in your hand and smite the rock, and out of it will gush forth waters
that will satisfy the thirst of every Israelite. You will discover that in the
midst of the flint of that rock I have buried fountains of waters. Now the
New Testament declares that the Rock that was smitten was Christ and the
waters that flowed from the smitten rock speak of the refreshing streams of
living water that flow from the cross at Calvary. Every thirsty soul that
has drunk, has gone away not only with his thirst quenched, but with a
well of water in his own being, springing up into everlasting life.

In closing, I want to leave the direct interpretation of the passage, and
apply its principle to our own lives. Many a life has been hard, many a
heart has been like flint, but the heart of stone can be changed to a heart of
flesh, and out of it can flow rivers of refreshing delight, when the individual
is willing to allow God to work a miracle on the stony heart. It is simply
amazing what God can do with a life that has been yielded to Him. I think

of a young man, who, filled with a desire to see life and possessed of some means, came to New York, hoping to do the town and make a huge success. Alas, what a broken, disappointed lad that fellow became in a short time. But today, that young man is busy, night after night, going from place to place witnessing to the joy of knowing Christ. No longer does the appetite of a depraved nature overpower him, but out of that heart flow rivers of living water. May He give you that same experience, if you have never yet had it.

PSALM ONE HUNDRED FIFTEEN

THE TWO GREAT SILENCES

THE 115th Psalm touches on two subjects which have provoked a tremendous amount of inquiry from almost the dawn of human history and multitudes still raise questions concerning them. The first subject is the silence of God, and the second, that of death and the grave. We can hardly imagine two more interesting subjects. Why does God keep silent? Has He ever spoken? Will He speak again? What happens at death? Why is the grave so silent?

It would be a tremendous task to try to discuss these subjects in a short period of twenty minutes. In order to conserve time, we shall read only a few verses; but I suggest that you read the entire Psalm at your leisure. You will find it profitable. We shall read the first nine verses, and then the last two:

> "Not unto us, O LORD, not unto us, but unto thy name give glory, for thy mercy, and for thy truth's sake.
> "Wherefore should the heathen say, Where is now their God?
> "But our God is in the heavens: he hath done whatsoever he hath pleased.
> "Their idols are silver and gold, the work of men's hands.
> "They have mouths, but they speak not: eyes have they, but they see not:
> "They have ears, but they hear not: noses have they, but they smell not:
> "They have hands, but they handle not: feet have they, but they walk not: neither speak they through their throat.
> "They that make them are like unto them; so is every one that trusteth in them.
> "O Israel, trust thou in the LORD: he is their help and their shield."

* * * *

"The dead praise not the LORD, neither any that go
down into silence.
"But we will bless the LORD from this time forth and
for evermore. Praise the LORD."

This Psalm was sung at the Passover season. It has a direct relation
to what transpired at that time and to some of the events which immediately
followed. Any understanding of what God did in Egypt, on behalf of the
Israelites, must bring a response of affirmation to what is found in the 1st
verse of our Psalm, where we read, "Not unto us, O LORD, not unto us,
but unto thy name give glory, for thy mercy and for thy truth's sake."
Israel could never boast of her own deliverance from Egypt. Israel
could boast only in the deliverance that God provided. Just so, no
individual can ever boast of what he has done; he can boast only in what
God has done on his behalf. Salvation is not the work of man. Salvation
is the work of the Lord. He is the author of it. He is the finisher of it.
He began it. He will perfect it. We are but clay in the hands of the potter.
Therefore we too can heartily join with the Psalmist in singing, "Not unto
us, O LORD, not unto us, but unto thy name give glory, for thy mercy,
and for thy truth's sake."

THE SILENCE OF GOD

Immediately following the expression of glory to God, we find this
question raised, "Wherefore should the heathen say, Where is *now* their
God?" Observe that little word *now*. Even the heathen, that is, Pharaoh
and the host of Egyptians, recognized and confessed that at *one time* God
did display His power on behalf of His people, the Israelites. There was
no doubt about it. The various plagues He visited upon Egypt, the manner
in which He indicated that there was a difference between the Egyptians and
the Israelites, were clear evidences that God was manifesting His power and
His presence on behalf of Israel. So the critic of the Christian message must
confess that there was a time during the ministry of our Lord Jesus Christ
on the earth, and shortly thereafter, when abundant evidence was given that
God ministered through Christ, and that Christ was glorified after His death
by the manifestations of the Holy Spirit's power on the behalf of the little
group of disciples who wrought miracles and accomplished wonders in the
name of the risen, exalted Christ. But just as the heathen asked concerning
Israel, "Where is *now* their God?" when God withheld the display of
miracles from among them; so likewise the critic of the Christian message,

seeing that there is no longer the active display of the miraculous, such as existed during Christ's ministry and the Apostolic days, today joins the chorus, "Where is *now* their God?"

THE VOICE OF THE SILENT HEAVENS

All will agree that the heavens are majestic. That man must be deaf and dumb and have a heart of stone who cannot feel a response in his soul to the message of creation, as he looks at the silent, majestic heavens on any night during this fall season of the year. Of those heavens the Psalmist said, "Day unto day uttereth speech, and night unto night sheweth knowledge. There is no speech nor language, where their voice is not heard." The silent heavens have a voice, and there is no speech nor language where the voice of the silent heavens is not heard. Yet, here was the question raised by the heathen, "Where is now their God?" Today, atheists and communists have great delight at our expense, as they chide us and amuse themselves with the question, "Where is now their God?" Actually, this is a simple question. It is not as difficult as it appears to the communists and atheists. The fact of the matter is that the answer appears in the very next verse of our Psalm, in the 3rd verse, where we read, "But our God is in the *heavens:* he hath done whatsoever he hath pleased." But notice, will you, the contrast that follows, "Their (that is, the heathen, and that goes for the communist and atheist as well) idols are silver and gold, the work of men's hands. They have mouths, but they speak not: eyes have they, but they see not: they have ears, but they hear not: noses have they, but they smell not: they have hands, but they handle not: feet have they, but they walk not: neither speak they through their throat. They that make them are like unto them; so is every one that trusteth in them."

So, in comparison with the self-made gods of the heathen, and the gods of materialism, such as communists and atheists worship, we have the God and Father of our Lord and Saviour Jesus Christ—the God of Abraham, Isaac, and Jacob. Any comparison must lead to a series of contrasts. The gods of the heathen are made with hands—the God of heaven is the eternal, life-giving Being, independent of man, not the work of man's hand. The majesty of God is so stupendous that it has never been given to man adequately to speak of God.

For almost two thousand years the heavens have been silent. As a result a number of people ask the question, "Where is now their God?" The answer is the same as is given in the 3rd verse of our Psalm, "our God is in the *heavens* . . ." Our Lord Jesus Christ, the God-Man, the manifestation of God in flesh, is now in the heavens, seated at the right hand of the eternal God. He is ever living to make intercession for those who love Him and serve Him. He is ever extending the hand of greeting to those who will receive Him, while He is still giving men an opportunity to demonstrate to their own satisfaction that they are utterly incapable of running their own lives, to say nothing about running the world. What a mess men have made! After two thousand long years of gospel preaching, after a hundred years of supposed advance in science, education, and philosophy, can you imagine anything comparable to our present situation? Probably the bloodiest civil war that has ever been fought is taking place in Spain today. It is almost unthinkable that men would do the things to their own countrymen that are being done today in Spain. What a situation we see in other sections of Europe, Asia, and Africa, or anywhere you wish to look! As for our own country, the less said the better. Yet, all the while, God is silent. Not a voice is heard from the heavens. Thus, man seems to think that because the heavens are silent, there is no God. Remember however that the Scripture says, "The fool hath said in his heart, There is no God." Do not assume that because God has been pleased to be silent, He is non-existent. *The silence of God is as majestic as His spoken word, and the work of God in the hearts of those who bow to His will today is more glorious than the miracles displayed in creation.*

WHY GOD IS SILENT

I have already intimated one reason for the silence of heaven. God has been extending to man every opportunity to satisfy himself that he is an abject failure as far as government is concerned. Another reason for the silent heavens is the fact that God is now enabling man to place faith in His spoken Word, and in His incarnate Word—Jesus Christ our Lord. Thus it is written, "God, who at sundry times and in divers manners spake in time past unto the fathers by the prophets, hath for the last time spoken unto us in his Son . . ." God has a right to be believed, especially as He has given abundant evidence in the perfection of the written Word and in the perfection of the incarnate Word, so that man is without excuse in rejecting God's testimony. How I wish I had time to develop this subject, but, if you are interested in it, my friend Dr. A. C. Gaebelein has just written a book entitled, "LISTEN: GOD SPEAKS." The trouble with us is that we do not listen. God has spoken in creation. God has spoken in His Word, and God has spoken in His Son. Those who have listened to His message have heard His voice. There has been a response in their breasts to the message of God, which, in turn, has brought them tremendous blessing. But, mark you, God will one day speak again. He is silent now, to be sure, but He will speak again. Then the silent heavens will be rent, and our Lord will come forth as the King of kings and the Lord of lords.

Of course, we do not know the day nor hour when that event will take place. But the Bible very clearly states that it shall take place, and what is more, it will come to pass when man least expects it. In the Word of God certain things are written that point as signs to the near approach of Jesus Christ our Lord. I believe that the coming of our Lord draweth nigh. I am sure that multitudes who love the Word of God and Jesus Christ our Lord, and who love man from the bottom of their hearts, earnestly desire the return of Christ, not only for the joy of seeing Him with these eyes of ours and being fully glorified by His grace, but in order that this poor old world may come to know an era of peace, and that mankind might be delivered from oppression. Well, so much for the subject of the silence of God.

Now let us look at the silence of death. In verse 16 of our Psalm, we read: ". . . the earth hath he given to the children of men." I cannot help but think of the terrific struggle that men must endure to have even the semblance of a comfortable living. If perchance we have a family, our eyes are focused on death as well as on life. We try to make every provision for our family, so that they will be cared for if death should suddenly call us. Every life insurance policy is a voice from the silent tomb. Every cemetery, every undertaking establishment, seems to cry out, You may be next! But then, what? Well, if it is a point of wisdom to prepare for the eventuality, as far as our loved ones are concerned, by building up an estate or leaving life insurance, and by bestowing the heritage of a godly life; what can be said about the folly of that man who does not make any preparation as far as his own soul is concerned? You come to the brink of an open grave and there you observe that the earth has been troubled; a hole has been dug so that it appears as if the bowels of the earth had opened to swallow their victim. The casket is lowered, the loved one is gone, but the earth is as silent about revealing its secret as the heavens are silent. "The dead praise not the LORD, neither any that go down into silence. But we will bless the LORD from this time forth and for evermore. Praise the LORD."

When the Bible speaks of the dead, it speaks of those who have not bowed the knee to the God of salvation. The phrase "the dead" brings a shudder in the breast of all men.

No apology is necessary for discussing the matter of death. It is something we all have to face. Like every other family, we have made that terrible journey to an open grave. But, above that plot today is a stone which bears a little inscription, a quotation from the Word of God—simple words, but oh, what they mean—"*At Home with the Lord*." Death is robbed of its sting, the grave is robbed of its silence, when the individual who has died has placed his or her faith in Jesus Christ and God's Word. That individual goes out of the here, into the presence of the Lord. I would ten thousand times rather know where I am going, if perchance death should meet me today, than to be in the shoes of any who think it is the sporting thing to take things as they come. One wonders however whether the sporting suggestion is the result of either refusing or dreading to face the fact of death.

THE OPENED GRAVES

Those graves, however, that have been so silent through the years, the Bible declares will some day burst forth with a message. Let me give you what the Word of God has to say regarding it. It is a quotation from the Apostle Paul's first letter to the Thessalonians, ". . . this we say unto you by the word of the Lord . . . the dead in Christ shall rise first: Then we which are alive and remain (until the coming of the Lord) shall be caught up together with them in the clouds, to meet the Lord in the air . . ." Did you notice that—"the dead in Christ."

There may be many divisions of social strata on the earth, but when it comes to the grave, there are only two divisions: either a man is in Christ, or he is out of Christ. The dead in Christ shall be raised first. That will take place at the coming of the Lord for His own. The Bible says that we who are on the earth when the Lord returns, shall be caught up in the air to meet Him, and later our Lord will return to this earth with His own, to take His place as the King of kings and the Lord of lords and institute what the Bible calls the Kingdom reign of our Lord Jesus Christ. He will rule this earth for one thousand years. At the end of that period "the rest of the dead" will be raised to face the "great white throne," when the books will be opened, containing the record of every man's life, and another book, the book of life, will be opened, which is the registry of heaven. The Bible says that "whosoever was not found written in the book of life was cast into the lake of fire." It should be noted however that the Bible further states that the dead, both small and great were judged according to their works. It is man's sin that sends him to hell.

PSALM ONE HUNDRED SIXTEEN

A PSALM WITH A MESSAGE FOR LIFE AND DEATH

NOW we come to the 116th Psalm, which reads:

"I love the LORD, because he hath heard my voice and my supplications.

"Because he hath inclined his ear unto me, therefore will I call upon him as long as I live.

"The sorrows of death compassed me, and the pains of hell gat hold upon me: I found trouble and sorrow.

"Then called I upon the name of the LORD; O LORD, I beseech thee, deliver my soul.

"Gracious is the LORD, and righteous; yea, our God is merciful.

"The LORD preserveth the simple: I was brought low, and he helped me.

"Return unto thy rest, O my soul; for the LORD hath dealt bountifully with thee.

"For thou hast delivered my soul from death, mine eyes from tears, and my feet from falling.

"I will walk before the LORD in the land of the living.

"I believed, therefore have I spoken: I was greatly afflicted:

"I said in my haste, All men are liars.

"What shall I render unto the LORD for all his benefits toward me?

"I will take the cup of salvation, and call upon the name of the LORD.

"I will pay my vows unto the LORD now in the presence of all his people.

"Precious in the sight of the LORD is the death of his saints.

"O LORD, truly I am thy servant; I am thy servant, and the son of thine handmaid: thou hast loosed my bonds.

"I will offer to thee the sacrifice of thanksgiving, and will call upon the name of the LORD.

"I will pay my vows unto the LORD now in the presence of all his people,

"In the courts of the LORD'S house, in the midst of thee, O Jerusalem. Praise ye the LORD."

This is an intensively personal Psalm. The pronouns *I* and *my* occur in every verse, except two. Usually, when a man frequently writes or speaks in the first person, we make a mental note of him and pay little attention to what he may have to say. If perchance the speaker is a preacher, it is decidedly unbecoming to have too many "I's" in his sermon. However, here is a Psalm where the use of the first person is not only acceptable, but delightful and essential. The Psalm could not be considered from any other viewpoint, for salvation and relationship to God must be intensely individual and personal.

"I LOVE THE LORD"

The first thing to notice is the fact that David said, "I love the LORD, because he hath heard my voice and my supplications." There is a New Testament passage of Scripture which declares that "If any man love not the Lord Jesus Christ, let him be Anathema Maran-atha." Anathema is merely a polite way of saying accursed, and Maran-atha refers to the return of Christ in glory, when the curse will be pronounced. Thus this could be translated, "If any man love not the Lord Jesus Christ, let him be accursed at the coming of our Lord in glory." These are solemn words. I have frequently said that I make no apology for what is found in the Word of God. If a man does not like what is written, he will have to settle that matter with the Lord Himself. I desire only to be a mouthpiece; to expound honestly the Word of God and tell you what it teaches. There is no more delightful occupation than to love the Lord, and just so, there is no more cruel fate than that which awaits the individual who despises the mercy of God and who does not love our Lord Jesus Christ.

There was a time in the life of almost every Christian when he did not like "to retain God" in his knowledge. What caused the change? I think David expressed it when he said, "I love the LORD, *because* he hath heard my voice and my supplications." Frequently we find that our difficulties drive us into the presence of God; in desperation we supplicate Him and cry out to Him. Then, when we observe that He has inclined His ear unto us and has definitely answered our prayer, it is the most natural thing in the world that affection should swell up in our breasts, which expresses itself in love to the Lord. Here David said, "The sorrows of death compassed me, and the pains of hell gat hold upon me: I found trouble and sorrow. Then called I upon the name of the LORD . . ." I think it was Spurgeon who said that if a man would preach to sorrowing souls, he would always preach to a full congregation.

ONLY BELIEVE, OR WHAT?

Last Sunday, quite by accident, I heard a man say something over the radio which filled my whole being with indignation. He is a prominent preacher, who takes delight in suggesting that his study of the Scripture at hand is apart from any doctrinal viewpoint. He might as well attempt to be a mathematician and cast the multiplication table out the window. He had delivered his address, and the few remaining moments were devoted to questions. Someone asked if it were true that all one had to do in order to be saved was to believe and that doing does not matter as much as believing. In responding, this clergyman said, "There is a great deal of falsity in the idea that all one has to do is believe." Then he went on to cast an aspersion upon the central fact and figure of Christianity. Speaking of the death of our Lord Jesus Christ upon the cross, he asked, "Do you rest back on an *isolated* transaction there on Calvary, and expect in some peculiar manner your salvation is secure?" Poor man! is that all he thinks of the death of Christ upon the cross? Is that all he has to offer to the sin-sick, sorrowing souls of mankind who cry out for peace, and who want to know if any provision has been made whereby they may approach a holy God and come to know Him? I dare say that when he gets to a place where the sorrows of death compass him and the pains of hell grasp hold of him, as David experienced; when he finds himself in troubles and sorrow, he will discover that the only place in the world where God has definitely given an answer to the sorrowing heart is at the place called Calvary, where the *divine* transaction concerning sin took place. There the "man of sorrows" bore our sorrows. There He was wounded for our transgressions and bruised for our iniquities. Many a soul has come to the cross with a conscience deadened by sin, with a body wrecked by sin's consequences, and with a soul that seemed to yield no response to righteousness and truth. Such a one found at the cross the balm for every human ill, the atonement for every sin. No wonder that into the breast of a redeemed man comes a love for his Redeemer. He looks up into the face of God and speaks in the language of the Scriptures, "Thanks be unto God for his indescribable gift." Should some casual observer be shocked at such an expression and ask "Why?" the answer would immediately be given, "We love Him, because He first loved us." So I would suggest to those who have troubles, and sorrows, and difficulties—go to the "man of sorrows"; to the One acquainted with grief. You will find as the Psalmist expressed in the 5th verse of the 116th Psalm, "Gracious is the LORD, and righteous; yea, our God is merciful." If perchance you have been brought low, it will encourage you to know that David said, "I was brought low, and he helped me." Because of that, David wrote in the 9th verse of this 116th Psalm, "I will walk before the LORD in the land of the living."

Another thing about this Psalm is tremendously interesting; in fact, it has made this Psalm one of the best known and most frequently quoted of all the writings of David. In the 10th and 11th verses, we read, "I believed, therefore have I spoken . . . I said in my haste, All men are liars." You know the old phrase which reads that if all men are liars then David must have been a liar. However, you will observe that David wrote, "I said in my haste, All men are liars." In other words, he spoke before he thought. It was when he was burdened with affliction. Before he looked up to the presence of God, he found everything and everybody about him to be a contradiction. That was not strange, for, even today, were you to pick up a half dozen books on a Bible subject, written by the six most learned men in that particular field, each absolutely dead as far as spiritual things are concerned, you would find that they would contradict one another. You, too, would almost conclude in your haste, as David did—that all men are liars. Man cannot be relied upon to give any information regarding God or man's relationship to God. There is only one book in the world that bears the impress of the hand of God and that vibrates with His breath. That Book is the Bible.

VOWS, AND PAYING THEM

Twice, in the 116th Psalm, David wrote, "I will pay my vows unto the LORD" and on each occasion he promised to do so in the presence of all the Lord's people. I do not think anyone will question me when I say that real, abiding joy in the knowledge of our Saviour depends upon our faithfulness to Him. Salvation does not depend upon us, it depends exclusively upon what Christ did on the cross: there is no doubt or question about that, but our joy in God depends upon our faithfulness to Him. Thus our Lord said, "If ye love me, keep my commandments" and "If ye abide in me, and my words abide in you, ye shall ask what ye will, and it shall be done unto you." I wonder how many people remember a time when they were in deep distress, when they cried out to God for deliverance; who, in their moments of anxiety promised God they would do certain things. That constituted a vow. Did you pay your vow, or did you forget all about it after God delivered you? If you forgot all about it, I urge you to follow the suggestion that David made in this Psalm, when he wrote, "I will pay my vows unto the LORD now . . ." Don't wait until tomorrow. Do it now, and do it in the presence of the Lord's people. The Bible encourages us to confess our faults one to another, thereby lending encouragement to each other.

But I raise the question: Does it pay to serve God and to meet our vows? I am thinking of a gentleman of whom I recently heard, who has borne a faithful testimony to his Lord and Saviour for many years. He is a Britisher, a sea captain. He commanded a vessel that plied between England and India. One day, just a short while before sailing time, he became suspicious about the cargo which was being stowed in his ship. He inquired for the manifest. It was not available. One of the officers of the line tried to quiet him by saying that everything was satisfactory; that he need not worry about a thing. The captain persisted, "Sir, I wish to know what is in that cargo." Finding the captain immovable, the information was finally given that it was a cargo of opium. Turning to the manager of the line, he said, "My orders are that the cargo be immediately unloaded." He was informed that his request was impossible. It was but a half-hour before sailing time and most of the passengers were already aboard. The captain insisted. He was a Christian gentleman. He said, "Sir, as long as I am captain of this ship, I insist that the cargo be unloaded. Either the cargo is unloaded or the captain is unloaded." Much to the surprise of the manager, the captain packed his belongings and walked down the gangplank. The passengers and others knew that some discussion was on, and when the captain reached the pier he was met by the president of the British & India Navigation Co., who immediately offered the captain the commodoreship of the British-East India Lines. That man had made a vow. He may not have expressed it audibly, but he vowed in his heart that, as he was a disciple of his Lord, he would be obedient to his Lord's commands. Did it pay? Do not assume because the cost of devotion to Christ sometimes appears decidedly large, that the price is too great to be paid. God has yet to be indebted to any man, and faithfulness to Him will always bring a double portion of blessing. No wonder the Psalmist said in verse 17: "I will offer to thee the sacrifice of thanksgiving, and will call upon the name of the LORD."

However, if sometime the Lord should not immediately reward faithfulness as He did in the case of Captain Carey, then what? What if it should appear as if God were indifferent to us? What if we have to pay the price of our lives as did, for instance, John and Betty Stam, almost two years ago in China. What then? The answer is given in the 15th verse, where we read, "Precious in the sight of the LORD is the death of his saints."

You will remember Stephen, who was stoned to death because of his faithfulness to the Lord Jesus Christ. What happened to him? He looked up to see the heavens opened, where he saw the glory of God, and Jesus standing on the right hand of God. While men stoned him to death, with the heavens open to his vision, he called upon God, saying, "Lord Jesus, receive my spirit." Wouldn't you have loved to have been in heaven that day, to observe the greeting that must have been extended to Stephen as he was received in the presence of his Lord. Observe that his Lord arose from the place where He previously sat down, at the right hand of His Father. He stood up. I am sure He stood up to receive one of His own. Ah, you say, but Stephen was a saint—I am not. To which I answer, "If you are a child of God you are a saint." Every Christian is a saint. Biblically speaking, a saint is one who has been set aside by the Lord for God. Of course, very often we do not act like saints. That is quite another matter; but every individual who embraces Christ as his Lord, thereby becomes one of the Lord's saints.

Here is a passage that maintains, "Precious in the sight of the LORD is the death of his saints." If we *now* have the Lord to hear the voice of our supplications, and if perchance death *should* visit us, our death is precious in the sight of the Lord. Then there is not very much left to worry about, is there? We might well join with David, saying, "Praise ye the LORD."

PSALM ONE HUNDRED SEVENTEEN

A DOXOLOGY THE WORLD WILL SOME DAY SING

MANY will agree with me that during the course of our series of meditations in the Book of Psalms it could never be said that we had any difficulty in getting sufficient material to give on these Psalms. Rather, we have had difficulty in finding sufficient time, so that at least some semblance of justice could be done. In our previous meditation we had to skip several verses of the 116th Psalm, but here we have a comparatively easy task, at least from the viewpoint of the number of verses to be found in a Psalm, for the 117th contains only two short verses; in fact, it is the shortest in the entire collection. Charles Haddon Spurgeon, that prince of British preachers, had this to say about the Psalm. "While it is very little in its letter, it is exceedingly large in its spirit; for, bursting beyond all bounds of race or nationality, it calls upon all mankind to praise the name of the Lord. In all probability it was frequently used as a brief hymn suitable for almost every occasion and especially if the time for worship was short. Perhaps it was also sung at the commencement or at the close of other Psalms, just as we now use the doxology. It would have served either to open a service or to conclude it. It is both short and sweet. The same divine Spirit which expatiates in the 119th Psalm here condenses His utterances into two short verses, but yet the same infinite fulness is present and perceptible."

The 117th Psalm reads:

> "O praise the LORD, all ye nations: praise him, all ye people.
>
> "For his merciful kindness is great toward us: and the truth of the LORD endureth for ever. Praise ye the LORD."

As far as I know, Israel was never a missionary people. Occasionally some Gentiles, observing that Israel worshipped the one true God, and recognizing that the worship of such a one coincided with the revelation of God in creation, joined forces with Israel in worshipping Jehovah God. During the time of the ministry of our Lord Jesus Christ there were certain proselytes who mingled with Israel; but strictly speaking, Israel was an exclusive company. They had no room for other than true-blooded descendants of Abraham, Isaac, and Jacob.

In the 23rd chapter of Deuteronomy, Moses gave certain instructions as to who might enter into the congregation of the Lord. He declared that an Ammonite or Moabite could not enter into the congregation of the Lord, even to their tenth generation. As for the Edomites or the Egyptians, if any children were born out of a union of an Israelite with an Egyptian, the children that were begotten could not enter into the congregation of the Lord until their third generation. We can appreciate, therefore, how exclusive a company of people Israel was. In fact, even to this day, that is one of the reasons why that nation has never been and never will be assimilated by other peoples.

IS THE LAW A MISSIONARY MESSAGE?

There are certain definite reasons for this situation. To begin with, God called Abraham, who at the time was a heathen and a worshipper of idols. He called him to leave his country, his family, and his friends, to go out to a land that God would show him. For obedience to His command, God promised that He would bless Abraham and make him a blessing, and make his name great; going so far as to say, ". . . in thee shall all families of the earth be blessed." Yet, from the time Abraham stepped out of Ur of the Chaldees, to the very hour of the ascension of our Lord Jesus Christ into glory, Israel never had a message *for* the Gentile world. Their entire history was a testimony *against* the Gentiles. Their very devotion, their worship, their national life, were all a testimony against the character and nature of the Gentiles. But, more specifically, Israel, from the time she embraced the law of Moses until the coming of Christ, had absolutely no message to give to the world; for the law is a message of condemnation—it is not a message of justification. The law is no gospel, for the law condemns wherever it is presented. Therefore, Israel had no reason to be a missionary people. They could not go out to the nations of the world and say, Embrace this law which we have embraced and you will find it a means of salvation. The Holy Spirit declared, through the pen of the Apostle Paul, that the law was not made for a righteous man. It was made for the ungodly and sinner. The law was given not to justify man but to condemn man and seal his lips. Thus it is written, "Now we know that what things soever the law saith, it saith to them who are under the law: that every mouth may be stopped, and all the world may become guilty before God."

While Israel never had a missionary message, the Psalms, the writings of Moses, and all the prophets, bore testimony to the fact that some day God would fulfill His promise to Abraham, when He said, ". . . in thee shall all families of the earth be blessed." It is to the day when this shall be fulfilled that this Psalm refers, when David wrote, "O praise the LORD, *all* ye nations: praise him, *all* ye people."

In the past generations, for a Gentile to come into the court of the temple was to defile that temple; but *here* the Psalmist invites all nations, and all people, to join with Israel in praising the Lord. The One who will bring this change to pass is the One of whom the prophet Isaiah wrote, when he said, "Behold my servant, whom I uphold; mine elect, in whom my soul delighteth; I have put my spirit upon him: he shall bring forth judgment to the Gentiles. He shall not cry, nor lift up, nor cause his voice to be heard in the street. A bruised reed shall he not break, and the smoking flax shall he not quench: he shall bring forth judgment unto truth. He shall not fail nor be discouraged, till he have set judgment in the earth: and the isles shall wait for his law."

Speaking to that One who undoubtedly is the Messiah, Isaiah was bold to write that the Father said, "I the LORD have called thee in righteousness, and will hold thine hand, and will keep thee, and give thee for a covenant of the people, for a light of the Gentiles; To open the blind eyes, to bring out the prisoners from the prison, and them that sit in darkness out of the prison house."

Here is a prediction from the writings of Isaiah concerning the universal Messiah, declaring that not only would He be a covenant of the people, that is, Israel, but He would also be a light to the Gentiles. This is the quotation that Simeon used, when that just and devout man who was waiting for the consolation of Israel saw our Lord in company with Mary and Joseph at Jerusalem, as the parents brought the child into the temple to do for Him after the custom of the law. Simeon took the child in his arms, and said, "Lord, now lettest thou thy servant depart in peace, according to thy word: for mine eyes have seen thy salvation, which thou hast prepared before the face of *all* people; a light to lighten the Gentiles, and the glory of thy people Israel."

While Israel under the law could never go to the Gentiles with the law of Moses, and say, Here is salvation, embrace it—yet through the coming of the Messiah, all the nations of the earth shall have an opportunity to praise Jehovah God and all the people will gather to laud and adore Him. When I think of that future day when Jew and Christian will gather round about the one and only Saviour who will be exalted in Jerusalem, I think of the prophet Zechariah, who wrote, "Thus saith the LORD of hosts; in those days it shall come to pass, that ten men shall take hold out of all languages of the nations, even shall take hold of the skirt of him that is a Jew, saying, We will go with you: for we have heard that God is with you." It is to that day that David referred, when he said, "O praise the LORD, all ye nations: praise him, all ye people. For his merciful kindness is great toward us: and the truth of the LORD endureth for ever. Praise ye the LORD."

THE MERCIFUL KINDNESS OF GOD

We have here two definite reasons for praising God. First, because of His merciful kindness. Isn't that interesting? Not only kindness, but merciful kindness. Not merely toward us, but great toward us. Second, because the truth of the Lord endureth forever. Now the very words "merciful kindness" presuppose that the individual upon whom it is bestowed is unworthy in his own name and has no right to receive the blessing of God. If we are to receive merciful kindness from God it is because we are desperately in need of it. We have no righteousness of our own. We have no ground upon which to stand in our own name, as mercy is that for which the guilty man cries out.

That brings us to what I believe is the first matter to be considered in any approach to God. I refer to the matter of the consciousness of the guilt of sin. Sin, of course, is not a pleasant thing to talk about. Yet it is an unavoidable subject.

A short time ago I referred to a recent, interesting book by Harvard's honored Professor of Philosophy, George Santayana, entitled "The Last Puritan." The book centers around a family by the name of Alden, a typical, wealthy New England family, steeped in self-righteousness, and yet with a few skeletons in the closet, that seemed like living beings pointing the finger of accusation at the remaining members of the family. Peter Alden married and had a boy whose name was Oliver. Much of Oliver's education was left to a German governess who occasionally took Oliver to the services at the Church of St. Barnabas. Oliver's mother would not go with them to St. Barnabas despite the nice music, because she said it was degrading "to call ourselves miserable sinners." The philosopher tritely adds, "The words might be old-fashioned but what if the thing was true? Would it not clear the air to confess it?" I believe that there are multitudes of people, probably more church people than non-church folk, who feel exactly as Oliver Alden's mother felt—go to church, yes, but let us go to a place where men and women are not referred to as miserable sinners; such words belong to a past age. But there is no denying the fact of sin.

It is because of our sinful state that the kindness of God is manifested toward us. That kindness is not offered through any reciprocal arrangement extended to individuals who, to use the popular phrase, try to "do good and be good." The kindness of God is called *merciful* kindness.

Our Psalm not only calls for praise to the Lord because of His merciful kindness, but also because the truth of the Lord endureth forever. Anyone with the slightest acquaintance with the testimony of the Bible concerning itself understands that the Psalmist was referring to the inspired writings, when he wrote of the truth of the Lord. There is no truth apart from the written Word. Pilate asked our Lord Jesus Christ, "What is truth?" but he failed to wait for the answer. He is very much like the current edition of college freshmen who are hypnotized by the solemn halls of learning and thoroughly drunk with the wine of human wisdom poured into them by their professors. The professors seem like little gods in the sight of freshmen, who learn to chant that "no intelligent person believes the Bible any longer." Even if that were a fact, it would never change the impregnable rock of Holy Writ. The opinions of men are as variable as the wind. They are no more stable than the sands of the seashore. When these opinions are couched in high sounding philosophical and scientific terms the average student finds himself a worshipper at the feet of his idols. But, with a monotone that is devastating, and which dashes into pieces the wisdom of this world like the constant pounding of the waves against the sinking bark, the Bible repeats, "the truth of the LORD endureth for ever."

Of course, nothing is farther from the truth than the statement that the consensus of scholarship is against the written Word of God. Pseudo-scholarship, yes, but all through the ages real scholarship has bowed before the revelation of God's Word, because of its evident truthfulness. We can have no more faithful guide in a changing world than the lamp of Scripture. Its light never dims, its joy never diminishes, its truth never changes, its power is still dynamic. Therefore, every individual who has bowed his knee to the Lord God, who worships God through Jesus Christ our Lord, praises God, not only because of His merciful kindness, but also because "the truth of the LORD endureth for ever."

PSALM ONE HUNDRED EIGHTEEN

THE REJECTED STONE

THE opening and closing verses of the 118th Psalm are identical. They read, "O give thanks unto the LORD; for he is good: because his mercy endureth for ever."

There are a few orators in our present generation to whom I delight to listen. I do not always agree with what they may have to say, but rather it is their oratory that thrills me. The premise from which they start, the development of their subject, the interweaving of arguments, and the final conclusion which comes back to the premise serves as a reminder of what a perfect speech ought to be. If such is the case in the utterance of a spoken message, then here, in the 118th, we have a perfect Psalm. It begins with an expression of thanks unto the Lord because of His goodness, and His mercy which endureth forever; then it goes on in its development of the

theme, finally coming back to the same premise as the message is brought
to a close.

AN ANTIPHONAL PSALM

Then, again, this is one of a series of antiphonal Psalms. That is a
big word, but it ought not to frighten anyone. Is simply means "responsive,"
as when one section sings a line or stanza and another answers, very much
like the reading of Scripture practiced in many churches today.

As we read this 118th Psalm, we can visualize the chief singer mount-
ing the rostrum with baton in hand, before him is a great host gathered to
sing the praises of the Lord. The chief singer cries out, "O give thanks unto
the LORD; for he is good: because his mercy endureth for ever." Then his
baton points to the section where Israel is gathered, as the maestro invites
Israel to say that "his mercy endureth for ever." Whereupon, he turns to
the priests, as he calls upon the house of Aaron to join, saying, "his mercy
endureth for ever" and, finally, with a big sweep, he invites all those that
fear the Lord to give thanks because the Lord's mercy endureth forever.

When we consider the 117th Psalm, we discovered that there were two
reasons for praising the Lord—first, because of His merciful kindness which
is great toward us, and, second, because His truth endureth forever. Such
being the case, is it any wonder that there should be a burst of antiphonal
praise, ascribing thanks unto the Lord because His mercy also endureth forever. How it thrills the heart of the sinner who has been redeemed by God's
grace, to know that God's mercy endureth forever. That cannot be said
about our mercy. We may occasionally deal with another on the basis of
human kindness, but invariably there is a limit to our mercy and kindness;
but not so with the mercy of the Lord. His mercy endureth forever.

The real heart of this Psalm is the statement which is found in verses
22 to 24, "The stone which the builders refused is become the head stone of
the corner. This is the LORD'S doing; it is marvelous in our eyes. This is
the day which the LORD hath made; we will rejoice and be glad in it."

From time to time I have stated that there are a number of Psalms we
call Messianic Psalms. In each of them, either the Messiah Himself speaks
or the substance of the Psalm concerns the Messiah. Sometimes the Psalm
is focused upon His coming in humiliation, which culminated in His death
on the cross, as we find for instance in the 22nd Psalm. Then there are
others that look beyond His first coming, when He was rejected, to His
exaltation at the right hand of His Father. We had an example of that type

of Messianic Psalm, when we considered the 110th Psalm, where God, speaking to His Son, said, "Sit thou at my right hand, until I make thine enemies thy footstool" and where we read, "The LORD hath sworn . . . Thou art a priest for ever after the order of Melchizedek." Then there are Psalms that look farther ahead into the future, to the time when the Messiah shall reign as King of kings and Lord of lords; when all the nations of the world will be obliged to bow the knee to Him in worship. The 2nd Psalm is a perfect example of that, when God cries out, "Yet have I set my king upon my holy hill of Zion."

In some cases a Psalm may have certain references to the experiences of the individual who wrote it, but it also looks beyond the writer to the eternal Christ. That, I believe, is what we have in this 118th Psalm. Some of the things David mentioned therein undoubtedly refer to himself, as, for instance when he said, "I called upon the LORD in my distress . . . The LORD is on my side; I will not fear: what can man do unto me?" or, as in the 16th and 17th verses, where we read, "The right hand of the LORD is exalted: the right hand of the LORD doeth valiantly. I shall not die, but live, and declare the works of the LORD." The same thing can be said for verse 18, where the Psalmist said, "The LORD hath chastened me sore: but he hath not given me over unto death." That, of course, could never be said of the Lord. He was given over to death. He did die, though He was raised from the dead. In fact, it is concerning His rejection that led to His death, that the Psalmist wrote, "The stone which the builders refused is become the head stone of the corner." Thus this 118th Psalm, though it undoubtedly describes some of David's experiences in his relation to the Lord, also has something to say about the Lord.

In the first Epistle of Peter, chapter 2, commencing with verse 6, we read, concerning the Lord Jesus, "Wherefore also it is contained in the scripture, Behold, I lay in Sion a chief corner stone, elect, precious: and he that believeth on him shall not be confounded. Unto you therefore which believe he is precious; but unto them which be disobedient, the stone which the builders disallowed, the same is made the head of the corner." Observe how the Holy Spirit, through the pen of the Apostle Peter, has gone to the 118th Psalm, in order to inform us that the 22nd verse refers to our Lord Jesus Christ, when it speaks of the rejected stone. To those who believe, He is precious, but "unto them which be disobedient, the stone which the builders disallowed, the same is made the head of the corner."

The stone, Jesus Christ, was rejected by the builders. The builders, of course, were the leaders of the people. Invariably, the people follow a leader like a flock of sheep. They seldom ask themselves the question, Is this leader one in whom we may have confidence? Will he direct us correctly? To the contrary, they will even follow him into a blind abyss. Thus the people who one day cried out, "Hosanna; Blessed is he that cometh in the name of the Lord . . ." readily followed their leaders who, later that same week, cried out, "Crucify him, crucify him" saying in effect, "We will not have this man to reign over us." The rejected stone, however, became the headstone of the corner. Do you know who made Him the headstone? The Psalmist told us in the very next verse, the 23rd. "This is the LORD'S doing; it is marvelous in our eyes."

THE CHANGE AT CALVARY

Were we to read carefully the record of the crucifixion of our Lord Jesus Christ, we would discover that a tremendous change came over the people during the time our Lord hung upon the cross. The mob mocked Him and His own forsook Him and fled, but as the minutes passed and all creation and the God of heaven gave evidence that they had something to say about the person who was dying upon that cross, the whole demeanor of the multitude changed: the mob fled and the leaders hid themselves, for the very earth seemed to crumble under their feet; yet the centurion, who dared not leave his post because he was charged with the care of the victim, bore effectual testimony of the Christ who was dying, and said, "Truly this was the Son of God." No one had thought so at the beginning of the crucifixion, but what a transformation took place as a result of the overwhelming evidence that God was interested in what was taking place on that cross. It was the Lord's doing. It is marvelous in our eyes. When a man's eyes are opened to what took place on that cross almost two thousand years ago, he increasingly marvels. He finds, moreover, that his whole outlook on life changes. He ceases to be indifferent to the things of God. He ceases to go along with the crowd. Very frequently he finds himself swimming against the stream, but above everything he is possessed of an abiding joy. As the Psalmist said, "This is the day which the LORD hath made; we will rejoice and be glad in it."

"THIS IS THE DAY . . ."

Some quote this passage and apply it to every day. I have some friends who, particularly on an unpleasant day, when it is raining and cold and the only comment that can be made about the weather is that it is disagreeable, immediately respond, "This is the day which the LORD hath made; we will rejoice and be glad in it." That is not doing justice to this passage of Scripture. I am absolutely convinced that we would never have a storm, we would never have an unpleasant day, were it not for the fact that sin entered into the world through Adam. The whole of creation was involved in that fall. That ought to be self-evident to any thinking man, for were you to drive out through the country at this season of the year, you would soon discover that the green is gone, the trees have lost their color, and the leaves have almost all fallen to the ground, and very soon the whole countryside will be barren and lifeless. I have always enjoyed the fall colorings, but I have never forgotten the comment my mother once made, while I was driving her through a certain section of New York State. It was the season of the year when the whole countryside was a blaze of color. I asked her if she thrilled over the sight, and, much to my surprise, she said, "No, I do not. It is the spring season of the year that brings joy to me for then all the earth seems ready to burst into newness of life; but the colorings of fall always remind me of the modern undertaker, who dresses up the body of the deceased so that the sight is not too gruesome. To me," said mother, "nature seems to be putting earth to sleep and the whole countryside speaks of death." Yes, creation was involved in the fall of man. There is nothing to rejoice about there: the only place of true joy is to be found in the Lord's doing on *that* day when the stone which the builders rejected became the headstone of the corner. Do you wonder why a Christian rejoices in the Lord's day, the first day of the week, which commemorates the resurrection of the Lord from the dead?

PROSPERITY—WHO BRINGS IT?

One final word, as we direct attention to the 25th verse, where the Psalmist said: "Save now, I beseech thee, O LORD: O LORD, I beseech thee, send now prosperity." It almost appears as if David knew something about the depression we have endured for nearly seven years—"O LORD, I beseech thee, send now prosperity." Strictly speaking, David was asking for a national deliverance of the people of Israel, but the principle in the case is identical to the application I hope to make. Observe to whom the Psalmist delivered his request. If, as I think, David was the writer of this Psalm, then he had none else to go to, for there was none higher than himself in his government. If someone else was the writer of the Psalm, then he did not place any confidence in the king's ability to bring prosperity to pass, for whoever wrote the Psalm knew that there was only one person who could send lasting prosperity and that was the One to whom he addressed his request, when he said , "O LORD, I beseech thee, send now prosperity."

Irrespective of what party affiliations you may have, or what candidate you intend voting for next Tuesday, neither one of them can bring lasting prosperity to this country. The only one who can send prosperity to the United States is the One to whom the Psalmist addressed his petition, when he said, "O LORD, I beseech thee, send now prosperity." What America needs more than anything else is a return to the God of the Scriptures, to a confession of national sins, to the bending of our national knees in prayer, that God Himself will send prosperity and send it *now*. Isn't it interesting to see how the Bible touches every part of our lives? It has a message for the present as well as the future. May we heed it now!

PSALM ONE HUNDRED NINETEEN—PART ONE
(VERSES 1 to 8)

DAVID'S DIARY—GOD'S DIARY

WE have finally come to the 119th Psalm in our series of meditations in this wonderful collection of inspired hymns. This is the longest Psalm. It is my judgment that David wrote it. I have not the slightest idea under what circumstances he composed it, or whether he followed, as some suggest, the idea of a diary, which he began in his youth and continued to his old age. Of one thing we can be sure: if this is David's diary, all the world has been invited to look at it. It is not the kind of a diary where the writer need be apprehensive lest others examine it. It certainly does not need to be locked up in any safe deposit box under the seal of the Court of the State. You know there are such diaries! And there are some newspapers that delight to get possession of those choice, tasty bits of comment that seem to satisfy the morbid curiosity of, sad to say, too many people of our land. If David kept a diary, and this 119th Psalm is it, then it gives us a splendid idea.

But may we first ask: does our mind run in the channels of this Psalm? Do we find ourselves again and again meditating upon the preciousness and the glory of the Word of God and the grace of God? Or, must we sadly confess that we very often find that our mind wanders into places where we would not dare permit our feet to enter?

Whether we keep a diary or not, God keeps one. In that wonderful little prophetic book of Malachi, we read this interesting statement in the 16th verse of the 3rd chapter, "Then they that feared the LORD spake often one to another: and the LORD hearkened, and heard it, and a book of remembrance was written before him for them that feared the LORD, and that thought upon his name." What a statement! There are a great number of writers in heaven. We might call them reporters, but in Scriptural language they are angels. Among their tasks is this— the keeping of books for them that fear the Lord and for those who think on His name. Let me complete the quotation from Malachi. The Lord says, "And they shall be mine," that is, those who think on His name, "And they shall be mine, saith the LORD of hosts, in that day when I make up my jewels; and I will spare them, as a man spareth his own son that serveth him." I know that this was written specifically to Israel, and I do not wish to rob Israel of any blessing that belongs to her, but I believe the principle is eternal and that we in this age, Gentiles in the flesh, to be true, but now members of the body of Christ, because we have been born again by the Spirit of God, I believe that we, too, have an intimate relationship to God. If God would keep a book of remembrance for those in Israel that thought on His name, what must be said for those who were Gentiles, outside of any covenant relationship with Him, and who now love Him, and delight to think on His name! Well, so much for the Lord's, as well as David's diary.

THE ALPHABET

There are twenty-two stanzas comprising this Psalm and each begins with one of the letters of the Hebrew alphabet, consecutively from *aleph* to *tau*. That brings us to another interesting matter, the subject of language or the matter of the alphabet. There was a time when all the world spoke the same language but, because those who were leaders in that age determined, by collective regimentation, to defy the eternal God to destroy the earth a second time with a flood, God dispersed the human race by co.. founding their tongues; the result of which was that the tower of Babel was never completed and the regimentation ended in the wildest type of individualism, for each man spoke a different tongue so that the others could not understand him. The alphabet is an interesting set of letters or characters. Human speech is invaluable; yet, in our own native tongue we require twenty-six letters to express our thoughts to each other, while in the Hebrew tongue they require but twenty-two. Thus, in this 119th Psalm, each one of the twenty-two letters of the alphabet introduces a stanza of the Psalm.

What does that convey to our minds? What was the Holy Spirit's intention but to remind us of the fact that language was devised primarily in order that man might converse with God, and, secondly, that he might converse with other men. If your tongue, and the alphabet at your disposal, is merely used for secular comments, sometimes even falling to a level of indecency, may I suggest that God never intended the alphabet to be used for such a purpose, and that it is just one more evidence of a sinful nature. Our mouths should be used to extol the glory of God and that we might acquire the language of heaven. Strange as it may appear, the twenty-six letters of the alphabet, which have been so effectively used by Satan as well as by the individual, are the very letters that God has taken into His own mouth, in order to convey to us, in our own language, the thoughts of His mind, the movements of His heart, and the purposes of His counsel. Thus, it is not surprising that this 119th Psalm in every one of its verses revolves around the Word of God. Let us read the first of the stanzas:

"Blessed are the undefiled in the way, who walk in the law of the LORD.

"Blessed are they that keep his testimonies, and that seek him with the whole heart.

"They also do no iniquity: they walk in his ways.

"Thou hast commanded us to keep thy precepts diligently.

"O that my ways were directed to keep thy statutes!

"Then shall I not be ashamed, when I have respect unto all thy commandments.

"I will praise thee with uprightness of heart, when I shall have learned thy righteous judgments.

"I will keep thy statutes: O forsake me not utterly."

Observe that in every one of these eight verses the Word of God is spoken of in a different way. In verse 1 it is the law of the Lord; in verse 2 it is His testimonies; in verse 3 His ways; in verse 4 His precepts; in verse

5 His statutes; in verse 6 His commandments; in verse 7 His judgments; and in verse 8 again His statutes. This brings us to the heart of the message, which is the Word of God. What a subject! It is absolutely inexhaustible. It defies the keenest intellect and it challenges the stoutest heart. The Word of God—what an expression! But what does the Psalmist mean, and what do we mean, by the term, the Word of God?

THE WORD OF GOD!

Has God ever spoken? Indeed He has! Where has He spoken? In His written Word. He has also spoken in creation, to be true, and He has spoken through His oral or living Word, our Lord Jesus Christ; but, more specifically, just now, we shall reduce the expression to mean the written Word, the Bible. This Book *is* God's Word. The Bible is—His commandments, His judgment, His law, His statutes, His inexorable word. He has said that it is forever settled in the heavens. He declares it to be perfect. He insists that the wise of this world stagger before it, while the foolish man, if he but be honest and acknowledge his sinfulness, will find that it abounds in simplicity as well as majesty and profundity. The greatest minds of every age have bowed before this wonderful Book—the Word of God. While there are more copies of it in the possession of man today than at any other period in human history, it is the most neglected book, the least known, and, I was about to say, the book least preached about from the pulpits of our land. There is a famine in the average church for the Word of God. Take our own city, the City of New York; go along Fifth Avenue or Park Avenue; go into the churches, go into one this Sunday, another the next, and so on, until you have covered them all. I dare say that were you to count on your fingers the number of churches where you felt assured that the man who was behind the pulpit was a man of God, expounding the Word of God, you might find that one hand had more fingers than you would need. That is a terribly sad commentary.

The other evening I was riding in the subway with a gentleman who knows the religious situation in this city as well as anyone. We talked about an individual, a young man, who has had a remarkable conversion. A derelict at one time, he is now gloriously saved, so that his major purpose in life is to witness for his Lord and to bring individuals into the presence of the Master. My friend said, concerning this man, that he brings more people to Christ in a week, than all the churches on Fifth Avenue do in the course of a year. I do not think that statement is exaggerated. Why do we have churches, if not for the express purpose of preaching the Word of God, which alone gives light to the darkened conscience of man?

The Word of God is sharp, sharper than any two-edged sword; yet it is a balm for the distressed mind and heart, and all the remedies on earth fade into insignificance when compared with the wonderful healing qualities of the Word of God. The most disturbed, the most perplexed, come to it to find peace and guidance. The new born babes in Christ come to it to enjoy the sincere milk of the Word. The young men, filled with hope and vitality, come to it for strength and inspiration. The older men, gray-haired, strong, weather-beaten, having gone through the conflicts of life and now mellowed, are the first to bear testimony to the truthfulness of the Word of God.

THE PERFECT LAW OF THE LORD

Let us took at what this 119th Psalm has to say about the Word of God. We shall limit our immediate comments to the first eight verses, which comprise the first stanza. In the first place, it is quite evident that the first four verses present an idealism to which none of us has attained. There is not a single one of us who has walked in the ways of the Lord; none can boast that he has kept His testimonies, or sought Him with a whole heart. Certainly, not a single one of us can say that we have done no iniquity, or that we have kept His precepts diligently. By the way, I remind you that in the Hebrew the little word "blessed," which is the first word of this Psalm, has in it the idea of happiness. We have not enjoyed that type of happiness. We do not know what it is to have perfection or to be undefiled. There is only one person who ever enjoyed that happiness, and that was the sinless, perfect Son of God. The best we can say was expressed by David in the 5th and 6th verses, when he wrote, "O that my ways were directed to keep thy statutes! Then shall I not be ashamed, when I have respect unto all thy commandments."

No, we cannot boast of perfection. We must acknowledge that we are defiled, that we have not kept His testimonies, that we have not sought Him with a whole heart, and in fact, instead of doing no iniquity, we have abounded in iniquity. We have not sought His precepts diligently; we have gone away from them. However, the moment the individual faces that record and suddenly becomes conscious of the righteousness of God and the perfection and holiness of God, his own sinfulness becomes overwhelming, so that he strives to hide himself from the eternal God. It is then that the gospel comes in as the greatest bit of news that the ear of man has ever heard—the good news that "though your sins be as scarlet, they shall be as white as snow; though they be red like crimson, they shall be as wool." When you have come to know and experience the forgiving grace of our Lord, then you will find that your whole attitude toward the Word of God will change. Whereas, previously, you ran away from His precepts, you now want your way directed by His statutes. You are no longer ashamed. A little while ago your heart was defiled, but now you have respect to His commandments. You now possess a song, whereas, previously you had a wail. Therefore you say, "I will praise thee with uprightness of heart, when I shall have learned thy righteous judgments." Furthermore, you are actuated by an urge that cries out, "I will keep thy statutes: O forsake me not utterly."

Observe that the Psalmist said, "forsake me not utterly." It seems that it is the lot of many devoted servants of God to experience at times a sense of despair, as if God had forsaken them. Let me give you an illustration of just such a case, out of the Book. The other morning, at our family devotions, we were reading the Book of Ruth. You remember the story. It will never be forgotten. The devotion of Ruth to her mother-in-law, Naomi, is but one of the interesting features of that story. Naomi sojourned in the land of Moab. While there, she went through some sad experiences. When she returned, accompanied by her daughter-in-law, to the land of Bethlehem from which she came, all the city came out to greet her, and said, "Is this Naomi?" She responded, "Call me not Naomi, call me Mara: for the Almighty hath dealt very bitterly with me. I went out full, and the LORD hath brought me home again empty: why then call ye me Naomi, seeing the LORD hath testified against me, and the Almighty hath afflicted me?" Little did Naomi understand, at that time, that her difficulties in the land of Moab were God's provisions and the evidences of His grace to get her back into Bethlehem, in order that He might bring about a union between Ruth and Boaz, out of whose loins would come David, the writer of this Psalm. Do not be discouraged if perchance your circumstances are disturbing and it appears as if God has forsaken you. When you come to the end of the road you will find that God has made wonderful provisions for you, to lead you into greater things. Then you will understand, just as Naomi learned, that your difficulties are God's appointments and the evidences of His grace.

PSALM ONE HUNDRED NINETEEN—PART TWO
(Verses 9 to 48)

THE INCREASING GREATNESS OF THE WORD OF GOD

WERE we to do justice to this Psalm, we would be obliged to devote at least one meditation to each stanza, but I have decided to take four or five stanzas together for the next few meditations and simply touch on the key verse of each stanza; and if not the key verse then the key thought, in order that we may gather some general impressions as to the theme of the stanzas and at the same time kindle a desire in the hearts and minds of those who listen to study this wonderful Psalm more carefully for themselves.

THE FACT OF SIN AND ITS CLEANSING

The second stanza begins with verse 9 and ends with verse 16. It is introduced by the second letter of the Hebrew alphabet. In the 1st verse of that section we are presented with the question, "Wherewithal shall a young man cleanse his way?" There can be no doubt that this question represents the key thought of the second stanza. There are some ideas flowing out of this question that are interesting. In the first place, one does not have to wait until he is aged to have need of cleansing, though, of course, it is true that the older a man gets the more sin is piled up against his record.

This idea was deftly expressed by the group who had gathered about our Lord Jesus Christ as they presented before Him a woman accused of adultery. They said she was caught in the very act. They said that Moses in the law commanded that she be stoned, yet they refrained from fulfilling the law in not stoning her. They wished only to place the responsibility upon His shoulders so that they might have something of which to accuse Him. If He excused the woman, they would say He was guilty of despising the law, and yet, if He upheld the law, where was His evidence of mercy? So His critics surely thought they had entrapped Him. At the beginning our Lord paid no attention to their accusations, but stooped down and with His finger wrote on the ground. I have not the slightest idea what He wrote, but, because of the continual prodding of the accusers, the Lord found it necessary to address them saying, "He that is without sin among you, let him first cast a stone at her." Again He stooped down and wrote on the ground. The record reads that "they which heard it, being convicted by their own

conscience, went out one by one, *beginning at the eldest,* even unto the last
. . ." So, you see, the older a man gets the more his conscience possesses
that with which to accuse him. Yet even the youngest member of the
group, that morning recognized his sinfulness by joining the procession,
leaving our Lord Jesus Christ alone with the accused woman. So youth
needs to be cleansed as well as old age.

But wherewithal shall a young man cleanse his way? Can he do so by
determination, solely? Indeed not! There can be only one answer to the
question. The Psalmist gave it when he added, "by taking heed thereto
according to *thy* word." The Word of God alone is powerful to keep a
young man and to cleanse his way. Wise is that young man who follows
the precedent of the Psalmist, expressed by him in the 11th verse, "Thy
word have I hid in mine heart, that I might not sin against thee."

Whether the sin is against another or against one's self, whether the sin
is in the body or out of the body, all sin strikes at the throne of God and,
in the final analysis, is treason against God. What better place therefore to
hide the Word of God than in our hearts, so that we sin not against God.
There are some people, many people in fact, who keep the Bible in their
minds. They have stored away a great many passages of Scripture. But
for what reason? Only the other day, I had luncheon with a friend who
commented on the frequency of quotation from the Scripture used by an
acquaintance who happens to be a trial lawyer. That lawyer hid the Word
of God in his mind. He did so in order to slay the accusers of his client or
to sway the jury about to weigh the evidence against his client. That man
never hid the Word of God in his heart. When the Word is stored in the
heart, the individual finds it a wonderful power in preserving him from
outbreaking sin.

SEEING "WONDROUS THINGS" AND TALKING ABOUT
"WONDROUS WORKS"

Now let us look at the third stanza. It begins with verse 17 and ends
with verse 24. I think the key verse is the 18th, which reads, "Open thou
mine eyes, that I may behold wondrous things out of thy law." The Psalmist recognized that human ability is in vain when it comes to understanding
God's Word. The New Testament has expressed this truth in the following
language, ". . . the natural man receiveth not the things of the Spirit of
God: for they are foolishness unto him: neither can he know them, because
they are spiritually discerned." The Bible defies and challenges the best

mind of the natural man. Once-born men are unable to see its beauties, its perfections, and its glory. Neither can they see that it is the revelation of God. It is only when a man has been born again, or twice-born, that the Holy Spirit opens the eyes of the mind, so that the individual can behold the wondrous things that are to be found in God's Word. So if you desire a knowledge of the Scripture, if you crave to behold its glories and its beauties, there is only one person who can unfold it to you, and that person is the Holy Spirit. It is His great joy to reveal the wondrous things that are hidden in the Word of God.

Let us continue into the next stanza, which begins with verse 25, and ends with verse 32. There the same thought seems to be expressed, as in the preceding stanza. The key verse of the fourth stanza is the 27th, which reads, "Make me to understand the way of thy precepts: so shall I talk of thy wondrous works." In verse 18, there was the cry, "Open thou mine eyes, that I may *behold* wondrous things out of thy law" but in verse 27 the Psalmist asked for an understanding of God's precepts, so that he might be able to *talk* of His wondrous works. In the first petition there is the desire for knowledge, and for an unfolding of the beauties of the Word of God, so that the individual's spiritual life may be fed and grow; whereas in verse 27 there is a desire to understand, in order to talk to others of the glories of God and His Word. Where there is an understanding, there is a desire to talk of the wondrous works of God. No wonder it is hard to keep a Christian quiet; I mean one who has feasted upon the Word of God, whose soul has been refreshed by the fountain of life, and whose eyes have beheld the beauties of God's Word. It is utterly impossible to seal that man's lips. A normal, healthy Christian experience involves the exercise of talking, even as it involves the delightful pleasure of feasting on spiritual food. We learn spiritual joys, not only for our own blessing, but that we may pass them on to others. In like manner a Christian is not normal, nor has he enjoyed a normal Christian experience, until he has spoken to others of the chief joy of his own heart.

In the current issue of "Time," there is an item entitled "Bibles," telling the story of how two men were assigned to the same room in a hotel in Boscobel, Wisconsin, as a result of which meeting no less than 1,300,000 Bibles have been given away. That was because a shoe salesman by the name of John H. Nicholson was putting into practice the 27th verse of the 119th Psalm—talking of God's "wondrous works"—when he turned to his new roommate, a paint salesman by the name of Samuel Eugene Hill, and said, "My custom is to read a portion of God's Word every night and give thanks for God's care over me during the day." Much to his joy, Hill answered, "I, too, am a Christian. Let us have our devotions together." Those of us who have had similar experiences, know the joy that those two salesmen experienced that night. Their meeting led to the formation of that splendid organization called "The Gideons," which distributes Bibles freely in hotel rooms and elsewhere.

THE FUTILITY OF SELF-DETERMINATION

Now let us proceed to the fifth stanza, which commences with verse 33 and ends with verse 40. Of that portion I should like to read verse 35, "Make me to go in the path of thy commandments; for therein do I delight." That seems a strange request, doesn't it? One would instinctively assume that if a man delighted to do a certain thing he would not need to be urged to do it. If a man enjoys playing a game of golf and he has the time available, you golfers (duffers as well as you who play in the low eighties) know it does not take much urging to accept an invitation to go out on the links with delightful companions. Thus it appears strange that the Psalmist, if he delighted in the path of obedience, should ask the Lord to "make" him to go in those paths. Yet David prayed definitely, "Make me to go in the path of thy commandments . . ." Upon closer examination we shall find that this is not strange, nor is it a contradiction. Rather it is a perfect expression of what takes place in the life of every individual who has sought to obey God. There seems to be in the human heart a tendency to leave the path of obedience. I was about to say it appears as if it is as natural for an individual to sin as it is for him to breathe. We are possessed of a nature whose sole desire is to express itself in disobedience and in sin. The Psalmist knew that, for he knew his own heart. So did George Robinson, who composed the words of that wonderful hymn, "Come, Thou Fount of Every Blessing," when he wrote:

> "O to grace how great a debtor
>   Daily I'm constrained to be!
> Let Thy goodness, like a fetter,
>   Bind my wand'ring heart to Thee:
> Prone to wander, Lord, I feel it,
>   Prone to leave the God I love;
> Here's my heart, O, take and seal it,
>   Seal it for Thy courts above."

He is a wise man who knows his own heart and who understands that he is unable to control his life, and therefore yields himself to God. I recall a phrase a friend of mine gave some years ago, which has been the source of much blessing to my heart. He said there is only one word for the unsaved person, and that word is *believe*. That is all one must do. "Believe on the Lord Jesus Christ," it is written, "and thou shalt be saved . . ." You can do nothing else, as nothing less is acceptable to God. So the word to be given to those who have not bowed the knee to Christ, who are still lost in their sin, who do not know what it is to have eternal life, is as clear as crystal and as simple as it is final. It is—Believe.

However, to those who have embraced the Lord Jesus Christ, who have trusted Him and who have put their faith in Him, there, too, is only one word that should characterize their life and that word is beautifully expressive. It is *yield*. "Yield yourselves unto God . . ." To yield a life means to turn over that life. That is what the Psalmist had in mind, when he asked, "Make me to go in the path of thy commandments." There is not a single Christian who will disagree with me when I say that there is no place of pleasure or joy comparable to that which is experienced when we walk in the path of obedience to the Lord. Some may say, if that be the case why do we leave the path of obedience? We too, have asked ourselves that question, yet the answer is well known. It is the human heart, which is so perverse that when left to itself for even one unguarded moment it walks in the path of disobedience. If this be the case, Christian, cease your struggle; cease trying to dominate your own life; and turn the task over to the One who was able to calm the waves and still the wind by His spoken word; who brought a great calm where there was a terrific storm. He can do for that heart of yours what He did to the Galilean lake.

THE UNANSWERABLE LOGIC OF GOD'S MERCIES

For our final comment, we go to the sixth stanza, which begins with verse 41 and continues to verse 48, and which reads:

> "Let thy mercies come also unto me, O LORD, even thy salvation, according to thy word.
> "So shall I have wherewith to answer him that reproacheth me: for I trust in thy word.
> "And take not the word of truth utterly out of my mouth; for I have hoped in thy judgments.
> "So shall I keep thy law continually for ever and ever.
> "And I will walk at liberty: for I seek thy precepts.
> "I will speak of thy testimonies also before kings, and will not be ashamed.

"And I will delight myself in thy commandments,
which I have loved.
"My hands also will I lift up unto thy commandments,
which I have loved; and I will meditate in thy statutes."

Too often the critic, the unbeliever, the agnostic, and the doubter have won the day with us because we were unable to answer their reproaches. Yet a clear knowledge of what the Word teaches will equip us with the answer for every dart. While argument and evidence of scientific character are all right in their place, they alone will rarely bring the individual to Christ. The most effective drawing power is the mercy of God, even His salvation, which is according to His Word.

This past week I had a letter from a gentleman who listens to our radio program, stating that he had been dealing with another man who insisted that if he could be given a satisfactory answer to the question, Where did Cain get his wife? he would believe the rest of the Bible. This gentleman said that he tried to answer him the best he knew how, and asked if I could help. I told him that I did not believe his skeptic friend would ever be satisfied, or would receive the Lord Jesus Christ and acknowledge the truth of the Word of God, even if he were thoroughly convinced as to where Cain got his wife. Of course, Cain married his sister. Whom else could he marry? The human race started with two people. Where, then, is this great difficulty? I responded to this man's letter, saying that with this question disposed of, there is no doubt but that the skeptic would seek to hide behind some other supposed difficulty.

Men are not brought to Christ by human persuasion or mental gymnastics. Men are brought to Christ by the vital ministry of the Spirit of God. As we who profess Christ yield ourselves to Him, so much the better are we able to answer the honest inquirer or the dishonest reproacher, as we present the Word of God to their heart and conscience.

The Psalmist wrote, in verse 46, "I will speak of thy testimonies also before kings, and will not be ashamed." David, you are correct; none need be ashamed of the Word of God. There is no necessity for an apology in our witness for Him, even if it be before kings, for there is no difference between the king and the commoner. They both have the same nature; they both commit the same sins; they both need the same Saviour. There is only one Saviour, as there is only one name given under heaven among men, whereby we must be saved, and that name is the most precious name, the name of the Lord Jesus Christ.

Psalm One Hundred Nineteen—Part Three
(Verses 49-88)

"A BOTTLE IN THE SMOKE"

W E have now come in the 119th Psalm to the seventh stanza, introduced by the Hebrew letter Zain and comprising verses 49 to 56. Let us read the first two verses of this stanza:

"Remember the word unto thy servant, upon which
thou hast caused me to hope.
"This is my comfort in my affliction: for thy word
hath quickened me."

I seriously question whether any child of God is exempt from affliction. In fact, if anyone has been exempt and has never known what affliction is, if I were that one I would be a little apprehensive of my relation to the Lord. In the New Testament letter to the Hebrews we learn that God exercises a paternal relationship over each of His children. Let me be clear once again, that, while God is the Creator of every individual, He has declared that He is the God and Father of all those who believe in Christ. Therefore He has a special intimacy with believers, quite distinct from His relationship as Creator to the rest of mankind. Concerning those who do believe, and who can therefore call God their Father, we read in the 12th chapter of Hebrews, the 6th verse, "For whom the Lord loveth he chasteneth, and scourgeth *every* son whom he receiveth." Note it says "every son." Not a single one is exempt. If we have never known affliction; if we have never known the corrective scourging of the Lord, we had better check up on our relationship with the Lord. It seems a peculiar privilege of the believer to endure affliction. David knew what it was to be afflicted, but he said that there was a certain thing which was his comfort in his affliction. What was it? The Word. Upon it, David based his faith and caused his hope to rest.

Isn't it interesting that David should call upon God to remember His own Word? You and I, therefore, have a right to remind God of His own promises, which are to be found in the Word, and confidently expect that God will deliver us out of our affliction through His steadfastness to His own Word. Human friends may bring their cheer and attempt to sympathize with us, and such sympathy should never be under-estimated, yet there is nothing in the world that brings joy and quietness to the human heart in the time of affliction, like the very Word of God itself.

REMINDING OUR HEARTS ABOUT OUR FEET

Now let us go to the next stanza, which comprises verses 57 to 64, the opening verse of which reads, "Thou art my portion, O LORD: I have said that I would keep thy words" and then verses 59 and 60, "I thought on my ways, and turned my feet unto thy testimonies. I made haste, and delayed not to keep thy commandments."

In the previous section David, as an afflicted child of God, asked God to remember His Word; in this section, David called upon his own heart to remember the Word of the Lord, and determined, by God's grace, to keep His Word. The other day I was talking to a friend who asked about another, and particularly concerning his relationship with the Lord. I said, "Well, he has the truth in his head. He has had the benefit of splendid Bible teaching, he knows what the truth is and what error is, but he has never allowed the Word of God to get into his feet." But David wrote in the 59th verse of this Psalm, "I thought on my ways, and turned *my feet* unto thy testimonies."

That brings us to the walk of a Christian. It is one thing to know doctrine and to have scripturally correct knowledge, and to be able to think clearly on spiritual subjects, but I am not sure how advantageous that is if our whole being is not permeated by the Word of God and the injunctions of this Word, so that our feet, as well as our minds, have become adjusted. I think there are a great number of Christians who are club-footed. Their heads are all right, but their feet are pointed in the opposite direction. I hope you won't mind strong language though I'm certain that if we will be honest with our own hearts and consciences we will confess that the words are soundly based on the teachings of the Word of God. We, as Christians, as professed followers of the Lord Jesus Christ, have absolutely no right to walk in the path of disobedience, or to walk in the path of this world. Our feet belong where the Lord traveled. We ought to take our position with the Lord whom we serve, but whom the world rejects. It is a depressingly sad sight to see a Christian walking in the ways of this world. If we are walking in such paths, David gave a good example as to what we should do, when he said, "I made haste, and delayed not to keep thy commandments."

GOLD AND SILVER

Now we go to the next section, which begins with verse 65 and ends with verse 72. We shall read the first and last verses of this stanza. Verse

65 reads, "Thou hast dealt well with thy servant, O LORD, according unto thy word" and verse 72, "The law of thy mouth is better unto me than thousands of gold and silver." Oh, yes, we can all respond with David, and say unto the Lord, "Thou hast dealt well with thy servant, O LORD, according unto thy word," but what about His Word being preferred above gold and silver? May I say something right here, which is decidedly personal. I have never known bitterness, nor disappointment, except when my heart has been disobedient to God. When something came in to spoil my fellowship with the Lord, a definite damper settled upon my spirit. No individual can enjoy the fulness of God's blessings, unless he is walking in the path of obedience. God must deal according to His Word. Who amongst us, who have professed Christ as our Saviour, but will acknowledge that even when we have been disobedient, God has dealt with us according to His Word. Thus we readily agree with David in saying, "Thou hast dealt well with thy servant, O LORD . . ." But what about the 72nd verse, "The law of thy mouth is better unto me than thousands of gold and silver"? How many can make a statement like that? How many, do you suppose, have said the opposite? Give me the gold and silver, Lord, six days of the week, and on the seventh I'll keep your Word. We may not have used those words audibly, but our life has spelled out each letter of it.

Now there is nothing wrong with gold or silver, despite the fact that a great many people think there is a passage of Scripture which reads, "Money is the root of all evil." But you will search the Scriptures in vain for any such idea or words. What you will find is this, ". . . the *love* of money is the root of all evil." Gold and silver stand us in good stead at times. They symbolize wealth, though we poor Americans can no longer lay our hands on gold—we have to be satisfied with paper money.

However, there is something that is infinitely more valuable than gold or silver; so much so, that David says it is worth more than thousands of silver and gold. That which is worth more is the law of God. Can we say what David said? If we can, we have learned the secret of two things. First, the indescribable peace of God; and second, the all-conquering spirit of contentment. The one enables us to enjoy fellowship with God, and the other to be at peace with ourselves and our neighbor. Thus it is written, "godliness with contentment is great gain. For we brought nothing into this world, and it is certain we can carry nothing out." The fact of the matter is that the New Testament declares that "they that will be rich fall into temptation and a snare, and into many foolish and hurtful lusts, which drown men in destruction and perdition." But they that love the law of the Lord never need worry about snares, hurtful lusts, destruction, or perdition. Such are the regular, special, and extra dividends that wealth receives; but godliness, contentment, and devotion to God's Word bring us dividends of eternal value, and, what is more, none can tax them away!

A SMALL LETTER AND A BIG SUBJECT

As we go into the tenth section, which comprises verses 73 to 80, we observe that the key verse is the first, which reads, "Thy hands have made me and fashioned me: give me understanding, that I may learn thy commandments." This section is introduced by the tenth letter of the Hebrew alphabet, which is Jod, which, by the way, is the smallest letter in their alphabet. While this letter reminds us of jots and tittles, it is a mistake to conclude that the section is occupied with trifling things. In fact, what could be more important than to give attention to the commandments of the Lord, whose hands have made and fashioned us.

Dr. Isaac Page, Field Director of the China Inland Mission, tells of an old Chinese gentleman who had come to know Christ, and who was accompanying him on one of his journeys in China. One morning Dr. Page was surprised to observe him bending over the earth, taking a little of the dirt in his hands and between his fingers, feeling it, and then dropping it to the ground. Dr. Page asked, "What are you doing?" Looking up into the face of Dr. Page, he answered, "Teacher, isn't it wonderful that I am made of the dust of this earth, and yet the Holy Spirit lives in me." That is enough to stagger any individual. It is almost too great to apprehend, and yet it is true. These bodies of ours have been fashioned by the hand of God. This life, which we call ours, is one of His gifts. We only possess it as long as He is willing that we should have it. When there is an understanding of this fact, there necessarily follows the petition, "give me understanding, that I may learn thy commandments."

"A BOTTLE IN THE SMOKE"

For our final comment, we go to the 11th stanza, comprising verses 81 to 88. In that section David is found to be in distress. His soul faints, his eyes fail him, his enemies have digged pits for him, and his persecutors wrongfully press him, so that he cries out, "I am become like a bottle in the smoke; yet do I not forget thy statutes." That is a strange simile, isn't it?

"I am become like a bottle in the smoke . . ." We will not be able to comprehend the significance of that comment, if we assume that David was talking about a glass bottle. Remember, our Lord said that men do not put new wine into old bottles or old wine into new bottles. Our Lord was not talking about glass bottles. When a bottle is made of glass, it does not make much difference what is put into it. Both our Lord and David were speaking of the skins that were used for holding wine. These skins, when empty, were hung up in the tents or homes of Israel. Were we to go to Palestine now and enter into the tent of an Arab, we would understand this simile. The tent wouldn't be a very attractive place. Our first impression would be of smoke and suffocation, so that we would be delighted to get outside again, to enjoy the clear air. It is not surprising that the tent is smoky, as the fire is usually made of wood. The place literally becomes dense with smoke. These bottles or containers, when they were hung up in a place that reeked with smoke, grew black and covered with soot, and the heat gave them the appearance of being wrinkled and worn. David, in this section of the Psalm, was in the throes of despondency. Everything had gone against him. He was in the thick of the battle. There was a haze about him, like smoke rising from a smouldering fire. He could not see or think clearly. He appeared to be in the midst of the conflict, so that he considered that he was hanging above the fire, and likened himself unto a bottle in the smoke. His face was lined, his skin was wrinkled and shriveled, his countenance was blackened with the soot; he had about reached the place of despair, except for the fact that he added, "yet do I not forget thy statutes."

A WAR AGAINST SPIRITUAL POWERS

The Christian is always in the midst of battle, though the Bible says that we wrestle not against flesh and blood, but against principalities, and powers, and spiritual wickedness in high places. Our warfare is terrific. It is with the powers of darkness. You who know nothing about it have not the slightest notion of what powers concentrate on the man who determines to live for God in this world. Let me illustrate what I mean. A preacher friend and I have been tremendously interested in a young man who has recently taken a definite stand for Jesus Christ. He is a graduate of one of our large eastern universities. His joy in his Saviour, the peace of mind and heart that he has received, and the absolute amazement that has possessed him over the glories of God's Word, have filled him with a desire that his friends and associates should get to know the same joy. As an effort toward this end, he communicated with the authorities of his alma mater, in order that they might extend an invitation to our mutual friend, so that he could address the student body of that college on the Scriptures and the Christ of the Scriptures. He was shocked at the response he received from his college, as the gentleman to whom he had written was a close friend of his. The letter suggested that this preacher was a back number, and that it was unwise to invite him to speak at the university, and if he must have a conservative, at least get one that's not an ignoramus. The young man was chagrined. He appeared bewildered. Why should his college take such a stand? But his preacher friend, whom both of us know to be one of the keenest and ablest men of the pulpit today, answered him by saying, "John, I'm not surprised, and you may just as well adjust yourself now to the inevitable, for our Lord said, 'If the world hate you, ye know that it hated me before it hated you. If ye were of the world, the world would love his own: but because ye are not of the world, but I have chosen you out of the world, therefore the world hateth you.'"

We, too, may be tempted to discouragement, as was David when he wrote, "I am become like a bottle in the smoke . . ." But, as David, so we rejoice by saying, "yet do I not forget thy statutes." The nation, or the individual, that forgets or discards or ridicules the statutes of God is much more in danger of the fire than a bottle in the smoke. After all, if one must choose, I'd rather be a bottle in the smoke than the wood in the fire.

PSALM ONE HUNDRED NINETEEN—PART FOUR
(Verses 89-128)

THE ETERNAL LIGHT OF THE WORD

IN many ways, the portion of the 119th Psalm to which we now come includes some of the most impressive expressions that are to be found in any part of the Scriptures. For instance, we begin with the section which commences with verse 89 and continues to verse 96, the opening verse of which reads, "For ever, O LORD, thy word is settled in heaven."

NO LIBERALISTS IN HEAVEN

This section is so impressive that we shall take time to read the eight verses comprising the stanza:

"For ever, O LORD, thy word is settled in heaven.
"Thy faithfulness is unto all generations: thou hast established the earth, and it abideth.

"They continue this day according to thine ordinances: for all are thy servants.

"Unless thy law had been my delights, I should then have perished in mine affliction.

"I will never forget thy precepts: for with them thou hast quickened me.

"I am thine, save me; for I have sought thy precepts.

"The wicked have waited for me to destroy me: but I will consider thy testimonies.

"I have seen an end of all perfection: but thy commandment is exceeding broad."

While there may be doubts in the minds of some people on earth as to the finality of God's Word, there is no question about it in heaven. The Psalmist said, "For ever, O LORD, thy word is settled *in heaven.*" There are no liberalists nor modernists in heaven.

I was looking at a Hebrew-English translation of this 89th verse, which reads, "To eternity, O LORD, standeth firm thy word in the heavens." Another translation gives it, "Thy word is set fast in the heavens." Now this does not mean that when an individual enters heaven (and you will, of course, realize by this time that I believe heaven is a literal place, not just the dream of religious fanatics), it does not mean that he ceases to possess an intellect, and that he becomes a machine, obeying the eternal God out of an exclusive sense of fear, much like a dog obeys his master. Anything of the kind is absolutely without the remotest justification, for, in the presence of God the believer possessed with the mind of Christ has greater facilities than ever for a contemplation of the trustworthiness as well as the perfections of the inspired Word.

It is rather significant that David should comment in this section upon the eternal steadfastness of the Word of God, when we consider that in the previous stanza he was in distress and in the bitterness of disappointment. He likened himself to a bottle in the smoke, so encompassed was he with trials and difficulties. That which proved to be his stay in the hour of trial was the Word of God; so out of his trial and sorrow of heart he enters into the joy and liberty and strength of the Word of God.

I wish we could comment on each verse of this stanza, as, for instance, commencing with verse 90, reading, "Thy faithfulness is unto all generations: thou hast established the earth, and it abideth. They continue this day according to thine ordinances: for all are thy servants."

But we must hasten to the thirteenth stanza, which commences with verse 97 and ends with verse 104. Observe verse 97, "O how love I thy law! it is my meditation all the day." Again, verse 99, "I have more understanding than all my teachers: for thy testimonies are my meditation" and, finally verse 103, "How sweet are thy words unto my taste! yea, sweeter than honey to my mouth!"

Occasionally I have heard from some who have stated that a study of the Scriptures has been somewhat dry to them. Certainly David never found it so, and let's not forget that David, in his day, possessed only a small part of the Scriptures that we have. I wonder if the difficulty some experience is due to their failure to love the Scriptures. The Psalmist said, "How sweet are thy words unto my taste!"—"O how love I thy law! it is my meditation all the day." David did not limit his meditation of God's Word to the Sabbath day. He was not satisfied to give only one day in seven to the Word of God. The fact is, the Word was David's constant companion, and in that law of the Lord did he meditate all the day.

Now notice verse 98, which immediately follows the declaration of David's love for the Word, and which reads, "Thou through thy commandments hast made me wiser than mine enemies . . ." I do not think that David was boasting, in the sense in which we are accustomed to think of boasting. I believe he was speaking the absolute truth, for, "The fear of the LORD is the beginning of wisdom . . ." There is no study which one could possibly engage in which will quicken the powers of perception and intelligence as much as a study of the commandments of the Lord. When we graduate from that school, if one ever does graduate, there is no question but that we possess wisdom exceeding that of our enemies. Invariably, as the individual meditates on the Scripture he develops an increasing appreciation of it. Such a man is amazed to observe the silly reasoning by men of unbelief.

We are living in a day when to confess that one believes in the Scriptures makes one almost sure to receive an invitation to be exhibited in the Smithsonian Institute, with the rest of the relics of a by-gone age. However, the fact remains that the wisest of this earth, devoid of spiritual life, express such idiotic fantasies when it comes to man's relationship with God, as to make them appear to be of a kindergarten age, rather than men of mature minds. If you wish to be wise, if you desire understanding, understanding more than the ancients, more than your present teachers, more than anyone in this world can give you, you will get it at the feet of our blessed Lord, with the Holy Spirit as your guide to lead you into all truth.

THE ETERNAL LIGHT

Now we enter the fourteenth stanza, which commences with verse 105 and ends with verse 112. This stanza begins with that familiar phrase, "Thy word is a lamp unto my feet, and a light unto my path." Charles Haddon Spurgeon has an interesting comment on this passage, when he writes, "The word of God is a lamp by night, a light by day, and a delight at all times." I think that that peerless preacher had the key to this passage. The Word of God is a lamp unto our feet, whenever we are called upon to tread unfamiliar pathways during the night season. In the high noon of human experience the Word is still equally important, for then it is a light unto our path. This world is in darkness; spiritual darkness. That darkness is so terrific, that even the presence of the Son of God as the light of the world could not penetrate it. Is that surprising? We learn this from the 1st chapter of John's Gospel, where we observe that "All things were made by him; and without him was not any thing made that was made. In him was life; and the life was the light of men. And the light shineth in darkness; and the darkness comprehended it not." Observe, that the darkness failed to comprehend the light. In other words, men failed to comprehend Christ. Do not reverse the order. It was not a case of the light not comprehending the darkness, nor of Christ failing to comprehend the depths of despair in the human soul. He know what was in man. He needed not that any should testify to Him of man. This world, and the men of this world, are in darkness. If we have light, surely it is not the light of intellect. If we have light, it is because Christ is the light. All light comes from the Word of God.

Some few years ago I had occasion to visit a doctor. While waiting for him, my eyes glanced over the books upon the table in the centre of the waiting room. I picked up a volume, a little booklet, which evidently was given to the physician by a friend at the time when that physician bade goodbye to his wife as she went out into the night of death. As I read through its pages, which abounded in the flowery language of philosophy, there was an exhortation to tread softly that weary road that leads to the open jaws of death. Through the use of sophistry, couched in the words which man's wisdom teacheth, it sought to ease the heart. When I finished reading it, I was impressed with its emptiness. Oh, it was beautifully written, it was as beautiful as a painted lily, but, like the lily, it lacked life. There was no warmth about it. Everything seemed to remind one of white sepulchres and cold stones. Man is absolutely lost in a dark labyrinth, when it comes to that thing we call death. But what a contrast with the individual who has the Word of God as a lamp unto his feet.

This past week I attended the funeral of a dear friend of mine; a man for whom I have had the greatest admiration. Were you to have asked me, in the days of his flesh, to point out to you a real Christian man in the city of New York, I would have pointed out that gentleman. Concerning him, my friend Dr. Harry A. Ironside, Pastor of the Moody Memorial Church, wrote that of all the men he knew he was the most Christlike. The family of that Christian man experienced the same emotions that well up in the breast of all humans when the hour of separation comes; yet they had a deep, abiding peace, which is the possession of every child of God. That peace comes from the Word of God, which has thrown light upon the darkest event in human history, when Christ said, "I am the resurrection, and the life: he that believeth in me, though he were dead, yet shall he live: and whosoever liveth and believeth in me shall never die." I challenge any to find words such as these in all the pages of human literature.

If you, this day, are nearing the close of your days (some of you, I know, are on beds of sickness, and some of you have just the faintest hold upon life), if you do not have the Word of God as a lamp unto your feet, I pray you, this moment, to receive the testimony of Christ, when He said, "I am the resurrection, and the life . . ." I urge you to put your confidence in Him. You will then have the inestimable joy of passing out of the here into the presence of the Lord, when He calls you to come up hither.

To you who are in the prime of life, who do not know what shadows are, possessed of vitality and keenness of intellect, may I suggest that even in the hour of greatest exuberance there is nothing comparable to the Word of God for throwing light upon your path. May you do as David did, when he wrote, in the 111th verse, "Thy testimonies have I taken as an heritage for ever: for they are the rejoicing of my heart."

"HOLD THOU ME UP . . ."

We now enter into the fifteenth stanza of this stupendous hymn. It commences with verse 113 and ends with verse 120. It begins, "I hate vain thoughts: but thy law do I love" and continues, "Thou art my hiding place and my shield: I hope in thy word." I believe the key verse of this section is the 117th, where we read, "Hold thou me up, and I shall be safe: and

I will have respect unto thy statutes continually." None of us possess the ability to keep ourselves. What the prophet said concerning Israel is true concerning the Gentiles, "All we like sheep have gone astray; we have turned every one to his own way . . ." If there is one characteristic a sheep possesses it is the ability to lose its way. It cannot keep the way or keep itself.

For our closing comment, I take you into the sixteenth section, which begins with verse 121 and ends with verse 128. We shall only comment on the 122nd verse, which reads, "Be surety for thy servant for good: let not the proud oppress me." I suppose that there are few who have not at some time or other gone surety for some friend or stranger. Those of you who have can probably all tell the same story. In that interesting book, The Proverbs, we read, "My son, if thou be surety for thy friend, if thou hast stricken thy hand with a stranger, thou art snared with the swords of thy mouth, thou art taken with the words of thy mouth." Perhaps Solomon knew about endorsing notes for some stranger or friend, and having them come back, like the cat with eight lives still to live! There is a further comment in Proverbs on this subject; it appears in the 15th verse of the 11th chapter and reads, "He that is surety for a stranger shall smart for it: and he that hateth suretiship is sure."

Yet, in this 119th Psalm, in the 122nd verse, David asked the Lord to be surety for him for good. If you will allow me to use commercial language to describe spiritual truth, David asked the Lord to endorse his note assuring him of an abundant entrance into the presence of God. The thing that is most amazing (and I mean every word of it) is the fact that God is perfectly willing to be surety for any man, stranger or friend. Oh, yes, our Lord smarted because of it. It was necessary that He pay the price. We were bankrupt, as far as having any rights or possessing the wherewithal to purchase a seat in the heavens was concerned, but the Lord Jesus Christ made the full payment, so that He endorses all those who will accept His payment as a full discharge of their obligations. It is incredible how few men there are who are willing to accept the Lord as their surety. And yet failure to do so means absolute bankruptcy and despair. I recommend the Lord Jesus Christ to you, as the endorser of your entrance into the kingdom of God.

PSALM ONE HUNDRED NINETEEN—PART FIVE
(Verses 129-136)

THE GLORY OF THE INCARNATE WORD

THE section we last touched upon, in our meditation on the 119th Psalm, covered the stanza commencing with verse 121 and ending with verse 128. We had time only to comment on the 122nd verse, which reads, "Be surety for thy servant for good: let not the proud oppress me." However there is another verse in that section which I feel must be considered. My attention was drawn to it on Friday of this past week, during a visit from a friend who listens each Sunday morning to this program, and who lives in York, Penna. He is a man with an infectious smile, so that you could pick him out of a crowd, feeling absolutely assured that he would respond affirmatively were you to ask him, Do you know the Lord as your Saviour? The verse to which he referred is the 126th, which reads, "It is time for thee, LORD, to work: for they have made void thy law." That is interesting, isn't it? The Psalmist informed the Lord that it was time for Him to work, and based the request on the fact that certain people, referred to by the editorial "they," had made void God's law.

THE LAW OF THE TEN COMMANDMENTS

There are so many thoughts that enter into one's mind upon considering this passage, that I would be tempted to devote a whole period to it, but I shall try to forbear. In the first place, let me be clear that I believe that' when the Psalmist speaks of the law, the commandments, the statutes, and God's precepts, he is not thinking primarily of the law of the Ten Commandments. Many people believe that such is the case. When one mentions the law of the Lord, immediately they assume that one must be referring to the Ten Commandments which were given to Moses. But that is not always so. When the Psalmist speaks of the law of the Lord in this Psalm, and the precepts of God and His testimonies, he is speaking of the entire revealed Word of God.

When David was living, he of course was under the law. We learn from the New Testament that the law was given by Moses, but grace and truth came by Jesus Christ; furthermore, that some people lived under the law, and other people outside the law. Those who were under the law were direct descendants of Israel, or who by choice had come within the camp of Israel. Those who lived outside the law were all the others, or the Gentiles. The law was the manifestation of God's requirements for the children of Israel, but if any believe that God gave the law in order that it might be kept, they miss its purpose entirely.

God gave the law in order to prove to man his utter incapability of meeting God's requirements. Please do not jump to a conclusion—it is not my own thought. What I have said is the exact teaching of the Holy Spirit, as expressed in the New Testament. To assure it, I take you to the 3rd chapter of that great letter to the Romans, where we read in the 19th verse, "Now we know that what things soever the law saith, it saith to them who are under the law . . ." For what purpose? "that every mouth may be stopped . . ." Not that every man might try to be good, but "that every mouth may be stopped, and all the world may become guilty before God. Therefore (note the conclusion) by the deeds of the law there shall no flesh be justified in his sight: for by the law is the knowledge of sin." The law, therefore, proves to man that he is utterly incapable of meeting the standards of God. The law, therefore, is a yardstick. A yardstick is used, not to stretch a piece of cloth, but to prove whether the cloth is thirty-six inches wide or less than that.

The law is also like a mirror. You do not stand before a mirror with the idea of having the mirror clean your face! You stand there in order to determine whether your face has any imperfections. And when you observe that it has, you proceed to use the proper cleansing methods to eliminate the imperfections and stains. So the law was given in order to reveal to man his utter incapability of meeting the requirements of God. The law is therefore called in the New Testament "the ministration of condemnation" and "the ministration of death." Anything that is a ministration of condemnation and of death is certainly nothing about which to enthuse.

However, my heart is enthused over the fact that now "the righteousness of God without the law is manifested, being witnessed by the law and the prophets; even the righteousness of God which is by faith of Jesus Christ unto all and upon all them that believe: for there is no difference . . ." My heart rejoices in the provision that God has made for my sin in the death of His Son, who alone met the righteous requirements of God.

If you think that this principle is solely a New Testament revelation, you are mistaken. The very principles of redemption which are enunciated and made clear in the New Testament are to be found in the Old Testament. I have sinned. My sin deserves condemnation. I cannot plead any merits of my own. I do not possess any. But Christ took my sin. He paid the price of my sin. God accepted the price He paid, and offered me His righteousness. What is more, because my sin has been charged to Christ it can never be charged to me again. Ponder that.

Now let us observe, from the 32nd Psalm, that David knew this same joy. He did not look to the law of the Ten Commandments for his salvation. Indeed, he did not. His joy was found in the fact, as we read in the 32nd Psalm, that "Blessed is he whose transgression is forgiven, whose sin is covered. Blessed is the man unto whom the LORD imputeth not iniquity . . ." Here David declared that happy is the man to whom God refuses to charge iniquity. Why? Because his transgression has been forgiven and his sin has been covered. And, by the way, the word "covered" is an atoning word, describing what takes place when the atoning blood covers our sin. This message of salvation, as well as the regulatory laws of God, is found in the entire written law of God. Well, so much for what the Psalmist meant by the use of the terms, law of the Lord, precepts of the Lord, etc. When he used these words he spoke of the entire written revelation of God, which is the delight of God's people.

"IT IS TIME FOR THEE, LORD, TO WORK"

But let us not get away from that wonderful 126th verse of the 119th Psalm—"It is time for thee, LORD, to work: for they have made void thy law." Of course, I believe that David was not only writing from the viewpoint of history, but he was speaking prophetically as well. You cannot make void the law of God or despise His Word, and expect that God will forever be silent. He may be silent for a long time, for His grace is beyond the imagination of any one of us. He is not willing that any should perish. Therefore, His patience is exactly like Himself—Godlike. However, there comes a day when it is high time for the Lord to work, and oh, what happens when He begins to work!

Occasionally I have mentioned that I am not a pessimist, but neither am I a confirmed ostrich, who sticks his head into the sand so that he cannot see the oncoming storm. If you think that everything is serene, you are just plain blind. No informed man feels any sense of security or serenity in the present day; certainly not any who are statesmen or political leaders. One treads softly today, for somehow the very ground under one's feet seems to have a give to it, as if it is ready to crumble or about to envelop one in quicksand. However, I know that just when everything seems darkest and men despise God's truth and His Word, making void His law, it is then time for the Lord to work.

Let me illustrate what I mean, by an event that took place last week which has attracted the attention of the whole world. The entire British Empire learned, probably to their surprise, that before any newspaper in their land commented upon the doings of their King, the Prime Minister had called upon him and acquainted him with the laws of the kingdom. The Prime Minister informed the British nation that he had heard from friends and from Britishers in America who had sent clippings of our newspapers, that a situation was developing which required that he, the Prime Minister, get to work. Before even the closest members of the Cabinet were aware, the Prime Minister had already concluded that it was time for him to *work* with the King, as it appeared that the King was traveling a road which would make void the law of God and of the nation.

So there will come a time when God will work; when He will no longer withhold His sword of justice; when He will rise to execute judgment and righteousness on the earth. It was not without import, as even our American newspapers noted, that in his note of abdication King Edward VIII made no reference to God, or to the fact that he was King by the grace of God alone.* By the way, I cannot help but comment, while we are on this subject, that the events of the past few weeks have made me, may I use the word, *admire* even more than before our King of kings and Lord of lords. There was a reaction in my heart and my mind as I read, for instance, from the editorial that appeared in the "New York Times" of December 11th, 1936, such words as these:

"It is a sad frustration of the hopes that had centered in Edward VIII. It was thought that he would be a democratic King, responsive to the social movements of his time and to the needs and aspirations of the British people. But all this high opportunity for service, this call to duty, he put aside in one mad surge of passion for a woman." That paper added, "This was unworthy of a true man and of the great tradition into which his inheritance had brought him."

---

* The omission of reference to King Edward as "Defender of the Faith" and "by the grace of God" in his instrument of abdication was explained in the House of Commons by Sir John Simon, Home Secretary, who said that these phrases are attached to the monarchy only after coronation. No one questions Sir Simon's knowledge of constitutional law, but it does seem that some explanation is required when one considers that these phrases "Defender of the Faith" and "by the grace of God" were used at the time of the proclamation of King Edward immediately after the death of his father.

One cannot avoid thinking of the multitudes of loyal British subjects who have been disappointed in their idol. Yet I do not know of a single soul who has bowed the knee to Jesus Christ and acknowledged Him as Lord, and given his allegiance to Him as King of kings and Lord of lords, who has ever found occasion to be disappointed in Him. The regal glory and the majestic character of the man Jesus Christ, whom God has declared to be King of kings and Lord of lords, calls forth increasing appreciation, as we observe the halting, faltering sons of men.

"THY TESTIMONIES ARE WONDERFUL"

Now let us go into the next stanza, which commences with verse 129 and continues to verse 136. There are so many good things in this section that we shall take time to read it in its entirety, even if we shall have only a moment or two to spend in it.

> "Thy testimonies are wonderful: therefore doth my soul keep them.
>
> "The entrance of thy words giveth light; it giveth understanding unto the simple.
>
> "I opened my mouth, and panted: for I longed for thy commandments.
>
> "Look thou upon me, and be merciful unto me, as thou usest to do unto those that love thy name.
>
> "Order my steps in thy word: and let not any iniquity have dominion over me.
>
> "Deliver me from the oppression of man: so will I keep thy precepts.
>
> "Make thy face to shine upon thy servant; and teach me thy statutes.
>
> "Rivers of waters run down my eyes, because they keep not thy law."

Observe verse 129, "Thy testimonies are wonderful: therefore doth my soul keep them." You who are acquainted with your Bible know that among the titles of the Messiah which Isaiah the prophet declared Him to have is the title *Wonderful*. It is, therefore, not surprising that the written Word is spoken of as wonderful, for there is a close harmony between the written Word and the incarnate Word, Jesus Christ the Lord. The written Word is wonderful—the person of Christ is wonderful. Because God's testimonies are wonderful, the Psalmist said, "my soul doth keep them." So, as the person of Christ fills the believer's heart and eyes with wonder, it causes him to bow before the Lord in yieldedness and in obedience to Him, saying, Lord, here am I, Thy will be done in me.

THE GEMS AND APPAREL OF THE KING

This past week a friend called at the office and left with me a booklet that had been prepared in anticipation of the coronation of the King of England. In that book there were little pieces of silk, dyed in the colors that are appropriate to the coronation season. These little strips of silk were pasted in the book and then, beside each, a little summary was carried describing the meaning of the colors and the gems they represent. I was thrilled when I read the booklet. I do not think I have ever seen more beautiful colors. There was the bright, deep, ruby red, which appears in all three of the King's crowns. To the spiritual mind, that conveys the thought of the glory of Christ, which is His death. Then there followed the lustrous blue of that great stone known as St. Edward's Sapphire, which clearly speaks of heavenly glories. Then came the pale cream of the pearl earrings of Queen Elizabeth, which reminds us of the parable of the pearl of great price, which our Lord told was sought out by Himself, as the merchantman who, when He had found it, went and sold all that He had and bought it. There was also the crown emerald, which somehow speaks to me of the green pastures into which the great Shepherd leads His sheep.

Then came the royal amethyst, the yellow sapphire, so rare and exquisite, and the delicate royal turquoise, all of which stones are to be found in the King's jewel-studded State sword. How these colors, in a sword, portray the grace of God in judgment; the amethyst speaking of sacrificial mercy, the yellow sapphire of godly judgment, and the turquoise of peace and serenity.

Then came the colors of the ceremonial robes; the imperial gold, revealed in the magnificent vestments worn by His Majesty, which, of course, declares to the Christian the fact that our Lord Jesus is the King of kings and Lord of lords. There was also the regal purple, the color of the trailing mantle worn by the King. It hardly seems necessary to recall to the spiritually minded that it was a purple robe which the soldiers placed upon Christ when they smote Him and bowed the knee in mock worship. But what a day it will be when He will be clad in a purple robe, and every knee shall bow and every tongue confess that Jesus Christ is Lord, to the glory of God the Father. Time almost fails me to tell of the deep blue dress of the Knight of the Order of the Garter and the expensive royal crimson, and, finally, the brilliant, radiant English scarlet, each of which colors unfold great truths to the spiritual heart, as we observe their usage in the Scriptures.

These colors, all in one booklet, were enough to dazzle one's eyes. It was not difficult to imagine the display that the gems themselves would make, and the glory of the garments that would be worn at the coronation. Yet a blind man would not be able to appreciate any of it. If you were to attempt to describe the colors to him, all would be in vain. So the spiritually blind, the man who has not been born again, and who has never received Christ as his Saviour and acknowledged Him as Lord, cannot see the wonders of the testimonies of God. To him, the Bible is a dry book; to him, it is not a book that reveals the glory, the majesty, and the wisdom of God. It is futile to try to explain it to him. However, I cannot imagine a single physically blind man who, if he learned of a positive, instantaneous cure for his blindness, but would run with the speed of a greyhound in order to accept the cure. Yet there is a cure for the spiritually blind—an absolute, sure cure! It never fails. It is a simple look, by faith, upon the Lamb of God on the cross of Calvary. Such a look will throw light into the darkened soul, will open the eyes of the understanding, and will give one that indescribable and overwhelming urge which possessed Thomas of old, that caused him to look up into the face of Jesus Christ and confess to Him, "My Lord and my God."

PSALM ONE HUNDRED NINETEEN—PART SIX
(Verses 137-176)

REJOICING IN THE WORD

IN the stanza of the 119th Psalm commencing with verse 137, there are two passages upon which we should comment. The first is verse 140, "Thy word is very pure: therfore thy servant loveth it." The other is the 142nd verse, "Thy righteousness is an everlasting righteousness, and thy law is the truth." That word "pure" in the Hebrew has in it the idea of refining, as for example when gold is purified through the refiner's fire. Someone has said concerning the Word of God that "it is absolutely perfect, without the dross of vanity and fallibility which runs through human writings. The more we try the promises, the surer we shall find them." I remember reading a statement to the effect that "pure gold is so fixed that if an ounce of it was set in the eye of a glass furnace for two months it would not lose a single grain." Those of you who have had any banking experience, particularly in the handling of gold coin or bullion, know that it is necessary to weigh the gold at regular intervals, because pieces of it chip off and a certain amount of deterioration takes place because the gold is not pure gold. So even with the most perfect of human words, there is still some dross in them. It is only the Word of God that is beyond the pale of criticism. It has stood the fires of its enemies for centuries, and is just as valid today, just as pure, and just as effective as the day it was written or spoken. It is still sharper than a two-edged sword. What is more, just as pure and eternal as is the Word, so perfect and everlasting is the righteousness of God with which He clothes every believing child of His.

Now note the first verse of the next stanza, verse 145, "I cried with my whole heart; hear me, O LORD: I will keep thy statutes." Devotion to the Lord and fellowship with Him is not a shallow thing. It is not something one ought to put on at Christmas or Eastertime, or even every Sunday. Devotion to the Lord, to be true, must be a vital part of an individual's life. Frequently that devotion will call forth a cry of anguish from the deepest recesses of our hearts. It is only when we have had such experiences that we are able to join with the Psalmist in expressing such anguish of heart as he did in the opening verses of the 42nd Psalm, when he cried, "As the heart panteth after the water brooks, so panteth my soul after thee, O God. My soul thirsteth for God, for the living God . . ."

A DIVINE COUNSELOR

In the next section, commencing with verse 153, you will observe that the Psalmist again reminded the Lord of his affliction, and wrote, "Consider mine affliction, and deliver me: for I do not forget thy law. Plead my cause, and deliver me: quicken me according to thy word." From this quotation we will observe that David knew something about the intercessory work of a divine counselor. Someone must have been the source of his difficulty; someone must have had the right to approach God to accuse David; while still another had the right of intercession, the right of an advocate, so that He, too, could go into the presence of God and plead the cause of His servant. I wonder if we have ever considered that David the Psalmist, and all the faithful in Israel, had an advocate with the Father, just as definitely as we have an advocate with Him now? Let us not forget that the tabernacle was planned after the pattern that God showed to Moses on the mount, and that the high priestly ministry and intercession on the behalf of the guilty were a part of the divine economy as expressed in the worship and the ritual connected with the tabernacle of the wilderness, erected by Moses of old.

If an individual should get into difficulty with the law of our land, knowingly or unknowingly, consciously or unconsciously, there is a certain feeling of assurance that all will be well, if one has a good attorney to plead his case. So the man or woman who has received Christ as his or her Saviour has a divine attorney in the presence of God, an advocate, who is called Jesus Christ the righteous. Interesting title, isn't it, in that connection? He pleads the cause of every believer in the presence of God His Father, whenever that believer has been subject to accusation by the one whom the Scripture speaks of as the accuser of the brethren.

PERPETUAL PRAISE

We must pass on rapidly in order to consider a few verses in the next to the last stanza, commencing with verse 161. Let me read three verses: first, the 162nd, "I rejoice at thy word, as one that findeth great spoil." The 164th, "Seven times a day do I praise thee because of thy righteous judgments" and the following verse, "Great peace have they which love thy law: and nothing shall offend them."

This is the season of the year when men rejoice because of God's faithfulness to His Word in the birth and incarnation of the Son of God. And wherever the gospel of Jesus Christ is preached, peace and contentment possess the souls of those who believe. "Great peace have they which love thy law . . ." No wonder that David, the Psalmist, said, "Seven times a day do I praise thee because of thy righteous judgments." David was a busy man. It is wonderful how much busy people accomplish. David was a king over a great people, he was a warrior, a marvelous musician, a great artist, a wonderful student of creation, the writer of Psalms and hymns, the father of a large family, a prophet of God, and the sweet singer of Israel. Yet he found time to praise the Lord, and to have fellowship and communion with Him, not just in the morning and evening, but *seven times* a day.

Once again, Christendom is about to celebrate Christmas. None of us care for the commercialism that surrounds the modern Christmas, but the fact remains that Christ did come into the world. There is no sight in the world that tugs at the heartstrings of an individual like the sight of a little babe in its crib. But this babe was the Son of God; He held the world in the palm of His hands, and yet, with all the naturalness of a little child, He was nourished and brought up by Mary and Joseph and was subject to them. The wildest imagination of the most gifted writer in the world could never have produced the scenes of the Nativity. It required God. Everything about it is Godlike. It was His gift to the world.

THE CLIMAX OF ALL REVELATION

But let us not forget that the manger led to the cross, the cross led to the tomb, and the tomb led to His exaltation at the right hand of God, where the babe of the manger is now Jesus Christ the Lord, "a Prince and a Saviour." It is only when you receive Him as your Lord and Saviour that you are able to take in the whole scope of His ministry and rejoice in His coming.

Finally, may I comment on the 172nd verse of the 119th Psalm, reading, "My tongue shall speak of thy word: for all thy commandments are righteousness." I have attempted to do that, in a measure, during these six messages on the 119th Psalm. I have sought to have my tongue speak of the glories of the incarnate Word and the written Word. I do trust that our contemplation and meditation have been well-pleasing in His sight, who is our strength and our Redeemer. And as a result of this meditation may it be that many have come to know the peace of God, that passeth all understanding.

PSALM ONE HUNDRED TWENTY

A PEACE-LOVING MAN IN A WARLIKE COMMUNITY

IT is interesting to notice how the Psalms vary in length. I suppose the Lord knew that as our experiences are not always the same, and as our stature varies, so we would not be particularly satisfied if everything were the same. Thus we have long Psalms and short Psalms and medium-sized Psalms, just as we have long days and short days, and good days and bad days. Life is a series of changes. You probably remember how the song writer phrased it, when he wrote, "Change and decay in all around I see . . ." The fact is, if you have not seen an individual for five or six years and you meet him unexpectedly on the street, you are obliged to look at him closely, and quite often your first comment will be, "My, but you have changed."

THE UNCHANGEABLE ONE

None of us stand still. We either go ahead or we lag behind. Yet it is tremendously comforting that through all the vicissitudes of life there is One who changes not. How that passage in the New Testament rings with a clarion note, "Jesus Christ the same yesterday, and to day, and for ever." He is the only One who does not change. And just as He is unchangeable, so the Word of God does not change. There is a marvelous unity between the written and the living Word, as I have so often mentioned before. Men may try to tear the Word of God apart, just as they have tried to find some fault with the person of Christ; but just as our blessed Lord comes out of each encounter more majestic than ever, so the Word of God, every time it is put through the furnace of criticism, comes out with its glories all the more accentuated.

This Psalm introduces a series of Psalms, each of which is called "A Song of degrees." We have been told that literally the word "degrees" means *ascents.* Thus these Psalms are songs of ascents, and they were to be used as Israel climbed the mountainside as they went up to Jerusalem to worship the Lord at the feasts of Jehovah. These Psalms might also be called Pilgrim Songs, as those who sung them were pilgrims. They were sojourners, and now they came back to that citadel of worship where there was quiet communion between kindred spirits around the great person of Jehovah God. Thus, while there is a plaintive note in these Songs of degrees, they have that about them which warms the cockles of the redeemed heart. Whether one is old or young or in the prime of life, the heart responds to the invitation, "Let us go into the house of the LORD."

Now that will do as an introduction. Let us look at the Psalm. It contains but seven verses. If one were to liken the 119th Psalm to a Thanksgiving dinner, then I suppose we ought to consider the 120th Psalm as a light breakfast, or perhaps what you good English folk would consider an "afternoon tea." It is short, with a little touch of the bitter and yet abounding with the sweet.

> "In my distress I cried unto the LORD, and he heard me.
> "Deliver my soul, O LORD, from lying lips, and from a deceitful tongue.
> "What shall be given unto thee? or what shall be done unto thee, thou false tongue?
> "Sharp arrows of the mighty, with coals of juniper.

"Woe is me, that I sojourn in Mesech, that I dwell in the tents of Kedar!

"My soul hath long dwelt with him that hateth peace.

"I am for peace: but when I speak, they are for war."

In some respects this is a strange Psalm. It appears as if the order is reversible, for just as much benefit can be derived by beginning with the 7th verse and reading upward to the first. Usually, in prayer, we enumerate our problems before the Lord and then we end with a note of praise that the Lord has heard and will deliver us. Here, however, the Psalmist began with an acknowledgment that God had heard his prayer and then enumerated his perplexities and difficulties. I wonder if that was not designedly done, in order that we, today, might appreciate the promise given in the 65th chapter of Isaiah, the 24th verse, where we read, "And it shall come to pass, that before they call, I will answer; and while they are yet speaking, I will hear." At any rate, David knew that there was only one person in all the world to whom he could go in distress for, said he, "In my distress I cried unto the LORD, and he heard me" just exactly as he had expected God to hear him. His distress was the result of association with deceitful people who possessed lying tongues. The world has not changed much since then, for there certainly are still a few people around who fit perfectly into that description.

LYING LIPS AND DECEITFUL TONGUES

Notice what the Psalmist said, "Deliver my soul, O LORD, from lying lips, and from a deceitful tongue." Then he went on to raise the question, "What shall be given unto thee? or what shall be done unto thee, thou false tongue?" and finally, he likened the darts of his enemies' tongues to "Sharp arrows of the mighty, with coals of juniper."

Someone has said that an unbridled tongue is the chariot of the devil, wherein he rides in triumph. One Mr. Greenbaum, whose name is almost forgotten, used a series of interesting contrasts in describing the tongue. Said he, "It (the tongue) is a little piece of flesh, small in quantity, mighty in quality. It is soft but slippery. It goeth lightly but falleth heavily. It striketh soft but woundeth sore. It goeth out quickly but burned vehemently. It pierceth deep and therefore healeth not speedily. It hath liberty granted easily to go forth, but it will find no means easily to return home, and being once inflamed with Satan's bellows, it is like the fire of hell."

Not a bad description, is it? The fact of the matter is, I wonder if it does not strike close home. I think that we would all do well to indulge in an open confession, and acknowledge that this little member has gotten us into difficulties all too frequently. You will also recall what the Apostle James had to say about this, when he wrote, "Even so the tongue is a little member, and boasteth great things. Behold, how great a matter a little fire kindleth! And the tongue is a fire, a world of iniquity: so is the tongue among our members, that it defileth the whole body, and setteth on fire the course of nature; and it is set on fire of hell."

A few weeks ago I had occasion to call on my dentist. I was ready to tell him about a tooth that was bothering me, and, just like all dentists, he put his fingers in my mouth and began talking, expecting me to answer him—you know what a job that is! I had developed a cavity and was struggling to describe its terrific size to him—or, at least, as it appeared to me while my tongue had investigated it. It is surprising how, with the aid of our tongue, a little bit of a hole in a tooth (hole is the proper word here, you know) can appear to be the size of a Grand Canyon. When my dentist finally took his fingers out of my mouth, I added, "I guess it is because these tongues of ours are so prone to exaggerate." Let us not forget, therefore, that this little member of ours is apt to get us into trouble and magnify a matter to an extent where it becomes a deceitful and a false tongue. No wonder the Psalmist said, "What shall be given unto thee? or what shall be done unto thee, thou false tongue?" As far as I know, the only remedy is a major operation!

We who have bowed the knee to the Lord Jesus Christ and have acknowledged Him as our Lord and Saviour, ought to be the last people in the world to allow our tongues to get us into difficulties. To us, there can be only one remedy, and that is confession before the Lord, coupled with a yieldedness to His Spirit. Of one thing we are sure: the Holy Spirit, as His title indicates, never exaggerates, never falsifies, never speaks ill-advisedly, but quietly glorifies the Lord Jesus Christ. And, as the Holy Spirit was given unto us to be our guide, certainly He can control our tongues, providing we allow Him to do so.

But the Psalmist, in the 120th Psalm, was not writing about the tongues of his fellow pilgrims; he was describing the lying tongues of those who lived in Mesech and in Kedar, for he said, in verse 5, "Woe is me, that I sojourn in Mesech, that I dwell in the tents of Kedar!" The distress of his heart is well expressed in verses 6 and 7, "My soul hath long dwelt with him that hateth peace. I am for peace: but when I speak, they are for war." David described himself as being in exile, living in the midst of his enemies.

Now we in this 20th century may not be able to fully grasp the significance of verse 5, where David said, "Woe is me, that I sojourn in Mesech, that I dwell in the tents of Kedar!" But the significance is understood, when we bear in mind that "Mesech was the son of Japheth; and the name here signifies his descendants, the Mosques, who occupied that wild mountain region which lies between the Caspian Sea and the Black Sea. Kedar was a son of Ishmael; and the name here signifies his descendants, the wandering tribes, whose 'hand is against every man, and every man's hand against them.' There is no geographical connection between these two nations; the former being upon the north of Palestine, and the latter upon the south. The connection is a moral one. They are mentioned together, because they were fierce and warlike barbarians. David had never lived on the shores of the Caspian Sea nor in the Arabian wilderness; and he means no more than this, that the persons with whom he now dwelt were as savage and quarrelsome as Mesech and Kedar. After a similar fashion, we call rude and troublesome persons, Turks, Tartars and Hottentots. David exclaims, 'I am just as miserable among these haters of peace, as if I had taken up my abode with those savage and treacherous tribes.'"

"I AM FOR PEACE . . ."

Now for a final comment. Let us look at the last verse, "I am for peace: but when I speak, they are for war." In the first place, I do not believe that any Christian loves war; indeed, he hates it. But how any intelligent Christian can subscribe to some of the foolish pacifism that periodically stirs some of the so-called leaders of the Christian church is simply beyond me. These men advocate a principle or policy between nations that not only is contra-Biblical but absolutely absurd; yet they have the temerity to palm it off as Christianity. What do you suppose would happen in New York, or any large city, if suddenly all traffic officers and all traffic signals were eliminated from the roads. Within ten minutes we would have chaos. But, further, we in this country have thousands of churches, millions of church members, and a history of 150 years of Christian preaching. In spite of that, suppose all police efforts were to be abolished; do you think you would be safe in any of the streets of the cities in our country? Of course not. Why? Because in the unregenerated heart of man there lies dormant all the impulses of crime and hatred that would revel and go on a rampage if given the license to do so. Every honest person would cry out for a power to cope with the forces of evil. Just so would it be in mass dealings of nations with nations in this hour of man's ascendency. Witness what took place in defenceless Ethiopia in the face of a mailed fist.

No, peace among men will not come that way. Do not misunderstand me, I believe that every legitimate means should be tried and even exhausted to maintain a spirit of good will between nations. But what I am saying is this: That our Lord knew more about human nature and national affairs than all of these self-styled religious pacifists combined, for He said that the age in which we live would be characterized by "wars and rumours of wars." A lasting condition of peace among the nations will never be enjoyed until He, the Prince of Peace, returns to this earth.

The human heart has not changed; it is still at enmity with God. Frequently it expresses itself not only in antagonism against God, but in war against its fellow men. Thus, in our efforts to live peaceably with all men, let us face reality and not cast dust in our eyes.

Just as man, individually, will never know peace in his heart and conscience until he receives the Lord Jesus Christ and makes Him Lord of his life, so nations will never know peace until the Prince of Peace reigns in righteousness and truth.

This is not a contradiction of David's viewpoint as expressed in this Psalm, when he said, "I am for peace: but when I speak, they are for war." David was a warrior, a mighty warrior, and yet would have made peace; but he found that there were others to contend with who were not amiable. They were men who possessed false tongues and lying tongues and who insisted upon disturbing the peace. All of this becomes exceedingly plain when we understand that this 120th Psalm was sung by a people in bondage, who found peace only in the worship of the Lord in the place He had appointed at Jerusalem. How those sorely tried pilgrims among Israel delighted to climb the mountains to Jerusalem, to there enjoy the peace of God.

What is even more important than peace among nations, is peace with God. When a man is at peace with God, he is at peace with his neighbor.

PSALM ONE HUNDRED TWENTY-ONE

A PSALM THAT LIFTS EVERY FOG

IN our series of meditations in the Book of Psalms, we come to the 121st Psalm, which certainly is a delightful piece of divine poetry. But it is more than poetry, for it contains eternal truth. It is for that reason that men and women have come to this Psalm again and again throughout the ages to find help and strength in the time of need.

This is the second in the series of Songs of degrees, which were intended for the Israelite, as he journeyed up the mountainside to Jerusalem to worship Jehovah God. We observed in our previous meditation that while a plaintive note is to be found in these songs, nevertheless, as the sojourners came back to their homeland, there was also a note of gladness to be heard. Now let us look at this 121st Psalm, every word of which is a jewel.

"I will lift up mine eyes unto the hills, from whence cometh my help.

"My help cometh from the LORD, which made heaven and earth.

"He will not suffer thy foot to be moved: he that keepeth thee will not slumber.

"Behold, he that keepeth Israel shall neither slumber nor sleep.

"The LORD is thy keeper: the LORD is thy shade upon thy right hand.

"The sun shall not smite thee by day, nor the moon by night.

"The LORD shall preserve thee from all evil: he shall preserve thy soul.

"The LORD shall preserve thy going out and thy coming in from this time forth, and even for evermore."

The very reading of the Psalm carries with it tremendous blessing and causes the redeemed heart to throb with joy. Can you imagine a great company of people marching up the hillsides of Judea, singing, "I will lift up mine eyes unto the hills, from whence cometh my help" and the reply, "My help cometh from the LORD, which made heaven and earth."

THE VALLEY vs. THE HILLS

From time immemorial man has associated the valley with disappointments, sorrows, and difficulties. Into every life there enters that which corresponds to the valley. It is only when one is down in the valley that he is able to look up. Let us not forget that. I think it was Dr. Pettingill who suggested that probably the reason God put so many of His saints on their backs was because they were thus better able to look up. You, of course, have observed that there is little or no effort involved in just lifting up the eye. The Psalmist said, "I will lift up mine eyes unto the hills, from whence cometh my help." If we are to get out of the valley of despair, we cannot expect to get any help by *looking around* to those who are likewise in the valley. Our help is found by *looking up* unto the hills, but, mark you, David was not so foolish as to assume that creation and the Creator are one. He never mixed them. There are some people who appear to revel in the fact that nature is their God. Thus they think it is so much more pleasant, particularly in the summertime, to talk a walk up the mountainside and over the hills and through the valleys, than to be in the house of the Lord. Oh, the air is too stuffy in a church building and outside we can breathe free air, we can enjoy nature—you know their line! Yet David never made a mistake like that, for he said, "My help cometh from the LORD, which made heaven and earth." From his place of despair in the valley he looked up unto the hills which spoke of God. But remember they only spoke *of* God: they were not *God*. He did not look to the hills for a message *directly*. He knew that the hills merely *witnessed to the glory* of the matchless Creator. Thus, in the 2nd verse, he added, "My help cometh from the LORD, which made heaven and earth."

I live in what we New Yorkers are pleased to call an apartment, but which more accurately should be described as a little box—so I enjoy, like most New Yorkers and other urbanites, taking a drive through the countryside. The eye is attracted to the beautiful houses and the magnificent gardens, but I am thinking this morning of some people who *own* those properties. You note I said "*own.*" They assume that these properties are their possessions, thus the rest of us poor mortals at times are not even permitted to look upon a display of the magnificent. I am thinking particularly of a place not far from Philadelphia, owned by one whom President Roosevelt has been pleased to call an "economic royalist." It is a beautiful, large place; but around the whole estate there is a wall at least twelve feet high and about a foot or probably eighteen inches wide. On top of this wall are broken pieces of glass and metals, as if to express the attitude of the occupant of that estate: This is my place; you are a stranger; keep out. As you come to the entrance, you observe a high iron gate. If it is your first trip past the estate, you may say, Now I will get a chance to see the beautiful gardens which must be within this estate. But, lo, as you approach, you discover that while the gate is made of iron bars, the "proprietor" has a huge steel plate behind the gate, so that you cannot even look through it. When I think of that place, I muse over this passage of Scripture, "My help cometh from the LORD, which *made* heaven and earth."

Some people may thing that *they* own the earth, but I hope you do not think I have gone mad by suggesting that they're mistaken—I'm part owner of it, because God *made* the earth as well as the heavens! But wait a minute, I'll explain. I believe on our Lord Jesus, and because God has been pleased to make our Lord heir of all things, including the earth, our Lord has been pleased to make me a joint-heir with Him, because I trust Him. So I never drive by one of those places without stopping to think that I own a part of them! The man who is occupying it now does not realize it, but because my Lord made heaven and earth and I am His and He is mine, why should I have a care? He has been pleased to give me, as He has given to every one who trusts Him, the glorious right to be a joint-heir with Him. Of course, I am not making the mistake of assuming that I *now* can have possession of it, for you will remember that our Lord is in exile. He has not yet begun to take His inheritance, but when He does, I will take up mine. So, you folk who feel that you have so little of this world's goods, do not assume that the problem will be solved by the distribution of wealth, by taxation, by old-age insurance, or any other means. That will not do you one bit of good; but put your trust in the Lord and your confidence in Him and you will be assured that some day He will say to you, "Fear not, little flock; for it is your Father's good pleasure to give you the kingdom."

THE NEVER-SLUMBERING GOD

Now let us continue in this wonderful Psalm. The Psalmist wrote, in verses 3 and 4, "He will not suffer thy foot to be moved: he that keepeth thee will not slumber. Behold, he that keepeth Israel shall neither slumber nor sleep." Of course, I understand that this Psalm was primarily intended for Israel. Maybe some good son of Israel ought to send a copy of it to Herr Hitler in Germany, for he seems to have arrived at the conclusion, in his warped thinking, that the keeper of Israel not only is slumbering, but sleeping very soundly, because it appears that He is indifferent to the people whom He called His own. The trouble with us is that we look upon things that are seen and not on the unseen. We are occupied with the temporal rather than with the eternal. And when we look at the temporal we are unable to see the purposes of God. But I still believe the Scripture, when the Psalmist said, ". . . he that keepeth thee will not slumber." You know, a person slumbers before he sleeps. Slumber is that few minutes of dozing off before one gets to sleep. When you slumber, the slightest noise will awaken you. However, the keeper of Israel neither slumbers nor sleeps. So, you good Israelites who are listening this morning, forget about looking to the nations for your help, for you will be disappointed. Why not look to God, the keeper of Israel. Believe me, though I am a Gentile in the flesh, I have no doubt that if your nation will get on its knees before God and humbly cry out to Him for deliverance and bow to His will, a million Hitlers will be like a Goliath before a David.

Now notice what the Psalmist said, concerning the provisions of the Lord, in verses 5 and 6, "The LORD is *thy* keeper: the LORD is *thy* shade upon thy right hand. The sun shall not smite thee by day, nor the moon by night." What care the keeper of Israel gives to His people! It must be evident to every loyal son of Israel that something is wrong with Israel, for she is not today enjoying the blessing of deliverance that God promised to her. As I have bowed the knee to Jesus Christ, I believe that the hour of deliverance for Israel, as well as for the world, will come when the Lord Jesus Christ Himself will rend the heavens and return as Israel's long rejected Messiah, and this world's King of kings and Lord of lords.

But I must not overlook a message for our present hour, for the principles of God are eternal, and men and women, irrespective of nationality, irrespective of birth, high or low, Jew or Gentile, may enjoy the provisions God promised here in this 121st Psalm. If you wish to know what it is to dwell in a sphere of eternal bliss and joy, then the answer is to be found in the opening phrase of the 5th verse, where the Psalmist said, "The LORD is thy keeper." That is the answer. If the Lord is thy keeper, then the Lord will be thy shade upon thy right hand, and because He is thy shade as well as thy keeper, "The sun shall not smite thee by day, nor the moon by night." Furthermore, the Lord will preserve you from evil, from this time forth and for evermore. But will you observe that all these blessings come by virtue of the fact that the Lord is thy keeper.

Occasionally, in dealing with souls in an attempt to lead them to the Lord Jesus Christ, I have heard them say, O, yes, I want to be a Christian, but I am afraid I will not last. I have no more confidence in my ability than I have in my own righteousness. If salvation, either past, present, or future, is dependent upon me, then I am doomed; but, because my salvation, to begin with is based on the fact of Christ's death and resurrection and continues on the promise of God and the intercession and ministry of our Lord Jesus Christ at the right hand of God now, I have no qualms nor doubts about the keeping power of my Lord. He said, "My sheep hear my voice, and I know them, and they follow me: and I give unto them eternal life; and they shall never perish, neither shall any man pluck them out of my hand." As if that were not sufficient, He added, "My Father, which gave them me, is greater than all; and no man is able to pluck them out of my Father's hand. I and my Father are one."

THE EVER-PRESENT GOD

We ought not to have a thought of fear, for the promises of God are yea and amen in Christ Jesus. The Lord shall preserve us from all evil; He shall preserve our soul. The climax of all this is expressed in the 8th verse, where we read, "The LORD shall preserve thy going out and thy coming in from this time forth, and even for evermore." George Mueller's name is a household word in Great Britain because of those great homes for orphans which he started by faith in the power and provision of God. On one occasion, George Mueller was crossing the Atlantic on a voyage from England to Canada. He knew the captain of the ship. The captain was a godly man. One day, while on board, George Mueller walked up to the bridge and addressed the captain, saying, "Captain, I have an appointment to speak at a meeting on Saturday afternoon in Quebec. What are the chances of your ship arriving in time?" The ship was then enveloped in a deep fog. The captain responded, "Absolutely impossible. Can't you see that fog? It has been necessary to cut down on the speed of the ship; it is absolutely impossible for us to be in time for your meeting on Saturday afternoon." "Very well," said George Mueller, "if you ship cannot get me there on time then God must have some other way of getting me there, for I have lived in fellowship with God for forty-five years and I have never missed an appointment, and God will not fail me on this occasion." The captain looked at him in absolute surprise, and if his expression could have spoken, he would have been heard to say, "Man, are you beside yourself? Here you are on the ocean, enveloped in a fog. How can you get to

Quebec except by this ship?" George Mueller then said to the captain,
"Suppose you allow someone else to take charge on the bridge while you
come downstairs with me to the chartroom, and let us pray." George
Mueller was the kind of a man you had to obey, and so the captain went
with him. They both knelt to pray. George Mueller p.ayed a short, simple
prayer, almost childlike, and when he had finished, the captain was about
to join in prayer, but George Mueller said, "Captain, there is no need for
you to pray. In the first place, I have prayed and God has already
answered my prayer. In the second place, you do not believe God, so why
pray? If you were to ask God to lift the fog, you would not believe that
He would do it, so why pray? God has answered my prayer. Go up to
the bridge and you will find that the fog has lifted." The captain went up
and sure enough, the fog was lifted and George Mueller arrived in Quebec
in time to keep his engagement.

God never changes. He is able to keep His Word, as when David said,
"The LORD shall preserve thy going out and thy coming in from this
time forth, and even for evermore." No man who has put his trust in God
and placed his life in God's keeping has found cause for disappointment.

PSALM ONE HUNDRED TWENTY-TWO

HOW PEACE IS MAINTAINED INDIVIDUALLY AND NATIONALLY, OR PRAYING FOR THE PEACE OF JERUSALEM

THIS Psalm, like so many others in the collection, has a definitely
Jewish atmosphere about it. But then, as some learned divine has
said, the New Testament is in the Old concealed, whereas the Old
Testament is in the New revealed. Not every part of the Bible was written
directly to us who are living in this age, but every part of the Bible was
written for our benefit. Thus we can safely go to this 122nd Psalm and
find a message for this particular hour. The fact of the matter is, that it
has a very important message, for the Psalm touches one of the really great
problems of the present hour. Let us read the Psalm:

> "I was glad when they said unto me, Let us go into the
> house of the LORD.
> "Our feet shall stand within thy gates, O Jerusalem.

"Jerusalem is builded as a city that is compact together:
"Whither the tribes go up, the tribes of the LORD
unto the testimony of Israel, to give thanks unto the
name of the LORD.
"For there are set thrones of judgment, the thrones of
the house of David.
"Pray for the peace of Jerusalem: they shall prosper
that love thee.
"Peace be within thy walls, and prosperity within thy
palaces.
"For my brethren and companions' sakes, I will now
say, Peace be within thee.
"Because of the house of the LORD our God I will seek
thy good."

To every devout Jew the city of Jerusalem symbolizes his acme of joy,
for there in that city "compact together," as the Psalmist said in the 3rd
verse, all of the great history of their people found its roots. It was there
that Solomon built his temple, David made it his own city, and it was
outside its walls that the Lord Jesus Christ was crucified. If you wish to
know how important that city is, consider that even in this present time
one has but to read the current magazines and newspapers to discover that
it is a city of trouble and disturbance, yet a place to which the eyes of the
world are turned for salvation—I mean national salvation.

WORSHIP—PLACE OR SPIRIT

In the course of our comments we shall not only touch upon the historical aspects of the Psalms, but we shall also drink of its spiritual wells
in order that our own souls may be refreshed. While we today do not have
a temple, or a certain city to which all devout pilgrims travel in order to
have kindred fellowship and to worship the one true God, yet in almost
every part of the globe there are little groups of people, and sometimes
larger groups, who gather as a company to worship and praise the Lord.
And I dare say that each member of each such company tastes of the joy
that possessed the Psalmist when he wrote, "I was glad when they said
unto me, Let us go into the house of the LORD." There can be no question but that the writer of this Psalm was occupied with that central place
of worship in Jerusalem; there was the house of the Lord.

You will remember that on one occasion our Lord discussed the subject
of worship with a woman of Samaria. A strange individual with whom to
discuss the subject of worship, you say; yet she raised a question when she

began to feel uncomfortable in the presence of our Lord, as His penetrating questions addressed to her brought a strange consciousness of sinfulness. She had observed the features of a Jew in the outward form of our Lord, and thus said to Him, "Our fathers (that is, the fathers of us Samaritans) worshipped in this mountain (that is, Mount Gerizim in Samaria); and ye say (that is, you Jews), that in Jerusalem is the place where men ought to worship." To this our Lord responded, and said, "Woman, believe me"! What an interesting way for our Lord to introduce His message. "Woman, believe me, the hour cometh, when ye shall neither in this mountain, nor yet at Jerusalem, worship the Father, Ye (Samaritans) worship ye know not what: we (Jews) know what we worship: for salvation is of the Jews. *But* the hour cometh, and now is, when the true worshippers shall worship the Father in spirit and in truth: for the Father seeketh such to worship him. God is a Spirit: and they that worship him must worship him in spirit and in truth." The woman was so amazed, not only at the dignity of the words used by our Lord, but also at their apparent truthfulness, that she turned to Him, and said, "I know that Messias cometh, which is called Christ: when he is come, he will tell us all things." To this our Lord answered, "I that speak unto thee am he."

Thus you will observe that our Lord maintained that a change had already taken place, so that it was no longer necessary for pilgrims to journey to Jerusalem in order to worship; no longer was even a building essential in order that men might worship the Lord, for the hour had already come when the true worshippers would worship God in the Spirit. This does not mean that a church building is unnecessary; but the fact of the matter is, a building is not the church; it is just a building. Scripturally, the church is a group of people, not a building. A church may meet in a building, but the church is a group of people who have acknowledged the Lordship of Christ and who have united themselves together in order to worship the Father in Spirit and in truth. So each redeemed heart can taste of the same joy that possessed the writer of this Psalm, when he said, "I was glad when they said unto me, Let us go into the house of the LORD."

In verse 2, we appreciate the fact that the Psalmist and his people were at that time pilgrims; and yet they were possessed of a hope that their feet should stand within the gates of Jerusalem. Concerning that wonderful city, the Psalmist said, "Whither the tribes go up, the tribes of the LORD, unto the testimony of Israel, to give thanks unto the name of the LORD. For there are set thrones of judgment, the thrones of the house of David." The balance of the Psalm contains a series of exhortations, for instance, "Pray for the peace of Jerusalem . . ." which, by the way, is a strange exhortation. Then follows the promise, "they shall prosper that love thee. Peace be within thy walls, and prosperity within thy palaces" and then the Psalmist said, "For my brethren and companions' sakes, I will now say, Peace be within thee."

Isn't it strange that the city of Jerusalem, which name literally means "the city of peace," requires that its pilgrims pray for its peace. Evidently the city itself is no guarantee of peace. Peace can only be enjoyed when proper relations with the Lord are maintained. I think this is important. May I repeat it? The city of Jerusalem, the city of peace, did not have peace in itself, but peace was there when proper relations with the Lord were maintained. Allow me to bring that principle down to the present day.

"YE MUST BE BORN AGAIN"

There is in our country today a distinguished Anglican clergyman. He has come to our shores as a guest, to participate in the celebrations of the 100th anniversary of the birth of D. L. Moody, which Christendom will officially celebrate this week. The gentleman to whom I refer is Bishop John Taylor Smith. During the war he was the Chaplain-General of the British forces. Dr. Ironside told me of something the bishop said in the course of some noonday meetings which were held in the Cathedral in Indianapolis, Indiana, a week or two ago. The bishop was impressing upon the minds of his audience the fact that one ought not to rest in any false sense of security and peace simply because they were members of a church or participated in recognized Christian worship. He urged them not to substitute religious service for new birth, remembering that it is still as true as ever that "Ye must be born again." Then he illustrated his point by saying, "Some time ago I was speaking in a cathedral in England. I was stressing the necessity of new birth to the congregation that was there gathered. Without referring to anyone specifically, I turned and said, pointing to the rector to my right, It is possible for a man to be a rector of a church and not be born again, and then, with a sweep of my left hand, pointing to the stall in which the archdeacon sat, I added, It is even possible for a man to be an archdeacon and yet not be born again." Within a week the bishop received a letter from the archdeacon, asking for the privilege of an interview. As both men sat down together, the archdeacon said, "Bishop, you found me out. I do not know what it is to be born again. I do not possess the joy of salvation that you and others seem to have. Pray tell me wherein I am wrong and what I must do."

So, too, Jerusalem is a city of peace, but peace is only enjoyed when there is right fellowship with Jehovah. The church of Jesus Christ on the earth, that is, the individual churches, are places of peace, at least that is what they were intended to be, but it is not sufficient that one be a church member or that one be religious. It is absolutely essential that a man be born again, for our Lord Jesus Christ said, "Except a man be born again, he cannot see the kingdom of God." So, in all kindliness, may I suggest that each of us examine himself to determine whether he has the correct relationship with the Lord Jesus Christ. Have we each, individually and personally, received Him as our own Saviour and acknowledged Him as Lord?

JERUSALEM—THE CITY

Now let us enter into another phase of this subject raised in the 122nd Psalm: the matter of praying for the peace of Jerusalem. Jerusalem is a marvelous city. I have never visited it. I hope to see it before the Lord comes, but if not, I know that I shall see it when the Lord returns. For a long time that city lay in ruins, but in recent years some strange things have taken place there. Anyone who possesses even the slightest knowledge of history knows how important the city of Jerusalem has been in the affairs of the world. It has been a citadel from which great law and peace have come, but it has also been a place of sorrow and terrible bloodshed and warfare. It was in that city that our Lord Jesus Christ was rejected, and it was outside the gates of that city that He was crucified. He prophesied that not a single stone of its great temple would be left one upon the other, and that the walls of the city would be broken down. It is a fact of history that the prophecy was fulfilled.

Once again Jerusalem has become front-page news, as multitudes of Jews have returned to the city and to Palestine, with great hopes and aspirations. But the presence of the Arabs makes that city a place of perpetual disturbance. One never knows when an outbreak will take place. There must be something about the city that makes it occupy such an important and recurring place in the thinking of man and in the history of the world. There is!

Will you observe that the Psalmist said in verse 5, *"there* (at Jerusalem) are set thrones of judgment, the thrones of the house of David."* Of course, at the present time those thrones have been demolished, but they will be set up again just as surely as there is a God in heaven. Though I have never seen the city, and though I am a Gentile in the flesh, I pray as earnestly for the peace of Jerusalem as any devout Jew. I love that city, and when there is peace within its walls there is also prosperity within the palaces of the people.

Let me digress for a moment, and in our mind leave Jerusalem and come back to our own country. All know that we are living in a day of great distress. We have been spared some of the things that other countries have suffered, yet I cannot help but think, in view of the dust storms of last year, and the present floods of the Ohio and Mississippi valleys, that have caused such frightful devastation, and of the millions of people out of work, and the thousands of others prevented from working because some individual appears possessed of a desire to have autocratic power in labor circles, and the class spirit that has raised its ghastly head lately, I say, I cannot help but do some serious thinking about our own country. For nearly ten years, here and there, men have raised their voices, calling attention to the dangers due to the inroads of the philosophy of communism in this country. Some of us have given them only a passive interest—we thought the situation was not serious, thought it never could be serious—it might develop in other countries, but *not here.* I am not so sure about that now! I repeat, conditions existing in our own land today are definite causes for deep concern and my earnest conviction is that there is only one possibility of our escaping serious trouble and that is by a return to the faith of our fathers, and to an earnest proclamation of the gospel of our Lord Jesus Christ. Unless this country returns to God, I frankly fear for it.

We will never enjoy real national prosperity, apart from right fellowship with God. As in the city of Jerusalem, there was peace within her walls and prosperity within her palaces only when there was peace and right fellowship with God, so, in a measure, the same principle is true in our day.

But Jerusalem some day will be the place from which our Lord Jesus Christ shall reign as the King of kings and the Lord of lords; then all the inequalities of life will be completely adjusted and peace and prosperity shall walk hand in hand. When that day comes, the world will know national deliverance. May the coming of our Lord Jesus Christ be hastened. But while our blessed Lord is in the presence of His Father, you and I can do much to make our dwelling here a joy to our own hearts and to the hearts of our fellow-men, by being faithful to our Lord Jesus Christ, and by preaching the gospel which still is the power of God unto salvation to everyone that believeth.

PSALM ONE HUNDRED TWENTY-THREE

CAN ALL MEN PRAY?

THE 123rd Psalm is a short Psalm containing only four verses.

"Unto thee lift I up mine eyes, O thou that dwellest in the heavens.

"Behold, as the eyes of servants look unto the hand of their masters, and as the eyes of a maiden unto the hand of her mistress; so our eyes wait upon the LORD our God, until that he have mercy upon us.

"Have mercy upon us, O LORD, have mercy upon us: for we are exceedingly filled with contempt.

"Our soul is exceedingly filled with the scorning of those that are at ease, and with the contempt of the proud."

There is a close relationship between this Psalm and the 121st. David opened the 121st Psalm by saying: "I will lift up mine eyes unto the hills, from whence cometh my help" but here in the 123rd he wrote, "Unto thee lift I up mine eyes, O thou that dwellest in the heavens." When we considered the 121st Psalm we called attention to the fact that David never made the mistake of confusing the Creator with creation, by thinking they were one and the same. Creation is the work of the Creator. Creation manifests the power, the wisdom, and the might of the Creator, but it is a mistake to look to nature or to creation for any help. Indeed, in the hour of distress we must go beyond creation to the Creator. I believe it was Charles H. Spurgeon who said, "It is good to have someone to look up to" and that "The Psalmist in this Psalm looks so high that he could look no higher."

WHO CAN PRAY?

Observe that it was the *Psalmist* who said, "Unto thee lift I up mine eyes . . ." In this particular Psalm the poet not only expressed his own privilege and relationship, but he used the plural in speaking of the people of God. He likened their relationship to God to that which exists between a servant and his master and a maiden and her mistress. "So," said he, "our eyes wait upon the LORD our God, until that he have mercy upon us."

In the Old Testament economy there was only one way to approach God, and that way was through the blood of the sacrifices of Israel. Israel was a commonwealth. Israel enjoyed a covenant relationship with God that no other nation enjoyed. As a result, a Gentile could not approach the presence of the God of Israel except he take his position as an Israelite. Now, however, under the New Testament economy, we have a slightly changed situation, but one which is equally as exclusive and inclusive as that which existed in the Old Testament economy. Our Lord Jesus Christ made a statement in the 14th chapter of the Gospel according to St. John, "I am the way, the truth, and the life: *no man cometh unto* the Father, but by me." Those words are so clear as to leave no possibility of mis-understanding. On the testimony of our Lord Jesus Christ, no man can come unto the Father but by Him.

God has a filial relationship with all the sons of men. As God, He is their Creator. They are the works of His hand. It was He who breathed into them the breath of life and, as a result, man became a living soul. But man, by virtue of sin, has separated himself from God. In fact, he himself has been alienated from God. The Lord God has laid down, as He has a perfect right to lay down, a basis upon which He will receive the worship and the petitions of men. On the testimony of the Word of God, that way is Jesus Christ and the basis is the death of Jesus Christ on the cross.

THE CRY OF THE HUMAN HEART

You will remember the cry of the human heart, so beautifully expressed by Job of old, that interesting character about whom the oldest book of the Bible was written. Job, after raising the question, How should man be just with God? came down to his own specific case and said, "If I wash myself with snow water, and make my hands never so clean; yet shalt thou plunge me in the ditch, and mine own clothes shall abhor me. For he (God) is not a man, as I am, that I should answer him, and we should come together in judgment. Neither is there any daysman betwixt us, that might lay his hand upon us both."

What a cry, and how true! Job was not so foolish as to rest upon a false philosophy of life. He knew that if he went to earth's clearest waters they could not make him clean. He was also conscious of the fact that a holy God could not come in contact with sin, and thus he cried out for a daysman, a redeemer, who might lay His hand upon God on the one side, and Job and others like him on the other side, and bring them together. That is exactly what our Lord Jesus Christ did. He is our daysman, He is our Redeemer. He came from God. He was as perfect as God. He could atone to God, for He was of like character. He was a man of sorrows and acquainted with grief, to be sure. He was tested in all points like as we, yet without sin. He could understand our trials. He could appreciate also our limitations, because He took upon Himself not the nature of angels, but the seed of Abraham. Thus He could stand betwixt us, that is, God on the one side and sinful man on the other. Snow water can never wash a man clean, nor can any chemical do better, as Jeremiah wrote in the 22nd verse of the 2nd chapter of his prophecy, "For though thou wash me with nitre, and take thee much soap, yet thine iniquity is marked before me, saith the Lord GOD." Therefore it is necessary for us to look for one who can be a redeemer. There is only one redeemer, the Lord Jesus Christ. There is only one thing that can cleanse from sin, and that is the blood of Jesus Christ.

In the Old Testament economy, God was preparing the children of Israel, and through them the rest of mankind, by teaching them that there was only one approach to a holy God, and that was by the blood of the sacrifice. Israel approached God through the sacrifices; and all those sacrifices were portraits, or types, of the one great sacrifice of our blessed Lord. God has decreed that no man can approach Him apart from our Lord Jesus Christ, but, blessed be His name He has promised to justify every man who comes in the name of Christ. To such He assures complete salvation and forgiveness of sin, and He declares that He has a personal relationship with each, so that they can look up into His face and cry, "Father God." Next to the precious name of my Lord, I know of no word in all language that conveys so much to my heart and mind and that so thrills my being as the word or title "Father God." God not only is the God and Father of our Lord Jesus Christ, He is also the God and Father of all those who believe in Him. Therefore, only those can lift up their eyes and address the holy One who dwells in heaven, who do so by virtue of the redemptive work of Christ.

The philosophy of this world rules out prayer. Some have even suggested that prayer is the occupation of weak-minded people. But prayer becomes a potent force in the life of the redeemed man or woman, and it is with tremendous joy that such a one enters into the presence of God to wait upon Him.

Now a further word regarding the 2nd verse, part of which we have already touched. There the Psalmist said, "Behold, as the eyes of servants look unto the hand of their masters, and as the eyes of a maiden unto the hand of her mistress; so our eyes wait upon the LORD our God, until that he have mercy upon us." You, of course, have observed that the position is that of a suppliant. The language is that of petition, and the relationship is that of a servant to his master, or a maiden to her mistress. Who ever heard of a servant commanding his master, or a maid her mistress? Such a condition could only be described as anarchy and chaos. It would be the wildest kind of presumption. What must be said, therefore, of the men or women who are so presuming as to insist that it is not necessary to come the way that God has decreed; that they will worship God in their own way and that God must accept their worship or do without it?

There is one thought in connection with this which I think is tremendously interesting. A man who has the proper viewpoint or perspective will always take the position of a servant before the Lord. He will never presume to be otherwise. Bear in mind that I am referring to those who have already received Christ. You cannot serve God unless you have been redeemed. It is written in the Scriptures, ". . . the plowing of the wicked, is sin." There is nothing wrong with plowing a field, but when a wicked man does it, it is sin. Everything he does is sin, because everything he does partakes of himself. Those who have been redeemed, and who have intimate relationship with God, are servants of the Lord. In that connection our Lord gave His disciples a wonderful revelation on the night of His betrayal, when He said, "Henceforth I call you not servants; for the servant knoweth not what his lord doeth: but I have called you friends; for all things that I have heard of my Father I have made known unto you."

You will recall how a man in the Old Testament was called a friend of God. I refer to Abraham. Abraham recognized that he was a servant of the Lord, but because of his love and devotion God called him a friend. The Lord also gave him the indescribable joy and privilege of entertaining an angel of the Lord as a guest. Every Bible student knows that the angel of the Lord was the direct representative of God. If you please, these visits of the Lord are called in theology "theophanies"—the appearance of God in the form of a man. The One who sat at Abraham's tent door was none other than the Lord Himself in His preincarnate state. Now notice the new relationship. "Henceforth," said the Lord, "I call you not servants; for the servant knoweth not what his lord doeth: but I have called you friends; for all things that I have heard of my Father I have made known unto you."

ALL-CONQUERING FAITH

Continuing in the 123rd Psalm, observe that the Psalmist, on behalf of his people, called upon God to display His mercy upon them. At that time they were filled with contempt and their souls were filled with the scorning of those who were at ease. The ways of the Lord, in the experiences of their life, were so contrary to reason that those who were at ease scorned them, while the proud looked upon the sons of Israel with contempt. Israel knew that the only place for her to be was on her knees before the Lord, crying out to Him for mercy, for when God's mercy is strong on the behalf of those that fear Him, then one can look up into the face of God, and with Job of old say, "Though he slay me, yet will I trust in him . . ."

A Christian is not devoid of disappointment. God makes the sun to shine upon the evil as well as the good and He causes the rain to fall upon the unjust as well as the righteous. We are men of common experience. There is no temptation come upon us which is not common to man, but the man of faith looks beyond circumstances to God.

PSALM ONE HUNDRED TWENTY-FOUR

CAN WE HAVE A UNITED CHRISTIAN CHURCH?

ON the 5th of February of this year it was my privilege to be in Chicago, attending a meeting commemorating the 100th anniversary of the birth of Dwight L. Moody. There were about fifteen thousand people crowded into the Colosseum. There was a chorus choir of two thousand voices, under the able direction of Dr. Bittikofer. Their singing was one of the most impressive things I have ever heard. It made me feel like immediately going to heaven to participate with that innumerable company of people who some day will join in one great burst of praise unto the Lord who has "redeemed us to God by His blood out of every kindred, and tongue, and people, and nation; and hast made us unto our

God a kingdom of priests . . ." If the singing of that chorus choir of two thousand voices could thrill a soul, what can be said of the sanctified joy that must have been Israel's portion when that nation, led by the sweet singers, chanted or sang this glorious hymn of praise unto the Lord.

THE LORD OR DESPAIR

As we read the Psalm, just imagine a host of people, among whom are pilgrims stooped with age, others vivacious with youth, with a great company of children; all joining in the singing of the words composing the 124th Psalm:

"If it had not been the LORD who was on our side, now may Israel say;

"If it had not been the LORD who was on our side, when men rose up against us:

"Then they had swallowed us up quick, when their wrath was kindled against us:

"Then the waters had overwhelmed us, the stream had gone over our soul:

"Then the proud waters had gone over our soul.

"Blessed be the LORD, who hath not given us as a prey to their teeth.

"Our soul is escaped as a bird out of the snare of the fowlers: the snare is broken, and we are escaped.

"Our help is in the name of the LORD, who made heaven and earth."

Here is an acknowledgment by the nation that it was a case of either the Lord or the blackness of despair. The matter of victory or defeat rested not upon the ability of the armies of Israel, but it rested upon the fact that the Lord was on the side of Israel. This Psalm is a thankful acknowledgment that the nation would have been swallowed up by the wrath of their enemies, and would have been deluged by the waters that would have overwhelmed them, were it not for the fact that the Lord was on their side. It is also a confession that the enemies of Israel outnumbered them and they were better equipped; and yet they were defeated, because on the side of Israel was none other than Jehovah. In this day of furious drives for armaments by the nations of the earth, it is well to bear in mind that the greatest victories were won by Israel when the Lord was on their side. In the last counsels by Joshua, the Israelites were urged to take heed unto themselves to see that they loved the Lord their God, for in so doing no man would be able to stand before them; in fact, one man of them would chase a thousand, for the promise was that the Lord their God would fight for them.

The entire world is now being swamped by a tidal wave of materialism and the hearts of many are filled with apprehension concerning the future. The whole earth appears to be in a state of turmoil as some of the nations of the earth seem bent on war, while the unrest in other nations resembles a war scare. It seems as if all the world is seated upon a keg of dynamite, with everybody playing around the keg with a lighted torch.

In the case of Israel in her glorious past, that nation knew what it was to be possessed of a spirit of apprehension. The inhabitants of the land of promise were like giants, so that some said that Israel appeared like grass-hoppers in comparison; indeed some thought that defeat was inevitable. Yet the grasshoppers smote the giants—and the land was conquered by the people of Israel because God was with them. They did not do it in their own power. The walls of Jericho fell, not because of the blasting of Israel, but because of the power of the word of God, who assured them that the walls would fall. The Lord was on the side of Israel.

There is the promise that "when the enemy shall come in like a flood, the Spirit of the LORD shall lift up a standard against him" but remember it is the Spirit of the Lord who shall lift up the standard against our enemy. I repeat, the 124th Psalm is an acknowledgment that the matter of victory or defeat rests solely upon the Lord. If it had not been for the Lord, then Israel would have been swallowed up by her enemies.

"A United Christian World"

Now let us draw an application from this Psalm to our present circumstances. When the crash of our pyramided prosperity took place in 1929, the whole world was shaken like a reed. Since then some voices have been heard suggesting that the collapse was inevitable, because of the materialism with which the people were possessed, but now that materialism had broken into bits and was found to be but a vapor, men would return to the verities of God and spiritual things. For a moment it seemed that men had learned a lesson. But what do we see today? It is acknowledged by some that we have turned the corner and are well on the road to another period of prosperity. Have men ceased to be materialists? Have the nations learned the lesson of 1929? Indeed not. Then what? What can be the hope of this particular hour?

An item appeared on the front pages of our newspapers this past week which I read with interest. It directed attention to the call raised by one of the richest men in this world, whose benefactions have been a tremendous aid to the sons of men. That distinguished gentleman suggested that only a "united Christian world could stem the rising tide of materialism, of selfishness, of broken traditions and crumbling moral standards and point the way out." He lamented the failure of the church visible, with its sects, still clinging to its denominationalism "in a drifting, disillusioned, discouraged world which sees in the church confusion rather than hope."

I wholeheartedly endorse the comments which that gentleman made and I agree with him that the world is on the brink of disaster as its very foundations are being shaken. I agree with him that the only thing for the church today is to bear a united testimony, so that she may be a bulwark against the raging storm. But let me be clear. There can be no united Christian church except it be founded on a solid rock.

The Apostle Paul, when he wrote to the Christians at Ephesus, exhorted them to endeavor " . . to keep the unity of the Spirit in the bond of peace." I am wholeheartedly for Christian unity if that unity is based on the deity of Christ, on the impregnable rock of Holy Writ, on the cardinal truth of the Christian faith revealed at the cross of Jesus Christ which towers "o'er the wrecks of time." I am for unity of the Christian church in bearing an effectual testimony to a world of moral failure when it invites the individual members of society to come to the "fountain filled with blood, drawn from Immanuel's veins," where sinners "plunged beneath that flood, lose all their guilty stains." What power the Christian church would have in this world if it would give faithful testimony concerning these verities of our faith.

Oh for another Dwight L. Moody to pack the largest auditoriums and preach in the simplest language the unsearchable riches of Christ, and to stir the ungodly to repentance toward God and faith in the Lord Jesus Christ. What a panacea such a revival would be for the distress of this world. But I cannot help but think that much of the responsibility for the spirit of materialism that is sweeping the world is due to the discordant note that has been heard all too frequently in the Christian church from those who have not been faithful to the gospel of Jesus Christ. You cannot undermine faith in the Scriptures; you cannot strip the robes of glory from the person of Jesus Christ and bring Him down to the level of mere

man; you cannot detract from the divine transaction at Calvary, the atoning work of God, and bring Calvary down to the level of a place of martyrdom of a religious zealot who gave his life merely in devotion to a principle; you cannot tear from the gospel of Jesus Christ, the dynamic power
to revolutionize and transform the lives of sinful men and bring the gospel
down to the level of a mere social message; you cannot do that and expect
that the church of Jesus Christ will be a potent force against the rising tide
of materialism.

"THE NAME OF THE LORD"

For our final comment, we go to the last verse of the 124th Psalm,
where we read, "Our help is in the name of the LORD, who made heaven
and earth." It is singular, and undoubtedly significant, that the Psalmist
should call attention to the *name* of the Lord, in the closing verse of this
Psalm, and say that our help is in that *name*. The angel Gabriel, when
announcing to the virgin Mary the glorious honor that had come to her,
said, concerning the child that she should bear, that His name would be
called Jesus, for He would save His people from their sins. The *name* of
the Lord Jesus is tremendously powerful. The disciples and the Apostles
knew the power of that *name*, as they commanded demons to come out of
afflicted men, for in each instance they commanded the demons not in their
own name, but in the *name* of the Lord Jesus Christ.

It is the testimony of the Scripture that God has highly exalted our
Lord and promised Him that ". . . at the name of Jesus every knee should
bow, of things in heaven, and things on earth, and things under the earth;
and that every tongue should confess that Jesus Christ is Lord, to the
glory of God the Father." I cannot be a pessimist, even in the midst of
what appears to be impending disaster, when I know that it is written that
God the Father has exalted the Lord Jesus Christ and promised Him that
every knee should bow and every tongue confess that He is Lord, and that
the sphere of that subjection is not limited alone to heaven, but to things
on the earth as well as things under the earth. Every creature will be
obliged to confess that Jesus Christ is Lord to the glory of God the Father.
I repeat, I cannot be a pessimist, for I am possessed of that glorious hope
that God will make good His promises to His own Son.

Now then, whether you believe the Bible or not—this promise that I
have just given, which appears in the 10th and 11th verses of the 2nd
chapter of St. Paul's letter to the Philippians, will not fail. You will be

made to bow the knee to Christ. But there is this difference: those who now bow the knee to the Lord Jesus Christ are given the gift of eternal life. Bowing the knee to Christ *now* brings tremendous profit. Bowing the knee to Christ by divine decree in the hereafter will not avail to the salvation of your soul.

PSALM ONE HUNDRED TWENTY-FIVE

THE SAFETY OF THOSE WHO TRUST GOD

Wgrave E are continuing our meditations in that series of Psalms, called the Songs of degrees, which begins with Psalm 120 and continues through to the 134th Psalm. Psalm 125 is a beautiful Psalm of five verses, which read:

> "They that trust in the LORD shall be as mount Zion, which cannot be removed, but abideth for ever.
> "As the mountains are round about Jerusalem, so the LORD is round about his people from henceforth even for ever.
> "For the rod of the wicked shall not rest upon the lot of the righteous; lest the righteous put forth their hands unto iniquity.
> "Do good, O LORD, unto those that be good, and to them that are upright in their hearts.
> "As for such as turn aside unto their crooked ways, the LORD shall lead them forth with the workers of iniquity: but peace shall be upon Israel."

When the temple of Solomon was built, the Israelites sang these songs as they mounted the steps of the temple. For that reason they are sometimes referred to as the "Stepping Psalms"—each Psalm seems to lead a step higher and causes one to further rejoice in the increasing revelation of divine truth.

Observe the security which is to be found in the opening verse of this 125th Psalm, "They that trust in the LORD shall be as mount Zion, which cannot be removed, but abideth for ever."

Practically all know that Mount Zion majestically represents the standing of the believer. As Mount Zion cannot be removed, neither is it possible for a believer to be moved. Mount Zion is the city of God. He has been pleased to call it His own place. He has said of those who trust in the Lord, that they will be as steadfast and immovable as Mount Zion.

SAFETY IN TRUSTING

In this Psalm is a promise that they who trust in the Lord will be steadfast, utterly immovable, and that they will abide forever. It is well to remember, however, that this promise is limited to those who trust in the Lord.

You who live in or near New York have undoubtedly enjoyed the Moody Conference which closed last Friday evening. Each of the speakers at that Conference brought great blessing by their ministry, but I must confess that Bishop Taylor Smith had a charm about him that was absolutely captivating. We sat together in my office one day and had some delightful fellowship. The bishop expressed himself in a manner that thrilled my heart. He said we need less religion and more regeneration in the pulpit, pew, and press. To trust the Lord is not a religious rite—it is a new birth. In fact, trusting the Lord begins with regeneration. I hope that is not too big a word for you who may not be acquainted with Bible language. To be regenerated is to be born again—is to have new life implanted in you and imparted to you—and it only comes by trusting the Lord. From the very moment an individual receives Christ and trusts Him for salvation he begins a life of trust. He goes on in confidence and abiding trust in the mercy of God, the goodness of God, and the power of God. Said the Psalmist concerning such, "They that trust in the LORD shall be as mount Zion, which cannot be removed, but abideth for ever."

How these words remind us or the language of our Lord Jesus Christ, when He spoke of His relationship with those who confess Him, under the imagery of a shepherd with his sheep. Said He, "I am the good shepherd, and know my sheep, and am known of mine . . . My sheep hear my voice, and I know them, and they follow me: and I give unto them eternal life; and they shall never perish, neither shall any man pluck them out of my hand." As if that were not sufficient security, He adds, "My Father, which gave them me, is greater than all; and no man is able to pluck them out of my Father's hand. I and my Father are one." If you have any doubts, or even a trembling heart, may the assurance of the words of our Lord and of the Holy Spirit through the Psalmist in this 125th Psalm be a source of comfort and strength to you. You have no right to a trembling heart, nor a doubting mind, nor a disturbed heart, if you trust in the Lord, for God is faithful to His Word. The Lord Jesus Christ said, ". . . they shall never perish, neither shall any man pluck them out of my hand." There may be some mountains that can be removed by the skill of an engineer, but there is one mountain that will abide forever; it is Mount Zion. Wonderful security, I repeat, is vouchsafed to those who trust in the Lord.

In the 2nd verse we get a still further revelation. The Psalmist wrote in that verse, "As the mountains are round about Jerusalem, so the LORD is round about his people from henceforth even for ever." In the 1st verse we have a picture of the trusting soul, absolutely immovable, and in the 2nd verse we have a description of the overshadowing power of God in the provisions He makes for those who trust in Him.

I believe that God created all things by our Lord and for Him. Thus, the more we know of creation, the more we will understand the goodness and the grace of God. In the choice of the land of Palestine and, particularly, the city of Jerusalem, I believe God placed those mountains about the city in order to impress Israel, and through Israel us, that in the very same manner He overshadows His people. With the Lord round about us we cannot possibly conceive of a more comfortable, peaceful, and safe place.

GOD'S HEDGE

Dr. Barnhouse has repeatedly stated that one of his favorite passages of Scripture is a statement which came from the lips of Satan, and which is found in that most ancient book—the Book of Job. Job was a just man, one who feared God and eschewed evil. He had a wonderful family and tremendous possessions, but above all his heart was right with God. The blessings, temporal and family, were all by-products of the blessings of God, because of that man's faithfulness. One day when the sons of God came to present themselves before the Lord, Satan came also among them to present himself, and Jehovah said unto Satan, "Whence cometh thou?" Satan answered, "From going to and fro in the earth, and from walking up and down in it." And the Lord said unto Satan, "Hast thou considered my servant Job, that there is none like him in the earth, a perfect and an upright man, one that feareth God, and escheweth evil?" Whereupon Satan had the audacity to say to God, "Doth Job fear God for nought?" (and now follow the words which Dr. Barnhouse likes so well) "Hast not thou made an hedge about him, and about his house, and about all that he hath on every side?" Satan knew very well that there was not a single opening in the hedge that God had placed about Job, the man who trusted God. Remember the words of our Psalm: "As the mountains are *round about* Jerusalem, so the LORD is *round about* his people from henceforth even for ever." If the Lord is round about you, if He encircles you, there is no break in the circle; and Satan knew that when he said, concerning Job, that the Lord had built a hedge about him, his house and *all that he had on every side.* There was not a single opening. This promise of steadfastness and the assurance of complete safety and shelter, however, is only given to those who trust in the Lord. It is given to none other.

In verse 3 we learn one of the reasons why God has so encircled His people, for there we read, "For the rod of the wicked shall not rest upon the lot of the righteous; *lest* the righteous put forth their hands unto iniquity." Now a rod is a symbol of power, of domination. The picture that is drawn for us in this verse is exactly the picture we have in the Book of Job. *The wicked* one is Satan; the *rod* of the wicked is Satan's power. He has the right to go up and down through the earth, but he cannot, without permission from the Lord, touch the righteous, those who trust the Lord. The reason he cannot touch them is to insure the righteous against putting forth their hands unto iniquity. In other words, were we to battle with Satan, not only would we succumb to defeat, but our hands would be defiled with iniquity. Some may smile and say, Sir, do you really believe in a personal devil? Without the slightest hesitancy I answer, Yes! One must be truly blind if one cannot see the evidence of Satan's handiwork in this world.

Occasionally I have seen preachers parade up and down the platform and rant with loud voices as if to challenge Satan to a duel. Whenever I have listened to that type of thing, I have felt that it would have been far better had the speaker spent more time in a study of the Word of God, from which he would have observed that we do not wrestle with flesh and blood, but against principalities and powers, and spiritual wickedness in high places; and because we wrestle not with flesh and blood, it is utterly foolish to meet the enemy of our soul with flesh and blood. One cannot break down the strongholds of Satan by any power of the flesh. There is only one way to meet the antagonist of our soul, and that is with the sword of the Spirit, which is the Word of God, the very thing which our Lord Jesus Christ used during His temptation in the wilderness.

We who have trusted the Lord for salvation have been taken out of the enemy's camp. We have been taken out of Satan's kingdom and dominion and we have been put into the kingdom of God's dear Son. We have been transferred to a safe place. We have been placed upon a rock that cannot be removed and we have been overshadowed by the Almighty. If

Satan at any time should disturb you with his darts, might I suggest that you do what Michael, the archangel, did when he met that great and tremendous creature, and said to him, "The Lord rebuke thee." The battle is the Lord's; it is not yours. If you will give it to Him, you will be the recipient of His victory.

WHO ARE GOOD?

In closing, let us look at verse 4, which is a prayer, "Do good, O LORD, unto those that be good, and to them that are upright in their hearts." Well, says someone, isn't that just what we have been saying— that so long as we do good and are good God will be good to us, and that salvation is not by faith, but by works? But wait a minute. We have no right to take this passage out of its context. The only way we will understand the passage is to keep it in its proper setting. The Psalm does not concern *anyone* except those who trust in the Lord. Those who trust in the Lord have the privilege of either walking in fellowship with Him, or walking in disobedience. Those who walk uprightly and in fellowship with the Lord always have the assurance that God will be good. But, "As for such as turn aside unto their crooked ways, the LORD shall lead them forth with the workers of iniquity . . ."

You may ask how that is possible. Let me take you to the New Testament, where we find, in the first letter to the Corinthians, that a certain member of the company of believers in Corinth was guilty of an immoral sin. The rest of the folk in Corinth, instead of being concerned about it, rejoiced in it, so that it greatly distressed the heart of the Apostle Paul, with the result that he wrote his first letter to that congregation, and said: When you come together again in the name of the Lord Jesus Christ, here is my suggestion, ". . . deliver such an one unto Satan for the destruction of the flesh, that the spirit may be saved in the day of the Lord Jesus." Did you observe that? Deliver such an one—the one who has already been washed in the blood of the Lamb, but who walked in the path of wickedness—deliver such an one unto Satan "for the destruction of the flesh, that the spirit may be saved in the day of our Lord Jesus Christ." Notice one further passage. In Paul's first letter to his friend Timothy, in the 1st chapter, commencing with the 18th verse, he gave a solemn charge to Timothy, when he wrote: "This charge I commit unto thee, son Timothy, according to the prophecies which went before on thee, that thou by them mightest war a *good* warfare; holding faith, and a *good* conscience (notice the word *good*); which some having put away concerning faith have made shipwreck: or whom is Hymenæus and Alexander; whom I have delivered unto Satan, that they may learn not to blaspheme."

How clear is the last part of this 125th Psalm in the light of the New Testament. "Do good, O LORD, unto those that be good, and to them that are upright in their hearts. As for such as turn aside unto their crooked ways, the LORD shall lead them forth with the workers of iniquity: but peace shall be upon Israel."

PSALM ONE HUNDRED TWENTY-SIX

LAUGHING MOUTHS AND SINGING TONGUES

THIS morning we will consider the 126th Psalm, which is the seventh in this series of Stepping Psalms. Anyone acquainted with the Scriptures knows that the Bible has a numerical structure and that each number carries its own significance. The number seven is invariably the number of perfection. Thus we shall expect to find the perfection of joy in this Psalm.

Frankly, we do not know exactly in what period of Israel's history this Psalm was written. Some say it was written after the Babylonian captivity; others hold an opposite view, claiming that the Psalm does not refer to the captivity of the people but to the captivity of the land. But whatever the period of history to which the Psalm refers, it certainly is pregnant with precious truth for the believer in this age. Dr. A. C. Gaebelein has a very apt expression which I think is excellent. He says, "A Psalm a day, keeps worry away." Thus, if you have a worry, try the remedy of "a Psalm a day" and see how quickly your worry will vanish away. Before we go any further, let us read this 126th Psalm in its entirety:

> "When the LORD turned again the captivity of Zion, we were like them that dream.
> "Then was our mouth filled with laughter, and our tongue with singing: then said they among the heathen, The LORD hath done great things for them.
> "The LORD hath done great things for us; whereof we are glad.
> "Turn again our captivity, O LORD, as the streams in the south.
> "They that sow in tears shall reap in joy.
> "He that goeth forth and weepeth, bearing precious seed, shall doubtless come again with rejoicing, bringing his sheaves with him."

GOD'S TURNING, AND OURS

It was Charles Haddon Spurgeon who suggested that the key thought of this Psalm centers in the words "turn" and "turned." These words appear in the 1st and 4th verses. In the 1st verse we learn that the Lord turned again the captivity of Zion, and in the 4th verse there is a prayer to the Lord to turn again the captivity of Israel.

The word "turn" is an interesting one. It means right-about-face, an entirely changed condition; and that is exactly what the Bible means by repentance or conversion. Conversion is a turning away *from* something *to* something else. The Scripture speaks of those who "turned *to* God *from* idols, to serve the living and true God; and to wait for his Son from heaven . . ." That is conversion. If you have never experienced this conversion in your life, you have yet to know what it is to be on the right path. But let us not forget that God can repent as well as man. It is written as early as the antediluvian age that " . . . it repented the LORD that he had made man on the earth, and it grieved him at his heart." When we read in the Scriptures that God repented it simply means that He changed His attitude or relationship.

Now let us notice what transpired when *God changed His attitude* toward Zion. We learn, first of all, that when the Lord did so the people of Israel were like those that dream, and the change was so marked and wonderful that the Psalmist said, "Then was our mouth filled with laughter, and our tongue with singing . . ." Even the heathen, by which the Psalmist meant other nations, as they observed the changed condition, said concerning Israel, "The LORD hath done great things for them." It is real conversion when others observe that the Lord has done great things for us. You notice I changed the pronoun from *them* to *us*, for while it is interesting and worthwhile to consider the change which took place in Israel and Jerusalem when the Lord once again smiled upon the people and the land, the thing that is more important is when that same experience is ours. When an individual has come to appreciate that God is not his enemy but his friend, and that God so loved him that He gave His only begotten Son to die for him, and that he may enter into intimate fellowship with God solely on the basis of what God did for him through Christ—that is enough to fill any mouth with laughter and any tongue with singing.

That reminds me of my friend "Mel" Trotter, of Grand Rapids, Michigan. What a testimony he gives! For the benefit of those who may not know "Mel" Trotter; he at one time was just an ordinary derelict of the street. He had sunk so low, even before he was thirty years of age, that he was absolutely a broken specimen of humanity. The craving for drink had a tremendous power over him. To look at him now you would never dream it was possible that he could have ever been in such desperate circumstances.

Upon entering a mission in Chicago in a drunken stupor, he was told that God loved him, that Christ died for him, and that the Holy Spirit would take possession of his life and live it for him if he would but yield to Christ. Mr. Trotter knelt in prayer and asked God to save him. That was many years ago.

You who heard him the other week on our radio program know how filled with laughter he is. Dr. Trotter is well known in the State of Michigan for the work that he has accomplished—going into the slum sections and telling the poor folk of the joy there is in Christ and that conversion can be a reality in every man's life. My heart was thrilled when I learned the other day of his ministry in England—for he sailed the day after our broadcast to participate in the D. L. Moody Centenary celebrations which are being held in the British Isles, as well as in our own country. In one week no less than 270 people came forward, definitely determined to receive Christ as thir Saviour. Is Dr. Trotter's mouth filled with laughter and his tongue with singing? A friend who has been close to Dr. Trotter for many years said that he is even more happy when he is sick, and that when he does not feel well physically it is a tonic to be in his presence.

Some of you may say, I never went to the depths that Dr. Trotter did. I would answer that it does not make any difference whether you did or not. There is only one thing acceptable to God, and that is perfection. Only One possessed it, and that was Jesus Christ. If you do not have perfection you are a sinner in the sight of God. Being a sinner, you need a Saviour. There is only one Saviour, and that is our Lord Jesus Christ. When you have been saved and have experienced the joy of eternal life in your breast, you cannot help but be glad. What is more, the changed life which results from that experience will be apparent to those who are around you. You will then say with the Psalmist, "The LORD hath done great things for us . . ."

I'm reminded of an incident I read about last week, which occurred in the life of Sir James Simpson who, you will remember, discovered chloroform. While that distinguished scientist lay ill with what proved to be his final illness, a friend visited him and asked what he considered his greatest discovery. Sir James Simpson answered, "My greatest discovery took place on Christmas Day of 1861, when I discovered that I was a lost sinner and that Jesus Christ was my Saviour." That, I assure you, is the greatest discovery any man can ever make.

THE UNIQUENESS OF CHRIST

Not only do we find joy and gladness in this Psalm, but we also find sorrow and tears. Here is a word of comfort and encouragement to those who sow in tears. They have the assurance that they shall reap in joy, and they have the comfort that "He that goeth forth and weepeth, bearing precious seed, shall doubtless come again with rejoicing, bringing his sheaves with him." I wonder if it is possible to experience real joy without knowing something of tears and sorrows. I am aware that the philosophy of this world rules out tears; in fact, the world's philosophy is expressed in the sentence, "It is the privilege of the great to conceal their tears." But the Scriptures read, "Jesus wept."

From the viewpoint of the philosophy of this world our Lord is an enigma. He is absolutely unique. It is utterly impossible to compare Him with anyone else. Dr. Otto Borchart in his work "The Original Jesus," speaking of the uniqueness of our Lord Jesus Christ, wrote, "This Holy One did not originate in the brain of sinners." Indeed, that is true. Our Lord Jesus Christ was not the product of the imagination of any age or any group of men. He was not even the product of the imagination of the writers of the four Gospels, for the Christ they present violates every conception of the philosophy of *their* day. Even our Lord's own friends, and possibly His relatives, considered Him with a big question mark. Thus it is not surprising, as Dr. Borchart affirms, that "the head doctor of a provincial lunatic asylum has dared to give it as his opinion that 'from the viewpoint of a psychologist' Jesus was insane." I suppose that will startle some, but it does not startle one who knows his Bible, for, in the 21st verse of the 3rd chapter of St. Mark's Gospel, we learn that the friends of our Lord Jesus said that He was "beside himself," which was just a polite way of saying He was insane.

It was not my intention to get so far away from our Psalm when I mentioned that our Lord also wept. But it is for that reason He can succor those who weep. If, for the moment, *you* are going through the valley of tears, may I assure you that God is true to His Word when He says that they "who sow in tears shall reap in joy."

WAGON-LOADS OF SHEAVES

But I want to spend a little time in the closing verse of this Psalm, where we read, "He that goeth forth and weepeth, bearing precious seed, shall doubtless come again with rejoicing, bringing his sheaves with him." This is a vivid picture of a farm scene. There is the sower, there is the field, there is the seed (called the precious seed), there is the rain that is needed (which is expressed in the word *weepeth*), and there are the wagon-loads of sheaves at the harvest time. You will recall that our Lord presented Himself as the sower. His greatest of all parables is to be found in the opening verses of the 13th chapter of Matthew's Gospel, where we read the story of the sower who went forth and, when he sowed, some seed fell by the wayside, some fell upon stony places, and some fell among thorns, but others fell in good ground and brought forth fruit. Then He told of the harvest, when some would reap terrible disappointment, while others would enjoy rapturous glory, shining forth as the sun in the kingdom of their Father.

In this Psalm we have the assurance that "He that goeth forth and weepeth, bearing precious seed, shall doubtless come again with rejoicing, bringing his sheaves with him." Now the seed is the Word of God. There can be no shadow of doubt about it. Our Lord said the seed was the Word of God. He that goeth forth with the seed is the sower of the seed. The first sower was Christ, but He has given to the sons of men, who have been redeemed by His blood, to be participants with Him in the harvest, and thus fellow laborers with Him in sowing the seed. Unless the seed is sown with weeping, we are not assured of a harvest. The Word of God is powerful, sharper than a two-edged sword; but the men who go forth bearing it must understand what it is to have their souls stirred even to tears in their effort to lead a soul to Christ. Unless the effort is baptized in prayer and real agony of soul one will not enjoy the experience of a great harvest. Those of us who are Christians, and who have yielded our lives to Him and are interested in the propagation of the gospel; if we go forth with the precious seed, weeping as we sow, we have the assurance that we will have wagon-loads of sheaves at the harvest time. Oh, what rejoicing that will bring!

There is one matter that we must stress; it is not our opinions we are to sow, it is the "seed of the Word." Our Lord said to the seventy unnamed disciples whom He sent forth two by two, "He that heareth you heareth me." It is only as the Word is preached that the seed is sown.

PSALM ONE HUNDRED TWENTY-SEVEN

A FAMILY PSALM

THE 127th Psalm reads:

> "Except the LORD build the house, they labour in vain that build it: except the LORD keep the city, the watchman waketh but in vain.
> "It is vain for you to rise up early, to sit up late, to eat the bread of sorrows: for so he giveth his beloved sleep.
> "Lo, children are an heritage of the LORD: and the fruit of the womb is his reward.
> "As arrows are in the hand of a mighty man; so are children of the youth.
> "Happy is the man that hath his quiver full of them: they shall not be ashamed, but they shall speak with the enemies in the gate."

I am sure all will agree that this Psalm runs contrary to the philosophy of the present day. If you live in a modern apartment, in a modern city, you will know that the 3rd verse does not apply to such a place. If it did, then the Psalmist would have had to say—Lo, dogs are an heritage of the Lord.

But let us examine the Psalm from the beginning. In the first place it is not clear who wrote the Psalm. It was either Solomon or David; at least, it was written for Solomon. Solomon was a wise builder. You remember he had a marvelous palace. But he also had in his breast a desire to build a house for the Lord. Thus one of the greatest buildings this world has ever seen was called Solomon's Temple. How interesting, therefore, to read, "Except the LORD build the house, they labour in vain that build it . . ." Ah, is it a possibility that God will join with us in labor and building? I am aware that labor is looked upon as something passé. Labor wants shorter hours, less work, and more pay. Yet the Psalm says, "Except the LORD build the house, they labour in vain that build it." Labor ought not to be unmindful of another Scripture which says that "the sleep of a labouring man is sweet . . ."

Irrespective of the application one may make of this 1st verse of the 127th Psalm, the principle applies in every sphere. We may look at the *building* of a house as being our home or family, or we may look at this *building* as the occupation at which we work, but to whatever sphere we apply it, God will build with us if we will let Him. When the Lord builds with us, such a building is on a solid foundation, but if He does not "they labour in vain that build it."

PRAYER AND PETITION

Again the Psalm said, "except the LORD keep the city, the watchman waketh but in vain." That contains a pertinent message for today. Many Christians are greatly distressed (and rightly so) regarding the things that are happening in this world and particularly in our own country. Take the problem now up for discussion in our own land: the matter of the Supreme Court. Some of us have been urged to petition our representatives. No one can take exception to that. Our representatives should know what we desire if they are to represent us properly. There is only one way through which they can accurately determine our wishes, and that is from our own expression. However, while a petition is desirable, prayer is infinitely more powerful. I repeat what I said on another occasion; I believe that our difficulties would soon be past if the godly people of this country would earnestly pray. I do not mean that we should thwart the purposes of God. I am aware of what the Scripture has to say about the conditions that will exist on earth just before the coming of the Lord. It is inevitable, therefore, that these things should come to pass. I do not wish to infer that we should pray that they might not come to pass but, rather, that we might understand that it is our right and privilege to pray about these governmental matters. Timothy was exhorted by the Apostle Paul "that, first of all, supplications, prayers, intercessions, and giving of thanks, be made for all men; for kings, and for all that are in authority; that we may lead a quiet and peaceable life in all godliness and honesty. For this is good and acceptable in the sight of God our Saviour; who will have all men to be saved, and to come unto the knowledge of the truth."

You will recall the case of Sodom and Gomorrah. God promised Abraham that if He found ten righteous men in those cities He would spare the cities for the sake of the ten righteous. He did not find them! There were not ten! I would fear for this country, were it not for the righteous men in it; were it not for the church of Jesus Christ; were it not for the men and women who have bowed their knee to the Lord Jesus Christ and who have power with God in prayer.

Now let us continue in our Psalm. We learn from the 2nd verse that "It is vain for you to rise up early, to sit up late, to eat the bread of sorrows: for so he giveth his beloved sleep." In other words, this constant, unending rising, sleeping, eating, and sorrowing is absolutely vanity. Some men cannot sleep. They are distressed by circumstances, by sin, by disappointments, by war, by fear, by a thousand and one other things. But the Psalmist said, "he (God) giveth his beloved sleep." Here is a sure cure for insomnia. Become one of His beloved.

"An Heritage of the Lord"

In the balance of the Psalm is painted a beautiful picture of a happy family scene. The Psalmist spoke of children as the heritage of the Lord. He spoke of them as the fruit of the union instituted and preserved by divine decree. He spoke of them as arrows that will protect the home against the darts of the enemy, and then he spoke of children as being a glory to the father of the household, who sits with his sons at the gate of the city, where the fact that his sons speak for their father assures absolute justice. Incidentally, the gate of the city was the place of adjudication of all disputes. It corresponded to our courtrooms. All this, the Psalmist declared, is the blessing of the man with children. Can you imagine what a world this would be without children?

My friend, Dr. Ironside, pastor of the Moody Memorial Church, of Chicago, returned from England this past week, after having participated in some of the D. L. Moody Centenary celebrations there. He told of an address which Mr. A. Lindsay Glegg of England gave at one of the meetings. Incidentally, A. Lindsay Glegg is a leading industrialist and financier. He is a godly man and one who loves the Lord Jesus Christ. By the way, wouldn't it be great if some of our leading industrialists and financiers were gospel preachers also? Dr. Ironside said that Mr. Glegg chose for his text the opening phrase of the 9th verse of the 6th chapter of St. John's Gospel, which chapter records the miracle by which our Lord fed five thousand men with five barley loaves and two small fishes. You will remember that our Lord, when He saw that great company, had compassion on them and asked Philip, one of His disciples, "Whence shall we buy bread, that these may eat?" Philip looked at the treasury and answered, "Two hundred pennyworth of bread is not sufficient for them, that every one of them may take a little." One of the other disciples, Andrew, Simon Peter's brother, overheard the conversation, and said, "*There is a lad here*, which hath five barley loaves, and two small fishes: but what are they among so many?" England's great financier took the phrase "There is a lad here" and proceeded to develop his subject from the viewpoint not only of the appeal of children to the Lord, but also of the Lord to children. He went on to say that in every crowd there is a lad. If there is a parade, there is bound to be a lad present. If there is a picnic, most certainly a lad will be there. If there is a fire, sure as life there is a lad present. You will always find a lad wherever there is a large gathering. When a lad gives his all to Christ, as did that lad in our Lord's day, what blessing results from it!

SORROW AND DISASTER

Talking of children at this time brings a note of sadness into our hearts and minds. It is a coincidence that we should be studying this Psalm this morning, when only a few days ago our country suffered one of its greatest disasters so far as children are concerned. There is much heartache and sorrow in many families and many homes this morning. There are perplexing questions arising in the minds and hearts of a great number of mothers and fathers in our land this Palm Sunday. The note of song which came so sweetly from the lips of children as our Lord rode into Jerusalem the first Palm Sunday is not heard this morning in hundreds of Texas homes. What can be said on an occasion of this kind? Not very much, I must confess. It is almost impossible for us to imagine the emotions that must be possessing these mothers and fathers, for only the other day there were happy, joyful homes where now there is sorrow and gloom. One is silenced in the presence of such sorrow.

Our Bible declares that God is love, and then proceeds to declare that God manifested His love in that, while we were yet sinners, Christ died for us. We should build our hope upon that impregnable rock of God's love, notwithstanding all circumstances to the contrary, and bring into captivity every thought to the obedience of Christ. In a time like this, oh to have the faith of Job, who said, "Though he slay me, yet will I trust in him . . . ."

Sometimes, either from failure to understand or from a desire to relieve themselves of responsibility, men speak of untoward acts as the acts of God. Let us not forget that our modern civilization, which has so completely ruled God out, is more often than not responsible for the things which happen. Our hearts go out to every bereaved family and to each stricken home. At the same time, one feels the urge to invite America to come back to God. One feels the need for a revival that will bring men and women to their knees, crying out to God for salvation!

In the hour of joy, or in the hour of perplexity, to whom shall we go? —to frail man? Ah, no, he is so weak there is no comfort in leaning upon him. To legislatures, which are in reality only a bundle of frail men? We might as well lean on a bundle of broken reeds. To whom shall we go? The disciples of our Lord both raised and answered the question when they said through Peter, "Lord, to whom shall we go? thou hast the words of eternal life." In our sorrows and our perplexities, therefore, let us cry out to God for His mercy.

PSALM ONE HUNDRED TWENTY-EIGHT

THE HOME THAT GOD DESIGNED

IN considering our message for this Easter morning, my first impulse was to disregard the consecutive order of the Psalms and give an address, wholly independent of the Psalms, on the theme "The Resurrection of the Lord Jesus Christ." It seems as natural to talk about the resurrection of our Lord on Easter Sunday as it is to breathe. Undoubtedly many of you will hear several sermons today on the resurrection. I caution you, however, to have sensitive ears, for you will no doubt hear such words as "immortality" and "resurrection," and similar words, but they will not have the remotest similarity to the Gospel records. Many will talk about the resurrection of the spirit of Jesus. Whatever that is, I do not know, but I do know that there is only one thing that dies, and that is the body. It was His body that was put into the tomb. When the women came to the sepulchre that early Sunday morning, the Scripture is both beautiful and clear in its comment, when we read, they "found not the *body* of the Lord Jesus." Our Lord had already taken possession of that body. He arose in that body. He met His disciples in that body, the very same body that a few days ago had been placed in the tomb, but now devoid of all blood, now a deathless, an immortal body. When the Bible speaks of the resurrection of our Lord Jesus Christ from the dead, it speaks of His physical, resurrection.

THE PROPHETS' TELESCOPE

While this Psalm does not speak directly of the resurrection of Christ, it does beautifully portray the happiness and joy that possess a family of believers as a result of the resurrection. But some may say, If David wrote this Psalm, he wrote it at least a thousand years before Jesus Christ came into this world. He could not be describing the blessedness of family life and the peace of a happy home because of the resurrection of Christ from the dead. Do you mean that this describes the benefactions that come from that resurrection?

To this I respond that I haven't a single doubt about it, for while David wrote long before our Lord came into this world, he foresaw the resurrection of Christ. That very subject was the theme of the Apostle Peter's message in the city of Jerusalem on the day of Pentecost, the record of which is found in the 2nd chapter of the Acts of the Apostles, particularly the 31st verse, where Peter, speaking about David and his Psalms, said, He seeing this before spake of the resurrection of Christ . . ." Surely, David saw the resurrection of Christ. Every one of the Old Testament prophets saw the resurrection of Christ. Our Lord said, "Abraham rejoiced to see my day: and he saw it . . ." Abraham knew that Christ would die and he knew that He would be raised again from the dead. You say, How is that possible? I will prove it to you in a moment. Abraham is seen going to Mount Moriah with Isaac, his only son, the son of his old age, the son of his love, the one in whom all the promises of God are yea and Amen; they all center in him. Yet God had said to Abraham, "Take now thy son, thine only son Isaac, whom thou lovest, and get thee into the land of Moriah; and offer him there for a burnt-offering upon one of the mountains which I will tell thee of." We cannot enter into the feelings which must have possessed Abraham and Isaac that day, as father and son conversed about the sacrifice, especially when Isaac said, "My father . . . Behold the fire and the wood: but where is the lamb for a burnt-offering?" With his eyes focused on Calvary, but with a range of two thousand years before Calvary was to come to pass in history, Abraham said, "My son, God will provide himself a lamb for a burnt-offering . . ." Abraham had full confidence in God. He knew that he would get his son back, and while he bound him, and laid him upon the altar upon the wood, and was about to slay him, God called out of the heavens, telling him to stay his hand. As Abraham looked about, he saw a ram caught in a thicket, and he offered that instead. When Abraham took his son from off the altar, it was a beautiful picture of the resurrection of Jesus Christ from the dead.

All of the Old Testament prophets and bards rejoiced in the typology that was apparent in the provision God had made for the sin of His people, the provision of the blood of the sacrifice. Only God can atone to God. So Jesus Christ offered Himself to God, first, in delight to do His Father's will, second, to save His people from their sins. As a result of the resurrection, both those who lived prior to the cross and those who have followed since the cross could have happy, joyful homes, because the peace of God rests upon the home where Jesus Christ is honored and believed.

A HAPPY HOME

This is a long introduction to our Psalm, but the fact of the matter is that it is also a partial exposition of it. So let us now read the 128th Psalm in its entirety. Again, it is one of the Songs of degrees which Israel sang as she journeyed up the mountainside to Jerusalem, on her festive days: and let us not forget that one of the important feasts days was the Passover.

> "Blessed is every one that feareth the LORD; that walketh in his ways.
> "For thou shalt eat the labour of thine hands: happy shalt thou be, and it shall be well with thee.
> "Thy wife shall be as a fruitful vine by the sides of thine house: thy children like olive plants round about thy table.
> "Behold, that thus shall the man be blessed that feareth the LORD.
> "The LORD shall bless thee out of Zion: and thou shalt see the good of Jerusalem all the days of thy life.
> "Yea, thou shalt see thy children's children, and peace upon Israel."

But I can hear some say: Is this an Easter Psalm? Indeed, it is! So much so, that the more I think of it the more my heart is thrilled over it. Life is interesting, life is wonderful; even though, to be true, it is sometimes hectic and even tragic. I challenge you to find anything in literature that can compare with this 128th Psalm in presenting such a beautiful blending of the spiritual and the domestic, of the eternal and the temporal, of the well-rounded life.

The Lord never intended us to spend all of our time in a formal church service. He knew that it was necessary to have seven days in the week; not only one. He so constituted us, that if we are to have the fullness of blessing we are to labor and to enjoy the labor of our hands; we are to be happy and have a happy home, and He knew that our eyes enjoy seeing good things. I have enjoyed life much more since I have come to know Christ as my Saviour than I did previously.

As I think of this Psalm, I think of the first Easter Sunday. The Psalm says, "Blessed is every one that feareth the LORD . . ." I have frequently stated that the word in the Hebrew which is translated in our English Bible as *blessed* could have just as well been translated by our English word *happy*. In fact, I have in my possession an English Old Testament translated from the Hebrew by Hebrews; a book used by the Hebrews of our day. In it, the opening verse of this Psalm reads, "Happy is every one that feareth the LORD: that walketh in his ways." Happy? Yes, that is the word.

But some may ask: Why does this Psalm make you think of the first Easter Sunday? On that Easter morning the disciples were the most dejected of men, when they first learned from the women who visited the sepulchre that they had not found His body, but reported seeing a vision of angels who had told them that Christ was risen from the dead. What a contrast between that Easter Sunday morning and the first Easter Sunday night. At night, the disciples were gathered in an upper room in Jerusalem. There was a table spread with broiled fish and a honeycomb. What a delicious supper! But no one wanted to touch it until the Lord came into the room, and said, "Peace be unto you." Then, knowing that they needed to have their bodies sustained as well as their spirits, He asked, "Have ye here any meat?" They pointed to the table. Then He, together with them, sat down and participated in the evening meal. Happiness? You do not know what happiness is until you have sat down in sweet fellowship with your Lord. This 128th Psalm begins with happiness and ends with peace— surely, it is a resurrection Psalm.

DOMESTIC HAPPINESS

In the 1st verse we have an obligation. If we are to have the happiness described and assured therein, it is necessary that we fear the Lord and walk in His ways. Again, the Lord knew how necessary labor was. Indeed, He knew more about the labor problem than any labor leader. He knew that idleness begets evil. He knew that men have a spirit, a soul, and a body. He knew that the spirit needed to be sustained by His own grace and the body needed to be supported by labor and the fruit of that labor. He knew that perfection of human joy comes with what is described in the 3rd verse of the 128th Psalm, where the Psalmist said, "Thy wife shall be as a fruitful vine by the sides of thine house: thy children like olive plants round about thy table." But the Psalmist has impressed us with the fact that this privilege is limited to a select group, for he said in the 4th verse, "Behold, that *thus* shall the man be blessed that feareth the LORD."

In considering the 127th Psalm, we found something similar to this Psalm; only in the former we had a description of a father surrounded by his sons, able to defend him. It described the family in relation to the outside world. Here, in the 128th Psalm, we have the inner side of domestic happiness: the one supplements the other.

It is surprising how frequently men have read this Psalm carelessly and quickly, without sensing its deep spiritual truth. As someone once said, "There is calm here, there is simple beauty here, but there are depths that no man has yet sounded." This Psalm is God's ideal of an earthly home. It is what every Christian home should be. I know sin has come in and marred human happiness and broken many homes, for sin cannot touch a thing without leaving its stain upon it.

But I believe that this Psalm also describes the future blessing that yet awaits this earth when the Lord, as the Prince of Peace and as David's greater Son, shall sit upon the throne of His Father. Then, as in Solomon's reign, only on a larger scale, Judah and Israel shall dwell safely, every man under his vine and under his fig tree, from Dan even to Beer-sheba. Thank God, that blessing will not be limited to Judah and Israel, but will include "all the Gentiles upon whom my name is called, saith the Lord . . ."

JERUSALEM, THE EARTH'S CENTER OF BLESSING

Finally, let us look at the 5th and 6th verses, where the Psalmist said, "The LORD shall bless thee out of Zion: and thou shalt see the good of Jerusalem all the days of thy life. Yea, thou shalt see thy children's children, and peace upon Israel." I freely acknowledge this is Israel's blessing. God speed the day when it shall literally be fulfilled.

"The LORD shall bless thee out of Zion . . ." said the Psalmist. All blessing which has come to man has come out of Zion, for out of Zion has come the lawgiver and the lifegiver. Today, in Jerusalem, multitudes are gathered; both Jew and Gentile. There is even peace this morning between the Arabs and the Jews in that city, though it is but an armistice; yet that armistice is a foretaste of what will take place in the future when all the nations of the earth shall bow before the Prince of Peace.

Some friends of mine are in Jerusalem this morning for their first visit. I would love to be there and still have this radio broadcast. I can think of nothing better than to be in the heart of that city on an Easter Sunday, beside the Lord's empty tomb, with a microphone before me, attempting to describe the city to you. That is a mere dream, but then, dreams have a way of coming true sometimes, don't they? At any rate, I told my friends that as they stand in the city and as the surrounding territory adds its increasing impression upon their hearts and minds of the glorious work of Christ, compelling them to lift up their hearts in prayer and thanksgiving to the Lord for His grace, to be sure to add that I, too, join with them in deep gratitude to the Lord for the death He died and for the blessing I have received out of Zion.

I can't be in Jerusalem this morning, but I do stand before this microphone and thank God that I can present to you my Lord and Saviour Jesus Christ and tell you that fullness of joy, of happiness, of peace, and of contentment, comes only by fearing the Lord and walking in His ways. Walking in His ways? Yes! Our Lord said, "I am the way, the truth, and the life: no man cometh unto the Father, but by me." Thus, if you walk in God's ways you must come by Jesus Christ. You must receive Him, believe Him, and revel in His fellowship. I trust that I have not been so wordy as to becloud the simple gospel message of peace.

Peace—do you have it? The peace of God that passeth all understanding comes out of the fact that we have peace with God. Do you have that peace? If not, then listen to the risen Lord, as He approached His disciples that first Easter Sunday night. With His hands outstretched, He said, "Peace be unto you." For a moment they were affrighted, thinking they had seen a mirage, or a spirit, or an optical illusion, but He said, ". . . handle me, and see; for a spirit hath not flesh and bones, as ye see me have." Christ gives peace! He offers peace through the blood of His cross. It is vouchsafed to us by the fact of His resurrection. Will you enjoy that peace by acknowledging His Lordship?

PSALM ONE HUNDRED TWENTY-NINE

"GRASS UPON THE HOUSETOPS" OR THE IMPENDING DOOM OF DICTATORS

THE 129th Psalm is as interesting as it is timely. It was written three thousand years ago, and yet the conditions which the Psalmist lamented still exist. In fact, the same people who found cause then to complain, and justly so, are, through their children, raising the same cry today.

The Psalm is occupied, primarily, with the lamentations of Israel, due to the affliction of her enemies, coupled with the hope that, as her enemies in previous ages had failed to obliterate them, so her future persecutors likewise will fail of that accomplishment.

While there is a note of sadness in this Psalm there is also a note of hope which culminates in a note of thanksgiving. When Israel leans upon the arm of flesh she fails, but when she learns upon the arm of God she triumphs; when she calls upon other nations in the time of her distress it aggravates her suffering, but when she calls upon the Lord, confessing her sin, then Israel is able to put to flight a thousand and one enemies.

As we read the Psalm, notice the repetition of the opening statement:

> "Many a time have they afflicted me from my youth, may Israel now say:
>
> "Many a time have they afflicted me from my youth: yet they have not prevailed against me.
>
> "The plowers plowed upon my back: they made long their furrows.
>
> "The LORD is righteous: he hath cut asunder the cords of the wicked.
>
> "Let them all be confounded and turned back that hate Zion.
>
> "Let them be as the grass upon the housetops, which withereth afore it groweth up:
>
> "Wherewith the mower filleth not his hand; nor he that bindeth sheaves his bosom.
>
> "Neither do they which go by say, The blessing of the LORD be upon you: we bless you in the name of the LORD."

The Psalmist said, "Many a time have they afflicted me from my youth, may Israel now say" and again, "Many a time have they afflicted me from my youth . . ." Why did the Psalmist repeat that phrase? Wasn't once sufficient?

In considering this subject, I would call your attention to the frequency with which our Lord introduced a pertinent statement by the familiar words, "Verily, verily, I say unto thee." Was it not sufficient for our Lord to say, "Verily, I say unto thee" instead of "Verily, verily, I say unto thee"? Why did He use the word "verily" twice? Our Lord was not a man of many words. Were you to look into the record you would find that His talks were all short, and each word was significant. He never indulged in superfluity of language. Then why did He say, "Verily, verily"?

For an answer we go to the 26th chapter of the prophecy of Isaiah, to observe something that is particularly true of the Hebrew language. In the 3rd verse of that chapter we read, in our English Bible, "Thou wilt keep him in *perfect peace*, whose mind is stayed on thee: because he trusteth in thee." If that passage had been translated literally, it would have read, "Thou wilt keep him in *peace peace*, whose mind is stayed on thee. In the Hebrew text the word "peace" is repeated. The answer, of course, is that in the Hebrew grammar there is no comparative or superlative degree such as we have in our English language. We think of a thing as great, then greater, and then greatest. In the Hebrew language, whenever the superlative is used the word is repeated, and that also holds good of the Aramaic in which our Lord spoke. Thus when Isaiah said, "Thou wilt keep him in peace peace, whose mind is stayed on thee" he referred to the superlative degree of peace. When our Lord said, "Verily, verily" He was giving a superlative message. When, therefore, the Psalmist repeated, "Many a time have they afflicted me from my youth" he called attention to the fact that it was an absolute truism. But the Psalmist added, in triumph, "yet they have not prevailed against me."

RETROSPECTION AND ANTICIPATION

The Psalmist was looking back into yesterday for sustaining courage for today, as well as hope for tomorrow. It was Alexander MacLaren, that princely Scotch preacher, who said, "The right use of retrospect is to make it the ground of hope. They who have passed unscathed through such afflictions may well be sure that any tomorrow shall be as the yesterdays were, and that all future assaults will fail as all past ones have failed . . . Israel's youth was far back in the days of Egyptian bondage, and many an affliction has he since met, but he lives still, and his existence proves that they have not prevailed against him. Therefore the backward look is gladsome, though it sees many trials. Survived sorrows yield joy and hope, as gashes in trees exude precious gums." How clear and encouraging are the words of that Scottish preacher.

There is a backward look that gives encouragement; but there is also given to the saints of God to look forward and forget the past. Lot's wife looked back and paid a terrific price for doing so. The Christian, as we learn from Paul the apostle, may forget the things that are behind, the unpleasant things, the sinful things, the disappointments, and the disobedience, for Paul said, ". . . this one thing I do, forgetting those things which are behind, and reaching forth unto those things which are before, I press toward the mark for the prize of the high calling of God in Christ Jesus."

When we urge retrospection, based on this 129th Psalm, we are not talking about a look at our disappointments, but a look back upon God's display of grace and power. Oh that Israel, in her present hour of difficulty, would do that and cry out to God in the language of this Psalm.

THE SUFFERING MESSIAH

The extent of Israel's suffering is graphically portrayed in the language of the 3rd verse, where we read, "The plowers plowed upon my back: they made long their furrows." So furious was the antagonism of the enemies of Israel, that they were not content with inflicting light punishment. Rather, they made long and deep their furrows.

This passage of Scripture reminds us of the physical sufferings of our Lord. The Roman soldiers inflicted the Roman scourge upon His bare back. Each time the lash fell upon His back, a piece of flesh was torn out, so that when the final thirty-ninth lash was laid upon Him His back could be likened unto a plowed field, where the furrows were made deep and long. In all of Israel's sufferings there is nothing to compare with His sufferings. Jeremiah, the lamenting prophet, expressed the sufferings of Christ poignantly, when he wrote, "Is it nothing to you, all ye that pass by? behold, and see if there be any sorrow like unto my sorrow, which is done unto me, wherewith the LORD hath afflicted me in the day of his fierce anger."

Isaiah presented Him prophetically, when he wrote, "He is despised and rejected of men; a man of sorrows, and acquainted with grief:" adding, "and we hid as it were our faces from him; he was despised, and we esteemed him not." But this was all because "he was wounded for our transgressions, he was bruised for our iniquities: the chastisement of our peace was upon him; and with his stripes we are healed."

"GRASS UPON THE HOUSETOPS"

The poetic language of this 129th Psalm is exquisite. Speaking about the enemies of Israel, the Psalmist said, "Let them be as the grass upon the housetops, which withereth afore it groweth up: wherewith the mower filleth not his hand; nor he that bindeth sheaves his bosom." Language could hardly be more powerfully descriptive and specific. The grass that grows upon the housetop is one thing, but the grass of the field is quite another. The grass of the field is used for the blessing of man, but the grass upon the housetop is absolutely valueless; it is so unimportant that even the mower pays no attention to it. It will wither before it grows up. Said someone: "The picture, of course, is Palestinian. There the roofs of the houses are plastered with a composition of mortar, tar, ashes, and sand, in the crevices of which grass often springs. The houses of the poor, in the country, are formed of a plaster of mud and straw, where the grass grows still more frequently." But what of it? Nobody pays any attention to it. It is not worthwhile plucking or cutting down. It will wither of itself. Oh, that Israel would only learn this lesson, then they would not waste their energy upon the oppressor, to the exclusion of knee exercise before the Lord.

The grass on the housetop is, of course, lifted above the grass of the field. It is on a higher plane, so to speak. But what of it? For a moment it is exalted, but the sun will scorch it and it will wither. What a figure of speech, in speaking of the oppressor! He may occupy the exalted position, momentarily. He may even be a dictator. He may be exalted above all, and the "grass of the field" may temporarily bow down before him, but the fact that he is on the housetop and lifted above the grass of the field is no assurance of his permanence. In fact, the sooner will he fall. He will wither even before he grows up.

What a lesson this Psalm also presents to the Christian of this age! We spend so much time fighting about this thing or that. We even assume that we can match wits and strength with the enemy of our soul. Let us give our enemies the privilege of basking in the sunlight of their self-exaltation and self-elevation: nothing more assures their quicker withering. How can we presume to battle with our enemy? Our strength is too weak to match his, and if it were possible for us to subdue him for the moment he would bob up in a thousand and one other ways overnight. But he has a time appointed unto him, when he will be assigned to the bottomless pit. At that time, all that will be necessary will be for the Lord to commission an angel to assign the enemy of our soul to his abode in the bottomless pit, in order that he may no longer deceive the nations of the earth.

The closing verse of this 129th Psalm is particularly significant concerning those who are oppressors. Such oppressors love crowds: they frequently indulge their fancy by arranging great gatherings, giving the populace the excitement of passing by a reviewing stand where these leaders enjoy exaltation. Those passing by the reviewing stand may gratify the human lust for power, by shouting "Heil" or its equivalent, but they do not pass the reviewing stand, saying, "The blessing of the LORD be upon you: we bless you in the name of the LORD." Indeed, no! There may be a time of forced obedience, but there is no voluntary blessing. The kind of salutation that bestows the blessing of the Lord upon one requires that the individual so blessed has himself proved a blessing. Even to this day, the Arabs use this very salutation when they pass by a cornfield or a fruit tree loaded with rich fruit. Invariably they will cry out, "Barak Allah" which is equivalent to saying, "The blessing of the LORD be upon you: we bless you in the name of the LORD." That type of blessing belongs to a fruitful vine or a fruitful field.

When a man's life yields the fruit of the Spirit, and when his life is lifted up in blessing, even the multitudes revere and honor that man and they spontaneously say, "The blessing of the LORD be upon you: we bless you in the name of the LORD." May we yield our life to Him, so that His fruit may be manifested in us, whereby our own associates may recognize the blessing of the Lord and in turn call us "blessed"!

PSALM ONE HUNDRED THIRTY

KNEELING DOWN AND STANDING UP

THE 130th Psalm presents a remarkable ascent from the depths of despair to the heights of glory. It parallels the experience of every individual who has ever come to know God in a personal and real sense. There can be no enjoyment of salvation until there is first an overwhelming consciousness of need. But let us read the Psalm, before commenting upon it:

> "Out of the depths have I cried unto thee, O LORD.
> "Lord, hear my voice: let thine ears be attentive to the voice of my supplications.
> "If thou, LORD, shouldest mark iniquities, O Lord, who shall stand?
> "But there is forgiveness with thee, that thou mayest be feared.
> "I wait for the LORD, my soul doth wait, and in his word do I hope.
> "My soul waiteth for the Lord more than they that watch for the morning: I say, more than they that watch for the morning.

"Let Israel hope in the LORD: for with the LORD
there is mercy, and with him is plenteous redemption.
"And he shall redeem Israel from all his iniquities."

It has been well said that "unless a man has been down in that black
abyss, he has scarcely cried to God as he should do" and "the beginning of
proper personal religion is the sense of personal sin." So we have two
important lessons to be learned from our meditation: the fact of sin and
the fact of salvation.

THE FACT OF SIN

I am afraid that many of the church-going people of our day have no
true conception of sin or salvation. Indeed, perhaps only a small percentage has experienced that consciousness of absolute depravity which causes
one to cry, as the Psalmist did, "Out of the depths have I cried unto thee,
O LORD."

But someone may ask: Is it necessary for one to go down, down, down
the ladder of moral depravity, in order to be a fit subject for God's redemption? Is it necessary to experience the vileness of sin, in order that one
may be a partaker of His salvation? Indeed not! It certainly is not to the
credit of any individual that he ride roughshod over the conventions of
life, and sin against his own body as well as against the Lord. However,
there must come into the life of every individual that consciousness of his
own sinfulness, that appreciation that he cannot stand in the presence of
God, if one is to enjoy the salvation of the Lord.

The whole trouble is, of course, that our standards are not the proper
standards. It is so easy to compare one person with another. We are not
as bad as John Jones or Sarah Smith—but that is not the true standard.
God Himself has provided the standard. When He sent His Son into the
world He revealed to man not only the way of salvation but He also revealed the standard of perfection. Unless you can equal the character of
Christ and the life of Christ you have come short of the glory of God. It
is useless to even try to maintain that standard, for the Bible is absolutely
clear that "all . . . have come short of the glory of God."

Bishop J. Taylor Smith in relating his own experience, said that it was
not the consciousness of sins that led him to Christ but the consciousness
of sin. Sins are the fruit of sin. As long as you have the same nature that
everyone else has, you have the capability for the vilest kind of sin that a

man has ever committed. The fact that you are able to control the expression of that nature of yours through religious observance, proper bringing up, or development of human character, does not change the fact. You still have a nature which is under the curse of God.

THE LIGHTED CANDLE

In mentioning Bishop Taylor Smith it brought to my mind one of his many interesting experiences. He was on board a vessel when a storm was about to break. The stewards suggested to the passengers that they clear the decks. The bishop was standing next to the smoking room and so walked into it. A group of men were gathered there. They evidently had been having a discussion, for the most boisterous one, when he observed the bishop, shouted, "Say there, sir, you are a clergyman. Can you answer me this question? If God gives a man a passionate nature, why should He hold the man responsible for the man's actions? Actually, isn't God responsible?" The bishop immediately lifted his heart in silent prayer to God that He would give him the proper answer, so that he would not be put to shame before that group of men. Then, addressing the man who quizzed him, he asked, "Will you concede that man is more than a body?" "Oh, yes." "That he possesses a soul and a spirit, in addition to his body?" "Yes."

Just then a steward walked through the smoking room carrying a lighted candle. Quick as a flash, the bishop said, "Do you see that candle? The Bible speaks of human life under the imagery of a candle. A candle is made of wax. It has an invisible stem in the center of it. When it stands perpendicularly it bears a light for the guidance of man. When a man realizes that his soul and his spirit are more important than his body he stands perpendicularly. He may feed his mind with good literature, or art, or music. He may fill his soul with a knowledge of God. In so doing he makes his body to be subservient to his spirit and soul. His life then throws a light for man's benefit.

"But when a man takes the horizontal position he thus places his body on the same level as his spirit and soul. The result is the same as when a candle is placed horizontally. The candle gives very little glow, much smoke, and throws off a distasteful stench. So, too, does the man who believes his body is equally as important as his soul and spirit.

"When a candle is reversed it does not yield any glow, rather, whatever light it did have goes out. So, too, is the experience of a man who reverses God's order by placing his body in the supreme place. Indeed, the

Bible states that such a man shall not live out half his days." The bishop's answer could not be controverted. May I raise the question: Are we living a perpendicular life, or a horizontal one, or have we entirely reversed the order?

KNEELING DOWN AND STANDING UP

No man will ever be able to stand up before he has knelt down. He must come to the place where, bowed down with the consciousness of his need, he will cry out to the Lord from the depths of his heart. A man who is conscious of his need knows full well that if the Lord should mark iniquity none could stand in His presence. If we are able to stand in God's presence it will be because we first bowed the knee to the Lord Jesus Christ. That statement excludes the possibility of anyone ever standing in the presence of God who has not embraced Jesus Christ and acknowledged Him Lord. It answers the question as to the status of the heathen and followers of other religions. It is a terrific statement. I would not make it, were it not that the Lord Jesus Christ Himself said, "I am the way, the truth, and the life: no man cometh unto the Father, but by me." Either our Lord was telling the truth or He was not. Either He was the Son of God and the way to God or He was an impostor. Logic demands that He be one or the other. That the disciples understood the words of the Lord Jesus Christ we know from the words of the Apostle Peter, when he said, "Neither is there salvation in any other: for there is none other name under heaven given among men, whereby we must be saved" but the name of Jesus Christ of Nazareth.

Such a statement is distasteful to some, and a decided shock to others. The first reaction might be to rebel against such words and decide to continue along the way one is already traveling. But it is just as futile to argue the matter as it would be to argue with a road map that indicated that the road to the left leads south to Florida and the road to the right leads north to Maine, and then insist that you will take the left road and get to Maine! Men have sense enough to follow a road map when they are driving an automobile. If only they would use the same intelligence in following the Word of God.

THE FACT OF SALVATION

So far we have discussed only one part of our subject—the fact of sin. Now let us look at the fact of salvation. In the 4th verse the writer beautifully expressed it: "But there is forgiveness with thee (the Lord), that thou mayest be feared." Here is assurance that there is forgiveness of sins with the Lord. In verse 7 we learn that there is mercy with the Lord and plenteous redemption. That is the Old Testament way of expressing the New Testament truth that the Lord is able to save unto the uttermost all those that come unto God by Christ. The sacrifice of Christ is sufficient; the blood He shed has such tremendous purchasing power that not only is it able to atone for the sins of those who have embraced Christ, but it is sufficient to atone for the sins of the whole world. That is what the Psalmist meant when he spoke of "plenteous redemption." We can never impoverish God by drawing upon His mercy.

But, mark you, there is no thought in either the Old or the New Testament that God dispenses the forgiveness of sins to the individual who has bowed his knee before Him in order that he may henceforth do as he pleases. Some have argued—Since there is plenteous redemption in Christ, since the blood of Jesus Christ is able to atone for past sins, and present sins, and future sins, we can live as we please. The New Testament declares, "God forbid. How shall we that are dead to sin, live any longer therein?" The Old Testament expresses the same idea, for in the 130th Psalm, the 4th verse, we read that ". . . there is forgiveness with thee, that thou (the Lord) *mayest be feared.*"

When the Scripture speaks of the fear of the Lord, it does not refer to that fear which genders fright, but rather that fear which genders awe and begets worship and devotion. It is not a spirit of terror. It is a spirit of love.

THE PEACE OF GOD

God has forgiven us our sins in order that we might have fellowship with Him. The greatest joy that can come to man is the joy which comes from *the knowledge of God.* I think I can illustrate that by another statement of Scripture. The Bible declares that we have peace *with* God through the blood of His sacrifice, but our Lord said to His disciples, who already had peace with God, "*my peace* I give unto you . . ." That is the peace *of* God. It is even greater than the former. In fact, the former was the means to effect the latter.

This peace, both with God and of God, passes all understanding. That does not mean that it is beyond the possibility of experiencing. The human brain, wonderful though it is, cannot fathom God's peace; it is outside its sphere and contemplation. But it is an experimental truth that every believer can testify is an accomplished fact. This peace has been made possible for, and given to us in order that we might fear and honor the Lord.

PSALM ONE HUNDRED THIRTY-ONE

LESSONS FOR ADULTS
FROM THE BEHAVIOR OF CHILDREN

WE are to consider the 131st Psalm. It contains three short verses. It has been called "the perfect miniature." Charles Haddon Spurgeon said that if the Psalms were compared to gems, the 131st should be likened to a pearl, and then added that "it will beautifully adorn the neck of patience." He further said, "It is one of the shortest Psalms to read, but one of the longest to learn."

The more one thinks of this Psalm the more convinced one becomes that we talk too much. Wordiness is not always a sign of depth of understanding. Which reminds me: one morning this past week I drove to the office in my car, accompanied by a friend. He told of attending a dinner of his law school the night before, at which two or three men, prominent in the public eye at present, graduates of the school, gave the principal addresses of the evening. Among them was the former Dean of the school, whom I'm sure you would know were I to mention his name. My friend said that if the Dean had limited his speech to what he said during the first ten minutes and the last five minutes, leaving out the middle part which took thirty-five minutes, he would have given a splendid talk. So wordiness, or the lack of it, is no test by which we can judge the depth of thought, the preparation that has gone into a message, or the benefits that can be derived from it. Surely we can learn many lessons from an examination of the Scriptures and the remarkable manner in which a thought is expressed therein with the use of a minimum of words.

When we considered the 130th Psalm we found it to be a perfect gospel message. In the 131st we have a further step in the pathway of faith, as it presents the blessedness of the man who possesses a meek and lowly spirit. The Psalm is marked by a tone of child-like simplicity which is simply delightful.

Someone has said that the writer of this Psalm "could assert his own lowliness without losing it." To boast of one's modesty, or even to speak of it, is commonly a sign that there is very little of which to boast. There are many kinds of pride, such as pride of possession, pride of wealth, pride of humility, etc., but, as others have said, pride of grace is the most odious. But let us read the Psalm:

> "LORD, my heart is not haughty, nor mine eyes lofty: neither do I exercise myself in great matters; or in things too high for me.
> "Surely I have behaved and quieted myself, as a child that is weaned of his mother: my soul is even as a weaned child.
> "Let Israel hope in the LORD from henceforth and for ever."

Lessons From Children

In preparation for this message, part of my reading included the introductory statements that appear in that splendid work entitled, "The Testimony of the Evangelists," written by Simon Greenleaf, Professor of Law at Harvard University, a generation ago. Every law student knows the position which Professor Greenleaf occupied. His work on Evidences is a classic. With the same keenness of mind and perception, that professor has taken the four Gospel records and subjected them to every test known to legal evidence. His conclusion is that the testimony of the Evangelists is true beyond any question. In the opening paragraphs of his great work, he calls attention to the fact that "it is essential to the discovery of truth that we bring to the investigation a mind freed as far as possible from existing prejudice, and open to conviction." Then he quotes a sentence from the pen of Lord Bacon, who wrote: "There is no other entrance to the kingdom of man, which is founded in the sciences, than to the kingdom of heaven, into which no one can enter but in the character of a little child." Professor Greenleaf further declares that "an examination of the Gospel record and the person of Jesus Christ should be pursued as in the presence of God and under the solemn sanctions created by a lively sense of His omniscience, and of our accountability to Him for the right use of the faculties which He has bestowed." Would to God more of our theological seminaries would do that; then we would have fewer unbelieving preachers in our pulpits.

Responsibility of God's Mouthpieces

As I read those lines by that learned gentleman, I was impressed with the responsibility that rests upon man to receive the testimony of God and the still greater responsibility that rests upon those men who are called to *present* the testimony of God.

The other evening our radio was turned on. I hardly paid any attention to it, as I was occupied with some reading for the moment, but suddenly I pricked up my ears—it was the March of Time program giving a re-enactment of the Black Tom explosion, which took place just twenty years ago! Quick as a flash, my memory resurrected that night in all its vividness. We were living in Brooklyn, N. Y., in the Bay Ridge section. It was in the early hours of the morning. We were suddenly awakened out of our sleep by a tremendous roar, and by the shattering of window-panes, and the glow of the sky. Again and again there was a loud burst. I hurriedly got into my clothes and rushed out into the street, to try to find out what it was all about. To my astonishment I saw people kneeling in the streets, crying out to God. What confusion—people shouting that the end of the world must be here! It was simply amazing to see the fear and the terror that took hold of people; and all that happened was a series of explosions—that was all.

The memory of that night will never leave my mind. It thoroughly convinced me that the overwhelming majority of people are in bondage. They have a sense of fear, and just as soon as something transpires which causes the ground under their feet to shake, they immediately assume that the hour of judgment has come. I raised the question in my mind that night, Why doesn't God speak to the world in a way that the whole world will know that He has spoken? Of course, I have since answered my own question as I have come to understand that God in His infinite wisdom has revealed Himself in an undeniable manner.

The revelation of God and the manner by which we enter into the kingdom of God is so clearly defined in the Scriptures that the wayfaring man, though he be a fool, need not err therein. But, in order to enter the kingdom of God, the heart must cease its haughtiness, the eyes must cease their lofty look; man must get down from his highly self-exalted position of "master of his fate" and come to the place where, as a child, he trusts and obeys God.

No man ever mastered any branch of science unless he was willing first to take the place of a babe and allow nature to reveal her secrets to him. Even so, no man can enter into the kingdom of God unless he is willing to become as a little child and allow God to unveil His revelation to him.

But let us look at a scene which beggars description. Here is a multitude round about our Lord. The disciples have formed an inner cordon about Him. Next are the Pharisees and lawyers, who seek to entrap Him, and then the multitudes who listen to our Lord with great eagerness. Suddenly some of the fathers and mothers, with their children, seek to break through the lines and come into the presence of our Lord, so that He may even *touch* their children. His disciples, enamoured by the wisdom of their Master, assume that He ought not to be annoyed by little children on such an occasion, and thus they rebuke the parents. But our Lord sees it, and is much displeased; not only displeased—but *much* displeased; whereupon He says to those disciples, "Suffer the little children to come unto me, and forbid them not: for of such is the kingdom of God. Verily I say unto you, Whosoever shall not receive the kingdom of God as a little child, he shall not enter therein." David knew the secret of all this, and for that reason he wrote the 131st Psalm.

GROWING IN GRACE

But in this Psalm David was not referring to the necessity of becoming a little child in order to *enter* into the kingdom of God. He had already entered in by that way. But now that he had entered, he was anxious about his behavior *inside* the kingdom of God. He wrote, "I have behaved and quieted myself, as a child that is weaned of his mother: my soul is even as a weaned child." Thus we discover that we can also learn much from children on the manner of growth in grace.

The word "behaved" which David used is an interesting word. It could just as well have been translated by our English word *adjusted* or *leveled*. It simply means that now that we are in the kingdom of God we should adjust ourselves to that standard. We could not adjust ourselves until we got inside, but now that we are inside we can adjust ourselves. That same truth is expressed in the New Testament under another symbolism, when the Apostle Paul urged the Philippians to work out their own salvation with fear and trembling, reminding them that "it is God which worketh in you both to will and to do of his good pleasure." To work out one's salvation is equivalent to behaving, adjusting, and quieting one's self, as when a child is weaned of its mother. If you will not misunderstand my language, there are a tremendous number of grown-up "old babies" among professing Christians. Yes, they have entered into the kingdom of God as a little child, but they are like unweaned babies, always crying for the world and never understanding that the cross not only was the means that God used for divine atonement, but, through that cross, the world is crucified unto us and we are crucified unto the world.

What is a monstrosity in the natural is equally a monstrosity in the spiritual. The strangest thing about it is that we recognize it in the natural world but we do not recognize it in the spiritual. While it is a delight for the mother to nurse her child, she is equally anxious to have that child develop and adjust itself, in order that it might be quieted even though it has been weaned. So, too, there are certain adjustments that are necessary to be made in the Christian life. I say necessary to be made, and I mean every word of it. True, there is nothing that we can do, or need do, in order to be saved, but now that we are saved our lives are not our own. We have been bought with a price, and we should glorify God in our bodies. That is the New Testament message; it is also the Old Testament message; it is the message of this 131st Psalm.

PSALM ONE HUNDRED THIRTY-TWO

FINDING A PLACE FOR GOD

IT would appear that the 132nd Psalm was written by King Solomon, David's son, for part of it is quoted by Solomon in connection with the dedication of the temple which bore his name. Yet it does not make a great deal of difference what human instrumentality was used by the Holy Spirit to write this or any other Psalm. The fact is that there is sufficient evidence in the Psalm itself whereby we know that it must have been inspired by the Holy Spirit of God. That is the reason the whole Bible is living and real today, despite the fact that much of it was written many thousands of years ago. Let us read the Psalm, and then we will comment on it.

"Lord, remember David, and all his afflictions:
"How he sware unto the LORD, and vowed unto the mighty God of Jacob;
"Surely I will not come into the tabernacle of my house, nor go up into my bed;
"I will not give sleep to mine eyes, or slumber to mine eyelids,
"Until I find out a place for the LORD, an habitation for the mighty God of Jacob.
"Lo, we heard of it at Ephratah: we found it in the fields of the wood.
"We will go into his tabernacles: we will worship at his footstool.
"Arise, O LORD, into thy rest; thou, and the ark of thy strength.

"Let thy priests be clothed with righteousness; and let thy saints shout for joy.

"For thy servant David's sake turn not away the face of thine anointed.

"The LORD hath sworn in truth unto David; he will not turn from it; Of the fruit of thy body will I set upon thy throne.

"If thy children will keep my covenant and my testimony that I shall teach them, their children shall also sit upon thy throne for evermore.

"For the LORD hath chosen Zion; he hath desired it for his habitation.

"This is my rest for ever: here will I dwell; for I have desired it.

"I will abundantly bless her provision: I will satisfy her poor with bread.

"I will also clothe her priests with salvation: and her saints shall shout aloud for joy.

"There will I make the horn of David to bud: I have ordained a lamp for mine anointed.

"His enemies will I clothe with shame: but upon himself shall his crown flourish."

It is, of course, apparent that this Psalm speaks of a dwelling-place for the Almighty God. The vow that the writer made clearly evidences this fact, for he wrote, "Surely I will not come into the tabernacle of *my* house, nor go up into *my* bed; I will not give sleep to *mine* eyes, or slumber to *mine* eyelids, until I find out a place for the LORD, an habitation for the mighty God of Jacob."

EXILING GOD

No one will question the value of a study of antiquity, for the pathway of former days is always the guide to the future. However, I am not so interested in fitting this Psalm to the temple that Solomon built (though it undoubtedly refers to that event) as I am in determining its application for our own lives in this day.

David had it in his heart to build a house for the Lord. It was to be a meeting-place, where God could commune with the children of Israel; a place in which to put the ark of the covenant and the other articles of furniture used in the tabernacle of the wilderness. He was not permitted to do so. That privilege was reserved for his son, King Solomon.

I used the word *privilege* advisedly, for surely it must be a privilege for a man to be given the opportunity of erecting a building where God promises to dwell. That privilege Solomon had. It causes one to raise the questions, Where is God's dwelling-place now? Can a man build Him a house today?

In answering, I remind you briefly of the history of God's dwelling-places upon the earth. From the opening words of the first book of the Bible one can observe that it is God's desire to dwell among His people on the earth. It was not very long, however, before His creatures *exiled* Him, refusing His domination and fellowship. One cannot have His fellowship apart from His domination. It is absurd to think otherwise. If He is God, then it is not given to man to dominate, but rather to be subservient. Some years later God promised Moses that He would dwell among the children of Israel. To this end He gave instructions, even to the minutest details, for the construction of a tabernacle in the wilderness. There God promised to tabernacle, or to dwell. Later, when Israel came into the Promised Land, God's dwelling-place became the temple but, as we learn from the testimony of our Lord Jesus Christ, the nation had already in that day made the house of God to be a den of thieves, so that once again God was *exiled* to the heavens.

He then took up His dwelling-place, or His tabernacle, in the person of our Lord Jesus Christ, in the body God had prepared especially for Him. This we learn from the 1st chapter of the Gospel according to St. John, where we are told that the Word (which is the very concept of God, the very expression of God) was made flesh, and dwelt among us, and we (that is, the disciples of our Lord) beheld His glory, the glory as of the only begotten of the Father, full of grace and truth. Thus God, in the person of Jesus Christ, dwelt with His people during His earth ministry. As the body of our Lord Jesus "tabernacled" the eternal God, so Christ's presence among the people was the dwelling-place of God. But again the people said, concerning Him, "We will not have this man to reign over us" and thus they also *exiled* Him to heaven.

It does seem startling that the God of heaven and earth, the Creator, should be exiled by His own creatures. It is even more astounding that God is willing to be exiled, in order that the desires and lusts of His creatures may be fulfilled. We have never seen a similar situation! Imagine, for example, a servant speaking to his master, and saying, Sir, I no longer desire to be your servant; I will not permit you to rule over me any longer; you leave this house and I will take possession of it. And, quietly, the master of the house leaves and goes into exile and permits the servant to dominate in the sphere which his own hands had created. You have never heard of such a situation!

But that is exactly what has transpired in man's relationship with God; yet God is still seeking a habitation where He may rest and dwell and abundantly bless. He wishes a place where He can clothe His priests with salvation and give His saints a song which will enable them to shout aloud with joy. He promises that He will clothe the enemies of His saints with shame. Isn't it strange, in the face of all of that, that man will still exile God and refuse His domination? Strange, it is true—but fact it is also.

When our Lord Jesus was born in Bethlehem, we read that there was no room in the inn for Joseph and Mary. In consequence, the Lord Jesus was born in a stable and cradled among the creatures of the field, who, by the way, recognized Him as their Master. During the wilderness experience, that period of forty days and forty nights when our Lord was tested by Satan, it is written that He "was with the wild beasts; and the angels ministered unto him." Thus, domestic beasts and wild beasts all recognized their Lord, their Creator. The angels recognized Him and ministered unto Him. But man, the creature of the dust, into whom God breathed the breath of life, to whom He gave an intellect and a reason, man exiled Christ and sent Him back into the heavens.

CAN MAN BUILD GOD A HOUSE?

In this Psalm Solomon vowed to God that he would not come into the tabernacle of *his* house, nor go up into *his* bed; he would not give sleep to *his* eyes nor slumber to *his* eyelids until he had found a place for the Lord; an habitation for the mighty God of Jacob.

Again I ask: Can man today build God a house? Where is the Lord's dwelling-place now? We are told that God is a Spirit, and they that worship Him must worship Him in spirit and in truth. Our Lord informed us that His Father seeketh such to worship Him.

We frequently, but erroneously, speak of a church building as "the house of the Lord," whereas, in fact, the church is not a building; it is a living organism, made up of individual members who compose what the Scripture calls "the body of Christ," of which He is the head. If we could only keep that thought clearly in our minds, we would not have so much difficulty in reconciling seemingly contradictory things in the religious world. A church building is just a meeting-place. The church is a living organism, made up of born-again men and women who have been baptized into it by the Holy Spirit. It does not make any difference what label is pasted on the individual, or of what particular body of Christians he may be a member. That has not the slightest thing to do with it. The dwelling-place of God today, collectively speaking, is in the body of Christ, which is the church of Jesus Christ. When a company of believing men and women gather together for worship, whether it be in a home or in a building set apart for that specific purpose, God is present and dwells with His people.

By the way, here is an interesting little thought on this subject which I would like to pass on to you. In Judaism, no meeting can be held unless ten men are present. Ten men constitute a synagogue. If there are less than ten men present a synagogue cannot function. It would be interesting to know the antecedent of that principle, but it may come from the fact that God promised Abraham that if He found ten righteous men in Sodom He would spare the city. However, under the New Testament economy the number has been reduced considerably, for our Lord said, "where two or three are gathered together in my name, there am I in the midst of them."

May I press this subject of God's dwelling-place a little closer home. In our Psalm, Solomon was seeking a proper place for God to dwell, and he wrote, "Lo, we heard of it at Ephratah: we found it in the fields of the wood. We will go into his tabernacles: we will worship at his footstool. Arise, O LORD, into thy rest; thou, and the ark of thy strength."

Observe that the word "it" refers to the ark of the covenant, that strange box which symbolized the presence of Jehovah among His people. For a while the ark rested in the home of Obed-edom, the Gittite. God blessed that home and all that pertained to it. He blessed it because of the presence of the ark. David finally removed the ark and arranged for its transportation to Jerusalem, where it was to be placed in the midst of the tent or tabernacle that he had pitched for it, from which place it was later transferred to the temple of Solomon.

Now think of the ark, symbolizing the presence of God, and Solomon saying, "We heard of it at Ephratah: we found it in the fields of the wood." Wherever that ark rested, there God dwelt. Wherever two or three gather in the name of the Lord, our Lord Jesus Christ is in the midst. That is His promise. Either it is a fact or it is a fallacy. Either it is a glorious experience or it is empty ceremonialism.

THE PRESENT CHRIST

But I said I wanted to bring this message closer home. If believers in Christ would recognize that wherever two or three people are gathered together in the name of our Lord, He is in the midst, every church dispute would fly away with the wind. I am sure of this—there would be no disputes, there would be no strained fellowship, there would be no disturbance. No one could have a controversy in His presence. How He must feel when Christians squabble among themselves, while He is right in the midst. What a travesty! When His position as the head of the church in the midst of His people is recognized, blessing flows from His presence. Then Christians enjoy spiritual fellowship one with the other. There we have the dwelling-place of God, collectively speaking, for today. Whenever a body of Christians meet together in the name of the Lord, irrespective of denominational labels, there is God's dwelling-place.

But, marvel of marvels, it is possible for God to take up His dwelling in the life of an individual believer. In the last book of the Bible, the book of The Revelation, in the 3rd chapter, the Lord has this to say, "Behold, I *stand* at the door, and knock: if any man hear my voice, and open the door, I will come in to him, and will sup with him, and he with me. To him that overcometh will I grant to sit with me in *my* throne, even as I also overcame, and am set down with my Father in *his* throne." Did you note the position of our Lord—standing at the door and knocking? The door, of course, can only be opened from the inside. You, the occupant, are always at home. If you can't hear His knock, you can hear His voice, for He says, ". . . if any man hear my voice, and open the door, I will come in to him, and will sup with him, and he with me." Would God that each of us might say with the Psalmist in this 132nd Psalm, "*I* will not come into the tabernacle of *my* house, nor go up into *my* bed; *I* will not give sleep to *mine* eyes, or slumber to *mine* eyelids, until *I* find out a place for the LORD, an habitation for the mighty God of Jacob."

Psalm One Hundred Thirty-Three

CHRISTIAN UNITY

IN the years during which it has been my privilege to give these meditations in this great Book of Psalms, I do not believe that I have ever approached a Psalm with more sorrow of heart and more concern of mind than the 133rd. At first glance this may seem strange for the Psalm is occupied with that spirit of unity which produces gladness, so that it ought to make the heart of every Christian throb with joy.

The Psalm was composed by David. Someone has said that it was written to present the benefits of the communion of saints. It contains only three verses, reading as follows:

> "Behold, how good and how pleasant it is for brethren to dwell together in unity!
>
> "It is like the precious ointment upon the head, that ran down upon the beard, even Aaron's beard: that went down to the skirts of his garments;
>
> "As the dew of Hermon, and as the dew that descended upon the mountains of Zion: for there the LORD commanded the blessing, even life for evermore."

Here is a Psalm speaking of gladness and pleasantry, as well as of something that is exceedingly precious—and yet I cannot approach this Psalm without feeling a deep burden and a sense of sorrow.

THE PRINCIPLE OF UNITY

How I wish it were possible that I might address my comments exclusively to those who have embraced Jesus Christ as their Saviour. Usually when there is a family discussion, non-members of the family are excluded. I have something on my heart that I feel is necessary to express to the members of the Christian family. You who are non-members may be a bit surprised at my frankness, though you probably are acquainted with the situation equally as well as I am. However, whether you listen or not, I hope you will appreciate that you are not tuning in on a family squabble, but rather a meeting of respective members of the family, in order to restore a spirit of unity and fellowship which will make true the words of our Psalm, when David said, "Behold, how good and how pleasant it is for brethren to dwell together in unity!"

No one takes exception to *the principle* expressed by the Psalmist— *it is* good, *it is* pleasant, to have brethren dwell together in unity. It is good, irrespective of what group of people is involved. It is good for capital and labor to dwell together in unity. It is good for any individual to enjoy the fellowship of other members of his group and preserve a spirit of unity. Such being the case, what an indictment it is against the Christian family when there are petty squabbles and when the spirit of discord and consequent disruption are present, as has been evident, particularly in recent years. I am not talking about Christendom as we know it today. I am not talking about the vast body of Christians and non-Christians gath-

ered together in one great melting-pot. I have no reference whatsoever to
that. I limit my comments to the body of Christ; to those who know that
their sins are forgiven, who know that they have eternal life through faith
in Jesus Christ, who know that they have passed out of death and into life,
and therefore know that the Lord Jesus Christ is their Saviour, and who
have acknowledged Him as their Lord.

All who are members of that body will agree that it is a serious question whether there has ever been a time in the entire history of the church
when there was less evidence of the unity of the Spirit in the bond of peace.
I am not talking of denominationalism. I am not interested in whether you
are a member of the Presbyterian or the Methodist or the Episcopal church,
or whether you are a member of an undenominational body. It does not
make any difference of what denomination or group you are a member. Since
you have been born again by the Spirit of God there is a family relationship between the members of the body of Christ which should express itself
in unity about the person of Christ, so as to cause each member of the body
to experience the goodness and pleasantness of such a relationship.

David knew what it was to have a divided family. He was the youngest of a large household and, as sometimes happens, the older members were
called upon to bow before the youngest; and that is no easy task. David's
brothers, urged on by jealousy, ridiculed and despised him when he challenged the uncircumcised Philistine. But, more than that, David knew
what it was to have division within his own family. He probably vowed as
a young man that when he had his own family he would determine by
everything within his power to avoid the causes that made for jealousy and
lack of unity in his father's household. Yet when David was a father he
discovered that there was controversy, deceit and rebellion among the members of his own family. He knew what it was to have his own son raise
his heel against him. When he learned of the death of that son in his
treachery and deceit, instead of showing a spirit of satisfaction that the
attempt had been thwarted, he cried bitter tears for the loss of his son,
Absalom. Thus David knew what it was to have disturbance within his
own household; yet he wrote, "Behold, how good and how pleasant it is for
brethren to dwell together in unity!" I think only such a man could write
about the pleasantness of unity, for he had experienced the bitter fires of
division.

I cannot say that I have any sympathy for the attempt which seeks
a united Protestant church. I am too well aware that there can be no united

church except on a solid foundation. I do not think it is possible to have unity between two groups of people, one of whom believes that Jesus Christ is the Son of God and the other believes that He is a mere man. I do not think it is possible to have unity between a group that looks upon the death of Jesus Christ on the cross as a divine transaction, wherein God made atonement for sin; and a group that looks on the cross and the death of Jesus Christ as that of a martyr or a good man who died for a cause. There can be no real fellowship between such groups—but there can be unity between every member of the body of Christ whose feet rest solidly upon the fact of the deity of Christ and upon the death which He died upon the cross.

God has so constituted us that no two of us are alike. That law is apparent in all creation. Take the grass of the field, for instance; no two blades of grass are identical, yet they have much of sameness about them. It is not expected that a man, when he is born again, will become a machine and necessarily see eye to eye about everything with everybody, but as there is a unity of design between the blades of grass, with consequent communion among them, so that they blanket a whole field and unitedly offer to men the blessings of a green earth, so, through united fellowship between all true believers in Christ who have been redeemd by His blood and who rejoice in the person of Jesus Christ, great blessing can result.

THE TEST OF SCRIPTURE

May I take you now to one or two New Testament passages of Scripture which will indicate that what I have said is amply attested to by the written Word. First, let us look at the 4th chapter of Paul's letter to the Ephesians, where Paul said,

> "I therefore, the prisoner of the Lord, beseech you that ye walk worthy of the vocation wherewith ye are called,
>
> "With all lowliness and meekness, with longsuffering, forbearing one another in love;
>
> "Endeavoring to keep the unity of the Spirit in the bond of peace.
>
> "There is one body, and one Spirit, even as ye are called in one hope of your calling;
>
> "One Lord, one faith, one baptism,
>
> "One God and Father of all, who is above all, and through all, and in you all."

I am particularly interested in two phrases contained in that exhortation; the first, "forbearing one another in love" and the second, "endeavouring to keep the unity of the Spirit in the bond of peace." If you have done the opposite, I do trust that the Holy Spirit will so crush your heart as to cause you to cry out before the Lord and repent of your sin. If you have spoken a word against your brethren in Christ; if you have been overbearing in hate instead of forbearing in love; if you have sought to disturb Christian fellowship instead of endeavoring to keep the unity. of the Spirit; you have sinned against the person of Jesus Christ your Lord.

In the 16th chapter of Paul's letter to the Romans, the Apostle gave a similar injunction. Beginning at the 17th verse, he said, "Now I beseech you, brethren, mark them which cause divisions and offenses contrary to the doctrine which ye have learned; and avoid them. For they that are such serve not our Lord Jesus Christ, but their own belly . . ." That is a strange expression, isn't it? Here we have a passage in which the Apostle Paul declared that there are some who make divisions, and Paul said: Mark those men and avoid them, for they do not serve the Lord. They serve their own selves.

Again, I take you to our Lord Jesus Christ, who is the fountain-head of all truth. In His great high priestly prayer, recorded in the 17th chapter of John's Gospel, our Lord said, "Neither pray I for these alone (that is, the Apostles gathered around Him), but for them also which shall believe on me through their word (that means us); that they all may be one; as thou, Father, art in me, and I in thee, that they also may be one in us: that the *world may believe* that thou hast sent me." What a responsibility rests upon each individual member of the body of Christ to observe a spirit of unity, in order that the world *may know* that our Lord Jesus Christ is the Son of God and was sent by Him to die for us.

Ah, but someone may say: So-and-so said this and that, and this man does not hold to all the truth; there are some things on which we disagree. Well, what of it? If a man holds to the truth of the inspired Word, to the truth of the deity, death, and bodily resurrection of Christ, and adheres to the simple gospel of Christ, and is walking in fellowship with his Lord, you should endeavor to keep with him the unity of the Spirit in the bond of peace. It is amazing to see the depths to which Christians will go in violating this passage of Scripture.

Recently I had dinner with a friend, a gracious gentleman, a man who loves the Lord Jesus Christ and who serves Him faithfully. He showed me a letter which he had received from a member of a committee under whose auspices he had recently conducted some meetings. These meetings were greatly blessed of the Lord and much good was accomplished. The committee was well pleased with his efforts and yet the letter stated that news had come to them that he had been guilty of stealing money from the collection plate in his own church. Now I know that one cannot do a work for God in this world without being subject to criticism. I have no idea where that lying information came from. It probably is useless to deny it —but I dare say that it was not an unsaved person who started that false rumor. It undoubtedly was a man or woman who professes to know Christ.

I do pray that our hearts and spirits may be melted. In the presence of this 133rd Psalm, which speaks of the blessings that exist when brethren dwell in unity, may we determine from now on, that instead of causing divisions we will endeavor to keep the unity of the Spirit in the bond of peace. Of one thing I am sure, the Holy Spirit always makes for unity amongst believers in Christ, for He dwells in every one of them.

THE DIVINE PRESCRIPTION

Well, so much for the exhortative part of this ministry. Let us look at the other side of the picture. David said that it is not only good and pleasant for brethren to dwell in unity, but it is so delightful that "It is like the precious ointment upon the head, that ran down upon the beard, even Aaron's beard: that went down to the skirts of his garments . . ."

Now what is it that David had in mind? When brethren dwell together in unity, when men and women gather in His name, one cannot enter the room without being conscious of a delightful odor of sweet fellowship. There is nothing cloying about that, nor effeminate. I have always liked a he-man. I happen to have a group of friends, men about my own age, who love the Lord Jesus Christ. When we get together we invariably have a marvelous time. Why? Because there is a unity of the Spirit. That does not mean that we do not find faults in each other or ourselves, and some-times there is no hesitancy in telling the other fellow his faults, but it is all done in the spirit of good fellowship. We would no more think of break-ing that fellowship than jumping off the Brooklyn Bridge. When that type of fellowship exists between believers in Christ even the world senses our possession of it.

Need I remind you who are acquainted with the Bible, that the ingredients that went into the oil with which Aaron was anointed were never used in like quantities for any other purpose. It was a prescription prepared by the divine Pharmacist to be used exclusively upon the high priest. No one else could even imitate it. The unity of the Spirit that exists between believers is of heavenly origin. It cannot be compounded by any of the earth's chemists. The world may try to imitate it, but they have never found the like ingredients, because the oil is a symbol of God's Holy Spirit.

God grant that each of us henceforth will manifest that spirit of true fellowship which the Lord intended us to possess.

PSALM ONE HUNDRED THIRTY-FOUR

THE NIGHT LIFE OF A CHRISTIAN

AT first thought I can appreciate that it may appear facetious to speak on the subject, "The Night Life of a Christian." We have been so accustomed to limiting "night life" to the "gay white way" as to entirely forget that there are marvelous mysteries in the night.

The 134th Psalm, which we are to consider, consist of three brief verses. An examination of our Bible will indicate that it is the last in the series of Songs of degrees. In previous broadcasts on these songs, we have discussed the import of this title. They were Psalms that were sung by the pilgrims of Israel as they journeyed up the mountainsides of Judea, and as they went to worship the Lord at Jerusalem. Some of them undoubtedly were sung before the temple was erected, while David reigned as king. They are called Songs of degrees, or Songs of ascent. It almost appears that each succeeding Psalm which comprises the series discusses a higher or deeper spiritual truth. In the 134th we arrive at the climax. It is in the nature of a grand finale.

THE SETTING OF THE PSALM

Robert Nisbet, in his description of the temple setting for this Psalm, wrote, "The last cloud of smoke from the evening sacrifice has mixed with the blue sky, the last note of the evening hymn has died away on the ear. The watch is being set for the night. The twenty-four Levites, the three priests, and the captain of the guard, whose duty it was to keep ward from sunset to sunrise over the hallowed precincts, are already at their several posts, and the multitudes are retiring through the gates, which will soon be shut, to many of them to open no more. But they cannot depart without one last expression of the piety that fills their hearts; and turning to the watchers on tower and battlement, they address them in holy song, in what was at once a brotherly admonition and a touching prayer:

'Behold, bless ye the LORD, all ye servants of the LORD, which by night stand in the house of the LORD.
'Lift up your hands in the sanctuary, and bless the LORD.'

"The pious guard are not unprepared for the appeal, and from their lofty heights, in words that float over the peopled city and down into the quiet valley of the Kedron, like the melody of angels, they respond (in the language of the last verse of our Psalm) to each worshipper who thus addressed them, with a benedictory farewell:

'The LORD that made heaven and earth bless thee out of Zion.' "

This quotation accurately presents the background of the Psalm. The twenty-four Levites, the three priests, and the captain of the guard were known as night watchers. They kept guard in the house of the Lord. As our Lord prophesied, the temple was later destroyed and not one stone was left upon another. Since Titus, the Roman General, destroyed the city, temple worship and night watchers have been things of the past. Yet one can come to this Psalm and find a message for his own circumstance and for this particular hour. Thus I have designated this address, "The Night Life of a Christian."

There is something captivating about the night, just as there is something dreadful about the night. Sometimes the quietness and stillness of the night plays havoc with the conscience, so that men seek to drown the stillness of night by wild participation in scenes of debauchery and fleshly lusts. Yet there is something grand and captivating about the night.

Just here I want to make mention, in passing, though we will come back to it later, of the promise the Lord gave to Cyrus, king of the Persians, one of the few Gentiles whom God honored during Old Testament times. The Lord had confided to Cyrus that He would uphold him by His right hand; He would subdue the nations before him; He would go before him and make crooked places straight, break in pieces gates of brass, and cut in sunder the bars of iron; and then the Lord concluded with this cryptic comment, which appears in the 3rd verse of the 45th chapter of Isaiah, "And I will give thee the treasures of darkness, and hidden riches of secret places, that thou mayest know that I, the LORD, which call thee by thy name, am the God of Israel. For Jacob my servant's sake, and Israel mine elect, I have even called thee by thy name: I have surnamed thee though thou hast not known me."

Oh for an hour to dig under the surface of that marvelous revelation of the Lord to Cyrus, the Gentile king! It is one of the great promises of Scripture. However, I want to keep to my subject: "The Night Life of a Christian."

Usually, the night is the season when we have laid aside the cares and labor of the day and when an opportunity is given for relaxation, contemplation, and enjoyment of the blessings of the day, but it is also the season when we may indulge in the almost priceless privilege of forgetting the disappointments and sorrows of the day. It is the time when the family is regathered. It is the time when, after a period of delightful fellowship, closing with prayer and meditations, one is cradled in the arms of the Lord while He administers to us the soothing anesthetic of sleep. I have, many a night, after completing my devotions and getting into bed, found myself thanking God for the pleasure and rest of sleep. It is wonderful to retire and feel like sleeping and then doze off and be thoroughly oblivious to anything that that is going on until the morning light breaks into the room. I believe that, too, was included in what God had in mind, when He said to Cyrus, "I will give thee the treasures of darkness, and hidden riches of secret places . . ." Yet there was much more in that promise.

"NIGHT IS NATURE'S GROWING TIME"

I am indebted to my friend, Dr. Ironside, for introducing me to the writings of that great Australian preacher, F. W. Boreham, whose essays are almost impossible to excel, if even to equal. He has written an article entitled, "Mushrooms on the Moor." Mr. Boreham had just finished reading G. K. Chesterton's "Victorian Age in English Literature," and was greatly distressed that Mr. Chesterton did not like mushrooms. Of course, Boreham was speaking figuratively. He referred to that writer's distaste for true spirituality, for the things of the night; for mushrooms, you know, grow at night and are harvested early the next morning. Mr. Boreham goes on to say that many fine things grow at night. "Indeed," said he, "Sir

James Crichton-Browne, the great doctor, in his lecture on 'Sleep,' argues that all things that grow at all grow in the night. Night is Nature's growing time." Boreham continues speaking of nightingales, the singers of the night; and mushrooms, the children of the night; and quotes from that wonderful line of Faber's which has been set appropriately to music: "Angels of Jesus, angels of light, Singing to welcome the pilgrims of the night!"

But I must give you another quotation from Boreham before leaving him. Speaking of Dan Crawford, the missionary to Africa who went home to be with his Lord a few years ago, he said that in Central Africa, if a young missionary attempts to prove the existence of God, the natives laugh, and point to the wonders of nature and exclaim, "No rain, no mushrooms!"

Since God has placed this principle in creation so that there is abundant testimony that it is necessary to have rain as well as sunshine, to have night as well as the light, why should we be surprised that into every Christian's life (if he is to grow in grace and in the knowledge of the Lord) there must come the rain, there must come the night as well as the light and sun, "for all things that grow at all grow in the night."

Our Psalm tells us that the servants of the Lord, by night stand in the house of the Lord. Did you note that it spoke of the night watchers as "servants"? We are children of God by faith in Jesus Christ. We had no more to do with our second birth than we had to do with our first birth. It was the operation of the Holy Spirit in conjunction with the Word of God. We were thus born again and made members of the household of faith.

There is, however, such a thing as growth in grace and in the knowledge of the Lord, whereby a child, a son, a member of the household of faith takes the position of a servant, thereby coming to understand the secrets of the Lord. Paul chose to be a bondslave of Jesus Christ. Paul had his night seasons.

Perhaps it surprises some to suggest that a servant is given to know the secrets of the Lord, for we are all too prone to conclude that sonship is higher than servitude, and in some respects it is, but I would remind you that it is written of our Lord, "Though he were a Son, yet learned he obedience by the things which he suffered . . ." Again, let us not forget the parenthesis that appears in the 9th verse of the 2nd chapter of John's Gospel, in the record of the first miracle of our Lord's public ministry, which took place at the marriage feast in Cana of Galilee. The water was changed to wine, but neither the governor of the feast nor the guests knew anything about it. They had no idea how it was made nor whence it was; but in parenthesis, in the Gospel record we read, "(but the servants which drew the water knew) . . ."

In addition to the servants that stood in the house of the Lord at night, there were also the shepherds who watched over their flock by night; the flock from which were chosen the lambs for the sacrifice. It was those shepherds, *in the night season,* to whom the gospel was first preached, when an angel said, " . . . behold, I bring you good tidings of great joy, which shall be to all people. For unto you is born this day in the city of David a Saviour, which is Christ the Lord." Indeed, if you wish to know the secrets of the Lord, you must know something about watching in the *night* season.

CRYING IN THE NIGHT SEASON

If it has pleased God to give you the experience of night life, when the stillness almost drives you to a point of desperation; when the unanswerable cries of your heart seem to rise to a ceiling of brass, only to reverberate without an answer, and to taunt you: I beg of you to appreciate that God is giving you the greatest blessing that can come into any life. "All things that grow at all grow in the night." God is about to reveal to you "the treasures of darkness and the hidden riches of secret places."

We are reminded of the 22nd Psalm, where we have the distressed cry of our Lord, as He prayed, "My God, my God, why hast thou forsaken me? why art thou so far from helping me, and from the words of my roaring? O my God, I cry in the daytime, but thou hearest not; and *in the night season,* and am not silent." It is impossible to read these words without some understanding of the anguish of heart and rending of spirit that must have been our Lord's when He uttered them. Imagine Him crying, "O my God . . ." That in itself is a cry of anguish, a cry of the crushed heart. But notice also, will you, the seasons of the despair, when he said, "I cry in the daytime, but thou hearest not; and in the night season, and am not silent." Though our Lord uttered that cry He was also conscious of the Father's purpose for He immediately added, "But thou art holy, O thou that inhabitest the praises of Israel." If our Lord Jesus Christ had a night season, it is small wonder that God graciously permits us to taste of it, for you will remember the word that our Lord said unto His disciples,

"The servant is not greater than his lord . . ." It is also written, "If we suffer, we shall also reign with him . . ." and Paul spoke about filling up "that which is behind of the afflictions of Christ . . ." These are hidden riches and treasures of darkness, in which the careless, indifferent Christian is refused participation.

We would do injustice to this 134th Psalm, however, if we failed to call attention to the fact that it abounds with blessing. Each verse contains the word "bless". Those of us who are spared or not permitted to endure the night seasons can at least encourage those who are enduring them by exhorting them to lift up their hands "in the sanctuary, and bless the LORD." May God grant that into each life there may come sustaining grace to avoid excesses in the day and to endure the silences of the night.

PSALM ONE HUNDRED THIRTY-FIVE

"WHAT KIND OF A GOD DO YOU HAVE?"

YOU who listened to that magnificent ceremony coming from Westminster Abbey early Wednesday morning appreciated, I'm sure, the great prominence which was given to our Lord and His Word throughout the entire proceedings. It was not so much the King who was being honored in his own right, as it was the King being honored as a representative of the Lord. Apart from the British national anthem, all the music and song was in praise of the great name of our Lord. Now observe the coronation theme in the opening verses of the 135th Psalm, which read:

> "Praise ye the LORD. Praise ye the name of the LORD; praise him, O ye servants of the LORD.
>
> "Ye that stand in the house of the LORD, in the courts of the house of our God.
>
> "Praise the LORD; for the LORD is good: sing praises unto his name; for it is pleasant.
>
> "For the LORD hath chosen Jacob unto himself, and Israel for his peculiar treasure.
>
> "For I know that the LORD is great, and that our Lord is above all gods."

It is not surprising, as we read these verses of the Psalm, that a strange emotion grips our being, urging us to join in a morning song of praise unto God.

IS GOD GOOD?

Let me comment on one or two things in the first part of this 135th Psalm before we go to the heart of the message of the Psalm. Observe that the Lord is said to be good. There are many people who curse God in this world, and there are many conflicting cross-currents and events that transpire even in one individual's life, so that it is small wonder that one raises a question about the *goodness* of God. Yet the Psalmist said, "Praise the LORD; for the LORD is good: sing praises unto his name; for it is pleasant."

In preparation for this message I happened to turn to a translation to which I have referred previously. It is an English version of the Old Testament by Hebrew scholars, and it is used in Hebrew synagogues. They have translated the 3rd verse of this Psalm, "Hallelujah; for the LORD is good: sing praises unto his name; for it is lovely." Somehow, I like the word "lovely" a little better than the word "pleasant." It seems more definitely to express the emotion of the heart of the redeemed individual as he enters into the courts of the Lord, beholding His beauty and praising Him from the depths of his being for His grace and goodness.

But someone may ask: Is God good at all times? If, perchance, we consider one who has been laid aside on a bed of sickness for an extended period, or others who have had bitter disappointments and trials in their life; if the night season endures for some for an unusual length of time, is it any wonder that one should raise the question: Is God good at all times?

In answering, I would suggest: Think of Job on an ash heap; a mass of boils from the top of his head to the soles of his feet, suffering the loss of friends, the loss of relatives, the loss of his children, the loss of his funds, the loss of all his possessions—was God good in his case? Did it not seem as if God was *hate* and that He wished to visit disappointments and sorrows upon a life, even a life which, beyond a shadow of doubt, was one of the finest that has ever been lived on this earth by a man. Job did not know that behind the scenes there was controversy between the two great powers of this universe, the power of good and the power of evil, which center in two great personalities—God on the one side and Satan on the other. Job did not know what we know now; that all the trials, losses, and disappointments which took place in his life, while sanctioned by the permissive will of God, were instigated by Satan in his attempt to prove that even a man like Job would curse God were it not for the fact that God had built a hedge about him.

Who knows but that behind the scenes of our disappointments and trials a similar controversy may be raging. In fact, were we, for a moment, to take our eyes off our circumstances and look to the future (I am talking now to believers in Christ—those who have been born again by the Spirit of God) and get a glimpse of the promises of the future, when we will be conformed to the image of His Son, there is no doubt that we would say in the words of St. Paul, ". . . that the sufferings of this present time are not worthy to be compared with the glory which shall be revealed in us." In our disappointment, in our sorrow, in our sickness, it is given to us to render the highest expression of service and devotion to our Lord by acknowledging that He is good, and by singing praises unto His name, which is indeed "lovely."

The God of Israel vs. the Gods of the Nations

But let us get to the heart of our message, in order that we may appreciate that the Psalm contrasts the gods made by men's hands with the eternal God, Jehovah Himself. We might raise the question: What kind of God do you worship; what kind of God do you have? Beginning with the 14th verse of our Psalm, we read:

> "For the LORD will judge his people, and he will repent himself concerning his servants.
> "The idols of the heathen are silver and gold, the work of men's hands.
> "They have mouths, but they speak not: eyes have they, but they see not;
> "They have ears, but they hear not; neither is there any breath in their mouths.
> "They that make them are like unto them: so is every one that trusteth in them.
> "Bless the LORD, O house of Israel: bless the LORD, O house of Aaron:
> "Bless the LORD, O house of Levi: ye that fear the LORD, bless the LORD.
> "Blessed be the LORD out of Zion, which dwelleth at Jerusalem. Praise ye the LORD."

What a series of contrasts! Here are the idols of the heathen, or the nations—silver and gold; oh, yes, very attractive, but they are the work of men's hands. To be sure they have mouths, eyes, and ears, but they neither speak, nor see, nor hear. What a contrast betwen such gods and the God and Father our Lord and Saviour Jesus Christ.

Will you notice particularly the 14th verse, which in our King James version reads, "For the LORD will judge his people, and he will repent himself concerning his servants." Again I turn to the Hebrew translation to which I have already alluded, and there I see it reads, "For the LORD will espouse the cause of his people, and concerning his servants will he bethink himself."

We are so prone to think of *judge* and *judging* in the sense of condemnation. One would almost think that the 1st verse of the 8th chapter of Paul's letter to the Romans was not in the Bible. You will remember that matchless declaration, "There is therefore now *no judgment* to them which are in Christ Jesus." (R. V.) If you who are in Christ are concerned about the judgment of your sin, you can forget it. You're wasting your time. God's promise is that there is even *now* no judgment to them which are in Christ Jesus. Make sure, however, that you are "in Christ." That is the only thing to be concerned about. If you are "in Him" and have received Him as your Lord and Saviour, there is no further judgment for sin, but "the LORD will espouse the cause of his people, and concerning his servants will he bethink himself." In other words, the Lord will *defend* the cause of His people. Isn't that exactly what we have in the 1st Epistle of John, where we learn that our Lord Jesus Christ is our Advocate with the Father and that He therefore, in the presence of God, *espouses* the cause of His people, answering every accusation of the enemy of our souls. What a God is our Lord!

But what about other gods, the gods of the nations? They may look like gods—they have mouths, eyes, and ears; every resemblance to reality but *life*. The Scripture declares that "They that make them are like unto them: so is every one that trusteth in them." What did the Psalmist mean by that? Just this, "There is . . . one God and Father of all, who is above all, and through all, and in you all." There is only one God. There can only be one. There is no room for another. That one God revealed Himself in Jesus Christ. He is *God*. No one else can appropriate that title without being an impostor.

THE CORONATION AND THE THRONE OF THE LORD

In closing, may I draw your attention to that great burst of antiphonal praise, found in the closing three verses of our Psalm, which read:

> "Bless the LORD, O house of Israel: bless the LORD,
> O house of Aaron:

> "Bless the LORD, O house of Levi: ye that fear the
> LORD, bless the LORD.
> "Blessed be the LORD out of Zion, which dwelleth at
> Jerusalem. Praise ye the LORD."

In these verses we find the chief singer in the midst, leading the vast congregation in an anthem of praise. He first calls to the house of Israel and bids them to bless the Lord, and then he points his baton to the house of Aaron and asks the priests to bless the Lord. Then he turns to the house of Levi, who minister and aid the priests, and he urges them to bless the Lord and, finally, with one great sweep of his hand, he invites all the multitudes who fear the Lord to join in this song of praise.

The closing verse is particularly appropriate, for it indicates the place where this great coronation anthem will be sung—"Blessed be the LORD out of Zion, which dwelleth at Jerusalem. Praise ye the LORD."

It was not our privilege to attend the ceremonies at Westminster Abbey. It was only given to us to listen in. We were not participants. However, there is coming a coronation of the King of kings and the Lord of lords, in which every child of God will participate; for the Lord will come with all His saints to be glorified in them. He will take up His abode at Jerusalem, and out of Zion shall go forth the law to all, and all mankind will tune in to the coronation of the King of kings and the Lord of lords.

PSALM ONE HUNDRED THIRTY-SIX

THE ETERNAL GREATNESS OF GOD'S MERCY

IT hardly requires more than a single reading to discover the theme of the 136th Psalm; for no less than twenty-six times does the Psalmist use the phrase "for his mercy endureth for ever." We shall not quote the phrase twenty-six times, but let us read the things about which the Psalmist wrote and which led him to add after each, the comment, "for his mercy endureth for ever."

> "O give thanks unto the LORD; for he is good: for his
> mercy endureth for ever.
> "O give thanks unto the God of gods . . .
> "O give thanks to the Lord of lords . . .
> "To him who alone doeth great wonders . . .
> "To him that by wisdom made the heavens . . .

"To him that stretched out the earth above the waters . . .

"To him that made great lights . . .

"The sun to rule by day . . .

"The moon and stars to rule by night . . .

"To him that smote Egypt in their firstborn . . .

"And brought out Israel from among them . . .

"With a strong hand, and with a stretched out arm . . .

"To him which divided the Red sea into parts . . .

"And made Israel to pass through the midst of it . . .

"But overthrew Pharaoh and his host in the Red sea . . .

"To him which led his people through the wilderness . . .

"To him which smote great kings . . .

"And slew famous kings . . .

"Sihon king of the Amorites . . .

"And Og the king of Bashan . . .

"And gave their land for an heritage . . .

"Even an heritage unto Israel his servant . . .

"Who remembered us in our low estate . . .

"And hath redeemed us from our enemies . . .

"Who giveth food to all flesh . . .

"O give thanks unto the God of heaven . . ."

Have you ever asked yourself the question, why such a Psalm was written; why it was made a part of the divine record; why it was not sufficient to make the statement once; why repeat the phrase "for his mercy endureth for ever"?

The Lord knew undoubtedly how hard of hearing we are and how often we need to be reminded of a matter in order to appreciate it. It ought to be sufficient for God to say a thing once to be believed, but the heart and mind of man are so dull as to make it necessary for Him to say the same thing again and again and again. And when it comes to His mercy, He needs remind us no less than twenty-six times in the course of one Psalm. Why? If there is one thing that man, generally speaking, does not seem to understand, it is the mercy of God. And well might man express himself in wonder at such mercy, for God is righteous and holy. He cannot excuse the guilty; He cannot even overlook sin unless He has exacted the payment for it, either from the individual or a substitute. Thus it seems almost impossible to believe that God's mercy should endure forever.

Mercy is a marvelous thing. Human mercy is one of the most precious things that we know anything about in man's dealings with man. If that can be said for human mercy, what can be said of divine mercy? But let us not forget the wide gulf between the two. For human mercy invariably means overlooking sin, but divine mercy is based on the righteous atonement for sin.

We learn from the 103rd Psalm that "the mercy of the LORD is from everlasting to everlasting upon them that fear him, and his righteousness unto children's children . . ." That statement gives us an insight into the extent of God's mercy, and upon whom it is poured out.

THE MERCY SEAT

Every informed Jew knows the meaning of "the mercy seat" which covered the ark of the covenant, on which the blood of the sacrifice was poured and from which God extended His mercy and held communion with the representative of the people. The mercy of God is based upon His righteousness, upon the atoning work that He Himself accomplished through the Lamb of God who beareth away the sin of the world. It is extended to those who fear Him. But more than that, the mercy of God is not extended for a temporary period when an individual might be sorely pressed, but the mercy of God is from everlasting to everlasting. It endureth forever.

That very mercy of God which was displayed in the offering of His Son, and which was manifested when our Lord answered the dying bandit on the cross, saying, "To day shalt thou be with me in paradise" continues today, and will always avail to those who fear God and who have bowed the knee to the Lord Jesus Christ. In mercy, God saved my soul; in mercy, He kept me unto the present hour; in mercy, He will bring me into His presence; and throughout all the years of eternity His mercy will endure.

He will never change His dealings with the one who has come under the shelter of the atoning work of our Lord Jesus Christ. Thus, the one who has received Christ is eternally saved, for the mercy of God is for eternity. Nothing can change it.

This 136th Psalm undoubtedly was a favorite among the children of Israel. I can easily imagine that it was set to a simple but catching melody. It is wonderful how a simple little thing finds a response in the redeemed heart. It was probably on the lips of every Israelite, humming, whistling, or singing it as a theme song of his life.

Charles Haddon Spurgeon summarized this Psalm excellently, by saying, "It commences with a three-fold praise to the triune God, then it gives us six notes of praise to the Creator, six more for the deliverance from Egypt, and seven upon the journey through the wilderness and the entrance into Canaan. Then we have two happy verses of personal gratitude for personal mercy, one to tell of the Lord's universal providence, and a closing verse to excite to never-ending praise."

It is hardly necessary to remind you that this is one of the songs of Zion that the captors of Israel delighted to plague Israel with, by asking them to sing it. We will discuss that more thoroughly when we come to that most wonderfully dirgeful Psalm, the 137th.

It is interesting and very often true that one can tell where another is *going* by the tunes he sings. The songs of Zion and Christian hymns have something about them that delight the heart. For instance, how many of us have enjoyed a thrill while traveling on a train or walking through the streets or waiting for someone, when suddenly we heard a tune of an old Gospel hymn either whistled or hummed. Immediately our hearts and minds responded and we concluded that undoubtedly that individual also loved the Lord.

CALVARY, THE FOUNDATION OF MERCY

Now let us examine the Psalm with a little care. We have already learned that it has several divisions, that it opens with a three-fold praise to the triune God, and that it praises Him for creation and the gifts and provisions that He has made for men through creation, that is, the sun to rule by day and the moon and the stars to rule by night. How poverty-stricken this world would be without the sun or the glittering heavens at night. But the Psalmist goes on to discover that in the dealings with the nation Israel, God has given much cause for thanksgiving. First and foremost is the reference to the Egyptian bondage as, of course, that was the beginning of God's dealings with Israel. Well might that nation constantly revert back to the Passover night.

Even so, a Christian never loses sight of the fact that it was Calvary and what God did at Calvary which was the beginning of all his Christian experience. It was there that God provided the unblemished lamb; it was there that God smote His first-born; it was there that Christ our Passover was slain for us. But the cross was the means to an end, just as the deliverance of the children of Israel from the Egyptian bondage was only the beginning and, likewise, the means to an end. After Egypt, there followed the journey through the wilderness and, finally, Israel's entrance into the Promised Land.

Just so, in the life of each Christian there comes a corresponding wilderness experience. He embarks on it immediately upon receiving Christ. The whole journey from the cross to glory is a wilderness period. The experiences that Israel had during that period we find to be typical of our own experiences. We find that certain powers, which interfere with our progress and growth in Christian life have to be conquered, even as Sihon, King of the Amorites, and Og, the King of Bashan had to be slain by the Israelites before they could enter into the land of Canaan. But, remember, it is God who provides the victory, even though He gives us the sword to wield.

When Israel arrived in Canaan she found still further cause for praise, for the land was given to her as a heritage. She did not work for it, she did not labor for it, it did not belong to her. It was given to her as a heritage. So those who have been redeemed by the blood of our Lord will some day be ushered into His presence in the glory and there discover an eternal heritage. We did not earn it, we did not work for it, it did not belong to us; but God gave it to us. It will be a heritage that beggars description, for we are heirs of God and joint-heirs with Jesus Christ.

If there is any one thing about this Psalm that I especially like, it is the 23rd verse, where the Psalmist said, "Who remembered us in our low estate . . ." and the 24th, "And hath redeemed us from our enemies . . ." There is such a thing as high estate and low estate in human relationships and in birth. But, in the sight of God, all men are equal "For all have sinned, and come short of the glory of God . . ." Before His bar, kings and queens, presidents and judges, lords and commoners are absolutely equal. The common man and the man of letters find, at the bar of God's justice, that all are absolutely equal, for all are of low estate. At God's throne, it is not a question of high birth or low birth, but new birth—Have you been born again?

Psalm One Hundred Thirty-Seven

HANGING HARPS UPON WILLOWS

WE are about to consider one of the most beautiful Psalms in the entire collection: the 137th. It has a plaintive note in it that cannot be matched in all of literature. Its depths of anguish, its moving determinations, its pathetic wail, and its perfection of imprecatory judgments are but a few of its many characteristics.

A few weeks ago, it was my pleasure to attend a concert by the *a cappella* choir of Northwestern University. Among the numbers they rendered was this 137th Psalm. The leading part was taken by a young Jewish student, who certainly knew how to sing the plaintive note, while the choir either hummed or softly sang the background. This number was beautifully accompanied by a gifted harpist. I do not know when I have listened to a selection, plaintive in character, that moved my being as that did. I would have given almost anything if it had been Sunday morning and we had had the 137th Psalm for our meditation.

SORROW'S SONG

But without the music and the accompanying harp, we shall endeavor to enter into the pathos of this ode, which reads:

> "By the rivers of Babylon, there we sat down, yea, we wept, when we remembered Zion.
> "We hanged our harps upon the willows in the midst thereof.
> "For there they that carried us away captive required of us a song; and they that wasted us required of us mirth, saying, Sing us one of the songs of Zion.
> "How shall we sing the LORD'S song in a strange land?
> "If I forget thee, O Jerusalem, let my right hand forget her cunning.
> "If I do not remember thee, let my tongue cleave to the roof of my mouth; if I prefer not Jerusalem above my chief joy.
> "Remember, O LORD, the children of Edom in the day of Jerusalem; who said, Rase it, rase it, even to the foundation thereof.
> "O daughter of Bablyon, who art to be destroyed; happy shall he be, that rewardeth thee as thou hast served us.
> "Happy shall he be, that taketh and dasheth thy little ones against the stones."

Note the past tense of the verbs used in the first three verses of the Psalm, which clearly indicates that this song must have been written after the experience of the Babylonian captivity. It is a rare occasion when either the nation or the individual can maintain a song in the midst of sorrow and trial. Usually it is not until after the trial is over and the sorrow has had its beneficent effect that the nation or the individual appreciates that sorrow, too, has its melody and its good work.

While Israel was in Babylon she wept. It was not until afterward that she was able to compose a song that expressed the emotions of the sorrowful heart.

Notice the movements of Israel while in Babylon. Led captive, made to do the work of slaves, Israel wended her way on the Sabbath days to the riverside where, resting from the toils of the week, there was nothing to do but weep as she thought of the glories and the liberties of Zion.

But why go to the riverside to sit down and weep? I think we can get the answer to that question by observing a New Testament passage which is found in the 16th chapter of the Acts of the Apostles, where we have the record of a part of the missionary activity of the Apostle Paul and his company of faithful fellow-workers. When they arrived at Philippi, which is the chief city of that part of Macedonia, they abode there certain days. On the Sabbath they "went out of the city *by a river side, where prayer was wont to be made;* and we sat down," said the writer of the Acts, the physician Luke, "and spake unto the women which resorted thither." Evidently the Israelites, away from Jerusalem, and particularly when living among the Gentiles, or in captivity, resorted to a riverside on the Sabbath for prayer, meditation, weeping, and wailing. How interesting, therefore, for the Apostle and his associates to be able to go down to the riverside on a Sabbath day and sit down with those who gather there, in order, not to weep with them, but to impart joy as they speak to them about the things of the Lord. However, one cannot impart that joy unless sent of the Lord, commissioned of the Lord, and equipped by the Lord. That is the business of a Christian ambassador.

In this 137th Psalm we have the distressed cry of a people who journeyed to the riverside, the place "where prayer was wont to be made," in order to weep as they contemplated the changed surroundings from the mountainsides of Zion.

HARPS AND WILLOWS

Observe also that when the Israelites were in captivity they hung their harps upon the willows. The music of a harp is beautifully exquisite. Man has always associated the harp with heaven and heaven's melodies. Many of us have anticipated from our youth the glories of heaven, which include a perfect harmony between the fingers gliding upon the strings of the harp and the heart from which the songs of Zion really begin. When a people are suffering because of their disobedience, there is nothing left to do but hang their harps upon the weeping willows by the side of the river.

How I wish Israel would come to the place where she would recognize that she never lost her song when she was faithful to her Lord, but she lost her melody and discarded her harp when she was disobedient to Jehovah, as she moved God to corrective judgment.

Notice, will you, the further irony of the situation and how the captors of Babylon rubbed salt into an open wound. We read in the 3rd verse, "there they that carried us away captive required of us a song; and they that wasted us required of us mirth, saying, Sing us one of the songs of Zion." Well might the Psalmist add, "How shall we sing the LORD'S song in a strange land?"

There is a time and a place for all things. The songs of Zion upon the lips of a defeated Christian—well, it just never happens! The man who goes his way through the world, mixes in with the system of this world, and loses sight of his place of separation—how can he sing the Lord's song in a strange land? How can he sing such songs as:

> "In the cross of Christ I glory,
> Tow'ring o'er the wrecks of time;
> All the light of sacred story
> Gathers round its head sublime."

Or that other equally splendid hymn:

> "When I survey the wondrous cross
> On which the Prince of glory died,
> My richest gain I count but loss,
> And pour contempt on all my pride."

Songs like that can only be sung when one is in fellowship with the Lord and His people.

And now let us examine that determination which is expressed in the 5th and 6th verses reading, "If I forget thee, O Jerusalem, let my right hand forget her cunning. If I do not remember thee, let my tongue cleave to the roof of my mouth; if I prefer not Jerusalem above my chief joy." Some people might consider this as nationalism run riot, but we will never be able to understand the patriotism of Israel unless we appreciate the spiritual significance of the city of Jerusalem.

Jerusalem was the city that God chose; the place where He engraved His name. It was called "the city of peace"; yet the bloodiest of battles have been fought in it. Jerusalem, spiritually speaking, is the center of the earth. It has had a magnificent history. It will yet see its greatest glory. The Israelites never dissociated the city from the worship of Jehovah; the two were one. In this dispensation the Christian has no such city, no such shrine. He is a stranger here, a pilgrim in a foreign land. His home is in the heavens, where his Lord now dwells. Thus the center of the Christian's life is in the heavens. It is for that reason that the Apostle Paul wrote, "Set your affection on things above, not on things of the earth. For ye are dead, and your life is hid with Christ in God. When Christ, who is our life, shall appear, then shall ye also appear with him in glory." But an instructed Jew looked to the city of Jerusalem; and what heaven is to us now, Jerusalem was to the Jew then. It ought still to be that to every Jew, and it shall be so in the future.

Sad indeed is that Israelite who has forgotten Jerusalem, who no longer remembers that city, and who prefers other things as his chief joy. Sad is the Christian who forgets the glory, and whose chief joy is other than fellowship with the Lord in the glory.

Let us get down to the point, instead of talking generalities. Truth is abstract, but truth should dominate every individual's life, so that every specific aspect of it is under control. If we have professed to know Christ, and yet our chief joy is other than the fellowship of our Lord, our life is powerless, it is fruitless, it is without purpose, and has no crowning joy. May I ask: Wherein do you walk, and where do you receive your joy? Your thoughts—do they run in the channels of this world? Your life's devotion and purpose—is it anything other than to glorify God? If it is, then I think it is about time you came to this 137th Psalm and but slightly paraphrasing the words of the Psalmist, say, "If I forget thee, O Lord, let my right hand forget her cunning. If I do not remember thee, let my tongue cleave to the roof of my mouth; if I prefer not the fellowship of my Lord above my chief joy."

IMPRECATIONS

Now a final word. We have spoken frequently of the criticism that has been lodged against imprecatory Psalms. Some men, who believe that they have a fairer sense of justice and mercy than the Psalmist, have taken particular pains to exaggerate and over-emphasize the imprecations of the Psalms. Some have also stated that the principle in the New Testament on this subject is entirely different from that which appears in the Old Testament. Those who express such a view evidently have overlooked many passages in the New Testament. For example, take the 6th chapter of The Revelation, commencing with the 9th verse, where we have the record of the opening of the fifth seal of the seven-sealed book. When that fifth seal was opened, John said, "I saw under the altar the souls of them that were slain for the word of God, and for the testimony which they held: And they (that is the martyrs) cried with a loud voice, saying, How long, O Lord, holy and true, dost thou not judge and *avenge* our blood on them that dwell on the earth? And white robes were given unto every one of them, and it was said unto them, that they should rest yet for a little season, until their fellow servants also and their brethren, that should be killed as they were, should be fulfilled." If that is not an imprecation, I do not know what constitutes an imprecatory cry.

So in this Psalm, as the writer looked back upon the sufferings of his people during the captivity, he asked the Lord to remember, and then he vented his imprecation upon that nation by saying, "O daughter of Babylon, who art to be destroyed; happy shall he be, that rewardeth thee as thou hast served us." You may take exception to the Psalmist's attitude, but anyone acquainted with Scripture knows that his prayer expressed perfect hatred.

PSALM ONE HUNDRED THIRTY-EIGHT

THE WORD OF GOD OR THE NAME OF GOD?

WE are now to consider the 138th Psalm which, to say the least, contains some important declarations. To begin with, this Psalm introduces a series of eight Psalms, all of which are written in the first person, and probably represent the last inspired writings of King David.

There is a time for united worship, united fellowship in suffering, and united prayer, as for example when in the 137th Psalm the Psalmist spoke for all the children of Israel who were carried away into captivity, when he wrote:

> "By the rivers of Babylon, there *we* sat down, yea, *we* wept, when *we* remembered Zion.

> "We hanged *our* harps upon the willows in the midst
> thereof.
> "For there they that carried *us* away captive required
> of *us* a song . . ."

Bearing one another's burdens and entering into each other's joys is an important part of Christian fellowship, but there is also such a thing as individual responsibility and individual worship. Except when God dealt with Israel as a nation, salvation has never been on the basis of multitudes, nations, or crowds. It is entirely an individual proposition. And as such is true in the case of our salvation, it is equally true in reference to our fellowship with God and our worship of the Lord. Note how decidedly personal David became, as he penned this Psalm which we are about to read:

> "I will praise thee with my whole heart: before the
> gods will I sing praise unto thee.
> "I will worship toward thy holy temple, and praise thy
> name for thy lovingkindness and for thy truth: for
> thou hast magnified thy word above all thy name.
> "In the day when I cried thou answeredst me, and
> strengthenedst me with strength in my soul.
> "All the kings of the earth shall praise thee, O LORD,
> when they hear the words of thy mouth.
> "Yea, they shall sing in the ways of the LORD: for
> great is the glory of the LORD.
> "Though the LORD be high, yet hath he respect unto
> the lowly: but the proud he knoweth afar off.
> "Though I walk in the midst of trouble, thou wilt re-
> vive me: thou shalt stretch forth thine hand against the
> wrath of mine enemies, and thy *right hand shall save
> me.*
> "*The LORD will perfect that which concerneth me:*
> thy mercy, O LORD, endureth for ever: forsake not
> the works of thine own hands."

Observe that the Psalmist said, "I will praise . . . I will sing . . . I will worship." In the first place, his thanksgiving is not half-hearted; it is from the very depths of his being and from his whole heart. Second he does not hesitate to sing his praise of the Lord before those whom he speaks of as "the gods." This may seem a queer expression to us, but in King David's time the people had not yet been entirely delivered from the worship of other gods. The heathen round about Israel who worshipped these gods were constantly a source of annoyance and sin to the children of Israel. Yet David said, "before *the gods* will I sing praise unto thee." He had no fear of these gods, for he well knew that while they had mouths, they could not speak; possessed of eyes, they could not see; having ears, they were unable to hear.

"THOU HAST MAGNIFIED THY WORD"

Notice also that the Psalmist said, "I will worship toward thy holy temple, and praise thy name for thy lovingkindness and for thy truth: for thou hast magnified thy word above all thy name." That declaration brings us to the heart of this message: in fact, to the key thought expressed in the Psalm. David's worship and praise were the result of God's lovingkindness and truth, the foundation of which was the fact that God has magnified His Word above all His name.

Our Lord told the Samaritan woman that they that worship God must worship Him in Spirit and in truth. When He said *in truth*, He was not talking about the blamelessness of the individual's life, but rather that whole body of revealed Scripture called *The Truth*. Worship, therefore, is primarily founded upon the Bible. When worship is not based on revealed truth, then it becomes what the Apostle Paul called *"will worship"* of which he wrote that it was a show of wisdom and neglect of the body. To intelligently worship God one must worship in God's accepted way. Therefore God rejects all worship which is offered in any other name than the name of the Lord Jesus Christ.

Our Lord declared Himself to be sent from God. He was "the way, the truth, and the life." He declared that no man could come unto the Father but by Him. He came to reveal the Father's will, the Father's name, and the Father's word. In the heart of that prayer He made a specific request on the behalf of those who had received Him. This request is expressed in the following words, "Sanctify them through thy truth, thy word is truth."

The Psalmist knew that God's Word was truth (though he did not have one-half of the revealed Word that we in this day possess) when he wrote that God had magnified His Word above all His name. Yet multitudes of men assume that it is sufficient to give respect to the name of God, while they still reject or neglect the Word of God, the Bible. David said that God had placed something even above His matchless name; and that which occupied that exalted position was the Word of God.

Why has God placed His Word even above His own name? It has often been said that a gentleman's word is as good as his bond. The reason, of course, is self-evident. A gentleman's word is truth. But there may be a time when even a gentleman is unable to keep his word, not for lack of determination, but by sheer inability of accomplishment. But God possesses all power, all knowledge, and all wisdom. He alone can see the end from the beginning. He alone knows our thoughts before we think them. When He speaks, it is evident that His Word must be true, for He has the power to fulfill His Word. No intelligent man thinks otherwise, but here we part company with a great multitude who have not yet come to the position where they recognize that God's Word is found alone in the book we call the Bible.

Again and again, the writers of the books of the Bible have spoken in the name of Jehovah God and have heralded their message, by saying, "Thus saith the LORD." Every writer was conscious that his pen was moved by the Holy Spirit of God and that what he wrote was not his own thoughts clothed in his own words. They all knew that the Holy Spirit had taken possession of their faculties and caused each to write the very words of God. Therefore it is written that ". . . holy men of God spake as they were moved by the Holy Spirit." It behooves man, therefore, to investigate the Word, the Bible, in order to determine its truthfulness and its message. Those who have given their lives to a study of this Book have found their hearts and minds repeatedly bowing before God, as they have entered into the wonders of Biblical revelation.

GOD'S RECORD OF HIS SON

In this Book, God is made to take the witness stand to give forth His testimony. Before His testimony is given, a logical argument is presented, that if we receive the witness of men, the witness of God is greater.

Then follows the witness of God which He hath testified of His Son. He that believeth on the Son of God hath the witness in himself. Contrariwise, he that believeth not God (that, of course, refers to those who have heard the testimony of God but who believe it not)—he that believeth not God hath made Him *a liar*. The words are strong, but they are the words of God.

It is well also to bear in mind the argument the Apostle Paul advanced in that wonderful New Testament letter to the Hebrews, when he wrote, "He that despised Moses' law died without mercy under two or three witnesses: of how much sorer punishment, suppose ye, shall he be thought worthy, who hath trodden under foot the Son of God, and hath counted the blood of the covenant, wherewith he was sanctified, an unholy thing, and hath done despite unto the Spirit of grace? For we know him that hath said, Vengeance belongeth unto me, I will recompense, said the Lord. And again, The Lord shall judge his people."

Well does the Apostle conclude by saying, "It is a fearful thing to fall into the hands of the living God."

The Psalmist, like every other child of God, knew something about suffering and disappointment, for he wrote, "In the day when I cried thou answeredst me, and strengthenedst me with strength in my soul." Again, the Psalmist knew something about the future hope of the world, when he said, "All the kings of the earth shall praise thee, O LORD, when they hear the words of thy mouth. Yea, they shall sing in the ways of the LORD: for great is the glory of the Lord." Again, the Psalmist knew something about the ways of the Lord in dealing with the sons of men, for he said, "Though the LORD be high, yet hath he respect unto the lowly: but the proud he knoweth afar off." Once more, the Psalmist knew what it was to experience deliverance from his enemies, when he wrote, "Though I walk in the midst of trouble, thou wilt revive me: thou shalt stretch forth thine hand against the wrath of mine enemies, and thy right hand shall save me."

What was vouchsafed to the Psalmist is the inalienable right of every believer in Christ. Some of us find ourselves in the midst of trouble, some know what it is to bear the wrath of enemies, but if God be true He will revive us in the midst of the day of trouble and He will put forth His hand against the enemies of His children.

Finally, the Psalmist, in this 138th Psalm, knew that one day he would be conformed to the image of God's Son, for he closed his Psalm of personal praise and personal faith by saying, "The LORD will perfect that which concerneth me . . ."

PSALM ONE HUNDRED THIRTY-NINE—PART ONE

A SEARCHING GOD, AND WHAT HE FINDS

ONE of the greatest Jewish scholars of all time, Aben Ezra, said of the 139th Psalm, that "it is the most glorious and excellent Psalm in the whole Book." The more I have studied and read the Psalms, the more difficult it becomes to choose one which I could call "the most excellent" Psalm. It would not be surprising if, in that glorious future day when we sit at our Lord's feet to hear Him unfold the Scriptures, we should conclude that the Psalms we now think least interesting contain nuggets we never dreamed were in them.

Whether I agree with Aben Ezra or not, this 139th Psalm is certainly an excellent and soul-searching Psalm. By the way, someone suggested that it would be a splendid custom were each Christian to read this Psalm every morning and every evening of his life.

"O LORD, thou hast searched me, and known me.

"Thou knowest my downsitting and mine uprising, thou understandest my thought afar off.

"Thou compassest my path and my lying down, and art acquainted with all my ways.

"For there is not a word in my tongue, but, lo, O LORD, thou knowest it altogether.

"Thou hast beset me behind and before, and laid thine hand upon me.

"Such knowledge is too wonderful for me, it is high, I cannot attain unto it.

"Whither shall I go from thy spirit? whither shall I flee from thy presence?

"If I ascend up into heaven, thou art there: if I make my bed in hell, behold, thou art there.

"If I take the wings of the morning, and dwell in the uttermost parts of the sea;

"Even there shall thy hand lead me, and thy right hand shall hold me.

"If I say, Surely the darkness shall cover me; even the night shall be light about me.

"Yea, the darkness hideth not from thee; but the night shineth as the day: the darkness and the light are both alike to thee.

"For thou hast possessed my reins: thou hast covered me in my mother's womb.

"I will praise thee; for I am fearfully and wonderfully made: marvellous are thy works; and that my soul knoweth right well.

"My substance was not hid from thee, when I was made in secret, and curiously wrought in the lowest parts of the earth.

"Thine eyes did see my substance, yet being unperfect; and in thy book all my members were written, which in continuance were fashioned, when as yet there was none of them.

"How precious also are thy thoughts unto me, O God! how great is the sum of them!

"If I should count them, they are more in number than the sand: when I awake, I am still with thee.

"Surely thou wilt slay the wicked, O God: depart from me therefore, ye bloody men.

"For they speak against thee wickedly, and thine enemies take thy name in vain.

"Do not I hate them, O LORD, that hate thee? and
am not I grieved with those that rise up against thee?
"I hate them with perfect hatred: I count them mine
enemies.
"Search me, O God, and know my heart: try me, and
know my thoughts:
"And see if there be any wicked way in me, and lead
me in the way everlasting."

Since the advent of hymns, and particularly our modern type of hymns, too many of them are superficial. Some, of course, are marvelous compositions in which the gospel has been beautifully interwoven; others have been born out of a devoted heart which sought to worship the Lord God; but it must be confessed that there are some hymns that really have no place in true Christian worship, such as the one which was so famous in the Billy Sunday campaigns, "The Brewers' Big Hosses Won't Run Over Me." One could go on and name other popular hymns, in which there is nothing distinctly Christian. However, a Psalm such as this 139th, moves our being and causes us to appreciate and enter into the secrets of worship.

A SEARCHING LOOK

Notice how David began when he ascribed his Psalm to the Lord: "O LORD, thou hast searched me, and known *me*." If you have your Bible open, you will observe that the last "me" is in italics, which indicates that it has been interpolated by the translators, in order to maintain the sense, but it does not appear in the original. At times, I like to drop the words which are in italics, because they often destroy the meaning. Thus the Psalm, as composed by David, reads, "O LORD, thou hast searched me, and known." In looking up another translation, I notice this verse reads, "O LORD, thou hast searched me through and thou knowest."

When God looks at the believer with that searching, piercing eye of His, the look does not bring fear into the heart. When the Lord searches the heart and life of one of *His own;* a child of His, precious in His sight, rest assured that it is not with an eye filled with determination to exercise His judicial prerogatives. True, there are times when it is necessary for God to deal in corrective measures with His disobedient child, but invariably His look is one of love.

Some of us have had, or have, parents whose love and affection beggar description. When we ever did anything that was displeasing to them, the mere look in their eye was enough to crush us. I have always felt sorry for the individual who did not have affectionate parents. I was walking through Central Park the other Saturday, when I saw a sight that went against my grain. I do not know what the little lad had done—he was only about four years of age—but, in a fit of anger, his mother grasped the boy by the hair of his head and pulled him until he screamed. I could not refrain from thanking God that the mother who bore me never resorted to such tactics in her corrective dealings with her children. Rather, her attitude and actions evidenced godliness.

"O LORD, thou hast searched me through." Notice that David was not writing about somebody else. In listening to a sermon, when a sharp arrow comes our way, it is easy to put up a shield of self-defense and convince ourselves that the arrow belongs to our neighbor; but it is quite another matter when God is looking at us; one cannot avoid that look. David was honest. He knew that when God looked at him there was no escape. But who wants to escape the searching eye of love?

But David continued to outline the extent of God's knowledge concerning himself, when he wrote, "Thou knowest my downsitting and mine uprising, thou understandest my thought afar off." In other words, the Lord knew all about David. He knew when he sat down and when he rose up. However, there is nothing of the "sit-down strike" character of this age in this 2nd verse. David was writing about that quiet hour when, separated from the world of things and activity, he sat down at the close of the day for contemplation and meditation.

The Lord also knew when David was moved by determination to go out to accomplish the dictates of his heart and mind. But more than that, David said that even before his thoughts were brought together coherently and expressed in words the Lord knew and understood about them. Such knowledge is overwhelming.

Note verse 4, where the Psalmist says, "For there is not a word in my tongue, but, lo, O LORD, thou knowest it altogether." Of course, all this is self-evident to the man who stops to consider the greatness of God. It ought to be a comfort and assurance to believers to know that God takes such minute interest in each individual's life. Oh, if we would only trust Him! It seems easier to worry and fret and have concern, than to believe that God is definitely interested in us. It is not surprising, however, for even the Psalmist, over and over again throughout the Psalms, gave expression to the cry of disappointment at the seeming neglect by the Lord. Yet when the Lord brought him through trial and difficulty, he had abundant evidence that the hour when he thought God was farthest away was the very hour when the Lord was nearest at hand.

A PLACE OF SAFETY

Now notice verse 5, where David said, "Thou hast beset me behind and before, and laid thine hand upon me." This is the very criticism that Satan lodged against God, concerning Job, for said Satan, "Hast not thou made an hedge about him . . .?" David said: Thou hast set a hedge before and behind me. In another Psalm he put it in a slightly different way, when he wrote that "The angel of the LORD encampeth round about them that fear him . . ." In this Psalm our Lord placed a hedge before and behind David and, as if that were not sufficient, the Psalmist said that the Lord also laid His hand upon him.

In the 10th chapter of St. John's Gospel, our Lord describes His Father's and His own relationship to individual believers under the imagery of a shepherd and his sheep. Said He, "My sheep hear my voice, and I know them, and they follow me: and I give unto them eternal life; and they shall never perish, neither shall any man pluck them out of *my hand*." It would appear, therefore, that in the palm of the hand of our Lord rests the power that keeps every believer. But, lest some might suggest that one palm was not sufficient and that someone could pluck a sheep out of His hand, our Lord adds, "My Father, which gave them me, is greater than all; and no man is able to pluck them out of my Father's hand. I and my Father are one." It does appear, therefore, that there is double protection given to the child of God. Not only is he in the palm of our Lord's hand, but the Father's hand likewise rests upon the believer. David knew about that, when he wrote, "Thou hast beset me behind and before, and laid thine hand upon me." That may appear to us as being a new truth, but David knew all about it. Oh, that we might enter into the joy of that preservation, and say with the Psalmist, "Such knowledge is too wonderful for me; it is high, I cannot attain unto it."

KNOWLEDGE TOO WONDERFUL

The knowledge of God's care and wisdom is awe-inspiring. If we want to enjoy a post-graduate course in knowledge, we must enter into a study and contemplation of the majesty and power of the Lord and of His love for His own. But we must know God first.

Last week while talking with my friend, Dr. Wilbur M. Smith, he told about a visit to his church by Dr. Howard A. Kelly, of Baltimore, Md. He went on to tell of the magnificent address which that scholarly gentleman delivered. But here is an interesting item that I think is particularly important for young people. Dr. Smith wished to impress the audience with the character and standing of Dr. Kelly, so, in introducing him he read part of the record of Dr. Kelly, which is to be found in "Who's Who in America" where no less than six inches of space are devoted to his honors and attainments, beginning with 1877, when, as a lad of nineteen, he graduated from the University of Pennsylvania with a Bachelor of Arts degree.

When Dr. Kelly rose to speak, he waved his hand as if to cast aside the record and said, "What does it all amount to—the greatest thing is for a man to know God and have eternal life." Dr. Kelly is a great figure in the field of scientific endeavor. He has written his name in the walls of Johns Hopkins University and Hospital. Devoted as he is to scientific research, he declared that evening, in the church of which my friend is pastor, "Science does not know the terms love, joy, peace, and the forgiveness of sins. Only in the Bible does one get an authoritative message about these things." How true!

PSALM ONE HUNDRED THIRTY-NINE—PART TWO

FLEEING AWAY FROM GOD OR FLEEING TO GOD

WE observed in our comments on the first six verses of the 139th Psalm, that David described God's searching eye and how wonderful such knowledge was to him. He wrote, "Such knowledge is too wonderful for me; it is high, I cannot attain unto it."

From the 7th verse down to the 12th, we get a wonderful dissertation upon the universal presence of God. In these verses, a man who already has found God and who already knows the Lord, is asking the question, "Whither shall I go from thy spirit? or whither shall I flee from thy presence?" Such being the case, what can be said about a man who does not know God? So we raise the question: Is it possible to flee from God or to hide one's self from the presence of God?

Here is a matter of deep concern to every individual. Whether we like it or not, the Bible says it is appointed unto men once to die, but after this, the judgment. We may dismiss it by saying that we do not believe the Bible. We can conclude that this was merely the expression of the Apostle

Paul; that it was only one man's idea; perhaps he was right or perhaps he was wrong. However, there is abundant evidence that it is utterly impossible for God to overlook sin or to withhold judgment. We are simply closing our eyes, if we cannot see the evidence of the judicial character, and the exercise of that character on the part of God in His dealings with the sons of men.

Whether we are ready or not, the fact is that *it is* appointed unto men once to die. We cannot controvert that; we must die. But after death— then what? Well, let's hear what the Psalmist had to say, "Whither shall I go from thy spirit? or whither shall I flee from thy presence?" Is it possible to find a place where the presence of God is not felt, or where the Spirit of God is not known either by His convicting or justifying ministry? David said, "If I ascend up into heaven, thou art there . . ." Even a skeptic is ready to agree that God dwells in the heavens, and so far no one will take exception to David. Man is accustomed to thinking that heaven is God's dwelling place; but he makes the mistake of thinking that God has no power over the earth.

But David also said, "if I make my bed in hell, behold, thou art there." The translators of our English version used the word "hell" to describe the underworld, the nether world. David was not talking about the eternal abyss of the wicked; he was talking about the graves of the dead. "If I make my bed in the nether world, behold, thou art there." In other words, David could not escape God, in death or in life.

Some men commit suicide, believing that they can thus get away from a disturbed mind and a distraught conscience, but what an awakening when they discover that God is everywhere. Making their bed in the nether world does not relieve their mind nor their conscience of the guilt of sin.

BUT WHAT ABOUT HELL?

But what about hell? Is there such a place? After all, it does not make any difference what anybody has to say about the subject; the most important thing is to know what God has to say about it. Among the things God has said about this place is that it was "prepared for the devil and his angels," that it is not occupied at the present, but that it will be occupied at some later date. Satan is not in hell now. His abode at present is in the heavens. He has not yet been cast out. He is the accuser of the brethren. He has a right to make accusations against the believer in Christ. He will, however, be dispossessed shortly, but he will not go out without a fight. The description of the encounter may be found in the 12th chapter of the book of The Revelation. There we learn that a war takes place in heaven. The record reads, ". . . Michael and his angels fought against the dragon; and the dragon fought and his angels, and prevailed not; neither was their place found any more in heaven. And the great dragon was cast out, that old serpent, called the Devil, and Satan, which deceiveth the whole world: he was cast out into the earth, and his angels were cast out with him." When the dragon saw that he was cast unto the earth, he persecuted Israel. Israel has suffered much in the years that have gone by since her rebellion, but her sufferings then and now are not to be compared with the sufferings she will endure when Satan is cast into the earth, for the Devil hates the Jew.

Thank God, the period when Satan will reign on this earth will not be long. It will come to an end when the Lord Jesus Christ is crowned King of kings and Lord of lords. Israel will then recognize her Messiah, as predicted in the prophecy of Zechariah. Then an angel will open the bottomless pit, and Satan and his angels will be bound and put into that pit or abyss for a period of one thousand years, during which our Lord will reign as King of kings and Lord of lords. After that, Satan is to be loosed from his prison and will go out to deceive the people. There will still be found a great army who will join with him. He will gather a great host to fight against the Lord and His people. Then fire will come down from God out of heaven and devour them, and the Scripture says, "And the devil that deceived them was cast into the lake of fire and brimstone, where the beast and the false prophet are, and shall be tormented day and night for ever and ever."

John then relates that he saw a great white throne erected and the dead, small and great, stand before God,

> "And the books were opened: and another book was opened, which is the book of life: and the dead were judged out of those things which were written in the books, according to their works.
> "And the sea gave up the dead which were in it; and death and hades delivered up the dead which were in them: and they were judged every man according to their works.
> "And death and hades were cast into the lake of fire. This is the second death."

The Bible says, "And whosoever was not found written in the book of life was cast into the lake of fire." And it is written of the people cast into the lake of fire, that they ". . . shall be tormented day and night for ever and ever."

FLEEING FROM GOD

One thing is sure, we cannot flee from God. We will never get away from Him. Infinitely better, therefore, is it to receive His mercy *now*. But the Psalmist continued and wrote, "If I take the wings of the morning, and dwell in the uttermost parts of the sea; even there shall thy hand lead me, and thy right hand shall hold me." Remember, David was talking about a man who knows God. He continued, "If I say, Surely, the darkness shall cover me; even the night shall be light about me. Yea, the darkness hideth not from thee; but the night shineth as the day: the darkness and the light are both alike to thee." Of course, every Christian knows this by experience; but mark you, if God is aware of the doings of His own, whether in light or in darkness, don't think for one moment that He does not know what is taking place in light or darkness when it comes to the unsaved, the wicked, and the sinner.

This message may appear to some as an attempt to scare people so that they will flee to God for salvation. To any such, I would remind you you of a passage of Scripture found in the prophecy of Ezekiel. Our Lord appeared before the prophet and said:

> "Son of man, I have made thee a watchman unto the house of Israel: therefore hear the word at my mouth, and give them warning from me.
> "When I say unto the wicked, Thou shalt surely die; and thou givest him not warning, nor speakest to warn the wicked from his wicked way, to save his life; the same wicked man shall die in his iniquity; but his blood will I require at thine hand.
> "Yet if thou warn the wicked, and he turn not from his wickedness, nor from his wicked way, he shall die in his iniquity; but thou hast delivered thy soul."

That statement was given specifically to Ezekiel, but the principle is universal and has never changed. I would be guilty of the blood of every man listening to this program, if I were unfaithful to God and failed to warn you as I have attempted to do.

How strange it is that if a man warns another about his sin and the necessity of receiving Christ in order to avoid judgment he is looked upon as a crape-hanger, whereas, if someone warns another against impending physical danger and thus saves a life that individual is a hero.

A few years ago some boys in an orphan home in Passaic, New Jersey, were watching a terrific rainstorm about seven o'clock in the evening. To their surprise, they saw a washout on the main-line tracks of the Erie Railroad, which are directly behind the orphan home. Realizing that the train was due shortly on its way up from New York City, six of the boys ran down the fire escape at the rear of the building and with raincoats and other articles of clothing as signal flags they rushed down to the track just in time to avoid disaster and prevent the loss of many lives. The boys were acclaimed, and rightly so. They were honored and rewarded for their devotion to the service of their fellow-men. If those boys, knowing what would have taken place, had taken an attitude of, Oh, well, we are safe, why worry about these other people, a disaster would have occurred, and they would have had the burden of the blood of those people upon their hearts and consciences! Why not, therefore, heed the warning of the Scripture to flee —not *from* God, but *to* God, and from the wrath to come?

Commencing with the 13th verse, David said:

> "For thou hast possessed my reins: thou hast covered me in my mother's womb.
> "I will praise thee; for I am fearfully and wonderfully made; marvellous are thy works; and that my soul knoweth right well.
> "My substance was not hid from thee, when I was made in secret, and curiously wrought in the lowest parts of the earth.
> "Thine eyes did see my substance, yet being unperfect; and in thy book all my members were written, which in continuance were fashioned, when as yet there was none of them."

David believed in divine creation! He was not an evolutionist. He knew he was made by the hand of God; that he was constructed by Him. He was urged to praise God, for he concluded that he was fearfully and wonderfully made. How wonderful is this life of ours! I think of the description that Bishop Taylor Smith gave some time ago on the Mid-Week Forum, when he said that if he were ever inclined to be cast down, which he never was, he would think of the loving kindness of the Lord in giving him this wonderful life. "Life," said he, "beyond our comprehension; the power of thought more wonderful than wireless telegraphy; the power of speech more wonderful than any instrument, any organ made by man; and the power of action. Take the human hand," said the bishop, "the most wonderful tool in the workshop of the world; or take those red rivers, the arteries; or the blue veins, the canals; or the nervous system, the telegraphic system. I have only touched the fringe of life, this gift of life, this wonderful life. The very thought of what God is, and has been to me, and done for me, makes my heart go forward toward Him."

What the bishop had to say about life, and the provisions that God has made in life caused his heart to go *forward to God.* Surely such a contemplation ought to drive men to the cross in adoration, worship, and praise of the Creator who has since become our Redeemer and Lord.

PSALM ONE HUNDRED THIRTY-NINE—PART THREE

PERFECT HATRED

THIS past week, I came across an interesting thing which I had not previously seen in the study of this 139th Psalm. It relates to the 5th verse, which reads, "Thou hast beset me behind and before, and laid thine hand upon me." Someone drew my attention to God's provision expressed in this verse, on the behalf of those who have bowed the knee to Him. The past is taken care of, the future, and the present. Concerning the past, the Psalmist said, "Thou hast beset me behind"; concerning the future, "thou hast beset me before"; and regarding the present, "thine hand (is) upon me."

It is so easy for us to be distressed by circumstances and to entirely lose sight of the fact that God is interested in our well-being and welfare. The Scripture says, "Be anxious for nothing; but in every thing by prayer and supplication with thanksgiving let your requests be made known unto God. And the peace of God, which passeth all understanding, shall keep your hearts and minds through Christ Jesus."

The Psalmist David was "down in the dumps" many times. He was so oppressed that he cried unto the Lord and begged Him to make haste and deliver him. He even raised the question, "Why hast thou forgotten me? why go I mourning because of the oppression of the enemy?" He encouraged his own soul by saying, "Why art thou cast down, O my soul? and why art thou disquieted within me? hope thou in God: for I shall yet praise him, who is the health of my countenance, and my God."

So let's remember that Christians are not exempt from the trials and disappointments of life. But isn't it good to know that as God has taken care of the past as well as the future, so, too, He has made provision for the present, for the Psalmist said, "Thou hast laid thine hand upon me."

PRECIOUS THOUGHTS

Beginning with the 17th verse, the Psalmist said, "How precious also are thy thoughts unto me, O God! how great is the sum of them! If I should count them, they are more in number than the sand: when I awake, I am still with thee." Evidently the Psalmist had occasion for making such a statement. He had disappointments, but he had also experienced deliverance, and times without number he had discovered that God's thoughts toward him were exceedingly precious, and when he stopped to count them they were more in number than the sand.

What childlike confidence is expressed in the phrase, "when I awake, I am still with thee." Usually when we awake we find our trouble is still with us, but here's a better phrase, "when I awake, I am still with thee."

Commencing with the next verse the Psalmist abruptly introduces an entirely opposite subject. He says, "Surely thou wilt slay the wicked, O God: depart from me therefore, ye bloody men. For they speak against thee wickedly, and thine enemies take thy name in vain. Do not I hate them, O LORD, that hate thee? and am not I grieved with those that rise up against thee? I hate them with perfect hatred: I count them mine enemies."

Is there such a thing as perfect hatred? What an expression—perfect hatred! The Bible speaks about perfect love, and tells us that "perfect love casteth out fear . . ." Evidently, there is an opposite side to perfect love. David said, "Do not I hate them, O LORD, that hate thee?"

Is it possible to hate God? Well, let us take a look at the 1st chapter of Paul's letter to the Romans, in which chapter he gives a divine "snapshot" of the human family. Beginning with verse 28 we discover that men did not like to retain God in their knowledge and, for that reason, God gave them over to a reprobate mind, to do those things which are not convenient. Then, we have a full length picture of man's indecencies, sin, and rebellion. Listen to the description, "Being filled with all unrighteousness, fornication, wickedness, covetousness, maliciousness; full of envy, murder, debate, deceit, malignity; whisperers, backbiters, *haters of God*, despiteful, proud, boasters, inventors of evil things, disobedient to parents, without understanding, covenantbreakers, without natural affection, implacable, unmerciful." And, as if that were not enough, the Holy Spirit adds, "Who knowing the judgment of God, that they which commit such things are worthy of death, not only do the same, but have pleasure in them that do them." Is it surprising, therefore, to discover that the man who loves God as David did must of necessity hate them that hate God, and he must hate them with a perfect hatred?

There is perfection in God's judgment, just as there is perfection in His love. Hate that finds its genesis in the rebellion of man, causes divine judgment. Perfect hatred is something quite different from the hatred born of a rebellious heart. It is only the new nature, which a man receives upon accepting Christ, that is able to express itself in perfection, both in love and hatred, because that nature is of divine character and is the extreme opposite of human nature.

While the Psalmist was speaking of his perfect hatred of the enemies of God, he turned to God, inviting Him to search him, saying, "know my heart: try me, and know my thoughts: and see if there be any wicked way in me, and lead me in the way everlasting." Thus, not only did the Psalmist write about his perfect hatred for the enemies of God, but he also laid his heart bare before the Lord, and asked Him to search him, try him, examine him, and lead him in the way everlasting.

That brings us to an important subject. I do not know who coined the phrase, "the sins of saints," but I do know that the only kind of saints God has ever had have been sinning saints. The only people God has had as His own are those who have been stumbling, stuttering, and disobedient. It becomes necessary for the child of God to constantly lay bare his heart before the Lord and ask Him to search it. If sin in a wicked man or an unsaved man is an abomination to God, what must it be when it is found in one of His children? Sin strikes at the very throne of God. Sin is rebellion against God and against His will. It is high treason against God. It is bad enough when it is found in the wicked, but it must be cutting to the divine heart when it is found in a believer.

In the First Epistle of John, the aged Apostle discussed two major problems affecting the Christian's life. The first is the matter of sin and the second the matter of love. They are the two great problems today confronting the individual Christian and the professing church of Jesus Christ on the earth.

We shall handle the latter first, before touching the former. The church of our Lord Jesus Christ, and we as individual members, have bitterly disappointed and sinned against God because of our failure to manifest love in our dealings one with the other. I am talking now exclusively about Christians. Again and again John calls upon believers to love one another. Our Lord said, "By this shall all men know that ye are my disciples, if ye have love one to another." If there is one thing that is necessary for believers to manifest in their dealings with one another, it is the perfection of love. There is a decisive statement found in this little Epistle of John, in which he, by the Holy Spirit, wrote, "Beloved, if God so loved us" (as to send His Son to be a propitiation for our sins), "we ought also to love one another . . . If we love one another, God dwelleth in us, and his love is perfected in us."

But what about the subject of sin? John wrote, "My little children, *these things* write I unto you, that ye sin not." What are the *things* about which he wrote? That our Lord was manifested to put away sin; that there was no darkness in Him, only light, and, "if we say that we have fellowship with him, and walk in darkness, we lie, and do not the truth; but if we walk in the light, as he is in the light, we have fellowship one with another, and the blood of Jesus Christ, his (God's) Son, cleanseth us from all sin."

John, of course, knew that the child of God would sin, and yet he wrote, "My little children, these things write I unto you, that ye sin not." But if a Christian sins, then what? John added, "And if any man sin, we have an advocate with the Father, Jesus Christ the righteous. And he is the propitiation for our sins: and not for ours only, but also for the sins of the whole world."

In this 139th Psalm I believe the Psalmist is occupied not only with the *expressions* of a sin nature, but with the very nature itself. He cannot trust himself to make an examination of his life. Thus he asks the Lord to do it. "Search me, O God, and know my heart: try me, and know my thoughts: and see if there be any wicked way in me . . ." He does not stop there. It is like going to a physician for an examination, so that he can determine whether there is disease in our members. When we go to a physician, we not only do so to determine whether we have a disease, for nine times out of ten we have already experienced some symptom and we are convinced something is wrong, but we go to have our case diagnosed, and to have the physician provide some healing balm for our illness. Thus David invited the Lord to examine him; but he was not satisfied with a diagnosis only; he wanted more than that, so he closed his Psalm by saying, "and lead me in the way everlasting."

PSALM ONE HUNDRED FORTY

HOW TO BEHAVE WHEN HATED

THE 140th Psalm contains much the same note we discovered in the closing verses of the preceding Psalm. In our last meditation we asked the question and discussed the subject, whether there is such a thing as perfect hatred as well as perfect love. In this 140th Psalm I believe we have an example of how a godly man should behave when he is the object of the hatred of his enemies.

Some of us have what might be called a dynamic nature, and if our ire should be aroused, my, what an explosion follows! David, however, refused to vent his wrath upon the heads of his enemies, but rather closeted himself with God and in prayer cried out to Him for deliverance from the hand of the enemy; the meanwhile leaving the matter of vengeance in God's hands.

One of the saddest aspects of present-day Christians is their un-christian attitude toward fellow-believers. It was Dr. Lewis Sperry Chafer, I believe, who said that there are two interesting names among the Devil's many titles. He is called the "accuser of the brethren," and again, he is spoken of as the "father of lies." If the Devil ever smiles, he must do so over the ease with which he succeeds in getting Christians to do his job as the accuser of the brethren.

"FRIENDLY ENEMIES"

David knew what it was to suffer at the hand of "friendly enemies." His chief enemy was King Saul, who was one of his own countrymen. Saul was an Israelite, David was an Israelite. Both Saul and David were under covenant relationship with God; but it was evident that God was about to exalt David and put down Saul, and, oh, the hatred that rose up in the heart of King Saul against David! David was a man of war. One would expect him to immediately return the hatred with a further expression of anger and vituperation, but David went into the presence of God and left his enemy in God's hands. But before we comment any further, let us read the Psalm:

> "Deliver me, O LORD, from the evil man: preserve me from the violent man;

> "Which imagine mischiefs in their heart; continually are they gathered together for war.

> "They have sharpened their tongues like a serpent; adders' poison is under their lips. Selah.

"Keep me, O LORD, from the hands of the wicked; preserve me from the violent man; who have purposed to overthrow my goings.

"The proud have hid a snare for me, and cords; they have spread a net by the wayside; they have set gins for me. Selah.

"I said unto the LORD, Thou art my God: hear the voice of my supplications, O LORD.

"O GOD the Lord, the strength of my salvation, thou hast covered my head in the day of battle.

"Grant not, O LORD, the desires of the wicked: further not his wicked device; lest they exalt themselves. Selah.

"As for the head of those that compass me about, let the mischief of their own lips cover them.

"Let burning coals fall upon them: let them be cast into the fire; into deep pits, that they rise not up again.

"Let not an evil speaker be established in the earth: evil shall hunt the violent man to overthrow him.

"I know that the LORD will maintain the cause of the afflicted, and the right of the poor.

"Surely the righteous shall give thanks unto thy name: · the upright shall dwell in thy presence."

Whether the opposition comes from within or from without, whether it comes from within the circle of our own friends and associates, or whether it comes from an entirely outside source, it is good to remember that the Scripture says (God speaking), "Vengeance belongeth unto me, I will recompence, saith the Lord." David, of course, knew that. He must have read from the book of the law that Jehovah had said, "To me belongeth vengeance, and recompence; their foot shall slide in due time: for the day of their calamity is at hand, and the things that shall come upon them make haste." David, therefore, did not take it into his own hands to pour out wrath upon the heads of his enemies. He knew that the Lord would maintain the cause of the afflicted and the right of the poor. He was perfectly content to allow the matter to rest in the hands of the Lord.

Note that not only did David pray for God's vengeance upon the evil man, but he did not even trust his own cunning in seeking deliverance from the hand of his enemy. He prayed the Lord to deliver him from the evil man and to preserve him from the violent man. The opening verse of this Psalm contains somewhat the same words used in the so-called Lord's Prayer, which our Lord gave to His disciples as a sample prayer. The passage to which I refer is, ". . . deliver us from evil: for thine is the king-dom, and the power, and the glory, for ever."

We are apt to think of evil in abstract terms. Evil is a "thing" to be true, but evil is a person as well. Lies, for instance, are "things," but there is a personality behind them and he is called the "father of lies." Evil is a "thing," but behind evil there is an "evil one." So whether we look at this Psalm from the viewpoint of referring to a man, or whether we believe it symbolizes Satan, the principle of our conduct should be the same in both cases. We should pray for deliverance and ask God to preserve us.

The extent to which David's enemies went is carefully depicted in this Psalm, when David said, "The proud have hid a snare for me, and cords; they have spread a net by the wayside; they have set gins for me." How much some men behave like Satan, and how ready an instrument Satan finds in people to do his work. Again and again, for instance, in David's case, Saul threw a javelin at him, but again and again God demonstrated that He covered David's head in the day of battle.

But let us get away from the direct application of this Psalm to an examination of the principles contained therein. In the first place, it is apparent that there is evil, mischief, and perverseness in the world. Second, we can clearly recognize the individual who is responsible for this evil and wickedness. The Psalm speaks of the evil man, the evil speaker, and the violent man.

Whether we like it or not, there is such a thing as sin in this world! What troubles and disappointments have followed in its wake! As there is sin in the world, there is a power and personality behind sin, called Satan. While we are not ignorant of his devices, we, in our own strength and cunning could never be a match for him. We therefore have to look to an-other, in order that the evil and the evil one may be overthrown.

Since God said, "Vengeance is mine, I will repay . . ." He can be trusted to maintain the cause of the afflicted. We can trust Him to avenge the adversary of our souls. But what about the poor and the afflicted? Are they not essentially a social problem rather than a spiritual one? We have a controversy raging throughout our land on this very problem. There are those who exploit the afflicted and the poor, while others insist they are seeking to maintain the rights of the poor and the afflicted. The crux of the problem is due to the inequalities that exist among mankind. There are those who afflict and there are those who are the afflicted ones, but I do not believe that man will ever be able to place a law upon the statute books that will eliminate the problem. We will never be able to have an economy that will be advantageous to all. We will never be able to put poverty out of this world. We might as well try to lift ourselves up by our own bootstraps. It is impossible. Thus poverty is not solely a social problem. But where man has failed, there is One who will maintain the cause of the afflicted and the right of the poor.

Again, poverty and affliction are no respecters of persons. We may be high or low, merchant or laborer, and yet be poor and afflicted. How Satan loves to afflict us! How he delights to acquaint those of us who love the Lord with the fact of our poverty; how he gloats in reminding us of our sinfulness. If you do not think there is a Satan, or an evil one in this world, that is excellent evidence that he has you in the palm of his hand and has lulled you to sleep. Dare to believe God's Word and the record concerning His Son, dare to follow our Lord Jesus Christ as a faithful servant, and you will soon find out whether there is such a one in this world as Satan. You will soon discover that one of his chief occupations is to remind you of your spiritual poverty, and how successful he is in afflicting you. Well, it is great to know that while he may succeed for a moment, we have a Lord who will maintain the cause of the afflicted and the right of the poor; who will some day give us the inestimable joy of dwelling in His presence.

SATAN'S DEATH WARRANT

If you are an afflicted person, I do trust that you may receive some encouragement from this meditation. Satan is a defeated enemy. I am indebted to my friend, Dr. Donald Barnhouse, for an excellent illustration of this fact. He was living in France when, one day toward evening, he walked up the mountainside. Across his path he beheld a huge snake. He pulled out his hatchet and decapitated it. As he did not believe that anyone else would pass by that path, and he expected to come back the next day, he left the axe-head in the earth between the severed parts of the serpent. Returning the next day he stopped to lift the axe-head out of the earth, when he noticed that there was still some life left in the serpent, whose tail wiggled a bit. But it was only the wiggle of a decapitated serpent! Our Lord Jesus Christ destroyed him who had the power of death, the enemy of our souls. He did that at Calvary. He signed Satan's death warrant there. Satan is, therefore, a decapitated serpent—but he still has a wiggle! The final execution of his judgment has not been accomplished. In the meanwhile, he wiggles! It is his delight to disturb the children of God, afflicting them, upsetting them, and trying to ensnare them. May we take courage in the knowledge that he will not prove finally successful, for the Lord will maintain the cause of the afflicted, and the right of the poor. Surely the righteous shall give thanks unto His name, and the upright shall dwell in His presence.

There are no poor people in heaven, no afflicted ones, no mortgage holder to disturb you with a threatened foreclosure; you'll dwell in the presence of God. Our Lord said, "In my Father's house are many mansions: if it were not so, I would have told you. I go to prepare a place for you. And if I go and prepare a place for you, I will come again, and receive you unto myself; that where I am, there ye may be also."

"Eye hath not seen, nor ear heard, neither have entered into the heart of man, the things which God hath prepared for them that love him." But, thank God, He has revealed them unto us by His Spirit. Therefore we rejoice in tribulation also, for we joy in God, who has so perfectly revealed Himself in Christ as loving us with an eternal love.

PSALM ONE HUNDRED FORTY-ONE

"KEEP THE DOOR OF MY LIPS"

WE are to consider the 141st Psalm, about which Alexander MacLaren wrote, "Part of it is hopelessly obscure, and the connection is difficult throughout." But he adds, "It is a prayer of a harassed soul, tempted to slacken its hold on God, and therefore betaking itself to Him. Nothing more definite as to author or occasion can be said with certainty." And yet it is generally agreed that David wrote the Psalm; in fact, a leading critic has conceded that it is one of the oldest of the Davidic Psalms. Whether that be so we do not know definitely; therefore, rather than spend our time with conjectures as to its historical setting, we shall read the Psalm and then draw from it a spiritual application that will assist us in our walk and fellowship with God. So let's read the Psalm:

"LORD, I cry unto thee: make haste unto me; give ear unto my voice, when I cry unto thee.

"Let my prayer be set forth before thee as incense; and the lifting up of my hands as the evening sacrifice.

"Set a watch, O LORD, before my mouth; keep the door of my lips.

"Incline not my heart to say any evil thing, to practise wicked works with men that work iniquity: and let me not eat of their dainties.

"Let the righteous smite me; it shall be a kindness: and let him reprove me; it shall be an excellent oil, which shall not break my head: for yet my prayer also shall be in their calamities.

"When their judges are overthrown in stony places, they shall hear my words; for they are sweet.

"Our bones are scattered at the grave's mouth, as when one cutteth and cleaveth wood upon the earth.

"But mine eyes are unto thee, O GOD the Lord: in thee is my trust; leave not my soul destitute.

"Keep me from the snares which they have laid for me, and the gins of the workers of iniquity.

"Let the wicked fall into their own nets, whilst that I withal escape."

Of one thing we can be absolutely sure: the Psalmist at this time was in difficulty and found himself in a greatly disturbed state of mind. Probably he had been slandered.

GOSSIP

Recently I sat with a preacher friend at a dinner table, when we talked of a mutual friend. The two had met, and the first man was quite anxious to invite the second man to come to his church and hold a series of meetings, but he was a bit apprehensive because he had heard that the second man demanded an excessive honorarium. It was questionable whether the church could afford to pay for this man's services. But my friend decided to discuss the matter with him, and the conversation went something like this—"You know, Dr. So-and-So, we would like to have you in our church for a week's meetings, but I am not sure that we can pay your fee. I understand you are one of those men who is never satisfied with less than five hundred dollars. We will be happy to have you come if you are willing to take whatever we can afford to give you." Our mutual friend turned and said, "Where did you get the impression that I am a five-hundred-dollar man? I have heard that same 'tale' about you!" And then they both roared with laughter.

Human nature hasn't changed. It seems to be latent in the breast of mankind to gossip and, of course, as gossip passes from the lips of one to the ears of another it increases and exaggerates in the minds of the second, third, fiftieth, and hundredth individual to whom it is told, and before long the molehill has grown into a mountain.

David knew something of slander. He knew what it was to be despised. He knew what it was to have men throw stones at him. Thank God, he had sense enough not to defend himself nor to throw stones back. Rather, he went into the presence of God and cried unto Him.

WHAT TO DO WHEN TRIED

We can do one of two things in the midst of disturbances. We may, as David did in this Psalm, go into the presence of God; or we may do as Peter did when he was deprived of his liberty because of preaching the gospel. Peter found himself in a prison, bound with two chains, between two soldiers, and the keepers before the door, keeping the prison. Yet he was so sound asleep that even the light of an angel, the message of the angel, and the smiting of the angel on his side did not awaken him. The angel had to go to the extent of raising him up, and saying, "Arise up quickly . . . Gird thyself, and bind on thy sandals . . . and follow me."

Now it is wonderful, when disturbing circumstances take place, to have the faith that the Apostle Peter had—to simply rest in the Lord and to sleep soundly—but all of us are not able to do that. Sometimes we can rest thus and at other times we are sorely distressed. God knows how we are constituted, He remembers that we are but dust. He knows that sometimes we can smile away our troubles, while at other times our troubles drive us to tears. In this case David was driven to his knees and he said, "LORD, I cry unto thee: make haste unto me; give ear unto my voice, when I cry unto thee. Let my prayer be set forth before thee as incense; and the lifting up of my hands as the evening sacrifice."

It is amazing to note the number of Psalms in which David finds cause to complain and thus is driven into the presence of God. That ought to be a source of comfort and cheer to those of us who are perplexed. We, too, can come into God's presence at any time. We can cry unto Him. We can ask Him to make haste to deliver us and to hear our voice. We can also be assured that God will answer our prayer and will provide a deliverance.

Then, too, notice how thoroughly the Psalmist prayed. In the 3rd verse he said, "Set a watch, O LORD, before my mouth; keep the door of my lips." He is a wise man who is able to do that—to keep a watch before his mouth. Wise, indeed, is that man; but most of us have stationed a dummy traffic officer at our lips, who cannot even blow a whistle when we let off steam! If you are constituted that way, may you take a lesson from the experiences of David and ask the Lord to set a watch before your mouth and keep the door of your lips. You ask, Will God do that for a man? Yes, He will. That does not mean that you will not be tempted to explode and let loose, but the proper place for the safety valve to perform its appointed task is in the private prayer room of the Christian.

"ANCIENT ORDER OF NATHANS"

Now let us look at verse 5, which is a concededly difficult passage of Scripture. Here David wrote: "Let the righteous smite me; it shall be a kindness: and let him reprove me . . ." David knew what it was to be reproved as, for instance, when Nathan, the prophet, came into his presence. But it is amusing how many think they belong to the "Ancient Order of Nathans."

A certain pastor had just returned from the annual meeting of the church denomination of which he was a member. He seemed to glory in the fact that he had grasped the opportunity during the course of the deliberations to rise to his feet, point a finger at the man whom he believed to be responsible for certain supposed difficulties and, shaking his finger in the face of that man, had said, "Thou art the man." I really felt sorry for that pastor, for it was evident as he related the incident that he had attempted to perform a spiritual ministry in the power of the flesh. It is only the servant of God, commissioned by the Lord, who can do that type of thing, and when he does so, if he performs it in the spirit of Nathan, instead of arousing an attack, he will bring the individual to his knees.

Let me illustrate what I mean. I learned of the following incident only the other day from my good friend, Dr. Wilbur M. Smith, of Coatesville, Pennsylvania. It seems that some years ago that great scholar, Sir William Ramsay, was invited by the Moody Bible Institute to give a series of lectures on his discoveries in the field of archæology. His address was heard by the student body of the Institute, presided over by the late dean, Dr. James M. Gray, a cultured and scholarly Christian gentleman. Sir William Ramsay, during the course of his address, made a statement to the effect that there is in the heart of every man the light of divinity, the life of God, and it needs only to be fanned into a flame. At the end of the address Dr. Gray rose to his feet, paid tribute to Sir William Ramsay's scholarship, but added in a courteous manner that he was not able to agree with the statement which I have just given, because it was in absolute contradiction to the Word of God, which declares that *all* have sinned and that *every* man is dead in trespasses and sins. But Dr. Gray spoke graciously, thus Sir William Ramsay did not take offense. Only a gifted man, led by the Holy Spirit, can do something like that. So let's not pass judgment nor throw stones at someone else, and may we reprove only when we are sure we are in the Spirit.

On the other hand, if you are the object of persecution, go into the presence of God as David did, and cry out as he did in the 8th verse and say, "But mine eyes are unto thee, O GOD the Lord: in thee is my trust; leave not my soul destitute."

Psalm One Hundred Forty-Two

"NO MAN CARED FOR MY SOUL"

IN our series of meditations in the Book of Psalms we arrive at the 142nd, which is a brief Psalm of seven verses. However, there is an introduction to the Psalm from which we gather certain facts: first, that it was written by David; second, that it is a Psalm of instruction, by which men of like passions can find a word of exhortation for similar experiences; third, we learn to what event in his life David refers; and finally we learn that this Psalm is in the nature of a prayer. With that in mind, understanding that inspired prayers are for instruction as well as for worship, let us read the Psalm, endeavoring to place ourselves in a similar position:

"I cried unto the LORD with my voice; with my voice unto the LORD did I make my supplication.

"I poured out my complaint before him; I shewed before him my trouble.

"When my spirit was overwhelmed within me, then thou knewest my path. In the way wherein I walked have they privily laid a snare for me.

"I looked on my right hand, and beheld, but there was no man that would know me: refuge failed me; no man cared for my soul.

"I cried unto thee, O LORD: I said, Thou art my refuge and my portion in the land of the living.

"Attend unto my cry; for I am brought very low: deliver me from my persecutors; for they are stronger than I.

> "Bring my soul out of prison, that I may praise thy
> name: the righteous shall compass me about; for thou
> shalt deal bountifully with me."

According to rabbinical tradition, David had a harp hanging by his couch, and over the strings of this harp the midnight breeze played music which David then wedded to words. Thus tradition would have us understand that the Book of Psalms contains the whole music of the heart of man swept by the hand of his Maker. I hasten to say, of course, that this is tradition, and tradition cannot be relied upon, but at least it contains some interesting information from which we can draw a certain conclusion. There is not an emotion nor an experience through which men go but the Psalmist has touched upon it or written about it in this wonderful collection of Psalms.

A DISTRESSED MAN

The 142nd Psalm is the prayer of a distressed man when he was in a cave; lonesome, dejected, and in the throes of despair. The exact place or hour in David's history to which he referred in writing this Psalm is not quite clear from the record. He was in a cave several times. However, it would not surprise me if David referred here to the time when he was in the cave of Adullam, to which place he had resorted in order to hide from King Saul. While in the cave of Adullam he was a dejected soul; nevertheless, ". . . when his brethren and all his father's house heard it, they went down thither to him. And every one that was in distress, and every one that was in debt, and every one that was discontented, gathered themselves unto him; and he became a captain over them: and there were with him about four hundred men."

But we cannot say with certainy that David referred to that experience, for in the 4th verse he wrote, "I looked on my right hand, and beheld, but there was no man that would know me: refuge failed me; no man cared for my soul." Perhaps David felt that despite the fact that there were four hundred with him, he was desperately alone because of the distress in which they, too, found themselves. Whether this be the experience to which David referred or not, does not change the fact that to the sons of men there come times of distress, grief, and disappointment, when one's soul is overwhelmed and it appears that no man cares for his soul.

Observe that the Psalmist wrote in the past tense. He was, therefore, describing an experience that was now happily over. He wrote, "I cried

unto the LORD with my voice . . . I poured out my complaint before him;
I shewed before him my trouble."

ECHOING THE CRY OF CHRIST ON THE CROSS

But now let us look at the Psalm with the idea that David is merely
echoing the cry of despair from the lips of the Christ of God. Certainly no
one will question the fact that our Lord was desperately alone. It can be
said of Him that no man cared for His soul. His own brethren had forsaken Him, His most intimate disciples had left Him, He was in the hands
of His enemies, even His Father had forsaken Him—He was desperately
alone. Truly He could say, "I looked on my right hand, and beheld, but
there was no man that would know me: refuge failed me; no man cared
for my soul. I cried unto thee, O LORD: I said, Thou art my refuge and
my portion in the land of the living." If this Psalm refers to the sufferings
of our Lord Jesus Christ, then it would not be amiss for us to spend a little
time in meditating upon those sufferings.

Our Lord knew that He would be left alone. Probably the most picturesque expression of loneliness is to be found in the 102nd Psalm where
the Psalmist said, "I . . . am as a sparrow alone upon the house top." He
told His disciples that every one of them would forsake Him. That was
part of the price which had to be paid in order to effect our ransom. It
is impossible for the human heart to grasp or fully appreciate the loneliness,
the suffering, the agony, and the dejection of the Son of God upon the cross.

Fortunately there were no photographers at the foot of the cross to
take pictures of the expressions of agony that must have been carved deeply
into the Lord's countenance. Of one thing we are sure—His face was in
such contortion that one could hardly recognize the face of a man. The
sight became too horrible for men to look upon, and when the earth began
to quake under their feet they smote their breasts and sought a place of
shelter. But the centurion, seeing the sight as only he could observe it,
being close enough to hear the agonizing cries, was forced by conviction to
acknowledge, "Truly this was the Son of God."

But someone may say, What has that to do with me? That event is
separated from me by a period of approximately nineteen hundred years.
Men have died before and since in a spasm of agony. Wherein is the death
of Jesus of Nazareth different from the death of any other man, and why

should I be interested in the agony He suffered? If such a question is honestly raised in the mind of a man, he deserves to have an answer.

"GOD COMMANDETH ALL ... TO REPENT"

The longer I live, the more confirmed is my conviction that the one message which is lacking in our modern gospel proclamation is the fact of judgment due to sin. When the Apostle Paul was in the city of Athens, the Athenians assumed that he would tickle their ears with the proclamation of a new or strange theory. But as he observed their ignorant religious worship of the unknown God, he declared that God ". . . commandeth all men everywhere to repent: because he hath appointed a day, in the which he will judge the world in righteousness by that man whom he hath ordained; whereof he hath given assurance unto all men, in that he hath raised him from the dead." Here is the message that needs to be proclaimed—God commands all men everywhere to repent. The word *command* is a very strong word. There are two ideas embodied in it: first, that of permanent command, and second of a command of perpetual force. Paul argues that there may have been a time when God overlooked the ignorance of man, but now, having perfectly revealed Himself in the person of Jesus Christ, every man is without excuse. Through Christ, God has exhibited Himself, His love, His hatred for sin; and now, having raised Him from the dead and having placed in His hands the exercise of judgment, He commands all men everywhere to repent.

Sin is a crime not only against one's self, but against God. We may escape the puunishment of sin here, but the death which our Lord Jesus Christ died is abundant evidence that sin must be punished. The agony which He suffered was the direct result of the fact that He was bearing the sin of the world and suffering its penalty. If the Bible be true in its presentation of the value of that death, then it cannot be controverted that God will exact the same penalty from every sinner who refuses to receive the death that Christ died as the atonement for his sins. I acknowledge that this sounds old-fashioned, but the Word of God declares it to be true.

There comes a time in every man's life when he must keep an engagement, whether he be prepared or not, with an individual who is called the angel of death. The majority of us refuse to think about it. We are disturbed when someone talks to us about it. But why wait until it is too late to heed the divine injunction?

PSALM ONE HUNDRED FORTY-THREE

THE COURT OR THE SANCTUARY

UR meditation is found in the 143rd Psalm, which reads as follows:

"Hear my prayer, O LORD, give ear to my supplications: in thy faithfulness answer me, and in thy righteousness.

"And enter not into judgment with thy servant: for in thy sight shall no man living be justified.

"For the enemy hath persecuted my soul; he hath smitten my life down to the ground; he hath made me to dwell in darkness, as those that have been long dead.

"Therefore is my spirit overwhelmed within me; my heart within me is desolate.

"I remember the days of old; I meditate on all thy works; I muse on the work of thy hands.

"I stretch forth my hands unto thee; my soul thirsteth after thee, as a thirsty land. Selah.

"Hear me speedily, O LORD: my spirit faileth: hide not thy face from me, lest I be like unto them that go down into the pit.

"Cause me to hear thy lovingkindness in the morning; for in thee do I trust: cause me to know the way wherein I should walk; for I lift up my soul unto thee.

"Deliver me, O LORD, from mine enemies: I flee unto thee to hide me.

"Teach me to do thy will; for thou art my God: thy spirit is good; lead me into the land of uprightness.

"Quicken me, O LORD, for thy name's sake: for thy righteousness' sake bring my soul out of trouble.

"And of thy mercy cut off mine enemies, and destroy all them that afflict my soul: for I am thy servant."

The opening verse of this Psalm is in contrast to that of the preceding Psalm. In the 142nd Psalm David said, "I *cried* unto the LORD with my voice . . ." Thus he wrote in the past tense, whereas in this Psalm he writes in the present tense; he is in the act of praying as he cries, "Hear my prayer, O LORD, give ear to my supplication . . ." Someone may raise the question, Why pray, anyway? If God is aware of our circumstances, and if He is omnipotent and omniscient, then certainly He has the power to alter our circumstances and we ought to be willing to merely trust Him, without praying.

Dr. Ironside relates an experience that he had some years ago while visiting among a company of Christians in a western state. They had some rather peculiar ideas. They came together weekly for the study of the Bible and for preaching, and to remember the Lord in observing His death, but they had no prayer meeting.

Dr. Ironside said to them, "Do you never have a prayer meeting?" A brother answered, "Oh, no, we have nothing to pray for." Dr. Ironside asked, "How is that?" "Why, God has blessed us 'with all spiritual blessings in heavenly places in Christ . . .' so we do not need to pray for spiritual blessings. We do not need to pray for temporal blessings, for we have everything we need. We are well cared for, we have all the land we know how to till. We do not need to pray for money, for we have plenty to keep us going. We do not need to pray for wives, for we are all married. We do not need to pray for children; I have thirteen and brother So-and-So has fifteen. We have nothing to pray for, so we just give God thanks." Dr. Ironside answered and said, "My dear brother, I wish, if for nothing else, that you would come together to pray for me." To that the gentleman responded, "We can do that at home. If we came together to pray, we wouldn't have anything to say." Dr. Ironside still responded, "But what about that word in Ephesians, the 6th chapter, 'Praying always with all prayer and supplication in the Spirit, and watching thereunto with all perseverance and supplication for all saints . . .'" and added, "Suppose you do nothing else but come together to remind one another of the Lord's dear children that you know, and spend an hour telling God about them." Still the good brother did not see it. Neither he nor the company with whom he was associated seemed to have any idea of what real prayer is.

Dr. Ironside continues his story, stating that some time later he was in Minneapolis when one day he tumbled over, and when he came to, he had a fever of 104 degrees and was on his back with typhoid fever for six weeks. When at last, a year later, he got back to the same place, the same brother said to him, "When we got the word that you were so very sick, we had two prayer meetings a week to pray for you, and our hearts were greatly burdened, but as soon as we got word that you were well enough to go home again we stopped." "Why did you stop?" Dr. Ironside asked. "When flat on my back, I did not have any trouble with the devil, but when strong and well I have to go out to face the foe and I need prayer far more." Then the brother looked in amazement and said, "I never thought of it that way." Well, that is one reason for praying, and not a bad one!

But most of us have experiences similar to those of David, so that we find ourselves constantly forced into the presence of God because of our circumstances. How good it is to have a God who can hear prayer.

Now note that David wrote, ". . . in thy sight shall no man living be justified." I think it was Captain Wallis who, in giving a definition of the word "justified," said that it meant "just-as-if-I-had-never-sinned." If you were to enter into the presence of God you could not enter as if you had not sinned. You have sinned. God has said, about the most religious nation under the sun, that their righteousnesses were as filthy rags in His sight. In other words, their best works were as rags in God's sight.

Now let me take you to the great "justification" Epistle of the New Testament—Paul's letter to the Romans. We read in the 20th verse of the 3rd chapter, "Therefore by the deeds of the law there shall no flesh be justified in his sight: for by the law is the knowledge of sin." If righteousness does not come by the law a man cannot justify himself in the presence of God. He is therefore in dire circumstances. But Paul, in his great argument, continues and declares, "But now the righteousness of God without the law is manifested . . . Even the righteousness of God which is by faith of Jesus Christ unto all and upon all of them that believe: for there is no difference . . . Being justified freely by his grace through the redemption that is in Christ Jesus . . ."

HOW MEN ARE JUSTIFIED

Notice how a person is justified. It is "freely." It is not stinted; it is not on the basis of purchase; it does not involve paying or buying anything or even praying. We are "justified freely by his grace through the redemption that is in Christ Jesus."

But someone will say, That does not seem fair. You mean to say that God will credit me with a righteousness which I have not earned and reject a righteousness which I have tried to earn?

No, *I* do not mean to say anything. What you and I may say on that subject isn't worth our breath. The thing that counts is what God has said. This principle of justification by faith alone in the integrity and Word of God is avowed from the beginning of Genesis to the end of The Revelation.

Does this mean that it does not make any difference what we do and that everything hinges on what we believe? Is a man justified simply because he believes in Jesus Christ, and thereafter he can do as he pleases? ABSOLUTELY NOT. We learn from the Scriptures that ". . . by grace are ye saved through faith; and that not of yourselves: it is the gift of God: not of works, lest any man should boast. For we are his workmanship, created in Christ Jesus *unto* good works, which God hath before ordained that we should walk in them."

Good works come after faith, not before. God requires that those who believe Him walk as becometh saints, and that they should work out their salvation which He has placed within them and work it out with fear and trembling. I trust I have made this quite clear.

MUSING ON THE WORK OF GOD'S HANDS

But let's continue in our Psalm. In the 5th and 6th verses the Psalmist, after relating his sorrow, disappointment, and the burden of his soul, gives us the panacea for such a spirit by saying, "I remember the days of old; I meditate on all thy works; I muse on the work of thy hands. I stretch forth my hands unto thee: my soul thirsteth after thee, as a thirsty land."

Last Wednesday evening Mrs. Olsen and I drove to Stony Brook, Long Island, in order to attend one of the conference meetings being held there. We saw a sunset that caused both of us to go into ecstacy. We had never seen a more marvelous sunset. The colors were dazzling. The setting sun lit up a great portion of the sky. It was one of the most awe-inspiring sights I have ever witnessed and I turned to my wife and said, "To think that there are some people who do not believe that there is a God." We were musing on the work of His hands. He had painted in the sky a work of art such as none of the geniuses of this world could put on canvas. As we thought of that sunset we thought of what went to make it up. Of course, you know it is utterly impossible to have such a profusion of color in such grandeur and splendor without the massing of clouds. It is as the sun is reflected upon the clouds that we get a glorious sunset.

So, too, if we are to experience a similar situation in our lives, there must be the clouds, to be sure, but there must also be the sun. Clouds are the common experiences of man. Suffering, disappointment, and difficulties are the lot of the righteous and of the unrighteous. At times it appears that the wicked prosper as a green bay tree, but a closer examination shows that the wicked are not without their clouds. Suffering is the common lot of man. From earliest childhood to the last illness, one's life is not without its clouds. But when a man knows the "Sun of righteousness"; when the Lord Jesus Christ is received into a life, He, as the Sun, can reflect His own glory through our clouds and make the common experiences of life to be illuminated with radiance so as to cause one to rejoice in the midst of disappointment.

Dr. Graham Scroggie, the great Scotch preacher, has given a homely illustration of the two views of the philosophy of life. He tells the story of two wooden buckets and the conversation which ensued between them. The one bitterly complained about its lot in life, and whined to the other that despite the many times he came up from the well filled, he had to go down empty every time, whereas the other bucket joyfully answered, "Every time I go down empty, I come up full." If you know the Lord Jesus you can draw joy out of the wells of salvation. You can make the common, ordinary experiences of life radiate with the reflection of His glory.

But I hasten to make one further comment before bringing our message to a close. In the 8th verse, the Psalmist wrote, "Cause me to hear thy lovingkindness in the morning . . ." You will remember the passage that says, "weeping may endure for a night, but joy cometh in the morning." Most of us must confess that we are so busy in the morning getting ready for our daily tasks that we give very few moments to the reading of His Word and a hurried recitation of prayer. We rarely stop to consider that prayer must be a two-way conversation if it is to be effective. How would you feel if someone called you on the phone, and before you could even say "Hello," they proceeded to talk, and talk, and talk, not giving you one chance to get a word in; and then the party at the other end of the line said "good-bye" and hung up. Yet we often pray like that. Hereafter let us make prayer a two-way conversation. Let us not do all the talking without hearing God's voice. If we once heard His "lovingkindness in the morning" we would want to hear it all the time.

PSALM ONE HUNDRED FORTY-FOUR

A PSALM FOR A DICTATOR

AT eleven o'clock last Thursday evening, for probably the twentieth time, I read the 144th Psalm, seeking a message from it for our meditation. Despite the fact that I had already completed my preparation for what I believed was to be my message on this Psalm, I was not satisfied with what I had prepared.

So as I read this 144th Psalm once again there flashed through my mind—here is a prayer in the form of a Psalm, presented by an absolute monarch, which might profitably be studied closely by our modern type of dictators, though they be pleased to designate us who are being regimented as my friends, my people, or comrades. Does not David in this Psalm, in its 2nd verse, speak of Israel as "my people," and does he not say that they are "subdued" under him? But the difference between David and our modern dictators is the difference between a godly, praying sovereign, and a godless, brutal egotist who thrives on the fanfare of class hatred and vituperation.

As we read this 144th Psalm observe how a beneficent monarch confesses that his source of strength, his hope of prosperity, and his desire for a happy, contented people is founded upon the overpowering mercy and goodness of God.

"Blessed be the LORD my strength, which teacheth my hands to war, and my fingers to fight:

"My goodness, and my fortress; my high tower, and my deliverer; my shield, and he in whom I trust; who subdueth my people under me.

"LORD, what is man, that thou takest knowledge of him! or the son of man, that thou makest account of him!

"Man is like to vanity: his days are as a shadow that passeth away.

"Bow thy heavens, O LORD, and come down: touch the mountains, and they shall smoke.

"Cast forth lightning, and scatter them: shoot out thine arrows, and destroy them.

"Send thine hand from above; rid me, and deliver me out of great waters, from the hand of strange children;

"Whose mouth speaketh vanity, and their right hand is a right hand of falsehood.

"I will sing a new song unto thee, O GOD: upon a psaltery and an instrument of ten strings will I sing praises unto thee.

"It is he that giveth salvation unto kings: who delivereth David his servant from the hurtful sword.

"Rid me, and deliver me from the hand of strange children, whose mouth speaketh vanity, and their right hand is a right hand of falsehood:

"That our sons may be as plants grown up in their youth; that our daughters may be as corner stones, polished after the similitude of a palace:

"That our garners may be full, affording all manner of store: that our sheep may bring forth thousands and ten thousands in our streets:

> "That our oxen may be strong to labour; that there be
> no breaking in, nor going out; that there be no com-
> plaining in our streets.
>
> "Happy is that people, that is in such a case: yea,
> happy is that people, whose God is the LORD."

Do you wonder why I say that this is a Psalm for a dictator? David prayed for prosperity and peace so complete that he added, ". . . that there be no complaining in our streets." Today the authority of dictators is effective only because any who dare to complain in the streets are immediately presented with their death warrant, or provided with a free ticket to Siberia.

Would that the world's leaders understood that they are like vanity and their days as a shadow that passeth away, and thus cast themselves before the throne of God to implore His blessing and His subjection of the people. Only then is a man fit to govern, as Cromwell declared in his day. No man ought to rule a people who has not himself bowed the knee to the Almighty God to confess his unworthiness and to implore *divine* guidance.

But enough of this—I am all too well aware of the fact that we do not have any dictators among our radio listeners this morning—so why spend our breath upon them? Instead we shall seek a personal message from this Psalm for our own selves, just as Professor Lewis of Drew Theological Seminary so ably sets forth in his work, "A Christian's Manifesto." Dr. Graham Scroggie told me that he considers that book one of the finest works on Christian apologetics published in our day. Speaking of the necessity, on the part of our preachers, to affirm the fact of *sin*, Professor Lewis says, "Your congregation will listen with pleasure and approval as you dilate on the sinfulness of the *absent* capitalist, or the *absent* banker, or the *absent* ward-boss, or the *absent* Congressman, or the *absent* war-monger. But what is the difference in principle between the act of the banker who steals a million and the act of a clerk who rides home on the street car without paying the fare because the conductor did not ask for it? The beam may be bigger than the splinter, but either will blind you."

LIFE—A BATTLEFIELD

To many, I am certain, the message of the 1st verse of our Psalm runs counter to their pet philosophy of the Christian life. I can picture the screwed-up faces that our modern "pink" Christians would make were one to rise up and declare, "Blessed be the LORD my strength, which teacheth

my hands to war, and my fiingers to fight . . ." But again, I can do no
better than to quote the words of Professor Lewis, whose former friends,
now turned critics, insist that he has sold out to the Fundamentalists, has
passed his creative period, and is becoming senile and conservative, even
suggesting that he has "slipped back into orthodoxy." Would God that
many more of our modern theologians would experience the same "slipping
back" into orthodoxy, but let's not forget that to be orthodox is to be guilty
of "straight thinking." Somehow I never object to being guilty of that
pastime. Professor Lewis declares, "An urgent need of the modern world
is to get some iron into its thinking about God. In our churches especially
people have been encouraged to suppose that divine Fatherhood means
divine Paternalism, with the result that God has been talked about as
though He were much the same kind of an individual as President Bill of
the local Rotary Club." Indeed, the professor continues, "Life is not a
playground—it is a battlefield."

Of course, our warfare is not carnal. We wrestle not against flesh and
blood, we war against principalities, against powers, against rulers of the
darkness of this world, and against spiritual wickedness in high places.

The 3rd verse of our Psalm reminds us of the 8th Psalm, where the
Psalmist, overawed by the resplendent heavens, cried out, "What is man,
that thou art mindful of him? and the son of man, that thou visitest him?"
Here, in this 144th Psalm, David raised somewhat the same question as he
wrote, "LORD, what is man, that thou takest knowledge of him! or the
son of man, that thou makest account of him!" David had in mind this
time not the matchless grace of God that makes His mind to be full of man,
but His inexhaustible patience in withholding judgment from the man whose
mouth speaketh vanity and whose right hand is a right hand of falsehood. We are so inclined to lose our patience and desire prompt judgment,
but God can afford to wait His time, knowing full well that man's day is
but a shadow.

Here then is a passage clearly stating that God takes knowledge of man
and makes account of him. The God who spun the universe into space, who
creates and recreates, who upholds all things by the Word of His power,
whose creation evidences the care of even the minutest detail, finds it not
difficult to take knowledge of man and make account of him.

I am thinking of a friend who, a few years had an audience with
Il Duce of Italy. For a time this friend was the editor of a New York
paper. He was a great authority on banking and finance. He was more

than a little surprised and a bit fussed, having responded to the question as to what he thought of Italy and its people, by saying that he was always an admirer of the Italian people, to hear the Dictator ask, as he opened a drawer of his desk, pulling out a number of clippings, all of which were from the editorial page of my friend's paper, "Then how do you account for these adverse editorials?" Fortunately, my friend was quick-witted, for with a twinkle in his eyes he answered, "Oh, they must have been written while I was away."

Do you think for one moment that God has less intelligence than man? Do you think that the God who ordained governmental authority, who decreed that rulers are not a terror to good works but to evil, and that rulers are the ministers of God for good, will not confront and demand an accounting from that very same Dictator, as He presents the case of Ethiopia to him? Do you think that the blood of untold thousands that has flowed from the bodies of Christians in Russia will not be avenged, when the commissars and the "Iron Man" of Russia stand before the bar of God's judgment? Do you think you will escape His all-piercing, all-searching eye? If so, then God is a myth, Christianity a fraud, the Bible a monstrosity, and man a creature of circumstances! No, a thousand times No!—for as the Apostle Paul declared in Athens, God "hath appointed a day, in the which he will judge the world in righteousness by that man whom he hath ordained; whereof he hath given assurance unto all, in that he hath raised him from the dead."

But let us continue with our Psalm. Note the 9th verse, which reads, "I will sing a new song unto thee, O God: upon a psaltery and an instrument of ten strings will I sing praises unto thee." Dr. Herbert Lockyer, of Liverpool, England, has an excellent sermon based on a phrase of this verse which he has entitled "An Instrument of Ten Strings."

It is evident that the instrument of which David was speaking was one that was used in the worship of Jehovah in Jerusalem. Music, whether instrumental or vocal, ought to be the expression of the worshipful heart in its devotion to the Lord. I am aware of its debasement in our modern jazz age. The new song of which David wrote was sung and played unto God. The Lord who alone giveth "songs in the night" can so adjust our lives that they will ring with melody unto the Lord. It is that thought which caused Dr. Lockyer to liken the instrument of ten strings to this body of ours, with its ten fingers.

INTELLIGENT HANDLING OF GOD'S WORD

In the latter part of the 144th Psalm, David prayed for God's blessing upon his people, that their sons might be as plants grown up in their youth; that their daughters might be as cornerstones; that their garners might be full; that their sheep and oxen might increase and be strong, and finally, that there be no complaining in their streets. Of such a people in such a state David said, "Happy is that people . . . yea, happy is that people, whose God is the LORD."

In David's time, and prior thereto, the godly Jew was rewarded with temporal blessings. Thus Abraham was rich, Jacob was rich, Joseph was rich, David was prosperous. Prosperity was the promise of God—it assured earthly blessings to an earthly people.

In our day, under the dispensation of grace, temporal prosperity is not assured the individual Christian for faithful service. Yea, it is written that they who will live godly in this age shall suffer persecution, and, if we suffer with Him we shall reign with Him. The Christian is a pilgrim here, he is a heavenly being, blessed with spiritual blessings in Christ, and assured of eternal life because of faith in Christ. Thus I have known of poor Christians, poor in this world's goods, but happy in the knowledge of their Lord.

Prosperity, therefore, is no assurance of happiness. There have been millionaries who have committed suicide because of their unhappiness. Adversity, poverty, and the like are no hindrance to happiness. The real reason for happiness springs from a knowledge of God as He is revealed in Christ.

PSALM ONE HUNDRED FORTY-FIVE—PART ONE

ETERNITY AND OUR OCCUPATION THEN

WERE we able to read the 145th Psalm in the Hebrew and see the Psalm in its original setting we would immediately recognize that each of the verses begins with a consecutive letter of the Hebrew alphabet. David undoubtedly devised the Psalm in that manner in order that one might readily grasp the contents of the Psalm and retain it in one's memory.

There are Psalms spoken of as "A Psalm of David," "A Psalm of Solomon," "A Psalm of Asaph," "A Psalm for the Sons of Korah," etc., but David puts his personal seal on this 145th Psalm and declares it is his. He does not call it "A Psalm of David," but speaks of it as "David's Psalm of praise." Here then was his choice for the expression of the adoration of his heart to God for His goodness and His benefactions. It is good to have a Psalm we can call our own or a portion of Scripture that is specifically ours. I do not know who originated the idea of autographing Bibles, but those who have attended Bible conferences have observed the beeline that is made to the preacher immediately after the service so that he may place his autograph in the Bibles of those attending the meetings. Invariably when I have been asked to autograph a Bible I have noticed that other names appearing in the Bible had a specific passage of Scripture following the name. I have, of course, followed the same procedure, for I, like every other lover of the Word, have a portion of Scripture I speak of as my own. It has meant so much to me in my own life that I call it mine. It happens to be a passage from the 13th chapter of St. Paul's letter to the Hebrews. It is in the form of a benediction, reading "Now the God of peace, that brought again from the dead our Lord Jesus, that great shepherd of the sheep, through the blood of the everlasting covenant, make you perfect in every good work to do his will, working in you that which is wellpleasing in his sight, through Jesus Christ; to whom be glory for ever and ever. Amen." David went through the Psalms and said concerning this 145th Psalm, "It is mine."

Observe that he began by praising the Lord, as he wrote, "I will extol thee, my God, O king; and I will bless thy name for ever and ever." Evidently David believed in immortality. Some people use the word "immortality" to describe the eternal character of the soul. Immortality refers to the body, that part of man which dies. The soul never dies in the sense of being destroyed, exterminated or extinguished. When the Bible says, "the soul that sinneth, it shall die," it speaks of the judgment of God against sin, which is separation from God and which was so graphically expressed by our Lord when He paid sin's penalty on the cross as He cried out, "My God, my God, why hast thou forsaken me?" Even the writer of the earliest book of the Bible, the Book of Job, took this view of immortality when he said, "For I know that my redeemer liveth, and that he shall stand at the latter day upon the earth; and though after my skin worms destroy this body, yet in my flesh shall I see God; whom I shall see for myself, and mine eyes shall behold, and not another . . ." Likewise David, though he knew that his flesh would see corruption and that he would be buried with his fathers, appreciated not only that he had an eternal soul but also that he would enjoy the glories of immortality which our Lord Jesus Christ has brought to light through the gospel. Thus he said, "I will extol thee, my God, O king; and I will bless thy name *for ever and ever*. Every day will I bless thee; and I will praise thy name *for ever ever*. Great is the LORD, and greatly to be praised; and his greatness is unsearchable."

The highest occupation of a man is to offer the worship of his heart to God. But why did David lay stress upon the "name" of God, for in the 1st and 2nd verses of this Psalm he said, ". . . I will bless *thy name* for ever and ever . . . I will praise *thy name* for ever and ever." When Moses received his commission to lead the children of Israel out of the Egyptian bondage he said, "Behold, when I come unto the children of Israel, and shall say unto them, The God of your fathers hath sent me unto you; and they shall say to me, What is his name? what shall I say unto them? And God said unto Moses, I AM THAT I AM: and he said, Thus shalt thou say unto the children of Israel, I AM hath sent me unto you." From that time forward the great eternal name of God, the I AM, was the most marvelous word that could fall from the lips of man. When we come into the New Testament, again and again we find that our Lord Jesus Christ appropriated that title to Himself. He said, "*I am* the bread of life . . ." He did not say, "I gave you the bread of life." He said, "I am the light . . ." "I am the way . . ." "I am the resurrection, and the life . . ." When He came to give His Father an accounting of His stewardship, as found in the 17th chapter of John's Gospel, we learn that one of the things that God had given Him to do during His earth ministry was to reveal the new name of God. It was then He said, "I have manifested *thy name* unto the men which thou gavest me out of the world: thine they were, and thou gavest them me; and they have kept thy word."

No wonder the heart of a redeemed individual vibrates with the music of heaven when he joins with David in the singing of this Psalm—"I will extol thee, my God, O king; and I will bless thy name for ever and ever. Every day will I bless thee; and I will praise thy name for ever and ever."

HEAVEN'S OCCUPATION

But I can hear some ask, Do you mean to say that you still maintain the notion of the medievalist that heaven's occupation consists solely of playing on a harp and walking up and down the streets of the Golden

City singing the songs of Zion? Is that all heaven is—a continuous song? I am very fond of music, and I love the singing of gospel music through the lips of redeemed people, yet I am frank to admit that if heaven consisted only of singing and walking the streets of gold it would have no great attraction for me. That is merely one feature of the heavenly life, which life some of us are already tasting here. There is another verse in this Psalm which more accurately reveals the occupation for eternity on the part of the redeemed soul. I refer to the 3rd verse, where David wrote, "Great is the LORD, and greatly to be praised; and his greatness is unsearchable." David did not say we could not search into God's greatness, but he said it is unsearchable. He did not say we have not a right to enter into it but that we will never come to the place where we will exhaust the greatness of our God.

In the 17th chapter of John's Gospel our Lord also revealed the occupation of eternity of those who have been redeemed. In the 24th verse of that chapter our Lord prayed: "Father, *I will* that they also, whom thou hast given me, be with me where I am; that they may behold my glory, which thou hast given me: for thou lovedst me before the foundation of the world." It will take an eternity, and even then we would have to acknowledge concerning the glory of our Lord Jesus Christ that His greatness is unsearchable.

THE UNBROKEN LINE OF TESTIMONY

It is not going to be possible for us to cover even in our usual "meditation" manner the complete 145th Psalm. We shall be satisfied to comment on the first seven verses:

"I will extol thee, my God, O king; and I will bless thy name for ever and ever.

"Every day will I bless thee; and I will praise thy name for ever and ever.

"Great is the LORD, and greatly to be praised; and his greatness is unsearchable.

"One generation shall praise thy works to another, and shall declare thy mighty acts.

"I will speak of the glorious honour of thy majesty, and of thy wondrous works.

"And men shall speak of the might of thy terrible acts: and I will declare thy greatness.

"They shall abundantly utter the memory of thy great goodness, and shall sing of thy righteousness."

Attempts have been made from time to time to blot out the memory of God. Russia in our day is an outstanding example of that principle, although it appears as if Germany desires to run Russia a close second. But David was a wise man. From the time that God took him from tending his father's sheep, through the various encounters with Saul, which culminated in his exaltation as King of Israel, and through the varied experiences of his reign, David had learned one thing—that it was impossible to blot out the memory of God from the hearts and minds of men. Those who attempt to do so are themselves plagued with a consciousness of the all-present God, as Dr. Ironside states in his new book, "Except Ye Repent," citing the infidel Altamont and reporting of him that he cried when dying, "O, thou blasphemed and yet indulgent God! Hell itself were a refuge if it hide me from Thy face." Evidently the infidel agreed that the 8th verse of the 139th Psalm was true where David said of God, ". . . if I make my bed in hell, behold, thou art there."

But in this 145th Psalm David was not concerned with the infidel nor those who seek to blot out the memory of God. Rather was he speaking of the line, that unbroken line of men and women from generation to generation, who have given testimony for God and have remained faithful to the revelation of God. "One generation shall praise thy works to another, and shall declare thy mighty acts." That is why Israel celebrates the Passover every year—that is why the Christian sits at the Lord's table celebrating a memorial of the sacrifice of the Lord Jesus—that is why every church building is in existence. But you could destroy every church building and yet you would find that one generation would praise the works of God unto another and declare His mighty acts. You cannot blot from the life of man that chain of testimony that has for its purpose the exaltation of God and the propagation of the great gospel that "God so loved the world, that he gave his only begotten Son, that whosoever believeth in him should not perish, but have everlasting life."

PSALM ONE HUNDRED FORTY-FIVE—PART TWO

THE ETERNAL KINGDOM

A S we continue our meditation in the 145th Psalm, covering verses 8 to 14, we find that the mercy of God, the righteousness of God, and His graciousness constitute the theme of this part of the Psalm:

> "The LORD is gracious, and full of compassion; slow
> to anger, and of great mercy.

"The LORD is good to all: and his tender mercies are over all his works.

"All thy works shall praise thee, O LORD; and thy saints shall bless thee.

"They shall speak of the glory of thy kingdom, and talk of thy power;

"To make known to the sons of men his mighty acts, and the glorious majesty of his kingdom.

"Thy kingdom is an everlasting kingdom, and thy dominion endureth throughout all generations.

"The LORD upholdeth all that fall, and raiseth up all those that be bowed down."

In considering that portion of the Psalm which we have just read, let us focus our attention first on one of the great parables our Lord uttered during His earthly ministry, the story commonly called "The Prodigal Son." Our Lord informed the publicans and sinners who drew nigh unto Him that ". . . there is joy in the presence of the angels of God over one sinner that repenteth." To illustrate, He told of a certain man who had two sons. The younger of them said to his father, "Father, give me the portion of goods that falleth to me." The father did not rebuke his son nor argue with him, but he gave to him his desires, for our Lord said, "And he divided unto them his living." It was not long after that the younger son gathered all together, and took his journey into a far country, and, as expected, wasted his substance with riotous living. As a result he ran into a "depression" as a sore famine beset the land. He was unable to get even a diet of bread and water. He had to satisfy his belly with the husks that the swine did eat. Our Lord added, "and no man gave unto him." What a decline—from the gaiety of his father's house to association with swine.

When that young fellow came to himself he began to reason. Notice that; so often men make the blunder of thinking that God expects a man to throw his reason to the wind and to take the statements of Scripture on the basis of sheer credulity. Nowhere in all Scripture does God appeal either to the ignorance of man or to his credulity. God appeals to man's reason and to his intelligence. Thus He said, "Come now, let us *reason* together . . ."

That young man in the pigpen reasoned aloud and said, "How many hired servants of my father's have bread enough and to spare, and I perish with hunger! I will arise and go to my father, and will say unto him, Father, I have sinned against heaven, and before thee, and am no more worthy to be called thy son: make me as one of thy hired servants."

After our Lord related the reasoning of the young man, He gave us a picture of the son departing from the pigpen, arising and going to his father; and then drew our attention to the father. Our Lord said that the father saw the lad while he was yet a great way off, and had compassion and ran and fell on his neck and kissed him. It was the son who broke in with the spoken word, not the father. The father never said a word to him. The son said, "Father, I have sinned against heaven, and in thy sight, and am no more worthy to be called thy son." The father seemed to pay no attention to the boy's message, but turned to his servants and said, "Bring forth the best robe, and put it on him; and put a ring on his hand, and shoes on his feet: and bring hither the fatted calf and kill it; and let us eat, and be merry: for this my son was dead, and is alive again; he was lost, and is found." And they began to be merry. Our Lord went on to tell about the elder son who was in the field, and how as he came nigh to the house he heard the music and dancing and called to one of the servants to find out the reason. When he learned the truth he became angry and refused to go into the house, but his father came out and entreated him and justified his actions toward the younger son.

That story is a perfect portrayal of God the Father's heart. There is nothing of cheap sentimentality about it. There is dignity, and compassion, and marvelous, moving mercy. One thing, in my judgment, stands out more than anything else and that is the silence of the father. He did not speak to his wayward son. He did not need to, for his actions spoke louder than words could. He did not rebuke the son, he did not even remonstrate with him, neither did he argue with him, but when he saw him a great way off he had compassion and ran out to meet him and fell upon his neck and kissed him. It was Charles Haddon Spurgeon who said, "The eyes of mercy are quicker than the eyes of repentance. Even the eye of our faith is dim compared with the eye of God's love . . . we read that the father ran. Slow are the steps of repentance, but swift are the feet of forgiveness." It was Dr. Scroggie who said that only once in all of Scripture do you find God in a hurry and that was when He ran out to meet the prodigal son.

"THE LORD IS GOOD TO ALL . . ."

With this parable as a background, let us now look at the 145th Psalm, reading from verse 8:

> "The LORD is gracious, and full of compassion; slow
> to anger, and of great mercy.

"The LORD is good to all: and his tender mercies are
over all his works."

Let us stop there and ask ourselves if these characteristics are manifested in the parable of the prodigal son. Certainly the father was gracious.
Who will question his compassion? And can any deny that he was slow
to anger? He did not rebuke his son. He did not even rebuke the elder
son, though he remonstrated with him. Certainly he was full of mercy.
He was good to the younger son, to the elder son, and to the servants,
and his tender mercies were over all his works. He supplied the provisions.
He provided the clothing. Over all his works there was the evidence of
tender mercies.

The fact that David wrote in the 9th verse of this 145th Psalm, "The
LORD is good to *all:* and his tender mercies are over all his works" has
led some people to assume that there is such a thing as "universal salvation"; that God's goodness will not permit Him to extend judgment or
punishment to sin. The parable of the prodigal son which we have just
related tells of a father's compassion toward a *repentant* son. Observe that
the father did not go to the pigpen to get his son! There was no evidence
of the father's compassion or demonstration of his mercy until the son came
to himself and gave evidence of true repentance by turning away from the
pigpen and wending his way to his father's house. To the repentant sinner God extends a welcome, compassion, and wonderful provisions. When
David said, "The LORD is good to all . . ." I do not believe that he
intended to include in the word *all* any who do not turn to God in repentance. Paul preached on Mars' hill that God "now commandeth all men
every where to repent . . ." and in his valedictory to the Ephesian elders
Paul said that he had testified of two messages—one, "repentance toward
God," and the other, "faith toward our Lord Jesus Christ." When men
refuse to receive the Father's remedy for sin then men must experience
isolation. Sin is a communicable disease. Sin's deadly germs are not
permitted to pass the threshold of the Father's house. God, therefore, has
provided an "isolation ward" where men who have refused His grace may
be separated.

THE POWER OF GOD

But let us continue with the Psalm, particularly verses 10 to 14, where
the Psalmist said:

"All thy works shall praise thee, O LORD: and thy
saints shall bless thee.

"They shall speak of the glory of thy kingdom, and
talk of thy power;

"To make known to the sons of men his mighty acts,
and the glorious majesty of his kingdom.

"Thy kingdom is an everlasting kingdom, and thy dominion endureth throughout all generations.

"The LORD upholdeth all that fall, and raiseth up all
those that be bowed down."

Here is a portion of Scripture from which every Christian gets a
blessing, ". . . thy saints shall bless thee," said David. "To make known
to the sons of men his mighty acts, and the glorious majesty of his kingdom." Thus, believers delight to talk about the glory of the Father's kingdom and the majesty of His power.

David undoubtedly referred to the same thing that the Apostle Paul
did when he said that the gospel of our Lord Jesus Christ is the *power* of
God unto salvation to everyone that believeth. It is in the gospel that God
reveals His *power*. It is for that reason the hymn writer wrote, "There is
power in the blood." As the gospel is preached and believed, the *power* of
God manifests itself in the life of the individual, so that he experiences a
spiritual resurrection. That *power* is tremendous. Paul prayed that Christians might know what is the exceeding greatness of God's *power* to us-
ward who believe, declaring that such *power* is the same which God wrought
in Christ when He raised Him from the dead and exalted Him to His own
right hand in the heavenly places.

But men of faith talk also about the glory of God's kingdom. The
words, "Thy kingdom is an everlasting kingdom," found in verse 13, are
engraved on the door of a mosque in Damascus, which was formerly a
Christian church. Originally they were plastered over by stucco, but the
stucco has dropped away, and the words stand out clearly defined. Dr.
F. B. Meyer, referring to this Psalm and to that historical fact, gleaned
from a world traveler, said, "They seem to be contradicted by centuries of
Mohammedanism; but they are essentially true. Just now," adds Dr.
Meyer, "the kingdom is in mystery; but soon it will be manifested."

Men have successfully laid a plaster cast over the declaration of this
Psalm: "Thy kingdom is an everlasting kingdom." For the present, the
kingdom of God is obscured. Men have reveled in their defiance of God
and basked in their man-made sunshine of exaltation. But just as time
wore off the stucco on the door of the former Christian church in Damascus
so time will effectively remove the plaster cast men have laid to obscure

the kingdom of God. Mussolini may glory in his dream of a revived Roman Empire, Hitler may rejoice in his present successes as a modern Pharaoh; but I could not avoid doing some thinking as I read a newspaper report of what took place this past week in Germany, in the stadium built for the Olympic games, where the crowds had gathered to hear the two dictators. It seems it rained; a cold, dismal rain. When Hitler finished he was sneezing, his voice had gone. Mussolini also was not so spry. He, too, had developed a "foghorn." When a little rain can "dampen" the effectiveness of two of the supposedly iron men of today, I think we are not only reasonable but rational when we rejoice in the Psalmist's majestic declaration, "Thy kingdom is an everlasting kingdom, and thy dominion endureth throughout all generations."

Dr. George McNeely, of Newark, has effectively said that the world needs a "dictator." God's choice is now in the heavens. He shall not always remain there; the plaster of stucco will drop, and out of those silent heavens shall come the One whose right it is to rule. When the rulers take counsel together against the Lord and against His anointed saying, "Let us break their bands asunder, and cast away their cords from us. He that sitteth in the heavens shall laugh: the Lord shall have them in derision. Then shall he speak unto them in his wrath, and vex them in his sore displeasure. Yet have I set my king upon my holy hill of Zion."

These and other passages of Scripture enable a Christian to maintain an equilibrium in these breath-taking days. A Christian looks up and rejoices. He does not look down or around and become morbid.

PSALM ONE HUNDRED FORTY-FIVE—PART THREE

THE OPEN HAND AND THE FULL MOUTH

WE come now to our third and final meditation in the 145th Psalm which will take in verses 15 to 21. Before we read, may we briefly review what we have previously said concerning this Psalm. In our first meditation we discussed the significance of the title. It is not *A* Psalm of David, but David's Psalm—it was his own. He delighted in this Psalm more than in any other for it expressed more perfectly the praise which was in his heart unto God. We also learned of a continuous word-of-mouth testimony, an unbroken line, whereby one generation praised the works of God to another and declared His mighty acts.

So as we come to the close of the Psalm, it is not surprising that David wrote, commencing with the 15th verse:

> "The eyes of all wait upon thee; and thou givest them their meat in due season.
> "Thou openest thine hand, and satisfiest the desire of every living thing.
> "The LORD is righteous in all his ways, and holy in all his works.
> "The LORD is nigh unto all them that call upon him, to all that call upon him in truth.
> "He will fulfil the desire of them that fear him; he also will hear their cry, and will save them.
> "The LORD preserveth all them that love him; but all the wicked will he destroy.
> "My mouth shall speak the praise of the LORD: and let all flesh bless his holy name for ever and ever."

David said, "Thou openest thine hand, and satisfiest the desire of every living thing." Incidentally, here is the solution to one of the great pressing problems of our day. Japan would not be in China this morning if it were not for a grasping hand. Japan's hand is open, but not to give, as is the hand of the Lord, described in this Psalm. Italy, France, and Germany would not be in Spain today if they had an open hand. We would not have problems in our own country that seem insurmountable and almost impossible of solution, if it were not for the grasping hand, either on the part of capital, or labor, or government. It may be a strange statement to make in this 20th century, but it is true—the world needs the open hand of God.

"THE EYES OF ALL WAIT UPON THEE . . ."

But let us look more closely at what the Psalmist wrote in this final portion of the Psalm. First, he said that the eyes of all wait upon God; second, that the Lord satisfies the desire of every living thing; again, that the Lord is righteous in all His ways, He is holy in all His works; and finally, He is nigh unto all them that call upon Him, who call upon Him in truth. That is enough to keep in mind for the moment. We will consider the balance later.

Note that none is exempt and that the Lord is able to meet the need and provide the solution for every one. The Psalmist has drawn a wonderful picture through the use of only seven words, "The eyes of all wait upon thee . . ." Let our sanctified imagination begin to work. Here God is upon His throne. About Him are the hosts of angelic beings—the cherubim, seraphim, the archangel, and the innumerable company of angels—the eyes of *all* wait upon the Lord. They receive their instructions from Him. They are obedient to His every word. Their life, their being, is bound up in Him. Look a little farther and see the host of the redeemed who are now present, or at home, with the Lord. There are Abraham, Isaac, Jacob, Moses, Elijah, Isaiah, David, Zechariah, Peter, James, John, Paul—we could go on, thousands, yea, millions, prominent and unheard of—all are gathered about the throne of God, and the eyes of *all* wait upon the Lord.

Come out of the heavens if you please, for a moment, and look at this massive creation, this world within worlds, this solar system which staggers the brains of men. What do we find? The eyes of all wait upon the Lord. They cover their courses in due season, never late, always on time. They perform with marvelous precision as they take their orders from their Creator—the eyes of *all* wait upon the Lord.

Now come down to earth itself. Here we see the grass and the flowers, the beasts of the field, the fish of the sea, and the birds of the air—the eyes of *all* wait upon the Lord. And finally there is man. Thank God, there are multitudes of men whose intelligence has not been dulled by the domination of sin, men who have been born again by the Spirit of God, whether in China, Japan, Russia, Germany, England, Switzerland, or the United States, whether they be black or white, yellow or brown—the eyes of *all* wait upon the Lord.

What a picture the Psalmist has given in just seven words, as the whole of creation waits upon the Lord. Note that it is the eyes that wait upon Him. There is expectancy, there is confidence, and there is adoration written in the expression of each eye. Above all, there is no failure on the part of God; for the Psalmist said, " . . . thou givest them their meat in due season."

Every high school student who has ever studied economics knows that there are three great principles in our economic structure, and in order to have a satisfied and contented nation there must be harmony among them. These three principles are production, distribution, and consumption. One day last week it rained in the Argentine—the wheat fields drank in the rain with joy—but there were some sad repercussions from that rain in the wheat pit at Chicago, the center of distribution. The price of wheat dropped a full five cents a bushel. There was gloom, there was disturbance, and there was disappointment, for the crowd that gathered about the pit was unable to keep prices up. The rain spoiled their plans. When we come to the homes of the land where consumption takes place, what a far cry from contentment, satisfaction, and a full mouth. Has God failed? A thousand times—NO. Has man failed? It is all too evident. Man mars everything he ever touches. Instead of an open hand, he has a grasping hand. Man is never satisfied until he gets all within his own control. Not so with the beneficent God, the Creator and Redeemer. He gives all their meat in due season. Do you want an example of it?

Let us go to a desert place in Bethsaida where there is a little spot of green grass. A multitude had gathered to hear our Lord. There were between fifteen and twenty thousand people present that day. They had been with Him all day as they had listened to Him speak and unfold the Scriptures. The close of the day drew near. The Lord was aware of the weariness of the multitude and that they needed to be sustained physically as well as spiritually. But His disciples, fearing trouble, urged Him to send the multitude away. Our Lord turned to Philip and asked, "Whence shall we buy bread, that these may eat?" Philip answered—We have only two hundred pennies; imagine feeding this multitude with two hundred pennyworth of bread! Andrew, Simon Peter's brother, broke in and said, "There is a lad here, who has five barley loaves, and two small fishes: but what are they among so many?" It was like a drop in the bucket compared to the ocean! Yet our Lord said—Make the multitude sit down, and give Me the five loaves and the two fishes. He took them, lifted up His eyes to heaven and gave thanks. Then He blessed the bread and brake it and gave to the disciples, and did likewise with the fishes. The disciples in turn brake the bread and gave to the multitudes; and while they divided and subtracted, the bread and fish were constantly being multiplied. After everyone had been fed, and well fed, our Lord ordered that nothing be wasted. He did not err, as did our much publicized Brain Trust, in destroying the provisions of a beneficent God. Rather, He said to His disciples, "Gather up the fragments that remain, that nothing be lost." God does not overlook even the crumbs. When the disciples had gathered them together they had twelve baskets full of fragments.

The eyes of all were upon our Lord that day and He gave them their meat in due season. The multitude recognized in Him a bread-giver and they wanted to make Him king. However, our Lord knew the fickleness of the mob. He knew what was in man and needed not that any should testify of man. He left them and went into a mountain Himself alone to pray. Our Lord knew that it was not because they had seen a miracle that they wanted to make Him king. He knew that the mob, which wanted to make Him king because their stomachs were full, would later cast their votes to crucify Him. But, the crowd made the mistake of thinking that our Lord was a bread-giver, whereas, in fact, *He was the Bread*. He said, ". . . my Father giveth you the true bread from heaven" and added, "I am the bread of God."

THE OPEN HAND

What a beneficent Creator God is. He opens His hand and satisfies the desire of every living thing. The open hand of God is a wonderful hand. He loved, and because He loved He gave His only begotten Son, and with His only begotten Son He has given us freely of all things. There is no change with Him. There is not even a shadow of turning with Him. There is no variableness with Him. He is the same constantly. He is always giving and pouring out.

If we desire to see the hands of God, let us look at the hands of Christ. He never touched anything but that His hands left a blessing. When He touched a blind man's eyes that man saw. When He touched the leper, He cleansed him of his leprosy. Wonderful hands! But look a little closer and we will see wound prints in those hands from the nails that were driven into the palms as He hung upon the cross. The print of the nails is a perfect portrayal of the wicked heart of man. Yes, Calvary was the divine atonement place, but it was also the place of human tragedy. We see in those wounds the love of God, and we revel in that love. But we see also our sin and the rebellion of our hearts.

But there is no unrighteousness with God. The Psalmist, with keen spiritual perception, observed the ways of God and wrote in the 17th verse, "The LORD is righteous in all his ways, and holy in all his works." At times it does not appear that God's ways are holy, but let us not forget that sin has marred the creation of God. He subjected all creation to vanity and the bondage of corruption because of man's sin. But He intends to gloriously liberate it. When we, therefore, see a riddle in the universe, let us remind ourselves that it is because of man's sin.

Now let us look at the 18th verse, which tells us to know how we can come close to God and how we can know Him. The Psalmist said, "The LORD is nigh unto all them that call upon him, to all that call upon him in truth. He will fulfil the desire of them that fear him; he also will hear their cry, and will save them." Notice that David had no objection to the use of the word *saved*. It is a good Biblical word, whether on the lips of a godly Jew or on the lips of a born-again Gentile.

Notice that the Lord is nigh unto *all* that call, to *all* that call upon Him in truth. There is a wide expanse in that statement and yet a narrow enclosure. The word *all* seems to embrace everyone. Salvation is to all—but the number dwindles as we discover that the word *all* is qualified by those who call upon Him *in truth!* Our Lord said that the Father was seeking worshippers, and that they who worship Him must worship Him in Spirit and in truth. It did not make any difference what color skin a man possessed or what his nationality happened to be, or his background. Man must worship God in Spirit and in truth. The Lord is nigh unto all that call upon Him. But if we are to call upon Him, we must call upon Him in truth. If we are to call upon God in truth, then we must call upon Him in Christ, for He said, "I am . . . the truth." There we have the exclusiveness of the Christian message, though it is all-embracing. That is the gospel. It is the message of salvation to those who receive. It is a message of condemnation to those who reject.

Notice also the prominence given by the Psalmist to the Lord. He is the center. He is the One who "does the doing." We are simply on the receiving end. He fulfills the desire of the heart. He hears the cry. He saves. In the 20th verse, David wrote, "The LORD *preserveth all* them that love him; but all the wicked will he destroy." There we have salvation and condemnation in one verse. We have preservation and destruction. Notice the basis upon which the preservation is offered. The Lord preserves all that *love* Him. Do we love God as He is revealed in Christ? If we do not, then something is wrong with us, for He is a lovable character. He was the "man of sorrows and acquainted with grief," yet He is the lovely One. He is the chief among ten thousand. He is the altogether lovely One.

Just as the Lord preserves all that love Him, losing none, so *all* the *wicked* will He destroy. None are exempt. If you do not now love Him, call now upon Him in Truth—receive His message, His Christ, come to know His salvation, and you will love Him just as multitudes have done.

Finally, in view of all this grace, what should be our attitude who have been redeemed, who have received Christ as Saviour? Could we do better than emulate David, "My mouth shall speak the praise of the LORD: and let all flesh bless his holy name for ever and ever."

Psalm One Hundred Forty-Six

HEAVEN'S LANGUAGE

T HE 146th Psalm, I am sure, will stir the emotions of every Christian. Like each of the remaining Psalms, it begins with the word *Halle-lujah*. In the King James version we have the phrase, "Praise ye the LORD," but when we turn to the Hebrew text we find only one word and that one word is *Hallelujah*. Here, therefore, are five *Hallelujah* Psalms.

People who use the word *Hallelujah* intelligently are those who possess a new life, an abundant life. This new life in Christ was imparted to them by the Holy Spirit who has taught them to use a language radically different from the language of this world. This new tongue has been called the language of Canaan. It is the language that is used in heaven. As long as we are going to heaven, might we not advisedly become accustomed to this language now? I am afraid some folk are going to find heaven a strange place. I refer to those who have trusted the Lord as their Saviour, but who have become indifferent to or have neglected the reading of the Word of God. They will not know the language. They will have to be instructed all over again, like some people I know who went to Paris this summer, but forgot to brush up on their French. The very first day in Paris they proceeded to order, in French, some chocolate ice cream. Their French must have been a bit rusty for the waiter brought hot chocolate instead! If we do not want an embarrassing experience like that when we get to heaven, we had better begin reading the Psalms of David and other portions of Scripture so that we will be able to use the language of heaven fluently when we get there. Let us now read the Psalm:

"Hallelujah. Praise the LORD, O my soul.

"While I live will I praise the LORD: I will sing praises unto my God while I have any being.

"Put not your trust in princes, nor in the son of man, in whom there is no help.

"His breath goeth forth, he returneth to his earth; in that very day his thoughts perish.

"Happy is he that hath the God of Jacob for his help, whose hope is in the LORD his God:

"Which made heaven, and earth, the sea, and all that therein is: which keepeth truth for ever:

"Which executeth judgment for the oppressed: which giveth food to the hungry. The LORD looseth the prisoners:

"The LORD openeth the eyes of the blind: the LORD raiseth them that are bowed down: the LORD loveth the righteous.

"The LORD perserveth the strangers; he relieveth the fatherless and widow: but the way of the wicked he turneth upside down.

"The LORD shall reign for ever, even thy God, O Zion, unto all generations. Hallelujah."

Does anyone wonder that David began this Psalm with the word *Hallelujah?* This past week I had a letter from a young man who stutters. Impediment of speech is a real handicap, but it is not a handicap in his case; it does not prevent him from praising the Lord. Indeed, you would go a long way to find a happier person—his letter literally burned with praise to God. His face expresses more quickly the thoughts of his heart than his tongue can speak them. As far as I know, he has no bank account. He is trusting in no man. He is trusting in the Lord. He looks to the Lord for sustenance, physically as well as spiritually, and he has great joy in the privilege that is his to do a real work of Gospel ministry in the giving out of tracts and booklets and in talking with seamen aboard ships. Who would think that a man who stutters could do work of that kind! I trust that relating this incident will effectively liberate some staid folk who have forgotten how to be joyful and happy and who think it is undignified to use the word *Hallelujah* or "Praise the Lord." Better get rid of your dignity and join that vast army of men and women who gather about the throne of God to praise Him for the indescribable joy of knowing His unspeakable gift, the Lord Jesus Christ, and who experience the unsurpassed peace of God in their hearts—a peace that passes understanding.

WHEN TO PRAISE GOD

Notice that David was not satisfied to wait until he got to heaven to praise God. In the 2nd verse, he said, "While I live will I praise the LORD: I will sing praises unto my God while I have any being." Now is the time to praise the Lord—while we are still here.

But there is also a word of exhortation from the pen of the Psalmist when he wrote, "Put not your trust in princes, nor in the son of man, in whom there is no help." In other words, don't be fooled even by a person who plays the part of Santa Claus, for vain is the help of man. "His breath

goeth forth, he returneth to his earth; in that very day his thoughts perish."
Whenever I hear or read the outbursts of those who think they are great
leaders of this world and who promise everything and anything, I think
of this passage, "His breath goeth forth, he returneth to his earth; in that
very day his thoughts perish." Better trust in God and place your confidence in Him. He never fails. We will also discover that the Psalmist
was correct when he wrote, "Happy is he that hath the God of Jacob for
his help, whose hope is in the LORD his God . . ."

Of course, the Psalms were written primarily for the godly Jew and
for the age in which they were composed—the reigns of David, Solomon,
and other great kings of Israel. But we learn from the New Testament
that these Psalms are intended for us as well; we can, therefore, learn something from them. Considering their Israelitish setting, it is not surprising
to find such a title of God as that which appears in the 5th verse and which
I quoted a moment ago. "Happy is he that hath *the God of Jacob* for his
help . . ." In the New Testament, the Lord is known as the God and
Father of our Lord Jesus Christ, while in the Old Testament He was known
as the God of Abraham, the God of Isaac, and the God of Jacob. In the
146th Psalm, David spoke of Him as the God of Jacob. If ever there was
a saint of God who was as crooked as a ram's horn it was Jacob. Even
his name revealed his character, for Jacob means "supplanter." By the
time God finished with him he not only made him a new man but He gave
him a new name, "Israel," which means "a prince with God." Because
Jacob was such a contrary rascal, there is no reason that we should try
to imitate him, though we must confess that more often than otherwise we
reveal the "Jacob" character rather than that of Israel. However, isn't it
good to know that a stumbling, faltering, unfaithful individual like Jacob,
who was constantly getting himself into trouble so that he had to outsmart
his associates as well as his enemies, could still have God so love him and
care for him as to delight to be named "The God of Jacob." We have no
desire to put a premium on sin, God forbid—the Apostle Paul disposed
of that subject once and for all when he wrote, "How shall we that are
dead to sin, live any longer therein?" What we are talking about is those
little eccentricities which most of us possess, that make us look like Jacob.
The Lord will never excuse us, even as He never excused Jacob, but neither
will He leave us nor neglect us. He will deal with us until we have been
delivered from the bondage of sin.

Commencing with the last phrase of the 7th verse certain works are ascribed to God. We learn that "The Lord looseth the prisoners: The LORD openeth the eyes of the blind: the LORD raiseth them that are bowed down: the LORD loveth the righteous: The LORD preserveth the strangers; (the LORD) relieveth the fatherless and widow. . . The LORD shall reign for ever . . . unto all generations."

OUR LORD'S SERMON

The first sermon that our Lord preached in his own native village of Nazareth is recorded in the 4th chapter of the Gospel according to St. Luke. All the townspeople were present at the synagogue. It was the Sabbath day, and our Lord entered into the synagogue as He was accustomed, for He had been brought up to attend the synagogue every Sabbath day. While in that place of worship there was delivered unto Him the scroll of the writings of the prophet Isaiah. Our Lord took it from the minister who passed it to Him, then He unrolled the sacred scroll until He found a certain portion. Then He began to read, "The Spirit of the Lord is upon me, because he hath anointed me to preach the gospel to the poor; he hath sent me to heal the broken-hearted, to preach deliverance to the captives, and recovering of sight to the blind, to set at liberty them that are bruised, to preach the acceptable year of the Lord." He stopped right there, in the middle of a verse, and then He closed the scroll and handed it back to the minister and sat down. The eyes of the multitude were fastened upon Him as our Lord began to say, "*This* day is *this* scripture fulfilled in your ears," and Luke says that all bare Him witness and wondered at the gracious words which proceeded out of His mouth. But they were offended in Him saying, "Is not this Joseph's son?" and they refused to receive Him or His message.

The very works that are ascribed to the Lord in this 146th Psalm are the things that are ascribed to the Messiah in the prophecy of Isaiah which our Lord read and which He said referred to Him. *He* loosed the prisoners, *He* opened the eyes of the blind, *He* raised them that were bowed down, *He* preserved the strangers, *He* relieved the fatherless and and the widows. What a wonderful Saviour is He! *He* loosed prisoners. If we have never been loosed, we are still prisoners. We are bound by sin. We have been led captive by the enemy of our soul. There is only one person who can deliver us and loose us. We cannot do it ourselves. The One who can is the Lord.

Psalm One Hundred Forty-Seven—Part One

FROM A BROKEN HEART TO A STARRY HEAVEN

THE fact that the last few Psalms begin with *Hallelujah* clearly indicates their character. These Psalms are not in the minor key, they are in the major key. They are like the closing strains of a great anthem, where all the various parts join together in one final burst of melody. The 147th Psalm also begins and ends with the word *Hallelujah*.

Before we consider the Psalm, I want to quote a line from the pen of Charles Haddon Spurgeon. He says, "The flow of the broad river of the Book of Psalms ends in a category of praise. Jehovah and happy praise should ever be associated in the mind of a believer."

So often I have found that people look upon religious profession as something that must be put on or affected and that which is put on is in the nature of a sanctified soberness that creates an impression that the religious man must be a somber, dignified, dirgeful, long-faced individual.

When the Israelites were in Palestine, enjoying the reigns of David and of Solomon, their music was pitched in the major key. They sang lustily and heartily. They were a happy people. They were happy because of their fellowship with Jehovah.

So a Christian, when he is in fellowship with the Lord, is a happy man. His heart contains a wellspring of joy. There is nothing sad about his countenance. He is full of life, full of joy; he has found happiness, and his song is in the major key and he sings *Hallelujah*.

Recently I learned that the word *Hallelujah* has been tabooed in Germany because it is a Hebrew word. Well, I thank God that as a child of Abraham "by faith" I love the word. I was born a Gentile in the flesh, I have been born again by the Spirit of God and am a member of a new body in which the middle wall of partition between Jew and Gentile has been broken down, and all are one in Christ Jesus.

The word *Hallelujah* means as much to a Christian as it does to any Jew. We love it, for it perfectly expresses, as perhaps no other word can do, the continuous praise of a heart that knows God.

But let's read the Psalm before making any further comment.

> "*Hallelujah:* for it is good to sing praises unto our God; for it is pleasant; and praise is comely.
> "The LORD doth build up Jerusalem: he gathereth together the outcasts of Israel.

"He healeth the broken in heart, and bindeth up their wounds.

"He telleth the number of the stars; he calleth them all by their names.

"Great is our Lord, and of great power: his understanding is infinite.

"The LORD lifteth up the meek: he casteth the wicked down to the ground.

"Sing unto the LORD with thanksgiving; sing praise upon the harp unto our God:

"Who covereth the heaven with clouds, who prepareth rain for the earth, who maketh grass to grow upon the mountains.

"He giveth to the beast his food, and to the young ravens which ..y.

"He delighteth not in the strength of the horse: he taketh not pleasure in the legs of a man.

"The LORD taketh pleasure in them that fear him, in those that hope in his mercy.

"Praise the LORD, O Jerusalem; praise thy God, O Zion.

"For he hath strengthened the bars of thy gates; he hath blessed thy children within thee.

"He maketh peace in thy borders, and filleth thee with the finest of the wheat.

"He sendeth forth his commandment upon earth: his word runneth very swiftly.

"He giveth snow like wool: he scattereth the hoar frost like ashes.

"He casteth forth his ice like morsels: who can stand before his cold?

"He sendeth out his word, and melteth them: he causeth his wind to blow, and the waters flow.

"He sheweth his word unto Jacob, his statutes and his judgments unto Israel.

"He hath not dealt so with any nation: and as for his judgments, they have not known them. *Hallelujah.*"

THE PRACTICE OF PRAISE

Mr. Spurgeon, whom I quoted earlier, suggests that the exhortation to praise may fitly be addressed to all those who owe anything to the favor of God. And who of us does not? Pay Him, we cannot, but praise Him, we will, not only now, but forever. "It is good," says Spurgeon, "to praise God, because it is right; good, because it is acceptable with God, beneficial to ourselves and stimulating to our fellows." Then he adds a comment which brings to my mind an illustration from an entirely different sphere. Spurgeon says that "the goodness of exercise is good argument with good men for its continual practice." In other words, if a man is to be efficient in the praise of God, and I use that word advisedly, he will not limit his visits to the house of the Lord to Easter Sunday and Christmas Day. Nor will he be content to go to church once on Sunday. Praise, perfect praise, requires continuous practice, just as a singer must continuously practise in order to perfect his or her singing.

Here's the illustration: I saw on the sporting pages of one of New York's great newspapers a picture of a young man in the act of kicking a football, and the picture was entitled "He never misses but still he practises." It was a picture of one of the members of a professional team who has a record of having gained 22 consecutive points after touchdowns. And despite that record, he was pictured diligently perfecting his skill in a workout for the next game.

I know some may not appreciate my bringing in an illustration from a football game in a Psalm program, but the Apostle Paul did not hesitate to do something of the same sort when he said:

"Know ye not that they which run in a race run all, but one receiveth the prize? So run, that ye may obtain.

"And every man that striveth for the mastery is temperate in all things. Now they do it to obtain a corruptible crown; but we an incorruptible.

"I therefore so run, not as uncertainly; so fight I, not as one that beateth the air:

"But I keep under my body, and bring it into subjection: lest that by any means, when I have preached to others, I myself should be disapproved."

If the Apostle Paul kept in training, I mean training for godliness, in order that he might not be disapproved by his Lord, how much more reason for us in this day to give attention to the practice of godliness and the exercise of prayer and praise in order that we may not be disapproved.

Dr. Ironside tells an amusing but pertinent story of how, when a young boy, he heard a certain preacher make the statement that "backsliding" always began at the knees. Dr. Ironside, as a little lad, thought of backsliding as lying on one's back on a sled, and he couldn't understand the preacher's figure of speech, or why it was that backsliding began at the knees. It didn't take him long to find out. When a Christian neglects knee exercise, when he forgets to pray, of course he forgets to praise—the two go hand in hand. Whenever there is a coldness developing in one's heart to God, it is because he has neglected praise.

As we will not be able to cover in this meditation more than a few verses of this Psalm let us limit ourselves to the following verses where the Psalmist said concerning the Lord:

> "He healeth the broken in heart, and bindeth up their wounds.
> "He telleth the number of the stars; he calleth them all by their names.
> "Great is our Lord, and of great power: his understanding is infinite."

There is a great sweep in these few verses—from the finite to the infinite. From the least man to the greatest of the constellations. It is a sweep from earth to heaven. No wonder the Psalmist said: "Great is our Lord, and of great power . . ." It is a wonderful link which he has forged between these two aspects of the character, power, and personality of God.

There are many who concede the power of God as revealed in creation. The scientist who takes his telescope and peers through the ceiling of the heavens to see those marvelous universes within universes is awed and amazed. He bows before the display of the magnificence of the infinite. But the God who placed all the universes in their respective orbits telleth the number of the stars. No scientist has ever been able to tell them, to count them, for that is the meaning of the word *tell*, just as we speak of a "bank teller" as the one who counts the money as it comes in and goes out. No scientist, by the aid of the most powerful telescope that has ever been invented, has been able to do more than to guess at the approximate number of the stars. As the telescope has become more perfected, men of science have been literally astounded by the myriads of stars within a given sphere, which is small compared with the entire heavens. Let us look at some of their "guesses."

Despite the plain statements of Scripture it was not until comparatively recent times that it was known that there were any more stars than could be seen and counted by the naked eye. Sir Arthur Eddington is of the opinion that one hundred thousand million stars make one galaxy, and one hundred thousand million galaxies make one universe. The number of stars in a universe, therefore, would be ten thousand trillion, or expressed in figures, 10 followed by 21 ciphers. That is equal to the number of drops of water in all the oceans of the world, or grains of fine sand sufficient to cover the whole of England and Wales to the depth of a foot, and each one of those stars comparable in size to our sun.

When some smart unbeliever tells us he does not believe the Bible, we should ask him, By what stretch of purely human imagination could the old Hebrew writers of the Bible have thought themselves justified in using a term which was not discovered to be true until three thousand years later?

But our Bible says—The Lord counteth the number of the stars, and He calls them all by their names. Do you think He forgets a single one? Some millionaire may forget about some of his investments and sometimes they turn up to surprise him and other times to plague him. But God is able to count the number of the stars and He calls them all by their names. Sometimes we run out of names, but the infinite wisdom of God provides a name for every one of the stars.

THE MINISTRY OF THE BROKEN HEART

There are some people who freely concede the infinity of God's wisdom. They are awed in the presence of a display of His power and yet they are unable to reconcile God's interest in a single human being. The God who can count the stars and give a name to each of them, who sees to it that they always revolve within their given orbit, certainly ought to be able to do as the Psalmist declared in this Psalm—He ought to be able to heal the broken hearted and bind up their wounds. I think that part of His ministry must give Him the greatest joy. I believe God is more occupied with the interests of a broken heart than He is with this massive universe. If He were not, then He would not have sent His only begotten Son into this world in order to reveal to us His own heart.

When one considers the words: "He healeth the broken in heart, and bindeth up their wounds" one cannot dismiss from his mind the story which our Lord Jesus Christ gave of the good Samaritan; and anyone acquainted with the Scripture readily recognizes Christ in the role of the good Samaritan.

What the Lord did in the story of the good Samaritan, He will do for us all, for—Great is our Lord, and of infinite power: and His understanding and wisdom is infinite. He has the panacea for the distressed spirit, the broken heart, and the wounded life. Why not stop trusting ourselves to quack physicians and place our case for eternity in the hands of the Great Physician?

SILVER-LINED CLOUDS

IN this meditation we shall attempt to cover the remaining verses of the Psalm, beginning with verse 6. I recall some time ago driving my automobile and coming to an intersection where some people were crossing. I stopped the car to give them the right of way. These pedestrians were evidently so surprised at such an experience that they looked up with a gracious smile and just as I was acknowledging it, I got a bump in the rear from one who was driving a car but evidently did not believe in courtesy. A few days ago I was driving with a friend when we were forced to weave in and out of traffic because of some careless parking, and in doing so my friend suggested that in New York, at least, if a man is to get anywhere, he has to look out for himself.

But in the 6th verse of the 147th Psalm we read, "The LORD lifteth up the meek: he casteth the wicked down to the ground," which reminds us of the passage which declares that "the meek shall inherit the earth;" but we would not guess in a thousand years that such was a fact. Look at China, for instance, or Spain, Germany, Italy and a number of other places of the earth. Certainly meekness does not characterize the nations of the earth today, nor their rulers, and as for inheriting the earth—leave it to the fellow who has a strong arm and a determined will and a bombastic voice. What's wrong? Is the Scripture incorrect? Why do not the meek inherit the earth? The answer, of course, is that this promise was never given to be applied generally to any age, but rather to a specific, particular age. Some day the meek shall inherit the earth and God will demonstrate that He does lift up the meek while He casts the wicked to the ground.

We need only to refer to one incident in the Old Testament for an example. It was said that Moses was the meekest man in the earth; but as for Pharaoh, his wickedness and his proud, haughty spirit were all too evident; yet it was Moses, the meek man, who gained the victory and it was the strong, wicked man who was cast to the ground.

But whatever the principle may be in the natural world, in the spiritual there can be no doubt that if we would be exalted, we must first be humbled, for the Lord resisteth the proud but giveth grace to the humble.

"GOD COVERETH THE HEAVENS"

The remainder of this Psalm is occupied with the great provisions which God has made in the earth for the benefit of beasts and birds, but primarily for the encouragement of Israel. When one looks at God's benefactions he cannot help but join with the Psalmist when he wrote, "Sing unto the LORD with thanksgiving; sing praise upon the harp unto our God. . . ."

Notice some of the things that God does, as stated in this Psalm. First, God covereth the heaven with clouds. When we see formations of clouds in the sky and when we see a beautiful sunset produced by the interplay of the sun upon the clouds, will we remember that they didn't just "happen"? They didn't come together without rhyme or reason or without power or personality behind them. Indeed, *God covereth* the heaven with clouds. By the way, that fact is interesting— I mean from a spiritual viewpoint. We all know that every cloud has a silver lining and the darkest cloud, if we were to go on the other side, would be illuminated with the glory of the sun. The aviator who rises above the clouds can see the silver lining. Why does God cover the heavens with clouds? I believe He does so in order to teach us that clouds may hide from us the face of the Lord, but they are only clouds. It is possible for the eye of faith to penetrate through the clouds to see the glory of God upon the face of the Lord Jesus.

Last Sunday upon completing the Psalm program my own heart was encouraged and my spirit was joyful as I mused afresh upon the wonders of God's grace, of how He who counts the number of the stars and calls them all by their names can heal the broken in heart and bind up their wounds! My spirit was as light as the air and my heart was filled with praise. But upon my return home, as I opened the door of our apartment, I noticed a telegram awaited me. Upon opening it I learned that the wife of a good friend of mine had passed away that morning. Immediately a cloud came over my spirit as I thought of the sorrow of heart of my friend and his family, caused by the loss of a devoted wife and mother. That man and that family found their spirits, on a glorious Lord's day morning, enveloped in the cloud of sorrow; but they also had the conscious joy that their loved one had gone into the presence of the Lord. And while they sorrowed, they did not sorrow as others who have no hope, for they believe even as did the Apostles and early Christians, that as Jesus died and rose again, even so also them which sleep in Jesus will God bring with Him, for we who are alive and remain unto the coming of the Lord shall not go before them which are asleep, for "the Lord himself shall descend from heaven with a shout, with the voice of the archangel, and with the trump of God: and

the dead in Christ shall rise first: Then we which are alive and remain shall
be caught up together with them" to meet the Lord in the air. The Apostle
Paul added "and so shall we ever be with the Lord." Finally, in closing
his message, Paul said, "Wherefore comfort one another with these words."

The clouds that envelop our spirits at times producing sadness and
sorrow of heart are common experiences of life. They are like the clouds
in the heavens which have been prepared by the hand of a beneficent
Creator. In the case of a Christian, these clouds have been prepared by the
hand of a loving, kind Father. If your spirit this morning is covered with
clouds, may you take courage in the knowledge that the One who covereth
the heaven with clouds is the One who prepares rain for the earth and
makes grass to grow upon the mountains. Those clouds are placed in the
heavens in order that they may draw up water and cast their refreshing
rain upon the earth that it may bring forth grass even upon the mountainside. So, if the Lord is pleased to allow the clouds of sorrow and disappointment to enter into our life, remember He also will cause the same
clouds to bring their refreshing rains, a benediction which will strengthen
others and provide encouragement to those who are distressed.

There is a wonderful passage on this subject in the New Testament,
in the 1st chapter of Paul's second letter to the Corinthians, where the
Apostle wrote, "Blessed be God, even the Father of our Lord Jesus Christ,
the Father of mercies, and the God of all comfort; Who comforteth us in all
our tribulation . . ." For what purpose? In order "that we may be able
to comfort them which are in any trouble, by the comfort wherewith we
ourselves are comforted of God. For as the sufferings of Christ abound in
us, so our consolation also aboundeth by Christ."

But look at the 10th and 11th verses of this Psalm where the Psalmist
said, "He (the Lord) delighteth not in the strength of the horse: he taketh
not pleasure in the legs of a man. The LORD taketh pleasure in them
that fear him, in those that hope in his mercy." Let us focus another portion of Scripture on this. In the Gospels, on several occasions we read that
God broke the silence of the heavens and said concerning the Lord Jesus
Christ, "This is my beloved Son, in whom I am well *pleased.*" The Father's
pleasure, therefore, was in His Son. It is not difficult to understand that,
for our Lord always did those things that were pleasing to His Father. He
was the perfect One. Isn't it remarkable, therefore, that it should be written that God does not take pleasure in the beauty of strength of a creature
like a horse, neither is His pleasure to be found in the perfect specimen of

physical man, for He taketh not pleasure in the legs of a man, but the very same pleasure which the Father found in His Son, He finds in those who fear Him and in those that hope in His mercy . That is a wonderful fact— God taking pleasure in you and me because we fear Him and hope in His mercy.

That brings up the question of our pleasure. In the case of the Lord, He delighted to do His Father's will. He found His pleasure in doing it. We who fear and hope in His mercy, where do we find our pleasure?

DARING TO TRUST GOD

We do not have time to comment specifically on the remaining facts found in this Psalm, which set forth the work of God on behalf of His people. Speaking of Jerusalem, the Psalmist said that God strengthened the bars of its gates and that He blessed Israel within it.

While I have on many occasions mentioned the fact that these Psalms refer specifically to Israel and that many of them apply to the reign of the Messiah, the King of kings, yet let us not forget that God's character never changes. He is the same, yesterday, today, and forever. What He was willing to do on the behalf of one people, He is willing to do on the behalf of all those who trust Him. Thus, when the Psalmist wrote concerning Israel and Zion, "He maketh peace in thy borders, and filleth thee with the finest of the wheat. He sendeth forth his commandment upon earth . . ." and so on, we must not limit the application of this principle to Israel exclusively.

If we carefully examine this Psalm we will observe a very interesting thing. There are no less than eleven verses out of a total of twenty which begin with the pronoun "He," and then there follow certain acts that God does. You see it is God who "does the doing." He giveth, He maketh, He sendeth, He casteth, He showeth, He dealeth. These are some of the things the Psalmist discusses in these verses.

It is a strange thing that man who trusts every other person and every other means, finds it difficult to trust God and the promises of God. It seems so hard for us to learn the lesson that we are to cast our burden upon the Lord and to rest assured that He not only can but does interpose His own power on the behalf of His own.

For example, these are hard times. Everyone in business will acknowledge that current problems are terrific. I think of a friend, a fine godly gentleman who has raised a splendid family. He has gotten along in years.

His hair is white. He has been a bulwark in Christian work and he is loved by a multitude. Yet that gentleman is facing a problem because of adversity in business. He finds himself bursting into tears frequently. What bothers him most is his testimony for the Lord. A cloud has enveloped his life at the moment, but do you think that the God who "giveth snow like wool . . ." who "casteth forth his ice like morsels . . ." will fail to come to his rescue, as He has come to the rescue of all who have dared trust Him? I doubt not. God never fails.

PSALM ONE HUNDRED FORTY-EIGHT

ALL THE WORLD TO PRAISE GOD

WE have a great Psalm to consider in this meditation. The 148th Psalm, like the others in the last group of Psalms, vibrates with praise. This Psalm also opens and closes with the word *Hallelujah*. No song that begins and ends with such a word can be devoid of praise. I am aware that there are those who cannot see the infinite beauties of God's revelation which are buried in these Psalms. Only last week my attention was called to an incident related by that great preacher, Dr. A. C. Dixon. Impressing his audience with the necessity for searching the Scriptures, he went on to say that "the Bible unsearched is a mine unworked" and that to learn the Word of God required diligent and persistent searching. Then he told of a man who died in an English almshouse who gave to his relatives an unproductive piece of land, so worthless that he did not have to pay taxes on it. The relatives searched it, and as a result they became millionaires. The pauper was rich without knowing it, and he was ignorant of the fact because he did not search his possessions. This Book, the Bible, is a mine of truth so precious that compared with it all the wealth buried in the earth is less than the few pennies of a pauper compared to the wealth of the richest man.

It is amazing how men neglect this mine, but the men who have searched it have found it to be the revelation of Almighty God. We should not allow any to tell us that it is only the ignorant and uneducated who believe the Scriptures. Someone recently said, "High scholarship is not incompatible with belief in the full inspiration and accuracy of Scripture," and to support this contention he quoted from the writings of Dean Burgon, one of the famous scholars of Oxford, who said, "I must be content with repudiating, in the most unqualified way, the notion that a mistake of any kind whatever is consistent with the texture of a narrative inspired by the Holy Spirit of God. The Bible is none other but the Word of God, not some part of it more and some part of it less so, but all alike the utterance of Him that sitteth upon the throne, absolute, faultless, unerring, supreme —(it is) 'The witness of God which He hath testified of His Son'!'"

That which impresses one upon a study of the Word and an examination of the lives of men and women who have believed it, is the great outstanding fact that here the ignorant and the learned, the wealthy and the poor, the man of high birth and the man of low birth, the master and the servant, the mistress and her maid, the mature man and the child—all find that which satisfies the craving of the human heart for a knowledge of God and the peace which passeth all understanding. It must be the Word of God!

This 148th Psalm is a perfect Psalm for a Sunday morning. Milton, in his "Paradise Lost," placed this Psalm on the lips of Adam and Eve as their morning hymn in the Garden of Eden. It reads:

> "Hallelujah. Praise ye the LORD from the heavens: praise him in the heights.
>
> "Praise ye him, all his angels: praise ye him, all his hosts.
>
> "Praise ye him, sun and moon: praise him, all ye stars of light.
>
> "Praise him, ye heavens of heavens, and ye waters that be above the heavens.
>
> "Let them praise the name of the LORD: for he commanded, and they were created.
>
> "He hath also stablished them for ever and ever: he hath made a decree which shall not pass.
>
> "Praise the LORD from the earth, ye dragons, and all deeps:
>
> "Fire, and hail; snow, and vapours; stormy wind fulfilling his word:
>
> "Mountains, and all hills; fruitful trees and all cedars:
>
> "Beasts, and all cattle; creeping things, and flying fowl:
>
> "Kings of the earth, and all people; princes, and all judges of the earth:
>
> "Both young men, and maidens; old men, and children:
>
> "Let them praise the name of the LORD: for his name alone is excellent; his glory is above the earth and heaven.

"He also exalteth the horn of his people, the praise of
all his saints; even of the children of Israel, a people
near unto him. Hallelujah."

Here is a Psalm which hardly requires a comment, for its message
is so apparent that all one ought to do is simply invite others to praise
the Lord. Yet we will venture to give a few suggestions regarding the
scope of this great Psalm.

THE PRAISE OF CREATED THINGS

Observe that the hosts within the heavens, those who are in the heights,
are called upon to praise Him together with all the angels, and all created
things such as the sun, the moon, the stars; the various forces of nature
such as fire, hail, snow, and vapors, even the mountains and hills and trees
are asked to join in this great burst of praise; the beasts and all the cattle
of the field, even creeping things and the fowl of the air; kings, princes,
judges, young men and maidens, old men and children are invited to praise
the name of the Lord.

There are many people who stumble over a portion of Scripture like
this, saying, How can trees praise God or how can dumb beasts join with
intelligent man in praising God? Wherein do fire and vapor have an articulate voice so that they can praise the Lord?

Let us not forget that on one occasion God used a dumb beast to
talk to a prophet. All God did was to loosen the cord of his tongue and
that enabled the ass to speak of the things he saw. The trees clap their
hands as their leaves touch one another and as the sweet music of the
wind blows through the forest. All things were made by our Lord and for
Him and all things praise Him. We have no imagination of what glory
possessed this original creation nor what glory was apparent in the Garden
of Eden in the reconstructed creation. All we can see is the remains of a
creation which has been subjected to bondage because of human sin. Yet
we can still see some of the beauties which must have existed in that glorious
age of creation as, for instance, when one picks up a rose. Yes, the thorns
are present, but there is also the beauty of the rose. One looks at the horse,
at the cattle, at the beasts of the field—and frequently finds an intelligent
look as if these dumb beasts want to express themselves so that we can
understand their thoughts. One can only lament the fact of man's sin and
remind his own heart that man has always marred whatever he has touched.
Man has left the impress of his sins and rebellion against God upon every-

thing with which he has come in contact, but the latent beauty is still there. How often have we heard a man, who has been suddenly transformed by the Spirit of God, say that even the grass appeared greener and the trees more beautiful and the flowers more fragrant, and that the heavens seemed to glitter more gloriously.

Dwight L. Moody used to tell the story of a friend whose wife was very fond of painting. For a long time that friend could never see any beauty in his wife's paintings. They all looked like a daub to him. One day his eyes troubled him, so he went to see an oculist. The man looked in amazement when the oculist said, "You have what we call a short and a long eye, and that makes everything a blur." The oculist gave him some glasses that just fitted him and then Moody's friend saw clearly. He understood for the first time why it was that his wife was so carried away with art. He then built an art gallery, and filled it with beautiful things, because everything looked so beautiful after he had had his eyes straightened out. Faithful Dwight L. Moody would bring his illustration to a climax by saying, "Now there are lots of people that have a long eye and a short eye, and they make miserable work of their Christian life. They keep one eye on the eternal city and the other eye on the well-watered plains of Sodom."

"HIS NAME ALONE IS EXCELLENT"

Commencing with verse 13 several reasons are given why all creation, man and beast, should join in praise of God. In this verse we read, "Let them praise the name of the LORD: for his name alone is excellent." We'll stop there. Do we know of any other name that abounds in excellency? Do we know of a single name of anyone who lived upon the earth against which there was not a single stain? Take the names of men prominent in this world today. Take the names of dictators, monarchs, or men of letters in the field of art and literature. We cannot mention a name about which there is no shadow. Go back into history. Napoleon, Bismarck, Alexander the Great, Nebuchadnezzar. Go on down the line to the very dawn of history, there is not a man in history against whom the finger of accusation cannot be pointed. Take the men of the Bible. Would we say that their names are "excellent"? Abraham was a liar, Noah was a drunkard, Moses lost his temper, Elijah was despondent, David was an adulterer and murderer, Peter denied his Lord. They were all men of like passions with us. Their names are great, but they are not excellent. But Jehovah possesses a name that *alone* is excellent. The Lord Jesus, the Jehovah of the Old

Testament, alone possesses excellency. How excellent is His name! The angel said, ". . . Thou shalt call his name JESUS: for he shall save his people from their sins." Simeon, when he saw the child, took Him up in his arms and blessed God, and said:

> "Lord, now lettest thou thy servant depart in peace, according to thy word:
>
> "For mine eyes have seen thy salvation,
>
> "Which thou hast prepared before the face of all people;
>
> "A light to lighten the Gentiles, and the glory of thy people Israel."

Wonderful, excellent name! At the name of the Lord Jesus, Satan wends his way as a defeated foe; at the name of the Lord Jesus, the heavens open to old men and children, young men and maidens, so that they may have the right to prayer and to a hearing before the throne of God. At the name of the Lord Jesus every knee shall bow and every tongue confess that He is Lord to the glory of God the Father. His name alone is excellent. He stands on the pages of history without a spot or wrinkle or criticism. No man has been able to accept His challenge, "Which of you convinceth me of sin?"

We are called upon to praise the Lord not only because His name alone is excellent, but because His glory is above the earth and the heavens. All things have been made subject unto Him, for, as the New Testament puts it, God hath

> ". . . raised him from the dead, and set him at his own right hand in the heavenly places,
>
> "Far above all principality, and power, and might, and dominion, and every name that is named, not only in this world, but also in that which is to come:
>
> "And hath put all things under his feet, and gave him to be the head over all things to the church,
>
> "Which is his body, the fullness of him that filleth all in all."

"THE HORN OF HIS PEOPLE"

Now all this is to be expected when one considers the majesty of God. Perfection must reside in the infinite God who has revealed Himself in Jesus Christ. That, to be true, is sufficient for praise and worship. But notice that the Psalmist closed this great hymn of praise by calling attention to the work of Jehovah on the behalf of His people, for we read, "He also exalteth the horn of his people, the praise of all his saints; even of the children of Israel, a people near unto him."

We do no injustice to Israel in making an application of this principle to the New Testament revelation. Israel will yet praise the horn of her salvation. Israel will yet sing this Psalm anew in her own land when her Messiah returns unto her. But we in this generation, Jew and Gentile alike, who have been redeemed by His precious blood, have been made nigh unto the Lord. In fact, the Scripture says, we are accepted in the beloved One. We are as near as He. Is this not sufficient for a continuous word of praise from the lips of a redeemed soul?

I am aware that some may say that this Psalm of praise may be splendid for those who are in a place of serene peace, but it is a far cry from reality when a life is encumbered with sorrows and cares. If we are Christians we have no right to foreboding. God help us to learn the lesson that Martin Luther did when in a time of much distress he, looking out of his window and seeing a blackbird sitting on a bough singing its very best in the midst of a pouring rain, said, "Why can't I, too, sit still and sing and let God think for me?"

PSALM ONE HUNDRED FORTY-NINE—PART ONE

A CONGREGATION OF DANCING SAINTS

WE come now to the next to the last Psalm in the Psalter. This is one more link in the final group of Hallelujah Psalms. Like the others in the chain, it opens and closes with the word Hallelujah.

This being Thanksgiving week, what better time is there to consider a Psalm of praise? I want to pass on a little thought which I received this past week. Speaking of what one ought to pay to God, a very gifted gentleman said, "The only coin which I can pay Him is that which comes from His own mint. I can give to Him only what He first gives to me, but I will try to pay Him in the only way He wants—by the praise of a devoted life; for if thanksgiving is good, thanksliving is better still."

While this 149th Psalm contains only nine verses and the proper place to begin is at the first verse, it is difficult to know where to begin and where to end our comments on this great Psalm. But let's read it:

"Hallelujah. Sing unto the LORD a new song, and his praise in the congregation of saints.

> "Let Israel rejoice in him that made him: let the children of Zion be joyful in their King.
>
> "Let them praise his name in the dance: let them sing praises unto him with the timbrel and harp.
>
> "For the LORD taketh pleasure in his people: he will beautify the meek with salvation.
>
> "Let the saints be joyful in glory: let them sing aloud upon their beds.
>
> "Let the high praises of God be in their mouth, and a twoedged sword in their hand;
>
> "To execute vengeance upon the heathen, and punishments upon the people;
>
> "To bind their kings with chains, and their nobles with fetters of iron;
>
> "To execute upon them the judgment written: this honour have all his saints. Hallelujah."

In this Psalm the chief singer mounts the rostrum and invites the "congregation of saints" to sing unto the Lord, to sing unto the Lord a new song, to sing His praises in the midst of the congregation. One of the great gifts that God bestows upon men is the ability to sing. Few have it— most of us do not. To be able to sing is to be able to lift one out of his environment and circumstances, to take the wings of the scales and mount up with a song. Songs are sung by *many* people and in *many* places. But here is a song which is sung in a specific place by a designated group of people. The singing is done by the congregation.

A short time ago in company with a friend I attended one of New York's *Fifth Avenue* churches. I remember being marvelously moved by the singing of the choir—much more so than by the message that was given by the minister. I do not, therefore, undervalue the singing of a choir, but there is nothing comparable to the singing from the heart by the entire congregation.

In this Psalm we find a congregation in which no one sings any lies, no voice is off key, and no heart out of tune. The congregation is composed of like-minded people called "saints." Some people would consider that a very queer congregation. Even the Bible calls saints a peculiar people, not in the sense of oddness, however, but from the viewpoint of value to the eternal God. So valuable are the saints to Him that it cost the blood of His own Son to purchase the congregation and to train the choir.

THE SONG

Now a word about this "new song," for we are aware that there are those who insist that this is a new day—we are living in a new world—we have new ideas about God, about sin, about salvation—we cannot sing the old songs—we must have new songs. This past week I have been greatly enjoying a rare book that was recommended to me by Dr. Scroggie. It is now out of print. I was particularly pleased to note that the copy I succeeded in getting came out of the library of that great English preacher, Dr. J. Stuart Holden. I came across a chapter in which the writer discussed the "all-sufficing Christ." He based his remarks on a text of Scripture appearing in the 6th chapter of St. John's Gospel where our Lord, seeing the mulitude departing because of the words He had spoken, turned to His bewildered disciples and asked, "Will ye also go away?" Peter answered, "Lord, to whom shall we go? Thou alone hast the words of eternal life." "In an age like this," said this interesting writer, "when doubt is everywhere, when remorseless hands are busy with attempts to pull down the most sacred and venerable beliefs, when the air is loaded with the *mephitic vapour of sceptical reasonings,* and I must breathe it whether I will or not; when covert sneers as well as open assaults on the faith meet me in books and magazines; when 'culture' ridicules me as being behind the age, and these repeated shocks produce an unsettlement within, loosening the stones of my faith-temple, if they do not overturn them altogether, so that I seem to have no longer the old comfort and the old certainty and the old rest that were once so sweet, I may surely ask myself, as Peter did, 'Supposing that I give up my faith in Christ, as I am tempted to do, what will I put in its place? Whom will I put in His place? What substitute for Christ and the old gospel will I find? What other message of peace will I get that will meet my need and satisfy it so well? If Christ is henceforth to be nothing to me (for if I doubt Him in one thing I must doubt Him in all), what other friend is there to whom, in my sin and sorrow, I can as safely and as comfortingly cling?' "

To every word of that quotation, the redeemed heart responds—Amen! But here let me read one more paragraph. "What other creed, what other gospel, what other hope will be so good for living men to live by, and dying men to die upon, as the old, long-tried, marvelous gospel of the crucified, risen, reigning Christ—that old gospel which still, in spite of a thousand attacks, is proving itself in the experience of tens of thousands of sinners, to be the only cure for a broken spirit, the only balm for a wounded conscience, the only pillow for a dying head—the gospel which is old as the very fall, yet new as the *new song* of the New Jerusalem—the gospel that tells me what I can never tire of hearing on earth, and what I shall know in heaven when it comes, *that Christ is enough for me, and that Christ is all?"*

You will find that the Scriptures frequently refer to this "new song." In the last book of the Bible we are given the substance of the song which will be sung by the redeemed congregation. It is found in the 5th chapter of The Revelation. The scene is in the heavens, the eternal God is on His throne. The Christ is presented as a Lamb, still bearing the scars of Calvary. He takes a book from the hand of God, which book is the title deed to earth's kingdoms. The great congregation gathers about the throne and falls down before the Lamb and they sing a new song saying, "Thou art worthy to take the book, and to open the seals thereof: for thou wast slain, and hast redeemed us to God by thy blood out of every kindred, and tongue, and people, and nation; and hast made us unto our God a kingdom of priests: and we shall reign over the earth."

The new song which will be sung in heaven is a song unto the Lord, extolling His worthiness and praising Him for His redemption which was accomplished by His blood.

There are some who refer to the gospel of the grace of God as a "bloody" religion. They do not like the blood. They prefer "the ethics of Jesus." They speak in admiring terms of the Teacher of Galilee, and the ethics of the Sermon on the Mount. But our Lord does not wish to be admired—He demands to be worshipped. We yield no ground to any man on "the ethics of Jesus" nor the teachings of the Sermon on the Mount—we rejoice in them, but if we did not first rejoice in the blood of the Lord Jesus "the ethics of Jesus" would condemn us to eternal banishment from the presence of the perfect God, whereas the blood of the Lord Jesus redeems us and enables us thereby to embrace the ethics of His teachings and discover in them the divine standards of life required of a regenerated believer. The man who despises the blood *here* will never sing about it *there.* The new song springs from the blood that was shed. One feels like saying, Hallelujah for the blood, for it ransomed me.

This new song in the 149th Psalm also has a part for Israel. The Psalmist said, "Let Israel rejoice in him that made him: let the children of Zion be joyful in their King." There is no room here for sadness or sorrow. The keynote is "rejoice . . . be joyful." The world has a Semitic problem on its hands today. It is a *hate* problem. Palestine is also a problem to the world. Israel is indigestible to the Gentiles. That is as God intended it to be, for God has put His seal upon Israel and designated

Israel as His earthly people. Israel will yet be the great proclamators of the glory of God and the kingship of the Messiah. In that day Israel again will "rejoice in him that made him . . ."

THE MUSIC AND THE DANCE

We have time to cover only the first three verses of our Psalm, so that for the remaining moments we shall consider the 3rd verse, which reads, "Let them praise his name in the dance; let them sing praises unto him with the timbrel and harp." Ah, say some—Then it is Biblical to dance and so the age old question of amusements is settled. Indeed it is! Even the "wise man" when he was out of touch with heaven said:

> "To every thing there is a season, and a time to every
> purpose under the heaven:
>
> "A time to be born, and a time to die; a time to plant,
> and a time to pluck up that which is planted;
>
> "A time to kill, and a time to heal; a time to break
> down, and a time to build up;
>
> "A time to weep, and a time to laugh; a time to mourn,
> and a time to dance."

But I can also hear some ask—Do you mean to say that *saints* dance, and that the Bible encourages them to do so? I do not know how anyone can read the 3rd verse of this 149th Psalm without experiencing a reverberation in his breast. The heart that is tuned to the melody of heaven vibrates with an emotion which is absolutely unique and which is sealed by the Spirit of God as being the enjoyment of the conscious presence of our Lord. But, wait a minute—I want to suggest something to those who think that this gives great license. Let's look at the kind of dancing that this Psalm discusses. Here is dancing by the congregation of the saints. Here is dancing accompanied by music played on the timbrel and harp, which music is praise unto God. Have you ever heard of a dance hall on this earth where one may dance to the tune of "Praise God, From Whom All Blessings Flow?" If you discover such a place, I'm sure you'll find there the liberty of the Spirit, but were you to step out on any dance floor and ask the orchestra leader to play a *hymn* he would look at you with a bewildered stare and say, "Buddy, you don't belong here. You're in the wrong place." And that would be putting his remarks mildly!

The Bible gives joys and pleasures to Christians, but those joys and pleasures are distinctly of a spiritual character, though they are often described by references to the experiences of the natural man. Heaven isn't a place for somber people. During the millennial reign of our Lord Jesus Christ on earth when Israel will be back in her home land, when the New Jerusalem will be above the old city, when there shall be close intercourse between heaven and earth, it will not be a time of sadness and sorrow—it will be a time of music and gladness. Some of us are enjoying that already!

May I clarify what I have just said, so that I shall not be misunderstood. My remarks regarding amusements were intended to be limited to those who have professed their faith in Christ. I am not a reformer, I am not interested in a crusade for "cleaner movies" or "more decent dancing," nor for a "whiter Gay White Way"—I am absolutely uninterested in the way this world amuses itself. As a Christian, my business is not to clean up this world; my business is something infinitely beyond that. I do not believe in reformation: I believe in regeneration by the Holy Spirit; not in changing lives, but in an imparting of the new life which is in Christ.

It is not our business to clean up "Sodom." Not that we do not hate vice and sin and civic corruption, but we know the futility of trying to clean up the natural man. Man must be born again ere he can enter the presence of God. And a born-again man, having been justified fully by God's grace, will endeavor by the power of God's Spirit to live soberly, righteously, and godly in this present evil world. Our business therefore as Christians is to shine as lights in this world, in the midst of a crooked and perverse generation and to hold forth the Word of life that we may rejoice in the day of Christ.

PSALM ONE HUNDRED FORTY-NINE—PART TWO

SINGING SAINTS ON SUFFERING BEDS

WE continue our meditation in the next to the last Psalm.
The first half of the 4th verse resembles the 11th verse of the 147th Psalm. At the time we dwelt on the 147th Psalm we considered the amazing suggestion that the Lord could take pleasure in any man or group of people. Now I happen to have a little youngster who has so completely filled my heart that with each passing day I wonder how I ever could have done without her. The smile on her face, the joyous expression that she manifests constantly, is enough to cause tears of joy to flow down one's cheeks. Of course I take pleasure in my child! If I, a human father, can take pleasure in my child, what pleasure must the Lord, who has an infinite capacity for love, take in His people. We stand amazed

at such love, by my little child does not stand amazed at my love. She takes it and rejoices in it.

In that connection I want to point out something that has been a great blessing to me. When John the Baptist inducted our Lord into His public ministry he cried, "*Behold* the Lamb of God, which beareth away the sin of the world." The word which John used and which is translated by our English word *behold* is an expression of amazement, so that what John cried was this, "Look—look in amazement—look in wonder—the Lamb of God, which taketh away the sin of the world." Well might we all stand amazed in the presence of Christ—the One who was always His Father's delight has become the Lamb of God foreordained before the foundation of the world—the Lamb for sinners slain. Now contrast this with another passage of Scripture written by the aged Apostle John in his first epistle, 3rd chapter, 1st verse, which reads, "*Behold*, what manner of love the Father hath bestowed upon us, that we should be called the children of God . . ." The word which is here translated *behold* is not exactly the same word that John the Baptist used. It is not a word intended to convey amazement or surprise; it is a word to indicate knowledge and assurance. It is translated many times in John's epistle by our English word *know*, so that what John literally wrote was this, "*Know* what manner of love the Father hath bestowed upon us, that we should be called the children of God." There is no amazement here—it is an invitation to enter into the joy of absolute assurance of God's love. No wonder that aged Christian who was once asked, "Do you not think it wonderful that the Lord of glory should stoop so low for you?" flashed back, "No, it was not wonderful for Him. It was just like Him."

TEARS OR PRAISE

It is strange how little we understand the grace of God. We seem to lose sight of the heart of God that was gloriously manifested in Christ. Isaiah referred to Him as the "man of sorrows." Why did He become the man of sorrows, if it were not for the fact that "He was to be the Man for sorrowers"? The weeping Saviour by His very tears should make us rejoice at the depth of love that God has for us. Some time ago I dealt with a gentleman, attempting to set before him God's plan of salvation. He was greatly conscious of his sin. His sin moved him to sobbing and tears, so that I was unable to present to him the goodness of God. I finally had to say, "As long as you cry I am unable to tell you what God has to say to you. Please cease your crying and read some passages of Scripture that I shall set before you."

Now tears are good. They may evidence a remorseful spirit and possibly a repentant heart. It is for that reason that someone has well said, "Tears for sin are good, but praise for the pardon of sin is better . . . It is good to fall at His feet daring no more than to touch His garment's hem, but it is better to go higher and lean upon His arm, and it is better still to sit down with Him even now in the heavenly places without any misgivings as to our right through His grace to be there. It is good to take the lowest place and be as the dogs that gather the falling crumbs, but better far to sit at our Father's table as in our Father's house and eat the children's bread." This is no time to mourn. "For the LORD taketh pleasure in his people . . ." It is a time to be glad and rejoice and allow Him to manifest His pleasure on our behalf.

But the Psalmist continued and wrote, "He will beautify the meek with salvation." We refrain from any reference to natural beauty, though we realize that some people assume that beauty can be purchased and put on as a thin veil so that some have suggested "beauty is only skin deep," yea, not even that deep! But the beauty of which the Psalmist spoke cannot be purchased in any beauty parlor. God is in the business of beautifying His people. The Psalmist said it is the meek whom God beautifies and that He beautifies them with salvation. Is it any wonder that the next verse reads, "Let the saints be joyful in glory: let them sing aloud upon their beds." But, you say, it is an easy thing for the saints to be joyful in glory. It is to be expected that heaven is a place where men rejoice. There will be no sorrow there. He shall wipe all tears away. Of course, the saints will be joyful in glory! But what can be said for the exhortation, "let them sing aloud upon their beds"? It is a great divide from the glory to a bed of pain, but here is a passage which bridges those two distant points. It is conceded that joy belongs to glory, but what is this—to sing aloud upon one's bed?

SUFFERING, SINGING SAINTS

Some most interesting letters which I have had recently from a number of our listeners have illuminated this truth to my mind. For instance, one letter came from a woman in Baltimore who thirteen years ago met with an accident which has forced her to be a shut-in ever since. Previously she was an active woman. She was standing on a safety platform about to get on a trolley to go to her home when the accident occurred which has made her a cripple for the rest of her life. With all that, her loved ones, including her husband, also have been taken away from her. But do you think that even such sorrow has deprived her of the joy of the Lord? She wrote that she goes about on what she calls her "kiddy-kar" which she described as a chair fastened to a platform, and on that platform are ball-bearing wheels. She rides from room to room attending to her home duties, which even include washing and ironing. That dear soul says she has one friend who is still with her and He has promised never to leave nor forsake her, and if she did not have that friend she could not bear all the burdens of this life. Of course, that friend is our Lord. She adds, "I do thank God that I can do what I can," referring to her ability to get around on her "kiddy-kar." So, you see, God's people can and do sing aloud upon their beds.

There is a woman living in Australia who for more than forty years has been a shining example of this principle. She has been a hopeless invalid—without arms, having only one leg—she has suffered frightfully and, while physicians have administered to her with great sympathetic helpfulness, they have been unable to arrest her disease without amputation of one leg and both arms. That dear soul, not satisfied to lie in bed and be ministered unto by others continuously, had someone arrange a contrivance whereby she is able herself to administer her medicines and can write on a contraption that is the most unique thing I have ever seen pictured. From that bed of pain have gone forth reams of letters to encourage believers everywhere, and some of God's choicest saints have found that bedroom the very vestibule of heaven, for that saint, by God's grace, sings aloud upon her bed.

Now look at the 6th verse, where the Psalmist wrote, "Let the high praises of God be in their mouth, and a twoedged sword in their hand." That is a sufficient equipment for any life. The Bible pictures the life of a Christian in this world as a warfare and the individual Christian as a soldier of Jesus Christ. The best kind of equipment for a soldier in the Lord's army is to have the high praise of God pour from his mouth and to have a two-edged sword in his hand. The Christian has only one offensive weapon. It is not argumentation. It is not his own wisdom nor his own powers of persuasion, neither is it his strength, for we wrestle not against flesh and blood, but against principalities and powers and spiritual wickedness in the high places. The weapon that a Christian has is "the sword of the Spirit." It is the Word of God. It is referred to in the Scriptures as sharper than any two-edged sword—powerful and quick. It pierces even to the dividing asunder of soul and spirit, joints and marrow, and is a discerner of the thoughts and intents of the heart.

GRACE AND JUDGMENT

We are not unmindful that it is and shall be the prerogative of God's people "to execute vengeance upon the nations, and punishments upon the people; to bind their kings with chains, and their nobles with fetters of iron; to execute upon them the judgment written," as the Psalmist declared in this Psalm. But that exercise of vengeance, that binding of those whom the Bible designates as the enemies of Christ, that execution of judgment, is not a resident force native in the individual Christian's life. It is a designated force which has been committed to him by God and will be exercised when he as an Associate Justice, with his Lord as Chief Justice, sits upon the great white throne and judges the world for its rejection of Christ and its sin against God. "This honour have all his saints"!

Let me make this a little clearer. The hour in which we live is the hour of God's grace. The born-again Christian is called upon to proclaim the grace of God. That grace tells about a Saviour who put away sin by the sacrifice of Himself, who thereby has brought salvation which is available to all men. And it teaches that upon receiving the Saviour, there is imparted unto us a new life by the Holy Spirit which enables us to "live soberly, righteously, and godly, in this present world; looking for that blessed hope, and the glorious appearing of the great God and our Saviour Jesus Christ . . ." Grace gives us no right *now* to express judgment or to execute vengeance. But as all judgment has been committed by God into the hands of His Son, He has ordained that the saints will, together with Him, judge the world of men and of angels. In the 6th chapter of 1st Corinthians the Apostle Paul wrote, "Do ye not know that the saints shall judge the world? . . . Know ye not that we shall judge angels?" We learn from the 20th chapter of the last book of the Bible, The Revelation, when that judgment is to take place.

It is a very solemn thing to consider that as Christians we shall sit with our Lord Jesus Christ upon the Great White Throne and judge the world. We with our Lord will examine the books containing the record of every man's life and the Lamb's book of life containing the list of names of all those who have voluntarily come under the shelter of the shed blood of our Lord. Every man who will stand before that throne and whose name is not found in the book of life will be cast into the lake of fire. I am not here to argue with any or give my views on the matter of the lake of fire. The language is too explicit to require any explanation by me. It is the final status of the unbelieving, Christ-rejecting world. I would much rather be on the throne with my Lord in the exercise of judgment than before the throne receiving the judgment of a condemned soul. No man will have a chance then to change his status.

Whether we are saved or lost—in heaven or hell—is determined before we leave this world, not after death—all commonly held notions to the contrary notwithstanding. That notion which so many people have of a general judgment day, when all men of all stripes will stand before God, and if their good deeds overbalance their evil they will enter into life and if not, they are lost, sounds religious, but it is *absolutely un-Biblical*.

PSALM ONE HUNDRED FIFTY

THE FINISHED SYMPHONY

THE mere reading of the 150th Psalm will thoroughly convince one that here is a great Psalm and a fitting climax to the great collection of Psalms. It seems as if the divine Spirit possessing the writer of the Psalms took up all the threads of emotions, experiences, and revelations which are found in the preceding Psalms and united these in one Psalm in order that there might be that cumulative and complete burst of praise which is due the eternal God. But before we comment any further, let us read the Psalm:

> "Hallelujah. Praise God in his sanctuary: praise him in the firmament of his power.
>
> "Praise him for his mighty acts: praise him according to his excellent greatness.
>
> "Praise him with the sound of the trumpet: praise him with the psaltery and harp.
>
> "Praise him with the timbrel and dance: praise him with stringed instruments and organs.
>
> "Praise him upon the loud cymbals: praise him upon the high sounding cymbals.
>
> "Let every thing that hath breath praise the LORD. Hallelujah."

A good friend who has been listening to our program regularly wondered what further comments might be made on the subject of praise. He suggested that he thought we had exhausted all that could possibly be said on that subject in our comments on the preceding Psalms which form the final cluster of *Hallelujah* Psalms in this collection. But I am sure that we will recognize that there is much yet to be said on this matter of praise.

PRAISE IN THE SANCTUARY

In the first place the Psalmist said, "Praise God in his sanctuary . . ." and second, "praise him in the firmament of his power"; then there follows that for which we are to praise Him, and an invitation to the various component parts of a great symphony orchestra to join in this song of praise. We will consider these individually.

First, let us consider the place where prayer or praise is wont to be made. We are to praise God in His sanctuary. There is no higher expression of service which a man can render to God than the act of worship. Man is a being created for worship. There never has been found a race of men which lacked this characteristic. Man is the only earthly creature that God made with this quality. God created man for His own enjoyment and that enjoyment is expressed in man's worship of God and his fellowship with Him. But what is worship? Sometimes it is expressed in the form of prayer and at other times in the singing of hymns; again in the pouring out of the heart and its affections upon the person of God, which at times may not be audibly expressed, but it may be that overwhelming consciousness of the grace of God that causes man to love Him and to enjoy His fellowship. It may express itself in a preaching service where the Word of God is exalted and the perfections and glories of Christ are presented. But above all, worship is praise and adoration unto God for His infinite grace and mercy.

Now God decrees that there is only a certain class of people who have the right to come into His presence and worship Him. That is so clearly apparent from a reading of the Scriptures that it hardly needs to be emphasized. In the Old Testament, the Israelites had the right of worship and there was a chosen seed among Israel which had the right to participate in the ordinances of worship, and finally there was one man chosen from among this tribe who, as the high priest, alone had the prerogative to enter into the very Holy of holies, there to make atonement for the sins which the children of Israel had committed during the preceding year. Controversy has raged over this exclusiveness of worship. It is to be seen for instance in our Lord's dealings with a Samaritan woman, the record of which is found in the 4th chapter of St. John's Gospel. This woman finding herself in an embarrassing position because of her sin, sought to sidetrack the conversation into religious lines. That is a pastime at which many are adept when the powerful conviction of the Holy Spirit makes them aware of their sinfulness. They try to calm that annoying status by seeking a discussion on religion rather than by acknowledging their sin and confessing Christ as their Saviour from sin. So this Samaritan woman discussed the subject of worship. She recognized in our Lord a Jew, so she said—Our fathers; that is, we Samaritans, tracing our ancestry back to Jacob, have maintained that the place for worship is at Mount Gerizim, in the land of the Samaritans, and we worship there, but you Jews say that in Jerusalem is the place where men ought to worship. Our Lord answered:

> "Woman, believe me, the hour cometh, when ye shall neither in this mountain, nor yet at Jerusalem, worship the Father.
>
> "Ye worship ye know not what: we know what we worship: for salvation is of the Jews.
>
> "But the hour cometh, and now is, when the true worshippers shall worship the Father in spirit and in truth: for the Father seeketh such to worship him.
>
> "God is a Spirit: and they that worship him must worship him in spirit and in truth."

Thus you see that in this conversation a transition is revealed by our Lord. He set His seal upon Jerusalem as the *place* of worship up until that hour. He acknowledged that Israel had the exclusive right of worship; that there was only one place at which God would accept worship, and that was at the temple in the city of Jerusalem. But our Lord said that now that time had passed, and it is now no longer a question of the place of worship: it is a question of the attitude. Irrespective of where a man may be—if he worships in Spirit and in truth, the worship is acceptable to God. Our Lord was not talking about the human spirit, He was referring to the Holy Spirit. When He talked about truth He was not speaking in abstract terms, He was talking of the personification of truth which He Himself is, for He said later, "I am the way, *the truth*, and the life: no man cometh unto the Father, but by me." So, while there has been a change whereby it does not make the slightest difference *where* a man might be worshipping, it is still true that worship is limited to an exclusive company of people—all who worship God in Spirit and in truth; in the Holy Spirit and in Christ.

This message, I realize, will disturb some people, but please remember that if it disturbs you your controversy is not with me, your controversy is with the Lord. I have merely expressed what is contained in His Book. I would not dare have the effrontery to intrude my own opinions on the subject of worship upon anyone. The One worshipped is the only One who has the right to set His own laws. It is my business as a believer in our Lord Jesus Christ to tell you exactly what the Word of God teaches.

THE TRUE SANCTUARY

The Psalmist wrote, "Praise God in his sanctuary . . ." You cannot praise Him in any other place. The sanctuary was formerly on earth. The temple in Jerusalem our Lord called "my Father's house" until He left it for the last time, and then He said concerning it, ". . . your house is left unto you desolate." I know that we speak of a church building as a sanctuary, but there is not the remotest justification in New Testament Scripture to sustain such a viewpoint. The sanctuary previously was in Jerusalem. When the leaders of Jerusalem rejected the Christ of God the sanctuary became *their* house, not the Father's house. There is no longer a sanctuary on earth. There is only one sanctuary in which God accepts the praise of His people, and that sanctuary is in the heavens. I will prove it by the Scriptures.

In the Epistle to the Hebrews the writer of that letter presents a contrast between the Aaronic priesthood and the priesthood of Christ. In the 8th chapter of his letter he presents a consummation of all that he had written previously by saying, "Now of the things which we have spoken this is the sum: We have such an high priest, who is set on the right hand of the throne of the Majesty in the heavens; a minister of the sanctuary, and of the true tabernacle, which the Lord pitched, and not man." In the 9th chapter of that same letter he declared that under the old covenant there were ordinances of divine service and an earthly sanctuary, which he described, but he added, "Christ being come an high priest of good things to come, by a greater and more perfect tabernacle, not made with hands, that is to say, not of this building; neither by the blood of goats and calves, but by his own blood he entered in once into the holy place, having obtained eternal redemption for us." We also learn that if our Lord were on earth He could not be a priest, for He was not of the tribe of Levi, but now He hath obtained a more excellent ministry than they because He is the mediator of a better covenant which was established upon better promises. Therefore, Christ is now entered into the holy place, the heavenly sanctuary where He as the Great High Priest intercedes for His people and presents to God the worship of His people. It is for that reason that Paul declared that we who were dead in trespasses and sins, who have been quickened by faith in Christ—God hath raised us up together and has made us sit together in heavenly places in Christ Jesus. Thus this heavenly place in which the believer now sits is the heavenly sanctuary. And it is there that praise is acceptable to God—within His sanctuary. Only the man who has been redeemed from his sin and justified by faith in Christ is a worshipper. He has not that right in himself, nor by virtue of his own perfection, but because of the perfection of Christ and the one sacrifice which our Lord made at Calvary. I trust that I have not been too involved in my language in describing the worship and the worshippers. I must add that there is nothing in this world that is so blessed, so peaceful, and so joyful as the worship of the Lord in His sanctuary.

The Psalmist continued and wrote, "praise him in the firmament of his power." Now that word "firmament" is a word which some people stumble over. It means *expanse*. I was looking at a Hebrew-English translation of this verse and I noted that it reads, "Hallelujah. Praise God in his sanctuary: praise him in the expansion of his power." May I put a New Testament scripture alongside of this Old Testament reference which will throw a flood of light on what is meant by *"the expansion of God's power."* In the letter to the Romans the Apostle Paul declared, "I am not ashamed of the gospel of Christ: for it is *the power of God* unto salvation to every one that believeth; to the Jew first, and also to the Gentile." The expanse of His power is the gospel of Christ—power, wonderful power, the very power that broke the jaws of death, raised our Lord Jesus Christ from the dead, caused Him to ascend into the very presence of God, and traverse in a flash a distance that is impossible to comprehend. That power, quiet in its working but terrific in its accomplishments, is expressed in the life of each individual who embraces the gospel of Christ. We therefore praise God in His sanctuary and we praise Him in the gospel. We praise God in His sanctuary when we worship Him. We praise Him in the gospel when we believe it, when we preach it, when we present it, when we live it.

THE SYMPHONY

The Psalmist continued, "Praise him for his mighty acts: praise him according to his excellent greatness." The final section of this Psalm presents a great symphony orchestra giving forth its praise to God. There is the trumpet, the psaltery and harp, the timbrel, the dance, stringed instruments and organs, loud cymbals and high sounding cymbals. These instruments played by sanctified hands are asked to praise God, which brings us to a great subject—the place of music in the worship of the Lord. I wish we had hours to discuss this subject, but we just have a few moments. Music was created by God. Musical instruments were made by man, but only because God had given to man a pair of hands and endowed him with the gift of heart and mind so that his hands could make a musical instrument, and of course it should be played in the worship of the Lord. These hands, which Bishop J. Taylor Smith called "the most wonderful tools in the workshop of the world," did not just evolve—they were made by God to praise God. I am aware that Satan and the natural man have taken these musical instruments and the great gift of music to use to their own debasement. That, however, does not deprive the Christian of the enjoyment of musical instruments and musical gifts, and they should be and can be used in the worship of the Lord God. If they cannot, then the 150th Psalm has no place in our Bible.

Someone has well said that there will be no music in hell unless you can call moaning, whining, and dirgeful expressions, music. Music belongs in heaven and in heaven there will be musical instruments—these great gifts will there be used for the glory of the Lord.

Now let us look at the last verse where the Psalmist wrote, "Let every thing that hath breath praise the LORD, Hallelujah." It is difficult for us to imagine a period when everything will praise God. In the animal kingdom there is the fear of man. Man himself is a creature of fear. He does not trust himself, and it is self-evident why he cannot. Everything we see round about us is a contradiction of this passage of Scripture. Whenever sin enters into the scene it brings contradictions; it brings a discordant note. But just as our Lord Jesus Christ conquered Satan on the cross and put away sin by the sacrifice of Himself, so when He returns, all creation, man and beast, will join in the praise of God.

I was greatly thrilled this week to receive a fine old volume on the Psalms from my friend, Dr. A. C. Gaebelein, who has been following these studies over the air whenever he has been near a radio. Dr. Gaebelein is beyond a doubt one of the giants of this generation in the exposition of Scripture. He presented me with this volume as a fitting gesture in coming to the last of the Psalms. It is a book printed in 1780, but first published in 1696. It is a version of the Psalms of David fitted to the tunes which were used in the churches of England. It was presented to His Majesty, the King of England, by Dr. Brady, a British Chaplain, and Mr. N. Tate, poet laureate in that year. Glancing through it I came to the 150th Psalm. I would like to read the Psalm as it appears in that book—

> "O praise the Lord in that blest Place
>   from whence his Goodness largely flows:
> Praise him in Heav'n, where he his Face
>   unveil'd in perfect Glory shows.
> Praise him for all the mighty Acts,
>   which he in our Behalf has done;
> His Kindness this Return exacts,
>   with which our Praise should equal run,
> Let the shrill Trumpet's warlike Voice
>   make Rocks and Hills his Praise rebound;
> Praise him with Harp's melodious Noise,
>   and gentle Psalt'ry's silver Sound.
> Let Virgin Troops soft Timbrels bring,
>   and some with graceful Motion dance;
> Let Instruments of various String,
>   with Organs join'd, his Praise advance.
> Let them who joyful Hymns compose,
>   to Cymbals set their Songs of Praise;
> Cymbals of common use, and those
>   that loudly sound on solemn Days.
> Let all, that vital Breath enjoy,
>   the Breath he does to them afford,
> In just Returns of Praise employ:
>   let ev'ry Creature praise the Lord."

This 150th Psalm could not better end than with the word *Hallelujah*.

CONCLUSION

A SWAN SONG ON THE PSALMS

WITH today's address I shall have given 204 radio messages on the Psalms. We began our broadcasts on February 18th, 1934. It was just like our good Lord to have arranged for Dr. Ironside, the beloved pastor of the Moody Memorial Church in Chicago, to be in New York at the time and he gave the first broadcast.

I do not know whether any preacher at any time ever gave a series of messages on the Psalms covering every one of them, but I think that this is the first time since they were written that a *broadcast* has been given on each of the Psalms.

Each message has taken twenty minutes to deliver. I have, therefore, spoken sixty-eight full hours on the Psalms. That is a lot of speaking, even for this very talkable age! I have never given less than four hours' study and preparation for each Psalm message. Frequently I have given twice that amount of time so that, apart from a background of study over the years, I have actually devoted more than one thousand hours during the past four and a half years, all concentrated on a study of the Book of Psalms.

There are 150 Psalms. It should be supposed that having spent one thousand hours of study in the Psalms one ought to know something about them, but I must confess that I know less about them now than when we began this series. At least, I thought I knew more when I started. As I have reviewed these Psalms, and particularly the messages I have given, it must be said that we have simply begun to scratch the surface. One kind gentleman who listens regularly to our broadcasts suggested that we begin an entire new series of studies in the Psalms, starting with Psalm 1 and going right through the book again. Well, that would be most interesting and, I am sure, it would prove profitable, for there are many, many things that we have not even so much as touched upon in our broadcasts on these wonderful, inspired hymns.

But let us not forget that the Book of Psalms is just one of the sixty-six books of the Bible. What a book is the Bible! Of one thing I am sure —I have received immeasurable blessing in my own soul through this series of meditations and judging from the letters received throughout the years many have been greatly blessed with these meditations. It is utterly impossible to find a book of any date, but particularly of antiquity, that has held the interest of humans as the Bible. It is another of the many evidences that this book is the inspired Word of God. It is living, and sharper than any two-edged sword.

It is also true, I think, that the people of God in periods of distress have gone to the Psalms more often than to any other book of the Bible. I do not know the author of these few lines, but whoever he be, he knew his Psalms, for he wrote:

> "Heavier the cross, the heartier prayer;
> The bruised reeds most fragrant are.
> If wind and sky were always fair,
> The sailor would not watch the star;
> And David's Psalms had ne'er been sung
> If David's heart had ne'er been wrung."

Martin Luther in his commentary on the Book of Psalms wrote: "All other books give us the words and deeds of the saints, but this gives us their inmost souls. It is 'the little Bible.' "

THE BEST KNOWN PSALM

Of course, the best known Psalm is the 23rd Psalm. When quoted by one whose heart has been the dwelling-place of the Lord it lifts that Psalm into a place of preeminence. My friend, Dr. Harris Gregg, I think, can quote the 23rd Psalm more feelingly than any other man I know.

"The LORD is my shepherd; I shall not want.

"He maketh me to lie down in green pastures: he leadeth me beside the still waters.

"He restoreth my soul: he leadeth me in the paths of righteousness for his name's sake.

"Yea, though I walk through the valley of the shadow of death, I will fear no evil: for thou art with me; thy rod and thy staff they comfort me.

"Thou preparest a table before me in the presence of mine enemies: thou anointest my head with oil; my cup runneth over.

"Surely goodness and mercy shall follow me all the days of my life: and I will dwell in the house of the LORD for ever."

There are only two persons in the 23rd Psalm apart from a slight intrusion by a group on the outside whom David called his "enemies." The Psalm is devoted exclusively to the Lord and to David, a man walking arm in arm with his Lord. Those of us who have had that experience acknowledge that it is the most blessed of any of the experiences of life. Think what it means that a man can look up into the face of the Lord and say, "The LORD is my shepherd . . ."—to have Him always as his guide even though he be called to go through the valley of the shadow of death— to have a hope steadfast and sure beyond the grave—to have a house there even if he has only a tenement flat here. What a fortunate person is the one who can really quote the 23rd Psalm from the bottom of his heart. May I ask, Do you, individually, know the Lord so personally that you can say "The LORD is my shepherd"?

A GREAT PSALM

But there are other Psalms that hold a warm place in my heart. If I were called upon to single out one Psalm above all others to leave with you as my closing testimony to this series of Meditations in the Book of Psalms I think I would choose the 84th Psalm where David said:

"How amiable are thy tabernacles, O LORD of hosts!

"My soul longeth, yea, even fainteth for the courts of the LORD: my heart and my flesh crieth out for the living God.

"Yea, the sparrow hath found an house, and the swallow a nest for herself, where she may lay her young, even thine altars, O LORD of hosts, my King, and my God.

"Blessed are they that dwell in thy house: they will be still praising thee. Selah.

"Blessed is the man whose strength is in thee; in whose heart are the ways of them.

"Who passing through the valley of Baca make it a well; the rain also filleth the pools.

"They go from strength to strength, every one of them in Zion appeareth before God.

"O LORD God of hosts, hear my prayer: give ear, O God of Jacob. Selah.

"Behold, O God our shield, and look upon the face of thine anointed.

"For a day in thy courts is better than a thousand. I had rather be a doorkeeper in the house of my God, than to dwell in the tents of wickedness.

"For the LORD God is a sun and shield: the LORD will give grace and glory: no good thing will he withhold from them that walk uprightly.

"O LORD of hosts, blessed is the man that trusteth in thee."

If you are able to say with the Psalmist, "The LORD is my shepherd," can you also truthfully say, "I had rather be a doorkeeper in the house of my God, than to dwell in the tents of wickedness," and can you also qualify that statement by saying, " . . . a day in thy courts is better than a thousand"?

We have all had interesting days in our lives. We call them Red Letter days; they stand out; they are milestones in our lives as we journey the pathway of life; we recall them with great pleasure—but can we say, looking into the face of God, "For a day in thy courts is better than a thousand"? If we can, then we know the secret of that fellowship which is available to every man, woman, and child who has received Jesus Christ as his or her Lord and Saviour.

A WORSHIP PSALM

But again, where is it possible to find a clarion call to worship as that which is found, for instance, in the 103rd Psalm? where David said:

"Bless the LORD, O my soul: and all that is within me, bless his holy name.

"Bless the LORD, O my soul, and forget not all his benefits:

"Who forgiveth all thine iniquities; who healeth all thy diseases;

"Who redeemeth thy life from destruction; who crowneth thee with lovingkindness and tender mercies;

"Who satisfieth thy mouth with good things; so that thy youth is renewed like the eagle's.

* * * *

"The LORD is merciful and gracious, slow to anger, and plenteous in mercy.

"He will not always chide: neither will he keep his anger for ever.

"He hath not dealt with us after our sins; nor rewarded us according to our iniquities."

Now notice what follows:

"For as the heaven is high above the earth, so great is his mercy toward them that fear him.

"As far as the east is from the west, so far hath he removed our transgressions from us.

"Like as a father pitieth his children, so the LORD pitieth them that fear him."

THE PENITENTIAL PSALM

But if you were to ask me what I consider to be the most remarkable statement in all the Word of God I would have to answer that it is found in the 51st Psalm. It is to this Psalm my own heart has often gone to find a message of exceeding joy. It is the Psalm to which the sinning saint has frequently made pilgrimage. He can so easily put himself into the Psalm. There is no cry of the human breast comparable to the cry of this 51st Psalm. Someone has said, "Rather be Atlas with the world on your shoulder, than David with God's hand on his conscience." May I ask, Who amongst us can honestly say we have never had the hand of God rest upon our conscience? What a privilege, therefore, to go into the very presence of God and cry out to Him in the language of the 51st Psalm.

"Have mercy upon me, O God, according to thy lovingkindness: according unto the multitude of thy tender mercies blot out my transgressions. Wash me throughly from mine iniquity, and cleanse me from my sin."

Of course, David understood that there was not a single thing in the world he could do for himself. What faith, what abounding, dynamic faith, to look up into the face of God and command Him, "Wash me throughly from mine iniquity, and cleanse me from my sin. For," said David, "I acknowledge my transgressions: and my sin is ever before me." Notice that David also recognized that every arrow of sin finally finds its lodging place in the heart of God for David said, "Against thee, thee only, have I sinned, and done this evil in thy sight . . ." Then as David examined his own heart he said, "Behold, I was shapen in iniquity; and in sin did my mother conceive me. Behold, thou desirest truth in the inward parts: and in the hidden part thou shalt make me to know wisdom."

God is not interested in our outward confessions of religiousness. He is not interested in frock coats or Sunday-go-to-meeting clothes which some people display as they enter into church, whether on Fifth or Park Avenue or Main Street. God is not the least interested in our clothes. *We are all nudists in His presence.* God looks at the heart. He looks at the inward parts. "Behold, thou desirest truth in the inward parts: and in the hidden part thou shalt make me to know wisdom."

Now follows what I consider the most remarkable if not the greatest passage on faith in all the Bible. "Purge me with hyssop, and I shall be clean; wash me, and I shall be whiter than snow." Here was a man whose fingers dripped with blood, whose conscience had the weight of God upon it, who had committed sin. He deserved to be ostracized: but who will cast the first stone? Our Lord said, "He that is without sin among you, let him first cast a stone . . ." But here in this 51st Psalm we find a man smeared with sin. Yet he looked up into the face of God and cried, "Purge me with hyssop, and I shall be clean: wash me, and I shall be whiter than snow." Those of you who are acquainted with your Bible will remember that the hyssop rested by the altar of sacrifice. It was a bunch of greens. David invited the Lord to take up that bunch of greens, to dip it into the blood of the sacrifice, and not to stop there but to take it and purge him with it.

We have heard much these days about purges, particularly in the political field, but this is a vital purge, a worthwhile purge, a purge to which we can all subscribe. "Purge me with hyssop and I shall be clean . . ." Purge *me*, not the other fellow. "Purge me . . . and I shall be clean: wash me, and I shall be whiter than snow."

We here, along the eastern seaboard, got more than a little taste of winter this past week. As most of us left our homes to go to business the morning after Thanksgiving, we saw the countryside as well as the city covered with newly fallen snow. There is nothing in this world that is as white as the driven snow. It is an awe-inspiring sight to see the country-side and the roofs of the city houses covered with snow before the muck and dirt of the city has rested upon it. It is a beautiful sight, all wonder-fully white. Imagine a man black with sin looking up into the face of God, asking God to wash him and make him whiter than snow. That is mar-velous faith! Sir, the thing that is so wonderful about it is this—if David had the right, every one of us possesses the same right. God can wash a black heart white, make it whiter than the driven snow through the blood of Jesus Christ, the blood He poured out on the cross of Calvary. God can take the hyssop, dip it into His precious blood and cleanse the one who receives Christ as his Lord and Saviour and make him whiter than newly fallen snow.

But David did not ask to be made white *as* snow. Indeed Dr. Forcey in his volume, "Sparrows and Men," correctly said, "David prayed in Psalm 51: 7 'Wash me, and I shall be whiter than snow.' For a long time people thought he did not know what he was talking about, but now we know from scientific data that snow at no time is pure. A great scientist has gone into the Polar Regions and tested the snow, as well as the ice-bergs. In all cases he found impurities. Another scientist examined with a powerful microscope the snow in the highest Alps and found impurities in it even there. There were particles of dust from the Grampian Hills of Scotland; soot from the smoke stacks of Manchester; microscopic bits of iron from the mills of Birmingham and the Krupp gun factories of Essen; and dust from the plains of Russia. So the snow was not pure. No snow is pure; but when God, through Christ, washes a sinful heart and life, He makes it *"whiter* than snow." If you have not had that experience I invite you to come under the shelter of it.

A PSALM FOR ISRAEL

Again, one cannot look across the horizon of this world without finding much cause for sadness, I mean as one looks at Israel and world conditions. It seems appropriate to bring our series of messages on these Hebrew Psalms to a close with a note on the Jewish question. Since the love of God is indescribable and the gift of God beyond description, so is the judgment of God. It is also irresistible. To Israel, therefore, let me read the 137th Psalm:

> "By the rivers of Babylon, there we sat down, yea, we wept, when we remembered Zion.

"We hanged our harps upon the willows in the midst thereof.

"For there they that carried us away captive required of us a song; and they that wasted us required of us mirth, saying, Sing us one of the songs of Zion.

"How shall we sing the LORD'S song in a strange land?

"If I forget thee, O Jerusalem, let my right hand forget her cunning.

"If I do not remember thee, let my tongue cleave to the roof of my mouth; if I prefer not Jerusalem above my chief joy

"Remember, O LORD, the children of Edom in the day of Jerusalem: who said, Rase it, rase it, even to the foundation thereof.

"O daughter of Babylon, who art to be destroyed; happy shall he be, that rewardeth thee as thou hast served us.

"Happy shall he be, that taketh and dasheth thy little ones against the stones."

THE CLOSING PSALM

And now for a Psalm in which all the world some day will join, the last Psalm, the 150th Psalm:

"Praise ye the LORD. Praise God in his sanctuary: praise him in the firmament of his power.

"Praise him for his mighty acts: praise him according to his excellent greatness.

"Praise him with the sound of the trumpet: praise him with the psaltery and harp.

"Praise him with the timbrel and dance: praise him with stringed instruments and organs.

"Praise him upon the loud cymbals: praise him upon the high sounding cymbals.

"Let every thing that hath breath praise the LORD. Praise ye the LORD."

——THE END——